A TEXT BOOK OF

Research Methodology

A TEXT BOOK OF

Research Methodology

A.K.P.C. SWAIN
Former Professor of Statistics and Chairman
Post Graduate Council
Utkal University, BHUBANESWAR
&
Former Visiting Faculty,
Xavier Institute of Management,
BHUBANESHWAR

KALYANI PUBLISHERS
LUDHIANA • NEW DELHI • NOIDA (U.P.) • HYDERABAD
CHENNAI • KOLKATA • CUTTACK • GUWAHATI • KOCHI

KALYANI PUBLISHERS

Head Office :
B-I/1292, Rajinder Nagar,
Ludhiana–141 008
Administrative Office :
4779, Ansari Road,
23, Daryaganj, **New Delhi**–110 002
Works :
B-16, Sector 8, **Noida** (U.P.)
Branches
1, Mahalakshmi Street,
T. Nagar, **Chennai**–600 017
110/111, Bharatia Towers, Badambadi
Cuttack–753 009 (Orissa)
3-5-1108, Narayanaguda,
Hyderabad–500 029
10/2B, Ramanath Mazumdar Street,
Kolkata–700 009
Arunalaya, 1st Floor, Saraswati Road
Pan Bazar, **Guwahati**–781 001
Convent Road, **Kochi**–682 035

KP-P-F3961 I G7. 5821-1

Second Revised Edition 2008

Reprinted 2009 2010

TYPESETTING & DIAGRAMS
(07-ATRM-AL)
At Gautam Graphic Printers,
Mai Hiran Gate, Jalandhar.

978-81-272-4172-8

PRINTED IN INDIA
At Kalyani Printings, B-15, Sector 8, NOIDA
and Published by Mrs. Usha Raj Kumar for
Kalyani Publishers, New Delhi-110 002

In memory of my parents

PREFACE

Second Edition

Research is an endeavour to discover facts by scientific study and is a course of critical investigation in a systematic manner. It encompasses a number of activities that are designed to help the researcher through information gathering and evaluation. In social science and business research it is necessary that the researcher should have a fairly good knowledge of research methods through which he can see things and analyse them in proper perspectives. Research is of importance to understand the reality and attain the truth. But this must be done scientifically to make the results based on critical and sound reasoning so as to make it useful for the decision maker, who need them in the decision making process. The social science researches in the present day have advanced rapidly to keep pace with the advancement in scientific data analysis.

In the business arena, the prime aim of research is to provide information to solve managerial problems by conducting an equiry of a management dilemma. Business research provides businesses with information about new technology, customers, their competitors and their overall industry. It is commonly used to identify business problems and opportunities, as well as to develop and evaluate the effectiveness of business strategies. The present day managers in a modern business environment have realised increased need for more and better information in face of intense global competition. Of course, there has been ever-increasing access to business communication technology to reach vital business research information sources. To cope with these environments, improved research methodology, research techniques and tools are forthcoming to solve intricate business problems in the complex business decision making environment. Besides, the managers face a host of economic, social and political factors, often interacting with each

While preparing the book, the author has referred to a number of authoritative books on research methodology, research papers, monographs, internet materials written by eminent authors and experts in relevant fields, to whom the author offers deep sense of appreciation and gratitude. Originality is maintained in the style of presenting and grouping the materials with the sole aim of making the book teacher-student friendly and informative.

In the present edition of the book the first three chapters of the first edition have been substantially revised, keeping in view the changing structure of the syllabi on research methodology. Further, in the final chapter, a few sections such as Technical Report writing, Instruction Manual, Technical proposal, etc. have been incorporated.

The chapters included in the book cover the syllabi of major business schools of the country in general and Bangalore University in particular. Besides business researchers, the book would no doubt be immensely helpful to social science researchers to learn research methodology to conduct research in their own fields.

Messrs Kalyani Publishers, Ludhiana deserve warmest thanks for their interest and sincere efforts in bringing out the publication in time.

My loving thanks go to my wife Smt. Harapriya Swain, sons Amar and Akash and daughter-in-law Samita for their constant encouragement to complete the book in the midst of pressing household and academic engagements.

Finally, I hope the faculty members and students of the business and social science schools will find the book useful and instructive. Comments and suggestions from all corners as regards the contents, presentations, oversight errors in formulae, statements and conclusions, etc. are cordially invited for corrections and improvements in the subsequent edition of the book.

2008 **A.K.P.C. Swain**

CONTENTS

Chapters	Pages

Chapters	Pages

Chapters	Pages

Chapters	*Pages*

CHAPTER 1

INTRODUCTION

1.1 SCIENCE AND SCIENTIFIC METHOD

Science may be defined as accumulation of systematic, organised and formula ed knowledge about real world situation. In reality, it is a method of approach to the entire empirical world in search of ultimate truth. To provide systematic knowledge, science has to state certain axioms, on the basis of which it deducts certain conclusions. The sole purpose of science is to know the mysteries of world in which man lives and the nature around it. The rational human mind asks certain questions and speculates certain visible phenomena and accumulates information to prove its speculation. Speculation when proved takes the form of a theory and ultimately the theory becomes facts. Thus the relationship between theory and fact is intricate in nature and inextricably mixed up.

A scientist, a person who pursuits science, promulgates his theory by defining types of data and facts to be abstracted and then puts this in a conceptual framework by which relevant phenomena are organised and systematised, if necessary in a comparative framework. Later, he condenses the facts to enable him to make empirical generalizations, prediction and then he either adds or negates or fills up the gaps in the existing state of knowledge. Facts initiate theories and if needed, either reformulate them or reject them for not subscribing to facts. In certain situations, facts reveal the direction to reorient, clarify and redefine the theory.

As science is knowledge, the pursuit of such knowledge requires proper understanding of its essence and the related and interconnected facts backed by rational explanation. The related facts then has to search for establishment of laws. The search for laws whether rational or empirical is one of the basic features of science and a scientist works towards this end.

The pursuit of knowledge extends to different spheres of science such as physical, natural, economic, social, political science, management, ethical etc. Some of these spheres are formal or deductive developed through definitions, axioms and dependent on self evident truths and conclusions are reached through deductive reasoning. For instance, pure mathematics is a deductive science. There are other sciences like economics, social, political science, management etc. which are empirical or inductive in nature and based on observed facts. Verification of assumed or established laws forms an important feature of empirical sciences in search for attainment of truth. In such empirical sciences there is every likelihood of incorporating new ideas and new facts so as to revise or correct already developed laws.

Science is the product of inquisitive human mind which connects the world of ideas to world of phenomena.

All the scientific ideas in human mind have been evolved in quest of what is reality and how best one is able to understand the same. The mysteries of nature for which man's knowledge is limited can only be realised through experiences and observations in a systematic and organised manner. One can reach the ultimate truth or at least can approach it through logic and empirical evidence.

The ***Structure of science*** may be defined in terms of the rules and procedures and the set of propositions accepted at a given point of time may be subjected to modification in the process of accumulation of facts, experiences and developments of thinking of logical mind.

Science may be classified in various ways :

(a) Pure and Applied

(b) Natural and Social

(c) Positive and Normative.

Pure science searches for laws and truth and in the process develops a system for the purpose of understanding the true state of nature. **Applied science** gathers such knowledge and applies to specific subject and issues. **Natural sciences** study natural phenomena such as Physics, Chemistry, Botany, Zoology, Geology etc. where as **social sciences** such as Economics, Sociology, Anthropology, Psychology, Management, Commerce etc. aim at increasing human comfort and welfare. **Positive science** studies pure and untainted facts, devoid of distortion and bias such as Physics, Chemistry, Biology, Ecology etc. **A normative science** is based on certain norms and standards for the judgement of phenomena and hence subjective in nature. For instance, ethics is a normative science based on concepts of certain ideals such as truth, morality, beauty and goodness etc. Of course these norms and standards are subject to different interpretations over period of time and space, sometimes overlooking eternal truth. **Social sciences** to certain extent are normative science interpreted from the point of view of human welfare.

On the whole **science provides systematic and organised knowledge** on certain specific subjects with certain objectivity and is essentially empirical in nature subject to critical judgement and discrimination. It is based on some general explanations and fundamental principles. It formulates theories leading to laws which are amenable to changes in light of new findings and facts. **Inductive science** generalizes from part to the whole and predicts future events based on laws of chance or probability. **Science is end neutral and objective in nature.**

The ***function of science*** is to establish laws governing the empirical events phenomena with which science is concerned and to make reliable prediction of unknown future events. **The scientific laws** either discover new vistas of knowledge or add to the existing laws or modify the established ones. It may sometimes end with controversies as to its interpretation, may open up new directions in search for advanced knowledge or standardise the whole approach of scientific thinking. The **scientific thinking** has three distinct features - discovery of truth devoid of personal bias and prejudices, exactness of end results and continuity and thoroughness. This is not concerned with isolated facts, but takes into account all available related facts to arrive at harmony in the face of chaos and diversities. **Science is a method of approach for a rational scientific thinking and susceptible to experience by man.**

Science, leaving apart its misuses, is primarily aimed at human welfare and thus plays a crucial role in the development of society and its environment at large.

The ***scientific method*** is a product of all logically trained minds and is the persuit of truth as determined by logical considerations.

The scientific method is a forerunner to achieve systematic knowledge and relates to a procedure and a mode of investigation facilitating the requirement of scientific knowledge based on certain **'articles of faith'**, summarised as

(a) reliance on empirical evidence and observed phenomena and ability for abstraction.
(b) defining certain basic concepts to systematise the acquired evidence and knowledge of a theoretical framework.
(c) clear objectivity to look at the empirical data.
(d) ethical neutrality.
(e) possibility for generalization
(f) prediction based on chance factor.
(g) methodology to collect empirical evidence, amenable to scientific analysis.

A scientist is confronted with a variety of phenomena in his universe for study. He abstracts from reality dealing with certain aspects of phenomena to gain systematic knowledge for the benefit of society. Each science has its own concepts for communicating its findings and develops a theoretical system of its own.

As concepts are developed as abstractions from reality, it is important that one should have clear objectives in mind for study, so as to develop concepts for them. Concepts in science must be communicable in the sense that their construction should be based on various components whose elements are derivable and can easily be classified without ambiguities. Concepts develop from shared experiences and give rise to development of a conceptual system. Terms and definitions of scientific terms used in development of a conceptual system should be clear so as to adequately describe the concept.

As knowledge accumulates, the meaning of concepts may change or be modified with the change in definitions. As time passes on, the science gets developed and many conceptual problems are bypassed and as a result re-definitions and re-conceptualization of the problems take place. Modern science and complexity of social structure and phenomena are always subservient to changing focus and thereby ushering new terms, definitions and concepts.

The *scientific method* involves collection of empirical evidences and observation of experimental results and in the process tests opinions and impressions through logical consideration for stable conclusions.

The *nature of scientific method* depends on nature and objective of a particular branch of science. Logical reasoning formulates necessary conditions for testing the validity of conclusions in different premises. Inference becomes valid if the scientific enquiry is based on **logical foundations and is free from subjective and experimental bias.**

The scientific method must have certain objectivity in search for truth, without having any subjective considerations otherwise the scientist wanders in wilderness and his pursuit of knowledge becomes truthless. **As truth is not subjective, the scientific method must adhere to ethical neutrality.**

As our knowledge about perceivable world is limited, the scientists adhere to prediction with the help of limited facts, assuming stochastic nature of phenomena. The scientific methods should be nurtured in such a way that the adopted methodology makes the prediction reliable to certain degree of confidence.

Scientific methods are varied in nature depending on the sphere of enquiry, objectivity, sources of observation and methods of verification.

The science is the product of thinking process of a scientist. If the tools of thinking are the minds of science, then the scientific attitude is the spirit. It is the attitude which drives a scientist to discover new vista of knowledge. The creative mind has brought about tremendous change in the development of science, resulting in spectacular inventions and discoveries in the twentieth century-influenced by folulore of imaginations, intuitions, cutriosity, suspicion, anguish, internal urge to know and self-doubt.

In business concern curiosity in many forms encourage managers persue persistent efforts to understand the relationship between productivity and worker's satisfaction.

The scientific enquiry occurs in the minds of many research workers with different motives and levels of thinking and who are full of excitement to explain new territory of knowledge, hither to unexplored or partially explored, with a hope to find order in the disordered world of ideas and drive to test established knowledge.

1.2 WHAT IS RESEARCH ?

Research in a general or formal sense means collecting information such as observing, asking questions, making experiments, etc. about something to reach decision in certain matter. In our daily lives we often make research or are involved in research at some level *e.g.* deciding menu for breakfast, lunch and dinner, for buying automobiles/personal computers, to find out more about a job vacancy, to vote for a political party, etc. In scientific terminology **research is an endeavour to discover facts by scientific method and is a course of a critical investigation.** It is a structured way of learning and a systematic and organised way of looking at facts with certain objectives/propositions in mind and using verifiable scientific methods to discover new knowledge or principles or laws governing the phenomena under review. It is an attempt to increase the sum of, what is known, usually referred to as a body of knowledge; by the discovery of new facts or relationships through a process of structured systematic enquiry, the research process. Thus, the scientific research is defined as systematic, controlled, empirical and critical investigation of hypothetical propositions about the presumed relations among natural phenomena. Because of systematic and controlled nature, the scientific research creates critical confidence in user's mind in respect of research outcomes. Further, it is empirical because the scientist must some how or other put his belief to a test outside himself, that is, the subjective belief must be checked against objective reality.

All research is based on a set of assumptions or factors that are presumed to be true and valid. By stating these assumptions, the researcher reduces potential criticism of the research, but without them, the research itself would not be possible.

A researcher is expected to be hypercritical of his own research results as well as those of others. After obtaining the research results the researcher should sit down to write the research reports to record his own research endeavour, besides meeting the needs of the sponsor as well as for the knowlege of the fellow research workers.

Thus, to sum up, research is a purposeful, precise and systematica search for new knowledge, skills, attitudes and values, or for the reinterpretation of existing knowledge, skills, attitude and values. It is concerned with seeking solutions to problems or answers to meaningful questions.

Research forms a cycle. It starts with a problem and ends with a solution to the problem. The problem statement is therefore the axis which the whole research revolves around, because it explains in short the aims of the research.

Every research has its own premises and perspectives. Research arises due to curiosity and aims at discovering truth and resolving contradictions in the area of study. Research is undertaken to discover answers to questions by applying the scientific method. With the discovery of new ideas and facts, old conclusions and theories are re-examined and may establish new empirical generalisations, falsifying the older ones. A good piece of research work gives rise to some problems requiring further research. Research is not an end to a problem and is rather the beginning in the sense tht a new research may be able to raise a new question.

1.2.1 Characterstics of Research

- Research originates with a meaningful question or a problem
- Research requires a clear articulation of a goal.
- Research follows a specific plan of proceedure.
- Research usually divides the principal problem into more manageable sub-problems.
- Research is guided by the specific research problem, question or hypothesis.
- Research accepts certain critical assumptions. These assumptions are underlying theories or ideas about how the world works.
- Research requires the collection and interpretation of data in attempting to resolve the problem that initiated the research.
- Research by nature is a cycle.

1.2.2 Research and Scientific method

Research refers to an inquiry into nature of, reasons for and the consequences of any particular set of circumstances whether under controlled experimental situations or existed as it is. Although the philosophy behind any research varies from discipline to another, the method used must adhere to characteristics of scientific method, which is the persuit of truth as determined by logical considerations and accompanied by the ideal of science, that is to achieve a systematic interrelation of facts.

The essential tenets of scientific method are :

- Direct observation of phenomena
- Clearly defined variables, methods and procedures.
- Empirically testable hypotheses
- Ability to rule out rival hypotheses
- Statistical rather than linguistic justification of conclusions.
- The self correcting process.

A good business research rests on

- sound reasoning
- empiricism.

A researcher has to act in this realm to play his role in a puzzle-solving activity of scientific method and scientific enquiry, encountering curiosity, doubt, barrier, suspicion or obstacle. He goes into struggles to state the problem, exercising his knowlege, experience, intellectual exercises, gathering facts including review of literature, exploring untrodden paths and having discussions with fellow research workers. He then proposes relevant hypotheses, deduce outcomes or consequences of hypotheses, formulates several rival hyptheses and conducts empirical tests, draws conclusions based on acceptance and rejection of the hypotheses, and finally feeds information back into the original problem, modifying it according to strength of evidence.

1.2.3 Purpose of Research

Many research studies are built upon the elements of the following purposes either individually or in combination.

The research purpose states what the study, its aims and goals are and what it hopes to discover or clarify.

- **Exploration :** Research is conducted to provide a beginning familiarity of a topic.
- **Description :** The purpose is to make careful and deliberate observations, aimed at providing accurate and precise description of situations and events.
- **Explanation—Causal or predictive :** The purpose is to focus why something occurs and in the process makes predictions and tests hypotheses.
- **Evaluation :** This includes elements of exploration, description and explanation with the purpose of evaluating policies, programmes and interventions.

More elaborately the purpose of research is

- to review and synthesize existing knowledge
- to investigate existing situations or problems.
- to provide solutions to a problem.
- to explore and analyse more general issues.
- to construct or create a new procedure or system.
- to explain a new phenomenon or to generate new knowledge.

Research purpose leads to **research strategy.** For instance if the research purpose is causal or predictive, the research strategy would involve using secondary data, survey techniques and classical experiments. For exploratory research, the research strategy consists of case study involving participant observations or a field study with in-depth interviewing.

1.2.4 Rationale of Research

Rationale specifies the reasons for conducting the research in light of current knowlege. It should include a well documented statement of the need/problem that is the basis of the project, the cause of this problem and its possible solutions. It is equivalent to the introduction in a research paper and it puts the project in the context. It should answer the question of 'why' and 'what'; why the research needs to be done and what will be its relevance.

In fact, in a research study the researcher needs to have a rationale for every aspect of the research study, beginning from formulation of the problem till the interpretation of results of study. That is why, research differs from other forms of inquiry in the sense that the researcher needs to justify virtually everything that he does.

1.2.5 Significance of Research

Research is a product of inquisitive human minds. It inculcates scientific and inductive thinking and promotes the development of logical habits of thinking and organisation. In olden days research was largely confined to physical and biological sciences. But in recent years due to advancement of science and technology, need for rapid economic and social development in global context and increasingly complex nature of business and government activities, significance of research results has been felt in many disciplines of knowledge-scientific, economic and social.

Research has become basis for planned economy and influenced the policies and programmes of the government to provide good governace and to allocate resources in budget to meet various needs of the people.

Research, in the present day market economy, is being undertaken in solving various operational and planning problems of business and industry.

Modernity has revolutionized the human nature accompanied by all its complexities, adding to a host of interacting social problems. As a result the social scientists are constantly at work to develop a body of principles that make possible the understanding and predicition of the whole range of human interactions. Because of increasing importance given to economic development with human face social scientists and economic scientists work together in an interdisciplinary research scenario to achieve this end.

Strategic research studies have assumed importance in the face of continuing misgivings and tensions vigible and brewing among different nationalities and governments and also splinter groups around the world in the political and economic arena and hence have given enough scope to strategic/defence/political analysts to work upon.

1.2.6 Desiderata of a Good research

A good research must be primarily of scientific nature and generate dependable data collected professionally with meticulous planning and design and can be relied upon by managers in their decision making process.

The characteristics of a good research are as follows :

(1) The problem of research must be clearly defined.

(2) The researcher/manager must have clear objectives and purpose in mind.

(3) It needs a detailed research proposal.

(4) Research design must be clearly formulated. Sampling design and method of data collection should be judiciously implemented.

(5) A good research needs to maintain ethical standards keeping in view of the study participants (units), organizations, clients and researchers. The scope of the research study, research methodology and limitations should have clear cut mention in the report.

(6) The research hypothesis should be unambiguously stated and the statisctical analysis and conclusions be made with reference to them.

(7) Research findings should be unambiguously presented in tables, graphs and words and logically organised in the report without much technical jargons, so as to facilitate the manager reaching a decision as to his problem. A good researcher always specifies the conditions under which his conclusions remain valid.

(8) Research results should conform to the needs and objectives of the manager and the statistical analysis should be directed towards this end. Sometimes a researcher goes beyond the data in hand and relies more on his past experiences and knowledge. Such interpolation of ideas should have been taken care of while designing the study and collecting the data.

(9) Research report would create greater confidence in the minds of the users if the researcher is a person of good knowledge, experience, reputation and integrity. This is the reason why some research reports mention information about the researcher and his associates for judging the degree of confidence warranted by the piece of research.

1.3 KINDS OF RESEARCH

Research is not confined to any single discipline or to any specified topic. In fact, there are different kinds of research covering various topics of interest, engulfing almost all disciplines enriching existing knowledge and exploring new vista of knowledge.

Some of them are briefed in the following :

- Scientific researches both basic and applied are carried out in physical, natural, biological, engineering, medical sciences involving whole range of sophisicated and specialist instruments and specialized technologies.
- Economic research relates to development of economic theory and principles and their applications towards welfare of man and its environment and society at large. It also studies economic problems and trends of development in different sectors economy.
- Business research is conducted in different functional areas of management such as marketing, production, finance and personnel to find solutions to several interacting decision making problems in day to day operations.

The topics of major areas in business research are :

- **Marketing :** Product identification, Demand estimation, Demand and supply analysis, Market segmentation, sales promotion programme, Product launching, Pricing, Design of distribution channel, Packaging, Design of advertisement, Buying behaviour, etc.

- **Production :** Forecasting, Capacity planning, Plant location and layout, Inventory control, Production scheduling, Single machine scheduling, Job-shop scheduing, Project mangement, Maintenance management, Quality control, Work design, etc.

- **Finance :** Models for break even analysis of multi-product, Economic evaluation of alternatives, capital Budgeting, Ratio analysis, Porfolio management, Plance of payment, Inflation, Deflation, Ecomomic growth models, etc.

- **Personnel/human resources management :** Manpower planning, Performance of appraisal systems, Conflict management, Incentive plans, Training methods, Change and resuffling of management, Labour disputes and wage settlement, Welfare programmes for workers, etc.

Social Research is quite a broad term encompassing all aspects of society and may involve different kinds of research from gathering information on the population and its habitat/social setting to attitude, interaction and behaviours of people in community or country. There are also researches concerning social work primaily aimed at developing weaker sections of our society in relation to their problems and aspirations.

Media research has assumed importance in view of rapid and revolutionary expansion media and communication studies. It involves looking at issues such as media content and audience and its overall impact on society and people at large. International understanding among various groups of people and nationalities gets channelised through the help of media and communication research.

Historical research looks at historical events of the past, economic and social upheavals and cultural movements and their impact on present day happenings and events.

1.4 TYPES OF RESEARCH

Research can be classified by different criteria:

Purpose of Research :

- **Exploratory.** The aim is to look for patterns, ideas or hypothesis rather than testing or confirming a hypothesis.

- **Descriptive.** This describes phenomena as they exist. It is used to identify and obtain information on the characteristics of a particular issue.

- **Analytical.** The reseacher goes beyond merely describing the characteristics, to analyse and explain why or how something is happening. Analytical research aims to understand phenomena by discovering and measuring causal relations among them.

- **Predictive.** Predictive research is concerned with forecasting the likelihood of a similar situation occurring elsewhere. It aims to generalise from the analysis by predicting certain phenomena on the basis of hypothesized, general relationships.

Process of Research :

• **Quantitative.** This usually starts with a theory or general statement proposing a general relationship between variables and the resarcher is likely to take an objective position. It is the systematic scientific investigation of quantitative properties and phenomena and their relationships. The objective of quantitative research is to develop and employ mathematical models, theories and hypotheses pertaining to natural phenomena.

• **Qualitative.** The investigator views the phenomena to be investigated as more personal. The emphasis is more on generating hypotheses from data collection rather than testing a hypothesis. The qualitative research is the examination, analysis and interpretation of observations for the purpose of discovering underlying meanings and patterns of relationships, including classifiation of types of phenomena and entities, in a manner that does not involve mathematical models.

Outcome of Research :

• **Basic or Pure.** It is also called fundamental research and is conducted primarily to improve our understanding of general issues, without any emphasis on its immediate application. The principal aim is to make a contribution to base of knowlege, usually for general good. Pure research is of theoretical nature and is conducted to add to our store of knowlege, test hypotheses, build theories and perhaps find some practical applications in future.

• **Applied Research.** This research resolves a particular problem and is carried out for practical reasons to produce findings that are applicable, practical and immediately useful. In business studies applied research deals with application of tools to various problems of research such as influence of various incentives provided in business. The problem solving nature of the applied research ends in answering certain specific research questions related to action, performance or policy needs. The applied research is directed more towards decision making of the managers or research sponsors.

Action Research :

Action research is regarded as research that is normally carried out by practitioners (persons that stand in the field work). It enables a researcher to investigate a specific problem that exists in practice. It requires that the researcher should be involved in the actions that take place, that is, the researcher, as expert, and the person standing in the practice, jointly decide on the formulation of research procedures allowing the problem to be solved.

Action research is characterized by the following features.

❒ Problem-aimed research focuses on a special situation in practice.

❒ Collective participation with the characteristic that all participants form an integral part of action research with the exclusive aim to assist in solving the identified problem.

❒ Type of empirical research where action research is characterized as a means to change the practice while research is going on.

❐ Outcome of research cannot be generalised. Action research is characterised by the fact that the problem solving cannot be generalised because it should comply with the criteria set for scientific character.

Logic of Research :

• **Deductive :** The research proceeds from general to specific. Deduction is a form of argument which is supposed to be conclusive, that is, the conclusion must necessarily follow from the reasons. In other words, the reasons are said to imply the conclusion and represent a proof. For a deduction to be correct, it must necessarily be true and valid.

• **Inductive.** The inductive argument proceeds from specific to general. There is no strength of relationship between reasons and conclusions in induction. Inductive argument induces to draw conclusions from one or more particular facts or pieces of information/evidence. The conclusion explains and is derived from facts and the facts support or corroborate the conclusions.

Nature of Research (Philosophical perspectives)

• **Positivist.** Deals with positive facts and observable phenomena.

Subscribes to the scientific method. Primary goal is not only description but prediction and explanation. Classification of substances and events, and observation of these, provide the basis for descriptive laws based on consistencies in patterns and properties. Characterised by absolute or varying degree of generalisability. Quantitative, as it draws on measurable evidence. Positivist research methods include.

Descriptive research (surveys, case studies, causal comparative studies, correlational studies, developmental studies, trend studies)

Experimental research (Deliberate manipulation of certain factors under highly controlled conditions. Purpose is to identify causal connections through keeping the levels of some variables constant and manipulating others)

Postulates in Positivist Research :

Postulates of natural kinds : all instances of classes and categories of phenomena exhibit the same properties.

Postulates of constancy : all phenomena remain the same or change only very slowly over time.

Postulates of determinism : There is orderliness and regularity in nature, constancy in terms of cause and effect.

• **Phenomenalist/Interpretivist :** Considers that each phenomena is unique and is controlled by' variables such as time, location and culture. No two situations are identical. No reliance on postulates of natural kinds, constancy or determinism. Essentially subjective, where the content of research and the way it is persued is, indicative of researchers intention. Outcomes are descriptions which are expressed in narrative and mainly in qualitative terms. Penomenology consists of case studies, experience surveys, focus studies, in-depth interviews, ethnography etc.

• **Critical Research.** Critical researchers assume that social reality is historically constituted and that it is produced and reproduced by people. Although people can conciously act to change their social and economic circumstances, critical researchers recognize that their ability to do so is constrained by various forms of social, cultural and political domination. The main tasks of critical research is seen as being one of social critique, where by restrictive and alienating conditions of the status quo are brought to light.

Note. The positivist and interpretivist paradigms rest on different assumptions about nature of the world and they require different instruments and procedures to find the type of data desired. This does not mean that the positivist never uses interviews nor that the interpretivist never uses survey.

Broadly positivism relates to quantitative appropach and interpretism relates to qualitative approach.

Interpretism proposes that there are multiple realities, not single reality of phenomena and these realities can differ across time and space.

The Measure of Control by Researchers :

Researches also may be classified as regards the measure of control by the researchers.

- ❒ library research
- ❒ field research
- ❒ laboratory research

Library research is based on secondary data available from library records, documents, monographs, reports, diaries, books, journals, magazines, internet data bases, etc.

Field research includes :

- ❒ Field Experiment
- ❒ Field Study
- ❒ Survey Study

Field experiments are conducted through expriments and quasi-experimental designs without much scientific rigor, but still provides a wealth of valuable information in natural setting.

Field studies have high degree of realism and are conducted in natural environments. Variables are not maniputated by the researcher and measurement of variables is less precise than in laboratory.

In survey studies data are collected in natural occurring environment through survey techniques (*e.g.* questionnaire, interviewing schedules, observations, etc.) The researcher has little or no control over variables in the study.

Laboratory researches are conducted in controlled conditions in the form of experiments. The experimenter has control over the assignment of subjects to conditions and the manipulation of independent variables. Measurement of behaviour is the most precise. Laboratory experiment is the best method for inferring cause-effect relationship.

1.5 RESEARCH METHODS AND RESEARCH METHODOLOGY

The terms–research methods and research methodology are sometimes used as though they were synonyms. But in real sense they are not. Methodology is the study of methods and deals with the philosophical assumptions underlying the research process, **while a method is a specific technique for data collection/data analysis/evaluation under those philosophical assumptions.**

There are a wide range of research methods available for answering every sort of research question, within every area of social and natural sciences. A combination of appropriate methods, to address carefully phrased research question (s), constitutes a research methodology. Research methodology covers the complete research project from literature review to writing up the final report and then being able to defend the work against assessment challenges and/or peer review. The appropriate research methods are those which address the specific research question phrased with the greatest reliability and validity, without ethical problems and which are most likely to enable you to write a competent research report with which the reader will have greatest confidence.

The major types of research methods vary in terms of the experimenter's corntrol over relevant variables and naturalness of setting. These differences have a direct bearing on critical issues such as what sort of conclusions we can make from the findings and how confident we are of the validity of these conclusions.

A research method is a strategy of enquiry which moves from underlying philosophical assumptions to research design and data collection. It influences the way in which the researcher collects data.

The choice of a particular method selected for conducting a research lays the foundation for how confidently we can claim to better understand the causes of the behaviour of interest. It is also fundamental to how likely our conclusions will generalise beyond the particular sample in the study.

Methodology in research refers to the process followed in planning and conducting a study. In the absence of knowledge about the methodology one cannot judge the quality and validity of the findings and conclusions presented by the researcher. Also, if one does not know the methodology followed by the researcher, he cannot replicate the study.

Research methodology is the structural process of research. It is the theoretical and philosophical assumptions underpinning the methods or the research design (the strategies for doing research).

More elaborately methodology should include

- ❒ recapitulation of the research problem
- ❒ the study settings/coverage
- ❒ the sample/test population
- ❒ any intervention
- ❒ data collection method and instruments.
- ❒ data analysis techniques including selection of statistical tools
- ❒ presentation of findings

Research methodology is concerned with

- ❒ how the design is implemented
- ❒ how the research is carried out
- ❒ solving the research problem systematically and scientifically.

Broadly research methods and logic and rationale behind the methods in context of research study, constitute the research methodology.

Research techniques are operational counterparts of research methods. A research method determines a set of research techniques. For instance, in case of library research method, data collection, is carried out by using techniques such as statistical compilations, manipulations, reference and abstract guides, content analysis, etc. Similarly in field research, personal interviewing may be chosen as a research technique of collection of data (instrument for data collection). In laboratory research different measurement techniques are used to take physical measurements.

1.6 RESEARCH DESIGN

A **research design** or designing a study streamlines the research. It is **basically a blue print of activities from the beginning of the research process till its completion, involving collection, measurement and analysis of data.** It starts from the purpose of the study and ends with the analysis of data and so to say a string of logic binding all elements of a research process.

There are many ways to design a research study depending on whether the research intends to adopt an experimental design, quasi-experimental design or non-experimental design, accompanied by specific research methods. Although experimental designs are more scientific, it is not always rigorously possible to control the extraneous variables in field research under natural conditions. However, quasi-experimental and non- experimental designs do help to produce a wealth of valuable information for research study even if they lack scientific rigor to examine cause-effect relationship.

A researcher is expected to be aware of the limitations of each design and avoid drawing unwarranted conclusions that are not supported by the design. Further, since the control that forms the basis of scientific investigation is not rigorously applied in non-experiemntal research, researchers should use caution to avoid drawing improper conclusion about the effect of one variable on another when conducting non-experimental investigation.

1.7 ETHICS IN RESEARCH

An important aspect of research is the respect and consideration shown to people who participate in the study. These people include managers/sponsors, the researcher and his colleagues and more importantly the subjects/respondents.

Research on humans to a large extent depends on volunteer subjects. Often, the products of research results in benefits to the society in the form of new methods of learning, innovation of new methods of production, distribution and marketing, new social welfare programmes and ways of conducting over affairs. However, it is not ethical to advance the society over the bones of our subjects. Here comes ethical concerns in areas of research.

There are **four areas of concern** where the rights and dignity of the subjects must be preserved.

These ethical issues are

- ***Consent***
- ***Harm***

- ❐ ***Privacy***
- ❐ ***Deception.***

Consent. This is the procedure by which research subjects choose whether or not they wish to participate in a research study. Consent involves three elements.

Capacity–defined as the ability to acquire or retain knowledge, and the authority, or legal qualification, to perform an act. Is the subject **able** to decide if he wants to participate ? Does a person who is mentally retarded have capacity.

Information–consists of insuring the subjects are told, and they understand, the purpose of the study and their roles as subjects.

Voluntariness–means that the subject chooses to be in the study of his free will and is free to withdraw from the study at any time. There must be no element of force, fraud, deceit, duress, ulterior form of constraint or coercion to get subject to participate.

The subject needs to be informed about the study and participate in the decision to be a subject as much as possible.

Harm. One of the most important issues in all of research ethics is that subjects not be harmed by the study. To avoid physical harm is obvious, but other areas such as psychological stress, personal embarrasment, humiliation etc. also need to be avoided. The dignity of the subject (be it human or animal) needs to be always a concern of the researcher.

Privacy. Every subject has the right to keep private the fact that he participated in the study and the right that the information divulged to the researcher not be leaked to him. The information collected may be used in the study and may perhaps be published, but it must be done in a way that insures individual's **anonymity.**

Violation of promise of privacy can result in harm to the subject. There is a trade off in science is need to know and the individual's right not to tell. Again there is rule about what is too private to ask about.

Deception. Deception in research involves the misrepresentation of facts related to the purpose, nature, or consequences of a research study. The omission of facts is the same as misrepresentation. Subjects need to be fully informed in order to give consent. If any part of the study is misrepresented, then either the subjects have not fully consented to the study or the researcher is morally in the wrong. The researcher can be successfully sued if harm comes to the subjects or if their privacy is violated.

1.8 DIFFERENT APPROACHES TO RESEARCH

Research is said to be a systematic and methodical process of inquiry, and investigation involving critical examination in seeking facts or principles, that increases knowledge and/or solves a particular problem. The motivation for research is the desire to know or understand for the sake of knowing (termed pure or basic research) or by the desire to know in order to use knowledge for practical concerns (termed applied research)

The reasonable and widely accepted approach to research of any variety is what is termed as **scientific approach/method, comprising of observation, hypothesis and verification.**

The scientific method is related to characteristics of science, which is a method of discovering **reliable knowledge** about nature. Reliable knowledge is knowledge that has a high probability of being true by reliable method. Reliable knowledge is justifiable **true belief.** The method used to justify scientific knowledge and thus making it reliable is called the **scientific method.** When one uses scientific method to study or investigate nature or the universe or any phenomena, one is really practising **critical thinking.** A critical thinking successfully leads to the most reliable answers to questions and solutions to problems. The critical thinking, an application of scientific thinking has been incorporated into all areas of study and types of investigation.

The scientific thinking is primarily based on three axioms :

Empiricism. The use of empirical evidence. Empirical evidence is evidence that others besides the researcher can experience and it is repeatable.

Rationalism. the practice of logical reasoning.

Skepticism. possessing a skeptical attitude, that is, constant questioning of beliefs and conclusions. Scientists and critical thinkers constantly examine the evidence, arguments and reasons for their beliefs.

1.8.1 Scientific and Non-scientific Approaches

Scientific method is really a philosophy of research, which has proven to be the most realiable method of thinking in human history and hence ideal for any research activities.

The scientific methods vary with research problems and also may vary at different stages of research. It is the persuit of truth determined by logical considerations and is supposed to be the most assured techiques for controlling a host of things and establishing **stable belief.** The scientific enquiry is based on systematic doubt and aims at discovering the actual facts and the rational interconnection of facts. It wants to establish general propositions through weighing evidence.

The scientific method of finding solutions involves controlled experimentation, capable of having broader generalisations.

The scientific approach to problem solving is carried out by the principles of scientific method. Therefore, the features of scientific approach are applicable *mutatis mutandis* to all methods.

The scientific approach has two elements :

- Procedural
- Personal

Observation, hypothesis and verification are three procedural components of scientific approach. Observation depending on knowledge, material and personal hunches, helps to build up hypotheses. A hypothesis, a tentative conclusion, guides the collection and processing of materials and direct investigation. Verification of the hypotheses through analytical tools and arriving at conclusion constitutes the final step of the scientific approach.

Personal component of the scientific research relates to the researcher himself. He needs to be personally qualified, imaginative, analytical, resourceful, skillful, persistent and ability to hold objective, scientific unbiased view and independent thinking, besides being man of integrity, honesty, truthfulness and strong morality.

Non-scientific approach to research involves conducting research without fully subscribed to scientific methods, *e.g.* quasi-experimental designs and non-experimental design, which lack rigorous scientific techniques. The results derived through non-scientific approaches do not involve broad generalisations. In social research the observations mostly relate to humans, human behaviour and social environment, which are complex and non-uniform in nature and thus reliable scientific data cannot be always be collected. However, in such situations the use of scientific method cannot altogether be ruled out. In social sciences, difficulties in taking observations and experiment may be reduced to a considerable extent by making the enquiry confined to a particular class whose behaviour is under study. The personal prejudices of an observer of human behaviour in social sciences can be minimised with the help of some standard techniques developed for the purpose. Even if human beings behave in a particular way with much individual variations, class variations are seen to be less prominent and hence the researcher is not prevented to make broad generalisations. Thus, the scientific method has been to some extent, successfully applied in the study of social phenomena and in predicting human behaviour.

Unlike experimental research, quasi-experimental research and non-experimental research, though not entirely non-scientific, lack scientific rigor necesaary to draw correlational or cause-effect conclusions about one variable on the other. Since the control that forms the basis of scientific investigation is not rigorously applied in non-experimental research. Researchers should use caution to avoid drawing improper conclusions about the effect of one variable on another when conducting non- experimental investigation. Nevertheless, non experiemental research is widely practised to take care of real world situation and does have educative and informative value in promoting knowledge. Organisations commonly conduct non- experimental research to produce a wealth of valuable information for future study and developing hypotheses.

1.8.2 Quantitative and Qualitative approaches

Two major approaches to research may be identified as

- ❒ **Quantitative approach**
- ❒ **Qualitative approach**

The quantitative approach is seen as an objective approach relying heavily on statistics and on the other hand the qualitative approach is seen as subjective and preferring language and description.

• Quantitative Approach

The basic beliefs of a **positivist** or **quantitative researcher** lead them to perceive the world as external and there is an objective reality that is not dependent of human interpretation. Nature is orderly and follows specific laws. Occurrences or events have causes which can be discovered. This approach relies on reasons behind various aspects of behaviour and investigates 'What', 'Where' and 'When'. In their general approach to research design, the quantitative researcher seeks to deduce cause and effect relationships to predict patterns of behaviour and then develops theory and uses this to explore the world. This theoretical framework identifies key variables and their relationships and associations.

Research methods used in quantitative approach are :

- **Descriptive research**
- **Correlational research**
- **Causal comparative research**
- **Experimental research**

Descriptive Research : invovles collecting data in order to test hypothesis or answer questions regarding the subjects of the study. Data are numerical, typically collected through questionnaires, an interview, or through observation.

Correlational Research : attempts to determine wether and to what degree, a relationship exists between two or more quantifiable (numerical) variables. It is used in predicting the value of one variable from the value of another. It is not cause-effect research.

Causal-comparative Research : attempts to establish cause-effect relationships among the variables of the study. This type of research usually involves group comparisons. The groups in the study make up the values of the independent variable, for example gender (males versus females). However, in causal-comparative research the independent variable is not under experimenter control.

Experimental Research : Causal-comparative research attempts to establish cause-effect relationship among the groups of subjects that make up the independent variable of the study, but in case of experimental research, the cause (the independent variable) is under the control of the experimenter. That is, the experimenter can randomly assign the subjects to the groups that make up the independent variable in the study. In the typical experimental research design the experimenter randomly assigns subjects to the groups or conditions that constitute the independent variable of the study and then measures the effect this group membership has on another variable, *i.e.* the dependent variable of the study.

The research sample size in a quantitative approach would be reasonably large, a sub-set of a larger population and a random sample with the same characteristics as that of the population.

Quantitative data analysis and interpretation is primarily deductive, a matter of proving or disproving the hypothesis or an assertion developed from a general statement.

• Qualitative Approach

Qualitative researchers approach their studies with a certain **paradigm or world view,** a basic set of beliefs or assumptions that guide their inquiries,

These assumptions are related to

- the nature of reality (the ontology issue)
- the relationship of the researcher to that being researched (epistemological issue)
- the role of values in the study (axiological issue)
- the process of research (the methodological issue)

Thus, the qualitative approach to research believes in realities. These realities are primarily subjective to the researcher and do not exist independent of humans, who interpret it. This **interpretivist** research is primarily exploratory and descriptive in purpose, designed to discover what can be learned about the area of interest. The interpretivist researcher views the world as a socio-psychological construct where there are multiple realities forming an inter-connected whole that can only be understood as those multiple realities. Occurrences and events have causes, which can be explored, but not completely explained.

Qualitative research involves an indepth understanding of human behaviour and the reasons that govern human behaviour. This investigates 'why' and 'how' of decision making.

Qualitative research approaches involve two broad types of research.

- **Historical research**
- **Qualitative research**

Historical research involves study of past events, *e.g.* factors leading toward independence movements in India, factors leading to industrial movements in Europe, trends in Geen revolution in India, etc. Qualitative research in general involves ethnographic research-collection of extensive narrative data (non-numerical data) on many variables over an extended period of time in natural setting, participant observation-researcher participates with the subjects being observed, case studies, focus studies, action research, content analysis, etc. The qualitative approach is descriptive an inductive, involves field work and the researcher is the primary instrument for data collection and analysis. The researcher builds abstractions, concepts, hypothesis and theories from details. The qualitative approach to research strategy is characterised by lower sample numbers, than quantitative research. Normally, forms of non-probability sampling such as purposive, judgement, convenience or snow ball are used. This approach is often time consuming as patterns slowly emerge. Also, what is true in one context may not be true for another and therefore data may need to be gathered in a variety of contexts, which takes both time and effort. The interpretivist also explores first and then develops theory thus allowing deeper explanations and in sights. However, some uncertainlty exists as it is possible that nothing of value may emerge. In qualitative approach the researcher is an active participant often immersing himself in a setting, becoming part of the group under study in order to understand meaning and significance. Typical techniques include participant observation, in-depth interviews, group interviews and documentation collection with an emphasis on field work. Data analysis and interpretation is an **ongoing activity** for the interpretivist researcher and in contrast to the functionalist analysis, that is, what is meaningful emerges from the data (inductive) and general principels are developed from specific observations.

The qualitative approach involves **conversation analysis**–to discover the implicit, unspoken assumptions existing in the society, semiotics–concerned with symbols and meanings, associated with content analysis, grounded theory method–theories generated from an examination of data.

Qualitative data are examined with respect to

frequencies : How often does a certain phenomenon or thing occur ?

magnitudes : How intense or how much does phenomenon happen ?

structures : What are various types of phenomenon under study ?

processes : Is there any order among the elements of structure ?

causes. What causes phenomona under study ?

consequences. What, if any, corsequences are there to phenomena ?

Qualitiative research also called **interpretive research/**naturalistic research/ phenomenological research comes from social and cutural anthropology; qualitative sociology; professional studies–education, law, business, nursing, health professions; poltical science and economics; journalism and media studies, field work in natural sciences; humanities and arts.

In this connection it is worth mentioning **five traditions of qualitative inquiry.**

These are :

- Biographical study
- Phenomenological study
- Grounded theory study
- Ethnography
- Case study.

A biographical study is the study of an individual and his/her experiences as told to the researcher or found in documents and archival material. Biographical writing has roots in different disciplines. The intellectual strands of this tradition are found in literary, historical, anthropological, psychological and sociological perspectives as well as in interdisciplinary views.

There are a number of biographical forms of research and the terms reflect different discipline perspectives, all forms representing an attempt to construct the history of life.

- biographical study
- auto-biography
- life history
- oral history

In a **biographical study,** the life history of an individual is written by some one, other than the individual being studied using archival documents and records. In an **autobiography** the life story is written by persons about themselves. The **life history** is an approach found in the social sciences and anthropology, where a researcher reports on an individual's life and how it reflects cultural themes of the society, personal themes, institutional themes and social histories. The investigator collects data primarily through interviews and conversations into the individual. An **oral history** is an approach in which the researcher gathers personal recoolections of events, their causes and their effects from an individual or several individuals.

Whereas a biography reports the life of a single individual, a phenomenological study describes the meaning of the lived experiences for several individuals about a concept or the phenomenon. Phenomenologists explore the structures of conciousness in human experiences : A phenomenological study has roots in philosophical perspectives, and data analysis proceeds through the methodology of reduction, the analysis of specific statements and themes, and search for all possible meanings. The researcher sets aside all prejudgments, bracketing his or her experiences and relying on intuition, imagination, and universal structures to obtain a picture of the experience.

A phenomenological study emphasizes the meaning of an experience for a number of individuals, but the intent of a **grounded theory study** is to generate or discover a theory, an abstract analytical schema of a phenomenon, that relates to a particular situation. This situation relates to one in which individuals interact, take actions, or engage in a process in response to a phenomenon. To study how people act or react to this phenomenon, the researcher collects primarily interview data, makes multiple visits to the field, develops and interrelates categories of information, and writes theoretical propositions or hypotheses or presents a visual picture of the society.

The centrepiece of grounded theory research is the development or generation of a theory closely related to the context of the phenomenon being studied. The process of data analysis in grounded theory research is systematic and follows a standard format such as **open coding, axial coding, selective coding, conditional matrix,** etc. In open coding the researcher forms initial categories of information about the phenomenon being studied by segmenting information. In axial coding, the investigator assembles the data in new ways after open coding. In selective coding, the researcher identifies a 'story line' and writes a story that integrates the categories in the axial coding model. As regards the conditional matrix, the researcher may develop and visually portray a conditional matrix that elucidates the social, historical and economic conditions influencing the central phenomenon.

An **ethnography** is a description and interpretation of a cultural or social group or system. The researcher examines the group's observable and learned pattern of behaviour, customs and ways of life. Ethnography involves prolonged observation of the group, typically through **participant observation** in which the researcher is immersed in the day to day lives of the people or through one-on-one interviews with members of the group. The researcher studies the meanings of **behaviour, language, and interactions of the culture-sharing group.** Ethnography has its genesis in cultural anthropology through early 20th century for studying comparative cultures specially primitive cultures. Recently, scientific approaches to ethnography have expanded to include schools or subtypes of ethnography with different theoretical orientations and aims such as structural functionalism, cultural and cognitive anthropology, cultural studies, marxism, ethnomethodology, post-modernism, etc.

A **case study** is an exploration of a **'bounded system'** or a case (or multiple cases) over time through detailed, in-depth data collection involving **multiple sources** of information. The system is bounded because it is bounded by time and place. It is the **case** being studied a program, an event, an activity or individuals. **Multiple sources of information** include observations, interviews, audio-visual material, and documents and reports. The **context** of the case involves situating the case within its setting, which may be physical setting or the social, historical, and/or economic setting for the case.

Although the quantitative/qualitative dichotomy may appear obvious in the distinction between two approaches, the division may not be regarded as clear cut as it seems and in fact these approaches **are not mutually exclusive.** The qualitative approach does provide necessary input for future quantitative research in the study area.

1.9 MANAGEMENT RESEARCH :

1.9.1 Meaning and Significance of Management Research

The research directed towards solving management/organizational problems is termed as **management research.** Management research revolves around managers and researchers, who work collaboratively to assess performance of on-going activities, develop predictors of performance and specify the conditions under which various approaches to research delivery are most effective.

The term management research is a broad one and is often used in two different, but overlapping ways :

Research for managers : Management research is research tailored to **specific management needs** and usually conducted at the request of managers. While it ideally informs theory and contributes to the development of knowledge, the priority is to answer specific questions defined in conjuction with managers, generally within time frames that meet their needs. The distinguishing feature of management research under this is the target audience not a particular subject area.

Research about management and organizations : In this context, management research is defined by **the subject of study.** For instance, it is research, about how organizations are structured and function, the practices of decision making, the factors that affect organizational operations. **The emphasis is on building knowledge.**

Business research is a systematic inquiry that provides information to guide managerial decisions in all aspects of marketing, production, finance and personnel. It is a process of planning, acquiring, analyzing and disseminating relevant data, information and insights provided to decision makers in ways to mobilize the organization to take appropriate and timely actions, that in turn maximize business performance in designated sectors.

The need for business research arises due to increased attention placed in recent year on enhancing **return on investment** (ROI) and requirement of organizational managers to know about what strategies (general approach an organization will follow to achieve its goals) and tactics (those specific, timed activities that execute a strategy) capture the highest return. Also, there is realisation among the managers about the need for a better understanding of employees, stake holder and customer behaviour in order to influence the desired metrics of interest. All these have given rise to innovation of sophisticated research methods and analytical techniques to solve the complex managerial issues.

The factors stimulating management research are

- Explosive growth and influence of company websites, e- commerce, electronic publications.
- Stakeholders, customers, workers, share holders and also general public demanding greater influence in decision making.
- Increasing global and domestic competitions.
- More aggresive government intervention to protect public from business practices.
- Complex decision making scenario involving a host of interacting variables.

- ❐ Improvement in quality theories and models to explain the strategic and tactical results in human resources, marketing operations and finance and thus providing managers with better knowledge.
- ❐ Greater computing power and speed, leading to lower cost of data collection, powerful computation, more integration of data, more and faster access to information, use of advanced analytical tools, data mining techniques, customized reporting.
- ❐ New perspectives on established research methodologies.

A researcher in order to become well versed with business research needs to understand how to identify quality information and to recognise the solid, reliable business research on which high risk decisions taken by manager can be based. Also understanding the relationship between the business research and information sources–decision support system and business intelligence, is critical for understanding how information drives the decision relating organizational activities, goals, strategies and tactics.

Research goals in business concern relate to sales, market share, return on investment, profitability, customer acquisition, customer statisfaction, customer retention, employee productivity, machine efficiency, etc.

Business research is often used to help a manager decide which of several tactics is likely to successfully execute the desired strategy.

Thus, in view of increasing advancement of technology in data acquisition and innovation of research methodologies, the managers are likely to have severe competitive disadvantages if they do not prepare themselves to advance up the hierarchy in the promotion of research.

1.9.2 Nature and Scope of Business Research

The business research is a systematic enquiry with defined objectives to provide information to business managers, entrepreneurs, technocrats and the heads of business and industrial establishments to solve technical and managerial problems. As the research methods necessarily need to be scientific, the characteristics of scientific methods are naturally to be associated with research methods. The study of research methods provides necessary knowledge and skill to solve the problems associated with decision making in the business world, which often may be complex in nature. During last decades due to increased scientific thinking to solve management problems and dilemma, varied research techniques have been evolved to help technology and business growth, keeping in view the timely market strategies in the face of global competitions, the knowledge of which reach the managers through advanced communication systems, not existent in earlier decades.

The factors which characterize the complexity of business decision making environment may be summarised as follows :

- ❐ Business environment is affected by a large number of variables and interaction among them makes the decision process more complex.
- ❐ The new concepts, theories and models are being increasingly applied, besides improving the older ones.

- ❒ Competition in global business environment has increased due to changing market economy.
- ❒ The government's concern and intervention in protecting the interests of the public is sometimes becoming aggressive to reign the managers.
- ❒ Net profit generated from a business concern is being closely watched by the workers, shareholders, customers and the general public to protect their self interests.
- ❒ Increasing use of computers in data mining and data warehousing has increased the responsibility of managers to work in a complex decision making system.
- ❒ Sophisticated research methods and tools for the collection, analysis and interpretation of data are ever increasing with the advancement of scientific thinking to cope with complex business decision making scenario.
- ❒ Advancement of communication system through the use of Internet has brought vast literature on the business world to the doorsteps of the managers to expand their knowledge horizon either for adoption or improvement in new techniques to their benefits.

Any decision in a business environment is always a decision under uncertainty, impregnated with certain amount of risk. This is because the information base is normally limited and the data may also sometimes lack quality. Further, the assumed models for the analysis may not be apporpriate and far from reality. This calls for need to develop skills in applying reliable and appropriate scientific methods to managerial decision making environment to minimize risk in the system.

A manager or a business executive is often confronted with a host of interacting decision-making problems in different functional areas of management such as marketing, production, finance, personnel etc., requiring the reliable data base and efficient analytical techniques to arrive at workable and relevant solutions.

The development of the scientific method in business lags behind the researches in physical sciences. This is usually the case with researches in social sciences where unlike the physical sciences, the concepts and the procedures have not reached rigorousity and perfection to an accepted level.

Researches in management sciences have picked up only recently because of competitive situations in global market and worldwide adherence and acceptance of market economy. As the world is moving away from the concept of power blocks and threats of world wars to a more open and liberalised world system where the welfare of whole mankind is the motto, advancement in research methods are no longer confined in close doors, although openness sometimes negates competitive advantage.

Although there is growing interest in business research around the world, funds, initiatives, patronisation and development of sophisticated techniques handling uncontrolled field data, generated by a host of interacting variables are not forthcoming in a big way compared to researches in natural or physical sciences. However, business researches have promising importance in world economy and managers tend to be interested in seeking advice from the researches in their decision making process with advantages pouring down from the computerisation of huge database and advancement of computer softwares to solve intricate business problems.

1.9.3 . Types of Business Research Studies

The research process begins with the need or dilemma in the mind of a manager. The manager must be specific in his intention so as to advise the researcher clearly and unambiguously to solve the problem posed by him and also to enable him to reach a decision.

Four broad types of research studies may be initiated in a business concern. These are :

- Reporting
- Descriptive
- Explanatory
- Predictive

A reporting study may be directed by a manager to prepare an evaluative account of his establishment/firm on its various aspects of information, which may be helpful for guidance on future occasion. Such types of studies call for knowledge and skill with information sources and officials responsible for maintaining such information and records. This may not be termed 'research' as such, but has great value in supplying information at right time. Such a study has little use in drawing inferences and conclusions and provides readymade information to all sections of employees, specially to the newly recruiting ones. Besides, if a manager of a big steel plant wants to choose a firm out of a number of supply firms, the researcher may collect relevant details about the financial status, credibility, quality of materials, cost and timeliness of supply etc. for the sake of information to the manager.

Descriptive study describes a subject, people or events and their characteristics and tries to answer certain questions relating to certain units of organisation as per requirement of a researcher and may or may not have objectives or potentiality for drawing inferences. An organisation having longitudinal database on employees, products, sales customers, suppliers, etc. may also contain significant information on some research variables. It may also further enlarge its database on certain other important aspects and problems to make the manager more knowledgeable about the business concern so as to enable him to take data based decisions including incorporation of certain changes in the system. The descriptive study has an important role in business research because of its coverage and versatility across disciplines and moreover has relevant input for use in a decision-making system of administrators, policy analysts for planning, monitoring and evaluating.

Descriptive study is not a research study and does not reflect answer on **'why'** questions but may provide sufficient input for developing thought process for future research, if any. For example, for a business concern the manager may like to have a detailed descriptive account of statistics relating to marketing section of the organisation and observe occurrence of certain event and interaction between certain variables of interest. However, descriptive study does not explain why at all event has occurred and why the variables interact among themselves in the manner as abserved.

Explanatory study as the name suggests goes beyond the description aspect and attempts to explain the reasons for the observed phenomena. For instance, if the falling sales of a business concern is linked to the inability to supply the materials to smaller outlets or wholesale customer in time, the descriptive study on sales leads to explanatory study. To sum up, the explanatory study moves in the direction of using existing theories and hypothesis to explain the occurrence of certain events or phenomena and to answer **'why'** and **'how'** questions.

If the researchers, besides providing explanation for certain phenomena that has occurred, is engaged in predicting **'when'** and **'what'** situations the phenomena would occur, the explanatory study results in a **predictive study**. **The predictive study** is performed under a theoretical model which is assumed to understand and explain the real life situations as close as possible. The business forecast concerning production, price, sales, profit, etc. is necessarily an important component of any business organisation. The globalisation of economy has made the business forecast more complex and baffling in the present day scenario of the world market.

1.9.4 Limitations of Business Research

The research is always intended to provide certain information to researcher on certain objectives in his chosen field of researach. As the research investigation is to have meaningful use in practice, it needs to be conducted in a scientific way to add value to research findings. Further it must adhere to characteristics of scientific research such as systematic, controlled, empirical, critical investigation of natural phenomena, guided by theory and hypothesis about the presumed relations among the factors defining the phenomena.

Business research has been widely talked now-a-days because of market economy and competitive business environment. Research finding cannot be made very much secret in the present day world because of advancement of electronic communication media and therefore often results in loss of certain advantages.

Business research is normally a social research with man at the centre stage and hence is often concerned with human attitudes, behaviour and performance, which are changing in nature.

Natural laws cannot prevail to the same extent as in business studies because of absolute dependence on human relations and social interactions guided and influenced by social institutions, environment, changing social conditions and also varied social forces whether national or international.

Business research unlike physical research generally faces uncontrolled conditions and morever social phenomena are not always determined by laws of nature and these factors make the business forecasts subject to error. The range of possibilities using control experiments in business studies like any other social science research is very much limited as compared to biological research. The replication being one of the basic principles for designing an experiment cannot be applied in social sciences.

Observation which is pre-requisite for scientific research is more difficult in social science research as compared to natural sciences. This is primarily because the observations in social science research are often subjective in nature and largely dependent on interpretation as the part of the observer.

The interacting variables in business scenario are difficult to be understood properly because of complex human behaviour which is volatile in nature. Moreover, all social phenomena cannot be perfectly scored or quantified for statistical analysis e.g. value, motive, attitude, etc.

In business researches, generlization of the theory is difficult to be established because of changing complex economic and social scenario.

Despite afore mentioned difficulties in carrying out reseaches in business environment, sophisticated techniques are being persistently innovated to make business research more helpful to business decision makers.

1.9.5. The Manager-Researcher Relationship

The manager may not necessarily be a researcher, although a manager sometimes possess sufficient knowledge and expertise to conduct his own researches to take certain decisions. But in most cases even if the managers possess an understanding of the issues to be studied, they may not be familiar with literature on the topic or with research methodology and statistics. Further, the managers may not be as concerned as the researcher about using systematic methods or advanced analytic techniques. However, the manager has the responsibility towards the management of research process and initiating the research. If the manager himself is not a researcher or alternatively does not have either time or talent to initiate the research process, the research work may be entrusted to a research organization or some research staff recruited for the purpose.

The delegation of responsibility to outside agencies sometimes seem to be wise because the outside agencies may have better knowledge and expertise in the posed research problem or may hire the expertise partly or fully from other sister concerns to solve the research issue. In any case there ought to be close liason and healthy interaction between the research users and researchers in every aspect of research in order that conclusions and recommendations derived from research findings will be useful to the manager/decision maker.

The role of manager is to specify his research problem clearly and provide researchers with information what he thinks proper and also facilitate access to company information. Alternatively, the manager may state the problems in terms of decision choices/alternatives and leave the requirements of information to be specified by the researcher.

Also, there may be occasions when both the manager and the researcher can jointly decide what information is needed. An effective manager-researcher relationship presupposes healthy professional interaction between them, realising their respective obligations and critical barriers as regards their responsibilities. The researcher must have to understand the problem well before he attempts to find answer to business questions and in case he needs certain clarifications about the problem, he must have interaction with the manager and his supporting staff.

When the researcher is conducting research for managers, the first challenge is to turn the manager's question or issue into good research question. Conversly, when researchers are developing their own research about management and organizations, they should frame the questions to be relevant to managers, over the long, if not the short-term.

Besides analysing the data, interpreting them and having conclusions on the problem specified, the researchers should point out implications that follow from such exercises in simple, clear and unambiguous terms which the decision maker likes to have. However, sometimes the researcher fails to meet the need of the decision maker because of the inability to understand the issues involved in the problem, lack of right approach to the problem, thought processes far away from reality and inability to report in concise and simple terms besides deficiency in required knowledge under consideration. It may also happen that the manager is looking to make changes, the researcher often approaches the study to prove or disprove hypotheses to build knowledge and/or theory and may not necessarily be looking for clear and obvious answers. A partnership between the researcher and manager will help bridge the natural differences in approach.

A good manager-researcher relationship facilitates the decision making process and may be hindered due to knowledge gap between the researcher and the manager and management's lack of understanding of research techniques and their appreciation, leading to stress in the minds of managers and researcher. To get rid of such unwelcome situation, the manager has to go to search for research generalist who can understand the problem well and communicate effectively with the manager to search out his needs and translate his needs to a research problem, requiring a solution.

A researcher to deal with a business organisation is expected to understand the corporate culture and socio-political situations in which the manager has to act in an organisation and his research findings should not create internal disharmony among the persons in the managerial cadre, so that research is blocked in future.

A congenial atmosphere and good understanding are to be created between the researcher and all sections of the management cadre to make the research an on-going process for a sound decision making system.

Finally, it may not be construed that a research is always necessary for any managerial decision. Business research has its value if it helps management make better decision in the prescribed time frame. An ideal business research results in increase of efficiency of the management towards a more profitable environement and less risky and does not create any by product managerial problems and is also worth incurring cost for research, otherwise its use may be questioned by those concerned. Sometimes, the management may have insufficient resources in terms of time, money and skill to conduct an appropriate study and in such situations there are valid reasons to avoid business research.

1.10 FOUNDATIONS–BASIC CONCEPTS AND CONNECTIONS

While conducting any research we ought to know what is required to understand, explain and predict phenomena. All questions occured in a researcher's mind require the use of certain concepts, constructs and definitions. These components and their underlying connections help us to understand the theory.

1.10.1 Concepts

The **concept** originates from the idea of classifying and categorising objects and events that have common characteristics. A concept is a generally accepted abstraction (collection of meanings or characteristics) of observed events, objects, conditions, situations and behaviours.

Concepts are, so to say, mental representations and are typically based on experience. Concepts can be of real phenomena (dogs, clouds, pain). Concepts can be of agree-upon phenomena (truth, beauty, justice, prejudice, value, etc.) When events occur or certain objects, conditions and behaviour are observed we try to abstract meanings from such reality and use certain words as labels to designate them and these are concepts. For example, when a person is having certain movements, we may like to mentally represent it whether he is walking, running or skipping etc. Such a concept is abstracted from his characteristics. The concept comes to have general use after being labelled by personal experience and subsequently through shared usage.

The importance of concepts stems from the fact that **all thoughts and communications make use of concepts, although we are barely aware of problems created by them.** This is because normal human communications are difficult when people use different languages. There are certain concepts where we may all agree to meaning of such concepts as dog, table, electric bulb, telephone, etc. We may encounter difficulties when we talk of concepts like household, retail transaction, leadership, personality etc. The concepts may not have eternal meaning and may change from time to time to express new ideas. In order that people communicate freely without confusion on thought processes, the concepts should be fairly known to persons involved.

In researches, **the concepts are of utmost importance because hypotheses are built upon by using concepts and measurement. Concepts are developed to test the hypothetical statements and further data are collected using concepts.**

It is necessary that the concepts should be developed clearly and unambiguously keeping the usage in mind. The confusion in developing concepts may be narrowed down by proper specifications.

In a survey to find out total income of families in a village, it is necessary that the respondents provide information, narrowing down concepts such as :

— Time period : weekly, monthly or annually.

— Before or after deduction of taxes.

— For salary and wages only or also includes dividends, interest and capital gains.

— Income in kind such as free house, free transport, lunches, etc.

1.10.2 Constructs

Constructs are theoretical creations that are based on observations but which cannot be seen either directly or indirectly. For example, things such as IQ, Leisure satisfaction, Quality of life, Environmental value, Job interest, Language skill, Presentation quality, etc. are constructs. These are said to **be images or ideas created by researchers for research purposes to help building a theoretical model.** To exemplify the relationship between constructs and concepts, let us consider a construct 'language skill'. Language skill construct may be thought of combining concepts such as vocabulary, syntax and spelling. **A construct is used to communicate the combination of meanings presented by concepts.** The researcher/analyst uses this as a label for the totality of concepts which have been formed empirically to be related. There are certain constructs like job satisfaction which is more complex and most abstract in nature and consists of concepts which are not entirely known to the researcher. Some constructs are most concrete and related concepts can be easily measured. For instance, 'presentation quality' is a construct which may be evaluated by concepts such as format, accuracy, manuscript error and typing speed. To sum up, concepts are meanings attached to observations and constructs are combination of concepts.

However, concepts and constructs should be generally acceptable to users and researchers as forms of communication of knowledge. If the propositions specifying the connection between concepts and constructs can be supported by empirical data, the researcher may think of developing a conceptual scheme. Concepts and constructs are product of intuition, keen observation, power of abstraction and analytical mind of the researcher and play a prominent role in social science research.

1.10.3 Definitions

A researcher's study get affected if there is confusion in the meaning of concepts. Sometimes words carry different meanings to different persons and hence their communications do not result in reliable data. This necessitates definitions to reduce the danger resulting from confusion. In research we must measure concepts and constructs and this requires more rigorous definitions. **Two types of definitions** occur in the minds of researchers.

- **Conceptual (theoretical) :** the words used in a theory; basically dictionary or common use.
- **Operational :** a definition that is stated in terms of measurement criteria for the characteristics, that is, how they are to be observed.

There are two types of operational definitions :

- **Directly measured :** IQ, weight, attitude.
- **Experimental :** the details of how subjects are treated differently, such as aggresive behaviour, frustrations, etc.

Operational definitions vary depending on purpose and the way we choose to measure the objects. For examples, definition is required for the physical objects like machine tool would be difficult from a highly abstract one like achievement motivation. It is important that the specification and procedures must be so clear and unambiguous that any qualified investigator would classify them in a similar manner.

Suppose we want, to classify workers according to status. Then, you merely ask their levels in the management and record it. You may also classify them according to their annual salary.

While dealing with operational definitions, one must not confuse it with concept or construct. Definition only provides limited insight into the object whereas concept or construct goes into something more concrete and deeper in meaning. However the problem of operational definition seems to be difficult when dealing with construct, which consists of a number of empirical referents. It is necessary to confirm whether the operational definition for a construct really measures what is intended to be measured. Thus, whether it is theoretical definition or operational definition, the purpose in research is basically the same, that is, it provides an understanding and measurement of concepts and constructs.

1.10.4 Variables

Variable is a measurable concept or construct or entity which varies and is assigned numerals or values.

- ❒ Variables may be either defined by conceptual definitions that explain the concept the variable is attempting to capture or operational definitions, that is, how the variable will be measured in practice.
- ❒ Variable is a lable or name that represents a concept or characteristic that varies (gender, weight, achievement, attitude, etc.)
- ❒ Variables are properties or characteristics of some event or object of person that can take different values or amounts and are the operationally defined measures of the concepts of a theory.

Objects are usually not considered as variables–but their characteristics are. As an example, transparency is not a variable (it is an object). The characteristics of the transparency are variables, *e.g.* colour, design, etc.

Consider the variable 'work effort' which can be defined conceptually as the amount of effort required to do the work, indicated by speed, hardness, effort, dexterity, repetitiveness, etc. Each of these aspects must have an operational definition, if it is to be measured.

A variable which is assigned with one unchanged value is termed as a constant. For example, annual income of a particular person Mr. X is a constant, but the annual income of families in a village is a variable, because it is likely to vary from one family to another.

A variable cannot always take indefinite values.

Broadly, a variable may be classified as :

- ❒ Discrete/discontinuous variable
- ❒ Continuous variable.

A discrete variable is assigned only with some specified values, for instance, the number of employees in business establishments, number of children in families, etc.

A continuous variable takes values within a given range/interval or in some cases an infinite set (*e.g.* income, expenditure, height, weight, etc.)

Some variables are quite concrete as height, weight, etc. and some can be more abstract like sense of well being, self esteem, strength of belief, IQ, etc.

Also, **variables are not always quantitative or numerical.** It may also be qualitative. The variable gender is a dichotomous qualitative variable having two attributes (text values)–male and female. **An attribute is a specific value on a variable**. If necessary, for ease in representation and analysis we may assign numerical values/codes (*e.g.* 0 and 1 or any two numerics) to the text values. The numerical codes have no other significance except identification (presence or absence) of the attribute. Dichotomous variable may be treated as nominal, however sometimes an ordinal quality may exist.

Examples : Gender-male, female; Race-black, white ; Agreement-yes, no; T/F-True, False; Value-high, low, etc.

Other dichotomous variables may be employment status, literary status, health status, etc. There may be polytomous variable : the variable 'agreement' might be defined as having five attributes

- 1 : strongly disagree
- 2 : disagree
- 3 : neutral

- 4 : agree
- 5 : strongly agree.

The variable educational status might be defined with

- 1 : Illiterate
- 2 : Below matriculation
- 3 : Matriculation
- 4 : Graduate
- 5 : Post-graduate

Discrete variables are also called **categorical variables.** A discrete variable can take a finite number of numerical values, categories, rankes, codes, etc. Nominal variables allowing only qualitative classification such as sex, marital status, when coded arbitrarily, are discrete variables. Ordered values of a variable in a meaningful sequence also give rise to discrete variable, such as socio-economic status–very low, low, medium, great, very great.

A quantitative variable can be transformed into a categorical variable called **dummy variable** by classifying the values of the variable into intervals. For example,

Monthly Income	***Code***
Below Rs 10,000	1
Rs 10,000–Rs. 20,000	2
Rs. 20,000–Rs. 40,000	3
Above Rs. 40,000	4

Continuous variable may be either interval scale or ratio scale variable.

As continuous variable is only measured in an interval, it can never be exactly measured and we can never be sure that the value we observed is correct. When we measure a person's height, we may only be able to measure to the nearest half centimetre. The true limits of a continuous variable are the values between which the reported value must fall. So determine the true limits, determine the unit of measure (how accurately one can measure). The true limits are then given by the observed value $\pm \frac{1}{2}$ (unit of measure). Continuuous variable falls along a continum and is not limited to a certain number of values. It has an infinite range of values between any two points.

• Independent and dependent variables

Researcher come across a number of variables either discrete or continuous in course of their studies. Naturally they are interested to know whether some relationships exist among these variables to throw light on certain proposition. Most researchers deal with at least two variables–one independent (IV) and the other dependent variable (DV). Independent variable is also termed as predictor (the presumed cause) and the dependent variable (the presumed effect).

Variables are not inheretly independent or dependent. In discreptive and exploratory studies, this distinction is not made.

The independent variable is that variable which the experimenter manipulates. But this is not true always because not all studies are experiments. Instead we merely collect data and observe how variables are related to each other.

The dependent variable is not necessarily caused by the independent variable. For instance, the height of a person is not necessarily always affected by the height of his father, because it may be affected by genetic factors and heights of forefathers, mother, etc

As the independent variable by virture of its relationship with the dependent variable explains the variation in DV, the independent variable is also called **explanatory variable.** In contrast, the DV is what we are studying, with respect to how it is related to or influenced by the IV or how it can be explained or predicted by the IV, it is sometimes called **response variable** or **criterion variable.**

The notions of indepedence and dependence getting into relationship between two variables put a researcher in a dilemma to take a logical decision depending on his imagination, empirical behaviour and natural conviction as to which variable is to be labelled as independent and which one is dependent. Sometimes, the researcher is faced with a symmetrical relationship, where the question of which is IV and which is DV is moot *e.g.* demand and price.

Moderating variable is a second independent variable which is thought to have some significant contribution to the relationship between one dependent variable and one independent variable. In a study of relationship between length of work week (four or five days a week) (IV) and the productivity (DV) we may like to know whether age difference among workers brings about differential patterns of relationship. In this case age of workers is a **moderating** variable.

Intervening variable is defined as a variable, which theoretically affects the observed phenomena, but cannot be seen, measured or manipulated and its effect is to be inferred from the effects of independent variable on the observed phenomena. For instance, job satisfaction may be treated as an intervening variable in the study of the effect of week length on the productivety

Control variables : Any variable that may affect DV should be controlled, that is measured and accounted for statistically or held constant (for example age, gender, socio-economic status, etc. could be control variables).

Confounding Variable

A confounding variable is an extraneous variable. It is a risk factor for the outcome variable and is associated with the predictor variable.

1.10.5 Measurement

Measurement is the assignment of numbers to things and expressed as a quantity. As a verb, measurement is making such observation. Measurement is fundamental in science. It is one of the things that distinguish science from psuedo science. Measurement is also essential in industry, commerce, engineering, construction, manufacturing, electronics, etc.

When you measure 'what are speaking about' and express it in numbers, you know something about it, but when you cannot express it in numbers, your knowledge is of a meagre and unsatisfactory kind, it may be beginning of knowledge, but you have scarcely in your thoughts advanced to the state of science (Lord Kelvin).

Measurement includes estimation of physical quantity such as distance, energy, temperature, time etc. It could also include such things as assessment of aptitudes, values, perceptions in survreys or testing aptitudes of individuals.

Measurement is the **process of observing and recoding the observations** that are collected as a part of research efforts. It is the assignment of numerals/symbols/numbers to observable phenomena according to rules. We can then carry out basic quantitative operations on these measurements such as counting. The nature of operations we can carry out will depend on the scale of measurement involved.

The result of a measurement is a **label/number** that reduces the uncertainty about the object. Thus, infact, we measure the values of a variable (characteristic) according to a rule. Objects are not variable, but their characteristics are.

Precision and exactness in measurement are vitally important. The measures are what are actually used to test hypotheses. A researcher needs good measures for both independent and dependent variables.

Measurement consists of two basic processes called **conceptualization** and **operationalization,** then an advanced process called determining the levels of measurement, and then even more advanced methods of measuring reliability and validity.

Four major levels/scales of measurement

- Nominal
- Ordinal
- Interval
- Ratio

Measuring Instruments

- Questionnaire
- Scales

Requirements for measuring devices

- Valid
- Reliable
- Precise

In order that the device is to be **valid,** it should measure what it purports to measure.

An instrument of measurement is said to **reliable** if the independent and comparable measures of the same object give similar results, provided the object being measured does not undergo change in between the measurements.

The measuring device is **precise** if it is capable of making distinctions in certain characteristics of objects.

Three kinds of phenomena requiring measurement

- Constants
- Variables
- Concepts or constructs

Three ways of measuring things

- Counting
- Ordering
- Classifying

Four broad categories of measurement used in social research :

Survey research. This includes the design and implementation of interviews and questionnaires.

Scaling. This involves consideration of major methods of developing and implementing a scale.

Qualitative research. This provides an overview of the boad range of non-numerical measurement approaches.

Unobtrusive measures. This provides a variety of measurement methods that do not intrude on or interfere with the context of research.

Three classes of things which can be measured :

- **direct** observables (height, weight, colour, etc.)
- **indirect** observables (through questionnaires that provide information on gender, age, income etc.)
- ***Constructs*** (e.g. IQ, leisure satisfaction, environemental values, etc.)

Conceptualization and Operationalization :

Conceptualization is the process of taking a raw idea and giving it a conceptual (or theoretical) definition.

- ***Conceptual definition***

❐ Defining ideas by using concepts

❐ Concepts : The unobservable properties of ideas.

For example, let us consider the idea 'participation'.

❐ [***General idea***] = Those activities by individual/group aimed at influencing a larger body/government.

❐ [***Conceptual definition***] = Voter turn out in the 2004 Parliament election.

The researchers take key words in their research question/hypothesis and finds a clear and consistent definition that is agreed upon by others in the scientific community. Conceptualization is often guided by the theoretical framework, perspectives, or approach the researcher is committed to. For example, a researcher having strong belief in marxism would have quite different conceptual definition for a hypothesis about social class than a non-marxist researcher.

Operationalization is the process of taking a conceptual definition and making it more precise by linking it to an operational definition.

- ***Operational definition.***

❐ ***Links :*** concepts to variables

❐ ***Variables :*** The observable properties of concepts.

EXAMPLE : Participation

[Conceptual definition] = Voter turnout in 2004 election.

[Operational definition] = The number of people who actually vote in 2004.

Operational definitions are usually things with numbers in them that reflect empirical or observable reality.

To sum up, **measurement is the assigment of values (not necessarily numbers) to empirical properties of concepts according to rules.**

What purposes does it serve ?

- Provides a set of procedures that tell us how to observe data.
- Bridges gap between theoretical concepts and empirical variables.

1.10.6 Levels of Measurement

When we observe and record a variable, it has characteristic that influence in determining what kinds of tools may be used to describe the variable, and what type of analysis may be used for inference about the variable. These characteristics are referred to as the levels/scales of measurement of the variable. In short, the level of measurement determines or constraints the types of descriptive and inferential statistics that may be applied to the variable. This refers to whether a particular measure permits one to perform mathematical operations on it. It specifies rules that define permissible mathematical operations that can be performed on a set of numbers produced by a measure.

The measuring instruments are scales. The scaling is the process of measuring or ordering entities with respect to quantitative attributes or traits. Certain methods of scaling permit estimation of magnitudes on a continuum, while other methods provide only the relative ordering of the entities.

Exactly how the measurement is carried out depends on the type of variable involved in the analysis. Different types of variable are measured differently. Thus, procedures for measurement or the process of assignment of numbers to data can be classified into four fundamental categories called **scale types** or just scales. These are also called four levels of measurement, associated with different types of variables, and also four ways of assigning numbers to data. All variables can be measured at one or more of four levels of measurement.

Stevens proposed four levels/scales of measurement.

The typology of measurement levels is such that

(*i*) anything that can be measured falls into one of the four types

(*ii*) the higher the type, the more precision in measurement and

(*iii*) every level up contains all the properties of the previous level.

The four levels/scale of measurement from lowest to highest are :

- Nominal (Nominal scale)
- Ordinal (Ordinal scale)
- Interval (Interval scale)
- Ratio (Ratio scale)

with associated variables termed as ***Nominal, Ordinal, Interval and Ratio variables***

Since, the results of measurement are observations (data), depending on the scale of measurement we may also **classify data** as

- Nominal data (measured at nominal level)
- Ordinal data (measured at ordinal level)
- Interval data (measured at interval level)
- Ratio data (measured at ratio level)

• Nominal measurement

The nominal level of measurement occurs when the observations do not have a meaningful numeric value, *e.g.* Hair colour, gender, religion, etc.

Names are assigned to objects as labels. Those names come from a given small set and are meant to identify categories used for classifying the data. They are the 'variable values'. For practical data processing the names may be numerals.

No quantitative information is conveyed by nominal measurement. Nominal scales are therefore qualitative rather than quantitative (*e.g.* religion, race, gender etc.).

Variables measured on a nominal scale are often referred to ***categorical or qualitative variables.***

No form of mathematical operations may be performed on nominal measures.

With a nominal measurement scale, there is no relative ordering of the categories–the assignment of numeric scores to each category, say in case of gender, Male = 0 and Female = 1, is purely arbitrary.

Nominal scale is the lowest level of measurement, only meant for categorising.

Nominal variables may be coded with numbes, but the magnitude of the number assigned is arbitrary. Changing the coding scheme will not change inference.

• Ordinal Measurement

Ordinal variables are used to represent observations that can be categorized and rank ordered.

The numbers assigned to objects represent the rank order (1st, 2nd, 3rd etc.) of the entities measured. The numbers are called ***ordinals.*** The concerned variables called ***ordinal or rank variables.*** Comparisons of greater and less can be made, in addition to equality and inequality. However, operations such as conventional addition and subtraction are still meaningless. Grades (A, B, C, D, E, F) referring to quality of material, examination scores are also ordinal measurements.

Measurements with ordinal scales are ordered in the sense that higher numbers represent higher scale values. However, the intervals between the numbers are not necessarily equal. For instance, suppose the marks secured by 4 students are 87, 65, 55, 25, which are ranked as 1st, 2nd, 3rd, and 4th. But the difference between marks secured by 1st and 2nd rank holders is not the same as the difference between marks secured by 2nd and 3rd rank holders. Rankings reflect more or less of something, but not how much more or less.

Nominal and ordinal variables together are called categorical variables because they classify into categories rather than count or measure.

When we assign numbers, to rank-ordered categories ranging from Low to High, we have an ordinal variable. For instance, soical class is an example of an ordical variable. Individuals can be classified with respect to their social class status as 'upper class', 'middle class' or 'working' class. We can say that a person in the category 'upper class' has a higher class status than a person in a 'middle class category, but we do not know the magnitude of the difference between between the categories, that is, we do not know how much higher,'upper class' is compared to 'middle class'. A student's level of standing freshman, junior and senior is ordinal. ***Subtraction cannot be done and distance does not make sense, like the classification according to social status.***

A researcher wishing to measure consumers' satisfaction with their microwave ovens might ask them to specify their feelings as either 'very dissatisfied', 'somewhat dissatisfied', somewhat satisfied' or 'very satisfied'. The items in this scale are ordered, ranging from least to most satisfied. This is what distinguishes ordinal from nominal scales. Unlike nominal scales, ***ordinal scales allow comparisions of the degree to which subjects possess the dependent variable.***

Further, consider a five point rating scale measuring attitude. The difference between a rating of 2 and a rating of 3 may not represent the same difference as the difference between a rating of 4 and a rating of 5. ***'here is no true zero point for ordinal scale since the zero point is chosen arb.'rarily.*** The lowest point on the rating scale is sometimes chosen to be 1. But it could also be 0 or –5.

• Interval Measurement

The numbers assigned to objects have all the features of ordinal measurements and in addition equal differences between measurements represent equivalent interval. That is, difference between arbitrary pairs of measurements can be meaningfully compared. ***The zero point is arbitrary. Ratios between numbers on the scale are not meaningful, so operations such as multiplication and division cannot be carried out directly.***

Variables measured at the interval level are called interval variables. Examples of interval measures are temperature in Celsius/Fahrenheit scale, constructed measures such as standardized intelligence tests (IQ). The interval measurement scale does not have a 'zero' value. In the Fahrenheit scale, for instance, 'zero' degrees does not mean there is no heat at all. Equal differences on this scale represent equal differences in temeprature, but a temperature of 30 degrees is **not** twice as warm as one of 15 degrees. GPA (Grade point average) is an interval measurement. Substraction can be done and distance makes sense. The distance between GPA 2.3 and 2.4 is the same distance as between 3.7 and 3.8. Ratios do not make sense because 4.0 is not twice as high as 2.0.

To sum up, the interval variables represent observations that can be categorized, rank ordered and have a unit of measure (implies that the difference between any two successive values is identical, *e.g.* shoe size, IQ score, Fahrenheit etc.) Further with an interval scaled variable, the value 0 does not represent the complete absence of the variable.

• Ratio Measurement

The numbers assigned to objects have all the features of interval measurement and also have ***meaningful ratios between arbitrary pairs of numbers.*** Operations such as multiplication and division are therefore meanigful. The ***zero value on a ratio scale is non-arbitrary. Variables measured at the ratio level are called ratio variables.*** Thus, Ratio variables represent observations that can be categorized, rank ordered, ***have an unit of measure and have a true zero.***

Most physical quantities, such as mass, length, or energy are measured on ratio scale. Social variables of ratio measure include age, length of residence in a given place, number of social/business organizations at a given time, etc. In social research most 'count' variables are ratio. Credit hours attended by a student for an acadmic course is a ratio measurement. A student who has completed 90 credit hours has twice as many as 45 credit hours. Zero credit hours completed by a student is meaningful.

Since in ratio measurement there is always an absolute zero (that is, natural zero point) that is meaningful, we can construct meaningful fraction (ratio) with a ratio variable.

Ratio measurement is said to be the highest level of measurement. Interval and Ratio variables are called **numerical variables** because they provide a 'number' which measures quantity (how much, how many) of something.

It is important to note that there is a hierarchy implied in the level of measurement idea. At lower levels of mesurement, assumptions tend to be less restrictive and data analyses tend to be less sensitive. In practice it is desirable to have a higher level of measurement (*e.g.* interval or ratio) rather than a lower one (nominal or ordinal).

Thus the hierarchy may be described as follows :

Ratio	Absolute zero . Distance is Meaningful. Fraction (ratio) is meaningful.
Interval	Distance is meaningful. Arbitrary zero point. Ratio has no meaning.
Ordinal	Attributes/characteristics can be ranked ordered, but not distance.
Nominal	Attributes are only named. No ordering. No distance

Why is level of measurement important ?

With the knowledge about the level of measurement one decides how to interpret data statistically from that variable.

Higher the level of measurement of a variable, the more powerful are the statistical techniques that can be used to analyse it. For instance, when you know that a measure is nominal, then you know that the numerical values are just codes for the names. Secondly, the knowlege of the level of measurement helps choosing an appropriate statistical analysis on the values that are assigned. For instance, if a measure is nominal, one would never try to average the data values or apply any statistical test on the data.

The four levels of measurement can usually be classified as follows :

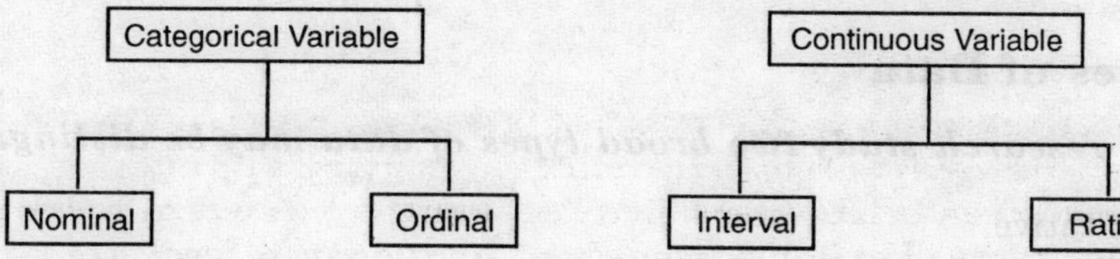

Level of measurement provides a framework for interpreting the categories of a variable. It tells us what sort of inferences we can make about cases assigned to different cateogries.

1.10.7 Validity and Reliability

Validity and reliability answer the question

How good are your measures ?

What is validity ?

- When a variable accurately/truthfully/correctly measures what it is supposed to measure.

What purpose does it serve ?

- Checks (theoretically) the correspondence between the measures we create and the concepts we are interested in .

What is reliability ?

- When a variable yields consistently similar results upon repeated tests.
- Can occur over time, across different situations, or between different instruments.

What purpose does it serve ?

- Checks (statistically) the performance of a measure.

Threats to validity :

- Systematic error
- ***Constant*** across the administration of a measurement instrument.
- Participant bias
- Researcher's bias
- Faulty design

Threats to reliability :

- Random Error
- Varies acrose the administration of a measurement instrument
- Setting
- Mood
- Data Entry

When dealing with measurement error it may be pointed out that random error is unavoidable, but systematic error can be controlled. The researcher when minimizing measurement error should see that random error does not exceed the systematic error.

1.10.8 Types of Data

In any research study two broad types of data may be distinguished :

- Qualitative
- Quantitative

If the data are in numerical form, it is said to be quantitative and if it is not, this is qualitative. There have been protracted arguments in favour of qualitative and quantitative data. The quantitative supporters argue that their data are hard, rigorous, credible and scientific. The qualitative proponents counter that their data is 'sensitive', 'nuanced', 'detailed', and 'contextual'. However, it may not be overlooked that qualitative and quantitative data are intimately related to each other. That is, all quantitative data are based upon qualitative judgements and all qualitative data can be described and manipulated numerically. For instance, consider a very common quantitative measure in social research–self esteem scale.

To develop such instruments the researcher has to make a number of judgements in constructing them :

- ❒ how to define self esteem ?
- ❒ how to distinguish them from other related concepts ?
- ❒ how to word potential scale items ?
- ❒ how to make sure the items to be understandable to the intended respondents ?
- ❒ what kind of contexts it could be used ?
- ❒ what kinds of cultural and language constraints might be present ?

The researchers using a scale should make judgements as to :

- ❒ how well does the scale measure the intended concept ?
- ❒ how reliable or consistent is it ?
- ❒ how appropriate is it for the research context and intended respondents ?

The respondents also make many judgements when filling out such a scale as regards their understanding of the phrases and words, need of the scale, time and energy at their disposal, etc.

The afore mentioned discussions indicate that however simple and straightforward the quantitative measure may seem, it is actually based on a number of qualitative judgements, made by different sections of people.

Collection of relevant data is crucial for testing research hypotheses and questions. No matter how well thought out the other aspects of study design are, if there are bias or errors in data collection or inappropriate data are collected, the study will lack scientific validity. Related to data collection are also issues of electronic data base design, entry, management and conversion to formats readable by statistical and other analytical software.

A common mistake usually made by inexperienced and not so knowledgeable investigators is the a prior failure to understand data types and their relationship to the

- ❒ research hypothesis/question being proposed and the
- ❒ best statistical methods used to test this hypothesis/question.

Thus, it calls for a worth while look at data types from two perspectives such as measurement and statistical analytic models. Measurement data type of qualitative nature includes nominal and ordinal scaled data (*e.g* Nominal qualitative data : 0 = Male, 1 = Female; Ordinal qualitative data : 1 = Illiterate, 2 = Below matriculation, 3 = Above matriculation).

Quantitative data relate to interval and ratio seated variable and may be either quantitative discontinuous such as number of ridges of finger tips or quantitative continuous such as stature = 165.2534 cm, weight = 92.23 kg etc. The metric measurements constitute quantitative data.

ILLUSTRATION : Determination of level of measurement of variables and data types (qualitative or quantitative)

Variable	Type	Level of measurement
Age	quantitative	ratio
Disposable income	quantitative	ratio
Sex	qualitative	nominal
Performance at school	quantitative	ordinal
Religious affiliation	qualitative	nominal
Body temperature	quantitative	interval

Properties of levels of data

Nominal. Classifies objects by type or characteristic (gender, models of vehicle etc.)

- ❒ categories are mutually exclusives
- ❒ no logical order.

Ordinal. Classifies objects by type or kind but also has order (military rank, letter grades etc.)

- ❒ cateogories are mutually exclusive
- ❒ logical order exists
- ❒ scaled according to amount of a particular characteristic it possesses.

Interval. Classified by type, logical order, but also requires differences between levels of a category are equal. (degrees in celsius, distance in kilometres, age in years)

- ❒ categories are mutually exclusive
- ❒ logical order exists
- ❒ scaled according to amount of a particular characteristic it possesses.
- ❒ differences between each level are equal
- ❒ no zero starting point.

Ratio. Same as interval, but has a true zero starting point (weight, length, age, etc.)

1.10.9 Deduction and Induction

In logic there are **two broad methods of reasoning** as the deductive and inductive approaches.

Deductive reasoning works from the more general to the more specific–informally called a 'top-down' approach. We might begins with thinking up a **theory** about our topic of interest. We then narrow down into more specific **hypothesis** that we can test. We narrow down even further when we collect **observations** to address the hypotheses. This ultimately leads to testing a hypothesis with specific data a **confirmation** (or not) of our original theories. Thus,

Theory → Hypothesis → Observation → Confirmation

Inductive reasoning works the other way, moving from specific observations to broader generalizations and theories. Informally we call this as 'bottom-up' apporach. In inductive reasoning we begin with specific observations and measures being to detect patterns and regularities, formulate some tentative hypotheses that we can explain, and finally end up developing some general conclusions or theories. Thus, in inductive reasoning

Observations → Pattern → Tentative hypothesis → Theory.

Inductive reasoning, by its very nature, is more open-ended and exploratory, especially at the beginning. Deductive reasoning is more narrow in nature and is concerned with testing or confirming hypothesis. Even though a particular hypothesis looks like purely deductive (*e.g.* an experiment designed to test the hypothesized effects of some treatment or some outcome), most social research involves both inductive and deductive reasoning processes at same time in the project.

1.10.10 Unit of Analysis

The unit of analysis is the major entity that is being analyzed in the study. It is the 'What' or 'Whom' that is being studied. In social science research, the most typical units of analysis are individual people. Other units of analysis can be groups (families, couples, classroom) social organizations (society, community) industrial/ business establishments, educational institutions (college, university), artifacts (books, photos, news papers etc), geographical units (towns, census wards, state), social interactions, social artifacts (speeches, plays). This is not to be confused with the unit of observation, which is the unit on which the researcher collects data. For example, a study may have unit of observation at the individual level but may have the unit of analysis at the neighbourhood level, drawing conclusions on neighbourhood characteristics from data collected from individuals. The type of analysis a researcher does in his studies determines the unit of analysis. If we have achievement scores of students in an educational institution and interested in comparing individual performances of students, the unit of analysis is the individual student. On the other hand, if we are interested in comparing performances in two classes, the unit of analysis is the group (the class room). In this case data that goes into analysis is the average (average performance) itself, and not the individuals' scores). That is, even though we have the data at the student level, we use aggregates/averages in the analysis and thus the unit of analysis is the group. In many social science researches hierarchies of analysis units have become usual phenomena, thus bringing hierachical modelling into the realm of statistical analysis.

1.10.11 Concept Mapping

Social scientists have developed a number of methods and processes that might be useful in helping to formulate a research project such as brain storming, nominal group techniques, focus groups, delphi techniques, etc. Concept mapping is yet another method, which is specially useful for research problem formulation. It is a structured process that can be used to help an individual or a group to describe their ideas about some topic in a pictorial form.

Although concept mapping is a general method, it is particularly useful for helping social researcher and research teams develop and detail ideas for research. It is especially valuable when the researchers want to involve relevant stakeholder groups in the act of creating the research project. In recent years concept mapping is used for many purposes such as strategic planning, product development, market analysis, measurement development etc.

What is a concept map ?

Concept mapping is a technique for visualizing the relationships among different concepts.

A **concept map** is a hierarchical diagram showing the relationship among a set of concepts. Concepts are connected with labelled arrows, in a downward-branching hierarchical structure. The relationship between concepts is articulated/explained in linking phrases/descriptive, words such as 'gives rise to' 'results in' or 'contributes to', etc. Thus, concept maps are spatial representation of ideas and their inter-relationships. The technique of concept mapping was first developed by Joseph D. Novak in 1970's and his research team at the Cornell University as a means of representing the emerging science knowlege of students. It has been subsequently been used as tool to increase meaningful learning in the sciences and other subjects as well as to represent the expert knowledge of individuals and teams in education, government and business.

Concept maps have their origin in the learning movement called constructivism, that is, 'learners actively construct knowlege'. Novak's work is based on cognitive theories of David Ausbel (assimilation theory) who stressed the importance of prior knowledge in being able to learn new concepts. In his book 'Learning to learn' Novak states that meaningful learning involves the association of new concepts and propositions into existing cognitive structures.

Concept mapping is a very useful tool for learning from written material.

While concept mapping requires significant time, it has benefits :

- ❐ outstanding tool for extracting knowledge
- ❐ creates great notes for later review
- ❐ reduces stress of learning.

Advantages of Concept Mapping

Visual representation has several advantages :

- ❐ Visual symbols are quickly and easily recognised
- ❐ Minimum use of text makes it easy to scan for a word, phrase or the general idea
- ❐ Visual representation allows for development of a holistic understanding that words alone cannot convey.
- ❐ Concept mapping helps represent the available information visually in a comprehensive clear manner. This is an easy way to gather and communicate information.
- ❐ Concept maps harness the power of our vision to understand complex information at-a-glance. The primary function of the brain is to interpret incoming information to make meaning, when information is presented in visual formats. This is why, a picture is worth a thousand words.

Using Concept Mapping

Concept mapping is a good method to organize information about a specific subject or problem. It arranges the existing information, in a form, of a web diagram, or 'concept map'. Typically a concept map consists of concepts enclosed in circles or boxes called nodes, linked by lines or arrows that may be labeled and illustrate relationships between concepts. The information structured in a concept map is more easily accessible; it can be quickly understood and shared with others. Concept map is an easy way to handle complex information. When starting to construct a concept map, it is important to define one or more central, most inclusive concepts for a certain problem or situation. This concept should be placed at the top of the map. More specific concepts should be arranged in the hierarchical fashion below the key concept.

After the preliminary concept map is constructed, it should be revised several times to arrive at a comprehensive structrue containing a number of principal and subordinate concepts with explicit links showing in which way the concepts are related to each other.

Concept maps are widely used in education and business for :

- Note taking and summarizing gleaning key concepts, their relationships and hierarchy from documents and source materials.
- New knowlege creation *e.g.*, transforming tacit knowledge into an organizational resource, mapping team knowledge.
- Institutional knowledge preservation (retention), e.g., eliciting and mapping expert knowledge of employees prior to retirement.
- Collaborative knowledge modeling and the transfer of expert knowlege.
- Facilitating the creation of shared vision and shared understanding within a team or organization.
- Instructional design : concept maps used as Ausubelian "advance organizers" which provide an initial conceptual frame for subsequent information and learning.
- Training : concept maps used as Ausubelian "advanced organizers" to represent the training context and its relationship to their jobs, to the organization's strategic objectives, to training goals.
- Increasing meaningful learning :
- Communicating complex ideas and arguments.
- Examining the symmetry of complex ideas and arguments and associated terminology :
- Detailing the entire structrue of an idea, train of thought, or line of argument (with the specific goal of exposing faults, errors, or gaps in one's own reasoning) for the scrutiny of others.
- Enhancing metacognition (learning to learn, and thinking about knowlege)
- Improving language ability
- Assessing learner understanding of learning objectives, concepts, and the relationship among those concepts

Construction of Concept Map

Concept mapping is a technique that allows the researcher to understand the relationships between ideas by creating a visual map of the connections. Concept maps allow the reaseacher.

- to see the connections between ideas the reasearcher already possesses.
- to connect new ideas to knowledge that the researcher already possesses.
- to organize ideas in a logical but not rigid structure that allows future information or viewpoints to be included.

Concept mapping looks like clustering (a type of free writing that is almost completely unstructured that works by free association), but it goes one step forward by revealing a clear relationship between the ideas that the researcher is writing about . It allows the researcher to see more complex relationships between ideas than just sequence and hierarchy.

To create a concept map, the researcher should first read widely on the research subject until he can list 10-15 key concepts or ideas and several examples. A concept is an abstract idea that is not limited to one place or time. An example is one instance of a concept. The following steps allow the researcher to build a concept map.

It may be remembered that one can create many different maps from the same list, depending on how the researcher interpret the relationships between ideas.

1. Transfer the concepts and examples to small pieces of paper.
2. Arrange the pieces of paper on a large sheet of paper or poster board, with the broadest or most abstract ideas at the top and the most specific ideas at the bottom. Do not include the examples yet.
3. If possible, arrange the concepts so that ideas go directly under ideas that they are related to (often this is not possible because ideas relate to several other concepts). At this point, you may wish to add concepts that help explain, connect, or expand the ideas that the researcher has.
4. Draw lines from upper concepts to lower concepts that they are related to, do the same for any related concepts that are on the same level. The researcher may decide to rearrange the pieces of paper during this stage.
5. The most important and most difficult step is about connecting lines, write words or phrases that explain relationship of the concepts.
6. Put the examples under the concepts they belong with, and conncet the concept to the example with a phrase like for example.

Applications of Concept Mapping

1. Creative Tool. Drawing a concept map can be compared to participating in a brainstorming session. As one puts ideas down on paper without criticism, the ideas become clearer and the mind becomes free to receive new ideas. These new ideas may be linked to ideas already on the paper, and they may also trigger new associations leading to new ideas.

2. Hypertext Design tool. As the World Wide Web becomes an increasing powerful and ubiquitous medium for disseminating information, writers must move from writing text in linear fashion to creating hypertext documents with links to other documents. The structural correspondence between hypertext design and concept maps makes concept mapping a suitable tool for designing the conceptual structure of hypertext.

3. Communication tool. A concept map produced by one person represents one possible way to structure information on ideas. A concept produced by a group of people represents the ideas of the group. Thus, concept mapping can be used as a communication tool for people to use to discuss concepts and the relationships between the concepts.

4. Learning tool. Novak's original work with concept mapping dealt with learning. Constructivist learning theory argues that new knowledge should be integrated into existing structures in order to be remembered and receive meaning. Concept mapping is also gaining inroads as a tool for problem solving in education.

5. Assessment tool. Concept maps can also be used as assessment tools. The research team of Novak found that an important by-product of concept mapping is its ability to detect or illustrate the 'misconceptions' learners may have as explanation of content matter.

EXAMPLE 1. (Concept Mapping page -McKenzie's Home Page)

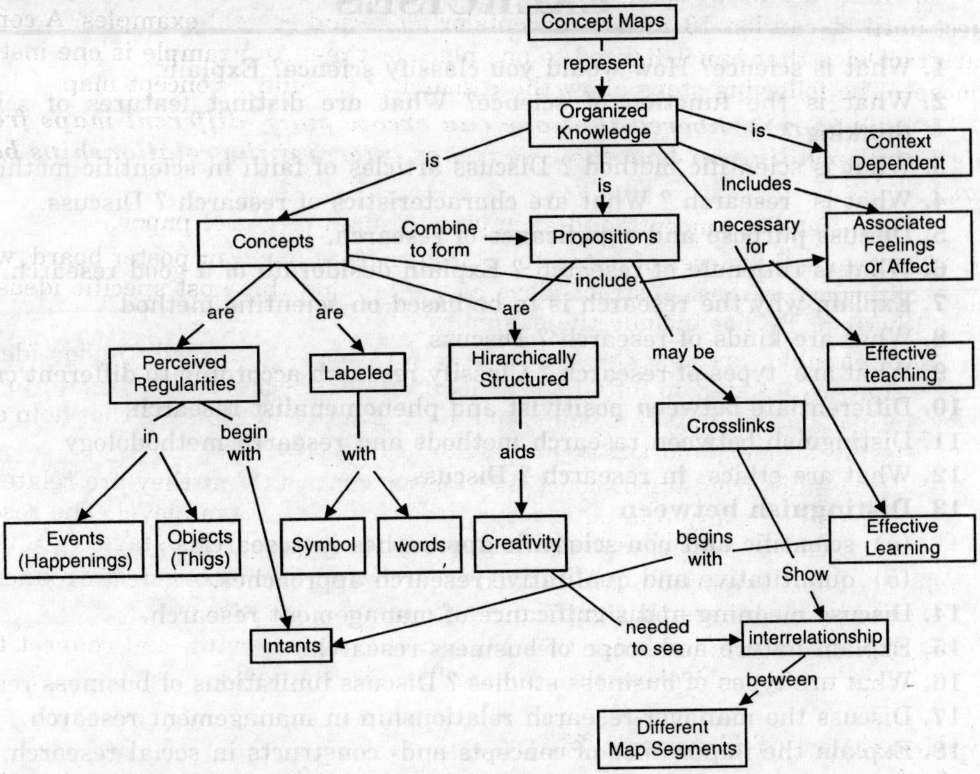

EXAMPLE 2. (Concept Mapping page-McKenzie's Home page)

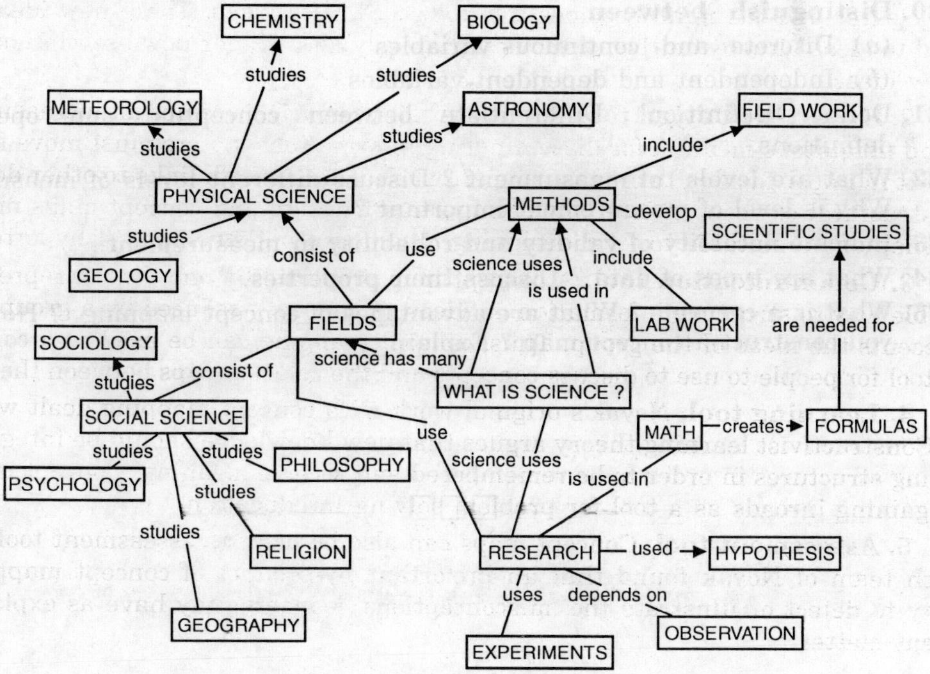

EXERCISES

1. What is science? How would you classify science? Explain.
2. What is the function of science? What are distinct features of scientific thinking ?
3. What is scientific method ? Discuss articles of faith in scientific method.
4. What is research ? What are characteristics of research ? Discuss.
5. Discuss purpose and significance of research.
6. What is rationale of research ? Explain desiderata of a good research.
7. Explain why the research is to be based on scientific method.
8. What are kinds of research ? Discuss.
9. What are types of research ? Classify research according to different criteria.
10. Differentiate between positivist and phenomenalist research.
11. Distinguish between research methods and research methodology.
12. What are ethics in research ? Discuss.
13. **Distinguish between**
    (*a*) scientific and non-scientific approaches in research.
    (*b*) quantitative and qualitative research approaches.
14. Discuss meaning and significance of management research.
15. Explain nature and scope of business research.
16. What are types of business studies ? Discuss limitations of business research.
17. Discuss the manager-research relationship in management research.
18. Explain the importance of concepts and constructs in social research.
19. Define variable and measurement. What are different types of variable ? Discuss.
20. **Distinguish between**
    (*a*) Discrete and continuous variables
    (*b*) Independent and dependent variables
21. Define 'Definition'. Differentiate between conceptual and operational definitions.
22. What are levels of measurment ? Discuss different levels of measurement. Why is level of measurement important ?
23. Indicate necessity of validity and reliability in measurement.
24. What are types of data ? Discuss their properties.
25. What is a concept ? What are advantages of concept mapping ? How would you construct a concept map ? Explain.

□□□

CHAPTER

2

THE RESEARCH PROCESS

2.1. INTRODUCTION :

The research process in social science researches is a sequential process involving a series of well defined steps. It is not necessary that each step should be completed before the next step is taken into action. The researcher before carrying out research at the behest of the manager/sponsoring authority or in his own interest should be clear about the purpose and objectives and then define a problem seeking solution and develop strategies for the same.

The research process starts with the doubts, dilemma, inquisitiveness, and curiosity occuring in the mind of a researcher or sponsoring authority and ends with the research output in the form of a report to be used by the sponsoring authority or the scientific community at large.

The simplified **overview of the research process** may be stated as follows, keeping in view the availability of resources both manpower and infrastructure within the budgetary constraints.

Phase 1. Problem formulation : Select the topic and develop the research question.

Phase 2. Designing the study : Examine alternative designs and select an appropriate one.

Phase 3. Data Collection : Implement the design and obtain data for processing and analysis.

Phase 4. Data Processing : Organise the data in preparation for analysis.

Phase 5. Data analysis : Manipulate the processed data to answer research questions.

Phase 6. Interpreting the findings : Determine what the results of the study signify.

Phase 7. Writing the research report : Include introduction, methodology and discussion.

2.2 COMPONENTS OF RESEARCH STUDY :

The research study comprises of

- Choosing the research problem, defining the area under study and objectives.
- Formulation of research questions/hypotheses.
- Collection of facts or observations through field studies or experimentation.
- Analysis and drawing conclusions after testing the formulated hypotheses.
- Developing a theory or empirical law.
- Writing the research report.

Criteria to judge the overall quality of study :

- Good research questions
- Appropriate research design
- Rigorous and feasible methods
- Qualified research team

2.3 RESEARCH PLANNING

Research plans depend on what information the manager/researcher needs to collect in order to make major decisions about a product, service, program etc.

The more focussed one is about what one wants to gain by research, the more effective and efficient he would be in his research.

The researcher has to make trade offs in the breadth and depth of information desired. The more breadth one usually wants, the less depth he gets in the process because of the resource constraints. For example, if one wants to examine a certain aspect of a product, service, program, etc., in great detail, he may not likely to get as much information about other aspects as well.

The following considerations may be taken up when designing research approach.

- For what purpose is the research being done *i.e.* what decisions are likely to be taken as a result of research ?
- Who are the audiences for the information from the research ? (*e.g.* funding agencies, upper management, employees, customers, etc.)
- What kinds of information are needed to make decisions ?
- From what sources should information be collected, *e.g.* households, organisations, institutions, industrial establishments, corporations, business houses, employees, customers, groups of employees or customers, certain documentation, etc ?

- ❒ How can that information be collected in a reasonable fashion, *e.g.* questionnaires, interviews, examining documentation, experiments, focus groups, etc. ?
- ❒ When is the information needed ? (*i.e.* by when must it be collected ?)
- ❒ What resources are available to collect information ?

2.3.1. Basic Steps in a Research Plan :

1. Identify the problem—purpose of study.
2. Surveying the literature.
3. State and formulate the problem clearly.
4. Formulate the research questions/hypotheses and define the basic concepts and variables.
5. Determine the information needs—objectives.
6. Construct the research design to maximise internal and external validity—ascertain types of data required and decide the type(s) of research.
7. Specify the data collection procedures.
8. Select the data analysis methodology.
9. State the underlying assumptions that govern the interpretation of results.
10. Execute the research plan. Preferably do a pilot study.
11. Evaluate the results and draw conclusions.
12. Writing the research report.

2.4. THE MANAGEMENT—RESEARCH QUESTION HIERARCHY :

When there is no question, one naturally expects no answer. The research starts in the inquisitive mind of a person in authority or in the mind of a researcher as to certain question. **This is the beginning of the start of a research process.**

The research process starts from the management/sponsor/the researcher dilemma and ends with certain conclusions, to be used by the concerned for decision making. In the business research the management dilemma originates from the performance factors—like sales, profits, employee turnover, manufacturing output, defective items, on-time deliveries, customer satisfaction, etc. and the identification is not very difficult one where the management is well alert about the internal activities. **Management research question** hierarchy differs according to performance factors of interest to manager.

The **management dilemma** needs to be translated into **management questions** to proceed with the research process.

For instance,

- ❒ What should be done to reduce cost of production ?
- ❒ What should be done to enhance sales in particular zone for a particular product ?
- ❒ What should be done to reduce after-service complaints ?
- ❒ What should be the welfare programmes to be undertaken in the area to meet the social commitment and to rehabilitate the displaced families.

- What strategies are to be adopted in the forthcoming labour negotiations ?
- Why does a particular department incur higher costs or higher level of discipline ?

The management question sets the research task in proper prospectives.

A poorly defined management question may misdirect research efforts.

Research question is the specific purpose of the management, stated in the form of a question. While formulating the research question the researcher is definitely benefited by the insight and expertise of the manager or sponsoring authority. If the research question is not properly defined or fails to be clearly defined, the researcher will need further exploration and revise the original question, if necessary. A research question may be broken down into sub-questions, which form the nucleus of the research itself and must be directly addressed by research instrument.

After finalisation of research question, the researcher moves to more specific questions revealing more specific process of information which the manager or sponsoring authority needs to know to answer the research questions. These specific questions are called **investigative questions,** which the researcher must answer satisfactorily to arrive at conclusions for the research question.

Before gathering data, the investigative questions should be reduced into **measurement questions** which are the questions to be asked to the respondents or observed on the units of study to elicit the required information. In all observational study these questions result in the observed data for subsequent analysis and reaching conclusions, helping management decision.

Thus, we may state the ***Management-Research question Hierarchy as Management Dilemma—Management question—Research question—Investigative question—Measurement Question—Management Decision.***

2.5. REVIEW OF LITERATURE :

One of the most important early steps in a research project is the conducting of literature review, that is, reviewing published research related to the purpose and objectives of the research study.

The literature review is designed to identify related research, to set the current research project within a conceptual and theoretical context..

A review of literature should relate to the hypotheses, definitions and operationalization of variables, methodology and data anlaysis that follow. It should summarize the results of previous studies that have reported relationships among the variables included in the proposed research.

An important function of the literature review is to provide a theoretical explanation of the relationships among the variables of interest. It is most important that the review explain what mechanisms link the variables. The review can also provide discipline information about related problems, intervention programs and target populations.

The literature review must address three areas :

1. Topic or problem area. This part of the literature review covers material directly related to the problem being studied. There will usually be at least two substantive areas reviewed because most research involves variables that have been studied in separate substantive areas.

For example, a study on some aspect of juvenile antisocial behavior suggests a review of the literatures on anti-social behavior, adolescent development and families at risk. As another example, research on the differential impact on males and females of intervention characteristics in a substance abuse program would require a review of the literature on substance abuse programs, the specific intervention characteristics in question, and pertinent research on gender differences. As another example, research on conceptualizations of work in high stress settings would suggest a review of literature on the stress factors in such settings, the concept of stress and the development of job-related attitudes.

2. Theory area. Investigators must identify the theory which relates to the problem area. Examples of such theories might be sex-role theory, theories of deviance, organisational theory, small group theory, family systems theory, or conflict theory. The theory area provides the theoretical "lens" through which the writer chooses to view and understand the problem. It provides guidelines of explaining the etiology of problems and the linking mechanisms that connect variables.

3. Methodology. Investigators must review the literature which is appropriate to various aspects of their closen method, including design, selection of subjects, and methods of data collection. This section describes research methods and measurement approaches used in previous investigations in the area. The content should be considered in designing the proposed research and used to support the choice of design and measurement techniques. Otherwise, the investigator must explain why/she/he has chosen method or approaches that have not used previously.

After reading the literature review, the reader should understand the problem area you have selected and the theoretical models, findings, methodologies, and measurement techniques that have been used in previous, related research efforts.

A good literature review has the following characteristics :

- ❒ Thorough and complete
- ❒ Logical
- ❒ Recent
- ❒ Original research
- ❒ Primary sources
- ❒ Critical appraisal
- ❒ Building case for new study

As regards conducting the literature review, the researcher should

- ❒ concentrate his efforts on the scientific literature and try to determine what the most credible research journals are in his topical area and start with those.
- ❒ perform the review early in the research process. The researcher is likely to learn a lot in the literature review that will help him in making the trade-offs he may need to face, like his predecessors and fellow research workers, facing similar trade-off decisions.

2.5.1. Need for the literature review :

1. The researcher might be able to find a study that is quite similar to the one he is trying to explore. Since all credible research studies have to review the literature themselves, he can check their literature review to enable him to get a quick-start on his own.
2. Secondly, prior research will help assure that he includes all of the major constructs in his study.
3. Thirdly, the literature review will help the researcher to find and select appropriate measurement instruments, taking clue from the measurement instruments used by other research workers in similar contexts.
4. Finally the literature review will help the researcher to anticipate common problems in his research context. He can use prior experience of others to devise ways to avoid common traps and pitfalls as regards measurement/response and non-response errors. A critical summary of research on a topic of interest helps the researcher to put a research problem in a context or to identify gaps and weaknesses in prior studies so as to justify new investigations.

2.6 RESEARCH PROBLEM

Research starts with a problem and the problem statement is the axis, around which the whole research revolves. The problem arises in the mind of a researcher as a product of his original thought processes due to gap in a particular field of research discovered by the researcher himself or suggested by the experts in the field. A review of the literature may help the researcher to find out the gap or invoke a new problem. Any problem whose solution is an impossibility or which posseses a trivial solution cannot be treated as a research problem. The choice of a good research problem depends on the intuition, knowledge and expertise of the researcher and it is necessary that solution to the research problem must add to the existing knowledge on the subject of the research study.

2.6.1. What is a research problem ?

Research starts with a problem and ends with a solution. The research problem is the demarcation of a problem area within, **a certain context involving the 'who' or 'what', the 'where', the 'when' and the 'why' of the problem situation.**

There are many problem situations that may give rise to research. Among them, three sources mostly contribute towards problem identification.

- ❐ Own (researcher's) intuition or experience, or that of others/research supervisors.
- ❐ Scientific literature. Going through certain findings of others and noticing deficiencies/gaps in certain field could lead to a research problem.
- ❐ Existing theories : Shortcomings in theories could be researched.

Research can thus be aimed at clarifying or substantiating an existing theory, at clarifying contradictory findings, at correcting a faulty methodology, at correcting the inadequate or unsuitable use of statistical techniques, at reconciling conflicting opinions, or at solving existing practical problems.

2.6.2 Identification of the Problem

The researcher should think on what caused the need to do the research (problem identification). The question should crop up in his mind : Are there questions about this problem to which answers have not been found up to the present ?

Research originates from a need that arises. It is necessary to make a clear distinction between the **problems** and **purpose.** The problem is the aspect, the researcher worries about, thinks about and wants to find a solution for. The purpose is to solve the problem, *i.e.* to find answers to questions.

If there is no clear problem formulation, the purpose and methods are meaningless.

To identify a problem the following considerations should be kept in mind.

- ❒ Outline the general context of the problem area.
- ❒ Highlight key theories, concepts and ideas current in this area.
- ❒ What appears to be some of the underlying assumptions of this area ?
- ❒ Why are these issues identified important ?
- ❒ What community or research needs to be solved or practical problems to be addressed ?
- ❒ Read round the area (subject) to get to know the background and to identify unanswered questions or controversies, and/or to identify the most significant issues for further exploration.
- ❒ The research topic, which comes under problem identification, should be important, relevant to priorities of policy and practice and specific about the question to be answered.
- ❒ Research questions contemplated to be posed should be narrow and specific and be posed in a way that can be answered by observable evidence.
- ❒ The emerging research study should be feasible in terms of time, money, and obtaining cooperation from relevant memers associated with study.
- ❒ The literature review should be ongoing to assist in selecting and clarifying the topic, in assisting to define the key concepts and other aspects of the research study.

2.6.3 Formulation of Research Problems

The formulation of a problem is far more often essential than its solution, which may be merely a matter of mathematical or experimental skill. (Albert Einstein and L. Infeld, 1938). To new possibilities, to regard old problems from a new angle requires creative imagination and marks real advance in science (The Evolution of Physics, 1938).

The research problem should be stated in such a way that it would lead to analytical thinking on the part of the researcher with the aim of possible concluding solutions to the stated problem. Problem formulation is the anchor of a research proposal. It applies to both problem driven or theory driven research.

- ❒ Research problems can be stated in the form of either questions or statements
- ❒ The research problem should always be formulated unambigously with regard to grammatically correct language and should be as completely as possible, avoiding meaningless words.
- ❒ Demarcating research field into manageable parts by dividing main problem into sub-problems is of utmost importance. Sub-problems are problems related to the main problem. They flow from the main problem and make up the main problem. They act as the means to reach the set goal in a manageable way and contribute to solving the problem.

Not every question can become research problem. A research problem has to indicate the possibility of empirical investigation–that is, of data collection and analysis. In order to make your research problem appropriate we need to follow some guidelines.

• Qualitative Research Problems

Problem formulation in qualitative research begins with selecting a general topic and methodology (ethnographic or an analysis of historical documents). The topic and methodology are interrelated and are selected interactively rather than in separate steps. Most qualitative research interests come from personal experiences and a long interest in a topic developed from accidents of current biography and personal history. The researcher begins by narrowing a general topic to a more definitive topic.

Qualitative research, in contrast to quantitative research, employs primarily **inductive reasoning.** Qualitative research problems are reformulated several times after researcher has begun data collection. Whereas, quantitative research problems are stated before data collection. The qualitative fresearch problem is stated initially when planning for the study, reformulated during beginning of data collection and also reformulated as necessary throughout data collection. The continuing reformulation of research problem reflects an emergent design. This emergent design allows qualitative research to build the findings from the data by analyzing and presenting data in increasingly abstract and synthesized forms. Reformulation of a research problem relates to changing data collection strategies to acquire the totality of the phenomena and then to study some aspects in greater depth. The specific research problem then emerges and is condensed toward the end of data collection. The condensed version of the research problem in most publications often is not exactly the same problem statement which initiated the research.

• Quantitative Research Problems

The quantitative research problems are formulated through **deductive logic,** that is, starting with a general construct or theory, then identifying some operational variables to quantify the general construct or theory, and finally deciding on variables to be observed.

Thus, it involves

- ❒ Review of the construct
- ❒ Identification of variables
- ❒ Operational definitions of variables.

2.6.4 Origin of Research Problem :

Where do research topics come from ?

The most common source of research ideas is the experience of **practical problems in the field.** Another source for research ideas is the **literature in the specific field.** Requests for proposals (RFPs) that are published by government agencies, also, act as a source of good research ideas. These RFPs describe some problems that the agency would like researchers to address, that is, they are handing the researcher an ideal. A RFP describes the problem that needs addressing the contexts in which it operates, the approach the sponsors would like the researcher to take to investigate to address the problem, and the amount they would be willing to pay for such research. The potential research funding available with sponsors get researchers to focus on a particular research topic. Further, many researchers also think up their own research topic synthesizing ideas of their own, influenced by their background, culture education and experiences.

Sometimes, exploratory research is required to help in the formulation of research problem.

Once the idea for a study takes off the researcher should think about whether the research study is feasible. Many of the arising problems involve making trade offs between rigor and practicality. There are several practical considerations which a researcher should take into account when deciding on the feasibility of research project.

These are :

- Time for completion
- Ethical constraint
- Needed co-operation
- Cost involved.

2.6.5 Statement of the Problem

The problem statement is the guiding theme of the proposal. This includes a statement of the **purpose of the study** and should specify **objectives.** The purpose of the study explains why the research is being conducted. It establishes the importance of the problem addressed by the research and why the research is needed. The **specification of objecitves** describes what the investigator hopes to accomplish with research. This makes the reader to visualize clearly about the questions to be asked, the kinds of answers expected, and the nature of the information to be provided by the proposed research.

The statement of the problem involves the demarcation and formulation, *i.e.* ***who/what/where, when, why.*** It usually includes the statement of hypothesis.

The problem statement should take into account the following considerations :

- Does the statement of the problem imply the possibility of empirical investigation ?
- Does the problem statement restrict the scope of the study ?
- Does the problem statement give the context in which the problem lies ?

In order to demonstrate that the problem is researchable, the statement of research problem should perform the following functions :

- ❒ The context of research
- ❒ The focus of research
- ❒ The significance of research
- ❒ The framework of research and conclusions.

The adequacy for problem statements visualizes the following specific research questions or hypothesis.

Quantitative questions :

1. Does the specific research purpose, question or hypothesis state concisely what is to be determined ?
2. Does the level of specificity indicate that the question or hypothesis is researchable ? Or do the variables seem amenable to operational definitions ?
3. Is the deductive logic of a research question or hypotheses with variables, precise ? Are the independent and dependent variables identified ?
4. Does the research question or hypothesis indicate the framework for reporting the results ?

Qualitative questions :

1. Do the foreshadowed problems or the condensed problem statement idndicate the particular case of some phenomena to be examined ?
2. Is the qualitative methodology appropriate for description of present or past events ?
3. Is the inductive logic of the research reasonably explicit ?
4. Does the research purpose (understanding of a social situation or grounded theory) indicate the framework for reporting the findings ?

2.6.6 Some Common Mistakes in Problem-formulation :

1. Collecting data without a well-defined plan or purpose, hoping to make some sense of it afterward.
2. Taking a "batch of data" that already exists and attempting to fit meaningful research questions to it.
3. Defining objectives in such general or ambiguous terms that your interpretations and conclusions will be arbitrary and invalid.
4. Undertaking a research project without reviewing the existing professional literature on the subject.
5. *Ad hoc* research, unique to a given situation, permitting no generalizations beyond the situation itself and making no contribution to the general body of educational research.
6. Failure to base research on a sound theoretical or conceptual framework.
7. Failure to make explicit and clear the underlying assumptions within your research, so that it can be evaluated in terms of these foundations.

8. Failure to recognize the limitations in your approach, implied or explicit, that place restrictions on the conclusions and how they apply to other situations.
9. Failure to anticipate alternative rival hypotheses that would also account for a given set of findings and which challenge the interpretations and conclusions reached by the investigator.

2.6.7. Evaluation of a Proposed Research Problem

Personal Considerations on the part of a researcher :

The researcher may ask himself :

1. Is the problem in line with my goal expectations and the expectations of others ?
2. Am I genuinely interested in this problem but free from strong biases ?
3. Do I possess or can I acquire the necessary skills, abilities, and background knowledge to study this problem ?
4. Do I have access to the tools, equipment, laboratories, and subjects necessary to conduct this investigation ?
5. Do I have the time and money to complete it ?
6. Can I obtain adequate data ?
7. Does the problem meet the scope, significance, and topical requirements of the institution of periodical to which I will submit my proposal ?
8. Can I obtain administrative support, guidance, and cooperation for the conduct of the study ?

Since interest is a tremendous stimulus to work in any form of endeavor, the researcher should select a problem that he has a consuming desire to solve. Maintaining the prodigious effort required in research is difficult if the researcher feels that his topic is meaningless and boring. An insatiable curiosity about a subject gives an investigator the extra enthusiasm and drive necessary to withstand the prolonged period of exacting work.

Social Considerations

1. Will the solution of this problem advance knowlege in the field appreciably ?
2. Will the findings be of practical value to educators, parents, social workers, or others ?
3. What will be the breadth of the application of the findings in terms of range of individuals, years of applicability, and areas of coverage ?
4. Will the investigation duplicate the work that has been or is being done adequately by someone else ?
5. If this topic has been covered, does it need to be extended beyond its present limits ?
6. Is the topic sufficiently delimited to permit an exhaustive treatment yet sufficiently significant to warrant investigating it ?
7. Will the conclusions of the study be of doubtful value because the tools and techniques available to conduct the inquiry are not adequately refined and sufficiently reliable ?
8. Will the study lead to the development of other investigations ?

When the researcher becomes interested in a topic he should locate and evaluate all studies relating to it that have been completed or are under way. If this survey reveals that his proposed problem has already been thoroughly explored, he will usually abandon it. He may persue the problem, however, if he doubts the validity of the conclusions reached by others, discover contradictory findings, believe new evidence or better techniques have been discovered that require a new investigation, or think that there are gaps to fill or extensions to be made in the organized body of knowledge.

Studies that are well written will typically make suggestions for future research in a given area. Systematically reading and evaluating published research can thus assists the researcher in the formulation of a research problem.

2.6.8 Checklist for Testing the feasibility of the Research Problem

		YES	NO
1.	Is the problem of current interest ? Will the research results have social, educational or scientific value ?		
2.	Will it be possible to apply the results in practice ?		
3.	Does the research contribute to the discipline under study ?		
4.	Will the research opt new problems and lead to further research ?		
5.	Is the research problem important ? Will you be proud of the result ?		
6.	Is there enough scope left within the area of research (field of research) ?		
7.	Can you find an answer to the problem through research ? Will you be able to handle the research problem ?		
8.	Will it be practically possible to undertake the research ?		
9.	Will it be possible for another researcher to repeat the research ?		
10.	Is the research free of any ethical problems and limitations ?		
11.	Do you have the necessary knowledge and skills to do the research ? Are you qualified to undertake the research ?		
12.	Is the problem important to you and are you motivated to undertake the research ?		
13.	Is the research viable in your situation ? Do you have enough time and energy to complete the project ?		
14.	Do you have the necessary funds for the research ?		
15.	Will you be able to complete the project within the time available ?		
16.	Do you have access to the administrative, statistics and computer facilities the research necessitates ?		
	TOTAL :		

2.7 RESEARCH QUESTION

Finding a research question is probably the most important task in the research process, because the question becomes the driving force behind the research from beginning to the end. Developing a good research question requires a great deal of thought and experience. Fine tuning of research question can be done after a preliminary **review of the literature** or a brief exploratory study. The refined research question will have a better focus and move the research forward with more clarity than the intially formulated question.

A research question is always stated in question form. It may start out being rather general become focused and refined later on, after one becomes familiar with the topic and on the basis of related review of the literature.

A well thought out and focused research question leads directly into hypothesis. The researcher when drawing conclusions should address to research questions. In the end the success of the research depends on how well one answers the questions.

It is important that the chosen question should satisfy certain criteria :

- ❒ It must be feasible with available resources–time, money and equipments
- ❒ It must not be too broad or general or ambiguous
- ❒ It should not have already been answered by previous research.
- ❒ It ought to be a clear statement or significant question that needs to be answered/investigated.
- ❒ It must be a question that can be answered through empirical means.
- ❒ It must be ethical.

What are the sources of research question ?

- ❒ Personal experience/thinking
- ❒ Profesional books
- ❒ Research articles in professional periodicals
- ❒ Teachers/Administrators/Managers
- ❒ Bibliographies
- ❒ Unpublished research by others.

It is advisable not to include too many research questions in a single study. However, it is very possible to address several related research questions in one study.

Research question identifies the research objective and key abstract concepts involved in the research.

No matter how well designed the methodology or sophisticated data analysis is, if there is problem with research question, the project is doomed from start.

A research question is a statement that identifies the phenomenon to be studied

To develop a strong research question the researcher should ask himself :

- ❒ Does he know the field and its literature ?
- ❒ What are important research questions in the field ?
- ❒ What areas need further exploration ?
- ❒ Could the present study fill the gap ?
- ❒ Has a great deal of research already conducted in this topic area ?

- ❒ Is the timing right to answer the question ? Is it hot topic or is it becoming obsolete ?
- ❒ Would funding sources be interested ?
- ❒ Will his study have a significant impact in the field ?

Research question emanates from research dilemma in the problem formulation. Research dilemma is what does concern the researcher ? For instance, a research dilemma may be 'rising IT costs'. The research question restating the dilemma in question form runs as 'Does the high costs of IT has any effect on the organisational productivity ?

A research problem can, sometimes, be broken up into a number of research questions.

- ❒ Developing a good research question requires a good deal of thought and experience and a good research is one that can be answered with available resources.
- ❒ The research question should be a clear statement about what to investigate. It should be specified before research is conducted and stated in reporting the results. A conventional approach is to reflect the research question in a purpose statement in the introductory part of the report. Given below is an example to show how it might be reflected in a purpose statement.

Research question. 'Is the quality of public sector and private sector employees different ?'

Purpose statement. 'The purpose of this study is to determine whether the quality of public and private sector of employees is different.'

The specification of research questions or hypotheses (*i.e.* what is to be studied) and research strategy (*i.e.* how to conduct the study) is an extremely important part of any research project. Research questions or hypotheses influence the strategy that is employed in order to either provide answers to the qquestions or verify/falsify hypotheses. What research strategy to use ought to depend on the nature of problem domain (*i.e.* sociology, management, mathematics, biology, etc.)

Formulation of precise research questions requires deep insights into the domain of study : Do the questions that are to be answered 'fit' the research domain ? Are they the ones most worthy of investigation ? To which degree will answering the questions contribute to any progress within the research area ? Do practitioners perceive the research questions to concern real problems ?

2.7.1 Types of Questions

There are three basic types of questions that research projects can address :

1. Descriptive. When a study is designed primarily to describe what is going on or what exists. Public opinion polls that seek only to describe the proportion of people who hold various opinions are primarily descriptive in nature.

2. Relational. When a study is designed to look at the relationships between two or more variables. A public opinion poll that compares what proportion of males and females say they would vote for a NDA or UPA political party candidate in the next presidential election is essentially studying the relationship between gender and voting preference.

3. Causal. When a study is designed to determine whether one or more variables (e.g., a program or treatment variable) causes or affects one or more outcome variables. If we did a public opinion poll to try to determine whether a recent political advertising campaign changed voter preferences, we would essentially be studying whether the campaign (cause) changed the proportion of voters who would vote NDA or UPA (effect).

Note : The three question types can be viewed as cumulative. That is, relational study assumes that you can first describe (by measuring or observing) each of the variables, you are trying to relate. And, a causal study assumes that you can describe both the cause and effect variables and that you can show that they are related to each other. Causal studies are probably the most demanding of the three.

2.8 THE HYPOTHESIS

In a research problem a variety of research questions arise in the minds of a researcher, who looks for some answers in the process of investigation. These qeustions may relate to either discovery of certain new facts or establishing relationship between variables or explaining particular situations and events, or predicting future events or generalizing existing results, whenever possible. While framing questions the researchers invariabley are not completely ignorant about the answers, however vague or approximate in nature these may be, before observing facts. Thus, in the event of haziness about answers, the researcher formulates questions in the form of his imaginable verifiable conclusion. This **imaginable verifiable conclusion is called a hypothesis.**

- Hypotheses are more specific predictions about the nature and direction of relationship between variables.
- The hypothesis starts, from a **proposition,** which is defined as a statement about a concept that may turn out to be true or false when referred to observable phenomena. When the propostion is suitably formulated for empirical verifiction, we name it as a hypothesis.
- The hypothesis is **a declarative tentative statement** and is **conjectoral** in nature.
- The generalization of a hypothesis results in establishment of theory. As profeser Northrop pointed out, the function of the hypothesis is to direct our research for order among facts.
- The suggestion formulated in the hypothesis may ultimately lead to the solution of the problem.
- The hypothesis in a way systematizes the proces of equiry and directs the researcher to collect relevant empirical data for its verification.
- It is a refinement of research problem and a most specific statement problem.
- It is a specific statement of prediction and describes in concrete (rather than theoretical) terms what the researcher expects will happen in his study.
- Hypothesis relates theory to observation and observation to theory.

2.8.1 Definition of Hypothesis

A hypthesis can be defined as a tentative explanation for certain behaviours, phenomena or events that have occurred or will occur, that is a possible outcome of the research or an educated guess about the research outcome which can be tested for possible acceptance or rejection

2.8.2 The Role of Hypothesis

- The hypothesis provides a tentative explanation phenomena under investigation and facilitates broadening the horizon of knowledge in an area of research. If identifies facts tht are relevant and those that are not.
- The hypothesis provides direction to the research investigation and enables the investigater to decide about the nature of the data to be collected for the purpose in the course of investigation.
- It suggests which form of design is likely to be most appropriate and provides the investigator a relational statement that is directly testable.
- The hypothesis provides a framework for reporting the conclusions of the research study.
- Hypotheses are more specific predictions about the nature and direction of relationship between two variables.

2.8.3 Nature of Hypothesis

The hypothesis is a clear statement of what is intended to be investigated. It should be specified before research is conducted and openly stated in reporting the results.

This allows to

- Identify the research objectives.
- Identify the key abstract concepts involved in the research
- Identify its relationship to both the problem statement and the literature review.

A problem cannot be scientifically solved unless it is reduced to hypothesis form. The hypothesis gives direction to the collection and interpretation of data.

It is a powerful tool of advancement of knowledge, consistent with existing knowledge and conducive to further enquiry.

It can be tested-verifiable or falsifiable.

Hypotheses are not moral or ethical questions. It is neither too specific nor too general. It is also considered valuable even if proven false. It is a prediction of consequences. A hypothesis can be directional or non-directional.

2.8.4 Types of Hypothesis

The hypothesis may be classified as

- Descriptive hypothesis
- Relational hypothesis

- ❒ Correlational hypothesis
- ❒ Causal hypothesis

Descriptive hypotheses are propositions that typically state the existence, size, form or distribution of some variable.

For instance, we might form the following hypothesis.

"Executives stay longer time in the office compared to other employees"

Relational hypothesis is used to describe a relationship between two variables. The relationship may be either an unspecified relationship or an explanatory/causal relationship.

The unspecified relationship gives rise to **correlational hypothesis** where the variables occur together in a specified manner without implying that one causes the other. Such weak links sometimes do exist when some basic causal forces act on both the variables without showing evidence for stranger linkage. When there is an implication and stronger reason that change in one variable causes or leads to change in other variables, the hypothesis on the relationship between two variables is called explanatory or causal hypothesis and the relationship is a cause–effect relationship.

Correlational hypothesis :

"Younger machinists (by under 30 years of age) are less productive than those who are older."

Explanatory/Causal hypothesis :

- ❒ Increase in family income leads to an increase in saving.
- ❒ Increase in petrol price leads to increase in Bus fare.

The Interpretation of causal hypothesis demands that the researcher must consider the direction of influence, which may not be always straight forward and hence might need the help of correct research design.

2.8.5 Theory and Hypothesis

A hypothesis refers to a provisional idea whose merit needs evaluation. For proper evaluation, the framer of a hypothesis needs to define specifics in operational terms. A hypothesis requires more work by the researcher in order to either confirm or disprove it. In due course a confirmed hypothesis may become part of a theory or occasionally may grow to become a theory itself.

A theory constitutes a set of concepts along with statements about the how and why of the relationships that exist among these concepts. Explanations embodied in theory apply to a wide range of phenomena. The statements are often hypothesis which are assumed to be true and some other which may be tested in subsequent studies. The inter–relationship proposed in the theory may help the investigator to state certain possible consequences, which could be logically assumed to follow and ultimately become bases of hypothesis which are subjected to empirical investigation.

Empirical hypothesis that experinmenters have repeatedly verified may become sufficiently dependable that, at some point in time, they become considered as 'proven'. Some people may succumb to the temptation to term such hypothesis as 'laws'. But such assertion is made mistakenly since by definition **an hypothesis explains and a law describes** (for example, a law can state "Matter can neither be created nor destroyed, only change in form"). More accurately, one could refer law as 'repeatedly verified' hypothesis or simply as 'adequately verified' or as 'dependable'.

2.8.6 Deductive and Inductive Hypothesis

A hypothesis can be tested either under the deductive reasoning principle of the scientific method or under inductive reasoning. If ideas and theories are truth, one can device controlled experiments and find evidences to support them (deductive reasoning). Alternatively, we may gather data and try to build hypothesis (inductive reasoning) and in this process we may land with large number of competing hypothesis which may or may not be true. This is called positive theorising which is a common way of looking at the outside world. In the event of not knowing which of the competing reasoning is true, we usually end up with the one which best fits our existing consideration.

Inductive reasoning has a major role to play in exploratory research in order to develop ideas and a hypothesis has to be tested to give scientific credence. The inductive hypothesis are formulated by the researcher as a genralisation from observed relationships. The researcher makes observations on variables, notices trends and relationships and then hypothesis, an explanation for the observed phenomena. Of course, the process of reasoning is facilitated by examination of past studies and literature review.

The deductive hypothesis are deduced from a theory or other hypothesis, where as the inductive hypothesis are derived from the observed phenomena.

2.8.7 Difference between Hypothesis and Problem.

Problems is a question and is not testable	Hypothesis can be tested.
Relation between variables in problem statement	Relation between variables in hypothesis
Is A related to B ?	If A, then B.
How are A and B related to C ?	If A and B, then C.
How is A related to B under conditions C and D ?	If A, then B under conditions C and D.

2.8.8 What is a good hypothesis ?

The researcher is expected to use his analytical thinking, level of knowlege from relevant literature, clarity of definitions and concepts and clear understanding of the objectives in research to formulate good and usable hypothesis.

A good hypothesis should fulfil the following objectives/criteria.

- The hypothesis must be conceptually clear and unambiguous and must have explanatory power. It must serve adequacy for its purpose.
- The hypothesis should have empirical referents. Total judgements and attitudes of the researcher should not play any role for its formulation.

- The hypothesis must be exact and spceific to enable its verification. In other words, it must be testable. Expressing hypothesis in general terms will not make it testable. It may be advisable to reduce the imprecise hypothesis into precise sub-hypothesis to make these testable and thereby increasing the validity of results.
- The hypothesis should give insight into a research question.
- A good hypothesis states a clearly and concisely as possible, the expected relationship (or difference) between two variables and defines these variables.
- A good hypothesis will lead to specific aims, that is, the steps the researcher is going to take to test his hypothesis.
- The hypothesis should be related to available techniques. The researcher must be aware of the techniques for the test of his hypothesis. This would help him to collect relevant facts accordingly.
- A hypothesis should be better than its rivals. That is, it must explain more facts and has greater range than other rivals and more power for discrimination. It should require few conditions and assumptions.
- The hypothesis should be related to body of theory or some theoretical operation. The researcher must assume that there are theoretical gains in existing knowledge in testing the hypothesis.

Wrong formulation of hypotheses and subsequenty collection of data for their verification will lead to wastage of time, labour and resources, without enhancing scientific knowledge.

The difficulties are :

- absence of any theoretical framework.
- lack of ability to utilise the theoretical framework logically.
- lack of acquaintance with available research techniques and literature to phrase the hypothesis properly.
- failure to formulate exact testable hypothesis free from ambiguities.

2.8.9. What is a Research Hypothesis ?

- The hypothesis states the researcher's expectations concerning the relationship between the variables in the research problem.
- The hypothesis is a refinement of the research problem. It is the most specific statement of the problem.
- The hypothesis states what the researcher thinks the outcome of the study will be.
- The researcher collects data that either supports the hypothesis or does not support it.
- The hypothesis is formulated following the review of related literature and prior to the execution of the study. The related literature leads the researcher to expect a certain relationship.
- A good hypothesis states as clearly and concisely as possible the expected relationship (or difference) between two variables and difines those variables in operational, measurable terms.

- A well-stated and defined hypothesis must be (and will be if well formulated and stated) testable. It should be possible to support or not support the hypothesis by collecting and analyzing data.

2.8.10. Scientific hypothesis vs. Statistical hypothesis

The hypothesis put to test in social research in general and management research in particular is not a scientific hypothesis, but rather a statistical hypothesis. For example, life exists in moon is a scientific hypothesis which can be established or not with certainty. But the statistical hypothesis is concerned with the behaviour of the observable random variable and tested on the basis of limited observations/results of visualized random experiments either man made or provided by nature. In testing a statistical hypothesis the researcher wishes to decide whether to reject or accept the hypothesis, set up for the purpose. Unlike the scientific hypothesis a statistical hypothesis does not establish the truth or fasity of the hypothesis with certainty. In most situations encountered in practice it becomes entirely impracticable to study the entire population to take correct decision. Instead, limited representative observations are selected by probability method from the propulation to put to statistical tests as to the unkown.

2.8.11 Research Hypothesis and Null hypothesis

Research hypotheses are substantive statistical hypotheses and are developed from observations, the related literature and/ or the theory involved in the research study. **A research hypothesis is a statement about the relationship one expects to find after the analysis of research results.**

Research hypothesis may be stated either **in a directional or non-directional form.** A directional hypothesis specifies the nature of relationship or expected difference that is predicted. But a non-directional hypothesis states only the existence of relationship or difference and never specifies the nature of expected findings.

Research hypothesis cannot be tested with the help of statistical techniques. In order that statistical tests are to be applied on empirical results, the research hypothesis must be transformed into another type of hypothesis called a **'null hypothesis'**, a hypothesis of no difference, which is opposite to what the investigator expects (research hypothesis) The reason for using null hypothesis is that it enables to distinguish the real difference from the observed difference due to chance only through staistical tests. If the null hypothesis is rejected, the **research hypothesis** (stated as **alternative hypothesis**) is expected to be true.

EXAMPLE : Null hypothesis (H_0) : There is no difference between old technology and new technology.

Alternative hypothesis (H_1 or H_A) : The two technologies have different effects.

2.8.12 Formulation of Hypothesis

The formulation of hypothesis may not occur automatically, but is usually preceded by many false starts, discussion with experts, study of literature, exploratory enquiries, vague statements etc. and may be developed at different stages beginning from common sense statements to the relationship between complex and abstract variables. A well grounded hypothesis indicates that the researcher has sufficient knowledge in the area to undertake investigation.

Although hypotheses are tools in the research process, they are not ends in themselves. We may come across studies in certain areas where little accumulated background is available and the investigator lacks insight into the scope of a problem, nature and behaviour of related variables. In such a situation it becomes difficult to state a meaningful hypothesis. For instance, to study certain phenomena or to seek to ascertain attitudes and opinions of groups, one often proceeds without hypothesis.

Formulation of a research hypothesis starts from a research question, keeping in mind the following points :

- Generate operational definitions for all variables, and
- formulate a research hypothesis keeping in mind,
  - expected relationship or differences.
  - operational definitions.
- Hypothesis can also be classified in terms of how they were derived.
  - Inductive hypothesis is a generalization based on observations.
  - Deductive hypothesis is derived from theory.
- A hypothesis can be directional or non-directional.
- Hypothesis can also be tested as research hypothesis or as statistical hypothesis.
- The statistical hypothesis consists of the null hypothesis (H_0), the hypothesis of no difference and the alternative hypothesis (H_1 or H_A) which is similar in form to the research hypothesis.

A well thoughtout and focussed research question leads directly into formulated hypothesis. Not all studies have hypotheses. In some studies there is no formal hypothesis, and perhaps the purpose of the study is to explore some area more thoroughly in order to develop some specific hypothesis or prediction that can be tested in future research.

2.8.13 Generation of Research Hypothesis

Problem statements become research hypotheses when constructs are operationalized.

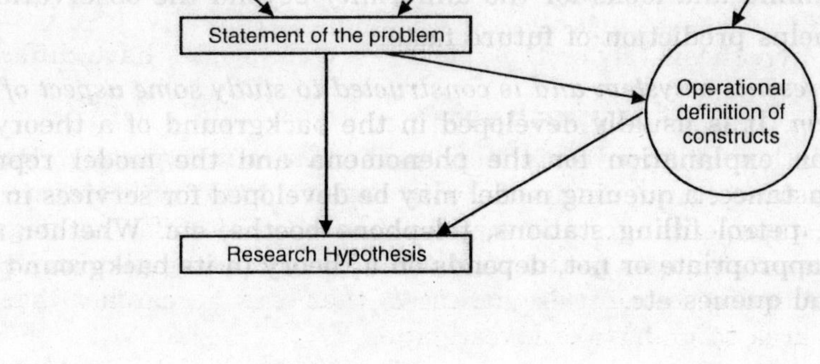

2.8.14 Testing the Hypothesis

A study usually begins with a research hypothesis which should be simple, clear and specific statement of the expected relationship between variables. One of the major requirements for putting up the hypothesis is that they must be testable, that is amenable to empirical verification. It may be pointed out here that research hypothesis transformed into null hypothesis are only testable through statistical procedures. The following steps may be observed while stating a hypothesis.

These are :

- ❒ State the relationship that should be observed if the research hypothesis is true.
- ❒ State the null hypothesis
- ❒ Select the research method to collect necessary observations reflecting the relationship.
- ❒ Collect and analyse the empirical data. Compute the test statistic.
- ❒ Determine with certain level of significance whether the evidence is sufficient enough to reject the null hypothesis.

2.8.15. Theory and Model

A theory is an attempt to explain a particular phenomenon.

Hypothesis plays an important part in the development of a theory, sometimes regarded as an important aspect of research. The distinction between hypothesis and theory needs to be considered in the realm of research. ***The theory is a set of systematically interrelated concepts, defintions and propositions to explain and predict certain phenomena.*** It is generally a complex abstraction involving multiple variables, whereas ***hypothesis is simple in nature and is based on limited propositions and may be concerned with certain aspect of the development of theory.***

Importance of the development of a theory originates from the following :

1. Being an abstraction, the theory narrows down the volume of facts needed for the study.
2. It suggests a meaningful approach to research and in the process suggests a system for the researcher.
3. Theory summarises the information collected, keeping the objectives of the study in mind and looks for the uniformity beyond the observations.
4. Theory helps prediction of future facts.

A model represents a system and is constructed to study some aspect of that system or the whole system. It is usually developed in the background of a theory. Thus, the theory provides an explanation for the phenomena and the model represents this phenomena. For instance, a queuing model may be developed for services in banks, post offices, bus stops, petrol filling stations, telephone booths, etc. Whether a particular queuing model is appropriate or not, depends on a theory in its background e.g. poisson queues, exponential queues etc.

Sometimes, models can be developed through the use of analogy and help building a theory. For instance, we may observe the data on heights of fathers and heights of sons develop a regression model and help formulating a theory that 'like father like son'.

2.9 RESEARCH OBJECTIVES

Goals are broad statements what the research proposal hopes to accomplish. Research objectives are specific types of data (qualitative) or data sets (quantitative), that are planned to develop or gather or that taken together, allow the researcher to answer research questions.

Research objectives are logically developed from research questions. It should be made clear that accomplishing these objectives will provide the researcher with the information he needs to address the research questions.

Objectives should be simple (not complex), specific (not vague) and stated in advance (not after the research is done).

The **objectives** of a research project are what is to be achieved by the study. These should be closely related to the statement of the problem and may be classified into **primary objectives and secondary objectives.** The **general objective** of a study states what researchers expect to achieve by the study in general terms. It is advisable to break down general objective into smaller, logically connected parts, referred to as **specific objectives.**

Specific objectives should systematically address the various aspects of the problem as defined under 'statement of the problem'. Specific objectives are statements of research questions.

Why should research objectives be developed ?

The formulation of objectives will help to

- **focus** the study
- **avoid** the collection of data which are not strictly necessary for understanding and solving the problem identified and
- **organise** the study in clearly defined parts or phases.

Properly formulated specific objectives will facilitate the development of research methodology and will help to orient the collection, analysis and interpretation and utilisation of data.

How should you state objectives ?

The objectives should :

1. cover the different aspects of the problem and its contributing factors in a **coherent way** and in a **logical sequence.**
2. state the objectives clearly phrased in operational terms, specifying exactly what you are going to do, where, and for what purpose.

3. be **realistic** considering conditions and situations at hand.
4. use **action verbs** that are specific enough to be evaluated.

(e.g. to determine, to compare, to verify, to calculate, to describe, and to establish)

Avoid use of vague non-action verbs such as : to appreciate, to understand or to study.

The researcher should keep in mind that when the research project is **evaluated,** the results will be compared to the objectives. If the objectives have not been spelled out clearly, the project cannot be evaluated.

After objectives are finalised, some more specific research questions, if necessary might be developed for different objectives.

Thus, the formulation of clear and comprehensive objectives is critical to the development of all the other components of a research design as well as to subsequent data analysis and report writing. The researcher should develop concise operational objectives that focus clearly on what the study hopes to accomplish and cover all parts of the study in logical order.

2.10 RESEARCH METHODS

A number of research methods are available which allow researchers to test hypothesis and theories and look for relationship between variables. Which type of research method is best ? This depends largely on the subject the researcher is exploring, the resources available and the theory or hypothesis being investigated. It is directly cannected with problem statement and goal of research.

The major types of research methods vary in terms of the experimenter's control over relevant variables and naturalness of the setting. These differences have a direct learning on critical issues such as what sorts of conclusions we can make from the findings and how confident we are of the validity of those conclusions.

Thus, we may classify research methods as

- ❒ Experimental Research
- ❒ Non-experimental Research

Experimental research methods are those in which the experimenter has control over

- ❒ assignment of subjects to conditions
- ❒ manipulation of the independent variable.

When the above conditions are not present, then the research methods are said to be **non-experimental** or simply **research study.**

In **non-experimental research** the investigator cannot manipulate the study variable or randomly assign treatments or subjects. The researcher has very little control over the research environment and in fact, often works with data collected long before the analysis was conducted. Non-experimental research lacks the scientific rigor necessary to draw conclusions about the effect one variable on another. Nevertheless, non experimental research is common and does have value.

Examples of commonly adopted non-experimental research are :

Descriptive Research, Case study Research, Correlation Research, Exploratory Research, Action Research, Ethnographic Research, etc.

Research can also be classified according to source of information :.

❒ primary sources and

❒ secondary sources.

Primary research is done by the researcher's own team and can be a focus group, survey, bench mark, etc. Secondary research is from another source such as a magazine, outside Survey, consultant, records, etc. The methodology used to gather the information, whether primary or secondary, determines the accuracy of the data.

Research methods can be categorized into two basic methods :

❒ Qulitative Research Method

❒ Quantitative Research Method

2.10.1 Qualitative Research

• As a scientific research it seeks answers to a question, systematically using a predefined set of procedures, collects evidence, produce findings that were not determined in advance and are applicable beyond the immediate boundaries of study. It provides a means for becoming more familiar with the phenomenon that fascinates us. It is also called interpretive research, naturalistic research, phenomenological research or descriptive research.

• Qualitative research is characterised by an emphasis on describing, understanding and explaining complex phenomena. It provides insights into setting of a problem generating ideas and/or hypothesis for later quantitative research and uncovers prevalent trends in thought and opinion.

• It is based on broad objectives, **usually with small samples** and results are not generalizable and is best used early to identify issues and again later in the process to validate.

• Qualitative research methods are valuable in conducting initial explorations to develop theories and to generate test hypothesis and moving toward explanations.

• Qualitative research involves field work. The researcher, who is the primary instrument for data collection and analysis, physically goes to people, setting, site or institution to observe or record behaviour in its natural setting.

• Qualitative research is descriptive in that the researcher is interested in process, meaning and understanding, gained through words and pictures.

• The process of qualitative research is more inductive in that the researcher builds abstractions, concepts, hypothesis and theories from details.

• Qualitative methods are also effective in identifying intangible factors, such as social norms, socio–economic status, gender roles, ethnicity and religion whose role in the research issue may not be readily apparent. That is, these are more discovery oriented.

• Qualitative research involves an in-depth understanding of human behaviour and the reasons that govern behaviour. **It investigates the 'why' and 'how' of decision making as compared to 'what', 'where' and 'when' of quantitative research.**

• **Qualititative research needs smaller but focused samples rather than large random samples as in case of quantitative research.**

• Qualitative research is less reactive, more naturalistic, and uses researcher as the instrument.

• It uses subjective data and stances as well as objective ones and involves triangulation method of data collection.

• Qualitative research most often is **grounded theory**, built from the ground up.

It generates data types in the form of field work, field notes, audio (and sometimes video) documents, recordings and transcripts, besides researcher's impressions and reactions. Qualitative research methods are designed to help researchers understand people and the social and cultural contexts within which they live.

The most common qualitative methods usually adopted in practice are :

❐ Secondary data analysis

❐ Participant observation-appropriate for collecting data on naturally occurring behaviours in their usual contexts.

- Complete participation
- Participant as observer
- Observer as participant
- Complete observation.

❐ Case studies and in-depth interviews-optimal for collecting data on individuals' personal histories, perspectives and experiences, particularly when sensitive topics are being explored.

❐ Focus groups-effective in eliciting data on the cultural norms of a group and in generating broad overviews of issues of concerning the cultural groups or sub-groups.

Besides there are other methods such as ***ethnography, sociometry, content analysis, historigraphy, photography, natural experiments etc.***

Firestone (1987) states that qualitative methods are built on a post positivist, phenomenological world view, and assumes that 'reality is socially constructed through individual or collective definitions of the situation. The purpose of qualitative research is to understand the current situation from the participant's perspective. Thus, Firestone concludes that it is important for the researcher to become ***'immersed in the phenomenon of interest'.***

Although qualitative research is a loosely defined category of research, it is being seen as a supplement to quantitative research and as a direct result, it has grown in importance in the ***field of management research.***

Sampling in Qualitative Research. It is not always possible or necessary to collect data from everyone in the community in order to get valid findings. In qualitative research, only a sample (that is, a subset) of a population is selected for any given study. The most common sampling methods used in qualitative research are purposive sampling, quota sampling and snow ball sampling. In **purposive sampling** participants are selected according to preselected criteria relevant to a particular research question. **Quota sampling** is sometimes considered as a type of purposive sampling in which one decides while designing the study how many people with which characteristics (*e.g.* age, class, sex, place of residence, profession, marital status, etc.) to include as participants. A third type of sampling — **snow ball sampling,** known as **chain referral sampling** is also considered as a type of purposive sampling. In this method participants or informants with whom contact has already been made; use their social network to refer the researchers to other people who could potentically participate in or contribute to the study.

- ❒ Produces more in-depth, comprehensive information.
- ❒ Uses subjective information and participant observation to describe the context, or natural setting, of the variables under consideration, as well as the interactions of the different variables in the context. It seeks a wide understanding of the entire situation.

Disadvantages

- ❒ The very subjectivity of the inquiry leads to difficulties in establishing the reliability and validity of the approaches and information.
- ❒ It is very difficult to prevent or detect researcher induced bias.
- ❒ Its scope is limited due to the in-depth, comprehensive data gathering approaches required.

2.10.2 Quantitative Research

Quantitiative research methods are research methods dealing with numbers and anything that is measurable, and are therefore to be distinguishable from qualitative methods. Counting and measuring are common features of quantitative methods.

Quantitative research is the systematic scientific investigation of quantitative properties and phenomena and their relationships. The relationship between variables is expressed using **effect statistics** such as correlations, relative frequencies or difference between means.

It is considered to be conclusive research and is used to test hypothesis, describe method or target population characteristics and check relationships among variables. The results lead to formal conclusions and recommendations to inform decision making.

The basic characteristics of quantitative research are :

- ❒ defined objectives that include hypotheses.
- ❒ focused research design that identifies 'who', 'how', 'what', 'why', 'when' (and sometimes even 'where')

❒ quantified data.
❒ large enough sample to allow generalization, projection of results.
❒ randomly selected respondents.
❒ structured data gathering techniques.
❒ statistical techniques used to recommend final course of action.

The **objective** of quantitative research is to develop and employ mathematical models, theories and hypothesis pertaining to natural phonomena the process of measurement is central to quantitative research because it provides the fundamental connection between empirical observations and mathematical expression of quantitative relationships. Quantifying relationships are of two types — **descriptive and experimental.** In a descriptive study no attempt is made to change the behaviour or conditions *i.e.* you measure things as they are. In an experimental study you take measurements, try some sort of intervention, then take measurements again to see what happened. A descriptive study establishes only associations between variables but an experiment establishes causality.

The Quantitative research is generally approached using scientific methods which include :

❒ The generation of models, theories and hypothesis.
❒ The development of instruments and methods of measurement.
❒ Experimental control and manipulation of variables.
❒ Collection of empirical data.
❒ Modelling and analysis of data.
❒ Evaluation of results.

• **Measurement is often pre-requisite for quantitative research** to express observations numerically in order to investigate causal relations or associations.

• Quantitative data are data which can be **sorted, classified, measured in a strictly 'objective' way** — they are capable of being accurately described by a set of rules of formulae or strict procedures which then make their definitions (if not always their interpretation) unambiguous and independent of individual judgement (Prof. David R. Harvey, 2002).

• Quantitative methods are **much more objective** than qualitative methods. The are essentially systematic and based on a **positivism perspective.** Firestone (1987) states that the positivist philosophy 'assumes that there are social facts with an objectivity reality apart from the beliefs of individuals.' He views quantitative methods as attempting to explain social changes through the use of objective measures and statistical analysis. Quantitative researchers put their emphasis on **procedures, methodologies and statistics.** They hope to reduce, if not eliminate, error and bias by using experimental design and correlational studies to achieve objectivity.

• Quantitative data are replicable. That is, it should be possible for the same data to be re-collected by another researcher in another place but for it to still measure the same thing *i.e.* results can be directly comparable. However, David Harvey (2002) argues that in practice **"many apparently quantitative data do depend critically on the way in which they were collected, who collected them, where they were collected and from whom they were collected."**

• Statistical methods are widely used in quantitative research in the fields of economics, social sciences and biology. Quantitative data using statistical methods typically begin with the collection of data based on theory and hypothesis. Causal relationships are studied by manipulating factors thought to influence the phenomena of interest while controlling other variables relevant to experimental outcomes.

The most common broadly stated quantitative research methods are :

- Experiments/quasi-experiments.
- Survey–mail, telephone, face to face interviews, on-line, etc.
- Field study–observing well defined events.
- Obtaining relevant data from management information systems.

The major disadvantages of quantitative research are as follows :

- Findings can be biased by researchers' perspectives.
- Research often tekes place in an Unnatural setting.
- Provides narrow, unrealistic information using measures which capture only a tiny proportion of the concept originally under study.
- The results of quantitative research may be statistically significant but are often humanly insignificant.
- Uses static and rigid approach and so employs an inflexible process.
- This can only be meaningfully employed when qualitative methods have shown that a simplification of identified relations is possible.

2.10.3 Basic Differences between Quantitative and Qualitative Research Methods

Quantitative and Qualitative research methods differ primarily in

- their analytical objectives.
- the types of questions posed.
- the types of data collection instruments used.
- the forms of data they produce.
- the degree of flexibility built into study design.
- size of the sample.

The key difference between quantitative and qualitative methods is their flexibility. Generally, **quantitative methods are fairly inflexible.** With quantitative methods such as surveys and questionnaires, for example, researchers ask all participants identical questions in the same order. The advantage of this inflexibility is that it allows for meaningful comparision of responses across participants and study sites. However, it presupposes a thorough understanding of the important questions to ask, the best way to ask them, and the range of possible responses.

Qualitative methods are typically more flexible – that is, they allow greater spontaneity and adaption of the interaction between the researcher and the study participant. For example, qualitative methods ask mostly 'open ended' questions that are not necessarily worded exactly the same way with each participant. With open-ended question, participants are free to respond in their own words, and these responses tend to be more complex than simply 'yes' or 'no'. In addition, with qualitative methods, the relationship between the researcher and the participant is often **less formal** than in quantitative research.

Participants have the opportunity to respond more elaborately and in greater detail with quantitative methods. Researchers have the opportunity to respond immediately to what participants say by tailoring subsequent questions to information, the participant has provided.

Qualitative research is largely **exploratory,** while the quantitative research is **conclusive.**

Qualitative research is phenomenological, inductive, holistic, subjective, process oriented in nature and takes into account anthropological world view with relatively lack of control, where as **quantitative research** is positivistic, deductive, particularistic, objective and outcome oriented, takes into account natural science world view and attempts to control variables.

Quantitative data are measurable while qualitative data cannot be put into context that can be graphed or displayed as a mathematical term.

A complete (typical) research plan includes both types of research – Qualitative and Quantitative. The mix depends on the stage of development, the research objectives, available funds, and other variables. Often, qualitative research such as focus group can be used to better identify what the issues are. Quantitative research is then employed to **determine** how prevalent the issue or need is.

Both qualitative and quantitative research methods look for bias, reliability, replicability, objectivity, scientific rigour, etc. Those who favour quantitative methods rely on statistical techniques aided by computational algorithms and software packages, whilst qualitative researchers view transcripts, interview recordings, notes of focus groups or participant research. Some researchers prefer to use qualitative methods in management research, stating that "in human enquiry it is much better to be deeply interesting than accurately boring". On the other hand if the quantitative methods are omitted in research, the causal relationships between variables and quantification and analysis of the variables to establish statistical properties and certainty of outcome will be blatantly missing. While recognising the advantages and disadvantages of both types of research methods, a researcher sould make use of a method, appropriate to the situation at hand. It may be mentioned here that quantitative measurements on qualitative assumptions about which constructs are worth measuring and conceptualising.

To conclude, quantitative methods have an objective approach, where data is controlled and measured, to address the accumulation of facts to determine the causes of behaviour. Qualitative methods view data from another's perspective and so doing to find understanding and meaning, here concerns centre on the changing and dynamic nature of reality. Combining both the methods ultimately strengthens the value of the research. However, **"all research approaches may have something to offer and there is no independent form of evaluating different strategies in any absolute terms."** In many areas of management research it may be prudent to verify quantitative results through qualitative methods.

TABLE – 2.1

Comparison of Quantitative and Qualitative Research Approaches

	Quantitative	Qualitative
General framework	Seek to confirm hypotheses about phenomena Instruments use more rigid style of eliciting and categorizing reponses to questions Use highly structured methods such as questionnaires, surveys, and structured observation	Seek to explore phenomena Instruments use more flexible, iterative style of eliciting and categorizing responses to questions Use semi-structured method such as in-depth interviews, focus groups, and participation observation
Analytical objectives	To quantify variation To predict causal relationships To describe characteristics of a population	To describe variation To describe and explain relationships To describe individual experiences To describe group norms
Question format	Closed-ended	Open-ended
Data format	Numerical (obtained by assigning numerical values to responses)	Textual (obtained from audiotapes, videotapes, and field notes)
Flexibility in study design	Study design is stable from beginning to end Participant responses do not influence or determine how and which questions researchers ask next Study design is subject to statistical assumptions and conditions	Some aspects of the study are flexible (for example, the addition, exclusion, or wording of particular interview question) Participant response affect how and which questions researchers ask next Study design is iterative, that is, data collection and research questions are adjusted according to what is learned

2.10.4 SOME SELECTED RESEARCH METHODS

• Descriptive Research

The term descriptive is self explanatory. It implies that the descriptive research describes, writes on and depicts. The aim of descriptive research is to verify formulated hypotheses that refer to the present situation in order to elucidate it.

Descriptive research is thus a type of research that is primarily concerned with describing the nature or conditions and degree in detail of the present situation. The emphasis is on describe rather their on judge or interpret or to determine cause–effect relationship between two variables.

Researchers who use this method for their research usually aim at

- ❐ demarcating the population (representative of the universe) by means of perceiving accurately research parameters, and
- ❐ recording in the form of a written report of that which has been perceived.

The aim of the latter is, that when the total record has been compiled, revision of the documents can occur so that the perceptions derived at can be thoroughly investigated.

Because the total population (universe) during a specific investigation can not be contemplated as a whole, researchers make use of the demarcation of the population or of the selection of a representative test sample. Test sampling therefore forms an integral part of descriptive research.

In descriptive research the following steps may be included :

- ❐ Problem selection and problem formulation. The research problem being tested should be explicitly formulated in the form of a question.
- ❐ Literature search.
- ❐ Problem reduction.
- ❐ Hypothesis formulation.
- ❐ Test sampling. The researcher should determine the size of the test sample.
- ❐ Information retrieval
- ❐ General planning
- ❐ Report planning

The five different types of descriptive approaches are :

1. Naturalistic observation. A technique which enables an investigator to unobtrusively observe and record naturally occurring behaviour.

2. Secondary record. A technique which enables an investigator to describe a given situation by using data that are gathered currently or previously.

3. Field study. A technique which allows an investigator to generate a description by collecting data through the use of participant observations, surveys, correlational studies, or longitudinal or cross-sectional studies.

4. Ex post facto studies. A technique which allows an investigator to describe a relationship between a given behaviour and a variable on which groups of subjects naturally differ, such as skin colour or gender.

5. Meta analysis. A technique which involves the quantitative analysis of the results of many studies in order to integrate and describe the overall picture presented by these studies.

Descriptive studies are observational because the researcher observes the subjects without otherwise interviewing.

The variants are :

- ❐ **Case :** Reports data on only one subject.
- ❐ **Case services :** Study of a few cases.
- ❐ **Cross sectional :** variables of interest in a sample of subjects are assayed once and the relationships between them are determined.

- **Prospective or Coport or longitudinal studies :** Some variables are assayed at the start of the study (*e.g.* dietary habits) then after a period of time the outcomes are determined (*e.g.* incidence of heart disease).
- **Case control studies :** These compare cases (subjects with a particular attribute) with controls (subjects without attribute). Comparison is made of the **exposure** to something suspected of causing the cases, for example volume of high intensity training. Case control studies are also called **retrospective,** because they focus on conditions in the past that might have caused subjects to become cases rather than controls.

• Exploratory Research

Exploratory research is a type of research conducted becuase a problem has not been clearly defined. Exploratory reseaarch helps determine the best research design, data collection methods and selection of subjects. Given its fundamental nature, exploratory research often concludes that a perceived problem does not actually exist.

Exploratory research often relies on secondary research such as reviewing available literature and/or data, or qualitative approaches such as informal discussion with experts, consumers, employees, management or competitors, and more formal approaches through in-depth interviews, focus graphs, projective methods, case studies or pilot studies.

The results of exploratory research are not usually useful for decision making by themselves, but they can provide significant insight into a given situation. Although the results of qualitative research can give some indication as to the 'why', 'how' and 'when' something occurs, it cannot tell us 'how often' or 'how many'.

Exploratory research is not typically generalizable to the population at large. In other words, the results can neither be generalized nor are representative of the whole population being studied.

Types of exploratory researches :

- Secondary data analysis
- Experience survey
- Focus group etc.

• Action Research

Action research is a reflective process of progressive problem solving lead by individuals working with others in teams, or as a part of a 'community of practice' to improve the way they address the issues and solve the problems.

Action research can also be undertaken by larger organisations or institutions, assisted or guided by professional researchers, with the aim of improving their strategies, practices and knowledge of the environments within which they practise.

Kurt Lewin (1946), the then Professor of MIT, first coined the term 'action of research' in a paper entitled "Action Research and Minority problems."

Action research challenges traditional social science, by moving beyond reflective knowledge created by outside experts sampling variables to an active moment-to-moment theorizing, data collecting and inquiring, occurring in the midst of emergent structure.

• Historical Research

Historical research, as the term implies, is research based on describing the past. This type of research includes for instance investigations like the recording, analysis and interpretation of events in the past with the purpose of discovering generalizations and deductions that can be useful in understanding the past, the present and to a limited extent, can anticipate the future. The researcher is dependent on the availability of documentary services of the original events that took place, which are of interest to the historians.

Historical research involves studying, understanding, and explaining past events in order to arrive at conclusions about causes, effects, or trends of what happened in past or what may happen in the future. Historical researchers work with primary documents, artifacts, and records found in archieves, libraries, other specialized institutional collections, and elsewhere. Historical researchers also use secondary sources which provide other people's descriptions of original events or sources.

- Internal evidence or criteria should be included that will explain the meaning of the data.

Although the chronological sequence of events should be precisely acknowledged, researchers should bear in mind the fact that mere compilation of chronological events is not considered research in itself. An investigation can only be regarded as scientific research when the researcher interprets the events that took place by pointing out their relationship to the problem investigated, and explaining their meaning.

Historical research involves steps such as the following :

- Recognizing an historical problem or identifying the need for certain historical knowledge.
- Gathering as much pertinent information about the problem or topic as possible.
- If appropriate, forming hypotheses to tentatively explain relationships between historical variables.
- Rigorously collecting and organizing evidence and verifying the authenticity of the information and sources, both primary and secondary.
- Selecting, organizing, analyzing and drawing conclusions about the most pertinent collected evidence.
- Recording conclusions in a meaningful narrative.

Lastly, it should be mentioned that historical research also encompasses research concerning the origin, development and influence of ideas of the past. For instance, in case of historical research on Marxism, the aspects like the origin, development and influence of communism, democracy, capitalism etc. can be mentioned.

• Case Studies

Case Studies involve in–depth examination of a single entity or a few.

A case study is a method in which the researcher studies an individual(s) or some activity in a unique setting as intensely as possible. The unique setting is important since the researcher is as interested in the context of the conditions surrounding the individual or activity as the individual or activity itself. What are the specific factors that set this person (or activity) apart from the others ? What is unique here ? Case study research is problem oriented and goes beyond studying an individual and certain behaviour traits. Communities, social groups, school systems, families, businesses, social service programs, hospitals, to mention a few, provide case study material. The case study is one of the favourite research methods of physicians, psychologists, organisational theorists. Business Schools use the case study method for much of its course material. Students analyze cases of business organizations; for example, why do they fail, why do they succeed, what were the causes and so on ? Common and necessary characteristics of almost every case study are extensive data collection and analysis, intense focus, detail orientation, both qualitative and quantitative methodologies, lengthy time commitment.

These are the preferred strategy when 'how' or 'why' questions are being posed when the investigators has little control over events, and when the focus is on contemporary phenomenon within some real life context.

Examples of possible case studies :

- Why has the University of Chicago produced so many Nobel Laureates ?
- Why is the leukemia rate so high in community X ?
- What are the career paths of women graduates of elite MBA programs who enter the Infosys empire ?
- How does lobbying group X influence Indo-USA Nuclear deal ?
- Why is the customer service program not working well in retail company X but is perceived quite favorably in a number of its peers in the region ?

Rather than looking at an entire population or a random sample, a case study usually focuses on a single individual or on small groups. Since the focus is rather narrow, case studies do not provide valid information about the population as a whole; the results therefore, cannot be generalized. Case studies do, however, provide useful anecdotes or examples to illustrate possible relationships and this helps follow-up research focusing on specific hypothesis, using proper sampling methods. As an example, a case study may ask "What is the effect of cigarette smoking on the manual factory workers? What is the effect of yogic exercises on the blood pressure level of a particular individual adult person ?

Advantages :

- provides detailed description of specific example *e.g.* business practices at a particularly successful company, leadership style of a respected leader.
- may spark development of a hypothesis for later testing by other methods.

Disadvantages :

- cannot draw firm conclusions about generalizing findings beyond the specific example.
- cannot test hypothesis.
- usually cannot establish cause-effect relationship.

• Ethnographic Research

Ethnography is a form of field research focusing on the sociology of meaning through close field observation of socio-cultural phenomena. Typically enthnographers focus on a community, selecting informants who are known to have an overview of the activities of community.

The ethnographic method starts with selection of a culture, review of the literature pertaining to the culture, and identification of variables of interest–typically variables perceived as significant by members of the culture.

The ethnographer, then goes about gaining entrance, which in turn sets the stage for cultural immersion of the ethnographic in the culture. It is not unusual for ethnographers to live in the culture for months even years. The middle stages of the ethnographic method involve gaining informants, using them to gain yet more informants in a chaining process, and gathering of data in the form of observational transcripts and interview recordings.

Data analysis and theory development come at the end, though theories may emerge from cultural immersion and theory – articulation by members of the culture.

Ethnographic methodologies vary and some ethnographers advocate use of structured observation schedules by which one may code observed behaviour or cultural artifacts for purposes of later statistical analysis. However, there has been extensive use of unstructured observations and conversations documents by detailed field notes forming the basis of this type of research.

Assumptions

- ❒ Ethnography assumes that the principal research interest is primarily affected by community cultural understandings.
- ❒ Ethnography assumes an ability to identify the relevant community of interest.
- ❒ Ethnography assumes that the researcher is capable of understanding the cultural mores of the population under study, has mastered the language or technical jargon of the culture, and has based findings on comprehensive knowledge of the culture.

Sociology and cultural studies also produce ethnography. Ethnographic methods have been used to study business settings, where groups of workers, managers and so on of different social categories participate in common social systems. Each group shows different characteristic attitudes, behaviour patterns and values.

Anthropologists have used ethnographic data to answer academic questions about consumers and consumption. Business, too, have found ethnographers helpful for understanding how people use products and services, as indicated in the increasing use of ethnographic methods to understand consumers and consumption or for new product development (sometimes called design ethnography). Education, performance studies, folklore, and linguistics and other fields which have made extensive use of ethnography.

Naturalistic/ethnographic inquiry is used when situations are unique or complex, when level of uncertainty about the questions to ask is high and when there is little or no theory to direct the investigator.

A subset of this type of inquiry involves participant observation in which the investigator becomes a part of setting or the process being studied.

• Survey Research

Survey research specifies a central focus, asks questions, and collects data. The more specific the question, the more focused the response. The principal methodology used in survey research is to ask a group of people a set of carefully selected questions to collect their views, values, beliefs on a topic, etc. Any one or agency can use a survey to determine what a population thinks or feels about a plan, issue, policy, event etc. Business bodies, the government, lobbying groups, political parties and countless other agencies all use surveys.

Survey research, usually, selects a representative sample of the population to be used for the study. A sample is a sub-section of a population that mirrors the traits of that population. Compared to a large population, a sample population is typically less expensive and more manageable and also involves less time to execute with less administrative arrangements.

The sample can be random, systematic, stratified or convenient.

Survey research uses many techniques to obtain responses and information.

- ❐ Interviewing
- ❐ Focus groups
- ❐ Questionnaire
- ❐ Telephone survey
- ❐ E-mail/Web panel survey

Advantages :

- ❐ data collected in naturally occurring environment.
- ❐ results of survey often yield new hypothesis to test by another method.
- ❐ several survey techniques are available (*e.g.* questionnaire, interviews, observations).

Disadvantages :

- ❐ little or no control over variables in the study.
- ❐ inferences made only through the use of complex statistical analysis.
- ❐ low return rates threaten representativeness of responses, thus biasing results.
- ❐ what people say does not always agree well with what they do.

• Observation Research

Interviews and/or questionnaire often encourage individuals, consciously or unconsciously, to provide biased information about themselves. Since an individual's recollections frequently cannot be trusted, a researcher may find the observational method or field work research, more accurate. Here, the researcher carefully watches how people act and behave in different situations.

The primary objective of observation approach is to systematically, but without questioning or communicating, collect data about individuals as they act naturally. Participants include humans, laboratory animals, indeed any beings (This research method is sometimes termed as naturalistic/enthnographic method).

The observation can be

❒ non-obtrusive (non-participant)

❒ obtrusive (participant)

Non-obtrusive observation is generally clandestine and always careful. The researcher studies a certain situation without being a participant in the group or organization. Examples of non- participant research include the following : sitting quietly by a conveyer belt in a factory floor observing the work processes and activities of the factory workers, studying the behaviour of the audience in a public meeting, etc. The critical dynamic of non-participant observation is that the observer does not interact in any way with the individual being observed.

Obtrusive or Participant observation : In participant observation the researcher joins the individual or group being observed. Everyone knows they are being observed and by whom in this forward and open method. Examples of participant observation include joining police patrols observing police activity as they make rounds, spending a month in a fishing vessel to know the lives of the fishermen, fishing in high seas, etc. Ethnographic researchers and anthropologists use this form of research and their written observations are the field notes.

Observation research, whether obtrusive or non-obtrusive, involves some of the most difficult research techniques. Observers require extensive training in observation methodologies, and in particular, how to report their findings.

• Field Research

A variety of research methods with diverse approaches are included in the category of field research.

These studies are conducted in the real world and free from the criticism of artificiality of environments, in which data are collected.

These are :

❒ naturalistic observation–direct observation (unobtrusive) of events as they occur in natural settings.

❒ archival research – studying information from already existing records made in natural settings.

❒ field surveys – asking direct questions to persons in natural settings.

❒ case study – making extensive observations of a single group or a person or any entity.

❒ program evaluation – conducting evaluations of applied procedures in natural settings.

❒ correlational studies; longitudinal and cross-sectional studies.

❒ field experiments – conducting experiments in natural settings where causal inferences are sought.

Advantages :

❒ high degree of realism because it is conducted in natural environment.

❒ data on large number of variables can be collected at the same time.

Disadvantages :

- variables not manipulated by researcher and hence no causality can be inferred.
- measurement of variables is less precise than in laboratory.

• Correlational Research

Correlational research attempts to determine whether and to what degree a relationship exists between two or more quantifiable (numerical) variables. Significant relationship between two variables does not imply that one variable causes the other. One can use the relationship to predict the value on one variable for a subject if he knows subject's value on the other variable. **Correlation implies prediction but not causation,** although correlational research is a first step in causal research. Correlation may be caused by some other variable or outside influence could be the cause of the mutual variation. Correlation studies have less control over the subjects, environment and thus have difficulty ruling out alternative explanation. Conducting surveys, directly observing phenomena and compiling research from earlier studies are some of the techniques for collecting data for correlational research.

Correlational Research :

- Describes relationship between variables.
- Hypotheses are formed to describe difference and relationships.

The investigator frequently uses the correlation coefficient to report the results of correlational research.

Examples :

- price and demand.
- intelligence and self esteem.
- mother's education and number of children.
- investment and profit.
- sales and advertisement expenditure.

• Ex. post-facto Research

The term 'ex post facto' according to Landman (1988) is used to refer to an experiment in which the researcher, rather than creating the treatment, examines the effect of a naturally occurring treatment after it has occurred. In other words it is a study that attempts to discover the pre-existing causal conditions between groups. In this study the researcher manipulates the independent variable whilst the dependent variable is controlled with the aim of establishing the effect of the independent variable on the dependent variable, that is, a cause-effect relationship. As this type of research involves group comparisons, the ex post facto research is alternatively termed as **Causal-Comparative Research.**

The groups in the study make up the values of the independent variable, for example, gender (male versus female), technical background versus non-technical background in the management code, or children with working mother versus children without working mother, etc. These could be independent variables. However, in causal comparative research the independent variable is not under experimental control, that is, the experimenter **cannot** randomly assign the subjects to a gender classification (say), but has to take the values of the independent variable as they come. The dependent variable is the outcome variable.

Examples of causal-comparative research :

- The effect of mother's working status on children's academic performance.
- The effect of technical/non-technical background on work efficiency among the management personnel.
- The comparative effectiveness of personalized instruction versus traditional instruction on computational skill.

• Experimental Research

In an experimental study the researcher takes measurement and try some sort of intervention and then takes measurements again to see what happened. Experimental research is the key to unconvering causal relationships between variables. In experimental research the experiments randomly assigns participants to one of two groups—**control grups and experimental group.** The control group receives no treatment and serves as a base line. Researchers manipulate the levels of some independent variables in the experimental group and then measure the effects. **Because researchers are able to control the independent variables, the experimental research can be used to find causal relationship between variables.** That is why, this type of research is termed, as **causal research,** 'the cause and the effect method', 'before and after design', 'control group design', etc.

Control is a fundamental characteristic of this type of research and as such control groups are a pre–requisite. Control groups are selected from a group of selected persons/experimental units, which are homogenous is nature and characteristics. Only difference is that they do not receive the same treatment.

The independent variable is the circumstances or characteristics which the researcher can manipulate in his effort to determine what their connection with the observed phenomenon is. This means that the researcher has direct control over the variable. The dependent variable, on the other hand, is the circumstances or characteristics that change, disappear or appear when the researcher implements the independent variable. For example, in an experiment concerning study methods and students performance, the dependent variable is student performance while the manipulation of study methods by means of different teaching methods, is the independent variable.

Another pre-requisite for experimental research is 'validity'.

- Internal validity
- External validity

Internal validity means that the perceived difference is the independent variable (characteristics that change) is a direct result of the manipulation of the obtained research results, and therefore possible to conclude.

External validity means that the results of the experimental research should be applied to similar situaton outside the experimental designs. The results of the experimental research can then be confirmed in similar situations and thus the findings are considered general.

Experimental researches may be classified into

- Laboratory experiment
- Field experiment

Laboratory experiment is conducted in laboratory under controlled environment.

Advantages :

- experimenter has greatest control over variables of influence, thus
- is best method for inferring causality.
- measurement of behaviour/outcome most precise.
- can most easily replicate.

Disadvantages :

- laboratory may lack realism.
- some phenomena cannot be studied in laboratory.
- limited generality of findings to the real world.

Field experiment is an experiment conducted in natural settings/environment.

Advantages :

- proper experimental design can suggest causal inferences.
- involves good realism because experiment is conducted in natural setting–thus generalization of results good.
- can address impact of complex behaviours in real-life contexts.

Disadvantages :

- less control.
- sometimes people (experimental units) refuse to participate.
- difficulty in getting access to a business or industrial setting for the experiment.

Field Experiments Versus Laboratory Experiments

The major difference between field experiment and laboratory experiment is that in field experiment there is a limited scope to control the variables, while laboratory experiment has adequate scope to rigorously control the variables. The randomization and manipulation of independent variable is difficult in field experiments. In fact the control of variables is the hallmark of laboratory experiment, other being the manipulation of variables independent variable(s). Apart from this other things are almost same – field experiments also require investigators who are specially skilled in that particular subject of study, field experiments can also establish causal relationship (direction of relationship included).

• Evaluation Research

In evaluation research a researcher formally and objectively appraises the outcome of the project, program, strategy, and so on. The researcher also carefully examines the chief factors that are positively or negatively influencing the performance of the activity. The primary objective is to gather data to facilitate making a decision regarding the future of the activity. Evaluation researchers employ a broad range of both qualitative and quantitative research methodologies. Such reserach is most commonly carried out in business, educational and non-profit organizations, as well as government agencies.

2.11 THE RESEARCH PROPOSAL

A proposal for a research study is an individual/researcher/organization's offer to offer a new product or improve the process of production or render useful services to a potential buyer/manager/sponsor. In a general social science arena the research proposal is submitted with a view to solve certain socio-economic problems or work in direction of achieving desired goals. It is intended to convince others that you have a worthwhile research project and that you have the competence and work plan to complete the study.

The objectives of the proposal delineate the ends or aims which the inquirer seeks to bring about a result of completing the research, development or evaluation undertaken. An objective may be thought of as either a solution or step along the way toward achieving the solution; and end to be achieved in relation to the problem.

The purpose :

- ❒ To present management/sponsor question in terms of research questions.
- ❒ To review the research efforts of others who have worked on similar or related research questions.
- ❒ To suggest research methodology and methods of data collection for solving the management question and also subsequent treatment of data and their interpretation.

A researcher's proposal must indicate the researcher's plan, services, past experiences, credibility in tackling the problem in best possible manner to withstand competition from other bidders.

A proposal is so to say a work plan, prospectus, outline, statement of intent or draft plan to convince the sponsor about the utility and significance of such research to solve the managerial problems and reach just solution. This also reflects the sincerity and ability of the researcher to solve the problem through the research process. A poorly planned, poorly elucidated or poorly organised research proposal does not exceed in getting it approved by the authority sponsoring the research.

A good research proposal depends on the healthy interaction between the researcher and manager and the level of understanding of the researcher about the problem at hand. If necessary, more than one round of discussions may be arranged between the manager and the researcher to revise the research questions.

For an outside research contract, the research proposals are submitted in response to a **Request for bid/proposal (RFP).**

A research proposal is also beneficial to the researcher to broaden his horizon of knowledge as to the project and logical steps involved in the execution. The review of literature helps him to get acquainted with previous approaches and provides necessary research input to revise his plan accordingly.

Besides educating both the researcher and the manager, a research proposal makes their interactions more fruitful and objective oriented with prime aim to solving management dilemma and helps research further in the same subject or related subjects.

A research proposal contains all key elements in the research process and includes sufficient information for the readers to evaluate the proposed study.

All research proposals must address the following questions :

❒ What do you plan to accomplish ?
❒ Why do you want to do it ?
❒ How are you going to do it ?

Writing a good research proposal results in satisfactory success in research endeavour, reflected in

Over all quality of study :

❒ Good research questions.
❒ Appropriate research design.
❒ Rigorous and feasible methods.
❒ Qualified research team.

Quality of the proposal

❒ Informative title.
❒ Self sufficient and convincing abstract.
❒ Clear research questions.
❒ Scholarly and pertinent background and rationale.
❒ Relevant previous work.
❒ Appropriate population and sample size.
❒ Appropriate measurement and intervention methods.
❒ Quality control.
❒ Adequate sample size.
❒ Sound analysis plan.
❒ Ethical issues well addressed.
❒ Tight budget.
❒ Realistic time table.

Quality of the Presentation

❒ Clear, concise, well organized.
❒ Helpful table of contents and sub-headings.

- Good schematic diagrams and tables.
- Neat and free of errors.

2.11.1 Types of Research Proposals

Research proposals may be subdivided into

- internal proposal
- external proposal

An internal proposal originates from the internal specialists of an organisation or firm.

External proposals sponsored by the government agencies, non- government/not-for-profit organisations, educational institutions, corporations, international aid institutions etc., can be further classified into ***solicited or unsolicited.***

As regards the level of complexity the proposals may be such as

- exploratory studies
- small scale studies
- large scale studies

The exploratory study generates the most simple research proposal and large scale studies necessistate complex research proposals.

Flowchart : Steps in the development of a research proposal

Questions you must ask	Step you will take	Important elements of each step
What is the problem and why should it be studied ?	Selection, analysis and statement of the research problem	problem identification, prioritising problems, analysis, justification
What information is available ?	Literature review	literature and other available information
Why do we want to carry out the researchh ? What do we hope to achieve ?	Formulation of research objectives	general and specific objectives, hypotheses
What additional data do we need to meet our research objectives ? How are we going to collect this information ?	Research Methodology	variables, types of study data collection techniques, sampling, plan for data collection, plan for data processing and analysis, ethical considerations pre-test or pilot study
Who will do what, and when ?	Work plan	human resources, timetable
What resources do we need to carry out the study ? What resources do we have ?	Budget	material support and equipment, money

How will the project be administered ? How will utilisation of results be ensured ?	Plan for project administration and utilisation of results	administration, monitoring, identification of potential users
How will we present our proposal to relevant authorities, community and the funding agencies ?	Proposal summary	briefing session and lobbying

2.11.2 Structure of a Research Proposal

1. Title. This should be concise and descriptive. Often titles are stated in terms of a functional relationship. However, if possible one may think of an information, but catchy title to create interest about the proposal.

2. Abstract. This is an informative abstract meant for the busy executives to grasp the essentials of the proposal. It should include the question, the rationale for the study, the hypothesis (if any), the method and the main findings. Descriptions of the method may include the design, procedures, the sample and any instrument that will be used.

3. Statement of the problem. The problem statement is the guiding theme of the proposal. It is a broad statement indicating goals of the project. This should include the statement of the purpose of the study and should specify its objectives. The importance of answering the management questions should be stated so as to emphasize the importance/benefit of the study in reader's mind.

4. Purpose of the study. This explains why the research is being conducted. It should also establish the importance of the problem addressed by the research and explains why the research is needed.

5. Objectives. This should describe what the investigator hopes to accomplish with the research. After going through this section the reader should be clear about questions to be asked, the kinds of answers expected, and the nature of the information to be provided by the proposed research.

6. Review of literature. This section reviews published research whether recent or historical related to the purpose and objective described above. A review of the literature should also relate to the hypothesis, definition and operationalization of variables, methodology and data analysis that follow. It should summarize the results of the previous studies that have reported relationships among the variables included in the proposed research. This is a critical summary of research on a topic of interest, generally prepared to put a research problem in context or to identify gaps and weaknesses in prior studies so as to justify a new invesgitation.

7. Research Design. Research design is the blueprint of the work plan towards obtaining relevant information for the project. It contains research methodology–methods of data collection, sample selection, measurement techniques, ethical requirements, administrative arrangements, etc. The particular choice of the design whether an idiographic, survey, quasi-experimental or experimental; whether cross-sectional or longitudinal; whether retrospective or prospective should also be specified.

Data Analysis. This section explains the method of handling data summarisation, procedures for analysis of data and theoretical basis for the selected statistical techniques, computer packages to be used. The objectives in view may need separate technique of analysis, which should also be described. The unit of analysis to be used should be specified and the reasons for such choice should also be explained.

After going through this section the reader should be able to know which considerations will guide the data analysis and in exactly what way the data are to be analyzed to meet each objective of the proposed study.

Data analysis should be specifically linked to the hypothesis so that it is clear how each hypothesis will be tested.

8. Contribution to knowledge. Any research is supposed to add to the existing knowledge. Hence, the research proposal should necessarily mention the nature and extent of knowledge added after the completion of the project and its effect on the society at large. This is needed to communicate a sense of enthusiasm and confidence about the merits of the proposal.

9. Limitations of the proposed study. A research study sometimes involves limitations as to area and scope and coverage of the study and the availability of research materials and also faces certain difficulties in getting desired information. It may be bound by time and resource constraints. Further, the statistical analysis may require certain assumptions to arrive at conclusions. These points must be taken care of while submitting a research proposal.

2.11.3 Common Mistakes in Proposal Writing

- ❐ Failure to provide the proper context to frame the research question.
- ❐ Failure to delimit the boundary conditions for research.
- ❐ Failure to cite landmark studies, if any.
- ❐ Failure to accurately present the theoretical and empirical contributions by other researchers.
- ❐ Failure to stay focussed on the research question.
- ❐ Failure to develop a coherent and persuasive argument for the proposed research.
- ❐ Too much details on minor issues, but not enough detail on major issues.
- ❐ Too much rambling – going "all over the map" without a clear sense of direction. The best proposals move forward with ease and grace like a seamless river.
- ❐ Too long or too short.
- ❐ Too many citation lapses and incorrect references.
- ❐ Slopping writing.

2.11.4 Ethics in Business Research

The contemporary social research needs to protect the rights of research participants. Business research also is no exception. It involves association and interaction of sponsor, researcher, respondents and others connected with research. All parties involved in research should exhibit ethical behaviour. Ethics are norms or standards of behaviour that guide and influence moral choices about our behaviour and relationship with others.

The adherence to ethics ensures that no one suffers adverse consequences from research activities and all individuals have right to privacy. Research should be undertaken in accordance with commonly agreed standards of good practice.

These fundamental and widely accepted principles should be honoured by participant respondents, the sponsor and the researcher and his team members and may be categorized as

- ❒ Voluntary participation.
- ❒ Beneficence – 'do positive good'
- ❒ Non-malfeasance – 'do no harm'
- ❒ Informed consent
- ❒ Confidentiality/Anonymity

The principle of voluntary participation requires that people not be coerced into participating into participating in research.

The terms beneficence and non-malfeasance refer to risk, harm and hazards which include emotional and mental distress and possible damage to financial and social standing as well as to physical harm.

Then comes the requirement of **informed consent.** This means that prospective research participants must be fully informed about the procedures and risks involved in research and must give consent to participate. Almost all research guarantees the participants' **confidentiality** – they are assured that identifying information will not be made available to anyone who is not directly involved in the study. The stricter standard is the principle of **anonymity** which essentially means that the participant will remain anonymous throughout the study – even to the researchers themselves. Of course, stronger guarantee of privacy is sometimes difficult to accomplish, especially when participants have to be measured at multiple time points.

As regards ethical issues concerning respondents the researcher should follow the following guidelines

- ❒ Explaining study benefits to the respondents.
- ❒ Explaining respondents rights and protections.
- ❒ Obtaining informed constent.
- ❒ Confidentiality/Anonymity

Right to privacy on the part of a respondent is a sensitive right, which the researcher must respect and guarantee. The privacy guarantee is important not only to validate the research findings, but also to protect respondents against real or imaginary harm cropping in the mind of a respondent. Once the researcher guarantees the confidentiality, it is ethical duty to protect that confidentiality.

There are several ways by which the researcher protects respondent confidentiality.

- ❒ All research should conform with legislation relating to data protection.
- ❒ Obtaining signed non-disclosure documents.

- ❒ Restricting access to respondent identification.
- ❒ Revealing the identity of the respondent only with written consent.
- ❒ Restricting access to data instruments where the respondent is identified, and all reasonable steps to be taken to ensure the confidential details are secure.
- ❒ Non-disclosure of data sets and no piracy of data set of one study for another.

Right to privacy also means that the respondent has also the right to refuse to be interviewed or refuse to answer any question in an interview. This requires the researcher should inform respondents about their right to answer any question/all questions in the study, obtain prior permission to interview respondents, schedule the field and nature of interview whether in person or on phone, limit the time required for participation in the interview and restrict observation to public behaviour only and no interference with privacy.

The research client or sponsor has to abide by ethical considerations in the research study. Some sponsors wish to undertake research without revealing themselves.

They may have right to several types of confidentiality such as

- ❒ sponsor non-disclosure
- ❒ purpose non-disclosure
- ❒ findings non-disclosure

Due to sensitive nature of the management dilemma or the research question, the sponsor may hire an outside consulting or research firm to conduct research without disclosing his identity (*e.g.* testing a new product idea or contemplating to enter the new market). The researcher should respect the desire of the sponser and adopt necessary safeguards.

Purpose non-disclosure involves protecting the purpose of the study or its details. When the company is testing a new idea, it may not like to disclose it before it is made patent.

Most research sponsors and companies would like to keep the research data and findings in secret till the management decision is made.

In addition to developing self-ethical behaviour the researcher also has responsibility towards his team members and should also see that his team members abide by the rules of ethics.

The researcher and his team members must protect the confidentiality of the sponsor's information and the anonymity of the respondents. The persons handling data should be required to sign confidentiality and non-disclosure declaration statement before proceeding with the assignment.

2.11.5 Steps in Conducting Research

❒ Identify a problem

—Need a researchable question

—Identify a researchable question ; Their must be sufficient information available.

—Question should be specific, not too broad, not too vague ; it should be testable.

❒ Review the literature

- **Form a hypotheses**
- **Identifying and labeling variables**
- **Constructing operational definitions**
- **Manipulating and controlling the variables.**
- **Constructing a research design.**
- **Identifying and constructing devices for observation and measurement.**
- **Constructing questionnaires and interview schedules.**
- **Conduct the experiment/collect data.**
- **Carrying out statistical analysis.**
- **Writing a research report.**

EXERCISES

1. What is a research process? How does it start and reach the ultimate goal ?

2. What are the components of research study ? What are criteria to judge the over all quality of study ?

3. What is a research plan ? Mention its basic steps.

4. Discuss the links between management dilemma, management question, research question, investigative question, measurement question and management decision.

5. Explain the importance of literature review in research.

6. What is a research problem ? How would you identify a research problem ?

7. How would you formulate a research problem ? How does a research problem originate ? Discuss.

8. Distinguish between qualitative and quantitative research problems.

9. What do you understand about 'statement of the problem' ? What are the considerations for the problem statement ? Discuss.

10. Mention common mistakes in problem formulation.

11. How would you evaluate a proposed research problem ?

12. What is a research question ? What are the sources of research question ? Explain basic types of research question.

13. What is a hypothesis ? Discuss role, nature and types of hypothesis.

14. Differentiate between theory and hypothesis.

15. Distinguish between deductive and inductive hypothesis.

16. What is a good hypothesis ? What are the characteristics of a good hypothesis.

17. What is a research hypotheses ? How would you formulate and test it ?

18. Distinguish between

(*a*) Scientific hypothesis and research hypothesis.

(*b*) Research hypothesis and null hypothesis.

(*c*) Theory and model.

19. What are research objectives ? What is the need for formulating research objectives ? How would you state objectives ?

20. Distinguish between experimental and non-experimental research methods.

21. How do qualitative research methods differ from quantitative research methods ? Discuss.
22. Discuss the need for descriptive research and mention different steps for the purpose.
23. Why do we conduct exploratory research ? What are types of exploratory researches ?
24. Discuss the advantages and disadvantages of case study research method.
25. What is ethnographic research ? Mention assumptions behind this type of research.
26. What is a research proposal? Classify the research proposal. Briefly mention structure of a research proposal.
27. Discuss ethics in business research.
28. Identify steps in conducting research.
29. Distinguish between field experiments and laboratory experiments.
30. Compare correlational research and causal comparative research.

□□□

CHAPTER

3

RESEARCH DESIGN

3.1 WHAT IS A RESEARCH DESIGN ?

Once the research problem is formulated unambigously and plan of the research is clearly specified, the next problem is to build up a **research design to streamline the research.** It determines 'what' and 'how' the researcher hopes to find the best solution to the problem. Research design is about organizing research activity, including collection of data, in ways that are most likely to achieve the research goals and objectives and thus is a plan for connducting the proposed research work.

A well thought out design helps in accelerating the research process and making it progress in a systematic manner so as to save time, cost and labour. A researcher having an ideal research design in mind is to translate the ideal model to a practical one which is a compromise dictated by a number of practical considerations.

• ***A research design is a string of logic that ultimately links the data to be collected and the conclusions to be drawn to the initial questions of study.*** It is a master plan specifying the methods of conducting research and what methods to be used.

The main design problems are :

(*a*) What questions to study ? Why ?

(*b*) What data are relevant ?

(*c*) What data to collect and how ?

(*d*) How to analyse and interpret the data ?

Thus, **the research design is basically a working plan/blue print** from **beginning to the end of a research study, involving collection, measurment and analysis of data.** The beginning rests in posing a set of research questions and the end is a set of conclusions about the questions.

- Research design concretises the research plan specifically before it is put to action, It is the plan and structure of investigations so conceived as to obtain answers to research questions.
- The research design indicates the steps that will be taken and in what squences they occur.

The **research strategy,** a subset of research design, includes elements of data collection and interpretation and emerges both from research purpose and question.

- Research design is an activity and a time based plan.
- It determines how to conduct research and takes into account of research questions and guides the selection of sources and types of information to be collected.
- It provides a framework for specifying relationship between variables, needed for the research study and systematically puts focus on procedures for every research activity from the beginning to end.
- A research design has five steps :
  - Purpose
  - Process
  - Data collection
  - Data analysis
  - Communication of findings
  - The research design tells the readers how the research was operationalized, as regards 'what', 'how' and 'why'.

An analogy :

Consider the design of a building construction. When constructing a building the ordering building materials and fixing the dates for completion of project stages will not carry any meaning until we know what sort of building-high rise office building/factory for manufacturing a machine/educational institution builiding/a residential home/a residential apartment block, is being constructed. Until this is done, we cannot sketch a plan, obtain permits, work out a work schedule or order materials.

Similarly, social research needs a design or structure before data collection or analysis can begin. A research design is **not just a work plan,** but a plan with all details that has to be done to complete the project. The work plan will flow from the project's research design.

The function of a research design is to ensure that the evidence obtained enables us to answer the initial question as unambiguously as possible. The research design is just like a complex system having different components, which should be examined separately and then combined together to come back into the system. A research design revolves around the research questions. Obtaining relevent evidence entails specifying the type of evidence needed to answer the research question, to test a theory, to evaluate a programme or to accurately describe some phenomenon. In other words, when designing research, we need to ask : given this research question (or theory) what type of evidence is needed to answer the question (or test the theory) in a **convincing** way ?

Before a builder or an architect can develop a work plan or order materials they can develop a work plan, or order materials, they must first establish the type of building required, its uses and the needs of the occupants. The work plan flows from these considerations. Similarly in social research the issues of sampling, method of data collection (*e.g.* questionnaire, observation, document analysis) and design of questions are all subsidiary to the matter of, what evidence do I need to collect ?

Often, the researchers start designing the questionnaires and begin interviewing before thinking what information they require to answer their research questions. Such endeavour without attending to design considerations in the beginning makes the conclusions weak and unconvincing and fails to answer the research questions.

3.2 NEED FOR RESEARCH DESIGN

- Research design systematizes the research operations.
- Advanced planning helps organizing data collection which involves the availability of field staff, time and money and devising solutions for possible field problems.
- A proper design of research study enhances the reliability of research results and minimizes any error that may upset the entire project.
- An appropriate design helps the researcher to systematically organising his ideas in a form which enable him to locate any flaws and inadequacies and thereby prompting him to revise the research design.

3.3 Structure of a Research Design

A research design consists of

- Problem identification
- Problem formulation
- Determination of Research design
    - Designing measurement
    - Instruments
    - Sampling; case studies
- Determination of data collection procedures
- Determination of Analytical procedures :
    - Data preparation
    - Data analysis
- Research reporting and evaluation.

3.4 Clsssification of Research Designs :

***The most common type of classification of research design is made according to research purpose*. Thus, the research designs are classified as :**

1. Exploratory research design
2. Conclusive research design
    - Descriptive research
    - Causal research

These research design are also termed as **basic research designs.**

A research design may also be distinguished according to other criteria:

- **Data collection techniques**
  - Personal observation
  - Interviewing
- **Period of study**
  - Cross-sectional
  - Longitudinal
- **Scope of Study**
  - Case studies
  - Statistical study.
- **Types of research questions :**
  - Explorative
  - Formal
- **Study environment :**
  - Field condition (Naturalistic)
  - Laboratory Condition
  - Simulation
- **Control of indepedent variables :**
  - Experimentai (manipulation, control and randomisation)
  - Quasi-experimental (manipulation, but no randomisation or no control group)
  - Non-experimental (no manipulation of independent variables)
- **Participants perceptions :**
  - Unbiased
  - Biased.
- **Occurence of independent variables (IV) and dependent variables (DV)**
  - Retrospective–study beings with DV and looks backward for cause and influence
  - Prospective–study begins with IV and looks forward for the effect.

Each of the research design can rely on one or more data collection techniques :

Primary data collection technique : This is an observation technique. The data are obstained by direct communication with subjects, e.g. survey techniques, interview or projective methods.

Secondary data collection technique : This essentially means reviewing literature and data sources, collected for some other purpose than the study at hand.

Whatever may be the data collection technique adopted for a study, it must satisfy the criteria of

- reliability
- validity

3.5 CHARACTERISTICS OF A GOOD RESEARCH DESIGN

A good research design has the following characteristic features :

- Objectivity
- Reliability
- Validity
- Generality

A research design should have clear cut **objectives** to be reflected in the collection, analysis and interpretation of observations.

Reliability refers to consistency to be checked throughout the series of taking observations. Precautions should be taken by different methods and relevant tests may be conducted for determining the reliability of responses.

The observations made on the units of enquiry must possess the characteristics of **validity** in the sense that the instruments or the questionnaires should measure what they purport to measure.

It is expected that a well planned research design should have the capability to **generalise the** findings of the study. The choice of the sampling design, the size of the sample and the method of taking observations ensuring reliability and validity lead toward generalizations.

3.6 FORMULATION OF A RESEARCH DESIGN

The formulation of a research design takes care of the following components.

(a) Title of the research study : The title of the study should be as precise as possible keeping in view of the objectives and scope of the study, expressed as far as possible in generalized terms.

(b) Statement of the problem ; its identification and formulation : The problem of the study is to be stated and posed in clear and unambiguous and precise terms.

(c) Review of literature : A brief review of the literature is to be given along with indications as to how far the present study would fill up the gap in the existing knowledge.

The research has to see what prior research has been conducted and what results were obtained.

In reviewing the literature, the researcher can gain information about

❒ Research methodology

❒ Study area frontiers and population

❒ Analysis techniques

Reviewing the literature helps the researcher refine his study question, data collection method and instrument and data analysis techniques.

(d) Area and scope of the study. As the scientific enquiries differ in their geographical, temporal and functional dimensions, it is essential that the research design should specify the subject area and coverage of the study both in respect of time and nature of data to be collected for the purpose.

(e) Objectives of the study. The objectives of the study are to be stated in precise terms of certain research questions for which answers are sought through scientific inquiries.

(f) Hypotheses. Hypotheses are product of the objectives of the study and should be stated unambiguously so that these can be rejected in the course of investigation to arrive at desired conclusion, close to things observable and to the body of the theory.

(g) Definition of concepts. Any scientific enquiry is embedded with certain concepts both formal and operational, which must be defined with utmost care before hand to enable the investigators to pose proper questions to respondents and collect relevant information. There should be specification of measures and scales at the design stage with prior specification and 'information needs'.

(h) Methods of data collection. Data collection is an important aspect of any type of research study. Inaccurate data collection can have impact on the results of a study and ultimately can lead to invalid results.

- Data may be collected either from primary sources or from secondary sources depending on the need of research project whether empirical or analytical.
- Information may be collected either on census (complete enumeration) or sample basis. Reasons for taking a decision on the matter depend on what is desired level of accuracy which decides whether to go for complete enumeration or for a sample study. If decided in favour of a sample study, then the question arises as to what should be the appropriate sampling design and what should be the sample size.

A sampling design refers to the method of selecting a sample to get a representative sample to estimate the desired population characteristic and to draw statistical conclusions.

Primary data may be collected either through the mailed questionnaires or introductory schedules or through participant observations. Construction of questionnaires and its pretest form an important component of design. Secondary data are collected from published sources, government reports, business research reports, personal diaries, etc.

The choice of the method whether quantitative or qualitative is prompted by the subject matter of study, the unit of enquiry and the scope of the study. It is expected that the researcher should keep the confidentiality of the collected data from the individuals and should be guided by ethical considerations.

(i) Data preparation, analysis and interpretation : After the collection, the data are put into statistical analysis, keeping in view the objectives of the study and the constructed hypotheses for the purpose. Towards this end, the raw data are to be processed by methods of condensation such as classification, tabulation and finding out certain statistical derivatives. Thus, at the design stage a data analysis and interpretation plan must be planned ahead.

(j) Research report writing : The researcher, finally, has to put his findings in a research report in a lucid way for the users whether in government, business or research organisations sponsoring the research study.

3.7 RESEARCH DESIGN VERSUS RESEARCH METHOD

Research design is different from a research method by which data are collected. Research design is a logical structure of an inquiry rather than a mode of data collection. There is nothing intrinsic about any research design that requires a particular method of data collection. Although cross-sectional surveys are frequently equated with questionnaires and case studies are often equated with participant observations, data for any design can be collected with any data collection method. How the data are collected is irrelevant to the logic of the design.

Failing to distinguish between design and method leads to poor evaluation of designs. Equating cross-sectional designs with questionnaires or case studies with participant observations, means that the designs are often evaluated against the strengths and weaknesses of the method rather than their ability to draw relatively unambiguous conclusions or to select between rival plausible hypotheses.

To make the distinctions between research designs and research methods and reasoning therefrom in a straight forward manner, it may be noted here that the research design may be any one of the following designs :

- ♦ Exploratory
  - ❒ Experiment
  - ❒ Case study
- ♦ Descriptive
  - ❒ Longitudinal design
  - ❒ Cross-sectional design
- ♦ Causal

Any one of these designs may use the following **methods of data collection** whether qualitative or quantitative, such as

- Questionnaire
- Interview (structured or loosely structured)
- Observation
- Analysis of documents
- Unobtrusive methods

Of course appropriateness of a particular method of data collection for a specified design is another matter for consideration.

Research design refers to the structure of an enquiry : it is a logical matter rather than a logistical one.

3.8 QUANTITATIVE AND QUALITATIVE RESEARCH (ARE THEY DESIGNS OR METHODS ?)

Sometimes, designs are equated with qualitative and quantitative research methods. Social surveys and experiments are frequently viewed as prime examples of quantitative research and are evaluated against the strengths and weaknesses of statistical, quantitative research methods and analysis. Case studies, on the other hand, are often seen as prime examples of qualitative research which adopts an interpretative approach to data, studies things within their context and considers the subjective meanings that people bring to their situation.

It is erroneous to equate a particular research design with either quantitative or qualitative methods. Yin (1993), a reputed social scientist and authority on case study design has stressed the irrelevance of the quantitative/qualitative distinction in case studies. That is, case study method (design) is not required to embrace any particular data collection method whether qualitative or quantitative.

3.9 BASIC RESEARCH DESIGNS

Social researchers look for answers two fundamental types of research questions :

What is going on (exploratory/descriptive research) ?

Why is it going on (explanatory/causal research) ?

A researcher needs to know where the design fits into the whole research process from framing a question to finally analysing and reporting data. Answers to 'What' questions are explored by exploratory research and quantitatively by descriptive research. Descriptive research initiates the 'why' questions in causal research.

Answering the 'why' questions involves developing causal explanations. Some causal explanations may be simple while others will be more complex.

The basic research designs differ according to

Objective

Characteristics

Method

They may be classified as (Fig 3.1)

- **Exploratory Research**
- **Conclusive Reserach :**
  - Descriptive Research (Cross-sectional/longitudinal)
  - Causal Research

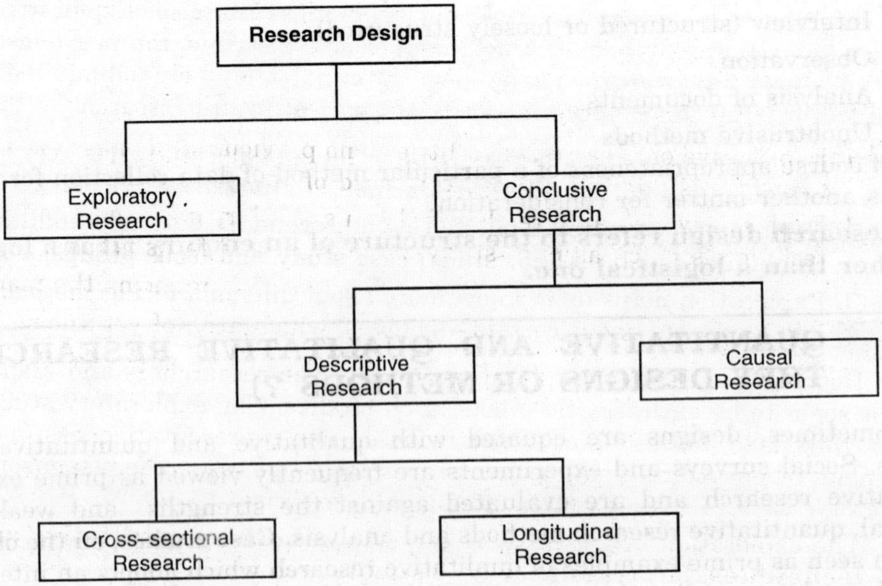

Fig. 3.1 Classification of Research Design.

TABLE 3.1

A Comparison of Basic Research Designs

	Exploratory	Descriptive	Causal
Objective :	Discovery of ideas and insights	Describe market characteristics or functions	Determine cause and effect relationships
Characteristics :	Flexible Versatile Often the front end of total research design	Marked by the prior formulation of specific hypotheses Preplanned and structured design	Manipulation of one or more independent variables Control of other mediating variables
Methods :	• Expert surveys • Pilot surveys • Case studies • Secondary data • Focus group	• Secondary data • Surveys • Panels • Observational and other data	• Experiments • Simulation

Among the basic research designs there is an increasing certainty in the problems defined as we move from exploratory to causal research. For instance, in market research we may distinguish between the degree of certainty associated with problems under different researches.

- **'Our sales are declining and we donot know why'.** *–Exploratory*
- **"What kinds of people buy our product ? Who buys our competitors' products ?"** *–Descriptive*
- **Would buyers prefer this new package design ?** *–Causal.*

3.9.1. Exploratory Research

Explorative research/studies is not an aimless exercise. Explorative studies are useful when the researcher does not have clear idea about the problems at hand and sometimes may have certain vague ideas in mind. They help delimit the problem and clearly outline the information needed as a part of future research.

- Explorative only exists when little or no previous study has ever been done and knowlege is minimal in a certain field of study.
- Exploratory research tends to rely on secondary data and qualitative research techniques such as pilot study, case study and focus groups.
- Exploration helps us to know more about dilemma facing the manager/sponsor and knolwege about certain variables, which are not yet known completely.

Despite the utility of exploratory studies, the researchers and managers usually do not seem to be enthusiastic about such studies. The exploratory studies are sometimes linked to biases like subjectiveness, non-representativeness, non-systematic design and hence diminising popularity among the researchers/sponsors. Of course, budgetory constraints may often inhibit such exercise.

The exploration in research is carried out **both by qualitative and quantitative techniques,** but relies heavily on qulitative ones.

Qualitative techniques emphasize on 'what' where as quantitative techniques attempt to find out 'how much'. Qualitative refers to meaning, analogy or model characterizing something, but the quantitative assumes a making and refers to measure it.

There are several approaches in qualitative research, which can be used in exploration'.

These are :

(*a*) In-depth interviewing (*b*) Participant observations, (*c*) Film, photographs, videotape, etc., (*d*) Case studies (*e*) Street ethnography (*f*) Expert interviewing (*f*) Document analyses (*h*) Proxemics and kinesics.

Four types of exploratory techniques are discussed in the following :

- ❒ Secondary data analysis
- ❒ Experience surveys
- ❒ The focus group
- ❒ Case studies

• Secondary data Analysis

Secondary data refer to data collected by others to suit their own research needs. A researcher needs to refer to any data sources which exist already that can be brought to bear on the problem at hand. To collect primary data for the same purpose sounds wastage of resources. He may also review prior studies and make use of historical data. Such endeavour will help the researcher.

- ❒ to have a look on the appropriateness of methodology.
- ❒ to search for an explanation of the theoretical rationale of the problem being studied.
- ❒ to be aware of the success stories about the past on the same or related subject along with deficiencies, if any, which may be taken care of in the present study.

The second source of secondary data is published documents by authors not connecte with the agency sponsoring the present study. In the present day world scenario large number of periodicals, journals and authoritative books on all disciplines including business studies may be helpful for exploratory research and the present status of the problem at hand. Further, advancement in electronic communication has brought the knowledge to the door step with all its development. Internet facilities in the computers provide rich source of seconday data base and the number of websites are available for the purpose with knowlege explosion. A creative mind with immense curiosity to proceed toward unknown will always get tips for further research from the secondary sources, which serve an excellent background to create new knowledge.

• Experience Surveys

Although published information forms an important sources of secondary data, it only covers a small fraction of information available in any organisation. Moreover, the internal data base of many organisation are rarely well organised and also a researcher, being an outsider in most cases may not have easy access to available information. It, then, becomes necessary to collect information from the experienced and knowledgeable persons in the area of study. This is achieved by an **experience survey** in which persons who matter are interviewed to know their views of important issues or aspects of the subject and to know the usually inaccessible, information 'where' and 'from whom' in th organisation. This needs the use of an extensive and flexible investigative format by the researcher to explore various aspects emerged during the interview. Such questioning endeavour by the researcher may help to contemplate a new hypothesis, discarding the older ones or at least produce new line of thinking intensifying the practicality of the study.

In a business research concerning a business organization, the researcher may enter into discussions with various segments of employees in getting information from sources that might be insightful.

• The Focus Group

In the applied social sciences including business studies, focus group discussions or group depth interviews are among the most widely used research tools. A focus group takes advantage of the interaction between a small group of people, made up of anywhere between 6 to 12 people with common characteristics and also having certain knowledge base or familiarly with a given topic. It must, however, be recognized that focus group discussion will only attract a certain types of participant, for the most part extroverts.

Participants will respond to and build on what others in the group have said. It is believed that this synergistic approach generates more insightful information, and encourages discussion participants to give more candid answers.

Focus groups are further characterized by the presence of a *moderator* and the use of a discussion guide. The moderator should stimulate discussion among group members rather than interview individual members, that is to say every participant should be encouraged to express his/her views on each topic as well as respond to the views expressed by other participants. In order to put focus group participants at ease, the moderator will often start out by assuring every one that there are no right or wrong answers, and that his/her feelings can not be hurt by any views that are expressed since he does not work for the organization for whom the research is being conducted.

Although the moderator's role is relatively passive, it is critical in keeping the discussion relevant. Some participants will try to dominate the discussion or talk about aspects that are of little interest to the research at hand. The type of data that needs to be obtained from the participants will determine the extent to which the session needs to be structured and therefore just how directive the moderator must be.

Although focus group sessions can be held in many different settings, and have been known to be conducted via *conference call*, they are most often conducted in special facilities that permit *audio recording* and/or *video taping* and are equipped with a *one-way mirror*. This observation of research process as it happens can be invaluable when trying to interpret the results. Many disparate views that are expressed in the course of 1 to 2 hours discussion make at times difficult to capture all observations on each topic. Rather than simply summarizing comments, possible avenues for further research or hypotheses for testing should be brought out.

It is a common practice to provide a *monetary incentive* to focus group participants. The incentive makes it easier to recruit participants, but can lead to 'professional' respondents. These professional participants by virtue of attending too many focus groups learn to anticipate the flow of the discussion. Some argue that these types of respondents no longer represent the population.

• Case Studies

Case studies are detailed investigations of individuals, groups, programs, policies, decisions, organizations and institutions or other social units. The researcher conducting a case study attempts to analyse the variables relevant to the subject under study. The principal difference between case studies and other research studies is that focus of attention is the individual case and not the whole population of cases.

Most studies search for what is common and pervasive. However, in the case study, the focus may not be on generalization but on understanding the particulars of that case in its complexity.

A case study focuses on a bounded system, usually under natural conditions, so that system can be understood in its own habitat.

The methods used in case study research is similar to those of naturalistic inquiry. However, the data collection is often more structured, using key informant interviews, structured observations of events and interactions and the collection and content analysis of relevant document (*e.g.* to help establish the facts, the assumptions, values and priorities, or to illuminate differences in perceptions). Case studies often also include quantitative data for background or to help generate questions to ask informants (*e.g.* data on demographics, health status, utilization, finances, etc.)

3.9.2. Conclusive Research

The **conclusive research** is meant to provide information that is useful in reaching conclusions or decision making.

- It relies both on primary and secondary data.
- It provides a reliable or representative picture of the population through the use of valid research instrument.
- In the case of formal research it will also test hypothesis.

Conclusive research can be sub-divided into two major categories :

- Descriptive or statistical reasearch
- Causal research

• Descriptive Research

Descriptive research or statistical research provides data about the population or universe being studied. But it can only describe the 'who, what, when, where, and how' of a situation, not what caused it. Therefore, descriptive research is used when the objective is to provide a systematic description, that is as factual and accurate as possible.

Descriptive research encompasses much goverment sponsored research including the population census, agricultural census, census of manufacturing industries, the collection of wide range of social indicators and economic information such as household expenditure patterns, employment surveys, industrial surveys etc.

Description can be **concrete or abstract**. A relatively **concrete** description might describe the ethnic mix of a community, the changing age profile of a population or the gender mix of a work place. Alternatively the description might ask more **abstract** questions such as. Is the level of social inequality rising ? How secular is the society ? How much poverty is there in the community ?

Good description provokes the 'why' questions of explanatory research. If we detect social polarization in last two decades, we are forced to ask 'why is this happening? This may help to develop elaborate theories for answering such questions.

Of course, description can degenerate to mindless fact gathering, sometimes called **abstracted empiricism.** Examples are many about unfocused surveys and case studies that report trivial information, fail to provoke any 'why' question or provide any basis for generalization.

It provides the number of times something occurs and lends itself to statistical calculations such as determining the average number of occurrences or central tendencies. One of the major limitations is that it cannot help determine what causes a specific behaviour, motivation or occurrence. As such it cannot establish a causal research relationship between variables, but may lead to causal questions.

As formalized studies, the descriptive studies serve, a variety of research objectives such as description of certain phenomena or characteristics, estimates of certain statistical derivatives–average, proportion etc., discovery of associations among different variables (correlational study)

Descriptive research may be classified into

- Cross-sectional research
- Longitudinal research

Cross sectional studies calls for data gathering at a single time and can be thought of as providing a 'snap shot' of the frequency and characteristics of an object at a particular point of time. It studies the relationship between variables at a point of time, for instance the relationship between income, locality and personal expenditure.

Longitudinal stdies are studies which observe the state of the world without manipulating it at several points in time.

The advantage of a logitudinal study is that it can track changes over time. Longitudinal studies include

- Cohort studies
- Panel studies

Cohort studies sample a cohort, defined as a group experiencing some event in a selected time period and studying them at intervals through time.

Panel studies sample a cross section and survey it at (usually regular) intervals.

A **retrospective** study is a longitudinal study that it looks back in time. For instance, a researcher may look up the medical records of previous years to look for a trend.

As longitudinal studies are observational, they have less power to detect causal relationships than do experiments. But because of the repeated observation at the individual level, they have more power than cross-sectional observational studies, by virtue of being able to exclude time-invariant unobserved individual differences, and by virtue of observing the temporal order of events.

• Causal Research

Causal research is a conclusive research and its objective is to determine which variable might be causing a certain behaviour *i.e.* whether there is cause and effect relationship between variables. In order to determine causality, it is important to hold the variable that is assumed to cause the change in the other variable(s) constant and then measure the changes in the other variable(s). This type of research is very complex and the researcher can never be completely certain that there are not other factors influencing the causal relationship, expecially when dealing with people's attitudes and motivations. There are often much deeper psychological considerations, that even the respondent may not be aware of.

The term *causation* is applied to situation where A 'produces' B or A 'forces' B to occur. But empirically one can never demonstrate A-B causality with certainty. We can not demonstrate A-B causal linkages deductively and empirical conclusions are inferences—inductive conclusions. Hence, probability statements are bound to be made on what we observe and measure and moreover it is not possible to observe and measure all the processes that may account for A-B relationship.

Causal relationship

In causal analysis one is interested to know how one variable affects or is responsible for changes in other variables. In business research the cause effect relationship is not very much explicit and we need to be more interested in understanding, explaining, predicting and controlling relationships between variables than searching about the causality.

We may visualize *three* types of relationship between two variables.

These are :

- ❒ Symmetrical
- ❒ Reciprocal
- ❒ Asymmetrical

A *symmetrical* relationship is one in which two variables fluctuate together, but we can not say that one is the cause of the other. For instance, correlation between low attendance in the office and active participation in company club may be the result of changes in outlook towards life style of the employees.

In a *reciprocal* relationship two variables mutually influence each other, *e.g.* reading of an advertisement and use of a brand of a product.

Asymmetrical relationship exists in researches, in which changes in one variable (independent variable) are responsible for changes in another variable (dependent variable). The identification of the variable, whether independent or dependent, often seems to be obyious to a researcher, but sometimes it is not so simple.

Some causal explanations may be simple while other will be more complex. Three types of causal relationship may be identified.

(a) Direct causal relationship. Phenomenon Y (*e.g.* income level) is affected by factor X (*e.g.* gender). We may argue that there is a direct effect of gender on income.

Gender ⟶ Income level

(b) Indirect causal relationship. A causal chain :

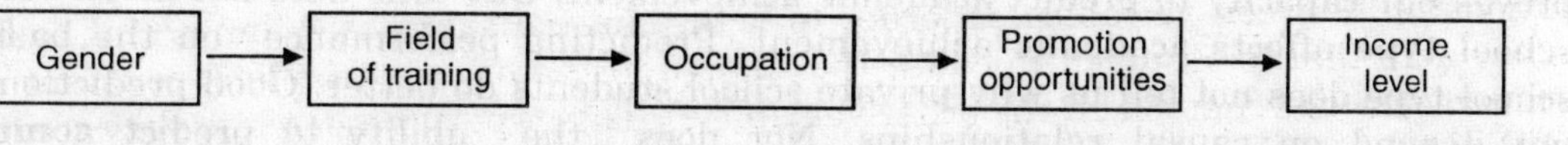

In this causal relationship (chain), gender affects choice of field of training which in turn affects occupational options, which are linked to opportunities for promotion, which in turn affect income level.

(c) A more complex causal model of direct indirect causal links may be represented as follows :

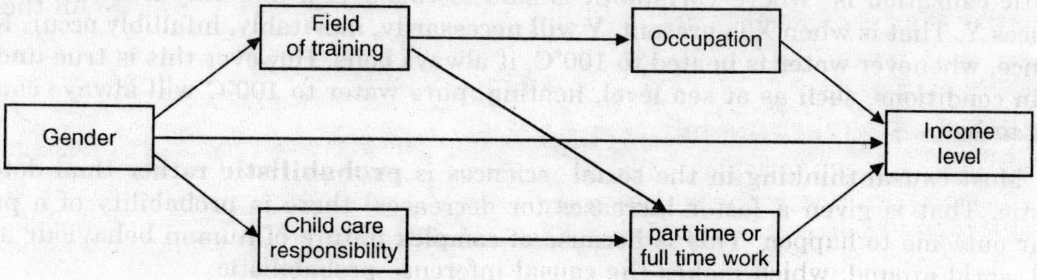

Exploring Cause-effect relationship :

The cause effect relationship between two variables may be determined by

- Experimentation
- Simulation

The **experimentation** is a highly controlled method, which allows the researcher to manipulate a specific independent variable to determine the effect of such manipulation on the dependent variables. It calls for a **control group** as well as an **experimental group** and subjects would be assigned randomly to either group. The experimentation may be conducted either under laboratory conditions or in the field (natural setting).

Another way of establishing causality between variables is through the use of **simulation.** Simulation like experimentation is a quantitative research technique and is the secondary research in nature. By changing one variable in the mathematical model, it is possible to note its effect on the other variable in the model equation.

Correlation, Prediction and Causation :

People often confuse correlation with causation. Two factors may co-vary. But it does not mean that one causes the other. Confusing causation with correlation also confuses prediction with causation. When two events or characteristics are correlated, we can predict one from the other. For instance, knowing the type of school attended improves our capacity to predict academic achievement. But this does not mean that the school type affects academic achievement. Predicting performance on the basis of school type does not tell us why private school students do better. Good prediction does not depend on causal relationships. Nor does the ability to predict accurately demonstrate anything about causality.

While we can observe correlation we cannot observe cause. We have to only infer cause. These inferences, however, are fallible and indirectly linked to observables. Because, our inferences are fallible, we must minimize the chances of incorrectly saying that a relationship causal when in fact it is not. One of the fundamental purposes of research design causal/explanatory research is to avoid invalid inferences.

The cause-effect relationship may be either deterministic or probabilistic. Deterministic causation is where variable X is said to cause Y, if and only if X invariably produces Y. That is when X is present, Y will necessarily, inevitably, infallibly occur. For instance, whenever water is heated to 100°C, it always boils. However this is true under certain conditions, such as at sea level, heating pure water to 100°C will always cause water to boil.

Most causal thinking in the social sciences is **probabilistic** rather than deterministic. That is given a factor increases (or decreases) there is probability of a particular outcome to happen. This is because of complex nature of human behaviour and social world around, which makes the causal inference probabilistic.

3.9.3 Research Design : A Sceptical Approach to Research

The need for research design stems from a sceptical approach to research and a view that scientific knowledge must always be provisional. The purpose of the research design is to reduce the ambiguity of much research evidence.

Good research designs will anticipate competing explanations before collecting data so that relevant information for evaluating the relative merits of these competing explanations is obtained.

In summary the researcher should adopt a sceptical approach to explanations. He should anticipate rival interpretations and collect data to enable the winnowing out of the weaker explanations and the identification of which alternative theories make most empirical sense. He also needs to ask what data would challenge the explanation and collect data to evaluate theory from this more demanding perspective.

3.9.4 Research Design : Plausible Rival Hypotheses

A fundamental strategy of social research involves evaluating plausible rival hypotheses. A researcher needs to examine and evaluate alternative ways of explaining a particular phenomenon. This applies regardless of whether the data are quantitative or qualitative, regardless of particular design (experimental, cross-sectional, longitudinal or case study) and regardless of the method of data collection (*e.g.* observation, questionnaire). The researcher's needs to develop mind set to anticipate alternative ways of interpreting findings and to regard any interpretation of these finidngs a provisional subject to further testing.

The central role of a causal research design is to minimise the chance of drawing incorrect causal inference from data. When designing research it is essential that we identify the type of evidences required to answer the research question in a convincing way. This means that we must simply collect evidence that is consistent with a particular theory or explanation. Research needs to be structural in such a way that the evidence also bears on alternative rival explanations and enables us to identify which of the competing explanations is most compelling empirically. It also means that we must not simply look for evidence that supports our favourite theory : we should also look for evidence that has the potential to disprove our preferred explanations.

EXERCISES

1. What is a research design ? What are its main problems ? Discuss.
2. What are the characteristics of a good research design ? Discuss.
3. Describe different components of a research design.
4. How would you classify research designs according to research purpose ? Discuss.
5. **Distinguish between :**
   (*i*) exploratory research and conclusive research.
   (*ii*) descriptive research and causal research.
   (*iii*) cross-sectional research and longitudinal research.
6. 'The uncertainty associated with the research problem, determines the research methodology'. Comment on this statement.
7. Distinguish between experimentation and simulation.
8. Explain types of causal relationship.
9. Classify exploratory techniques.
10. Write notes on (*i*) Focus group (*ii*) Conclusive research (*iii*) Experience survey.

□□□

CHAPTER

4

MEASUREMENT PROBLEMS AND SCALING TECHNIQUES

4.1. What is measurement ?

Measurement is the foundation of any scientific investigation.

Everything we do begins with the measurement of whatever we want to study. In our everyday life we come across measurement of certain objects or things such as height, weight or a feature of a physical object. We may also like to measure the personality and attitude of a person or his preferences towards certain objects or phenomena. As per dictionary meaning, to measure is to discover the extent, dimensions, quantity or capacity of something, especially by comparison with a standard.

Measurement denotes the assignment of certain numbers or symbols to empirical events, objects in compliance with a set of well developed and meaningful rules in a systematic fashion. The measuring process starts with

- ❒ Selection of observable events.
- ❒ Development of certain mapping rules, *i.e.* scheme of assigning numbers to measurable events.
- ❒ Application of mapping rules to each observation under consideration.

The assignment of numbers or symbols are done in such a way that the relationships of numbers/symbols reflect the relationships of the attitudes of things being measured. To observe gender we may either use symbols F and M for females and males respectively. Alternatively, we may use the number 0 (zero) for female and 1 (one) for male. A mapping rule can reflect both qualitative and quantitative concepts.

A particular **procedure** of assigning numbers or symbols to measure something is called a **scale of measurement.**

A scale may be defined as a continuum from highest to lowest points

having certain other intermediate points between these two extremes. Scales are primarily used to measure attitudes, values and other characteristics of objects. They measure the degree to which an individual possesses certain characteristics of interest.

The question now arises as to what one really measures. Broadly speaking, it is **the variable which we measure.** The researcher measures the variable/construct, classified as objects or as properties. The objects denote things such as table, chair, people, books, automobiles, plants etc. or less concrete ones like genes, attitudes, neutrons. **Properties** are characteristics of objects. For instance, physical properties of a person may be his/her height, weight etc. and psychological properties may be attitude, personality, behaviour, etc. and social properties may include leadership ability, religion, class classification or status. A research study covers these and many other properties an individual/object. However, in practice a researcher does not measure either object or property but the indicants of the properties or indicants of properties of objects. These concepts are so much intermixed that one thinks as if he is observing the objects or properties directly. There are certain objects/events like 'motivation to succeed', problem solving ability, etc., whose properties are not easy to be measured. In these situations one needs to search for some indicants to measure them indirectly. To make the indicants operationally free from disagreement and controversies is an important aspect in any behavioural research study.

4.2. Data types and measurement scales

A researcher devises certain *mapping rules* and then translates the observation of property indicants using this rule. Thus, several types of data whether qualitative or quantitative are generated for each variable/concept/construct considered for the purpose, depending on assumption about mapping rules. Each data type is based on certain underlying assumptions about how numbers/symbols correspond to real world observation.

Mapping rules **may have following characteristics :**

- Classification : Numbers used to group and classify.
- Order : Numbers are ordered.
- Distance : Differences between numbers are ordered. No unique origin.
- Origin : The number series has a unique origin indicated by zero.

Combination of mapping rules—classification, order, distance and origin give rise to classification measurement scales according to properties or four levels of measurement of a variable such as

- Nominal (categorical)
- Ordinal (rank)
- Interval
- Ratio

The level of measurement of a variable is a classification, proposed to describe the nature of information contained in their numbers assigned to objects and therefore within the variable. **The levels of measurement/scales generate four types of data—nominal, ordinal, interval and ratio.** These levels or scales were proposed by Stanley Smith Stevens in 1946 article 'On the Theory of Scales of Measurement'. Different mathematical operations on variables are possible, depending on the level or scale at which a variable is measured. The scales are distinguished on the basis of relationships assumed to exist between objects having different scale values.

Nominal scale

A nominal scale classifies or categorizes objects, individuals into two or more categories. Nothing is accounted to decide which object goes into which category. In nominal scale categories are mutually exclusive. It is a simple method of classification or labelling rather than an arrangement on a continuum scale. For example, classification of individuals according to sex, religion, caste, communities etc. is done with a nominal scale. The label numbers do not stand for quantities. Hence, nominal data do not provide quantitative information.

Nominal Scale

- ❒ Not really a scale ; it does not scale any dimension.
- ❒ It simply labels objects. Example : Gender : Male—1, Female—2

Categorical data are measured on nominal scales which merely assign labels to distinguish categories. In research activities a Yes/No scale is nominal. Here, there is no order and there is no distance between Yes and No.

Ordinal Scale

An ordinal scale is one in which data can be ordered in some way—either high to low or from low to high. Ordinal numbers specify relative position of items in a group. Thus ordinal scale provides ranks to individuals such as 1st, 2nd, 3rd .... along a specified continuum. It only indicates individual's position but nothing at all about distances between positions. Ordinal variables are also called *Rank variables.* In social science research attitudes like preference, conservatism or prejudice and social class can be represented by ordinal scale.

Ordinal Scale

- ❒ Numbers are used to place objects in order and rank them.
- ❒ But, there is no information regarding the differences (intervals) between points on the scale.

Interval scale (Cardinal scale)

An interval scale has all the characteristics of an ordinal scale with an additional feature that the distances between points on the scale are ideally equal for equal units.

It not only orders the individuals but also measures the distance between them. For example, temperature from 20°C to 30°C is the same as interval —5°C to 5°C. This means that as per the measure system, the expansion of mercury changes by equal amounts for equal numerical units.

Interval scale

- ❒ A interval scale is a scale on which equal intervals between objects represent equal differences.
- ❒ The interval differences are meaningful.
- ❒ But we cannot defend ratio relationships.

However, it may be pointed out here that the temperature 20°C cannot be considered as twice as hot as 10°C.

Interval scale does not measure the relative magnitude, but involves the use of numbers to represent equal intervals in different segments on a continuum.

The numbers assigned to objects have all the features of ordinal measurements and in addition equal differences between measurements represent equal intervals. That is, differences between arbitrary pairs of measurements can be meaningfully compared. Operations such as addition and subtraction are therefore meaningful. The zero point is arbitrary. Ratios between numbers on the scale are not meaningful, so operations such as multiplication and division cannot be carried out directly. *Variables measured at the interval level are called Interval Variables.* Examples of interval measures are the year, month and date in calenders and temperatures in Celsius (°C) scale or Fahrenheit (°F) scale. Interval measures commonly used in social scientific research are constructed measures such as standardized Intelligence Quotient tests (IQ).

Ratio scale

An interval scale having an actual or true zero point is called a *Ratio scale.* Examples of ratio scale are : distance, income, height, age etc. On the basis of ratio scale are compared both differences in scores and the relative magnitude of scores. For example, in a ratio scale absence of height means no height and absence of weight represents zero weight. The weights 10 kg, 15 kg, 20 kg, 25 kg of four items indicate the weight of 3rd item is twice as heavy as the first item. The difference between the weights of 1st and 2nd item is the same interval as the difference between 2nd and 3rd and between 3rd and 4th item. Ratios can be formed between any two given values on the scale. Then, a ratio scale involves the use of numbers to represent equal distances from a known zero point by the researcher. The numbers assigned to objects have all the features of interval measurement and also have meaningful ratios between arbitrary pairs of numbers. Operations such as multiplication and division are therefore meaningful. The zero value on a ratio scale is non-arbitrary. Variables measured at the ratio scaled are called *Ratio variables*. Social variables of ratio measure include age, length, place of residence in a given place, number of industrial establishments at different points of time.

Ratio scale

- ❒ Has a true zero point.
- ❒ Ratios are meaningful.
- ❒ Physical scales of time, length and volume are ratio scales.
- ❒ We can say 20 seconds is twice as long as 10 seconds.

Interval and/or ratio measurement are sometimes called *'true measurement'*. Only ratio or interval scales can correctly be said to *hav units of measurement.*

Measurement scales assume importance in social and business research because they relate to type of statistics, that can be used for the analysis of data. For instance, the only kind of measure of central tendency appropriate to nominal measurement is the Mode, but no notion of standard deviation exists. The central tendency of an *ordinally* measured variable can be represented by its Mode or its Median. Ordinal data would use non-parametric statsitics. These include rank order correlation, non-parametric analysis of variance and further, modelling techniques can also be used with ordinal data.

The central tendency of a variable measured at the interval level can be represented by its mode, its median or its arithmetic mean; the mean gives the most information. Interval scale data can use parametric statistical techniques such as mean and standard deviation; correlation coefficient, regression, analysis of variance, factor analysis along with a wide range of multivariate and modelling techniques.

The central tendency of a variable measured at the ratio level can be represented by its mode, its median, its arithmetic mean or its geometric mean; however as with an interval scale, the artithmetic mean gives the most useful information. All statistical treatments and modelling can be applied to a variable measured in ratio scale. Thus, the following observations are worth mentioning in the context discussed above :

- ❒ The underlying construct or variable being measured defines the scale of measurement, not the numbers themselves.
- ❒ Statistical procedures use numbers without considering the underlying constructs that are measured.
- ❒ Measurement is the foundation but whether or not satisfies can be interpreted depending on research design issues.

4.3. Sources of measurement error

An ideal study should be designed and implemented with precise and unambiguous measurement of variables which are hardly attainable in their entirety. Hence, certain types of error are likely to occur in the process of measurement, some of which are systematic while the remainder may be random or erratic.

True differences among the respondents or measurements may be contaminated by the following major sources of error :

- ❒ the respondent.
- ❒ the situational factors during interview or measurement session.
- ❒ the measurer/interviewer.
- ❒ the instrument used for data collection.

4.4. Characteristics of sound measurement

The quality of data depends on sound measurement tool. Thus, the question arises as to what are the characteristics of sound measurement ? There are *three major criteria* for evaluating a measuring instrument : *reliability, validity and practicality.*

Reliability and validity

Whenever a research social scientist discusses measurement in the form of scales, tests, surveys, etc. the question arises as to whether the measures are reliable and valid.

Reliability implies the extent to which a measuring device is consistent in measuring whatever it measures. In case of surveys, the questionnaire should produce the same results when administered on the same respondents at different times and when different investigators/ observers measuring the same trait come up with same ratings. Reliability is conceived with estimates of the degree to which a measurement is free of random or unstable error. Reliable instruments are robust, that is, they work well at different times under different conditions.

Validity refers to the extent to which one instrument measures what it is intended to measure or what one thinks it is measuring. Validity is always specific to the particular purpose for which the instrument is being used. It requires the measurement tool to be sensitive to all the nuances of meaning in the variable and to changes in nuances in meaning over time. The difficulty in meeting the test of validity is that usually one does not know what the true differences are. The concept of validity is an important aspect for which the researcher should be careful in defining variables and designing the study. It may be possible for a measuring instrument to be reliable without being valid. But validity presupposes reliability.

The relationship between reliability and validity can be best understood by illustrating with use of weight measurement scale. If the scale measures weight correctly, then it is both reliable and valid. But if there is constant bias in the measurement that is the weighing machine overweighs you by three kg., then the scale is reliable but not valid. If the scale erratically measures the weight, it is not reliable and therefore cannot be valid. Therefore, if a measurement is not valid, it does not matter if it is reliable because it does not measure what the designer purports to measure towards solving his research problem. In this example, reliability is not as valuable as validity, but reliability is much easier to assess.

Reliability is affected by random errors creeping into measurement. Random errors arise from a number of sources. These are :

- errors inherent in the instrument.
- imprecise scoring procedures.
- ambiguous questions.
- errors inherent in the administration of the instrument (inexperienced persons may depart from standardized procedures).
- pupil error (fluctuations in motivation, interest, fatigue, physical condition, anxiety and other mental and emotional factors).

Reliability procedures are concerned with determining the degree of inconsistency in scores due to random error in scores. It is assumed that every test score (X) consists of two parts—true test score (T) and random error in measurement (E). Thus,

$$X = T + E$$

Mathematically, the variance of the observed score of a large group of subjects, the variance of true scores and variance of their errors of measurement are related by

$$\sigma_x^{\ 2} = \sigma_t^{\ 2} + \sigma_e^{\ 2}$$

Reliability is defined as

$$\gamma_{xx} = \frac{\sigma_t^{\ 2}}{\sigma_x^{\ 2}}$$

that is, ratio of the true score variance to the observed score variance in a set of scores. In other words, reliability is the progression of the variance in the observed score, that is free from error of measurement. This is called *Coefficient of reliability,* which may be alternatively expressed as

$$\gamma_{xx} = 1 - \frac{\sigma_e^{\ 2}}{\sigma_x^{\ 2}}$$

which ranges from 1 to 0 (γ_{xx} is 1 when there is no error and 0 when measurements are all error). The coefficient close to 1 indicates high reliability.

Reliability can be estimated from the observed scores by correlating the scores on same individuals on different occasions or with different sets of equivalent items. Reliability indices may be computed by following procedures such as : (*a*) Test- Retest Reliablity (*b*) Equivalent-Forms Reliability. To estimate the reliability of a test, it is required to administer the test to the same group of individuals on two occasions and compute the correlation coefficient from the paired scores. This correlation coefficient is called **Test-Retest Reliability Coefficient** and also sometimes referred to as **coefficient of stability** because it is indicative of the consistency of subjects. **Alternatively,** reliability may be estimated by *alternate or parallel forms technique* where one correlates the results of equivalent forms of the test administered to the same individuals rather than correlating the results of two administrations of the same test to the same group, which may be biased by the recall effect in the responses. The resulting coefficient of reliability may be termed as **coefficient of equivalence.**

Besides the above techniques there are certain other procedures to compute measures of reliability which are designed to determine whether the items in a test are measuring the same thing. These are called the **internal consistency procedures** which take into account only a single administration of one form of a test.

Some of these procedures are :

(*a*) split-half reliability, which artifically splits the test into two halves and correlates the individual scores on two forms.

(*b*) procedures to assess inter-item consistency or homogeneity of items *e.g.* Kuder-Richardson procedures.

Certain factors do affect the reliability coefficient :

(*i*) Reliability of a test is a function of the length of the test. That is, longer the test the greater its reliability.

(*ii*) Reliability is a function of group heterogeneity. The reliability coefficient increases as the heterogeneity of the test subjects increases.

(*iii*) The reliability of a test is partly a function of ability of the test subjects.

(*iv*) Reliability depends on the nature of the variables being measured.

(*v*) Reliability is in part a function of the specific technique used for its estimation.

Validity is purpose specific. A test/measurement that has validity in one situation may not be valid in a different situation or for a different purpose. Here comes question of relevant evidence. What is relevant depends on the nature of the research problem and the researcher's is judgement.

The means for determining validity may be grouped into the following categories :

(*a*) Content validity

(*b*) Construct related validity

(*c*) Criterion related validity

The content validity of a measuring instrument (measurement scale) is the extent to which it provides adequate coverage of the investigative questions guiding the study. The content related evidence shows how far a sample of items is representative of some defined universe or domain of content.

Construct related validity focuses its attention on the test score measure of psychological trait or construct, which is not directly measurable but can only explain observable effects. To evaluate construct validity we consider both theory and the measuring instrument used for the purpose. If we are interested in measuring the effect of industrial exhibition on sales promotion, the way in which exhibition operationally defined would have to correspond to empirically grounded theory. **First,** the construct has to be meaningful in a theoretical sense, and then we would investigate the adequacy of the instrument.

The criterion validity refers the success of measures used for prediction or estimation. The criteria selected for measurement should be relevant, free from bias, reliable and available, so that they can really be valid for prediction or estimation of certain characteristics. There are certainly difficulties in estimating validity. For instance, consider the estimation of family income. Although true income does exist for every family, it is difficult to get this figure in practice. Even if the criterion is conceptually clear, it may be unavailable due to different reasons.

Practicality

Besides the scientific requirements of reliability and validity for the measurement process, the researcher needs practicality as an operational requirement. Practicality has been defined as economy, convenience and interpretability. Any research project needs certain budget and therefore the measuring device for the data collection must be guided by economic factors. Further, it must be convenient to be applied in practice.

4.5. Selection of Measurement Scales

Social science researcher devises scaling procedure for the assignment of numbers (or symbols) to a property of objects so that the characteristics of numbers get associated with the properties in question. In practice, numbers are assigned to the indicants of the properties of objects. While selecting a measurement scale the researcher has to consider the following points for a decision.

These are :

- Research objectives
- Response types
- Degrees of preference
- Data properties
- Number of dimensions
- Method of construction.

The researcher generally has two **objectives** in collecting information from respondents. He may be required to observe the characteristics of respondents. Alternatively he may use the respondent as judges to collect information on objects or indicants in question. For instance, he may like to study the attitude of respondents towards a development programme of the government to obtain information on attitudinal differences. Secondly, he may be interested to know how the respondents rate different governmental programmes *i.e.* to study differences in acceptance level.

The measurement scales can be classified according to **nature of responses** received from the respondents. A *rating scale* is used when the respondents score on an object or on its indicant without comparing with other objects. A *ranking scale* is used when the respondent participant makes comparison among two or more indicants or objects. *Categorization* requires the respondents to classify or categorize objects/indicants in question in groups or categories.

Measurement scales may **involve preferences or non-preference evaluation.** Individual respondent may be asked to choose the object he prefers. Alternatively, the respondent may be asked to judge which object possesses more of same characteristic without showing any personal preference for any object.

Measurement scales may be distinguished as to **properties of data,** generated by each scale-nominal, ordinal, interval or ratio. These levels of measurement describe the nature of information contained within numbers assigned to objects/variables. This is a matter of concern because the type of statistical treatment given to the data depends on properties of data.

Measurement Sales may be either **unidimensional or multidimensional.** In a unidimensional scale the researcher seeks to measure only one attribute of the respondent/object, while in multidimensional scaling an object is described in an attitude space of n-dimensions. For instance, the promotability of an employee in a business organisation may be better expressed by three dimensions such as performance, technical knowledge and team work.

Measurement scales may be classified according to methods of construction. **Five** approaches may be considered while constructing a measurement scale.

These are :

- **Arbitrary.** A scale is custom-designed to measure a property or indicant.
- **Consensus.** Judges evaluate the items to be included.
- **Item analysis.** Measurement scales are tested with a sample of respondents.
- **Cumulative.** Scales are chosen for their conformity to a ranking of items with ascending or descending discriminating power.
- **Factoring.** Scales are constructed from inter-correlations of items from other studies. In factoring common factors account for relationships. The relationships are measured statistically through factor analysis or cluster analysis.

4.5.1 Response Methods

Rating Scales

Rating scales are widely used in management and social science research. A researcher used rating scales to judge properties of objects in that reference to similar objects such as classifying objects like/dislike, approve/disapprove, Yes/No, other classification using even more categories. A rating scale question requires a person to rate a product or brand along a well defined evenly placed continum.

As to the number of scale points there is no such hard and fast rule. However some researcher that move points on a rating scale provide an opportunity for greater sensitivity of measurement.

Some examples of rating scales are given below :

1. **Simple category scale.** Data-nominal

This relates to dichotomous question which provides two options usually a "Yes/No" question.

Example : 'I plan to purchase a personal computer in the next 12 months' Yes ☐ No ☐

2. **Multiple choice single response scale.** Data : Nominal

Example. "What newspaper do you read most often for financial news."?

❒ Hindusthan Times

❒ Times of India

❒ Indian Express

❒ Financial Times

❒ Deccan Herald.

3. **Multiple choice multiple response scale.** Data : Nominal

Example : Check any of the sources you consulted to prepare for CAT examination.

☐ Online Coaching ☐ Coaching Centre

☐ Postal Coaching ☐ Faculty Members of Management Institutes.

☐ Entrance test books and periodicals

4. **The Likert Type rating Scale.** Data : Interval

Rating scale questions are used when building a survey that requires a person to rate a product or a brand along a well dyfined, evenly spaced continuum. Rating scales are often used to measure the direction and intensity of attitudes.

Example : When considering your last service experience at our dealership, would you say that your experience was

❒ Delightful

❒ Excellent

❒ Satisfactory

❒ Unsatisfactory

❒ A failure

5. **Multiple Choice the likert type scale.** Data : Ordinal or interval.

This is a series of questions all of which has the same answer scale.

Example : When considering your last service experience at our dealership, would you say that your experience was

	Delightful (5)	Excellent (4)	Satisfactory (3)	Unsatisfactory (2)	A Failure (1)
Customer service representative	☐	☐	☐	☐	☐
Timeliness of service	☐	☐	☐	☐	☐
Over all experience	☐	☐	☐	☐	☐

6. **The Semantic Differential Scale.** Data- interval

The semantic differential scale asks a person to rate a product, brand, or company based upon a seven point rating scale that has two bipolar adjectives at each end :

Example :

Attractive .... Unattractive
Simple .... Complicated
Stylish .... Out of fashion
High Quality .... Low Quality

7. **The Stapel Scale.** Data-Ordinal or Interval.

The stapel scale is another variant of the multiple choice question that asks a person to rate a brand/product/service according to a certain characteristic on a scale from –5 to 5, indicating how well the characteristic discribes the product or service.

Example : When thinking about management courses in ABC Institute of Management the word 'innovative' aptly describes or poorly describes the Institute ?

Describes poorly	(—5)	(—4)	(—3)	(—2)	(—1)	(0)	(+ 1)	(+2)	(+3)	(+4)	(+ 5)
Innovations	☐	☐	☐	☐	☐	☐	☐	☐	☐	☐	☐

8. **The Constant Sum Scale.** (Data - ratio)

The constant sum scale question produces what is assumed to be a ratio measurement data. Ratio data is the most powerful of all measurement scales because it is characterized by an absolute zero point and an equal interval scale.

Constant sum data is obtained by asking the respondent to "Assign 100 points or percent across the answer options so as to reflect your degree of preference, importance or other evaluation". Typical questions might include identifying not only liking or preference, but attribute strength or intention to buy, look for a new job and so forth.

Example : When thinking for the reasons you purchased *'Target- Find'* data mining software, please rate the following reasons according to their relative importance.

- ❒ Seamless integration with other software
- ❒ User friendliness of software
- ❒ Ability to manipulate algorithms
- ❒ Level of pre-and post-purchase service
- ❒ Level of value for the price.
- ❒ Convenience of purchase/quick delivery

Note : Values/scores must add up to 100.

9. **Graphic Rating Scale.** The graphic rating scale is created to enable researchers to discern five differences. This makes it possible to have infinite number of ratings. Further, the respondent checks his response at any point along a continuum. The score is a measure of length (milimetres) from either end point. This creates interval data. Such rating scale also creates difficulties in coding and analysis. Other graphic rating scales use pictures, icons or other visuals to communicate with rates, thus creating a varied data types.

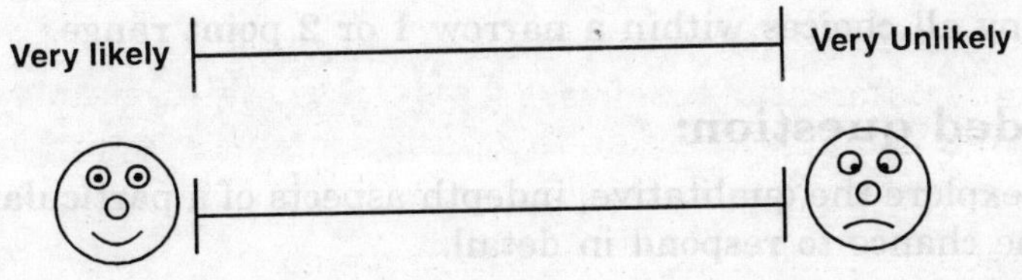

Such rating scales are often used with children with more limited vocabulary.

Errors associated with rating scales

The rates using rating scales have tendencies to commit errors of the following types :

- ❒ Leniency
- ❒ Central tendency
- ❒ Halo effect

The error of leniency occurs when a respondent is either a 'easy rater' a 'hard rater.' Sometimes the raters are inclined to rate the people higher to whom they know well or rate the objects higher having familiarity.

Sometimes, there is also opposite in the sense that the rater rates lower the acquaintances, having the knowledge towards positive leniency. Such positive leniency can be taken care of by adopting an asymmetrical rating scale to anticipate it. If a rater expects that mean rating will be hear 'good', he may use one unfavourable term and say four favourable terms such as "poor, fair, good, very good, excellent."

The error of **central tendency** arises when the rater are reluctant to give extreme judgements. This occurs when the rater does not know the object well and likes to take the middle path. To counter such error the raters may adjust the strength of descriptive adjectives, space the intermediate descriptives farther apart, use more points in the scale, etc.

The **halo effect** is the systematic bias that the rates introduces by carrying over the generalized impression from one rating to another. If the first question answered by a student gets a good rating, this impression is usually carried out by the examiner (rater) for the second question answered by the student.

Halo is a pervasive error and is very difficult to control. To counteract halo effect it is advisable to rate one trait at a time for all subjects/respondents or not to put all traits together in the same page of the questionnaire, preferably one trait per page.

Ranking Scales

In ranking scales the rater compares two or more objects and makes choices among them. The rank order question provides more powerful data than a simple multiple choice question for selecting nominal or categorical items. Ordinal scales apply order to the data. Unlike rank order data, most multiple choice scales do nor permit us to say that one item is greater than another. The rank order question provides direction and relative position, but not absolute difference. That is, rank order data indicate order, but do not tell us how much one item is preferred over another. The rank order question is a powerful tool because respondents often misue traditional rating scales, indicating ties and evaluating all choices within a narrow 1 or 2 point range.

The open ended question:

It seeks to explore the qualitative, indepth aspects of a particular topic or issue. It gives a person the chance to respond in detail.

"What product or service were you looking for that were not found on the website" ?

The demographic question :

The demographic questions are used to identify characteristics such as age, gender, income, race, place of residence, number of children and so forth. For instance, such questions help to classify the difference between users and non-users.

Rank order data uses an answer format that requires the respondent to assign a rank position for the first, second..... up to the *n* th item to be ordered. This format of assigning position numbers is very versatile. Respondents may be asked to rank a specified subset from the list (such as their first, second and third choices from a list) or to rank all items in the list. Typical questions might include identifying preference rankings, attribute association strength, first to last, oldest to youngest, or relative position (most, next most, and so forth, until either a set of items is ordered or all items may are ordered).

Some examples on rank order scaling are given below :

1. Paired Comparison Scale. (Data-ordinal) In paired comparison scale the respondent can express attitudes unambiguously by choosing between two objects.

Example :

"For each pair of 4 mini cars listed below, place a check (√) beside the one you would most prefer if you had to choose between the two."

—Maruti	— Maruti
—Indica	— Alto
—Maruti	— Alto
—Santro	— Santro
—Indica	— Indica
—Santro	— Alto

2. Forced Ranking Scale. (Data-Ordinal) The forced ranking scale lists attributes that are ranked relative to each other. The method is faster than the paired comparison and is usually more motivating to the respondent. However, the respondent may become careless in ranking a large number of items. For instance, we may like to rank certain set of brands or products based on a specific attribute or characteristics.

As regards fuel efficiency rank the following mini cars.

—Indica
—Maruti
—Santro
—Alto

3. Comparative Scale. (Data : Ordinal) Sometimes a manager or researcher is interesting in bench marking and hence calls for a standard by which other programs, processes, brands, points of sale or people are compared. The comparative scale is best suited for such comparison if the respondents are familiar or knowledgeable with the standard.

Example : 'Compared to the previous mutual fund's performance, the present one is :

Superior		About the same		Inferior
$\overline{1}$	$\overline{2}$	$\overline{3}$	$\overline{4}$	$\overline{5}$

4.5.2 Measurement Scale Construction

Arbitrary Scaling

For a given topic of interest or reasearch question we select a number of items (points of information) for inclusion in the study. From this set we select a sample of items, that we believe throw light on a research question. Suppose the research question is related to image of a company having a major steel plant in a region. Let us consider the following questions with relevant 4 items.

How do you regard company X ?

1. As a place to work ? Bad .... Good.
2. Recruitment of local persons ? Bad .... Good.
3. Concern for initiating welfare projects in the region ? Bad .... Good.
4. Ecological concern ? Bad .... Good.

Suppose we decide to score these items on a 5 point scale 1 to 5, depending on the degree of favourableness. Points of each company or for individuals may be computed to determine how they compare to others. If you add the total scores for these four items, each company would receive 4 to 20 points for each respondent. Further, the attitude scores of each individual are computed to study differences among individual respondents.

Arbitrary scales are easy to construct and happen to be inexpensive and are highly specific. Such a design of scale is subjective and is dependent on the insight and ability of the researcher to choose a sample of representative meaningful items. There is no guarantee that the respondents will have same frame of mind and reference. There has been great effort in recent years in developing other construction techniques to take care of deficiencies in arbitrary scales.

Consensus Scaling

In this scaling procedure, a panel of judges select the items and evaluate them, keeping in view the (*a*) the relevance of the topic/research question (*b*) potential of the items for ambiguity (*c*) the level of attitude represented by items. Such type of construction of scale is known as **Thurstone equal appearing interval scale,** which is a interval rating scale for attitude measurement. Consensus scaling is rarely used in management research because of cost, time and staff requirements.

Item Analysis Scaling

Item analysis scaling procedure is a technique by which an item is evaluated to know how well it discriminates between those persons whose total score is high and those persons whose total score is low. In this procedure the mean scores for each scale item for high score group and low score group are computed. Then, the items means are statistically tested and some items having highest significant differences among themselves are selected for inclusion in the final scale. The most popular scale using item analysis approach is the **summated or Likert scale,** which is easy and quick to construct.

Cumulative Scaling

Given total score on cumulative scales, it is possible to estimate which items were answered positively and negatively. Scalogram is a scale of this type and scalogram analysis is a procedure for determining whether a set of items forms a unidimensional scale. Cumulative scale is a measurement scale that assumes that when you agree with a scale item, you will also agree with items that are less extreme. **Guttman scaling** is sometimes known as *Cumulative scaling* or *Scalogram analysis*. The purpose of Guttman scaling is to establish a one-dimensional continuum for a concept you wish to measure. This is a procedure to determine whether a set of items can be rank-ordered on an unidimensional scale. It utilizes the intensity structure among several indicators of a given variable. Statements are listed in order of importance. The rating is scaled by summing all responses until the first negative response in the list.

Factor Scaling

Factor scaling includes a variety of techniques which deal with multi-dimensional universe and brings out underlying dimensions/factors that have not been identified in exploratory research. These techniques are designed to inter-correlate items to detect their level of dependence. One of the techniques is the **semantic differential** (SD) method which is based on *factor analysis* and is developed to measure the people's reactions to stimulus words and concept in terms of ratings on bipolar scales defined with contrasting adjectives at each end. An example of an SD scale is

Good —	—	—	—	—	—	— Bad
3	2	1	0	1	2	3

0—neutral
1—slightly
2—quite
3—extremely.

4.6. A Comparison of Scaling Techniques and their Construction

The scaling techniques commonly employed in business/social science research can be classified into two broad types. These are

- Comparative Scaling Techniques
- Non-comparative Scaling Techniques.

With **comparative scaling techniques** the stimulus objects/items are directly compared with each other. For instance, a respondent might be asked whether they prefer 'Maruti' or 'Indica' car. Comparative scale data must be inspected in relative terms and have only ordinal or rank order properties. That is why, the comparative scaling is sometimes termed as *non-metric scaling*. Comparative scales are easily understood and applied. Small difference between stimulus objects can be detected easily.

In **non-comparative scaling** each object/item is scaled independently of the others in the stimulus set. For instance, the respondents are asked how they rate 'Maruti', say on a 6-point scale. (1 = not at all preferred, 6 = greatly preferred). The resulting data are generally assumed to be in interval or ratio scale. Non comparative scaling is the most widely used scaling technique in marketing research.

Comparative scales are :

- ❒ Pairwise comparison scale
- ❒ Rank-order scale
- ❒ Constant sum scale
- ❒ Q-Sort scale
- ❒ Guttman scale

Non-comparative scales :

- ❒ Continuous rating scale
- ❒ Likert scale
- ❒ Thurstone scale
- ❒ Itemized rating scales
- ❒ Semantic differential scale
- ❒ Stapel scale

4.6.1. Comparative Scales :

(a) Paired comparison scaling : In paired comparison scaling a respondent is presented with two objects/items and asked to select one according to certain criterion. The data are ordinal (rank-order) in nature. If there are say 4 items, then there would be 6 paired comparisons. Suppose the researcher presents 6 pairs of toothpaste brands (Colgate, Forhans, Pepsodent, Closeup). For each pair the respondent is asked to indicate one of the two brands of toothpaste in the pair he would prefer for personal use.

Colgate	☐	Close up	☐
Forhans	☐	Colgate	☐
Pepsodent	☐	Forhans	☐
Colgate	☐	Pepsodent	☐
Forhans	☐	Pepsodent	☐
Close up	☐	Close up	☐

Suppose the respondent scores 1 for his preference in the pair and zero for the other, and as such the number of times a brand is preferred, is obtained by the summing the 1's. Thus, for each respondent we have four scores for four brands. The researcher sums scores for all respondents and divides the total score for each brand by the number of respondents to get average score for each brand for comparison among different brands. Further, the researcher might also compute the percentage of respondents prefering one brand to the other. It may be mentioned here that there are several ways of analyzing paired comparison data and further several modifications of the paired comparison technique have been suggested in the literature.

Paired comparison scaling is useful when the number of brands is limited, because it requires direct comparison and overt choice. However, with a large number of brands/stimuli/objects the number of comparisons become unwieldy.

(b) Rank-order scale : In rank order scaling the respondents are presented with several objects simultaneously and asked to order or rank them according to some criterion. This procedure of scaling is commonly used to measure preference for brands as well as attributes.

Suppose it is required to rank the various brands of toothpaste in order of preference. From the list of brands assign the rank 1 to the most preferred and then choose the second most preferred brand to get the rank 2 and continue ranking till all the brands are exhausted. The criterion of preference is subjective and ranking scales are more difficult than rating scales because they involve comparison among several alternatives and hence require more attention and mental effort. The ranking technique may force the respondents to make choices they might not otherwise make. Sometimes the researcher wonders whether he is measuring a real relationship or one that is artificially contrived.

	Brand	*Rank Order*
1.	Colgate	—
2.	Gleem	—
3.	Pepsodent	—
4.	Close up	—
5.	Forhans	—

***(c)* Constant sum scaling :** In constant sum scaling the respondents are required to allocate a constant sum of units among a set of stimulus objects with respect to some criterion fixed by the researcher. For instance, the respondents may be asked to allocate say 100 points to attributes of a toilet soap in a way that reflect the importance they attach to each attribute. If an attribute is not of any importance to the respondent, he may assign it zero points. The sum of all the points is constant 100. Hence, the scale is so named. The attributes are scaled by counting the points assigned to each one attribute by all the respondents and dividing the total points by the number of respondents. A hypothetical illustration is given below to show average response of three groups of respondents where the attributes of a bath soap are under contention.

	Attribute	Average Response		
		Group 1	Group 2	Group 3
1.	**Mildness**	10	5	6
2.	**Lather**	2	4	15
3.	**Price**	45	20	9
4.	**Fragrance**	15	2	16
5.	**Packaging**	8	5	8
6.	**Moisturizing**	3	5	18
7.	**Cleaning power**	12	50	20
8.	**Shrinkage/Longeivity**	5	9	8
		100	100	100

The main advantage of the constant sum scale is that it allows fine discrimination among the attributes with less time for making a decision. The use of large number of stimulus objects/units may cause confusion while allocating points to the units.

***(d)* Q-Sort scaling :** This technique was developed to discriminate among a relatively large number of objects or characteristics simultaneously. The objects are sorted into piles based on similarity with respect to some criterion. For example, the respondents are given, say 100, attitude of statements/characteristics/objects on individual cards and asked them to pile or group them into say 11 piles ranging from those with higher preference to those with lower preference. The number of objects to be placed in each pile is to be pre- fixed so as to follow an approximate normal distribution of objects in the whole set. After placing all the cards into the piles, the respondent is asked to rank-order only those objects/characteristics in the most preferred pile.

***(e)* Guttman scaling :** Guttman scaling is a comparative scaling technique developed by Louis Guttman in 1944. It is sometimes known as **Cumulative scaling** or **Scalogram analysis.** The purpose of Guttman scaling is to establish a one-dimensional continuum for a concept we wish to measure. An attitude is said to be **unidimensional** only if it yields a cumulative scale—the items are related to one another in such a way that a respondent who agrees with item 2, also agrees with item 1 and who agrees with item 4 also agrees with items 1, 2 and 3. Thus, the respondents who agree with a particular item has a higher score than those who disagree with it. This technique therefore presupposes the arrangement of items to satisfy the aforesaid requirement. In practice, we would seldom expect to find this cumulative pattern perfectly. So we use scalogram anlysis to examine how closely a set of items corresponds with this idea of cumulativeness.

The steps for the construction of Guttman scale are as follows :

1. Define the focus. The first step in the construction of a scaling method is to define the focus.

2. Develop the items. Develop a large set of items/statements that reflect the concept. An expert may be consulted, if necessary.

3. Rate the items. Consult a group of judges to rate the statements/items in terms of how favourable they are to the concept under question, and not asking the judges whether they personally agree with the statement. They are simply asked to make a judgement (Yes/No) about how the statement is related to the construct of interest.

4. Develop the cumulative. The key to Guttman scaling is in the analysis. We construct a matrix or table that shows the responses of all the respondents on all of the items. We then sort this matrix so that respondents who agree with more statements are listed at the top and those agreeing with fewer are at the bottom. For respondents with same number of agreements, we sort the statements from left to right from those that most agreed to those that fewest agreed to. Such an arrangement and review are made with a view to sort out items that best approximate the cumulative property. Thus, we obtain scale items and scale scores associated with them. A respondent is presented with the scale items in same order and asked to check items with which they agree.

Example of Cumulative Technique

	Agree with item			**Disagree with item**		
Score	**3**	**2**	**1**	**3**	**2**	**1**
3	√	√	√	X	X	X
2	X	√	√	√	X	X
1	X	X	√	√	√	X
0	X	X	X	√	√	√

Note : For each agreement the response score is 1.

While constructing a cumulative scale the researcher must ascertain whether the concerned items form a unidimensional scale. In this connection one ought to analyse the reproducibility of the responses—the proportion of responses that actually follow the pattern of cumulative technique.

A hypothetical perfect Guttman scale consists of a unidimensional set of items that are ranked in order of difficulty from least extreme to most extreme position. An important property of Guttman's model is that a person's entire set of responses to all items can be predicted from their cumulative score because the model is deterministic.

4.6.2. Noncomparative Scales

(*a*) Continuous rating scale : In continuous rating scale, sometimes referred to as a *graphic rating scale,* respondents rate the objects by placing a mark on the appropriate place on a line which runs from one extreme of the criterion variable to another. The respondents are not restricted to selecting from marks previously set by the researcher. That is, the respondent has only two extreme points in a horizontal or vertical scale and he shall have to place a mark between these points. In this type of scaling, one object is rated at a time and is not compared with others.

Illustration 1.

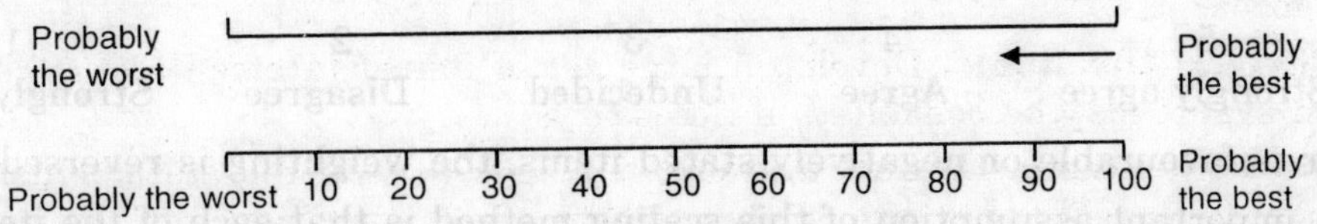

Once the respondent has provided the rating on a scale, the researcher divides the line into as many categories he likes and assigns scores based on the categories into which the ratings of the respondent fall.

The continuous rating scale is easy to construct. But the scoring may be cumbersome and unreliable.

(*b*) **Likert Scale :** A Likert scale is a type of psychometric scale (attitude scale) often used in questionnaires and is the most widely used scale in survey research. It asks the respondents to specify their level of agreement to each of a **list of statements.** It was named often Rensis Likert, who invented the scale in 1932. The statements should constitute a representative sample of all the possible opinions or attitudes about the object and half of them should express a clearly favourable attitude and the other half clearly unfavourable. If necessary, some expert opinion may be sought for to select the statements needed to highlight the topic.

A typical test item in a Likert scale is a **statement,** the respondent is asked to indicate his degree of agreement with the statement. Traditionally, a five-point scale is used, however many researchers/ psychometricians advocate using a **seven or nine-point scale.**

Likert scaling is a **bipolar scaling method,** measuring either positive or negative response to a statement. Sometimes, Likert scales are used in a forced choice method where the middle option of "Neither agree nor disagree" is not available.

Likert scale may be subject to distortion from several causes.

Three types of biases due to respondents may occur :

- Central tendency bias
  (extreme response categories may be avoided)
- Acquiescence response bias
  (agree with statements as presented)
- Social desirability bias
  (protraying themselves or their group in a more favourable light)

After the questionnaire is completed the score on each item is summed together, to create a test score for the respondent. Hence, Likert scales are often called **summative scales.**

Data from Likert scales can be analysed by a number of ways using non-parametric tests—Mann Whitney test, the Wilcoxon signed rank test and the Kruskal-Wallis test. Median is preferred over mean because of the ordinal quality of the scale and the lack of a true zero.

Data from Likert scales are sometimes reduced to the nominal level by combining all agree and disagree responses into two categories of 'accept' and 'reject'.

Illustration 2.

"Ice cream is good for breakfast"

5	4	3	2	1
Strongly agree	Agree	Undecided	Disagree	Strongly disagree

For unfavourable or negatively stated items, the weighting is reversed.

An important assumption of this scaling method is that each of the items (statements) measures some aspect of a single common factor, otherwise the items cannot legitimately be summed to get an overall score for a respondent. Thus, the resulting scale is unidimensional.

Item analysis picks out best items (statements) through three statistics such as : (*i*) an item discriminating index. (*ii*) number of percentage of respondents marking each choice to each item. (*iii*) item mean and standard deviation. After the good items are selected by a preliminary group of respondents, the researcher should try out the revised scale with a different group of subjects/respondents and again check the discriminating power of the items.

After an attitude scale is constructed, its reliability must be determined and validity must be established. An easiest way to check the validity is to determine the extent to which the scale is capable of discriminating between two groups, whose numbers are known to have different attitudes to items.

Likert scale is useful for a manager when the organization plans to conduct an experiment or undertake a program of change or improvement in administration.

(*c*) Thurstone scale : Thurstone scale, named after Louis Leon Thurstone (1928), is a way of measuring people's attitudes along a single dimension by asking them to indicate that they agree or disagree with each of a large set of statements (*e.g.* 100) that are about that attitude. The statements are designed to be parallel in construction, but some toward one end of the scale and some toward the other end, and each trying to indicate the attitude in a slightly different way.

Thurstone scaling method assigns specific scale values to attitude items. It is different from the Likert scaling in a sense that while Likert scales assess attitudes by asking questions to respondents to indicate their intensity of agreement—disagreement with **each** of a series of statements concerning a topic/concept, Thurstone scales present a bunch of statements about a concept which range from very favourable to very unfavourable through a neutral to the respondents and asking them to select from these statements those which nearly reflect their own attitude.

The procedure of Thurstone scales is also known as the method of equal—appearing intervals, since the objective is to obtain a unidimensional scale with **interval properties.**

The following steps are to be undertaken to construct Thurstone scales :

1. Generate a large number of statements (usually 50 to 100) that express widely both positive or negative/favourableness or unfavourableness towards the attitude object, including neutral statements.
2. Such a set of statements are then presented to a panel of judges/knowledgeable persons about the object to classify them according to their degree of favourableness or unfavourableness. This is, usually, done with an 11-category bipolar scale with 'very favourable' at one end, 'very unfavourable' at

the other and a neutral position in the middle. The judges are advised to use all the points on scale rather than bunching them into a few categories.

3. Then, compute the mean value/median value of scale values for each item from the distribution of all the judges' ratings—showing the number of judges who placed the item into each of the 11 categories. Compute also a measure of variation either Standard deviation (σ) or Quartile deviation (QD). If the judges agree highly with ratings, σ or QD will be low. Poor agreement among judges will result in high σ or QD.
4. After average scale values and σ or QD are computed for each statement, those statements are selected which represent points on the favourable—unfavourable continuum in an evenly distributed manner from 1 to 11. The statements having high variability of ratings among the judges are to be rejected. As far as possible, scale values are to be chosen with equal increments to attain interval measurement. In case two or more statements/items have the same or nearly the same value, the one with less σ or QD is to be retained.
5. Finally, the scale so constructed is presented to the respondents to obtain their scores (scale values) against the items agreed upon. It may be mentioned here that the items are randomly ordered in the final form. Of course, the scale values are **not** shown in the form lest these will bias the responses and the respondents are only asked to check only the statements.

For instance, if a respondent agrees with statements having scale values 1.8, 2.3, 3.4 and 4.5, his attitude score is $\frac{1.8 + 2.3 + 3.4 + 4.5}{4} = 3.0$. The amount of spread in the scale values of the items checked by any respondent may be taken as a measure of the extent to which the respondent has a clearly defined attitude on a concerned topic. It may be mentioned here that an individual with a well defined attitude tends to check only statements very close in scale values.

Likert scales *Vs.* Thurstone scales :

The Likert scales are simpler to construct as compared to Thurstone scales. They are more reliable. As regards Thurstone scales, they permit more absolute interpretation of the scale scores compared to Likert scales which permit scores to be interpreted on a relative basis only and the ranking of the individuals in terms of the degree of favourableness of their attitude toward a particular topic/object. Besides involving lot of work for the construction of the scale, Thurstone's technique requires participation of judges who may find it difficult in rating the statements/items independently of their own attitude towards the object/topic.

(*d*) **The Semantic Differential (SD) Scale** : The Semantic Differential (SD) scale measures people's reactions to stimulus words and concepts in terms of ratings on bipolar scales defined with contrasting adjectives at each end. An example of a Semantic differential scale is given below :

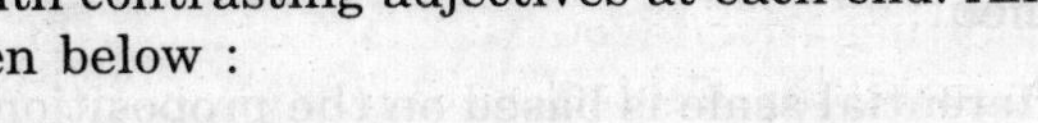

Usually, the position marked 0 is labelled neutral, the 1 position is labeled 'slightly', the 2 position 'quite' and the 3 position 'extremely'. A scale like this one measures directionality of a reaction (*e.g.* good vrs bad) and also intensity (slight through extreme). Typically, a person is presented with **some concept of interest** such as City Traffic, Railways, ABC Company, etc. and asked to rate it on a number of such scales. Ratings are combined in various ways to describe and analyze the person's feelings.

The Semantic differential scale measures the psychological meanings of an attitude object. Managers use this scale for brand image and other marketing studies and organizational studies. The procedure is also an insightful procedure for comparing the images of competing brands, stores or services. Respondents are asked to rate each attitude object in turn on a number of five or seven point rating scales, bounded at each end bipolar adjectives or phrases. Some researchers also use unipolar scales. The respondent chooses end point only if that adjective is closely descriptive of that object. With unipolar scales, the mid-point is simply a step on the scale from 'sweet' to 'not sweet', whereas on a bipolar scale it is a neutral point. A researcher may use as many as 15 to 25 semantic differential scales for each attitude object.

A number of basic considerations are involved in SD methodology :

1. Bipolar adjective scales are a simple, economical means for obtaining data on people's reactions. In market studies the pairs of adjectives or phrases are selected carefully to be meaningful in the market being studied and often correspond to product or service attributes. Exploratory research may be required to ensure that important attributes are represented and described in words that are familiar to respondents.
2. The negative or unfavourable pole is sometimes on the right side and sometimes on the left. The rotation is necessary to avoid the **halo effect,** in which the location of previous judgments on the scale affect subsequent judgments because of respondent's carelessness and seriousness to the issue at hand.
3. The category increments are treated as interval scales, so that group mean values can be computed for each object on each scale.
4. Ratings on bipolar adjective scales tend to be correlated, and three basic dimensions of response account for most of the co-variation in ratings. The three dimensions, which have been labelled Evaluation, Potency and Activity (EPA), have been verified in an impressive variety of studies.
5. Some adjective scales are almost pure measures of the EPA dimensions; for example, good-bad for Evaluation, powerful-powerless for Potency and fast-slow for Activity.

   Measurements of a concept on the EPA dimensions are referred to as the *concept's profile.*
6. EPA measurements are appropriate when one is interested in affective responses. The EPA system is notable for being a multivariate approach to affect measurement.

The Semantic differential scale is based on the proposition that an object can have several dimensions of connotative meaning. The meanings are located in multidimensional property space, called *Semantic space*. The *connotative* meaning of an object for an individual is the term's association with the individual. *Denotative* meaning of the term is its *dictionary* meaning.

The scale values on different bipolar rating scales are totalled and then averaged to obtain a total score, which measures the meaning of the object and the individual's reaction/perception to the object. Individuals then can be compared on the basis of their total scores.

The semantic differential technique, when applied to attitude measurement produces apparently good reliability values and correlates fairly with other attitude scaling techniques. However, the Semantic differential technique is obsessed with the fact that the respondents may have tendency towards response bias in the sense that they use the extreme ones ignoring the middle scale values. Further, there may be problems of interpreting middle point on the scale.

The semantic differential has several advantages. Besides providing **interval** data, it is an efficient and easy way to secure attitude from a large sample, measured in both directions and intensity. Its versatility makes the semantic differential a popular rating scale in marketing research. It has been widely used in comparing brand, product and company images. It has also been popularly used to develop advertising and promotion strategies and in new product development studies.

Illustration 3. *Semantic-differential scales for (Assam Tea) :*

Low price	—	—	—	—	High price
Consistent quality	—	—	—	—	Spotty quality
Poor flavour	—	—	—	—	Good flavour
Bitter	—	—	—	—	Not bitter
Light colour	—	—	—	—	Dark colour.

(*e*) The Stapel Scale : The Stapel scale, named after its developer, Jan Stapel is a unipolar rating scale with 10 categories numbered from —5 to +5 *without* a neutral point zero. Respondents are asked to indicate the object by selecting a numerical response category. The higher the positive score, the better the adjective phrase describes the object. The less accurately one thinks of the phrase describing the object, the larger the *minus* number he should choose.

Illustration 4.

Stapel Scale (*Assam Tea*)

	+5		**+5**		**+5**
	+4		**+4**		**+4**
	+3		**+3**		**+3**
	+2		**+2**		**+2**
Price	**+1**	*Flavour*	**+1**	*Consistent*	**+1**
	–1		**–1**	*Quality*	**–1**
	–2		**–2**		**–2**
	–3		**–3**		**–3**
	–4		**–4**		**–4**
	–5		**–5**		**–5**

The data obtained by using a Stapel scale can be analyzed in the same way as Semantic differential data. The Stapel scale produces results similar to the semantic differential. The main advantage of the Stapel scale is that it does not require adjectives/phrases to assure bipolarity and can be administered over the telephone.

However, some researchers feel that the Stapel scale is confusing and difficult to apply.

Basic Non comparative Scales

Scale	Basic Characteristics	Examples
Continuous rating scale	Place a mark an a continuous scale	Reaction to TV Commercials
Itemized Rating Scales :		
Likert Scale	Degree of agreement as1 (strongly disagree) to 5 (Strongly agree) scale	Measurement of attitudes
Semantic differential	Seven–Point scale with bipolar labels	Brand Products and Company images
Stapel Scale	Unipolar ten–point scale, –5 to +5, without a Neutral point (Zero)	Measurement of attitudes and images

4.7. Noncomparative Itemized Rating Scale Decisions

The researcher is required to take **six major decisions** when constructing the noncomparative itemized rating scales.

These are :

- The number of scale categories.
- Balanced *Vs.* unbalanced scale.
- Odd or even number of categories.
- The nature and degree of verbal description.
- The physical form of the scale.

(*a*) Number of Scale Categories : The greater the number of categories, the finer the discrimination among stimulus objects that is possible. On the other hand, all respondents might not be able to handle a large number of categories. Of course, there is no optimal number of categories. Knowledge about the object and nature of the object largely determine the number of categories. Sometimes the mode of data collection has a relevance in his decision. For example, telephone interviews may confuse the respondents in case large number of categories are used. Further, there may be space limitations in mail questionnaires.

(*b*) **Balanced Vs. Unbalanced Scales :** In *balanced scale* **equal** number of favourable and unfavourable categories are used. The scale should be balanced to obtain objective data. If the distribution of responses are likely to be skewed, an *unbalanced scale* with more categories in the direction of skewness may seem to appropriate. However, in data analysis, the nature and degree of unbalance in the scale should be taken into account.

(*c*) **Odd or Even Number of Categories :** With an odd number of categories the middle scale position is designated as a neutral point. The prime position and labelling of a neutral category can have a significant effect on the response. The Likert scale is a balanced rating scale with an odd number of categories and a neutral point. The decision depends on whether some of the respondents may be neutral on the response being measured. If the researcher wants to force the respondent not to remain neutral, a rating scale with an even number of categories.

(*d*) **Forced Vs. Nonforced Scales :** A rating scale where 'no opinion' option is not provided, is called a *Forced scale.* In such a situation sometimes a respondent may mark middle scale position. If a large number of respondents adopt this technique of utilising the middle position of the scale, this may distort measures of central tendency and dispersion. If the researcher is justified in expecting 'no opinion' position of respondents, he may use *nonforced scale* with a 'no opinion' category.

(*e*) **Nature and Degree of Verbal Description :** The nature and degree of verbal description associated with scale categories varies as per the requirement of the researcher and can have an effect on the response. The scale categories may be verbal, numerical or even pictorial description. The researcher must decide whether to label each scale category, some scale categories or only extreme ones. Verbal description of each category may not improve accuracy or reliability of the data. The labelling of scale categories is supposed to reduce scale ambiguity.

The strength of adjectives used to label the scale categories may influence the distribution of responses. For instance, the respondents are less likely to use extreme scale categories such as 'completely disagree', 'completely agree' because of strong anchors. Alternatively, weak anchors produce uniform or flat distributions.

(*f*) **Physical form or Configuration :** A number of options are available as to physical form of a scale. Scales can be presented either vertically or horizontally. Categories can be expressed by boxes, discrete lines, or units on a continuum and may or may not have numbers assigned to them. The numerical descriptions may be positive, negative or both.

In marketing research two unique scale configurations such as the thermometer scale and the smiling face scale are used to make it more attractive and specially useful for children. For the thermometer scale, the higher the temperature, the more favourable the evaluation/attitude. Similar, happier faces indicate more favourable evaluations.

Classification of Attitude Rating Scales :

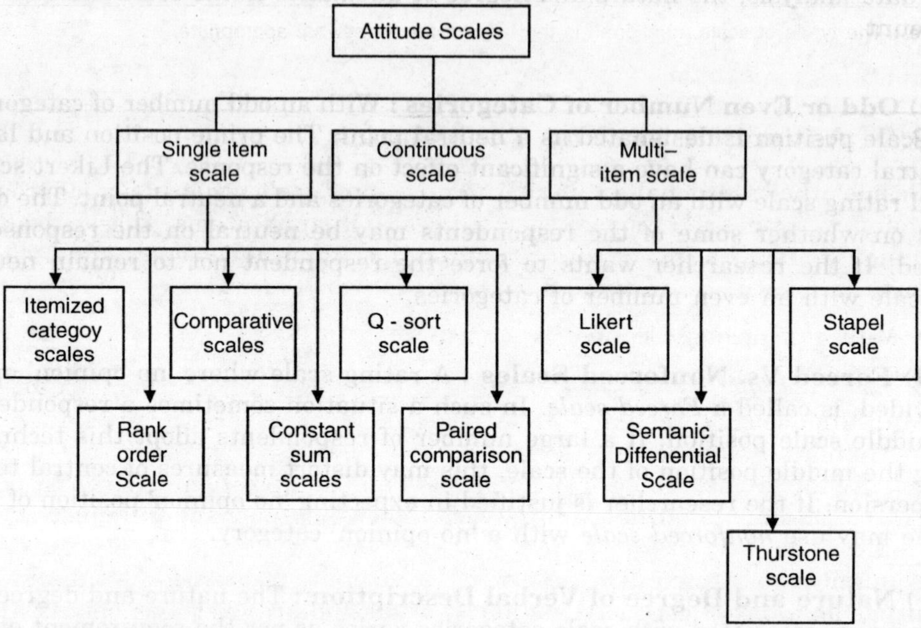

4.8. Choosing an Appropriate Scale

The choice of a scale is not a very easy proposition. There are a number of scaling techniques available to a researcher, each with its own strengths and weaknesses. However, the researcher's choice should be shaped by (*i*) the specific information that is required to satisfy the research objectives, (*ii*) the adaptability of the scale to the data collection method and budget constraints, and (*iii*) the compatibility of the scale with the structure of the respondent's attitude.

Appropriate applications of some attitude scales are presented below :

Attitude Component	Appropriate Type of Scale
Knowledge :	
Awareness	Itemized category
Attribute beliefs	Itemized category, semantic differential (Rank order, constant sum, Likert)
Attribute importance	Itemized category, constant sum (Rank order, Likert)
Affect or liking :	
Overall preferences	Itemized category, constant sum (Rank order, Likert, semantic differential)

Specific attribute	Itemized category, semantic differential (Rank order, constant sum, Likert)
Action :	
Intentions	Itemized category, constant sum (Rank order, Likert)

Note : The types of scale mentioned in the bracket are somewhat appropriate.

4.9. Advanced Scaling Techniques

Besides the traditional scaling techniques, new scale construction approaches are forthcoming to handle specific management research applications. These advanced scaling techniques make use of complex computer algorithms and require an understanding of multivariate statistics. In this convection it is worth mentioning.

- Multidimensional Scaling
- Conjoint analysis

Multidimensional scaling (MDS) consists of multivariate techniques, used to measure human perceptions and preferences towards some stimuli (objects), like products, organisations, places, events, brands etc. and positioning them in perceptual space. The MDS handles ordinal input (with interval output) and fully metric (interval) and non-metric modes.

A number of techniques are used to compute *proximities* as input data. A proximity is an index of perceived similarity or dissimilarity between objects. Given certain number of objects the respondents are asked to judge in pairs of possible combinations as to their similarity. The ranked or rated relationships are then represented as points on a map in multidimensional space.

From a non-technical point of view, the purpose of multidimensional scaling (MDS) is to provide a visual representation of the pattern of proximities (i.e. similarities or distances) among a set of objects. Thus, given a matrix of perceived similarities between various brands of a product (air freshners, toilet soaps, minicars, etc.) or between various of cities/organisations/places/events, etc., the objects that are perceived to be very similar to each other are placed near each other on the map and objects that are perceived to be very different from each other are placed far away from each other on the map.

Conjoint analysis is another collection of techniques, used to measure complex decision making that requires multi-attribute judgements. For instance, in a real purchase situation the consumers do not make choices based on a single attribute and examine a range of features or attributes and then make judgements or trade-offs to determine their final purchase choice. Conjoint analysis examines these trade-offs to determine the combination of attributes that will be most satisfying to the consumer. In other words by using conjoint analysis a company can determine the optimal features for their product or service.

To sum up, the value of conjoint analysis is that it predicts what products or services people will choose and assesses the weight, people give to various factors that underlie their decisions. As such, it is one of the most powerful, versatile and strategically important research techniques available for business research.

EXERCISES

1. What is measurement ? Explain its role in scientific investigation.
2. What are scales ? Mention their relationships with data. Distinguish among different scales based on levels of measurement.
3. What are characteristics of good measurement ? Discuss.
4. What are major considerations for selecting a measuremnet scale ?
5. Explain the concepts of reliability and validity. What is the relationship between them ?
6. Distinguish between rating scales and ranking scales with examples. Discuss the situations where they will be more appropriate.
7. Discuss the classification of measurement scales according to methods of construction.
8. What are comparative scaling techniques ? How do they compare with non-comparative scaling techniques ? Discuss.
9. Explain constant sum scaling with an example.
10. Explain the steps for construction of Guttman scale.
11. What is Liket scale ? How is it constructed ? Explain.
12. Explain the construction of Thurstone scale. How is it different from Likert scaling.
13. Discuss the semantic differential scale methodology.
14. What are major decisions to be taken for constructing non-comparative itemized rating scales ?
15. **Write short notes on :**
    (*a*) Stapel scale
    (*b*) Q-sort scale
    (*c*) Constant sum scale.
16. How would you choose an appropriate scale ? Discuss.
17. Write notes on (*i*) Multidimensional scaling (*ii*) Conjoint Analysis.
18. What are data properties ? Explain briefly.
19. What are sources of measurement error ?
20. Distinguish between unidimensional scale and multidimensional scale.

□□□

CHAPTER

5

SOURCES AND METHODS OF COLLECTION OF DATA

5.1 Sources of data :

Once the research design is finalised, the next task of the researcher is to collect accurate and reliable data from different sources to achieve research objectives. There are different types of data and methods of collection to suit the research problem and the research process. An appropriate method of collection of data depends on the research design as well as the nature of research-exploratory or conclusive (descriptive or causal). While exploring the research problem one may consider many different types of information sources ; some may be more valuable than others. Information from different sources may be categorized into three *broad* sources or levels.

- primary sources
- secondary sources
- tertiary sources,

depending on their originality and their proximity to the source of origin.

The designations of primary, secondary and tertiary data sources differ between disciplines or subjects.

5.1.1 Primary Sources :

The primary sources data are original works of research or raw data without analysis, interpretation or pronouncement. The primary sources are based on the following definitions :

- original materials on which research is based.
- first formal appearance of results in the print or electronic literature.
- information in original form.

- earliest writings
- original thinkings, report on discoveries or share of new information.

Some examples of primary sources are :

- scientific journal articles reporting experimental research results.
- proceedings of meetings, conferences and symposia
- dissertation or theses (may also be secondary)
- sets of data such as census statistics, economic statistics, labour statistics, etc.
- works of literature
- diaries and autobiographies
- interviews, surveys and field work and experiments
- internal sources such as inventory records, personnel records, purchasing requisition forms, statistical control charts, etc.
- letters and correspondences
- speeches
- newspaper articles (may be secondary)
- government documents
- photographs
- original documents
- internet communications on e-mail.

5.1.2 Secondary Sources :

Secondary sources are less easily defined than primary sources. These are works that interpret the primary data. It is not always easy to distinguish primary from secondary sources. A news paper article is a primary source if it reports events, but a secondary source if it analyses and comments on those events. In science secondary sources are those which simplify the process of finding and evaluating the primary literature. Thus, we may have some definitions as to secondary sources.

- describe, interpret, analyze and evaluate the primary sources.
- comment on and discuss the evidence provided by primary sources.
- works which are one or more steps removed from the event or, information they refer to being written after the fact with the benefit of hindsight.

Some examples of secondary sources :

- bibliographies (may also be tertiary)
- biographical works
- commentaries
- dictionaries, encyclopedias (may also be tertiary)
- dissertations or theses
- handbooks and data compilations
- history
- indexing and abstracting tools used to locate primary and secondary sources.
- journal articles (may also be primary)
- monographs

- ❒ newspaper and popular magazines
- ❒ review articles and literature reviews.
- ❒ text books (may be tertiary)
- ❒ treatises, works of criticism and interpretation

5.1.3 Tertiary Sources :

Tertiary sources are regarded as interpretation of secondary sources, but are not easily distinguished from secondary sources and are generally defined as :

- ❒ Works which list primary and secondary sources in a specific subject area.
- ❒ Works which index, organize and compile citations and show how to use secondary sources.

Some examples of tertiary sources :

- ❒ almanacs and fact books
- ❒ bibliographies (may also be secondary)
- ❒ chronologies
- ❒ dictionaries and encyclopedias (may also be secondary)
- ❒ directories
- ❒ guide books, manuals, etc.
- ❒ hand books, and data compilations
- ❒ indexing and abstracting tools used to locate primary and secondary sources (may also be secondary)
- ❒ text books (may also be secondary)
- ❒ internet search engines.

5.2 Secondary Data :

Secondary data are information gathered for some other purposes other than the purpose under consideration. A variety of secondary information sources is available to the researcher gathering data in an industry, potential product applications and the market place. Secondary data are also used to gain insight into the research problem.

Secondary data may be classified in terms of its sources - either *internal or external*. Internal or in-house data are secondary information acquired within the organisation where and for whom research is being carried out. External secondary data are obtained from outside sources.

* *Advantages of using secondary data*

1. The secondary research process takes less time to complete the work because data can be collected in matter of days.
2. These are easier to collect because the researcher needs only to locate the source of the data and extract the required information.
3. Secondary research is generally less expensive than primary research. This does not make use of specialised and highly trained personnel.
4. Some information can be obtained only from secondary data.

* *Disadvantages of using secondary data* :

1. Secondary information pertinent to the research topic is either not available or is only available in insufficient quantities. The researchers have no knowledge of how the data were collected, nor do they have any control over it.
2. Some secondary data may be of questionable accuracy and reliability.
3. Data may be in a different format or units than is required by the researcher.
4. Much secondary data may be outdated and in market studies may not reflect current market conditions.

As a general rule, a thorough research of the secondary data should be undertaken prior to conducting primary research. The secondary information will provide a useful background and will identify key questions and issues that will need to be addressed by the primary research.

* Internal data sources :

Internal secondary data are usually an inexpensive information source for the company conducting research, and is the place to start for existing operations. Internally generated production data, sales and pricing data, inventory, employee data, etc. can be used as a research source. The use of this data is to define the competitive position of the firm both in production and sales and man power, an evaluation of a strategy the firm has used in the past for gaining a better understanding of the problems of the company pertaining to research area - production, sales, marketing, man power requirement, incentives to be awarded to employees, competition facing from other firms, investment potential, financial problems, new ventures in business, etc. Accounting records can be used to evaluate the success of various marketing strategies such revenues from a direct marketing campaign. The principal virtues of these data are ready availability, reasonable accessibility on a continuing basis and relevance to the organisation's situation.

* External data sources

External data sources include :

- ❒ Government reports and publications.
- ❒ Reports of statistical agencies
- ❒ Trade associations' data
- ❒ General business publications
- ❒ Magazines and newspaper articles
- ❒ Compilation and directories
- ❒ Annual reports
- ❒ Academic publications
- ❒ Library sources
- ❒ Computerised bibliographies/data bases
- ❒ Syndicated services.

Published data are by far the most popular source of marketing information. Besides being readily available, they are often sufficient to answer the research question.

For instance, a marketing manager studying developments in tobacco industry will use trade association data to learn how the total consumption of tobacco is broken down, by type of customers belonging to different classes, geographical area, type, brand name and distribution client. A person starting a new shop in a locality may use the census data to know the family characteristics and income levels to support the likely location for the shop.

Applications of secondary data :

- Demand estimation
- Monitoring the Environment
- Segmentation and Targeting
- Developing a Business Intelligence

Demand estimation is a key determinant of the allocation of marketing resources - sales effort, service coverage, communication activity, etc. to different regions/segments/ territories.

Secondary data can be effectively used to monitor the environment in which the company is functioning. The marketing environment in recent days is quite volatile because of the changing attitudes, fashions and tastes of customers. To have up-to-date knowledge of latest developments the company has to be in constant touch with newspapers, magazines and periodicals.

Market segmentation is common among businesses seeking to improve their marketing efforts. An effective segmentation demands that firms group their customers into relatively homogeneous groups. Demographic and lifestyle characteristics data may be consulted in such endeavour.

A business intelligence system contains data on environment and the competitors and is an integral part of the marketing decision support system. Data on environment can be obtained from various sources and data on competitors can be obtained from annual reports, press releases, patent, business magazines, etc.

5.2.1. Exploring Secondary Data

As mentioned earlier there are a number of sources (information types) of secondary data, each with a special function. However, there are five information types, generally used by business researchers. These are :

* *Indexes and Bibliographies*

Any library maintains the Indexes and bibliographies which help identifying and locating a single book or journal article from among the millions published under relevant topics and subjects. The most important bibliography in any modern library is its **online catalog.** There are also specialized indexes and bibliographies, specially maintained concerning business topics. These serve useful purposes for literature search to find authors and titles of prior works on the topic of interest to a researcher.

* *Dictionaries*

Dictionaries serve certain purposes which are well known. We use them to verify spelling or grammar usage or to define certain terms. Specialized Dictionaries have also been prepared for specialised disciplines such as business, natural and physical sciences, biological sciences, social sciences, etc. which define words, terms, or jargon, information on people, events or organizations connected with the discipline.

A growing number of such dictionaries and glossaries are now available on the web, such as Dictionary of Business and Management.

* *Encyclopedias*

These provide background or historical information on a topic or to find names and terms that enhance the capability of the researchers to search results from other sources.

* *Handbooks*

A handbook is a collection of facts unique to a topic. Handbooks include statistics, directory information, glossary of terms and other relevant data including laws and regulations relevant to the topic.

* *Directories*

Directories are fact finding records which help finding names and addresses as well as other data relevant to a discipline. Many directories are now available in printed format and also can be downloaded from the websites.

Source evaluation

A researcher, when beginning to collect information on any topic should conduct a **source evalution** so that the materials collected serve his research purpose efficiently.

The source evaluation consists of evaluating

- ❒ Purpose
- ❒ Scope
- ❒ Authority
- ❒ Audience
- ❒ Format

Purpose

The purpose of the source is what the author or a group of authors is trying to accomplish. The purpose may be to enlighten and broaden the knowledge or to entertain the readers within a particular field or discipline. The authors might also trying to establish credibility for company's image and for websites. Sometimes the purpose of a source is to make search process easier for those who would like to buy certion products. Once the purpose of the source is determined the researcher will also want to determine whether the source provides bias information or balanced presentation of information.

Most researchers expect company websites to be biased in favour of the company. However, one can expect sources offered by independent organizations to be more balanced.

Scope

Scope is interlinked with purpose of the source. It relates to date of publication, time period covered by the source, in what extent and in what depth the topic is covered, whether material covered is local, national or international, whether the source is bibliographic, how comprehensive is it, etc.

Authority

A major concern to the information user as regards source is the authority of the source. Primary source is supposed to be more authoritative. In any source both the author and the publisher are indicators of the authority. Therefore, the source to present impression of reliability should contain the name of the author and his credentials as regards his position, educational background, previous publications, etc. Web resources are not always reliable and hence the researcher should check the credentials of the site.

Audience

Audience is an important factor which should be taken into account to evaluate a source and this initimately linked with the purpose. The researcher while visiting any source should evaluate how far the source is helpful towards his topic of interest, because some sources may have text book orientation, some may be towards a variety of research needs or some may be simply for educating audience.

Format

Formating may vary from source to source, but in general relates to how the information is presented and how easy to locate a specific piece of information. In the printed source the arrangement of information whether alphabetical or hierarchical or chronological has an impact on the retrieval of information.

The format of an electronic source or website is generally related to its design.

5.2.2 Searching a Bibliographic Database

In a bibliographic database—**online catalog of a library**, each record is a bibliographic citation to a book or a journal article.

There are several bibliographic database available to business researchers. Most of these databases offer numerous purchase options both in amount and type of coverage, sometimes including abstracts and short-summaries.

What is a Database ?

In computing, a **database** can be defined as a structured collection of records or data that is stored in a computer so that a program can consult it to answer queries. The records retrieved in answer to queries become information that can be used to make decisions. The computer program used to manage and query a database is known as a **database management system (DBMS).**

The central concept of a database is that of a collection of records, or pieces of knowledge. Typically, for a given database, there is a structural description of the type of facts held in that database : this description is known as a **schema.** The schema describes the objects that are represented in the database, and the relationships among them. There are a number of different ways of organizing a schema, that is, of modeling the database structure : these are known as **database models** (or data models). The model in most common use today is the **relational model,** which in layman's terms represents all information in the form of multiple related tables each consisting of rows and columns (the true definition uses mathematical terminology). This model represents relationships by the use of values common to more than one table. Other models such as the hierarchical model and the network model use a more explicit representation of relationships.

Database management systems are usually categorized according to the data model that they support : relational, object-relational, network, and so on. The data model will tend to determine the query languages that are available to access the database.

The process of searching bibliographic databases and retrieving results are as follows :

1. Select a database appropriate to a topic.
2. Construct a **search query/**search statement—Review and evaluate search results, modify search query.
3. Save results of your search.
4. Retrieve articles not present in the database.
5. Supplement your results with information from web sources.

Note :

1. Judicious selection of database is necessary to save time in search process. Library's online catalog, a biblographic database will help identification. A librarian can suggest one or more database for the topic of search.
2. For articles not available in full text online, retrieval will normally require the additional step of searching the online catalog to determine the availability and its location.

5.2.3 Searching the World Wide Web

A website is a collection of web pages, images, videos and other digital assets and hosted on a particular domain or subdomain on the world wide web.

A web page is a document, typically written in HTML, that is almost always accessible via HTTP, a protocol that transfers information from the website's server to display in the user's web browser.

All publicly accessible websites are seen collectively as constituting the "World Wide Web".

The World Wide Web is a vast information treasure covering a large variety of information sources pertaining to a variety of disciplines and the business researcher, therefore, should not overlook such important data source. Till 2007 there are over 110 million websites in total on the world wide web, providing millions of pages of data which are publicly available.

The pages of websites can usually be accessed from a common root URL, called the homepage and usually reside on the same physical server.

The first on-line website appeared in 1991 and on 30 April, 1993, CERN announced that the World Wide Web would be free to any one.

Organised by function a website may be

- a personal website
- a business website
- a government website
- a non-government website
- a non-profit organisation website

Websites a written in or dynamically converted to **HTML** (Hyper Text Markup Language) and are accessed using a software program called **a web broser,** also known as an HTTP server and these terms can also refer to the software that runs on these systems and that retrieves and deliver the web pages in response to requests from the website users.

A static website is one that has web pages stored on the server in the same form as the user will view them.

A dynamic website is one that has frequently changing information or collates information on the hop each time a page is requested. For example, it would call various bits of information from a database and put them together in a pre-defined format to present the reader with a coherent page.

The searching and retrieving reliable information on the web is great deal more problematic than searching a bibliographic database. This is because there are no standard database fields, subject hierarchies not carefully defined, no cross reference, no selection criteria and in general no rules.

These are many varieties of websites, each specialising in a particular type of content or use and they may be classified in any number of ways.

A few such classifications might include :

- Corporate website used to provide background information about a business, organization, or service.
- Commerce site or e-commerce site : for purchasing goods, such as Amazon. Com.
- Development website ; a site whose purpose is to provide information and resources related to software development.
- Data base site ;
- Directory site ;
- Employment site ;
- Information site ;
- Personal home page
- Search engine site : a site that provides general information and is intended as a gateway or look up for other sites, e.g. Google, Yahoo, etc.
- Web portal : a site that provides a starting point or a gateway to other resources on the Internet or an Intranet.

Some websites may be included in one or more of these categories. However, the extraordinary amount of information to be found on it provides compelling reasons for the researchers to use it as an information source.

The basic steps to searching the web are similar to those outlined for searching a bibliographic database. These are :

1. Select a search engine or directory
2. Determine your search option
3. Construct a search query
   - Review and evaluate search results
   - Modify the search query, if necessary
4. Save those valuable results of your search.
5. Supplement your results with information from non-web sources.

A number of search engines are available, but they work differently and their working procedures are not easy to determine. Some websites may be included in one or more of these categories :

5.2.4 Search Engine

A search engine is an information retrieval system designed to help find information stored on a computer system, such as on the world wide web, inside a corporate or proprietary network, or in a personal computer. The search engine allows one to ask for content meeting specific criteria (typically those containing a given word or phrase) and retrieves a list of items that match those criteria. This list is often sorted with respect to some measure of relevance of the results. Search engines use regularly updated indexes to operate quickly and efficiently.

Search engine usually refers to web search engine, which searches for information on the public web. Some research engines also mine data available in newsgroup, databases or open directories. Unlike web directories, which are maintained by human editors, search engines operate algorithmically or are a mixture of algorithm and human input.

The first-tool used for searching on this interest was **Archie**, created in 1990, followed by Gopher, in 1991. While Archie indexed computer files, gopher indexed plain text documents. The first web search engine was **Wandex**, a now defunet index collected by the World wide web wanderer, a **Web crawler** developed in 1993. The first 'full text' crawler based search engine was web crawler, came out in 1994. Soon after, many search engines appeared and vied for popularity. These included Excite, Infoseek, Inktome, Northern Light and Alta Vista. Later, the directories integrated or added on search engine technology for greater functionality.

Around 2001, the **Google** search engine rose to prominenee. Its success was based in part on the concept of link popularity and Page Rank. The number of other websites and webpages that link to a given page is taken into consideration with Page Rank, on the premise that good or desirable pages are linked to more than others.

In 2002, **Yahoo !** acquired **Inktomi** and in 2003 **Yahoo !** acquired **overture**, which owned All the Web and Alta Vista. Despite owning its own search engine, Yahoo! launced its own search engine based on the combined technologies of its acquisitions and providing a service that gave pre-eminence to the web search engine over the directory.

The most recent major search engine is **MSN Search**, owned by **Microsoft**, which previously relied on others for its search engine listings. In 2006, Microsoft migrated to a new search platform—**Window Live Search**, retiring the MSN search name in the process

Challenges faced by search engines

- The web is growing much faster than any present technology search engine can possibly index.
- Many web pages are updated frequently, which forces the search engine to reviset them periodically.
- Dynamically generated sites may be slow and difficult to index or not indexable.
- Sometimes the engines cannot get what the person is looking for.
- Secure pages (content hosted on HTTPs URLs) pose a challenge for crawlers which either cannot browse the content for technical reasons or won't index it for privacy reasons.

How search engines work ?

A search engine operates, in the following order

1. Web crawling
2. Indexing
3. Searching

Web search engines work by storing information about a large number of web pages, which they retrieve from the WWW itself. These pages are retrieved by a Web crawler (sometimes also known as a **spider**)—an automated Web browser which follows every link it sees. Exclusions can be made by the use of robots. txt. The contents of each page are then analyzed to determine how it should be indexed (for example, words are extracted from the titles, headings, or special fields called **meta tags**). Data about web pages are stored in an index database for use in later queries. Some search engines, such as Google, store all or part of the source page (referred to as a **cache**) as well as information about the web pages, whereas others, such as Alta Vista, store every word of every page they find. This cached page always holds the actual search text since it is the one that was actually indexed, so it can be very useful when the content of the current page has been updated and the search terms are no longer in it. This problem might be considered to be mild form of linkrot, and Google's handling of it increases usability by satisfying user expectations that the search terms will be on th e returned webpage. This satisfies for principle of least astonishment since the user normally expects the search terms to be on the returned pages. Increased search relevance makes these cached pages very useful, even beyond the fact that they may contain data that may no longer be available elsewhere.

When a user comes to the search engine and makes a query, typically by giving key words, the engine looks up the index and provides a listing of best-matching web pages according to its criteria, usually with a short summary containing the document's title and sometimes parts of the text. Most search engines support the use of the boolean terms AND, OR and NOT to further specify the search query. An advanced feature is proximity search, which allows users to define the distance between keywords.

The usefulness of a search depends on the relevance of the **result set** it gives back. While there may be millions of webpages that include a particular word or phrase, some pages may be more relevant, popular, or authoritative than others. Most search engines employ methods to rank the results to provide the "best" results first. How a search engine decides which pages are the best matches, and what order the results should be shown in, varies widely from one engine to another. The methods also change over time as Internet usage changes and new techniques evolve.

Most Web search engines are commercial ventures supported by advertising revenue and, as a result, some employ the controversial practice of allowing advertisers to pay money to have their listings ranked higher in search results. Those search engines which do not accept money for their search engine make money by running search related ads alongside the regular search engine results. The search engines makes money everytime someone clicks on one of these ads.

The vast majority of search engines are run by private companies using proprietary algorithms and closed databases, though some are open source.

Categories of Search Engines

The **search engines** may be categorised as :

1. General search engines.
2. Metasearch engines
3. Regional Search engines
4. People search engines
5. Google search engines
6. Yahoo! based search engines
7. Windows—live—based search engines
8. Job search engines
9. News search engines
10. Multimedia search engines.
11. Accountancy search engines
12. Medical search engines
13. Property search engines
14. Business search engines
15. Geographic search engines
16. Social search engines, etc. and many others

The **General search engines** include :

- ❒ Baidu
- ❒ Exalead
- ❒ Gigablast
- ❒ Google
- ❒ Windows Live search (formerly MSN Search)
- ❒ Yahoo ! Search, etc.

Metasearch engines

- ❒ Hot Bot
- ❒ Brainboost
- ❒ Meta Crawler
- ❒ Myriad Search
- ❒ Bioinformatic—Harvester, etc.

Business search engines include :

- ❒ Thomasnet (United States)
- ❒ Business. Com
- ❒ Nexis (Lexis Nexis)

Accountancy search engines :

- ❒ IFAC net

News search engines :

- ❒ Google News
- ❒ Magportal
- ❒ Topix. net
- ❒ Yahool ! News

Regional search engines :

- ❒ Baidu, China
- ❒ Rediff, India
- ❒ Accoona, China/US
- ❒ Yandex, Russia
- ❒ Ansearch, Australia/US/UK etc.

Multimedia search engines :

- ❒ blink X
- ❒ Picsearch
- ❒ Podscope, etc.

Comparison shopping search engines :

- ❒ MSN shopping
- ❒ My Simon
- ❒ Nex Tag
- ❒ Shopping. Com
- ❒ Shopzilla
- ❒ Froogle, etc.

Geographic search engines

- ❒ Geoportail
- ❒ Google Maps
- ❒ Map Quest
- ❒ Windows Live Maps
- ❒ Yahoo ! Maps

Google-based search engines :

- ❒ AOL search
- ❒ My space Search
- ❒ Netscope

Yahoo! —based search engines :

- ❒ Alta Vista

- All the web
- Good search

Job search engines :

- Naukri. Com (India)
- Bixee. Com (India)
- Hotjobs. Com (USA)
- Monster. Com (USA)
- Career Builder. Com (USA)
- Recruit . net (International), etc.

Answer-based search engines

- Answers. Com
- Ask Me Now
- Google Answers
- Lexxe
- Lycos iQ
- Yahoo ! Answers

Vertical Search engines

Vertical search engines or specialized search engines which specialize in specific context categories or that search within a specific media. Popular search engines like Google or Yahoo ! are very effective when the user searches for websites, webpages or general information vertical search engines enable the user to find specific types of listing thus making the search more customized to the user's needs.

5.2.5 Data Mining—Mining Internal Sources

An organization's own historical data is often ignored or underutilized source of information in the exploratory phase. The research may choose to ignore such data because of his ignorance about existence of historical data, time and budget constraints and lack of an organized archive. However, digging of historical data through data archieves forms an important function for the researcher to put his research findings on realistic footings with knowledge and information about the past.

A **data warehouse** is an electronic single organizational repository of databases that organizes large volumes of data into categories to facilitate retrieval, interpretation and sorting by end users. The data warehouse is the authoritative repository of all the fact and dimension at an atomic level.

The data warehouse provides an accessible archive to support dynamic organizational intelligence applications. The key words here are dynamically accessible. Data in a data warehouse must be continually updated to ensure that managers have access to data appropriate for real-time decisions. The **data mart** is a specific subject oriented, repositary of data designed to answer specific questions for a specific set of users. So an organization could have multiple data marts, serving the needs of marketing, sales, operations, collections, etc.

The more accessible the databases that comprise the data warehouse, the more likely a researcher will use such databases to reveal underlying pattern. It is to be noted that data in a data warehouse were once primary data collected for a specific purpose. When a researcher data-mine a company's data warehouse, all the data contained within that database becomes secondary data and pattern revealed may be used for other purposes of the researcher than originally intended. The critical factor leading to use of a data warehouse is that a data analyst can perform complex queries and analysis (such as data mining) on the information without slowing down the operational systems. The data warehouse contains raw material for management's decision support system. Data warehouses become a distinct type of data base during late 1980's and early 1990's.

While operational systems are optimised for simplicity and speed of modification (on line transaction processing, or OLTP) through heavy use of database normalization and an entity—relationship model, the data warhouse is optimised for reporting analysis (online analytical processing or OLAP). Frequently data in data ware houses is heavily denormalised, summarized and/or stored in a dimension—based model but this is not always required to achieve acceptable query response times.

Data Warehouse architecture

The term data warehouse architecture is primarily used to day to describe the overall structure of a Business Intelligence system. Other historical terms include Decision support systems (DSS), Management information systems (MIS), and other. The data warehouse architecture describes the overall system from various perspectives such as data, process and infrastructure needed to communicate the structure, function and interrelationship of each component. The infrastructure or technology perspective details the various hardware and software products used to implement the distinct components of the overall system.

Data Storage Methods

In OLTP on line transaction processing systems relational database design use the discipline of data modeling and generally follow the **Codd rules** of data normalization in order to ensure absolute data integrity. Using these rules complex information is broken down into its most-simple structures (a table) where all of the individual atomic level elements relate to each other and satisfy the normalization rules.

Designing the data warehouse data Architecture synergy is the realm of Data Warehouse Architects. The goal of a data warehouse is to bring data together from a variety of existing databases to support management and reporting needs. There are two leading approaches to organizing the date in a data warehouse.

- The dimensional approach
- The normalized approach

In the 'dimensional' approach, transaction data is partitioned into either a measured 'facts' which are generally numeric data that captures specific values or dimensions which contain the reference information that gives each transaction its context. As an example, a sales transaction would be broken up into facts such as the number of products ordered, the price paid, and dimensions such as date, customer, product, geographical location and sales person. The main advantage of a dimensional approach is that the data warehouse is easy for business staff with limited information technology experience to understand and use. Also, as the data is pre-joined into the dimensional form, the data warehouse tends to operate quickly. The main disadvantage of the dimensional approach is that it is quite difficult to add or change later if the company changes the way in which it does business.

The 'normalized' approach uses database normalization. In this method, the data in the data warehouse are stored in normal form. Tables are grouped together by **subject areas** that reflect the ganeral definition of the data (customer, product, finance etc.) The main advantage of this approach is that it is quite straight forward to add new information into the database and the primary disadvantage of this approach is that because of the number of tables involved, it can be rather slow to produce information and reports.

Advantages of using data warehouses

There are many advantages to using data warehouses. Some of these are :

- Enhances end user access to a wide variety of data.
- Business decision makers can obtain various kinds of trend reports e.g. item wise sales in a particular area for past years.

Concerns in using data warehouses

- Extracting, cleaning and loading of data is time consuming
- Problems with compatibility with systems already in place.
- Security could develop into a serious issue, especially if the data warehouse is web accessible.

Data Mining

The term data mining has been defined as "the non-trivial extraction of implicity, previously unknown and potentially useful information from data" and the "science of extracting useful information from large data sets or databases" stored in data marts or data warehouses. Similar to traditional concept of mining to search beneath the surfaces for valuable ore, data mining searches large data bases for indispensable information for managing an organisation.

Data mining government or commercial data sets for national security or law enforcement purposes has also raised privacy concerns.

There are many legitimate uses of data mining. For example, a database of prescription of drugs taken by people could be used to find combinations of drugs exhibiting harmful interactions. Since the detection occurs on rare occasions, a great deal of data would need to be examined to discover such interaction. Essentially, data mining gives information that would not be available otherwise. It must be properly interpreted to be useful. If involves sorting through large amounts of data and picking out relevant information.

Data mining identifies trends within data that go beyond simple analysis. Through the use of sophisticated algorithms, users have the ability to identify key attributes of business processes and target opportunities.

Data mining has gone through a number of evolutionary steps, such as :

- Data Collection
- Data Access
- Data Navigation
- Data Mining

Data Mining Techniques

Numerous techniques are used in data mining, often they are used together, but broadly depending on nature of data available and the nature of information sought for. The major techniques are :

- ❒ Data visulaization
- ❒ Clustering
- ❒ Induction
- ❒ Neural network
- ❒ On line Analytical Processing

Data Visualisation

Data visualisation makes it possible for the analyst to gain a deeper, more intuitive understanding of the data and as such can work well along side data mining. Data mining allows the analyst to focus on certain patterns and trends and explore in depth using visualisation. On its own data visualisation can be overwhelmed by the volume of data in a database but in conjunction with data mining can help with exploration.

Data visualisation uses two types of interactive queries :

- ❒ Via a query language, usually available to end user.
- ❒ Using online analytical processing (OLAP) tools for complex queries

Cluster Analysis

Clustering is often used as the first step in data mining. Clustering and segmentation basically partition the database so that each partition or group is similar according to some criteria or metric. Clustering/segmentation in databases is the process of separating a data set into components that reflect a consistent pattern of behaviour. Once the pattern have been established they can then be used to 'deconstruct' data into more understandable subsets and also they provide sub-groups of a population for further analysis or action which is important when dealing with very large databases. For example a database could be used for profile generation for target marketing where previous response to mailing campaigns can be used to generate a profile of people who responded and this can be used to predict response and filter mailing lists to achieve the best response.

Induction

A database is a store of information but more important is the information which can be inferred from it. There are **two** main inference techniques available :

- ❒ Deduction
- ❒ Induction

Deduction is a technique to refer information that is a logical consequence of the information in the database.

Induction is a technique to infer information that is generalized from the database.

Induction has been used in the following ways within data mining.

* *Decision trees*

Decision trees are simple knowledge representation and they classify examples to a finite number of classes, the nodes are labelled with attribute names, the edges are labelled with possible values for this attributes and the leaves labelled with different classes. Objects are classified by following a path down the tree, by taking the edges, corresponding to the values of the attributes in an object.

* *Rule Induction*

A data mine system has to infer a model from the database, that is, it may define classes such that the database contains one or more attributes that denote the class of a tuple *i.e.* the predicted attributes while the remaining attributes are the predicting attributes. Class can then be defined by condition on the attributes. When the classes are defined the system should be able to infer the rules that govern classification in other words the system should find the description of each class.

Neural networks

Neural networks are an approach to computing that involves developing mathematical structure with the ability to learn. The methods are the result of academic investigations to model nervous system learning Neural networks have the remarkable ability to derive meaning from complicated or imprecise data and can be used to extract patterns and detect trends that are too complex to be noticed by either humans or other computer techniques.

Since neural networks are best at identifying patterns or trends in data, they are suited for prediction or forecasting needs including :

- ❒ sales forecasting
- ❒ industrial process control
- ❒ customer research
- ❒ data validation
- ❒ risk management
- ❒ target marketing, etc.

Neural, networks use a set of processing elements (or nodes) analogous to neurons in the brain. These processing elements are interconnected in a network that can then identify patterns in data, once it is exposed to the data. This distinguishes neural networks from traditional computing programs that simply follow instructions in a fixed sequential order.

On line Analytical Processing

A major issue in information processing is how to process larger and larger databases, containing increasingly complex data, without sacrificing response time. The client/server architecture gives organizations the opportunity to deploy specialized servers which are optimized for handling specific data management problems. Untill recently organizations have tried to target relational database management systems (RDBMs) for the complete spectrum of database applications.

OLAP (on-line analytical processing) was a term coined by E.F. Codd in 1993 and was defined by him as the dynamic synthesis, analysis and consolidation of large volumes of multidimensional data. The requirements/rules for an OLAP system are :

- ❒ multidimensional conceptual view
- ❒ transparency
- ❒ accessibility
- ❒ consistent reporting performance
- ❒ client/server architecture
- ❒ generic dimensionality
- ❒ multi-user support
- ❒ unrestricted cross dimensional
- ❒ intuitive data manipulation
- ❒ flexible reporting
- ❒ unlimited dimension and aggregation levels

OLAP database servers use multidimensional structures to store data and relationships between data.

OLAP database serves support common analytical operations including : consolidation, drill down, and 'slicing and dicing".

OLAP servers have the means of storing multidimensional data in a compressed form. This is accomplished by dynamically selecting the physical storage arrangements and compression techniques that maximise space utilization.

In conclusion OLAP servers logically organize data in multiple dimensions which allows users to quickly and easily analyze data relationships.

Other data mining techniques include **Association** which is the process used to recognize and understand patterns in the data. The goal is to find, across large numbers of small transactions, trends that can be used to understand and exploit natural buying patterns. The most common form of association is **market basket analysis** and its variant **sequence based analysis.**

Fuzzy logic, genetic algorithms and fractal transforms are used in more complex mining operations :

The data mining involves a **five** step process :

- ❒ sample
- ❒ explore
- ❒ modify
- ❒ model
- ❒ assess

Most data mining efforts are focussed on developing highly detailed models of some large data set. Sometimes, a researcher feels that some one's data mining efforts result in discovering patterns or causal relationships which may seem unfounded.

Data dredging or data fishing techniques may be used to scan the data for any relationships. Cross validation is a common approach to evaluating the fitness of a model generated via data mining, where the data is divided into a training subset or test subset to respectively build and then test the model. Common cross validation techniques include *holdout method, k-fold cross validation* and the *leave-one-out method.*

5.2.6 Government Publications

In a democratic state, information about governments own activities in different social and economic sectors is of crucial importance to all citizens, whether common man, academicians or researchers. The Indian government has expanded it statistical activities many fold after independence. A large number of planning and policy making institutions have been founded in addition to regulatory bodies (Reserve Bank of India, Ministry of Commerce, Ministry of Finance etc.) The government has become the largest respository of data and information. It publishes a large number of documents in a diffused manner. The publications include reports of regulatory bodies, legislative agencies, experts groups, results of surveys and census operations (*i.e.* statistical publications).

Of late, government agencies in India have made efforts to disseminate information through the internet. National Informatics Centre (NIC) has developed websites in which one can get an overview of working of different agencies and implementation of development programmes.

Government Documents : Major Groups

The governments at all levels *i.e.* municipal, district, state and union, publish thousands of documents in a year. The Indian government reports can be divided into the following major groups.

- **Administrative Reports.** These are generally published annually containing summary records of etc activities and achievements of government agencies.
- **Statistical publications.** Results of statistical operations such as sample surveys, censuses and statistical series derived out of administrative records of regulatory agencies of government come under this category.
- **Commission and Committee Reports.** Ministries, departments and their sub-ordinate bodies frequently appoint commitees and commissions consisting of one or more members. The purpose is to enquire into various problems or to elicit expert opinion on certain issues. The finding are recorded and published as reports.
- **Research Reports.** The results of government sponsored research projects fall under this category. Many government agencies have their own research wing. Some of these assign their research projects to autonomous institutions.

In addition, there are certain other categories of publications, which are required to carry out judicial, legislative and administrative responsibilities of the state. They are:

- Bills, Acts, Laws, Codes, etc.
- Laws Reports and Digests
- Rules and Regulations, and
- Records of Proceedings (e.g. Lok Sabha and Rajya Sabha (Houses of Indian Parliament)).

There is another category of documents, which are published regularly through normal trade channel ; and treated as reference sources by the librarians. Examples are:

- India : A reference Annual
- Statistical Abstract

- Mass Media in India
- Publications of Ministry of Information and Broadcasting.
- Publications on Science technology, agriculture, socio economic planning.
- The Gazette of India
- Budget of India
- Economic Survey
- National Accounts Statistics

Statistical Publications

India has a federal structure of government with a division of responsibilty for administration between the central government and states. In most cases, statistical data collection programmes are organized basically at the state level and national statistics are built up from below. Much of the statistical activity is now concurrent and this has helped in coordination of statistical programmes at center by the apex body *i.e.* Ministry of Statistics and Programme Implementation (MOSPI) a special unit of the central government. MOSPI has two major constituent units. They are :

- Central Statistical Organization (CSO)
- National Sample Survey Organization (NSSO)

Central Statistical Organization (CSO) co-ordinates the statistical activities of central and state agencies and keeps a close liason with international agencies.

Major databases developed by CSO include :

- National Accounts Statistics (NAS)
- Annual Survey of Industries (ASI)
- Index of Industrial Production (IIP)
- Economic Census (EC)
- Consumer Price Index for Urban Non-manual employees.

National sample survey organization (NSSO) conducts multi-subject household surveys in randomly selected villages and urban blocks spread all over the country.

The subject on which NSSO conducts sample surveys include household consumption, employment, unemployment, manufacturing and trade, agriculture, social sectors, housing conditions, prices (including data on rural credit) etc.

NSSO has played a key role in building up a sound database covering several sectors of the company and providing valuable inputs in planning and policy formulation. Apart from conducting socio- economic surveys, Field Operations Division of NSSO undertakes fieldwork for ASI and follow up surveys for EC, besides collection of price data from rural and urban sectors. Thus, in certain statistical endeavors, it works in close cooperation with CSO and other bodies. The databases created by NSSO in recent years are available in electronic form.

Registrar General of India (RGI) is one of the premier statistical agencies in India responsible for conducting population census and registration of births and deaths in the country. Census of India database is considered to be the largest respository of data. It contains data in various forms, which include classification of persons by sex and age, marital status, rural/urban residence, educational standards, economic activities etc. The census schedule is the main apparatus for collection of data. During the last five decades, several changes have been introduced in census schedule to reflect socio-economic conditions of population. The databases pertaining to vital events (i.e. birth and death) are collected through Vital Registration System (VRS).

Directorate General of Commercial intelligence and Statistics (DGCIS) has created a foreign trade database. The database developed by DGCIS is basically a byproduct of regulatory mechanism of the government.

Statistics of India's foreign trade are complied according to general system. All goods entering the customs area by land, sea or air whether for hom consumption or for subsequent re- exportation are called imports. All goods which are products of the country and which leave the customs frontiers are called exports. Goods, which were previously imported and are subsequently exported, are called "re-exports." Recently time lag in foreign trade data has been reduced considerably as a result of computerized processing.

Directorate of Economics and Statistics (DES) is the apex body for agriculture statistics in India. Though agricultural statistics is primarily the responsibility of states, DES is the co-coordinating agency for data collection and processing of results. DES develops advance estimate database pertaining to area and yield through a Timely Reporting Scheme (TRS) and General Crop Estimation survey (GCES). Agricultural Census is conducted every five years by DES ; and it provides data on land holdings.

The Labour Bureau is responsible for developing database on labour and employment. Data are collected from different regulatory agencies and statistical organizations like NSSO, RGI, etc.

The RBI is responsible for developing database on banking and finance. The source of data for RBI is statistical return submitted by banks. According to Banking Regulation Act, 1949 every banking company is required to submit a monthly return to RBI showing overall assets and liabilities as well as data pertaining to their business operations. RBI also conducts ad-hoc surveys on banking business particularly in rural areas and in the process collects additional information.

Department of Education, Ministry of Human Resource Development is responsible for population of education statistics at all India level. The principle sources of data are Directorate of Education in states, Univeristy Grant Commission, All India Education Surveys conducted periodically by National Council of Educational Research and Training (NCERT), New Delhi, and population census data of RGI.

In India, just five years ago, the only way to disseminate statistical data to the users was by printed reports. All statistical agencies disseminated data through print media in the form of serials or ad-hoc publications almost always at subsidized rates or free of cost and sometimes on no-profit no loss basis. The vast myriad of statistical publications are released all over the country in a dispersed manner have found place in many government libraries by virtue of 'free mailing list' culture of the government. Even now, most of these reports do not have adequate bibliographical details and it becomes difficult to process them properly for the purpose of maintaining in the library. In the year 2000, a national policy on the dissemination of statistical data has been approved. According to this policy, researchers can have access to unpublished data in electronic form. However, in order to maintain confidentiality provision, (Statistics Act 1953). The unit level data (i.e. a household or an enterprise) is to be released after deleting identification marks.

Administrative/Working Group Reports, Committees and Commission Reports and Other Similar Publications

Apart from statistical publications, the government at levels publishes a large number of volumes in the form of reports. Social scientists believe that reports are intrinsically less reliable than official records that normally remain buried in files ; as they contain some intention of justifying the actions and minimizing the failures of the concerned organizations. Liberaries such as The National Library, Calcutta, Central Secretariat ; Planning Commission; Ministry of Industry and Commerce ; etc (all located in New Delhi) have a strong collection of government reports.

Most of the committee/commission reports, working group/task force/expert group recommendations and administration reports (i.e. annual reports of working of different government bodies) are unpriced publications. Therefore, they are not available through traditional trade channel. However, there are a number of government reports published with a price tag. Most of the prominent social science libraries in India acquire government reports from agents who deal with official publications where as libraries attached to government departments and institutions directly funded by the government have the privilege of getting complimentary copies of reports through the government's free mailing list' system. Priced reports are supplied to the libraries on an 'as and when published' basis by agents.

Some of the government reports are published as serials; and there are gaps in their collection is in most of the libraries. Serials by definition are published in successive parts and intended to continue indefinitely. They are different from monographs for they continue and change. Normally monograph entries stay unchanged once they are made but all characteristics of serial may alter during its lifetime. There is no bibliographical control for these compilations at any level of government. A majority of these reports remain confined to government offices and are never distributed. In fact, diversity of practices in government offices with regard to printing, distribution and announcement of government reports has generated a genuine demand for coordination and integration of bibliographic activities.

Most of the reports are distributed among priority users with the help of a mailing list. Maintenance and revision of a mailing list is normally done by a junior level official. As a result, analysis or judgement is not applied as to what names are to be placed on the list. This means that potential users of a report may not get an opportunity to consult it. During 1976's and 1980's many government publications were indiseriminately marked as 'for official use' or 'for restricted circulation.'. There is an urgent need to launch an awareness campaign to increase the distribution and use of government reports. User's group from academic institutions and research units must be associated with this campaign.

Access to unpublished Records

There are mainly two aspects of public access to government information. One is access to published data and the other is unpublished administrative and other records. One can have access to published information through print media or through the concerned department/ministry. It is difficult to have access to unpublished records. The provisions of *Official Secrets' Act (1923)* empower the officials to without information from the public.

There are quite a few reasons why information collected by the government is not made available. It is argued that some of this information is obtained on the condition that its confidential nature will be respected. It is also said that personal information acquired for the purpose of doing a specific statutory duty should not be made available for other purposes. These principles are embodied in *Collection of Statistics Act. 1950*. And finally, it is often said that the primary task of a government agency is to carry out its statutory responsibilities and that dissemination of information collected in the course of these duties may be a burden on resource and also a deviation from their main activities. This argument loses credibility when one considers the need for open government. It is now believed that all rights in a democratic society extend from one's ability to access information and citizens should have ready access to information in order to keep government accountable.

Government Information and Electronic Media

Recent advances in Information and Communication Technology (ICT) has made it possible to develop and disseminate information in various forms and means of media on local, national, and international level. ICT has produced marvels like the Internet, Word Wide Web, Interactive Multimedia, CD-ROMs, on-line digital libraries etc. The viewpoint that electronic governance can bring greater transparency and simplicity in governmnets' relationship with business and public now has a wider acceptance. In addition, 64th and 73rd Amendment of Indian Constitution has made provisions for *Gram Panchayat* (i.e. Village Assembly) based administration. A citizen can now participate in decision-making process for which the person is required to be information literate. The government has initiated plans and programmes to provide access to official information through electronic media.

Almost all the government ministries, departments, subordinate offices and government funded autonomous organizations have their websites on the Internet created by the NIC (National Informatics Centre, India), (http://www.nic.in). The spheres of activity, plans and programmes of different ministries and departments are made public through their website. For example, The Planning Commission has put all important plan documents and other publications on its website. Similarly, statistics wing of Ministry of Statistics and Programme Implementation (MOSPI) has a website which contains annual report of the Ministry. It also contains information about publications released by MOSPI and the necessary guidelines for obtaining the publications. The latest macro-economic indicators and socio-economic statistics released by MOSPI have also been included. Reserved Bank of India (RBI) has a website which provides access to information on many subjects like (*a*) money market operations (*b*) RBI rules (*c*) statement by RBI on recent developments in the foreign exchange markets. In most of the cases, the website of a government department also include a profile of the Minister in charge, administrative set up and a report of the working of the organization.

Concluding Remarks

In India, the government is the largest producer of data and information. Reports, serials and other publications are released in a dispersed manner by the government.

There is an urgent need for a coordinating agency which can monitor the publishing activity. A proper bibliographical control is also necessary. Following measures can be taken to activate the use of government publications.

- ❒ Sharing of access/collection development responsibilities based on subject strength of libraries or geographic considerations.
- ❒ Identification of government information holdings through on-line catalogues, union lists and other locator systems.
- ❒ Provision for feedback mechanism for information creator and access providers to evaluate.

Websites

Directory of official websites of the government of India have nearly 2000 websites in number, having categories such as Arts/Entertainment, Business, Employment, Government, Education Directories—Business Directories, Science and Environment, Transportation, Travel and Tourism, etc. Some of the important websites are available at :

1. www.business line India.com
2. IndiaBusinesswebsiteswww.dinesh.com
3. www.gateway to India.com
4. www.planetIndia.com
5. www.CensusIndia.net
6. www.Indiadata.com
7. www.Demographic.net
8. www.Capitaline.com

Business directory contains information on exporters, manufacturers and suppliers of products and services.

Major Business Publications in India with Online Resources

The following links will take you to the most important sources of financial news available in India and on the Internet :

www.economictimes.com. *The Economic Times* is a major daily covering economics and finance from the Times of India Group, a leading newspaper organization in India that reports on new economy companies, infrastructure, economic indicators, finance, stocks, Forex, and commodities.

www.business-standard.com. *The Business Standard* is another major financial newspaper from the Anand Bazaar Patrika Group. They update their Internet edition at midnight.

www.financialexpress.com. *The Financial Express* is a financial daily from the leading Indian Express Group that covers the Indian economy generally, as well as tracks financial issues and stock markets.

www.hinduonnet.com/bline. *Business Line* is a business newspaper from the Hindu Group, a leading newspaper group of South India.

www.businessworldindia.com This site provides an online business journal with searchable archives.

www.india-today.com/btoday/index.html *Business Today* is a magazine from the major magazine group India Today.

www.indeconomist.com/ *The Industrial Economist* is South India's oldest business magazine.

www.epw.org.in *The Economic and Political Weekly* is another leading source for financial information.

www.business-leaders.com/This is an online magazine aimed particularly at corporate leaders and management.

5.3 PRIMARY DATA

Primary data collection becomes necessary when the researcher cannot or fails to obtain data from secondary sources. Researchers are interested in primary data about demographic/ socio-economic characteristics, attitudes/opinions/interests, awareness/knowledge, intentions, motivations and behaviours for reaching marketing decisions, even otherwise for other decision purposes. In primary research, data are collected specifically for the study at hand. It can be obtained either by the investigator *observing* the subject(or phenomenon) being studied or *communicating* directly or indirectly with the subject or through *experimentation* under controlled conditions. Primary sources of data for qualitative research are

- ❒ people (individuals/groups)
- ❒ organisations/institutions
- ❒ settings and environments
- ❒ objects, artifacts, media products
- ❒ events, happenings

Sources of data for quantitative research are causal and non-causal studies both in field (naturalistic) and laboratory involving counting and/or measuring the characteristic or phenomena under consideration.

Qualitative and quantitative research are not mutually exclusive and moreover most research draws data on both methods. Both the approaches can generate qualitative and quantitative data. The difference between two methods is in the overall form and the emphasis, and objective of the study. Measurement often plays a more important role in quantitative research compared to qualitative research.

Research techniques for collecting primary data may be grouped as :

- Qualitative research techniques
- Quantitative research techniques

5.3.1 Qualitative Research Techniques :

Qualitative research is particularly helpful in identifying the scope of research that should be persued to fully understand the views, opinions and attitudes that may be encountered. It also allows to probe in depth how consumers reach a decision in the buying process. Qualitative research can even lead to formulating the hypothesis that will be tested through quantitative research.

Survey instruments can be pretested in part using qualitative research techniques. The qualitative techniques such focus groups are also ideal for generating new ideas, fine tuning concepts and testing advertisements, promotion programmes.

Qualitative research has the following characteristics, distinguishing it from quantitative research. These are :

- The data are usually gathered using less structured research instruments.
- The findings are more in-depth since they make greater use of open-ended questions.
- The results provide much more detail on behaviour, attitude and motivation.
- The research is more intensive and more flexible, allowing the researcher to probe since he has greater latitude to do so.
- The results are based on smaller sample sizes and are often not representative of the population.
- The research can usually not be replicated or repeated, giving it low reliablility.
- The analysis of results is much more subjective.

Because of the nature of the interaction with the respondents, the training and level of expertise required by the person engaging in the direct communication with the respondents must be quite high.

The most common *qualitative research techniques* are :

- Experience survey
- Case study
- Pilot study
  - In-depth interview
  - Focus group
  - Brain Storming
  - Panels
  - Projective techniques

The Experience Survey

Any time a researcher or decision-maker needs to gain greater insight into a particular problem, he or she is likely to question knowledgeable individuals about it. This is usually done through an informal, free-flowing conversation with any one who is believed to be able to shed light on the question both within the organization and outside it. Such an approach is referred to as an *experience survey*. It is only meant to help formulate the problem and clarify concepts, not develop conclusive evidence.

People seen as providing the insight necessary are not only found in the top ranks of an organisation or amongst its 'professional' staff, but can also involve frontline employees. In an experience survey, respondents are not selected randomly nor are they representatives of the organization or department within which they work. Rather, they are knowledgeable, articulates and thoughtful individuals.

The Case Study

The case study is a comprehensive description and analysis of one or a few situations that are similar to the one being studied, the emphasis is on an entire organisation with great attention paid to detail in order to understand and document the relationships among circumstances, events, individuals, processes, and decisions made.

In order to obtain the information required, it is usually necessary to conduct a depth interview with key individuals in the organization as well as consulting internal documents and records or searching press reports.

Observation of actual meetings, sales calls or trips, negotiations etc. can also prove insightful, since "actions speak louder than words" even when it comes to understanding how decisions are made in an organization or why some organizations are more successful than others.

The case study method as a social research method was first introduced by Frederic Le play (1806-1882). It is a way of organizing social/organizational/institutional data so as to preserve the unitary character of the unit being studied. Even if it is not a scientific method, it is a healthy first step in scientific procedure. When individual cases club together to reveal uniformities, types and patterns of behaviour, its scientific significance increases.

The case study is a form of qualitative descriptive research and derives valuable data from participant observations, non- participant observations, structured schedules, all sorts of documents, historical records, diaries, letters etc. without scientific and adequate sampling design.

The case studies are difficult to generalize because of their inherent subjectivity and also because they are based on qualitative data which can be generalized only in a particular context. Thus, case studies are seldom comparable in 'pluralistic universe of discourse' because of this subjectivitly and this is the major shortcoming with the case study method.

Many good research designs have some recourse to case analysis even if final report does not show any indication. The finalisation of questionnaire gets facilitated by the experience accrued from the case studies.

The case studies provide a wider range of personal experience to the researcher to understand the dynamics of social/organizational structure and processes.

For preliminary researches in any field, most researchers use some form of case studies for the purpose of group or process analysis and for getting deeper insight into the problem.

Even if it is not possible to provide the case study method a status of a particular technique for eliciting data, it is to be recognised as a mode of organising data in terms of some chosen unit such as individual, group, organization, community or some delimited social process.

The usefulness of case study data stems from the fact that acquaintance with particular is the beginning of knowledge scientific or otherwise.

Case studies bring out the presence of new variables and other new questions for further research and emphasize detailed contextual analysis of a limited number of events or conditions and their relationships. Case study is a sort of qualitative research method to examine contemporary real life situations and provide the basis for the application of ideas and extension of methods.

Yin (1993) and Stake (1995) have developed certain robust procedures for effective application of case study methodology. Whether the study is experimental or quasi-experimental the data collection and analysis methods are known to hide certain details of information and the case studies are so designed as to bring out the details from the view point of the participant by using multiple sources of data. Most case study advocates point out that case studies produce much more detailed information than what is available through a statistical analysis. They are also of the view that although statistical methods might be able to deal with situations where behaviour is homogeneous and routine, case studies are needed to deal with creativity, innovation and context.

Case study research helps understanding a complex issue or object and can extend experience or add strength to what is known through previous research.

Case studies may be classified into

- *Illustrative case studies* : These are primarily meant to make unfamiliar familiar and to give readers a common language about the topic in question.
- *Exploratory (pilot) case studies* : These are undertaken before implementing a large scale investigations with view to identify questions and investigation and select types of measurement.
- *Explanatory case studies* : These look into possible case- effect relationship and may be used for long causal investigations.
- *Cumulative case studies* : These serve to aggregate information from several sites and units at different times and allow for greater generalization without additional cost or time being expanded on new, possibly repetitive studies.
- *Critical instance case studies* : These examine a situation of unique interest with little or no interest in generalizability.

Yin (1994) have listed *six primary sources* of evidence for data collection in the case study protocol.

These are :

- documentation
- direct observations
- archival records
- participant observation
- interviews
- physical artifacts

He has suggested *three principles* of data collection for case studies

- use of multiple sources of data
- create a case study data base
- maintain a chain of evidence

The rationale for using multiple sources of data is the *triangulation of evidence*. Triangulation increases the reliability of data and the process of gathering it. In the context of data collection, triangulation serves to corroborate the data gathered from other sources. The cost of using multiple sources and the investigator's ability to carry out the task, should be taken into account prior to deciding on the use of this technique.

The design of data bases (data and the report of the investigator) should be such the other researchers would be able to use the material based on the descriptions contained in the documentation.

In recommending that a chain of evidence be maintained, Yin (1994) provided an avenue for the researcher to increase the reliability of the study. The procedure is to have an external observer follow the derivation of evidence from initial research questions to ultimate case study conclusions.

The following *steps* may be suggested for conducting a case study research.

❒ Determine and define the research questions
❒ Select the cases and determine data gathering and analysis techniques
❒ Prepare to collect data
❒ Evaluate and analyze the data
❒ Prepare the report.

Case study data are generally treated confidential in nature. These are carefully synthesized with possibility follow-up action. However, caution must be exercised in transforming case study lessons to other situations : there is no 'formula' that can be applied, but rather a context that must be understood and interaction among the individuals that must be appreciated.

Case studies vs. statistical studies :

Statistical studies are designed for breadth rather than depth. The prime aim is to infer on population characteristics by taking a sample. Hypotheses are tested quantitatively and generalizations about the findings are presented subject to representativeness of the sample and the validity of the design.

Case studies place more emphasis on a full textual analysis of fewer events or conditions and their interrelations. Although hypotheses are often used, the reliance on qualitative data makes the support or rejection more difficult. By emphasizing on details the case studies provide valuable insight for problem solving, evaluation and strategy. These details are secured from multiple sources of information.

Although some argue that case studies can be treated as 'scientifically worthless' because they do not meet minimum design requirements for comparison, they have a significant role in research studies.

It is known that important scientific propositions have the form of universalization and the universalization can be falsified by a single counter instance. Thus, a single well designed case study can provide a major challenge to a theory and in the process provide a source of new hypothesis and construct simultaneously.

The Pilot Study

When data are collected from a limited number of subjects selected from the population targeted by the researcher, this is referred to as a **pilot study.** A pilot study can also take the form of a trial run. For instance, an advertising campaign is tested in a specific market before it goes nation-wide to study the response by potential consumers.

In a pilot study, the rigorous standards used to obtain precise, quantitative estimates from large, representative samples are often relaxed, since the objective is to gain insight into how subjects will respond prior to administering the full instrument.

There are four major qualitative research techniques that can be used as a part of a pilot study.

These are :

- In-Depth interview
- Focus group (or group depth interview)
- Brain storming
- Panel
- Projective technique.

In-depth Interview

In-Depth interviews are an unstructured and direct way of obtaining information on a one-one-basis. They are also called **individual depth interviews.** A depth interview is an unstructured, direct, personal interview in which a single respondent is probed by a highly skilled interviewer to uncover underlying motivation, beliefs, attitudes, and feelings on a topic. For instance, suppose the researcher wants to probe 'How do you feel about shopping at department stores/super market ?" Then he encourages the individual subject/respondent to talk freely about his attitude toward department stores. After some initial questions to develop favourable interaction, he uses an unstructured format to probe elaborately into his attitudes, depending on his answers. It may be mentioned here that probing helps in uncovering underlying or hidden information and is an integral part of depth interviews.

There are three depth interviewing techniques that have gained popularity in market research.

- laddering
- hidden issue questioning
- symbolic analysis.

Laddering presupposes interviewers trained in specific probing techniques with a view to develop a meaningful 'mental map' of the consumer's view toward a target product with an ultimate goal to combine the mental maps of consumers having similar views to reflect upon the reasons why people purchase particular product. In laddering the line of questioning proceeds from product characteristics to user characteristics. It provides the way to go deep into consumer's deep underlying psychological and emotional reasons that affect the purchasing decisions rather than only 'quality' and 'low price'.

In hidden issue questioning the focus is not on socially shared values, but on personal 'sore spots' ; not on personal life styles but on deeply felt personal concerns.

Symbolic analysis is a technique for conducting depth interviews in whcih the symbolic meaning of objects is analyzed by comparing them with their opposities. This implies that before learning what something is, the researcher attempts to learn what is is not. Investigations rest on studying attitude toward a usage of an imaginary 'non-product', 'non-products' which is/are logical opposites of a product.

The success of the depth interview depends on how efficiently the interviewer plays his role. Thus, the interviewer should avoid appearing superior while facing the respondent, look detached and objective, yet personable, ask questions in an informative manner, not accept 'yes' or 'no' answers and probe the respondent.

Advantages :

- uncovers greater depth of insights than focus groups.
- easy to determine reponses of an individual respondent unlike focus groups.
- free exchange of information that may not be possible in focus groups, where social pressure might encourage the respondent unwillingly to conform to group response.

Disadvantages :

- Skilled interviewers may be difficult and expensive to find.
- the lack of structure of the interview makes the results succeptible to the interviewer's influence.

- Quality and completeness of the interview depend heavily on the skill of the interviewer.
- Data may be difficult to be interpreted without the help of skilled psychologists.
- Number of depth interviews may be restricted due to time and cost involved.

The Focus group (group method interview)

A focus group is an interview conducted by a *trained moderator* with a small group of respondents. *The moderater* leads the discussion. The main purpose of focus groups is to become wise and to gain insights by listening to a group of people about issues of interest to the researcher. Sometimes it so happens that free flowing discussions among the members of the focus group bring out some unexpected and even suprising findings.

Focus groups are the most familiar and important qualitative research procedure in market research studies.

A focus group generally consists of 8 to 12 members and should be homogeneous in terms of demographic and socio-economic characteristics or common characteristics to avoid conflict among group members on side issues. Participants in the focus groups should be clearly screened so that professional focus group participants are not selected, because their participation may lead to serious validity problems.

The moderator plays a key role in the success of a focus group. He must have capability to establish rapport with the participants to keep the discussion live and moving forward, and to probe the respondents to elicit insights about the issues at hand. Further, the moderator plays a centrol role in the analysis and interpretation of focus group data. Therefore the moderator should have the necessary skill, expertise, knowledge of the discussion topic and an understanding of the nature of the group dynamics.

The physical setting for the focus group is no less important for the discussion. It should be held in a relaxed, informal atmosphere to encourage spontaneous comments. The meeting of the focus group should have 1 to 3 hours duration with provision of light refreshments served before the session or in between the discussion to develop an informal atmosphere to explore in depth their feelings, attitudes, beliefs, ideas and insights regarding the topics of concern. Focus group interviews are invariably recorded, often on videotape for subsequent replay, transcription and analysis. Videotaping has another advantage of showing facial expressions and body movements of the participants to gauge certain aspects of their feelings and attitudes. It is a common practice to provide monetary incentive to focus group participants.

Online focus groups are emerging as an important focus groups with the advancement of Internet and computer applications.

In the past, focus groups were called as "focussed interviews" or "group depth interviews". The technique was developed after World War II to evaluate audience response to radio programmes. The use of focus groups in social research is not as frequent as in market research, and more recently in medical research. In the last 20 years, government agencies, non-governmental organisations (NGOs), academics, business organisations, public health organisations, educational and environmental organisations were quick to make use of focus groups. A focus group has been defined differently by several social scientists. Some define focus group as *"a group of individuals selected and assembled by researchers to discuss and comment on, from per-*

sonal experience, the topic that is subject of research". A focus group relies on interaction within the group based on topics that are supplied by the researcher. Thus, a focus group could be defined as a group or panel of people having common interest on a common/specific issue or focussed issue, brought together by a researcher (moderator in this case) to elucidate information by way of interaction among them. The main purpose of organising a focus group is to use organised group discussion to gather opinions about a specific issue from a small group of selected individuals. In other words, it aims at capturing participants attitudes, feelings, beliefs, experiences and reactions to a particular issue in a way that is not possible in any other methods, may it be one to one observation interview or questionnaire surveys. It provides information on (a) how groups of people think or feel about a particular topic, (b) throws greater insight into why certain opinions are held, (c) help improve the planning and design of new programmes, (d) provide a means of evaluating existing programmes and (e) help developing strategies for outreach.

Thus, some of the important features of a focus group are; (i) organised discussion, (ii) collective activity, (iii) social events and (iv) interaction. The moderator or facilitator introduces the topic and encourages the group to discuss it among themselves.

It must be noted here that focus group discussions are not the same as 'group interviewing'. In group interviewing a group of persons are interviewed at a time and the emphasis is being laid on questions and responses between the researchers and participants. On the contrary in a focus group, discussions are held among the participants on a particular issue. Further, it must be borne in mind that focus group is not a method which can provide information on individuals, events changed over time and information generally applicable to other groups of people.

The Role of Moderator

If facilitated well, the focus group method can generate detail information. Therefore, the role played by a moderator/facilitator is very critical and assumes great importance in conducting the discussion. Moderators should have charateristics that are similar to the participants and be skilled in group processes.

- Prior to discussion the moderator should greet the participants and begin small talk on any issue other than the one to be discussed by the group.
- During the meeting moderator needs to promote debate by asking open questions. Some times the moderator is required to probe for details and carry forward the discussion in case the discussion has reached a minor conclusion.
- Moderators always try to keep the discussion focussed on the main issue. As a general rule, a moderator should pause for five seconds after a participant talks before beginning to talk. This five seconds pause provides other participants to react.
- While encouraging every one to participate in the discussion, moderators should avoid head nodding, and short verval responses such as "ok", "yes", "correct" "that's good" etc. In other words a moderator should not show so much approval to any one participant's view. The moderator should restrain himself/herself from giving own opinion.
- Moderators should be prepared for any eventualities such as no one showing up, group does not want to talk, space is inadequate, early questions take up too much time etc.

- To be a good moderator, one should possess good interpersonal skill, be a good listner with cool temperament, pleasing personality, non-judgemental and adaptable.
- He/She must have the quality to regulate the discussion on the lines of desired objectives of the research. For this, moderators should be mentally alert, listen well, and think quickly on their feet. All questiones should be memorised.

Although all participants are given the chance to speak, some participants may be allowed to continue if they are answering the question and giving new and useful information. Thanking them for their inputs the moderator should control dominant talkers and insist humbly quiet participants to share their view points. The output of the session is a list of ideas and behavioural observations with recommendations of the moderator.

- Before concluding the session the moderator shall have to summarise the key points of the discussion and ask for confirmation. Finally, the session comes to an end after the vote of thanks is proposed to the participants.

Where can it be used ?

Focus groups can be used at the preliminary of exploratory stages of a study. It can be used either to evaluate or develop a particular programme of activities during a study or to assess its impact or to generate further avenues of research after a programmes has been completed. Focus groups can be used as a method or as a complements to other methods, especially for triangulation and cross checking. Focus groups also can help develop hypotheses and questions and concepts for questionnaire and interview schedule.

In the past decade, a large number of focus group research have emerged which involve the community members in the research process. Topics in these studies are mainly related to policy development, community development, or prevention of drug use etc. In business or manufacturing concern the topic of objective may be a new product or proudct concept or a marketing strategy.

How to form focus groups :

Most focus groups are homogeneous. They are located through informal network of colleagues, community agencies, and the target group. Sometimes the researchers advertise to attract wide range of opinions and participation.

Types of focus groups

Depending on the setting of meeting place, the focus groups may be classified as

- Traditional focus groups
- Telephone focus groups
- On line focus groups
- Videoconferencing focus groups

In traditional focus group the participants meet face to face in a comfortable setting where they are observed by the sponsoring client.

When it is difficult to recruit desired participants who are often busy; target group members are rare ; the issues are sensitive and require confidentiality ; there is need for nation wide representation for certain issues ; modern telephone conferencing facilities are available, telephone focus groups can be particularly effective.

An emerging advanced communication technology facilitating exploratory research is to approximate the group dynamics using e- mail, websites, usenet news groups or an Internet chat room. It has also made possible to do 'live' voice-chats on line, thus reducing the cost associated with telephone focus group. However online forum discussions are unlikely to represent average participants. Another non face-to-face focus group is conducted via video conferencing. This results in significant saving in arranging focus group and reduces travel time for the facilitator and the client. Further, more focus groups can be accomplished in a shorter time. However, there is certain barrier between the moderator and participants, although less so than telephone focus groups. It may be pointed here that video conferencing facilities are not widely available except in large business concerns, corporations and establishments.

Advantages :

1. Focus group provides the benefits of direct interaction and group processes. Here people naturally interact and are influenced by others and hence it has high face validity. As an exploratory research tool it has the ability to quickly and inexpensively grasp the core issues of the topic.
2. This is one of the few research tools available for obtaining data from children or from those who are illiterate.
3. Data can be collected quickly and at a lower cost than if individuals interviwed separately. Groups can be assembled at a very short notice.
4. It requires less time to prepare and is comparatively easy to conduct and is extremly flexible. It can be used with wide range of topics, individuals and settings.
5. Interpersonal communication and direct interaction with the respondents allow clarification, follow up questions and probing verbal responses. Thus, the focus groups best enable the exploration of surprise information and new ideas.
6. Since focus group uses own language, the respondent's deeper levels of meaning to a particular issue can be obtained. It provides a manager, researcher or client with a chance to observe reactions to their research questions in an open ended group setting and to get into a greater depth of understanding, helped by a facilitator.
7. Results are easy to understand and more accessible to common audience and policy makers than complex statistical analysis of survey data.

Disadvantages :

Like other methods of research focus group has also some inherent limitations, some of which can be overcome by careful planning and moderating.

1. Moderators have less control over the group and hence lack control over the information produced.
2. Data produced are relatively chaotic in nature and are produced through qualitative devices, lacking sampling accuracy.
3. If the group size is small, it is difficult to generalise to larger populations.
4. The effectiveness of this method depends largely on the efficiency and skill of the moderator who is expected to be knowledgeable about group dynamics.
5. Results may be biased due to the presence of dominant members.

6. Data generated are not confidential or anonymous because views are shared openly in a group.

Brain Storming

Brain storming is an effective means to generate lots of creative ideas in group to solve a problem. Therefore, the term 'brainstorming' has become a commonly used word in the English langauge as a generic term for creative thinking over a problem and has sought for the best solution possible. In 1941 Alex Osborn, an advertising executive, found that business meetings were inhibiting the creation of new ideas and hence, proposed some new rules to help stimulate them. He used the term "think up" to describe the process he developed and later came to be known as "brainstrorming". He explained the process of brainstorming in his book entitled *Applied Imagination* (1953).

The dictionary meanings of 'brainstorm' include the following (a) A sudden inspiration, (b) A bright idea, (c) A severe outburst of excitement, often as a result of transitory disturbance of cerebral activity and (d) A sudden mental aberration. According to Osborn, brainstorm means using the brain to storm a creative problem and to do so 'in commando fashion', each stormier audaciously attacking the same objective. Thus, he defines, "brainstorming is a technique by which a group attempts to find a solution for specific problem by amassing all the ideas spontaneously by its members".

Thus, brainstorming is a process of developing many creative solutions to a problem. It works by focusing on a problem and then coming up with the best possible solutions to it. The whole idea of brainstorming is that other people's remarks in a group would act to stimulate your own ideas in a sort of chain reaction of ideas. In the process, the experience and creativity of all members of the group are topped effectively towards solution of a problem. When the individual member's perception or idea reaches its limit, another member's creativity and experience can carry the idea further. Therefore, it is said that more indepth ideas are better developed in a group brainstorming than individual brainstorming. Individual brainstorming although is best for generating many ideas, yet it often becomes less effective at developing and giving a proper shape to those ideas.

Basic Rules of Brainstorming :

Brainstorming has *four* basic rules. They are as follows :

(i) *Generate as many solutions as possible.* More the ideas generated the better are the chances to arrive at something innovative.

(ii) *Build on each other's ideas.* Ideas do not have to be completely new, it is perfectly fine to 'pinch' or expand or 'hitchhike' or build on other people's ideas.

(iii) *Wild ideas are encouraged.* The more odd, weird, impossible or crazy ideas that are generated, the better are the chances of coming up with a truly original solution.

(iv) *No criticism is allowed.* There is no such idea as a dumb idea. There are no such thing right or wrong ideas in brainstorming. Evaluation and judgement are deferred until later.

Conducting Brainstorming Sessions

Step by Step : Group brainstorming needs the following steps to be followed for conducting the brainstorming session effectively.

Step I. The 'problem' must be clearly defined so that everyone understands the problem and is in agreement with the way it is worded. It must be borne in mind that the 'problem' posed is not necessarily negative.

Step II. There should be a time limit. However, larger groups may need more time to get every one's ideas out.

Step III. While everyone prescribe/suggest solutions to the problem, there must be a person assigned with the responsiblity to write down all the ideas as they occur.

Step IV. There must be absolutely no criticizing of ideas no matter how impossible or how silly an idea is, it must be recorded. If ideas are criticised or participants feel that they have to face criticism, there wouldn't be free flow of ideas. Any idea may seem to be silly initially, but later it may prove to be ideal one or may lead to better ideas that are good.

Step V. Once the time is over five best ideas should be selected. All the selected ideas must have the approval of the brainstorming session.

Step VI. Five criteria should be laid down for making a judgement of ideas best suited for solving the problem. Criteria preferably should start with the word 'should' for example, it should be cost effective, it should be completed before such date, etc.

Step VII. Once criteria are decided each idea is scored in a 0 to 5 points scale depending upon how will it meet the criteria. Then, addition is made to arrive at the aggregate score for each criterion.

Step VIII. The ideas with the highest score will best solve the problem.

However, a record of all ideas with their respective scores should be kept in record for future use in case the selected solution is found not be workable.

It is worth mentioning that thinking as a group using brainstorming can certainly produce ideas, but individual thinking is much better at generating ideas and fresh directions. Once the ideas have been formed at the individual level, a group may be better able to develop the idea.

What is brainstorming used for ?

Since its invention, brainstorming as a technique of creative thinking for better solution to a focussed problem has spread throughout the world. Nearly all the largest companies, charities, government organisations, non-governmental organisation (NGOs) and educational institutions, use it. In brief, brainstorming has been used to develop the following :

(i) Advertising campaigns, (ii) Marketing strategy and methods, (iii) Research and development procedures, (iv) Research techniques, (v) Patents, (vi) Physical products, (vii) Written documents and articles, (viii) Processes, (ix) Government policies, (x) Consumer research, (xi) Management methods, (xii) Investment decisions, (xiii) New industries, etc.

Advantages :

1. Using the basic rules of brainstorming people's natural inhibitions are reduced.

2. New ideas come up with surprisingly with little effort.
3. Through group brainstorming silly ideas could turn to be very useful and problem solving.
4. Draws on groups' knowledge and experience.
5. Spirit of cooperation is created.
6. One idea can spark off other ideas.
7. Used to develop new products, services, new techniques or even one's personal life.

Disadvantages :

1. It is often applied ineffectively because of poor training and lack of access to quality training materials.
2. If it is not managed well, criticism and negative evaluations may occur.
3. Further, it should be noted that this method does not, on its own, suffice as a data collection or analysis method. This method is commonly used in combination with other methods, for example, to start a focus group session.

Panels

When it is important to collect information on trends, whether with respect to consumer preferences and purchasing behaviour or changes in business climate and opportunities, researchers may decide to set up a panel of individuals which can be questioned or surveyed over an extended period of time.

There are essentially *three* different types of panels :

- Consumer Panels
- Nominal Group Technique
- Delphi Method.

The most common uses for panels are :

- Trend monitoring and future assessment.
- Test marketing and impact assessment.
- Priority setting for planning and development.

There are some clear advantages to using panels. These include the fact that recall problmes are usually minimized and that it is even possible to study the attitudes and motivation of non- respondents. However, it must also be recognized that maintaining panels is a constant effort. Since there is a tendency for certain people to drop out (those that are too busy, professionals, senior executives, etc.), this can lead to serious bias in the type of respondents that remain on the panel. Participants can also become too sensitized to the study objectives, and thus anticipate the responses they "should" be giving.

Consumer Panels :

When researchers are interested in detailed information about purchasing behaviour or insight into certain leisure activities, they will often resort to panels of consumers. A panel will allow the researcher to track behaviour using same sample over time. This type of longitndinal research provides more reliable results on changes that occur as a result of life cycle, social or professional status, attitudes, and opinions. By working with the same panel members, intentions can be checked against action, one of the more problematic challenges that researchers face when studying planned purchases or intentions to engage in certain behaviour (e.g. going on trips, visiting certain sites, participating in sports, etc.)

But looking at the trends is not the only use for panels. They can also provide invaluable insight into product acceptance prior to the launch of a new product or service or a change in packaging, for instance Paneles, whether formally established or tracked informally through common behaviour (e.g. membership in a club, purchase of a specific product, etc.) can also be used to study the reaction to potential or actual events, the use of promotional materials or the search for information.

Compared to the depth interview and the focus group, a panel is less likely to exaggerate the frequency of a behaviour or purchase decision or their brand loyalty. Although panels only require sampling once, maintaining the panel can be both time consuming and relatively costly as attribution and hence finding replacements can be quite high. In order to allow researchers to obtain more detailed follow-up information from panel members, they are usually paid for their services. At the same time, this can introduce a bias into the panel, since the financial incentive will be more or less important depending on the panelists' economic status.

Possibly one of the more interesting advantages of panels is that they can provide significant insight into non-response as well as non-participation or decisions not to purchase a given product.

The Nominal Group Technique

The Nominal Group Technique (NGT) is a structured group method for working towards consensus. Originally developed as an organizational planning technique by Delbecq, Van de Ven and Gustafson in 1971, the nominal group technique is a consensus planning tools that helps prioritize issues. Later, this method has been used and is being used in different fields. In this technique, participants are brought together for a discussion session led by a moderator.

The nominal group technique is preferably used when normal group dynamics of conformity might possibly distort decision making and problem solving in a group. The very purpose of NGT is to eliminate social and psychological dynamics of group behaviour which tend to inhibit individual creativity and participation in group decisions. By using this method the group avoids the normal problems of a few individuals doing all the talking, the rest listening and very few people taking the time to actually think about the issue at hand. The nominal group brings people together to generate ideas and to gather information from the participants about a specific concern more effectively and creatively than when people interact to discuss, brainstorm and exchange information, so as to identify problems and priorities, issues or actions. In this method group consensus is reached by providing each participants with an equal voice. Individual participants make their independent judgements through written responses to problems. Thus, NGT can be used when specific problems arise.

The Nominal Group Technique includes mainly *five* steps.

❒ Generation of ideas

❒ Round-Robin

❒ Discussion and clarification

❒ Voting on priorities

❒ Plan of action.

Generation of ideas **:** The topic is presented to session participants with a list of questions/problems, issues or actions that need to be ranked as clearly as possible. They have had an opportunity to ask questions or briefly discuss the scope of the topic. After five to ten minutes time are allowed to them to think over the issues, they are asked to write down ideas/responses based on questions posed. However, the solutions suggested must be defensible and practicable. It is required that the group members should work silently and independently.

Round Robin **:** After the time limit allowed to generate ideas and to write down is over, each participant reads out and elaborate on one of his ideas/responses with the best one first and the facilitator notes these responses on a *flipchart.*

Discussion and Clarification **:** Each idea listed on the chart is discussed in order and clarified for a limited period of time and in the process duplicate ideas are brought together and the individual ideas are numbered.

Voting on Priorities **:** Once the ideas are numbered, the participants are asked to vote/rank the ideas/responses according to their relative importance. These rankings are collected from all participants and aggregated. For example,

Response	Participant 1	Participant 2	Participant 3	Sum of ranks
A	ranked Ist	ranked 2nd	ranked 2nd	5 = ranked 1st
B	ranked 3rd	ranked Ist	ranked 3rd	7 = ranked 3rd
C	ranked 2nd	ranked 3rd	ranked Ist	6 = ranked 2nd
D	ranked 4th	ranked 4th	ranked 4th	12 = ranked 4th

Sometimes these results are given back to the participants in order to stimulate further discussions, and perhaps a readjustment in the over all rankings assigned to various responses. This is done only when group consensus regarding the prioritization of issues is important to the overall research or planning project.

Plan of Action :

The group discusses its plan of action based on the outcome of vote in order to reach at the final group agreement on how to deal with the original issue/question.

The maximum size of the nominal group should not be more than 10 people.

Advantages :

1. The NGT is best used for small group meetings.
2. A heterogeneous group can move toward a definite group conclusion/group consensus.
3. Since verbal interaction is not allowed, there is less of an opportunity for powerful individuals to have control/influence over other group members.
4. A large number of ideas are likely to emerge from the participants in a short period of time.
5. It stimulates creative thinking and effective dialogue among the participants and allows for classification of ideas.

Disadvantages :

1. Use of NGT is not suitable for meetings to provide routine, meetings and called to co-ordinate or negotiate.

2. This technique may produce judgements inferior to the judgement of the most knowledgeable group member.
3. The most serious problem with the technique is that participants feel awkward about restriction in their interaction. As a result most common that it is the process not to reach the consensus.

The Delphi Method

The Delphi Method was originally developed by the RAND Corporation in 1969 for technological forecasting. It is a group decision process about the likelihood that certain events will occur. In recent times it is also used for environmental, marketing and sales forecasting.

The Delphi Method makes use of a *Panel of experts*, selected based on the areas of expertise required. The notion is that well informed individuals, calling on their insights and experience, are better equipped to predict the future than theoretical approaches or extrapolation of trends. Their responses to a series of questionnaires are anonymous, and they are provided with a summary of opinions before answering the next questionnaire. It is believed that the group will converge toward the best response through this consensus process. The mid-point of responses is statistically categorized by the median score. In each succeeding round of questionnaires the range of responses by the panelists will presumably decrease and the median will move toward what is deemed to be the 'correct' answer.

The Delphi method is designed to encourage to debate, independent of personalities. Anonymity is required in the sense that no one knows who else is participating. As the responses are anonymous, the pit-falls of ego, domineering personalities and the 'bandwagon' or 'halo effect' in responses are all avoided. Further, to eliminate the force of oratory and pedagogy, the reasons giyne for extreme opinions were synthesized by the researchers to give them all equal 'weight' and then feed back to the group as a whole for further analysis. Thus, aspects like anonymity and feedback represent the two irreducible elements of the Delphi method. The Delphi technique requires a co-ordinator to organise requests for information, information received, and to be responsible for communication channel to link the co- ordinator with each of the participants. In Delphi method, keeping panelists for the numerous rounds of questionnaires is at times difficult. Further and perhaps more troubling the future developments are not always predicted correctly by iterative consensus nor by experts, but at times by 'off the wall' thinking or by 'non-experts'.

Advantages :

One of the greatest virtues lies in its simplicity ; advanced mathematical skills are not required for design, implimentation and analysis of a Delphi study. The Delphi method has a number of advantages.

These are :

1. It is said that 'two heads are better than one'. Generally, a group response is not only acceptable but also found to the truth than of any one individual.

The Delphi technique offers the advantages of group response without the disadvantages sometimes experienced with group problem solving or decision making.

2. In Delphi study a selected respondent panel comprising a mix of experts can provide a broad analytical perspective on any particular issue.
3. Anonymity for the experts is one of the basic characteristics of Delphi study and it is maintained through out the entire process. As a result, a number of problems in communication which arise from face to face interactions among the experts are avoided without any difficulty. Further, it does not allow any group member to dominate the group.
4. Another advantage of the technique in the fact that the responses can be elicited from a geographically dispersed panel of experts without bringing the panel of experts together.
5. Delphi technique as a method of data collection is considered to be inexpensive as compared to other available methods dealing with the group problem solving or decision- making.
6. In the Delphi technique the expert participants are more likely to generate reasoned, independent, and well considered opinions in the absence of exposure to the 'persuasively stated opinions of others'. Since panel members do not ever participate in a face to face discussion there is no peer pressure, irrelevant or biased communication and the danger of one or more individuals', opinions being swayed by a more dominant or more experienced individual.
7. Another advantage of the Delphi technique lies in its efficiency and flexibility, expecially in age of modern communication where technologies such as e-mail and the Internet have been proved to be less expensive and more effective. Thus, the time and money invested in this method is minimal.
8. It reduces time pressure and allows for more reflection and contemplation of response. With the use of questionnaire, it is possible to capture a wide range of interrelated variables and multi-dimensional facts.
9. The Delphi method has been found to be an effective way to conduct research when the responses being sought are value judgements rather than factual information. Although it is more difficult to assess the correctness of value judgements, it is generally agreed upon that value judgements are not all equal but can infact be more 'right' or more 'wrong'.

   Delphi is particularly useful for studies that call for subjective judgement rather than precise statistical analysis.
10. Delphi method provides an opportunity to reach consensus among groups hostile to each other.

Disadvantages :

1. The reliabilityof Delphi results depend on unbiased selection of right experts. There is no clearly defined method of assessing which expects and indeed how many should be included in a study. Some experts selected, may not be willing to participate in the study and substituted new experts may not possess desirable level of expertise in the chosen field of study.
2. The co-ordinator makes the review of responses and tries to eliminate extreme positions and force a middle-of-the road consensus and hence, the expected result may be lowest common denominator.

3. Another point worth mentioning is that the facilitator may be tempted to make very influential decision that may not always be clear-cut and more over the facilitator decides when an acceptable degree of consensus has been reached and what questions should be put to the experts. There is a possibility that the facilitator may misuse his role and responsibility.
   Also, it is not always easy to make a firm decision when studying a large and complex system.
4. Delphi should not be used when any of the following three critical conditions are not present : adequate time, participant skill in written communication and high participant motivation. It is, thus, naturally a pre condition that the participants must be knowledgeable and able to clearly communicate their ideas. A high degree of motivation is needed to offset the tendency for participant drop out as the study progresses. Because there is no direct contact between participants, those who are not highly motivated and interested in the subject at hand may feel isolated or detached from the process.
5. In Delphi study judgements are those of a selected group of people and to that extent it may not be representative.
6. The Delphi technique is relatively more time consuming than the other group process methods such as working groups etc. and therefore it is expensive.
7. Participant drop out can be a problem in Delphi studies. The failure to allow participants to adequately contribute their own perspectives to the problem or issue at hand or failure to properly recognize or reward participants can have negative impact on results.
8. Finally, Delphi technique like other group techniques is not free from bias. The biases in Delphi studies can occur from poorly worded or leading questions or selective interpretation of the results. However, this problem can be overcome by using a facilitation team or an unbiased facilitator who has no stake in the results of the study.

In spite of all the disadvantages, Delphi technique in social science and business studies has the potential for being used and can be modeled in number of ways.

It can be used as output, input, or designated as a evaluation tool. Delphi technique is flexible and can be developed into a tool for the examination of the effectiveness of policy processes, as well as a vehicle for the formulation, development and assessment.

PROJECTIVE TECHNIQUES

Both focus group and depth interviews are direct approaches in which the true purpose of the enquiry is disclosed to the respondents or becomes obvious to them. Projective techniques are different from the above techniques in that they attempt to disguise the purpose of the enquiry to the respondents. Further, deeply held attitude and motivations are often not verbalized by respondents when questioned directly. Indeed respondents may not even be aware that they hold these particular attitudes, or may feel that their motivation reflect badly on them. A projective technique is an unstructured, indirect form of questioning that encourages respondents to project their underlying motivation, beliefs, attitudes or feelings regarding the issues under consideration. Projective techniques allow respondents to project their subjective or true opinions and beliefs on to other people or even objects. The respondents' real feelings are then inferred from what he says about others. That is, the respondents are asked to interpret the behaviour of others rather than describe their own behaviour. While interpreting the behaviour of others, respondents indirectly project their own motivations, attitudes, beliefs or feelings into the situation. Thus, the respondents attitude are uncovered by analysing their responses regarding others, that are deliberately unstructured, vague and ambiguous.

Projective techniques are normally used during individual or small group interviews. They incorporate a number of different research methods. Among the most commonly used are

- ❒ Association Techniques
- ❒ Completion Techniques
- ❒ Construction Techniques
- ❒ Expressive Techniques

Association Techniques

In *association techniques*, an individual is presented with a stimulus and asked to respond with the first thing that comes to mind. Word association is the best known among the association techniques. In word association, respondents are presented with a list words, one at a time, and asked to respond to each with the first word that comes to mind.The words of interest called *test words* are interspersed with other words to disguise the purpose of the study. For instance, super bazar study, the test words may be 'location', 'parking', 'shopping', 'quality', 'price' etc.

The list is read quickly to avoid allowing time for defense mechanisms to come into play. Responses are analysed by calculating (i) the frequency of each word given as response (ii) amount of time elapsed before a response is given (iii) the respondents who do not respond within a stipulated period of time.

An individual's pattern of responses and the details of the response are used to determine the person's underlying attitudes or feelings or emotions on the topic of interest.

Completion Techniques

In *completion techniques*, the respondent is asked to complete an incomplete stimulus situation. Common completion techniques used in marketing research are :

- ❒ sentence completion
- ❒ story completion

Sentence completion is similar to word association technique. Respondents are asked to complete incomplete sentences with first word or phrase that comes to mind, thus indicating their feelings, attitudes or emotions.

As compared to word association technique the respondents can be provided with a more directed stimulus. Sentence completion may provide more information about the respondent's (subject's) feeling than word completion. However, sentence completion technique is not as disguised as the word association technique to guess the purpose of the study. A variation of sentence completion is paragraph completion in which the respondent is asked to complete the paragraph beginning with the stimulus phrase. Another variation may be story completion where the respondent is directed towards a particular topic and given a part of the story, but not any hint about the ending. He is then required to give the conclusion in his own words. The respondents' completion of the story may reveal their underlying feelings and emotions.

Construction Techniques

Construction techniques are closely related to completion techniques, and require the respondent to construct a response in the form of story, dialogue or description.

Two main construction techniques are (i) *picture response* (ii) *cartoons.*

The *picture response technique* is a Thematic Apperception Test (TAT) which consists of a series of pictures of ordinary as well as unusual events.

The respondents are asked to react to these pictures and tell stories of these pictures. Their individual personalities will be reflected in the interpretation of these pictures. For instance, an individual may be characterized as impulsive, creative, imaginative and so on. The TAT is used because themes are elicited through the subject's perceptual interpretation (apperception) of pictures.

In *Cartoon Tests* cartoon characters are shown in a specific situation related to the problem under study. The respondents are asked to indicate what one character would comment on another character. The responses would indicate respondents' feelings, beliefs and attitudes toward the situation.

Expressive Techniques

Respondents are presented with a verbal or visual situation and are asked to comment on feelings and attitudes of others toward the situation and not their own attitudes or feelings. Two expressive techniques that need to be mentioned in the present discussion are

- Role playing
- Third person technique

In *role playing technique* the respondents are asked to play the role depicting the behaviour of some one else and thereby projecting his own feelings into the role. This can be uncovered by analyzing the responses.

In *third person technique* the respondents are presented with a verbal or visual situation and are asked then to relate the beliefs and attitudes of a third person, who may be his friend, neighbour, collague or a typical person. The researcher believes that while projecting the feelings and attitudes of a third person, he would indirectely convey his own beliefs and attitudes.

Advantages and Disadvantages of Projective Techniques

Projective techniques score advantage over the unstructured direct techniques like focus groups and depth interview in that they may elicit responses from the respondents without making them aware of the purpose of the study, because there may be some respondents who would be unwilling or unable to give their opinions if they know the purpose.

As regards disadvantages projective techniques require the services of highly trained interviewers as well as the expertise of skilled clinical psychologists to help devise the tests and analyze and interpret them correctly. Further, some projective techniques such as role playing require the respondnets to engage in unusual behaviour, for which they may not be forthcoming to participate.

5.3.2 Quantitative Research Techniques

Quantitative research is most commonly encountered as part of a formal or conclusive research, but is also **sometimes used when conducting exploratory research.**

Quantitative research techniques are part of primary research. These differ from qualitative research in the following ways.

- The data are usually gathered using more structured research instruments.
- The results provide less detail on behaviour, attidue and motivation.
- The results are based on larger sample sizes that are representative of the population.
- The research can usually be replicated or repeated and give it high reliability ; and
- The analysis of the results is more objective.

The most common ***quantitative research techniques*** include

- *Observation*
- *Survey (Participant communications)*
- *Experimentation*

A. Observation

Observation is a primary method of collecting information by human, mechnical, electrical or electronic means. The researcher may or may not have direct contact or communication with the people whose behaviour is being recorded. **Observation techniques can be part of both qualitative and quantitative research techniques.**

Observation becomes a part of scientific enquiry when it is conducted specifically to answer a research question. It is systematically planned and executed, uses proper controls and provides a reliable and valid account of what happened. It is versatile in nature and is an indispensable primary source method. Collection of data through observation involves

- Visual observation
- Listening
- Reading
- Smelling
- Touching

Thus, observation includes the full range of monitoring behavioural and non-behavioural activities and conditions and can be classified as

Behavioural observation

- Non-verbal analysis
- Linguistic analysis

- Extralinguistic analysis
- Spatial analysis

Non-behavioural observation

- Record analysis
- Physical condition analysis
- Physical process analysis

Record analysis involves observation of historical/current and public/private records. A researcher might like to inspect current financial records and economic data of the company and look into content analysis of competitive advertising and the analysis of personnel records.

Physical condition analysis involves

- Store audits of merchandise availability
- Studies of inventory conditions
- Analysis of financial statements.

Process analysis includes

- Time/motion studies of manufacturing process
- Analysis of traffic flows in a distributing system
- Financial flows in the banking system

Non-verbal behaviour includes body movement, motor expressions and even exchanged glances.

Linguistic behaviour of the observed individuals is a frequently used form of behaviour observation. For example, some persons utter certain murmuring words in a discussion platform which indicate their behaviour pattern in accepting or rejecting certain events or situations. Further, linguistic behaviour is also marked in the interaction processes that occur between two people or in small groups.

Sometimes extralinguistic behaviour also is accounted as an important means of communication. There are certain dimensions of extralinguistic behaviour such as

- Vocal (pitch, loudness, etc.)
- Temporal (rate of speaking, durance of utterence and rhythm)
- Interaction (tendencies to interrupt, dominate or inhibit)
- Verbal stylistic (vocabulary, pronounciation style and peculiarities, dialect, characteristics of expressions)

Spatial behaviour relates to a person's relationship to others in a spatial set up, that it, how people organize territory around them and maintain discrete distances between themselves and others. How sales persons approach the customers in the market place and how people conduct themselves in a crowded market place and its effect on them are examples of spatial behavioural relationship.

The Observer-Participant Relationship

Observation as a method of collection of data depends to some extent on the observer - participant relationship, although it is less pronounced compared to interviewing method of data collection. The relationship may be viewed from three perspectives :

- direct observation or indirect observation
- presence of observer known or unknown to the participant
- role played by the observer.

Direct observation occurs when the observer is physically present at the spot and monitors what takes place. The observer is in a position to react to and report aspects of events and situations and behaviours as they occur. He has also the scope to shift the places, change the focus of the observations or concentrate on some unusual and unexpected events, if he comes across. It has a marked disadvantage that the obsever may be overloaded with events as they occur more quickly and sometimes may be required to re construct the events which he failed to record. Alos, the fatigue, boredom and distracting events can reduce the accuracy and completeness of observation, thus affecting the reliablity of the observations, so observed.

Indirect observation occurs when the observer does not record the events, but the recording is done by mechanical, photographic, or electronic means. It is less flexible compared to direct observation, besides being less biased and less erratic inaccuracy. Another factor influencing the observer - participant relationship concerns the participants, aware of the observer's presence at the situation. There is every likelihood that the activity patterns of the participants may be upset at the presence of the observer, but soon they may be unconcerned after they are engaged in absorbing activities. However, the potential bias arising out of awareness of the participants as to the presence of the observer is a matter of concern which should never be lost sight of. To get rid of such a situation the observers may use concealment to shield themselves from the object of their observation and as such mirrors, hidden cameras or microphones may be used for the purpose. However, such an approach may not be appreciated because of ethical reasons.

A modified approach in the study of selling methods the observer may accompany the sales person and observe while the sales person makes calls to customers. It is necessary that real motive of the observer may be hidden from both the sales person and the customer.

Now the question arises whether the observer should participate in the situation while observing. Participant observation occurs when the observer enters into the situation and acts both as an observer and a participant. Thus, participant observation puts dual responsibility on the part of the observer. Recording can interfere with participation, and participation can intefere with observation. The obsever's role may influence the way the participants act and therefore might bias the results. Therefore, participant observation is less popular in business research.

How to conduct an observational study ?

Observation as a method of data collection is used in almost all research studies, at least in exploratory stage. Sometimes this is resorted to as an intermediary when the researcher moves from research questions to investigative questions.

If the researcher intends to study something other than exploratory, he may go for systematic observation employing standardized procedures, skilled observers, schedules for recording the results of observation and utilise other devices with some scientific procedures, commonly adopted in collection of primary data.

Classification of observation methods :

There are *six* ways of classifying observational methods :

- *Participant and non-participant observation* depending on whether the researcher chooses to be part of the situation, he is studying or observing.
- *Obtrusive and unobtrusive observation* depending on whether the subjects being studied can detect the observation (e.g. hidden microphones or cameras observing behaviour and doing garbage audits to determine consumption are examples of unobtrusive observation).
- *Direct and indirect observation*, depending on whether the behaviour is being observed as it occurs or after the fact, as in case of TV viewing.
- *Observation in natural or contrived settings*, whereby the behaviour is observed (usually unobtrusively), when and where it is occurring, while in the contrived setting the situation is created to speed up the behaviour.
- *Disguised and non-disguised observation*, depending on whether the subjects being observed are aware that they are being studied or not.
- *Structured and unstructured observation*, which refers to whether guideliness or a check list being used for the aspects of the behaviour that are to be recorded.

Structured observation presupposes a well formulated problem and the knowledge of the clear and specific definition of the units to be observed and the type of data to be collected. This method is primarily adopted when the researcher has in mind to describe a problem or to test a causal hypothesis. In practical situation it is not always possible to plan out the nature and unit of observation before hand, which is most often the case with exploratory studies, where the researcher is unable to structure his observations because there is likelihood of changes in what he observes. The unstructured observation is flexible enough to take account for changes in focus from time to time.

Content specification of observations

'What we intend to observe e.g. specific conditions, events or activities, determines the observational reporting system and corresponds to measuresment questions. Besides observing on major variables, we may also observe other variables that may affect them. Keeping these in view we then select those items that we plan to observe.

Observation may be at either a factual or an inferential level depending on whether we would like to have descriptive data or causal data.

Who should be an observer ?

The general guidelines for the selection of an observer are :

- ❒ *Concentration* : The observer should have ability to function in a setting full of distractions.
- ❒ *Detail-oriented* : The observer should have ability to remember details of an experience/event.
- ❒ *Unobtrusive* : The observer should have ability to blend himself with the setting and not stand as distractive.
- ❒ *Experienced* : An experienced observer would be able to extract more information from an observational study.

Data Collection :

The researcher needs the details of data collection plan to serve his goal. Before embarking on data collection he must take into account the answers to the following questions.

❒ (Who) Who is a participant ? What qualifies a participant to be observyered ? Does he need an introduction or criteria ? Who is entrusted with responsibilities for the various aspects of the study ? Who is to take care of ethical issues involved in the study.

❒ (What) What are to be observed ? The characteristics of observation may be selected behaviour of the participants or time point sample in quality control inspection or an act established by the needs of the study such as
—expressed thought,
—physical movement
—facial expression
—motor skill, etc.

❒ (When) When should we go for observation ? For instance, if we are interested in studying out of stock position in a supermarket, the exact timings of observation may be an important factor because this is related to arrival time of the inventory to the store and buying peak periods.

❒ (How) How are the data going to be observed ? Whether more than one observer are needed ? Is it observed directly ? How will the observers tackle different situations that may occur sometimes quite unexpectedly ? What steps the observers take, if they are challenged in the midst of taking observations ?

❒ (Where) Where will the observer take the observation ? Is it within a spatial confine ? Observers often face unlimited variations in conditions. A trained observer may be able to know or try to explore the best place where he can take the observation conveniently.

Advantages of the Observational Methods :

1. Observation is the only method available to gather certain types of information such as study of records, mechanical processes, information from inarticulate participants.
2. It enables to collect the original data at the time they occur and does not depend on reports by others.
3. It is possible to collect information that most participants would ignore because of different reasons. Some facts which cannot be reported correctly can be obtained by keen observation.
4. It can capture the whole event as it occurs in its natural environment. Observation is less restrictive than most primary collection methods.
5. Paricipants seem to accept an observational intrusion better than they respond to direct questioning.
6. Casual observation plays an important role in explantory research. Managers continually monitor such variables as competitive prices and advertising activity, the length of tlines of customers waiting for service, trade journals on executives' disk's, etc. to identify research problems and opportunities. Systematic observation can supplement other methods of observation

7. Observation may be the least expensive and most accurate method of collecting behavioural data, e.g. traffic patterns in city roads and lanes, customers arrival in super markets, etc.
8. Observational technique might sometimes be taken as only research alternative. For instance, in case of study of physiological phenomena or study of young children who cannot articulate their preferences or motives, say, for toys, observations help research in these areas.

Limitations of the Observational Methods :

1. The observational method presupposes that the observer normally must be at the scene of the event at the time of its occurrence.
2. Managers sometimes on the basis of small sample observations jump into conclusions in a decision making process. Further, the results are not necessarily representative of what would be found in the population and there may be certain ambiguity in the results.
3. The observation technique does not provide us with any insight into what the person may be thinking or what might motivate a given behaviour/comment.
4. When people are being observed, whether they are aware of it or not, the ethical issues arising there from must be considered by the researchers. Particularly with advances in technology, cameras, microphones have made it possible to gather a significant amount of information about verbal and non-verbal behaviour of customers as well as employees that might easily be considered to be an invasion of privacy or abusive, particularly if the subject is unaware of being observed, yet the information is used to make decisions that impact him.
5. The observations supposed to be most reliable are restricted only to information that can be learned by overt action or surface indicators.
6. The research environment is more likely suited to subjective assessment and recording of data than experimental controls and principles of taking observations.
7. Observations are of limited value to know about the past and also may not have predictive value.
8. Observations cannot gather information on attitudes, intentions, opinions or preferences.
9. They are often more costly and time consuming and may yield biased results, if there are sampling problems or if significant observer subjectivety is involved.

B. Survey Methods (Participant Communication)

To survey implies casting of eyes or mind over something i.e. observation or inquiry into something's condition i.e. communication. The communication approach involves surveying people through any medium of communication directly or indirectly and recording responses for analysis. As a primary data collection technique, the survey with communication approach is popular for its versatility. It is *more efficient and economical than observational technique.* Participant communication survey that uses telephone, mail or the Internet as the medium of communication can expand its geographical coverage at a fraction of the cost and time required by observation. This is the most appropriate method where participants are uniquely qualified to provide desired information. It is convenient to collect information through questions about subjects that are exclusively internal and related to the participants such as attitudes, opinions, expectations, and intentions. This is possible if right questions are asked of participants. It allows for standardilization and uniformity both in questions asked and in methods of approaching subjects.

One of the major weakenesses of communication approach is that quality information obtained from the participants depend heavily on the willingness of the participants to co-operate. Further, the participants might not have adequate knowledge about the question, might fail to understand the question fully or may not have an opinion on the topic of concern. Sometimes a participant may wish to impress or please the researcher by providing the kind of response the researcher is looking for. This adds to response error or bias.

The interviewer can (inadvertently) influence the response elicited through comments made or by stressing certain words in the question itself. In interview surveys, the interviewer can also introduce bias through facial expression, body language or even clothing. This is termed as *interviewer bias.*

Another consideration which is worth noting in consideration of response rate. Depending on the method chosen, the length of the questionnaire, the type and motivation of the respondent, the type of questions - their structure, content and order, the time of day or place and whether respondents were informed to expect the survey or offered an incentive can all influence the response rate obtained. Proper questionnaire design and question wording can help increase the response rate.

* Telephone Interviewing :

The telephone inteview is a unique mode of communication to collect information from participants. The telephone can be helpful in arranging personal interviews from a long distance at a reasonable cost. When calls are made from a single location, a fewer yet more skilled interviewers may be necessary. It results in cuts in travel costs and administrative savings from trainings and supervision. It makes it easier to collect information from widely scattered participants.

With the widespread use of computers, telephonic interviewing can be combined and thus effectively facilitating the immediate entry of the responses into data files by means of terminals, personal computers, or voice data entry.

The researcher may also arrange computer - administered telephone survey where there is no interviewer, but the computer calls the phone number, conducts the interview, places the data into a file for later tabulation and terminates the contact. This mode of interview offers the advantage of privacy.

More interviews can be conducted in a given time period because no time is lost in travelling and locating respondents. Respondents can be contacted even during leisure hours/evening hours specially for working women. Repeated call backs at different times of the day can be made at very low cost.

As compared to interviews or mail surveys, the telephone interview brings a faster completion of a study and even takes a day or two days for the entire field work. Further, interviewer's bias arising out of physical appearence, body language and actions of the interviewer is much reduced through telephone surveys. The behavioural norms work towards telephone interviews in the sense that if some one is present, a ringing phone is usually answered and thus reduces error due to non-contact and cost involved there in. The telephone is a particularly effective method for gaining access to hard to reach people such as busy executives. There are also certain advantages in undertaking telephone interviewing. These are inaccessibility of households lacking telephone facilities, inaccurate telephone numbers, limitation of interview length, limitations on the use of complex questions in the absence of face to face with the interviewer, ease of interview termination, less participant involvement, distracting physical environment of the respondent (if any), etc.

* *Self Administered Survey*

Any survey technique that requires the respondent to complete the questionnaire him/herself is referred to as a *self-administered survey*. In this method no interviewer is involved.

The most common ways of distributing these surveys are through the use of mail, fax, news-papers/magazines and increasingly the internet or through the place of purchase of a good or service (hotel, restaurant, store etc.). They can also be distributed in person, for instance as part of an intercept survey (e.g. the respondent participates without interviewer assistance usually in a predetermined environment such as a shopping complex, etc.) Depending on the method of survey administration, there are a number of sampling frame considerations, such as who can or cannot be reached by fax or internet, or whether there is a sample bias.

Self administered questionnaire has become a part of modern living and has become a medium of self assessement. Self- administered mail surveys work best when a specific group of individuals is contacted for information and a high response rate can be expected in such a case.

Mail surveys are not only delivered by Indian postal service, but also by fax and courier service. Other delivery modalities include computer - delivered (e-mail) and intercept studies. Computer-delivered self administered questionnaires use organisational intranets, the internet or online services to reach their participants. Intercept studies may use a traditional paper questionnaire/pamphlets or a computer - delivered survey.

The self-administered mail surveys have the following advantages :

- ❒ Potential anonymity of the respondent, which can lead to more truthful or valid responses.
- ❒ Questionnaire can be filled out at convenience of the respondents.
- ❒ In the absence of interviewer, the error due to interviewer is eliminated.
- ❒ Self-administered surveys of all types typically cost less than personal interviews because cost of reaching a geographically dispersed sample is drastically reduced, although mail surveys are not necessarily cheap.
- ❒ The researcher can contact participants who might otherwise be inaccessible.

In business studies the major corporate executives may not be accessible to reach in person or by telephone, as the secreteries, office managers and assistants may limit the access. But the researchers can often access these special participants by mail or computer either directly or ranked through assistants/operators.

The limitations of the self-administered mail surveys are as follows :

- There is no control over who actually fills out the questionnaire
- The respondent may very well read part or all of the questionnaire before filling it out, thus potentially biasing his/her responses.
- Researchers normally do not expect large amount of information and can not probe deep into topics.
- Participants may refuse to co-operate with long and/or complex mail, computer delivered ones or intercept questionnaire unless they perceive that some personal benefits may accrue to them.
- Some part of the questionnaire may be left answered because of disinterest or lack of understanding about the questions.
- One of the most important disadvantage of self-administered surveys is their low response rate.

Several practical suggestions may be put forward to improve response rate, thereby reducing non-response error. These are :

1. A well written covering letter of appeal, personalized to the extent possible, that stresses why the study is important and why the particular respondent should fill in the questionnaire.
2. If the respondents are interested in the topic and/or the sponsoring organization, they are more likely to participate in the survey. These aspects should be mentioned in the covering letter.
3. Ensuring confidentiality and/or anonymity and providing the name and contact number of the lead researcher and/or research sponsor, should the respondent wish to verify the legitimacy of the survey or specific questions.
4. Providing due date that is reasonable but not too far off or phoning at least one reminder.
5. Follow up with non-respondents.
6. Providing a postage paid envelope or reply card.
7. Providing an incentive, particularly monetary, even if only a token.
8. A well designed, visually appealing questionnaire.
9. A shorted questionnaire where the wording of questions has been carefully considered.
10. An envelope that is eye-catching and personalized. Advance notification either by phone or mail.

In recent days several high technology systems have been developed to facilitate data collection. Some of these are :

- Computer - assisted personal interviewing (CAPI)
- Computer - assisted telephone interviewing (CATI)
- Audiocomputer - assisted self interviewing (ACASI)
- Telephone audio computer assisted self interviewing (T-ACASI)
- Computer-assisted recorded interviewing (CARI).

* Interview Methods (Personal Interviewing)

Personal interviews (or face to face interviews) are a direct communication primary research collection technique. A personal interview is a two way conversation initiated by an interviewer to obtain information from a participant.

Interview may be either formal or an informal one or some mixture of both formal and informal. In formal interviewing a set of questions are asked and the answers are recorded in a structured and standardised form. In less formal variants, the interviewers are at liberty to vary the sequence of questions, explain their meaning, add additional questions and even change the wordings to secure valid answers.

Nature of Interview :

An interview is said to be a conversation between the interviewer and the respondent for eliciting certain required information on the basis of certain objectives of the survey. Interview is generally conducted with the help of a structured questionnaire constructed for the purpose.

The interview is not a straight forward one and the attainment of a successful interview is a complex one.

Three broad concepts may be taken as necessary conditions for a successful interview.

- ❐ Accessibility
- ❐ Cognition
- ❐ Motivation

The accessibility of the required information to the respondent is a major requisite for the respondent to answer the question. This may be due to forgetfulness of the respondent or inability to grasp the question in the way it is put or framed.

The cognition or understanding by the respondent of what is required of him. When he is asked to play the role of an informant, he must, establish means of deciding what is relevant information and also what is terms of reference. The role of the interviewer is to teach the respondent about the realization of his role what is expected of him after explaining him the objective of the survey.

The third requirement of a successful interview is motivation on the part of the respondent to provide accurate answer to the questions. This depends on his initial decision to co-opreate and then continue it with the progress of the interview.

The role of all interviewers is to build up a rapport with the respondent so that the effect of factors tending to decrease level of motivation is reduced.

Factors reducing the level of motivation are :

- ❐ embarassment at ignorance
- ❐ dislike of the interviewer content
- ❐ fear of consequences
- ❐ suspicions about the interviewer

Factors which increase the level of motivation are :

- ❐ curiosity
- ❐ lonelinness
- ❐ politeness
- ❐ feeling of duty
- ❐ interest in the enquiry

- helping attitude
- liking the interviewer.

An interview is an interaction process involving two individuals - *the interviewer and the respondent* and as such the success of the interview depends on the healthy interaction between them in an atmosphere of cordiality and responsibility. The increase in accuracy of the interview data can be effected by careful interviewer training. The selection of interviewers is an important part of conducting personal interviews. The interviewers must be trained in the art of interviewing to avoid to give vent to his views while interviewing and to develop capacity in probing and to put him in such a way that is least likely to influence respondents answers and to improve the quality of recording answers.

The Interviewer's task :

The main task of all interviewers is to locate the respondents, obtain interviews with them and record answers in structured formats.

Locating the respondents depends on the interest of the interviewers to go around to meet the people and more important is that the interviwer should be enthusiastic about interviewing.

If sampling method is adopted, the interviewer should be careful enough to locate the respondents in the lists who come under sampling and should have proper addresses and other information. In quota sampling the interviwer should judiciously choose the respondents required for the investigation.

When the interviewer is set to obtain an interview, his introduction approach increases the respondent's motivation to co-operate and so also increases the response rate. The form of the interview opening is crucial to win over those who are less willing to co-operate. The interviewer's interest in the survey, his conviction of its value can go long way to affect the response rate.

Asking question is an art which either can be acquired through training or personal initiative. It is necessary that steps should be taken to obtain unformity in the asking of questions and recording answers. The interviewers should be trained to cover all questions in the order with no more elucidation and probing than what is explicitly allowed and further, should resist to make unauthorised variations in the wording. If complete uniformity could be achieved and interviewer acted like machines,. answers could be regarded as independent of the way the questions are asked. However, the interviewers are not machines, their personality, voice, looks, pronunciations, etc. vary and no amount of instructions can bring about uniformity. Further, the importance of interviewing uniformity itself varies with the type of questions. In this respect opinion questions are more sensitive than factual questions.

Kahn and Cannell have distinguished five principal symptoms of inadequate response. These are :

- partial response
- non-response
- irrelevant response
- inaccurate response
- verbalized response (when the respondent fails to understand the question)

The interviewer is expected to take these symptoms into account and devise ways to obtain satisfactory response from the respondents.

The decision as to devise and develop instruments for participant communication and to plan for collection of data should take into account the management-research question hierachy. The process of starting from general management dilemma to specific measurement questions passes through four question levels :

- ❒ Management questions
- ❒ Research question
- ❒ Investigative question
- ❒ Measurement question

Investigative questions point out the researcher's informative needs and if necessary exploratory investigations may help the researcher to facilitate the understanding of the researcher about the problem.

The design of an instrument for collection of data through participant communication has the following strategic concerns

- ❒ What type of data is needed to answer the management questions ?
- ❒ What will be the communication approach ?
- ❒ Whether there will be structured or unstructured questions ?
- ❒ Whether the questioning will be disguised or undisguised ?

Data types (Nominal, ordinal, interval, ratio) determine the type of analytical procedure to be adopted for the analysis of data. Communication approach relates to whether the participants are to be communicated through telephone, mail, computer, personal interview or combination of these. Besides communication method, it is also desirable to fix the place where to interact with the participants - home, office or the neutral place, etc. The dispersion of participants, the availability of trained interviewers and budget limitations might dictate mail surveys where the participants received the instrument either at home or place of work.

* Questionnaire–Instrument for participant communication

Questionnaire or interview schedule (an alternative term for questionnaire used in an interview) is

- ❒ a systematic list of questions
- ❒ a set of stimuli to which the respondents are exposed in order to observe their verbal behaviour under these stimuli
- ❒ refers to a device for securing answers to questions by using a form which the respondent fills in himself or the interviewer fills in on behalf of the respondents.

The questionnaire is an essential instrument for participant communication and its design is of paramount importance for the sucess of investigation.

Although broadly the questionnaire and recording schedules are somewhat similar in structure, in some respects they are different. The recording schedule is a fairly formal decument, because the efficiency of the interviewer comes to account in handling the document. But the mail questionnaire is to be constructed with caution, which can be operated smoothly by the respondents. In both the cases the document should be accompanied with all necessary instructions and definitions and should be in codified form to aid the processing of data.

In designing either questionnaire or recording schedule, care should be taken for the convenience of data analysts, interviewers and respondents. Lay out and printing should be such that editing and coding can proceed smoothly when documents are put for processing and analysis.

Objectives of a Questionnaire :

Any questionnaire may have three specific objectives. First, it must translate the information needed into a set of specific questions that the respondents can and will answer. whether this objective can be achieved and the desired information would be obtained are difficult in practice and pose a challenge to the researcher.

Secondly, a questionnaire must uplift, motivate, and encourage the respondent to become involved in the interview, to cooperate and to complete the interview. While designing a questionnaire, the researcher, in his own interest, should try to minimize respondent fatigue, boredom, incompleteness, refusal and other forms of non-response. A well designed questionnaire has a definite role in motivating the respondents and increase the response rate.

Third, a questionnaire should have inherent strength in minimising response error. Care should be exercised so that the respondents do not tend to provide inaccurate answers.

Design process for a questionnaire

A questionnaire design has no theory in its background. It has some logical and practical steps.

1. Specify the information needed.
2. Specify the type of interviewing
3. Determine the content of individual questions.
4. Design the questions to overcome the respondent's inability and unwillingness to answer.
5. Decide on the question structure.
6. Determine the question wording
7. Arrange the question in proper order.
8. Identify the form and lay out.
9. Reproduce the questionnaire.
10. Pretest the questionnaire.

The first step in the design process for a questionnaire is to specify information need, as specified in the research design.

The type of interviewing method influences questionnaire design. The design of a questionnaire varies with the method 'how the questionnaire is administered ?' In personal interviews, respondents see the questionnaire and interact face to face with the interviewer, which is easy to administer lengthy, complex and varied questions. In the telephone the respondents interact with the interviewer but they do not see the questionnaire and the questions transmitted through telephone must be short and simple ones. Mail questionnaires are self administered, so the questions must be simple and detailed instructions must be provided. In computer assisted personal interviewing, (CAPI), complex skip patterns and randomisation of questions to eliminate order bias can be easily accommodated. Internet questionnaires share the same characteristics CAPI, but e-mail questionnaires have to be simple. Questionnaires designed for personal and telephone interviews should be written in conversational style.

'What to include in individual questions' is an important decision in designing a questionnaire. It is necessary that every question should contribute to the information needed or serve some specific purpose.

In certain situations some questions may be asked that are not directly related to the information, that is needed. It is therefore useful to ask some neutral questions at the beginning of questionnaire to build up involvement and rapport, particularly when the questionnaire is sensitive or controversial. Sometimes, filter questions are asked to disguise the purpose or sponsorship of the project (e.g. questioning about brand of interest in market research). Further, sometimes several questions are needed to obtain the required information in an unambiguous manner.

Researchers should not assume that respondents can provide accurate or reasonable answers to all questions. The researcher should attempt to overcome the respondents' inability to answer certain questions and should not ask about topics on which they are not informed. Even if respondents are able to answer a particular question, they may be unwilling to answer because too much effort may be required, the situation or context may not seem appropriate for disclosure, no legitimate purpose will be served by disclosure of information or the information requested may be sensitive. Respondents may be encouraged to provide information for which they are unwilling.

A question may be either unstructured or structured. Unstructured questions are open-ended questions that respondents answer in their own words. Structured questions specify the set of response alternatives and the response format and may be multiple choice, dichotomous or a scale. In multiple-choice questions, the researcher provides several possible answers and the respondents are asked to select one or more of the alternatives. A dichotomous question has only two response alternatives (e.g. yes or no, agree or disagree etc.)

Question wording is the translation of the desired question content and structure into words that respondents can clearly understand and react upon. It is therefore desirable that the researcher should resort to using ordinary and unambiguous words, besides avoiding leading or biased questions, implicit alternatives and implicit assummptions, and generalisations and estimates.

Determining the order of questions is another important matter for consideration in designing a questionnaire. The opening questions can be crucial in gaining the confidence and co- opeation of respondents and hence should be interesting, simple and non-threatening. Questions relating to opinions can be good opening questions. Difficult questions that are sensitive, embarassing, complex or dull should be placed in the later part in the sequence. After rapport has been established, it would be easier to receive answers on these questions and the respondents would be less likely to object. Questions should be asked in logical order.

The format, spacing and positioning of questions can have significant effect on the results of the study. In questionnaire design, assigning code to every possible response, dividing a questionnaire into several parts and numbering of the questions in each part, etc are pre-requisites of a good questionnaire.

How a questionnaire is reproduced for administration has a significant effect on the responses from the respondents. The questionnaire should be reproduced on good quality paper and should not look shabby.

Pretesting of the questionnaire is necessary to identify and eliminate potential problems in the design of the questionnaire.

Pretesting is carried out on a small sample of respondents. As a general rule no field survey should be undertaken without pretesting. A pretesting invariably improves the design of a questionnaire. Pretests are always undertaken by personal interviews, even if the actual survey is undertaken by mail, telephone, or electronic means, because it helps the interviewers observing respondents' reactions and attitudes.

Question Structure :

Both questionnaires and interview schedules contain three types of measurement questions.

- ❒ Administrative questions
- ❒ Classification questions
- ❒ Target questions

Administrative questions identify the participant, interviewer, location of interview and conditions. Classification questions are generally socio-demographic variables that allow the participants to be grouped suitably so that the patterns and differentials can be studied for possible analytical studies. Target questions address the investigative questions set for a specific study.

The type of interview also affects the question structure. If the interviews are unstructured in nature, the interviewer's task is to encourage the participant to open up and share in-depth as much information as possible.

Interviews with participants in focus groups are guided by the interviewer-moderator who generally has a set of specific points to be discussed at length by the participants. If necessary, he might prompt the group members to come to the points and interact among themselves.

Types of Questions

1. *Contigency questions* : A question that is answered only if the respondent gives a particular response to a previous question. This avoids asking questions of people that do not apply to them.
2. *Matrix questions* : Identical response categories are assigned to multiple questions. The questions are placed one under the other, forming a matrix with response categories along the top and a list of questions down the side. This is an efficient use of page space and respondent's time.
3. *Scaled questions* : Responses are graded on a continuum.
4. *Closed ended questions* (Structured) : Respondents' answers are limited to a fixed set of responses. Most scales are closed ended. Other types of closed ended questions include :
   - ❒ *Dichotomous questions* : The respondent answers with a 'yes' or a 'no'.
   - ❒ *Multiple choice* : The respondent has several option from which to choose.

5. *Open ended questions (unstructured)* : No options or predefined categories are suggested. The respondent supplies their own answer without being constrained by a fixed set of possible responses. Examples of types of open ended questions include :
   - ❒ Completely unstructured
   - ❒ Word association
   - ❒ Sentence completion
   - ❒ Story completion
   - ❒ Picture completion
   - ❒ Thematic apperception test—Respondents explain a picture or make up a story about what they think is happening in the picture.

Another consideration in designing a questionnaires is whether the purpose of the study should be *disguised*. A disguised question is designed to cancel the question's true purpose, if the researcher feels that the respondents will respond differently them they would if they know about the sponsor and the objectives of the study.

Question Content

Four questions need to be addressed while deciding about *question content*. These are :

- ❒ Should this question be asked ?
- ❒ Is the question of proper scope and coverage ?
- ❒ Can the participant be able to answer the question adequately ?
- ❒ Will the participant be able to answer the question willingly ?

The question designer should justifiably think whether the framed question significantly contribute towards answering nesearch questions. A good question designer knows the value of learning more from fewer questions.

The question should have power to reveal the motivations for particular behaviours or attitudes of the participants. This will be achieved by asking them 'Why'. The simple question may be inadequate to probe the range of most causal relationships. Sometimes, two or three questions may be necessory for studying product use behaviour. Questions are also inadequate if they do not provide the information needed to interprete the responses.

If the question requested is heavy with content, it may be necessary that it should be broken into two or more questions. Although it is desired to reduce the overall number of questions, the designer should not try to ask double-barreled questions i.e. two or more questions in one that the participant might need to answer differently to preserve the accuracy of the data.

To test the precision of the question the researcher should ask 'whether the question asks precisely what he wants and needs to know ?'

Even if the question may address the topic, it should be asked in such a way that the participant will be able to frame an answer or reasonably can determine the answer.

Sometimes the participants tend to co-operate in interviews and assume that giving any answer is more helpful than denying knowledge of a topic. Their desire to impress the interviewer results in giving answers based on no information. To counter such tendencies of the respondents to respond at any cost, filter questions are used to qualify a participant's knowledge.

The question designer should consider the participants' information level to determine the content and appropriateness of a particular question.

The question should so framed so as not to overtax participants' recall ability. Participants are not expected to recall much of the events occurred in the distant past.

Proper balance should be maintained between general and specific questions. Too often participants are asked to recall individual use experiences over an extended time and to average them out to provide answers. Such questions need to be avoided because these would encourage substantial response errors. It may also contribute to higher refusal rate and higher discontinuation rate.

The ability of participants to answer adequately is often distorted by questions where content is biased by what is included or omitted. The researcher is expected to look into these aspects while framing a questionnaire.

Sometimes the participants have the information, but are unwillingly to part with because of the sensitive nature of information. Further, they may be unwilling to give correct answers for ego reasons. It is seen that many exaggerate their incomes and their assets while others do not like to reveal because of tax reasons. The designer should try to avoid such direct questions and obtain estimated answers using alternative indirect methods of questioning.

Question wording :

It is a matter of great concern when participants fail to understand a question, which is so painstakingly coined by the researcher. This problem arises partially due to lack of a *shared vocabulary* and difficulty in understanding long and complex sentences and uncommon phrases.

A question designer should look into the following criteria before finalising a question to be administered.

- ❒ Is the question stated in terms of a shared vocabulary ?
- ❒ Does the question require vocabulary with a single meaning ?
- ❒ Does the question contain unsupported or misleading assumption ?
- ❒ Does the question contain biased wording ?
  Bias wording leads to distortion of responses.
- ❒ Is the question correctly personalized ?
  The personalizing questions most likely change responses.
- ❒ Whether adequate alternatives have been provided within the question ?
  Each alternative is to be stated explicitly to avoid bias.

Responses strategy

The questionnaire is to be framed, keeping in view the degree and form of structure imposed on the participant.

The response strategies to be taken care of by the designer include

- ❒ unstructured response
- ❒ structured response

The decision in this regard depends on

- ❒ Objectives of the study
- ❒ Participant's level of information about the subject matter of study and the degree of attainment in the thought process.
- ❒ Communication skill
- ❒ Participant motivation

If the objective of the question is to classify the participants according to a point of view, the closed question will serve the purpose.

Open ended questions are appropriate when the objective of the question is to discover the opinion and degree of knowledge of the participant. The designer should go for the use of open-ended questions when the interviewer does not have a clear idea of the level of information of the participant. If the researcher thinks that the participant understands the topic well and his level of information is predictable and stronger group of vocabulary closed questions would be preferable.

Closed questions require less motivation and answering them is less threatening to participants. The response alternatives sometimes provide clear suggestion as to which answer is appropriate and thus the closed questions may be biased. However, in large scale surveys, closed questions are generally preferred, because they

- ❒ reduce the variability of response
- ❒ make fewer demands on interviewer skill
- ❒ less costly to administer
- ❒ easier to code and analyse the data

Types of response strategies :

Free-response strategy :

In free-response strategy the interviewer pauses for all answers (in non-face to face interview) or the participant is asked to record his answer in his/her own words in the space provided on a questionnaire.

In dichotomous response strategey the participant has to choose one of the two alternative responses. Multiple-choice questions are appropriate where more than two alternatives are available for the participant to choose one amongst them and usually generate nominal data.

Check list response strategy is a logical choice when the designer wants a participant to give multiple responses to a single question, i.e., checking (√) all that reply.

Rating Response Strategy :

Rating questions ask the participant to rate or position each factor on a comparison scale, either verbal, numeric, or graphic.

Ranking Response strategy :

The ranking question is an ideal choice when the relative order of the alternatives is important.

Logical order and sequencing :

Question should be asked in a logical order. The designer of questionnaire should take into account this aspect while framing questions. All the questions that deal with a particular topic should be asked before beginning a new topic. This will help the participants switch over their train of thought. Branching questions direct the respondents to different places in the questionnaire based on how they respond the questions at hand. This ensures that all possible contigencies associated with the main question are covered. They also help reduce interviewer and respondent error and encourage complete response.

The following points should be kept in mind for sequencing the questions.

- Questions should flow logically from one to the next.
- The researcher must ensure that the answer to a question is not influenced by previous question.
- Questions should flow from the more general to the more specific.
- Questions should flow from the least sensitive to more sensitive.
- Questions should flow from factual and behavioural questions to attitudinal and opinion questions.
- Questions should flow from unaided to aided questions.
- According to the *three stage theory* (also called sandwitch theory), initial questions should be screening and rapport questions, in the second stage all the product specific questions and in the last stage the demographic questions.

Selecting an optimal Method

The choice of a communication method is dependent on research objectives. Each method has its own strengths and weaknesses. If the investigative questions call for information from hard-to-reach or inaccessible participants, the telephone interviews, mail surveys or computer delivered surveys should be considered. For a quick survey, mail surveys may be avoided because of lack of control over the returns. If there is need for extensive questioning and probing, the personal interview is the best choice.

Most of the time the choice of a method becomes apparent. In case manager's needs for information outweigh internal resources, the assistance from research vendors of survey related services having specialized expertise, a large field team and other infrastructure facilities may be sought for.

Outsourcing :

Outsourcing is the practice of using an outside firm to handle the work that might otherwise be performed within a company.

Outsourcing became a part of business lexicon during 1980's and often refers to the delegation of non-core operations from internal production to an external entity specialising in management of that operation. This concept has also come to play in business researches in global scenario. Outsourcing :

- Involves a degree of two way information exchange, co-ordination and trust between the outsourcer and the client.
- Controls capital expenditure and enables the company to direct more of capital into revenue generating activities.

- Increases efficiency in avoiding higher expenses, slower response times and spending too much energy and 'mind share' on peripheral tasks by exploiting available infrastructure and expertise of the outside provider.
- Lets the company to focus human resources talent where it needs most and thereby reduces labour costs.
- Saves time to start the project quickly by availing the research help/output from outside sources without hiring right people, training them and utilising the research results.
- Allows focus on core business in view of limited resources, limited time and attention.
- Helps small business and individuals who cannot afford to match the resources of big companies, by providing access to business researches having outsourcing facilities.
- Expects the outsourcing providers to assume and manage and avoid risk in their areas of expertise.

Outsourcing is criticised on the following grounds :

- It is sometimes criticised as to quality of the outsourced service.
- It often raises security question concerning companies giving outside access to sensitive internal business information.
- It often threatens the availability of jobs for highly qualified experts in the field.

Outsourcing Survey Services :

Commercial suppliers of research services vary from full-service operations to speciality consultants. Sometimes managers, with a view to keep confidentiality of the results affecting the competitive advantage prefer to bid only a phase of the project and the rest of the project-study may be handled by organization's staff members, possessing unique knowledge of the product or service.

However, the different aspects of a project such as exploratory work, design, sampling, data collection or processing and analysis may be contracted separately as a whole by using a **request for proposal** (RFP) to describe their requirements and seek competitive bids.

Research firms may offer special advantages which are not available at in-house. These consist of centralized-location interviewing, focus group facilities, computer-assisted facilities etc., which may be desirable for certain research needs. Besides some reputed firms possess professionally trained staff with vast experience of management research and efficient data processing and satistical analysis capabilities to cater to specialized research needs. Some research vendors, also, have specially designed software for interviewing and data tabulation.

Panel suppliers provide another type of research service with emphasis on longitudinal survey findings. Panels, using same participants over time, can track trends in attitude towards issues or products, product adoption, consumption behaviour and other interests. Thus, panel suppliers can produce data from different sources such as personal and telephone interviews, mails, diaries etc. for longitudinal studies of all varieties.

C. EXPERIMENTATION

What are experiments ?

An experiment is "a trial or special observation made to confirm or disprove something doubtful, especially one under conditions determined by the experimenter ; an act or operation undertaken in order to discover some unknown principle or effect or to test, establish or illustrate some suggested or known truth'. Thus, experiments are studies involving intervention by the researcher beyond that is required for measurement. The intervention lies in manipulating some variable in a setting and observe how it affects the subjects being studied e.g. people or physical entities, situations, events etc.

The variable that can be manipulated, changed or altered by the experimenter, independently of any other variable is called an *independent variable.* The independent variable is hypothesized to have the causal influence. Thus, one way of establishing causality between variables is through the use of *experimentation.*

The cause and effect relationship between variables can also be studied by *simulation* technique.

The variable whose value is dependent on the experimenter's manipulation is termed as *dependent variable*. It is the criterion or the standard by which the results of the experiment are judged. Changes in the dependent variable are presumed to be the effect of changes in the independent variable.

In any experiment there is at least one independent variable (IV) and one dependent variable (DV) in a causal relationship. It is hypothesized that in some way the 'IV' causes the 'DV' to occur.

Dependent variables are measured on the *test units*, which are individuals, organizations or other entities such as consumers, stores or geographical areas etc. whose response to the independent variables or treatments is being examined. For instance, the independent variables are treatments which may include price levels. package designs and advertising themes, and the dependent variables may include sales, profits, market shares, etc.

While considering causal relationship between independent and dependent variable the experimenter comes across some other variables termed as *extraneous variables* that affect the response of the test units. These variables can confound or influence the dependent variable measures in a way that weakens or invalidates the results of the experiment. For instance in experiments conducted on departmental stores, the extraneous variables include store size, store location, competitive scenario, age of the stores etc.

Thus, an experiment is conducted when the researcher manipulates one or more independent variables and measures their effect on one or more dependent variables, while controlling for the effect of extraneous variables and in the process attempts to establish causality.

Through experimental procedure scientific data are collected in a sptematic way in order to maximise the chance of answering an hypothesis correctly (Confirmatory research) or to provide material for generation of new hypothesis (exploratory research). Confirmatory research will normally involve formal significance testing where as exploratory research will normally involve looking for patterns in the data, and may not involve formal significance testing. However there may be some overlap between these two types of experiment.

What is Causality ?

Causation implies change in one variable will produce a change in another. Experiment is an usual process to infer causal relationship. When we want to determine whether some treatment causes some outcome or outcomes, essentially we want to assess the proposition "If X, then Y".

If there is causal relationship we have to simultaneously address two propositions.

If X, then Y and If not X, then not Y

Unfortunately, this is not true always, because there may be lot of other reasons, other them the program of experimentation for why you observed the outcome.

Where the event A is positively correlated with the event B, it is sometimes mistaken that A is the cause of B.There are four possible explanations of why the observed correlation exists.

1. A is the cause of B
2. B is the cause of A
3. A and B have a common cause C.
4. The correlation is coincidence.

To show that A is the cause of B, one needs to show that explanations 2 to 4 are mistaken.

The basic principle of causal analysis is to find causes that you can treat rather than treating symptoms. A root cause in the causal analysis is to search for basic reason why something happens and can be quite distant from the original effects.

What is an experimental design ?

Experimental design is a set of procedures that specify.

(*i*) the test units/experimental material which are to be divided into subsamples.

(*ii*) what independent variables/treatements are to be manipulated ?

(*iii*) what dependent variable are to be observed/measured ?

(*iv*) how the extraneous variables/experimental errors are to be controlled.

Advantages of Experiments

The causality cannot proved with certainty, but the probability that one variable being linked to another could be established convincingly through experimentation. Major advantages of experiments are :

- The researcher can manipulate the independent variables.
- The contamination from extraneous variables can be controlled more effectively.
- As regards convenience and cost of experimentation it scores superiority over other methods.
- Replication-repeating the experiment with different subject groups leads to computation of average effect of the independent variable across people, situation and times.

Disadvantages

- Artificiality of laboratory environment. Sometimes subjects' perception of a contrived environment is affected by improved situation
- Generalization using non-probability samples can create problems despite random assignment.
- Sometimes cost of experimentation can outweigh the available resources.
- Experimental studies of the past is not feasible. The experiments are only targeted for the present problems and the predictions are difficult.
- The management research is often concerned with study of people which puts limits to types of manipulations.

Steps for conducting an Experiment

An experiment needs to be scientifically planned and executed to establish causality. However, in order to make the experiment line up to its potential, much depend on the resourcefulness and creativeness of the researcher. For the success of an experiment certain logical steps to be taken up by the researcher in order to make his endeavour successful. These are :

- Selection of relevant variables.
- Specification of levels of treatments
- Control of the experimental environment/material
- Choice of the experimental design.
- Selecting and assigning subjects.
- Pilot testing, revising and testing.
- Analysis of data.

Selection of Variables

A research problem starts with a hierarchy of questions starting with the management problem. The researcher translates an amorphous problem into questions/hypotheses to state the objectives of research. The hypotheses must also be operationalized, so that concepts are transformed into variables to make them measurable and subject it to testing. For instance, let us consider the problem of sales presentation to describe a particular product benefits so that through the introduction of message it leads to improved retention of product knowledge. In this case the researcher might put a hypothesis as to whether the benefits module placed in the introduction part of the presentation produce better retention of product knowledge than those where the benefit module is placed in the conclusion.

In this problem the researcher needs to select variables that best operationalise concepts such as sales presentation, product benefits, retention and product knowledge.

The challenging jobs put before the researcher are :

- Select variables that are the best-operational representation of the original concepts.
- Determination of the number of variables to be involved in the experiment.
- Select or design appropriate measures.

Specification of Levels of Treatments

The treatment levels of the independent variable are to be decided by the researcher to make distinctions between different aspects of the treatment condition. For example, if the income of a person is hypothesized to have effect on buying habits, it might be divided into high, middle and low ranges to represent three levels of the independent variable.

The levels assigned to an independent variable should be based on simplicity and commonsense.

Control Group

Sometimes an independent variable is tested with several levels and it may be necessary to use a **control group** which could provide a base level for comparison. The control group composed of subjects who are not exposed to the independent variable in contrast to those who receive experimental treatment (manipulation of independent variable).

Control of the Experimental Environment

Referring to sales presentation experiment, a number of extraneous variables such age, gender, race, dress, communication competence and also many other characteristics related to the presenter, message or the situation may surface in the experiment. These extraneous variables have the potential to distort the effect of the treatment on the dependent variable and hence must be controlled or eliminated. Besides the experimental environment i.e. the physical environment to the experiment needs to be kept constant for uniformity and consistency, e.g. the introduction of the experiment to the subjects, arrangement of the place of experiment, the time of administration, experimenter's contact with the subjects, administration of the experiment etc.

Choice of Design

In the conduct of the experiment the experimeter must apply his expertise to choose the right type of experimental design, which will best suited to the goals of the research.

The right choice of the experiment improves the probability that the observed change in the dependent variable by the manipulation of the independent variable and not by any other factor and also helps the generalizability of results of the experiment.

Selecting and Assigning Subjects

The subjects selected for the experiment should be representative of the population to which the generalization of study's results relate. This requires the adoption of random sampling and random assignment of subjects to groups.

Pilot Testing, Revising and Testing

These procedures are similar to those considered for the collection of primary data in field surveys. Pilot testing is intended to reveal errors in the design and improper control of the extraneous variable and experimental environment. Pre-testing the instruments brings about refinement for the final test. The experiment should be timed so that the subjects are not sensitized to the independent variable by factor in the environment.

Analysis of Data

If adequate planning and pre-testing are undertaken, the experimental data are expected to be in proper order and fit for statistical analysis. The analysis may not be always easy, but with proper specification of the model assumed before start of the experiment, orderly arrangement of data pertaining to levels of treatment condition backed by pretests and post tests to make the experiment more scientific devoid of controllable errors, the choice of statistical techniques may be simplified.

Validity in experimentation

The researcher, conducting an experiment, should aim at

- ❐ drawing valid conclusions about the effects of independent variables on the study variables, termed as *internal validity.*
- ❐ making valid generalizations across persons, setting, times, etc, termed as *external validity.*

Internal validity refers whether the manipulations of the independent variables or application of treatments to subjects manifest effects on the dependent variables.

External validity refers to whether the cause-effect relationship established in the experiment can be generalized beyond the experimental situation, over space, times, events and subjects.

In an experimental design the experimenter/researcher should seek for both internal and external validity. In applied marketing research we often have to trade one type of validity for another. Sometimes a researcher conducts his experiment in a controlled environment to control extraneous variable, but for such a step there is every possibility of reducing external validity. However, if an experiment lacks internal validity, it may not be meaningful to search for generalizing the results to claim external validity.

Extraneous variables

Extraneous variables come on the way of exploring or determining cause-effect relationship and hence becomes a very important factor for consideration when an experimenter starts conducting an experiment. In order to isolate the effect of the independent variable on the dependent variable, the researcher must rule out alternative explanations. In other words only the independent variable can be allowed to vary. The term extraneous variable is used to refer to any other factor that might affect the dependent variable.

The following *categories* may be considered to classify the extraneous variables. These are among many *threats to internal validity.*

❐ History

History refers to occurrence of events that are external to the experiment, but occur unexpectedly at the time of the experiment, thus affecting the dependent variables.

❒ Maturation

Maturation effects associated with extraneous variables are attributable to changes in test units themselves that occur with the passage of time. These changes are not due to effect of the independent variables, but changes coming over the test units to affect the dependent variables. Market studies that span several months are vulnerable to maturation.

❒ Testing effects

Testing efforts are caused by the process of experimentation. When a dependent variable at two point of time, say, one before the application of treatment and the other after the application of the treatement, there may be carry over effect between two observations on the dependent variable. For instance, if an experiment is conducted to measure the effect of advertisement on attitude toward a particular brand of product, the respondents pre treatment attitude and post treatment attitude might not show any difference. From this result one should not jump into conclusion that advertisement has no effect on the attitude of respondents. An alternative explanation might be that the respondents tried to maintain consistency between their pre and post treatment attitudes.

❒ Instrumention

The changes may be brought about in the measuring instrument, in the observers, or in the scores themselves. Instrumentation effects are likely to come up when the interviewer measures pre and post treatment effects. Further, effectiveness of interviewers can be different at different times.

❒ Statistical regression

Statistical regression effects occur when respondents with extreme attitude scores come closer to average score during the course of the experiment. It is seen that people with extreme attitude have more room for change, so variation is more likely to occur between pre and post treatment measurement. This is a *confounding effect* on the results because the observerd difference may be attributable to statistical regression rather than to change in attitude.

❒ Selection Bias

The heterogeneity of test units/respondents before the exposure to treatments conditions may result in varying differences in the effects between pre and post treatment measurements.

If test units self-select their own groups or the researcher uses his personal judgement to assign test units to groups, the selection bias also occurs.

❒ Mortality

Mortality refers to extraneous variable attributable to the loss of test units during the course of experiment. This loss may be due to death, absence, closure, refusal, drop out of the test units.

Internal validity creates confusion about whether the experimental treatement (X) or extraneous factors are the source of observed differences, where as the external validity is concerned with the interaction of experimental treatment with other factors and the resulting impact on the ability to generalize (and across) times, space or persons. The major threats to external validity are the following possibilities of interactions. The first one is the reactive effect produdced by sensitizing the subjects before the application of treatment (X)/ experimental stimulus. This before-measurement effect can be particularly significant in experiments where the independent variable refers to change in attitude. Secondly, the selection of test subjects may also cause threats to external validity. It may so happen that the population from which one selects subjects may not be the same as the population to which the experimenter wishes to generalize the results. For instance, if the experiment is on the study of effect of incentives given to sales persons on the sales in department stores, the question arises as to whether the results can be extended to other stores over time and space. Further, if the subjects are aware of their role in the experiment, what would be its effect on the results ?

Internal validity can be taken care of by careful design of experiments. But external validity is a matter of generalization and is a part of inductive process by extrapolating beyond the data collected, requiring more careful thoughts.

Control of Extraneous Variable

Extraneous variables provide alternative explanation to experimental results. They affect the internal and external validity of the experiment. Unless they are controlled before or during the experiment, the dependent variables are bound to be affected. Because of this reasons they are also termed as *confounding variables.* Different ways of controlling extraneous variables which may be due to either random or non- random causes are :

❒ Randomisation

Randomisation refers random assignment of test units to experimental groups.

❒ Matching :

Matching is a method of controlling extraneous variables that involves matching test units on a set of key background characteristics before assigning them to the treatment conditions.

❒ Statistical Control

Statistical control involves measuring extraneous variables and removing its effect on the dependent variable by an adjustment of the dependent variable.

❒ Design Control

The researcher can choose suitable design for the experiment to control specific extraneous variables.

Experimental Research Designs

Experimental designs vary widely in their power to control contamination of the relationship between independent and dependent variables. Thus, we may classify experimental designs as

❒ Pre-experimental designs
❒ True experimental designs
❒ Quasi-experimental designs
❒ Statistical designs

Pre-experimental designs do not employ randomisation procedures to control for extraneous variables.

In true experimental designs the experimenter can randomly assign test units and treatments to experimental groups.

Quasi-experimental designs apply part of the procedures of true experimental designs, but lack experimental control.

Statistical designs apply all basic principles of experimental designs including randomisation.

Pre-experimental Designs

Pre-experimental designs are devoid of randomisation. Three specific designs are included in this group.

- One shot case study
- Pretest-post test design
- Static group design.

One-shot case study :

Let X denote the treatment X. A single group of test units are exposed to X. A single mesurement (O_1) on the dependent variable is taken.

Such a study does not provide comparison of O_1 with an observation, when X was absent. O_1 might have been affected by many extraneous variables and lack of control of these variables undermines the internal validity.

One Group Pretest-Postest Design :

A group of test units is taken. The treatement X is applied to them. Pre-treatment measurement O_1 and Post-treatment measurement O_2 are taken. There is no control group.

The treatment effect is computed as $O_2 - O_1$. The extraneous variables remain largely uncontrolled.

Static Group Design :

The static group is a two group experimental design. One group is called the experimental group (EG) and the other group (CG).

- EG is exposed to treatment X
- CG is not exposed
- Measurement on both groups are made only after the application of treatment.
- Test units are not assigned at random.

Symbolically

EG :	X	O_1
CG :	-	O_2

The treatment effect is now measured as $O_1 - O_2$

This difference may be contaminated by two extraneous variables - selection and mortality, besides other extraneous variables. Because test uits are not randomly assigned, the selection bias may be likely to be present and further some test units may withdraw from the experiment group.

True Experimental Designs

In true experimental design

(*i*) the test units are randomly assigned to experimental groups.

(*ii*) the treatments are randomly allocated to experimental groups.

Pretest- Post test Control Group Design :

This design consists of adding a control group to the one-group pre test-post test design.

Assign the subject to either of the groups by a random procedure (R).

$$\begin{array}{lllll} EF & R: O_1 & X & O_2 \\ CG & R: O_3 & - & O_4 \end{array}$$

The effect of the treatment (experimental variable) is measured as

$$E = (O_2 - O_1) - (O_4 - O_3)$$

This design controls most of the extraneous variables. Selection bias is eliminated by randomisation.

However, the interactive effect, which occurs due to the effect of pretest measurement on the reaction of units in the experimental group to the treatment.

Post test-only Control Group Design :

In this design pretest measurements are not taken. It is symbolized as

$$\begin{array}{lll} EG: R & X & O_1 \\ CG: R & & O_2 \end{array}$$

The treatment effect is obtained as

$$E = O_1 - O_2$$

Quasi-experimental Designs :

In this group of designs the experiment/researcher can control when measurements are taken and on whom they are taken. But, the researcher lacks control over the scheduling of the treatments and further he is unable to expose test units to the treatments randomly.

Quasi-experimental designs are useful when true experimental designs can not be used. Moreover, they are quicker to execute and less expensive. Popular forms of this design are

- ❒ Time series Design
- ❒ Multiple Time Series Design.

Time Series Design :

In the time series design a series of periodic measurements are taken on the dependent variable for a group of test units. The treatment is then aplied and again periodic measurements are continued.

$$O_1\ O_2\ O_3\ O_4\ O_5 \times O_6\ O_7\ O_8\ O_9\ O_{10}$$

There is no randomisation of test units to treatments and the timing of treatment allocation. Further, which test units are exposed to the treatment may not be within the researcher's control.

In practice, the researcher makes a few observations to establish a base line, do the intervention by applying a treatment and then makes a few more observations. Just how many observations are to be made on either side of the interventions is determined by the stability of the data.

The major threat to internal validity of the time series is history. That is, a criticism that the results obtained would have occurred with or without experimental intervention is difficult to define with data from the simple time series experiment. Further, time series quasi-experiments can have any number of outcomes and the search for stability may be difficult at times.

Multiple Time Series Design :

This is a time series design except that another group of test units is added to the design to serve as control group.

$$EG : O_1\ O_2\ O_3\ O_4\ O_5 \times\ O_6\ O_7\ O_8\ O_9\ O_{10}$$
$$CG : O_1\ O_2\ O_3\ O_4\ O_5\quad O_6\ O_7\ O_8\ O_9\ O_{10}$$

The design provides some information about what might have happened to your experimental group had the experimental treatment not been applied. Since naturally-ocurring groups are used instead of randomisation, one has less confidence in the equivalence of the two groups ; still the addition of the control group does add some credibility to any positive results by helping to rule out potential rival explanations based on extraneous factors.

Statistical Designs

Statistical designs are randomised designs and allow examination of the effects of different treatment levels of an experimental (independent) variable and also measure the effects of two or more independent variables at various levels.

In statistical designs *factor* is widely used to denote an *independent variable*. A factor may be divided into treatment levels for application to test units. Further, different factors may be applied at different levels simultaneously. The combination of levels of different factors are termed as *factorial treatment combinations*. These levels may be (i) male and female (ii) large, medium and small, (iii) no training, brief training or (iv) different levels of fertilizers such as nitrogen, phosphate and potash, etc.

An experimenter, besides dealing with one or more experimental/active factors (independent variables) may consider another factor, termed as *blocking factor*, the experimenter can only identify and classify the test units into groups, having internal homogeniety. In research the blocking factors may be gender, age group, customer status, organizational rank, etc.

Test unit may be an individual, organization, geographic market, machine type, mix of materials, etc. Blocking factor is an extraneous variable, which can be controlled to provide more precise estimates of effects of independent variable on the dependent variable.

Statistical designs consist of a series of basic experiments that allow for statistical control analysis of extraneous variables vis-a-vis other variables-independent and dependent. These designs have the following advantages :

- ❒ The effects of more than one independent variable can be measured.

- **Specific extraneous variables can be statistically controlled.**
- **Economic designs can be formulated when each test unit is measured more than once.**

The **principal aspects of statistical designs** *are* :

- **The layouts of the experiment by which the treatment levels are assigned to test units/subjects**
- **The techniques that are used to analyze the results of the experiment.**

The **basic statistical designs** often used in practice are :

- Completely randomised design.
- Randomised complete Block design.
- Latin square design.

These basic designs can be applied to both

- Single factor experiments
- Multi factor experiments (popularly termed as *factorial experiments*)

Basic Principles of Design of Experiments :

The advantage of experimental approach is that it allows control to examine the cause-effect relationship by answering the question 'What causes something to occur ?' The cause is the stimulus/independent variable and the effect is the response/dependent variable. In order to isolate the effect of the independent variable on the dependent variable, the researcher/experimenter must rule out alternative explanations provided by the extraneous variables. In other words only the independent variable can be allowed to vary. The term extraneous variable is used to refer to any other factor that might affect the dependent variable and contribute to the experimental error.

The variability in experimental material is almost universal. Replication (repetition of the set of treatments) in the experiment is or should be practised in nearly all experimental work. Two conditions are necessary to obtain a valid estimate of experimental error-**replication and randomisation.**

When variability in experimental material is small and the observations are not costly, an elaborate experimental design is not required. The experimenter simply takes the results from a large number of readings and observes the relationships or mean differences.

When there is considerable variation from observation to observation on the same material and it is not feasible to take large number of observations, the experimenter is forced to refine his experimental techniques and (or) to use an experimental design which allows for unbiased estimates of the true treatment differences with a specified degree of precision. It is, therefore, necessary that a probability statement be attached to treatment differences, if influences beyond data are to be made. To make possible probability statements, replication and randomisation are two required conditions for an experimental design. Also, randomisation and replication are necessary to obtain a valid estimate of the error variation. A valid estimate of the error variance (or experimental error variance) makes possible statements concerning the percentage of errors committed by the experimenter when he states that treatment means are different when the differences are actually chance sampling fluctuations and that treatment means do not differ when they actually do differ by more than some specified value.

Thus, regardless of the size of relative variability, there are certain basic principles to be followed for conducting an experiment. These are :

- *Randomisation* : guarantees validity of estimates and their unbiasedness
- *Replication* : helps provide a source of estimate of error which can be used to compare treatments.
- *Local control* : helps to reduce sampling variation in the comparisons by eliminating some sources of such variations.

In order to have a valid error term for testing the difference among treatments an experimental design of radomised nature and replication of treatments is a necessity. Such a procedure allows for the calculation of unbiased estimates of treatment differences and an appropriate error variance. As pointed out by R.A.,Fisher the correct error variance for testing the variation among the tretment means in one which contains "all the sources of variation inherent in the variation among treatment means except the portion of the variance due specifically to the treatments themselves."

Selection of an Experimental Design :

The selection of an experimental design of the randomised nature necessitates knowledge of the variability of the material/units under test and the selection of the number of replicates to be used is determined by the minimum size of the treatement difference which the experimenter wishes to detect.

There are *four* ways in which variability of treatement means may be reduced :

(*i*) selection of more homogeneous material.

(*ii*) stratification/grouping of experimental material into homogeneous subgroups.

(*iii*) increasing the number of observations or replications.

(*iv*) measurement of one or more characteristics in order to use regression technique.

The selection of homogeneous experimental reduces experimental error and this facilitates easy detection of treatment differences. If it is impracticable to obtain a single, homogeneous group of material, several small groups of homogeneous material may be obtained for the experimentation leading to more complex design incorporating large number of replications, thereby reducing the experimental error.

Another method used for the reduction of experimental error is to measure a related variate or variates and using covariance analysis. If the cost of observing such ancillary variate is not high, the covariance technique may prove extermely useful. Thus, if the variability in the experimental material is not easily controllable, then it is advisable to measure an ancillary variable and use covariance or regression technique to remove the initial variability, thus reducing the experimental error variance.

Completely Randomised Design (CRD)

Completely Randomised Design is the basic and the simplest of all experimental designs. In this design no blocking technique is utilized to control the extraneous variables. Different treatment levels of a factor (independent variable) are assigned to experimental units/test units at random. The number of test units receiving different treatment levels (in short treatments) may be equal or unequal. That is, the number of repetitions for any one treatment may vary. The completely randomized design is usually selected when the variation over all of the experimental material is relatively small. Due to non-availability of large amount of homogeneous material the design is suited only for small number of treatments. When large number of treatmens are included, a relatively large amount of experimental material must be used and such material might not be all homogeneous resulting in the variation among treatment responses. If the variation over the experimental material is relatively large, it is possible to selecte more efficient designs than the completely randomised one resulting in more precise estimate of treatment means with the same number of replicates.

Illustration 1.

Suppose we are interested in judging the sales performances of four graduate toppers of four business schools of same grade.

The experiment can be conducted with four treatments (toppers A, B, C, D of four business schools) and weekly sales for five weeks (say) as replications (which may not always necessarily be equal).

Randomised Block Design (RBD)

In a Randomised Block Design (RBD) only one extraenous variable (Blocking factor), that might influence the dependent variable, is controlled. The test units are blocked or grouped on the basis of the extraneous variable. The researcher has a prime responsibility to identify and measure the blocking variable. In each block or group, the treatments/treatment levels are randomly allotted to test units. As all the tretments are accomodated in each block, the design is also called **Randomised Complete Block Design (RCBD),** developed in 1925. Since then the design has become extremely popular in scientific experiments. In RBD, the randomisation is restricted in the sense that the treatments are allotted at random to experimental units/test units within each group/stratum/block, but not over entire experimental material. Also, the variation among the blocks is removed from the variation among replicates within treatments. Therefore, if it is designed to control one source of variation by grouping the experimental material one should select the RBD rather than Completely Randomised Design (CRD). The block/strata/groups in RBD are the replicates.

The chief advantages of the Randomised Block Design are :

Accuracy :

This design is seen to be more accurate than the completely randomised design with the help of blocking because the variation among blcoks is eliminated from total variation due to extraneous variables.

Flexibility :

No restriction is put on the number of treatments and the number of replicates in the experiment.

Ease of analysis :

The statistical analysis is simple and rapid. Any number of treatments can be omitted from the experiments without complicating it.

The chief disadvantage of RBD is that it is not suitable for experimenting with large number of treatments for which certain Incomplete Block Designs may be adopted.

Illustration

An experiment may be conducted to study the effect of four different machines on output. Each machine is worked upon by a given number of workers, say five workers. Five homogeneous groups of four workers are selected. Four machines are assigned at random to workers in each group. This is a RCBD with four treatments and five replications.

Latin Square Design :

A Latin Square design is an improvement over Randomised complete block design and allow the researcher to statistically control two non-interacting extraneous variables (Blocking variables) as well as to manipulate the independent variable. Each of the blocking variables is divided into same number of levels, so also the independent variable. Rows and Columns of the latin square represent the levels of two blocking variables. The levels of the independent variable are then assigned to the cells in the square, formed by grids of rows and columns. In a 4 × 4 Latin square, there are 16 cells. Each level of the independent variable occurs only once in each row and once in each column and further treatment levels are randomly assigned to these cells.

Rows	**Columns**			
	1	**2**	**3**	**4**
1	A	B	C	D
2	B	C	D	A
3	C	D	A	B
4	D	A	B	C

Method of arrangement in a k × k Latin square :

(*i*) Assign letters to first row at random; This results in k! permutations of the letters in the first row.

(*ii*) Assign remaining (k - 1) lettes at random in the first column resulting in (k - 1)! permutations of these letters.

(*iii*) Continue the process until all rows and columns are filled, excluding letters which have already appeared in a row or in a column.

Advantages and Disadvantages :

The major advantage of Latin square design is that it controls more of the variation than the CRD or the RBD with a two way stratification or grouping of the experimental material.

As regards disadvantage it has a major restriction that the number of rows, number of coloums and the number of treatments must be equal. Further, for large number of treatments the latin square is seldom used.

Illustration

A latin square design (4 × 4) may be adopted if we are considering sales performances of graduates of 4 business schools across 4 weeks of a month and 4 sections of a Departmental Store.

Factorial Experiment

When the researcher is interested in testing the number of treatments/different levels of a factor, not necessarily related to each other, it is a common practice to use the basic experimental designs such as Completely Randomised Design/Randomised Complete Block design or Latin squares, for example, varieties, types of processes, brands or fertilizer treatments etc.

Frequently, we know that several factors may affect the response variable/dependent variable in which we are interested and we wish to estimate the effects of each of the factors and how effect of one factor varies over the levels of other factors. For instance, suppose a sales mananger wants to study the effect of sales person (Male/Female), sales person (trained/untrained) as well as sales region (North/South) on its quarterly revenue in rupees, then he is to design a $2 \times 2 \times 2 = 2^3$ factorial experiment. Such an experiment allows studying the effect of each factor on the response variable, while requiring fewer observations than by conducting seperate experiments for each factor independently. Further and most important is that it also allows studying the effect of interaction between factors on the response variable.

Factorial experiment, in itself, is not considered as an experimental design. Any of the experimental designs may be used for the factorial experiment.

In a factorial experiment we are not generally interested in factorial treatment means, but with effects and interactions. Consider a 2^2 factorial experiment with 2 factors a and b, each at 2 levels (a_0, a_1), (b_0, b_1) respectively. The factorial treatment combinations are (a_0, b_0), (a_1, b_0), (a_0, b_1) and (a_1, b_1). The main effect of the factor '*a*', denoted by the capital leter A is defined as

$$A = \frac{1}{2} [\{(a_1 b_0) - (a_0 b_0) + (a_1 b_1) - (a_0 b_1)\}]$$

= Average of the effect of '*a*' at b_0 level of *b* and effect of '*a*' at b_1 level of *b*.

Symbolically, A is written as

$$A = \frac{1}{2} (a_1 - a_0) (b_1 + b_0)$$

The two factors on the right hand side are symbolically multiplied to obtain relevant treatment combinations with + or - signs

Similarly

$$B = \frac{1}{2} [\{(a_0 b_1) - (a_0 b_0)\} + \{(a_1 b_1) - (a_1 b_0)\}]$$

If the factor '*a*' does not interact with factor '*b*', then

$\{(a_1 b_0) - (a_0 b_0)\}$ and $\{(a_1 b_1) - (a_0 b_1)\}$ should be essentially the same. In case they differ, we have the interaction effect AB, defiend as

$$AB = \frac{1}{2} [\{(a_1 b_1) - (a_0 b_1)\} - \{(a_1 b_0) - (a_0 b_0)\}],$$

which may be symbolically expressed as

$$AB = \frac{1}{2} (a_1 - a_0) (b_1 - b_0),$$ which is also equal to BA.

Laboratory experiments Vrs. Field experiments/surveys

Laboratory environment is an artificial one, where as field environment is natural one in which all forces act (*e.g.,* market conditions, etc.) without much constraints.

The laboratory experiments can be conducted with high degree of control, carefully monitored by the experimenter. Further, a laboratory experiment tends to produce same results, if repeated under identical conditions, then leading to high internal validity. Also, small number of test units are required for laboratory experiments. It is also generally less expensive. As regards disadvantages of laboratory experimetns, the artificially created environment may cause reactive error, that is, the respondents react to the situation itself, rather than to the independent variable. Also, the respondents might cause demand artifacts, a phenomenon in which the respondents being aware of the experiment respond accordingly. The laboratory experiments are likely to have lower external validity than the field experiments, because laboratory experiments are conducted in artificial environment, diminishing the ability to generalize the results.

In contrast a survey in field environment is used to find association between the effects of some variable, which is not usully under the control of the scientist, and some characteristics of the subjects being investigated.

The researcher can easily conduct laboratory experiments and can control more variables compared to field experiments with more complex designs. However, laboratory and field experiments play complementary roles in marketing research.

Limitations of experimentation

Experiments are becoming increasing popular in business studies, specially in marketing research. However, there are certain limitations with respect to

- time
- cost
- administration.

Experiments can be *time consuming* if one is interested in measuring long term effect of a treatment, such as a marketing strategy/advertising campaigns. Further the test subjects may move out and the situations may not remain the same through out the period.

Experiments are often *expensive* because of cost of making observations/measurement in different groups.

Experiments can be *difficult to administer* in a field environment because it is generally difficult to control the effects of the extraneous variables. In marketing research it may not be always possible to obtain co-operation from all concerned in the experiment and competitors may deliberately contaminate the results of experiment.

EXERCISES

1. What are different sources of data ? Discuss with the help suitable examples.
2. Distinguish between primary data and secondary data with examples. What are advantages and disadvantages of secondary data ?
3. Distinguish between internal and external data sources.

4. Discuss applications of secondary data for taking business decisions.

5. Distinguish betwen qualitative and quantitative research techniques for collecting primary data.

6. Explain the importance of the case studies in collection of primary data.

7. What is a pilot study ? What does it achieve ? Discuss.

8. Distinguish between case studies and statistical studies.

9. What is in-depth interview ? Explain different depth interviewing techniques.

10. Discuss the focus group as a useful method of collecting primary dates. Mention its merits and demerits along with its sphere of applications.

11. What is brain storming ? Is it an effective means to generate useful input for the business research ? Discuss its basic rules.

12. Discuss different types of panels for collecting primary data. Mention their uses.

13. Explain the nominal group technique in collection of data. Mention its advantages and disadvantages.

14. What is the delphi method ? Explain its advantages and disadvantages.

15. What are projective techniques ? Explain different types of projective techniques.

16. What are the most common quantitative research techniques in primary data collection ? Discuss.

17. Explain observation as a primary method of collecting information. Discuss the observer—participant—relationship in this context.

18. How would you conduct an observational study ? Explain different observation methods. Who should be an observer ?

19. Discuss advantages and limitations of the observation methods.

20. What are survey techniques ? Mention their characteristics. Explain different survey techniques with examples.

21. Discuss the merits and demerits of self administered surveys and suggest steps for improving response rate.

22. What are characteristics of personal interviews ? Discuss.

23. What is a questionnaire ? Mention its objectives. What are practical steps for designing a questionnaire ?

24. What are experiments ? Explain their characteristics, advantages and disadvantages.

25. What is an experimental design ? What do you mean by validity in experimentation ?

26. What are basic principles for conducting an experiment ? Discuss their importance.

27. How would you control extraneous variables in designing an experiment ? Discuss.

28. What are different types of experimental research designs ? Discuss.

29. What are characteristics of statistical designs ? Differentiate between Completely Randomised design and Randomised Block Design.

30. Explain utility of Latin square design. How does it differ from Randomised Block Disign ? Mention its advantages and disadvantages.

31. What is a factorial experiment ? How does it differ from experiments where factors are varied one at a time ?

32. Distinguish between laboratory experiments and field experiments. What are the limitations of experimentation ?

33. What is outsourcing ? How does it help business research ?

34. Mention information types in business research.

35. What is a database ? How would you search a bibliographic database ?

36. What is a search engine ? How does it work ?

37. Explain the terms : Data warehouse, Data Marts, Data Mining.

38. Write a Note on Government India publications ?

39. What is CSO ? Mention major databases developed by CSO.

40. (*a*) What is a Website ? Mention different types of Websites.

(*b*) Write a note on World Wide Web.

□□□

CHAPTER

6

PROCESSING OF DATA (DATA PREPARATION AND PRESENTATION)

6.1. Introduction

Once the data are received from the field, the researcher has an important duty to prepare data for subsequent statistical analysis. First, the researcher has to edit the data for diagnosing possible errors in reporting and missing ones, writing the answers by the interviewes/respondents, to check the consistency in answers and coding errors, if any, etc. It is desirable that the scrutiny process should begin while the field data are in flow without waiting for the entire data to be received. Such a process is called *editing of data*. This is required to save time and also to dispense with mistakes while hurrying up for the data processing.

Sometimes, it becomes necessary to classify the unstructured responses into a limited number of categories by providing numeric codes. Although the classification of responses to a number of categories sacrifices some data in detail, this has a role to play in easy statistical analysis. Further, identification particulars for the respondents and qualitative information when translated into numeric codes help data processing. Thirdly, the researcher should also look into new and more efficient ways of speeding up the research process by adopting appropriate data entry methods. Data entry converts information collected from secondary or primary sources to a medium for viewing and manipulation.

Thus, data preparation consists of three important steps :

- Editing
- Coding
- Data entry

The raw data are often in bulky form and are difficult to be comprehended easily for ready reference. This calls for devising certain suitable methods for processing of data such as condensing/ summarizing data for easy comprehension and providing directions for subsequent analysis in computing required statistical derivatives and applying further statistical treatment.

The most prominent and universally adopted data processing methods which present data in summary form are :

- classification
- tabulation
- graphical representation
- diagrammatic representation of data, etc.

6.2. EDITING

Editing is the review of the questionnaire with the objective of increasing accuracy and precision. It is needed to detect and if possible, to eliminate errors in the filled in questionnaires. Editing work, although uninteresting and dull in nature, is no doubt necessary for faultless analysis of survey data.

There are three points—completeness, accuracy and uniformity, to be checked while editing the data.

Completeness. While checking the questionnaires for completeness it should be remembered that there is an answer to every question. If not, the answer should be deduced from other data. Alternatively, the interviewer may be asked to fill up the answer from memory. If the answer is such, for example, in case of open question, that neither the person in charge of editing nor the interviewer is able to fill up, this may be referred back to the concerned respondent.

Further care must be taken to see that the answers are legible enough to facilitate coding.

Accuracy. Besides checking that all questionnaires are provided with answers, one must try to check whether answers are accurate. Inconsistencies in answers should be looked for and resolved. Inaccuracy may be due to carelessness or concious attempt to give misleading answers on the part of respondents. Carelessness and non-deliberate noting of wrong answers by the interviewer due to stress and strain of interviews may also result in inaccuracies.

The questionnaires with unsatisfactory responses may be returned to the field, where the interviewers recontact the respondents. This approach is feasible when for business and industrial marketing surveys the sample sizes are small and easily identifiable. However, there may be certain changes in response due to time factor and the mode of questionnaire administration.

If returning to the field to correct the unsatisfactory responses and to fill up the missing values is not feasible, the editor may assign seemingly appropriate values to unsatisfactory responses.

Alternatively, the editor may discard the unsatisfactory responses. Of course, discarding is advisable only when the unsatisfactory responses are few in number.

Uniformity. While editing the schedules, efforts should be made to check whether the interviewers have interpreted questions and instructions uniformly. In case of lack of uniformity etc. editing staff may try to make correction or refer back the schedules to the respondents or omit the schedules from analysis.

6.3. CODING

After editing the data it may be required in most surveys to put the results in quantitative form by coding the answers before summarization and analysis begin. This may also be conveniently carried out at the time of editing.

The purpose of coding in surveys is to put the answers into a particular question into meaningful and unambiguous categories to bring out essential pattern, concealed in the mass of information. Essentially, *coding means assigning a code, usually a number, to each possible response to each question.*

Coding helps the researcher to reduce several replies to a few categories as per the requirement of the analysis. In coding categories, partition a set of information using certain rules. The code includes an indication of the column position (field) and data record it will occupy. For instance, gender may be coded as M (male) or F (female. Alternatively, male may be coded as 1. and female as 2.

A *field* represents a single item of data, such as sex of the respondent. A *record* consists of related fields such as sex, marital status, age, household size, occupation etc. All the data for a respondent are contained in a *single record*. Sometimes more than one record may be necessary.

Coding of structured questions is relatively easy and simple because the response options are predetermined. The researcher assigns a code for each response to each question and specifies the appropriate record and column in which the response codes are to appear.

The coding of unstructured or open ended questions is more complex. Respondents' verbatim responses are recorded on the questionnaire. Codes are then developed and assigned to these responses. As codes are to be attached to categories, **these should be appropriate to the research problem and purpose, besides being collectively exhaustive, mutually exclusive and derived from one classification principle, termed as coding rules.**

The respondent code and the record number should appear on each record in the data. However, the record code can be dispensed with if there is only one record for each respondent. The following additional codes should be included for each respondent : project code, interviewer code, date and time codes, etc.

Code Book Construction

A code book or coding scheme contains each variable, along with specification for the application of coding rules to the variable. It is used by the researcher as a guide to make the data entry less prone to error and more efficient. It provides a source for locating the positions of the variables in the data file during statistical analysis.

Coding Closed Questions

The responses to closed questions include scaled items and others for which answers can be anticipated. When codes are established in the beginning of the research process, it is possible to precode the questionnaire. Precoding is helpful for data entry without going through intermediate steps for completing the coding sheet.

Coding Open-ended Questions

Closed questions can be easily handled by the researchers for coding. As regards open-ended questions the researcher should note the varieties of answers and after preliminary evaluation, response categories can be settled down/created for coding. Although most responses could be accounted for by the derived categories, an other category might be established to meet the coding rule exhaustiveness. It is to be noted that open questions are more difficult to code since answers are not prepared in advance. However, they do encourage disclosure of complete information without restriction imposed by prior suggestive answers.

Another systematic method for analyzing open questions is **content analysis** which provides quantitative description of the manifest content of a communication. It uses preselected sampling units to produce frequency counts and other insights into data pattern.

Don't Know (DK) Answers

The Don't know response poses special problems if it is frequent and substantial in nature. When the DK response group is small, it is not troublesome.

Most DK responses may be due to

- legitimate reasons when the respondent does not know the answer.
- due to researcher's failure to get appropriate information.

Which may be due to defective formulation of questions, lack of rapport between the researcher and the respondent and wilful avoidance on the part of the respondent to answer certain questions (because of confidentiality in nature and lack of motivation/concern for the success of the research)

The best way to deal with undesired DK response is to design the better questions at the beginning. To minimize the DK response rate, the researcher should identify the questions which may invite DK response and design them accordingly. However, the interviewer must use his ingenuity to deal with it in the field and the undesired DK response may be avoided by cultivating proper rapport, which will motivate the respondent. Certain DK responses may be indirectly assessed through other correlated questions for which the respondent has the answers.

At the tabulation stage a few DK responses do not pose any problem as to how they are handled and may probably be kept in a separate category. If the DK response is legitimate, it should remain in a separate category, which may have some research value. In any case if the researcher is not sure how to treat it, the DK responses should be kept in a separate category and let the reader make the decision.

Transcribing

Transcribing data involves transferring the coded data from the questionnaire or coding sheets onto a computer for subsequent data treatment.

Data Cleaning

The data collected through questionnaires may contain certain inconsistencies and also missing responses. Thus, there is need for **consistency checks** to make corrections for out of range and logically inconsistent data and also for extreme values.

Missing responses correspond to unknown values of the variable because of ambiguous answers provided by the respondents and also because the interviewers fail to record answers properly.

The treatment of missing responses may be made by

- substituting a neutral value such as mean response, etc.
- substituting an imputed response by studying the pattern of responses
- deleting the missing responses from the analysis either by discarding the respondents/cases having missing responses
- taking into account only available responses for each question.

6.4. Data Entry

Data entry implies conversion of information gathered from secondary or primary sources to a medium for viewing and manipulation. Keyboarding helps the researchers who need to create a data file immediately and store it in a minimum space on a variety of media.

The researcher can make use of a PC image scanner and with the help of *optical character recognition programs* can transfer printed text into computer files in order to edit and use it without taking recourse to retyping. Optical scanning instruments serves the researchers more efficiently. Optical scanners process the marked-sensed questionnairs and store the answers in a file. This method is often associated with standardised and preprinted forms and has been largely adopted by designers for data entry and preprocessing.

Optical mark recognition (OM) is a more flexible format and uses a spreadsheet style interface to read and process user created forms.

Data analysis through the computer has made the task of a researcher easier than the situation decades ago. The statistical packages like SPSS/SAS/S-plus/Mini tab etc. are available to make routine calculations and also for sophisticated statistical analysis. To facilitate the use of statistical packages a full screen editor, where an entire data can be edited or browsed is a viable means for data entry.

For large research projects involving large bulk of data base programs serve as valuable data entry devices. A **data base** is a collection of data organized for computerized retrieval. A company's personnel records is an example of a data base storing information in several files such as salary, official position, education, special training, if any, benefits, incentives, home and family. The data can also be separated so that the users can see those parts pertaining to their needs.

Researchers make use of data base entry having large amounts of linked data by retrieving and tabulating in different ways over time. Further, the data base can store data into a set of linked files that allow the data to be easily sorted. Descriptive statistics and tables can be easily generated from within the data base.

Spreadsheets are a specialized type of data base. It provides an easy to learn mechanism for organizing and tabulatng data and computing simple statistics. Data entry on a spread sheet uses numbered rows and letter columns with a matrix of thousands of cells into which an entry may be placed.

Spread sheets have also the provision that you can type numbers, formulas and text into appropriate cells. Many statistics programs for personal computers and also charting and graphic applications have provision for data editors, similar to **Excel spread sheet.** Spread sheet is a very convenient and flexible means for entering and viewing data and also facilitates subsequent applications.

A **dataware** house organizes large volumes of data into categories to facilitate retrieval, interpretation and sorting by end-users.

6.5. Condensation/Summarization of Data

Numerical data collected in an enquiry are usually in raw and bulky form difficult to be easily comprehensible and grasped and therefore need certain methods to bring about condensation or summarization of data. There are different ways of presenting data in summary form.

These are :

(*a*) classification

(*b*) seriation

(*c*) tabulation

(*d*) graphical representation of data

(*e*) diagrammatic representation of data

6.5.1. Classification of data

Classification is a process by which the data are arranged according to resemblances, affinities, internal homogeneity and common characteristics. This process is fore runner to the tabular, graphical and diagrammatic representation of data. For example, in a socio-economic enquiry, data can be classified according to age, sex, educational qualification, religion, caste, income group, occupation, etc.

Advantages of Classification

1. Classification brings a simple look to the data by grouping voluminous and heterogeneous data into homogeneous groups and by putting it in an orderly and condensed form, and as a result, significant features of data become more explicit, by ignoring unnecessary details.
2. Classification helps comparison among difficult groups. For instance, we may be interested to study literacy rates between sex groups—male and female. Further, we may like to study the changes in income according to education.
3. Classification according to different criteria facilitates the drawing of inferences about the underlying relationship among these criteria.
4. Classification is the first step in carrying out different processes of condensation of data *e.g.* tabulation, diagrammatic representation, graphical representation etc.

Kinds of Classification

Statistical data may be classified according to different characteristics.

These are :

(i) Qualitative Classification. In this method statistical data are classified according to characters *i.e. attributes*. For example, in the study of human populations, the data may be classified according to sex, caste, literacy, religion, occupation, etc. Further, classification may be done with the help of two or more attributes giving rise to two way or multi-way classified data, *e.g.* Rural-Urban and Male-Female, Rural-Urban and Literates-Illiterates, Male-Female and Workers-Non-workers, etc.

(ii) Spatial Classification. Classification of data according to geographical areas is called *spatial classification*, *e.g.* statewise classification of population into different demographic categories, level of industrialization and urbanization. Classification of world population according to countries, etc.

(iii) Chronological Classification. In chronological classification the data are classified according to different time periods, *e.g.* population of India for different census periods, State budget over different years, crime rates over years, vital rates over years, etc.

(iv) Quantitative Classification. Quantitative data such as age, height, weight, production, income, expenditure intelligence scores, number of children, marks etc. can be classified according to class intervals which have upper and lower limits. The number of observation falling in each class interval is called **frequency** of that class. The classification of data according to class-intervals showing frequency in each class interval form **frequency distribution.**

6.5.2. Seriation of Data

A systematic arrangement of data is called *seriation.* The seriation gives rise to statistical series, which has close connection with classification.

The statistical series are of three types :

(*i*) Time series
(*ii*) Spatial series
(*iii*) Frequency series

In a time series the data are arranged systematically according to time. (Table 6.1). In a spatial series the data are arranged according to geographical areas (Table 6.2). Frequency series relates to seriation of certain phenomenon, which can be classified according to class intervals (Table 6.3)

Table 6.1 Foreign Direct Investment in India

Year	*Foreign Direct Investment (in million US dollars)*
1999	2155
2000	2339
2001	3904
2002	2146

Source. Asian Development Outlook, 2003

Table 6.2 Statewise sugar production (in lakh tonnes) in 2004-2005

States	*Production*
Andhra Pradesh	9.8
Bihar	2.5
Gujarat	8.0

Haryana	4.0
Karnatak	10.4
Maharashtra	22.2
Punjab	3.2
Tamilnadu	1.1
Uttar Pradesh	50.4
Others	5.4
Total	117.0

Source. Economic Survey

TABLE 6.3

Distribution of household population in a sample survey NFHS-2

Age group in years	*Number (frequency)*
6-9	1101
10-14	1318
15-19	1155
20-29	2003
30-39	1702
40-49	1153
50+	1871
Total	10,303

Source. NFHS–2

6.5.3. Tabulation

After classification of data the next step in the process of summarization of data is to put the classified data in rows and columns having special characteristics on a piece of paper. Such representation of data in orderly and easily comprehensible fashion is called **tabulation.**

Classification is a pre-requisite for tabulation.

Salient features of a Table :

1. A faultless table should have a table number, table title and sub-titles for rows and columns in the body of the table. The source of data used in the table and foot-notes, if any, should be mentioned, just below the final horizontal line of the table.
2. A good table should be simple to understand, readily comprehensible, compact, complete and self explanatory.
3. The numerical figures represented in the table should be such that it would be possible to compare the related figures without waiting for further calculation. (*e.g.* summary tables).
4. A good table should be of proper size and shape with proper spacings for rows and columns and should have attractive get up.
5. The data incorporated in the table should be ordered alphabetically, geographically or chronologically or according to magnitude depending upon the necessity to facilitate ready comparison.

Types of Table

As the process of tabulation presupposes a particular type of classification, there is one to one correspondence between of classification and tabulation.

The statistical tables may be constructed in different manner depending upon the objectives, scope, nature and extent of coverage of enquiry.

(i) Classification of tables according to purpose :

In large scale enquiries two types of tables are popularly used. These are :

(*a*) General purpose tables

(*b*) Summary tables

General purpose tables, sometimes termed as *reference tables* or information tables are *detailed tables*, providing in a systematic manner, usually in chronological order, all information connected with the enquiry. These tables are also termed as **Master Tables**. The detailed tables prepared in census reports belong to this class.

The **summary tables** are **special purpose tables** which are constructed or derived from **Master Tables** with certain specific purpose and are useful for analytical and comparative studies involving the study of relationship among variables.

Calculation of analytical statistics like ratios, percentages, index numbers, etc. are incorporated in these tables.

(ii) Classification of tables according to nature of data :

Nature of data collected in the course of an enquiry may suggest two alternative types of tables. These are

(*a*) Primary tables

(*b*) Derived tables

The *primary tables* represent data in original form without arithmetical rounding up and derivatives, where as the *derived tables* contain condensed figures or entries, for example, ratios, percentages, etc. from the primary tables.

(iii) Classification of tables according to characteristics :

According to the number of characteristics used in the construction, the tables can be classified as *simple table* relating to one way classified data, *two way table,* corresponding to two-way classified data, three way table, etc.

ILLUSTRATION 1. (Simple Table)

TABLE 6.4

Growth Rate of Gross Domestic Product in 2004 (% per year)

Country	**Percentage**
India	6.5
China	8.8
Pakistan	6.4
Bangladesh	5.5
Sri Lanka	5.0
Singapore	8.1

Source : Asian Development Outlook, 2004

ILLUSTRATION 2. (Multi-way table)

TABLE 6.5
Labour Force Participation Rates (LFPR) by sex and sector in India (1999-2000)

Education Level	Rural		Urban	
	Male	Female	Male	Female
Literate below secondary	86.38	36.84	81.96	17.85
Secondary and higher secondary	74.66	19.47	68.23	12.72
Graduates and above	89.90	41.00	85.40	30.20

Source : N.S.S.

ILLUSTRATION 3.

General format of a table :

Table number
Title
Head note (Row Headings and Column Headings)
Body of the Table
Foot note (if any)
Source note (if any)

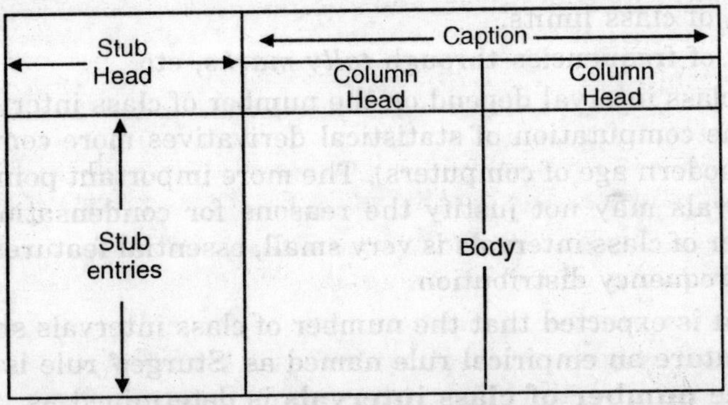

A general format of a table is given in Illustration 3. An ideal table should have (1) title (2) stub (3) caption (or box head) (4) body.

(iv) Frequency Table and its construction

In the presence of bulky data, making it difficult for ready comprehension, it is a general practice to classify the data according to class intervals and then constructing a frequency table, a popular method of condensation/summarisation of data. This sort of technique of condensation is not without pitfalls. If the class intervals are very evide, there is every likelihood that the essential features of data may be concealed behind the summarization, thus making the statistical analysis deceptive and arriving at conclusions, which are far from reality.

Consider monthly income data of 1000 households in a large community. Suppose 250 households have monthly income between 3000 and 4000 rupees. The interval written as Rs. 3000 — Rs. 4000 is called a *class interval* with Rs. 3000/- as the *lower limit* and Rs. 4000/- as the *upper limit*. The difference between the upper limit and the lower limit is defined as *size of the class interval* or *length of the class interval*.

The class intervals may be either continuous or discontinuous. Considering income data the intervals such as

1000-2000, 2000-3000, 3000-4000, 4000-5000, ... are continuous class intervals and intervals such as

1000-1999, 2000-2999, 3000-3999, ... etc. are discontinuous class intervals.

What should be the nature of class intervals either continuous or discontinuous depends on the variable whose values are under consideration for the construction of frequency distribution. For example, if the researcher wants to construct frequency distribution of the heights of individuals, it is suggested that one should use continuous class intervals because height is regarded as a continuous variable. Further, if examination scores or marks (taking only integer values) are under consideration, one should necessarily take the help of discontinuous class intervals. However, in practice, the researchers in general do not make any distinction between continuous and discontinuous while forming frequency distribution for data generated by a discontinuous variable. In forming frequency distribution with continuous class intervals, a rule must be formed whether to include the upper limit of the class in the concerned interval or in the succeeding one. It may be mentioned here that all continuous random variables are discontinuously observed.

The *principal steps* in the construction of frequency distribution are :

(*i*) decision as to number and size of class intervals.

(*ii*) selection of class limits.

(*iii*) counting of frequencies through *tally marks*, etc.

Size of the class interval depend on the number of class intervals. Too many class intervals make the computation of statistical derivatives more complicated and tedius (of course not in modern age of computers). The more important point is that large number of class intervals may not justify the reasons for condensation/summarization of data. If the number of class intervals is very small, essential features of the data may be concealed in the frequency distribution.

In practice it is expected that the number of class intervals should not exceed 15. In statistical literature an empirical rule named as 'Sturges' rule is mentioned. According to this rule the **number of class intervals** is determined as

$$I = 1 + (3.222 \log_{10} N),$$

where N is the number of observations.

Hence, the **size of the class interval** is found as

$$i = \frac{X_{max} - X_{min}}{I},$$

X_{min} and X_{min} are maximum and minimum values in the set of observations.

After class limits of the class intervals are fixed, the number of observations falling in each class interval is counted by using 'Tally marks', which is an oldest method of counting in groups of five observations (~~||||~~).

For instance, given the following observations (number of years of executive experience)

21, 25, 12, 19, 8, 6, 20, 19, 22

18, 17, 9, 11, 14, 12, 13, 12, 10, 14
10, 11, 13, 13, 11, 15, 16, 18, 17, 15, 18

The frequency distribution is shown in Table 6.6.

TABLE 6.6.
FREQUENCY DISTRIBUTION

	Tally Mark	Frequency
5 — 10	|||	3
10 — 15	~~||||~~ ~~||||~~ |||	13
15 — 20	~~||||~~ ~~||||~~	10
20 — 25	||||	4
Total		30

The frequency distribution may consist of equal sized class intervals or unequal class intervals. The equal sized class intervals help comparison of frequencies in different class intervals. The beginning and end class intervals may be either open or closed. In open ended class intervals the beginning class interval is written as 'Less than the lower limit' of the succeeding class interval and the end class interval is expressed as 'Greater than or equal to' the upper limit of the preceding class interval.

ILLUSTRATION 4. A frequency distribution of marks secured in 'statistics' examination with open ended class intervals.

Class Interval	Frequency
< 30	5
30 — 40	10
40 — 50	18
50 — 60	12
60 — 70	8
70 — 80	5
≥ 80	2
Total	60

ILLUSTRATION 5. ***A frequency distribution with discontinuous class interval.***

Class Interval	Frequency
0 — 29	5
30 — 39	10
40 — 49	18
50 — 59	12
60 — 69	8
70 — 79	5
Total	58

ILLUSTRATION 6. ***Frequency distribution with continuous class intervals.***

Class Interval	Frequency
0 — 30	5
30 — 40	10
40 — 50	18
50 — 60	12
60 — 70	8
70 — 80	5
Total	58

Relative frequency and cumulative frequency

Relative frequency *is defined as the ratio of frequency in a particular class intervals the total frequency in a data set.*

Cumulative frequency *is the consecutive addition of class frequencies when the class intervals in a frequency distribution are either in increasing or decreasing order.* The computations of relative frequency and cumulative frequency are shown in Table 6.7.

TABLE 6.7.

Class Interval (Salary in Rs.)	Number of employees (f)	Relative frequency	Cumulative frequency (greater than type)	Cumulative frequency (less than type)
7,000—9,000	14	$\frac{14}{237} = 0.0591$	14	237
9,000—11,000	49	$\frac{49}{237} = 0.2067$	63	223
11,000—13,000	101	$\frac{101}{237} = 0.4262$	164	174
13,000—15,000	43	$\frac{43}{237} = 0.1814$	207	73
15,000—17,000	14	$\frac{14}{237} = 0.0591$	221	30
17,000—19,000	10	$\frac{10}{237} = 0.0422$	231	16
19,000—21,000	6	$\frac{6}{237} = 0.0253$	237	6
Total	237	1.0000		

Naturally, sum of the relative frequency must be equal to unity. The greater than type cumulative frequency column shows that there are 14 employees whose salaries are less than Rs. 9000/-, 63 employees whose salaries are less than Rs. 11000/-, and so on, where as the less than type cumulative frequency column shows that there are 237 employees whose salaries are more than Rs. 7000/-, 223 employees whose salaries are more than Rs. 9000/- and so on.

6.5.4. Graphical Representation of Data

The graphs provide an alternative method of representing data in a condensed and summary form. **A graph is a scale-dependent geometrical figure and provides a visual presentation of statistical data.** As compared to tables the graphs point out more vividly the nature, characteristics and variability in data and also inherent relationship among different phenomena. They facilitate comparison of spatial and time series data.

Graphs are immensely useful to depict economic relationship explicitly through lines and have become indispensable tools for economic analysis (*e.g.* price vrs demand, income vrs expenditure, time vrs population, time vrs agricultural production, economic development vrs population growth, etc.)

Graphs with more than two variables lose their ready recognisability and are not in common use.

Techniques of Construction

The graphs are plotted against background of a **grid** *i.e. a network of horizontal and vertical lines*. The grids may form squares or rectangles. The variation in magnitude are shown in two directions : horizontal direction (*i.e.* along X- axis) and vertical direction (*i.e.* along Y-axis). **As a convention, the dependent variable is usually represented in Y- axis and independent variable along X-axis.** The scales used for both the axes may be same or different. However, the choice of scales depends on the maker and should be of moderate size for ready comprehension and should be such that it would be possible to draw the graph on a limited piece of paper. After the axes are drawn the points are plotted referring to the pointed values and then joined by lines or curves. An ideal graph should be self explanatory and drawn neatly with indication of scales on both axes and a clear and unambiguons title, head note, foot notes and source note at suitable places in the body. All descriptions used in graph should be written horizontally.

Types of graphs

According to the nature of data represented, the graphs may be classified as :

(*i*) graphs with time series or historigram (Fig. 6.1).
(*ii*) graphs with two variables other than time series graph (Fig. 6.2).
(*iii*) frequency graph (histogram) (Fig. 6.3)

ILLUSTRATION 7. ***Represent time series data in Table 6.8 graphically***

TABLE 6.8
Foreign Investment Inflows (in million US dollars)

Year	Direct Investment (in million US dollars)
1996-97	2821
1997-98	3557

1998-99	2462
1999-00	2155
2000-01	4029
2001-02	6131
2002-03	4660

Source : Reserve Bank of India

Solution. Time series graph is shown in Fig. 6.1

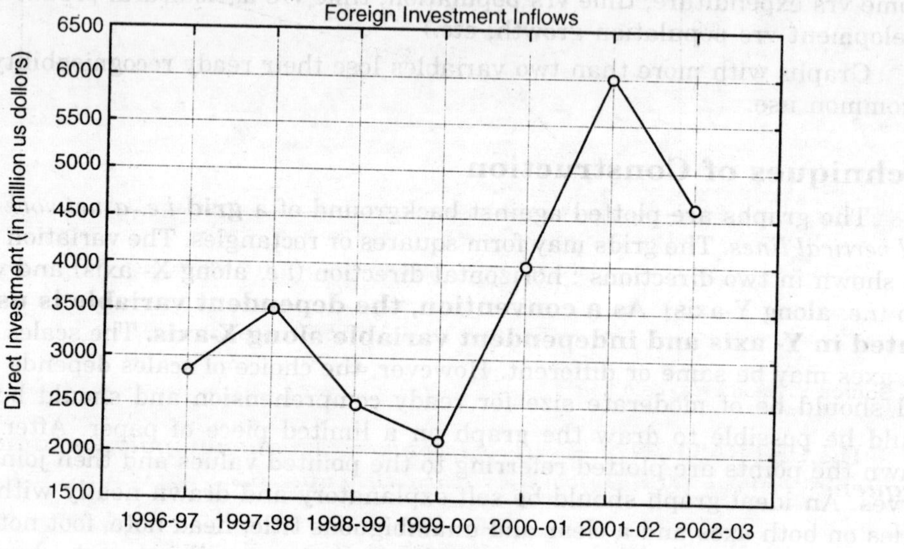

Fig. 6.1 Time series graph

Source : Reserve Bank of India

ILLUSTRATION 8. ***Draw two variable graph using data in Table 6.9.***

TABLE 6.9
Expenditure on advertisement vrs. sales

Expenditure on advertisement in thousand Rs.	**Sales (in thousand Rs.)**
16	260
17	280
19	290
23	310
25	340

Source : Hypothetical

Solution : Fig. 6.2.

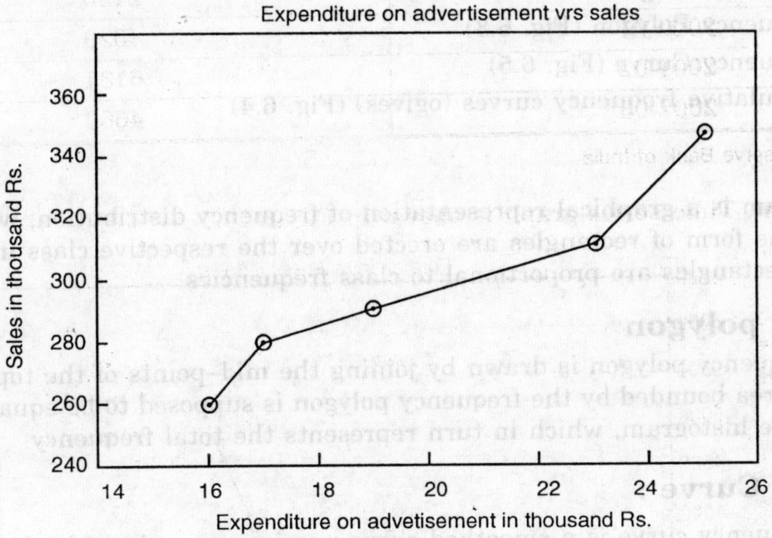

Fig. 6.2 Two variables graph

Source : Hypothetical data

ILLUSTRATION 9. ***Draw histogram, frequency polygon and cumulative frequency curves (Ogives), using data in Table 6.7.***

TABLE 6.10
Frequency distribution of monthly basic salary of employees in a business establishment

Class Interval (Rs.)	Frequency	*Cumulative Frequency (greater than type)*	Cumulative Frequency (less than type)
7000-9000	14	14	237
9000-11000	49	63	223
11000-13000	101	164	174
13000-15000	43	207	73
15000-17000	14	221	30
17000-19000	10	231	16
19000-21000	6	237	6

Solution : Fig. 6.3 and Fig. 6.4.

Inspection of the graphs of frequency distribution often brings out features that are not immediately apparent from the data themselves. Aside from the fact that such a graph presents a good over all picture of the data, it can also emphasize irregularities and unusual features such as outliers.

Important frequency graphs are :

- Histogram (Fig. 6.3)
- Frequency Polygon (Fig. 6.3)
- Frequency Curve (Fig. 6.5)
- Cumulative frequency curves (ogives) (Fig. 6.4)

Histogram :

Histogram is a graphical representation of frequency distribution, where the frequencies in the form of rectangles are erected over the respective class intervals. The areas of the rectangles are proportional to class frequencies.

Frequency polygon

The frequency polygon is drawn by joining the mid–points of the tops of the rectangles. The area bounded by the frequency polygon is supposed to be equal to the area bounded by the histogram, which in turn represents the total frequency.

Frequency Curve :

The frequency curve is a smoothed curve passing approximately through the extreme points of the frequency polygon and the area bounded by the frequency curve and the X-axis represents the total frequency.

Cumulative Frequency Curve :

The cumulative frequency curve is drawn by plotting cumulative frequencies greater than type/less than type against the lower class limits/upper class limits of the class intervals. The cumulative frequency curves are also called **ogives**.

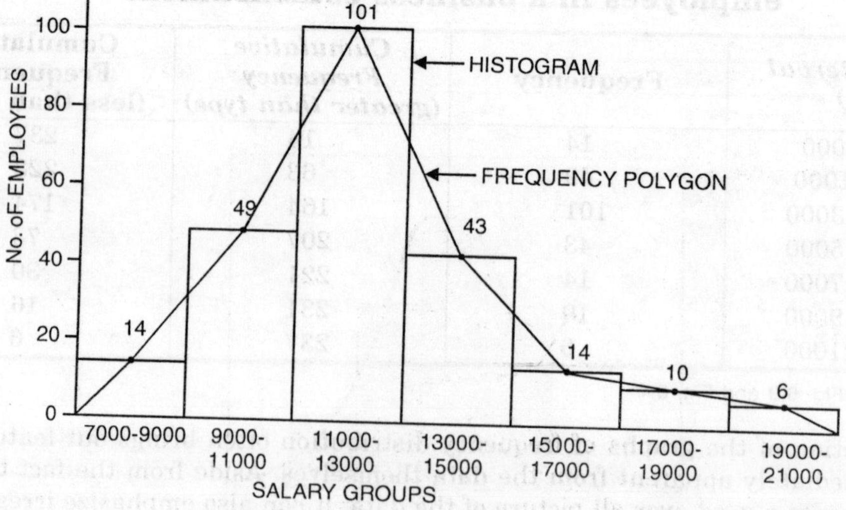

Fig. 6.3. Histogram and Frequency Polygon

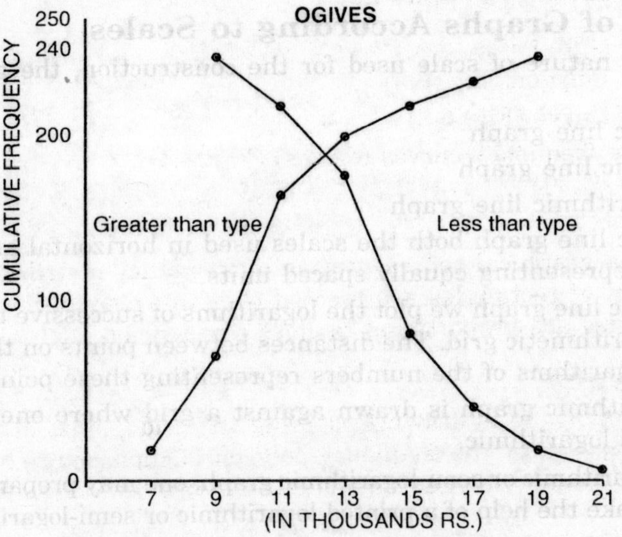

Fig. 6.4. Cumulative Frequency Curves.

ILLUSTRATION 10. ***Given below the frequency distribution of number of defective electronic tubes in 20 lots, each of size 100.***

Draw a histogram and superimpose a smoothed frequency curve.

TABLE 6.11

Frequency distribution of defective tubes

Class Interval (Defective tubes)	Frequency of Lots
0–5	1
5–10	5
10–15	7
15–20	5
20-25	2
Total	20

Solution : Fig. 6.5.

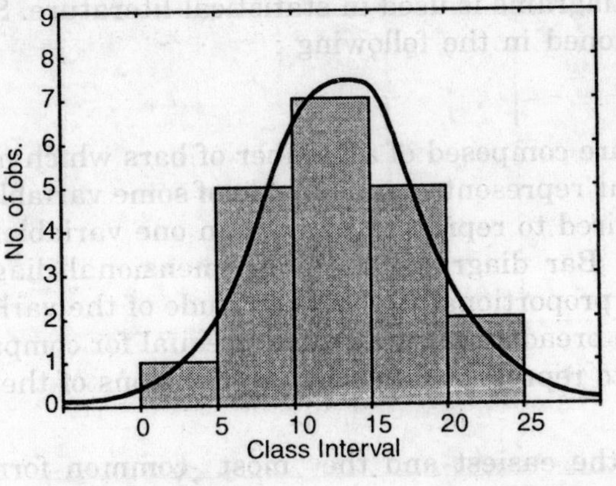

Fig. 6.5. Histogram and Frequency Curve.

Classification of Graphs According to Scales

According to nature of scale used for the construction, the graphs may be classified as

(*a*) arithmetic line graph

(*b*) logarithmic line graph

(*c*) semi-logarithmic line graph

In arithmetic line graph both the scales used in horizontal and vertical axes are arithmetic scales representing equally spaced units.

In logarithmic line graph we plot the logarithms of successive units (both in X-axis and Y-axis) on an arithmetic grid. The distances between points on this scale are distances between the logarithms of the numbers representing these points.

A semi-logarithmic graph is drawn against a grid where one scale is arithmetic and the other scale logarithmic.

To draw a logarithmic or semi-logarithmic graph, one may prepare the grid to be used for the purpose or take the help of a printed logarithmic or semi-logarithmic graph papers.

6.5.5. Diagrammatic Representation of Data

Besides graphical representation of data, **diagrams provide an alternative technique of visual representation of statistical data in a summary or condensed form.** Diagrams are easy to understand. They enable the data to be grasped quickly and facilitate ready comparison over time and space. The study of data by diagrams is a great attraction to a layman.

Types of Diagrams

Diagrams consist of various geometrical figures like rectangles, squares, circles, cubes, etc. and also pictures. These are suitably shaded and coloured and marked to make them more attractive and readily comprehensible.

While constructing a diagram it should be remembered that the diagram should be of normal size and drawn with proper scale, neatly and as accurate as possible.

Every diagram should have a serial number, title and sub-titles and a scale. The choice of a particular diagram to represent given statistical data depends on the nature of data and type of users for whom it is meant.

A large variety of diagrams is used in statistical literature. Some of the commonly used diagrams are mentioned in the following :

(a) Bar Diagrams

The bar diagrams are composed of a number of bars which may be either horizontal or vertical and each bar represents a magnitude of some variable with respect to time or space. When it is required to represent more than one variable, a group of bars may be used for the purpose. Bar diagrams are one-dimensional diagrams. The height or length of the bar is made proportional to the magnitude of the variable. The bars should be equally spaced and the breadths should be made equal for comparison. Further, a bar may also be sub divided to represent different sub-divisions of the total magnitude represented by the bar.

Bar diagrams are the easiest and the most common form of diagrams representing business and economic data.

The important bar diagrams generally used in practice are :

(*i*) Simple bar diagram
(*ii*) Compound or component bar diagram
(*iii*) Percentage bar diagram
(*iv*) Multiple bar diagram
(*v*) Deviation bar diagram

Simple bar diagrams represent aggregate values of a single phenomenon. Compound bar diagrams consist of sub-divided bars and each sub-division represents a component of the aggregate. In percentage bar diagrams each component is expressed as the percentage of the total.

A **Pareto Chart** is a bar diagram showing groups of error causes arranged by their frequencies of occurrence. This is used in quality/system improvement process and is constructed by simply counting data from observations.

Multiple bar diagrams consist of multiple bars representing aggregates of two or more interrelated phenomena.

Deviation bar diagrams are used to show certain quantities which have both positive or negative values, *e.g.* profit and loss, surplus and deficit, import and export, etc. For ready recognisability the positive and negative values are shown in opposite directions.

ILLUSTRATION 11. (Simple Bar Diagram)

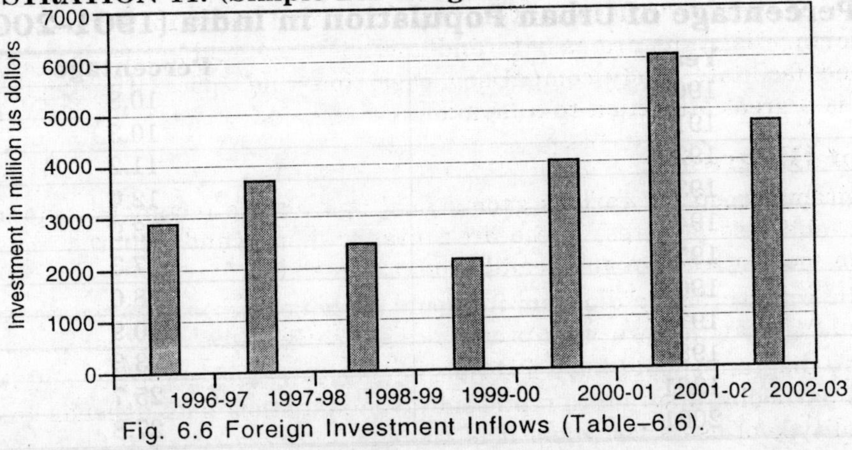

Fig. 6.6 Foreign Investment Inflows (Table–6.6).

ILLUSTRATION 12. (Multiple Bar Diagram)

Draw Multiple Bar Diagram using data in Table 6.12.

TABLE 6.12

Trends in Foreign Institutional Investment

Period	Gross Purchase (Rs. Billion)	Gross sale (Rs. Billion)
1999-00	568.56	467.34
2000-01	740.51	641.16
2001-02	499.20	411.5
2002-03	470.50	443.71
2003-04	1448.50	990.94

Source. Reserve Bank of India

Solution. Multiple bar diagram shown in Fig. 6.7.

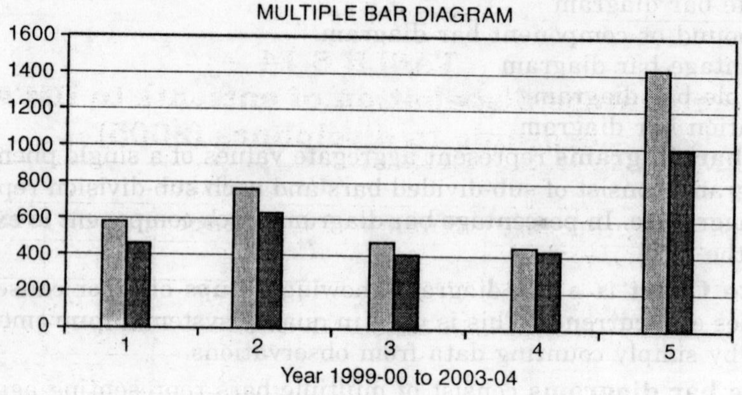

Fig. 6.7 Gross purchase/sales

ILLUSTRATION 13. ***Draw percentage bar diagram using data in Table 6.13***

TABLE 6.13
Percentage of Urban Population in India (1901–2001)

Year	Percentage
1901	10.8
1911	10.3
1921	11.2
1931	12.0
1941	13.9
1951	17.3
1961	18.0
1971	10.9
1981	23.3
1991	25.7
2001	27.8

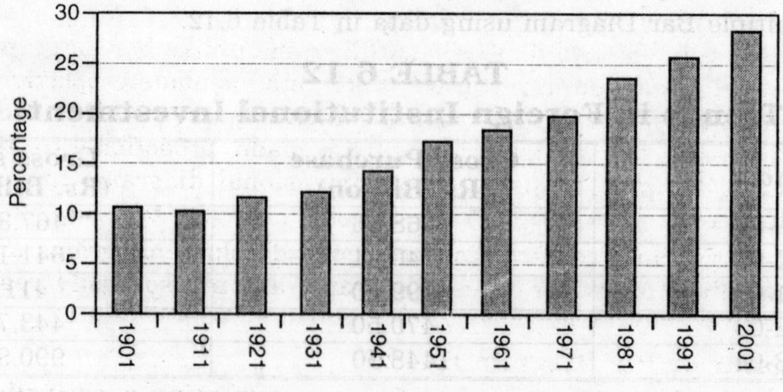

Fig. 6.8. Percentage of urban population in India (1901–2001).

ILLUSTRATION 14. ***Draw compound bar diagram using data in Table 6.14***

TABLE 6.14
Percentage distribution of entrants to IIM's according to disciplines (2005)

IIM	Percentages					
	Engineering	**Commerce**	**Science**	**Arts**	**Others**	**Total**
Ahmedabad	76	15	4	3	2	100
Bangalore	77	11.5	3.1	1.6	6.8	100
Kolkata	77	10	6	3	4	100
Indore	62.5	17.9	8	2.7	8.9	100
Kozhikode	73	13	5	4	3	100
Lucknow	74.89	12.79	7.31	1.83	3.19	100

Source : Business Today, April, 24, 2005

Solution Fig. 6.9

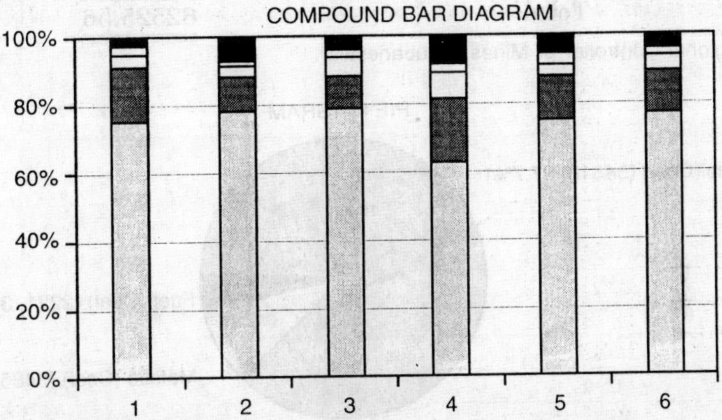

Fig. 6.9. Percentage distribution of entrants to IIM's according to disciplines, 2005

(*b*) Area and Volume Diagrams :

Area diagrams are two dimensional diagrams unlike bar diagrams. The area of each geometrical figure (square, rectangle, circle, etc.) is made proportional to the magnitude it represents. Three dimensional diagrams are called **volume diagrams** where the volume of the geometrical figure is made propotional to the given magnitude. The most common forms of three-dimensional diagrams are cubes, spheres, cylinders, cones, etc.

The calculation and construction of area and volume diagrams are cumbersome and time consuming. Moreover, these diagrams are not so easily readable like bar diagrams.

(*c*) Angular or Pie Diagram :

Sub-division of a total numerical figure representing a particular quantitative phenomenon into different segments can be well represented with the help of a **pie diagram**, which resembles a Pie (a particular type of British sweet dish). The total magnitude is made equivalent to the angle at the centre of the circle *i.e.* 360° and each component is represented by an angle, whose magnitude is a fraction of this amount. The sectors so formed by the division of total angle at the centre of a circle are also called **angular diagrams.**

Pie diagrams are generally used to show the sub-division of total agricultural production in a country, government budget expenditure under different heads, net domestic product from different sources, area irrigated under different sources of irrigation, etc. However, pie diagrams are not as effective as the bar diagrams in showing comparison among different components of an aggregate. It is **not** advisable to show large number of sub- divisions in a pie diagram, because that will not make the comparison readily comprehensible.

ILLUSTRATION 15. ***Draw pie diagram to represent value of Minerals produced in India (2003-2004) in Crores Rupees***

	India
Fuel (Coal)	54818.29
Metallic	5486.14
Non-Metalic	2221.13
Total	62525.56

Source : Regional Controller of Mines, Bhubaneswar.

PIE DIAGRAM

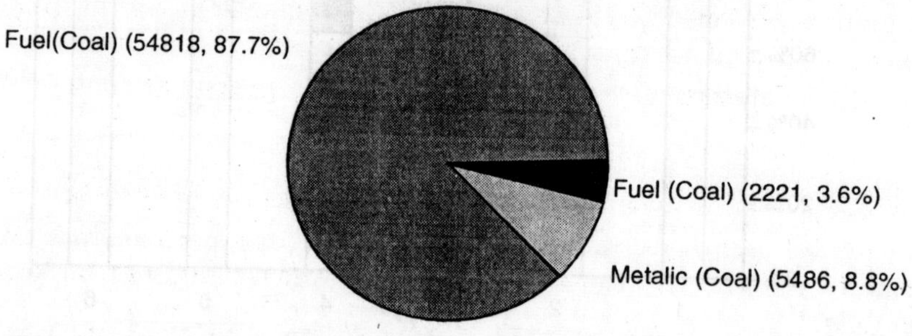

Fig. 6.10. Value of minerals produced in India, 2003-2004 in crores of rupees

(*d*) Pictorial Diagrams :

Pictorial diagrams are most popular and attractive, though not very accurate method of representing statistical facts. Appropriate proportionate pictures and symbols are used to represent different types of data.

(*e*) Statistical Maps

Maps showing statistical facts on geographical or regional basis are called **statistical maps** or **cartograms**. The statistical factss are represented region wise through the help of different diagrams discussed earlier and also through different shades and colours. Regional variations are better marked and easily understood through statistical maps.

Choosing a Diagram :

There is no rigid rule as to which diagram should be used for representing a particular data. However, the nature of data, ease in comparison and type of users determine the choice. Further, Certain conventional and specialised uses make the task easier.

Bar diagrams are the simplest of all diagrams and are generally used to denote changes in one phenomenon.

Compound or component bar diagrams consist of sub-divided bars representing sub-divisions of a given phenomenon. It is desired that different components of each bar should be kept in some order for easy comparison.

Percentage bar diagrams are used when each component of a bar is expresed as the percentage of the aggregate. Relative changes are better shown in such diagrams.

Multiple bar diagrams are used to show changes in absolute values of two or more interrelated phenomena.

A pie diagram is popularly used to represent different propositions or percentages of a single aggregate.

Squares and circles are size diagrams and may be used to represent size figures. For example, plan outlays for different plan periods, agricultural production of different year or countries, etc. may be represented by such diagrams.

The three dimensional diagrams such as cubes, cones, rectangular solids, etc. are preferred when the difference between the smallest and largest size values is very large. Pictorial diagrams look attractive and are generally used to make the layman more conscious of the facts represented by data and their importance at a first glance. Much accuracy cannot be expected to be achieved through pictorial diagrams.

Cartograms or statistical maps are meant for geographical comparison of data.

EXERCISES

1. A company collects large volume of data on the performance of sales of his various products throughout the country and attitude of buyers towards its products.
What are the major steps the company should adopt towards data preparation for its subsequent analysis ?

2. Write a note on data entry formats and its utility in data preparation.

3. Describe different methods for the condensation/summarization of data.

4. What is classification of data ? What are objectives of classification ?

5. Explain with examples different kinds of classification.

6. What is seriation of data ? Distinguish between different methods of seriation with examples.

7. Discuss salient features of a table ? Differentiate between (*i*) general purpose tables and summary tables (*ii*) primary tables and derived tables. (*iii*) simple table and two way table.

8. What is a graph ? Mention technique of its construction and its utility in data analysis.

9. (*a*) Distinguish between different types of graphs with examples.

(*b*) Differentiate between historigram and histogram.

(*c*) Explain construction of important frequency graphs.

10. What are the advantages and limitations of diagrammatic presentation of data ?

11. What are major considerations in choosing a suitable diagram for data representation ? Discuss.

12. Differentiate between graphical and diagrammatical representation of data and their relative advantages and limitations.

13. What are different types of bar diagrams ? Explain their methods of construction.

14. Distinguish between circular diagram and pie diagram and their spheres of application.

15. The following data relate to business environment of National Agricultural Co-operative Marketing Federation of India, Ltd. (NAFED) during 2002-2003. Represent the data by suitable diagrams.

TABLE 6.15

Out right purchase and sales of NAFED (quantity in MT and value in crores of rupees)

Sl. No.	Commodity	Purchases		Sales	
		Quantity	Value	Quantity	Value
1	Foodgrains	437876	243	74,112	45
2	Pulses	47502	72	40,253	65
3	Oilseeds	83239	118	1,11,085	150
4	Horticulture	21047	9	6,745	3
5	Spices	3243	16	2,601	10
	Total	592907	458	2,34,796	273

Source. Annual Report 2002-2003, NAFED.

16. The following Table 6.14 shows the Labour Force Participation Rates (LFPR) for educated persons by sex and sector in India in 1999-2000.

TABLE 6.16

Educational Level	Rural		Urban	
	Male	Female	Male	Female
Literate below secondary	86.38	36.64	81.96	17.85
Secondary and higher secondary	74.66	19.47	68.23	12.72
Graduates and above	89.80	41.00	85.40	30.20

Source. National Sample Survey Organisation. The LFPRs for the person of age 15 years above.

Represent the table by suitable diagrams.

17. As per 1991 census data released by the office of Registrar general, India there were 10.26 and 1.03 million working children (Main and Marginal) in rural and uirban sector respectively belonging to both the sexes. These data relate to age group 5-14 years.

Out of 10.26 million workers in rural sector 8.13 million were main workers and 2.13 million marginal workers ; among 8.13 million main workers 4.96 million were males and 3.17 million females ; among 2.13 million marginal workers 0.50 million were males and 1.63 million females.
Further, out of 1.03 million working children in urban sector 0.95 million were main workers, out of which 0.25 million were females and among the marginal workers 0.05 million were females.
Represent the above data in a suitable table.

18. Represent graphically following vital rates over years based on Sample Registration System (office of the Registrar General, India) by sector in India.

TABLE 6.17

Year	Birth Rate			Death Rate			Natural Growth Rate		
	Rural	Urban	Total	Rural	Urban	Total	Rural	Urban	Total
1971	38.9	30.1	36.9	16.4	9.7	14.9	22.5	20.4	22.0
1981	35.6	27.0	33.9	13.7	7.8	12.5	21.9	19.2	21.4
1991	30.9	24.3	29.5	10.6	7.1	9.8	20.3	17.2	19.2
2001	27.1	20.2	25.4	9.0	6.3	8.4	18.0	13.9	17.0

19. Represent the following population data of India relating to 1991 and 2001 census by bar diagrams.

TABLE 6.18 (a) Population of India (in Millions)

1991		2001	
Male	Female	Male	Female
439.23	407.07	531.28	495.74

TABLE 6.18 (b) Literates per thousand population in India

1991			2001		
Male	Female	Total	Male	Female	Total
641	393	522	759	542	654

Source. Office of the Registrar General, India.

20. Compare graphically the expenditure (in rupees) incurred on education, health and social security and welfare services in India.

TABLE 6.19. : Expenditure (in rupees) on education, health and social security and welfare services in India

Year	Education	Health	Social Security and Welfare Services
1990–91	236	54	58
1991–92	256	57	64
1992–93	283	64	69

1993–94	309	70	79
1994–95	353	76	94
1995–96	400	85	114
1996–97	455	98	121
1997–98	508	112	132
1998–99	634	137	145
1999–00	701	156	160
2000–01	793	167	182

21. The following data relate to monthly expenditure of two families under different heads. Represent the data by suitable diagrams.

TABLE 6.20

Item of Expenditure	Family A (Expenditure in Rs.)	Family B (Expenditure in Rs.)
Food	5,000	5,400
Clothing	2,500	1,600
Rent	3,000	2,500
Education	2,000	1,600
Fuel and lighting	1,500	1,400
Others	500	500
Total	14,500	13,000

22. The following table shows the number of operational holdings by size classes—All India.

Draw (*a*) Histogram

(*b*) Frequency polygon

(*c*) Cumulative frequency graph.

TABLE 6.21 : Number of Operational Holdings by Size Clases

Category	Size of Holding (in hectares)	Number of holdings (Million)
Marginal	0–1.0	63.39
Small	1.0–2.0	20.09
Semi-Medium	2.0–4.0	13.92
Medium	4.0–10.0	7.58
Large	10.0 and above	1.65
Total	—	106.64

Source. Govt. of India, Ministry of Agriculture, Agricultural Statistics at a glance.

23. Compare the Agricultural growth Rates (1980–96) of the following countries is by a suitable diagrammatic reprosentation.

TABLE 6.22

Country	Growth Rate in %
China	5.86
Pakistan	4.00
USA	3.86
Thailand	3.70
Malaysia	3.39
Indonesia	3.23
India	3.10

24. Represent the following data relating to India's foreign trade by deviation bars.

TABLE 6.23

Year	Imports	Exports
1959–60	961	940
1960–61	1087	648
1961–62	958	677
1962–63	981	709

25. Graphically represent the Gross National Product (GNP) in crores of rupees and per capita National income (in rupees) at 1993-94 prices.

TABLE 6.24

Year	GNP (Rs. Crore) at 1993-94 prices	Per Capita National Income (Rs.) at 1993-94 prices
1991–92	6,91,143	7,212
1992–93	7,26,375	7,433
1993–94	7,69,265	7,690
1994–95	8,24,816	8,070
1995–96	9,96,961	8,489
1996–97	9,59,360	9,007
1997–98	10,05,945	9,244
1998–99	10,70,774	9,650
1999–00	11,36,840	10,068
2000–01	11,82,246	10,306
2001–02	12,57,043	10,754
2002–03	13,09,917	11,014

Source. Central Statistical Organisation.

26. The following table gives the frequency distribution of weekly wages of 200 workers of a factory.

TABLE 6.25

Monthly Wages in Rs.	Number of Workers
1500–2000	30
2000–2500	35
2500–3000	40
3000–3500	55
3500–4000	25
4000–4500	10
4500–5000	5
Total	200

(*a*) Draw ogives for the above data and determine from the graph the number of workers having monthly wages above Rs. 3,250 and number of workers having monthly income below Rs. 2,750.

(*b*) Draw histogram and frequency polygon.

27. What is coding ? How would you code closed questions and open-ended questions ? Explain.

28. Explain the terms : Transcribing, Data Cleaning, Data Entry.

29. Write a note on data editing.

30. How would you deal with 'Don't know answers' in survey findings ? Discuss.

31. How would you construct a frequency distribution ? Explain.

32. What are ogives ? What do they indicate ? Where do they intersect ?

□□□

CHAPTER

7

BASIC DESCRIPTIVE STATISTICS

7.1. Introduction

What is statistics ? *The object of statistics is information. The objective of statistics is the understanding of information contained in the data.*

Famous statistician-scientists Professor Egon Pearson and Professor Sir Maurice Kendall have defined statistics as *'the study of collective character of population and the science of collective and group properties'* besides a very much meaningful definition from a famous psychologist S.S. Stevens who referred to statistics as *'a straight forward discipline designed to amplify the power of common sense in the discernment of order amid complexity.'* This complexity further found place in the writings of Sir Maurice Kendall, when he described statistics as 'the matrix of quantitative knowledge of nearly everykind, as the principal instrument yet devised by man for bringing within his grasp the terrifying complexity of things and relations between things, and a powerful illuminant, of the process of rational thought itself.'

Variability and uncertainty are two sides of the same coin and together are the hallmark of a statistical problem. It is this which gives statistics right entry to almost everysphere of human endeavour. In the words of Professor R.A. Fisher the statistical science is a peculiar aspect of human progress which gave 20th century its special character, turning towards statisticians in its more important activities.

The gambling instinct is deeply embedded in the human psyche. Much of the excitement of life is derived from uncertainty. From the games of chance to investment plans we are constantly engaged in choice and chance. That is why, business environment around the world look towards statistics discipline to seek caution and judicious decisions in the face of uncertainty, which is a product of random phenomena, much of which can only be approximated, presumably in best possible manner.

With this back ground the **function of statistics** is to collect observations on phenomena of interest, summarize the information, ignoring unnecessary details to avoid bulkiness and unweildy nature of data and finally to compute necessary statistical derivatives to describe the data, highlighting its essential features.

Besides the classification, seriation and tabulation of data and their representation through graphs and diagrams, there may be further necessity of calculating certain important statistical derivatives (numerical quantities) like percentages, rates, ratios, indices, averages/measures of location/measures of central tendency, measures of variation/dispersion and analytical ones such as differences, correlation coefficient, regression coefficient, etc. to lead to ultimate reduction of data. Such reduction to some numerical quantities is useful for the sophisticated analysis and interpretation of data.

Thus, descriptive statistics provides a clear, concise, useful and informative picture of a mass of numerical figures.

In modern days statistics is no longer restricted to only descriptive statistics, but has entered into arena of scientific disciplines dealing with inductive methods. Inductive reasoning rests on reasoning from partial to the general and is a powerful tool for prediction and to take decision under uncertainty. This has given rise to theory of statistical inference, which aims at deriving conclusions on the basis of insufficient observations, a part of totality of all possible observations. Inductive statistics has been playing a very useful role in the analysis of many diverse problems in economics, business and social studies. Calculation of descriptive statistics is always fore-runner to the analysis with inductive methods.

7.2 Rate, Ratio and Proportion :

Rates, ratios and proportions are relative numbers for better understanding of sets of data over time and space. Rate is a most commonly used measure to indicate the speed of occurrence of events in the population. Rates express the number of events (E) occurred in a population of size P referred to a given period of time and is computed as

$$\text{Rate} = \frac{E}{P}.$$

Sometimes a constant 100 or 1000 is multiplied with rate to make it a fraction of 100 or 1000 rather than fraction of unit.

The concept of rate is associated with dynamic phenomena such as growth, birth, death, prevalence of disease etc. The economic growth, industrial growth, agricultural growth, business growth and demographic growth rates are most popular terms in socio-economic studies. Rate is a special ratio indicator towards rate of change of certain phenomena generally over period of time such as rate of economic growth, rate of interest, literacy rate, infant mortality rate, saving rate, unemployment rate, inflation rate, labour force participation rate etc.

In the business profession broad use is made of ratios and percentages to simplify numbers and make comparison more lucid. Ratio is a comparison of two numbers or measurements. For instance, in business studies we may discuss 'current ratio', which compares current assets with current liabilities. The ratio of one number x to another number y is written as x divided by y, *i.e.* $\frac{x}{y}$. Thus, ratio is a fraction and the fundamental laws of fractions may be applied to ratios. Financial analysis of firm data contains discussions on a number of financial ratios such as

$$\text{Current ratio} = \frac{\text{Current assets}}{\text{Current liabilities}},$$

$$\text{Quick ratio} = \frac{\text{Current Assets} - \text{Inventory}}{\text{Current Liabilities}},$$

$$\text{Debt ratio} = \frac{\text{Total Debt}}{\text{Total Assets}}, \text{ etc.}$$

In demographic studies we come across some important ratios such as sex ratio, maternal mortality ratio, dependency ratio, etc.

Sometimes it is useful to express ratios as percentages. A ratio is changed to percent by multiplying 100 with the ratio and then adding a symbol %.

A data set pertaining to observations on a variable has some intrinsic characteristics which can be best depicted by certain basic statistical measures. These measures besides providing estimates, help comparison with similar data and provide basis for making inferences about the characteristics of sampled population to which the data belong. As these measures describe the characteristics of data, they are called *descriptive statistics*, which may be broadly classified into :

- *Measures of central tendency / measures of central location.*
- *Measures of dispersion / variation.*
- *Measures of shape / skewness and kurtosis.*

7.3. Measures of Central tendency

The measures of central tendency are types of measures which show the average of the values/central values, in the data set and are also called measures of location average. These measures are Arithmetic Mean, Median, Mode, Geometric Mean and Harmonic Mean.

Arithmetic Mean

The arithmetic mean of a set of values is the sum of values divided by the total number of values and represents the average of the values in the data set.

For example, if we have monthly income of five households in a locality, given by Rs. 6,000, Rs. 8,000, Rs. 6,500, Rs. 4,500, Rs. 5,500, the average or arithmetic mean or simply mean income of these five households is defined by

$$\text{Arithmetic Mean} = \frac{\text{Sum of incomes of five households}}{\text{Number of households}}$$

$$= \frac{6{,}000 + 8{,}000 + 6{,}500 + 4{,}500 + 5{,}500}{5} \text{ Rs.}$$

$$= \text{Rs. } 6{,}100$$

Given a set of observations (ratio or interval data) $X_1, X_2, \ldots, X_n$,

Arithmetic Mean (A.M.) :

$$\overline{X} = \frac{X_1 + X_2 + \ldots + X_n}{n}$$

$$= \frac{\Sigma X_i}{n}$$

Median

Median is another measure of central location which divides a set of data into two equal parts and is the middle most value. Half of the values lie below the median and half above the median. To compute the median from a data set, the values are to be ordered either from lowest to highest or from highest to lowest.

Mode

Sometimes we may be interested in the most typical or the most frequent value in the data array or the value around which maximum concentration of items occurs. This value is called **Mode.** A garment manufacturer may like to know the size of men's shirts that has the maximum demand in the market, so that his production will have to concentrate around this shirt size. In a series of 6 observations—10, 15, 18, 15, 20, 15, the modal value is 15, because it is the most frequent value.

In the foregoing illustration, the monthly incomes of the households may be ordered as

Rs. 4,500, Rs. 5,500, Rs. 6,000, Rs. 6,500, Rs. 8,000

The median is the value of middle most observation *i.e.* $\frac{5+1}{2}$th observation *i.e.* value of 3rd observation, *i.e.* Rs. 6,000/-. There is no mode, because each value accurs only once in the series.

If the number of observations in the data array is even, the mean of two middlemost values is taken as the median. For instance, given a set of ordered observations 27, 35, 40, 42, 48 and 52, the median value is (40 + 42)/2 = 40

Thus in a set of n ordered observation, the value of $\frac{n+1}{2}$th observation is the median value, if n is odd. In case n is even, there is no middle most value. However, the average of the values of $\frac{n}{2}$th observation and $\left(\frac{n}{2}+1\right)$th observations may be approximately taken as the median value.

Arithmetic mean has a major disadvantage as a measure of central tendency in the sense that it is affected by extreme values *i.e.* outliers. For example, suppose we have observed four values—5, 8, 10 and 117. The Arithmetic mean is (5 + 8 + 10 + 117)/4 = 35, which does not seem to be a good average representing central value because values of three of the four observations —5, 8, 10 are much less numerically compared to the average 35. In such a situation one may compute median which is $\frac{8+10}{2}$ *i.e.* 9

Geometric Mean and Harmonic Mean :

Given a set of observation $X_1, X_2 \ldots\ldots X_n$., the geometric mean is defined by

$$\text{G.M.} = (X_1 \cdot X_2 \ldots . X_n)^{\frac{1}{n}}, \quad X_i > 0 \text{ for all } i$$

and the harmonic mean is defined by

$$\text{H.M.} = \frac{n}{\frac{1}{X_1} + \frac{1}{X_2} + ... + \frac{1}{X_n}},$$
$$X_i \neq 0 \text{ for all } i.$$

Note. Geometric mean and harmonic mean are useful measures to average rates and ratios and are not much affected by outliers.

Further,

$$\text{A.M.} > \text{G.M.} > \text{H.M.}$$

For example, given four observations 5, 8, 10 and 117,

$$\text{A.M.} = \frac{5 + 8 + 10 + 117}{4} = 35$$

$$\text{G.M.} = (5 \times 8 \times 10 \times 117)^{\frac{1}{4}} = (46{,}800)^{\frac{1}{4}}$$
$$= 14.71$$

and the Harmonic Mean,

$$\text{H.M.} = \frac{1}{\frac{1}{4}\left(\frac{1}{5} + \frac{1}{8} + \frac{1}{10} + \frac{1}{117}\right)} = 9.23$$

We have seen that the arithmetic mean is affected by extreme values in the data set. The effect is reduced substantially if geometric mean or harmonic mean is used as a method of averaging.

Geometric mean is the appropriate average of distributions which tend to be logarithmic in form. It is the correct average of percentage rate of increase and ratios.

The harmonic mean is useful when data are given in terms of rates. Sometimes, it is convenient to deal with data in kilometres per hour, units purchased per rupee, or units produced per hour.

The computation of geometric mean requires the values to be non zero positive, where as for the computation of harmonic mean, values must not be zero in magnitude.

EXAMPLE 7.1. A machine was purchased for Rs. 1,50,000/- in year 2000. Depreciation on the diminishing balance was charged @ 40% in the first year, 25% in the second year and 15% per annum during the next three years. What is the average depreciation charged during the whole period ?

Solution :

Since we are interested in finding the average rate of depreciation, geometric mean will be the most appropriate average.

TABLE 7.1.

Year	Diminishing Value (for a value of Rs. 100) X	Log X
2000	100 — 40 = 60	1.77815
2001	100 — 25 = 75	1.87506

2002	100 — 15 = 85	1.92941
2003	100 — 15 = 85	1.92941
2004	100 — 15 = 85	1.92941
		Σ log X = 9.44144

$$\text{Geometric Mean} = \text{Antilog}\left(\frac{\Sigma \log X}{N}\right)$$

$$= \text{Antilog}\left(\frac{9.44144}{5}\right)$$

$$= \text{Antilog}\,(1.8883) = 77.32$$

With the diminishing value Rs. 77.32, the depreciation will be

100 — 77.32 = 22.68%

Note : The geometric mean is the most appropriate measure of central tendency in averaging ratios and percentages.

EXAMPLE 7.2. In a factory a unit of work is completed by A in 5 minutes, by B in 8 minutes, by C in 7 minutes, by D in 10 minutes. Find the average number of units of work completed per minute.

Solution :

Harmonic mean is an appropriate method of averaging in the present problem.

Calculations :

TABLE 7.2.

X	1/X
5	0.200
8	0.125
7	0.143
10	0.100
	Σ 1/X = 0.568

Hence, the average number of units computed per minute is computed as

$$\text{Harmonic mean} = \frac{n}{\sum_{i=1}^{n} \frac{1}{X_i}}$$

$$= \frac{4}{0.568} = 7.04$$

Note : The harmonic mean is useful for computing the average rate of increase of profits, or average speed at which a journey has been performed, or the average price at which an article has been sold.

7.4. Measures of Dispersion/Variability

Dispersion implies spread or variability in the values of the items in the given data array. Suppose five households have monthly income Rs. 6,000, Rs. 6,500, Rs.

8,000, Rs. 4,500, Rs. 5,500. As these monthly incomes are not equal, there exists variation in the data set and some measures of variation/dispersion are required to measure the amount of variation/dispersion. If the five households have same monthly income, there is no variation or dispersion among the values and as such any measure to depict variation/dispersion ought to have zero value only.

Suppose there are n observations (interval or ratio data) having the values

$$X_1, X_2, \ldots, X_n.$$

The methods computation some important measures of dispersion are stated below.

Variance (σ^2) :

$$\sigma^2 = \frac{(X_1 - \overline{X})^2 + (X_2 - \overline{X})^2 + \ldots + (X_n - \overline{X})^2}{n}$$

$$= \frac{1}{n} \sum_{i=1}^{n} (X_i - \overline{X})^2, \text{ where } \overline{X} = \frac{1}{n} \Sigma X_i$$

Standard deviation (σ)

$$\sigma = \sqrt{\frac{1}{n} \sum_{i=1}^{n} (X_i - \overline{X})^2},$$

where $\overline{X}$ is the arithmetic mean

Mean Absolute Deviation (MAD) :

$$\text{M.A.D.} = \frac{1}{n} \sum_{i=1}^{n} |X_i - \overline{X}|$$

Note : If a constant quantity is either added to or subtracted from $X_1, X_2, \ldots X_n$, the standard deviation and mean absolute deviation remain unchanged. Further, if a $X_1, X_2, \ldots, X_n$ are divided by a constant quantity say c, the standard deviation or mean deviation of the reduced data is to be multiplied by c for the final results.

Range (R) :

$$R = X_{max} - X_{min},$$

where X_{max} and X_{min} are maximum and minimum values in the set of observations. The range measures the spread of the data and is a very approximate measure.

Mean difference (Δ)

$$\Delta = \frac{1}{n(n-1)} \sum\sum_{i \neq j}^{n} |X_i - X_j|$$

The mean difference attributed to Gini, measures the intrinsic spread of the distribution independently of any central value.

Quartile deviation

The median divides the data array into two equal parts *i.e.* 50% of the observation lie above median and 50% lie below the median. The first quartile (Q_1) in an ordered data array is the value above which 75% of the values lie and below which 25% of the values lie. The second quartile (Q_2) is the median. The third quartile (Q_3) is the value below which 75% of the values lie and above which 25% of the values lie. Thus, the interquartile range is Q_3—Q_1.

The quartile deviation is

$$\text{Q.D.} = \frac{Q_3 - Q_1}{2}$$

EXAMPLE 7.3. Let us consider an example on monthly incomes of 10 households. The observations are :

Rs. 9,000, Rs. 7,500, Rs. 6,500, Rs. 8,600, Rs. 6,000, Rs. 7,400, Rs. 8,400, Rs. 9,500, Rs. 7,200, Rs. 6,800.

$$\text{Arithmetic Mean } (\overline{X}) = \Sigma X_i/n = \frac{76,900}{10}\text{ Rs.} = \text{Rs. } 7,690.$$

$$\text{Median (M)} = \text{Value of } \frac{n+1}{2}\text{th item}$$

$$= \text{value of } \frac{11}{2} (= 5.5)\text{th item}$$

$$= \text{Average of values of 5th and 6th item}$$

$$= \frac{\text{Rs. } 7,400 + \text{Rs. } 7,500}{2}$$

$$= \text{Rs. } 7,450/-$$

$$\text{Standard deviation } (\sigma) = \sqrt{\frac{1}{n}\sum_{i=1}^{n}(X_i - \overline{X})^2} = \sqrt{\frac{1}{n}\sum_{i=1}^{n} X_i^{\,2} - \overline{X}^2}$$

$$= \sqrt{\frac{1}{10}(60,311)\,10^4 - 5,91,361 \times 10^2}$$

$$= \sqrt{6,03,11,000 - 5,91,36,100} = \sqrt{11,74,900}$$

$$= \text{Rs. } 1,083.93$$

Mean absolute deviation (MAD) from mean

$$= \frac{1}{n}\sum_{i=1}^{n} | X_i - \overline{X} |$$

$$= \frac{1}{10}[1310 + 190 + 1190 + 910 + 1690 + 290 + 710 + 1810 + 490 + 890]$$

$$= \frac{1}{10}(9480) = \text{Rs. } 948$$

Range :

$$X_{max} - X_{min} = \text{Rs. } 9500 - \text{Rs. } 6000 = \text{Rs. } 3500$$

Mean absolute deviation from median

$$= \frac{1}{n}\sum_{i=1}^{n} | X_i - M |$$

$$= \frac{9{,}100}{10} = \text{Rs. } 910$$

Mean Difference :

$$MD = \frac{1}{n(n-1)} \sum\sum_{i \neq j}^{n} | X_i - X_j |$$

$$= \frac{61200}{10 \times 9} = \text{Rs. } 680$$

Quartile Deviation :

$$Q_1 = \text{Value of } \frac{n+1}{4}\text{th item in an ordered series.}$$

$$= \text{Value of } \frac{10+1}{4}\text{th item}$$

$$= \text{Value of 2.75th item}$$

$$= \text{Average of the values of 2nd item and 3rd item}$$

$$= \frac{\text{Rs. } 6{,}500 + \text{Rs. } 6{,}800}{2} = \text{Rs.}6{,}650/-$$

$$Q_3 = \text{Value of } \frac{3(n+1)}{4}\text{th item in an ordered series}$$

$$= \text{Value of } \frac{3 \times 11}{4}\text{th item}$$

$$= \text{Value of 8.25th item}$$

$$= \text{Average of the values of 8th and 9th item} = \frac{\text{Rs. } 8{,}600 + \text{Rs. } 9{,}000}{2}$$

$$= \text{Rs. } 8{,}800$$

$$\text{Interquartile Range} = Q_3 - Q_1 = \text{Rs. } 8{,}800 - \text{Rs. } 6{,}650 = \text{Rs. } 2{,}150$$

Quartile deviation = Semi-inter quartile Range

$$= \frac{Q_3 - Q_1}{2} = \text{Rs. } 1{,}075$$

Relative measures of dispersion

The measures of dispersion are measured in the same unit of the original set of observations. When it is required to compare the variations in two or more sets of data having varying units of measurement, it is desirable to construct some measures which are independent of the units of measurement. For example, if it is required to compare the veriations in annual income of households in a locality and the variations in size of the households in the same locality, the comparison with usual measures of dispersion lands into difficulties because the annual income is measured in rupees and the household size is measured in numbers.

The most popular relative measure of dispersion/variation is the coefficient of variation which is computed as

$$\text{Coefficient of variation (C.V.)} = \frac{\text{Standard deviation}}{\text{Mean}}$$

usually expressed in percentage. The coefficient of variation is meaningful if the variable is measured on a ratio scale.

In the foregoing Illustration the standard deviation is computed to be Rs. 1083.93 where as the mean is Rs. 7690/-

Therefore, the coefficient of variation is

$$\text{C.V.} = \frac{1083.93}{7690} \times 100$$

$$= 14.10\%.$$

Other *relative measures of dispersion* are :

(*i*) $\dfrac{\text{Mean Absolute Deviation (from mean)}}{\text{Mean}} = \dfrac{948}{7,690} = 0.1233$

(*ii*) $\dfrac{\text{Mean Absolute Deviation (from median)}}{\text{Median}} = \dfrac{91}{7,450} = 0.1221$

(*iii*) $\dfrac{Q_3 - Q_1}{Q_3 + Q_1} = \dfrac{8,800 - 6,650}{8,800 + 6,650} = \dfrac{2150}{15450} = 0.1392$

(*iv*) Coefficient of Range $= \dfrac{\text{Max. Value} - \text{Min. Value}}{\text{Max. Value} + \text{Min. Value}} = \dfrac{9500 - 6000}{9500 + 6000} = 0.2258.$

EXAMPLE 7.4. Monthly earnings of the employees of two factories in a locality are as follows :

Compute the arithmetic means and compare the variability in the monthly earnings

1st Factory Income of employees in 000' Rs. (X_1)	2nd Factory Income of employees in 000' Rs. (X_2)
4.2	2.5
2.5	3.2
5.2	5.5
6.4	3.5
3.8	6.2
7.5	8.0

8.2	4.2
4.5	6.5
	3.5
	8.5
	2.5

Solution :

$$\overline{X}_1 = \frac{\Sigma X_1}{n} = \frac{42.3}{8} = 5.29,\ \overline{X}_2 = \frac{\Sigma X_2}{n} = \frac{54.1}{11} = 4.92$$

$$\sigma_1 = \sqrt{\frac{\Sigma X_1{}^2}{n} - \left(\frac{\Sigma X_1}{n}\right)^2} = \sqrt{\frac{305.47}{8} - (5.29)^2}$$

$$= \sqrt{38.18 - 27.98} = 3.19$$

$$\sigma_2 = \sqrt{\frac{\Sigma X_2{}^2}{n} - \left(\frac{\Sigma X_2}{n}\right)^2} = \sqrt{\frac{930.82}{11} - (4.92)^2}$$

$$= \sqrt{84.62 - 24.21} = 7.77$$

$$CV\ (X_1) = (\sigma_1/\overline{X}_1) \times 100$$

$$= \frac{3.19}{5.29} \times 100 = 60.3\%$$

$$CV\ (X_2) = (\sigma_2/\overline{X}_2) \times 100$$

$$= \frac{4.92}{7.77} \times 100 = 63.3\%$$

There is more variability in the monthly earnings of the employees of the second factory compared to the monthly earnings of the employees of the first factory.

7.5. Computation of statistical derivatives from frequency distribution

While computing statistical derivatives from a frequency distribution, it is assumed that frequency in a class interval is lumped up in **mid-value** (middle of the class interval) or **class mark.**

Because of such assumptions involved in the process of computation of statistical derivatives from a frequency distribution, computations with the help of grouped frequency distribution might not be exact as compared with computations from the ungrouped data.

7.5.1. Measures of Central Tendency/Location

Arithmetic Mean

Let $X_1, X_2, \ldots\ldots, X_k$ represent the mid values of k class intervals with frequencies $f_1, f_2, \ldots\ldots, f_k$.

The arithmetic mean of X is defined as

$$\text{A.M.} = \overline{X} = \frac{f_1 . X_1 + f_2 . X_2 + ... + f_k . X_k}{f_1 + f_2 + ... + f_k} = \frac{\sum_{i=1}^{k} f_i X_i}{\sum_{i=1}^{k} f_i}$$

If X_1, X_2, ..., X_k are measured from a fixed point A, define $d_i = X_i - A$. Then,

$$\text{A.M.} = \overline{X} = A + \frac{f_1 . d_1 + f_2 . d_2 + ... + f_k . d_k}{f_1 + f_2 + ... + f_k}$$

$$= A + \frac{\sum_{i=1}^{k} f_i d_i}{\sum_{i=1}^{k} f_i}.$$

If further a scale factor c is introduced, define

$$d'_i = \frac{X_i - A}{c}$$

Then,

$$\text{AM} = A + c \frac{\Sigma f_i d_i'}{\Sigma f_i}$$

Weighted Arithmetic Mean :

When the items, whose values are included in the calculation of arithmetic mean, are not of equal importance, it is advisable to calculate the weighted mean instead of unweighted simple mean by attaching some numerical coefficients or weights to values of items. If w_1, w_2, ..., w_n are weights of n items in a series, whose values are $x_1, x_2, ..., x_n$, then the weighted mean is calculated as

$$\bar{x}_w = \frac{w_1 x_1 + w_2 x_2 + \ldots + w_n x_n}{w_1 + w_2 + .. + w_n} = \frac{\Sigma w_i x_i}{\Sigma w_i}$$

If $w_1 = w_2 = ... = w_n = w$ (say),

then $$\bar{x}_w = \frac{w(x_1 + x_2 + \ldots + x_n)}{nw} = \frac{x_1 + x_2 + \ldots + x_n}{n} = \bar{x}$$

A rational choice of weights depends upon a valid criterion or values of a related variable. Use of arbitrary weights leads to wrong conclusions.

The arithmetic mean calculated from a frequency distribution is nothing but a weighted mean with $w_i = f_i$.

The weighted arithmetic mean finds application in the calculation of standardised rates.

ILLUSTRATION 1. *The following data show the number of years of executive experience in a large business establishment.*

TABLE 7.3.

Class Interval	f	Mid-Value X	d = X–12.5	$d' = \frac{X-12.5}{5}$	$f.d$	$f.d'$
5—10	3	7.5	—5	—1	—15	—3
10—15	13	12.5	0	0	0	0
15—20	10	17.5	5	+ 1	50	10
20—25	4	22.5	10	+ 2	40	8
Σ	30	—	—	—	75	15

$$\text{A.M.} = \frac{f_1 \cdot X_1 + f_2 \cdot X_2 + f_3 \cdot X_3 + f_4 \cdot X_4}{f_1 + f_2 + f_3 + f_4}$$

$$= \frac{3\,(7.5) + 13\,(12.5) + 10\,(17.5) + 4\,(22.5)}{3 + 13 + 10 + 4}$$

$$= \frac{450}{30} = 15$$

A.M. (changing the origin or taking deviation from 12.5)

$$= A + \frac{\Sigma f_i\, d_i}{\Sigma f_i}$$

$$= 12.5 + \frac{75}{30} = 12.5 + 2.5$$

$$= 15$$

A.M. (changing origin and using scale factor c)

$$= A + c\,\frac{\Sigma f_i\, d_i'}{\Sigma f_i}$$

$$= 12.5 + 5\left(\frac{15}{30}\right)$$

$$= 12.5 + 2.5 = 15$$

Median

Median is a type of average/measure of central tendency and is a value of the concerned variable, which divides the frequency distribution into two equal parts.

As exact value of the median is not possible to locate in a grouped frequency distribution, it is required to use a numerical interpolation formula such as

$$\boxed{\text{Median} = M_e = l_1 + \frac{l_2 - l_1}{f}\,(m - c),}$$

where l_1 = lower limit of the median class
l_2 = upper limit of the median class
f = frequency in the median class
$m = \frac{N}{2}$, where N is the total frequency
c = cumulative frequency in the class preceding the median class.

TABLE 7.4

	Class Interval	f	Cumulative frequency
	5 — 10	3	3
median class →	10 — 15	13	16
	15 — 20	10	26
	20 — 25	4	30
		30	

Median = X_{Me}

$$= l_1 + \frac{l_2 - l_1}{f}(m - c)$$

$$= 10 + \frac{15 - 10}{13}(15 - 3)$$

$$= 10 + \frac{5}{13} \times 12 = 10 + \frac{60}{13}$$

$$= 10 + 4.62 = 14.62$$

Note : (*i*) In the computation of median the class intervals should be ordered and continuous. In case of discontinuous class intervals, these intervals should be made continuous by adding 0.5 to the upper limit and subtracting 0.5 from the lower limit. (*ii*) The median is not affected by extreme values and also can be determined for the open-end distributions; whether the class intervals are equal or unequal. (*iii*) The median can not be computed as exactly as the mean and its reliability can not be so readily estimated.

Mode

The modal class is the class for which the frequency is maximum. To compute mode from the grouped frequency distribution with continuous class intervals, the numerical interpolation formula is to be adopted. As such,

$$X_{MO} = l_1 + i\,\frac{\Delta_1}{\Delta_1 + \Delta_2}$$

l_1 = lower limit of the modal class
i = size of the class interval
Δ_1 = difference between frequency in the modal class and the preceding class.
Δ_2 = difference between frequency in the modal class and the succeeding class.

Thus,

$$X_{MO} = 10 + 5.\frac{|13 - 3|}{|13 - 3| + |13 - 10|}$$

$$= 10 + 5 \frac{10}{10+3}$$

$$= 10 + \frac{50}{13} = 10 + 3.84$$

$$= 13.84.$$

Note : Like the median, the mode is not directly influenced by extreme items or by open-end distributions. It is only a rough estimate and has several short comings. For example, it can not be treated algebraically or tested for reliability.

Comparison of Arithmetic Mean, Median and Mode

For any frequency distribution the mean, median and mode may not be the same. They have different spheres of application. For the distribution having extreme values, the mean may not be taken as an appropriate measure. Moreover for distribution with open ended class intervals, arithmetic mean may not be justified as a good measure of average because of difficulties in locating mid-value for the open ended class intervals. In such situations median is usually preferred as an average. As a measure of average or central tendency mode is not very popular one, but may be used when the frequency in a particular class interval is very high and frequencies in other class intervals are negligible in number. In such situation mode may be preferred over both median and mean. Both median and mode use numerical interpolation formula, assuming that the frequency curve is a continuous one. For a symmetrical frequency distribution mean, median and mode are the same values. That is, the value that occurs most frequently and the value that divides the data in half are identical with the computed arithmetic mean. However, if we were to add a few high values or low values to same distribution, then it would be pulled up to the right or left, as the case may be, resulting either in positive or negative skewness. As the mean is influenced by each and every value, the additional high values would tend to increase the mean (*i.e.* move to the right on the continuous scale). The median which is a positional measure is responsive only to the number of items in the distribution. It would shift slightly to the right but only because of the number of items added, not because of their magnitude. The mode probably would remain exactly where it was previously. Thus, in a positively skewed distribution mean > median > mode and for a negatively skewed distribution mean < median < mode.

The choice between arithmetic mean and the median depends on the nature of the frequency curve. If the distribution is bell shaped and symmetrical or flat topped one with few extreme values, the arithmetic mean is the best choice, because it is less affected by sampling fluctuations. If the distribution is sharply peaked, i.e. the data cluster markedly at the middle or if there are abnormally small or larger values, the median has smaller sampling fluctuations than the arithmetic mean. That is, clustering around the median makes it more accurate and extreme values inflate the arithmetic mean.

However, the arithmetic mean should ordinarily be used because it is simple to calculate, rigidly defined, based on all observations and amenable to further statistical treatment, unless nature of data strongly prohibits its use.

Geometric Mean

$$\text{G.M.} = \left(X_1^{f_1} . X_2^{f_2} .... X_k^{f_k}\right)^{\frac{1}{f_1 + f_2 + ... + f_k}}, \quad X_i > 0 \text{ for all } i.$$

Harmonic Mean

$$\text{H.M.} = \frac{f_1 + f_2 + ... + f_k}{\sum_{i=1}^{k} f_i \left(\frac{1}{X_i}\right)}$$

with $X_i \neq 0$

7.5.2. Measures of Dispersion/Variation

Besides the measures of central tendency, a measure of dispersion is an important characteristic of a frequency distribution indicating amount of variability in the data set. Two series or two frequency distributions may have same average, but different amount of variability. In business research like any other field of research the variability in the data set creates interest in the minds of analysts as to sources of variation and their further statistical treatment.

Various measures of dispersion or variation are variance, standard deviation, mean absolute deviation, range, quartile deviation, mean difference, etc. A good measure of dispersion should be based on all observations, rigidly defined, simple to understand, easy to calculae, less affected by sampling fluctuations and amendable to algebraic treatment. Due to their origin from the concept of distance, the measures of dispersion are always measured in positive quantities. A zero value for the measure implies and is implied by no variation.

Variance as a measure of dispersion is **measured in squared units** unlike other measures which preserve the original unit of measurement.

Variance, standard deviation and mean absolute deviation are computed with reference to a central position—a measure of central tendency.

Variance :

$$\sigma^2 = \frac{1}{\Sigma f_{ii}} \sum_{=1}^{k} f_i (X_i - \overline{X})^2$$

Standard Deviation :

$$\sigma = \sqrt{\frac{1}{\Sigma f_i} \sum_{i=1}^{k} f_i (X_i - \overline{X})^2},$$

where $\overline{X} = \frac{1}{\sum_{i=1}^{k} f_i} \sum_{i=1}^{k} f_i X_i$

Mean Absolute Deviation

$$\text{MAD} = \frac{1}{\sum_{i=1}^{k} f_i} \sum_{i=1}^{k} f_i \mid X_i - \overline{X} \mid$$

Note : Both standard deviation and the mean absolute deviation are invariant under the change of origin. If scale is changed, then the scale factor c is multiplied with the reduced standard deviation and mean absolute deviation.

Quartile Deviation

$$Q_i = l_1 + \frac{l_2 - l_1}{f}(q_i - c), \quad (i = 1, 2, 3)$$

where l_1 is the lower limit of the ith quartile class and l_2 is the upper limit of the ith quartile class; f is the frequency in the ith quartile class and c is the cumulative frequency in the class preceding the ith quartile class; $q_i = i \cdot \frac{n}{4}$.

Quartile Deviation is then defined by

$$\text{Q.D.} = \frac{Q_3 - Q_1}{2}$$

ILLUSTRATION 2.

Size of firm in crores of rupees	Number of firms
0—1	13
1—2	20
2—3	10
3—4	5
4—5	2
Total	50

Table 7.5
Computations of standard deviation, mean deviation and quartile deviation

Class Interval	f	Cum f	Mid-value X	f.X	X — $\bar{X}$	f.(X – $\bar{X}$)	(X – $\bar{X}$)^2	f.(X – $\bar{X}$)^2
0—1	13	13	0.5	6.5	—1.26	16.38	1.59	20.67
1—2	20	33	1.5	30.0	—0.26	5.20	0.07	1.40
2—3	10	43	2.5	25.0	0.74	7.40	0.55	5.50
3—4	5	48	3.5	17.5	1.74	8.70	3.03	15.15
4—5	2	50	4.5	9.0	2.74	5.48	7.51	15.02
Total (Σ)	50		—	88.0 $\bar{X}$ = 1.76	—	43.16	—	57.74

$$\sigma = \sqrt{\frac{57.74}{50}} = \sqrt{1.1548} = 1.0746$$

$$\text{MAD} = \frac{43.16}{50} = 0.8632$$

$$Q_1 = 0 + \frac{1-0}{13}(12.5 - 0)$$

$$= \frac{1}{13}(12.5) = 0.9615$$

$$Q_3 = 2 + \frac{3-2}{10}(37.5 - 33)$$

$$= 2 + \frac{1}{10}(4.5) = 2.045$$

$$\text{Quartile Deviation} = \frac{Q_3 - Q_1}{2}$$

$$= \frac{2.045 - 0.9615}{2} = 0.5418$$

LORENZ CURVE

It is a graphical method to study dispersion in special areas like income distribution, wage distribution, profit distribution etc., in economic and business studies. **Lorenz** curve was devised by Lorenz to study inequalities in the distribution of income, which resembles an ogive. Gini's coefficient is a summary statistics of the Lorenz curve.

For the construction of Lorenz curve, we have the following computations with the frequency distribution (Illustration 6).

The value of the variable and the corresponding frequencies are cumulated and expressed as percentages. On the x-axis per cent cumulative frequencies are represented and on the y-axis per cent cumulative values are represented. The paired values, per cent cumulative frequencies and per cent cumulative values are plotted and the resulting points are joined by a smooth free hand curve. The plotted graph will always deviate from the line of equal distribution which makes an angle of 45° with both the axes. The curve always lies below the line unless the distribution is uniform in which case the curve coincides with the line. The greater the distance of the curve from the line of equal distribution, the greater is the variability. Thus, the measure of variability is provided by the distance of the curve from the line of equal distribution. A frequency distribution is more variable than the other, if its curve deviates from the line of equal distribution more than the curve shown by the other frequency distribution.

ILLUSTRATION 3. *The following table represents the distribution of daily income of households in two different communities A and B of a locality. Draw the Lorenz curves and compare the variability.*

TABLE 7.6

Daily Income (Rs.)	Number of Households	
	Community A	Community B
450	30	45
550	50	66
600	70	75
700	20	54
800	20	45
900	10	15
	200	300

SOLUTION :

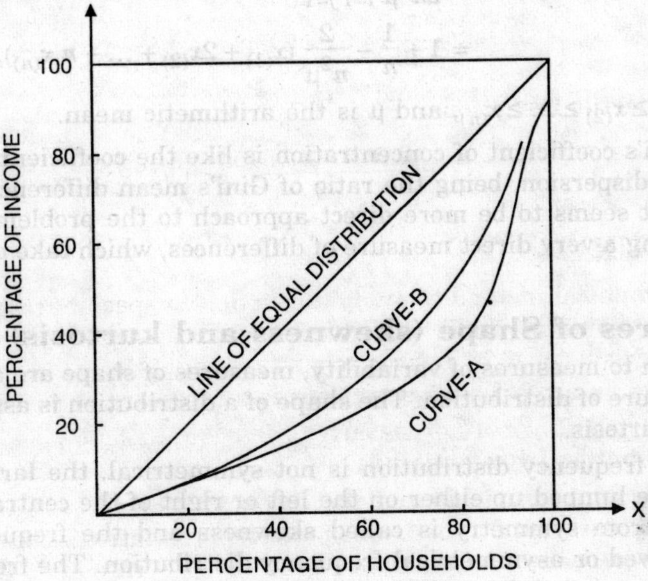

Fig. 7.1. Lorenz Curves

TABLE 7.7

Daily Income (Rs.)	Cumu-lative Income (Rs.)	Cumu-lative %	Community A			Community B		
			No. of House-holds	Cumu-lative	Cumu-lative %	No. of House-holds	Cumu-lative	Cumu-lative %
450	450	11.25	30	30	15	45	45	15
550	1000	25.00	50	80	40	66	111	37
600	1600	40.00	70	150	75	75	186	62
700	2300	57.50	20	170	85	54	240	80
800	3100	77.50	20	190	95	45	285	95
900	4000	100.00	10	200	100	15	300	100

The Lorenz curves are shown in Fig. 7.1 both for community A and community B. It is seen that the curve for community B is nearer to the line of equal distribution than the curve for the community A. Hence, the community A is more variable according to daily income of its households compared to the community B.

Gini's Coefficient of Concentration

Gini's coefficient of concentration in case of a set of n values of x, say $x_1, x_2, \ldots, x_n$ is exactly $\frac{1}{2}$ of the relative mean difference and is defined as

$$G = \frac{1}{2n^2\mu} \sum_{i=1}^{n} \sum_{j=1}^{n} |x_i - x_j|$$

$$= 1 + \frac{1}{n} - \frac{2}{n^2\mu}(x_{(1)} + 2x_{(2)} + \ldots + n\, x_{(n)}),$$

When $x_{(1)} \geq x_{(2)} \geq \ldots \geq x_{(n)}$, and μ is the arithmetic mean.

Thus, Gini's coefficient of concentration is like the coefficient of variation, a relative measure of dispersion, being the ratio of Gini's mean difference to twice the arithmetic mean μ. It seems to be more direct approach to the problem of measurement of inequalities, being a very direct measure of differences, which take care of the difference in every pair.

7.5.3. Measures of Shape (skewness and kurtosis)

In addition to measures of variability, measures of shape are also useful in understanding the nature of distribution. The shape of a distribution is assessed by examining skewness and kurtosis.

When the frequency distribution is not symmetrical, the larger fraction of total frequency may be lumped up either on the left or right of the central axis of symmetry. Such deviation from symmetry is called skewness and the frequency distribution is termed as a skewed or asymmetrical frequency distribution. The frequency distribution which is skewed towards left is called positively skewed distribution and the distribution which is skewed towards right is called a negatively skewed frequency distribution. For example, the frequency distribution of land holdings according to size is an asymmetrical distribution and is positively skewed having larger number of households belonging to lower holding sizes category. Further, the distribution of break down of machines is a negatively skewed distribution having higher number of break downs among the older machines. The well known measures of skewness are :

(*i*) $\dfrac{Q_3 + Q_1 - 2\,M}{Q_3 - Q_1}$, M being the median, Q_1 and Q_3 being the first and third quartile respectively.

(*ii*) $\dfrac{\text{Mean} - \text{Mode}}{\text{Standard deviation}}$

(*iii*) $\dfrac{3\,(\text{Mean} - \text{Median})}{\text{Standard deviation}}$

(*iv*) $\sqrt{\beta_1} = \sqrt{\dfrac{\{\Sigma f_i\,(X_i - \overline{X})^3/\Sigma f_i\}^2}{\{\Sigma f_i\,(X_i - \overline{X})^2/\Sigma f_i\}^3}} = \sqrt{\dfrac{\mu_3^{\,2}}{\mu_2^{\,3}}}$,

where $\mu_3 = \dfrac{1}{\Sigma f_i} f_i\,(X_i - \overline{X})^3$ and $\mu_2 = \dfrac{1}{\Sigma f_i}\Sigma f_i\,(X_i - \overline{X})^2$

For a symmetrical distribution mean, median and mode coincide and as such measure of skewness is zero. Also, $\Sigma f_i\,(X_i - \overline{X})^3 = 0$.

For a positively skewed distribution this measure $(\sqrt{\beta_1})$ is positive and for a negatively skewed distribution the measure is negative. The sign of $\sqrt{\beta_1}$ is determined by the sign of $\Sigma f_i (X_i - \overline{X})^3$.

If the distribution is positively skewed (asymmetrical), Mean > Median > Mode and for negatively skewed one, Mean < Median < Mode.

Kurtosis refers to the **peakedness of the frequency distribution,** compared to bell shaped symmetrical normal distribution. Thus, we may distinguish between flat topped and peaked frequency distributions, comparing with the normal one. A measure of kurtosis (β_2) which is a positive number is defined as

$$\beta_2 = \frac{\mu_4}{\mu_2{}^2},$$

where

$$\mu_4 = \frac{1}{\Sigma f_i} \Sigma f_i (X_i - \overline{X})^4$$

$$\mu_2 = \frac{1}{\Sigma f_i} \Sigma f_i (X_i - \overline{X})^2$$

Note : The measures of skewness and kurtosis are independent of the units of measurement. For a normal symmetrical distribution $\sqrt{\beta_1} = 0$ and $\beta_2 = 3$. In general $\beta_2 \geq 1$.

Some Graphical Examples of Frequency Curves (Frequency distribtions)

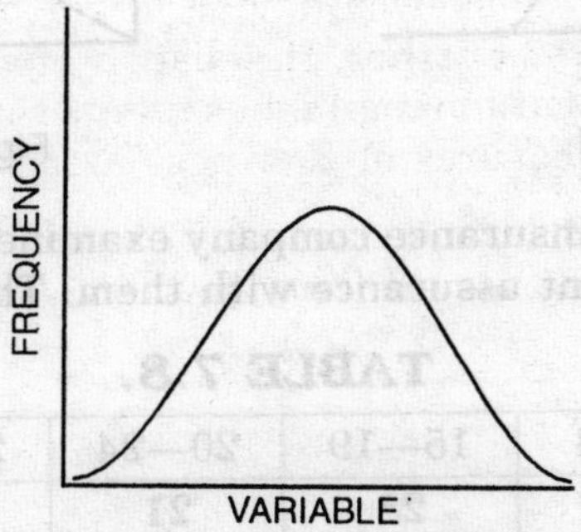

Fig. 7.2. Symmetrical

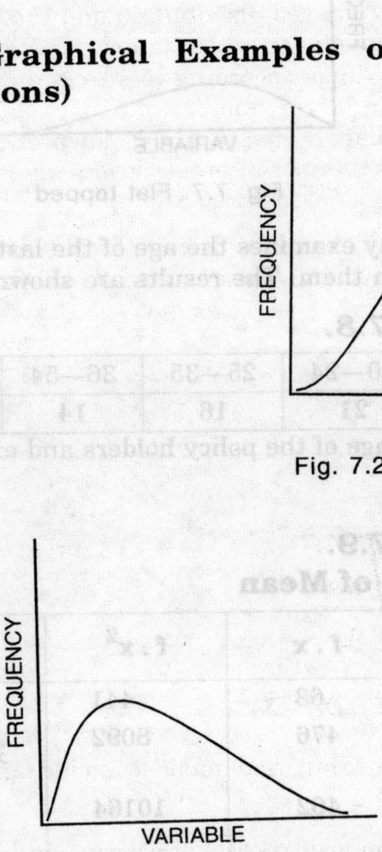

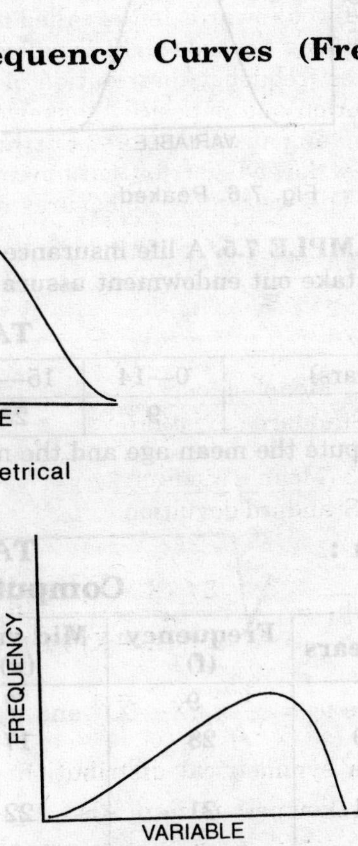

Fig. 7.3(a) Positively asymmetrical (Skewed) Fig. 7.3(b) Negatively asymmetrical (Skewed)

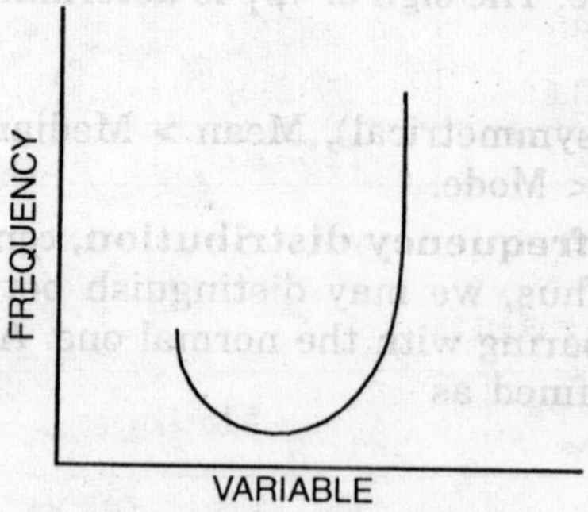

Fig. 7.4. J-Shaped

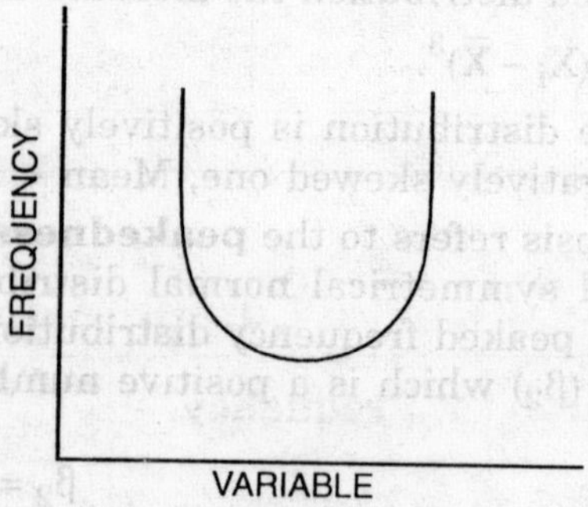

Fig. 7.5. U-Shaped.

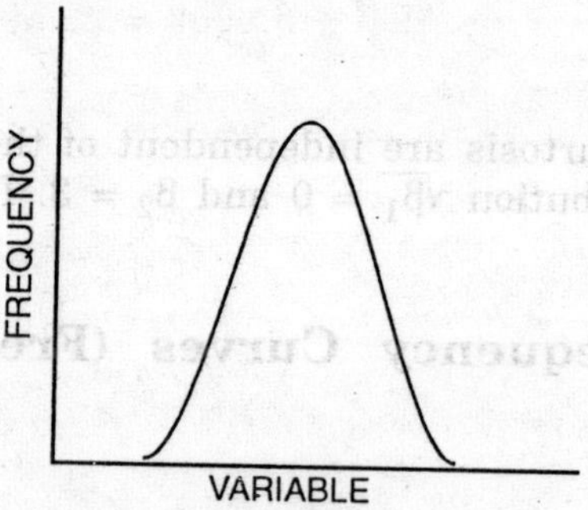

Fig. 7.6. Peaked

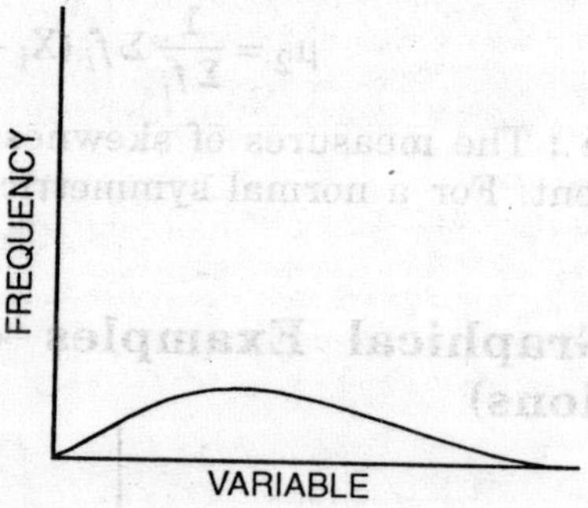

Fig. 7.7. Flat topped

EXAMPLE 7.5. A life insurance company examines the age of the last 100 policy holders to take out endowment assurance with them. The results are shown below :

TABLE 7.8.

Age (in years)	0—14	15—19	20—24	25—35	36—54	55—79
Frequency	9	28	21	16	14	12

Compute the mean age and the median age of the policy holders and examine the data

Solution :

TABLE 7.9.
Computation of Mean

Age in Years	Frequency (f)	Mid value (x)	f . x	f . x^2	Mean
0—14	9	7	63	441	Mean
15—19	28	17	476	8092	$\bar{x} = \frac{\Sigma fx}{\Sigma f}$
20—24	21	22	462	10164	$= \frac{2915}{100}$

25—35	16	30	480	14400	= 29.15
36—54	14	45	630	28350	
55—79	12	67	804	53868	
Total	100	—	2915	115315	

TABLE 7.10.
Computation of Median

Age (in years)	Frequency	Cumulative frequency	Median
— .5—14.5	9	9	Median $\mu_0 = l_1 + \frac{l_2 - l_1}{f}(m—c)$
14.5—19.5	28	37	
19.5—24.5	21	58	$= 19.5 + \frac{5}{21}(50—37)$
25.5—35.5	16	74	
35.5—54.5	14	88	$= 19.5 + 3.0952 = 22.5952$
54.5—79.5	12	100	

$$\text{Variance } \sigma^2 = \frac{\Sigma f(x-\bar{x})^2}{\Sigma f}$$

$$= \frac{\Sigma fx^2}{\Sigma f} - \left(\frac{\Sigma fx}{\Sigma f}\right)^2$$

$$= \frac{115315}{100} - \left(\frac{2915}{100}\right)^2$$

$$= 1153.15 — 849.7225$$

$$= 303.4275$$

$$\text{Standard deviation } \sigma = \sqrt{303.4275}$$

$$= 17.4192$$

$$\text{Coefficient of variation (CV)} = \frac{\text{Standard Deviation}}{\text{Mean}} \times 100$$

$$= \frac{17.4192}{29.15} = 59.76\%$$

An empirical measure of skewness

$$= \frac{3\text{ (Mean} - \text{Median)}}{\text{Standard deviation}}$$

$$= \frac{3\,(29.15 - 22.5912)}{17.4192}$$

$$= 1.13$$

Conclusion

The mean age and median age of the policy holders are 29.15 and 22.59 years respectively. The standard deviation of age is 17.42 years and the coefficient of variation is 59.76%. As mean is greater than the median, the age structure of the policy holders is positively skewed, that is, majority of policy holders belongs to lower age groups.

EXAMPLE 7.6. Given below the frequency distribution of salary of 237 employees in a company.

Compute the mean, median, mode and the standard deviation.

TABLE 7.11.

Class Interval (Salary in Rs.)	Frequency (f)	Mid-value (x)	$u = \frac{x - 14000}{2000}$	f . u	f . u^2
7000—9000	14	8000	—3	—42	126
9000—11000	49	10,000	—2	—98	196
11000—13000	101	12,000	—1	—101	101
13000—15000	43	14,000	0	0	0
15000—17000	14	16,000	1	14	14
17000—19000	10	18,000	2	20	40
19000—21000	6	20,000	3	18	54
Total	237	—	—	—189	531

• Arithmetic Mean $\bar{x} = 14000 + 2000\,(\Sigma fu/\Sigma f)$

$$= 14000 + (2000)\left(-\frac{189}{237}\right)$$

$$= \text{Rs. } 12405/-$$

$$\text{Standard Deviation } \sigma = 2000\sqrt{\frac{\Sigma fu^2}{\Sigma f} - \left(\frac{\Sigma fu}{\Sigma f}\right)^2}$$

$$= 2000\sqrt{\frac{531}{237} - \left(\frac{-189}{237}\right)^2}$$

$$= 2000\sqrt{2.2405 - (0.7975)^2}$$

$$= \text{Rs. } 2533.38$$

TABLE 7.12.
Computations for Median

Class Interval	Frequency	Cumulative frequency
7000—9000	14	14
9000—11000	49	63
11000—13000	101	164
13000—15000	43	207
15000—17000	14	221
17000—19000	10	231
19000—21000	6	237
Total	237	—

$$n = \text{Total frequency} = 237$$

$$m = \frac{n}{2} = \frac{237}{2} = 118.5$$

The median lies in the class interval 11,000 and 13,000. Thus,

$$\text{Median} = l_1 + \frac{l_2 - l_1}{f}(m—c)$$

$$= 11{,}000 + \frac{13000 - 11000}{101}(118.5—62)$$

$$= 11{,}000 + \frac{2000 \times 55.5}{101} = \text{Rs. } 12099$$

Mode lies in the class interval 11,000—13,000

$$\text{Mode} = l_1 + i\,\frac{\Delta_1}{\Delta_1 + \Delta_2}$$

$$= 11{,}000 + 2{,}000\,\frac{|\,101 - 49\,|}{|\,101 - 49\,| + |\,101 - 43\,|}$$

$$= 11{,}000 + 2{,}000\,\frac{52}{52 + 58} = \text{Rs. } 11{,}945$$

7.6 Exploratory data analysis :

One of the major advantage in forming a frequency distribution and its graphical display through histogram is to bring out essential features hither to concealed in the data. A histogram although displays the shape, location and variability of the data, it does not give due regard to individul observations grouped into class intervals in a frequency distribution and thus making them indistinguishable. There are certain graphical displays, which seem to be more informative than the histogram in the initial stage of the data analysis and may be useful in a later occasion for the construction of a frequency distribution and corresponding histogram. In the following we consider two of these procedures :

(*a*) Stem and Leaf plot.

(*b*) Box Plot/Box Whisker Plot.

The Stem and Leaf Plot :

Let $x_1, x_2, \ldots, x_n$ be the observations in the data array. To construct a stem and leaf plot, divide each number into two groups of digits—first few digits form stem and the remaining digits form leaf.

For example, consider the data consisting of number of defectives in 20 lots of electronic tables, each lot hving 100 tubes. If for a particular lot the number is 12, then of two digits in 12, 1 is taken as stem and 2 as leaf. Once the stems are chosen, they are listed in the left hand margin of the display and leaves against each stem on its right hand side in order in which they are placed in the data set. For easy visualization stems and leaves may be separated by a vertical line.

ILLUSTRATION 4. *Number of defectives in 20 lots of electronic tubes manufactured by Company A and Company B*

Company A	**Company B**
12, 5, 6, 9, 11,	20, 8, 9, 9, 13,
9, 13, 18, 20, 22,	15, 19, 4, 21, 18
21, 20, 17, 13, 14	6, 8, 10, 12, 11
15, 16, 12, 7, 8.	9, 15, 14, 13, 11.

TABLE 7.13
Stem and Leaf Display (Company A)

Stem	Leaf	Leaf–Ordered	Frequency
0	5,6,9,9,7,8	5,6,7,8,9,9	6
1	2,1,3,8,7,3,4,5,6,2	1,2,2,3,3,4,5,6,7,8	10
2	0,2,1,0	0,0,1,2	4
		Total	20

TABLE 7.14
Stem and Leaf Display (Company B)

Stem	Leaf	Leaf–Ordered	Frequency
0	8,9,9,4,6,8,9	4,6,8,8,9,9,9	7
1	3,5,9,8,0,2,1,5,4,3,1	0,1,1,2,3,3,4,5,5,8,9	11
2	0,1	0,1	2
		Total	20

Inspection of stem and leaf plots show that for both companies A and B the maximum number of defectives lie between 10 and 19.

In order to find a central value like median, it is necessary to order the leaves in stem and leaf plot. Since the number of observations is even, the median is the average of 10th and 11th value in ordered form, that is, the median

$$= \frac{13+13}{2} = 13 \text{ (for Company A)}$$

$$= \frac{11+12}{2} = 11.5 \text{ (for Company B)}$$

and the quartiles

$$Q_1 = \frac{9+9}{2} = 9 \quad \text{(for Company A)}$$

$$= \frac{9+9}{2} = 9 \quad \text{(for Company B)}$$

$$Q_3 = \frac{17+18}{2} = 17.5 \quad \text{(for Company A)}$$

$$= \frac{15+15}{2} = 15 \quad \text{(for Company B)}$$

Interquartile Range :

$$Q_3 - Q_1 = 17.5 - 9 = 8.5 \quad \text{(for Company A)}$$

$$= 15 - 9 = 6 \quad \text{(for Company B)}$$

The Box Plot

A **box plot** graphically displays summary information contained in the quartiles. A centre half of the data between the first and third quartiles is represented by a rectangle. A line is drawn through the **box** at the second quartile (Median). Both the ends of the box are extended up to the extreme values by lines, which are called **Whiskers.** Therefore, sometimes **box plot** is also termed as **Box-Whisker** plot. Thus, looking at the box plot we can visualize nature of distribution of observations (symmetrical or asymmetrical) along with the locations of minimum value, maximum value, first quartile, second quartile (median) and the third quartile.

ILLUSTRATION 5. *Using the data given in Illustration 7 for Company A and Company B the Box-plots are shown in Fig. 7.8 and Fig. 7.9.*

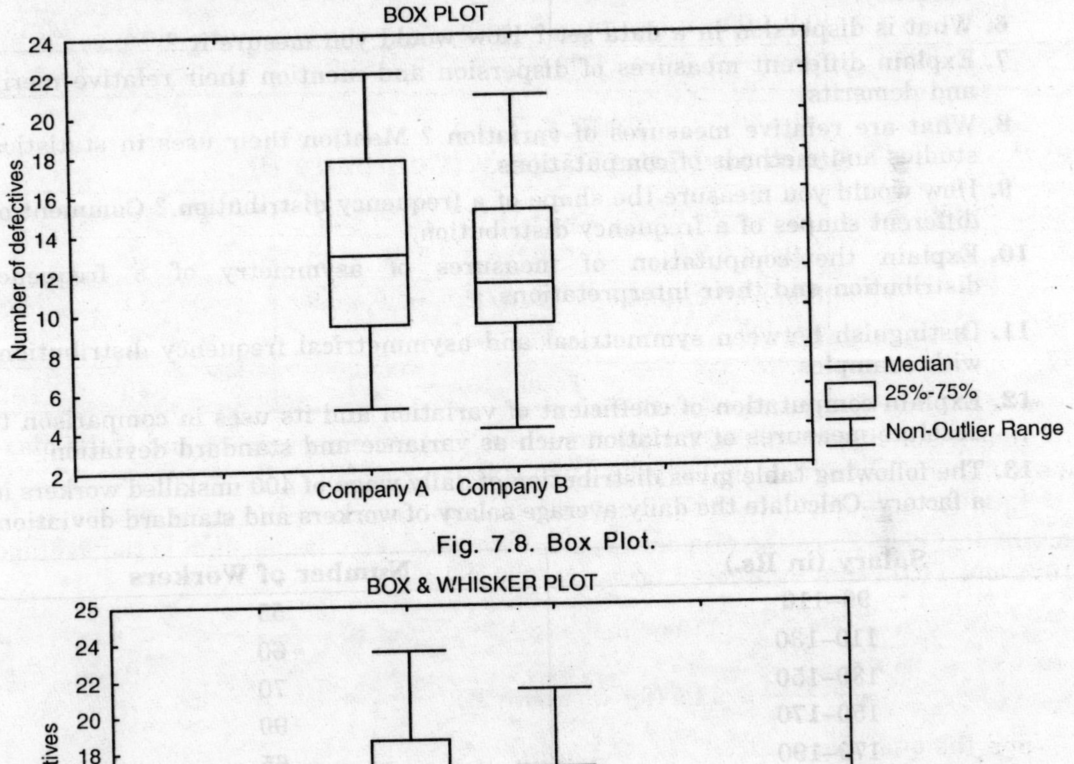

Fig. 7.8. Box Plot.

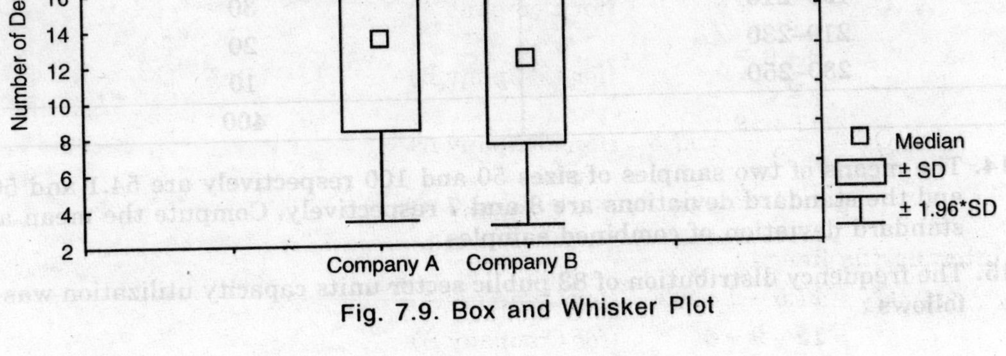

Fig. 7.9. Box and Whisker Plot

EXERCISES

1. Differentiate between rate and ratios and discuss their importance in descriptive statistics.

2. What is a frequency distribution ? Explain the construction of a frequency distribution from grouped data. Mention its Characteristics.

3. Distinguish between relative frequency and cumulative frequency and their interpretations.

4. What are measures of central tendency ? Mention their relative advantages and disadvantages.

5. Compare the arithmetic mean and the median as measures of central tendency.

6. What is dispersion in a data set ? How would you mesure it ?

7. Explain different measures of dispersion and mention their relative merits and demerits.

8. What are relative measures of variation ? Mention their uses in statistical studies and methods of computations.

9. How would you measure the shape of a frequency distribution ? Comment on different shapes of a frequency distribution.

10. Explain the computation of measures of asymmetry of a frequency distribution and their interpretations.

11. Distinguish between symmetrical and asymmetrical frequency distributions with examples.

12. Explain computation of coefficient of variation and its uses in comparison to absolute measures of variation such as variance and standard deviation.

13. The following table gives distribution of daily wage of 400 unskilled workers in a factory. Calculate the daily average salary of workers and standard deviation.

Salary (in Rs.)	Number of Workers
90–110	55
110–130	60
130–150	70
150–170	90
170–190	65
190–210	30
210–230	20
230–250	10
	400

14. The means of two samples of sizes 50 and 100 respectively are 54.1 and 50.3 and the standard deviations are 8 and 7 respectively. Compute the mean and standard deviation of combined samples.

15. The frequency distribution of 83 public sector units capacity utilization was as follows :

Capacity-Utilization (Percentage)	Number of Units
Less than 50	15
50–60	14
60–70	6
70–80	10
80–90	11
90–100	7
More than 100	20
Total	83

Compute median, quartiles, mean absolute deviation from the median and quartile deviation.

16. Out of a sample of 230 companies the inventory sales ratio was found as follows.

Inventory Sales Ratio (Percentage)	No. of Companies
0.1–5.0	2
5.1–10.0	4
10.1–15.0	9
15.1–20.0	12
20.1–25.0	38
25.1–30.0	61
30.1–35.0	44
35.1–40.0	35
40.1–45.0	25
Total	230

(*a*) Draw histogram.

(*b*) Compute arithmetic, median and mode.

(*c*) Compute relative measures of dispersion and coefficients of skewness.

17. What are the considerations involved in the construction of a frequency distribution ? Discuss.

18. Monthly expenditure (in Rs.) of 15 households in a locality are given below. Compute arithmetic mean, median, standard deviation, mean absolute deviation and quartile deviation.
3240, 3129, 2540, 1895, 2100, 2795, 2835, 1645, 3495, 1260, 2925, 1750, 3560, 2675, 1950.

19. An economy grows at the rate of 2% in the first year, 2.5% in the second year, 3% in the third, ..., and 10% in the tenth year. What is the average rate of growth of the economy ?

20. (a) If the income distribution in a particular region is symmetric then will the symmetry be affected if income of every one is increased ?

(*i*) by Rs. 100 ?

(*ii*) by certain proportion.

(b) What happens to the symmetry of the income distribution if the income of every one becomes square of what it is ?

21. For the following frequency distribution find the range and quartile deviation, standard deviation and mean absolute deviation.

x	10	15	20	25	30	35	40	80
f	6	17	29	38	25	14	9	2

22. Compare arithmetic mean, geometric mean and harmonic mean as measures of central tendency and explain the situations where they would be more appropriate to be computed.

23. Following is the table showing I.Q. of 100 students. Calculate the mean, median and mode and comment on the frequency distribution.

Class	55–64	65–74	75–84	85–94	95–104	105–114
Frequency	1	2	9	22	33	25

Class	115–124	125–134	135–144
Frequency	8	3	2

24. Compare the variability of temperature of two regions, given below.

Region	Temperature in Degree Farenheit				
A	90	98	106	114	122
B	120	130	84	126	70

25. The following statistical measures relate to production in three factories.

	A	B	C
Arithmetic Mean	800	780	820
Median	800	790	810
Mode	800	810	790
Standard Deviation	20	40	60
Quartile Deviation	14	28	40

Compare the production features of three factories.

26. Draw the Lorenz curve for the following data concerning two companies and interpret them.

Daily Income Rs.	Company A No. of Persons	Company B No. of Persons
150–300	250	150
300–450	100	80
450–600	80	65
600–750	30	55
750–900	25	40
900–1050	10	35
1050–1200	5	20

27. The value of two shares of Rs. 10. quoted in a stock market from January to December of a year are given.

Share X	9 8	10 9.5	9.5 11.6	10.5 10.7	11 9.4	11.5 10.2
Share Y	8 9	10.5 7.5	9.2 7	8.4 11	10.5 10	11.5 11.5

Compare the coefficient of variations.

28. Explain Gini's coefficient of concentration and its application.

29. The number of runs scored by cricketers A and B during 5 test matches consisting of 10 innings are as follows :

Make a comparative study of their batting performances.

Cricketer A :	5	0	26	97	66	112	89	102	24	15
Cricketer B :	51	45	47	60	58	39	35	71	50	65

30. The following data are the monthly rental prices of 10 unfurnished 3-room flats in the center of a large city and also in the outskirt area.

City Centre

Rs. 6,000, Rs. 6,500, Rs. 6,800, Rs. 5,500, Rs. 4,550, Rs. 5,250, Rs. 6,100, Rs. 5,800, Rs. 5,400, Rs. 7,000.

Outskirt Area

Rs. 4,500, Rs. 3,800, Rs. 4,200, Rs. 4,600, Rs. 2,900, Rs. 3,400, Rs. 3,200, Rs. 4,000, Rs. 3,400, Rs. 3,500.

Form Box whisker plot and describe the shape. Comment on the distribution of results in two areas.

□□□

CHAPTER

8

ELEMENTS OF PROBABILITY THEORY AND PROBABILITY DISTRIBUTIONS

8.1 Introduction

The Theory of Probability, first originated in the 17th century through the works of Galileo, Huygens, Pascal, Fermat and Bernoulli to solve the problems faced by gamblers in their games of chance, provided thoughts to the scientists to study the statistical regularities in the random phenomenon encountered by them. Thus, the mathematical framework came to picture to take care of probabilistic and uncertain problems. Demoivre, Laplace and Gauss pioneered further development of the probability theory.

In recent days, probabilistic conclusions have made significant impact on all scientific researches concerning random events. Social researchers have, also, not lagged behind to apply probabilistic techniques to analyse and predict socio-economic development, human attitude, behaviour, emotions, social interactions in probabilistic or uncertain frameworks.

In the present chapter certain probability concepts are studied to help understand the statistical principles involved in the analysis and interpretation of statistical data.

Sample space

Statistical events relate to results of certain random experiments. *All possible outcomes of a random experiment constitute elements of a set called Sample Space (S).*

Randam Experiment

An experiment is an operation resulting in two or more outcomes. When the nature of the outcome is not predetermined and depends on chance, the concerned experiment is called a **random experiment.** Two or more outcomes are said to be equally likely, if any one of them cannot be expected to occur in preference to the others.

An event

An event is a subset of the sample space. This subset may constitute one or more possible outcomes.

An event is said to be *simple* if it corresponds to a single possible outcome of an experiment, *e.g.* a coin is tossed once. The simple events are Head and Tail.

A joint occurrence of two or more simple events is called a *compound event*, e.g. a coin is tossed twice. The appearence of two heads is a compound event.

Two events are said to be *mutually exclusive* if the occurrence of one prevents the occurrence of the other. That is, two mutually exclusive events cannot occur simultaneously in the same trial, e.g. a coin is tossed once. Head and Tail are mutually exclusive outcomes.

A number of events are said to be *mutually exclusive and exhaustive* if they are pairwise mutually exclusive and all together constitute the entire sample space, e.g. a fair die is rolled once. Let A be the event of having odd score and B be the event of having even score. A and B are mutually exclusive and exhaustive.

8.2. Definition of probability

Probability is the chance that a particular event can happen and logically depend on the possible outcomes constituting the sample space. Intuitively, the probability of an event should be a positive proper fraction and probability of a sure event should be equal to unity and also the probability that a particular event can never happen, naturally, should be equal to zero.

8.2.1. Classical definition

If an experiment or trial results in n possible outcomes and in k of the outcomes an event A is said to happen, then the probability of the happening of the event A is defined as

$$P(A) = \frac{\text{Favourable number of outcomes for happening of the event A}}{\text{Exhaustive number of outcomes}}$$

$$= \frac{k}{n}, \text{ which is} \leq 1.$$

The classical definition rests on three basic assumptions :

(*i*) The outcomes are exhaustive

(*ii*) The outcomes are mutually exclusive

(*iii*) The outcomes are equally likely.

Probability of not happening of the event A, that is, happening of $\bar{A}$, called the *complement of A* equals

$$P(\bar{A}) = 1 - P(A)$$

Thus, (*i*) $0 \le P(A) \le 1$

(*ii*) $P(A) + P(\bar{A}) = 1$

Limitation

The classical definition presupposes that the outcomes are equally likely, which may not be always true.

To remove deficiencies in the classical definition, the *axiomatic* definition is stated below.

8.2.2. Axiomatic definition

Let S be a finite sample space $\{e_1, e_2, ..., e_n\}$ and A is an event consisting of *elementary events* $\{e_1, e_2, ..., e_k\}$; $e_i \cap e_j = \phi$.

The probability of the event A is defined with the help of *three* axioms. Let $p_i = P(e_i)$ be a non-negative weight attached to the *i*th elemantary event $(i = 1, 2, ..., n)$.

Axioms :

(*i*) $0 \le P(e_i) \le 1$

(*ii*) $P(e_1 \cup e_2) = P(e_1) + P(e_2)$

(*iii*) $P(S) = 1$, where

$$S = e_1 \cup e_2 \cup .... \cup e_n$$

$$\begin{aligned} P(A) &= P(e_1 \cup e_2 \cup .... \cup e_k) \\ &= P(e_1) + P(e_2) + ... + P(e_k) \\ &= p_1 + p_2 + ... + p_k \end{aligned}$$

If $p_1 = p_2 = ... = p_n = \dfrac{1}{n}$,

$$P(A) = \frac{k}{n}.$$

Thus, classical definition is a *special case* of the axiomatic definition.

Mathematically, it sounds logical when we toss a coin once and say that the probability of getting a 'Head' is one half. But does it happen when we toss a coin twice ? Can we realise the results that once there will be 'Head' and the other will be 'Tail' ? Perhaps it will not be always true.

Here comes the empirical/statistical definition to get us out of the contention.

8.2.3. Empirical/Statistical definition

The statistical definition is due to Von Mises. If S_n is the number of occurrences of an event A in *n* independent repetitions of an experiment under identical conditions, the *relative frequency* $\dfrac{S_n}{n}$ hovers around a constant with increasing *n*, because of statis-

tical regularities governing the phenomenon. This constant is approximately taken as the probability of the random event A.

$$P(A) = \frac{S_n}{n},$$

when *n* increases indefinitely and hovers around a constant value, surely less than unity.

ILLUSTRATION 1.

Experiment : Tossing of an unbiased coin twice

Possible outcomes : Head—Head (e_1)

Head—Tail (e_2)

Tail—Head (e_3)

Tail—Tail (e_4)

Sample space : S = $\{e_1, e_2, e_3, e_4\}$

Outcome or Elementary event : $e \in S$

Event (A) : Subset of S *i.e.*

$$A = \{e_2, e_3\};\ A \subset S$$

Assuming that equal weights (1/4) attached to all outcomes (elementary events or sample points),

$$P(e_1) = P(e_2) = P(e_3) = P(e_4) = \frac{1}{4}$$

$$P(A) = P(e_2 \cup e_3) = P(H\,T) + P(T\,H)$$

$$= \frac{1}{4} + \frac{1}{4} = \frac{1}{2}.$$

ILLUSTRATION 2.

Experiment : A die is rolled once.

Possible outcomes : Number on the upper face of the die :

$e_1(1), e_2(2), e_3(3), \ldots, e_6(6)$

Sample space : S = {1, 2, 3, 4, 5, 6}

Outcomes or Elementary events :

{1}, {2}, {3} .... {6}

Event A : Obtaining an even score {2, 4, 6}.

Assume that equal weights are attached to the sample points in the sample space.

That is, $P(e_i) = \frac{1}{6}$ (i = 1, 2, 3, ..., 6).

Thus,

$$P(A) = P(e_2 \cup e_4 \cup e_6)$$

$$= P(e_2) + P(e_4) + P(e_6)$$

$$= \frac{1}{6} + \frac{1}{6} + \frac{1}{6} = \frac{3}{6} = \frac{1}{2}.$$

ILLUSTRATION 3. In a large scale sample survey it was found that out of 1000 couples interviewed, 650 had jointly taken decision on financial matters. Thus, the relative frequency or the probability that a decision taken by a couple is a joint decision is

$$P(A) = \frac{650}{1000} = 0.65$$

8.2.4. Determination of weights attached to the sample points in the sample space

The experimental situation faced in tossing of an unbiased coin or rolling of a die cannot be universally accepted. Assumptions about attaching uniform weights to sample points may not be always justified. Even if we do not know any reason to suggest that one outcome is more likely than the other, it is not appropriate to attach equal probabilities/weights to the sample points/elementary events.

Consider an experiment of determining the sex of a new born baby. Suppose in 1000 births 535 are boys and 465 are girls. Then it is more appropriate to assign probability 0.535 to the outcome boy and 0.465 to the outcome girl. Such conclusion based on statistical observations is not a static conclusion and might vary from country to country and from one environment to another depending on genetic consideration.

8.3. Probability Laws

8.3.1. Additive Law of Probability

If A and B are two events, not necessarily mutually exclusive

$$\begin{aligned} P(A \cup B) &= P\,(A \text{ or } B \text{ or both}) \\ &= P(A) + P(B) - P(A \cap B) \\ &= P(A) + P(B), \text{ if A and B are mutually exclusive} \end{aligned}$$

ILLUSTRATION 4. A sample survey of 500 households in a locality shows the number of households having safety toilet facilities and unattached (to living rooms) cattlesheds.

Compute the probability of having safety toilet facilities or unattached cattlesheds or both in the locality.

	Attached cattlesheds	Unattached cattlesheds	Total
Safety toilets	275	75	350
No safety toilets	125	25	150
Total	400	100	500

Let A be the event of having safety toilets and B be the event of unattached cattlesheds.

$$P(A) = \frac{350}{500}, \quad P(B) = \frac{100}{500}$$

$$P(A \cap B) = \frac{75}{500}$$

$$P(A \cup B) = P(A) + P(B) - P\,(A \cap B)$$

$$= \frac{350}{500} + \frac{100}{500} - \frac{75}{500}$$

$$= \frac{375}{500} = 0.75.$$

ILLUSTRATION 5. A die is rolled once. What is the probability of obtaining either 4 or 6 ?

Let A be the event of getting a score 4 and B the event of getting a score 6.

Then, $P(A \text{ or } B) = P(A) + P(B) - P(A \cap B)$

$$= \frac{1}{6} + \frac{1}{6} + 0 = \frac{2}{6} = \frac{1}{3}.$$

8.3.2. Conditional Probability

The probability of happening of a particular event A, gives information about the occurrence of another event B is known as the *Conditional probability* $P(A|B)$. That is, instead of searching for outcomes for the happening of A in the entire sample space, we need to search only among the sample points in the subject accounting for the happening of the event B.

Thus, the conditional probability of happening of A given that B has actually happened is defined as

$$P(A|B) = \frac{P(A \cap B)}{P(B)}, \text{ provided } P(B) \neq 0.$$

8.3.3. Multiplicative Law of Probability

If in an experiment both A and B simultaneously occur,

Then $P(A \cap B) = P(B)\, P(A|B)$.

This is known as *Multiplicative rule/law of probability.*

8.3.4. Statistical Independence

The events A and B are said to be *statistically independent* if the happening of A does not depend on the happening of B.

That is, $P(A \cap B) = P(A \text{ and } B)$

$= P(A) . P(B)$

Also, $P(A|B) = P(A)$.

ILLUSTRATION 6. Consider 300 mining centres surveyed to study the availability of safe drinking water and occurrence of gastric disorders

		Safe drinking water		
		Available	*Not available*	*Total*
Gastric disorders	Yes	25	90	115
	No	175	10	185
	Total	200	100	300

Now, P (gastric disorder | safe drinking water not available)

$$= \frac{\text{P (Gastric disorder and no safe drinking water)}}{\text{P(No safe drinking water)}}$$

$$= \frac{90/300}{100/300} = \frac{90}{100} = 0.9$$

ILLUSTRATION 7. A box contains 5 white balls and 10 green balls. Two balls are drawn one after another without replacement.

The probability of both the drawn balls are green is computed as follows :

Let A_g be the event that first ball is green and B_g be the second ball is green. Then,

$$P(A_g \text{ and } B_g) = P(A_g)\, P(B_g \mid A_g)$$

$$= \frac{10}{15} \cdot \frac{9}{14} = \frac{3}{7} = 0.42.$$

ILLUSTRATION 8. In a clinic, six deliveries are to be conducted. Assuming that the probability of having a male child is $\frac{1}{2}$, find the probability that all the children to be born will be of the same sex.

Solution :

Let A be the event that all the six births $A_1, A_2, ..., A_6$ are males and B be the event that all the six births $B_1, B_2, ..., B_6$ are females. A and B are independent events. Thus we have,

$$P(A) = P(A_1)\, P(A_2) \,....\, P(A_6)$$

$$= \frac{1}{2} \cdot \frac{1}{2} \cdot \frac{1}{2} \cdot \frac{1}{2} \cdot \frac{1}{2} \cdot \frac{1}{2} = \left(\frac{1}{2}\right)^6 = \frac{1}{64}$$

$$P(B) = P(B_1)\, P(B_2) \,....\, P(B_6)$$

$$= \frac{1}{2} \cdot \frac{1}{2} \cdot \frac{1}{2} \cdot \frac{1}{2} \cdot \frac{1}{2} \cdot \frac{1}{2} = \left(\frac{1}{2}\right)^6 = \frac{1}{64}.$$

Therefore, the required probability is

$$P(A \text{ or } B) = \frac{1}{64} + \frac{1}{64} = \frac{1}{32} = 0.031$$

Note :

1. If there are more than two events, say, A, B and C, then

$$P(A \cap B \cap C) = P(A \text{ and } B \text{ and } C)$$
$$= P(A)\, P(B \mid A)\, P(C \mid A, B).$$

2. A, B and C are said to be mutually independent, if

(*i*) $P(A \cap B) = P(A) \,.\, P(B)$

(*ii*) $P(A \cap C) = P(A) \,.\, P(C)$

(*iii*) $P(B \cap C) = P(B) \,.\, P(C)$

(*iv*) $P(A \cap B \cap C) = P(A) \,.\, P(B) \,.\, P(C)$

It may be mentioned here, *pairwise independence does not imply mutual independence.*

Example 8.1. It is found that in manufacturing a certain article, defects of one type occur with probability 0.1 and defect of a second type with probability 0.05. (Assume independence between types of defects). What is the probability that

(*a*) an article does not have both kinds of defects ?

(*b*) an article is defective ?

Solution :

Let A be the event that defects of the first type occur and B be the event that defects of the second type occur.

$$P(A) = 0.1 \text{ and } P(B) = 0.05$$

(*a*) Now, probability that both types of defects occur

$$= (0.1)(0.05) = 0.005.$$

Thus, the probability that both kinds of defects do not occur = 1 — 0.005 = 0.995

(*b*) The probability that an article is defective

$$= P(A) + P(B) - P(A \cap B) = P(A) + P(B) - P(A) \,.\, P(B)$$

$$= 0.1 + 0.05 - 0.005 = 0.145.$$

Example 8.2. A machine consists of two parts P_1 and P_2. The manufacturing process of each part is such that probability of defect in P_1 is 0.05 and that in P_2 is 0.02. What is the probability that the assembled machine (i) will not have any defect (ii) will have at least one defect ?

Solution :

Let A be the event that the part P_1 is free from defect.

$$P(A) = 1 - P(\text{part } P_1 \text{ is defective})$$

$$= 1 - 0.05 = 0.95.$$

Let B be the event that the part P_2 is free from defect

$$P(B) = 1 - P(\text{part } P_2 \text{ is defective})$$

$$= 1 - 0.02 = 0.98.$$

The two events A and B are independent.

Let E be the event the assembled part will not have any defect.

$$\text{Then, } P(E) = P(A \cap B)$$

$$= P(A)\, P(B \mid A)$$

$$= P(A)\, P(B)$$

$$= (0.95)(0.98) = 0.8740$$

Let E_1 be the event the assembled part will have at least one defect.

$$P(E_1) = 1 - 0.8740 = 0.126.$$

Example 8.3. Two different digits are selected at random from the digits 1, 2, ..., 6. If the sum is odd, what is the probability that 4 is one of the digits selected ?

Solution :

Let A be the event that its sum is odd. In order that the sum would be odd, one of 2 digits must be odd. There are 3 odd digits and 3 even digits, which can be selected in $3C_1$ nd $3C_1$ ways respectively. Hence, the event A consists of 3 × 3 = 9 sample points in the conditional sample space.

Under the assumption that A has occurred, let B be the event that 2 is one of the digits chosen. If one digit 4, the other must be odd and can be selected in 3C = 3 ways out of 3 odd digits. Hence B ∩ A consists of 3 sample points.

$$\therefore\ P(B \mid A) = \frac{P(B \cap A)}{P(A)} = \frac{3}{9} = \frac{1}{3}$$

8.4. Bayes' Rule

Suppose an event A can happen if one of the mutually exclusive and exhaustive events B_1 and B_2 occur

Now, $A = (A \cap B_1) \cup (A \cap B_2)$

where $A \cap B_1$ and $A \cap B_2$ are mutually exclusive

Therefore,
$$P(A) = P(A \cap B_1) + P(A \cap B_2)$$
$$= P(B_1)\,P(A \mid B_1) + P(B_2)\,P(A \mid B_2)$$

If we want to know the probability of the happening of the event B_1, given that A has actually happened, we write

$$P(B_1 \mid A) = \frac{P(A \cap B_1)}{P(A)}$$
$$= \frac{P(B_1)\,P(A \mid B_1)}{P(B_1)\,P(A \mid B_1) + P(B_2)\,P(A \mid B_2)}$$

Such a method of calculating probability in the given instance is called *Bayes' Rule or Bayes' formula*, named after Thomas Bayes.

Generalization :

If B_1, B_2, ..., B_k are mutually exclusive events, then

$$P(B_i \mid A) = \frac{P(B_i)\,P(A \mid B_i)}{\sum_{i=1}^{k} P(B_i)\,P(A \mid B_i)},$$

for $i = 1, 2, ..., k$

The probabilities $P(B_i)$ are called Priori or a Prior probabilities while $P(B_i \mid A)$ are called 'a Posteriori' probabilities.

Example 8.4. In a bolt factory machine A, B, C manufacture respectively 15%, 30% and 55% of the total. Of their output 5, 4, 3 percents are defective bolts. A bolt was selected at random. What are the probabilities that it was manufactured by machines A, B and C ?

Solution :

Let D be the event that the bolt is defective.

$$P(A) = 0.15 \quad P(B) = 0.30 \text{ and } P(C) = 0.55$$

Further, $P(D \mid A) = 0.05$, $P(D \mid B) = 0.04$ and $P(D \mid C) = 0.03$

Now,
$$P(A \mid D) = \frac{P(A)\,P(D \mid A)}{P(A)\,P(D \mid A) + P(B)\,P(D \mid B) + (P(C)\,P(D \mid C)}$$
$$= \frac{(0.15)\,(0.05)}{(0.15)\,(0.05) + (0.30)\,(0.04) + (0.55)\,(0.03)}$$
$$= \frac{0.0075}{0.036} = 0.2083$$

Similarly, $P(B \mid D) = 0.3333$

and $P(C \mid D) = 0.4583$

Example 8.5. An acturial recruitment company places advertisements in three publications with probabilities 0.2, 0.3 and 0.5 respectively.

The probability that the recruitment company gets an inquiry from an advertisement in the first publication is 0.001. The probabilities for the other two publications are 0.002 and 0.004 respectively.

Given that the company has just received an enquiry, calculate the probability that it came from an advertisement in the first publication.

Solution :

Let A be the event that an advertisement is placed in publication A. Let B be the event that an advertisement is placed in publication B. Let C be the event that an advertisement is placed in publication C.

Let E be the event that an enquiry is received.

Thus, we have

$$P(A) = 0.2,\ P(B) = 0.3,\ P(C) = 0.5$$
$$P(E \mid A) = 0.001$$
$$P(E \mid B) = 0.002$$
$$P(E \mid C) = 0.004$$

The required probability is

$$P(A \mid E) = \frac{P(E \mid A)\, P(A)}{P(E)}$$
$$= \frac{P(E \mid A)\, P(A)}{P(E \mid A)\, P(A) + P(E \mid B)\, P(B) + P(E \mid C)\, P(C)}$$
$$= \frac{(0.001)\,(0.2)}{(0.001)\,(0.2) + (0.002)\,(0.3) + (0.004)\,(0.5)}$$
$$= 0.0714.$$

8.5. Random Variable

A variable having a probability distribution is termed as a *random variable.*

Random variables may be classified into two types :

- Discrete random variable.
- Continuous random variable.

Definition : A random variable is a numerical (real) valued function defined on a sample space.

The variable is called a random variable because its value is determined by the random outcome of an experiment, that is, outcome which depends on chance only. As all possible outcomes of an experiment, constitute a sample space, it is thus natural that it must be defined over the sample space.

A discrete random variable is defined over a *discrete sample space*, whose elements are finite such that number of heads falling in a coin tossing experiment, number of children in a family, number of workers in a factory, etc. If the sample space has infinite number of sample points, for example, all possible heights, weights, temperatures, pressure, income of individuals, machine errors, etc., such a sample space is called a *Continuous sample space* and the variable defined over it is called a *Continuous random variable.* Roughly speaking, a discrete random variable takes on specified values whereas a continuous random variable assumes all values in some interval (a, b), where

a and b may be $-\alpha$ and $+\alpha$. In most of the situations met in practice, the continuous random variables involve measured data and the discrete random variables involve count data.

8.5.1. Discrete random variable and probability distribution

Interest of an experimenter while performing a random experiments or looking at one such rests in associating a numerical description to the experimental outcomes. In a hypothetical situation let us toss one coin twice and note the outcomes. The experiments might be interested in observing number of heads on the throw. The possible outcomes are

$$(HH, HT, TH, TT),$$

with associated probabilities $\left(\frac{1}{4}, \frac{1}{4}, \frac{1}{4}, \frac{1}{4}\right)$. Thus, the numerical description associated with elementary events after counting the number of heads is (2, 1, 1, 0). Thus,

> A discrete random variable is a numerically valued function defined over the discrete sample space.

If X is taken, as a random variable standing for the number of heads in the throw of a coin twice.

To calculate P(X = 2), P(X = 1) and P(X = 0), we find out the elementary events, which give rise two heads, one head and zero head and

$$P(X = 2) = P(HH) = \frac{1}{4}$$

$$P(X = 1) = P(HT \text{ or } TH) = P(HT) + P(TH)$$

$$= \frac{1}{4} + \frac{1}{4} = \frac{1}{2}$$

$$P(X = 0) = P(TT) = \frac{1}{4}$$

> A set of ordered pairs $\{x, p(x)\}$ is called the Probability mass function or Probability distribution of the random variable x, where
> $$P(X = x) = p(x) > 0 \text{ and } \Sigma\, p(x) = 1$$

In the coin throwing example,

x :	0	1	2
$P(X = x)$:	$\frac{1}{4}$	$\frac{1}{2}$	$\frac{1}{4}$

define the probability distribution of X.

8.5.2. Continuous random variable and Probability distribution

A continuous random variable is characterized by a distribution function

$$F_X(x) = P(X \le x) = \int_{-\infty}^{x} f(x)\, dx, \quad -\infty < x < +\infty$$

$$f(x) = \frac{d\,F(x)}{dx} \text{ is called the Probability density function of } x, -\infty \le x \le +\infty.$$

F(x) is a montonous increasing function of x; $0 \le F(x) \le 1$ for all x;

$$\int_{-\infty}^{+\infty} f(x)\,dx = 1 \quad (-\infty \le x \le +\infty)$$

Continuous probability models have found important applications in physical, engineering, management and social sciences.

8.5.3. Expected value and variance of probability distribution of a random variable

The expected value of a random variable X denoted as E(X), which is also called the mean of a random variable X or its probability distribution. The expected value of rth power of X is called rth moment of X (r = 1, 2, 3, 4, ...). The moments define the location, spread, shape etc. of a probability distribution.

Discrete Case :

If the discrete random variable X takes values $x_1, x_2, ..., x_k$ with probabilities $p_1, p_2, ..., p_k$, then

$$E(X) = p_1 \times x_1 + p_2 \times x_2 + ... + p_k \times x_k$$
$$= \sum_{i=1}^{k} p_i x_i, \quad \text{with} \quad \sum_{i=1}^{k} p_i = 1,$$

provided E (|X|) is finite.

The variability in the values taken by the random variable X is measured by computing

$$V(X) = E\,[X - E(X)]^2$$
$$= \sum_{i=1}^{k} p_i (x_i - E(X))^2$$

Alternatively,

$$V(X) = E(X - E(X))^2 = E(X^2) - [E(X)]^2$$
$$= \sum_{i=1}^{k} p_i x_i^2 - \left(\sum_{i=1}^{k} p_i x_i\right)^2$$

The standard deviation of X is defined as

$$\sigma_x = \sqrt{V(X)}.$$

Continuous Case

If the continuous random variable X has the probability density function $f(x)$, the expected value of X is defined as

$$E(X) = \int_{-\infty}^{+\infty} x f(x)\, dx \;;\; -\infty \le x \le +\infty, \text{ with } \int_{-\infty}^{\infty} f(x)\, dx = 1$$

$$\text{or} \quad = \int_{a}^{b} x f(x)\, dx \;;\; a \le x \le b, \text{ with } \int_{a}^{b} f(x)\, dx = 1.$$

provided E(|X|) is finite. The variance of X

$$V(X) = \sigma_x^2 = E(X - E(X))^2$$

$$= \int_{-\infty}^{\infty} [x - E(X)]^2 f(x)\, dx$$

$$= \int_{-\infty}^{\infty} x^2 f(x)\, dx - \left[\int_{-\infty}^{+\infty} x f(x)\, dx\right]^2$$

$$\therefore \quad \sigma_x = +\sqrt{V(X)}.$$

Note :

(*i*) $E(aX + b) = a\,E(X) + b$, where a and b are constants. If X= 0, $E(b) = b$.
That is, E (constant) = Same constant.

(*ii*) $V(aX + b) = a^2\, V(X)$, the variance of a constant being zero.

(*iii*) A mathematical measure of skewness of a random variable or its probability distribution is defined by $\sqrt{\beta_1} = \sqrt{\mu_3^{\,2}/\mu_2^{\,3}}$, where

$\mu_3 = E(X - E(X))^3$ and $\mu_2 = E(X - E(X))^2$. The sign of $\sqrt{\beta_1}$ is determined by sign of μ_3.

(*iv*) A mathematical measure of Kurtosis

$$\beta_2 = \mu_4/\mu_2^{\,2}, \text{ where } \mu_4 = E(X - E(X))^4 \text{ and}$$
$$\mu_2 = E[X - E(X)]^2.$$

8.6. Important Discrete Probability Distributions

8.6.1. Binomial distribution

This is a discrete probability distribution and has many everyday applications. It has the following properties :

(*i*) Each observation being a product of a trial may be classified into two mutually exclusive and collectively exhaustive cases, usually named *success and failure.*

(*ii*) The trials are independent and the probability of success p or failure $(1-p)$, is constant from trial to trial.

The number of success (X) in a series of n independent trials is a discrete random variable having binomial probability mass function.

Binomial probability mass function

$$P(X = x) = \binom{n}{x} p^x (1-p)^{n-x};\ x = 0, 1, 2, \ldots, n$$

It may be verified that

$$\sum_{x=0}^{n} P(X = x) = \sum_{x=0}^{n} \binom{n}{x} p^x (1-p)^{n-x} = 1$$

Further,

$$P(X < x) = \sum_{r=0}^{x-1} \binom{n}{r} p^r (1-p)^{n-r}$$

$$P(X \geq x) = \sum_{r=x}^{n} \binom{n}{r} p^r (1-p)^{n-r}$$

$$P(X = x) = \frac{n-x+1}{x} \cdot \frac{p}{q} \cdot P(X = x-1).$$

ILLUSTRATION 9. In Integrated Rural Development Programme, 5 persons are allotted with a trade and are given loan facilities to improve economic status. Past records show that the success rate is 60%.

Solution :

The probability that exactly three beneficiaries are successful is

$$P(X = 3) = \binom{5}{3} (0.6)^3 (0.4)^2$$

$$= 0.3456$$

The probability that at least three beneficiaries are successful is

$$P(X \geq 3) = P(x = 3) + P(X = 4) + P(X = 5)$$

$$= \sum_{x=3}^{5} \binom{5}{x} (0.6)^x (0.4)^{5-x}$$

$$= 0.4669$$

The probability that no beneficiary becomes successful is

$$P(X = 0) = \binom{10}{0} (0.6)^0 (0.4)^5$$

$$= 0.01024.$$

Characteristics of the Binomial Distribution

A binomial distribution is characterized by two parameters n and p. If $p = 0.5$, the binomial distribution will be symmetrical regardless of how large or small the value of n. If $p \neq 0.5$, the binomial distribution becomes a *skewed or asymmetrical* one.

The mean μ of the binomial distribution or expected value of the binomial variable X with parameters n and p, symbolically denoted by $B(X : n, p)$ is given by

$$\mu = E(X) = np$$

The variance σ^2 of the binomial distribution is given by

$$\sigma^2 = E(X - np)^2 = npq, \text{ where } q = 1 - p.$$

Standard deviation $\sigma = \sqrt{npq}$

Suppose $n = 5$ and $p = 0.6$

Then $E(X) = 5 \times 0.6 = 3$

Standard deviation of X $\sigma = \sqrt{npq}$

$$= \sqrt{5 \times 0.6 \times 0.4} = \sqrt{1.20}$$

$$= 1.1 \text{ approx.}$$

Skewness :

$$\pm\sqrt{\beta_1} = \pm\sqrt{\frac{(1-2p)^2}{npq}} = \pm\sqrt{\frac{[1-2\,(0.6)]^2}{5\,(0.6)\,(0.4)}} = \pm\sqrt{\frac{0.04}{1.20}} = \pm\, 0.1825$$

The sign of skewness is —ve because $\mu_3 = npq\,(q - p)$ is negative.

Kurtosis :

$$\beta_2 = 3 + \frac{1-6\,pq}{npq} = 3 + \frac{1-6\,(0.6)\,(0.4)}{5\,(0.6)\,(0.4)}$$

$$= 3 + \frac{1-1.44}{1.20} = 3 - .3667 = 2.6333.$$

8.6.2. Poisson Distribution

The Poisson distribution is a discrete probability distribution with many practical applications.

The Poisson probability distribution can be derived from Binomial distribution by putting $np = \lambda$ (finite) and tending n to infinity. This distribution is more suited to situations where the probability of occurrence of an event in finite interval is very small, the expected number of occurrences is finite and the number of intervals is very large. For example, number of accidents at a busy crossing road, number of printing mistakes per page in a book, arrival of telephone calls on a switch board and arrival of persons in a queue etc. are poisson random variables.

Poisson probability mass function :

$$P(X = x) = e^{-\lambda}\frac{\lambda^x}{\lfloor x} \quad ; \quad x = 0, 1, 2, \ldots, \infty\ ; \lambda > 0$$

$$\sum_{x=0}^{\infty} e^{-\lambda}\frac{\lambda^x}{\lfloor x} = 1 \quad ; \quad e = 2.71828$$

The expected value or mean of X is

$$E(X) = \lambda,$$

and the variance of X is

$$V(X) = \lambda$$

Standard deviation of X is $\sigma = \sqrt{\lambda}$

The Poisson distribution is a positively skewed and leptokurtic distribution with $\sqrt{\beta_1} = \sqrt{\frac{1}{\lambda}}$ and $\beta_2 = 3 + \frac{1}{\lambda}$.

$$P(X \le x) = \sum_{r=0}^{x} e^{-\lambda} \frac{\lambda^r}{\underline{|r}}$$

$$P(X < x) = \sum_{r=0}^{x-1} e^{-\lambda} \frac{\lambda^r}{\underline{|r}}$$

$$P(X \ge x) = \sum_{x}^{\infty} e^{-\lambda} \frac{\lambda^r}{\underline{|r}}; \; P(X = x) = \frac{\lambda}{x} P(X = x - 1).$$

Symbolically, the probability distribution of the Poisson random variable X may be written as $P(x : \lambda)$

Example 8.4. At a petrol filling station 0.3 customers arrive per minute on the average. What is the probability that exactly 3 customers will arrive during a 5 minute span ?

Solution :

Assume Poisson distribution during 5 minute span on the average $0.3 \times 5 = 1.5$ customers will arrive for service

Therefore, $\lambda = 1.5$

The required probability is

$$P(x : \lambda) = P(3 : 1.5)$$

$$= e^{-1.5} \frac{(1.5)^3}{\underline{|3}} = (0.223)\,(0.5625)$$

$$= 0.1254.$$

Example 8.5. The average number of calls received per minute in a railway enquiry booth during busy hours is 3. Find the probability that

(*i*) more than 5 calls are received.

(*ii*) at best 2 calls are received.

Solution :

Let X be the number of calls received.

(*i*) $P(X > 5) = 1 - P(X \le 5)$

$$= 1 - \left[\sum_{x=0}^{5} e^{-3} \frac{3^x}{x\,!}\right]$$

$$= 1 - e^{-3} \sum_{x=0}^{5} \frac{3^x}{x\,!}$$

$$= 1 - 0.0498 \left[\frac{3^0}{0\,!} + \frac{3^1}{1\,!} + \frac{3^2}{2\,!} + \frac{3^3}{3\,!} + \frac{3^4}{4\,!} + \frac{3^5}{5\,!}\right]$$

$$= 1 - 0.0498\,[1 + 3 + 4.5 + 4.5 + 3.37 + 2.02]$$

$$= 1 - 0.0498\,(18.39) = 1 - 0.9158 = 0.0842$$

(*ii*) $P(X \le 2) = P(X = 0) + P(X = 1) + P(X = 2)$

$$= 0.0498 \left(\frac{3^0}{0\,!} + \frac{3^1}{1\,!} + \frac{3^2}{2\,!}\right)$$

$$= 0.4233.$$

Example 8.6. Compare the binomial probability of getting 2 successes in a series of 100 independent trials when the probability of a success is 0.05 with the corresponding Poisson approximation.

Solution :

Now $B(x : n, p)$

$$= B(2 : 100, 0.05), \text{ where } n = 100, p = 0.05$$
$$= \binom{100}{2}(0.05)^2 (0.95)^{98} = 0.081$$

Further, $P(x : \lambda) = P(2 : 5)$, since $\lambda = 100 \times 0.05 = 5$

$$= e^{-5} \frac{5^2}{2\,!} = 0.084$$

It is to be noted that the difference between the true binomial probability and the Poisson approximation is as small as 0.003.

Example 8.7. Compute $P(X < 8)$ if X is the number of deaths amongst a group of 500 policy holders. Each policy holder has a 0.01 probability of dying independently of any other policy holder.

Solution :

We have a binomial distribution with $n = 500$ and $p = 0.01$. Since n is large and p is small we could use a Poisson approximation.

The required probability using binomial distribution is

$$\begin{aligned} P(X < 8) &= P(X \le 7) \\ &= P(X = 0) + P(X = 1) + P(X = 2) + P(X = 3) + P(X = 4) \\ &\quad + P(X = 5) + P(X = 6) + P(X = 7) \\ &= 0.00657 + 0.03318 + 0.08363 + 0.14023 + 0.17600 \\ &\quad + 0.17635 + 0.14696 + 0.10476 = 0.86768 \end{aligned}$$

Following Poisson approximation

$$\lambda = n \,.\, p = 500\,(0.01) = 5$$

The approximate probability may be calculated by referring to cumulative Poisson tables or adding individual terms as

$$P(X \le 7) = \sum_{x=0}^{7} e^{-5} \frac{5^x}{x\,!} = 0.86663.$$

8.7. Normal distribution

A continuous probability distribution which has revolutionized the statistical theory is the *normal distribution*, which was discovered by Demoivre in 1753 as an approximation to the binomial distribution. Gauss (1809) rediscovered this distribution from the law of distribution of errors. The equation of the normal curve is of exponential type and the description of the distribution as *'normal'* is due to Karl Pearson, a famous British Biometrician.

The normal curve is bell-shaped and symmetrical in nature. The three measures of central tendency—Mean, Median and Mode are the same. The normal random variable X has an infinite range $-\infty < X < +\infty$. The normal distribution is characterized by two parameters μ and σ, which are the mean and standard deviation of the normal distribution. Its measure of skewness $\sqrt{\beta_1} = 0$, being a symmetrical distribution and coefficient of kurtosis $\beta_2 = 3$.

The Normal distribution :

$$f(X \mid \mu, \sigma) = \frac{1}{\sqrt{2\pi}\,\sigma} e^{-\frac{1}{2\sigma^2}(X-\mu)^2}, \quad -\infty \le X \le +\infty$$
$$-\infty \le \mu \le \infty, \ \sigma > 0.$$

μ = Mean = Median = Mode

σ = Standard deviation; $\sigma > 0$

e = constant approximated by 2.71828

π = constant approximated by 3.14159

$$\int_{-\infty}^{+\infty} f(x \mid \mu, \sigma)\, dx = 1$$

$$\int_{-\infty}^{\mu} f(x \mid \mu, \sigma)\, dx = 0.5 = \int_{\mu}^{\infty} f(x \mid \mu, \sigma)\, dx$$

The Quartiles Q_1 and Q_3 are given by

$$Q_1 = \mu - 0.6745\,\sigma, \quad Q_3 = \mu + 0.6745\,\sigma.$$

The calculation of the distribution function $F(x) = P(X < x)$ of the normal probability distribution is tedious and time consuming. Further, if tables need to be prepared for ready use, this number would be very large and thus making the task almost impossible. To get rid of these difficulties by virtue of a transformation formula any normal random variable X with parameters μ and σ can be converted to a standard normal random variable Z. Thus,

$$Z = \frac{X - \mu}{\sigma}$$

The mean of Z is zero and variance is unity. The probability density of Z is given by

$$f(z) = \frac{1}{\sqrt{2\pi}} e^{-\frac{1}{2}z^2}, \quad -\infty < z < +\infty$$

with $\int_{-\infty}^{+\infty} f(z)\, dz = 1$.

Normal probability integral tables have been prepared in statistical literature to compute $\Phi(z) = \int_{-\infty}^{z} f(t)\, dt$ for various values of z.

Due to symmetrical property of standard normal distribution,

$$P(Z < 0) = P(Z > 0) = 0.5$$
$$P(Z < -t) = P(Z > t);\ t > 0$$
$$P(-t < Z < 0) = P(0 < Z < t);\ t > 0$$

This also implies

$$P(X < \mu) = P(X > \mu) = 0.5$$

Further,
$$P(\mu - \sigma < X < \mu + \sigma) = P(-1 < Z < 1) = 0.6826$$
$$P(\mu - 2\sigma < X < \mu + 2\sigma) = P(-2 < Z < 2) = 0.9544$$
$$P(\mu - 3\sigma < X < \mu + 3\sigma) = P(-3 < Z < +3) = 0.9973$$

The probability curve of the normal distribution reveals that the tails of the distribution tapers towards the horizontal axis and

$$P(|X - \mu| > 3\sigma) = 0.0027$$

That is, very small probability is located in the tail areas of the normal distribution.

In many applications of statistical theory we often come across distributions which are at least approximately normal such as distribution of errors, distributions of biological and demographic variables. Some random variables in biological, social and economic fields due to a multitude of independent causes often follow the normal law.

Note : In Table A–1, $P(Z > z)$ with $z \geq 0$ has been computed.

ILLUSTRATION 10. Given a normal distribution with $\mu = 100$, $\sigma = 10$

Probability that the normal random variable X is greater than 75 is

$$P(X > 75) = P\left(\frac{X-\mu}{\sigma} > \frac{75-100}{10}\right)$$
$$= P(Z > -2.5) = 0.9938$$
$$P(X < 70) = P\left(\frac{X-\mu}{\sigma} < \frac{70-100}{10}\right)$$
$$= P(Z < -3) = 0.0013$$
$$P(75 < X < 85) = P\left(\frac{75-100}{10} < \frac{X-\mu}{\sigma} < \frac{85-100}{10}\right)$$
$$= P(-2.5 < Z < -1.5)$$
$$= 0.0606$$
$$P(X < 80 \text{ or } X > 100)$$
$$= P(X < 80) + P(X > 100)$$
$$= P(Z < -2) + P(Z > 0)$$
$$= 0.0228 + 0.5 = 0.5228$$

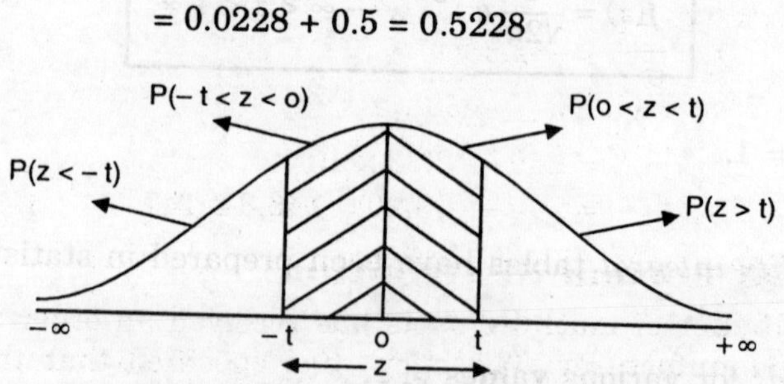

Fig. 8.1. Standard Normal Distribution.

ILLUSTRATION 11. Given a normal distribution with mean $\mu = 75$ and $\sigma = 9$. Find X_0 such that

(*i*) $P(X < X_0) = 0.10$

(*ii*) $P(X > X_0) = 0.70$

Solution :

Now,

$$(i)\ P\left(\frac{X-\mu}{\sigma} < \frac{X_0 - 75}{9}\right) = 0.10$$

From standard normal probability distribution table,

$$\frac{X_0 - 75}{9} = -1.28$$

$$\Rightarrow \quad X_0 = 63.48$$

$$(ii)\ P\left(\frac{X-\mu}{\sigma} > \frac{X_0 - 75}{9}\right) = 0.70$$

$$\Rightarrow \quad \frac{X_0 - 75}{9} = -0.52$$

$$\Rightarrow \quad X_0 = 70.32$$

ILLUSTRATION 12. A statistical analysis of 1000 long distance telephone calls made from the State Secretariat indicates that lengths of these calls are normally distributed with mean $\mu = 240$ seconds and standard deviation $\sigma = 40$ seconds.

(*a*) What percentage of these calls lasted less than 180 seconds ?

(*b*) What is the probability that a particular call lasted between 180 and 300 seconds ?

(*c*) What is the length of a particular call if only 1% of all calls are shorter ?

Let X be the duration of call.

$$P(X < 180) = P\left(Z < \frac{180 - 240}{40}\right)$$

$$= P(Z < -1.5) = 0.0668$$

$$P(180 < X < 300) = P(-1.5 < Z < 1.5)$$

$$= 0.8664$$

$$P(X < X_0) = 0.01$$

$$\Rightarrow \quad P\left(Z < \frac{X_0 - \mu}{\sigma}\right) = 0.01$$

Therefore,

$$\frac{X_0 - \mu}{\sigma} = -2.33$$

$$\Rightarrow \quad X_0 = \mu - 2.33\,\sigma$$

$$= 240 - 2.33 \times 40$$

$$= 240 - 93.20 = 146.8 \cong 147.$$

8.7.1. Application of normal distribution

Exmple 8.8. A supplier of machine parts has received an order to supply piston rods to an automobile manufacturer. The client has specified that the rod diameter should lie between 2.541 and 2.548 cm. Accordingly, the supplier has been looking for the right kind of machine. He has identified two machines both of which can produce a mean diameter of 2.545 cm. The standard deviations of the diameter produced from the machine 1 and 2 are 0.003 and 0.005 respectively. Further, machine 1 costs Rs. 3.3 lakhs more than machine 2. The supplier is confident of making a profit of Rs. 100/- per piston rod, however, a piston rod rejected will mean a loss of Rs. 40/-.

The supplier questions whether he should go for the better machine with an extra cost.

Solution :

Assume that the diameters of the piston rods produced by the machining process is normally distributed.

For machine 1, the diameter is N (2.545, 0.003), and

For machine 2, the diameter is N(2.545, 0.005).

If D denotes the diameter, the probability of acceptance of a piston rod produced by machine 1 is given by

$$P\left(\frac{2.541-2.545}{0.003} < \frac{D-2.545}{0.003} < \frac{2.548-2.545}{0.003}\right)$$

$$\Rightarrow \quad P(-1.33 < Z < 1) = 0.7479$$

Hence, the probability of rejection is

$$1 - 0.7479 = 0.2521$$

Thus, the expected profit if machine 1 is used is

$$= 100 \times 0.7479 - 40 \times 0.2521$$
$$= \text{Rs. } 64.706$$

Similarly, if machine 2 is used, the probability of acceptance is

$$P\left(\frac{2.541-2.545}{0.005} < \frac{D-2.545}{0.005} < \frac{2.548-2.545}{0.005}\right)$$
$$= P(-0.8 < Z < 0.6) = 0.5138$$

Hence, the probability of rejection is

$$1 - 0.5138 = 0.4862$$

Then, expected profit per piston rod if machine 2 is used

$$= 100 \times 0.5138 - 40 \times 0.4862$$
$$= \text{Rs. } 31.932$$

Thus, we see that expected profit per piston rod is more if machine 1 used. As machine 1 costs more, it would be profitable if machine 1 produces more piston rods.

To find the break even production level, let n denote the number of rods produced. Then,

$$n\,(64.706 - 31.932) = 3{,}30{,}000$$

or $\quad n = 10{,}069$

This implies that it is advisable to go for machine 1, only if the production level is higher than 10,069. Such a conclusion will be feasible only if there is enough demand for the rods.

Normal approximation to Binomial distribution

When n is very large, the Binomial probabilities can be approximated to a normal distribution. This is derived from the fact that, if X is a Binomial variable with parameters n and p, the limiting form of $Z = \frac{X - np}{\sqrt{npq}}$ is standardised normal as $n \to \infty$ or very large n, with mean zero and variance unity. For large n, the calculation of partial sums of the Binomial probabilities becomes a difficult and time consuming affair and hence, in such case the normal approximation can be used without losing much accuracy. If n is not large, approximation will be good provided p is reasonably close to 1/2.

As the continuous normal distribution is used to approximate the discrete Binomial distribution, each x (number of success) is replaced by the corresponding interval from $x - \frac{1}{2}$ to $x + \frac{1}{2}$ to account towards correction for continuity. Such correction is referred to as Continuity Correction. $P(X = x) \cong P\left(x - \frac{1}{2} \leq X \leq x + \frac{1}{2}\right)$ and $P(a \leq X \leq b) \cong P\left(a - \frac{1}{2} \leq X \leq b + \frac{1}{2}\right)$.

Example 8.9. Suppose that 20% of the products made in a certain factory are defective, so that thcy have to be inspected carefully before these are released to the market. Find the probability of obtaining

(*a*) at most 15 defectives, (*b*) exactly 15 defectives,

in a lot of 100 chosen for inspection.

Solution :

(*a*) Assuming the conditions of Binomial distribution to hold, the required probability is

$$\Sigma\, B\,(x : n, p)$$

$$= \sum_{x=0}^{15} B\,(x : 100, 0.20), \text{ where } n = 100 \text{ and } p = 0.20$$

$$= 0.1285$$

To approximate the Binomial probability by normal approximation, we take

$$\mu = np = 100 \times 0.20 = 20$$

$$\sigma^2 = np\,(1-p) = 100\,(0.20)\,(0.80) = 16$$

Using Continuity correction

$$\Sigma\, B(x : 100, 0.20)$$

$$\cong P\left[Z < \frac{15.5 - 20}{4}\right], \text{ Z being a standard normal variable.}$$

$$= P\,(Z < -1.13)$$

$$= 0.1292.$$

Thus, it is seen that difference between true Binomial probability and normal approximation is only 0.0007.

(*b*) The probability of getting exactly 15 defectives through Binomial distribution is

$$B\,(15 : 100, 0.20) = 0.481$$

To use normal approximation, we make the continuity correction of representing 15 by means of the interval 14.5 to 15.5.

Thus, $B\,(15 : 100, 0.20)$

$$\cong P\left[\frac{14.5 - 20}{4} < Z < \frac{15.5 - 20}{4}\right]$$

$$= 0.0454$$

8.7.3. Normal Approximation to Poisson Distribution

If X is a Poisson variable with parameter λ, then the limiting form of $\frac{X-\lambda}{\sqrt{\lambda}}$ as $\lambda \to \infty$ follows a standardized normal distribution. In using the normal approximation to a Poisson distribution we take recourse to same consideration for approximating the distribution of a discrete random variable with the distribution of a continuous random variable. Hence, some care must be taken with the end points of the intervals involved. This is because for a continuous random variable X, P(X = 5) = 0, while for a discrete random variable this probability may be non zero positive. Hence, the correction for continuity may be applied as in case of normal approximation to Binomial distribution to improve approximation.

8.8. Independence of random variables

Definition : Two discrete random variables X_1 and X_2 are said to be independent if their joint probability mass function is factorised into their individual mass functions, that is,

$$p_{x_1 x_2}(x_1, x_2) = p_{x_1}(x_1)\, p_{x_2}(x_2), \text{ for all } x_1 \text{ and } x_2.$$

Two continuous random variables X_1 and X_2 are said to be independent if their joint probability distribution function is factorised into their individual distribution functions

$$F(x_1, x_2) = F_{X_1}(x_1)\, F_{X_2}(x_2), \; -\infty < x_1 < +\infty, \; -\infty < x_2 < +\infty.$$

8.9. Expectation of sum and product of two independent random variables

$$E(X_1 + X_2) = E(X_1) + E(X_2),$$
$$V(X_1 + X_2) = V(X_1) + V(X_2)$$
$$E(X_1 X_2) = E(X_1)\,.\,E(X_2)$$

Note : If X_1 and X_2 are not independent,

$$E(X_1 + X_2) = E(X_1) + E(X_2)$$
$$V(X_1 + X_2) = V(X_1) + V(X_2) + 2\,\text{Cov.}(X_1, X_2),$$

where $\text{Cov.}(X_1, X_2) = E[\{X_1 - E(X_1)\}\{X_2 - E(X_2)\}]$,

which vanishes if X_1 and X_2 are independent.

8.10. The Weak law of large numbers

Consider a sequence of independent random variables $X_1, X_2, \ldots, X_n$ with means $\mu_1, \mu_2, \ldots, \mu_n$ and variances $\sigma_1^2, \sigma_2^2, \ldots, \sigma_n^2$ respectively.

Let $$T = X_1 + X_2 + \ldots + X_n$$

$$\bar{X} = \frac{T}{n} = \sum_{i=1}^{n} X_i/n$$

$$E(\bar{X}) = \sum_{i=1}^{n} \mu_i/n = \bar{\mu}$$

$$V(\bar{X}) = \frac{1}{n^2} \sum_{i=1}^{n} \sigma_i^2$$

Applying Chebyshev's inequality,

$$P[|\bar{X} - \bar{\mu}| \geq \epsilon] \leq \sum_{i=1}^{n} \sigma_i^2 / n^2 \epsilon^2$$

This implies $P(|\bar{X} - \bar{\mu}| > \epsilon) \to 0$ as $n \to \infty$

If $\mu_1 = \mu_2 = ... = \mu_n = \mu$ say, and

$\sigma_1^2 = \sigma_2^2 = ... = \sigma_n^2 = \sigma^2$, say

$$E(\bar{X}) = \mu, \; V(\bar{X}) = \sigma^2/n.$$

The Chebyshev's inequality reduces to

$$P(|\bar{X} - \mu| > \epsilon) < \frac{\sigma^2}{n\epsilon^2}.$$

That is, $\bar{X} \xrightarrow{P} \mu$ as $n \to \infty$.

This result is a milestone in the development of statistical theory, known as the *Weak law of large numbers.* This law indicates that whatever may be the form of the distribution, the mean of independent and identically distributed random variables $\bar{X}$ will tend to their common expected value μ as the number of random variables increases.

Note. If X is a random variable with mean μ and variance σ^2, then for any value of $K > 0$ $p(|X - \mu| \geq k) \leq \frac{\sigma^2}{k^2}$, which is called Chebyshev's inequality.

8.11. Central limit theorem

Let $X_1, X_2, ..., ...$ be independently and identically distributed random variables having common mean μ and finite variance σ^2.

Let $S_n = X_1 + ... + X_n$.

Then $$\lim_{n \to \infty} P\left(\frac{S_n - n\mu}{\sigma\sqrt{n}} \leq z\right) = \Phi(z), \; -\infty < z < +\infty$$

where $\Phi(z)$ is the cumulative distribution function of the *standard normal distribution.*

This result has a far reaching consequence in statistical inference. The random variable X_i can be discrete, continuous or neither of these. The specific requirements are that the mean and variance of X_i must exist.

Applications

Let X_i takes values 1 and 0 with respective probabilities p and $1-p$. Then

$$P(S_n = r) = \binom{n}{r} p^r (1-p)^{n-r}$$

Thus, as discovered by DeMoivre (1667-1754) and Laplace (1749-1827)

$\underset{n \to \infty}{\text{Lt}} \; P\left[\frac{S_n - np}{\sqrt{np(1-p)}} \leq z\right] = \Phi(z)$, that is, $\frac{S_n - np}{\sqrt{npq}}$ is asymptotically normally distributed with mean zero and variance unity.

Further, let $X_1, X_2, ...$ be independent random variables each having a Poisson distribution with parameter λ. Then

$$S_n = X_1 + X_2 + ... + X_n$$

has mean $n\lambda$ and variance $n\lambda$

The Central limit theorem implies that

$$\lim_{n \to \infty} P\left[\frac{S_n - n\lambda}{\sqrt{n\lambda}} \le z\right] = \Phi(z), -\infty < z < +\infty$$

Example 8.10. Let $X_1, X_2, ..., X_n$ be n independent normal variables with same mean μ and variance σ^2. Compute $P(\bar{X} < 15)$ for $n = 5$, $\mu = 20$ and $\sigma^2 = 5$.

Solution :

The mean $\bar{X} = \frac{1}{n}(X_1 + ... + X_n)$ is normally distributed with mean μ and variance $\frac{\sigma^2}{n}$.

Thus,
$$\begin{aligned} P(\bar{X} < 15) &= P\left(Z < \frac{15-20}{5/\sqrt{5}}\right) \\ &= P(Z < -2.236) \\ &= 1 - \Phi(2.236) = 0.0127 \end{aligned}$$

Example 8.11. Suppose n is large, say equal to 50 and there is no assumption about the distribution of the random variables, except that they have finite mean μ and variance σ^2. The mean of the random variables $X_1, X_2, ..., X_n$ is asymptotically normally distributed with mean μ and variance $\frac{\sigma^2}{n}$. For $\mu = 20$ and $\sigma^2 = 25$,

$$\begin{aligned} P(\bar{X} > 22) &= P\left(\frac{\bar{X}-\mu}{\sigma/\sqrt{n}} > \frac{22-20}{5/\sqrt{50}}\right) \\ &= P\left(Z > \frac{2}{\sqrt{.5}}\right) = P(Z > 2.828) \\ &= 1 - \Phi(2.828) = 0.00234 \end{aligned}$$

Example 8.12. A random sample of size 100 is taken from an infinite population having mean 76 and variance 256. What is the probability that the sample mean $\bar{X}$ will be between 75 and 78 ?

Solution :

Applying Central limit theorem, $Z = \frac{\bar{X}-\mu}{\sigma/\sqrt{n}}$ is asymptotically normally distributed, as the sample size is large *i.e.* 100.

Here
$$n = 100$$
$$\mu = 76$$
$$\sigma^2 = 256 \Rightarrow \sigma = 16$$

Thus,
$$\begin{aligned} &P(75 < \bar{X} < 78) \\ &= P\left(\frac{75-\mu}{\sigma/\sqrt{n}} < \frac{\bar{X}-\mu}{\sigma/\sqrt{n}} < \frac{78-\mu}{\sigma/\sqrt{n}}\right) \end{aligned}$$

$$= P\left(\frac{75-76}{16/\sqrt{100}} < Z < \frac{78-76}{16/\sqrt{100}}\right)$$
$$= P(-0.625 < Z < 1.25)$$
$$= \Phi(1.25) - \Phi(-0.625)$$
$$= 0.8944 - 0.2660 = 0.6284.$$

EXERCISES

1. (*a*) Define a sample space and an event.

(*b*) Describe sample space for the following random experiments.

(*i*) A card is drawn from a well-shuffled pack of playing cards.

(*ii*) A ball is thrown in the air.

(*iii*) A coin is tossed twice.

(*iv*) A six-faced die is rolled.

(*v*) Occurrence of accidents at a busy crossing.

(*vi*) Choosing a bolt from a box consisting of 400 bolts.

(*vii*) Choosing a student from a class consisting of 10 boys and 20 girls.

(*viii*) A student appears at an examination.

(*ix*) Five candidates contesting in an election.

2. A bag contains 6 red balls and 4 white balls. Two successive draws of 3 balls are made without replacement. Find the probability that the first drawing will give 3 white balls and second 3 red balls. (**Ans.** 1/5)

3. In a single throw of two dice, find the probability of getting a score of (*i*) ten (*ii*) twelve on the two dice. (**Ans.** 1/2, 1/36)

4. A box contains 400 bolts of which 40 are defectives. Find the probability that a bolt chosen at random from the box is not defective. (**Ans.** 0.9)

5. Find the chance of throwing an even score in a single throw with two dice.

6. The following table gives distribution of wages of 1000 workers.

Wages (in Rs.)	120–140	140–160	160–180	180–200	200–220	220–240	240–260
No. of Workers	12	115	478	200	142	35	18

An individual is selected at random from the above group. What is the probability that his wages are (*i*) under 180 (*ii*) above 220 (*iii*) between 160 and 240. (**Ans.** $\frac{605}{1000}, \frac{53}{1000}, \frac{855}{1000}$)

7. The following table traces life history of 200 personal computers installed in an engineering college.

Life (in Year)	0	1	2	3	4	5
Number Working in Order	200	180	160	120	100	80

Find the probablity that a computer after installation will be in order till the completion of 5th year. (**Ans.** 0.4)

8. Six dice are rolled simultaneously. Find the probability of getting 20 points. (**Ans.** $\frac{462}{5184}$)

9. A M.B.A. degree holder applies for a job in two computer firms, say X and Y. The probability of his being selected in firm X is 0.8 and being rejected in firm

Y is 0.6. The probability of at least one of his applications being rejected is 0.6. What is the probability that he will be selected in one of the two firms ?

(**Ans.** 0.8)

10. There are 10 cards marked with numbers 1 to 10. One card is selected at random. What is the probability that it is divisible by 2 or 5 ? (**Ans.** 0.5)

11. A card is drawn from a well-shuffled pack of playing cards. What is the probability that it is either a diamond or a queen ?

(**Ans.** $\frac{4}{13}$)

12. The following table shows the results of 250 MBA graduates passing out from an Institute of Business Management.

Sex/Grade	**First Class**	**Second Class**	**Total**
Male	100	50	150
Female	60	40	100
Total	160	90	250

One of these students is to be selected at random for employment. What is the probability of selecting a first class male student ? (**Ans.** 0.625)

13. A consignment of 15 television sets contains 4 defectives. The radios are selected at random, one by one and examined. The ones examined are not put back. What is the probability that the 9th one examined is the last defective ?

(**Ans.** 8/195)

14. The chances of accidents in factories—A, B and C are 0.60, 0.40 and 0.20 respectively. Find the probability that an accident may happen in (i) at least one of them (ii) all of them. (**Ans.** 0.808 ; 0.048)

15. Assuming that sex ratio in a community is $\frac{1}{2}$, find the probability that in a family of 6 children (*a*) all children will be of the same sex (*b*) three of them will be boys and two girls.

(**Ans.** $\frac{1}{32}$; $\frac{5}{8}$)

16. Two cards are drawn with replacement from a full pack of 52 cards. What is the probability :

(*i*) that both cards are spades ?

(*ii*) that cards are either two hearts or two diamonds ?

(**Ans.** $\frac{1}{16}$; $\frac{1}{8}$)

17. The odds in favour of A winning a game against B are 5 : 2. If three games are played, what are the odds in favour of A's winning at least once ?

(**Ans.** 0.977)

18. The chances of A, B, C being Chief Minister are 2 : 3 : 4. The probability that the government aided housing programme will be introduced is 0.5, 0.8 and 0.3 respectively.

(*a*) What is the probability that there will be a government aided housing programme ?

(*b*) If the housing programme has been introduced, what is the probability that the appointed Chief minister is (*i*) A (*ii*) B (*ii*) C ?

(**Ans.** (*a*) 0.93 (*b*) $\frac{5}{23}$, $\frac{12}{23}$, $\frac{6}{23}$)

19. The marketing manager of a toy manufacturing company is considering the marketing of new toy.

In the past, 40% of toys introduced by the company have been successful and 60% unsuccessful. Before the toy is marketed, a market research is conducted and a report either favourable or unfavourable is compiled. In the past 80% of the successful toys received a favourable market research report and 30% of the unsuccessful toys received a favourable market research report.
What is the probability that the toy will be successful if it receives a favourable report ? (**Ans.** 0.64)

20. How many tosses of a coin is needed so that the probability of getting at least one head is 0.875 ?

21. Distinguish between discrete and continuous random vriables with examples.

22. Define Mathematical expectation of a random variable.
If a business concern makes a profit of 2 lakhs of rupees by introducing a new product with probability 2/5 and incurs a loss of rupees one lakh with probability 3/5, what is mathematical expectation of his gain ?
(**Ans.** $\frac{1}{5}$ Lakh of rupees)

23. A consignment of 30 radio contains 4 defectives. A random sample of 5 is selected from this consignment. If X denotes the number of defectives, find the probability function of X and hence find E(X) and V(X).

24. Let Y denote the profit that a man makes in business. He may earn Rs. 2,800 with probability 0.5. He may lose Rs. 1,500 with probability 0.3. He may neither earn nor lose with probability 0.2. Calculate the mathematical expectation of Y.

25. If 20% of a large consignment of eggs are bad, what is the probability distribution of number of bad eggs in a box consisting of half dozen eggs chosen at random ?

26. A hawker visits daily 5 localities to sell his goods. The probability of selling at each place is 0.3. Given the observed frequency distribution of the hawker's number of sales per day for 120 days.

Number of Sales per Day	0	1	2	3	4	5
Frequency	15	50	34	13	5	3

Calculate the expected frequencies assuming that a binomial distribution provides a good fit.

27. During war one ship out of 9 was sunk on an average in making a voyage. Find the probability that : (*a*) exactly 3 (*b*) at least 3 out of a convoy of 6 ships would arrive safely.

28. Distinguish betwen Binomial probability distribution and Poisson probability distribution and their spheres of application with examples.

29. Assume that the chance of an individual coal miner being killed in a mine accident in a year is $\frac{1}{1400}$. Calculate the probability that a mine employing 350 miners there will be at least one fatal accident in a year. (**Ans.** 0.2202)

30. At a petrol filling station 0.3 customers arrive per minute on the average. What is the probability that exactly 3 customers will arrive during a 5 minute span ? (**Ans.** 0.1254)

31. A Car hire firm has 2 cars, which it hires out day by day. The number of demands for a car on each day is distributed as a Poisson distribution with mean 1.5.

Calculate the proportion of days on which

(*a*) neither car is used.

(*b*) some demand is refused.

(*c*) only one car is demanded.

32. A skilled typist on routine work kept a record of mistakes made per day during 300 working days.

Mistakes per Day	0	1	2	3	4	5	6
Number of Days	143	90	42	12	9	3	1

Calculate the frequencies of a Poisson series which has the same total frequency and mean as the above distribution.

33. What are the characteristics of a normal distribution ? Discuss. Mention its importance in statistical analysis.

34. In final MBA examination 10% of the candidates scored 60 or more marks and 30% scored 40 or less marks. Find the mean and standard deviation of marks, assuming marks are normally distributed. (**Ans.** 45.82, 11.08)

35. A television set lasts on the average 2 years with standard deviation 0.5 without any repair. Find the probability that a television set will last

(*a*) less than a year.

(*b*) more than 2.5 year.

Assume that the life of a television set is normally distributed.

(**Ans.** 0.0228 ; 0.1587)

36. Given that, the switch board of a consultant's office receives on the average 0.9 calls per minute. Find the probability that during the span of 15 minutes.

(*a*) at most 5 incoming calls.

(*b*) exactly 6 incoming calls will be received.

Compare these probabilities with normal approximations.

[**Ans.** 0.008 (Normal approx 0.015), 0.011 (Normal approx : 0.013)]

37. What is the central limit theorem ? Explain its applications in statistical analysis.

38. For a normal distribution the median is 89 and the first quartile is 75.5. What is the value of the standard deviation ?

39. The marks secured by a large group of statistics students are assumed to be normally distributed with mean 65 and standard deviation 5. What is the probability that a student will have mark over 70 ?

40. The daily sales of a certain item are normally distributed with mean Rs. 8,000 and standard deviation of Rs. 1,000.

(*a*) What is the probability that on a given day the sales will be less than Rs. 8,500 ?

(*b*) What percentage of days will the sales be between Rs. 8,200 and Rs. 8,600 ?

(*c*) What proportion of days will the sales be within 10% of the population mean ?

□□□

CHAPTER 9

SAMPLING TECHNIQUES

9.1 What is a Survey ?

A survey is a process by which certain quantitative / qualitative facts pertaining to certain field of enquiry are collected to throw light on the objectives of a research problem. This may be related to any discipline needing scientific investigation. Thus, we may talk of economic surveys, business surveys, social surveys, market surveys, industrial surveys, agricultural surveys, geological surveys, environmental surveys, bovine surveys, epidemiological surveys, health and demographic surveys, family planning surveys etc.

A survey is a planned observation of objects that are not themselves deliberately treated or controlled by the observer. 'Nature' is assumed to have applied the treatments/stimulus and all that the analysts can do it to observe the consequences.

A survey may be either exploratory or based on certain specific objectives and forms a basis for further investigation.

Some surveys are conducted on regular basis and there are also **ad hoc surveys** which are conducted depending on the problems at hand. Further, surveys may be either **census surveys or sample surveys.** Census surveys take into account all the units of the enquiry whereas as sample surveys deal with a part of it. Again, surveys may be alternatively classified as **descriptive and analytical surveys.** *The descriptive surveys are broadly fact finding surveys whereas analytical surveys deal with interrelations among different variables of interest, levels of different factors and their interaction such as factorial surveys, comparison of different domains and groups etc.* There are also hybrid investigations being combination of both descriptive and analytical.

9.2 Population and Sample

In our day–to–day life we come across certain situations where we continuously or otherwise take a decision based on a limited facts or limited number of units, which is a part or fraction of totality of facts/units. This **totality or aggregate of units on which observations are made is called population**—a term having broad meaning in statistical investigation such as population of human beings, cattle population, population of cities/villages/households, plant population, fish population, population of factories/industrial establishments, consumers of certain product, population of departmental stores, population of workers, etc.

Survey of complete enumeration of population of interest is called **Census.** A **sample** is a subset of the population and the survey based on sample is termed as **sample survey.**

A possible problem in the sample survey is that **the sample size** which may need to be very large if information is wanted for very rare population characteristics and many very small groups in the population. In general, the size of the sample depends on the inherent variability in the population and the cost of making an observation.

9.2.1 When is a census appropriate ?

A census is appropriate when the population size itself in quite small. For instance, if the researcher is interested in conducting a study on the problems of fertilizer plants in the country, it is advisable to contact all fertilizer firms. A census is also appropriate if information is needed from every individual object in the population such as population census, industrial census, agricultural census, etc. Further, if the cost of making an incorrect decision is high or if sampling errors are high, then a census may be more appropriate. Also, if the cost of making an observation is negligibly low or not a matter of concern and it is possible to complete the survey within a reasonable period of time, one may think of a census study for more reliable results.

9.2.2 When is a sample study appropriate ?

Sampling is the best course to adopt if the population size is large and if both the cost and time associated with obtaining information from the population is high. In a sample study it is possible to employ qualified and trained interviewers, which are always available in a limited way, to collect higher quality information. Further, organisation of field work and supervision of interviewers become easier. Unlike complete surveying a large population, quick decision is arrived at with a sample study. Besides in destructive tests, the sampling procedure is always to be preferred over the complete enumeration.

Sampling in business studies plays an important role in decision making. For instance, if a company is interested to obtain the reactions of employees towards certain workers' welfare programmes, a sample of employees may be adequate. Further, if a researcher is interested in obtaining consumer response from all over the world to a new advertising theme for an international soft drink brand, a census is not a sensible proposition.

9.2.3 Sampling unit

The unit of the population, which is liable to be sampled for investigation is called a **sampling unit.** The sampling unit may be a single individual unit (or element) like a person, industrial establishment, institution, etc. or a cluster of units such as households, village, class, school, community groups, etc. A researcher has a prime duty to decide **what should be the appropriate sampling unit** for collecting necessary information conveniently.

9.2.4 Sampling frame

The list of units in the population from which a random sample can be selected is called a **frame**. It may be list of households, pay roll registers, attendance sheets, list of ration cards, village maps, list of voters, revenue records, city maps showing wards, aerial photo maps, list of magazine subscribers, list of PAN cards, list of retail hardware stores, list of industrial establishments, etc.

Drawing of a random sample presupposes **existence of unambigous error-free frame.**

Errors associated with a frame are :

- Inadequacy
- Inaccuracy
- Out of date
- Subject to duplication

The description of frame does not necessarily require to enumerate all population members. It may be sufficient to specify the procedure by which each sampling unit can be located. For instance, in a study on mine workers in mining industries in a country, it would be convenient and feasible to sample mining centres for which a frame may be readily available or can be constructed with ease.

9.2.5 Target population and Survey population

As sampling is intended to gain information about a population, it is necessary to identify the population properly and accurately. If the population is defined improperly, the research may lead to wrong findings and inappropriate results.

Target population consists of all elements (units) about which we wish to make certain inference, *e.g.* to study toy buying habits in toy stores, the children going to nursery schools.

Actual population surveyed (*e.g.* all households in a region having children going to nursery schools) is the **survey population**. This actual population is surveyed for the purpose to reach target population. Ideally, survey and target populations should coincide, but hardly this is so because of non- availability of frames for the target population and difficulties in obtaining necessary information from the elements of target population. If the research objectives are well thought out, the definition of the target population will be clear and unambiguous as well.

9.2.6 Purpose of sampling

The main reason for drawing a sample from a defined population is to **infer about population characteristics** (termed **population parameters**) such as mean (average), total, ratio, percentage, variance, standard deviation, coefficient of variation, etc.

Finite population parameter value would be known exactly if a census of the survey population is carried out.

The sample quantities calculated on the basis of sample observations to represent the population characteristics are called **estimators** or their numerical values called **estimates**. Thus, **estimates are functions of sample values** to represent unknown population characteristics under estimation. For instance, if we are interested in estimating average income of employees in a factory, the computation of average income of the employees in a random sample from the population of employees is an estimate for the purpose.

9.2.7 Probability (Random) sampling and Non-probability sampling

The selection of a sample from a population is called **sampling** and the procedure of selection of sample is termed as **sampling design**.

A sample may be either a **random sample** (probability sample) or a **non-random sample** (non-probability sample). In random sampling, not to be construed with haphazard sampling, every unit of the population has a definite chance or probability of being selected, whereas in non-random sampling, no probability is attached to the unit for selection. Examples of non-random sampling are quota sampling, judgment sampling, convenience sampling, purposive sampling etc. In these sampling methods, the sampler uses his discretion depending on his need and purpose to select a sample. The major disadvantage associated with non- random sampling is that one cannot calculate or estimate the sampling error from the sample. However, such sampling procedures are sometimes adopted in exploratory surveys and in opinion surveys where quick results are needed.

Although the non-probability sampling does not involve random selection like probability sampling, it does not necessarily mean that non-probability samples are not representative of the population. It may be mentioned here that if proper probability sampling designs is not adopted, there is every likelihood that we may turn up with a non-representative sample, even if the sample is a probability sample.

9.2.8 Steps in Sampling

- Determination and fixation of the population under consideration, depending on the objectives.
- Construction of the frame of the identifiable sampling units.
- Determination of sample size.
- Choice of the appropriate sample design.
- Selection of a sample.

9.2.9 Major Steps in a sample survey

The conduct of a sample survey usually consists of the following major steps :

- planning
- execution
- processing and analysis of data
- writing of the report.

During planning stage the entire operations beginning from the determination of objectives and fixation of population under enquiry till the finalisation of report, should be kept in mind before execution of the survey.

The questions as to

(*i*) the types of data to be collected

(*ii*) the appropriate precision to be fixed for the sample results.

(*iii*) the methods of data collection-physical measurement, personal interviews, mailed enquiry, transcription from secondary sources such as official and non-official records either in printed or manuscript forms, diaries and notes, etc.

(*iv*) the determination of sampling frame and its construction, if a suitable one does not exist.

(*v*) sample size.

(*vi*) determination of sampling units

(*vii*) selection of sampling design

(*viii*) organization of field work,

are some of the major considerations for conducting any survey.

Another aspect which may require special attention is about the determination of (*i*) **survey period**, that is time period during which the survey data are to be collected,

(*ii*) **reference period,** the time period to which the data for all units should refer,

(*iii*) **the reporting period,** which may coincide or be a part of the reference period for which the required statistical information is collected for the units at a time.

Processing of data and its subsequent analysis should be carried out, keeping in view the objectives with which the survey was started.

The report should be written in a lucid style, exhibiting the analysis depending on the objectives and survey data only. The content should also vary according as whether the report is to be used by the decision making authorities or for the purpose of research.

9.3. Errors in sample surveys

Observations are always prone to errors; may it be measurement error, reporting error, response error, etc. These errors creep into the estimates, computed from the sampled observations.

Two types of errors occur in the sampling process. These are :

❒ *Sampling errors*

❒ *Non-sampling errors*

The sampling error is an inevitability when a probability sample is observed from a population instead of canvassing the whole population and is related to the deviation of the sample estimate from its corresponding population parameter. **As the sample size increases, the sampling error decreases and becomes zero for census or complete enumeration.**

Non-sampling error is a type of error occurring in statistical investigation irrespective of whether the investigation is based on a sample or there is complete enumeration. It is likely that the magnitude of non-sampling error may be more in complete enumeration, enumerating much larger number of units.

Both sampling and non–sampling errors need to be controlled and reduced to a level at which their presence does not defeat or obliterate the usefulness of the final sample results.

Non-sampling errors arise due to one or more of the following factors :

- Errors in coverage by the use of defective frame/imprecise and wrong definitions/inadequate data specification/duplication or omission of units due to faulty frames, etc.
- Errors due to observation—response errors and measurement errors.
- Errors due to non-response or non-observation of units.
- Errors in processing and analysis of data.
- Errors in preparation of reports or dissemination of findings.

Non-sampling errors cannot be effectively estimated, but may be controlled to a reasonable extent, while implementing survey operations and analysis of data, by taking precaution at every stage of the survey.

Unlike the control of sampling error which decreases with increase in sample size, non–sampling error may increase with increase in sample size and if not properly controlled it can be more damaging than sampling error for large scale surveys. Thus,

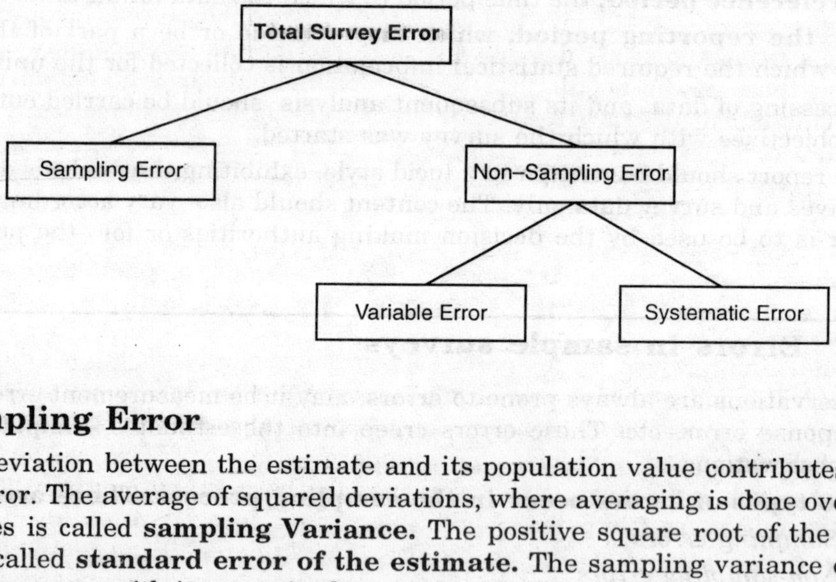

9.3.1 Sampling Error

The deviation between the estimate and its population value contributes towards sampling error. The average of squared deviations, where averaging is done over all possible samples is called **sampling Variance.** The positive square root of the sampling variance is called **standard error of the estimate.** The sampling variance or **standard error** decreases with increase in the sample size. The sampling error is caused due to random sampling from a population. If there is no sampling and we completely enumerate the population, the sampling error becomes zero and hence also the sampling variance/standard error of the estimate.

Accuracy and Precision :

A sampling design is the method of drawing a sample from a defined population. The ultimate test of a good sample is how well the sample represents the characteristics of the population it purports to measure, that is, a true representative of the population.

In order that a sample is a valid one, the derived estimate must be relatively **accurate** and **precise.**

Accuracy is the degree to which the bias is absent from the sample. The bias may arise due to faulty measuring devices, errors due to interviewers, errors due to respondents, etc. by which the measured/calculated value differs from its actual (true) value. Thus, the accuracy is the degree of conformity of the measured value to the true value. Some of the elements in the sample may show upward bias in measurement and some others may show downward bias and such variations may offset each other, bringing about some balancing effect in the final results.

Another aspect of bias which affects the accuracy is non- representativeness of the sampled elements from the population, which may occur due to sampling from a faulty frame. For instance, in a survey of business establishments, if some large establishments are knowingly avoided in the sampling process because of lack of accessibility to information needs, the final results involve inaccuracies.

Precision is associated with measured values. Precision is a measurement of how closely the analytical results can be duplicated. It is the degree to which further measurements or calculations will show the same or similar results. In sampling process no sample will fully represent the population in all respects and hence sample quantities/numerical descriptors that describe the samples may be expected to differ from those of the populations because of fluctuations inherent in the sampling process. This is called **sampling error** and is measured mathematically by the sampling variance of the estimate. It is a general practice to report sampling error by the standard error of estimate, which is defined as the positive square root of the sampling variance. This is relevant because the standard error is expressed in the same unit as that of the estimate, unlike the sampling variance, which is expressed in squared units. Sometimes the term **'efficiency'** is used analogous to **'precision'** and is defined as the **inverse of the sampling variance.**

Two estimators can be compared as regards their precision or efficiency. An estimator which is more precise or efficient is more reliable. As the estimates vary, sometimes largely, as regards their magnitude, it is advisable to compute **Relative Standard Error** (RSE), which is the standard error expressed as the percentage of the estimate itself, and use it in preference to the standard error, when comparing variability of different estimates of different magnitudes. That is, the RSE places SE in the context of the estimate. For instance, an estimate 0.01 with standard error 0.1 is certainly not preferred compared to an estimator 0.5 with standard error 0.1.

However, the **standard error can be computed only in case of probability sampling,** where units are selected depending on laws of chance or probability. **In case of non-probability sampling** such as quota sampling, purposive sampling, convenience sampling, judgement sampling, etc. **the standard error cannot be computed** or estimated from the sample itself.

The results of a measurement can be accurate but not precise, precise but not accurate or both; if a **result is both accurate and precise, it is called valid.**

9.3.2 Non-sampling Errors

Observation Errors

In field surveys, the observational errors occur when the observations made on the units of enquiry are not the true values of the observations. Errors of observation may be classified as

- *Measurement errors*
- *Response errors*

Measurement errors occur due to faulty measuring devices and inefficiency of the investigators to use the measuring devices and lack of knowledge about the measurement. These errors affect the results of the study and unless the errors of measurement are controlled and kept between the accepted limits, this is likely to affect and vitiate the survey results substantially leading to wastage of time and resources to get unreliable findings.

Reason for such errors are :

- Inadequate instructions to field staff.
- Inadequate supervision of enumerators.
- Inadequately trained and inexperienced field staff.

In social science research surveys there is possibility of large amount of response errors in the interviewing to elicit correct answers from the respondents. Every individual (unit of enquiry) has a true value, which is independent of the survey, the way the question is asked and by whom. Suppose an enquiry is made on the age of the individuals. If the respondent says truthfully he is 25 years old but the interviewer carelessly or due to some reasons writes 22 or 28 years' then this a response error. If the respondent conceals his age or unable to tell the correct age, the interviewer takes note of this, then this is also a response error. The respondents may be subject to memory lapses, willfully provide wrong answers to keep personal prestige on sensitive issues, inability to provide correct answers, carelessly answering the questions put by the interviewer.

Response error does not apply only to sample surveys and can arise whatever be the coverage of the population. Some response errors may be self-compensating for each interviewer, while others may be systematic either fully or partly to leave an overall net bias. Sometimes failure on the part of the interviewer in understanding questions or wrongly putting the questions to the respondent elicits wrong answers. Success of an interview in getting reliable information from the respondents depends on cordial interaction between the interviewer and the respondent, both understanding clearly the utility of data and interest in survey.

The unwillingness and sometimes inability of the respondents to give correct answer and more so on sensitive issues is a potential source of error. This, of course, is not independent of the interviewer or of the way questions are asked. Personal characteristics, views or expectations of the interviewers and in some cases interviewer's judgement and discretion also add to response errors. Thus, **the response errors may be broadly due to (a) interviewers (b) respondents.**

The **specification error** occurs when the concept implied by the question is different from the underlying construct that should be measured.

Errors due to Interviewers

(i) *Art of asking question*

Interviewer is expected to act on instruction to keep to the wording and order on the schedule and to ask questions in the stated manner. It is likely that the interviewers may move out of the scope to produce interviewer's bias. The likelihood of interviewers disobeying instructions is dependent on the construction of the questionnaire. If the questionnaire is very long and the questionnaire does not proceed smoothly and logically from one topic to another, the interviewer may be treated to simplify the questions and change the order. Thus, it is necessary that the interviewer is to be provided with a *workable questionnaire.*

(ii) *Probing*

Differential method of probing to elicit right type of answer from the respondents gives scope for the operation of response errors.

(iii) *Recording the answer*

Apart from carelessly recording or studying the answer, the interviewer may record incorrectly or ambiguously when open question are put to respondents. If the respondent gives a long answer, the interviewer might be tempted to select the part of the answer which fits best with other answers.

(iv) *Coding*

Interviewers are often required to code answers on the spot of interview. If the codes are not properly understood by the interviewer or the answers are ambiguous, the interviewer's judgement on the matter may lead to response error.

(v) *Cheating*

There is possibility of cheating on the part of the interviewers, if they do not have right type of attitude and responsibility towards the assigned job or lack morale connected with remuneration, working hours, difficulty of questionnaires. Most survey organisations have developed techniques to prevent cheating, which is a serious type of response error.

Errors due to Respondents

The respondents' attitude, ignorance and characteristics contribute towards response errors.

These are :

- ❒ Unwilling to answer or having habit of giving evasive answers.
- ❒ Inability to answer because of personal characteristics or question wording or unacquainted questions.
- ❒ Willfully giving wrong answers because of non-cooperative attitude or to maintain secrecy on sensitive issues or due to fear of reprisals on supplying information.

- Memory lapses to answer questions relating to long past.
- Adverse reactions to personality or age or social status of the interviewer.

Response error and its relationship to the conditions of the survey

Response error not only depends on the interviewer, the respondent and their interaction, but also the conditions of the survey. These are :

The length of questionnaire :

Very lengthy questionnaire makes both interviewer and respondent less attentive and the information elicited from the respondents may tend to be inaccurate.

- *The order of questions*
- *Question structure*
- *Question content*
- *Question wording*

Interviewer instruction :

The training given to the interviewers and the clarity of instructions imparted to the interviewers will help to determine the accuracy of information collected in the survey.

Designated respondent :

The accuracy of information may depend on the person from when it is collected. In household surveys, it is sometimes specified that information must be supplied by the head of the household, sometimes from his wife, sometimes from any adult member of the household. Any wider latitude given to the interviewer for the choice of respondent may lead to response error because every member of the household is not expected to answer every question correctly.

Place and time of interview :

The physical location of the place of interview may have an influence upon response errors. Some respondents may like to give answer to some personal questions or sensitive questions at a secluded place maintaining privacy. Some respondents may not like the presence of a third person. Interviews should be conducted by the interviewers at a time when the respondents feel at ease to answer the questions and the working or busy hours of the respondents must be avoided so that the respondents feel it comfortable to permit some time for the interview.

Interest in the survey :

The willingness as well as accuracy of the response in certain cases depends on the respondents' interest in the enquiry which will, in turn, help the interviewer to elicit reliable answers.

Sponsorship :

The interest of the respondents may sometimes vary according to the organisation which conducts the enquiry.

Detection of response errors

The potential sources of response errors are not exhaustive. No satisfactory methodology has been developed to measure their sizes and also to what extent they can cancel out and to what extent they affect the survey results.

The investigator has a responsibility to check the accuracy of information supplied by the respondents against data from other sources, whenever feasible from individual records he may assess the response error to arrive at gross errors, that is, total response errors and also net error after some response errors cancel out. It may be mentioned here that only net error creates a bias in survey results. Of course from researcher's point of view, the individual response errors should be tried to be minimized. The detection of procedural errors-failure to ask all the questions, insufficient probing to obtain correct answers, failure to record accurately and completely-is an important component of raising the quality of field work.

Usual methods to detect response errors in surveys are as follows :

(a) Record checks. Individual validity checks are designated to ascertain how close the answer recorded on the schedule is to the individual true value. Records or documents of some kind can be used to check the individual responses. For example, both records and documents would help in checking the age returns, doctor records for illness, employers' record on wages etc.

Record checks may not be always authentic because the records may themselves be incomplete and inaccurate. Errors may also creep in due to mismatching between individual's survey and record data and no follow–up action will be to reconcile differences.

(*b*) Consistent checks : Consistent check is to ask for the same information in two or more ways. For example, to know the age of a respondent, one may ask 'When he was born' and 'How old he is' and discrepancy between these two answers may be checked.

(*c*) Re-interviewing : A more straight forward way of checking the accuracy of a measurement is to repeat it. Re-interview checks are also known as **quality checks** or **post-enumeration surveys.**

Control and measurement of response errors

The questions may arise : What should be done to keep response error to the minimum ? Some *specific possibilities* are mentioned below :

(*a*) Selection, training and supervision of interviewers

The proper choice of 'error free' interviewers depends on the skill and experience of the interviewers and also the nature and type of survey. The same set of interviewers might not fit in all types of surveys. Quality and effective supervision is necessary to keep the interviewers in right track and under control.

(*b*) Control of interview

There are certain danger spots in the interview where response errors may be of substantial magnitude. If the open questions would result in many errors, it is advisable to use pre-coded questions. If probing of the interviewer results in misgivings in the minds of the respondents, perhaps probing should be more strictly controlled.

The stricter the instructions imparted to the respondents, the less scope is left to the interviewer to apply his judgement and discretion.

(*c*) Increasing the number of interviewers

Interviewer variance can be reduced by selecting, training and supervising the field staff efficiently so as to achieve maximum uniformity in their performance. An alternative way may be to decrease its effect by increasing the number of interviewers, engaged for the survey work. Since the contribution of interviewer variance is a function of number of interviewers, increasing the number of interviewers will have added problems in accepting low skilled interviewers and spending less on their training and supervision and thus resulting in increased response errors.

(*d*) Interviewer-respondent matching

The quality of interview depends on the healthy interaction between the interviewer and the respondent. A less educated working class person may react, sometimes, unfavorably when the questions about his education are asked by highly qualified interviewers. Of course, there is no guarantee that high degree of rapport between the interviewer and the respondent would always lead to unbiased answers. Therefore, there is no case for interviewer-respondent matching unless there is reasonable doubt about reliable answers.

(*e*) Analytical methods

Statisticians have developed some theoretical models by which the response variance due to interviewers and due to other components can be segregated and measured with a suitable sampling design.

Consistent checks like asking same question twice in different ways on, the questionnaire and also by some other intricate methods will certainly be helpful in comparing the information and thereby assessing the magnitude of response error. The behavior of the respondents can also be studied by comparing information over different reference periods. Even if, the researcher is not able to assess exactly the magnitude of response error, the methods discussed here along with other suitably devised methods can reduce it to an accepted level so as not to undermine the survey accuracy.

Non-response Errors

Non–response is regarded as a problem for the survey of human populations. But in a wider context this may be regarded as ***non- observation of certain units which are duly included in the sample***. This may be due to deaths, absence, refusal to cooperate, failure to contact, omissions, unsuitable for interviews etc. With a well designed survey it is usually possible to keep the level of non-response down to a reasonable level, so as not to vitiate the survey results. It may be pointed out here that some amount of non-response are often present in a survey enquiry and researcher should not have undue worry about the scientific nature of enquiry.

There are two types of non-responses—*unit nonrespnse and item non-response.* Unit non-response implies that no information is obtained from certain sample units. This may be because respondents refuse to participate in the survey when contacted or they cannot be contacted. Item non–response refers to a situation where for some units the information collected is incomplete. Item non–response is therefore, evidenced by gaps in the data record for responding sample units. Reasons may be due to refusals, omissions by enumerators and incapacity.

There are **six sources of non-response :**

(*i*) *Unsuitable for interview.* Some units may not be interviewable because they may be deaf or unfamiliar with the language of the interview schedule. Some respondents may also be non-co-operating.

(*ii*) *Movers.* Certain units may have moved out either within the same area or to another area.

(*iii*) *Refusals.* Some people have tendencies to refuse to answer survey questions with the view that they do not find any reason to be disturbed to answer them and more so to face strangers.

(*iv*) *Long absence.* As selection of sampled units does not envisage the presence of the units at home during interview period, some amount of non-response sometimes do occur and recalling may not be possible.

(*v*) *Temporary absence.* Some people might not be present at the time of calling by the interviewer and to compensate this they may be contacted by recalling.

(*vi*) *Deaths or extinct or non-existent.* Some people may not be found due to deaths and some industrial units in industrial surveys may not be existing at the time of taking the observations due to sudden and unexpected closures.

Magnitude of non-response and its control

Large magnitude of non-response is certainly not welcome and the surveyor must sufficiently contemplate on the issues before processing the survey results. Some usable techniques depending on the type of non-respnse may be thought of to improve the response rate. Substituting for the non-respondents may not solve the problem because the substitution only improves the position of respondent class and bias or deficiencies in results due to non-respondents remain as they are. The only advantage accompanying the method of substitution is to keep the sample size intact and to keep sampling errors to their estimated magnitude. Further, in stratified sampling if the non-response rate varies in the strata, substitution helps proper representation. However, the substitution should be taken at random from the reserve list prepared and drawn together with the initial sample.

Before adopting substitution other possibilities, if possible to improve response rate, should be adopted. There is nothing which can tackle the people who have moved out but may be tracked down on a later date. The surveyor should win over the persons who are going to answer and thus it may be possible to try to keep rapport with the units concerned in order to make the interview period as brief as possible, sometimes with the financial reward. However, there may be some hard core left out, who will refuse to answer under any circumstance and this number is not expected to be very large. Experienced interviewers are expected to get a better response rate than the inexperienced ones. People those who are absent during survey period can be contacted after it is over. People who are out at time of call may be sizeable and can be recalled, which is a standard practice. Call backs may be done on all the non- respondents or on a sub-sample of them. An ingenious method of overcoming the not-at-home problem in interview surveys was suggested by Politz and Simmons. The essence of the technique rests in sub-dividing the population into groups constructed according to the probability of their being found at home by the interviewer.

Errors in Coverage

In most area surveys primary sampling units are generally called enumeration areas. If the demarcation of enumeration areas are not properly carried out, some units may be either duplicated or omitted in the second stage frame. Imperfect frames can bias the estimates in the following ways : If the units are not represented in the frame but should have been part of the frame, this results in zero probability of selection for those units omitted from the frame. On the other hand, if some units are duplicated, this results in overcoverage with such units having larger probabilities of selection. Errors associated with the frame may result in both over coverage and under coverage.

It is important to emphasize that neither the magnitude nor the effect of coverage errors is easy to estimate because it requires information not only external to the sample but also, by definition, external to the sampling frame used.

Non-coverage denotes the failure to include some sample units of a defined survey population in the sampling frame. Because such units have zero probability of selection, they are effectively excluded from the survey results. This non–coverage does not refer to deliberate and explicit exclusion of sections of a larger population from the survey population, because survey objectives and practical difficulties determine such deliberate exclusions. Therefore, defining the survey population should be part of the clearly stated essential survey conditions.

Non-coverage is often associated with problems of incomplete frames. Omissions might occur while preparing the frame and also due to faulty execution of survey procedures. Thus non coverage refers to the negative errors resulting from failure to include elements that would, under normal circumstances, belong to the sample. Positive errors of over coverage also occur due to inclusion in the sample of elements that do not belong there.

The non–coverage errors may be caused by the use of faulty frames of sampling units. If the frames are not updated or old frames are used as a device to save time or money, it may lead to serious bias.

Non coverage errors differ from non-response, which result from failure to obtain observations on some sample units, due to refusals, failure to locate addresses or find respondents at home and losses of questionnaires.

Further, there may be sample selection and implementation errors due to distortions within the sampling frame, *e.g.* the wrong application of the selection procedures and selection probabilities. An inappropriate substitution of the selected units by others, also causes this type of error.

Processing Errors

Processing errors comprise :

- Editing errors
- Coding errors
- Data entry errors
- Programming errors etc.

These errors arise during data processing stage. For example, in coding open ended answers related to economic characteristics, coders may deviate from the laid out procedures in coding manuals, and therefore assign wrong codes to occupations. In addition, the weighting procedures may be wrongly applied during the processing stage, etc.

Reporting Errors

The researcher after analysis of data should sit down with the findings at hand to write a report, keeping in view the objectives and the research questions. The conclusions obtained should be based on available scientific statistical techniques, devoid of confusion and errors in analysis.

There is a caution to remember that the interpretation should not go beyond what the data contain and certain probability statements should be attached to the findings, whenever appropriate. It may be mentioned that the analysis and interpretation go together and moreover the interpretative ideas govern the task of analysis.

The general purpose of the report is both for upward and downward communication. The report must be objective and based on facts collected through enquiry. Subjective expression of ideas and opinions must be avoided. The typographical errors should be thoroughly checked. The style should be simple, direct and easily readable.

Systematic Errors Vrs Variable Errors :

The nonsampling errors may be classified as

- Systematic errors
- Variable errors

The systematic errors are generally non–compensating errors and therefore tend to agree, whereas the variable errors are compensating errors that tend to disagree (cancelling each other).

The variable component of an error arises from chance (random) factors affecting different samples and repetition of the survey. When the variable errors are caused only by sampling errors, variable error squared equals sampling variance. The deviation of the average survey value from the true population value is the **bias.** Both variable errors and biases can arise either from sampling or nonsampling operations. The variable error will measure the divergence of the estimator from its expected value and it comprises both sampling variance and nonsampling variance. The difference of the expected value of the estimator from its true value is total bias and comprises both sampling bias and non-sampling bias.

Systematic error occurs when there is binding either to consistently under report or over report in a survey. For example, in areas where there are no birth certificates, there is tendency among men/women to exaggerate. This will result in systematic bias of the average age in the male population, producing higher average than what the true average age should be and in case of female population a lower average than the true average.

9.3.3. Effect of Sample size on errors in sampling

The sampling error in an estimate is measured by computing the sampling variance or standard error of the estimate. If the sample size increases, the sampling variance, which is inversely proportional to sample size, decreases and so also the standard error of the estimate. The sampling variance of the stimate becomes zero when n = N, *i.e.* the sample size is equal to the population size or in other words there is census or 100% sampling. It would also be zero, when all values in the population are the same. Either the sampling variance or the standard error gives us an idea of the likelihood that the estimate is near the true value in the population. **A lower standard error implies that the estimate is more reliable.**

The non-sampling error unlike the sampling error is likely to increase with the increase in the sample size and can only be controlled by taking precautions/checks at every stage of the sample survey beginning from the planning stage till the writing of the report.

9.3.4 Determination of sample size

The number of sampling units enumerated in a sample survey is called **the size of the sample,** usually denoted by the small letter, 'n'. Its maximum value is the size of the population (N). If $n = N$, there is no sampling and we have 100% enumeration or complete enumeration or census. The larger the sample size, there is more likelihood of the sample giving proper representation to the population. Its determination depends on

- ❒ Variability in the population
- ❒ Cost of observing sampling units and other associated costs relating to survey operations

The variability in the population implies variability among the values observable characteristics of the population. A population having larger variability requires a large sample to be selected. Further, if the sample size is large, it costs more for the sample survey operations. Then, it is advisable for the investigator to have reasonable compromise between variance and cost functions in determination of sample size. Both variance and cost depend on the nature of the sampling unit.

In practice, the variance of the values in the population is not known in advance and hence the investigator may have to choose an approximate value from a past survey conducted on the same or similar population observing the same characteristic or another characteristic closely related to the characteristic under considereation. Alternatively, the investigator may conduct a pilot survey-a small scale survey prior to the execution of the main survey to as certain approximately the variance of the population.

Once the variance is known or estimated, the sample size can be determined by taking into consideration the margin of error, **assumed** to be tolerated between the population parameter and its representative sample estimate with the help of a derived formula, stated in later sections of this chapter.

9.4 Types of Probability (Random) Sampling Designs

In sample surveys the researcher resorts to different *sampling designs* depending on:

- ❒ nature of population
- ❒ simplicity in adoption
- ❒ availability of frame
- ❒ representativeness
- ❒ nature of sampling unit
- ❒ cost of enumeration
- ❒ precision criterion

The *common sampling designs* adopted in sample surveys are :

- Simple random sampling
- Stratified random sampling
- Systematic sampling
- Cluster sampling
- Multistage sampling
- Double sampling

The simple random sampling is the simplest of all sampling designs in which every unit has equal probability of being selected. That is why, the simple random sampling is termed as **equal probability sampling**. However, for a very much heterogeneous population a simple random sampling may not give best results in providing precise estimation. The simple random sampling is also called *unrestricated random sampling*.

Stratified random sampling rests in sub-dividing the entire population into groups, preferably homogeneous groups/administrative divisions/any convenient groups etc. and drawing simple random sample from each group. These groups are termed as *strata*. In surveys of business establishments, one may form strata with large, medium and small establishments.

Systematic sampling in simple and easy to execute and may be applied without much loss in accuracy in the absence of a frame. In this sampling procedure the first unit in an ordered list of units is selected with simple random sampling and the rest of the units are selected by the pre–determined pattern. A common use of systematic sampling is in telephone surveys.

Cluster sampling is a variant of simple random sampling where the sampling unit is not an element, but a group of elements, termed as a cluster. It is a convenient method of sampling when the frame for the individual elements is not available, but frame with clusters as sampling units is available.

Multi-stage sampling is carried out at different stages. For instance, in two stage sampling the population is visualized to consist of first stage units/primary units, which are clusters of second stage/secondary units. Thus, in two–stage sampling a random sample of first stage units is selected at the first instance and in the second stage the first stage units are sampled, that is, from each first stage unit selected, a sample of second stage units or ultimate units is selected. Further stages may be added to the sampling process, if necessary. In large scale sample surveys, it is usual practice to use multistage sampling, primarily because of cost considerations arising out of travel from one unit to another and for the time constraint. For instance, for surveys concerning shopping establishments under unorganised sector in a city, one may select a random sample of city wards and from each selected ward, a random sample of shops may be selected. In multi-stage sampling one may not construct the frame for the entire population, if it is not available. Instead he may construct the frames for the wards in the first stage, in case these are not available.

Sometimes it may be convenient and economical to collect information from a larger sample and then use this information as the basis for selecting a sub-sample for further detailed study on the subject of interest. This is termed as **double sampling** (sometimes named **two phase sampling**). This technique was developed to take advantage of the relationship between the variable of interest and some easily or cheaply measured and highly correlated auxiliary variable. A larger sample is selected to observe the auxiliary variable and a smaller sub-sample or independent sample to observe the variable of interest with sole purpose of increasing the efficiency of the sample estimate. In stratified random sampling it is necessary that the stratum weights need be known in advance. In case stratum weights are not-known, a preliminary large sample may be selected from the entire population to estimate the weights/strata sizes. In the second phase independent samples are selected from strata constituted in the first phase. This is termed as **double sampling stratification.**

In acceptance sampling if it is inconclusive to take a decision on the basis of first sample either to accept or reject the lot, a second sample may be taken to break the deadlock and arrive at a decision, if possible.

Two phase sampling may be extended to **multi-phase sampling** when samples in different phases are selected to meet different objectives with ultimate aim of studying the subject of interest or estimating the parameters of the main variable under study.

In sample surveys there may be more than one characteristic of interest and the sample which is best for estimating one characteristic may not be optimum for others. For instance, in a business survey for estimating the average sales of retail stores one may also be interested in estimating total employment, total wages paid, total inventory, ratio of wages paid to sales i.e. percentage of gross receipts spent for wages, ratio of inventory to sales. Further, one may also be interested in estimating such characteristics by size group (Large, Medium and Small) of stores. A sample design which is developed in a compromise manner, keeping in view all the characteristics in question is termed as **multi-purpose sample.**

In **inverse sampling,** sampling is carried out until a pre-determined number of units possessing the rare attribute A occurs in the sample. In simple random sampling there may not be any guarantee of inclusion some units possessing a rare attribute of interest. Suppose we are interested in estimating the proportion (P) of a rare attribute A. If the sample size n is required to attain m—the number of units in the sample possessing A, then the estimate of P is given by $p = \dfrac{m-1}{n-1}$.

While discussing about probability sampling, it may be worth pointing out here that probability sampling may not be always equal probability sampling. There might arise occasions when the researcher might like to adopt **unequal probability sampling** designs. For instance, when we are interested to draw a sample of business establishments to study on the working conditions of the employees, it may be appropriate to select the business establishments probability proportional to size of the establishment depending on the number of employed workers which may not be always equal in size. Thus, we come across **probability proportional to size sampling** which is an unequal probability sampling design.

9.5 Types of Non-probability/Non-random Sampling

Non-probability sampling is also termed as **Non-random sampling** and the sampling is carried out with some other considerations rather than involving random selection.

Some commonly adopted non-probability sampling procedures are :

- *Purposive sampling*
- *Judgement sampling*
- *Convenience sampling*
- *Quota sampling*
- *Modal Instance sampling*
- *Expert sampling*
- *Snowball sampling*

In Purposive sampling we sample with a purpose in mind. That is, we have certain predefined group(s) in mind and attempt is made to seek members of this group to be included in the sample. For example, if the purpose is to study the buying habits of females between 30-40 years old in a super-market, we may interview persons of this category coming out of the supermarket, depending on their consent.

Purposive sampling can be very useful for situations where you need to reach a targeted sample quickly.

In Judgement sampling an *expert* uses judgement to identify representative samples. For instance, the members of different community associations in a city may provide a representative sample of city dwellers. A sample of side walk vendors would be best available through judgement sampling. Further, a judgmental sample is likely to be more reliable and representative than a probability sample. However, a judgemental sample should be honestly judged, otherwise unwelcome bias might creep into the results, thereby vitiating the results.

To obtain information quickly and inexpensively, **a convenience sample** may be employed. In this procedure the respondents or the sampling units are contacted depending on the convenience of the interviewer/investigator, keeping in view the general representativeness of the population in question.

In Quota sampling we observe/contact the responding units non- randomly according to some fixed quota. Prior to taking observations one has to decide the specific characteristics on which the quota will be based *e.g.* gender, age, education, size of the business establishment, type of workers, managerial cadre etc. Quota sampling is the non-probabilistic analogue of stratified random sampling. It is typically used to assure that smaller groups are adequately represented in the sample. As in case of stratified random sampling we may have proportional quota sampling and non–proportional quota sampling depending on whether we attach equal importance to each group or some should be extensively sampled to get the correct picture of the situation. However, it involves interviewer's bias, which cannot be estimated.

In statistics, the mode is defined as the value which occurs most often in a frequency distribution. In sampling, when we select a **Modal Instance sample,** we are actually sampling the most frequent case or the typical case. In public opinion polls, it may be necessary to sample typical respondents depending on their age, education, income, attitude, status in the population. In a survey on working conditions in a firm having an overwhelming number of daily labourers, we should concentrate more on this category than sampling from a handful of highly paid workers.

Expert sampling involves the assembling of a sample of persons with known or demonstrable experience and expertise in some area. Often we may be required to convene such a sample under the auspices of a 'panel of experts'. There may be two reasons for taking up expert sampling. The first reason may be that this is the best way of eliciting views of persons who have specific expertise. In this case, expert sampling is essentially just a specific sub-case of purposive sampling. The other reason as to why you should opt for expert sampling is that the opinions of experts might provide evidence for the validity of another sampling approach, you have chosen. The advantage of expert sampling is that you are not out on your own trying to defend your decisions, but you have some acknowledged experts to back you.

The disadvantage is that even the experts can be, and often may go wrong.

Snowball sampling is a form of judgement sampling that is very appropriate when it is necessary to reach small specialized populations. First, we begin by identifying someone who meets the criteria for inclusion in the study and then we ask them to recommend others who they may know and also meet the criteria. Although this method would hardly lead to representative samples, there are at times when it may be the best method available. Snowball sampling is especially useful when the researcher is trying to reach populations that are inaccessible or hard to find. For instance, suppose a planning group wants to sample people who are very knowledgeable about a specialized new technology and even specialized magazines might not have many readers of this category. Under such circumstances, the researcher might identify a respondent or a few respondents of this category and take him (or them) to identify one or more others in the field.

One inherent problem in this type of sampling is that those who are socially visible are more likely to be selected.

9.6 Basic Sampling Designs

9.6.1 Simple Random Sampling (SRS)

In a simple random sampling every unit of the population has equal chance of being selected. This method of sampling is also called **equal probability sampling.** A simple random sample may be drawn with or without replacement.

Probability of the selection of a sample s of size n out of a finite population of size N ($n < \text{N}$), is

$$\text{P}(s) = \frac{1}{\binom{\text{N}}{n}}, \text{ if the sampling is done without replacement (SRSWOR)}$$

$$= \frac{1}{\text{N}^n}, \text{ if the sampling is done with replacement (SRSWR).}$$

This may be regarded as a definition of simple random sampling. Further, in both SRSWOR and SRSWR the probability of selecting any specified unit at any specified draw is the same and is equal to $\frac{1}{\text{N}}$. The probability that a particular unit is included in a sample of size n is $\frac{n}{\text{N}}$, which is also termed as **sampling fraction.**

Method of drawing a simple random sample (SRS) :

Suppose the finite survey population is of size N. Then the units of the population are serially numbered from 1, 2, ..., N and N chits are prepared with one number written on each chit (without duplication). These N chits are placed in a bowl and are well shuffled. Then n chits are drawn one after another using lottery mehod. Thus, a simple random sample of size n is selected. If the chit already drawn is not replaced in the bowl, the sample is said to be drawn without replacement (SRSWOR) and in case it is replaced, a with replacement simple random sample (SRSWR) is obtained.

There are also other methods of drawing a simple random sample with the help of some predetermined random mechanism such as experiment with dice, coin, generation of random numbers with some mathematical random functions, etc.

A method which is widely convenient to be adopted in practice is a method of drawing by refering to a **Random Number Table,** containing random numbers arranged in rows and columns, generated by a random mechanism.

ILLUSTRATION 1. Suppose there are 30 units in a population and it is required to select a simple random sample of size 5. Number the units serially from 1 to 30. Choose a two digit number at 30, rejecting 00, 31-99, from any point from the Table and then continuously proceeding either in horizontal or in vertical direction in groups of two digits till we get 5 distinct numbers. The units corresponding to these 5 numbers constitute a simple random sample without replacement of size 5. If we start seeing the two digit random numbers from the beginning of the extract of a random number table, given below the chosen numbers are

03, 11, 04, 24, 09 and other selected numbers from 31-99 are rejected

An Extract from a Random Number Table

03991	10461	93716	16894	98953
73231	39528	72484	82474	25593
38555	95554	32886	59780	09958
18065	81616	18711	53342	44276
17546	73704	92052	46215	15917
06253	07586	16120	82641	22820
32643	52861	95819	06831	19640

Source : Random digits, Statistical Survey Techniques, Jessen, R.J. (1978)

If the sampling is done with replacement, any two digit random numbers appearing for the second time or subsequently are not rejected, but in case of simple random sampling without replacement this is rejected.

However, such a procedure is wasteful of numbers, that is, rejections become more numerous as it has happened in the present case.

A more efficient procedure might be as follows :

Divide the highest two digit number (because the population size is a two digit number) 99 by the population size *i.e.* 30. The remainder is 9. The valid random numbers are now 01—90. Now, select a two digit number as before from the Random Number Table. If it is less than 30, accept it as it is and if it is greater than 30, but is less than or equal to 90, divide it by 30 and the remainder is the serial number of the unit selected into the sample. In case the remainder is zero, the 30th unit is selected.

This process is continued until a distinct set of 5 units (sample size) is selected. The random numbers 00, 91-99 are rejected in the process. Because if these random numbers are taken into account the principle of equal probability of selection is violated.

Estimation of Population Mean and Total :

Let there be N units—$U_1, U_2, \ldots, U_N$ in the population having values $Y_1, Y_2, \ldots, Y_N$ respectively corresponding to character y (survey variable). For a SRSWOR of size n, let the sample values be $y_1, y_2, \ldots, y_n$. Finite population parametric values and their sample estimators are given below.

Parameter	Estimator
Population Mean : $\overline{Y} = \frac{1}{N}\sum_{i=1}^{N} Y_i$	Sample Mean : $\overline{y} = \frac{1}{n}\sum_{i=1}^{n} y_i$
Population total $Y = \sum_{i=1}^{N} Y_i$	Estimate of population total : $\hat{Y} = N\overline{y}$
Population variance : $S^2 = \frac{1}{N-1}\Sigma(Y_i - \overline{Y})^2 = \frac{N}{N-1}\sigma^2$	Sample variance : $s^2 = \frac{1}{n-1}\sum_{i=1}^{n}(y_i - \overline{y})^2$
Sampling variance of $\overline{y}$ in srswor : $V(\overline{y}) = \left(\frac{1}{n} - \frac{1}{N}\right)S^2 = \frac{N-n}{N-1}\cdot\frac{\sigma^2}{n}$	Estimator of $V(\overline{y})$ in srswor : Est. $V(\overline{y}) = \left(\frac{1}{n} - \frac{1}{N}\right)s^2$.
Sampling variance of $\hat{Y}$: $V(\hat{Y}) = V(N\overline{y}) = N^2 V(\overline{y})$	Estimator of $V(\hat{Y})$: Est. $V(\hat{Y}) = N^2$ Est. $V(\overline{y})$.

Note

(i) Finite population (or descriptive) parameter is a quantity whose value would be known **exactly** if a census of the survey population was carried out.

(ii) In SRSWOR $\overline{y}$ is an unbiased estimator of $\overline{Y}$

$$V(\overline{y}) = \left(1 - \frac{n}{N}\right)\frac{S^2}{n} = \left(1 - \frac{n-1}{N-1}\right)\frac{\sigma^2}{n}$$

Here, $\left(1 - \frac{n}{N}\right) = (1 - f)$ is called finite population correction factor (f.p.c.), where $f = \frac{n}{N}$ (i.e. sampling fraction).

$$\text{Est. } V(\overline{y})_{SRSWOR} = (1 - f)\frac{s^2}{n}$$

(iii) In SRSWR $\overline{y}$ is also an unbiased estimator of $\overline{Y}$, But

$$V(\overline{y})_{SRSWR} = \frac{\sigma^2}{n}, \text{ where } \sigma^2 = \frac{1}{N}\sum_{i=1}^{N}(Y_i - \overline{Y})^2$$

Further an unbiased estimator of $V(\bar{y})$ is given by

$$\text{Est } V(\bar{y})_{SRSWR} = \frac{s^2}{n}$$

(*iv*) To estimate the population mean $\overline{Y}$, simple random sampling without replacement is more efficient than the simple random sampling with replacement.

ILLUSTRATION 2. The following are the sizes of 12 holdings (in acres) selected by SRSWOR from a population of 500 holdings. Obtain an unbiased estimate of average size of holding in the population along with an estimate of its standard error.

Sample Data :	3.5	8.2	6.4	4.2	12.5	5.5
	4.5	2.5	10.5	2.8	6.5	8.5

Let y_i be the value of the ith observation in the sample, $i = 1, 2, ..., 12$. Then the sample average is an unbiased estimate of the average holding size in the population and is given by

$$\bar{y} = \frac{\sum_{i=1}^{n} y_i}{n} = \frac{\text{Total of sample values}}{12}$$

$$= \frac{3.5 + 8.2 + 6.4 + 4.2 + 12.5 + 5.5 + 4.5 + 2.5 + 10.5 + 2.8 + 6.5 + 8.5}{12}$$

$$= \frac{75.6}{12} = 6.3 \text{ acres}$$

Now, $n = 12$

$N = 500$

$$s^2 = \frac{\Sigma (y_i - \bar{y})^2}{n-1} = \frac{\Sigma y_i^2 - n\bar{y}^2}{n-1}$$

$$= \frac{583.68 - 12\,(6.3)^2}{12 - 1} = \frac{583.68 - 476.28}{11}$$

$$= \frac{107.4}{11} = 9.7636$$

Therefore, $\text{Est. S.E. } (\bar{y}) = = \sqrt{\left(\frac{1}{n} - \frac{1}{N}\right)s^2}$

$$= \sqrt{\left(\frac{1}{12} - \frac{1}{500}\right)} (9.7636) = 0.89 \text{ acres.}$$

Estimation of sample size

To determine the sample size, one will have to answer the following questions :

(*a*) **First,** how large an error in the estimate can be tolerated before the inference drawn from the sample results will lead to wrong action ?

(*b*) **Secondly,** what risks are we willing to take that the results of the sample are in error by more than that amount ?

The first question relates to the specification of **a margin of error *d*** and the second relates to specification of a **small probability (risk) α for wrong action.**

If we require to estimate the population mean $\overline{Y}$ by the sample mean $\bar{y}$, then n is so selected

$$P(|\bar{y} - \overline{Y}| \geq d) = \alpha$$

Assuming $\bar{y}$ to be normally distributed with standard error $\sigma(\bar{y}) = \sqrt{\left(\frac{1}{n} - \frac{1}{N}\right) S^2}$, for a given α

$$d = Z_{\alpha/2} \sqrt{\left(\frac{1}{n} - \frac{1}{N}\right) S^2},$$

where $Z_{\alpha/2}$ is the $\left(\frac{\alpha}{2}\right)$th percent point of the standard normal distribution

Thus, we have,

$$n = \frac{\left(Z_{\alpha/2} \cdot \frac{S}{d}\right)^2}{1 + \frac{1}{N}\left(Z_{\alpha/2} \frac{S}{d}\right)^2}$$

The expression for n has a distinct disadvantage in the sense that the finite population standard deviation S is not known. In practice, S may be estimated from the past surveys or pilot surveys.

ILLUSTRATION 3. How large a sample should be taken from a population of 2000 units so that sample estimate of $\bar{y}$ differs from its true value $\overline{Y}$ by a quantity less than 20 with probability 0.95 ? It is given that the estimate of population variance is 10,000.

Solution :

$$S = \sqrt{10,000} = 100, \; d = 20$$
$$Z_{\alpha/2} = 1.96$$

$$n = \frac{\left(1.96 \cdot \frac{100}{20}\right)^2}{1 + \frac{1}{2000}\left(1.96 \cdot \frac{100}{20}\right)^2} = \frac{96.04}{1 + \frac{1}{2000}(96.04)}$$

$$= \frac{96.04}{1 + 0.048} = \frac{96.04}{1.048} = 91.64 \cong 92$$

Alternative Methods

(*i*) Suppose we are required to ensure *e*% coefficient of variation for the estimation of the population mean $\bar{y}$ in SRSWOR, then putting

$$e = \text{Coefficient of variation of } \bar{y}$$

$$= \sqrt{\frac{N-n}{N-1}}\ \frac{C}{\sqrt{n}};\quad C = \frac{\sigma}{\bar{Y}}$$

The sampling size n can be solved out as

$$n = \frac{NC^2}{(N-1)\,e^2 + C^2}$$

(*ii*) Assuming a linear cost function

$C^* = C_0 + n\,C_1$, where C^* is total cost allocated for the survey, C_0 is the overhead cost and C_1 is the cost of enumeration of one unit

$$n = \frac{C^* - C_0}{C_1}$$

Estimation of proportion

Sometimes a researcher is interested in estimating qualitative characteristics such as proportion or percentage of units in the population having certain characteristic or attribute or belonging to certain defined class. For example, one might be interested to estimate the proportion of households below the poverty line or having facilities for safety toilets/safe drinking water or proportion of total expenditure of rural poor households spent on food items, etc.

Suppose N_1 = number of units having characteristics C and N = total number of units in the population.

Then, population proportion is

$$P = \frac{N_1}{N}$$

In a simple random sample of n units, n_1 units have the characteristic C. Then P is estimated by

$$p = \frac{n_1}{n}$$

The sampling variance of p is

$$V(p) = \frac{N-n}{N-1}\cdot\frac{PQ}{n}, \text{ where } Q = 1 - P.$$

An unbiased estimate of $V(p)$ is

$$\text{Est. } V(p) = \frac{N-n}{(n-1)N}\ pq, \text{ where } q = 1 - p$$

$$\text{Estimated S.E. } (p) = \sqrt{\frac{N-n}{(n-1)N}\ pq}$$

ILLUSTRATION 4. In a survey of 800 households a simple random sample of 75 households gave an estimated proportion of households having safety latrines equal to 0.85. Compute the estimated standard error. What size of the simple random sample is needed if it is desired to estimate the proportion with a discrepancy of 0.01 at the 95% probability level ?

Solution

$$p = 0.85,\ N = 800,\ n = 75$$

$$V(p) = \frac{N-n}{(n-1)N}\, pq = \frac{800-75}{(75-1)\,800}\,(0.85)\,(0.15)$$

$$= \frac{725}{59200}\,(0.1275) = 0.001561$$

$$S.E.(p) = +\sqrt{0.001561} = 0.0395$$

Now,
$$n = \frac{\left(\dfrac{Z^2_{\alpha/2}\, PQ}{d^2}\right)}{\dfrac{N-1}{N} + \dfrac{1}{N}\cdot\dfrac{Z^2_{\alpha/2} PQ}{d^2}}$$

$$= \left\{(1.96)^2\,\frac{(0.85)\,(0.15)}{(.01)^2}\right\} \Big/ \left\{\frac{799}{800} + \frac{1}{800}(1.96)^2\,\frac{(0.85)(0.15)}{(.01)^2}\right\}$$

$$= \frac{4898.04}{0.99875 + 6.12255} \cong 688$$

9.6.2. Stratified Sampling

In this method the finite population is divided into sub-groups called **strata.** From each stratum independent samples are selected following any sampling design. Before drawing stratified samples it must be ensured that the relevant frame along with the sizes of sub-groups are known.

Formation of strata is generally effective by making the **strata as homogeneous as possible** within themselves by the use of suitable auxiliary variable termed as stratification variable. This might bring about a possible increase in efficiency of the estimator of the parameter of the whole finite population. For instance, to estimate the per capita monthly income of the employees of an organization, we may divide the heterogenous population into homogeneous groups such as Grade I, Grade II, Grade III and Grade IV employees and then sample each group independently. However, stratification may also be adopted due to other reasons.

Reasons for stratification

The stratification may be adopted due to following reasons :

(*i*) To reduce the heterogeneous population into homogeneous groups so that the variation within the stratum is made as less as possible, whereas the variation between strata is made as large as possible.

(*ii*) For administrative convenience to conduct the survey operations in a population covering a large geographical area.

(*iii*) To make comparison among different segments of the population having special characteristics.

(*iv*) To conduct survey on a population where sampling problems vary from one segment to another.

Description

Let there be N units in the population grouped into L strata having known sizes $N_1, N_2, \ldots, N_L$ such that $N_1 + N_2 + \ldots + N_L = N$.

Let y be the character under study. The measurement or value attached to N units are

$$
\begin{array}{llll}
Y_{11} & Y_{12} & \cdots & Y_{1N_1} \\
Y_{21} & Y_{22} & \cdots & Y_{2N_2} \\
\ldots & & & \\
\ldots & & & \\
Y_{L1} & Y_{L2} & \cdots & Y_{LN_L}
\end{array}
$$

Suppose a simple random sample of size $n_i = (i = 1, 2, .., L)$ is selected from the ith stratum.

$$n_1 + n_2 + \ldots + n_L = n.$$

The sample values are

$$
\begin{array}{llll}
y_{11} & y_{12} & \cdots & y_{1n1} \\
y_{21} & y_{22} & \cdots & y_{2n2} \\
\ldots & & & \\
y_{21} & y_{22} & \cdots & y_{Ln_L}
\end{array}
$$

Estimate of Population Mean/Total

An estimate of population mean $\bar{Y}$ is given by

$$\bar{y}_{st} = \sum_{j=1}^{L} \frac{N_i}{N} \bar{y}_i,$$

where $\bar{y}_i = \frac{1}{n_i} \sum_{j=1}^{n_i} y_{ij}$

and an estimate of population total is

$$\hat{Y} = N\bar{y}_{st}$$

The sampling variance of $\bar{y}_{st}$ is

$$V(\bar{y}_{st}) = \sum_{i=1}^{L} \left(\frac{N_i}{N}\right)^2 \left(1 - \frac{n_i}{N_i}\right) \frac{S_i^2}{n_i}$$

Standard error of $\bar{y}_{st}$ is

$$\text{S.E.}(\bar{y}_{st}) = \sqrt{V(\bar{y}_{st})}$$

The estimate of $V(\bar{y}_{st})$ is obtained by substituting

$$S_i^2 = \frac{1}{N_i - 1} \sum_{j=1}^{Ni} (Y_{ij} - Y_i)^2, \ (i = 1, 2, \ldots, L)$$

by its unbiased sample estimate

$$s_i^2 = \frac{1}{n_i - 1} \sum_{j=1}^{n_i} (y_{ij} - \bar{y}_i)^2, i = 1, 2, \ldots L$$

in the variance formula.

The sampling variance of the estimate of population total *i.e.* $N\bar{y}_{st}$ is computed as $N^2V(\bar{y}_{st})$, which is estimated as N^2 Est. $V(\bar{y}_{st})$.

Allocation of sample to different strata :

After defining the strata, the sampler is required to decide on the number of units to be chosen from each stratum. This is called **problem of allocation.** Different types of allocations are available in statistical literature. These are described below.

(a) Proportional allocation

Let $N_1, N_2, \ldots, N_L$ be the sizes of strata in the population and $n_1, n_2, \ldots, n_L$ be the sample sizes allocated to strata respectively

$$\frac{n_1}{N_1} = \frac{n_2}{N_2} = \ldots = \frac{n_L}{N_L} = \frac{n}{N}$$

That is, sampling fractions in each stratum are the same and as such equal to overall sampling fraction. This is called **proportional allocation.**

Thus, $$n_i = n\left(\frac{N_i}{N}\right), i = 1, 2, .., L$$

As n_i varies as N_i, take a larger sample from a larger stratum.

(b) Neyman allocation

If the strata variances are unequal, it is logical and also can be mathematically derived to make the sample size n_i to vary as $N_i S_i$ (i = 1, 2, ..., L), where S_i is the stratum standard deviation in the ith stratum.

Thus, $$n_i = n \frac{N_i S_i}{\sum_{i=1}^{L} N_i S_i}; i = 1, 2, \ldots, L.$$

Note. Neyman allocation is always more efficient than proportional allocation and is obtained by minimising $V(\bar{y}_{st})$ s.t. $\Sigma n_i = n$.

(c) Optimum allocation

Often it is noticed that the cost for observing a unit varies from stratum of stratum. In such a situation it is necessary to allocate samples to strata such that n_i varies as $\frac{N_i S_i}{\sqrt{C_i}}$, where C_i is the cost of observing a unit from the ith stratum. Thus, the optimum sample sizes are

$$n_i = n \frac{\dfrac{N_i S_i}{\sqrt{C_i}}}{\sum \dfrac{N_i S_i}{\sqrt{C_i}}}, \ (i = 1, 2, ..., L)$$

This optimum allocation is obtained by minimising V $(\bar{y}_{st})$ s.t. fixed cost C = $C_0 + \sum_{i=1}^{L} C_i n_i$, C_0 being overhead cost.

Note. Neyman allocation or Optimum allocation requires the advance knowledge of the population standard deviation which is generally not practicable. However, approximate optimum sample sizes in the strata may be determined by substituting some guessed estimates of S_i from past surveys or pilot surveys in the formula.

The formula for finding out the optimum n_i indicates the following conclusions. A larger sample is taken in a given stratum if the stratum is larger or if the stratum is more variable or if the sampling is cheaper in the stratum.

ILLUSTRATION 5. A rural block in a district was divided into three strata. The following table gives the number of villages (N_i), and standard deviation (S_i) of area under rice crop for different strata :

Stratum No.	**Number of villages**	**Standard deviation S_i (hectares)**	**Cost for enumeration per village (C_i)**
1	15	25	Rs. 30
2	10	20	Rs. 40
3	30	16	Rs. 20

If a sample of 20 villages is to be drawn, compute (*i*) Proportional (*ii*) Neyman and (*iii*) Optimum allocations.

Solution

(*i*) Proportional allocation :

$$n_1 = n \frac{N_1}{N} = 20 \cdot \frac{15}{55} \cong 5$$

$$n_2 = n \frac{N_2}{N} = 20 \cdot \frac{10}{55} \cong 4$$

$$n_3 = n \frac{N_3}{N} = 20 \cdot \frac{30}{55} \cong 11$$

(*ii*) Neyman allocation

$$n_1 = n \frac{N_1 S_1}{\Sigma N_i S_i} = \frac{20(15 \times 25)}{1055} \cong 7$$

$$n_2 = n \frac{N_2 S_2}{\Sigma N_i S_i} = \frac{20(10 \times 20)}{1055} \cong 4$$

$$n_3 = n \frac{N_3 S_3}{\Sigma N_i S_i} = \frac{20(30 \times 16)}{1055} \cong 9$$

(*iii*) Optimum allocation :

$$n_1 = n \frac{\dfrac{N_1 S_1}{\sqrt{C_1}}}{\sum \dfrac{N_i S_i}{\sqrt{C_i}}} = \frac{20(68.4653)}{207.4194} \cong 7$$

$$n_2 = \frac{20(31.6228)}{207.4194} \cong 3,$$

$$n_3 = \frac{20(107.3313)}{207.4194} \cong 10$$

ILLUSTRATION 6. To estimate the total amount of daily sales (in 000' Rs.) in non-organized business establishments located in a township, the area was divided into four zones. From each zone a simple random sample of establishments was selected. Let y be the amount of daily sales in thousands of rupees. Through a census it was ascertained that there were 90 establishments in non-organized sector in the survey area. Further, the number of business units in 4 zones were 20, 30, 25 and 15 from which simple randam samples of size 6, 10, 8 and 6 respectively were selected.

The summary statistics with usual notations are given below.

N = total number of business establishments in the population.

$N_1 = 20$, $N_2 = 30$, $N_3 = 25$ and $N_4 = 15$, where N_i is the member of business units in *i*th zone ($i = 1, 2, 3, 4$). $n_1 = 6$, $n_2 = 10$, $n_3 = 8$ and $n_4 = 6$, n_i being size of the sample selected from *i*th zone, $i = 1, 2, 3, 4$. $\bar{y}_1 = 10$, $\bar{y}_2 = 12$, $\bar{y}_3 = 10$ and $\bar{y}_4 = 8$, where $\bar{y}_i$ is the sample mean sales in the *i*th zone ($i = 1, 2, 3, 4$).

Further, $s_1^2 = 6$, $s_2^2 = 8$, $s_3^2 = 9$ and $s_4^2 = 4$ where s_i^2 is the sample variance for the *i*th zone ($i = 1, 2, 3, 4$)

Then, the estimate of total sales in the urban area

$$= N\bar{y}_{si} = N \sum_{i=1}^{4} \left(\frac{N_i}{N}\right) \bar{y}_i$$

$$= 90 \left[\frac{20}{90}(10) + \frac{30}{90}(12) + \frac{25}{90}(10) + \frac{15}{90}(8)\right]$$

$= 90\ (10.3333) = 929.997$ thousands of rupees.

$$\text{Est. V}(N\bar{y}_{si}) = N^2 \Sigma \left(\frac{N_i}{N}\right)^2 \left(\frac{1}{n_i} - \frac{1}{N_i}\right) s_i^2$$

$$= (90)^2 \left[\left(\frac{20}{90}\right)^2 \left(\frac{1}{6} - \frac{1}{20}\right)(6) + \left(\frac{30}{90}\right)^2 \left(\frac{1}{10} - \frac{1}{30}\right)(8) + \left(\frac{25}{90}\right)^2 \left(\frac{1}{8} - \frac{1}{25}\right)9) + \left(\frac{15}{90}\right)^2 \left(\frac{1}{6} - \frac{1}{15}\right)(4)\right]$$

$$= 8100\ (0.1639) = 1327.59$$

Est. S.E. ($N\bar{y}_{si}$) = $\sqrt{1327.59}$ = 36.4361 thousands of rupees.

Therefore, the estimate of total daily sales of the non-organised business establishments in the township is Rs. 9,29,997 with estimated standard error Rs. 36,436.

Comparison of Stratified Random Sampling with Simple Random Sampling

Stratified random sampling may not be always more efficient than simple random sampling. If the values of n_i's are far from optimum, there is likelihood that stratified sampling would have a higher variance.

However, if the f.p.c. is ignored, then

$$V(\bar{y}_{st})_{opt.} \le V(\bar{y}_{st})_{prop.} \le V(\bar{y})_{random.}$$

The optimum allocation refers to Neyman-optimum allocation.

If f.p.c. cannot be ignored or neglected.

$$V(\bar{y})_{random} = V(\bar{y}_{st})_{prop.} + \frac{N-n}{n\,N(N-1)} \times \left[\Sigma N_i (\bar{Y}_i - \bar{Y})^2 - \frac{1}{N}\Sigma (N - N_i)\, S_i^2\right]$$

The proportional stratification gives a higher variance than simple random sampling if

$$\Sigma N_i (\bar{Y}_i - \bar{Y})^2 < \frac{1}{N}\Sigma (N - N_i)\, S_i^2$$

9.6.3 Systematic Sampling

One of the operationally more convenient and simple method of sampling is the systematic sampling. Suppose the population consists of N units serially numbered from 1 to N and a sample of size n is selected such that $N = nk$, where k is an integer. k is called **sampling interval**. Systematic sampling consists of selecting a number at random between 1 and k (both inclusive) and then selecting every kth number thereafter to get a sample of n numbers. The units corresponding to these numbers constitute a systematic sample of size n.

A systematic sampling is also performed by arranging N units into n rows and k columns and then selecting one of the columns out of k columns at random. Each column is said to be a cluster of n units, having the same probability $\frac{1}{k}$ of being selected.

The main difference between a simple random sample and a systematic sample is that only one of the units in a systematic sample is selected at random and the rest (n—1) units are selected according to a predetermined pattern, but in simple random sampling all the n units are selected with equal probability. The main disadvantage with the systematic sampling is that the sampling variance of the estimate cannot be estimated, because only one uit is selected at random.

The systematic sampling is found to be useful in sampling of natural populations like forest surveys to estimate the volume of timber and fish surveys to estimate catch of fish in certain fishing zones. This may also be used conveniently in human settlements arranged in rows.

As regards efficiency, systematic sampling is more efficient than simple random sampling when **intraclass correlation is negative** and also when there is linear trend in the population. If the units of the population are in random order, the systematic sampling has the same efficiency as that of the simple random sampling and the variance of the estimate can be approximately estimated by assuming the sample to be a simple random sample.

If N is not a multiple of n, a feature which invariable happens, the theory of systematic sampling fails and the disturbance caused by such a situation may be negligible if n exceeds 50 and hence may be ignored. Even if n is small, such a disturbance is unlikely to be large in practice.

If $N \neq nk$, a method known as **Circular systematic sampling** has been suggested in sampling theory literature. This method has been successfully used in the Indian National Sample Survey for sampling villages, households, plots, etc. for its different rounds of surveys. According to this method a random number is chosen between 1 to N and the unit corresponding to the random start and every kth unit thereafter in a cyclical manner, till a sample of n units is obtained where k is the integer nearest to (N/n).

When $N = nk$, an unbiased estimate of the population mean $\overline{Y}$ is given by

$$\bar{y}_{sy} = \frac{1}{n}\sum_{j=1}^{n} y_{ij} = \bar{y}_{i0},$$

where $y_{i1}, y_{i2}, \ldots, y_{in}$ are n observations of the ith systematic sample.

$$V(\bar{y}_{sy}) = \frac{1}{k}\sum_{i=1}^{k} (\bar{y}_{i0} - \overline{Y})^2$$

If the units of the population are arranged at random, the estimated variance of $\bar{y}_{sy}$ can be approximated by the estimated variance in simple random sampling.

ILLUSTRATION 7. In a Metro-building complex there are 500 flats numbered from 1 to 500. It is desired to select a systematic sample of 20 flats to estimate the total number of inmates in the complex.

Solution :

Here $N = 500$, $n = 20$. Hence the sampling interval $k = \frac{N}{n} = \frac{500}{20} = 25$.

The procedure to select a systematic sample of size 20 is to select one integer at random from 1 to 25 and suppose this number is 12. The 12th flat in the serially listed flats is selected and then every 25th one. Thus, the serial numbers of the flats selected in the systematic sample are

12, 37, 62, 87, 112, 137, 162, 187, 212, 237, 262, 287, 312, 337, 362, 387, 412, 437, 462, 487.

Now observe the number of inmates in these 20 flats. Suppose these are :

2, 4, 3, 2, 4, 5, 4, 3, 2, 3 5, 4, 4, 2, 6, 3, 4, 5, 3, 2

The estimate of number of inmates in the complex is

$$N\bar{y}_{sy} = (500)\left(\frac{70}{20}\right) = 1750.$$

9.6.4 Cluster Sampling

It is not always convenient to sample the elements (units) of the population because of the travel cost and organisational problems involved in the field work and also due to absence of required frame. In such a situation the sampler may divide the population into units, which are not elementary units but cluster of elements, called *cluster units* for which frame is available. For instance, in business surveys, instead of selecting the business units for study, the city wards, which are clusters of business units may be sampled. Suppose there are N clusters in the population and n clusters are selected by simple random sampling. Then, these clusters are completely enumerated as regards elements constituting clusters. This is called **cluster sampling.** If the clusters are again sampled, the resulting sampling is called **Two–stage sampling.** For instance in a business survey in a city, the wards may be taken as clusters and in cluster sampling all the sampled wards are completely enumerated with respect to business units. If wards are sampled to have business units for observation, the resulting sampling design is a two stage sampling.

Thus, the reasons for adopting cluster sampling may arise due to

(*a*) desire to lower the field costs.

(*b*) absence of satisfactory sampling frame for the elements in the whole population.

In connection with clustering it may be said that whether or not a particular aggregate of units should be called a cluster depends on circumstances and decision as to right unit of enquiry. Further, clustering may not necessarily be natural aggregates such as villages, households, cities, schools, hospitals, electoral constituencies, human settlements industrial centres, business units, etc., but it may also be grids imposed on maps. Cluster sampling in certain form is sometimes termed as **area sampling.**

Area sampling methods have been applied to national populations and even smaller areas where there are well-defined political or natural boundaries.

Estimator of population mean

Let Y_{ij} be the value of the jth unit of the ith cluster $i = 1, 2, \ldots N; j = 1, 2, \ldots, M$. For a simple random sample of size n clusters, an unbiased estimator of population mean $\overline{Y}$ is given by

$$\overline{y}_c = \frac{1}{n}\sum_{i=1}^{n} \overline{Y}_{i\,.},$$

where $$\overline{Y}_{i\,.} = \frac{1}{M}\sum_{j=1}^{M} Y_{ij}$$

$$V(\overline{y}_c) = \left(\frac{1}{n} - \frac{1}{N}\right) S_b^2,$$

where $$S_b^2 = \frac{1}{N-1}\sum_{i=1}^{N} (\overline{Y}_{i\,.} - \overline{Y})^2,$$

$$\text{Est } V(\overline{y}_c) = \left(\frac{1}{n} - \frac{1}{N}\right) s_b^2,$$

where $$s_b^2 = \frac{1}{n-1} \sum_{i=1}^{n} (\overline{Y}_{i\cdot} - \overline{y}_c)^2$$

If the clusters are of unequal sizes, that is, the ith cluster has size M_i (i = 1, 2, ..., N), a number of estimators may be suggested and the reader is advised to refer any sampling theory text book.

Efficiency of Cluster Sampling :

To make a comparison of estimator $\overline{y}_c$ with $\overline{y}$ based on a simple random sampling without replacement of nM elements from NM elements in the population, we have the relative efficiency of cluster sampling given by

$$\text{RE} = \frac{\left(\frac{1}{nM} - \frac{1}{NM}\right) S^2}{\left(\frac{1}{n} - \frac{1}{N}\right) S_b^2} = \frac{S^2}{MS_b^2}$$

$$= \frac{1}{1 + \frac{N(M-1)}{N-1}\delta},$$

where $$\delta = 1 - \frac{S_w^2}{S^2},$$

S^2 = Total variance in the population,

and S_w^2 = Pooled within cluster variance.

For large N,

$$\text{RE} = \frac{1}{1 + (M-1)\delta}$$

δ is positive or negative depending on whether pooled within cluster variance is smaller or greater than the total variance in the population.

Note. Statistical efficiency for cluster samples is usually **lower** than for simple random samples because clusters are usually homogeneous. Economic efficiency is often great enough to overcome this weakness.

9.6.5. Two–Stage Sampling :

Two stage sampling may be carried out due to convenience in sampling and also due to saving of time and the cost of the survey, although there happens to be loss of efficiency due to two stage sampling over uni-stage sampling. In large scale sample surveys adoption of multi-stage sampling is a usual phenomenon. In household surveys concerning a large area, the area may be divided into number of clusters according to geographical or administrative divisions or according to any characteristic called *primary stage units* (p.s.u.) from which a certain number of clusters are selected following any sampling design and then from each selected cluster or p.s.u., certain number of households called *secondary stage units* (s.s.u.) are selected using any sampling design. The two stage sampling in the present instance enables the researcher to locate the households in some of the clusters rather than spreading over the entire area requiring complete frame. If necessary, the entire area may be sub-divided into differet regions called strata and then from each stratum a two-stage sample is selected and thereby resulting in a *stratified two-stage sampling design.* Two stage sampling design may be extended to multi-stage sampling design, if more than two stages are necessary.

Estimation of Population Mean

Let Y_{ij} be the value of the characteristic under study for the jth second stage unit of the ith first stage unit; $j = 1, 2, \ldots M$, $i = 1, 2, \ldots, N$, Then,

Further, the mean per second stage unit of the ith first stage unit is

$$\overline{Y}_{i.} = \frac{1}{M}\sum_{j=1}^{M} Y_{ij}$$

The population mean $$\overline{Y} = \frac{1}{NM}\sum_{i=1}^{N}\sum_{j=1}^{M} Y_{ij}$$

$$= \frac{1}{N}\sum_{i=1}^{N} \overline{Y}_{i\cdot}$$

Now, select a simple random sample of size n from the N first stage units and then select a simple random sample of m second stage units from each of the selected first stage units.

Let $$\overline{y}_{io} = \frac{1}{m}\sum_{j=1}^{m} y_{ij}$$

$$\overline{y} = \frac{1}{nm}\sum_{i}\sum_{j} y_{ij} = \frac{1}{n}\Sigma\,\overline{y}_{i.}$$

the sample mean based on nm–units in the sample.

We find, $\overline{y}$ is an unbiased estimate of $\overline{Y}$.

$$V(\overline{y}) = \left(\frac{1}{n} - \frac{1}{N}\right)S_b^2 + \frac{1}{n}\left(\frac{1}{m} - \frac{1}{M}\right)S_W^2,$$

where $$S_b^2 = \frac{1}{N-1}\Sigma(\overline{Y}_{i.} - \overline{Y})^2,$$

and $$S_W^2 = \frac{1}{N}\sum_{i=1}^{N} S_i^2 = \frac{1}{N(M-1)}\sum_{i=1}^{N}\sum_{j=1}^{M}(Y_{ij} - \overline{Y}_{i.})^2$$

$$\text{Est. } V(\overline{y}) = \left(\frac{1}{n} - \frac{1}{N}\right)s_b^2 + \frac{1}{N}\left(\frac{1}{m} - \frac{1}{M}\right)s_w^2,$$

where $$s_b^2 = \frac{1}{n-1}\sum_{i=1}^{n}(\overline{y}_{i.} - \overline{y})^2$$

and $$s_w^2 = \frac{1}{n} \sum_{i=1}^{n} s_i^2 = \frac{1}{n(m-1)} \sum_{i=1}^{n} \sum_{j=1}^{m} (y_{ij} - \bar{y}_{i.})^2.$$

Note. (*i*) If $n = N$, two stage sampling reduces to stratified random sampling.

(*ii*) If $m = M$, two stage sampling corresponds to cluster sampling.

The relative efficiency is

$$\text{R.E.}\ (\bar{y}) = \frac{V(\bar{y})_{\text{SRSWOR}}}{V(\bar{y})_{\text{two stage}}}$$

$$= \frac{1}{1 + \delta_c (m-1)}$$

where δ_c represents the intra class correlation within first stage units.

The problem of dealing with unequal first stage units is a bit complicated and the practitioner may refer to any sampling theory text book for treatment.

Note. If the first stage units are of unequal sizes M_i $(i = 1, 2, ..., N)$ we may sub-sample varying size of second stage units m_i $(i = 1, 2, ... n)$ from each of the selected first stage units.

An unbiased estimator is given by

$$\hat{Y}_1 = \frac{1}{n} \sum_{i=1}^{n} \frac{M_i}{\bar{M}} \bar{y}_{i.},$$

where $$\bar{M} = \frac{1}{N} \sum_{i=1}^{N} M_i, \text{ and}$$

$$\bar{y}_{i.} = \frac{1}{m_i} \sum_{j=1}^{m_i} y_{ij}$$

$$V\left(\hat{Y}_1\right) = \left(\frac{1}{n} - \frac{1}{N}\right) S_u^2 + \frac{1}{nN} \sum_{i=1}^{N} \left(\frac{M_i}{\bar{M}}\right)^2 \left(\frac{1}{m_i} - \frac{1}{M_i}\right) S_{iy}^2$$

$$= \left(\frac{1}{n} - \frac{1}{N}\right) \frac{1}{N-1} \sum \left(\frac{M_i}{\bar{M}} \bar{Y}_{i.} - \bar{Y}\right)^2 + \frac{1}{nN} \sum_{i=1}^{N} \left(\frac{M_i}{\bar{M}}\right)^2 \left(\frac{1}{m_i} - \frac{1}{M_i}\right) S_{iy}^2,$$

where $$S_{iy}^2 = \frac{1}{M_i - 1} \sum_{j=1}^{M_i} (Y_{ij} - \bar{Y}_{i.})^2$$

EXERCISES

1. What is a survey ? Distinguish between descriptive and analytical surveys.
2. Define population and sample. Discuss the situations where census survey and sample survey are appropriate.
3. What is a sampling unit ? Discuss types of sampling unit.

4. What is a sampling frame ? Mention its necessity in a sample survey. What are different types of frame ? What are possible errors associated with frame ? Discuss.

5. Differentiate between target population and survey population with examples.

6. Why do you sample a population ? Discuss.

7. Distinguish between probability sampling and non-probability sampling with examples.

8. What are errors in a sample surveys ? How can they be controlled ?

9. Differentiate between accuracy and precision in a sample survey. Discuss with suitable examples.

10. (*a*) What are types of non-sampling erors ? How would you control them ? Discuss.

(*b*) Distinguish between sampling error and non-sampling error.

(*c*) What would be sampling error in a complete enumeration survey ?

(*d*) How would you reduce the sampling error ? Discuss.

(*e*) Distinguish between response and non-response errors with examples.

(*f*) Explain quota sampling and judgement sampling.

(*i*) Can you compute or estimate sampling error in convenience sampling ? Give reasons of your answer.

11. Explain errors due to respondents and non-respondents. Mention the role of interviewer in controlling them. How would you detect-response errors ? Discuss.

12. Write notes on :

(*a*) Errors in coverage

(*b*) Processing errors

(*c*) Reporting errors

13. What are major criteria in determining an appropriate sampling design ?

14. Discuss different types of non-probability sampling.

15. Explain merits and demerits of non-probability sampling.

16. How would you determine the sample size ? Discuss with respect to simple random sampling.

17. Define simple random sampling. Mention its characteristics.

18. Discuss different methods of drawing a simple random sample.

19. How would you estimate population mean and total by drawing a simple random sample from a finite population ? Give expressions for sampling variance and estimates of standard error.

20. What is stratified random sampling ? What are reasons for stratification ? Discuss.

21. A sample survey is conducted to study the working conditions of employees in cement factories in the country. What is the appropriate sampling design for the purpose ? How can this be conducted ? Discuss.

22. Discuss the problems of allocation of units to different strata in a stratified sampling.

23. Distinguish between proportional allocation and Neyman allocation and state reasons for their adoption.

24. What is systematic sampling ? Discuss the situation when this sampling is to be adopted ? Mention its relative merits and demerits.

25. Compare cluster sampling with simple random sampling of elements.

26. Discuss the situations when two stage sampling is to be preferred over single stage sampling.

27. Mention the uses of double sampling.

28. Is stratified sampling always more efficient than unrestricted random sampling ? Discuss.

29. What is inverse sampling ?

30. What is a multi-purpose sample ?

31. How do you select a sample ? Breifly mention salient steps.

32. What are major steps in conducting a sample survey ? Breifly discuss.

33. Out of 250 industrial units in an industrial estate, a simple random sample of 30 units were selected, of which 5 of them wre seen to be incurring losses. Estimate the number of losing concerns among the industrial units in the population and estimate its standard error.

34. The daily number of absentee workers in a factory over 25 working days, a random sample from 300 working days in a year is given below. Compute the estimate of number of absentee workers in the year under review and estimate its standard error.

2, 0, 5, 3, 4
1, 2, 2, 1 , 0
2, 0, 3, 1, 1
1, 2, 4, 1, 0
2, 3, 2, 1, 2

35. Briefly explain the importance of sample size in a sample survey.

□□□

CHAPTER

10

PARAMETRIC STATISTICAL INFERENCE (PROBLEMS OF ESTIMATION AND HYPOTHESIS TESTING)

10.1. Introduction

Besides interpreting the collected data through descriptive statistics, a researcher might like to infer from his findings based on certain quantitative information in the light of certain hypothesis or even otherwise about the true unknown characteristics of the population *i.e.* the aggregate of units under study. Depending on the availability of time, resources both human and finance, measurement techniques and inherent feasibility and more so objectives of the study, the researcher may cover the *entire population* or a part of it called a *sample*. If the inference or decision is made on the basis of a sample, the decision is said to be made *under uncertainty* and in this situation the researcher has to devise statistical techniques/procedures so that the decision does not go far away from reality even if the probability statements are associated.

Statistical inference is broadly classified into *two areas of inferential procedures,* representing two different aspects of ignorance about populations, whether finite or infinite—

- **Problems of Estimation**
- **Hypothesis Testing.**

The problem of estimation arises when the reasearcher wants to estimate some unknown population characteristics, termed as *Parameters* of the population. For instance, we may like to estimate average daily output in a factory, average daily sales in grocery stores in a city, average annual income of the employees in government departments/business establishments etc.

The unknown population parameter may be either estimated by a single numerical value (called *Point estimate*) or by an interval having defined lower and upper limits (called *Interval estimate*). Thus, an interval estimate is a range of values to estimate an unknown population parameter. A point estimate, sometimes, may be nearer to the true value (parameter) or may be faraway from that. Hence, we cannol know how wrong it is and moreover one cannot be certain about its reliability. Such short-coming is somewhat compensated by interval estimate which gives a range within which the true value is likely to lie with certain probability. Thus, the theory of estimation is broadly classified as :

- *Point estimation.*
- *Interval estimation.*

The **theory of testing of hypotheses** in decision-making process helps us to know whether hypothesis stated on the parameter(s) of a population is tenable on the basis of a random sample from the concerned population. For instance, a quality manager may like to know whether proportion of defectives in the lot supplied by Vendor-1 is less than the proportion of defectives in the lot supplied by Vendor-2; a manager may like to know whether advance training incentives given to workers have increased the output in a factory, whether the recruitment of management graduates from reputed business management institutes has improved the business environment in the company leading to increased sales and thereby profits, etc.

10.2 Problems of estimation

Point estimation

Let us consider sampling from an infinite population having probability density $f(x, \theta)$, where θ is the only parameter usually unknown and the observed sample values are $x_1, x_2, \ldots, x_n$. These n observations may be regarded as single observations from n identical populations generated by n independently and identically distributed random variables $X_1, X_2, \ldots, X_n$.

Let t be a function of sample observations $x_1, x_2, \ldots, x_n$. In statistical language t is called a *statistic.* It t is chosen as an approximate/representative value of θ, then t is called an *estimator* of θ. An *estimate* is a numerical description of an estimator, but sometimes both the terms are used in statistical literature without any distinction.

> If t, a function of sample observations, is used by a researcher to represent the unknown population characteristic θ, t is called an estimator of θ.

t, being a function of random sample values, is also a random variable which varies from sample to sample. For instance, to estimate average daily sales in 50 Department stores in a city on a particular day, we may take a random sample of 10 stores, say, and then compute sample average sales for the purpose. This sample average might not be the same, if we select another sample of size 10 and then compute the sample average. In fact, there will be $50\ C_{10}$ = 10, 272, 278, 170 possible samples and the chosen sample is one of them. Some of these sample averages might be equal to population average when all 50 stores are taken into account, but *not* all sample averages.

In sampling from an infinite population, there would be infinite number of possible samples, all providing sample estimates of the population characteristic.

The variations in the values of t give rise to a probability distribution of t, termed as *sampling distribution of t*.

> **Sampling Distribution :**
> The probability distribution of the statistic t is defined as the sampling distribution of t.

Now, the question arises as to how much variable is the estimator t ? Naturally, this is to be decided by looking at the sampling distribution of t. Thus, the variance of the sampling distribution is popularly termed as *sampling variance* of t and positive square root of sampling variance is called *standard error* of t.

> **Standard Error :**
> The standard deviation of the sampling distribution of t is called standard error of t.

The reliability or efficiency of t as an estimator of the unknown population characteristic θ is measured by its sampling variance or standard error. If all possible values of t closely concentrate around the true value θ, then t is supposed to be an ideal estimator of θ.

Properties of estimator

Three important properties may be associated with one estimator. These are :

- Unbiasedness
- Consistency
- Efficiency

Theoretically, t is said to be an unbiased of θ, if

$$E(t) = \theta$$

This implies that any single value of t may not be equal to θ, but if its long-run average is equal to θ. Then, t may be said to have a desirable property such as *unbiasedness*. However in practice, it may not be always possible to obtain an unbiased estimator of θ. In such circumstances we may get satisfied with the property of *consistency* associated with the estimator t. Thus, t is said to be a consistent estimator of θ, if for infinitely small $\in$,

$$\text{Prob}\{| t - \theta | \le \in\} \to 1 \quad \text{as } n \to \infty$$

That is, if the sample size is large, the deviation between t and θ will be minimal in probability. This will be possible if $V(t) \to 0$ as $n \to \infty$.

The property of efficiency is linked up with the variance of the estimator. An unbiased estimator is said to be efficient, if it has the minimum possible variance among all unbiased estimators. Thus, if t and t_1 are both unbiased estimators of θ, then t would be more efficient than t_1, if

$$\boxed{V(t) < V(t_1)}$$

In case t is not an unbiased estimator of θ, then

$$E(t) \neq \theta$$

and t is said to be a *biased* estimator of θ with bias $B(t) = E(t) - \theta$. The bias may be either positive or negative. The sampling variation in t is measured by computing mean square error (MSE) of t, that is,

$$\boxed{\begin{aligned} MSE(t) &= E(t - \theta)^2 \\ &= V(t) + \{E(t) - \theta\}^2. \end{aligned}}$$

Interval Estimation

The technique of estimating θ in an interval rather than with a single sample value t rests in finding the lower limit L and the upper limit U such that

$$\boxed{P(L < \theta < U) = 1 - \alpha}$$

where α is a small fraction. L and U depend on sample observations and usually computed with the help of a statistic t, which is a function of sample observations. The interval having shortest length *i.e.* U—L should be the appropriate choice. Toward constructing an interval in which θ is likely to lie with certain probability we define a pivotal quantity

$$\boxed{Z = \frac{t - \theta}{\sqrt{V(t)}},}$$

whose distribution is supposed to be known.

Then, we compute z_1 and z_2 such that

$$\boxed{P(z_1 < Z < z_2) = 1 - \alpha}$$

If it is possible to write down the inequality $z_1 < Z < z_2$ in the form $t_1 < \theta < t_2$, where t_1 and t_2 are some functions z_1, z_2 and the x's, but not of θ, then we can assert

$$\boxed{P(t_1 < \theta < t_2) = 1 - \alpha, \text{ for all } \theta,}$$

α being a small fraction. This assertion that θ lies in the interval t_1 and t_2 with certain probability $(1 - \alpha)$ is called a *Confidence statement* on θ. The greater the probability $(1 - \alpha)$, the more confident we feel that the interval $[t_1, t_2]$ would cover the parameter θ. The interval t_1 to t_2 is therefore called a *Confidence interval* for θ, with t_1 and t_2 as the lower and upper *confidence limits* respectively. The fraction $(1 - \alpha)$ is called the *Confidence coefficient.* Thus, the confidence interval is an interval with a *measure of reliability.*

10.2.1. Estimation of Population Mean

Infinite Population

Consider a random sample of size $n \rightarrow X_1, X_2, ..., X_n$ from an infinite population having probability density $f(X|\mu, \sigma^2)$, where μ is the population mean and σ^2 is the population variance, but the form of the population is not known.

Compute the sample mean

$$\overline{X} = \frac{1}{n} \sum_{i=1}^{n} X_i$$

$$E(\overline{X}) = \frac{1}{n} \sum_{i=1}^{n} E(X_i) = \frac{1}{n} \sum_{i=1}^{n} \mu = \frac{n\mu}{n}$$

$$= \mu.$$

Thus, $\overline{X}$ is an unbiased estimator of μ.

$$V(\overline{X}) = V\left(\frac{X_1 + ... + X_n}{n}\right)$$

$$= \frac{1}{n^2}[\sigma^2 + ... + \sigma^2] = \frac{n\sigma^2}{n^2}$$

$$= \frac{\sigma^2}{n}.$$

Standard error of $\overline{X} = \frac{\sigma}{\sqrt{n}}$.

Note : Thus, we arrive at two important results. First, if the population is infinitely large, the expected value of sample mean is equal to the population mean and secondly the sampling variance of the sample mean is the variance of the population divided by the sample size.

$$\boxed{\begin{array}{c} E(\overline{X}) = \mu \\ V(\overline{X}) = \sigma^2/n \end{array}}$$

As the sample size n increases, the average value of *sample means* tends to be close to the true population mean. Further, if sample size is increased, the variance of $\overline{X}$ gets reduced and all possible sample means cluster closely around the population mean μ.

The standard deviation of the sampling distribution of $\overline{X}$ is called the *Standard error of mean*. The standard error indicates the extent to which the observed value of sample mean can be away from the true value, due to sampling errors. For example, if the standard error is small, we are reasonably confident that the observed value of the sample mean cannot be very far away from the true value.

Finite Population

Consider a simple random sample (without replacement) of size $n \to X_1, X_2, ..., X_n$ from a finite population U of size N.

The sample mean $\overline{X}$ is an unbiased estimator of the population mean μ. The sampling variance of the sample mean $\overline{X}$ is

$$\boxed{V(\overline{X}) = \frac{N - n}{n(N-1)}\sigma^2},$$

where $$\sigma^2 = \frac{1}{N} \sum_{i=1}^{N} (X_i - \mu)^2$$

An unbiased estimate of $V(\overline{X})$ is given by

$$\text{Est } V(\overline{X}) = \frac{N-n}{Nn} s^2,$$

where $$s^2 = \frac{1}{n-1} \sum_{i=1}^{n} (X_i - \overline{X})^2$$

Thus, estimated standard error of $\overline{X}$ is

$$\boxed{\text{Est. S.E. } (\overline{X}) = \sqrt{\frac{N-n}{N}} \frac{s}{\sqrt{n}}}$$

In case of drawing a simple random sample *with replacement,* the sample mean $\overline{X}$ is still an unbiased estimator of the population mean μ. But $V(\overline{X}) = \frac{\sigma^2}{n}$ and Est. $V(\overline{X}) = \frac{s^2}{n}$. Est. S.E. $(\overline{X}) = \frac{s}{\sqrt{n}}$.

Normal Population (known variance σ^2)

Consider $X_1, X_2, ..., X_n$ as a random sample from a normal population with mean μ and known variance σ^2.

The sample mean $\overline{X} = \frac{1}{n} \Sigma X_i$ is an unbiased estimator of μ with variance σ^2/n. This is the most efficient of all unbiased estimators of μ. $\overline{X}$ is normally distributed with mean μ and variance σ^2/n.

The standard normal variate is defined as

$$\boxed{Z = \frac{\overline{X} - \mu}{\sigma/\sqrt{n}}}$$

$$E(Z) = 0 \text{ and } V(Z) = 1.$$

The shortest confidence interval for μ is the equal tail interval given by

$$\left(\bar{x} - z_{\alpha/2} \frac{\sigma}{\sqrt{n}}, \bar{x} + z_{\alpha/2} \frac{\sigma}{\sqrt{n}}\right),$$

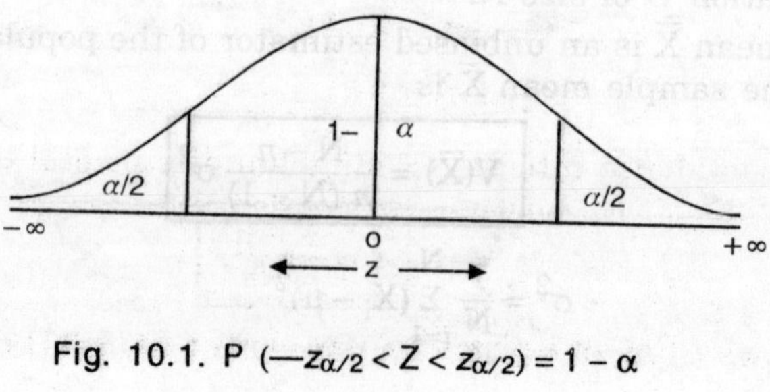

Fig. 10.1. P $(-z_{\alpha/2} < Z < z_{\alpha/2}) = 1 - \alpha$

where $z_{\alpha/2}$ is the value of the standard normal variable Z, above which we find an area of $\alpha/2$, *i.e.*

$$P(-z_{\alpha/2} < Z < z_{\alpha/2}) = 1 - \alpha.$$

Example 10.1. Suppose it is known that the weight of cement in packed bags is distributed normally with a standard deviation of 0.2 kg. A sample of 16 bags is picked up at random and the mean weight of cement in these 16 bags is only 49.5 kg.

What is the estimate of average weight of packed cement bags in the cement store ? Construct a 90% confidence interval for the mean weight of cement in packed bags.

Solution :

Let X be a random variable representing the weight of cement in a packed bag. Assume that X is distributed normally with a standard deviation of 0.2 kg.

The estimate of the average weight of the cement bag is the sample mean $(\overline{X})$ 49.5 kg.

The standard error of the Mean is computed as

$$\text{S.E. }(\overline{X}) = \frac{\sigma}{\sqrt{n}} = \frac{0.2}{\sqrt{16}} = \frac{0.2}{4} = 0.05 \text{ kg.}$$

For a 90% confidence interval, the lower limit

$$= \overline{X} - 1.645\frac{\sigma}{\sqrt{n}}$$

$$= 49.5 - 1.645\,(0.05) = 49.4178 \text{ kg.}$$

and the upper limit

$$= \overline{X} + 1.645\frac{\sigma}{\sqrt{n}}$$

$$= 49.5 + 1.645\,(0.05) = 49.5822 \text{ kg.}$$

Thus, 90% confidence interval is given by (49.4178, 49.5822)

Normal Population (unknown variance σ^2)

If a random sample $X_1, X_2, \ldots, X_n$ is said to be drawn from a normal population with unknown mean μ and unknown variance σ^2, the sample mean $\overline{X}$ is also an unbiased estimator of the population mean μ.

$$V(\overline{X}) = \frac{\sigma^2}{n},$$

which cannot be computed unless σ^2 is estimated from the sample itself.

Thus, the estimate of sampling variance $V(\overline{X})$ is given by

$$\text{Est. } V(\overline{X}) = \frac{s^2}{n},$$

where $$s^2 = \frac{1}{n-1}\sum_{i=1}^{n}(X_i - \overline{X})^2$$

Also, $$\text{Est. S.E. }(\overline{X}) = \frac{s}{\sqrt{n}}.$$

To derive confidence interval for μ, define the pivotal quantity

$$\boxed{t = \frac{\overline{X} - \mu}{s/\sqrt{n}},}$$

which follows Student's *t*-distribution with $v = (n-1)$ degrees of freedom.

Example 10.2. The mean and standard deviation of the grade points of a random sample of 10 final year MBA students of a college were calculated to be 5.8 and 0.5 respectively. Assuming the normal distribution of grade points, find the 95% confidence interval for the mean grade point of the entire final year class.

Solution :

The point estimate of μ (mean of the normal population) is $\overline{X} = 5.8$

The 95% confidence interval for μ can be constructed by appealing to the *t*-distribution with 9 d.f. and is given by

$$\overline{X} - t_{\alpha/2}\frac{s}{\sqrt{n}} < \mu < \overline{X} + t_{\alpha/2}\frac{s}{\sqrt{n}}$$

That is, $5.8 - (2.262)(0.5/\sqrt{10}) < \mu < 5.8 + (2.262) \times (0.5/\sqrt{10})$

$\Rightarrow$ $5.4423 < \mu < 6.1577.$

Note :

Degree of freedom refers to the number of independent variates entering into the construction of estimates obtained from the set of observations. In case of sample variance s^2, it is $(n-1)$ because of the only constraint $X_1 + X_2 + ... + X_n = n\overline{X}$.

The student *t*-distribution is a symmetrical distribution and looks like a standard normal distribution with slightly more peaked. This distribution is more variable than the standard normal distribution with variance equal to $(n-1)/(n-3)$. Being a symmetrical distribution, its skewness is zero, whereas the coefficient of kurtosis is greater than 3 *i.e.* $\beta_2 = 3\,(n-3)/(n-5)$.

The distribution entirely depends on its degrees of freedom $\upsilon = (n-1)$ and if $\upsilon \to \infty$, the *t*-distribution tends to normality.

For the application of *t*-distribution, it is pre-requisite that the sample must come from a normal population.

For samples of size $n \geq 30$, s^2 provides a reasonably good estimator of σ^2 and $\frac{\overline{X} - \mu}{s/\sqrt{n}}$ is approximately distributed as a standard normal variable.

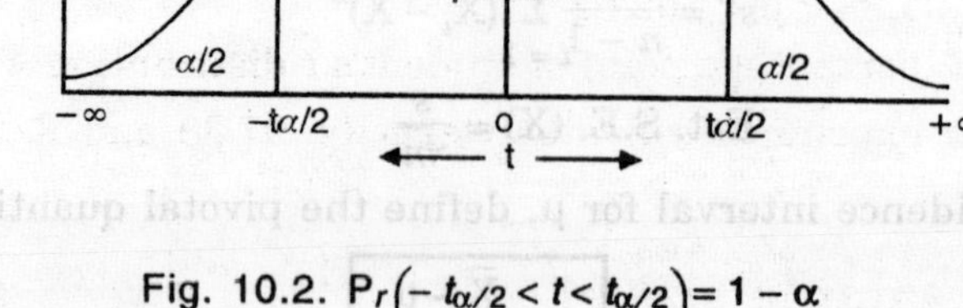

Fig. 10.2. $P_r\left(-t_{\alpha/2} < t < t_{\alpha/2}\right) = 1 - \alpha$

The probability that in random sampling the value of *t* falls between two specified values is equal to the area under *t*-curve between two ordinates corresponding to the specified values. Table A–2 gives the value of $|t|$, read as modulus of t, with probability α being exceeded in random sampling. This table can also be used to find those t-values above which we find a specified area α*.

To calculate the confidence interval of μ with confidence level $(1-\alpha)$, we find $t_{\alpha/2}$ such that

$$P_r\left[-t_{\alpha/2} < \frac{\overline{X}-\mu}{s/\sqrt{n}} < t_{\alpha/2}\right] = 1-\alpha$$

Thus, the confidence interval for μ with unknown variance σ^2 is given by

$$\overline{X} - t_{\alpha/2\,,\,n-1}\frac{s}{\sqrt{n}} < \mu < \overline{X} + t_{\alpha/2\,,\,n-1}\frac{s}{\sqrt{n}}.$$

Example 10.3. The weekly expenditure of 7 households in a village on milk or milk products are Rs. 98, 102, 104, 98, 100, 102 and 96. Find a 95% confidence interval for the mean expenditure, assuming an approximate normal distribution. Estimate also an average weekly expenditure on milk products.

Solution :

The sample mean and standard deviation for the data on expenditure are :

$$\overline{X} = \frac{\Sigma X_i}{n} = \frac{98+102+104+98+100+102+96}{7}$$

$$= \frac{700}{7} = 100 \text{ Rs.}$$

$$s^2 = \frac{1}{n-1}\,\Sigma\,(X_i - \overline{X})^2 = \frac{1}{6}\,[48] = 8$$

The standard error of the estimate

$$\sigma_{\overline{x}} = \sqrt{\frac{s^2}{n}} = \sqrt{\frac{8}{7}}$$

$$= 1.0690$$

Hence, the 95% confidence interval for μ is

$$\overline{X} - t_{0.025}\frac{s}{\sqrt{n}} < \mu < \overline{X} + t_{0.025}\frac{s}{\sqrt{n}}$$

or $$100 - (2.45)\frac{2.83}{\sqrt{7}} < \mu < 100 + (2.45)\frac{2.83}{\sqrt{7}}$$

which simplifies to

$$97.38 < \mu < 102.62$$

where $t_{0.025}$ = 2.5% percentage point of student's t-distribution = 2.45.

That is, the mean expenditure lies between Rs. 97.38 and Rs. 102.62 with 95% confidence.

Determination of sample size

Given a prescribed confidence level $(1-\alpha)$ and length of confidence interval $\leq 2\,d$, how large a sample is required to achieve these ?

We choose the smallest n such that

$$d \geq z_{\alpha/2} \frac{\sigma}{\sqrt{n}}$$

or

$$n \geq z_{\alpha/2}^2 \frac{\sigma^2}{d^2}.$$

Thus, if we estimate μ by taking $\overline{X}$, based on a sample of size

$$n \geq z_{\alpha/2}^2 \left(\frac{\sigma^2}{d^2}\right),$$

then we are (1—α) 100% confident that the error in our estimate $\overline{X}$ is at most d.

If σ^2 is not known, the inequality to determine n is given by

$$n \geq t_{\alpha/2}^2 \left(\frac{s^2}{d^2}\right)$$

Example 10.4. An efficiency expert wishes to determine the average time that it takes to complete a job in a computer centre. How large a sample will he need to be 95% confident that his sample average will be within 15 seconds of the true average ? Assume that it is known from previous studies that σ = 25 seconds.

Solution :

$$d = 15, \sigma = 25$$

$$1 - \alpha = 0.95, z_{\alpha/2} = 1.96$$

Therefore

$$n \geq z_{\alpha/2}^2 \left(\frac{\sigma^2}{d^2}\right)$$

$$= (1.96)^2 \frac{25^2}{15^2} = (3.8416) \frac{625}{225}$$

$$= 10.67 \cong 11.$$

Non-normal population

Consider a sample of size n, $X_1, X_2, \ldots, X_n$ from a non-normal population with mean μ and known variance σ^2.

The sample mean $\overline{X}$ is an unbiased estimator of μ with standard error $\sigma/\sqrt{n}$.

But what's about finding a confidence interval for μ ?

Toward this end, we state a very important theorem in statistics called *Central limit theorem*. This theorem states that given a distribution with finite mean μ and finite variance σ^2, the sampling distribution of the sample mean approaches a normal distribution with mean μ and variance σ^2/n as the sample size n increases, no matter what the shape of the original distribution is. It is to be remembered that n is the sample size for each mean and not the number of samples, which is assumed to be infinite in a sampling distribution.

Central limit theorem

Let $X_1, X_2, \ldots, X_n$ be a sequence of random variables with expected value μ and variance σ^2.

Define $S_n = X_1 + X_2 + ... + X_n$

$E(S_n) = n\mu$ and

$V(S_n) = n\sigma^2$

Then, the distribution of

$$Z_n = \frac{S_n - n\mu}{\sigma\sqrt{n}}$$

converges towards the standard normal distribution N(0, 1) as $n \to \infty$.

That is, if $\Phi(z)$ is the cumulative distribution function of N(0, 1), then for every real number z, we have

$$\lim_{n \to \infty} P(Z_n \le z) = \Phi(z)$$

or equivalently

$$\lim_{n \to \infty} P\left[\frac{\overline{X}_n - \mu}{\sigma/\sqrt{n}} \le z\right] = \Phi(z),$$

where $\overline{X}_n = \frac{S_n}{n} = \frac{X_1 + X_2 + ... + X_n}{n}$.

Thus, if the sample size is large, a confidence interval for the population mean can be constructed with the help of a normal distribution, even if the parent distribution is not normal.

10.2.2. Estimation of difference between two population means

(*a*) **Known variances :** Suppose we have two independent samples of sizes n_1 and n_2 from two normal populations with means μ_1 and μ_2 and known variances σ_1^2 and σ_2^2 respectively.

The point estimate of $\mu_1 - \mu_2$ is given by $\overline{X}_1 - \overline{X}_2$.

The sampling distribution of $\overline{X}_1 - \overline{X}_2$ is normal with mean $\mu_1 - \mu_2$ and variance $\frac{\sigma_1^2}{n_1} + \frac{\sigma_2^2}{n_2}$.

Define

$$Z = \frac{(\overline{X}_1 - \overline{X}_2) - (\mu_1 - \mu_2)}{\sqrt{\frac{\sigma_1^2}{n_1} + \frac{\sigma_2^2}{n_2}}},$$

Z is a standard normal variate. We, now, assert with probability (1 — α) that Z will lie between $-z_{\alpha/2}$ and $z_{\alpha/2}$. That is,

$$P_r[-z_{\alpha/2} < Z < z_{\alpha/2}] = 1 - \alpha.$$

On simplification, the (1 — α) 100% confidence interval for $\mu_1 - \mu_2$ is

$$(\overline{X}_1 - \overline{X}_2) - z_{\alpha/2}\sqrt{\frac{\sigma_1^{\,2}}{n_1} + \frac{\sigma_2^{\,2}}{n_2}}$$

$$< \mu_1 - \mu_2 < (\overline{X}_1 - \overline{X}_2) + z_{\alpha/2}\sqrt{\frac{\sigma_1^{\,2}}{n_1} + \frac{\sigma_2^{\,2}}{n_2}}.$$

(*b*) Unknown but equal variances

If $\sigma_1^{\,2}$ and $\sigma_2^{\,2}$ are not known, let us consider the case when $\sigma_1^{\,2} = \sigma_2^{\,2} = \sigma^2$.

The point estimate of $\mu_1 - \mu_2$ is $\overline{X}_1 - \overline{X}_2$ with standard error

$$\sqrt{\sigma^2\left(\frac{1}{n_1} + \frac{1}{n_2}\right)}$$

As σ^2 is not known, this can be estimated by

$$s^2 = \frac{(n_1 - 1)\, s_1^{\,2} + (n_2 - 1)\, s_2^{\,2}}{n_1 + n_2 - 2},$$

where $s_1^{\,2}$ and $s_2^{\,2}$ are unbiased estimates of σ^2 from first and second samples respectively.

Define,

$$t = \frac{(\overline{X}_1 - \overline{X}_2) - (\mu_1 - \mu_2)}{s\sqrt{\frac{1}{n_1} + \frac{1}{n_2}}}$$

***t* has a Student's *t*-distribution with $\upsilon = n_1 + n_2 - 2$ degrees of freedom. We can now set**

$$P_r\left[-t_{\alpha/2,\, n_1+n_2-2} < \frac{(\overline{X}_1 - \overline{X}_2) - (\mu_1 - \mu_2)}{s\sqrt{\frac{1}{n_1} + \frac{1}{n_2}}} < t_{\alpha/2,\, n_1+n_2-2}\right]$$
$$= 1 - \alpha.$$

Thus, the $(1 - \alpha)$ 100% confidence interval of $\mu_1 - \mu_2$ is given by $(\overline{X}_1 - \overline{X}_2) - t_{\alpha/2,\, n_1+n_2-2} \cdot s\sqrt{\frac{1}{n_1} + \frac{1}{n_2}}$

$$< \mu_1 - \mu_2 < (\overline{X}_1 - \overline{X}_2) + t_{\alpha/2,\, n_1+n_2-2} \cdot s\sqrt{\frac{1}{n_1} + \frac{1}{n_2}}$$

If both n_1 and n_2 are *not* less than 30, the sampling distribution of $\overline{X}_1 - \overline{X}_2$ is approximately normal with mean $(\mu_1 - \mu_2)$ and variance $\frac{s_1^{\,2}}{n_1} + \frac{s_2^{\,2}}{n_2}$. Hence, the confidence interval for $(\mu_1 - \mu_2)$ may be based on

$$Z = \frac{(\overline{X}_1 - \overline{X}_2) - (\mu_1 - \mu_2)}{\sqrt{\frac{s_1^2}{n_1} + \frac{s_2^2}{n_2}}},$$

which follows an approximate standard normal distribution for large n_1 and n_2.

Example 10.5. A random sample of 340 male and 460 female employees is selected from large organizations in a city. Mean daily wages of males and females are computed to be Rs. 250 and Rs. 200 respectively whereas the sample standard deviations for males and females are found to be Rs. 30 and Rs. 20 respectively.

Compute a 95% confidence interval for the difference between average daily wage of male and female employees.

Solution :

Assuming normality and further assuming the difference between sample standard deviations and population standard deviations to be negligibly small for large samples, the statistic

$$Z = \frac{(\overline{X}_1 - \overline{X}_2) - (\mu_1 - \mu_2)}{\sqrt{\frac{s_1^2}{n_1} + \frac{s_2^2}{n_2}}}$$

is approximately standard normal.

Given $\overline{X}_1 = \text{Rs. } 250, \overline{X}_2 = \text{Rs. } 200$

$s_1 = \text{Rs. } 30, s_2 = \text{Rs. } 20$

Thus, the 95% confidence interval for $(\mu_1 - \mu_2)$ is given by

$$(\overline{X}_1 - \overline{X}_2) - z_{0.025}\sqrt{\frac{s_1^2}{n_1} + \frac{s_2^2}{n_2}} < (\mu_1 - \mu_2)$$

$$< (\overline{X}_1 - \overline{X}_2) + z_{0.025}\sqrt{\frac{s_1^2}{n_1} + \frac{s_2^2}{n_2}}$$

On relevant substitutions and $z_{0.025} = 1.96$,

$$46.3244 < \mu_1 - \mu_2 < 53.6756$$

(*c*) Situations arise when the observations in two samples occur in pairs so that the two observations are related. Thus, the samples are not independent and moreover the variances of two populations may not necessarily be equal. For instance, to determine the effectiveness of technical training programme on the output of workers, we take a random sample of n workers and observe their output before and after training.

Let d_i (i = 1, 2, ..., n) be the difference observed between the observations in the ith pair, assumed to be a random sample from a normal population with mean μ_d and variance σ_d^2.

The point estimate of μ_d is given by $\overline{d} = \frac{1}{n}\sum_{i=1}^{n} d_i$, with estimated standard error

$$s_d = \sqrt{\frac{1}{n-1} \sum_{i=1}^{n} (d_i - \bar{d})^2}$$

Define

$$\boxed{t = \frac{\bar{d} - \mu_d}{s_d/\sqrt{n}}},$$

which follows Student's t-distribution with (n—1) degrees of freedom.

(1—α) 100% confidence interval of u_d is given by

$$\bar{d} - t_{\alpha/2,\, n-1}\frac{s_d}{\sqrt{n}} < \mu_d < \bar{d} + t_{\alpha/2,\, n-1}\frac{s_d}{\sqrt{n}}.$$

Example 10.6. A random sample of 10 overweight persons were prescribed some Yogic exercises and diet program. After an expiry of 3 months the difference (in kg) between initial weight and weight after 3 months are noted as given below.

2, 2.5, 1.5, 3, 2.2, 1.8, 3, 2.5, 1.8, 2.4

Compute a 95% confidence interval for the true difference between average weights.

Solution :

Let d_i stands for the difference between weights

$$\bar{d} = \frac{1}{n} \sum_{i=1}^{n} d_i = \frac{22.7}{10} = 2.27 \text{ kg}$$

$$s_d^2 = \frac{1}{n-1} [\Sigma d_i{}^2 - n\, \bar{d}^2]$$

$$= \frac{1}{9} [53.83 - 10\,(2.27)^2]$$

$$= \frac{1}{9} [53.83 — 51.53] = \frac{2.3}{9}$$

$$= 0.2556$$

Hence, $s_d = 0.5055$

The 95% confidence interval for μ_d (true difference between average weights) is

$$\bar{d} - t_{\alpha/2,\, n-1}\frac{s_d}{\sqrt{n}} < \mu_d < \bar{d} + t_{\alpha/2,\, n-1}\frac{s_d}{\sqrt{n}}$$

That is,

$$2.27 — (2.26)\frac{0.5055}{\sqrt{10}} < \mu_d$$

$$< 2.27 + (2.26)\frac{0.5055}{\sqrt{10}}$$

or $2.27 — 0.31613 < \mu < 2.27 + 0.3613$

or $1.9087 < \mu_d < 2.6313.$

Example 10.7. Samples of two types of electric bulbs were tested for length of life and the following data were recorded :

Type 1	Type 2
$n_1 = 5$	$n_2 = 7$
$\overline{X}_1 = 1200$ hrs	$\overline{X}_2 = 1030$ hrs
$s_1 = 35$ hrs	$s_2 = 40$ hrs

Estimate the difference between average lengths of life of two types of electric bulbs.

Assuming normality, compute 95% confidence interval for the difference between population mean length of life of two types of bulbs (Assume that the standard deviation of life for the two types is the same).

Solution :

$$s^2 = \frac{(n_1 - 1)\, s_1^{\,2} + (n_2 - 1)\, s_2^{\,2}}{n_1 + n_2 - 2}$$

$$= \frac{(5-1)\, 35^2 + (7-1)\, 40^2}{5 + 7 - 2} = 1450$$

$$\therefore \quad s = \sqrt{1450} = 38.08 \text{ hrs}$$

$$1 - \alpha = 0.95$$

A 95% confidence interval for $(\mu_1 - \mu_2)$ is

$$(\bar{x}_1 - \bar{x}_2) - t_{\alpha/2,\, n_1 + n_2 - 2},\, s\sqrt{\frac{1}{n_1} + \frac{1}{n_2}}$$

$$< (\mu_1 - \mu_2) < (\bar{x}_1 - \bar{x}_2) + t_{\alpha/2,\, n_1 + n_2 - 2},\, s\sqrt{\frac{1}{n_1} + \frac{1}{n_2}}$$

which reduces to

$$(1200—1030) — (2.23)(38.08)\sqrt{\frac{1}{5} + \frac{1}{7}}$$

$$< (\mu_1 - \mu_2) < (1200—1030) + (2.23)(38.08)\sqrt{\frac{1}{5} + \frac{1}{7}}$$

or $\quad 120.28 < \mu_1 - \mu_2 < 219.72.$

Note : If population variances are not known to be equal, this should be tested with the help of 'F' test (to be discussed later on) before constructing confidence interval using student's t-distribution.

Example 10.8. An advertising agency claims that advertisement in a local daily newspaper increased sales of a product. In order to test this claim, the following experiment was conducted. Twelve major cities in the country were selected and in each city largest wholesale shop dealing with the product was chosen. From each of the 12 shops, monthly sales figures before and after the introduction of the advertisement in the local daily newspaper were collected.

The following table gives the required information collected from the shops.

Monthly sales in Rs. in thousands

Shop	Before Advertisement	After Advertisement
1	83	90
2	83	90
3	81	80
4	93	90
5	89	92
6	84	88
7	88	90
8	61	63
9	64	70
10	51	54
11	71	78
12	90	86

Do you agree with the advertising agency's claim ?

Solution :

Let $d_i = x_i - y_i$

d_i is assumed to be normally distributed with mean μ_d and variance $\sigma_d{}^2$. H_0 : $\mu_d \leq 0$, H_1 : $\mu_d > 0$ (one-tailed test)

Shop	$d_i = x_i - y_i$
1	—7
2	—7
3	1
4	3
5	—3
6	—4
7	—2
8	—2
9	—6
10	—3
11	—7
12	4

Compute $\quad \bar{d} = \frac{1}{n}\sum_{i=1}^{n} d_i = -2.75$

$$s_d{}^2 = \frac{1}{n-1}\left[\Sigma\, d_i{}^2 - \frac{(\Sigma\, d_i)^2}{n}\right]$$

$$= \frac{1}{11}\left[251 - \frac{(-33)^2}{12}\right] = \frac{1}{11}(251 - 90.75)$$

$$= \frac{1}{11}(160.25) = 14.5682$$

$$s_d = \sqrt{14.5682} = 3.82$$

$$t = \frac{\bar{d} - 0}{s_d/\sqrt{n}} = \frac{-2.75}{(3.82)/\sqrt{12}} = \frac{-2.75}{1.1018} = -2.50$$

$$|\,t\,| = 2.50$$

The table value of t at 5% level with 11 degrees of freedom = 1.796

As the calculated value of $|t|$ exceeds the tabulated value, H_0 is rejected. That is, the advertisement in the local daily newspaper has increased the sales.

10.2.3. Estimation of Variance of a Normal Population

(*a*) **Unknown mean μ :**

A point estimate of the population variance σ^2 is provided by

$$s^2 = \frac{1}{n-1} \sum_{i=1}^{n} (X_i - \overline{X})^2,$$

having (n—1) degrees of freedom.

An interval estimate of σ^2 can be established by defining a statistic

$$\chi^2 = \frac{(n-1)\, s^2}{\sigma^2}$$

which has a χ^2-distribution (Chi-square distribution) with $\upsilon = (n-1)$ degrees of freedom. Thus, the sampling distribution of s^2 is a constant times χ^2–distribution.

We can, then find $\chi^2_{1-\alpha/2}$ and $\chi^2_{\alpha/2}$ such that

$$P_r\,(\chi^2_{1-\alpha/2} < \chi^2 < \chi^2_{\alpha/2}) = 1 - \alpha,$$

where $\chi^2_{1-\alpha/2}$ and $\chi^2_{\alpha/2}$ are the values of the Chi-square distribution with $\upsilon = (n-1)$ degrees of freedom having area of $1 - \alpha/2$ and $\alpha/2$ respectively to the right. The values of χ^2_α have been tabulated for various fixed values of α and for values of υ from 1 to 30 (Table A–3).

Substituting $\frac{(n-1)\, s^2}{\sigma^2}$ in place of χ^2, we have

$$P_r\left[\chi^2_{1-\alpha/2} < \frac{(n-1)\, s^2}{\sigma^2} < \chi^2_{\alpha/2}\right] = 1 - \alpha$$

i.e.,

$$P_r\left[\frac{(n-1)\, s^2}{\chi^2_{\alpha/2}} < \sigma^2 < \frac{(n-1)\, s^2}{\chi^2_{1-\alpha/2}}\right] = 1 - \alpha$$

Thus, the (1 — α) 100% confidence interval of the variance σ^2 is given by

$$\frac{(n-1)\,s^2}{\chi^2_{\alpha/2}} < \sigma^2 < \frac{(n-1)\,s^2}{\chi^2_{1-\alpha/2}}$$

Note : For values of $\upsilon \geq 30$,

$$\sqrt{2\chi^2} - \sqrt{2\upsilon - 1}$$

is asymptomatically a standard normal variate.

(*b*) **Known** μ **:**

The point estimate of σ^2 is given by

$$\hat{\sigma}^2 = \frac{1}{n}\sum_{i=1}^{n} (X_i - \mu)^2$$

An interval estimate of σ^2 is established with the aid of a statistic defined by

$$\chi^2 = \frac{n\hat{\sigma}^2}{\sigma^2}$$

which follows a χ^2-distribution with *n* d.f.

Proceeding as in case of unknown μ, the $(1 - \alpha)$ 100% confidence interval is given by

$$\frac{n\,\hat{\sigma}^2}{\chi^2_{\alpha/2}} < \sigma^2 < \frac{n\,\hat{\sigma}^2}{\chi^2_{1-\alpha/2}}$$

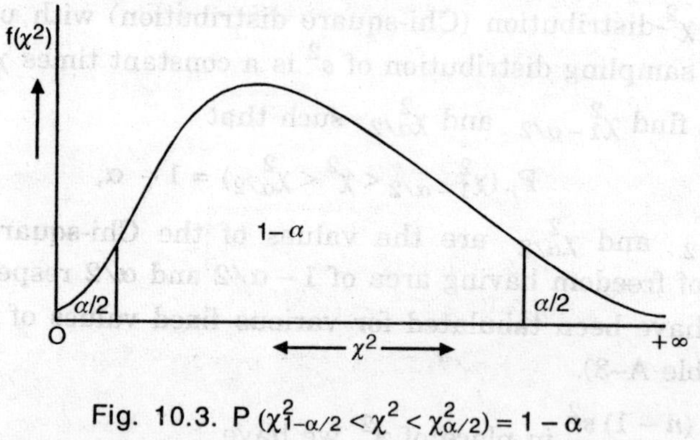

Fig. 10.3. $P(\chi^2_{1-\alpha/2} < \chi^2 < \chi^2_{\alpha/2}) = 1 - \alpha$

Example 10.9. The following are the weights (in kg) of 100 bags of milk powder distributed by a certain dairy centre.

20.5, 20.4, 21.0, 20.8, 20.5, 21.0, 19.8, 20.0, 20.2

Find a 95% confidence interval for the variance of all such bags of milk powder distributed by the dairy centre.

Solution :

To calculate the sampling variance, we subtract 20 from each observation (as the variance is unaltered by the change of origin)

$$s^2 = \frac{1}{n-1}\Sigma(X_i - \overline{X})^2$$

$$= \frac{1}{n(n-1)}[n\Sigma X_i^2 - (\Sigma X_i)^2]$$

$$= \frac{10(4.02) - 5^2}{10 \times 9} = \frac{40.2 - 25}{90} = 0.1689$$

Thus, s^2 is an estimate of variance in the population.

$1 - \alpha = 0.95$, using χ^2-table with 9 d.f.

$$\chi^2_{0.025} = 19.02$$

$$\chi^2_{0.975} = 2.70$$

The 95% confidence interval is

$$\frac{(n-1)s^2}{\chi^2_{0.025}} < \sigma^2 < \frac{(n-1)s^2}{\chi^2_{0.975}}$$

which becomes

$$\frac{9(0.1689)}{19.02} < \sigma^2 < \frac{9(0.1689)}{2.70}$$

or $$0.0799 < \sigma^2 < 0.5630.$$

10.2.4. Estimation of variance ratio from two normal populations

Let σ_1^2 and σ_2^2 be the population variances of first and second normal populations from which the samples of size n_1 and n_2 are selected. If μ_1 and μ_2 (population means of two populations) are not known, the unbiased estimators of $\sigma_1^{\ 2}$ and $\sigma_2^{\ 2}$ are given by $s_1^{\ 2}$ and $s_2^{\ 2}$ respectively, where $s_1^2 = \frac{1}{n_1 - 1}\Sigma(X_{1i} - \overline{X}_1)^2$ and $s_2^2 = \frac{1}{n_2 - 1}\Sigma(X_{2i} - \overline{X}_2)^2$.

A consistent point estimate of $\sigma_1^{\ 2}/\sigma_2^{\ 2}$ is given by the ratio $s_1^{\ 2}/s_2^{\ 2}$ of the sample variances.

To calculate a confidence interval for $\sigma_1^{\ 2}/\sigma_2^{\ 2}$, we define a statistic

$$\boxed{F = \frac{s_1^{\ 2}}{\sigma_1^{\ 2}} \Big/ \frac{s_2^{\ 2}}{\sigma_2^{\ 2}},}$$

which has Snedecor's F-distribution with $\upsilon_1 = n_1 - 1$ and $\upsilon_2 = n_2 - 1$ d.f.

Hence, we may write

$$P_r\,[F_{1-\alpha/2}(\upsilon_1, \upsilon_2) < F < F_{\alpha/2}(\upsilon_1, \upsilon_2)] = 1 - \alpha,$$

where $F_{1-\alpha/2}(\upsilon_1, \upsilon_2)$ and $F_{\alpha/2}(\upsilon_1, \upsilon_2)$ are the values of the F-distribution with υ_1 and υ_2 degrees of freedom, leaving areas of $1 - \alpha/2$ and $\alpha/2$ respectively to the right, (Table A–4).

Substituting for F and then simplifying, we have

$$P_r\left[\frac{s_1^{\ 2}}{s_2^{\ 2}} \cdot \frac{1}{F_{\alpha/2}(\upsilon_1, \upsilon_2)} < \frac{\sigma_1^{\ 2}}{\sigma_2^{\ 2}} < \frac{s_1^{\ 2}}{s_2^{\ 2}}, \frac{1}{F_{1-\alpha/2}(\upsilon_1, \upsilon_2)}\right] = 1 - \alpha.$$

It may be verified that

$$F_{1-\alpha/2}(\upsilon_1, \upsilon_2) = \frac{1}{F_{\alpha/2}(\upsilon_2, \upsilon_1)}$$

Thus, we write

$$P_r\left[\frac{s_1^2}{s_2^2}\frac{1}{F_{\alpha/2}(\upsilon_1, \upsilon_2)} < \frac{\sigma_1^2}{\sigma_2^2} < \frac{s_1^2}{s_2^2} F_{\alpha/2}(\upsilon_2, \upsilon_1)\right] = 1 - \alpha$$

Hence, the required confidence interval is

$$\left[\frac{s_1^2}{s_2^2} \cdot \frac{1}{F_{\alpha/2}(\upsilon_1, \upsilon_2)} < \frac{\sigma_1^2}{\sigma_2^2} < \frac{s_1^2}{s_2^2} F_{\alpha/2}(\upsilon_2, \upsilon_1)\right]$$

If μ_1, μ_2 are known, the confidence interval for $\frac{\sigma_1^2}{\sigma_2^2}$ is derived by defining

$$F = \frac{\hat{\sigma}_1^2}{\sigma_1^2} \Big/ \frac{\hat{\sigma}_2^2}{\sigma_2^2},$$

where $$\hat{\sigma}_1^2 = \frac{1}{n_1}\sum_{i=1}^{n_1}(X_{1i} - \mu_1)^2$$

and $$\hat{\sigma}_2^2 = \frac{1}{n_2}\sum_{i=1}(X_{2i} - \mu_2)^2,$$

which has an F-distribution with $\upsilon_1 = n_1$ and $\upsilon_2 = n_2$ d.f.

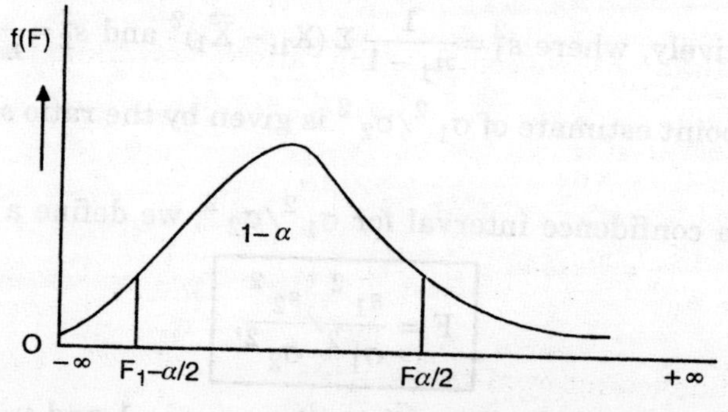

Fig. 10.4. $P_r\left[F_{1-\alpha/2}(\upsilon_1, \upsilon_2) < F < F_{\alpha/2}(\upsilon_1, \upsilon_2)\right] = 1 - \alpha$

Note : F-distribution is a positively skewed one with mode at $\left(\frac{1}{2}\upsilon_1 - 1\right) : \left(\frac{1}{2}\upsilon_2 + 1\right)$, mean equal to $\frac{\upsilon_2}{\upsilon_2 - 2}$ and variance equal to $\frac{2\upsilon_2^2(\upsilon_1 + \upsilon_2 - 2)}{\upsilon_1(\upsilon_2 - 2)^2(\upsilon_2 - 4)}$, which is approximately $2\left(\frac{1}{\upsilon_1} + \frac{1}{\upsilon_2}\right)$.

F statistic can be expressed in terms of the ratio of two Chi- square variates. The degrees of freedom of F contain the degrees of freedom of both numerator and denominator. As a matter of convertion the degrees of freedom of the denominator follows that of the numerator, while stating the degrees of freedom of F.

For large υ_1 and υ_2, $\frac{1}{2}\log_e F$ is asymptotically normally distributed with mean $\frac{1}{2}\left(\frac{1}{\upsilon_2}-\frac{1}{\upsilon_1}\right)$ and variance $\frac{1}{2}\left(\frac{1}{\upsilon_2}+\frac{1}{\upsilon_1}\right)$

Example 10.10. The following data represent the running times of films, produced by two motion picture companies. Construct a 98% confidence interval for the ratio of variances of running times of films produced by the two companies.

Time in minutes

Company I	103	94	110	87	95		
Company II	97	82	120	92	125	88	105

Solution :

Let $\sigma_1^{\ 2}$ and $\sigma_2^{\ 2}$ represent the population variances and $s_1^{\ 2}$ and $s_2^{\ 2}$ represent the sample variances of running times of films produced by two companies. n_1 = number of observations on company I = 5, n_2 = number of observations on company II = 7

Now, $$s_1^{\ 2} = \frac{\Sigma\,(X_{1i}-\overline{X}_1)^2}{(n_1-1)} = 78.7$$

and $$s_2^{\ 2} = \frac{\Sigma\,(X_{2i}-\overline{X}_2)^2}{(n_2-1)} = 263.24.$$

As $s_2^{\ 2}$ is greater than $s_1^{\ 2}$, we compute the ratio $s_2^{\ 2}/s_1^{\ 2}$ and take its help to compute the confidence interval of $\frac{\sigma_2^{\ 2}}{\sigma_1^{\ 2}}$.

Thus, $$\frac{s_2^{\ 2}}{s_1^{\ 2}} = 3.3448$$

$(1—\alpha)$ 100% confidence interval for $\frac{\sigma_2^{\ 2}}{\sigma_1^{\ 2}}$ is

$$\frac{s_2^{\ 2}}{s_1^{\ 2}}\cdot\frac{1}{F_{\alpha/2}\,(\upsilon_2\,,\upsilon_1)} < \frac{\sigma_2^{\ 2}}{\sigma_1^{\ 2}} < \frac{s_2^{\ 2}}{s_1^{\ 2}}\,F_{\alpha/2}\,(\upsilon_1\,,\upsilon_2)$$

where $\upsilon_2 = n_2 - 1$ and $\upsilon_1 = n_1 - 1$

Now, $\upsilon_2 = 7 — 1 = 6$

$\upsilon_1 = 5 — 1 = 4$

$$\frac{s_2^{\ 2}}{s_1^{\ 2}} = 3.3448,\ 1 — \alpha = 0.98$$

$$F_{\alpha/2}(\upsilon_2, \upsilon_1) = F_{0.01}(6, 4) = 15.21$$
$$F_{\alpha/2}(\upsilon_1, \upsilon_2) = F_{0.01}(4, 6) = 9.15$$

Thus, the 98% confidence interval

$$3.3448\left(\frac{1}{15.21}\right) < \frac{\sigma_2^{\ 2}}{\sigma_1^{\ 2}} < (3.3448)\,(9.15)$$

or $$0.2199 < \frac{\sigma_2^{\ 2}}{\sigma_1^{\ 2}} < 30.6049.$$

10.2.5. Estimation of proportion

In binomial experiment with number of trials n and population proportion of successes P, the number of successes actually observed is r. The sample proportion $p = \frac{r}{n}$ is an unbiased estimator of P.

The estimator p is subject to sampling distribution and

$$E(p) = P$$
$$V(p) = \frac{PQ}{n}, \quad Q = 1 - P.$$

$\frac{PQ}{n}$ measures the accuracy of the sample proportion as an estimate of P.

As P is not known, $\frac{pq}{n}$, $(q = 1 - p)$ may be taken as a consistent estimate of $\frac{PQ}{n}$.

Now question arises : How shall we construct a confidence interval for P ? In many practical problems dealing with estimation of proportion in binomial distribution, the sample size is generally very large. Hence, for n sufficiently large, the distribution of p is approximately normally distributed with mean P and variance $\frac{PQ}{n}$.

Hence, we may define

$$Z = \frac{p - P}{\sqrt{\frac{PQ}{n}}},$$

which is approximately distributed as a standard normal variable. Therefore, we can assert that

$$P_r(-z_{\alpha/2} < Z < z_{\alpha/2}) = 1 - \alpha$$

That is, $$P_r\left[-z_{\alpha/2} < \frac{p - P}{\sqrt{\frac{PQ}{n}}} < z_{\alpha/2}\right] = 1 - \alpha$$

or $$P_r\left[p - z_{\alpha/2}\sqrt{\frac{PQ}{n}} < P < p + z_{\alpha/2}\sqrt{\frac{PQ}{n}}\right]$$

Thus, (1 — α) 100% confidence interval is

$$p - z_{\alpha/2}\sqrt{\frac{PQ}{n}} < P < p + z_{\alpha/2}\sqrt{\frac{PQ}{n}}.$$

When n is large, very little error is introduced by substituting p for P under the radical (square root) sign

Thus,

$$P_r\left[p - z_{\alpha/2}\sqrt{\frac{pq}{n}} < P < p + z_{\alpha/2}\sqrt{\frac{pq}{n}}\right] \cong 1—\alpha$$

Hence, an approximate (1 — α) 100% confidence interval is

$$p - z_{\alpha/2}\sqrt{\frac{pq}{n}} < P < p + z_{\alpha/2}\sqrt{\frac{pq}{n}}$$

Example 10.11. If in a random sample of 600 MBA students drawn from business schools throughout the country, 360 are sons of businessmen, compute the 90% confidence interval for the proportion of all MBA students who are sons of businessmen ?

Solution :

Let P be the proportion of all MBA students who are sons of businessmen. The point estimate of P is

$$p = \frac{360}{600} = 0.6$$

$$1 — \alpha = 0.90$$

The 90% confidence interval of P is

$$p - z_{\alpha/2}\sqrt{\frac{pq}{n}} < P < p + z_{\alpha/2}\sqrt{\frac{pq}{n}},$$

which reduces to

$$0.6 — 1.645\sqrt{\frac{0.6\,(1-0.6)}{600}}$$

$$< P < 0.6 + 1.645\sqrt{\frac{(0.6)\,(1-0.6)}{600}},$$

where $z_{\alpha/2} = 1.645$

or $0.5671 < P < 0.6329$

10.2.6. Estimation of the difference between two proportions (Large samples)

Consider two independent samples of size n_1 and n_2 from two binomial populations with proportion of successes P_1 and P_2 respectively. Let the proportion of successes in each sample be p_1 and p_2 respectively.

A point estimate of the difference $P_1 - P_2$ is given by $p_1 - p_2$.

$$E(p_1 - p_2) = P_1 - P_2$$

$$V(p_1 - p_2) = \frac{P_1Q_1}{n_1} + \frac{P_2Q_2}{n_2},$$

where $Q_1 = 1 - P_1$ and $Q_2 = 1 - P_2$

We have $p_1 - p_2$ as approximately normally distributed with mean $P_1 - P_2$ and variance $\frac{P_1Q_1}{n_1} + \frac{P_2Q_2}{n_2}$.

Define

$$Z = \frac{(p_1 - p_2) - (P_1 - P_2)}{\sqrt{\frac{P_1Q_1}{n_1} + \frac{P_2Q_2}{n_2}}}$$

which follows an approximate standard normal distribution.

Thus, we can assert

$$P_r(-z_{\alpha/2} < Z < z_{\alpha/2}) = 1 - \alpha$$

or

$$P_r\left[-z_{\alpha/2} < \frac{(p_1 - p_2) - (P_1 - P_2)}{\sqrt{\frac{P_1Q_1}{n_1} + \frac{P_2Q_2}{n_2}}} < z_{\alpha/2}\right] = 1 - \alpha$$

Thus, the $(1 - \alpha)$ 100% confidence interval of $P_1 - P_2$ is given by

$$(p_1 - p_2) - z_{\alpha/2}\sqrt{\frac{P_1Q_1}{n_1} + \frac{P_2Q_2}{n_2}}$$

$$< P_1 - P_2 < (p_1 - p_2) + z_{\alpha/2}\sqrt{\frac{P_1Q_1}{n_1} + \frac{P_2Q_2}{n_2}}$$

When n_1 and n_2 are large, very little error is introduced by substituting p_1 and p_2 for P_1 and P_2 respectively.

Thus, an approximate $(1 - \alpha)$ 100% confidence interval for $P_1 - P_2$ is

$$(p_1 - p_2) - z_{\alpha/2}\sqrt{\frac{p_1q_1}{n_1} + \frac{p_2q_2}{n_2}}$$

$$< P_1 - P_2 < (p_1 - p_2) + z_{\alpha/2}\sqrt{\frac{p_1q_1}{n_1} + \frac{p_2q_2}{n_2}}.$$

Example 10.12. A poll is taken among dwellers of a city (both males and females) to determine the feasibility of an urban development programme. If 2400 out of 5000 male city dewellers favour the proposal and 1500 out of 2500 females favour it, find a 99% confidence interval for the true difference in the proportions favouring the urban development programme.

Solution :

Let P_1 and P_2 be the true proportions of city males and city females respectively, favouring the proposal. Hence,

$$p_1 = \frac{2400}{5000} = 0.48$$

$$p_2 = \frac{1500}{2500} = 0.60$$

The point estimate of $P_2 - P_1$ is

$$p_2 - p_1 = 0.60 - 0.48 = 0.12$$

$$1 - \alpha = 0.99,\ z_{\alpha/2} = z_{0.005} = 2.58$$

Therefore, the 99% confidence interval of $P_2 - P_1$ is

$$(p_2 - p_1) - z_{\alpha/2}\sqrt{\frac{p_2 q_2}{n_2} + \frac{p_1 q_1}{n_1}}$$

$$< P_2 - P_1 < (p_2 - p_1) + z_{\alpha/2}\sqrt{\frac{p_2 q_2}{n_2} + \frac{p_1 q_1}{n_1}}$$

or $$0.12 - (2.58)\sqrt{\frac{(0.48)\,(1-0.48)}{5000} + \frac{(0.60)\,(1-0.60)}{2500}}$$

$$< P_2 - P_1 < 0.12 + 2.58\sqrt{\frac{0.48\,(1-0.48)}{5000} + \frac{(0.60)\,(1-0.60)}{2500}}$$

or $$0.12 - 0.03117 < P_2 - P_1 < 0.12 + 0.03117$$

or $$0.08883 < P_2 - P_1 < 0.15117$$

10.2.7. Determination of sample size in estimating proportion

Suppose sample proportion p is computed from a sample size n to estimate population proportion P. We further like to assert that

$$P\,[\,|\,p - P\,| \le d] = 1 - \alpha$$

That is, $$P\left[\frac{|\,p - P\,|}{\sqrt{\frac{PQ}{n}}} \le \frac{d}{\sqrt{\frac{PQ}{n}}}\right] = 1 - \alpha$$

Assuming that $\frac{p - P}{\sqrt{PQ/n}}$ is asymptotically normally distributed, put

$$\frac{d}{\sqrt{PQ/n}} = z_{\alpha/2}$$

Thus, simplifying $$n = \frac{z^2_{\alpha/2}\,PQ}{d^2}$$

As an illustration,

$P = 0.60$ (guessed value)

$d = 0.03$

$z_{\alpha/2} = 1.96$ for $\alpha = 0.05$

Therefore, $$n = \frac{(1.96)^2\,(0.6 \times 0.4)}{(0.03)^2}$$

$$= \frac{3.8416 \times 0.24}{0.0009}$$

$$= 1024.43 \equiv 1024.$$

It may be stated here that the higher the degree of confidence, the greater will be the sample size.

Example 10.13. A random sample of 400 inhabitants in a large residential area indicated that 240 favoured that the Municipal Corporation grants the approval for the construction of a shopping complex in their area. Establish the 90% confidence limits for the true proportion of the population who support the shopping complex.

Solution :

Let P be the population proportion. The sample proportion p is computed as

$$p = \frac{240}{400} = 0.6$$

The 90% confidence interval is given by

$$p \pm z_{\alpha/2} \sqrt{\frac{pq}{n}}, \text{ where } \alpha = 0.10$$

That is, $$0.6 \pm 1.648 \sqrt{\frac{(0.6)\,(0.4)}{400}}$$

or $$0.6 \pm 0.0404.$$

Therefore, lower confidence limit for the true proportion is 0.5596 and the upper confidence limit 0.6404.

10.3. Hypothesis Testing :

The theory of testing of hypothesis is a very important branch of decision theory. As such, the testing of hypothesis is an innovative statistical instrument in the hands of researchers to provide statisfactory probable answers to management questions translated into research questions. *A hypothesis is a statement/assumption/proposition, which is under verification.* The hypothesis may be classified into two types :

- *Scientific hypothesis*
- *Statistical hypothesis.*

In scientific hypothesis, we either reject or accept the hypothesis entirely without attaching any probability statement. For instance, 'life exists on moon' is a scientific hypothesis which can be either established or not with certainty. But the statistical hypothesis is concerned with the behaviour of an observable random variable and is tested on the basis of limited results of a random experiment. In testing a statistical hypothesis the researcher either rejects or accepts the hypothesis formulated for the purpose on the basis of a random sample from the population in question. As the decision is based on the basis of a sample, the inference is bound to be a decision under uncertainty and hence becomes probabilistic.

Regardless of the type of research process, all research begins with a generalised idea in the form of a research question or a hypothesis. A research question usually is posed in the beginning of a research effort or in a specific area of study that has had little formal research. A research question may take the form of a basic question about some issue or phenomena or a question about the relationship between two or more variables. For example, a research question might be : "Do flexible work hours improve employee's productivity ?" or "How do flexible hours influence employees' work ?"

A hypothesis differs from a research question; it is more specific and makes a prediction. It is a tentative statement about the relationship between two or more variables. The major difference between a research question and a hypothesis is that a hypothesis predicts an experimental outcome. For example, a hypothesis might state : "There is a positive relationship between the availability of flexible work hours and employee productivity".

Hypotheses provide the following advantages :

- They determine the focus and direction for a research effort.
- Their development forces the researcher to clearly state the purpose of the research activity.
- They determine what variables will not be considered, as well as those that will be considered.
- They require the researcher to have an operational definition of the variables of interest.

Thus, we can define *a statistical hypothesis as an assumption*, which may or may not be true, concerning one or more populations as regards their parameters. Its test is based on experimental results/field observations, which are supposed to be product of random process.

Testing of hypothesis is very much helpful in examining validity or otherwise of the economic theories such as wage increase leads to rising prices, etc. In market studies we may be interested to know whether new pack of a product results in increase in sales; whether new innovative technique results in increased production. Sometimes statistical testing is required by a manufacturing concern to promote some sort of a statement concerning the average life of its product.

The hypothesis which is tested for the purpose of rejection is called **Null hypothesis** (H_0), which is usually taken as opposite to **research hypothesis** posed by the researcher, called **Alternative hypothesis (H_1)**. A null hypothesis H_0 is always one of status quo or no difference. The alternative hypothesis, H_1, is a statement of what a statistical hypothesis test is set up to establish.

The selection of null hypothesis is an important problem in testing of hypothesis. The null hypothesis should be exact and free from ambiguities and is set up for possible rejection. By acceptance or rejection of null hypothesis we should understand that the rejection of a null hypothesis under test means that it is false while the acceptance of the null hypothesis implies that we have no evidence against it. Because of this reason the researcher/statistician should choose the null hypothesis which has strong likelihood of being rejected. For example, if he is interested in testing whether the new system of marking the students in the examination is better than the old one, he should put the null hypothesis that the new system is **not** better than the old one and then set out to reject this contention.

As the test is to be based on experimental results, it should be possible to divide all possible experimental results (W) into two classes—Acceptance class (W—w) and Rejection class (w). A random sample of n observations ($X_1, X_2, ..., X_n$) constitute a point in n-dimensional sample space (W). If this point falls in w, we reject the hypothesis otherwise accept it. If the probability distribution of the random variables under the hypothesis being tested is known, it is possible to determine such a region (w) equal to a pre-assigned small fraction α. That is, P(X ∈ w H) = α. The rejection region is popularly called the **Critical region.** The choice of the best critical region, in other words, the best decision rule has been given by Neyman and Pearson (1933) by invoking two types of errors committed in testing a statistical hypothesis and more importantly the *critical values are demarcated on the real line (unidemsional).*

These are errors of first kind or **Type I error** and error of the second kind or **Type II error**. The Type I error is said to be commited when we wrongly reject the hypothesis under test *i.e.* the null hypothesis when it is true. Type II error is commited when we wrongly accept the alternative hypothesis *i.e.* a hypothesis which is different from one under test. These errors are measured in terms of probabilities and are given as follows :

Type I error = $P(X \in w \mid H_0) = \alpha$, (say)

Type II error = $P(X \in W — w \mid H_1) = \beta$, (say)

The probability of rejecting a false hypothesis is called **Power of the test.**

Thus, power of the test γ = 1-Type II error = $(1—\beta)$.

As α and β can not be simultaneously minimized, we fix the size of critical region(w) that is, α and choose the critical region from among possible ones which maximises power of the test. The type I error is often considered to be more serious and therefore more important to avoid.

Decision

		Reject H_0	**Don't reject H_0**
Truth	H_0	Type I Error	Right Decision
	H_1	Right Decision	Type II Error

10.3.1. Steps for testing of hypothesis

Let θ be the parameter indexing the probability density function $f(x, \theta)$.

1. Set up a null hypothesis $H_0 : \theta = \theta_0$
2. Set up an alternative hypothesis either one-sided such as $H_1 : \theta < \theta_0$ or $\theta > \theta_0$ or two sided $\theta \neq \theta_0$.
3. Specify the Type-I error (probability of rejecting the null hypothesis) equal to a small fraction α, which is usually fixed at 0.01 or 0.05.
4. Select an appropriate test statistic, a function of sample observations and establish objective criteria for choice between H_0 and H_1.
5. Draw a random sample from the population.
6. Compute the test statistic.
7. Evaluate the sample evidence in consonance with the established criteria.
8. Take decision as to course of action (acceptance of H_0 or H_1).

10.3.2. Test of significance

Test of hypothesis can be viewed as a problem of test of significance. To expand the idea further, the testing of hypothesis $H_0 : \theta = \theta_0$ is equivalent to testing the hypothesis that there is no difference between the true value θ and the hypothesized value θ_0.

As the hypothesis is to be tested on the basis of a random sample, from a defined population, we formulate a statistic T (function of sample observations) and then examine whether the observed value of T is likely to come from the probability distribution (sampling distribution) of T under the null hypothesis. If the divergence between the observed statistic T and the hypothesized population value is too large to have occurred due to chance causes only or if the observed value is significantly different from what we expect from the probability distribution, the hypothesis is rejected. The probability of getting the divergence more extreme than the observed one or in other words the probability that the observed result is exceeded in random sampling is called **P-value** for a test or **exceedence probability.** The probability on the basis of which the divergence between the observed value and the hypothetical value is regarded as significant is called the **level of significance.** *This probability is the Type I error* (α) which is also the size of the *Critical region*, usually, tail areas of the sampling distribution of the test statistic. The *critical region* is the area or areas of the sampling distribution of a statistic that will lead to the rejection of the null hypothesis if the computed value of the statistic falls in this region. Alternatively,

- H_0 would be rejected at level α for any $\alpha \geq$ P-value.
- H_0 would not be rejected at level α for any $\alpha <$ P-value.

10.3.3. One-tailed and two-tailed test

If the critical region of a test is located on one of the tails of the sampling distribution of the test statistic, the test is called a *one-tailed test*. If both the tails are considered for the critical region, then the test is called a *two-tailed test.*

Whether one should go for a one-tailed test or two-tailed test depends on the structure of the alternative hypothesis. That is, for a one-sided alternative *i.e.* $H_1 : \theta > \theta_0$ or $H_1 : \theta < \theta_0$, we should choose one-tailed test (right tail for $H_1 : \theta > \theta_0$ and left tail for $H_1 : \theta < \theta_0$). Further, for a two-sided alternative such as $H_1 : \theta \neq \theta_0$, we should choose two-tailed test, *i.e.* the critical region is located on both the tails of the sampling distribution of the test statistic.

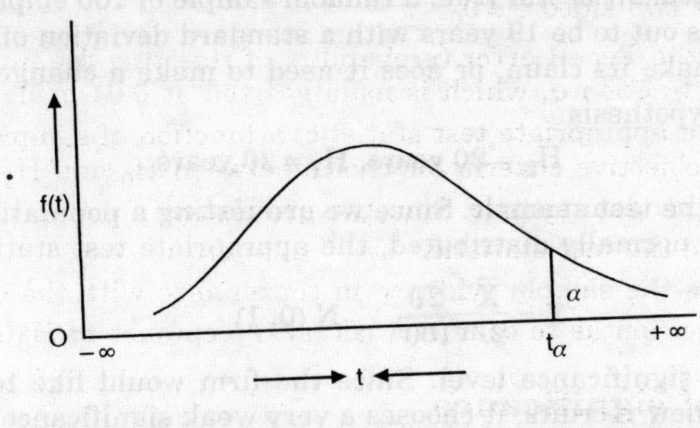

Fig. 10.5. Right-tailed critical region (test).

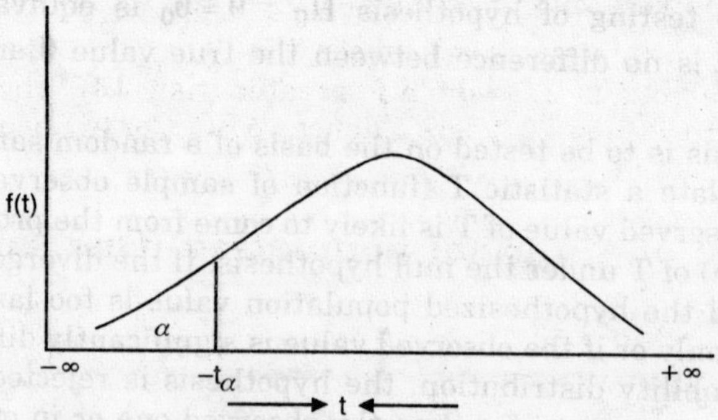

Fig. 10.6. Left-tailed critical region (test).

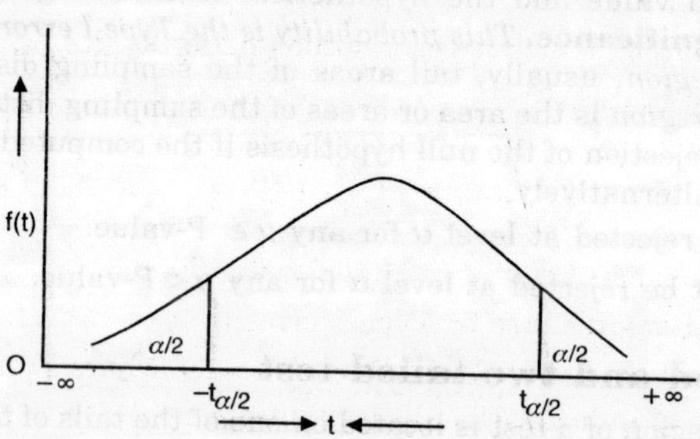

Fig. 10.7. Two-tailed critical region (test).

Illustration

Suppose ABC Corporation is a company that is focused on a stable work force that has very little turnover. ABC Corpn. has been in business for 50 years and has more than 10,000 employees. The company has always promoted the idea that its employees stay with them for a very long time, and it has used the following line in its recruitment brochures. "The average tenure of our employees is 20 years". Since ABC Corpn. is not quite sure if that statement is still true, a random sample of 100 employees is taken and the average age turns out to be 19 years with a standard deviation of 2 years. Can ABC Corpn. continue to make its claim, or does it need to make a change ?

1. **State the hypothesis**

$$H_0 = 20 \text{ years}, \ H_1 \neq 20 \text{ years}$$

2. **Determine the test statistic. Since we are testing a population mean of a variable that is normally distributed, the appropriate test statistic is**

$$Z = \frac{\overline{X} - 20}{2/\sqrt{100}} \sim N(0, 1)$$

3. **Specify the significance level. Since the firm would like to keep its present message to new recruits, it chooses a very weak significance level *i.e.* α = 0.05. Since this is a two-tailed test, the critical values of Z are +1.96 and —1.96.**

4. State the decision rule. If $Z \geq +1.96$ or ≤ -1.96, H_0 is rejected.
5. Calculations.
6. Since the calculated Z is 2.5, which is greater than 1.96, the null is rejected. The mean tenure is not 20 years. Hence, ABC Corpn. needs to change its statement.

10.3.4. Test of mean of a normal population (One sample test)

(*a*) **Known variance** (σ^2).

$H_0 : \mu = \mu_0$

against $H_1 : \mu > \mu_0$ (one sided alternative)

or $H_1 : \mu < \mu_0$ (one sided alternative)

or $H_1 : \mu \neq \mu_0$ (two sided alternative)

Given a random sample of size n observations being $X_1, X_2, \ldots, X_n$.

Compute the test statistic

$$z = \frac{\overline{X} - \mu_0}{\sigma/\sqrt{n}},$$

which is N(0, 1) variable. Let the computed value be z.

For a given level of significance or Type I error α

(*i*) $H_1 : \mu > \mu_0$, Reject H_0 if $z > z_\alpha$ in favour of $\mu > \mu_0$, where z_α is the αth percentage point of the standard normal distribution.

(*ii*) $H_1 : \mu < \mu_0$, Reject H_0 if $z < -z_\alpha$

(*iii*) $H_1 : \mu \neq \mu_0$, Reject H_0 if $|z| > z_{\alpha/2}$, where $z_{\alpha/2}$ is $(\alpha/2)$th percentage point of standard normal distribution.

P-Value for Z test :

H_1 : upper tailed $\mu > \mu_0$,

$P = 1 - \Phi(z)$

H_1 : Lower tailed $\mu < \mu_0$,

$P = \Phi(z)$

H_1 : two tailed $\mu \neq \mu_0$

$P = 2(1 - \Phi(z))$

(*b*) **Unknown variance** (σ^2)

Random sample : $X_1, X_2, \ldots, X_n$

Compute the sample mean

$$\overline{X} = \Sigma X_i / n$$

and sample variance

$$s^2 = \frac{1}{n-1} \sum^{n} (X_i - \overline{X})^2$$

Compute the test statistic,

$$t = \frac{\overline{X} - \mu_0}{s/\sqrt{n}}$$

(*i*) $H_1 : \mu > \mu_0$, Reject H_0, if $t > t_{\alpha, n-1}$

(*ii*) $H_1 : \mu < \mu_0$, Reject H_0, if $t < -t_{\alpha, n-1}$

(*iii*) $H_1 : \mu \neq \mu_0$, Reject H_0 if $| t | > t_{\alpha/2, n-1}$

$t_{\alpha, n-1}$ is the αth percentage point of Student *t*-distribution with (*n*—1) degrees of freedom, since the sampling distribution *t* is Student's *t*-distribution with (*n*—1) degrees of freedom.

Example 10.14. On the basis of retail sales in an area, a market analyst states the hypothesis that average annual income is Rs. 50,000/-. The population standard deviation of incomes in the area is known to be Rs. 5,000/-. In a random sample of 100 households the average annual income was found to be Rs. 48,000/- . On the basis of sample evidence, shall we accept the assertion of the market analyst at 5% level of significance ?

Solution :

Assume that incomes of the households are normally distributed with mean μ and standard deviation σ.

$$H_0 : \mu = \text{Rs. } 50{,}000$$
$$H_1 : \mu \neq \text{Rs. } 50{,}000$$

Given σ = Rs. 5000, n = 100, sample mean $\overline{X}$ = Rs. 48,000/-

Under H_0, $\overline{X}$ is normally distributed with mean μ_0 = Rs. 50,000/- and standard error $\sigma/\sqrt{n}$ = Rs. $5000/\sqrt{100}$

Define the normal statistic

$$| Z | = \frac{|\overline{X} - \mu_0|}{\sigma/\sqrt{n}} = \frac{| 48{,}000 - 50{,}000 |}{5{,}000/\sqrt{100}}$$

$$= 4.$$

The tabulated value of Z at 5% level of significance or the critical value (for a 2-tailed test) is 1.96.

As the calculated value of the statistic Z exceeds the critical value, the null hypothesis is rejected and we conclude that the assertion of the market analyst is probably wrong.

Suppose $H_0 : \mu \leq \text{Rs. } 45{,}000$

$H_1 : \mu > \text{Rs. } 45{,}000$

$$Z = \frac{\overline{X} - \mu_0}{\sigma/\sqrt{n}} = \frac{48{,}000 - 45{,}000}{5{,}000/\sqrt{100}}$$

$$= \frac{3{,}000}{500} = 6$$

The tabulated or critical value of Z for one tailed test with α = 0.05 is 1.648.

Thus, the H_0 is rejected and we conclude that the observed difference might not have occurred due to chance.

Example 10.15. The Alpha Manufacturing Company wishes to promote some sort of a statement concerning the average life of its product. In fact, the Sales Manager wishes to advertise to the effect that the average life is 5 years. His assertion is based on the following sample evidence and simulated tests of the product under varying conditions of use :

$\overline{X} = 55$ months (average life)

$s_x = 6$ months

$n = 16$

Test at 5% level of significance whether the assertion of the Sales manager is corroborated by sample evidence.

Solution :

$$H_0 = \mu = \mu_0 = 60 \text{ months}$$

$$H_1 : \mu \neq \mu_0$$

Assuming that the life of the product to be normally distributed, compute the statistic under H_0,

$$|\,t\,| = \frac{|\,\overline{X} - \mu_0\,|}{s_x/\sqrt{n}} = \frac{|\,55 - 60\,|}{6/\sqrt{16}}$$

$$= 3.33$$

The tabulated value of t (2-tailed test) with n—1 = 16—1=15 degrees of freedom at 5% level of significance is 2.13, which is less than the computed value 3.33.

Thus, the null hypothesis that the average life of the product is 60 months is rejected.

10.3.5. Test of difference between means of two normal populations N (μ_1, σ_1^2) and N (μ_2, σ_2^2)–Two sample test

(*a*) σ_1^2 **and** σ_2^2 **are known**

$H_0 : \mu_1 - \mu_2 = \Delta = 0$

$H_1 :$ (*i*) $\Delta > 0$

or (*ii*) $\Delta < 0$

or (*iii*) $\Delta \neq 0$

Sample from first population :

$$X_{11}, X_{12}, \ldots, X_{1n_1}$$

Sample from second population

$$X_{21}, X_{22}, \ldots, X_{2,n_2}$$

Compute the sample means as

$$\overline{X}_1 = \Sigma X_{1\,i/n_1}$$

and $$\overline{X}_2 = \Sigma X_{2\,i/n_2}$$

Compute the test statistic under H_0,

$$Z = \frac{\overline{X}_1 - \overline{X}_2}{\sqrt{\frac{\sigma_1^{\;2}}{n_1} + \frac{\sigma_2^{\;2}}{n_2}}}$$

(*i*) $H_1 : \Delta > 0$

Reject H_0, if $z > z_\alpha$

(*ii*) $H_1 : \Delta < 0$

Reject H_0 if $z < -z_\alpha$

(*iii*) $H_1 = \Delta \neq 0$

Reject H_0 if $| z | > z_{\alpha/2}$

(*b*) $\sigma_1^{\;2}$ **and** $\sigma_2^{\;2}$ **are unknown**, but $\sigma_1^{\;2} = \sigma_2^{\;2} = \sigma^2$ (say)

Estimate σ^2 by

$$s^2 = \frac{\Sigma (X_{1\,i} - \overline{X}_1)^2 + \Sigma (X_{2\,i} - \overline{X}_2)^2}{n_1 + n_2 - 2}$$

Under the null hypothesis, compute the test statistic

$$t = \frac{\overline{X}_1 - \overline{X}_2}{\sqrt{s^2\left(\frac{1}{n_2} + \frac{1}{n_2}\right)}}$$

which follows Student's t distribution with $n_1 + n_2 - 2$ degrees of freedom.

Example 10.16. A random sample of size 25 taken from a normal population with a standard deviation $\sigma_1 = 5.2$ has a mean $\overline{X}_1 = 81$. A second random sample of size $n_2 = 36$ taken from a different normal population with a standard deviation $\sigma_2 = 3.4$, has a mean $\overline{X}_2 = 76$. Test the null hypothesis at 0.05 level of significance $H_0 : \mu_1 = \mu_2$ against the alternative $H_1 : \mu_1 > \mu_2$.

Solution :

Compute the test statistic under H_0,

$$z = \frac{\overline{X}_1 - \overline{X}_2}{\sqrt{\frac{\sigma_1^{\;2}}{n_1} + \frac{\sigma_2^{\;2}}{n_2}}} = \frac{81 - 76}{\sqrt{\frac{(5.2)^2}{25} + \frac{(3.4)^2}{36}}}$$

$$= 4.22$$

This value exceeds the critical value $z_{0.05} = 1.648$

Hence, the null hypothesis is rejected in favour of the alternative hypothesis.

Example 10.17. A Production Manager wants to compare two manufacturing processes with the following data

$n_1 = 100$ $\qquad\qquad$ $n_2 = 100$

$\overline{X}_1 = 110 \qquad \overline{X}_2 = 115$

$\hat{\sigma}_1^2 = 400 \qquad \hat{\sigma}_2^2 = 225$

Is there a significant difference between two processes, using $\alpha = 0.05$?

Solution :

Compute the test statistic under H_0,

$$|Z| = \frac{|\overline{X}_1 - \overline{X}_2|}{\sqrt{\frac{\hat{\sigma}_1^{\,2}}{n_1} + \frac{\hat{\sigma}_2^{\,2}}{n_2}}}$$

As n_1 and n_2 are large, the deviations of estimated values of variances from true values are likely to be negligible. Assuming observations on two manufacturing processes to be normally distributed, Z follows a standard normal distribution.

Thus, $$|z| = \frac{5}{\sqrt{\frac{400}{100} + \frac{225}{100}}} = \frac{5}{\sqrt{4 + 2.25}}$$

$$= \frac{5}{2.5} = 2$$

The table value of $z_{0.025} = 1.96$.

Hence, two manufacturing processes are significantly different.

Example 10.18. The following measurements show the heat producing capacity of the coal produced by two mines (in million calories per tonne)

Mine 1 :	8260	8130	8350	8070	8340
Mine 2 :	7950	7890	7900	8140	7920
	7840				

Test at 1% level of significance whether the coal produced by two mines have the same average heat producing capacity. (Assume normality of observations)

Solution :

Let X_1 and X_2 stand for the measurement of heat producing capacity of Mine 1 and Mine 2 respectively.

$$n_1 = 5, n_2 = 6, \overline{X}_1 = 8230, \overline{X}_2 = 7940$$

$$\Sigma (X_1 - \overline{X}_1)^2 = 63{,}000$$

$$\Sigma (X_2 - \overline{X}_2)^2 = 54{,}600$$

$H_0 : \mu_1 = \mu_2$ (where μ_1 and μ_2 represent population average heat producing capacity of coal from Mine 1 and Mine 2 respectively)

$H_1 : \mu_1 \neq \mu_2$

Assume equality of variances, *i.e.* $\sigma_1^{\,2} = \sigma_2^{\,2}$. Now the estimate of common variance

$$s^2 = \frac{\Sigma (X_1 - \overline{X}_1)^2 + \Sigma (X_2 - \overline{X}_2)^2}{n_1 + n_2 - 2}$$

$$= \frac{63{,}000 + 54{,}600}{5 + 6 - 2} = 13066.67$$

The appropriate test statistic is

$$|\, t \,| = \frac{|\, \overline{X}_1 - \overline{X}_2 \,|}{\sqrt{s^2 \left(\frac{1}{n_1} + \frac{1}{n_2} \right)}}$$

$$= \frac{8230 - 7940}{\sqrt{13066.67 \left(\frac{1}{5} + \frac{1}{6} \right)}} = 4.19$$

Since this value of t exceeds 3.25, the value of $t_{0.005}$ (for a two tailed test) for 5 + 6 — 2 = 9 degrees of freedom, the null hypothesis is rejected and we conclude that the average heat producing capacity of the coal from two mines is different.

10.3.6. Test of population proportion

Let P be proportion of certain attribute in a population. For a random sample of size n, let r be the number of individuals having the specified attribute.

Compute $p = \frac{r}{n}$

Then p is an estimate of P.

$$V(p) = \frac{PQ}{n}, \text{ where } Q = 1 - P.$$

To test the null hypothesis

$$H_0 : P = P_0$$

against alternative $H_1 : P \neq P_0$

Compute the test statistic under H_0,

$$\boxed{Z = \frac{p - P_0}{\sqrt{pq/n}}}$$

which for large n, has an approximate standard normal distribution.

We reject H_0 if

$$|\, z \,| > z_{\alpha/2}.$$

Example 10.19. It is hypothesized that 10% of the families in a city plan to buy new automobiles this year. A sample of 2,000 families interviewed in a city-wide survey indicated that 160 planned to purchase new cars this year. Do you accept the hypothesis at 0.01 level of significance ?

Solution :

$$H_0 : P = 0.10$$
$$H_1 : P \neq 0.10$$

The estimated value

$$p = \frac{160}{2000} = 0.08$$

Now, $$| Z | = \frac{| p - 0.10 |}{\sqrt{\frac{pq}{n}}}$$

is asymptotically normally distributed.

Thus,

$$| z | = \frac{0.02}{\sqrt{\frac{(0.08)(1-0.08)}{2000}}}$$

$$= \frac{0.02}{0.0063} = 3.175$$

The tabulated value $z_{\alpha/2} = z_{0.005} = 2.58$

As the calculated value 3.175 exceeds the critical value 2.58, the null hypothesis is rejected.

10.3.7. Test of equality of two population proportions

Let P_1 and P_2 be the population proportions in two populations.

The null hypothesis under test is

$$H_0 : P_1 = P_2$$

against alternative $\quad H_1 : P_1 \neq P_2$

Select random samples of size n_1 and n_2 from two populations and compute the sample estimates p_1 and p_2.

Under the null hypothesis, the estimate of common proportion P is

$$p = \frac{n_1 p_1 + n_2 p_2}{n_1 + n_2}$$

The variance of difference between two proportions in the samples is

$$V(p_1 - p_2) = PQ\left(\frac{1}{n_1} + \frac{1}{n_2}\right)$$

$$\text{Estimate of } V(p_1 - p_2) = pq\left(\frac{1}{n_1} + \frac{1}{n_2}\right)$$

Under null hypothesis, for large samples n_1 and n_2

$$Z = \frac{p_1 - p_2}{\sqrt{pq\left(\frac{1}{n_1} + \frac{1}{n_2}\right)}}$$

is a standard normal variate. To test H_0, reject H_0, if $| z | > z_{\alpha/2}$.

Example 10.20. In two large industrial establishments a random sample of 100 business executives from each establishment shows that the proportions of technical-cum-management degree holders were 0.65 and 0.70 respectively.

Test whether the proportions are significantly different at 5% level of significance.

Solution :

Let P_1 and P_2 be the proportions of technical-cum-management degree holders in two establishments

Null hypothesis : $P_1 = P_2$

against alternative hypothesis : $P_1 \neq P_2$

Now $p_1 = 0.65,\ p_2 = 0.70$

$n_1 = 100,\ n_2 = 100$

Under the null hypothesis, the pooled estimate of proportion is given by

$$p = \frac{n_1 p_1 + n_2 p_2}{n_1 + n_2}$$

$$= \frac{100\,(0.65) + 100\,(0.70)}{200}$$

$$= 0.675$$

$$q = 1 - 0.675 = 0.325$$

Now an estimate of $\sigma_{p_1 - p_2}$ can be obtained using

$$\sigma_{p_1 - p_2} = \sqrt{\frac{pq}{n_1} + \frac{pq}{n_2}}$$

$$= \sqrt{\frac{(0.675)\,(0.325)}{100} + \frac{(0.675)\,(0.325)}{100}}$$

$$= 0.0662$$

As sample sizes are large, we compute normal statistic

$$|Z| = \frac{|\,(p_1 - p_2) - 0\,|}{\sigma_{p_1 - p_2}} = \frac{0.05}{0.0662}$$

$$= 0.7553$$

The critical value obtained from the normal table is 1.96 (for $\alpha = 0.05$). Hence, we fail to reject the hypothesis and as such the difference between two proportions is not statistically significant.

10.3.8. The Chi-square tests of hypothesis

(*a*) Test of Variance (σ^2) of a Normal Population :

$$H_0 : \sigma^2 = \sigma_0^{\,2}$$

$$H_1 : \sigma^2 > \sigma_0^{\,2} \text{ or } \sigma^2 < \sigma_0^{\,2} \text{ or } \sigma^2 \neq \sigma_0^{\,2}.$$

For a random sample of size n —$X_1, X_2, \ldots, X_n$ from a normal population, compute test statistics

$$\chi^2 = \frac{\Sigma\,(X_i - \mu)^2}{\sigma_0^{\,2}}, \text{ if } \mu \text{ is known}$$

$$= \frac{\Sigma\,(X_i - \overline{X})^2}{\sigma_0^{\,2}}, \text{ if } \mu \text{ is not known.}$$

To test the hypothesis H_0 against alternative

(*i*) $H_1 : \sigma^2 > \sigma_0{}^2$, Reject H_0 if $\chi^2 > \chi_\alpha{}^2$

(*ii*) $H_1 : \sigma^2 < \sigma_0{}^2$, Reject H_0 if $\chi^2 < \chi^2_{1-\alpha}$

(*iii*) $H_1 : \sigma^2 \neq \sigma_0{}^2$, Reject H_0 if $\chi^2 > \chi^2_{\alpha/2}$ or $< \chi^2_{1-\alpha/2}$

Note. For random samples of size n from a normal population with variance σ^2, the sampling distribution of s^2 has the mean σ^2 and the variance $2\sigma^4/(n-1)$.

For large samples from normal populations

$$s^2 \geq \sigma_0^2\left[1 + Z_\alpha\sqrt{\frac{2}{n-1}}\right]$$

is an approximate critical region of size α for testing the null hypothesis $\sigma^2 = \sigma_0^2$ against the alternative $\sigma^2 > \sigma_0^2$.

Example 10.21. In a cement godown, the handling of cement bags reduces actual content of cement in the bags. On a random sample of 15 bags from the godown, the sample estimate of the variance is computed to be 0.75 kg^2. It is known that more than 0.50 kg^2 weight loss per bag will lead to customers' complaint.

Test whether the manager of the godown will face the customers' complaint ?

Solution :

Assume weight loss due to handling of cement bags to be normally distributed.

$$H_0 : \sigma^2 \leq 0.50$$

$$H_1 : \sigma^2 > 0.50$$

The sample estimate of σ^2 is

$$s^2 = 0.85$$

The Chi-square statistic to test the variance

$$\chi^2 = \frac{(n-1)\,s^2}{\sigma^2} \text{ (with } n\text{—1 degrees of freedom)}$$

$$= \frac{(15-1)\,(0.75)}{0.50}$$

$$= 21$$

The table value of Chi-square with 14 degrees of freedom at 0.01 level of significance is 29.141.

(*b*) **The Goodness-of-fit Test**

Besides testing a hypothesis that the variance of a normal distribution has a given value, there are other applications of Chi-square test. For instance, consider a population having k classes and the probability that in random sample of n units any unit is classified under ith class is p_i, whereas the observed number falling into ith class is n_i (i = 1, 2, ..., k). Thus,

$$n_1 + n_2 + ... + n_k = n$$

$$p_1 + p_2 + ... + p_k = 1$$

$$E\,(n_i) = n\,p_i$$

Karl Pearson showed that

$$\chi^2 = \sum_{i=1}^{k} \frac{(n_i - n\,p_i)^2}{n\,p_i} = \sum_{i=1}^{k} \frac{(O_i - E_i)^2}{E_i}$$

followed an approximately Chi-square distribution with (*k*—1) degrees of freedom, provided $n\,p_i \geq 5$, *i.e.* no expected frequency is less than 5; O_i is the observed and E_i is the expected frequency. The expression for Chi-square is a measure of discrepancy between O_i and E_i. If $\chi^2 = 0$, the sample data exactly fits the population.

Large discrepancy results in large value of χ^2, signifying the lack of agreement between the observed and expected frequencies. By comparing the calculated value of χ^2 with the percentage point from the theoretical χ^2-distribution with (*k*—1) degrees of freedom at a given significant level, we determine whether the sample may reasonably be regarded as drawn from a certain hypothetical population specified by the hypothesis. Thus, the χ^2-test is a means of judging the credibility of a hypothesis concerning a population with the help of a random sample drawn from it.

In other words Chi-square goodness-of-fit test is a test for comparing a theoretical distribution such as Normal, Poisson, Binomial, etc. with the observed data from a sample.

Suppose at a busy traffic crossing the probability of having an accident is very small because of the presence of traffic police and electronic signal arrangements, but in course of daily observation for a year we find certain number of accidents do occur in spite of all precautionary arrangements. In such circumstances one might like to know for efficient traffic planning as to the probability of having one accident days, two accident days, etc. As such, to put the observed data in a probability framework, we may fit a Poisson theoretical probability distribution to the observed data and compute the required probabilities—a long run relative frequency interpretation and then calculate expected frequencies for each class and finally make a Chi-square test of goodness-of-fit to find whether the data statistically conforms to assumed Poisson distribution with its only parameter λ made equal to the observed mean of the frequency distribution. If the fit is good, we may proceed to compute the required probabilities. If the fit is not good, we may try with another theoretical frequency distribution which best approximates the observed one.

The degrees of freedom for chi-square distribution is (*k*-*p*-1), where *k* is number of classes and *p* is the number of parameters estimated. In filling a poisson distribution *p* = 1, because λ is the only parameter to be estimated.

Example 10.22. An automobile manufacturer, while planning the production schedule for the next model, is interested to know as to how many different colours of the car should be produced. Past data show that the preference for black, red, blue and white colours is in the ratio 20 : 30 : 25 : 25. The present sales record shows that out of 2500 cars sold to date 550 were black, 650 red, 700 blue and 600 white.

Based on this sample of 2500 sales the production manager wants to know whether there has been substantial change in the consumers' preference for colour of cars, so that the next production schedule can be made accordingly.

Solution :

H_0 : There is no shift in the preference, that is, the observed colour preference coincides with the expected pattern.

H_1 : The observed colour preference does not coincide with the expected pattern.

The Chi-square statistic is calculated as

$$\chi^2 = \sum_{i=1}^{k} \frac{(O_i - E_i)^2}{E_i}$$

$O_1 = 550, O_2 = 650, O_3 = 700, O_4 = 600$

$$E_1 = 2500\left(\frac{20}{100}\right) = 500$$

$$E_2 = 2500\left(\frac{30}{100}\right) = 750$$

$$E_3 = 2500\left(\frac{25}{100}\right) = E_4 = 625$$

Hence, $\chi^2 = \frac{(550-500)^2}{500} + \frac{(650-750)^2}{750} + \frac{(700-625)^2}{625} + \frac{(600-625)^2}{625} = 28.33$

The degrees of freedom for the test = k—1 = 3

For $\alpha = .05$, $\chi^2_{0.05} = 7.81$. As the calculated value of χ^2 exceeds the table value, we conclude that there has been shift in the colour preference of the customers.

(*c*) **Test of Independence**

Situations may arise when both the population and sample are classified according to several attributes but the probability distribution of these classifications are not known. For example, each adult individual male in the city may be classified as a smoker or non-smoker and also suffering from lungs disease or not. Further, each household may be classified into annual household income and also according to size of the holding. We are interested in examining whether there exists some sort of dependency or relationship between individual's smoking habits and suffering from lung disease, or between annual household income and size of the holding. The appropriate null hypothesis to be set up is that two attributes are independent of each other. Such a test is called the **Test of independence.** If rejected, the test will indicate the dependence of one attribute on the other, but not its degrees of association. If the hypothesis is not rejected, the observed sample data are consistent with the null hypothesis that two attributes are independent.

The table showing the classification of the sample according to different attributes is called a *Contigency table.*

Let us consider the test of independence in a 2 × 2 contigency table. Let N members of the population be classified according to two attributes—having smoking habit (A) and suffering from lungs disease (B). A has two classes A_1 and A_2 and B has two classes B_1 and B_2. N_{ij} is the number of persons belonging to the ith classification of A and jth classification of B (i = 1, 2 and j = 1, 2)

Smoking habit	**Lungs disease**		**Total (N_{io})**
	Suffering (B_1)	**Not suffering (B_2)**	
Smokers (A_1)	N_{11}	N_{12}	$N_{1.}$
Non-smokers (A_2)	N_{21}	N_{22}	$N_{2.}$
	$N_{.1}$	$N_{.2}$	N

Define $p_{ij} = \frac{N_{ij}}{N}$ $(i = 1, 2, \text{ and } j = 1, 2)$

For a random sample of size n is selected from the above population, the sample classification is given an follows :

	B_1	B_2	Total
A_1	n_{11}	n_{12}	$n_{1.}$
A_2	n_{21}	n_{22}	$n_{2.}$
	$n_{.1}$	$n_{.2}$	n

n_{ij} represents the observed frequency corresponding to ith classification of B and is called (ij)th Cell frequency or Class frequency.

$$\hat{p}_{ij} = \frac{n_{ij}}{n} \quad (i = 1, 2; j = 1, 2)$$

is an unbiased estimate of p_{ij}

Define
$$u = \sum_{i=1}^{2} \sum_{j=1}^{2} \frac{(n_{ij} - n\,\hat{p}_{i.}\,.\,\hat{p}_{.j})^2}{n\,\hat{p}_{i.}\,.\,\hat{p}_{.j}}$$
$$= \sum_{i=1}^{2} \sum_{j=1}^{2} \frac{(O_{ij} - E_{ij})^2}{E_{ij}}$$
$$= \Sigma\Sigma \frac{\left(n_{ij} - \frac{n_{i.}\,.\,n_{.j}}{n}\right)^2}{n_{i.}\,.\,n_{.j}},$$

where $\hat{p}_{i.} = \frac{n_{i.}}{n}$, $\hat{p}_{.j} = \frac{n_{.j}}{n}$,

Under the hypothesis of independence u follows approximately a χ^2-distribution with $(2 — 1)(2 — 1) = 1$ degree of freedom

The formula for u is simplified if we put $n_{11} = a$, $n_{12} = b$, $n_{21} = c$ and $n_{22} = d$. Thus, u becomes

$$u = \frac{n\,(ad - bc)^2}{(a + b)\,(c + d)\,(a + c)\,(b + d)}.$$

Similarly, the test statistic u may be calculated for a $r \times c$ contigency table, where there are r classifications of A and c classification of B.

The degrees of freedom of χ^2 for a $r \times c$ contigency table is $(r—1)\,(c—1)$.

Conditions for the validity of χ^2-test :

1. The sample size n should be large in order to make Chi-square test approximately valid.
2. No expected cell frequency should be less than 5. If it so happens, one or more classes should be combined together to obviate the difficulty in approximation.
3. The constraints on cell frequencies should be linear. The test is based on the assumption that marginal row and columns totals of the contigency table is fixed.
4. Sum of the observed frequencies is equal to the sum of the expected frequencies.

5. For moderate values of the total sample size and specially when any of the expected frequency is less than 5, Yates has proposed a correction, known as *Yates correction for continuity* to improve approximation in case of a 2×2 contigency table. The corrected statistic becomes

$$u = n \cdot \frac{\left\{ | \, ad - bc \, | - \frac{n}{2} \right\}^2}{(a+b)(c+d)(a+c)(b+d)}$$

Example 10.23. In an evaluation of Integrated Rural Development Programme (IRDP), it was required to investigate whether incremental income derived by the beneficiarcies is dependent upon the supervision of the programme. On this aspect the following data were obtained in a random sample of 630 beneficiaries. Use 0.01 level of significance to test whether the incremental income is dependent upon the supervision.

	Supervision	No Supervision	Total
Incremental income	227	196	423
No incremental income	25	182	207
Total	252	378	630

Solution :

The χ^2-statistic is computed as

$$\chi^2 = \frac{n\,(ad - bc)^2}{(a+b)(c+d)(a+c)(b+d)}$$

$$= \frac{630\,(4134 - 4900)^2}{423.\,207.\,252.\,378}$$

$$= 100.16$$

This χ^2 computed value exceeds the critical value 6.635 of $\chi_{.01}{}^2$ at 1 degree of freedom. Hence, the null hypothesis of the independence of incremental income and supervision is rejected at 1% level of significance and thus we conclude that the incremental income is highly dependent upon the supervision.

Example 10.24. In a family planning study a random sample of 500 married business executives were classified according to the profession of their wives and the number of children they have, as follows :

Number of Children

Profession	0—1	2—3	Above 3	Total
Housewife	15	80	160	255
Teacher	22	60	62	144
Lawyer	15	15	5	35
Business Executive	55	9	2	66
Total	107	164	229	500

Test the hypothesis of independence of profession of wives and the number of children.

Solution :

Computation of expected cell frequencies

Profession	0—1	2—3	Above 3	Row Total
Housewife	15 (54.57)	80 (83.64)	160 (116.79)	255
Teacher	22 (30.82)	60 (47.23)	62 (65.95)	144
Lawyer	15 (7.49)	15 (11.48)	5 (16.03)	35
Business executive	55 (14.12)	9 (21.65)	2 (30.23)	66
Column Total	107	164	229	500

The expected cell frequencies are shown in the brackets. The expected frequency corresponding to first row and first column is $\frac{255 \times 107}{500} = 54.57$,

corresponding to first row and second column is $\frac{255 \times 164}{500} = 83.64$,

corresponding to first row and third column is $\frac{255 \times 229}{500} = 116.79$ and so on.

The value of χ^2-statistic is

$$\chi^2 = \sum_{i=1}^{12} (O_i - E_i)^2/E_i$$

$$= \frac{(15-54.57)^2}{54.57} + \frac{(80-83.64)^2}{83.64} + \frac{(160-116.79)^2}{116.79} + \ldots\ldots + \frac{(2-30.23)^2}{30.23}$$

$$= 219.3593$$

This value exceeds the critical value 16.812 of $\chi^2_{0.01}$ at (4—1) (3—1) = 6 degrees of freedom.

Hence the null hypothesis of independence of profession of wives and the number of children is rejected at 1% level. Thus, we conclude that the number of children born is dependent on the profession of wives.

(*d*) **Test of Homogeneity**

Suppose we have k samples of sizes $n_1, n_2, \ldots, n_k$ from k different populations. Each sample is classified according to a particular criterion into say r classes. It is required to test the null hypothesis that the samples are homogeneous *i.e.* they come from the same population.

Classification according to a sample

A/Population	1	2	...j...	k	Total
A_1	n_{11}	n_{12}	n_{1j}	n_{1k}	$n_{1.}$
A_2	n_{21}	n_{22}	n_{2j}	n_{2k}	$n_{2.}$
:					
A_i	n_{i1}	n_{i2}	n_{ij}	n_{ik}	$n_{i.}$
:					
A_r	n_{r1}	n_{r2}	n_{rj}	n_{rk}	$n_{r.}$
Total	n_1	n_2	n_j	n_k	n

Under the hypothesis (H_0) there is a single probability distribution of attribute in the population represented by $(p_1, p_2, ... p_r)$.

The expected frequency in the *j*th sample for the *i*th classification of A is

$$n_j p_i \; (i = 1, 2, ..., r; j = 1, 2, ... k)$$

The discrepancy between the observed and the expected frequency in the *j*th sample for the *i*th classification of A is

$$(n_{ij} - n_j p_i), \; i = 1, 2, ..., r \; ; \; j = 1, 2, ..., k$$

Construct the test statistic

$$u = \sum_{i=1}^{r} \sum_{j=1}^{k} \frac{(n_{ij} - n_j p_i)^2}{n_j p_i},$$

which is approximately distributed as χ^2 with $(r—1)\, k$ degrees of freedom as n becomes large.

If p_i is not known, it is estimated from the sample as

$$\hat{p}_i = \frac{n_{i.}}{n},$$

which is approximately used in u, because $\hat{p}_i \to p_i$ as $n \to N$ (size of population.) Thus, the test of the null hypothesis can be carried out by calculating

$$u = \sum_{i=1}^{r} \sum_{j=1}^{k} \frac{(n_{ij} - n_j \cdot \hat{p}_i)^2}{n_j \cdot \hat{p}_i},$$

which is distributed as χ^2 with $(r — 1)\,(k — 1)$ degrees of freedom. If $u > \chi^2_{\alpha, (r-1)(k-1)}$, the null hypothesis is rejected at 100 α% level of significance, otherwise accepted.

Example 10.25. The following table summarises the result of the two types of investigations (by mail and by interview) and the complete enumeration by an independent organization.

Type of Music	Persons with first preference		Percentage of persons with first preference
	Mailing method	Interview method	From complete enumeration
Classical	9	35	20
Folk	51	55	30
Cinema songs	90	110	50
Total	150	200	100

Examine by appropriate test whether the results of types of investigation (by mail and interview) are consistent.

Solution :

$$p_1 = 0.2,\ p_2 = 0.3,\ p_3 = 0.5$$
$$n_1 = 150$$
$$n_2 = 200$$
$$n_1 p_1 = 150 \times .2 = 30$$
$$n_1 p_2 = 150 \times .3 = 45$$
$$n_1 p_3 = 150 \times .5 = 75$$
$$n_2 p_1 = 200 \times .2 = 40$$
$$n_2 p_2 = 200 \times .3 = 60$$
$$n_2 p_3 = 200 \times .5 = 100$$
$$\chi^2 = \sum_{i=1}^{3} \sum_{j=1}^{2} \frac{(n_{ij} - n_j p_i)^2}{n_j p_i}$$

Substituting the relevant values in the expression for χ^2 we have,

$$\chi^2 = \frac{(9-30)^2}{30} + \frac{(35-40)^2}{40} + \frac{(51-45)^2}{45} + \frac{(55-60)^2}{60} + \frac{(90-75)^2}{75} + \frac{(110-100)^2}{100}$$
$$= 14.7 + 0.625 + 0.8 + 0.417 + 3 + 1$$
$$= 20.542$$

The tabulated value of Chi-square with (3—1) (2—1) = 2 degrees of freedom at 1% level of significance is 9.210. The null hypothesis that the results of investigation—mail and interview are consistent is rejected.

Test of independence *Vs.* Test of goodness-of-fit

A test of independence is employed when the manager/researcher wants to know whether there are associations between two or more attribute variables in a given study. A Chi-square statistic is computed from a cross tabulated data and this statistic has an approximate theoretical Chi-square distribution. Hence, the test of independence is carried out with the help of Chi-square test.

On the other hand when the manager wants to know whether the observed frequency distribution of a study variable conforms to a postulated theoretical distribution, a Chi-square goodness-of-fit test is employed.

10.3.9. Testing of equality of two population variances

In many situations it may be required to compare two variances to know whether one is larger than the other or they are equal.

We have seen that while testing the equality of two population means, the test statistic is based on the difference between the concerned sample means. However, for testing the equality of two population variances, the ratio of sample variances is the test statistic.

Consider two independent sets of observations from two normal populations with variances σ_1^2 and σ_2^2 respectively such as :

$$X_{11}, X_{12}, ..., X_{1n_1}$$
$$X_{21}, X_{22}, ..., X_{2n_2}$$

The null hypothesis

$$H_0 : \sigma_1^2 = \sigma_2^2$$

The alternative hypothesis

$$H_1 : \sigma_1^2 > \sigma_2^2$$

or $$H_1 : \sigma_1^2 \neq \sigma_2^2$$

The sample estimates of σ_1^2 and σ_2^2 are s_1^2 and s_2^2 respectively where

$$s_1^2 = \frac{1}{n_1 - 1} \Sigma (X_{1i} - \overline{X}_1)^2, \text{ and}$$

$$s_2^2 = \frac{1}{n_2 - 1} \Sigma (X_{2i} - \overline{X}_2)^2$$

Compute the test statistic

$$\boxed{F = \frac{s_1^2}{s_2^2},}$$

which under null hypothesis follows a theoretical 'F' distribution with $n_1 - 1$ and $n_2 - 1$ degrees of freedom.

Reject H_0 at 100 α% level of significance, in favour of

$$H_1 : \sigma_1^2 > \sigma_2^2 \text{ if } F > F_{\alpha, (n_1 - 1), (n_2 - 1)},$$

where $F_{\alpha, n_1 - 1, n_2 - 1}$ is 100 α% percentage of the F-distribution.

Reject H_0 at 100 α% level of significance in favour of $H_1 : \sigma_1^2 \neq \sigma_2^2$ if $F > F_{\alpha/2, n_1 - 1, n_2 - 1}$ or $F < F_{1 - \alpha/2, n_1 - 1, n_2 - 1}$

To compute $F_{1 - \alpha/2, n_1 - 1, n_2 - 1}$, we use the equality to refer to the published F-table which only provides percentage points corresponding to upper tail areas of the F-distribution. That is,

$$F_{1 - \alpha/2, n_1 - 1, n_2 - 1} = \frac{1}{F_{\alpha/2, n_2 - 1, n_1 - 1}}$$

Example 10.26. To study the variability in monthly income among Class I officers and class IV employees of an organization, two random samples were taken from two groups of employees and the following data were obtained :

n_1 = size of the sample from the group of officers = 10

s_1 = standard deviation of income among the officers = Rs. 1200

n_2 = size of the sample from the group of class IV employees = 20

s_2 = standard deviation of income among the class IV employees = 800

Test the hypothesis that $\sigma_1{}^2 = \sigma_2{}^2$ against the alternative $\sigma_1{}^2 > \sigma_2{}^2$. Use 0.05 level of significance.

Solution :

Assume that samples have come from normal populations.

Construct the F-statistic

$$F = \frac{s_1{}^2}{s_2{}^2} = \frac{(1200)^2}{(800)^2} = 2.25$$

Since $\quad \upsilon_1 = n_1 - 1 = 10 - 1 = 9$

$\upsilon_2 = n_2 - 1 = 20 - 1 = 19$

The value of F with 9 and 19 degrees of freedom for the 5% critical point is 2.42 (for one-tailed test).

Then F = 2.25 is not significantly large and we have no reason therefore to suspect the validity of the $H_0 : \sigma_1{}^2 = \sigma_2{}^2$.

10.3.10. Test of Equality of Several Means of Normal Populations

Suppose there are k independent normal populations with means μ_i $(i = 1, 2, .., k)$ and common variance σ^2.

It is required to test the null hypothesis

$$H_0 : \mu_1 = \mu_2 = . . = \mu_k$$

For instance, we may be interested to test whether k machines have same average output. In agricultural experiment we may like to test whether different fertilizers produce same effect on yield of a certain crop.

The alternative hypothesis is $H_1 : \mu_i$'s are **not** all equal.

Random samples of size n_i from the ith population are taken $(i = 1, 2, ..., k)$.

The measured values are

$$x_{i1}, x_{i2}, ..., x_{in_i} \quad (i = 1, 2, .., k).$$

Define sample mean of the ith sample as $\bar{x}_i$ $(i = 1, 2, .., k)$ and sample variance of the ith sample as s_i^2 $(i = 1, 2, .. k)$,

where $$\bar{x}_i = \frac{1}{n_i} \sum_{j=1}^{n_i} x_{ij}$$

$$s_i^2 = \frac{1}{n_i - 1} \sum_{j=1}^{n_i} (x_{ij} - \bar{x}_i)^2$$

An unbiased estimator of σ^2 is obtained by pooling several sample variances. That is,

$$\hat{\sigma}_1^2 = \frac{(n_1 - 1)\, s_1^2 + (n_2 - 1)\, s_2^2 + \dots + (n_k - 1)\, s_k^2}{n_1 + n_2 + .. + n_k - k}$$

The pooled mean

$$\bar{x} = \frac{n_1\bar{x}_1 + n_2\bar{x}_2 + .. + n_k\bar{x}_k}{n_1 + n_2 + .. + n_k}$$

If H_0 is true, $\bar{x}_i$ $(i = 1, 2, .., k)$ should not differ significantly from each other and also from the overall mean $\bar{x}$. A measure of discrepancy, if any, is given by

$$\hat{\sigma}_2^2 = \frac{\sum_{i=1}^{k} n_i\, (\bar{x}_i - \bar{x})^2}{k - 1}$$

would also provide an alternative unbiased estimator of σ^2.

Under H_0 :

$$F = \frac{\hat{\sigma}_2^2}{\hat{\sigma}_1^2} = \frac{\frac{1}{k-1}\,\Sigma n_i\, (\bar{x}_i - \bar{x})^2}{\frac{1}{\Sigma n_i - k}\,\Sigma\Sigma (x_{ij} - \bar{x}_i)^2}$$

has theoretical F–distribution with (k–1) and $(\Sigma n_i - k)$ degrees of freedom. Therefore, compute the statistic F from the sample. If $F > F_\alpha\,(k - 1, \Sigma n_i - k)$, H_0 is rejected at $\alpha\%$ level in favour of H_1, otherwise there is no reason to suspect the null hypothesis about the equality of population means.

EXAMPLE 10.27. The following are the numbers of mistakes made in five successive weeks by four technicians working for a medical laboratory.

Technician	Number of Mistakes				
1	13	16	12	14	15
2	14	16	11	19	15
3	13	18	17	14	18
4	18	11	14	15	12

Test at the 0.05 level of significance whether the differences among the four sample means can be attributed to chance.

SOLUTION

$$\bar{x}_1 = \frac{70}{5} = 14.0,\quad \bar{x}_2 = \frac{75}{5} = 15.0,\quad \bar{x}_3 = \frac{80}{5} = 16.0,\quad \bar{x}_4 = \frac{70}{5} = 14.0$$

$$\bar{x} = \frac{70 + 75 + 80 + 70}{20} = \frac{295}{20} = 14.75$$

$$\hat{\sigma}_1^2 = \Sigma(x_{1i} - \bar{x}_1)^2 + \Sigma(x_{2i} - \bar{x}_2)^2 + \Sigma(x_{3i} - \bar{x}_3)^2 + \Sigma(x_{4i} - \bar{x}_4)^2$$

$$= \frac{10 + 34 + 22 + 30}{16}$$

$$= \frac{96}{16} = 6$$

$$\hat{\sigma}_2^2 = \frac{\sum_{i=1}^{4} n_i (\bar{x}_i - \bar{x})^2}{4 - 1}$$

$$= \frac{n_1 (\bar{x}_1 - \bar{x})^2 + n_2 (\bar{x}_2 - \bar{x})^2 + n_3 (\bar{x}_3 - \bar{x})^2 + n_4 (\bar{x}_4 - \bar{x})^2}{3}$$

$$= \frac{5 (14 - 14.75)^2 + 5 (15 - 14.75)^2 + 5 (16 - 14.75)^2 + 5 (14 - 14.75)^2}{3}$$

$$= \frac{13.75}{3} = 4.5833$$

$$F = \frac{\hat{\sigma}_2^2}{\hat{\sigma}_1^2} = \frac{4.5833}{6.0} < 1$$

Hence, H_0 cannot be rejected. Thus, we have no reason to suspect the equality of means of populations.

10.3.11. Test for Equality of Variances from Several Normal Populations

Given k independent samples of sizes $n_1, n_2, \ldots, n_k$ from k normal populations having variances $\sigma_1^2, \sigma_2^2, \ldots, \sigma_k^2$ respectively. We are interested in testing the null hypothesis.

$$H_0 : \sigma_1^2 = \sigma_2^2 = \ldots = \sigma_k^2$$

against H_1, that at least one of the equality sign does not hold good.

Let $s_1^2, s_2^2, \ldots, s_k^2$ be the variances of k independent samples.

A pooled estimate σ^2 obtained by pooling the variances of the k samples is

$$s^2 = \frac{v_1 s_1^2 + v_2 s_2^2 + \ldots + v_k s_k^2}{v_1 + v_2 + .. + v_k}$$

where $v_i = (n_i - 1)$.

Compute the statistic

$$B = \frac{2.3062}{C}\left[v \log_{10} s^2 - \Sigma v_i \log_{10} s_i^2\right],$$

where $$v = \sum_{i=1}^{k} v_i$$

and $$C = 1 + \frac{1}{3(k-1)}\left[\Sigma \frac{1}{v_i} - \frac{1}{v}\right]$$

For reasonably large $n_1, n_2, ..., n_k$, B is approximately distributed as χ^2 with $(k-1)$ degrees of freedom. Hence, the test of H_0 can be carried out with the help of χ^2–test.

This test procedure is known as **Bartlett's test** for homogeneity of variances.

EXAMPLE 10.28. Test whether the estimates 4.2, 3.9, 7.2 and 8.1 of the population variance based on 4, 7, 6 and 3 degrees of freedom respectively may be regarded as homogeneous.

SOLUTION.

TABLE

s_i^2	v_i	$v_i s_i^2$	$\log_{10} s_i^2$	$v_i \log_{10} s_i^2$
4.2	4	16.8	0.6232	2.4928
3.9	7	27.3	0.5911	4.1377
7.2	6	43.2	0.8573	5.1438
8.1	3	24.3	0.9085	2.7255
Total	20	111.6	—	14.4998

$$s^2 = \frac{\Sigma v_i s_i^2}{\Sigma v_i} = \frac{111.6}{20} = 5.58$$

$$v = \Sigma v_i = 20$$

$$\log_{10} s^2 = 0.7466$$

$$C = 1 + \frac{1}{3(k-1)}\left[\Sigma \frac{1}{v_i} - \frac{1}{v}\right]$$

$$= 1 + \frac{1}{3 \times 3}(0.89 - 0.50) = 1.043$$

$$B = \frac{2.3026}{C}\left[v \log_{10} s^2 - \Sigma v_i \log_{10} s_i^2\right]$$

$$= \frac{2.3026}{1.043}\left[(20)(0.7466) - 14.4998\right]$$

$$= (2.2077)(0.4322) = 0.9542$$

The computed value of B is less than the critical value 7.815 of $\chi^2_{0.05}$ at 3 degrees of freedom. Hence, the null hypothesis cannot be rejected and thus the variances may be regarded by homogeneous.

EXERCISES

1. What are problems in statistical inference ? Discuss its importance in research.
2. Distinguish between point estimate and interval estimate with examples.
3. Explain the terms :
   Population, sample, parameter, statistic and estimator.

4. What is sampling distribution of a statistic ? Why does it arise ? How would you meaure the sampling variability of a statistic ? Discuss.

5. What is an estimator ? Explain its properties. How does it differ from an estimate ?

6. What does a confidence interval indicate ? Explain with an example. Is it a better alternative than point estimation ?

7. A random sample of size 30 was selected from a normal population with mean μ and standard deviation 5.

The sample mean computed from the sample is $\bar{x}$ = 65.8 kg.

Answer the following :

(*i*) What is the estimate of μ ?

(*ii*) What is the standard error of the estimate ?

(*iii*) Compute 95% confidence interval for μ.

8. In a sample of 80 item taken from a large consignment 10 items were found to be defective. Find the estimate of proportion of defectives in the population along with is standard error. Also compute 90% confidence interval for the population proportion.

9. A manager wishes to estimate average time required by a machinist to complete a particular job. He observed the working of 20 machinists and found that average time required for the sample workers was 10 minutes with estimated standard deviation 3 minutes. Compute 95% and 99% confidence intervals for the unknown population mean and comment. (Assume normality).

10. Explain shortcoming that occurs in a point estimate but not in the interval estimate. What measure is associated with an interval estimate to compensate such shortcoming ?

11. What are criteria for a good estimator ? Explain.

12. Why does a decision maker resort to sampling technique rather than surveying entire population ? Mention its disadvantages.

13. The following is a sample of eight observations from normal population.

75.3, 83.2, 84.8, 72.6
68.3, 76.4, 58.5, 81.2

(*a*) Find the estimate of population mean.

(*b*) Estimate the standard error of the sample mean.

(*c*) Compute a 98% confidence interval for the population mean.

(*d*) How does the confidence interval change if the normal population has standard deviation equal to 5 ?

14. Given a population with a standard deviation of 8.6, what size of sample is needed to estimate the mean of the population within ± 0.5 with 99 percent confidence.

15. A management institute is considering raising tuition fees to improve the academic curriculum in face of rising cost of education and wants to determine what percentage of students favour the increase. The institute needs to be 90% confident that the percentage has been estimated to within 2% of the true value. How large a sample is needed to guarantee this accuracy regardless of the true percentage ?

16. For a test market, find the sample size needed to estimate the true population of prospective buyers satisfied with new brand of minicar within ± 0.04 at the 95% confidence level. Assume that you have no strong feeling about what the proportion is.

17. In a Pizza fast food shop the owner wantd to know the average time required for a customer to get the service, so that he can increase the number of wokers to boost the sale and facilitate the customers. For this purpose observations were made to serve 15 customers and the results are follows (in minutes).
25, 20, 21, 18, 28, 25, 30, 24, 22, 28, 26, 25, 30, 32, 22.
(*a*) Estimate the average service time.
(*b*) Estimate the standard error.
(*c*) Compute 99% confidence interval of the true average.

18. It was known from the past experience that the standard deviation of the annual earnings of entire population of 500 fresh management graduates is about Rs. 30,000. How large a sample size should the university take in order to estimate the mean annual earnings of last year's class within Rs. 10,000 and at a 95% confidence level ?

19. Compute the 95% confidence intervals for the following data for the population mean and comment on your findings. Assume that the samples have come normal populations. The sample mean happens to be the same in all the cases.
(*i*) $\sigma = 9,\ n = 25$
(*ii*) $\sigma = 9,\ n = 40$
(*iii*) $\sigma = 9,\ n = 60$
(*iv*) $\sigma = 4,\ n = 25$
(*v*) $\sigma = 4,\ n = 40$
(*vi*) $\sigma = 4,\ n = 60$

20. The personnel manager of a firm selects graduate trainees from two universities university–1 and university–2. After training the performance index for a sample trainees from two universities were comported on a 0–10 scale. The sample sizes for the university–1 and university–2 were 25 and 36 respectively. Mean performance index of the sample from university–1 was 7 and the sample from the university–2 was 6. The variance of the performance index of the trainees the university–1 is 9 and that of the trainees from the university–2 is 4 (as per the performance index of previous batches of trainees from the two universities).
Construct a 95% confidence interval for the difference between their mean performance in the populations.

21. The proportions of woman shoppers in random samples of shoppers on the 1st and 4th Sunday evenings from a city super market were found to be 0.35 and 0.25 respectively. The sample size on both the evenings was 50.
Construct 98% confidence interval for the difference in proportions in two populations.

22. The weight of fertilizer bags produced by a fertilizer company follows normal distribution with mean μ and variance σ^2. A randam sample of 8 fertilizer bags gives sample variance $s^2 = 0.36\ (\text{kg})^2$.
Construct 95% confidence interval for the population variance σ^2.

23. A random sample of 10 small scale industries in Region–1 and 15 small scale industries in Region–2 were selected and their annual sales (in lakhs of rupees) were noted. The sample variances of the annual sales in two regions were computed to be $s_1^2 = 100$ (Lakh of Rs.)^2 and $s_2^2 = 144$ (Lakhs of Rs.)^2 Assuming that the annual sales in both the regions are normally distributed with unknown variance σ_1^2 and σ_2^2 respectively, construct 98% confidence interval for the ratio of population variances that is, σ_1^2/σ_2^2.

24. What is a hypothesis ? Distinguish between research hypothesis and statistical hypothesis. Discuss utility of testing of hypothesis in business research.

25. What are errors likely to be committed in testing a statistical hypothesis ? Discuss.

26. Differentiate between Null hypothesis and Alternative hypothesis.

(*i*) Type I error and Type II error.

(*ii*) Critical region and acceptance region.

(*iii*) One tailed test and two tailed test.

27. Discuss salient steps in testing a statistical hypothesis.

28. A manufacturer of two wheelers claims that his product gives average mileage of 80 km. per litre of petrol with standard deviation of 15 km. However, on a random sample of 12 two wheelers, when tested, gave average mileage of 75 km. Is the manufacturer's claim justified ?

29. Two door to door salesmen A and B are working in a certain region. Their performances during a month were observed. Their previous performances for a long period showed standard deviation of sales amount to be Rs. 140 and Rs. 180 respecting. From a sample suvey conducted by the marketing section of the Head Office the following results were obtained. State whether there is any significant difference in the average sales between two salesmen.

	A	B
Number of Sales	200	150
Average Sales (Rs.)	3500	2700

30. Two brands of electric bulbs were required to be compared as regards their life span and the following data were obtained from a sample survey for the purpose.
Is there any significant difference in the mean life of two brands ?

	Mean Life	Standard Deviation	Sample Size
Brand A	2,500 hrs.	230 hrs.	15
Brand B	2,300 hrs.	300 hrs.	20

31. 500 manufacturing parts produced by Machine–A were inspected and 15 were found to be defective. Furthe, 800 manufacturing parts were produced by Machine–B and 15 were found to be defective. Can it be concluded at 5% level of significance that Machine–B's profromance is better than that of Machine–A ?

32. A coin was tossed 300 times and the Heads figured 120 times. Can you suggest that the coin is an unbiased one at 5% level of significance ? State the null and alternative Hypotheses.

33. The following 10 observations show the scores of Mr. A in 10 test innings in cricket maches.

25, 45, 54, 60, 90

0, 30, 42, 65, 85

Test at 1% level of significance that the population standard deviation $\sigma = 25$. (Assume Normality of Scores)

How does the test change if we assume that the average score of Mr. A as per the past history is about 50 ?

34. The arrival rates of customers at the Housing loan counter of a Nationalised Bank are given below.

Arrival Rate (X)	Observed Frequency (f)
0	2
1	6
2	18
3	12
4	8
5	3
6	1
Total	50

Test whether the given data follow Poisson distribution.

35. 500 families are classified according to poverty level both by per capita monthly income and monthly per capita consumer expenditure method and the results are given below.

Per Capita Income	MPCE	
	BPL	**APL**
BPL	8	23
APL	11	458

Test whether two methods of determining BPL category are consistent. Use 1% level of significance.

36. A production supervisor is interested in knowing if number of breakdowns on four machines is independent of experience of the workers.

Machines

Types of Workers	A	B	C	D
Experienced	14	10	12	9
Inexperienced	12	8	14	6

Can you say that breakdown is dependent on experience ?

37. An automobile company wants to know whether the colour of the new model car is dependent on the age group of the prospective buyers ? The relevant data from a survey are given below :

Age Group (in Years)

Colour	Below 25	25–50	Above 50
Black	20	8	10
White	35	12	30
Red	15	20	12
Silver Grey	10	40	28
Total	80	80	80

Analyse the data and draw conclusions.

38. (*i*) What is a chi-square test ? Mention its applications.

(*ii*) What is chi-square test of independence ? State the situations where the test is applied.

(*iii*) What is chi-square test of goodness of fit ? Mention its sphere of application with examples.

(*iv*) Write short notes on :

(*a*) Yates' correction for continuity.

(*b*) Degrees of freedom.

(*c*) Level of significance.

(*d*) Chi-square distribution.

(*e*) Chi-square test of homogeneity.

39. What are precautions to be adopted while applying the chi-square test ?

40. Determine on the basis of following sample data whether the true proportion of shoppers favouring detergent A over detergent B is the same in all three cities. Use 5% level of significance.

Number Favouring Detergent A	Number Favouring Detergent B	
220	180	400
280	220	500
135	165	300

41. Suppose that a random sample from a normal population with known variance σ^2 is to be used to test the null hypothesis $\mu = \mu_0$ against the alternative hypothesis $\mu = \mu_1$, where $\mu_1 > \mu_0$ and that the probabilities of type I and type II errors are to have pre-assigned values α and β. Then the required sample size

$$n = \frac{\sigma^2 (Z_\alpha + Z_\beta)^2}{(\mu_1 - \mu_{0)}^2}.$$

Find n when $\sigma = 9$, $\mu_0 = 15$, $\mu_1 = 20$, $\alpha = 0.05$ and $\beta = 0.01$.

42. A pertrol filling station claims that 20 percent of all four wheeler owners buy Extra Premium Brand Petrol. Test this claim at $\alpha = 0.01$, if a random check indicates that 58 out of 200 owners buy Extra Premium Brand.

43. In a random sample, the time which 30 women took to complete the written test for their driver's license had a variance of 6.4 minutes. Assuming normality, test the null hypothesis $\sigma^2 = 8$ against the alternative $\sigma^2 < 8$ at the level of significance $\alpha = 0.05$.

44. The following are the scores obtained in a personality test by samples of ten male MBA graduates and 12 female MBA graduates.

Male Graduates	88	68	77	82	63	80	78	71	73	75		
Female Graduates	73	72	65	68	74	74	69	71	71	68	70	73

Assuming that data can be looked upon as independent random samples from two normal populations, test the null hypothesis $\sigma_1^2 = \sigma_2^2$ against alternative $\sigma_1^2 > \sigma_2^2$ at the level of significance $\alpha = 0.05$ (σ_1^2 and σ_2^2 male and female graduates respectively.)

45. (*a*) What is a test of significance ? How does it compare with the test of hypothesis ?

(*b*) Explain P-value of a test and mention its significance in testing a hypothesis.

□□□

CHAPTER

11

NONPARAMETRIC TESTS

11.1. Introduction

In the foregoing sections we have discussed testing of hypothesis on the parameters indexing the probability distribution of the random variables in question. It is assumed that the concerned probability distribution is known before hand. But there may be situations when we have no complete information on the nature and form of the distribution of the variable under consideration and we are still interested in testing hypothesis on certain characteristics of the population, not exactly the parameters of the population. Such problems are tackled by nonparametric methods or distribution free methods as discussed in statistical literature.

There are certain advantages and disadvantages associated with nonparametric methods. **The advantages** are :

- ❐ No assumption is required as to form of the distribution.
- ❐ Nonparametric tests are suitable and can be used for nominal and ordinal data *i.e.* for ranked, scaled or rated data submitted for analysis and are based on order relationship among the observations.
- ❐ Nonparametric tests are simple to understand and easier to execute for analysis and make less stringent demands of the data.
- ❐ Exact inference can be made when the assumptions underlying parametric tests are not met.
- ❐ These tests involve no or less restrictive assumptions when compared to parametric tests.

The main disadvantages are :

- ❐ Non-parametric tests throw away information and are based on limited information on population under sampling.
- ❐ As compared to parametric tests, they are less efficient, particularly when sample size is small or the normality of observations holds good.

- The null hypothesis is loosely and broadly set up and as such conclusions are less precise. Because the procedures are non-parametric, there are no parameters to describe and it becomes more difficult to make quantitative statements about the actual difference between populations.

Nonparametric tests may be categorized as

- **One sample tests**
  - One sample sign test
  - Kolmogorov-Smirnov test
  - Run test
- **Two sample tests**
  - Two sample sign test
  - Median test
  - Mann-Whitney U test (Wilcoxon Rank-sum test)
- **K-sample tests**
  - Median test
  - Kruskal-Wallis test

11.2 One sample tests

11.2.1. Sign test : The sign test is designed to test a hypothesis about the location most often the median of a continuous population distribution. It does not require the assumption that the population is normally distributed. In many applications, the test is used in place of *t*-test when normality assumption is questionable.

Let X be a continuous random variable with median $\tilde{\mu}$.

That is, $P(X \le \tilde{\mu}) = P(X > \tilde{\mu}) = 0.5$ Suppose that the null hypothesis and alternative hypothesis on median $\tilde{\mu}$ are

$$H_0 : \tilde{\mu} = \tilde{\mu}^\circ$$

$$H_1 : \tilde{\mu} \ne \tilde{\mu}^\circ \text{ (two sided)}$$

or

$$H_1 : \tilde{\mu} > \tilde{\mu}^\circ \text{ (one sided)}$$

$$H_1 : \tilde{\mu} < \tilde{\mu}^\circ \text{ (one sided)}$$

Given a random sample of size n — $X_1, X_2, \ldots, X_n$ from a continuous population, form the differences

$$(X_i - \tilde{\mu}^\circ),\ i = 1, 2, \ldots, n$$

and note the number of positive and negative signs. Let r^+ denote the number of positive differences and r^- the number of negative differences.

Under the null hypothesis we expect half the x's to be above median and half below.

Let Y denote the number of positive differences. Then Y has a binomial distribution with parameters n and p. The test thus reduces to

$$H_0 : p = \frac{1}{2} \text{ against } H_1 : p > \frac{1}{2} \text{ or } p < \frac{1}{2} \text{ or } p \ne \frac{1}{2}.$$

Case 1. $H_1 : p > \frac{1}{2}$

Let r_α stand for $\alpha\%$ critical point of the binomial distribution. If $r^+ \geq r_\alpha$, reject H_0, where r_α is the smallest integer such that

$$\sum_{r_\alpha}^{n} \binom{n}{x} \left(\frac{1}{2}\right)^n \leq \alpha$$

Note : Because of the discrete nature of the binomial distribution, a critical value r_α cannot be chosen with level of significance exactly equal to α, when ties occur, that is x_i equals $\tilde{\mu}^\circ$, making the difference Y_i zero, these should be set aside and the sign test is to be based on remaining data.

Case 2. $H_1 : p < \frac{1}{2}$

The critical region is placed at the left tail of the $B\left(n, \frac{1}{2}\right)$ distribution. As such if $r^+ \leq r'_\alpha$, where r'_α is the lower $\alpha\%$ critical point of $B\left(n, \frac{1}{2}\right)$, the H_0 is rejected where r'_α is the largest integers such that $\sum_{0}^{r'_\alpha} \binom{n}{x} \left(\frac{1}{2}\right)^n \leq \alpha$.

Case 3. $H_1 : p \neq \frac{1}{2}$

The critical region is halved and placed at both the tails of binomial distribution. Thus, the critical region is $r^+ \geq r_{\alpha/2}$ and $r^+ \leq r'_{\alpha/2}$, defined by $r^+ \geq r_{\alpha/2}$ and $r^+ \leq r'_{\alpha/2}$ where $r_{\alpha/2}$ and $r'_{\alpha/2}$ are the smallest and the largest integers respectively such that

$$\sum_{r_{\alpha/2}}^{n} \binom{n}{x} \left(\frac{1}{2}\right)^n \leq \alpha/2 \text{ and } \sum_{0}^{r'_{\alpha/2}} \binom{n}{x} \left(\frac{1}{2}\right)^n \leq \alpha/2.$$

Alternatively, if $P(Y \geq r^+) \leq \alpha/2$, the H_0 is rejected.

Large sample sign test

If sample size n is large, say > 25, one can approximate binomial distribution to normal distribution. That is, $Y \sim B(n, p)$ leads to

$Z = \dfrac{Y - np}{\sqrt{np(1-p)}}$, a standard normal variable asymptotically for large n.

Thus, $H_0 : p = \frac{1}{2}$ against alternatives $H_0 : p > \frac{1}{2}$ or $H_1 : p < \frac{1}{2}$ or $H_1 : p \neq \frac{1}{2}$ can be tested by appealing to percentage points of the standard normal distribution.

Alternative method

Denote $r = \min(r^+, r^-)$

(*i*) For a two-sided test,

if $r \leq r_\alpha{}^*$, H_0 is rejected in favour of $p \neq \frac{1}{2}$.

(*ii*) If $r^- \leq r_\alpha{}^*$, H_0 is rejected in favour of $p > \frac{1}{2}$.

(*iii*) If $r^+ \leq r_\alpha{}^*$, H_0 is rejected in favour of $p < \frac{1}{2}$.

The level of significance of a one-sided test is one half of the value shown for a 2-sided test.

A P-value Method

1. Choose $r = \max(r^+, r^-)$.
2. Choose table of binomial distribution to find probability of observing a value of r or higher, assuming $p = \frac{1}{2}$. If the test is one-sided, this is the P-value.
3. If the test is a two-sided, double the probability obtained in (2) to obtain P-value.

Example 11.1. On a survey of a random sample of 3-Star hotels, the waiting times (in minutes) for a medium standard lunch to be served are 25, 35, 32, 34, 28, 28, 35, 31, 20. Test $H_0 : \tilde{\mu} = 30$ against $H_1 : \tilde{\mu} > 30$ at 5% level of significance.

Solution :

$H_0 : \tilde{\mu} = 30$

$H_1 : \tilde{\mu} > 30$

X	25	35	32	34	28	28	35	31	20
$X - \tilde{\mu}$	–5	+ 5	+ 2	+ 4	–2	–2	+ 5	+ 1	–10
Sign	–	+	+	+	–	–	+	+	–

r^+ = Number of (+) signs = 5

r^- = Number of (–) signs = 4

$n = 9$

Now the hypotheses are restated as

$$H_0 : p = \frac{1}{2}, \quad H_1 : p > \frac{1}{2}, \alpha = 0.05$$

From Table in the Appendix

$r_{0.05} = 1$ (for one-sided test)

Since r^- (= 4) is not less than $r_{0.05}$ (= 1), we cannot reject the null hypothesis.

Alternatively, $P(Y \leq 4) = \sum_{r=0}^{4} \binom{9}{r} (0.5)^r (0.5)^{9-r}$

$$= \left(\frac{1}{2}\right)^9 \left[\binom{9}{0} + \binom{9}{1} + \binom{9}{2} + \binom{9}{3} + \binom{9}{4}\right]$$

$$= \left(\frac{1}{2}\right)^9 (1 + 9 + 36 + 84 + 126) = \frac{256}{512}$$

$$= 0.5$$

Since $P(Y < 4)$ is greater than 0.05 (the level of significance) H_0 cannot be rejected.

Example 11.2. On a particular day the number of outside orders received by a random sample of 8 fast-food centres in a city are

14, 12, 10, 18, 25, 16, 13, 8

Test the hypothesis $H_0 : \tilde{\mu} = 15$ against alternative $\tilde{\mu} < 15$.

Solution :

$$n = 8, r^+ = 3, r^- = 5, \alpha = .05$$

The critical region $r^+ < r_\alpha{}^*$

From the Table A–5 in the Appendix

$$r_{0.05} = 1$$

Thus $$r^+ \nless r_{0.05}$$

Hence, H_0 is accepted.

Note : The critical number shown for 0.10 level of significance for a 2-sided test corresponds to one half of 0.10 *i.e.* 0.05 level of significance for a one-sided test.

Example 11.3. The hours of relief provided by analgesic drugs in 10 patients suffering from arthritis are as follows :

2.0, 2.6, 2.8, 2.6, 3.2, 4.0, 2.5, 2.8, 3.4, 3.0

Test the hypothesis H_0 : median hours $(\tilde{\mu}) = 3$ against alternative $H_1 : (\tilde{\mu}) \neq 3$.

Solution :

$$H_0 = \tilde{\mu} = 3$$
$$H_1 : \tilde{\mu} \neq 3$$

X	2.0	2.6	2.8	2.6	3.2	4.0	2.5	2.8	3.4	3.0
$X - \tilde{\mu}$	—1.0	—0.4	—0.2	—0.4	+ 0.2	+ 1.0	—0.5	—0.2	+ 0.4	0
Sign	—	—	—	—	+	+	—	—	+	omit

Solution :

$$n = 9 \text{ (omitting the zero difference)}$$
$$r^+ = 4, r^- = 6$$
$$r = \max(r^+, r^-) = 6$$

Now $$P(Y \geq r) = P(Y \geq 6) = \sum_{x=6}^{9} \binom{9}{x} \left(\frac{1}{2}\right)^9$$

$$= \left(\frac{1}{2}\right)^9 \sum_{x=6}^{9} \binom{9}{x} = \left(\frac{1}{2}\right)^9 \left[\binom{9}{6} + \binom{9}{7} + \binom{9}{8} + \binom{9}{9}\right]$$

$$= \left(\frac{1}{2}\right)^9 [84 + 36 + 9 + 1]$$

$$= \frac{130}{512} = 0.2539$$

Now since $2P(Y \geq r) = 2 \times 0.2539 = 0.5078$, which is greater than the level of significance $\alpha = 0.05$, the null hypothesis H_0 cannot be rejected.

Example 11.4. The following data constitute a random sample of 30 measurements of the octane rating of a certain kind of petrol.

99.0, 102.3, 98.0, 98.5, 97.0, 99.0
101.2, 101.3, 102.5, 104.6, 96.9, 98.2
95.0, 96.7, 98.0, 100.5, 98.9, 99.5
99.2, 100.8, 102.6, 103.7, 97.2, 95.9
100.2, 98.4, 96.5, 100.4, 101.6, 100.6

Test the null hypothesis

$$H_0 : \tilde{\mu} = 100 \Rightarrow p = \frac{1}{2}$$

against

$$H_1 : \tilde{\mu} > 100 \Rightarrow p > \frac{1}{2}$$

Solution :

$$n = 30$$

$$r^+ = 13, r^- = 17$$

$$r = \text{Max}\,(r^+, r^-) = 17$$

Apply normal approximation

$$Z = \frac{17 - \frac{n}{2}}{\sqrt{n/4}} = \frac{17 - 30/2}{\sqrt{\frac{30}{4}}}$$

$$= \frac{2}{2.7386} = 0.7303$$

The critical value at 5% level of significance is 1.648, which is greater than the computed value of Z *i.e.* 0.7303, the H_0 is accepted.

11.2.2. One-sample Wilcoxon signed-rank test

Wilcoxon test is more efficient for testing a hypothesis about median of a distribution than the sign test, provided the distribution is continuous and symmetric. This test takes into account both the signs and magnitudes (ranks). This test is used in place of *t*-test, when normality assumption is questionable.

Consider a random sample $X_1, X_2, ..., X_n$ of size n from a continuous and symmetric distribution, having median $\tilde{\mu}$.

The null hypothesis under test is

$$H_0 : \tilde{\mu} = \tilde{\mu}_0$$

Then, under H_0, the difference $d_i = X_i - \tilde{\mu}_0$ comes from a continuous distribution which is symmetric about zero. Thus, the positive d_i's and negative d_i's have same probabilities to occur. Next, rank (from smallest to largest) the absolute differences $|d_i|$, ignoring zero d_i's. The tied ranks are given value which is the average of ranks if there had been no ties. Let $T(d_i)$ = rank of $|d_i|$.

Let T^+ be the sum of the ranks of the positive d_i's and T^- be the sum of the ranks of the negative d_i's. Let m is the number of non-zero d_i's and $m \le n$. Thus $T^+ = \sum_{d_i > 0} T(d_i)$ and $T^- = \sum_{d_i < 0} T(d_i)$.

$$T^+ + T^- = \frac{m(m+1)}{2}.$$

T^+ and T^{-1} have identical distributions, each being symmetric about $\frac{m(m+1)}{4}$ and ranges from 0 to $\frac{m(m+1)}{2}$.

Note : This test can also be applied when the observations in a sample of data are ranks, that is, ordinal data rather than direct measurements.

To test $H_0 : \tilde{\mu} = \tilde{\mu}_0$

$H_1 : \tilde{\mu} > \tilde{\mu}_0$

We reject H_0 for *small* values of

$$T^- = \sum_{d_i < 0} T(d_i)$$

If $H_1 : \tilde{\mu} < \tilde{\mu}_0$, let

$$T^+ = \sum_{d_i > 0} T(d_i)$$

and reject H_0 for small values of T^+. For $H_1 : \tilde{\mu} \ne \tilde{\mu}_0$, we double the appropriate one sided p-value.

If T_α is such that $P(T \le T_\alpha) = \alpha$, being chosen level of significance, then reject H_0, if

$T^- \le T_{2\alpha}$, for alternative $H_1 : \tilde{\mu} > \tilde{\mu}_0$

$T^+ \le T_{2\alpha}$, for $H_1 : \tilde{\mu} < \tilde{\mu}_0$

$T^+ \le T_\alpha$ or $T^- \le T_\alpha$, for $H_1 : \tilde{\mu} \ne \tilde{\mu}_0$

or $T \le T_\alpha$, $T = \text{Min}(T^+, T^-)$

Note : For $H_1 : \tilde{\mu} > \tilde{\mu}_0$, reject H_0 for large values of T^+ or equivalently, T^- is too small. Similar arguments hold good for other critical regions.

Define $I_k = \{1$ if for some i, $|d_i|$ has rank k and $d_i > 0$

0, otherwise

Then, $T^+ = \sum_{k=1}^{n} k I_k$; I_k is binomial with $p = 1/2$

$$E(T^+) = \sum_{k=1}^{n} k\, E(I_k) = \frac{1}{2} \sum_{k=1}^{n} k = \frac{n(n+1)}{4}$$

$$V(T^+) = n(n+1)(2n+1)/24$$

For $n > 25$, T^+ and T^- are approximately normally distributed with mean $\frac{n(n+1)}{4}$ and variance $n(n+1)(2n+1)/24$. For small samples the critical values are given in Table A–9.

11.2.3. Kolmogorov-Smirnov test

The Kolmogorov-Smirnov test is used to test whether the empirical cumulative distribution function of a continuously distributed random variable (F_x) with a theoretical distribution function (F_0). This serves the same purpose as the Chi-square goodness of fit test. The K-S test is generally more efficient than the Chi-square goodness of fit test for small samples. This one sample test is based on computing maximum absolute difference D between the empirical cumulative distribution of a random sample of size n and a specified theoretical cumulative distribution. If the maximum absolute difference or the distance is not significant, then the observed distribution is well described by the theoretical distribution.

Let $X_1, X_2, ..., X_n$ be a random sample from a continuous distribution function $F(x)$.

Define the empirical distribution of a random variable X as

$$F_n(x) = \frac{\text{Number of observations } X_j \le x}{n}$$

The K-S statistic for the test of goodness of fit is

$$D_n = \sup_x \mid F_n(x) - F_0(x) \mid,$$

which tests

$$H_0 : F(x) = F_0(x) \text{ for all } x$$

against $\quad H_1 : F(x) \neq F_0(x)$ for some x.

Reject H_0, if $D_n > D_{n,\alpha}$ at $\alpha\%$ level of significance.

For one-sided alternatives such as $H_1 : F(x) \ge F_0(x)$ or $H_1 : F(x) \le F_0(x)$, the K-S statistics are respectively

$$D_n^+ = \sup_x [F_n(x) - F_0(x)] \text{ and}$$

$$D_n^- = \inf_x [F_n(x) - F_0(x)]$$

The K-S statistics D_n, D_n^+ and D_n^- are distribution free, provided, $F_0(x)$ is an absolutely continuous distribution function.

Advantages :

(*i*) The distribution of K-S statistic does not depend on the underlying theoretical cumulative distribution, being tested under null hypothesis.

(*ii*) K-S test is an exact test unlike Chi-square test of goodness of fit which depends on an adequate sample size for the approximation to be valid.

(*iii*) K-S test does not require the distributional assumptions about the sampled population. It is truly non-parametric and distribution free. But, it is used to test the normality of the sampled observations.

Disadvantages :

(*i*) It only applies to continuous distribution.

(*ii*) It tends to be more sensitive near the centre of the distribution than at tails.

(*iii*) Perhaps the most serious limitation is that the distribution must be fully specified. That is, if the location, scale and shape parameters are estimated from data, the critical region of the K-S test is no longer valid.

The critical values of D_n for $\alpha = 0.01$ and 0.05 for various sample sizes (n) are given in Table A–6.

Example 11.5. The number of telephone calls received by a switch board in successive 5 minute interval at a business centre is given below :

Number of calls (x)	0	1	2	3	4	5
No. of 5-minute interval (f)	4	10	8	5	2	1

Test whether a Poisson distribution can be best fitted to data.

Solution :

The sample mean $\bar{x} = \frac{\Sigma xf}{\Sigma f} = \frac{54}{30} = 1.8$

The estimate of Poisson parameter λ is $\hat{\lambda} = 1.8$

H_0 : Poisson distribution is a good fit, H_1 : Not a good fit.

x	f_0	Observed relative f	Expected Probability	Cumulative obs. rel. f	Expected cumulative probability	$\lvert F_n - F_0 \rvert$
0	4	0.1333	0.1653	0.1333	0.1653	0.0320
1	10	0.3333	0.2975	0.4666	0.4628	0.0038
2	8	0.2667	0.2678	0.7333	0.7306	0.0027
3	5	0.1667	0.1607	0.9000	0.8913	0.0087
4	2	0.0667	0.0723	0.9667	0.9636	0.0031
5	1	0.0333	0.0260	1.0000	0.9896	0.0104
≥ 6	0	0	0.0104	1.0000	1.0000	0.0000

Now for $D_{30} = \sup_x \lvert F_{30}(x) - F_0(x) \rvert = 0.0320$

Since tabulated value of $D_{30,\,0.05} = 0.218$, H_0 is accepted.

11.2.4. Run test (Test of Randomness)

Sometimes we may require to know whether the sample observations which have been assumed to have been taken from a continuous population is really random in nature. For this purpose we may observe the order in which the observations have been obtained and then count the number of runs and perform the test of randomness.

Suppose in a milk bottling plant, the containers are sealed automatically by machines and a sample of 25 containers on the production line is taken for checking whether the bottling is defective or non-defective. As an illustration noting the defective item with symbol '*d*' and non-defective one with symbol '*n*', the units in their order of production are arranged as

n n n d n n d d n d n n n d d d n n d d n n d n d

Null hypothesis H_0 : arrangement is random

H_1 : arrangement is not random

Compute the number of 'runs' in the arrangement, where *a run is defined as a* sequence of identical letters preceded and followed by a different letter or by no letter at all.

In the present illustration, the number of runs $r = 14$

Let n_1 denote the number of letters of one type say '*d*' and n_2 denote the number of letters of the second type '*n*'. Under H_0,

$$E(r) = \frac{2\, n_1 n_2}{n_1 + n_2} + 1$$

$$V(r) = \frac{2\, n_1 n_2\, (2 n_1 n_2 - n_1 - n_2)}{(n_1 + n_2)^2\, (n_1 + n_2 - 1)}$$

If n_1 and n_2 are large *i.e.* say not less than 10,

$Z = \dfrac{r - E(r)}{\sqrt{V(r)}}$ is approximately distributed as a standard normal variable.

Thus, in the present illustration

$$E(r) = 13.32 \quad V(r) = 5.8109$$

$$z = \frac{14 - 13.32}{\sqrt{5.8109}} = 0.2821$$

At 5% level of significance, the critical value of z is 1.96, the H_0 cannot be rejected and as such there is no reason to suspect the randomness of observations.

Note : The run test can be used to test the randomness of samples having measurement data by counting the runs above and below the median. The critical values of run test are given in Table A–14.

11.3. Two Sample Tests

11.3.1. Two-sample sign test

The single sample sign test can be applied to paired sample observations, for instance, before and after observations, effectiveness of two drugs on individuals, effectiveness two diets, two types of promotional advertisements, etc. Two sample sign test is a non-parametric alternative to the paired *t*-test.

Let (X_{1j}, X_{2j}) $j = 1, 2, ..., n$ be n paired observations from two continuous populations. Now compute the differences $D_j = X_{1j} - X_{2j}$, $j = 1, 2, ..., n$ and test the hypothesis using sign test with n differences that two populations have the common median that is, $H_0 : \tilde{\mu}_1 = \tilde{\mu}_2$ against alternative $H_1 : \tilde{\mu}_1 > \tilde{\mu}_2$ or $H_1 : \tilde{\mu}_1 < \tilde{\mu}_2$ or $H_1 : \tilde{\mu}_1 \neq \tilde{\mu}_2$.

Let r^+ denote the number of D_j's greater than zero. r^+ follows binomial distribution $B(X : n, p)$ with parameters n and p; where n is the sample size (number of trials) and p is the probability of success or getting a positive (+) D_j.

Thus, we may like to have

Test 1. $H_0 : \tilde{\mu}_1 = \tilde{\mu}_2$ or $p = \frac{1}{2}$

$H_1 : \tilde{\mu}_1 > \tilde{\mu}_2$ or $p > \frac{1}{2}$ (One-tailed test)

Test 2. $H_0 : \tilde{\mu}_1 = \tilde{\mu}_2$ or $p = \frac{1}{2}$

$H_1 : \tilde{\mu}_1 < \tilde{\mu}_2$ or $p < \frac{1}{2}$ (One-tailed test)

Test 3. $H_0 : \tilde{\mu}_1 = \tilde{\mu}_2$ or $p = \frac{1}{2}$

$H_1 : \tilde{\mu}_1 \neq \tilde{\mu}_2$ or $p \neq \frac{1}{2}$ (Two-tailed test)

For Test—1, if P ($X \geq r^+$) is more than α (the significance level), the null hypothesis H_0 is accepted, otherwise reject it. For Test—2, if P ($X \leq r^+$) is more than α, accept H_0, otherwise reject H_0. For Test—3 if P ($X \geq r^+$) is more than $\alpha/2$ (two-tailed test), accept H_0, otherwise reject H_0.

For large n, normal approximation is to be used.

Example 11.6. The hours of relief provided by analgesic drugs in 12 patients suffering from arthritis. Is there any evidence that one drug provides longer relief than the other ?

Case	Drug A	Drug B	Case	Drug A	Drug B
1.	2.0	3.5	7	14.9	16.7
2.	3.6	5.7	8	6.6	6.0
3.	2.6	2.9	9	2.3	3.8
4.	2.6	2.4	10	2.0	4.0
5.	7.3	9.9	11	6.8	9.1
6.	3.4	3.3	12	8.5	20.9

Solution :

H_0 : That the median difference is zero.

H_1 : Drug B provides longer relief.

Compute actual differences (Drug B — Drug A). There are 9 positive differences, *i.e.* $r^+ = 9$.

$$P(X \geq r^+ \mid H_0 \mid) = P(X \geq 9) = 0.019,$$

which is less than 0.05 (level of significance).

Hence, H_0 is rejected and we conclude that Drug B provides longer relief than Drug A.

Note. Sign test is applied to data given as pairs or is comprised of two independent samples that are randomly paired.

11.3.2. Two Sample Wilcoxon signed-rank test (Matched Samples)

Like the paired *t*-test for correlated samples, the Wilcoxon signed rank-test applies to two sample designs involving repeated measures, matched pairs or 'before and after' measures.

This test for paired observations is more powerful than the sign test for paired observations since the former takes into account of the magnitude of the difference between the members of a pair.

Let (X_{1j}, X_{2j}) $j = 1, 2, ..., n$ be a collection of paired observations from continuous distributions that differ only with respect to location parameter mean or median. Assume that the distribution of the differences $D_j = X_{1j} - X_{2j}$ is continuous and symmetric.

To use Wilcoxon signed rank test, the differences are first ranked in ascending order of their ***absolute values*** and then ranks are given the signs of the differences. Ties are assigned average ranks and zero differences are omitted.

Let T^+ = Sum of ranks corresponding to positive differences,

T^- = Sum of negative ranks

and $T = \min(T^+, T^-)$

Let $\Delta = \tilde{\mu}_1 - \tilde{\mu}_2$ = Difference between location parameters for two populations.

For $H_1 : \tilde{\mu}_1 > \tilde{\mu}_2$, reject H_0 at α% level of significance if $T^- < T_{2\alpha}$.

For $H_1 : \tilde{\mu}_1 < \tilde{\mu}_2$, reject H_0 if $T^+ < T_{2\alpha}$.

Further, $H_1 : \tilde{\mu}_1 \neq \tilde{\mu}_2$, reject H_0 if $T < T_\alpha$

Note 1 : $P(T < T_\alpha) = \alpha$.

Note 2 : It may be generally concluded that the Wilcoxon signed rank test will never be much worse than the *t*-test and in many cases where the population is non-normal, it may be superior.

Example 11.7. Considering an example on the hours of relief provided by two analgesic drugs to 12 patients, apply Wilcoxon-signed rank test to test whether drug B provides longer relief.

Solution :

Case	Drug X_B	Drug X_A	$d = X_B - X_A$	$\lvert d \rvert$	Rank	Rank with sign	Remarks
1.	3.5	2.0	+ 1.5	1.5	5.5	5.5	
2.	5.7	3.6	+ 2.1	2.1	9	9	T^+ = Sum of
3.	2.9	2.6	+ 0.3	0.3	3	3	positive
4.	2.4	2.6	—0.2	0.2	2	—2	ranks = 71
5.	9.9	7.3	+ 2.6	2.6	11	11	T^- = Sum
6.	3.3	3.4	—0.1	0.1	1	—1	of negative
7.	16.7	14.9	+ 1.8	1.8	7	7	ranks = 7
8.	6.0	6.6	—0.6	0.6	4	—4	
9.	3.8	2.3	+ 1.5	1.5	5.5	5.5	
10.	4.0	2.0	+ 2.0	2.0	8	8	
11.	9.1	6.8	+ 2.3	2.3	10	10	
12.	20.9	8.5	+ 12.4	12.4	12	12	

$$H_0 : \mu_B = \mu_A, \quad H_1 : \mu_B > \mu_A$$

Now $T^- = 7$, $T_{2\alpha}$ for $\alpha = 0.05 = 17$ (Table A–10)

As $T^- < T_{2\alpha}$, H_0 is rejected and hence drug B is more effective than drug A.

11.3.3. Median test

The Median test is used to test the null hypothesis that the two independent samples are from identical distributions against alternative that they have different location parameters (Median). The alternatives may be either one-sided or two-sided.

Let there be two samples of sizes n_1 and n_2 from two distributions.

Now, order the entire $N = n_1 + n_2$ observations from two samples and determine the combined sample median (m). Then, count the number of observations in two samples that lie below m and the number and those which do not. This classification can be put into a 2 × 2 contigency table.

2 × 2 Contigency Table

Samples	Observations		Total
	$< m$	$\geq m$	
Sample 1	n_{11}	n_{12}	R_1 (= n_1)
Sample 2	n_{21}	n_{22}	R_2 (= n_2)
Total	C_1	C_2	N

If n_1 and n_2 are small we may compute exact probability of the distributions over cells with fixed marginal totals *i.e.* R_1, R_2, C_1 and C_2. This probability is given by

$$P = \frac{R_1\,!\,R_2\,!\,C_1\,!\,C_2\,!}{n_{11}\,!\,n_{12}\,!\,n_{21}\,!\,n_{22}\,!\,N\,!}$$

For moderately large n_1 and n_2 we may compute the, chi square test statistic (as computed for test of independence) such as

$$\chi^2 = \frac{(n_{11}\,n_{22} - n_{12}\,n_{21})^2\,N}{R_1\,!\,R_2\,!\,C_1\,!\,C_2\,!},$$

which is distributed as theoretical Chi-square distribution with 1 degree of freedom. If the computed value of χ^2 exceeds the tabulated value of Chi-square with 1 degree of freedom at α% level of significance, H_0 is rejected.

As regards the computation of exact probability, we compute P for the observed ones in 2 × 2 table and also for less likely distributions (in one direction). Denote the sum of these probabilities as P^*. So the exact probability of getting the observed distributions or less likely ones in either direction is by symmetry, $2P^*$.

If $2P^*$ exceeds α, the chosen level of significance, the null hypothesis cannot be rejected, against two sided alternatives. For one sided alternative P^* is to compared with α.

Example 11.8. Two batches of salesmen obtained the following scores after the final training. Use median test to test the null hypothesis that scores for two batches have come from identical populations having same median, at 5% level of significance.

Batch 1 : 24, 26, 30, 32, 34, 35, 36, 40

Batch 2 : 20, 22, 25, 29, 38

Solution :

From the combined samples the median is computed as 30.

The 2 × 2 contigency table is shown below :

Table 1

Batch	Observations		Total
	< 30	≥ 30	
Batch 1	2	6	8
Batch 2	4	1	5
Total	6	7	13

The exact probability computed from the observed 2 × 2 table is

$$P = \frac{6!\,7!\,8!\,5!}{2!\,6!\,4!\,1!\,13!} = 0.0816$$

Another less likely distribution (in one direction) may be constructed from the observed 2 × 2 table as

Table 2

Batch	Observations		Total
	< 30	≥ 30	
Batch 1	1	7	8
Batch 2	5	0	5
Total	6	7	13

The probability for such a less likely distribution shown in Table 2 is

$$P_1 = \frac{6!\,7!\,8!\,5!}{1!\,7!\,5!\,0!\,13!} = 0.0047$$

The exact probability of getting the observed table or more extreme tables in one direction is therefore

$$P^* = P + P_1 = 0.0816 + 0.0047 = 0.0863$$

So the exact probability of getting the observed distribution or less likely ones in either direction is by symmetry is $2P^*$

$$= 2 \times 0.0863 = 0.1726$$

As $2P^*$ is greater than α *i.e.* 0.05, the null hypothesis fails to be rejected and there is no evidence to suspect the null hypothesis. Hence, the samples have come from two identical populations.

11.3.4 The Wilcoxon Rank sum W-test/Mann-Whitney U-test

Let $X_1, X_2, ..., X_{n_1}$, be a random sample drawn from a population with continuous cumulative distribution function $F_X(x)$ and $Y_1, Y_2, ..., Y_{n_2}$ be another random sample from a different population having continuous distribution function $F_Y(x)$. Two populations are independent.

We are interested in testing the null hypothesis

$H_0 : F_X(x) = F_Y(x)$ for all x, that is, the samples have come from identical/same continuous populations.

The alternatives may be set as

$$H_1 : F_X(x) \neq F_Y(x) \text{ for some } x$$

or

$$H_1 : F_X(x) > F_Y(x) \text{ for some } x$$

Suppose in particular two continuous populations have the same shape and spread, but possibly differ in a location parameter say means. Then we want to test

$$H_0 : \mu_x = \mu_y$$

against

$$H_1 : \mu_x \neq \mu_y$$

or

$$H_1 : \mu_x > \mu_y.$$

Arrange $n_1 + n_2$ observations from lowest to highest and rank them. If two or more observations are tied, then use mean of the ranks that would have been assigned if the observations differed.

Let W_1 and W_2 be the sum of ranks in the first and second samples respectively, *i.e.* sum of ranks assigned to x's and y's respectively. If the null hypothesis is true, the means of ranks assigned to values of two samples would be more or less the same. Instead of comparing the means of ranks, we may compare the sums of the ranks taking into account the difference in the sizes of samples. If there is an appreciable difference between the means of the two populations, most of the lower ranks are likely to go to the values of one sample while most of the higher ranks are likely to go to the values of the other sample. The test statistic may be either W_1 or W_2 and the tests based on W_1 and W_2 are equivalent since

$$W_1 + W_2 = \frac{(n_1 + n_2)(n_1 + n_2 + 1)}{2},$$

or

$$W_2 = \frac{(n_1 + n_2)(n_1 + n_2 + 1)}{2} - W_1$$

When $H_0 : \Delta = \mu_x - \mu_y = 0$ is true, the distribution of W_1 is symmetric about its mean $\frac{n_1(n_1 + n_2 + 1)}{2}$.

For one-sided test of $H_0 : \Delta = 0$ against $H_1 : \Delta > 0$ at the level α, reject H_0 : if $W_2 < W_{\alpha : n_1, n_2}$ where $W_{\alpha : n_1, n_2}$ is the lower 100 α% point of the null distribution of W_2 with sample sizes n_1 and n_2 in Table A–12. We reject H_0 in favour of $H_1 : \Delta < 0$ if $W_1 \leq W_{\alpha : n_1, n_2}$

For two-sided test, we reject H_0 at the level α if $W = \text{Min}(W_1, W_2) < W_{\alpha : n_1, n_2}$

$$E(W_1) = \frac{n_1(n_1 + n_2 + 1)}{2}, \quad V(W_1) = \frac{n_1 n_2 (n_1 + n_2 + 1)}{12}$$

For large samples, we define the test statistic

$$Z = \frac{W_1 - n_1(n_1 + n_2 + 1)/2}{\sqrt{n_1 n_2 (n_1 + n_2 + 1)/12}},$$

which has, under H_0 an asymptotic N(0, 1) distribution as min $(n_1, n_2) \to \infty$.

Mann-Whitney proposed a test with the same assumptions as those of Wilcoxon. Although the test statistics are different, but the tests are equivalent. Wilcoxon test uses ranks while the Mann- Whitney test makes use of a count.

To test $H_0 : \Delta = 0$, Mann and Whitney defined the statistic

$$U = \sum_{i=1}^{n_1} \sum_{j=1}^{n_2} \phi(x_i, y_j)$$

where

$$\phi(x_i, y_j) = \begin{cases} 1 \text{ if } x_i > y_j \\ 0 \text{ otherwise} \end{cases}$$

U_1 is the number of y_j precedes x_i among all (x_i, y_j) pairs. Mann and Whitney showed that in case there are no ties,

$$W_1 = U_1 + \frac{n_1(n_1+1)}{2}$$

$$W_2 = U_2 + \frac{n_2(n_2+1)}{2}$$

Thus, $$U_1 = W_1 - \frac{n_1(n_1+1)}{2}$$

and $$U_2 = W_2 - \frac{n_2(n_2+1)}{2}$$

Hence $$U_1 + U_2 = (W_1 + W_2) - \frac{n_1(n_1+1)}{2} - \frac{n_2(n_2+1)}{2}$$

$$= \frac{(n_1+n_2)(n_1+n_2+1)}{2} - \frac{n_1(n_1+1)}{2} - \frac{n_2(n_2+1)}{2}$$

$$= n_1 n_2.$$

Both U_1 and U_2 lie between 0 and $n_1 n_2$.

For $H_1 : \Delta > 0$, U_1 will tend to be larger than U_2 and hence H_0 is rejected for *large values U_1 or small values U_2*. For $H_1 : \Delta < 0$, we reject H_0 for *small values of U_1*, while for the two-sided alternatives $\Delta \neq 0$, we reject H_0 for small values of min (U_1, U_2) that is, reject H_0, if computed value is less than the tabulated value. We have, $E(U_1) = \frac{n_1 n_2}{2}$ and

$$V(U_1) = \frac{n_1 n_2 (n_1 + n_2 + 1)}{12}$$

For large samples,

$$Z = \frac{U_1 - \frac{n_1 n_2}{2}}{\sqrt{\frac{n_1 n_2 (n_1 + n_2 + 1)}{12}}}$$

has an asymptotic standard normal distribution N(0, 1) as min $(n_1, n_2) \to \infty$ and as such we perform large sample normal test. The critical values of U for different values of n_1 and n_2 (size of large sample) have been tabulated in Tables A–13(*a*) and A–13(*b*).

Example 11.9. The following are the marks secured by two batches of salesmen in the final test taken after the completion of training. Use U-test with $\alpha = 0.02$ to test the null hypothesis that the samples are drawn from identical distributions against the alternative that the distributions differ in location only.

Batch A : 26, 27, 31, 26, 19, 21, 20, 25, 30
Batch B : 23, 28, 26, 24, 22, 19

Solution :

$$n_1 = 6, n_2 = 9$$
$$n = n_1 + n_2 = 15$$

Arrange all the 15 observations in ascending order and rank them.

Batch A(X)*	26 (10)	27 (12)	31 (15)	26 (10)	19 (1.5)	21 (4)	20 (3)	25 (8)	30 (14)
Batch B(Y)*	23 (6)	28 (13)	26 (10)	24 (7)	22 (5)	19 (1.5)			

*Figures in brackets show the ranks of the combined samples.

W_1 = Sum of the ranks for Batch A

$= 10 + 12 + 15 + ... + 14 = 77.5$

W_2 = Sum of the ranks for Batch B

$= 6 + 13 + 10 + ... + 1.5 = 42.5$

Check : $W_1 + W_2 = 77.5 + 42.5 = 120$

which is equal to sum of ranks in the combined samples.

U_1 = number of $X_i > Y_j = 31$

U_2 = number of $X_i < Y_j = 20$

From the Table 13(*a*) and 13(*b*) in Appendix, we find for the larger sample size $n_2 = 9$ and size of the smaller sample $n_1 = 6$ for a two-tailed test at the level 0.02, the critical value is 7.

Since Min $(U_1, U_2) = 20$, which is greater than 7, we have no reason to suspect the null hypothesis. Thus, the null hypothesis is accepted.

W-test

$$W_1 = 77.5$$
$$W_2 = 42.5$$
$$W = \text{Min}(W_1, W_2) = 42.5$$
$$W_{\alpha : 9, 6} = 31, \text{ with } \alpha = 0.05$$

As neither W_1 nor W_2 is less than $W_{0.05}$, the null hypothesis cannot be rejected against two-sided alternatives.

Example 11.10. Many States are considering lowering the blood-alcohol level at which a driver is designated as driving under the influence (DUI) of alcohol. An investigator designed the following test to study the effect of alcohol on reaction time.

Four participants consumed a specified amount of alcohol. Another group of four participants consumed the same amount of non-alcoholic drink, a placebo. The two groups did not know whether they were receiving alcohol or the placebo. The participants' reaction times (in seconds) in a series of simulated driving situations are reported in the following table. Does it appear that alcohol consumption increases reaction time ?

Treatment	Reaction time (seconds)
Alcohol	1.45, 3.07, 1.11, 1.27
Placebo	0.90, 0.37, 0.61, 1.97

Solution :

$$n_1 = n_2 = 4, n = n_1 + n_2 = 8$$

We rank all 8 observations together as

Time	0.37	0.61	0.90	1.11	1.27	1.45	1.97	3.07
Rank	1	2	3	4	5	6	7	8

We see that the reaction times are higher for alcohol group. The idea of rank tests is to look at the rank of the observations. We replace each observation by its rank and we retain as the ordering of observations. We make no other use of numerical values. Working with ranks instead of numerical outcomes, allows us to abandon specific assumptions about the shape of the distribution.

The reduced data set (Ranks) :

Treatment	Reaction time			
Alcohol	6	8	4	5
Placebo	3	1	2	7

If alcohol consumption increases reaction time we expect that the ranks of the reaction times of the alcohol group to be larger than the ranks of the reaction times of the Placebo group.

$$W_1 = \text{Sum of ranks for Alcohol group} = 23$$
$$W_2 = \text{Sum of ranks for Placebo group} = 13$$
$$U_2 = W_2 - \frac{n_2\,(n_2+1)}{2} = 13 - \frac{4\,(4+1)}{2} = 3$$

The critical value of W_2 is $W_{.025}$ (for one sided test) = 10 hence H_0 cannot be rejected (Table A–12).

11.3.5. Two sample Kolmogorov-Smirnov test

Suppose two independent random samples are selected from two continuous populations having distribution functions F and G.

$$F : X_1, X_2, \ldots, X_m$$
$$G : Y_1, Y_2, \ldots, Y_n$$

Denote F_m and G_n as the empirical distribution functions of the x-sample and the y-sample respectively.

We are required to test the null hypothesis that two distributions are identical *i.e.* $H_0 : F(t) = G(t)$ for all t, against two sided alternatives, say, $H_1 : F(t) \neq G(t)$ for some t.

The test statistic according to Kolmogorov and Smirnov is

$$D_{m,n} = \underset{-\infty < t < \infty}{\text{Max}} \;|\, F_m(t) - G_n(t) \,|$$

If the hypothesis is true, one expects the value of D_{mn} to be small, while a large value of D_{mn} may be taken as an indication against the null hypothesis that the distributions are identical.

The two sample K-S test is one of the most useful and general non-parametric methods for comparing two samples, as it is sensitive to differences in both location and shape of the empirical cumulative distribution functions of the two samples.

Example 11.11. The following data represent the life time (hours) of batteries for two different brands :

Brand A : 40, 30, 40, 45, 55, 30

Brand B : 50, 50, 45, 55, 60, 40

Are these brands different with respect to average life ?

Solution :

Apply the Kolmogorov-Smirnov two-sample test to test H_0 : that the population distribution of length of life for the two brands is the same against two sided alternative.

x	$F_6^*(x)$	$G_6^*(x)$	$\lvert F_6^*(x) - G_6^*(x) \rvert$
30	2/6	0	2/6
40	4/6	1/6	3/6
45	5/6	2/6	3/6
50	5/6	4/6	1/6
55	1	5/6	1/6
60	1	1	0

$$D_{6,6} = \underset{x}{\text{Sup}} \mid F_0^*(x) - G_0^*(x) \mid = 3/6$$

The critical value at α = .05 is

$$D_{6,6,0.05} = 4/6 \text{ (Table A–7)}$$

As the computed value does not exceed the tabulated value, we accept H_0 that population distribution for the length of life for the two brands is the same.

11.4. K-Samples tests

There may arise situations when we are interested to compare more than two independent samples (k samples) from k continuous populations. The null hypothesis is that the k independent samples have come from the same or identical populations.

11.4.1. The H-test or the Kruskal-Wallis test

This is a generalization of U-test and it enables to test the null hypothesis that k independent samples have come from the same or identical continuous populations.

The test procedure is to rank all the observations jointly. Let R_i be the sum of the ranks of n_i observations in the ith sample. Let $n_1 + n_2 + ... + n_k = n$.

Construct the statistic

$$H = \frac{12}{n(n+1)} \sum_{i=1}^{k} \frac{R_i^2}{n_i} - 3(n+1),$$

which has an approximate *Chi-square distribution* with (k—1) degrees of freedom.

The calculated H value is to be compared against the Chi-square value with (k—1) degrees of freedom at a given significance level of size α.

If the value of H is more than the tabulated value of Chi-square, then reject the null hypothesis; otherwise accept the null hypothesis.

Example 11.12. The following are the final examination grades of samples from three groups of students who were taught communication English by three different methods—class room instruction and language laboratory, only class room instruction and only self study in language laboratory.

First Method : 94, 88, 91, 74, 87, 97

Second Method : 85, 82, 79, 84, 61, 72, 80

Third Method : 89, 67, 72, 76, 69

Use H-test at the 0.05 level of significance to test the null hypothesis that the three methods are equally effective.

Solution :

Suppose the three populations under consideration may possibly differ in their location parameters, say μ_1, μ_2 and μ_3. Then set up null hypothesis $H_0 : \mu_1 = \mu_2 = \mu_3$ against alternative H_1 : not all of them are equal.

Rank all the 18 observations in ascending order from the lowest to the highest and find the sum of the ranks corresponding to each method. As such, denoting R_1, R_2 and R_3 as sums of ranks for the three methods, we have

$R_1 = 17 + 14 + 16 + 6 + 13 + 18 = 84$

$R_2 = 12 + 10 + 8 + 11 + 1 + 4.5 + 9 = 55.5$

$R_3 = 15 + 2 + 4.5 + 7 + 3 = 31.5$

$n_1 = 6, n_2 = 7$ and $n_3 = 5$; $n = n_1 + n_2 + n_3 = 18$

Now
$$H = \frac{12}{n(n+1)} \Sigma \frac{R_i^{\,2}}{n_i} - 3(n+1)$$

$$= \frac{12}{18 \times 19}\left(\frac{84^2}{6} + \frac{55.5^2}{7} + \frac{31.5^2}{5}\right) - 3 \times 19$$

$$= 6.6662$$

As the calculated value 6.6662 exceeds the tabulated value of χ^2 with $(k - 1) = 2$ degrees of freedom at 5% level of significance *i.e.* 5.991, H_0 is rejected and we conclude that three methods are not equally effective.

Note : The ranks with ties have been replaced by average of the ranks.

The modified formula for H with tied ranks is given by

$$H = \frac{\dfrac{12}{n(n+1)} \Sigma R_i^{\,2}/n_i - 3(n+1)}{1 - \dfrac{\Sigma (T_i^{\,3} - T_i)}{n^3 - n}},$$

where k = number of categories

n = number of cases in the sample

n_i = number of cases in the ith category

R_i = sum of ranks in the ith category

T_i = number of ties in the ith category.

Thus, the revised value of H in the foregoing example is then

$$H = \frac{6.6662}{1 - \dfrac{2^3 - 2}{18^3 - 18}} = \frac{6.6662}{1 - \dfrac{6}{5814}}$$

$$= \frac{6.6662}{1 - 0.001} = 6.6729$$

11.4.2. K-samples Median Test

We have k independent random samples $n_1, n_2, ..., n_k$ from k continuous different populations.

The problem is to test

H_0 : k independent samples are drawn from populations having the same median.

H_1 : Not all the populations have same median.

Procedure

1. Pool the observations in k samples and find the median of the combined observations.
2. Construct a $k \times 2$ contigency table for the pooled observations, showing the number of observations in each sample falling above or below the combined median.

Sample

	1	2	3	....	k	Total
Above Median	n_{11}	n_{21}	n_{31}	....	n_{k1}	$n.1$
Below Median	n_{12}	n_{22}	n_{32}	....	n_{k2}	$n.2$
Total	n_1	n_2	n_3	....	n_k	n

3. Compute the probability

$$P = \frac{{}^{n_1}C_{n_{11}} \quad {}^{n_2}C_{n_{21}} \quad ...... \quad {}^{n_k}C_{n_{k1}}}{{}^{n}C_{n.1}}$$

4. If the computed value of the probability P is more than the level of significance level α, accept the null hypothesis, otherwise reject it.
5. For large samples compute the Chi-square statistic from the k×2 Contigency table. If the computed value of χ^2 exceeds the tabulated value of χ^2 with (k—1) degrees of freedom at α% level of significance, the H_0 is rejected, otherwise accepted.

Example 11.13. The yearly sales revenue of three competing products is shown below :

Yearly Sales Revenue (crores of rupees)

Product 1	Product 2	Product 3
10	8	15
30	25	40
50	45	35
42	38	55
28	32	48

Check whether there is a significant difference between the yearly sales revenues of the three competing products using the median test at a significance level 0.01.

Solution :

H_0 : Samples have come from identical populations having the same median.

H_1 : Samples are not from the populations with the same median.

Arrange all the observations in the samples in increasing order and compute the median. The median is found to be 35. Make $k \times 2$ contigency table as follows :

	Product 1	Product 2	Product 3	Total
Above or equal to Median	2	2	4	8
Below Median	3	3	1	7
Total	5	5	5	15

Compute $$P = \frac{{}^5C_2 \; {}^5C_2 \; {}^5C_4}{{}^{15}C_8}$$

$$= \frac{10 \times 10 \times 5}{9 \times 5 \times 11 \times 13} = 0.078$$

As P is greater than the level of significance 0.01, the null hypothesis is accepted.

EXERCISES

1. Distinguish between parametric and non-parametric tests of hypotheses. Mention their relative merits and demerits.
2. Test the hypothesis that the median of a continuous distribution is $\tilde{\mu} = 15$ against the alternative that $\tilde{\mu} \neq 15$. Ten observations were taken as follows :
   12, 10, 16, 18, 17, 8, 14, 20, 122, 22
3. Suppose 12 consumers were asked to taste cups of tea with tea liquor first added to the cup and milk first added to the cup. The ratings of 12 consumers are given below.

Ratings of Consumers

Tea Liquor First Added to the Cup (A)	25	30	32	38	44	28	35	49	51	34	37	18
Milk First Added to the Cup (B)	20	28	35	40	42	30	32	45	48	29	33	25

Use sign test to test the hypothesis A tastes better than B.

4. The following data indicate the life time of two kinds of electric bulbs, when used continuously.

Brand A	586	641	625	630	590	600	650	540	610	640	635	520
Brand B	620	644	615	570	580	541	670	628	539	649	669	652

Use Mann-Whitney test to test the hypothesis that there is no significant difference between the life times of two brands.

5. The waiting times (in minutes) for 20 patients at a clinic for consultation are given below.
   Test the randomness of the data.
   12, 20, 14, 18, 15, 22, 20, 15, 19, 17, 10, 12, 10, 14, 11, 8, 21, 13, 14, 16

6. Two random samples of 12 boys and 14 girls have the following I.Q's.

Boys	110	112	108	97	99	98	102	105	120	118	114
Girls	100	111	121	123	117	120	115				

Test the hypothesis that the boys and girls are equally intelligent, at the 0.01 level.

7. A die is rolled 50 times and the following table gives the outcomes.

Face Number	1	2	3	4	5	6
Frequency	7	8	9	8	8	10

Test the hypothesis that the die is balanced.

8. (*a*) The marks obtained by the students in a class have the following frequency distribution.

Marks	Less than 40	41–50	51–60	61–70	71–80	81–90	91–100
Number of Students :	5	10	35	20	15	8	5

Test the goodness of fit of normal distribution by pearson's chi-square test and Kolmogorov simirnov statistic.

(*b*) The bust measurements of 100 womern are given below. The mean and standard deviation before classification are 36 and 2 respectively. Test whether or not a normal distribution is a good fit. Can you generalize your findings ?

Measurements	30 or Less	31–32	33–34	35–36	37–38	39 or More
Frequency	10	15	30	30	10	5

9. The percent reduction in cavities due to 3 different tooth pastes is given in the following table :

Brand A	50	42	40	30	35	36	38	29
Brand B	28	34	26	27	31	24		
Brand C	37	32	47	39	33			

Test the hypothesis that all the tooth pastes are equally effective in reducing cavitics. Choose an appropriate level of significance.

10. Emission of gamma particles by a radioctive source at 5 minutes a intervals is given below :

Number of emissions (x)	0	1	2	3	4	5	6	7
Number of 5 Minutes Interval	20	65	50	45	30	20	15	5

Test whether or not a poisson distribution is a good fit.

11. Compare sign test and Mnn-Whitney U test as two methods of non-parametric tests.

12. **Write notes on :**

(*a*) Median test

(*b*) Wilcoxon test.

□□□

CHAPTER 12

ANALYSIS OF VARIANCE

12.1 Introduction

Once experimental data are collected from a properly designed experiment, the next duty of the experimenter is to analyse the data keeping in view the experimental factors under consideration.

The experiments, which are repeatable, are conducted with certain objectives in mind under controlled conditions, as far as possible, in order to draw certain inference from the population based on experimental data, usually few in number.

It is assumed that the observations are results of the effects of multitude of factors controllable and uncontrollable. The factors are also termed as independent variables. The controllable independent variables potentially affect the response variable (dependent variable) whose values are observed. The independent variables which are uncontrollable cannot be set before hand, but only observed as a part of response measurements.

The independent variables (controllable) may either be quantitative such as amount of fertilizers applied to increase crop production, number of I/O operations performed by a job, the percentage of cotton in the fibre affecting the tensile strength of a synthetic fibre, firing temperature affecting the density of a brick, etc. or qualitative such as types of detergents to compare their cleansing action, different types of advertising stimuli to study the shopping propensity, different discount schemes to study their effect on the sales, different methods teaching aids on performance of students, etc.

The controllable factors are sometimes called **treatments**. A particular value of a factor is called a **level.** The uncontrollable factors cause random variations called random errors or experimental errors in the responses and their presence is due to random causes (non-assignable causes), the nature of which can only be guessed or approximated by the experimenter.

The analysis appropriate to the experimental data is carried through the analysis of variance (ANOVA).

> **The analysis of variance essentially consists in partitioning the total variation in an experiment into components ascribable to different sources of variations due to the controllable factors and error.**

The analysis of variane is used to compare the means of more than two populations. It uncovers and studies the main and interaction effects of classification or independent variables on one or more dependent variables. ANOVA has found extensive applications in psychological and agricultural research and can also be used in business management, especially in consumer behaviour and marketing management problems. Industrial experiments may be conducted to identify the source of potential problems in the production process and identify whether variation in measured output values is due to variation between various manufacturing processes, or within them. By varying the factors in a predetermined pattern and analysing the output, one can use statistical techniques to make an accurate assessment as to the cause of variation in-a manufacturing process. Analysis of variance technique is also a useful tool for the social scientist to assess whether the effectiveness of an AIDS Awareness campaign/election campaign varies depending on geographical location, campaign media and usage of celebrities in the campaigns.

12.2 Analysis of Variance Model

The analysis of variance is conducted with the help of a model called *Analysis of variance Model.* The usual model is an *additive model* where the value of a response variable is composed of certain additive components due to different controllable factors and random error. For instance, let us consider the study of the effect of two controllable factors on a response variable. The appropriate analysis of variance model may be put as

$$y_{ij} = \mu + \alpha_i + \beta_j + e_{ij},$$
$$i = 1, 2, \ldots, k$$
$$j = 1, 2, \ldots, r$$

μ = a fixed effect general mean.

α_i = effect of ith level of factor A.

β_j = effect of jth level of factor B.

e_{ij} = random error associated with response corresponding to ith level of A and jth level of B.

Analysis of variance model may be classified as

- Fixed Effect Model
- Random Effect Model
- Mixed Effect Model

In a *fixed effect Model* the effects such as α_i 's and β_j's are unknown constants, also called parameters. In a *random effect model* all effects excepting the additive constant μ are the random variables. Finally, a model in which some of the effects are fixed and some are random variables (excepting the additive constant and random error) is called a *mixed model.*

In the following sections we shall discuss only fixed effect models for one way and two way classified data.

The inferences made from the analysis of variance are :

(*a*) estimation of unknown constants/parameters.

(*b*) testing hypothesis/hypotheses on the parameters.

The estimation of parameters is carried out by the *method of least squares*. The least square estimators provide best linear unbiased estimators, under the assumptions enshrined in the model such as additivity of the effects, linearity of the model, independence and homoscedasity of the errors. However, for the testing of hypotheses on the parameters, that is, the equality of effects, etc. the normality assumption on the random error is required to simplify the test procedures.

12.3 One Way Classified Data (one way analysis of Variance)

When the observations derived from are experiment are classified according to levels of a single factor, such data are called one way classified data. The design of such an experiment is called completely randomised design. In this design the experimental materials/units are supposed to be uniform in nature and different levels of a factor/treatments are applied to groups of exprimental units at random, not necessarily of equal size. The observation on the response variable is assumed to consists of three additive components a general mean effect (fixed), effect of the level of a factor and an effect of random uncontrolled component.

Theoretical formulation :

Let there be k independent random samples of sizes $n_1, n_2, ..., n_k$ from k normal populations.

$$\text{Population } 1 : y_{11}, y_{12}, ..., y_{1n_1}$$

$$\text{Population } 2 : y_{21}, y_{22}, ..., y_{2n_2}$$

$$\vdots \qquad \vdots$$

$$\text{Population } k : y_{k1}, y_{k2}, ..., y_{kn_k}.$$

X_{ij} are all independent normal random variables with means μ_i and the common variance σ^2.

Assume the model

$$y_{ij} = \mu_i + e_{ij};\ i = 1, 2, ..., k, \text{ and } \alpha = 1, 2, ..., n_i$$

μ_i's are constant and $e_{ij} \sim N(0, \sigma_e^2)$.

Further, assume

$$\mu_i = \mu + \alpha_i,\ (i = 1, 2, ..., k),$$

where μ is the grand mean and α_i is the effect of the *i*th level of factor A or say *i*th treatment effect. α_i's are such that $\sum_{i=1}^{k} n_i \alpha_i = 0$.

The null hypothesis under test is

$$H_0 : \mu_1 = \mu_2 = ... = \mu_k \text{ or equivalently } H_0 : \alpha_i = 0 \text{ for all } i.$$

The alternative hypothesis

$$H_1 : \alpha_i \neq 0 \text{ for at least one } i.$$

The total variation in sets of observations is measured by computing Total sum of squares

$$\text{TSS} = \sum_{i=1}^{k} \sum_{j=1}^{n_i} (y_{ij} - \bar{y})^2; \text{ where } \bar{y} = \Sigma\Sigma y_{ij} / \sum_{i=1}^{k} n_i$$

$$= \sum_i \sum_j (\bar{y}_i - \bar{y})^2 + \sum_i \sum_j (y_{ij} - \bar{y}_i)^2,$$

where $\bar{y}_i = \frac{1}{n_i} \sum_{j}^{n_i} y_{ij}$

Thus, $$\text{TSS} = \sum_{i=1}^{k} n_i (\bar{y}_i - \bar{y})^2 + \sum_{i=1}^{k} \sum_{j=1}^{n_i} (y_{ij} - \bar{y}_i)^2$$

= Sum of squares due to treatment (SST)
+ Sum of squares due to error (SSE)

The degrees of freedom (df) carried by SST is $k-1$, because out of deviations $(\bar{y}_i - \bar{y})$ $i = 1, 2, \ldots, k$, only $(k-1)$ are independent. Further, the degrees of freedom carried by SSE is

$$\sum_{i=1}^{k} (n_i - 1) = \sum_{i=1}^{k} n_i - k$$

The mean square due to treatments (MST) is defined as

$$\text{MST} = \frac{\text{SST}}{d.f.} = \frac{\text{SST}}{k-1}$$

and the mean square error is defined as

$$\text{MSE} = \frac{\text{SSE}}{d.f.} = \frac{\text{SSE}}{\Sigma n_i - k}$$

The null hypothesis is tested by computing the ratio

$$F = \frac{\text{MST}}{\text{MSE}},$$

which (under H_0) is distributed as Snedecor's F distribution with $(k-1)$ and $(\Sigma n_i - k)$ degrees of freedom. If the computed value of F exceeds the theoretical/tabulated value of $F_{(k-1), (\Sigma n_i - k)}$ at $\alpha\%$ level of significance, then H_0 is rejected at that level. In practice α is chosen as 0.05 or 0.01. When the H_0 is rejected at 0.01 level, the differences among treatment effects are said to be highly significant. The acceptance of H_0 implies that the given set of observations does not show any evidence against the null hypothesis.

The test of H_0 may also be conducted by summarizing the computations in a analysis of variance table.

Table 12.1 Analysis of Variance

Sources of Variation	Sum of squares	d.f.	Mean squares	F	$F_{5\%}$ or $F_{1\%}$
Due to Treatments	$SST = \Sigma n_i (\bar{y}_i - \bar{y})^2$	$k-1$	$MST = SST/k-1$	$\frac{MST}{MSE}$	
Error	$SSE = \Sigma \Sigma (y_{ij} - \bar{y}_i)^2$	$\Sigma n_i - k$	$MSE = SSE/(\Sigma n_i - k)$		
Total	$\Sigma \Sigma (y_{ij} - \bar{y})^2$	$\Sigma n_i - 1$			

The estimates of μ and α_i are obtained by minimising

$$D = \sum_{i=1}^{k} \sum_{j=1}^{n_i} (y_{ij} - \mu - \alpha_i)^2,$$

with respect to μ and α_i $(i = 1, 2, ..., k)$, using the condition $\sum^{k} n_i \alpha_i = 0$.

The minimising equations (obtained by differentiating D with respect to μ and α_i $(i = 1, 2, ..., k)$) are

$$\Sigma \Sigma y_{ij} = (\Sigma n_i)\mu$$

$$\sum_{j=1}^{n_i} y_{ij} = n_i \mu + n_i \alpha_i \quad (i = 1, 2, ..., k).$$

The solutions of above equations give the estimates of μ and α_i $(i = 1, 2, ..., k)$.

Thus $$\hat{\mu} = \sum_{i=1}^{k} \sum_{j=1}^{n_i} y_{ij} \Big/ \sum_{i=1}^{k} n_i = \bar{y}_{oo}.$$

and $$\hat{\alpha}_i = \bar{y}_{io} - \bar{y}_{oo}, \ (i = 1, 2, ..., k)$$

where $$\bar{y}_{io} = \frac{\sum_{j=1}^{n_i} y_{ij}}{n_i}.$$

Suppose we are interested in testing the equality of two treatment effects, say α_i and α_j. The relevant statistic.

$$t = \frac{\hat{\alpha}_i - \hat{\alpha}_j}{\sqrt{MSE\left(\frac{1}{n_i} + \frac{1}{n_j}\right)}}$$

$$= \frac{\bar{y}_{io} - \bar{y}_{jo}}{\sqrt{MSE\left(\frac{1}{n_i} + \frac{1}{n_j}\right)}}$$

which has Student's t-distibution with error degrees of freedom *i.e.* $\left(\sum_{i=1}^{k} n_i - k\right)$.

If $|t| > t_{\alpha/2, \Sigma n_i - k}$, $H_0 : \alpha_i = \alpha_j$ is rejected at the level α. Alternatively, we compute the critical difference defined by

$t_{\alpha/2, \Sigma n_i - k} \sqrt{\text{MSE}\left(\dfrac{1}{n_i} + \dfrac{1}{n_j}\right)}$, which is called *least significant difference* (l.s.d) and if $|\bar{y}_{io} - \bar{y}_{jo}|$ is greater than *lsd*, then $H_0 : \alpha_i = \alpha_j$ is rejected at the 100 α% level of significance. If n_i's are equal, common *l.s.d.* can be employed.

If F-test in the analysis of variance reveals that the hypothesis cannot be rejected, the test of significance of difference between two treatment means is not required to be undertaken.

Using critical difference (CD) a *bar diagram* can be drawn to show all effects which do not differ among them significantly *one bar*.

Other procedures for testing the significance between two estimated treatment effects are student Newman Keuls range test, Duncan multiple range test, Scheffe's S and T methods, etc. In the following we shall explain only New man-Keuls method. The method runs as follows :

Arrange the estimates of treatment effects in ascending order. To test the significance difference between two estimates of treatment effects compute the absolute difference between two estimates ($\hat{\alpha}_i$ and $\hat{\alpha}_j$) and compare it with upper α percent point of the Student's critical range given by

$$W_t = q_{\alpha, t, p} \sqrt{\frac{\text{MSE}}{n}},$$

where t = number of estimates between two estimates under comparison +2.

p = number of degrees of freedom associated with MSE

n = equal sample of size on which the estimates are based.

When sample sizes are unequal, an approximate average value of n_i's may be employed.

The values of $q_{\alpha, t, p}$ have been given in Table A–17 (*a* and *b*) in the Appendix.

Non-parametric Methods in the Analysis of variance :

In the one way analysis of variance the e_{ij}'s are assumed to be normally and independently distributed with mean zero and variance σ_e^2. These assumptions about the error terms make applicable the F-test in the analysis of variance. If, however, normally assumption is avoided one may apply the Kruskal Wallis test a non parametric alternative to F- test which requires only that e_{ij}'s have the same continuous destribution for all treatments, i = 1, 2, ...k.

Suppose that $n = \sum_{i=1}^{k} n_i$ is the total number of observations.

Rank all the observations from smallest to largest and assign the smallest observation rank 1, the next smallest rank 2 ... and the largest rank n.

If the null hypothesis $H_0 : \alpha_1 = \alpha_2 = \ldots = \alpha_k$ is the the true, n observations come from the same distribution and all possible n ranks to the k samples are equally likely, then we would expect the ranks, 1, 2, ...,n to be mixed throughout the k samples. If the null hypothesis is not true, some samples will consist of observations having predominentely small ranks and other samples will consist of predominentely large ranks.

Let R_{ij} denote the rank of observations y_{ij}. Let

$$R_{i\bullet} = \sum_j R_{ij}, \text{ the total of } n_i \text{ ranks in the } i\text{th treatment and}$$

$$\overline{R}_{i\bullet} = \frac{1}{n_i} \sum_{j=1}^{n_i} R_{ij}$$

Thus, under H_0,

$$E(R_{ij}) = \frac{n+1}{2}$$

and

$$E(\overline{R}_{i\bullet}) = E\left[\frac{1}{n_i} \sum_{j=1}^{n_i} R_{ij}\right]$$

$$= \frac{n+1}{2}.$$

The Krusral- Wallis test measures the divergence of the actual observed average ranks $\overline{R}_{i\bullet}$ from their expected value $\frac{n+1}{2}$. If this difference is large, then the null hypothesis H_0 is rejected.

The test statistic is

$$H = \frac{12}{n(n+1)} \sum_{i=1}^{k} n_i \left(\overline{R}_{i\bullet} - \frac{n+1}{2}\right)^2$$

$$= \frac{12}{n(n+1)} \sum \frac{R_{i\bullet}^2}{n_i} - 3(n+1).$$

For small samples, tables may be prepared for the critical values. For large samples H has approximately a chi-square distribution with $(k-1)$ degrees of freedom.

Thus, for large samples, reject H_0 if

$$H > \chi^2_{\alpha, k-1}$$

at approximate significance level α.

Note : When observations are tied, assign an average rank to each of the tied observations.

Example 12.1 Suppose it is desired to test the effect of computer aided instruction on the performance of M.B.A. students. The students were grouped into three sections A, B, C each having six students. Section–A students were taught in the conventional method, Section B received completely computer aided instructions and Section C were taught in a mixed approach. The following test scores were obtained.

Test at 5% level of significance whether the mean effects of three methods of instructions are the same.

Table 12.2

Sec A	Sec B	Sec C
63	76	86
68	72	74
65	74	77
70	78	84
60	73	79
69	68	75

SOLUTION

$$G = 1311; \frac{G^2}{18} = 95484.5$$

Total sum of squares

$$= \Sigma\Sigma y_{ij}^2 - \frac{G^2}{nk}$$
$$= 96275–95484.5$$
$$= 790.5$$

Between section sum of squares

$$= \sum_{i=1}^{k} \frac{y_{i\bullet}^2}{n} - \frac{G^2}{nk}$$
$$= 96021.833–95484.5$$
$$= 537.333$$

Within sum of squares

= Error sum of squares

= Total sum of squares – between section sum of squares

= 790.5 – 537.333

= 253.167

H_0 : Three methods of instructions have equal mean effect

H_1 : Not all methods of instructions have equal mean effects.

Table 12.3
Analysis of Variance

Source	d.f.	S.S.	M.S.	F	$F_{5\%}$
Between sections	2	537.333	268.6665	15.9183	3.68
Within sections (Error)	15	253.167	16.8778		
Total	17	790.500	–	–	

As $F > F_{0.05, (2, 15)}$ H_0 is rejected.

Now question arises which two sections differ in their mean performances and which do not.

Let the mean performances of three sections be

$\bar{T}_A$	$\bar{T}_B$	$\bar{T}_C$
65.83	73.50	79.17

Arrange the mean performances in increasing order and in the present situation are in ascending order.

Thus, $$l.s.d. = t_{0.05, 15}\sqrt{\frac{2MSE}{6}}$$

$$= 2.131\sqrt{\frac{2 \times 16.8778}{6}}$$

$$= 5.05.$$

It may be seen that all

$$|\bar{T}_A - \bar{T}_B|,\ |\bar{T}_B - \bar{T}_C| \text{ and } |\bar{T}_A - \bar{T}_C|$$

are greater than 5.05.

Hence, there exists significant differences among all pairs of treatment means. It is therefore desirable to choose the method having highest treatment mean (mean performance). In the present example, it is the mixed approach to instruction methods.

Newman-Keuls methods.

Arrange the treatment means in increasing order

$\bar{T}_A$	$\bar{T}_B$	$\bar{T}_C$
65.83	73.5	79.17

Compute the standardised range :

$$\bar{T}_A \text{ vrs } \bar{T}_B : q_{\alpha, t, p}\sqrt{\frac{MSE}{n}}$$

$$= q_{0.05, 2, 15}\sqrt{\frac{16.8778}{6}}$$

$$= 3.01\ (1.6772) = 5.04$$

$$\bar{T}_A \text{ vrs } \bar{T}_C : q_{r, t, p}\sqrt{\frac{MSE}{n}}$$

$$= q_{0.05, 3, 15}\sqrt{\frac{16.8778}{6}}$$

$$= 3.67\ (1.6772) = 6.15$$

$$\bar{T}_B \text{ vrs } \bar{T}_C : q_{\alpha, t, p}\sqrt{\frac{MSE}{n}}$$

$$= q_{0.05,\,2,\,15}\sqrt{\frac{16.8778}{6}}$$
$$= 3.01(1.6772) = 5.04.$$

All pairs of treatment means are significantly different from each other.

Kruskal-Wallis Test.

Rank all observations from smallest to highest. The ranks are shown in the brackets for three sections.

Table 12.4

Sec A	Sec B	Sec C
63 (2)	76 (13)	86 (18)
68 (4.5)	72 (8)	74 (10.5)
65 (3)	74 (10.5)	77 (14)
70 (7)	78 (15)	84 (17)
60 (1)	73 (9)	79 (16)
69 (6)	68 (4.5)	75 (12)
Sum of ranks : 23.5	60	87.5

* Figures inside brackets indicate ranks.

Compute

$$H = \frac{12}{n(n+1)}\sum_{i=1}^{k}\frac{R_{i.}^2}{n_i} - 3(n+1)$$

$$= \frac{12}{18(18+1)}\left[\frac{(23.5)^2}{6} + \frac{60^2}{6} + \frac{(87.5)^2}{6}\right] - 3(19)$$

$$= \frac{12}{342}(1968.0832) - 57$$

$$= 69.0555 - 57 = 12.0555$$

Now $\chi^2_{0.05,\,2} = 5.99$

Hence, H_0 is rejected at 5% level of significance.

12.4 Two way classified Data (Two way analysis of variance)

Suppose we have a two way classified data corresponding to p levels $\alpha_1, \alpha_2, \ldots, \alpha_p$ of factor A and q levels $\beta_1, \beta_2, \ldots, \beta_q$ of factor B. The observations can be represented by the linear model.

$$y_{ij} = \mu + \alpha_i + \beta_j + e_{ij}, \begin{cases} i = 1, 2, \ldots, p \\ j = 1, 2, \ldots, q \end{cases}$$

where μ is an over all mean, α_i is the effect of ith level of A and β_j is the effect of jth level of B. e_{ij}'s are independently and normally distributed with mean zero and variance σ_e^2 for all (i, j).

Some times one of the factors acts like a local control to provide homogeneous conditions/materials for the comparison among the effects of the other factor. For example, suppose that we wish to compare the effect of p different chemicals on the strength of a particular fabric. It is known that the effect of chemicals varies from one specimen fabric to another. Therefore, we may select a number of specimens (q) of fabric and compare all p types of chemicals with in the relatively homogeneous materials provided by each piece of fabric.

The general experimental disign which generates a two way classified data is called a *Randomised block design* or sometimes called a *Randomised complete block design* investigates the p levels of a single factor (A) applied in q blocks which one relatively internally homogeneous. These q blocks may be regarded as the q levels of the second factor (B).

In the present problem suppose we are interested in testing the equality of the effects $\alpha_1, \alpha_2, ..., \alpha_p$.

That is, $H_0 : \alpha_1 = \alpha_2 = ... = \alpha_p = 0$(say) $\quad H_1$: Not all α_i's are equal.

$$\text{Defining } \frac{\Sigma\Sigma y_{ij}}{pq} = \bar{y}_{oo}$$

$$\sum_{j=1}^{q} \frac{y_{ij}}{q} = \bar{y}_{io} \; (i = 1, 2, ..., p)$$

and

$$\sum_{i=1}^{p} \frac{y_{ij}}{p} = \bar{y}_{jo}, \; (j = 1, 2, ..., q)$$

Total sum of squares

$$= \sum_{i=1}^{p}\sum_{j=1}^{q} (y_{ij} - \bar{y}_{oo})^2$$

$$= \Sigma\Sigma(\bar{y}_{io} - \bar{y}_{oo})^2 + \Sigma\Sigma(\bar{y}_{oj} - \bar{y}_{oo})^2 + \Sigma\Sigma(y_{ij} - \bar{y}_{io} - \bar{y}_{oj} + \bar{y}_{oo})^2$$

= Sum of squares due to A

+ Sum of squares due to B

+ Sum of squares due to error.

Symbolically,

$$\text{T.S.S.} = \text{S.S.A} + \text{S.S.B} + \text{S.S.E.}$$

The degrees of freedom of total sum of squares is $pq-1$ which breaks down to $pq-1 = (p-1) + (q-1) + (p-1)(q-1)$, where $(p-1)$, $(q-1)$ and $(p-1)(q-1)$. are degres of freedom of SSA, SSB and SSE respectively.

The null hypothesis

$H_0 : \alpha_i = 0$ for all i or equality of all effectsd $\alpha_1, \alpha_2, ..., \alpha_p$ is tested by the ratio

$$F = \frac{MSA}{MSE},$$

which follows a theoretical F–distribution with $(p-1)$ and $(p-1)(q-1)$ degrees of freedom.

If $F > F_{\alpha}, \{(p-1), (p-1)(q-1)\}$, H_0 is rejected at 100 α % level of significance.

The results of analysis of variance may be summarised in an analysis of variance table (Table 12.5).

Table 12.5 : Analysis of Variance

Source	d.f.	SS	M.S.	F	F5% or F1%
Due to A	$(p-1)$	$SSA = q\Sigma(\bar{y}_{io} - \bar{y}_{oo})^2$	$MSA = \frac{SSA}{p-1}$	$\frac{MSA}{MSE}$	
B	$(q-1)$	$SSB = p\,\Sigma(\bar{y}_{oj} - \bar{y}_{oo})^2$	$MSB = \frac{SSB}{q-1}$	$\frac{MSB}{MSE}$	
Error	$(p-1)(q-1)$	By Subtraction (SSE)	$MSE = \frac{SSE}{(p-1)(q-1)}$	–	
Total	$pq-1$	$\Sigma\Sigma(y_{ij} - \bar{y}_{oo})^2$	–	–	

Computational Forms of Sum of Squares :

Total sum of squares

$$= \sum_{i=1}^{p}\sum_{j=1}^{q}(y_{ij} - \bar{y}_{oo})^2$$

$$= \Sigma\Sigma\, y_{ij}^2 - \frac{G^2}{pq},$$

where
$$G = \sum_{i=1}^{p}\sum_{j=1}^{q} y_{ij}$$

$$S.S.A. = \sum_{i=1}^{p}\sum_{j=1}^{q}(\bar{y}_{io} - \bar{y}_{oo})^2$$

$$= \sum_{i=1}^{p}\frac{y_{i.}^2}{q} - \frac{G^2}{pq}$$

$$S.S.B. = \sum_{i=1}^{p}\sum_{j=1}^{q}(\bar{y}_{oj} - \bar{y}_{oo})^2$$

$$= \sum_{j=1}^{q}\frac{y_{oj}^2}{p} - \frac{G^2}{pq},$$

where
$$y_{io} = \sum_{j=1}^{q} y_{ij}$$

$$y_{oj} = \sum_{i=1}^{p} y_i$$

$$y_{oo} = \Sigma\Sigma\, y_{ij}$$

Test of Hypothesis

To test

$H_{0A}: \alpha_1 = \alpha_2 = \ldots = \alpha_p$ against H_{1A} : Not all α's are equal the test statistic is

$$F = \frac{MSA}{MSE},$$

If $F > F_{\alpha\,(p-1),\,(p-1)(q-1)}$

the H_0 is rejected at 100 α% level of significance.

Further to test

$H_{0B}: \beta_1 = \beta_2 = \ldots = \beta_q$

against H_{1B}: Not all β's are equal the test statistic is

$$F = \frac{MSB}{MSE},$$

If $F > F_{\alpha,\,(q-1),\,(p-1)(q-1)}$,

H_0 is rejected at 100 α% level of significance.

Critical Difference of Least Significant Difference :

The critical difference for testing the difference between estimates of $\hat{\alpha}_i$ and $\hat{\alpha}_j$ is

$$C.D. = t_{\alpha/2,\,(p-1)(q-1)} \sqrt{\frac{2MSE}{q}}$$

Further, the C.D. for testing the significant difference between estimates of $\hat{\beta}_i$ and $\hat{\beta}_j$ is

$$C.D = t_{\alpha/2,\,(p-1)(q-1)} \sqrt{\frac{2MSE}{p}}.$$

Example 12.2 Four different technological alternatives to manufacture a product were tested in four plants and the relevant data consisting of hourly output (in units) corresponding to each technology and plant are noted below.

Investigate whether the output differs according to technologies.

Table 12.6

		Technology			
		T_1	T_2	T_3	T_4
Plant	P_1	73	68	74	71
	P_2	72	57	75	45
	P_3	55	38	68	40
	P_4	75	40	75	72

SOLUTION

Let Y_{ij} be the output corresponding to ith technology and jth plant, i = 1, 2, 3, 4 and j = 1, 2, 3, 4.

Let $$T_i = \sum_{j=1}^{4} Y_{ij}\,;\; i = 1, 2, 3, 4$$

$$P_j = \sum_{i=1}^{4} Y_{ij};\; i = 1, 2, 3, 4.$$

and $$G = \sum_{i=1}^{4} \sum_{j=1}^{4} Y_{ij}$$

$$T_1 = 275\,,\; T_2 = 203\,,\; T_3 = 292\,,\; T_4 = 228,$$

$$P_1 = 286\,,\; P_2 = 249,\; P_3 = 201,\; P_4 = 262,\; G = 998$$

Total sum of squares $= \Sigma\,\Sigma\, Y_{ij}^2 - \dfrac{G^2}{16}$

$$= 65280 - \frac{(998)^2}{16}$$

$$= 65280 - 62250.25$$

$$= 3029.75$$

Sum of squares due to technologies

$$= \sum_{i=1}^{4} T_i^2/4 - \frac{G^2}{16}$$

$$= \frac{254082}{4} - \frac{(998)^2}{16}$$

$$= 63520.5 - 62250.25$$

$$= 1270.25$$

Sum of squares due to plants

$$= \sum_{j=1}^{4} P_j^2/4 - \frac{G^2}{16}$$

$$= \frac{252842}{4} - 62250.25$$

$$= 63210.5 - 62250.25$$

$$= 960.25$$

Table 12.7 : Analysis of variance

Source	d.f.	S.S.	M.S.	F	F5%
Due to :					
Technologies	3	1270.25	423.42	*4.77	3.86
Plants	3	960.25	320.08	3.60	3.86
Error	9	799.25	88.80		
Total	15	3029.75	–	–	–

Analysis shows that the technologies differ significantly with respect to output. But there is no significant difference among the plants.

The critical difference among the technology means ($\overline{T}_i - \overline{T}_j$)..

$$C.D. = t_{0.025,\,9}\sqrt{\frac{2\,MSE}{q}}$$

$$= 2.262\sqrt{88.80\left(\frac{2}{4}\right)} = 15.0724$$

Bar diagram :

$\overline{T}_3$	$\overline{T}_1$	$\overline{T}_4$	$\overline{T}_2$
73	68.75	57	50.75

There are no significant differences between $\overline{T}_3$ and $\overline{T}_1$, $\overline{T}_1$ and $\overline{T}_4$ and $\overline{T}_4$ and $\overline{T}_2$.

12.5 Analysis of Latin Square design :

In the randomised complete block design the restriction is imposed that all treatments/factors must appear together in a block, an equal number of firms rather than being allotted at random over the whole experimental area as in the completely randomised design. For the latin square design, two restrictions are imposed; namely, that for an experimental area divided into rows and columns or along two sources of variation each treatment must appear once in a row and once in a column. Thus, for latin squares, the treatments are grouped into replicates in two ways, once in rows and once in columns. Through the elimination of row and column effects from the within treatment variation, the residual or error variance may be considerably reduced.

Latin square designs have a wide variety of applications in experimental work concerning industrial, agricultural, educational, medical, marketing and sociological experimentation.

		Group on first factor		
		1	2	3
Group on second factor	1			
	2			
	3			

Since the latin square design requires as many replicates as treatments, the design is seldom used for more than ten to tewelve treatments.

With two way stratification or grouping the latin square controls more of the variation than the completely randomized design or the randomised complete block design. As a result of two way elimination of variation, error mean square is often made smaller. Latin square design requires the number of experimental units to be a perfect square and further the number of treatments has to be limited to the number of each way of grouping or alternatively to the number of rows and columns.

An experiment with a latin square design can be conducted with any one of the possible arrangements of the latin squares.

A square is said to be standard of the first row and first column are ordered alphabetically or numerically.

Two standard squares are said to be conjugate if the rows of one are the columns of the other.

A square is self conjugate if its arrangement in rows and columns is the same.

Standard squares :

2 × 2 latin square :

A	B
B	A

3 × 3 latin square.

A	B	C
B	C	A
C	A	B

4 × 4 latin square :

A	B	C	D
B	C	D	A
C	D	A	B
D	A	B	C

A	B	C	D
B	A	D	C
C	D	B	A
D	C	A	B

A	B	C	D
B	D	A	C
C	A	D	B
D	C	B	A

A	B	C	D
B	A	D	C
C	D	A	B
D	C	B	A

For a 2 × 2 latin square there are 2 possible arrangements and for a 3 × 3 latin square there are 3! (3!–1) = 12 arrangements, of which 11 are non-standard squares.

In case of a 4 × 4 latin square, there are 4 standard squares and for each standard square there are 4! (4!–1) ! = 144 possible arrangements, resulting in a total of 576 possible arrangements.

For a 5 × 5 latin square there are 25 standard squares and 6 self conjugate squares, resulting in 56 standard squares. Thus, there are 56 × 5!(5–1)! = 56(2 8 8 0 161,280 possible arrangements.

The number of possible arrangements increases rapidly as the size of the latin square increases.

In designing an experiment as a latin square, one of the possible arrangements is selected at random. Alternatively, say, for a 3 × 3 latin square randomize the arrangement of the three columns and of the last two rows of the standard square and for a 4 × 4 latin square, select one of the four standard squares at random and then randomize the arrangement of columns and the last three rows.

Statistical Analysis. Let Y_{ijk} denote the value corresponding to ith row, jth column and kth treatment. The assumed additive model for a $t \times t$ latin square design is

$$Y_{ijk} = \mu + \rho_i + \gamma_j + \tau_k + e_{ijk} \quad i, j, k = 1, 2, ..., t.$$

μ = general mean effect

ρ_i = the effect of ith raw

γ_j = the effect of jth column

τ_k = the effect of kth treatment

e_{ijk} = random error.

μ, ρ_i, γ_j, and τ_k are fixed constants and e_{ijk}'s are normally and independently distributed with mean zero and constant variance σ_e^2. Assume $\Sigma \rho_i = 0, \Sigma \gamma_j = 0$ and $\Sigma \tau_k = 0$.

Possible hypothesis under test :

$$H_{OR} : \rho_1 = \rho_2 = \ldots = \rho_t$$

H_{1R} : Row means are not all equal

$$H_{OC} : \gamma_1 = \gamma_2 = \ldots = \gamma_t$$

H_{1C} : Column means are not all equal.

$$H_{OT} : \tau_1 = \tau_2 = \ldots = \tau_t$$

H_{1T} : Treatment means are not all equal

Total sum of squares

= Sum of squares due to rows
+ Sum of squares due to columns
+ Sum of squares due to treatments
+ Sum of squares due to error.

Symbolically,

T.S.S. = SSR + SSC + SST + SSE

Computations of sum of squares :

$$\text{T.S.S.} = \Sigma\Sigma\Sigma Y_{ijk}^2 - \frac{G^2}{t^2},$$

$$\text{S.S.R.} = \sum_i \frac{Y_{i\bullet\bullet}^2}{t} - \frac{G^2}{t^2},$$

$$\text{S.S.C.} = \sum_j \frac{Y_{\bullet j\bullet}^2}{t} - \frac{G^2}{t^2},$$

$$\text{S.S.T.} = \sum_k \frac{Y_{\bullet\bullet k}^2}{t} - \frac{G^2}{t^2},$$

where

$$Y_{i\bullet\bullet} = \sum_j \sum_k Y_{ijk},$$

$$Y_{\bullet j\bullet} = \sum_i \sum_k Y_{ijk},$$

$$Y_{\bullet\bullet k} = \sum_i \sum_j Y_{ijk},$$

$$G = \sum_i \sum_j \sum_k Y_{ijk}$$

Table 12.8 : Analysis of variance

Source	degrees of freedom	S.S.	M.S.	F	$F_{5\%}$ or 1%
Due to Rows	$t-1$	S.S.R	$MSR = \frac{SSR}{t-1}$	$\frac{MSR}{MSE}$	
Columns	$t-1$	S.S.C	$MSC = \frac{SSC}{t-1}$	$\frac{MSC}{MSE}$	
Treatments	$t-1$	S.S.T	$MST = \frac{SST}{t-1}$	$\frac{MST}{MSE}$	
Error	$(t-1)(t-2)$	(By Subtraction)	$MSE = \frac{SSE}{(t-1)(t-2)}$		
Total	t^2-1	T.S.S.	–	–	–

Null hypotheses	Test statistics
H_{OR}	$F = \frac{MSR}{MSE}$
H_{OC}	$F = \frac{MSC}{MSE}$
H_{OT}	$F = \frac{MST}{MSE}$

If the calculated value of F exceeds the theoretical value of F with $(t-1)$ and $(t-1)(t-2)$ degrees of freedom at $\alpha\%$ level of significance, then, the corresponding null hypothesis is said to be rejected at that level.

The estimated standard error of a difference between two treatment means is obtained from the formula

$$\sqrt{\frac{2\,(\text{error mean square})}{t}}$$

Example 12.3 A production manager wants to test the efficacy of 4 production machines, ($\mu_1, \mu_2, \mu_3, \mu_4$), 4 operators (A, B, C, D) and 4 brands of raw materials (B_1, B_2, B_3, B_4) as regards hourly production volumes through a Latin square design.

The relevant data are given below. Analyse the data and draw conclusions.

Table 12.9
Brands of raw materials

Machines		B_1	B_2	B_3	B_4
	M_1	A = 12	B = 10	C = 8	D = 15
	M_2	B = 8	C = 6	D = 13	A = 11
	M_3	C = 7	D = 13	A = 11	B = 9
	M_4	D = 10	A = 9	B = 8	C = 7

Let Y_{ijk} be the production volume corresponding to ith machine, jth brand of raw material and kth worker.

SOLUTION

The model of the Latin square design is assumed as

$$Y_{ijk} = \mu + M_i + B_j + W_k + e_{ijk};\ i, j, k = 1, 2, 3, 4,$$

where μ is the overall mean effect,

M_i is the effect of ith machine

B_j is the effect of jth brand of raw materials

W_k is the effect of kth greator e_{ijk} is the random error.

μ, M_i, B_j and W_k are the fixed effects and $e_{ijk} \sim N(0, \sigma_e^2)$

Assume further $\sum_i M_i = \sum_j B_j = \sum_k W_k = 0.$

Hypotheses under test are :

$$H_{OM} : M_1 = M_2 = M_3 = M_4$$

against H_{1M} : Not all M's are equal

$$H_{OB} : B_1 = B_2 = B_3 = B_4$$

against H_{1B} : Not all B's are equal

$$H_{OW} : W_1 = W_2 = W_3 = W_4$$

against H_{1W} : Not all W's are equal.

Now,

$$G = Y_{\bullet\bullet\bullet} = \sum_i \sum_j \sum_k Y_{ijk} = 157$$

$$Y_{1\bullet\bullet} = 45\ Y_{2\bullet\bullet} = 38\ Y_{3\bullet\bullet} = 40\ Y_{4\bullet\bullet} = 34$$

$$Y_{\bullet 1\bullet} = 37\ Y_{\bullet 2\bullet} = 38\ Y_{\bullet 3\bullet} = 40\ Y_{\bullet 4\bullet} = 42$$

$$Y_{\bullet\bullet 1} = 43\ Y_{\bullet\bullet 2} = 35\ Y_{\bullet\bullet 3} = 28\ Y_{\bullet\bullet 4} = 51$$

where $$Y_{i\bullet\bullet} = \sum_j \sum_k Y_{ijk}$$

$$Y_{\bullet j\bullet} = \sum_i \sum_k Y_{ijk}$$

$$Y_{\bullet\bullet k} = \sum_i \sum_j Y_{ijk}$$

Total sum of squares

$$= \sum \sum \sum Y_{ijk}^2 - \frac{G^2}{16}$$

$$= (12)^2 + (10)^2 + (8)^2 + (15)^2 + (8)^2 + (6)^2 + (13)^2 + (11)^2 + \ldots + (10)^2 + (9)^2 + (8)^2 + (7)^2 - \frac{(157)^2}{16}$$

$$= 1637 - 1540.5625 = 96.4375$$

Sum of squres due to machines

$$= \sum_{i=1}^{4} \frac{Y_{i\bullet\bullet}^2}{4} - \frac{G^2}{16}$$

$$= \frac{(45)^2 + (38)^2 + (40)^2 + (34)^2}{4} - \frac{(157)^2}{16}$$

$= 1556.25 - 1540.5625$

$= 15.6875$

Sum of squares due to brands of raw materials

$$= \sum_i \sum_k \frac{Y^2_{\bullet j \bullet}}{4} - \frac{G^2}{16}$$

$$= \frac{(37)^2 + (38)^2 + (40)^2 + (42)^2}{4} - \frac{(157)^2}{16}$$

$= 1544.25 – 1540.5625$

$= 3.6875$

Sum of squares due to workers

$$= \sum_i \sum_j \frac{Y^2_{\bullet\bullet k}}{4} - \frac{G^2}{16}$$

$$= \frac{(43)^2 + (35)^2 + (28)^2 + (51)^2}{4} - \frac{(157)^2}{16}$$

$= 1614.75 - 1540.5625$

$= 74.1875$

Sum of squares due to error

= Total sum of squres
– Sum of squares due to machines
– Sum of squares due to brands of raw materials
–Sum of squares due to workers.

$= 96.4375 – 15.6875 – 3.6875 – 74.1875$

$= 2.8750$

Table 12.10 : Analysis of Variance

Source	d.f.	S.S.	M.S.	F	$F_{5\%}$
Due to : Machines	3	15.6875	5.2292	10*.912	4.76
Brands	3	3.6875	1.2292	2.565	4.76
Workers	3	74.1875	24.7292	51.605	4.76
Error	6	2.8750	0.4792		
Total	15	96.4375			

*indicates significant at 5% level.

Conclusion : The null hypotheses H_{OM} and H_{OW} are rejected at 5% level of significance. As such there exist significant differences among the machines and workers.

Further, the brands of raw materials do not differ significantly as the correspoding F-ratio is less than the theoretical value of F with 3 and 6 degrees of freedom at 5% level of significance.

The estimated standard error of a difference between two means corresponding to two workers from the formula

$$= \sqrt{\frac{2\text{ (error mean square)}}{t}}$$

$$= \sqrt{\frac{2(0.4792)}{4}}$$

$$= \sqrt{0.2396} = 0.4895$$

The means of workers are :

$$\overline{T}_A = 10.75$$

$$\overline{B}_B = 8.75$$

$$\overline{T}_C = 7.0$$

$$\overline{T}_D = 12.75$$

The ordered worker means are :

$\overline{T}_D$	$\overline{T}_A$	$\overline{T}_B$	$\overline{T}_C$
12.75	10.75	8.75	7.0

The critical difference between two means is

$$t_{0.05,\,6}\sqrt{\frac{2\text{ (error mean square)}}{t}}$$

$$= (1.943)\ (0.4895) = 0.9511$$

The comparison of the observed difference between means of two workers with the critical difference shows that all workers differ significantly among themselves.

As regards the effect of machines, it may be seen that the effects of M_2 and M_3 do not differ significantly. (The standard error of the difference between two machine means is the same as the standard error of the difference between two worker means *i.e.* $\sqrt{\frac{2\text{(error mean square)}}{t}} = 0.4895$.)

Efficiency of Latin Squares

It may be of importance whether row classification or column classification or both have lead to increased precision in the experiment. Let us write down the mean squares in a general analysis of variance table

Table 12.11

Due to	d.f.	Mean square
Rows	$t-1$	R
Columns	$t-1$	C
Treatments	$t-1$	T
Errors	$(t-1)\ (t-2)$	E
Total	$t^2 - 1$	

The efficiency of Latin squares relative to randomised blocks made up by rows is estimated by $\frac{C+(t-1)E}{tE}$

Similarly, the relative efficiency of the Latin square to randomised blocks made up of columns is estimated by $\frac{R+(t-1)E}{tE}$.

The relative efficiency of the Latin square relative to complete or unrestricted randomisation is estimated by $\frac{R+C+(t-1)E}{(t+1)E}$.

12.6 Analysis of Factorial Experiements

For testing a number of treatments, not necessarily related to each other, experiments may be conducted with one of the basic experimental designs such as completely randomised design, Randomised complete block design and Latin square design. For example, if we are interested to study effect of different production processes on production, different advertisement techniques on sales, different methods of training/teaching methods on performances, different type brands on tread loss, different types of companies as regards their quarterly averages of the earnings per share (EPS), regional differences on sales, different fertilizers on yield, different varieties of paddy on quantity produced, etc. we may use one of the basic designs.

Sometimes we come across treatments/factors which are applied at two or more levels in combination with levels of other factors.

Such combinations of the levels of different factors are called factorial treatment combinations. It is frequently observed that several factors may effect the characteristic in which we are interested and we wish to estimate the effects of each of the factors and how the effect of one factor varies over the level of other factors.

Thus, the question arises whether we should study one factor at a time at different levels, keeping other factors at constant level or alternatively study several factors simultaneously and estimate characteristic for each combination of the factors. The former proceedure is required to establish a law and the later are to suggest possible response relations and to solve many technological problems, besides studying main effects of the factors and interaction effect among factors. The choice between the two procedures is largely a quesion of the nature and stage of the research.

Factorial experiments are experiments which incude all combinations of several different sets of treatments or "factors". Information is thus simultaneously obtained on the responses to different factors, and also on the effects of changes in the level of each factor on the responses to others.

If the effects of some or all of the factors vary with changes in the other factors, the factors are said to interact. The estimates obtained from a factorial experiment will be the average of the effects of each factor in conjunction with the different levels of other factors. At the same time estimates of the actual amount of the variation may be obtained by taking the differences of the effects of one factor at the different levels of other factors. In such circumstances a set of experiments involving single factors will lead to misleading results to an extent depending on the degree of variation in the effects.

2^2 Factorial experiment

Suppose there are two factors a and b, each at two levels (a_0, a_1) and (b_0, b_1) respectively. This results in $2 \times 2 = 2^2$ factorial experiment. The 4 factorial treatment combinations are

$$a_0b_0,\ a_0b_1,\ a_1b_0 \text{ and } a_1b_1.$$

The average effect of the factor 'a' called the **main effect A** is estimated by

$$A = \frac{1}{2}\{(a_1b_1 - a_0b_1) + (a_1b_0 - a_0b_0)\}$$

or symbolically,

$$A = \frac{1}{2}(a_1 - a_0)(b_1 + b_0).$$

Similarly, the average effect of the factor 'b', termed as **main effect B** is estimated by

$$B = \frac{1}{2}\{(a_1b_1 - a_1b_0) + (a_0b_1 - a_0b_0)\} \text{ and symbolically represented as}$$

$$B = \frac{1}{2}(a_1 + a_0)(b_1 - b_0)$$

If there is no effect of the factor 'b' on factor 'a', then $(a_1b_1 - a_0b_1)$ should be the same as $(a_1b_0 - a_0b_0)$. If these two differences differ, there is said to be **interaction** between the factor 'a' and factor 'b', which is measured by

$$AB = \frac{1}{2}[\text{effect of '}a\text{' at the level } b_1 - \text{effect of '}a\text{' at the level } b_0]$$

$$= \frac{1}{2}[(a_1b_1 - a_0b_1) - (a_1b_0 - a_0b_0)]$$

$$= \frac{1}{2}[a_1b_1 - a_0b_1 - a_1b_0 + a_0b_0], \text{ symbolically written as } \frac{1}{2}(a_1 - a_0)(b_1 - b_0)$$

Note : While estimating the main effect and interaction it may be noted that the addition and substraction operations are carried out **not** with the treatment combinations, but with the responses attached to the treatment combinations.

It may be verified that

$$BA = \frac{1}{2}[\text{effect of '}b\text{' at the level } a_1 - \text{effect of '}b\text{' at the level } a_0]$$

$$= \frac{1}{2}[(a_1b_1 - a_1b_0) - (a_0b_1 - a_0b_0)]$$

$$= \frac{1}{2}[a_1b_1 - a_1b_0 - a_0b_1 + a_0b_0]$$

$$= AB$$

It may be seen that A, B and AB are estimated by three **mutually orthogonal contrasts** such as

$$(A):\ +a_1b_1 + a_1b_0 - a_0b_1 - a_0b_0$$

$$(B):\ +a_1b_1 - a_1b_0 + a_0b_1 - a_0b_0$$

$$(AB):\ +a_1b_1 - a_1b_0 - a_0b_1 + a_0b_0$$

Note : (*i*) A linear function of observations $(X_1, X_2, \ldots X_n)$

$$C_1X_1 + C_2X_2 + \ldots + C_nX_n$$

is said to be a contrast, if $\sum_{i=1}^{n} C_i = 0$

(*ii*) The contrasts $C_1X_1 + C_2X_2 + \ldots + C_nX_n$ and $d_1X_1 + d_2X_2 + \ldots + d_nX_n$ are said to be orthogonal if $\sum_{j=1}^{n} C_i d_i = 0$.

$$\text{Sum of squares due to A} = \frac{(\text{Contrast determining A})^2}{\text{Sum of squares of the coefficients in the contrast.}}$$

$$= \frac{\{[a_1b_1] + [a_1b_0] - [a_0b_1] - [a_0b_0]\}^2}{4}$$

where $[a_1b_1]$ denotes the response corresponding to the treatment combination (a_1b_1), ... and so on.

Similarly, the sums of squares due to B and AB can be derived.

Sum of squares due to B

$$= \frac{\{[a_1b_1] - [a_1b_0] + [a_0b_1] - [a_0b_0]\}^2}{4}$$

Sum of squares due to AB

$$= \frac{\{[a_1b_1] - [a_1b_0] - [a_0b_1] + [a_0b_0]\}^2}{4}$$

Total sum of squares, representing variation in a set of four observations is defined by

$$\text{T.S.S.} = [a_1b_1]^2 + [a_1b_0]^2 + [a_0b_1]^2 + [a_0b_0]^2$$

$$- \frac{\{[a_1b_1] + [a_1b_0] + [a_0b_1] + [a_0b_0]\}^2}{4}$$

It may be verified that

$$\text{T.S.S.} = \text{S.S.A} + \text{S.S.B} + \text{S.S.AB}.$$

T.S.S. carries 3 degrees of freedom. S.S.A., S.S.B and S.S. AB carry one degree of freedom each.

No degrees of freedom is left to estimate error. This happens because there is no replication for the treatment combinations in the 2^2 factorial experiment. Hence, the tests of null hypotheses

H_{OA} : There is no effect of A

H_{OB} : There is no effect of B.

H_{OAB} : There is no effect of AB.

cannot be made in practice. This requires replication of the 2^2 factorial experiment.

Now consider the analysis of a 2^2 experiment with r replications, conducted in a randomised block design.

The sum of squares for the main effects and interactions from r replicates are :

$$\frac{[A]^2}{4r} = \frac{[(A)_1-(A)_0]^2}{4r}$$

$$[B]^2/4r = \frac{[(B)_1-(B)_0]^2}{4r}$$

and $$[AB]^2/4r = \frac{[(AB)_0-(AB)_1]^2}{4r},$$

where
$$(A)_0 = a_0b_0 + a_0b_1$$
$$(A)_1 = a_1b_0 + a_1b_1$$
$$(B)_0 = a_0b_0 + a_1b_0$$
$$(B)_1 = a_0b_1 + a_1b_1$$
$$(AB)_0 = a_0b_0 + a_1b_1$$
$$(AB)_1 = a_0b_1 + a_1b_0$$

Table 12.12 Analysis of variance

Source	d.f.	S.S.	M.S.	F
Due to : Replication	$r-1$	$\Sigma R_i^2/4 - G^2/4r$		
A	1	$[A]^2/4r$,	SSA/1	MSA/MSE
B	1	$[B]^2/4r$	SSB/1	MSB/MSE
AB	1	$[AB]^2/4r$	SSAB/1	MSAB/MSE
Error	$3(r-1)$	By subtraction	SSE/$3(r-1)$	
Total	$4r-1$	$\sum_{i=1}^{r}\sum_{j=1}^{4} y_{ij}^2 - \frac{G^2}{4r}$	G being the grand total of observations.	

The F-ratios are compared with the tabulated (theoretical) F values with 1 and $3(r-1)$ degrees of freedom at a chosen α level of significance either to reject or to accept the hypotheses under consideration.

When the number of factors is large, the treatment combinations also become large in number and hence the computation of sum of squares for main effects and interaction become more cumbersome. To simplify the computations one may use Yate's algorithm for the purpose.

Let us rename the treatment combinations in 2^2 experiment

$$(a_0b_0) \to (1)$$
$$(a_1b_0) \to a$$
$$(a_0b_1) \to b$$
$$(a_1b_1) \to ab$$

and form the Yate's table as follows

Table 12.13

Treatment Combinations	Col 1	Col 2	Effect Total
(1)	(1) + a	(1) + a + b + ab	G
a	$b + ab$	a–1 + ab–b	[A]
b	a–1	$b + ab$–(1) –a	[B]
ab	ab–b	ab–b–a + 1	[AB]

The column 1 has four entries. The first entry is obtained by adding first two observations and the second entry by adding next two observations. The third entry is obtained by subtracting first observation from the second and the fourth entry by subtracting third observation from the fourth. The column 2 is obtained by the similar procedure. The second column provides the effect totals as mentioned.

Note. While writing treatment combinations for the application of Yates' algorithm, an order should be followed in the sense that lower case letters corresponing to factors should be introduced one at a time, followed by their combinations with the previous entries. For instance, for a 2^2 factorial experiment, with two factors a and b the treatment combinations in order are (1),. a, b, ab; for a 2^3 factorial experiments with three factors a, b and c, the treatment combinations are (1), a, b, ab, c, ac, bc, abc, for a 2^4 factorial experiments with four factors a, b, c, d, the treatment combinations are (1),a, b, ab, c, ac, bc, abc, d, ad, bd, abd, acd, bcd, $abcd$.

Example 12.4. A company wishes to assess the contribution of its employees in a 0–10 scale in terms of value addition to its business operations. In this connection, the UG qualification and work experience of the employees are considered to be the factors.

The corresponding ratings of the employees are shown in the following Tables.

Replication–1

		UG degree	
		Engineering a_0	Commerce a_1
Work experience	Less than 5 years b_0	5	4
	5 years and above b_1	9	6

Replication–2

		UG degree	
		Engineering a_0	Commerce a_1
Work Experience	Less than 5 years b_0	6	4
	5 years and above b_1	10	7

Replication–3

		UG degree	
		Engineering a_0	Commerce a_1
Work experience	Less than 5 yeras b_0	6	5
	5 year and above b_1	9	8

Analyse the experiment using Yates' algorithm and draw your conclusions.

SOLUTION

The data relate to a 2^2 factorial experiment conducted in randomised block design with three replications. The factors are :

a : UG degree–Engineering degree (a_0) and commerce degree (a_1)

b : Work experience – Less than 5 years (b_0) and 5 years and above (b_1).

Observed totals (over three replications)

$(a_0b_0) \rightarrow (1) = 17$

$(a_1b_0) \rightarrow a = 13$

$(a_0b_1) \rightarrow b = 28$

$(a_1b_1) \rightarrow ab = 21$

Grand total G = 79

r = number replications = 3

Table 12.14

Yates Algorithm

Treatment Combinations Col 1	Observed total Col 2	Col 3	Col 4	Effect Total
(1)	17	30	79	G
a	13	49	–11	[A]
b	28	–4	19	[B]
ab	21	–7	–3	[AB]

Total sum of squares

$$= \sum\sum\sum y_{ijk}^2 - \frac{G^2}{r.2^2}$$

$$= 565 - \frac{79^2}{12}$$

$$= 565 - 520.083 = 44.917$$

Replication totals :

$R_1 = 24.$

$R_2 = 27$

$R_3 = 28$

Sum of squares due to replications

$$= \frac{R_1^2 + R_2^2 + R_3^2}{4} - \frac{G^2}{r.2^2}$$

$$= \frac{(24)^2 + (27)^2 + (28)^2}{4} - 52.083$$

$$= 522.250–52.083 = 2.167.$$

Sum of squares due to A

$$= \frac{[A]^2}{r.2^2} = \frac{(-11)^2}{12} = 10.083$$

Sum of squares do to B

$$= \frac{[B]^2}{r.2^2} = \frac{(19)^2}{12} = \frac{361}{12} = 30.083$$

Sum of squares due to AB

$$= \frac{[AB]^2}{r.2^2} = \frac{(-3)^2}{12} = 0.750$$

Error sum of squares

= Total sum of squares
– Sum of squares due to replications
– Sum of squares due to A
– Sum of squares due to B
– Sum of squares due to AB
= 44.917 – 2.167–10.083–30.083
–0.750 = 1.834

Table 12.15
Analysis of Variance

Source	Degree of Freedom	S.S.	M.S.	F	$F_{5\%}$
Due to : Replications	2	2.167	1.084	3.54	5.14
A	1	10.083	10.083	32*.951	5.99
B	1	30.083	30.083	98*.310	5.99
AB	1	0.750	0.750	2.451	5.99
Error	6	1.834	0.306		
Total	11	44.917	–		

Conclusions : (*i*) Effects of replications are not significant.

(*ii*) The main effects A and B are significant.

(*iii*) The interaction effect AB is not significant.

Thus, there is significant effect of under graduate degree as well as that of the work experience and further the interaction effect undergraduate degree with work experience is not significant.

EXERCISES

1. What is analysis of variance ? Explain its utility in statistical analysis. Suggest its application in solving business decisions.
2. What are models in analysis of variance ? How does it help in analysis data ? Explain.
3. What are the types of models used in analysis of variance ? Explain with examples.
4. Explain the inferences made from the analysis of variance.
5. Distinguish between analysis of one way and two way classified data.
6. Explain the theoretical formulation of one way analysis of variance and structure of analysis of variance table.
7. What are the assumptions, made in the analysis of variance ? Discuss.
8. State the null hypothesis in two way analysis of variance and explain how it is tested.
9. The output of 4 workers on 5 days of a week from Monday to Friday are given below,

   W_1 : 22, 26, 25, 29, 31
   W_2 : 25, 22, 27, 26, 28
   W_3 : 26, 24, 31, 32, 35
   W_4 : 28, 21, 30, 30, 25

   Use analysis of variance technique to test whether there is significant difference among the weekly average out put of four workers.
10. State the model with assumptions used for analysing data from a Randomised Block Design. Give the structure of the analysis of variance table and the related tests.
11. The following are the cholesterol contents in milligrams per package, which four laboratories obtained for packages of three similar diet foods.

		Diet food		
		A	B	C
Laboratories	1	3.4	2.6	2.8
	2	3.0	2.7	3.1
	3	3.3	3.0	3.4
	4	3.5	3.1	3.7

Analyse the data with a two way analysis of variance and test the null hypotheses concerning the diet foods and the laboratories at the 0.05 level of significance.

11. Three varities of paddy A, B, C were treated with four different fertilizers 1, 2, 3 and 4.
    The yields of paddy per plot in kg. were as under :

Fertilizers	Varieties of Paddy		
	A	B	C
1	55	72	67
2	64	66	53
3	58	68	65
4	52	57	58

Perform an analysis of variance of the data and interpret the results.

12. **A company recruited 5 salesmen, who were sent to 4 different regions for selling cosmetics. The sales in thousand rupees per month are given below.**

		Sales men				
		A	B	C	D	E
Regions	R_1	30	25	28	35	40
	R_2	28	35	32	45	42
	R_3	32	30	30	29	35
	R_4	50	55	45	35	50

Carry out an analysis of variance and draw conclusions.

13. **The yields of number of test plots under 3 different fertilizers are given below. Test the hypothesis that all the fertilizers are equally effective as far as the yields are concerned.**

A	31, 28, 32, 30, 31, 28, 31
B	32, 35, 35, 36, 29, 30
C	35, 30, 29, 27, 28

14. **The percentage reduction in cavities due to 3 different toothpastes is given in the following table.**

Brand A	50, 29, 28, 29, 45, 42, 30, 35
Brand B	28, 33, 31, 30, 41, 41, 28
Brand C	30, 32, 31, 28, 47, 31

Test the hypothesis that all the toothpastes are equally effective in reducing cavities.

Choose an appropriate size of the critical region for the problem.

15. What is a latin square design ? How does it differ from a Randomised complete Block Design ? State its limitations.

Give the structure of the analysis of variance table and related tests of significance.

16. Under a faculty improvement programme of the University Grants Commission four faculty experts (A, B, C and D) were involved in the programme consists of four subjects and four batches of young faculty members. Average performance of the participants were computed on a 0–10 scale.

Batch

Subject	1	2	3	4
1	A 10	B 6	C 6	D 5
2	B 7	C 6	D 5	A 5
3	C 2	D 3	A 6	B 4
4	D 6	A 5	B 3	C 4

(*a*) Identify the design and write down the model.

(*b*) Analyse the data and draw conclusions.

16. Differentiate among Completely Randomised Design, Randomised Complete Block Design and Latin square Design and mention their respective spheres of application.

17. What are factorial experiments ? Mention their advantages over experiments where one factor is experimented at a time. Write down contrasts for a 2^2 factorial experiment.

18. For a factorial experiment with three factors N, P and K each at two levels, the design and yield per plot are given below. Analyse the experiment.

Replicate 1

(1)	*pk*	*nk*	*np*	*n*	*k*	*npk*	*p*
25	24	32	30	25	24	35	27

Replicate 2

(1)	*pk*	*np*	*nk*	*k*	*n*	*npk*	*p*
28	24	29	32	34	29	33	30

Analyse the data and draw conclusions.

19. Performance of executives in two business organisations were studied with three factors each at two levels. The factors are

Sex : Male, Female (M,F)

Educational Qualification : Engineering degree with and without management degree (E, EM)

Experience : Below three years and above three years (W1, W2)

Performances were assessed in a 0–10 scale.

Organisation 1

	E		EM	
	Male	Female	Male	Female
W_1	5	5	6	5
W_2	6	5	8	7

Organisation 2

	E		EM	
	Male	Female	Male	Female
W_1	6	5	6	6
W_2	7	7	7	8

Analyse the data using Yates' algorithm and draw inferences.

20. Describe Yates' algorithm and structure of analysis of variance table.

□□□

CHAPTER

13

CORRELATION AND REGRESSION ANALYSIS

13.1 Introduction

In social science research and also in its extension to business research, we come across certain variables which seem to have statistical relationship/association among them, for example, between age of husband and age of wife, height of father and height of son; family income and percentage spent on food items, sales revenue and advertising expenditure, price and sales, aptitude score and productivity index of workers in a factory, price and demand, price and supply, age and sum assured, rainfall and yield, etc. Thus, the relationship between two or more variables is termed as **correlation**, which may also be considered as **covariation** among variables.

'Association' also refers to relationship between two variables and has given rise to a wide variety of coefficients which measure **the strength of relationship.** However, we use the term 'association' to describe relationship between two variables in which at least one of the variables is dichotomous, nominal or ordinal. **Correlation is a type of association when both the variables are measured in interval/ratio scale.** The concept of correlation is a subset of the concept of association.

Most coefficients of association vary from 0 (indicating no relationship) to 1 (indicating perfect positive relationship) or to –1 (indicating perfect negative relationship).

Measures of association may be differentiated as to whether they are :

- Symmetric or Asymmetric
- Directional or Nondirectional
- PRE (Proportional Reduction in Error) or Not PRE.

Symmetric indicates measures of association that produces the same result regardless of which of the two variables is independent and which is the dependent variable. Asymmetric indicates measure of association where the researcher has to pay attention to which is the independent and which is the dependent variable.

Directional refers to a measure of association that can produce positive and negative results. Most of the meaures of association are directional. Nondirectional refers to a measure of association that cannot detect the direction of an association. A measure of association designed for use with nominal data will be nondirectional because a nominal scale of measurement generates data which do not indicate rankings (i.e. no direction).

Proportional Reduction in Error (PRE) measures are essentially ratios of a measure of error in predicting the values of one variable based on the knowledge of that variable and the same measure of error applied to prediction based on the knowledge of an additional variable. That is,

$$\text{PRE} = \frac{\left(\begin{array}{c}\text{No. of errors using}\\ \text{one variable}\end{array}\right) - \left(\begin{array}{c}\text{No. of errors using}\\ \text{one more variable}\end{array}\right)}{\text{No. of errors using one variable}}$$

PRE is a desirable characteristic that all measures should possess and help us to interpret the results more meaningfully.

Concept of Concordance

The bivariate random variable pairs (X_i, Y_i) and (X_j, Y_j) are said to be concordant if $(X_i - X_j)(Y_i - Y_j) > 0$,

i.e. X and Y change in the same direction.

The pairs are said to be **discordant** if

$$(X_i - X_j)(Y_i - Y_j) < 0$$

i.e. X and Y change in the opposite direction :

For **tied** pairs

$$(X_i - X_j)(Y_i - Y_j) = 0$$

i.e. either $X_i = X_j$ or $Y_i = Y_j$ or both factors are zero.

Let us consider joint distribution of two variables X and Y. Let X be an independent variable with **three** values and let Y be a dependent with **two** values, with *a*, *b*, ..., *f* being the cell counts in the resulting table, illustrated below.

		x		
		1	2	3
y	1	*a*	*b*	c
	2	*d*	e	f

Type of Pair	Number of Pairs	Symbols
Concordant	$a(e+f)+b(f)$	P
Discordant	$c(d+e)+b(d)$	Q
Tied on X	$ad+be+cf$	X_0
Tied on Y	$a(b+c)+bc+d(e+f)+ef$	Y_0

The measures of association may be classified according to underlying concepts involved in the computation. These are :

1. Chi-square based measures :

❒ Phi

❒ Contingency coefficient C

❒ Cramer' V, etc.

2. Concordance based measures :
- ❒ Gamma (Goodman–Kruskal's gamma)
- ❒ Somer's *d*
- ❒ Kendall's Tau–*b* and Tau–*c*, etc.

3. Rank based measures :
- ❒ Spearman's Rank Correlation Coefficient.
- ❒ Kendall's Rank Correlation Coefficient.

4. PRE measures :
- ❒ Lambda (λ)
- ❒ Goodman–Kruskal's Tau
- ❒ Uncertainty Coefficient.

5. Product moment measure :
- ❒ Pearson's Correlation Coefficient (*r*)

The measures of association may also be classified according to measurement scales–Nominal, Ordinal, Interval, Ratio.

* Nominal by Nominal
- ❒ Phi (ϕ)
- ❒ Contingency Coefficient C
- ❒ Cramer's V
- ❒ Goodman–Kruskal Tau. (τ)
- ❒ Lambda (λ)

* Ordinal by Ordinal
- ❒ Gamma
- ❒ Yule's Q
- ❒ Somer's *d*
- ❒ Kendall's Tau–*b* and Tau–*c*
- ❒ Spearman's Rho.

* Two Interval/Ratio Variables
- ❒ Pearson's *r*

* Interval/Ratio—Dependent Variable and Nominal/ Ordinal—Independent Variable
- ❒ Eta (η)

13.2 Measurement of Linear Correlation

When two variables are involved in the study of correlation, the nature and extent (magnitude) of correlation may be observed by plotting the bivariate data in a graph, popularly called **Scatter diagram**. If the scatter diagram shows linear band (sloping downward or upward) the correlation is said to be **linear correlation** or simple correlation. If the scatter diagram shows curvilinear/non linear band, the correlation is said to be **curvilinear.**

If the scattered diagram shows linear band of scatter points, depicting an approximate linear relationship (either increasing or decreasing), Karl Pearson, a famous British biologist suggested an absolute measure of linear relationship called Karl Pearson's correlation Coefficient/Product moment correlation Coefficient/linear or simple correlation coefficient, usually denoted by r, which is the ratio of covariance between two variables to the product of standard deviations of two variables.

The coefficient of correlation r lies between –1 +1 and is indepenent of the units of measurement of two variables. If $r = -1$, the correlation is said to be perfect negative and if $r = +1$, the correlation is said to be perfect positive. If $r = 0$, there is no linear relationship between two variables, but there may be other type of relationship.

Suppose two variables under consideration are X and Y. If the increase in X (or Y) gives rise to increase in Y (or X) or decrease in the values of X (or Y) gives rise to decrease in values of Y (or X), the correlation is said to positive and as such $r > 0$.

Alternatively, if increase in the values of X (or Y) corresponds to decrease in the values of Y(or X), or vice versa, the correlation is said to be negative and as such $r < 0$.

Thus, the **correlation coefficient is an absolute measure of relationship and determines to the extent two variables are linearly related.** Correlation is high, if the scattering of the data points in the scatter diagram can be summarized by a straight line. The examples of two variables which are supposed to have high positive correlation are (height, weight), (income, expenditure on food items), (expenditure on advertisement and sales), (net profits, market value of shares), etc.

The negative correlated variables are expenditure and savings, level of education of mother and number of children born, price and demand, etc.

The interpretation of the coefficient of correlation, as a measure of linear relationship between two variables is only a statistical interpretation and has nothing to do with cause- effect relationship. Sometimes a third variable might affect both the variables under study to cause a similtaneous upward or downward movement. For instance, the correlation coefficient between the increase of salaries of teachers and the consumption of imported liquor in a city over a period of years may be very high. This may be due to general policy of the Government to bring about a steady rise in the salaries of employees of all types and increase in the consumption of foreign liquor, which is the result of increasing buying power. Thus, the presence of high correlation merely reflects the general upward trend in both series and does not signify association between them. Such correlation coefficient indicates no sensible correlation and is called **non-sensical correlation or spurious correlation.**

The study of correlation coefficients necessitates familiarity with the field of application as well as the nature of the concerned variables. Correlation analysis is used to measure the strength of relationship/association between numerical variables.

The value of correlation coefficients nearing +1 or –1 may be interpreted as very high positive or negative correlation (strong relationship) and nearing zero is considered very low (weak relationship).

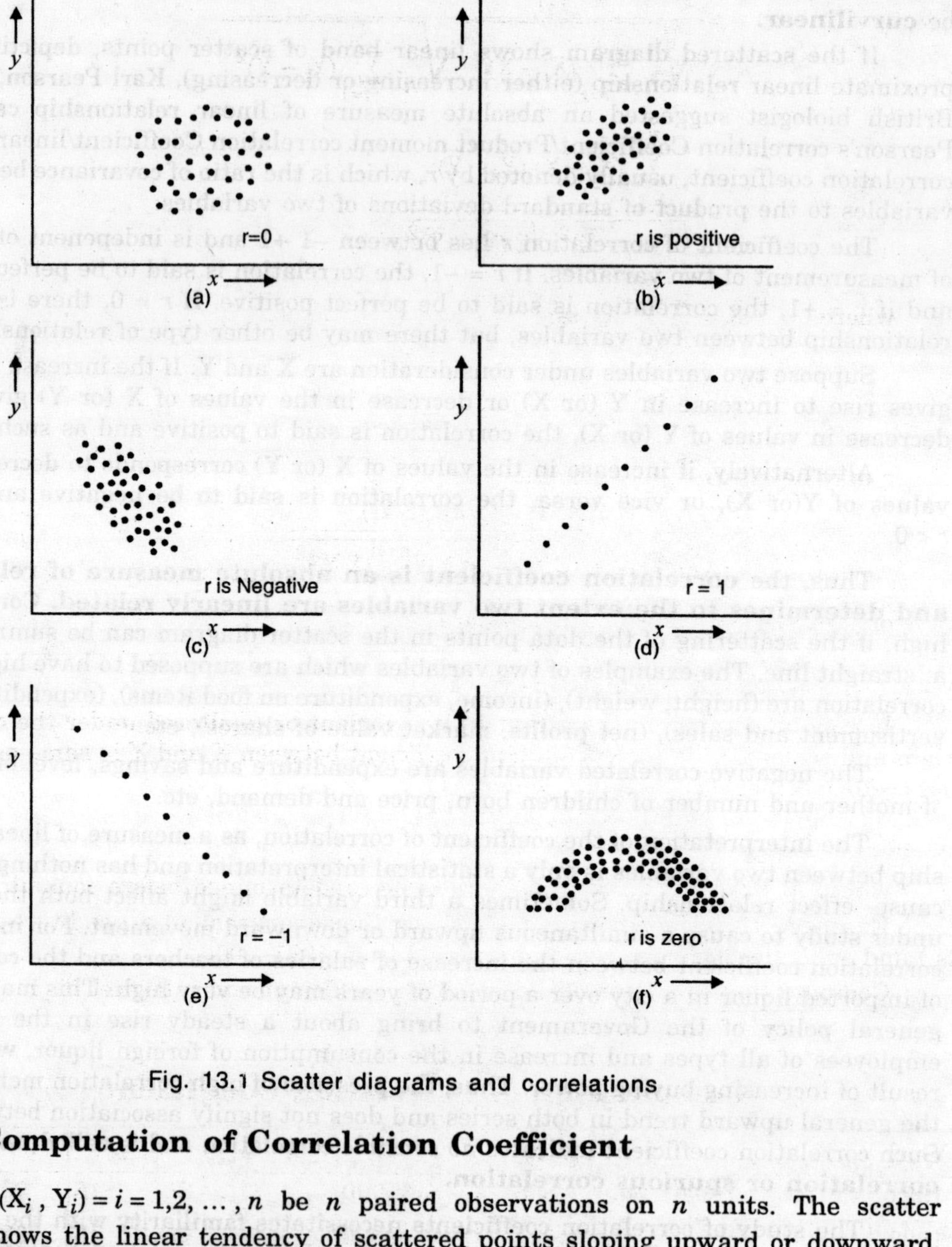

Fig. 13.1 Scatter diagrams and correlations

13.2.1. Computation of Correlation Coefficient

Let $(X_i, Y_i) = i = 1, 2, \ldots, n$ be n paired observations on n units. The scatter diagram shows the linear tendency of scattered points sloping upward or downward. Then, **Karl Pearson's Correlation Coefficient** r, sometimes called **Product Moment Correlation Coefficient,** is computed as

$$r = \frac{\text{Covariance (X, Y)}}{\text{(standard deviation of X) (standard deviation of Y)}}$$

$$= \frac{\frac{1}{n}\sum_{i=1}^{n}(X_i - \overline{X})(Y_i - \overline{Y})}{\sqrt{\frac{1}{n}\sum_{i=1}^{n}(X_i - \overline{X})^2}\sqrt{\frac{1}{n}\sum_{i=1}^{n}(Y_i - \overline{Y})^2}}$$

$$= \frac{\sum_{i=1}^{n}(X_i - \overline{X})(Y_i - \overline{Y})}{\sqrt{\Sigma(X_i - \overline{X})^2}\sqrt{\Sigma(Y_i - \overline{Y})^2}}$$

where $\overline{X} = \frac{1}{n}\sum_{i=1}^{n} X_i$ and

$$\overline{Y} = \frac{1}{n}\sum_{i=1}^{n} Y_i .$$

r may be alternatively computed as

$$r = \frac{n\,\Sigma X_i Y_i - (\Sigma X_i)(\Sigma Y_i)}{\sqrt{n\,\Sigma X_i^2 - (\Sigma X_i)^2}\sqrt{n\,\Sigma Y_i^2 - (\Sigma Y_i)^2}}$$

or $= \frac{\Sigma\, dx\, dy}{\sqrt{\Sigma\, dx^2}\sqrt{\Sigma\, dy^2}}$, where

$$dx = X_i - \overline{X} \text{ and } dy = Y_i - \overline{Y}$$

It may be pointed out here that 'r' is invariant or unaltered under the change of origin and scale, that is the correlation coefficient between X and Y is same as correlation coefficient between u and v, where

$$u = \frac{X - A}{B} \quad v = \frac{Y - C}{D},$$

where A, B, C and D are constants to be predetermined before computation.

Example 13.1 The following table shows the advertisement expenditure X (in 000' Rs.) and sales (in 000's) for two years period from 1991–2000.

Compute the Karl Pearson's correlation coefficient and interpret it.

TABLE—13.1
Computation of Correlation Coefficient

Year	X	Y	X^2	Y^2	XY	u	v	u^2	v^2	uv
1991	50	700	2500	4900×10^2	35000	4	30	16	900	120
1992	50	650	2500	4225×10^2	32500	4	25	16	625	100
1993	50	600	2500	3600×10^2	30000	4	20	16	400	80
1994	40	500	1600	2500×10^2	20000	2	10	4	100	20
1995	30	450	900	2025×10^2	13500	0	5	0	25	0

1996	20	400	400	1600×10^2	8000	−2	0	4	9	0
1997	20	300	400	900×10^2	6000	−2	−10	4	100	20
1998	15	250	225	625×10^2	3750	−3	−15	9	225	45
1999	10	210	100	441×10^2	2100	−4	−19	16	361	76
2000	5	200	25	400×10^2	1000	−5	−20	25	400	100
Total	290	4260	11150	21216×10^2	151850	−2	26	110	3136	561

Note. $u = \dfrac{X - 30}{5}, v = \dfrac{Y - 400}{10}$

$$r = \frac{n \Sigma u_i v_i - (\Sigma u_i)(\Sigma v_i)}{\sqrt{n \Sigma u_i^2 - (\Sigma u_i)^2}\sqrt{n \Sigma v_i^2 - (\Sigma v_i)^2}}$$

$$= \frac{10 \times 561 - (-2)(26)}{\sqrt{10 \times 110 - (-2)^2}\sqrt{10 \times 3136 - (26)^2}}$$

$$= \frac{566.2}{(10.47)(55.39)}$$

$$= 0.976$$

If we calculate the value of r without changing the origin and scale, we have

$$\Sigma X = 290, \Sigma Y = 4260$$
$$\Sigma X^2 = 11,150, \Sigma Y^2 = 21216 \times 10^2$$
$$\Sigma XY = 151,850$$

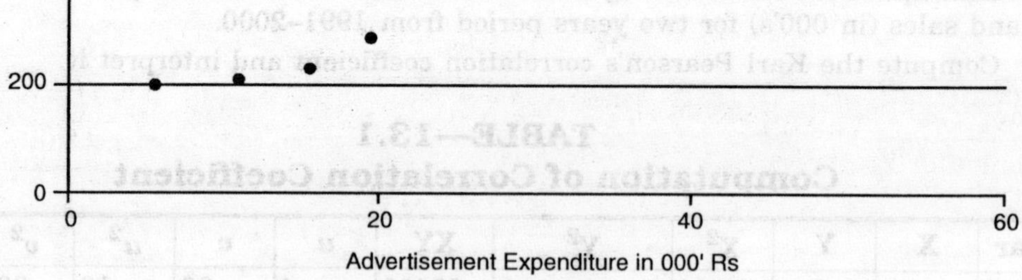

Fig. 13.2. Scatter diagram.

Therefore, $$r = \frac{n \Sigma XY - (\Sigma X)(\Sigma Y)}{\sqrt{n \Sigma X^2 - (\Sigma X)^2}\sqrt{n \Sigma Y^2 - (\Sigma Y)^2}}$$

$$= \frac{10 \times 151850 - (290)(4260)}{\sqrt{10 \times 11150 - (290)^2}\sqrt{10 \times 21216 \times 10^2 - (4260)^2}}$$

$$= \frac{1518500 - 1235400}{\sqrt{111500 - 84100}\ \sqrt{21216000 - 18147600}}$$

$$= \frac{283100}{\sqrt{27400}\ \sqrt{3068400}} = \frac{283100}{165.5294 \times 1751.6849} = \mathbf{0.976}$$

Interpretation : There is high degree of positive correlation betwen advertisement expenditure and sales.

13.2.2 Coefficient of determination

The square of the correlation coefficient *r* indicates another aspect of the relationship between X and Y. Thus, r^2 stands for the proportion of the variation in one variable (X or Y) explained by the variation in other (Y or X).

In Example 13.1, $r^2 = (0.976)^2 = 0.9526$

That is, 95.26% of the variation in Y (or X) explained by the variation in X (or Y).

13.2.3 Rank Correlation Coefficient

When $(X_{(i)}, Y_{(i)})$ $i = 1, 2, \ldots, n$ are the ranks of the values corresponding to two variables X and Y, the product moment correlation coefficient between the ranks is computed as

$$r_s = 1 - \frac{6\,\Sigma\, d_i^2}{n^3 - n},$$

where $d_i = X_{(i)} - Y_{(i)}$,

called **Spearman's rank correlation coefficient**–a non- parametic measure of relationship.

r_s is sensitive only to the ordinal values of two variables and ignores monotonous curvilinearity. r_s preserves all properties of the correlation coefficient and lies between −1 and +1.

Example 13.2. Suppose the ranks obtained by a set of 8 students in a sociology test and a statistics test are as follows.

Table 13.2

Ranks for Sociology test (X)	1	2	3	4	5	6	7	8
Ranks for Statistics test (Y)	3	1	2	4	6	8	5	7

d_i : −2, 1, 1, 0, −1, −2, 2, 1

$$r_s = 1 - \frac{6\,\Sigma\, d_i^2}{n^3 - n}$$

$$= 1 - \frac{6 \times 16}{8^3 - 8} = 1 - \frac{96}{504}$$

$$= 1 - 0.19 = 0.81$$

Thus, we may conclude that there is a high degree correlation between the performance in sociology and statistics.

Note 1. When two or more items have the same rank, a correction is to be applied to Σd_i^2. Suppose there are two items whose rank is 3, then the write $3\frac{1}{2}$ to each so that the sum of the ranks of these two items is 7. The mean of the ranks is unaffected, but the standard deviation is affected. Thus, correction is needed for Σd_i^2. That is, Σd_i^2 is increased by $\frac{(t^3 - t)}{12}$ for each tie, where t is the number of items in each tie.

Note 2. The primary purpose of correlation to establish an association between the variables. The presence of association does not imply causation, but the existence of causation certainly implies association. Statistical evidence can only establish the presence or absence of association. Correlation analysis besides showing the extent of association, is helpful to select independent variables.

Note 3. Be careful when using the correlation coefficient. One should remember the following rules for practical purposes.

The result of the calculation, (r) is a measure of linear relationship/association between X and Y, as it exists in any given set of number of pairs. Even when there is high value of (r), it does not mean that X and Y are related in any way as cause and effect. It is possible to obtain a high degree of correlation with no causal connection whatsoever. It is also not impossible that two variables which are not related may both be related to a third variable. This could cause the first two variables to show a statistical association when there are not necessarily any real cause and effect.

Do not draw any conclusion based on the correlation coefficient until it is tested for significance. When r is not significant, it may be either due to a genuine lack of linear correlation or inadequate data.

If $r = 0$, it implies there is no linear relationship between X and Y, but there may be any non-linear relationship.

13.2.4. Nonlinear Association

Some scatterplots have curved patterns. Such scatterplots are said to show *non-linear association* between the two variables. The **correlation coefficient** does not reflect nonlinear relationships between variables, only linear ones. For example, even if the association is quite strong, if it is nonlinear, the correlation coefficient r can be small or zero.

Suppose there is a deterministic relationship between the two variables : Y = sin(X). (The plot is half a period of the sine function). Even though the association is perfect-one can predict Y exactly from X–the correlation coefficient r is exactly zero. This is because the association is purely nonlinear, Fig. 13.3.

In Fig. 13.4 the correlation coefficient is reasonably large (0.71), because there is an overall trend in the data. However, the correlation coefficient still does not show how strongly associated the variables are, because the pattern of their relationship is curved (nonlinear).

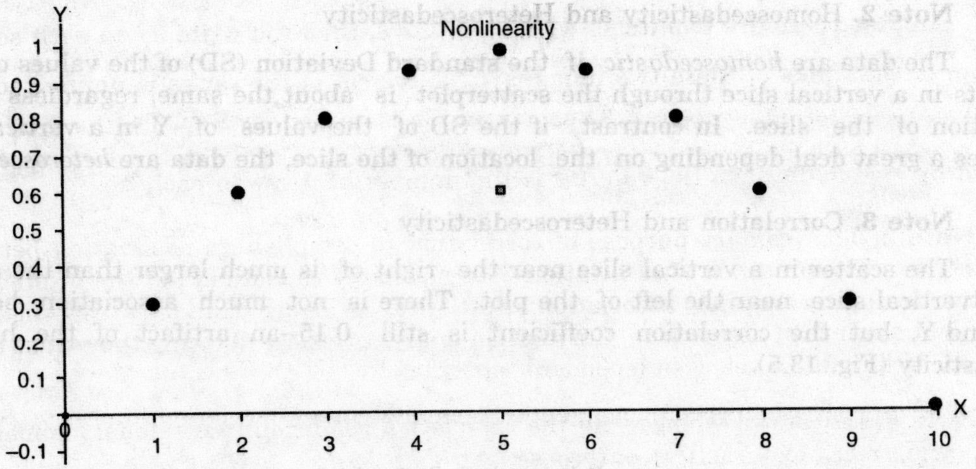

Fig. 13.3 $r = 0$

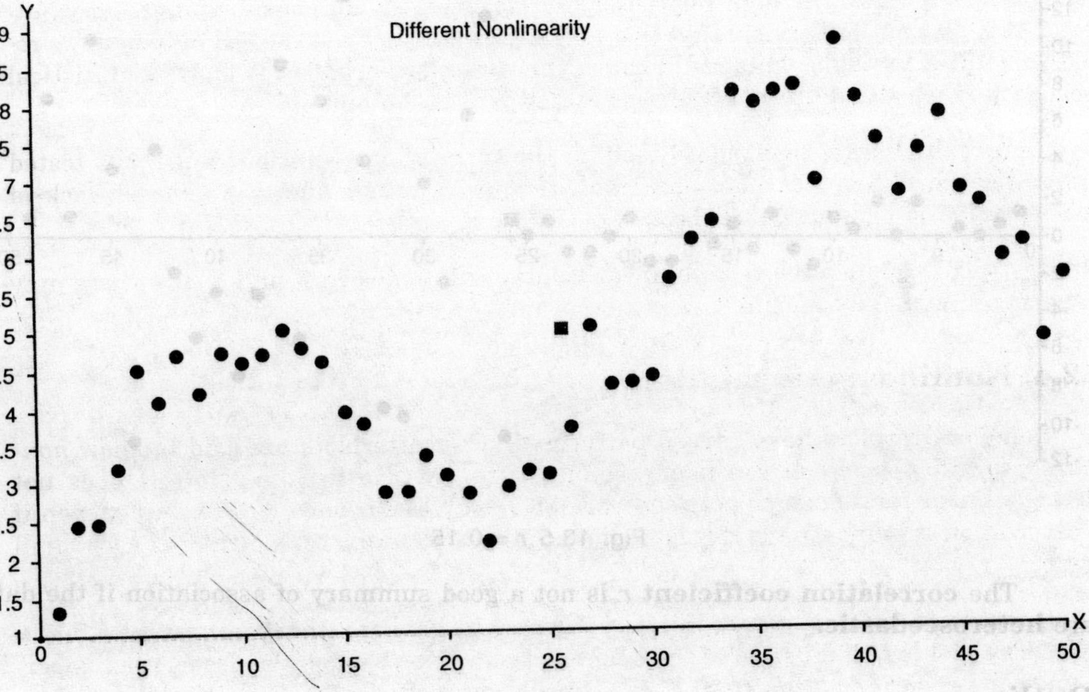

Fig. 13.4 $r = 0.71$

Note 1. Correlation and Association :

The correlation coefficient r measures only linear association : how nearly the data fall on a straight line. It is not a good summary of association if the scatterplot has a nonlinear (curved) pattern.

Note 2. Homoscedasticity and Heteroscedasticity

The data are *homoscedastic* if the standard Deviation (SD) of the values of Y for points in a vertical slice through the scatterplot is about the same, regardless of the location of the slice. In contrast, if the SD of the values of Y in a vertical slice varies a great deal depending on the location of the slice, the data are *heteroscedastic.*

Note 3. Correlation and Heteroscedasticity :

The scatter in a vertical slice near the right of is much larger than the scatter in a vertical slice near the left of the plot. There is not much association between X and Y, but the correlation coefficient is still 0.15--an artifact of the heteroscedasticity (Fig. 13.5).

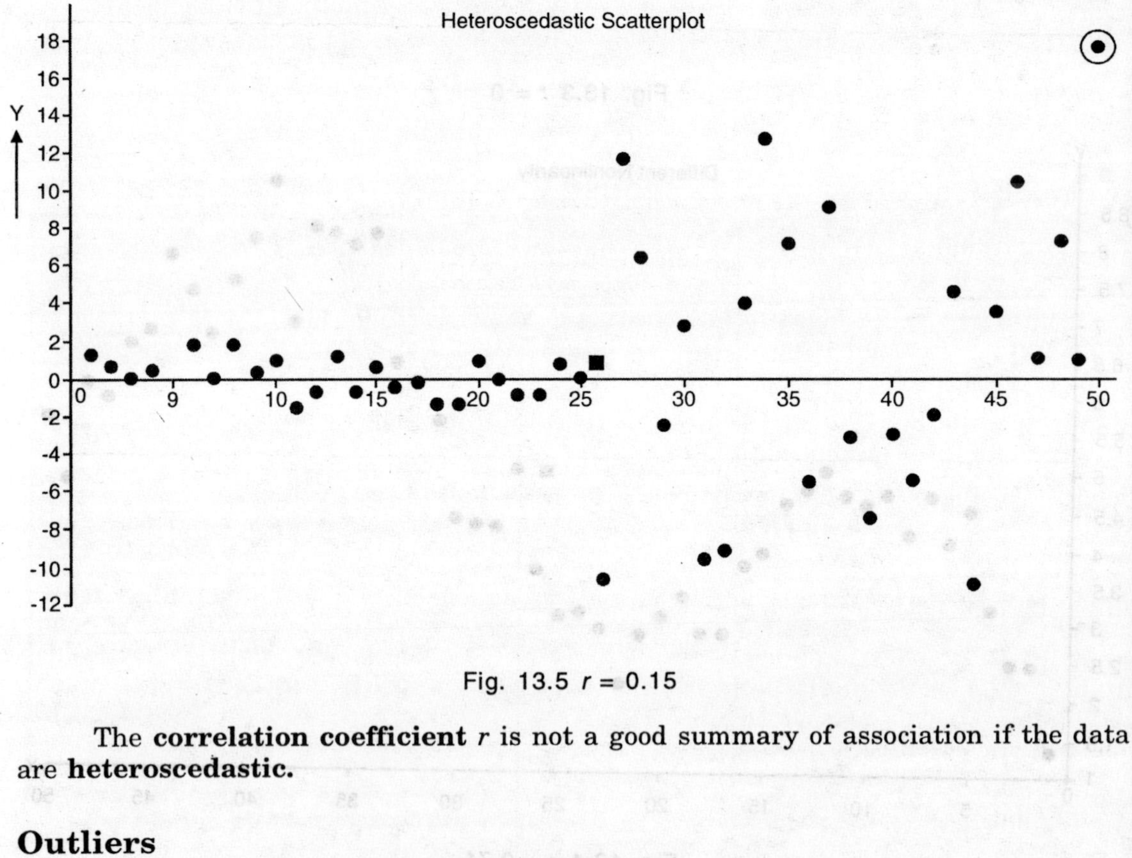

Fig. 13.5 $r = 0.15$

The **correlation coefficient** r is not a good summary of association if the data are **heteroscedastic.**

Outliers

A datum that does not fit the overall pattern in the data is called an **outlier**. A single outlier that is far from the **point of averages** can have a large effect on the correlation coefficient. The outlier makes the correlation coefficient nearly one; without it, the correlation coefficient would be nearly zero. Also,the outlier makes the correlation coefficient nearly zero; without it, the correlation coefficient would be nearly one (Fig. 13.6 and Fig. 13.7).

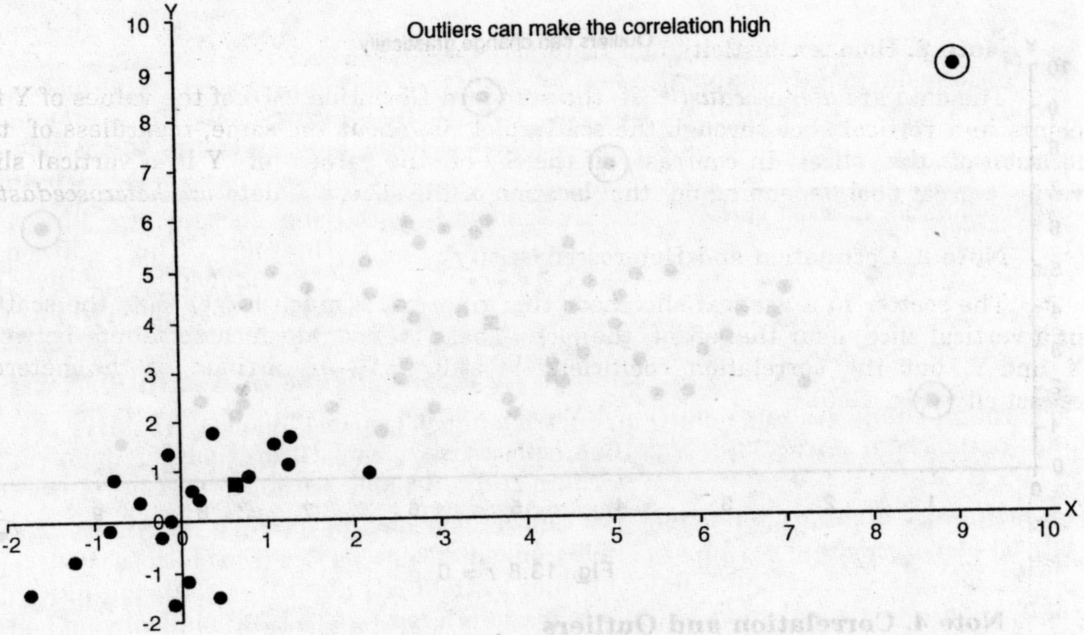

Fig. 13.6 $r = 0.92$

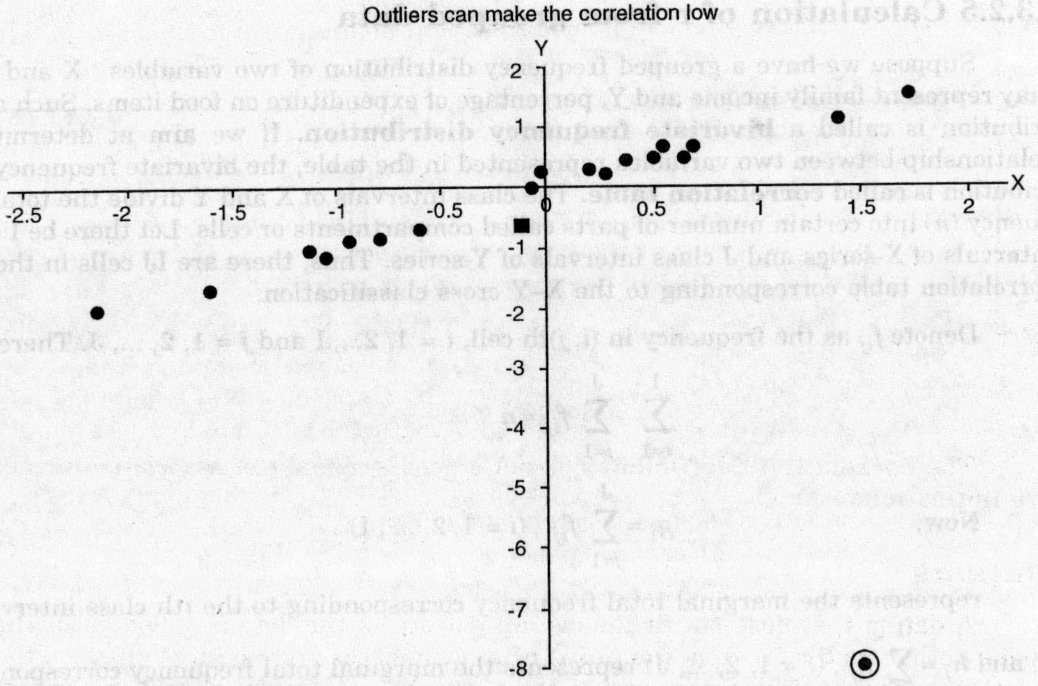

Fig. 13.7 $r = 0.08$

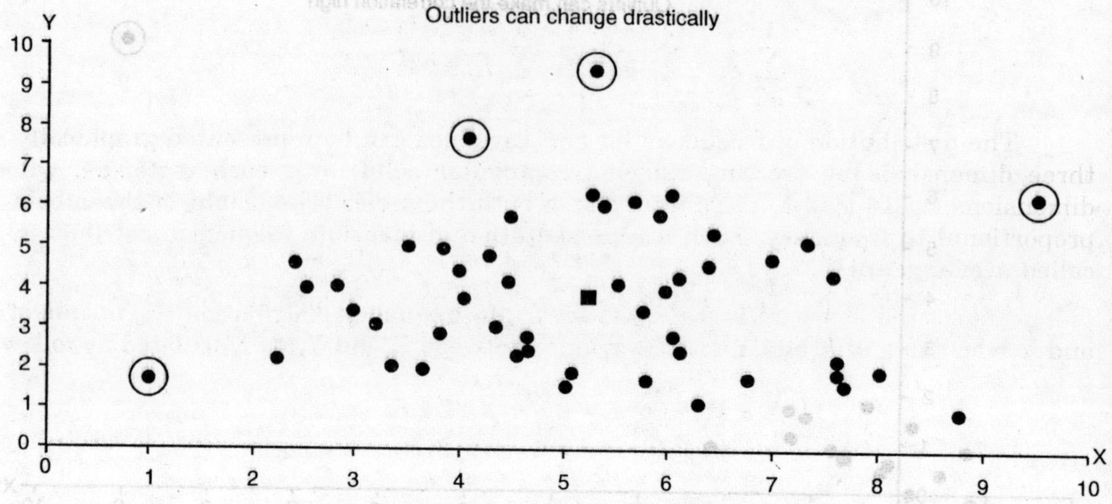

Fig. 13.8 $r = 0$

Note 4. Correlation and Outliers

The **correlation coefficient** r is not a good summary of association if the data have outliers.

13.2.5 Calculation of r from grouped data

Suppose we have a grouped frequency distribution of two variables : X and Y. X may represent family income and Y, percentage of expenditure on food items. Such a distribution is called a **bivariate frequency distribution.** If we aim at determining relationship between two variables represented in the table, the bivariate frequency distribution is called **correlation table.** The class intervals of X and Y divide the total frequency (n) into certain number of parts called compartments or cells. Let there be I class intervals of X-series and J class intervals of Y-series. Thus, there are IJ cells in the cal-correlation table corresponding to the X–Y cross classification.

Denote f_{ij} as the frequency in (i, j)th cell, $i = 1, 2, \ldots I$ and $j = 1, 2, \ldots, J$. Therefore,

$$\sum_{i=1}^{I} \sum_{j=1}^{J} f_{ij} = n$$

Now,
$$g_i = \sum_{j=1}^{J} f_{ij}, \; (i = 1, 2, \ldots, I)$$

represents the marginal total frequency corresponding to the ith class interval of X, and $h_j = \sum_{i=1}^{I} f_{ij}$, $(j = 1, 2, \ldots, J)$ represents the marginal total frequency corresponding to the jth class interval of Y.

It may be varified that

$$\sum_{i=1}^{I} g_i = \sum_{j=1}^{J} h_j = \sum_{i=1}^{I} \sum_{j=1}^{J} f_{ij} = n.$$

The distribution of frequency for two variables can be represented graphically in three dimensions by erecting cuboid (rectangular solid) over each rectangle, whose dimensions correspond to class intervals of both the series. The height of the cuboid is proportional to frequency. Such a representation of bivariate frequency distribution is called **stereogram**.

Among the characteristics of the bivariate frequency distribution the means of X and Y, variances of X and Y and covariance between X and Y are calculated as follows:

$$\overline{X} = \text{Mean of X} = \Sigma\Sigma f_{ij} X_i / \Sigma\Sigma f_{ij}$$

$$= \frac{\Sigma g_i X_i}{\Sigma g_i}$$

$$\overline{Y} = \text{Mean of Y} = \frac{\Sigma\Sigma f_{ij} Y_j}{\Sigma\Sigma f_{ij}} = \frac{\Sigma h_j y_j}{\Sigma h_j}$$

$$\sigma_x^2 = \text{Variance of X}$$

$$= \frac{\Sigma\Sigma f_{ij} (X_i - \overline{X})^2}{\Sigma\Sigma f_{ij}} = \frac{\Sigma g_i (X_i - \overline{X})^2}{\Sigma g_i}$$

$$\sigma_y^2 = \text{Variance of Y}$$

$$= \frac{\Sigma\Sigma f_{ij} (Y_i - \overline{Y})^2}{\Sigma\Sigma f_{ij}} = \frac{\Sigma h_j (Y_j - \overline{Y})^2}{\Sigma h_j}$$

$$\sigma_{xy} = \text{Covariance between X and Y}$$

$$= \frac{\Sigma\Sigma f_{ij} (X_i - \overline{X})(Y_j - Y)}{\Sigma\Sigma f_{ij}}$$

$$= \frac{\Sigma\Sigma f_{ij} X_i Y_j - n\overline{X}\,\overline{Y}}{\Sigma\Sigma f_{ij}}$$

Thus,

$$r = \frac{\text{Covariance between X and Y}}{\sqrt{\text{var X}}\sqrt{\text{var Y}}}$$

$$r = \frac{\Sigma\Sigma f_{ij} X_i Y_j - n\overline{X}\,\overline{Y}}{\sqrt{\Sigma g_1 X_i^2 - n\overline{X}^2}\sqrt{\Sigma h_j Y_j^2 - n\overline{Y}^2}}$$

Table–13.3
Bivariate Frequency Table

Y \ X	X_1	X_2	....	....	X_I	Row Total
Y_1	f_{11}	f_{21}	.	.	f_{I1}	h_1
Y_2	f_{12}	f_{22}	.	.	f_{I2}	h_2
.	.	.	.	.	.	
.	.	.	.	.	.	
.	.	.	.	.	.	
Y_J	f_{1J}	f_{2J}	.	.	f_{IJ}	h_J
Column Total	g_1	g_2	..	...	g_I	Grand Total = n

Example 13.3 Compute the coefficient of correlation between age and sum assured from the following data.

TABLE–13.4

Age group (Y)	Sum assured in 000' Rs. (X)				Total
	5	10	15	20	
20–30	2	3	4	6	15
30–40	–	2	3	5	10
40–50	–	2	2	3	7
50–60	5	8	3	2	18
Total	7	15	12	16	50

Solution

Let X denote the sum assured and Y denote the age group.

Transform $u = \dfrac{X - 15}{5}$

and $v = \dfrac{Y - 15}{10}$

TABLE–13.5
Computation of Correlation Coefficient

Age Mid-Value	x : 5	10	15	20	Total			
(y) (v)	u : –2	–1	0	1	h	hv	hv^2	$v\,(\Sigma uf)$
25 –2	2 (4)	3 (2)	4 (0)	6 (–2)	15	–30	60	2
35 –1	– (2)	2 (1)	3 (0)	5 (–1)	10	–10	10	–3
45 0	– (0)	2 (0)	2 (0)	3 (0)	7	0	0	0

55 1	5 (–2)	8 (–1)	3 (0)	2 (1)	18	18	18	–16
Total *g*	7	15	12	16	50	–22	88	–17
gu	–14	–15	0	16	–13			
gu^2	28	15	0	16	59			
$u(\Sigma\, vf)$	–2	0	0	–15	–17			

Now,

$$r = \frac{\Sigma\,\Sigma\, f_{ij}\, u_i\, v_j - n\,\bar{u}\,\bar{v}}{\sqrt{\Sigma\, g_i\, u_i^2 - n\bar{u}^2}\,\sqrt{\Sigma\, h_j\, v_j^2 - n\bar{v}^2}}$$

$$= \frac{-17 - 50\left(\frac{-30}{50}\right)\left(\frac{-22}{50}\right)}{\sqrt{59 - 50\left(\frac{-13}{50}\right)^2}\,\sqrt{88 - 50\left(\frac{-22}{50}\right)^2}}$$

$$= \frac{-22.72}{\sqrt{55.62}\,\sqrt{78.32}} = -\,0.3442$$

13.2.6. Testing for the significance of the correlation coefficient

Once the correlation coefficient has been calculated from sample data, a question arises to know whether the correlation coefficient, so computed is statistically significant.

The required statistic to test the significance of the observed correlation coefficient r is

$$t = \frac{r}{\sqrt{1-r^2}}\sqrt{n-2},$$

which follows Student's *t*-distribution with $(n–2)$ degrees of freedom under the null hypothesis $H_0 : \rho = 0$, where ρ is the correlation coefficient in the population.

Illustration

Suppose $r = 0.45$, $n = 10$.

To test the null hypothesis $H_0 : \rho = 0$ against alternative hypothesis $H_1 : \rho > 0$,

$$t = \frac{r}{\sqrt{1-r^2}}\sqrt{n-2} = \frac{0.45}{\sqrt{1-(0.45)^2}}\sqrt{10-2}$$

$$= \frac{0.45}{0.8930}\sqrt{8} = 1.4253$$

The tabulated value of t with $n - 2 = 8$ degrees of freedom at 5% level of significance is 1.86.

As the computed value of t *i.e.* 1.42 is less than the tabulated value of t, *i.e.*, 1.86, the computed sample value of r is not statistically significant, *i.e.* not significantly different from zero (no correlation).

Example 13.4. The following data pertain to length of service (in years) and the annual income for a sample of ten employees in a business organisation.

Table–13.6

Length of service in years (X)	Annual income in thousand rupees (Y)
6	14
8	17
9	15
10	18
11	16
12	22
14	26
16	25
18	30
20	34

Compute the correlation coefficient between X and Y and test its significance at levels of 0.01 and 0.05.

Solution

$$\Sigma X = 124 \qquad \Sigma Y = 217$$

$$\Sigma X^2 = 1722 \qquad \Sigma Y^2 = 5131$$

$$\Sigma XY = 2959$$

$$r = \frac{n\,\Sigma XY - (\Sigma X)(\Sigma Y)}{\sqrt{n\,\Sigma X^2 - (\Sigma X)^2}\sqrt{n\,\Sigma Y^2 - (\Sigma Y)^2}}$$

$$= \frac{10\,(2959) - (124)\,(217)}{\sqrt{10(1722) - (124)^2}\sqrt{10(5131) - (217)^2}}$$

$$= \frac{2682}{\sqrt{1844}\;\sqrt{4221}} = \frac{2682}{2789.90}$$

$$= 0.9613$$

To test $H_0 : \rho = 0$ against alternative $H_1 : \rho > 0$, compute

$$t = \frac{r}{\sqrt{1 - r^2}}\sqrt{n - 2} = \frac{0.9613}{\sqrt{1 - (0.9613)^2}}\sqrt{10 - 2}$$

$$= \frac{0.9613}{0.2755}\sqrt{8} = 9.8692$$

The tabulated value of t with n–2 = 8 degree of freedom at 0.01 level is 2.90 and at 0.05 level is 1.86.

As the calculated value of t exceeds the tabulated values of t at both 1% and 5% levels of significance, the null hypothesis H_0 is rejected and the sample value r is significantly different from zero.

Note. When $n \geq 30$, under $H_0 : \rho = 0$ the distribution of r is approximately normal with mean zero and standard error $\frac{1}{\sqrt{n-1}}$. Therefore $\frac{r}{\text{S.E.}(r)} = r\sqrt{n-1}$ is approximately standard normal and can be used to test H_0.

To test $H_0 : \rho \neq 0$, Fisher defined a variable

$$Z = \frac{1}{2}\log_e \frac{1+r}{1-r} = 1.1513 \log_{10} \frac{1+r}{1-r}$$

and a quantity

$$\zeta = \frac{1}{2}\log_e \frac{1+\rho}{1-\rho} = 1.1513 \log_{10} \frac{1+\rho}{1-\rho}$$

The distribution of Z is approximately normal with mean ζ and standard error $\frac{1}{\sqrt{n-3}}$. Hence $(Z-\zeta)\sqrt{n-3}$ has an approximate standard normal distribution and the test can be done accordingly.

(*c*) $H_0 : \rho_1 = \rho_2$. Let r_1 and r_2 be the sample correlation coefficients from samples of size n_1 and n_2 drawn from the bivariate normal populations with correlations ρ_1 and ρ_2 respectively.

Compute $$Z_i = \frac{1}{2}\log_e \frac{1+r_i}{1-r_i} \quad (i = 1, 2)$$

and $$\zeta_i = \frac{1}{2}\log_e \frac{1+\rho_i}{1-\rho_i} \quad (i = 1, 2)$$

The sampling distribution of $(Z_1 - Z_2)$ is approximately normal with mean $(\zeta_1 - \zeta_2)$ and standard error $\sqrt{\frac{1}{n_1-3} + \frac{1}{n_2-3}}$

Thus, the normal theory test can be applied to test $H_0 : \rho_1 = \rho_2$, by using

$$z = \frac{Z_1 - Z_2}{\sqrt{\frac{1}{n_1-3} + \frac{1}{n_2-3}}},$$ which is standard normal.

(*d*) Suppose that k independent samples of n_i $(i = 1,2,\ldots, k)$ pairs of values give correlation coefficients r_i $(i \; 1,2,\ldots, k)$.

Defining Z_i $(i = 1,2,\ldots, k)$ as before and with $\overline{Z} = \frac{\Sigma (n_i - 3) Z_i}{\Sigma (n_i - 3)}$

$\sum_{i=1}^{k} (n_i - 3)(Z_i - \overline{Z})^2$, is approximately distributed as χ^2 with $(k-1)$ degrees of freedom.

If the calculated value of χ^2 exceeds $\chi^2_{\alpha,\, k-1}$, the hypothesis of homogeneity of correlation coefficients is rejected at 100 α% level of significance, otherwise accepted.

Example 13.5. Independent random samples of 15, 22, 34 and 25 pairs of values gave correlation coefficients 0.45, 0.62, 0.52 and 0.56 respectively.

Test the hypotehsis that the samples have come from equally correlated populations.

Solution

$$r_1 = 0.45, n_1 = 15$$
$$r_2 = 0.62, n_2 = 22$$
$$r_3 = 0.52, n_3 = 34$$
$$r_4 = 0.56, n_4 = 25$$

Compute $Z_1 = 0.4854, Z_2 = 0.7246, Z_3 = 0.5769, Z_4 = 0.6321$

$$\bar{Z} = \frac{51.3823}{84} = 0.6117$$

Now, the χ^2 statistic

$$\Sigma (n_i - 3)(Z_i - \bar{Z})^2 = 0.4793$$

This value is less than the critical value 7.82 of $\chi^2_{0.05}$ at 3 degrees of freedom. Therefore, the null hypothesis is accepted or in other words the samples have come from equally correlated populations.

Example 13.6. The following data are the monthly salaries y and the grade point average x for students who have obtained a bachelor's degree in business administration with a major in information systems.

Table–13.7

GPA (x)	Monthly Salary (Rs. in hundreds) (y)
2.6	33
3.4	36
3.6	40
3.2	35
3.5	39
2.9	36

Compute the linear correlation coefficient between GPA and monthly salary and test its significance at 5% level.

Solution

$\Sigma x = 19.2$ $\qquad$ $\Sigma y = 219$

$\Sigma x^2 = 62.18$ $\qquad$ $\Sigma y^2 = 8027$

$\Sigma xy = 705.1$

$$r = \frac{\Sigma xy - \frac{(\Sigma x)(\Sigma y)}{n}}{\sqrt{\Sigma x^2 - \frac{(\Sigma x)^2}{n}}\sqrt{\Sigma y^2 - \frac{(\Sigma y)^2}{n}}}$$

$$= \frac{705.1 - \frac{(19.2)(219)}{6}}{\sqrt{62.18 - \frac{(19.2)^2}{6}}\sqrt{8027 - \frac{(219)^2}{6}}}$$

$$= \frac{705.1 - 700.8}{\sqrt{62.18 - 61.44}\sqrt{8027 - 7993.5}} = \frac{4.3}{\sqrt{0.74}\sqrt{33.5}}$$

$$= \frac{4.3}{4.979} = 0.8636$$

The coefficient of determination $r^2 = .7458$

Thus, 74.58% of variations in monthly salary (y) is explained by the variations in GPA (x).

To test the significance of the sample correlation coefficient r, compute

$$t = \frac{|r|}{\sqrt{1 - r^2}}\sqrt{n - 2} = \frac{0.8636}{\sqrt{1 - 0.7458}}\sqrt{6 - 2}$$

$$= \frac{0.8636}{0.5042}\sqrt{4} = 3.4256$$

The tabulated value of t with 4 degrees of freedom at 5% level of significance is 2.78. Thus, the null hypothesis that there is no correlation between GPA and monthly salary is rejected. The sample r is significatly different from zero.

13.3 Linear Regression Lines

Suppose scattered points in the scatter diagram indicates an approximate linear relationship between two variables X and Y. A line which best summarizes the scattering is called **line of regression**, which is approximated in such a way that the sum of the squared deviations of the scattered points from the proposed regression line measured is kept as low as possible. A mathematical technique termed as **method of least squares** solves this problem. Thus, in computing a regression line with two variables X and Y, one is taken as independent variable, say X and the other variable Y, assumed as dependent variable. Of course, the choice depends on the value of variables as decided by the researcher.

Regression analysis is used primarily for the purpose of prediction and the line of regression predicts the value of dependent variable (response variable) for a given value of independent variable (explanatory variable)

Suppose the aptitude scores and productivity indices of seven workers are as follows:

TABLE–13.8

Workers	1	2	3	4	5	6	7
Aptitude score (X)	9	12	16	18	20	23	25
Productivity index (Y)	23	24	22	25	30	28	32

The best fitted straight line may be found as

Y = 16.7001 + 0.5455X

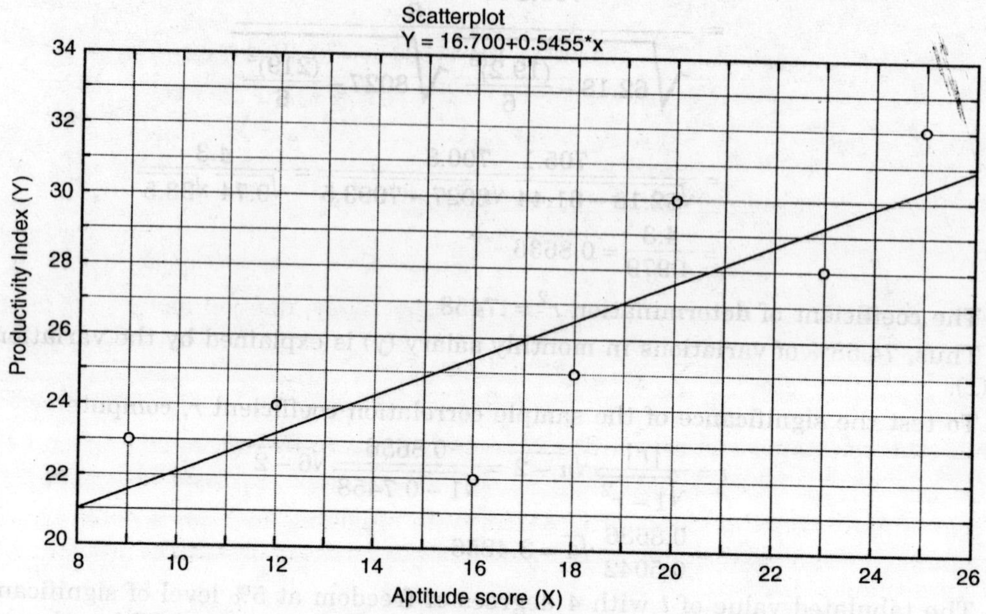

Fig. 13.9 Scatter diagram and Regression line

13.3.1 Fitting of Regression Line

Given n paired observations (X_i, Y_i), $i = 1, 2, \ldots, n$, suppose the functional relationship for the purpose of finding a statistical relationship between the dependent variable Y and independent variable X is

$$Y = \alpha + \beta X$$

Any paired observation (y_i, x_i) follows the model

$$Y_i = \alpha + \beta X_i + e_i,$$

where e_i is a random error. $E(e_i) = 0$, $V(e_i) = \sigma_e^2$ (Constant)

e_i and e_j are independent and as such Cov. $(e_i, e_j) = 0$ for $i \neq j$, e_i's are independently distributed uncorrelated normal variables.

α and β are not known in practice and are to be estimated from the given data. Method of least squares demands that estimates of α and β are to be so chosen to make

$$D = \sum_{i=1}^{n} e_i^2 = \sum_{i=1}^{n} (Y_i - \hat{\alpha} - \hat{\beta} X_i)^2, \text{ minimum.}$$

By using minimization techniques, the estimates of α and β are found as

$$\hat{\beta} = \frac{\frac{1}{n} \cdot \sum_{i=1}^{n} (X_i - \overline{X})(Y_i - \overline{Y})}{\frac{1}{n} \sum_{i=1}^{n} (X_i - \overline{X})^2} = \frac{\Sigma (X_i - \overline{X})(Y_i - \overline{Y})}{\Sigma (X_i - \overline{X})^2}$$

$$= \frac{\text{Covariance between X and Y}}{\text{Variance of X}}$$

$$\hat{\alpha} = \hat{Y} - \hat{\beta}\overline{X}$$

where $\overline{X}$ and $\overline{Y}$ are the means of X and Y respectively, defined as

$$\overline{X} = \frac{1}{n} \sum_{i=1}^{n} X_i \text{ and } \overline{Y} = \frac{1}{n} \sum_{i=1}^{n} Y_i$$

Thus, the estimated regression line of Y on X is given by

$$\hat{Y} = \hat{\alpha} + \hat{\beta}X,$$

Where $\hat{\beta}$ indicates the **slope of the line** (rate of change in Y for a given change in X) called regression coefficient of Y on X and $\hat{\alpha}$ is the estimate of **intercept** of the line where it cuts the *y*-axis.

The equation to the **regression line depicts the average relationship between two variable with Y as the dependent variable and X as the independent variable.** This equation helps predicting the value of Y for a given value of the independent variable X.

If X is assumed to be a dependent variable and Y an independent variable, then the estimated regression line of X on Y is computed as

$$\hat{X} = \hat{\alpha}_1 + \hat{\beta}_1 Y,$$

where
$$\hat{\beta}_1 = \frac{\text{Covariance between Y and X}}{\text{Variance of Y}}$$

$$= \frac{\Sigma (X_i - \overline{X})(Y_i - \overline{Y})}{\Sigma (Y_i - \overline{Y})^2}$$

$$\hat{\alpha}_1 = \overline{X} - \hat{\beta}_1 \overline{Y}.$$

Notes :

(*i*) The regression lines intersect at a point whose co-ordinates are $(\overline{X}, \overline{Y})$.

(*ii*) If two regression lines intersect at a right angle, *r* is zero.

(*iii*) The closer the regression lines, greater is the degree of correlation.

(*iv*) Upward slope of regression line implies positive correlation and downward slope implies negative correlation.

(*v*) The regression coefficient indicates a value by which one variable changes corresponding to a unit change in the other variable and is given by the slope of the concerned regression line.

(*vi*) Regression Analysis is to be undertaken where there is **definite direction** of dependency where as the **correlation analysis** is more suitable for cases when we have no clear idea of the direction of dependency.

13.3.2 Relation between $\hat{\beta}$, $\hat{\beta}_1$ and r

It may be verified

$$\hat{\beta}.\,\hat{\beta}_1 = \frac{(\text{Covariance between } y \text{ and } x)}{(\text{Variance } x)\ (\text{Variance of } y)}$$
$$= r^2$$

Further, $\hat{\beta}$, $\hat{\beta}_1$ and r have the same sign (+ve or –ve), depending on whether the covariance is +ve or negative. They have the common numerator and the denominators are always positive. A positive value of the regression coefficient indicates the value of the dependent variable increases or decreases with the increase or decrease of the independent variable and a negative value of the regression coefficient indicates that the value of the dependent variable decreases (or increases) with the increase (or decrease) in the value of the independent variable.

13.3.3 Can there be always two regression lines ?

The answer is 'no'. Before computing regression line, the researcher should be convinced that the regression line can be meaningfully interpreted. For example, in the study of time series where one of the variables is a time variable, (t), it would not be meaningful to compute the regression line of t on u_t (value at time t).

13.3.4 How good is the Regression ?

Once the regression line is obtained it is necessary to know how good the fit is. This can be examined by the examination of errors in fitting the regression line.

If Y_i is the ith data point and $\hat{Y}_i$ its predicted value by the regression equation, then we can write the deviation.

$$Y_i - \hat{Y}_i = (Y_i - \overline{Y}) - (\hat{Y}_i - \overline{Y})$$

$$\sum_{i=1}^{n} (Y_i - \hat{Y}_i)^2 = \sum_{i=1}^{n} (Y_i - \overline{Y})^2 - \sum_{i=1}^{n} (\hat{Y}_i - \overline{Y})^2, \text{ which may be written as}$$

$$\sum_{i=1}^{n} (Y_i - \overline{Y})^2 = \sum_{i=1}^{n} (\hat{Y}_i - \overline{Y})^2 + \sum_{i=1}^{n} (Y_i - \hat{Y}_i)^2$$

Sum of squares about the mean

= Sum of squares due to the regression + Sum of squares due to deviation from regression (Residual).

It may be verified,

$$r^2 = \frac{\text{Sum of squares due to regression}}{\text{Sum of squares about mean}}$$

$$= \frac{\sum_{i=1}^{n} (\hat{Y}_i - \overline{Y})^2}{\sum_{i=1}^{n} (Y_i - \overline{Y})^2} = 1 - \frac{\Sigma\,(Y_i - \hat{Y}_i)^2}{\Sigma\,(Y_i - \overline{Y})^2}$$

$$= 1 - \frac{\text{Sum of squares due to deviation from regression}}{\text{Sum of squares about mean}}$$

As such, $\sum_{i=1}^{n} (Y_i - \hat{Y}_i)^2 = (1 - r^2) \sum_{i=1}^{n} (Y_i - \overline{Y})^2$

If $\hat{Y}_i$'s move closer to Y_i's *i.e.* the scattering of points in the scatter diagram becomes closer to the regression line, r tends to be close to 1 or –1. If r = +1 or –1, the scattered points in the scatter diagram exactly lie on the line.

Now, $$100\, r^2 = 100 \frac{\Sigma (\hat{Y}_i - \overline{Y})^2}{\Sigma (Y_i - \overline{Y})^2}$$

indicates percentage of total variation in Y's explained by the regression line. If r = 0.8, then 64% of the variation in Y is explained by the regression line of Y on X and same percentage of variation in X is also explained by the regression line of X on Y.

Note. Given two independent bivariate samples, it is possible to have different r's and identical slopes and also different slopes with similar r's.

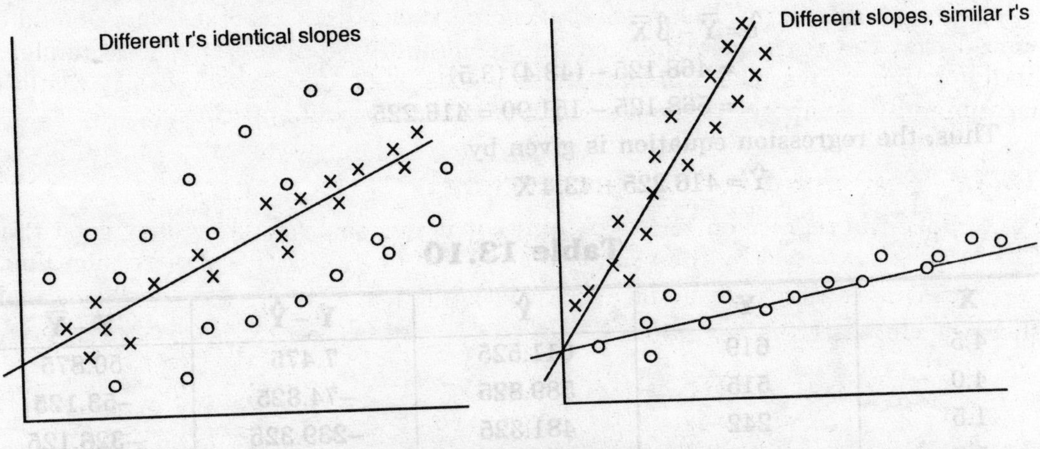

Fig. 13.10 Scatter diagrams.

Example 13.7. The cost of maintenance of tractors seems to increase with the age of tractor. The following data are collected. Calculate the linear regression of the cost of maintenance on the age of tractors.

Table–13.9

Age in years (X)	Monthly Cost (Rs.) (Y)	X^2	XY
4.5	619	20.25	2785.50
4.0	515	16.0	2060.00
1.5	242	2.25	363.00
5.0	845	25.0	4225.00
5.5	997	30.25	5483.50

0.5	127	0.25	63.50
1.0	150	1.00	150.00
6.0	1050	36.00	6300.00
Total : 28	4545	225.25	21430.5

$$\overline{X} = \frac{28}{8} \qquad \Sigma X^2 = 225.25$$

$$\overline{Y} = \frac{4545}{8} \qquad \Sigma XY = 21430.5$$

The estimate of slope of the regression line is computed as

$$\hat{\beta} = \frac{n\,\Sigma XY - \Sigma(X)\,\Sigma(Y)}{n\,\Sigma X^2 - (\Sigma X)^2}$$

$$= \frac{8 \times 21430.5 - (28)\,(4545)}{8 \times 225.25 - (28)^2} = \frac{171444 - 127260}{1082 - 784}$$

$$= \frac{44184}{1018} = \mathbf{43.40}$$

$$\hat{\alpha} = \overline{Y} - \hat{\beta}\,\overline{X}$$

$$= 468.125 - (43.4)\,(3.5)$$

$$= 568.125 - 151.90 = 416.225$$

Thus, the regression equation is given by

$$\hat{Y} = 416.225 + 43.4\,X$$

Table 13.10

X	Y	$\hat{Y}$	$Y - \hat{Y}$	$Y - \overline{Y}$
4.5	619	611.525	7.475	50.875
4.0	515	589.825	–74.825	–53.125
1.5	242	481.325	–239.325	–326.125
5.0	845	633.225	211.775	276.875
5.5	997	654.925	342.075	428.875
0.5	127	437.925	–310.925	–441.125
1.0	150	459.625	–309.625	–418.125
6.0	1050	676.625	373.373	481.875
Total : 28	4545	4545	$\Sigma (Y-\hat{Y})^2 =$ 556745.955	$\Sigma (Y-\overline{Y})^2 =$ 973984.875

$$\Sigma (Y - \hat{Y})^2 = 556745.955$$

$$\Sigma (Y - \overline{Y})^2 = 973984.875$$

Coefficient of determination

$$= 1 - \frac{\Sigma (Y - \hat{Y})^2}{\Sigma (Y - \hat{Y})^2}$$

$$= 1 - 0.5716 = 0.4284$$

Example 13.8 For computation of linear trend of Daily sales in a shop over first 11 days of a month we have the following data. Compute the regression equation for trend.

Table 13.11

Days t	**Daily sales (in 000' Rs.)** u_t	**Change the origin to 1951** (t)	$t.u_t$	t^2
1	972	–5	–4860	25
2	964	–4	–38516	16
3	955	–3	–2865	9
4	950	–2	–1900	4
5	945	–1	–945	1
6	946	0	0	0
7	941	1	941	1
8	930	2	1860	4
9	934	3	2802	9
10	927	4	3708	16
11	933	5	4665	25
Total Σ	10397	0	13976–14426	110

SOLUTION. Assume the linear regression

$$u_t = \alpha + \beta t$$

The least square estimates of α and β are as follows :

$$\hat{\beta} = \frac{11\,\Sigma\, tu_t - (\Sigma t)\,(\Sigma\, u_t)}{11\,\Sigma\, t^2 - (\Sigma\, t)^2}$$

$$= \frac{11\,\Sigma\, t\, u_t}{11\,\Sigma\, t^2} = \frac{\Sigma\, t\, u_t}{\Sigma\, t^2} = -\frac{450}{110}$$

$$= -4.091$$

$$\hat{\alpha} = \overline{u}_t - \overline{\beta}\,\overline{t}$$

$$= \frac{10397}{11} - (-4.091)\,(0)$$

$$= 945.18$$

The regression equation for trend is

$$u_t = 945.18 - 4.091\, t$$

13.3.5 Examination and interpretation of Regression line :

In the regression analysis the least square criterion is used to fit the linear model

$$Y = \alpha + \beta X + e$$

With assumptions about probability distribution of e. α and β were estimated by minimising the sum of squares of the errors of residuals $\Sigma\,(Y_i - \alpha - \beta\, X_i)^2$, which involves the solution of two simultaneous equations which are called **least square equations**.

However, the precision of estimates of α and β and estimated regression line can be obtained by incorporating certain assumptions in the basic model.

$$Y_i = \alpha + \beta X_i + e_i, \; i = 1 \; .... , n,$$

The relevant assumptions are

(*i*) e_i is a random variable with mean zero and variance σ_e^2 (unknown), that is, $E(e_i) = 0$ and $V(e_i) = \sigma_e^2$. Further, e_i and e_j are independent for $i \neq j$, i.e. Cov. $(e_i, e_j) = 0$.

Thus $E(Y_i) = \alpha + \beta X_i$,

$V(Y_i) = \sigma_e^2$ and Y_i and Y_j $(i \neq j)$ are independent.

(*ii*) e_i is normally distributed with mean zero and variance σ_e^2.

e_i and e_j are not only uncorrelated but also independent.

Thus, we may summarize the assumptions of regression as (*i*) Normality (*ii*) Homoscedasticity (*iii*) Independence of errors.

The first assumption, normality requires that the error around the line of regression be normally distributed.

The second assumption, homoscedasticity requires that variation around the line of regression be constant for all values of X. This means that errors vary the same amount when X is low as when X is high value. The homoscedasticity assumption is important for using the least square method of determining regression coefficients. If there are serious departures from this assumption, either data transformations or weighted least square methods can be applied.

The third assumption, independence of errors, requires that the errors be independent for each value of X. This assumption is particularly important when data are collected over a period of time with possibility of autocorrelation.

The following problems occur while fitting a regression line. These are :

(*i*) standard error of the slope $\hat{\beta}$ and the confidence interval for $\hat{\beta}$.

(*ii*) standard error of the intercept $\hat{\alpha}$ and a confidence interval for $\hat{\alpha}$.

(*iii*) standard error of $\hat{Y}$, the predicted value

(*iv*) significance of regression.

(*v*) percentage of variation explained.

Standard Errors of $\hat{\alpha}$ and $\hat{\beta}$

Now, $$V(\hat{\beta}) = \frac{\sigma_e^2}{\Sigma (X_i - \overline{X})^2}$$

Thus, $$\text{S.E.}(\hat{\beta}) = \frac{\sigma_e}{\sqrt{\Sigma (X_i - \overline{X})^2}}$$

If σ_e^2 is not known, which is usually so, it can be estimated from the given data as

$$s_e^2 = \frac{\Sigma (Y_i - \hat{Y}_i)^2}{n-2}$$

Alternatively, s_e^2 may be computed as

$$s_e^2 = \frac{\Sigma Y_i^2 - \hat{\alpha}\,\Sigma Y_i - \hat{\beta}\,\Sigma X_i Y_i}{n-2}$$

Then, 100(1 – α)% confidence interval for β is given by

$$\hat{\beta} \pm t_{n-2\,,\,\alpha/2} \frac{s_e}{\sqrt{\Sigma\,(X_i - \overline{X})^2}}$$

where $t_{n-2\,,\,\alpha/2}$ is the (α/2)th percentage point of t-distribution with (n–2) degrees of freedom, which is the degrees of freedom of residual sum of squares.

Further, $\hat{\alpha} = \overline{Y} - \hat{\beta}\overline{X}$

Hence, $$V(\hat{\alpha}) = \sigma_e^2 \left[\frac{1}{n} + \frac{\overline{X}^2}{\Sigma\,(X_i - \overline{X})^2}\right]$$

$$= \frac{\sigma_e^2\,\Sigma X_i^2}{n\,\Sigma\,(X_i - \overline{X})^2}\text{. Thus, S.E. }(\hat{\alpha}) = \sigma_e \left[\frac{1}{n} + \frac{\overline{X}^2}{\Sigma(X_i - \text{Xar})^2}\right]^{\frac{1}{2}}$$

Thus, the 100(1–α)% confidence limits for $\hat{\alpha}$ are given by

$$\hat{\alpha} \pm t_{n-2\,,\,\frac{\alpha}{2}} \left[\frac{\Sigma X_i^2}{n\,\Sigma\,(X_i - \overline{X})^2}\right]^{\frac{1}{2}} . \, s_e$$

Interval Estimation of Predicted Values :

The dependent variable $\hat{Y}$ is written as

$$\hat{Y} = \hat{Y} + \hat{\beta}(X - \overline{X})$$

$\hat{Y}$ and $\hat{\beta}$ are uncorrelated random variables. Thus the variance of the predicted mean value of Y, $\hat{Y}_k$ at a specific value X_k of X is

$$V(\hat{Y}_k) = V(\overline{Y}) + (X_k - \overline{X})^2\, V(\hat{\beta})$$

$$= \frac{\sigma_e^2}{n} + \frac{(X_k - \overline{X})^2}{\Sigma\,(X_i - \overline{X})^2}\,\sigma_e^2$$

Hence, the estimated standard error for the predicted mean value of Y for a given X_k is

$$\text{Est. } s.e.\ (\hat{Y}_k) = s_e \times \left[\frac{1}{n} + \frac{(X_k - \overline{X})^2}{\Sigma\,(X_i - \overline{X})^2}\right]^{\frac{1}{2}}$$

The interval estimate for the mean of Y is

$$\hat{Y}_k \pm t_{n-2,\,\alpha/2} s_e \left[\frac{1}{n} + \frac{(X_k - \overline{X})^2}{\Sigma(X_i - \overline{X})^2}\right]^{\frac{1}{2}}$$

This is a minimum when $X_k = \overline{X}$ and increases as we move X_k away from $\overline{X}$ in either direction. In other words, the greater distance an X_k is (in either direction) from $\overline{X}$, the longer is the error one may expect to make when predicting from the regression line **the mean value of Y at X_k i.e. $\hat{Y}_k$**. This is natural since we expect the best prediction in the middle of our observed range of X, with predictions becoming worse as we move away from the range of observed X values.

The prediction interval estimate for an individual response Y_k is

$$\hat{Y}_k \pm t_{n-2,\,\alpha/2}\, s_e \sqrt{1+\frac{1}{n}+\frac{(X_k-\overline{X})^2}{\Sigma(X_i-\overline{X})^2}}$$

13.3.6. Test of hypothesis about the slope (regression coefficient)

A test of hypothesis about the regression coefficient is performed by testing the null hypothesis.

$$H_0 : \beta = \beta_0$$

against alternative $H_1 : \beta \neq \beta_0$.

The appropriative the statistic is

$$t_0 = \frac{\hat{\beta}-\beta_0}{\text{S.E.}\,(\hat{\beta})} = \frac{\hat{\beta}-\beta_0}{\sqrt{\text{MSE}/\Sigma\,(X_i-\overline{X})^2}}$$

which under H_0 has Student's t-distribution with $(n–2)$ degrees of freedom.

We reject $\quad H_0 : \beta = \beta_0$ if

$$|t_0| > t_{\alpha/2\,,\,n-2}$$

Note. When $\beta_0 = 0$, the null hypothesis relates to test of significance of regression function. As such, the test of regression function can be carried out by the Student's t-test mentioned above with $\beta_0 = 0$.

Alternatively, the test of regression function can be carried out by the F-test in the analysis of variance Table.

Table 13.12
Analysis of Variance

Source	**Degrees of freedom**	**Sum of squares**	**Mean Squares**	**F**
Regression	1	$SSR = \Sigma\,(\hat{Y}_i - \overline{Y})^2$	$MSR = \frac{SSR}{1}$	$\frac{MSR}{MSE}$
Deviation from Regression	n–2	$SSE = \Sigma\,(Y_i - \hat{Y}_i)^2$	$MSE = \frac{SSE}{n-2}$	
Total	n–1	$SST = \Sigma\,(Y_i - \overline{Y})^2$		

$F = \frac{MSR}{MSE}$ follows the theoretical F- distribution with 1 and $(n–2)$ degrees of freedom under $H_0 \,.\, \beta = 0$.

If the computed value of F exceeds $F_{\alpha, 1, n-2}$ at $\alpha\%$ level of significance, the null hypothesis is rejected and we conclude that the regression is significant.

13.3.7. Test of hypothesis about the intercept (α)

$$H_0 : \alpha = \alpha_0$$
$$H_1 : \alpha \neq \alpha_0$$

The appropriate statistic is

$$t_0 = \frac{\hat{\alpha} - \alpha_0}{\sqrt{\text{MSE}\left[\frac{1}{n} + \frac{\overline{X}^2}{\Sigma (X_i - \overline{X})^2}\right]}}$$

Reject H_0 : if $|t_0| > t_{\alpha/2, n-2}$

Example 13.9. Compute the regression line of productivity index (Y) on aptitude score (X) from data given in Table–13.6, and test the regression function using analysis of variance table.

Solution

$$\Sigma X = 123 \qquad \Sigma Y = 184$$
$$\Sigma X^2 = 2359 \qquad \Sigma YX = 3341$$

$$\hat{\beta} = \frac{\Sigma YX - (\Sigma X)(\Sigma Y)/n}{\Sigma X^2 - (\Sigma X)^2/n}$$
$$= \frac{3341 - (123)(184)/7}{2359 - (123)^2/7}$$
$$= \frac{3341 - 3233.1428}{2359 - 2161.2857} = \frac{107.8572}{197.7143}$$
$$= 0.5455$$
$$\hat{\alpha} = \overline{Y} - \hat{\beta}\overline{X} = \frac{184}{7} - (0.5455)\left(\frac{123}{7}\right)$$
$$= 26.2857 - 9.5852$$
$$= 16.7005$$

The regression line of productivity index on aptitude score for workers is computed as

$$Y = 16.700 + 0.546\, X$$

Table–13.13
Analysis of Variance

Source	Degrees of freedom	Sum of Squares	Mean Squares	F	$F_{5\%}$
Regression	1	58.838	58.838	11.064	6.61
Residual	5	26.590	5.318		
Total	6	85.428			

Conclusion. As the computed value of F exceeds the tabulated $F_{5\%}$ value with (1,5) degrees of freedom, the regression function is significant.

13.3.8. Test of Significance of regression

Table–13.14
Analysis of Variance

Source	Degrees of Freedom	Sum of Squares	Mean Squares	F
Due to Regression	1	$SSR = \Sigma(\hat{Y}_i - \overline{Y})^2$	$MSR = \frac{SSR}{1}$	$\frac{MSR}{MSE}$
Deviation from Regression	$n-2$	$SSE = \Sigma(Y_i - \hat{Y}_i)^2$	$MSE = \frac{SSE}{n-2}$	
Total	$n-1$	$\Sigma(Y_i - \overline{Y})^2$	–	–

$F = \frac{MSR}{MSE}$ follows an F-distribution with 1 and $(n-2)$ degrees of freedom under $H_0 : \beta = 0$.

If the computed value of either t or F at a prescribed level of significance is greater than tabulated values of t or F (as the case may be) the null hypothesis is rejected and we conclude that the regression is significant.

Example 13.10. The different interest rates charged by some financial institutions may reflect how stringent their standards are for their loan appraisal; that is the lower the rate, the higher the standards (and hence lower the default rate). The following data were collected from a sample of financial companies that were selected at random.

Table 13.15

Interest rate (%) (x)	Default rate (per 1000 loans) (y)
7.0	38
6.6	40
6.0	35
8.5	46
8.0	48
7.5	39
6.5	36
7.0	37
8.0	44
$\Sigma x = 65.1$	$\Sigma y = 363$

$\Sigma x^2 = 476.31$, $\Sigma y^2 = 14{,}811$

$\Sigma xy = 2652.5$

(*a*) Find the equation of the regression line of y on x

(*b*) Interpret the slope of the regression line

(*c*) Calculate the coefficient of determination

(*d*) Calculate 95% confidence interval for the mean default rate when the interest rate is 8%.

Solution

$$n = 9, \bar{x} = \frac{65.1}{9} = 7.23$$

$$\bar{y} = \frac{363}{9} = 40.33$$

$$S_{xx} = \sum_{i=1}^{n} (x_i - \bar{x})^2 = \Sigma x_i^2 - \frac{(\Sigma x_i)^2}{n}$$

$$= 476.31 - \frac{65.1)^2}{9} = 5.42$$

$$S_{yy} = \Sigma (y_i - \bar{y})^2 = \Sigma y_i^2 - \frac{(\Sigma y_i)^2}{n}$$

$$= 14811 - \frac{(363)^2}{9} = 170$$

$$S_{xy} = \Sigma (x_i - \bar{x})(y_i - \bar{y})$$

$$= \Sigma x_i y_i - \frac{(\Sigma x_i)(\Sigma y_i)}{n}$$

$$= 2652.2 - \frac{(65.1)(363)}{9}$$

$$= 26.8$$

Therefore, $\hat{\beta} = \frac{S_{xy}}{S_{xx}} = \frac{26.8}{5.42} = 4.94$

$$\hat{\alpha} = \bar{y} - \hat{\beta}\bar{x}$$

$$= 40.33 - (4.94)(7.23)$$

$$= 4.61$$

Thus, the equation of the regression line of y on xl is

$$Y = \hat{\alpha} + \hat{\beta}x$$

$$= 4.61 + 4.94\,x$$

The value 4.94 of slope $\hat{\beta}$ indicates that the default rate increases by 4.94 (per 1000 loans) as the rate of interest increases by 1%.

The coefficient of determination

= square of the correlation coefficient

$$= r^2 = \frac{S_{xy}^2}{S_{xx}\,S_{yy}} = \frac{(26.8)^2}{(5.42)(180)} = 0.78$$

Then, 78% of the variation in y is explained by the variation x.

When $x = 8$, the estimated mean is

$$\hat{Y} = 4.61 + (4.94)(8)$$
$$= 44.13$$

The variance σ_e^2 is estimated by

$$\hat{\sigma}_e^2 = \frac{1}{n-2}\left[S_{yy} - \frac{S_{xy}^2}{S_{xx}}\right]$$

$$= \frac{1}{7}\left[170 - \frac{(26.8)^2}{5.42}\right]$$

$$= 5.354$$

Variance of the mean response when $x = 8$, is given by

$$\left[\frac{1}{n} + \frac{(x_0 - \bar{x})^2}{S_{xx}}\right]\hat{\sigma}_e^2$$

$$= \left[\frac{1}{9} + \frac{(8 - 7.23)^2}{5.42}\right](5.354)$$

$$= (0.111 + 0.109)(5.354) = 1.178,$$

so that standard deviation is 1.085

5% value of t for 7 d.f. is 2.365.

Thus, the required confidence interval is

$$44.13 \pm (2.365)(1.085)$$

or 41.6 and 46.7 (per 1000 loans).

Example 13.11. The following data show the number of hours that ten administrative officers worked and number of files disposed by them in a certain LIC office.

Table 13.16

Hours worked (x) :	4	9	10	14	4	7	12	22	1	17
No. of files disposed (y) :	31	58	65	73	37	44	60	91	21	84

Fit a linear regression model $Y = \alpha + \beta x$ and estimate the average number of files disposed by an officer who worked 14 hours.

Assuming the usual normal linear regression model,

(*a*) Test the null hypothesis $\beta = 3$ against $\beta > 3$ at 0.01 level of significance.

(*b*) Calculate a two sided 95% confidence interval for β.

Solution

$$n = 0$$

$\Sigma x = 100,$ $\qquad \Sigma y = 564,$

$\Sigma x^2 = 1376,$ $\qquad \Sigma y^2 = 36,562$

$$S_{xx} = \Sigma x^2 - \frac{(\Sigma x)^2}{n}$$

$$= 1376 - \frac{100^2}{10} = 376$$

$$S_{yy} = \Sigma y^2 - \frac{(\Sigma y)^2}{n}$$

$$= 36562 - \frac{(564)^2}{10}$$

$$= 4752.4$$

$$S_{xy} = \Sigma xy - \frac{(\Sigma x)(\Sigma y)}{n}$$

$$= 6945 - \frac{(100)(564)}{10}$$

$$= 1305$$

$$\hat{\beta} = \frac{S_{xy}}{S_{xx}} = 3.471$$

$$\hat{\alpha} = \bar{y} - \hat{\beta}\bar{x}$$

$$= 21.69$$

The equation to the regression line

$$Y = \hat{\alpha} + \hat{\beta}x$$

$$= 21.69 + 3.471x$$

When $x = 14$

$$\hat{Y} = 21.69 + 3.471 \times 14$$

$$= 70.284 \cong 70$$

Test $H_0 : \beta = 3$

$$H_1 : \beta > 3$$

The residual variance

$$\hat{\sigma}_e^2 = \frac{1}{n-2}(S_{yy} - \hat{\beta}S_{xy})$$

$$= \frac{1}{8}(4752.4 - 3.471 \times 1305)$$

$$= \frac{(222.745)}{8} = 27.8431$$

Hence, $\hat{\sigma}_e = 5.277$

Define the statistic

$$t = \frac{\hat{\beta} - \beta}{\hat{\sigma}_e}\sqrt{S_{xx}}$$

$$= \frac{3.471 - 3}{5.277}\sqrt{376}$$

$$= \frac{0.471}{5.277}(19.3907) = 1.731$$

For 8 degrees of freedom the table value of t for one tailed test is 2.896

Hence, H_0 cannot be rejected .95% confidence interval for β given by

$$\hat{\beta} \pm t_{\alpha/2\,,\,n-2} \frac{\hat{\sigma}_e}{\sqrt{S_{xx}}}$$

$$2.84 < \beta < 4.10 \text{ for } t_{\alpha/2\,,\,n-2} = 2.306$$

Comparison of two simple regression equations :

Consider two sets of bivariate data $\{y_{ij}, x_{ij}\}$, $j = 1,2,\ldots,n_i$, $i = 1,2$ producing two least square regression equations

$$y = \alpha_1 + \beta_1 x$$

and $$y = \alpha_2 + \beta_2 x$$

where $$\hat{\alpha}_i = \bar{y}_i - \hat{\beta}_i \bar{x}_i \text{ and}$$

$$\hat{\beta}_i = \frac{\sum_{j=1}^{n_i} (x_{ij} - \bar{x}_i)(y_{ij} - \bar{y}_i)}{\sum_{j=1}^{n_i} (x_{ij} - \bar{x}_i)^2}, \; i = 1, 2.$$

Assuming y for each x to be normally distributed, with means $\alpha_1 + \beta_1 x$ and $\alpha_2 + \beta_2 x$ and common variance σ_e^2,

$$E(\hat{\beta}_1 - \hat{\beta}_2) = \beta_1 - \beta_2$$

$$E(\hat{\alpha}_1 - \hat{\alpha}_2) = \alpha_1 - \alpha_2$$

$$V(\hat{\beta}_1 - \hat{\beta}_2) = V(\hat{\beta}_1) + V(\hat{\beta}_2)$$

$$= \sigma_e^2 \left\{ \frac{1}{S_{xx}^{(1)}} + \frac{1}{S_{xx}^{(2)}} \right\},$$

where $$S_{xx}^{(i)} = \sum_{j=1}^{n_i} (x_{ij} - \bar{x}_i)^2$$

$$V(\hat{\alpha}_1 - \hat{\alpha}_2) = V(\hat{\alpha}_1) + V(\hat{\alpha}_2)$$

$$= \sigma_e^2 \left\{ \frac{1}{n_1} + \frac{1}{n_2} + \frac{\bar{x}_1^2}{S_{xx}^{(1)}} + \frac{\bar{x}_2^2}{S_{xx}^{(2)}} \right\}$$

An unbiased estimator of σ_e^2, is given by the pooled value

$$s_e^2 = \frac{\Sigma (y_{1j} - \hat{\alpha}_1 - \hat{\beta}_1 x_{1j})^2 + \Sigma (y_{2j} - \hat{\alpha}_2 - \hat{\beta}_2 x_{2j})^2}{n_1 + n_2 - 4}$$

Note

(*i*) $\dfrac{(n_1 + n_2 - 4)\, s_e^2}{\sigma_e^2}$ is distributed as χ^2 with $n_1 + n_2 - 4$ degrees of freedom.

(*ii*) $\bar{y}_1, \bar{y}_2, \hat{\beta}_1, \hat{\beta}_2$ and s_e^2 are distributed independently of each other.

To test the hypothesis

$$H_{01} : \beta_1 = \beta_2$$

The appropriate statistic is

$$t = \frac{\hat{\beta}_1 - \hat{\beta}_2}{s_e \sqrt{\frac{1}{S_{xx}^{(1)}} + \frac{1}{S_{xx}^{(2)}}}},$$

which is distributed (under the H_{01}) as Student's t-distribution with $n_1 + n_2 - 4$ degrees of freedom.

Further, to test the hypothesis $H_{02} : \alpha_1 = \alpha_2$,

the appropriate statistic is

$$t = \frac{\hat{\alpha}_1 - \hat{\alpha}_2}{s_e \sqrt{\frac{1}{n_1} + \frac{1}{n_2} + \frac{\bar{x}_1^2}{S_{xx}^{(1)}} + \frac{\bar{x}_2^2}{S_{xx}^{(2)}}}}$$

which is distributed as Student's t-distribution with $n_1 + n_2 - 4$ degrees of freedom.

13.4 Polynomial Regression

It is sometimes observed that the scatter diagram indicates the scattering of points along a curve rather than a along a straight line. In such a situation it is desirable to search for an appropriate non-linear regression. The polynomial regression equation of degree p of Y on X is of the form

$$Y = B_0 + B_1X + B_2X^2 + \ldots + B_p X^p,$$

where all the powers of X are positive integers and the coefficients $B_0, B_1, \ldots, B_p$ are constants, which for any specific problem are estimated from the data. The choice of the degree p of the regression equation is at the disposal of the analyst and should be decided roughly by looking at the scatter diagram or by looking at the residuals after fitting regression equations of different degrees.

The method of fitting a polynomial regression equation to a given set of data is explained by taking p = 2. Thus, the equation of the polynomial of degree 2 involving the dependent variable Y and independent variable X is written as

$$Y = B_0 + B_1X + B_2X^2,$$

which is called on equation of **second degree** or **parabola**.

Given n paired values on (Y, X), the method of least square gives the following normal equations

$$n\hat{B}_0 + \hat{B}_1 \Sigma X + 2\hat{0}B_2 \Sigma X^2 = \Sigma Y$$

$$\hat{B}_0 \Sigma X + \hat{B}_1 \Sigma X^2 + \hat{B}_2 \Sigma X^3 = \Sigma YX$$

$$\hat{B}_0 \Sigma X^2 + \hat{B}_1 \Sigma X^3 + \hat{B}_2 \Sigma X^4 = \Sigma YX^2$$

On solving we get the estimates of B_0, B_1 and B_2 and hence write down the estimated parabolic regression equation as

$$\hat{Y} = \hat{B}_0 + \hat{B}_1 X + \hat{B}_2 X^2$$

In this equation, the first regression coefficient $\hat{B}_0$ represents the Y-intercept, the second regression coefficient $\hat{B}_1$ represents the linear coefficient and the third regression coefficient $\hat{B}_2$ represents the quadratic or curvilinear effect.

The coefficient of correlation R_0, sometimes termed as **index of correlation** between the observed Y's and the expected Y's (read from the regression curve) is given

$$R_0 = \sqrt{\frac{\Sigma(\hat{Y} - \overline{Y})^2}{\Sigma(Y - \overline{Y})^2}} = \frac{\sigma_{\hat{Y}}}{\sigma_Y}$$, which is never negative.

The coefficient R_0 indicates the closeness with which the points of the scatter diagram approximate to the regression curve. R_0^2 is called the coefficient of multiple determination.

Example 13.12. Fit a second degree polynomial to the following data and compute the coefficient of multiple determination and estimate the drying time for varnish additive of 6.5 gms.

Table–13.17

Amount of Varnish additive (gms) (*x*)	Drying time (in hours) (*y*)
0	12.0
1	10.5
2	10.0
3	8.5
4	7.0
5	8.0
6	7.5
7	8.5
8	9.0

Solution

The fitted second degree polynomial regression equation is

$$\hat{Y} = 12.879 - 1.7813\, X + 0.1737\, X^2$$

Standard error of estimate = 0.5005

Index of correlation $R_0 = 0.9617$

$$R_0^2 = 0.9249$$

Test of regression function :

Compute the ratio of mean square due to regression to mean square due to deviation from regression F = 36.9251

P-value for F(2, 6) = 0.000424

Hence, the polynomial regression function is highly significant (statistically). The estimated drying time for varnish additive of 6.5 gms is 7.9485.

Example 13.13. The following data are given on y = ultimate shear strength of a rubber compound (psi) and x = curve temperature (°F).

Table–13.18

Y	770	800	840	810	735	640	590	560
X	280	284	292	295	298	305	308	315

(a) Fit a polynomial of the second degree to the data.

(b) Test for the significance of regression.

(c) Test the hypothesis that $B_2 = 0$

Solution

The fitted polynomial regression is given by

$\hat{Y} = -26219.1 + 189.205\,X - 0.331\,X^2$, with $R^2 = 0.873$ (P-value 0.006)

Table–13.19
Analysis of Variance

Source	df	Sum of squares	Mean Square	F	P-Value
Regression	2	70283.847	35141.924	17.204	0.006
Residual	5	10213.028	2042.606		
Total	7	80496.875			

Coefficients	Standard Error	t	P-Value
$\hat{B}_0 = -26219.1$	11910.696	–2.201	0.079
$\hat{B}_1 = 189.205$	80.240	2.258	0.065
$\hat{B}_2 = -0.331$	0.135	–2.453	0.058

The polynomial regression is found to be significant at less than 1% level.

To test $H_0 : B_2 = 0$ against $H_1 : B_2 \neq 0$

Compute $t = \dfrac{|-0.331|}{0.135} = +2.453$

The tabulated value (theoretical value) of t with 5 degrees of freedom at 5% level (two tailed test) is 2.571. Thus, H_0 is not rejected.

However, P-value is 0.058.

13.5 Time series regression

Suppose we have a time series data (t, u_t) for n time periods, where u_t is the dependent variable, varying with time t. It is desired to determine the straight line trend, when fitted to a time series.

Assume the trend equation

$$u_t = a + bt;\ t = 1, 2, \ldots n$$

The method of least squares determines the following normal equations

$$\Sigma u_t = na + b\,\Sigma t$$

$$\Sigma t\,u_t = a\,\Sigma t + b\,\Sigma t^2$$

Solving the above equations, we estimate a and b and hence estimate linear trend as

$$u_t = \hat{a} + \hat{b}t$$

Illustration 1. Odd number of time points

Table–13.20

Census years	Population (India) in crores (u_t)	t	$t.u_t$	t^2
1961	43.9	–2	–87.8	4
1971	54.8	–1	–54.8	1
1981	68.3	0	0	0
1991	84.4	1	84.4	1
2001	102.7	2	205.4	4
Total	354.1	0	147.2	10

Thus, we have

$$\Sigma t = 0, \qquad \Sigma u_t = 354.1$$

$$\Sigma tu_t = 147.2, \qquad \Sigma t^2 = 10$$

Substituting these values in normal equations

$$354.1 = 5a + b \times 0$$

$$147.2 = a \times 0 + b \times 10$$

Solving the equations

$$\hat{a} = \frac{354.1}{5} = 70.82$$

$$\hat{b} = \frac{147.2}{10} = 14.72$$

Therefore, the equation to the straight line trend is given by

$$u_t = 70.82 + 14.72\,t$$

Illustration 2. Even number of time points

Table 13.21

Census year	Pop. India in crores (u_t)	t	$t.u_t$	t^2
1951	36.1	–3	–108.3	9
1961	43.9	–2	–87.8	4
1971	54.8	–1	–54.8	1

1981	68.3	1	68.3	1
1991	84.4	2	168.8	4
2001	102.7	3	308.1	9
Total	390.2	0	294.3	28

$$\Sigma t = 0, \Sigma u_t = 390.2,$$

$$\Sigma t.u_t = 294.3, \Sigma t^2 = 28$$

Normal equations :

$$390.2 = 6a + b \times 0$$

$$294.3 = a \times 0 + b \times 28$$

Solving the equations

$$\hat{a} = \frac{390.2}{6} = 65.03$$

$$\hat{b} = \frac{294.3}{28} = 10.51$$

$$u_t = 65.03 + 10.51\, t$$

13.6 Exponential Regression

Let y be the dependent variable and x be the only independent variable.

(*i*) Assumed regression relationship is

$$y = ab^x$$

Given a paired values (x, y), direct application of least square method is not easy to solve out for the constants in the regression. Hence taking logarithmic transformation of both sides of the regression equation, we have a linear regression form

$$\log y = \log a + x \log b$$

Now, we may rewrite the equation as

$$Y = A + Bx,$$

where $Y = \log y$; $A = \log a$

$X = x$; $B = \log b$

The least square equations are

$$\Sigma Y = n\hat{A} + \hat{B}\Sigma X$$

$$\Sigma YX = \hat{A}\Sigma X + \hat{B}\Sigma X^2$$

On solving we have

$$\hat{A} = \overline{Y} - \hat{B}\overline{X}$$

and $$\hat{B} = \frac{\Sigma YX - n\overline{Y}\overline{X}}{\Sigma(X - \overline{X})^2}$$

Thus, $$\hat{a} = \text{Antilog}(\hat{A})$$

and $$\hat{b} = \text{Antilog}(\hat{B})$$

Finally we have the fitted regression equation

$$\hat{y} = \hat{a}(\hat{b})^x$$

An index of correlation between y and x is given by

$$R = +\sqrt{\frac{\Sigma(\hat{y}-\bar{y})^2}{\Sigma(y-\bar{y})^2}}$$

(*ii*) Suppose the exponential relationship between y and x is of the type

$$y = ax^b$$

which is termed as log–log relationship *i.e.* the relationship between log y and log x is linear. We may fit the linear relation of the type

$$\log y = \log a + b \log x$$

i.e. $$Y = A + BX$$

After estimating A and B from the least square equations, we obtain

$$\hat{a} = \text{Antilog}(\hat{A})$$

$$\hat{b} = \hat{B}$$

Example 13.14. Given the following data on population of India during census years, fit a exponential trend.

$$P_t = ab^t.$$

Table–13.22

Census years t	Population (in crores) P_t
1951	36.1
1961	43.9
1971	54.8
1981	68.3
1991	84.4
2001	102.7

Solution

$$P_t = ab^t$$

$$\log P_t = \log a + t \,.\, \log b$$

or $$\log P_t = A + t.B$$

We have the following computations

Table–13.23

Year	t	P_t	log P_t	$t.\log P_t$	t^2
1951	–3	36.1	1.5575	–4.6725	9
1961	–2	43.9	1.6425	–3.2850	4
1971	–1	54.8	1.7388	–1.7388	1
1981	+1	68.3	1.8344	1.8344	1

1991	+2	84.4	1.9263	3.8526	4
2001	+3	102.7	2.0114	6.0342	9
Total : Σ	0	–	10.7109	2.0249	28

The least square equations are

$$\Sigma \log P_t = 6A + B\,\Sigma t$$

$$\Sigma t \,.\, \log P_t = A\,\Sigma t + B\,\Sigma t^2$$

On substitution

$$10.7109 = 6A + B \times 0$$

$$2.0249 = A \times 0 + B \times 28$$

$$\hat{A} = 1.78515 \,;\; \hat{B} = 0.0723$$

$$\therefore \quad \hat{a} = \text{Antilog}\,(\hat{A}) = 60.95$$

$$\hat{b} = \text{Antilog}\,(\hat{B}) = 1.180$$

Thus, the estimated exponential regression is

$$\hat{P}_t = (60.95)\,(1.180)^t$$

Table–13.24

t	P_t	$\hat{P}_t$	Residual $P_t - \hat{P}_t$	$P_t - \overline{P}_t$
–3	36.1	37.10	–1.00	–28.93
–2	43.9	43.77	0.13	–21.13
–1	54.8	51.65	3.15	–10.23
1	68.3	71.92	–3.62	3.27
2	84.4	84.87	–0.47	19.37
3	102.7	100.14	2.56	37.67

Mean $\overline{P}_t = 65.03$

$$\text{Index of Correlation} = +\sqrt{1 - \frac{\Sigma\,(P_t - \hat{P}_t)^2}{\Sigma\,(P_t - \overline{P}_t)^2}}$$

$$= +\sqrt{1 - \frac{30.8183}{3192.9934}} = +\sqrt{0.9903}$$

$$= .9951$$

13.7 Non-Parametric Measures of Association

Non-parametric measures of association are non-parametric statistics which do not assume the form of distribution of the variable under consideration. Parametric statistics assume (1) that the distribution characteristics of sample's population are known (e.g. mean, standard deviation, normality) and (2) that the data being analyzed are at the interval or ratio level. Frequently these assumptions cannot be met. Commonly this occurs with nominal or ordinal-level data (for which there are no measures of means or standard deviations). Also, continuous data may be so severely skewed from normal that it cannot be analyzed using regular parametric methods. In these cases we cannot perform analysis based on means and standard deviations. Instead it would be appropriate to use non-parametric methods which neither assume form of the distribution of the data nor do they rely on estimates of population parameter such as the mean in order to describe a variable's distribution. Non-parametric tests often are called *distribution free or parameter free statistics.*

3.7.1. Categorized (Nominal) Data—Association in 2 × 2 Tables

The categorized data imply data presented in the form of frequencies falling into certain specific categories or classes. The problem under discussion to compute statistical relationship/association between two or more variables where at least one of the variables is a dichotomy, nominal or ordinal. The concept of variable used here is in the most-general sense. A **contingency table** of frequencies classified according to values of the variables in question is used to summarise categorical data.

The tables showing the classification of attributes are called **contingency tables.**

Consider the problem of inter-dependence between two attributes A and B represented in 2 × 2 table in which N individuals are classified both according to presence or absence of certain attribute A, and presence or absence of another attribute B. Denote the presence of attribute A and α respectively and the presence and absence of attribute B by B and β, respectively. Thus, the numbers falling into four possible sub-groups called cells may be represented by 2 × 2 table or four fold table, historically called 2 × 2 contingency table, as

	B	not-B	Totals
A	(AB)	(Aβ)	(A)
not-A	(αB)	(αB)	(α)
Totals	(B)	(β)	N

Obviously (A) = (AB) + (Aβ)

(B) = (AB) + (α B)

(α) = (αB) + (αβ)

(β) = (A β) + (αβ)

Denote N = (A) + (α)

= (B) + (β)

= (AB) + (Aβ) + (αB) + (αβ)

For simplicity of notations we may write the above 2 × 2 table as

a	b	$a+b$
c	d	$c+d$
$a+c$	$b+d$	N

If there is no association between A and B, it is natural to think that the possession of A is irrelevant to the possession of B. Hence, there must be same proportion of A's among B's as among the not B's. Thus, two attributes A and B are said to be unas sociated or independent if

$$\frac{(AB)}{(B)} = \frac{(A\beta)}{(\beta)} = \frac{(AB)+(A\beta)}{(B)+(\beta)}$$

That is,
$$\frac{a}{a+c} = \frac{b}{b+d} = \frac{a+b}{a+b+c+d}$$

or
$$\frac{a}{a+c} = \frac{b}{b+d} = \frac{a+b}{N} \quad \ldots(1)$$

It therefore follows that

$$\frac{c}{a+c} = \frac{d}{b+d} = \frac{c+d}{N}$$

$$\frac{a}{a+b} = \frac{c}{c+d} = \frac{a+c}{N}$$

$$\frac{b}{a+b} = \frac{d}{c+d} = \frac{b+d}{N}$$

From (1) it follows that

$$a = \frac{(a+b)\,(a+c)}{N}$$

If in any given table

$$a > \frac{(a+b)\,(a+c)}{N},$$

there must be more A's among B's than among not B's. We say that A and B are positively associated (simply associated). Alternatively, if

$$a < \frac{(a+b)\,(a+c)}{N},$$

A and B are negatively associated

13.7.2. Measures of Association in 2 × 2 tables (Nominal Data)

Yule defined two coefficients to measure the association between two dichotomous attributes A and B.

(*i*) Coefficient of Association

$$Q = \frac{ad-bc}{ad+bc} = \frac{(AB)\,(\alpha\,\beta)-(A\,\beta)\,(\alpha\,\beta)}{(AB)\,(\alpha\,\beta)+(A\,\beta)\,(\alpha\,\beta)}$$

Q is symmetrical. It requires dichotomous data, which may be nominal or higher level.

Q = 0, if A and B are independent

= 1 (bc = 0), there is complete association.

= –1 (ad = 0), there is complete disassociation.

Q defines null relationship as statistical independence.

(*ii*) Coefficient of Colligation :

$$Y = \frac{1-\sqrt{\dfrac{bc}{ad}}}{1+\sqrt{\dfrac{bc}{ad}}} = \frac{\sqrt{ad}-\sqrt{bc}}{\sqrt{ad}+\sqrt{bc}}$$

Yule's Y is symmetrical.

Y requires dichotomous data which may be nominal or higher.

Y defines null relationship as statistical independence.

However, Y has no easily expressible interpretation.

13.7.3. The Relative Risk Coefficient (RR) :

Risk is a common measure of association for dichotomous variables. It is widely used in medical studies of risk factors such as relation of a treatment to heart attacks. While common in health related studies, risk is applicable to any situation in which the independent (column) variable is a treatment or cause and the dependent variable in an outcome (effect). SPSS package gives the relative risk estimates where treatment/control is given in rows (independent) and effect is given in columns (dependent).

Illustration 1.

	Attack	No Attack
Treatment	$a = 80$	$b = 420$
Control	$c = 100$	$d = 400$

The risk of a treated person getting an attack $= \dfrac{a}{a+b} = \dfrac{80}{5100} = 0.16$

The Risk of a control person getting an attack is $= \dfrac{c}{c+d} = \dfrac{100}{500} = 0.20.$

The relative risk (RR) is the ratio of two ratios $= \dfrac{0.16}{0.20} = 0.80$

That is, the relative risk of heart attack after treatment (among treated group) is 80%.

Note :

(*i*) RR for the given data means that the treatment group has 80% of the risk of the control group.

(*ii*) RR is zero and a null relationship exists when a/c = b/d, which corresponds to the conditions of independence and balance. RR is maximum when the treatment/effect cell aproaches 0 (cell *a*) and others are non-zero, which corresponds to a condition of weak monotonicity.

(*iii*) Risk is an **asymmetric** measures. Different coefficients will result depending on which is the independent variable.

(*iv*) Dichotomous data are assumed, of nominal level or higher.

(*v*) Risk does not vary from 0 to plus or minus 1 as do most measures of association. As risk in the treatment group approaches 0 for > 0 risk in the control group, RR approaches 0. Further, as risk in the treatment group approaches 0 for > 0 in the treatment group, RR approaches infinity.

Relative Risk Reduction (RRR) :

$$RRR = 1 - RR$$

The Relative Risk Reduction in the present illustration implies that the treatment reduces risk by 20%.

Th Odd Ratio :

❒ The Odd Ratio is related to relative risk. The odds being treatment group heart attack victim are $\frac{a}{b} = \frac{80}{420} = 0.19$.

The Odds being control group heart attack victim are $\frac{c}{d} = \frac{100}{400} = 0.25$.

The **Odd Ratio is the ratio of these two odds.** That is,

$$\text{Odds Ratio} = \frac{(a/b)}{(c/d)} = \frac{0.19}{0.25} = 0.76$$

Interpretation. The odds ratio signifies that the chance of getting a heart attack after treatment is 76% of the chance in the control group without treatment.

The odds ratio = 1 implies that two variables are independent. The larger the odds ratio above 1, the more effect the independent has on the dependent.

The farther below 1.0 the odds ratio is, the more the negative association between the two.

As regardfs the test of significance, the null hypothesis that odds ratio = 1.0 (independence), can be tested using Cochran's test.

The odds ratio is an asymmetric measure. Different coefficients will result depending on which is the independent (column) variable.

13.7.4. Measures of Association (Ordinal data)

Gamma (γ) : When data level is ordinal or higher, *Goodman and Kruskal* suggested a symmetric mesure Gamma which varies form –1 to +1, based on the difference between concordant pairs (P) and discordant pairs (Q). The concept of concordant pairs is illustrated in the following illustration. Thus, **Gamma** is computed as

$$\textbf{Gamma } (\gamma) = \frac{P - Q}{P + Q}$$

Illustration 2.

		Industry Size (x)		
		Small	**Medium**	**Large**
Type of Manager (y)	Weak	a = 10	b = 5	c = 2
	Strong	d = 10	e = 15	f = 20

$$\begin{aligned} P &= a(e+f) + bf \\ &= 10(15+20) + 5(20) \\ &= 450 \end{aligned}$$

$$\begin{aligned} Q &= c(d+e) + bd \\ &= 2(10+15) + 5(10) \\ &= 100 \end{aligned}$$

$$\text{Gamma } (\gamma) = \frac{P - Q}{P + Q} = \frac{450 - 100}{450 + 100} = 0.636$$

Since Gamma has a known sampling distribution approximating normal for large samples, it is possible to compute its standard error for large samples and hence the test of significance.

Gamma is the surplus of concordant pairs over discordant points, as a percentage of all pairs ignoring ties.

Under statistical independence gamma will be zero, otherwise it may also be zero when P = Q.

Gamma is a symmetrical measure. It will compute the same coefficient value regardless of which is the independent (column) variable.

Gamma assumes both variables to be ordinal or higher.

For a 2 × 2 table, gamma equals Yule's Q.

Computation of Gamma

Gamma assumes that both of the variables consist of ordered set of categories. To understand the computation of Gamma, consider pairs of cases. Imagine four individuals –A, B, C and D classified under income and education as given below

	Education (X)		
Income (Y)	**High**	**Medium**	**Low**
High	A		
Medium		C	
Low	B		D

Note. Both the variables are arranged from High to Low. These four individuals form six possible pairs (A, B), (A, C), (A, D), (B, C), (B, D) and (C, D).

A has more education and income than C. This is what is called a **concordant** pair. A is higher on both variables income and education than C. The AD pair is also concordant.

A is higher on both education and income than D. And CD pair is also concordant. C has more education and income than D.

However, C has more income than B, but C has less education than B. This is what is called **discordant pair**. C is higher on one variable (education) and lower on the other variable (income).

When we look at the AB pair we see another possibility. A has more income than B, but A and B are tied on education. This is what is called a **tied pair**. The BD pair is also tied.

Gamma ignores all tied pairs and therefore tends to inflate the value of gamma.

$$\text{Gamma} = \frac{\text{Number of concordant pairs} - \text{Number of discordant pairs}}{\text{Number of Concordant pairs} + \text{Number of discordant pairs}}$$

If there are more concordant pairs than the discordant pairs, the Gamma is positive and hence this is called **positive relationship.** If the number of discordant pairs is greater than the number of concordant pairs gamma is negative and there is **negative relationship.** That is, large (small) values of one variable go with small (large) values of the other variable.

Kendall's tau–b (τ_b)

This is a refinement of gamma that considers tied pairs. A tied pair occurs when subjects have the same value on the X-variable, on the Y-variable or on both. For a given sample size N, there are $\frac{N(N-1)}{2}$ pairs of observations. After concordant pairs and discordant pairs are removed, the remainder are tied tau b does not have a PRE interpretation, but does provide a range of –1.0 to +1.0 for square tables. It may be calculated as

$$\tau_b = \frac{P - Q}{\sqrt{\left(\frac{N(N-1)}{2} - T_x\right)}\sqrt{\left(\frac{N(N-1)}{2} - T_y\right)}}$$

where $T_y = \sum_{i=1}^{r} \frac{m_{i} \cdot (m_{i.} - 1)}{2}$, where $m_{i.} = i$ th row total, $i = 1, \ldots, r$

and $T_x = \sum_{j=1}^{c} \frac{m_{.j}\ (m_{.j} - 1)}{2}$, where $m_{.j} = j$th column total, $j = 1,2,\ldots, c$

tau–b requires binary or ordinal data.

Kendall's *tau* – c (τ_c)

This is another adjustment to the basic P–Q relationship of gamma and is suitable for tables of any size

$$\tau_c = \frac{2m\,(P - Q)}{N^2\,(m - 1)},$$

where m is the smaller number of rows or columns.

There is no simply intuitable meaning which can be attached to tau, although it is a symmetrical measure which will yield the same coefficient magnitude regardless of which of two variables is considered the independent (column) variable.

τ_c is designed for use where at least one of two variables is ordinal in level. τ_c varies from –1 to +1 and was specifically designed to be able to attain these bounds for non-square tables.

Somers' *d*

This is a modified gamma, modified to penalise for pairs tied on X only, in directional (asymmetric) hypothesis in which X causes or predicts Y and to penalise for pairs tied on Y only, in hypotheses in which Y causes or predicts X.

Thus, to compute Somers' d :

$$d_{yx} = \frac{P - Q}{P + Q + Y_0}, \text{ if X causes Y}$$

$$d_{xy} = \frac{P - Q}{P + Q + X_0}, \text{ if Y causes X}$$

Here,

$$P = \text{Number of concordant pairs}$$
$$Q = \text{Number of Discordant pairs}$$
$$Y_0 = \text{Pairs tied on Y}$$
$$= \frac{N(N-1)}{2} - P - Q - T_x$$
$$X_0 = \text{Pairs tied on X}$$
$$= \frac{N(N-1)}{2} - P - Q - T_y$$

Thus,

$$d_{yx} = \frac{P - Q}{\frac{N(N-1)}{2} - T_x}$$

$$d_{xy} = \frac{P - Q}{\frac{N(N-1)}{2} - T_y}$$

Illustration 3.

Computations of tau-*b*, tau-*c* and Somers' d :

		x			
		Small	Medium	Large	Total
y	Weak	10	5	2	17
	Strong	10	15	20	45
	Total	20	20	22	62

$$P = 450,\ Q = 100$$

$$\frac{N(N-1)}{2} = \frac{62(62-1)}{2} = 1891$$

$$T_x = \frac{20(20-1)}{2} + \frac{20(20-1)}{2} + \frac{22(22-1)}{2}$$
$$= 190 + 190 + 231 = 611$$

$$Y_y = \frac{17(17-1)}{2} + \frac{45(45-1)}{2}$$
$$= 136 + 990 = 1126$$

$$\text{Thus, } \tau_b\ (tau-b) = \frac{P - Q}{\sqrt{\frac{N(N-1)}{2} - T_x}\ \sqrt{\frac{N(N-1)}{2} - T_y}}$$

$$= \frac{450 - 100}{\sqrt{1891 - 611}\ \sqrt{1891 - 1126}}$$

$$= \frac{350}{\sqrt{(1280)\ (765)}} = 0.3537$$

$$\tau_c\ (tau-c) = \frac{2m\ (P - Q)}{N^2\ (m-1)}$$

$$= \frac{(2)(2)(450 - 100)}{(62)^2 (2-1)}$$

$$= \frac{1400}{3844} = 0.3642$$

Somers' d :

If x causes y,

$$d_{yx} = \frac{P - Q}{\frac{N(N-1)}{2} - T_x} = \frac{350}{1891 - 611}$$

$$= \frac{350}{1280} = 0.2734$$

If y causes x,

$$d_{xy} = \frac{P - Q}{\frac{N(N-1)}{2} - T_y} = \frac{350}{1891 - 1126}$$

$$= \frac{350}{765} = 0.4575$$

13.7.5. Measurement of Association in $r \times c$ contigency table (Chi-square based) :

Consider a $r \times c$ contigency table with r rows and c columns. Let n_{ij} be the frequency in the cell corresponding to ith row and jth column.

If two variables are independent the frequency in (i, j)th cell would be $\frac{n_{i.}\, n_{j}}{N}$, where $n_{i.} = \sum_j n_{ij}$ and $n_{.j} = \sum_i n_{ij}$.

The deviation from independence in (i,j)th cell in then measured by

$$D_{ij} = n_{ij} - \frac{n_{i.}\, n_{j}}{N}$$

A coefficient of association is therefore defined as

$$\Sigma\, D_{ij}^2 / (n_i \,.\, n_j),$$

called a **square contingency,**

$$\chi^2 = \sum_i \sum_j \frac{D_{ij}^2}{(n_{i.}\, n_{.j}/N)}$$

χ^2 is not a convenient measure of association because its upper limit increases as N increases. Therefore some modified forms of coefficient of association, proposed by Karl Pearson and others are given below.

Note. The significance of measures of strength of association based on Chi-square can be tested using approximate Chi-square tests.

(a) Phi Coefficient. Phi is a chi-square based measure of association and both variables are nominal and dichotomous, introduced by 2×2 contigency tables. It may be pointed out that the size of the chi- square coefficient depends on the strength of relationship and sample size. Phi coefficient eliminates by dividing chi-square by N, the sample size and taking the square root.

That is,

$$P = \sqrt{\frac{\chi^2}{N}}$$

Phi is sometimes called Pearson's **Coefficient of mean square contingency.**

When computing phi, note that Yates' correction to chi-square is **not** used. Phi can handle larger tables but is often used as a measure of association in 2 × 2 table formed by true dichotomies. For larger tables the maximum value of phi depends on table size, maximum value being $\sqrt{k-1}$, where k = the no. of rows or columns, which is smaller and can exceed 1.0 making phi a **not** suitable measure of association.

In a 2 × 2 table, phi can be interpreted as symmetric percent difference, measuring the percent of concentration of cases in the diagonal.

Phi defines perfect association as predictive monotonicity and defines null relationship as statistical independence.

The significance of phi is same as for chi-square.

Phi is a symmetrical measure and is used with nominal data, though for 2 × 2 tables, data may be ordinal.

(b) The Contingency Coefficient (Pearson's C). The contingency coefficient is an adjustment to phi, intended to adopt it to tables larger than 2 × 2.

Thus, Pearson defines C as equal to the square root of chi-square divided by chi-square plus N, the sample size. That is,

$$C = \sqrt{\frac{\chi^2}{\chi^2 + N}}$$

C has a maximum approaching but never totally reaching 1.0 only for large tables and some researchers recommend it only for 5 × 5 tables or larger. For smaller tables it will underestimate the level of association when all observations are on the diagonal of a table.

By dividing C by C_{max} one gets adjusted C, named C^*, which varies from 0 to 1 regardless of table size, making it a much more useful measure. Thus, C^*, termed as **Sakoda's adjusted Pearson's C** is defined as

$$C^* = \frac{C}{\sqrt{\frac{k-1}{k}}}$$

where k = number of rows or columns, whichever is **smaller**.

Pearson's C may be viewed as a nominal approximation to Pearsonian coefficient correlation r.

The significance of C is the same as for chi-square.

C and C^* define a null relationship as statistical independence. However, the smaller the table the more C (but not C^*) will be less than 1.0 regardless of monotonicity.

C and C^* are symmetrical measures and may be used with nominal data or higher.

C and C^* can reach 1.0 only when the two variables have equal marginals.

(c) Tshuprow's T. T is a chi-square based measure of association which reaches 1.0 in square tables where row marginals and identical to column marginals. T is equal to the square root chi- square divided by sample size N times the square root of the number of degrees of freedom in the table, that is,

$$T = \sqrt{\frac{\chi^2}{N\sqrt{(r-1)(c-1)}}}$$

Where r is the number of rows and c is the number of columns. Because T is less than 1.0 for non-square tables, it is little used and is not supported by major statistical packages.

For a 2 × 2 table T = phi and the significance of T is same as for chi-square.

T is a symmetrical measure and it does not matter which is the independent (column) variable.

At the data level, T may be used with nominal data or higher.

(d) Cramer' V. Cramer's V is the most popular of the chi-square based measures of nominal association because it gives good norming from 0 to 1 regardless of table size, where row marginals equal column marginals. V equals the square root of chi square divided by sample size N time m, which is the smaller of (row–1) or (column–1). That is,

$$V = \sqrt{\frac{\chi^2}{Nm}}$$

Cramer's V tends to be lower than phi or C.

For a 2 × 2 table, V = phi.

V can reach 1.0 only when two variables have equal marginals.

V is also a symmetrical measure and may be used with nominal data or higher.

(e) Likelihood Ratio χ^2. This is a goodness-of-fit statistic similar to Pearson's χ^2. For large samples both the statistics are equivalent.

An advantage with the likelihood ratio Chi-square is that it can be subdivided into interpretable parts that add up to total.

Thus,

LR Chi-square

$$= -2 \sum_i \sum_j f_{0ij} \; l_n \left(\frac{f_{eij}}{f_{0ij}} \right)$$

13.7.6. PRE Measures :

(a) **Lambda (λ).** Lambda, also known as **Goodman-Kruskal lambda** is a PRE (proportionate reduction in error) measure. This means that its value reflects the percentage reduction in errors in predicting the dependent given knowledge of the independent. This probability is defined as the chance that an observation is in a category other than the most common (modal) one. That is, with no knowledge of the independent, a blind forecaster would guess that each observation of the dependent would have the value its modal category. Thus, the marginal of the modal category is the number of correct guesses one would expect by chance. This forms the denominator of the equation for lambda. The numerator reflects the number of correct guesses knowing the independent variable.

Lambda, in its asymmetric form is given by

$$\text{Lambda} = \frac{[\text{Sum}\,(f_i) - F_d]}{(N - F_d)},$$

where f_i is the largest frequency for each class of the i classes of the independent variable and F_d is the largest marginal value of the dependent variable and N is the sample size.

Since lambda has a known sampling distribution (it is asymptotically normal) it is possible to compute its standard error and hence significance. Lambda divided by its standard error gives the coefficient used to compute P_λ, the probability or significance level of the computed lambda value.

Interpretation

Lambda is the percent, one reduces errors in guessing the value of the dependent variable when one knows the value of the independent variable. Specifically, lambda is the surplus of errors made when the marginals of the dependent variable are known, minus the number of errors made when the frequencies of the dependent variable are known for each class (value) of the independent variable as a percentage of errors of the first type. A lambda is 0, indicates that knowing the distribution of the independent variable is of no help in estimating the value of the dependent variable, compared to estimating the dependent variable solely on the basis of its own frequency distribution.

Lambda defines 'perfect relationship' as predictive monotonic or higher and defines 'null relationship'. This differs from most measures of association, which use the criteria of strict monotonicity and statistical independence respectively.

SPSS package computes the significance of lambda.

The usual version of lambda is asymmetric.

Lambda may be used with nominal level data or higher. That is, lambda is unaffected by the ordering of columns of the independent variable.

Lambda generally varies from 0 to 1.

(b) The Uncertainty Coefficient or Theil's U. The uncertainty coefficient, also called the **entropy coefficient** varies from 0 to 1 and has a proportionate reduction in error interpretation based on information theory. UC is the percent reduction in error in accounting for the variance in the dependent variable, where variance is defined in terms of entropy. Though lambda and UC are both PRE measures of nominal association, UC is differentiated in that its formula takes into account the entire distribution rather than just the modal distribution upon which lambda focuses and is therefore sometimes preferred for this reason.

The formula for UC (R | C), which is the uncertainty coefficient for predicting the row variable on the basis of column variable is given below, with its variants :

$$UC(R|C) = [H(X) + H(Y) - H(XY)]/H(Y)$$

$$UC(C|R) = [H(X) + H(Y) - H(XY)]/H(X)$$

$$UC_{symmetric} = 2\,[H(X) + H(X) - H(XY)]/[H(X) + H(Y)]$$

where X is the column variable
Y is the row variable
N is sample size

r_j are the raw totals (marginals) for rows 1, ..., J

c_k are the column totals (marginals) for columns 1, ..., K

n_{jk} is the cell count for row j, column k.

l_n is the symbol for natural log function.

$$H(X) = -\sum_{j=1}^{J} [(r_j/N)\, l_n\, (r_j/N)$$

$$= \text{entropy for UC(C | R)}$$

$$H(Y) = -\sum_{k=1}^{K} (c_k/N)\, l_n\, (c_k/N)$$

$$= \text{entropy for UC(R | C)}$$

$$H(XY) = -\sum_{j=1}^{J}\sum_{k=1}^{K}\left[\left(\frac{n_{jk}}{N}\right) l_n \left(\frac{n_{jk}}{N}\right)\right]$$

Interpretation. The uncertainty coefficient is the percent reduction in uncertainty in predicting the dependent variable based on knowing the independent variable. When UC = 0, the independent variable is of no help in predicting the dependent variable.

The uncertainty coefficient defines 'perfect relationship' as predictive monotonic or higher and defines 'null relationship' as statistical independence.

SPSS and other statistical packages report the significance of uncertainty coefficient.

The uncertainty coefficient is an asymmetric measure. It will have different value depending on which is dependent and which is independent variable. The statistical packages give output for **three** versions of UC–row independent, column independent and the symmetric version averaging the first two. Nonetheless, whereas asymmetric has a clear PRE meaning, symmetric UC does not, other than being an average of the two asymmetric UC's.

Data may be nominal level or higher.

For historical reason, the uncertainty coefficient was often computed in terms of predicting the column variable from the row variable *i.e.* UC(C | R) as opposite to the social science where column variable is taken as independent variable *i.e.* UC(R | C).

(c) Goodman and Kruskal tau (τ). The Goodman and Kruskal tau (τ) is obtained by using the principle of proportional reduction in error. Like λ, this is a directional measure of association with different values depending on whether rows or columns of a cross-classification table are dependent. τ has limits of zero (no association) and 1 (complete or perfect association). SPSS package has the facilities of cross tabulation and computations of λ and τ along with their statistical significance.

Let us consider the computation of τ for **rows dependent**. The principle underlying τ is to determine the proportional reduction in error by using two rules. The method is to predict the actual frequencies in the table for each value of the dependent variable.

Rule 1. is to determine the number of errors of prediction **without** using the information on the **independent** variable. This results in E_1, the number of errors of prediction for each value of the dependent variable, using only **row totals.**

Rule 2. The information about the independent variable (in each column) is used to predict the frequencies for each value of the dependent variable. This results in a second set of error of prediction, E_2.

The proportionate reduction of errors, defined as τ, is

$$\tau = \frac{E_1 - E_2}{E_1}$$

Formula :

If R_i is the row total for row i of the table and N is the total number of cases in the table, the number of errors using Rule 1 is

$$E_1 = \sum_i \left(\frac{N - R_i}{N} \times R_i \right)$$

Then, for each column j, use the same procedure and add all the errors and term this E_{2j}. That is, for column j, the number of errors of prediction is

$$E_{2j} = \sum_j \left(\frac{C_j - O_{ij}}{C_j} \times O_{ij} \right),$$

where C_j is the column total for column j and O_{ij} is the number of cases in row i and column j. The sum of these $E_2 = \sum_j E_{2j}$.

The value of τ is the proportional reduction in error

$$\tau = \frac{E_1 - E_2}{E_1}$$

Comparison between Goodman-Kruskal Lambda (λ) and Goodman-Kruskal tau (τ) :

The basic concept behind the computation of Lambda statistic centres around the use of **modal value** of a nominal variable to predict the value of the variable for any given case.

As regards the strategy of prediction in the computation, tau uses the information of the frequencies distribution of both dependent and independent variables.

Example 13.15. Compute Phi, C, C*, T and V.

Vote/Party	UDF	LDF	Total
Voted	20 (*a*)	10 (*b*)	30
Didn't Vote	5 (*c*)	25 (*d*)	30
Total	25	35	N = 60

$$\chi^2 = \frac{N(ad - bc)^2}{(a+b)(c+d)(a+c)(b+d)}$$

$$= \frac{60(500 - 50)^2}{30 \times 30 \times 25 \times 35} = \frac{108}{7}$$

$$\text{Thus, phi } (\phi) = \sqrt{\frac{\chi^2}{N}}$$

$$= \sqrt{\frac{108}{7 \times 60}} = 0.5071$$

Further, *Pearson's Contigency Coefficient*

$$C = \sqrt{\frac{\chi^2}{\chi^2 + N}}$$

$$= \sqrt{\frac{15.4286}{15.4286 + 60}} = \sqrt{\frac{15.4286}{75.4286}}$$

$$= 0.4523$$

Sakoda's adjusted Pearson's C,

$$C^* = \frac{C}{\sqrt{\frac{k-1}{k}}} = \frac{0.4523}{\sqrt{\frac{(2-1)}{2}}} = \frac{0.4523}{0.71}$$

$$= 0.637$$

Tshuprow's T :

For 2 × 2 table, T = Phi.

Cramer's V :

$$V = \sqrt{\frac{\chi^2}{\text{Min }\{(r-1)\ ,\ (c-1)\}\ N}}$$

= Phi, for a 2 × 2 table.

Example 13.16. Computations for Lambda (λ) and Goodman Kruskal (τ) Statistics

Basic degree at managerial level (x) Independent

Efficiency (y)	Arts	Science	Engineering	Total
High	4	8	5	17
Medium	42	17	21	80
Low	19	20	14	53
Total	65	45	40	150

Computation of Goodman-Kruskal (τ) with Rows dependent (y) :

Rule 1 :

For **row 1**, the number of errors of prediction is $\frac{150-17}{150} \times 17 = 15.07$

For **row 2**, the number of errors of prediction is $\frac{150-80}{150} \times 80 = 37.33$

Fro **row 3**, the number of errors of prediction is $\frac{150-53}{150} \times 53 = 34.27$

Thus, the total number of erros of prediction is $E_1 = 15.07 + 37.33 + 34.27 = 86.67$

Rule 2.

Begin with column 1, the errors of predictions for the three rows are :

$$\frac{65-4}{65} \times 4 = 3.75$$

$$\frac{65-42}{65}\times 42 = 14.86$$

$$\frac{65-19}{65}\times 19 = 13.45$$

Thus, the errors for the **1st Column**

$$E_{21} = 3.75 + 14.86 + 13.45$$
$$= 32.06$$

For column 2, the errors of prediction for the three rows are :

$$\frac{45-8}{45}\times 8 = 6.58$$

$$\frac{45-17}{45}\times 17 = 10.58$$

$$\frac{45-20}{45}\times 20 = 11.11$$

Thus, the errors of prediction for the **second column**

$$E_{22} = 6.58 + 10.58 + 11.11$$
$$= 28.27$$

For column 3, the errors of prediction for the three rows are :

$$\frac{40-5}{40}\times 5 = 4.38$$

$$\frac{40-21}{40}\times 21 = 9.98$$

$$\frac{40-14}{40}\times 14 = 9.10$$

Thus, the total errors for the **third column** is

$$E_{23} = 4.38 + 9.98 + 9.10$$
$$= 23.46$$

For **Rule 2,** the total number of errors of prediction for efficiency (y) is the sum of the above errors

$$E_2 = E_{21} + E_{22} + E_{23}$$
$$= 32.06 + 28.27 + 23.46$$
$$= 83.79$$

Calculation of τ :

$$\tau = \frac{E_1 - E_2}{E_1} = \frac{86.67 - 83.79}{86.67}$$

$$= \frac{2.88}{86.67} = \mathbf{0.0332}$$

Computation for Lambda :

The largest frequencies in the 1st Column, 2nd Column and 3rd Column of the independent variable (x) are 42, 20 and 21 respectively.

Thus $f_1 = 42$, $f_2 = 20$ and $f_3 = 21$

F_d = largest marginal value of the dependent variable (y)

= 80

N = 150

Therefore,

$$\text{Lambda } (\lambda) = \frac{(\Sigma f_i) - F_d}{N - F_d}$$

$$= \frac{(42 + 20 + 21) - 80}{150 - 80}$$

$$= \frac{83 - 80}{70} = \frac{3}{70} = 0.0429$$

13.7.7 Eta (η) Coefficient

Eta (η) measures of association is used when one variable is measured on an interval/ratio scale (e.g. income) and the other variable has a limited number of categories (e.g. gender)

- value ranges between 0 and 1.
- values close to 1 indicate a strong relationship between two variables.
- values close to zero indicate little or no relationship.

η^2 computes proportion of variance in the dependent variable explained by the group (categorical) variable. That is,

$$\eta^2 = \frac{SSB}{SST},$$

where, SSB = Sum of squares between groups.

SST = Total sum of squares.

$\eta = \sqrt{\eta^2}$ is termed **correlation ratio,** indicating magnitude of relationship between the dependent variable and the group (categorical) variable.

Eta is often useful to measure non-linear relationship and is computed as

$$\text{Eta} = +\sqrt{\frac{SSR}{SST}}$$

where SSR = Sum of squares due to regression

SST = Total sum of squares

The statistic Eta is interpreted similar to the pearson r, but can never be negative. However, even though *r* is the same when we regress *y* on *x* or *x* on *y*, two possible values for eta can be obtained.

13.7.8 Point-Biserial Correlation Coefficient (r_{pb}) :

The point-biserial correlation coefficient, referred to as r_{pb}, is a special case of Pearson in which one variable Y is quantitative (Continuous) and the other variable X is dichotomous and nominal. The calculations simplify since typically the values 1 (presence) and 0 (absence) are used for dischotomous variable X.

The Pearson's formula r_{xy} on simplification becomes

$$r_{pb} = \frac{Y_1 - Y_0}{s_y}\sqrt{\frac{n_1 n_0}{n(n-1)}}$$

where Y_1 = mean value on the continuous variable Y for all data points in group 1.

Y_0 = mean value on the continuous variable Y for all data points in group 2.

n = total sample size

n_1 = number of data points in group 1.

n_0 = number of data points in group 2.

13.7.9 Biserial Correlation Coefficient (r_b)

Another measure of association, the biserial correlation coefficient, termed r_b, is similar to the point biserial, but puts quantitative data against ordinal data, with an underlying continuity but measured discretely as two values (dichotomous).

This measure is appropriate for a $t \times 2$ frequency table, where dichotomy may relate to some quantitative character, but the other classification relates to a variable.

If the two characters are denoted by A and y respectively, then the frequency table may be laid out as follows :

TABLE 13.25

$t \times 2$ frequency table

y-Class / A-Class	Class 1	Class 2 ..	Class t	Total
A_1	f_1	f_2 ...	f_t	f
A_2	$n_1 - f_1$	$n_2 - f_2$....	$n_t - f_t$	$n - f$
Total	n_1	n_2.......	n_t	n

It will be assumed that the A-classes arise from the division of the range of a continuous variable x by a point, say h, the class A_1 corresponding to values greater than h and the class A_2 to values less than or equal to h. Assume that x and y jointly follow bivariate normal distribution.

The biserial correlation coefficient is computed as

$$r_b = (Y_1 - Y_0) \cdot \cdot \frac{pq}{Y} / s_y ,$$

where Y_0 and Y_1 are the Y score means for data pairs with x score of 0 and 1, respectively, $q = 1 - p$ and p are the proportions of data a pairs with x scores of 0 and 1, respectively, and s_y is the standard deviation for the y-data and Y is the height of the standardized normal distribution at the point z, where P $(Z < z) = q$ and P $(Z > z) = p$. Since the factor involving p, q and the height is always greater than 1, the biserial is always greater than the point-biserial.

13.7.10 Rank-Biserial Coefficient

The rank-biserial correlation coefficient, r_{rb} is used for dischotomous nominal data vrs rankings (ordinal). The formula is usually expressed as

$$r_{rb} = 2(Y_1 - Y_0)/n$$

where n is the number of data pairs, and Y_0 and Y_1 , again, are the Y score means for data pairs with x score of 0 and 1, respectively.

As regards computation of correlation coefficient between different types of variables, some common choices may be stated as follows :

Table 13.26

Y \ X	Quantitative (Interval) X	Ordinal X	Nominal X
Quantitative (Interval) Y	Pearson r	Biserial r_b	Point Biserial r_{pb}
Ordinal Y	Biserial r_b	Spearman rho	Rank Biserial r_{rb}
Nominal Y	Point Biserial r_{pb}	Rank Biserial r_{rb}	Phi, C, Lambda

13.7.11 Rank based measures of association

(a) Spearman's **Rank Correlation Coefficient (Rho)**

It is a popular non-parametric measure of association between two ordinal variables (X and Y).

If the data are not ranked, convert data on X to ranks and also convert data on Y to ranks : that is, $X_{(1)}$, $X_{(2)}$,..... and $Y_{(1)}$, $Y_{(2)}$,..... in ascending or descending order.

The Pearson's product moment correlation is used to compute correlation between Y and X (using ranked values), termed as Spearman's Rank Correlation coefficient (r_s). If there are no tied ranks $X_{(i)}$ and $Y_{(i)}$, the Spearman's rank correlation coefficient is computed as

$$r_s = 1 - \frac{6\Sigma d_i^2}{n(n^2-1)}, \text{ where } d_i = (X_{(i)} - Y_{(i)}),\ i = 1, 2, \ldots n$$

r_s lies between -1 and +1 and preserves all properties of Pearson's r But like Perason's r it does **not** assume linearity of relation between X and Y. The test of significance of r_s is similar to that of r.

Illustration :

Case	A	B	C	D	E	F	G	H
Rank by Height	1	2	3	4	5	6	7	8
Rank by Weight	3	4	1	2	5	7	8	6

Difference between ranks (d_i) :

–2,–2,2,2,0,–1,–1,2

$$\Sigma d_i^2 = 4+4+4+4+0+1+1+4$$

$$= 22$$

$$r_s = 1 - \frac{6\Sigma d_i^2}{n(n^2-1)}$$

$$= 1 - \frac{6 \times 22}{8(8^2-1)}$$

$$= 1 - \frac{132}{504} = 0.738$$

The value of Spearman's rank correlation coefficient shows that there is moderately strong positive correlation between height rank and weight rank. This indicates that as a person's height rank increases, so too his weight rank.

(*b*) **Kendall tau rank Correlation Coefficient**

The Kendall tau rank correlation coefficient or Kendall's τ_a is used to measure the degree of correspondence between two rankings.

Kendall's coefficient, compared to Spearman's correlation coefficient, has an intuitively simple interpretation. Its alegbraic structure is much simpler than that of the Spearman coefficient. It can be computed either from the actual observations or from observations converting them to ranks. The strength of relationship between two variables as shown by the correlation coefficient implies the strength of the tendency of two variables X and Y to move in the same (or opposite) direction. The Kendall's tau measures this tendency in a very direct and easily understood way.

Let (X_i, Y_i) and (X_j, Y_j) be pairs of bivariate observations. If $(X_i - X_j)$ and $(Y_i - Y_j)$ have the same sign, we shall say that the pair is concordant, if they have opposite sign, the pair is discordant. Let P stand for the number of concordant pairs and Q stand for the discordant pairs. Compute S = P — Q, known as Kendall's S. Large positive value of S indicate a strong positive relationship and a large negative value of S indicates a strong negative relationship.

As S lies between $-\frac{n(n-1)}{2}$ and $\frac{n(n-1)}{2}$, where $\frac{n(n-1)}{2}$ being the total number of pairs, $\frac{2S}{n(n-1)}$ lies between –1 and +1. +1 occurs if all the $\frac{n(n-1)}{2}$ pairs are concordant and –1 if all the $\frac{n(n-1)}{2}$ pairs are discordant.

Thus, Kendall's tau, known as tau $-a(\tau_a)$ is computed as

$$\tau_a = \frac{P - Q}{\frac{n(n-1)}{2}}$$

$$= \frac{4P}{n(n-1)} - 1 \text{ (Assuming no ties)}$$

Further, Goodman—Kruskal Gamma (γ), is defined as $\gamma = \frac{P - Q}{P + Q}$, (Neglecting ties).

Example 13.17. Suppose we rank a group of 8 people by height and weight where A is tallest and third heaviest and so on.

Person	A	B	C	D	E	F	G	H
Rank by Height	1	2	3	4	5	6	7	8
Rank by weight	3	4	1	2	5	7	8	6

The data show there is some correlation between the two rankings.

The persons have been ranked from 1 to 8 according to height. As regards weight ranking the first entry 3, has five higher ranks to the right of it, the contribution to P of this entry is 5. The second entry is 4 and there are four higher ranks to the right of it and the contribution to P is 4. Continuing this way we find $P = 5 + 4 + 5 + 4 + 3 + 1 + 0 + 0 = 22$

Thus $\tau = \frac{4 \times 22}{56} - 1 = 0.57$

Thus, there is positive correlation between the ranking, but less strong than Spearman's rho. The same value for τ is obtained by computing concordant (P) and discordant (Q) pairs among the paired ranks.

13.7.12 The Choice of Measures

With many measures of association/correlation it is rather confusing to choose the appropriate one. The basic rules in choosing measures are :

1. Choose the measure which is appropriate for the level of measurement obtained by the variables. Never use Pearson *r* for nominal scale data.
   (*a*) Statistics appropriate for lower level of measurement can be used for higher level of measurement, e.g. contingency coefficient can be used to describe interval scale.
   (*b*) However, using statistics designed for lower level of measurement one will under utilize the amount of information available in the data. If we use ordinal measures of correlation for interval scale data, the data will be treated as ordinal only and the interval nature of the data will be ignored.
2. If we want to compare correlation or association across different pairs of variables, try to use measures which give intuitive meaning, such as lambda, uncertainty coefficient, gamma, Eta, Spearman's Rank and Pearson's r.
3. If it is required to test the significance or correlation, try to use statistics whose significance can be tested, such as Eta, Kendall's tau-b and tau-c, Spearman's Rank correlation coefficient, Pearson's r, etc.
4. Theoretically, for different types of measures there would be different types of correlation statistics, regarded to be most suitable. In a single research report, it would not be advisable to use many different types of correlation statistics that more generally applicable, though not necessarily the most suitable. Cramer's V, Kendall's tau-C and Pearson r would be most generally applicable correlation statistics for nominal, ordinal and interval scale measures.

EXERCISES

1. What are bivariate data ? Given a bivariate table, what information does it contain ?

2. What is a scatter diagram ? How would you interpret it ? Discuss.

3. What is correlation ? Discuss different kinds of correlation with examples.

4. Define linear correlation ? How is it measured ? Discuss.

5. Explain the computation of Karl Pearson's Correlation Coefficient. How would you interprete a given correlation coefficient ?

6. Discuss the properties of the linear correlation coefficient.

7. Differentiate between covariance and linear correlation coefficient.

8. What is rank correlation coefficient ? Does it differ from linear correlation coefficient ? Bring out its usefulness and limitations.

9. Compute the correlation coefficient from the following data and comment on its value. Compute coefficient of determination and interpret.

Price (Rs.)	95	80	85	75	90	98
Sales (Unit)	450	500	520	600	480	400

10. Compute a measure of linear relationship between aptitude score and productivity index of 10 workers ?

Sl. No. of Worker	Aptitude score (X)	Productivity Index (Y)
1	16	25
2	14	22
3	18	30
4	20	32

5	25	35
6	24	30
7	28	32
8	30	40
9	35	45
10	22	30

11. The following data relate to the gross investment as a percentage of National Income and the percentage of growth in National Income in 10 selected countries of the world. Compute the Karl Pearson's Correlation Coefficient and Spearman's rank correlation coefficient. Compare these two correlation coefficients and comment.

Sl. No. of Countries	Gross investment (%)	National Income growth (%)
1	19.2	3.4
2	18.7	3.2
3	20.5	3.8
4	25.4	6.2
5	21.8	5.2
6	26.0	6.0
7	28.5	7.5
8	17.4	2.8
9	17.4	3.2
10	22.5	4.5

12. What is coefficient of determination ? What does it indicate ? Explain.

13. Calculate coefficient of correlation between sales (in lakhs of rupees) and profit (in lakhs of rupees) from the following bivariate frequency table.

Profit (rupees in lakhs)	Sales (rupees in lakhs)				
	80–90	90–100	100–110	110–120	120–130
50–55	1	3	8	5	2
55–60	2	2	10	6	4
60–65	1	5	12	10	6
65–70	0	3	6	2	4

14. What are regression lines ? What do they indicate ? What indication do you get about nature or regression lines from the scatter diagram ? Explain.

15. Compare the coefficient of correlation and regression lines as statistical measures in bivariate data analysis.

16. Compare the Karl's Pearson's correlation coefficient and regression coefficients as regards their methods of computations and applications.

17. The following data show the scores of 12 students in mid-term and final examination.

Mid. term examination	Final examination
71	82
65	58
85	88
58	48
64	76
87	80
80	89
73	77
54	65
68	80
93	89
49	62

(*a*) Find the least square equations which will enable us to predict a student's final examination score leased on his mid- term score.

(*b*) Predict the final examination score of a student who received a score of 60 in the mid-term examination.

18. Given below the average ODI score and average test score of 10 batsmen of the country. Compute the regression lines and the coefficient of determination.

Sl. No. of batsmen	ODI score	Test score
1	32.5	54.2
2	28.5	35.7
3	30.5	29.4
4	45.8	55.6
5	25.2	38.0
6	50.4	30.2
7	29.5	18.2
8	15.3	20.2
9	34.8	35.6
10	26.7	42.9

19. Raw materials used in the production of a synthetic fibre is stored in a place which has no humidity control. Measurement of the relative humidty in the storage place and the moisture content of a sample of the raw material (both in percentages) on 10 days yield the following results.

(*a*) Fit a least square regression line to predict the moisture content in terms of humidity.

(*b*) Estimate the moisture content when the relative humidity is 38 percent.

Humidity	Moisture Content
45	13
52	14
37	11

42	13
34	11
29	8
50	15
46	12
41	10
33	9

20. Fit an exponential regression curve of the form $y = \alpha \beta^x$ to the following data on growth of cactus grafts under controlled environment conditions.

Weeks after grafting	Height (in cm.)
1	5.0
2	6.1
4	12.6
5	18.5
6	23.9
8	46.5

21. The following data are given on the unit cost of producng certain electronic components and the number of units produced.

Lot size (x)	Unit Cost (y) in Rs.
50	5040
100	2540
250	1150
500	400
1000	250

Fit a power function $y = \alpha x^{\beta}$ and estimate the unit cost for a lot of 350 components.

22. Suppose an agronomist wants to study the relationship of different levels of fertilizers (in kg.) on the yield (in kg.) of tomato in plots of size 100 square meters. Different rates of fertilizers are assigned to plots at random.

Plot	Fertilizer application rate	Yield
1	0	8
2	0	10
3	10	16
4	10	20
5	20	40
6	20	45
7	30	54
8	30	60
9	40	52
10	40	58

(*i*) Assuming a curvilinear relationship between the application rate and tomato yield compute the least square regression.

(*ii*) Plot the scatter diagram along with the estimated curve.

(*iii*) Predict the average yield of tomatoes for a plot where 50 kg. of fertiliser has been applied.

(*iv*) Test the significance of regression.

(*v*) Interpret the meaning of multiple determination R^2.

(*vi*) Compute the adjusted R^2.

23. Compute the coefficients of association from the following 2×2 contingency table.

	Drug A	Drug B	Total
Relief from cold	30	35	65
No relief	15	10	25
Total	45	45	90

Test the hypothesis that drugs are equally effective at 5% of significance.

24. By using the method of least squares fit the following non- linear regressions to the given data.

(*i*) $y = ab^x$ (*ii*) $y = a + bx + cx^2$

(*iii*) $y = a + \dfrac{b}{x}$

x	1	2	3	4	5	6
y	5	8	10	15	13	9

Compute the coefficients of determination and comment.

25. Given the following contingency table, compute

(*i*) the mean square contingency

(*ii*) coefficient of contigency

and test if there is any evidence of association.

	B_1	B_2	B_3	B_4
A_1	8	12	18	24
A_2	10	13	20	28
A_3	10	15	22	30

26. Test for independence between a person's ability in mathematics and his interest in statistics from the following the data. Use the 0.01 level of significance.

		Ability in mathematics		
		Low	**Average**	**High**
Interest in Statistics	Low	63	42	15
	Average	58	61	31
	High	14	47	29

27. The following table gives the distribution of items of production and also the number of defective items according to size groups.
Is there any correlation between size and defect in quality ?

Size group	15–16	16–17	17–18	18–19	19–20
Number of items	190	250	320	340	360
No. of defective items	150	158	175	190	130

28. Compute the linear regression equation of maintenance cost on age of cars from the following data.

Age of Cars in yrs.	Maintenance cost in thousands of Rs.
2	3
4	6
5	8
6	10
8	15
10	25

Test the significance of regression

29. The following table shows the assessed value and the settling price of 8 houses, constituting a random sample of all the houses sold recently in a metropolitan area.

Assessed Value (Rs. in lakhs)	Setting price (Rs. in lakhs)
40.3	62.8
25.4	30.2
10.7	12.4
20.5	25.2
18.2	22.3
30.4	45.7
18.5	24.6
21.2	28.2

Compute the linear correlation coefficient using analysis of variance technique and test its significance.

30. Regression equations between two variables X and Y are as follows :

$$3X + 2Y - 26 = 0$$

$$6X + 6Y - 35 = 0$$

Find (*i*) the means (*ii*) the regression coefficients (*iii*) the coefficient of correlation between X and Y.

31. (*a*) Interpret the coefficients in regression lines.

(*b*) Can there be always two regression lines ? Explain.

(*c*) Given the regresson coefficients, how would you compute the correlation coefficient ?

(*d*) What is the difference between the product moment correlation coefficient and the rank correlation coefficient ?

(*e*) Point out the merits of Spearman's rank correlation coefficient compared to Karl Pearson's coefficient of correlation.

(*f*) Distinguish between correlation and causation.

(*g*) How would you test the significance of sample correlation coefficient ?

(*h*) Discuss various measures of ordinal association in 2×2 contingency table.

(*i*) Distinguish between coefficient of correlation and coefficient of contingency.

32. Explain the concepts :

(*a*) Perfect positive correlation

(*b*) Non linear correlation

(*c*) Spurious correlation

33. (*a*) How would you test the significance of the linear regression function by forming an analysis of variance table ? Discuss.

(*b*) How would you test the significance of linear regression coefficient and regression intercept ? Explain.

34. Given the following time series of the number of passangers (in millions) using a particular air line, fit an exponential trend model.

Year	1990	1991	1992	1993	1994	1995	1996	1997
Passangers	31.5	33.5	36.8	39.1	41.5	43.7	45.5	46.8

35. Fit a quadratic trend model to the following data :

Year	1990	1991	1992	1993	1994	1995	1996	1997	1998	1999
Passengers (in million)	30.0	31.0	33.5	36.5	42.0	49.1	57.5	68.5	80.0	92.0

Estimate the number of passangers in the year 2000.

36. Two groups of males and females were subjected to a personality test and their score-distributions are given below. Find the association between sex and personality using biserial and point-biserial correlation.

Score	Frequency	
	Males	Females
71–80	5	3
61–70	15	12
51–60	27	23
41–50	12	10
31–40	9	8
21–30	2	4
Total	70	60

37. Two judges rank a number of hotels of the same category as regards their level of hospitality. Measure the association between the Judgements of the two judges by using Spearman's correlation coefficient.

Ranks	Hotels									
	1	2	3	4	5	6	7	8	9	10
Judge A	5	1	4	2	7	8	6	3	10	9
Judge B	4	2	3	5	6	10	9	1	8	7

38. A company manufacturing machine parts would like to develop a model to estimate the number of worker–hours required for production runs of varying lot size. A random sample of 10 production runs (2 for each lot sizes 20, 30, 40, 50, 60) is selected with the following results :

Lot Size	Worker—Hours
20	50
20	55
30	72
30	68
40	87
40	95
50	108
50	114
60	138
60	145

(*a*) Draw a scatter diagram.

(*b*) Compute a linear regression relationship.

(*c*) Interprete Y intercept and slope.

(*d*) Predict the average number of worker-hours required for production run with a lot of size of 45.

(*e*) Set up a 95% confidence interval estimate of the average worker-hours for a lot size of 45.

(*f*) Set up a 95% prediction interval of the worker-hours of an individual lot size of 45.

39. Answer the following :

(*a*) If coefficient of determination $r^2 = 0.70$, what does it indicate ?

(*b*) If SSR = 36 and SSE = 4, find SST, then compute the coefficient of determination r^2.

(*c*) If SSR = 66 and SST = 95, compute the coefficient of determination r^2.
(*d*) If SSE = 20 and SST = 50, compute the coefficient of determination r^2.

40. Explain the following terms :
(*a*) Method of least squares.
(*b*) Standard error of estimate.
(*c*) Confidence interval.
(*d*) Prediction interval
(*e*) Homoscedasticity.
(*f*) Independence of errors.

41. (*a*) Find r if $b_{yx} = 0.8$ and $b_{xy} = 0.46$.
(*b*) Compare the meanings of r and r^2.

42. Given that the variance of $x = 9$, and the regression equations are

$$8x - 10y + 66 = 0$$
$$40x - 18y = 214$$

Find (*i*) r and variance of y.
(*ii*) the means of x and y.

43. Discuss the effect of outliers on the magnitude of correlation coefficient.

44. Distinguish between association and correlation. Explain the computation of Chi-square based measures of association based on 2×2 contingency table.

45. Differentiate between Spearman's rank correlation coefficient and Kendall's rank correlation coefficient.

46. What are concordance based measures of association ? Discuss.

47. What are PRE measures of association ? Discuss.

48. Explain the computation of Gamma, Yule's Q, Somer's d, Kendall's tau-a. tau-b and tau-c.

49. Explain the Relative Risk coefficient.

50. Explain the computation of Theil's coefficient of association.

51. Distinguish between Lambda and Goodman-Kruskal tau-τ.

52. What is Eta coefficient as a measure of association ? Explain.

53. What notes on :
Point-biserial coefficient, Biserial correlation coefficient, Rank biserial coefficient.

54. What is likelihood ratio chi-square based measure of association ?

55. Write a note on the choice of measures of association.

□□□

CHAPTER

14

MULTIPLE REGRESSION ANALYSIS

14.1 INTRODUCTION

Multiple linear regression is the simplest of all the multivariate statistical techniques and is a straight forward generalization of simple regression.

In multiple regression we deal with one dependent response variable and many independent explanatory variables. We seek to explain variation in one dependent variable in terms of other independent variables which we can observe. It is inherently a correlational technique and cannot tell is anything about underlying causal relationship, if any. For the application of multiple regression technique a random sample from some well defined population is observed for both dependent and independent variables. The dependent variable should be measured on an interval, continuous scale. The independent variables should be measured on interval scales. However, categorical and dummy variables can be acceptable as independent variables in multiple regression analysis. To test the efficiency of regression function, the distribution of all the variables should be normal. If they are not normal, this can often be corrected by using an appropriate transformation (e.g. logarithmic transformation of all the measurement.)

The relationship between the dependent variable and the independent variable should be linear. Although the independent variables can be correlated, there must be no perfect (or near perfect) correlations among them, a situation called **multicollinearity,** which adversely affects the estimates of partial regression coefficients and their variances.

The search for regression relationship involving a number of independent variables is a common phenomena in economic, social and business studies and in fact in all branches of scientific research. Some examples of dependent variables. (response variables) and independent variables (predictors/explanatory variables) are given below:

Dependent Variable	Independent Variables
Crop Yield	Rainfall, Temperature, Fertilizer
Annual Sales revenue	Sales force, Annual advertising expenditure, Number of products introduced
Score	IQ, Number of hours studied
Weekly net profit in restaurant	Traffic Count, Seating capacity
Hardness of steel	Copper content, Annealing temperature
Percent effectiveness of a pain reliever	Types of medications present in each capsule.
Productivity Index	Annual training expenditure, Cash incentives to employees.
Infant mortality Rate	Total fertility Rate, Female literacy
Efficiency of management trainees	Academic performances, Leadership abilities, IQ level.
Age of marriage of girls	Education level, Parents' education Number of siblings, Parents' annual income.
Performance of a firm in a particular industry	Size (number of employees) and Age of firm.
Sex Ratio (Female to Male Ratio)	Literacy rate, Differential mortality, Female labour participation, Sex ratio at birth.

14.2 The Multiple Regression Model

Let $X_1, X_2, \ldots, X_k$ denote k predictors (explanatory) variable to be investigated for their relationship with a response variable Y.

A multiple linear regression model is a hypothetical relationship involving Y and $(X_1, X_2, \ldots, X_k)$ and is defined by $Y = \beta_0 + \beta_1 X_1 + \beta_2 X_2 + \ldots + \beta_k X_k + \epsilon$, where $\beta_0, \beta_1, \ldots, \beta_k$ are called parameters or constants of the regression model. β_0 defines the interecept ; $\beta_0, \beta_1, \ldots \beta_k$ are called **partial regression coefficients** of predictors. The regression coefficient of a predictor quantifies the amount of linear trend in Y. It is the amount of change in Y corresponding to one unit change in a predictor while all other predictors one held fixed at some specified levels. If the scatter plot of Y with a predictor suggests a non-linear trend, then the predictor suitably transformed may preserve the linearity.

Further, ϵ is a random error/disturbance with $E(\epsilon) = 0$ and constant variance $V(\epsilon) = \sigma_e^2$.

As such,

$$E(Y) = \beta_0 + \beta_1 X_1 + \ldots + \beta_k X_k,$$

That is, $\beta_0 + \beta_1 X_1 + \ldots + \beta_k X_k$ is hypothesized as mean of Y.

14.2.1. Fitting of Regression Model :

Consider a random sample of n units. For each unit, a vector of $(k + 1)$ observations is recorded on $(k + 1)$ random variables Y (dependent) and $X_1, X_2, ..., X_k$ (independent).

Thus, from the model $Y_i = \beta_0 + \beta_1 X_{1i} + ... + B_k X_{ki} + \in_i$, $i = 1,2,.....,n$.

where $\in_i$ are values of an unobserved error term, $\in$ and the unknown parameters $\beta_0, \beta_1,.....\beta_k$ are constants.

Assumptions :

The error terms $\in_i$ are mutually independent and identically distributed with mean = 0 and constant variances.

i.e.
$$E(\in_i) = 0, V(\in_i) = \sigma_e^2$$

This is so, because the observations $Y_1, Y_2, ...Y_n$ are a random sample, they are mutually independent and hence the error terms are also mutually independent.

Normality assumptions on $\in_i$ may be imposed to validate the tests of significance.

❒ The distribution of the error term is independent of the joint distribution of $X_1, X_2, ..., X_k$.

❒ The unknown parameters $\beta_0, \beta_1, ..., \beta_k$ are constants.

Let the fitted line be $\hat{Y}_i = \hat{\beta}_0 + \hat{\beta}_1 X_{1i} + ... + \hat{\beta}_k X_{ki}$, the estimates $\hat{\beta}_0, \hat{\beta}_1, ..., \hat{\beta}_k$ are chosen by minimizing the sum of squared residual

$$S = \sum_{i=1}^{n} (Y_i - \hat{Y}_i)^2$$

This is done by differentiating S partially with respect to $\hat{\beta}_0, \hat{\beta}_1, ..., \hat{\beta}_k$ and setting each derivative equal to zero to obtain the **least square or normal equations.** $\hat{\beta}_0, \hat{\beta}_1, ..., \hat{\beta}_k$ are therefore called **least square estimates.**

Thus the minimizing equations (least square equations) are given by

$$\Sigma Y_i = n\hat{\beta}_0 + \hat{\beta}_1 \Sigma X_{1i} + \hat{\beta}_2 \Sigma X_{2i} + ... + \hat{\beta}_k \Sigma X_{ki}$$

$$\Sigma Y_i X_{1i} = \hat{\beta}_0 \Sigma X_{1i} + \hat{\beta}_1 \Sigma X_{1i}^2 + \hat{\beta}_2 \Sigma X_{1i} X_{2i} + ... + \hat{\beta}_k \Sigma X_{1i} X_{ki}$$

$$\Sigma Y_i X_{1i} = \hat{\beta}_0 \Sigma X_{2i} + \hat{\beta}_1 \Sigma X_{1i} X_{2i} + \hat{\beta}_2 \Sigma X_{2i}^2 + ... + \hat{\beta}_k \Sigma X_{2i} X_{ki}$$

....

$$\Sigma Y_i X_{ki} = \hat{\beta}_0 \Sigma X_{ki} + \hat{\beta}_1 \Sigma X_{1i} X_{ki} + \hat{\beta}_2 \Sigma X_{2i} X_{ki} + ... + \hat{\beta}_k \Sigma X_{ki}^2$$

These equations can now be solved for $\hat{\beta}_0, \hat{\beta}_1, \hat{\beta}_2, ..., \hat{\beta}_k$ However, to simplify the procedure, we may express $\hat{\beta}_0$ in terms of $\hat{\beta}_1, \hat{\beta}_2, ..., \hat{\beta}_u$ from the first equation and then substitute it in the remaining equations of solve for $\hat{\beta}_1, \hat{\beta}_2, ..., \hat{\beta}_k$.

From the first equation $\hat{\beta}_0 = \overline{Y} - \hat{\beta}_1 \overline{X}_1 - \hat{\beta}_2 \overline{X}_2, ... - \hat{\beta}_k \overline{X}_k$

Eliminating $\hat{\beta}_0$ from rest of the equations and writing lower case letters as deviations from respective means we have

$$\Sigma yx_1 = \hat{\beta}_1 \Sigma x_1^2 + \hat{\beta}_2 \Sigma x_1 x_2 + ... + \hat{\beta}_k \Sigma x_1 x_k$$

$$\Sigma yx_2 = \hat{\beta}_1 \Sigma x_1 x_2 + \hat{\beta}_2 \Sigma x_2^2 + ... + \hat{\beta}_k \Sigma x_2 x_k$$

$$\vdots \quad \vdots \quad \vdots \quad \vdots \quad \vdots \quad \vdots$$

$$\Sigma yx_k = \hat{\beta}_1 \Sigma x_1 x_k + \hat{\beta}_2 \Sigma x_2 x_k + ... + \hat{\beta}_k \Sigma x_k^2$$

The solutions of above k equations give us the expressions for the estimates $\hat{\beta}_1, \hat{\beta}_2, ..., \hat{\beta}_k$.

The estimated relationship can be expressed by

$$\hat{Y} = \hat{\beta}_0 + \hat{\beta}_1 X_1 + \hat{\beta}_2 X_2 + ... + \hat{\beta}_k X_k$$

Denote the standard error of $\hat{Y}$ for specified values of predictors by *s*.

An estimate of σ_e is s_e, given by :

$$s_e = \sqrt{\frac{\Sigma(Y - \hat{Y})^2}{n-k-1}}$$

Note : $s_e^2 = \frac{1}{n-k-1}\Sigma(Y - \hat{Y})^2$ is an unbiased estimate of σ_e^2.

The number $(n - k - 1)$ is deviation from referred to as the number of degrees of freedom of the regression.

14.2.2 Test of regression Coefficient

To test the null hypothesis $H_0 : \hat{\beta}_i = \hat{\beta}_{io}$ against alternative $H_1 : \beta_i \neq \beta_{i0}$, the *t*-statistic is defined as

$$t = \frac{\hat{\beta}_i - \hat{\beta}_{io}}{s(\hat{\beta}_i)},$$

(where $s(\hat{\beta}_i)$ = estimated standard error of $\hat{\beta}_i = s_e/\sqrt{(\Sigma x_i^2)}$, which is distributed as Student's *t* distribution with $(n - k - 1)$ degrees of freedom.

14.2.3 Test of equality of two regression coefficients

Consider the problem of testing the hypothesis concerning the equality of two regression coefficients, say $\beta_1$and β_2

That is,

$H_o : \beta_1 = \beta_2$ (or equivalently, $\beta_1 - \beta_2 = 0$) against $H_1 : \beta_1 \neq \beta_2$ or $\beta_1 > \beta_2$ (or $\beta_1 < \beta_2$)

The appropriate test statistic

$$t = \frac{\hat{\beta}_1 - \hat{\beta}_2}{s(\hat{\beta}_1 - \hat{\beta}_2)},$$

where $s(\hat{\beta}_1 - \hat{\beta}_2)$ is the estimated standard error of $\hat{\beta}_1 - \hat{\beta}_2$

We have

$$V(\hat{\beta}_1 - \hat{\beta}_2) = V(\hat{\beta}_1) + V(\hat{\beta}_2) - 2\text{ Cov. }(\hat{\beta}_1, \hat{\beta}_2).$$

$$s(\hat{\beta}_1 - \hat{\beta}_2) = \sqrt{\text{Est. } V(\hat{\beta}_1 - \hat{\beta}_2)}$$

14.2.4 Test of Regression Function

Write the total variation in $Y_1, Y_2, ..., Y_n$ as total sum of squares

$$\sum_{i=1}^{n}(Y_i - \overline{Y}^2) = \sum_{i=1}^{n}(\hat{Y}_i - \overline{Y})^2 + \sum_{i=1}^{n}(Y_i - \hat{Y}_i)^2$$

= Sum of squares due to regression + Sum of squares due to deviation from regression (Residual sum of squares or error sum of squares)

That is, TSS = SSR + SSE

TABLE–14.1
Analysis of Variance

Source	Degree of Freedom	Sum of Squares	Mean Squares	F
Due to regression	k	$SSR = \Sigma(\hat{Y}_i - \overline{Y})^2$	$MSR = \Sigma(\hat{Y}_i - \overline{Y})^2$	$\frac{MSR}{MSE}$
Residual (Deviation from regression)	$n-k-1$	$SSE = \Sigma(Y_i - \hat{Y}_i)^2$	$MSE = \frac{\Sigma(Y_i - \hat{Y}_i)^2}{n-k-1}$	
Total	$n-1$	$TSS = \Sigma(Y_i - \overline{Y})^2$	—	

The overall goodness of fit of the regression model i.e. whether the regression model is at all helpful in predicting the values of y is made by testing the regression function under the null hypothesis.

$$H_0 : \beta_1 = \beta_2 = ... = \beta_k = 0 \text{ (say), against } H_1 : \text{At least one } \beta_i \neq 0.$$

which can be carried out with F-statistic, that is F = MSR/MSE., computed from the analysis of variance, which follows the theoretical F-distribution with k and $n-k-1$ degrees of freedom. Thus, if the computed value of F is greater than theoretical (tabulated) value of F with k and $n-k-1$ degrees of freedom at a chosen level of significance, say, at 5%, then H_0 is rejected, that is, the regression involving the dependent variable Y and the set of independent variables or predictors $X_1, X_2, ..., X_k$ is statistically significant.

14.3 Multiple Correlation Coefficient

The Correlation between Y and the group of predictors $(X_1, X_2, ...X_k)$ is termed as multiple correlation (R) and is defined as

$$R^2 = \frac{\Sigma(\hat{Y} - \overline{Y})^2}{\Sigma(Y - \overline{Y})^2}, \hat{Y} = \frac{SSR}{TSS}$$

That is, R^2 is the ratio of explained to the total sum of squares. R is a measure of the strength of the linear relationship between Y and the set of variables $X_1, X_2, ...X_k$. It is the highest possible simple correlation between Y and linear combination of $X_1, X_2, ...X_k$.

Alternatively, $$R^2 = 1 - \frac{\Sigma(Y - \hat{Y})^2}{\Sigma(Y - \overline{Y})^2} = 1 - \frac{SSE}{TSS}$$

and $$0 \leq R^2 \leq 1$$

Since the multiple correlation coefficient between Y and $(X_1, X_2, ...X_k)$ is the correlation between Y's and its estimated values from the fitted regression equation, **it cannot be negative.**

Hence, $0 \le R \le 1$

When the values of R is close to zero, the regression equation barely predicts Y better than sheer chance. A value of R close to 1 indicates a very good fit :

Coefficient of multiple determination :

100 R^2 indicates percentage of variation in Y explained by the multiple regression equation and is termed as **coefficient of multiple determination.**

Adjusted $R^2(\bar{R}^2)$

Two regression functions can be differentiated with the help of the computed values of R^2 from these equations. The inclusion of more independent variables in the fitted regression function improves the value of R^2 and hence the goodness of fit. However, the comparison of different regression functions with varying number of independent variables will not be very much appropriate in the sense that $\Sigma(Y - \hat{Y})^2$ is based on varying number of degrees of freedom. Thus, there is need for the correction for the computation of R^2.

Hence, the relation

$$R^2 = 1 - \frac{\Sigma(Y - \hat{Y})^2}{\Sigma(Y - \overline{Y})^2} = 1 - \frac{SSE}{TSS}$$

neeeds to be corrected as

$$\bar{R}^2 = 1 - \frac{\Sigma(Y - \hat{Y})^2/(n - k - 1)}{\Sigma(Y - \overline{Y})^2/(n - 1)}$$

$$= 1 - \frac{MSE}{MST},$$

where k is the number of independent variables.

Thus, $$\bar{R}^2 = 1 - \frac{n - 1}{n - k - 1}\left[\frac{\Sigma(Y - \hat{Y})^2}{\Sigma(Y - \overline{Y})^2}\right]$$

$$= 1 - \frac{n - 1}{n - k - 1}(1 - R^2),$$

which is termed as adjusted R^2.

Prediction : Regression equations can be used to obtain predicted/fitted values of the dependent variable for given values of the independent variables.

Test of Multiple Correlation Coefficient

To evaluate the significance of the observed multiple correlation coefficient R, We compute F-ratio

$$F = \frac{R^2}{1 - R^2} \cdot \frac{n - k - 1}{k},$$

where k is the number of independent variables.

If $F > F_{\alpha, (k-1), (n-k-1)}$, the coefficient R is significant at 100 α % 10 level of significance.

14.4 Beta Regression Coefficients

The partial regression coefficients β's are simply weights expressing the influence of the independent variables as they are combined into an estimate of the dependent variable. The magnitude of the regression coefficients depends upon the scales of measurement used for the dependent varible Y and the explanatory variables (X_1 , X_2 ,.... , X_k) included in the regression equation. Unstandardised regression coefficients cannot be compared directly because of differing units of measurement and different variances of the x–variables.

Further, $X_1 X_2$,..., X_k may be different and as such their variances may also differ greatly. As such $\hat{\beta}$'s do not indicate the actual comparative significance of each independent variable. It is therefore necessary to **standardize** the variables for meaningful comparisons. As a consequence of this we define a measure called the **'beta coefficient'** (standardized regression coefficient), which recognize the dissimilarity of the units and their variances.

The beta coefficients can be obtained by multiplying certain ratios of standard deviations with the original estimated partial regression coefficient such as

$$\hat{\beta}_i^* = \hat{\beta}_i \left(\frac{s_{xi}}{s_y} \right), \ (i = 1, 2, ..., k).$$

Alternatively, the beta coefficients can be solved out from the linear equations with simple correlations rather than variance and covariances. That is, they are **the partial regression coefficients among the standardised variables.**

For instance, with two independent variables X_1 and X_2, the linear equations are:

$$r_{yx_1} = \hat{\beta}_1^* + \hat{\beta}_2^* \ r_{x_1 x_2}$$

$$r_{yx_2} = \hat{\beta}_1^* \ r_{x_1 x_2} + \hat{\beta}_2^*$$

The standardized regression coefficient measures the impact of a unit change in the standardized value X_i on the standardized value of Y. The larger the magnitude of standardized $\hat{\beta}_i$ the more X_i contributes to the prediction of Y. However, the regression equation itself should be supported in terms of unstandardized $\hat{\beta}_i$ so that the prediction of Y can be made directly from X-variables.

The **betas** provide a more accurate idea of the relative importance of the independent variable rather than *partial regression coefficients* in regression analysis. The standard error of **betas** can be obtained through the standard error of partial regression coefficients.

14.5 Coefficient of Partial Correlation

The regression coefficients such as β's occurring in the regression model may be referred to as net regression coefficients or sometimes called **partial regression coefficients.** They reflect the net regression of the dependent variable Y upon the respective independent variable after the impact of the remaining independent variables theoretically held constant.

Thus, the partial regression coefficients can be symbolically written as :

$$\beta_1 = \beta_{yx_1 \cdot x_2, x_3 ..., x_k}$$

$$\beta_2 = \beta_{yx_2 \cdot x_1, x_3, \ldots, x_k}$$

....

$$\beta_k = \beta_{yx_k \cdot x_1, x_2, \ldots x_{k-1}}$$

and can be expressed a function a simple regression coefficients.

Partial correlation is the direct result of the concept of partial regression or net regression. It measures the association between a dependent variable and a single independent variable, holding other independent variables theoretically constant. Thus, we may write symbolically $\rho_{yx_1 \cdot x_2, \ldots, x_k}$ (or $r_{yx_1 \cdot x_2, \ldots x_k}$) as population (or sample) partial correlation coefficient between the dependent variable Y and independent variable X_1, holding other independent variables theoretically constant. It is a measure of linear association between two variables after adjusting for the linear effect of a group of other variables. If the number of other variables is 1, the partial correlation coefficient is called the first order coefficient. If the number of other variables is equal to 2, the partial corr. coefficient is called the second order coefficient and so on. Unlike multiple correlation coefficient $-1 \leq r_{yx_1 \cdot x_2, \ldots x_k} \leq +1$

Test of Significance of Observed Partial Correlation

The sampling distribution of a sample partial correlation coefficient from a multivariate normal population is same as that of a simple correlation coefficient from a bivariate normal population.

Under the hypothesis $H_0 : \rho_{yx_1 \cdot x_2, \ldots, x_k} = 0$

$$t = \frac{r_{yx_1 \cdot x_2, \ldots, x_k}}{\sqrt{1 - r_{yx_1 \cdot x_2, \ldots, x_k}}} \sqrt{n-k-2}$$

is distributed as Student's t-distribution with $(n - k - 2)$ degrees of freedom. Thus, the test can be performed accordingly.

Illustration 1.

Consider a linear regression model with two independent variables X_1 and X_2. The dependent variable Y is related to independent variables X_1 and X_2 as

$$Y = \beta_0 + \beta_1 X_1 + \beta_2 X_2 + \varepsilon$$

where $\beta_0, \beta_1, \beta_2$ are constants (parameters) and ε is a random error or distubance with mean zero and variance σ_e^2.

Given a random sample of n observations in triplets (Y, X_1, X_2) and the problem is to fit a multiple regression model to the data.

The observation when put in the model are written as

$$Y_i = \beta_0 + \beta_1 X_{1i} + \beta_2 X_{2i} + \varepsilon_i \ (i = 1, 2, .., n).$$

ε_i's are independently and identically distributed with mean zero and variance. Very often normality of the ε_i's are assumed to help tests of hypothesis on the unknown constants/parameters.

Suppose the fitted linear regression is

$$\hat{Y}_i = \hat{\beta}_0 + \hat{\beta}_1 X_{1i} + \hat{\beta}_2 X_{2i}$$

Applying least square technique, we choose $\hat{\beta}_0$, $\hat{\beta}_1$ and $\hat{\beta}_2$ so as to minimize

$$S = \sum_{i=1}^{n} \varepsilon_i^2 = \sum^{n} (Y_i - \hat{Y}_i)^2$$

$$= \Sigma(Y_i - \hat{\beta}_0 - \hat{\beta}_1 X_{1i} - \hat{\beta}_2 X_{2i})^2$$

Differentiating S with respect to $\hat{\beta}_0$, $\hat{\beta}_1$ and $\hat{\beta}_2$ and setting each derivative equal to zero,

$$\frac{\partial S}{\partial \hat{\beta}_0} = -2\Sigma(Y_i - \hat{\beta}_0 - \hat{\beta}_1 X_{1i} - \hat{\beta}_2 X_{2i}) = 0$$

$$\frac{\partial S}{\partial \hat{\beta}_1} = -2\Sigma X_{1i}(Y_i - \hat{\beta}_0 - \hat{\beta}_1 X_{1i} - \hat{\beta}_2 X_{2i}) = 0$$

$$\frac{\partial S}{\partial \hat{\beta}_2} = -2\Sigma X_{2i}(Y_i - \hat{\beta}_0 - \hat{\beta}_1 X_{1i} - \hat{\beta}_2 X_{2i}) = 0$$

These lead to Normal equations

$$\Sigma Y_i = n\,\hat{\beta}_0 - \hat{\beta}_1 \Sigma X_{1i} - \hat{\beta}_2 \Sigma X_{2i}$$

$$\Sigma Y_i X_{1i} = \hat{\beta}_0 \Sigma X_{1i} + \hat{\beta}_1 \Sigma X_{1i}^2 + \hat{\beta}_2 \Sigma X_{1i} X_{2i}$$

$$\Sigma Y_i X_{2i} = \hat{\beta}_0 \Sigma X_{2i} + \hat{\beta}_1 \Sigma X_{1i} X_{2i} + \hat{\beta}_2 \Sigma X_{2i}^2$$

The estimated regression equation

$$\hat{Y} = \hat{\beta}_0 + \hat{\beta}_1 X_1 + \hat{\beta}_2 X_2$$

where

$$\hat{\beta}_0 = \overline{Y} - \hat{\beta}_1 \overline{X}_1 - \hat{\beta}_2 \overline{X}_2$$

$$\hat{\beta}_1 = \frac{\Sigma(Y - \overline{Y})(X_1 - \overline{X}_1)\Sigma(X_2 - \overline{X}_2)^2 - \Sigma(Y - \overline{Y})(X_2 - \overline{X}_2)\Sigma(X_1 - \overline{X}_1)(X_2 - \overline{X}_2)}{\Sigma(X_1 - \overline{X}_1)^2 \Sigma(X_2 - \overline{X}_2)^2 - \left[\Sigma(X_1 - \overline{X}_1)\ (X_2 - \overline{X}_2)\right]^2}$$

$$= \frac{\Sigma y x_1\ \Sigma x_2^2 - \Sigma y x_2\ \Sigma x_1 x_2}{\Sigma x_1^2\ \Sigma x_2^2 - (\Sigma x_1 x_2)^2}$$

$$= \frac{r_{yx_1} - r_{yx_2}\ r_{x_1 x_2}}{1 - r_{x_1 x_2}^2} \cdot \frac{\sigma_y}{\sigma_{x_1}}$$

and $$\hat{\beta}_2 = \frac{\Sigma(Y - \overline{Y})\ (X_2 - \overline{X}_2)\ \Sigma(X_1 = \overline{X}_1)^2 - \Sigma(Y - \overline{Y})\ (X_1 - \overline{X}_1)\ \Sigma(X_1 - \overline{X}_1)\ (X_2 - \overline{X}_2)}{\Sigma(X_1 - \overline{X}_1)^2\ \ \Sigma(X_2 - \overline{X}_2)^2 - \left[\Sigma\ (X_1 - \overline{X}_1)\ (X_2 - \overline{X}_2)\right]^2}$$

$$= \frac{\Sigma y x_2\ \Sigma x_1^2 - \Sigma y x_1\ \Sigma x_1 x_2}{\Sigma x_1^2\ \Sigma x_2^2 - (\Sigma x_1\ x_2)^2}$$

$$= \frac{r_{yx_2} - r_{yx_1}\ r_{x_1 x_2}}{1 - r_{x_1 x_2}^2} \cdot \frac{\sigma_y}{\sigma_{x_2}}$$

It may be seen that

$$E(\hat{\beta}_0) = \beta_0,\ E(\hat{\beta}_1) = \beta_1 \text{ and } E(\hat{\beta}_2) = \beta_2$$

$$V(\hat{\beta}_1) = \frac{\sigma_e^2\ \Sigma\, x_2^2}{\Sigma\, x_1^2\ \Sigma x_2^2 - (\Sigma x_1 x_2)^2}$$

$$V(\hat{\beta}_2) = \frac{\sigma_e^2 \, \Sigma x_1^2}{\Sigma x_1^2 \, \Sigma x_2^2 - (\Sigma x_1 x_2)^2}$$

$$Cov(\hat{\beta}_1, \hat{\beta}_2) = -\frac{\sigma_e^2 \, \Sigma x_1 x_2}{\Sigma x_1^2 \, \Sigma x_2^2 - (\Sigma x_1 x_2)^2}$$

$$V(\hat{\beta}_0) = \overline{X}_1^2 V(\hat{\beta}_1) + \overline{X}_2^2 V(\hat{\beta}_2) + 2\, \overline{X}_1 \overline{X}_2 \; Cov(\hat{\beta}_1, \hat{\beta}_2) + \frac{\sigma_e^2}{n}$$

The expected value of the sum of squares of the observed y's from the fitted equation is

$$E\left[\sum_{i=1}^{n} \varepsilon_i^2\right] = E\left[\sum_{i=1}^{n} (Y_i - \hat{\beta}_0 - \hat{\beta}_1 X_{1i} - \hat{\beta}_2 X_{2i})^2\right]$$

$$= (n-3)\sigma_e^2$$

Hence, an unbiased estimate of σ_e^2 is given by

$$\hat{\sigma}_e^2 = \frac{\sum_{i=1}^{n} (Y_i - \hat{\beta}_0 - \hat{\beta}_1 X_{1i} - \hat{\beta}_2 X_{2i})^2}{n-3},$$

where (n-3) refers to degrees of freedom of the deviation from regression.

Relationship between partial regression coefficients and simple regression coefficients.

$$\hat{\beta}_{yx_1.x_2} = \frac{\hat{\beta}_{yx_1} - \hat{\beta}_{yx_2} \hat{\beta}_{x_2x_1}}{1 - \hat{\beta}_{x_1x_2} \hat{\beta}_{x_2x_1}}$$

The partial correlation coefficient between y and x_1 can be expressed in terms of simple correlation coefficients like γ_{yx_1}, γ_{yx_2} and $\gamma_{x_1x_2}$.

Thus,

$$r_{yx_1.x_2} = \sqrt{\hat{\beta}_{yx_1.x_2} \hat{\beta}_{x_1y.x_2}}$$

$$= \frac{r_{yx_1} - r_{yx_2} \, r_{x_1x_2}}{\sqrt{(1 - r_{yx_2}^2) \; (1 - r_{x_1x_2}^2)}} \qquad -1 \le r_{yx_1.x_2} \le +1$$

$r_{yx_1.x_2}$ is called the **first order partial correlation coefficient** because the effect of only one independent variable x_2 has been eliminated or kept constant in a trivariate population consisting of y, x_1 and x_2.

The coefficient of determination $(r)^2$ or the coefficient of multiple determination (R^2) indicates the proportion of total variance in the dependent variable that is explained by the variance of the regression equation. Similarly, the squared coefficient of partial correlation is called **coefficient of partial determination**.

For example, suppose a multiple regression relationship with two independent variables (x_1, x_2) is under consideration.

Suppose further,

(*i*) total variance to be accounted for Y expressed in percentage is 100%.

(*ii*) variance accounted for the regression with X_2 only is $r^2_{yx_2}$ = 34%.

Then *unaccounted or unexplained variance* is (100–34) % = 66%.

Again suppose variance accounted for by multiple coefficient of determination is R^2 = 61%. Thus, unexplained variance in multiple correlation is (100–61)% = 39%

Hence, reduction in variance by including r_{yx_1} in the multiple correlation is (66–39) % = 25%.

Thus, percent reduction in *unaccounted variance* is $\frac{27}{66} \times 100 = 41\%$

That is, $r^2_{yx_1 \cdot x_2}$ = 0.41 is called coefficient of partial determination.

Note : (*i*) It may be theoretically proved that R^2 is always greater than $r^2_{yx_1}$, $r^2_{yx_2}$, $r^2_{yx_1 . x_2}$ and $r^2_{yx_2 . x_1}$.

(*ii*) The coefficient of partial determination measures the percentage reduction in the unexplained variance by including r_{yx_1} in the multiple correlation that is attributable to covariation with the given independent variable represented by the coefficient.

(*iii*) Theoretically, for two independent variables x_1 and x_2,

$$R^2 = (1 - r^2_{yx_2})\ (1 - r^2_{yx_1 \cdot x_2}),$$

which shows

$$R^2 > r^2_{yx_2} \quad \text{and also } R^2 > r^2_{yx_1 . x_2}$$

(*iv*) Further,

$$R^2 = \frac{r^2_{yx_1} + r^2_{yx_2} - 2\, r_{x_1x_2}\, r_{yx_1}\, r_{yx_2}}{1 - r^2_{x_1x_2}}$$

Illustration 2 :

Suppose $r_{yx_1} = 0.768$, $r_{yx_2} = 0.719$ and $r_{x_1 x_2} = 0.520$

Therefore, $$R = r_{y(x_1, x_2)} = \sqrt{\frac{r^2_{yx_1} + r^2_{yx_2} - 2r_{yx_1}\, r_{yx_2}\, r_{x_1x_2}}{1 - r^2_{x_1x_2}}}$$

$$= \sqrt{\frac{0.5255}{0.7296}} = \sqrt{0.7299} = 0.854.$$

Thus, the coefficient of multiple determination = R^2 = 0.7299.

$$r_{yx_1.x_2} = \frac{r_{yx_1} - r_{yx_2}\, r_{x_1x_2}}{\sqrt{1 - r^2_{x_1x_2}}} = \frac{0.768 - (0.719)\,(0.520)}{\sqrt{1 - (0.520)^2}}$$

$$= \frac{0.39412}{0.85417} = 0.4614$$

$$r_{yx_2.x_1} = \frac{r_{yx_2} - r_{yx_1}\, r_{x_1x_2}}{\sqrt{1 - r^2_{x_1x_2}}} = \frac{0.719 - (0.768)\,(0.520)}{\sqrt{1 - (0.520)^2}}$$

$$= \frac{0.31964}{0.85417} = 0.3742$$

The coefficients of partial determination are :

$$r^2_{yx_1.x_2} = 0.2129$$

and $$r^2_{yx_2.x_1} = 0.1400$$

14.6 The main questions which the multiple regression answers :

1. How well do the regressors, taken together, explain the variation in the dependent variable ? This is assessed by the value of R^2_{adj} $(\overline{R}^2)$.
2. Are the regressors, taken together, significantly associated with the dependent variable ? This is assessed by the statistic F in the 'Analysis of variance'.
3. What relationship does each regressor have with the dependent variable when all other regressors are held constant ? This is answered by looking at the regression coefficients.
4. Which independent variable has most effect on the dependent variable ? It is not possible to give a fully satisfactory answer to this question, for a number of reasons. The chief one is that we are always looking at the effect of each variable in the presence of all the others ; since the independent variables need not be independent, it is hard to be sure which one is contributing to a joint relationship.

   However, the usual way of addressing the question is to look at the **standardised regression coefficients** or **beta weights** for each variable ; these are regression coefficients we would get if we convert all variables (independent and dependent) to z-scores before doing the regression.
5. Are the relationships of each regressor with the dependent variable statistically significant, with all other regressors taken into account ? This is answered by looking at the t-values in the table of regression coefficients. The degrees of freedom for t are those for the residual in the ANOVA table.

14.7 Selecting the independent variables (regressors)

Identifying potentially useful independent variables (x) is not always easy. Usually, people who are experts in the area under study may be called on to provide a list of possible x-variables. The data (y) will be collected at selected levels of these x- variables.

Often many x-variables are identified than actually needed to form a good model.

Some subsets of the x's are often so closely related to one another that each provides about the same information about y, hence only one variable from the subset is needed in the model. Identifying such redundancies is the major challenge in variable selection.

One selection procedure which may be used is to do **all possible regressions.** This means fitting every possible submodel of the full model involving all independent variables. Then a 'good' sub model is selected based on some criterion related to the model fits. Some criteria often used are :

1. Small s_e^2 (error mean square)

2. Large R^2 (squared multiple correlation coefficient)

Unfortunately the full model always give the smallest s_e^2 and the largest R^2. What is a 'good' submodel will be one that is a compromise between the desires to optimise s_e^2 and R^2, and use as few x- variables as possible. Usually more than one 'good' submodel will emerge, and a decision to select one must somehow be made.

One technique that is sometimes used to help in this direction is **data splitting.** This means dividing the dat^ into two parts. The first part is used to compute all possible regressions (or some other method). The second part of the data are used to see how well various sub models predict 'future' observations *i.e.* the y's in this second subset. This technique can help sort out the better of the 'good' submodels. Most often the data are split by dividing them in half. If there are too few observations to split, a statistic named PRESS may be used. For each of the 'good' submodels do the following : For each of the n data elements in turn, delete one element, fit the model using $(n-1)$ remaining data elements, and use the fit to predict the y of the deleted observation. Call the prediction $\hat{y}_i^*$ and y_i, the observation deleted. Then

$$\text{PRESS} = \Sigma(y_i - \hat{y}_i^*)^2$$

Submodels with small PRESS are preferable. PRESS may be used in conjunction with all possible regressions to decide between two or more 'good' submodels, or PRESS can be used alone to help select a useful subset of the x's.

It must be emphasized that a 'best' subset of independent variables is not-defined, so doesn't exist. Thus, we may look for 'good' subsets and then select one of these as our model.

A competitor technique to all possible regressions and PRESS is the use of the C_p statistic defined as

$$C_p = \frac{\text{SSE}_p}{s_e^2} - (n-2p),$$

where SSE_p is the error sum of squares due to fitting the sub-model containing p-parameters (including β_0) and s_e^2 is the error SS due to fitting all available x-variables. 'Good' submodels have C_p which is nearly p *i.e.* $C_p \simeq p$. This technique is especially good at helping to avoid selecting **over specified** model having redundant x-variables.

There are some numerical algorithms available which automate the subset selection process. Some of these are discussed in the following :

1. Backward Elimination. Start with all the variables in the model $Y = \beta_0 + \beta_1 X_1 + ... + \beta_k X_k + \varepsilon$ and drop the least significant, one at a time, until you are left with only 'significant' variables.

The variable selected for deletion is the one that causes least increase in error sum of squares of the full model.

In other words the variable that is least significant that is one with largest. P-value is removed and the model is refitted. Each subsequent step removes the least signficant variable in the model until all remaining variables have individual P-values smaller than some value such as 0.05 and 0.01.

2. Forward Selection. The algorithm begins with the empty model $y = \beta_0 + \epsilon$ and extends model by attempting to add one term at a time.

The variable selected at each stage is the one that causes largest decrease in Error sum of squares of the full model. That is, choose the independent variable which explains the most variation in the dependent variable. Choose a second variable which explains the most residual variation and thus recalculate the regression coefficients. Continue until no variables 'significantly' explain residual variation.

In other words, the variable that has the smallest P-value when it is the only predictor in the regression equation is placed in the model.

Each subsequent step adds the variable that has the smallest P-value in the presence of the predictors already in the equation. Variables are added one at a time as long as their P-values are small enough, typically less than 0.05 and 0.01.

3. Stepwise Regression. Stepwise regression is a sequential process for fitting the least square model where in each step a single explanatory variable is either added or removed from the model in the next fit.

The algorithm combines the steps of forward selection and backward elimination. It begins with the model $y = \beta_0 + \epsilon$ and does a forward selection step. If a variable is added then the current model is (if X_j added)

$$y = \beta_0 + \beta_1 X_j + \epsilon$$

Now a backward elimination (modified) step is made. If an x-variable is deleted then the current model has one fewer terms. Otherwise it is unchanged and a forward selection step is made.

Thus, alternating foward and backward steps are made until no variable is added to the current subset in a forward step and no variable is deleted in the following backward step. Then the algorithm stops and the current subset at that time compromise the selected model.

Stepwise regression is similar to forward selection except that variables are removed from the model if they become non-significant as other predictors are added.

Partial F-test Criterion – Choice of an explanatory variable

In a multiple regression model, it is advisable to use those explanatory variables which are useful in predicting the dependent variable. If it is found that some of the explanatory variables are not helpful in making the prediction, it could be deleted from the multiple regression model.

The **partial F-test Criterion** involves determining the contribution to regression sum of softwares made by each explanatory variable after all other explanatory variables have been included in the model. Reasonably, an explanatory variable is included only if it significantly improves the model.

Thus, to determine the contribution of the variable X_i, assuming that all other variables are already included, we have SSR (X_i | all variables X_i) = SSR (all variables including X_i) - SSR (all variables except X_i)

The partical F-test criterion for determining the contribution of the independent variable X_i is given by

$$F = \frac{\text{SSR}(X_i \mid \text{all variables except } X_i)}{\text{MSE}} = \frac{\text{MSR}(X_i \mid \text{all variables except } X_i)}{\text{MSE}}$$

which follows F-distribution with 1 and $n - k - 1$ degrees of freedom.

14.8 Checking Model Assumptions

The assumption is usually made in the multiple regression model are :

1. $E(\epsilon_i) = 0$ for all i
2. $V(\epsilon_i) = \sigma_e^2$ all i
3. ϵ_i is normally distributed for all i.
4. The ϵ_i are independent.

Since the residual $e_i = Y_i - \hat{Y}_i$ are estimates of the ε_i, they are used to detect violations.

1. E (ϵ_i) = 0 (Model Adequacy). If a linear regression model fits well to the data this assumption will not be seriously violated. In the multiple regression case, plot $e_i = (Y_i - \hat{Y}_i)$ against each of the independent variable X_i. A noticeable curvature or non-linearity present in this plot may indicate a more complicated relationship such as a polynomial. In this case a transformation of the y-variable or the particular x_i variable may be attempted.

2. V(ϵ_i) = σ_e^2 (Constant error Variance). Plotting residuals $e_i = Y_i - \hat{Y}_i$ versus predicted values $\hat{Y}_i$ will show significant heterogeneity if it exists. Non-constant variance will make the width of confidence and prediction intervals too wide or too narrow depending on the variance at the considered x value.

Transformations to stablize variance are possible, and a technique called weighted least squares can be used to overcome some of the adverse effects of heterogeneity of variance.

3. ϵ_i Normal. A Normal probability plot of the residuals or better the studentized residuals $(Y_i - \hat{Y}_i)/s_e$ versus percentiles from the standard normal distribution. If this plot shows a substantial deviation from linearity the normality assumption about ϵ's is seriously in doubt. Particularly one should look for one of the patterns that indicate that the error distribution deviates from a normal distribution.

Also Histogram plots and Box plots of residuals can show skewness in distribution which indicates non-normality, (lack of symmetry to be specific).

Serious violation of this assumption does not impact point estimate, but distributional assumptions for t and F tests are not valid and these tests may be seriously invalidated. An available remedy is again to try a transformation of the y-variable.

4. Independent $\in_i$ (Uncorrelated) : This is not so easy to check. Let us consider about a check only when the observations have a time-oriented sequence. For observations taken over time serial correlation measures the tendency of successive adjacent $\in$'s to be similar (positive serial correlation) or dissimilar (negative correlation). Independence gives zero serial correlation.

A statistic which estimates serial correlation is the **Durbin–Watson statistic.** Let $\hat{\in}_t$ be the residual for the observation at time t. Then

$$D = \sum_{t=1}^{n-1} (\hat{\in}_{t+1} - \hat{\in}_t)^2 / \Sigma \hat{\in}_t^2$$

When there is no serial correlation E(D) = 2.0 and the observed value of D outside the interval (1.5, 2.5) suggests non-zero serial correlation.

A good idea is to try to avoid dependence of $\in$'s, when collecting the data. It is advisable to introduce randomness as much as possible in the process of data collection and try to avoid taking observations where one depends on the value obtained for another.

14.9 Multicollinearity

In practice, the problem of multicollinearity occurs when some of the x variables are highly correlated. Multicollinearity can have significant impact on the quality and stability of the fitted regression model. A common approach to multicollinearity problem is to omit explanatory variables. For example, if X_1 and X_2 are highly correlated (say correlation greater than 0.9), then the simplest approach would be to use only one of them, since one variable conveys essentially all the information in the other variable. The simplest method for detecting multicollinearity is the correlation matrix, which can be used to detect if there are large correlations between pairs of explanatory variables.

Consider two independent variables X_1 and X_2 regressions on the dependent variable Y. That is $Y = \beta_0 + \beta_1 X_1 + \beta_2 X_1 + \in$. Suppose there is perfect correlation between the sample values of X_1 and X_2 either perfect negative or positive correlation that is, $X_2 = a + bx_1$ (b is either positive or negative). Then, the least square estimate of β_1 is $\hat{\beta}_{yx_1.x_2} = \dfrac{\hat{\beta}yx_1 - \hat{\beta}_{yx_2} \hat{\beta}_{x_2x_1}}{1 - r^2_{x_1x_2}} = \dfrac{0}{0}$, which is indeterminate. Similarly the estimate $\hat{\beta}_{yx_2x_1}$ is not determinate.

As $r^2_{x_1x_2}$ goes near to unity, the estimate then becomes very sensitive to the actual value of $r^2_{yx_1 . x_2}$.

Further, Var ($\hat{\beta}_{yx_1.x_2}$)

$$= \frac{\sigma_e^2 \, \Sigma(X_2 - \overline{X}_2)^2}{\Sigma(X_1 - \overline{X}_1)^2 \, \Sigma(X_2 - \overline{X}_2)^2 - \{\Sigma(X_1 - \overline{X}_1)(X_2 - \overline{X}_2)\}^2}$$

$$= \frac{\sigma_e^2 \, . \, b^2 \, . \, \Sigma(X_1 - \overline{X}_1)^2}{0}$$

which becomes infinite.

Thus, it may be made clear that if the correlation between X_1 and X_2 is high but not perfect, the expression for $\hat{\beta}_1$ will become ratio of two very small numbers, so that the estimate of β_1 will become highly uncertain while the denominator in Var $(\hat{\beta}_1)$ will approach zero and so that the variance of $\hat{\beta}_1$ will become very large.

Note : It is sometimes suggested that the presence of 'high' standard errors in the estimated coefficients should give adequate warning that there is multcollinearity.

14.10 Autocorrelation

One of the basic assumption in the regression analysis is the independence of the errors. This assumption is likely to be violated when data are collected over periods of time because a residual at any one point in time may tend to be similar to residuals at adjacent points in time. Thus, positive residuals would be more likely to be followed by positive residuals and negative residuals would be more likely followed by negative residuals. Such a pattern in the residuals is called **autocorrelation** (serial correlation). When substantial autocorrelation is present in a set of data, the validity of a fitted regression model may be in serious doubt.

Autocorrelation can be detected and measured by using the **Durbin-Watson statistic.**

This statistic measures the correlation between each residual and the residual for the time period **immediately preceeding** the one of interest. Thus, the Durbin-Watson statistic popularly known as D—W statistic is defined as :

$$D = \frac{\sum_{t=2}^{n} (e_t - e_{t-1})^2}{\sum_{t=1}^{n} e_t^2},$$

where $e_t = \hat{\epsilon}_t$ = residual at time period t

Interpretation of D

When successive residuals are positively autocorrelated, the value of D will approach zero. If the residuals are not correlated, the value of D will be close to 2. If there is negative autocorrelation, D will be greater than 2 and could even approach its maximum value of 4.

The problem of interest to know while using Durbin-Watson statistic is the determination of when the autocorrelation is large enough to make D statistic fall sufficiently below 2 to cause concern about the validity of the model.

The critical values of the D—W statistic depend on

(*a*) n, the number of observations

(*b*) α, the significance level

(*c*) p, the number of independent variables in the model.

To provide the method to use the critical values of D-W statistic an extract of the table of Durbin-Watson statistic is given below with $\alpha = 0.05$, n = 15, 16, 17, 18, 19, 20 ; p = 1, 2, 3, 4.

TABLE–14.2. An Extract of the Critical Values of Durbin-Watson Statistic : α = 0.05

	p = 1		p = 2		p = 3		p = 4	
n	d_L	d_U	d_L	d_U	d_L	d_U	d_L	d_U
15	1.08	1.36	0.95	1.54	0.82	1.75	0.69	1.97
16	1.10	1.37	0.98	1.54	0.86	1.73	0.74	1.93
17	1.13	1.28	1.02	1.54	0.90	1.71	0.78	1.90
18	1.16	1.39	1.05	1.53	0.93	1.69	0.82	1.87
19	1.18	1.40	1.08	1.53	0.97	1.68	0.86	1.85
20	1.20	1.41	1.10	1.54	1.00	1.68	0.90	1.83

In the Durbin-Watson table two values are shown for each combination of α (level of significance), n (sample size) and p (number of independent variables in the model). The first value, d_L represents the lower critical value when there is no autocorrelation in the data. If D is below d_L, we conclude that there is positive autocorrelation among the residuals . The second value d_U, represents the upper critical value of D, above which we would conclude that there is **no** evidence of autocorrelation among the residuals. If D is between d_L and d_U, we are unable to arrive at a definite conclusion.

14.11 Multiple Regression Equation in Matrix notation

The multiple regression model is written as

where $\underline{Y} = \underline{X}\,\underline{\beta} + \underline{\in}$

$$\underline{X} = \begin{bmatrix} 1 & X_{11} & X_{21} & \dots & X_{k_1} \\ 1 & X_{12} & X_{22} & \dots & X_{k_2} \\ \vdots & \vdots & \vdots & \vdots & \vdots \\ 1 & X_{1n} & X_{2n} & \dots & X_{kn} \end{bmatrix}, \quad \underline{Y} = \begin{bmatrix} Y_1 \\ Y_2 \\ \vdots \\ Y_n \end{bmatrix},$$

$$\underline{\beta} = \begin{bmatrix} \beta_0 \\ \beta_1 \\ \vdots \\ \beta_k \end{bmatrix} \text{ and } \underline{\in} = \begin{bmatrix} \in_1 \\ \in_2 \\ \vdots \\ \in_n \end{bmatrix}, \text{ with } E(\underline{\in}) = 0 \text{ and } Cov(\underline{\in}) = \sigma_e^2 I.$$

The least square estimates of the regression coefficients are given by $\hat{\underline{\beta}} = (\underline{X}'\underline{X})^{-1}\underline{X}'\underline{Y}$, which is the solution of minimizing equation $\underline{X}'\underline{Y} = \underline{X}'\underline{X}\,\hat{\underline{\beta}}$

It is assumed that $\underline{X}'\underline{X}$ is non-singular so that the inverse exists.

$$E(\hat{\beta}_i) = \beta_i \ (i = 0,1,2,\dots,k)$$

$$V(\hat{\beta}_i) = C_{ii}\,\sigma_e^2 \text{ for } i = 0, 1, 2, \dots, k$$

$Cov(\hat{\beta}_i, \hat{\beta}_j) = C_{ij}\,\sigma_e^2$ for $i \neq 0,1,2,\dots,k$,

where C_{ij} is the element in ith row and jth column of the matrix $(\underline{X}'\underline{X})^{-1}$.

In matrix notation $E(\hat{\underline{\beta}}) = \underline{\beta}$ and

$$Cov(\hat{\underline{\beta}}) = \sigma_e^2 (X'X)^{-1}$$

14.12 Regression with qualitative Explanatory (predictor) variables :

Sometimes, explanatory variables for inclusion in a regression model are not in interval scale, but may be nominal or ordinal variables. Such variables can be used in the regression model by creating 'dummy' (or indicator) variables.

Suppose a dependent variable Y is linearly regressed on dichotomous/indicator variable X as

$Y = a + bX,$

where Y = income of an individual

X = a dichotomous variable (dummy/indicator) coded as

0, if female

1, if male.

Suppose the estimated regression equation is

$$\hat{Y} = \hat{a} + \hat{b}X$$

Thus, $\hat{Y} = \hat{a}$, if $X = 0$

$= \hat{a} + \hat{b}$, if $X = 1$

That is, the estimated average income for females is $\hat{a}$ (sample mean) and $(\hat{a} + \hat{b})$ is estimated average income for males.

The regression coefficient $\hat{b}$ is therefore, $\hat{Y}_{male} - \hat{Y}_{female}$

In fact, females are considered as the reference group and males' income is measured by how much it differ from females' income.

Consider a trichotomous variable X

$$Y = a + b X$$

where Y = percentage of work time spent on teaching

X = Trichotomous variable 'rank' with three modalities (categories)

1 = Professor

2 = Reader

3 = Lecturer

We create **two dummy** variables

$X_1 = 1$, if rank is professor

0, if otherwise

$X_2 = 1$, if rank is Reader

= 0, if otherwise

Thus, we have created two dummy variables to represent a trichotomous variable. If we create a third dummy variable X_3 (score 1 if rank = Lecturer and score 0 otherwise), the parameters of the regression equation cannot be estimated uniquely. This is because if the score of any respondent on X_1 and X_2 is known, it would always be possible to predict score on X_3 For example, if a respondent has score 0 on X_1 (not Professor) and 0 on X_2 (not Reader), then the respondent is certainly a lecturer (i.e. score 1 on X_3). This represents a situation of perfect multicollinearity. Hence, the general rule for creating dummy variable is Number of dummy variables = Number modalities (categories) minus 1.

The statistical significance of regression coefficients and multiple R^2 is determined in the same way as for interval scale explanatory variables.

Thus, if a qualitative predictor has C categories, then we need to define (C – 1) qualitative indicator variables. First, a **base line category** is selected. No indicator variable is defined for it. For each of the remaining categories there is an indicator variable taking 1 if the unit belongs to this category and 0 otherwise. When all the (C – 1) indicator variables are 0, it means that the observations come from the baseline category.

Example 14.1

The electric power consumed each month(y) by a chemical plant is thought to be related to the average ambient temperature (x_1), the number of days in the month (x_2), the average product purity (x_3) and tons of product produced (x_4). Some historical data are available and are presented in the following.

Y	X1	X2	X3	X4
240	25	24	91	100
236	31	21	90	95
290	45	24	88	110
274	60	25	87	88
301	65	25	91	94
316	72	26	94	99
300	80	25	87	97
296	84	25	86	96
267	75	24	88	110
276	60	25	91	105
288	50	25	90	100
261	38	23	89	98

(*a*) Fit a multiple regression model.

(*b*) Test for significance of regression.

(*c*) Test $H_0 : \beta_3 = 0$ and $\beta_4 = 0$

Solution

Analysis (SPSS Output)

Descriptive Statistics

	Mean	Std. Deviation	N
Y	278.7500	24.5991	12
X_1	57.0833	19.4069	12
X_2	24.3333	1.3027	12
X_3	89.3333	2.2697	12
X_4	99.3333	6.4291	12

Correlations

		Y	X_1	X_2	X_3	X_4
Pearson Correlation	Y	1.000	.751	.803	.049	-.009
	X_1	.751	1.000	.660	-.288	-.024

	X_2	.803	.660	1.000	.113	-.025
	X_3	.049	-.288	.113	1.000	.079
	X_4	-.009	-.024	-.025	.079	1.000
Sig. (1-tailed)	Y	.	.002	.001	.440	.489
	X_1	.002	-	.010	.182	.471
	X_2	.001	.110	.	.364	.469
	X_3	.440	.182	.364	.	.404
	X_4	.489	.471	.469	.404	.
N	Y	12	12	12	12	12
	X_1	12	12	12	12	12
	X_2	12	12	12	12	12
	X_3	12	12	12	12	12
	X_4	12	12	12	12	12

Variables Entered/Removed[b]

Model	Variable Entered	Variables Removed	Method
1	$X_{4a}X_1, X_3X_2$	.	Enter

a. All requested variables entered.

b. Dependent Variable : Y

Model Summary

Model	R	R Square	Adjusted R Square	Std. Error of the Estimate
1	.863[a]	.745	.599	15.5793

a. Predictors : (Constant), X_4, X_1, X_3, X_2

ANOVA[b]

Model	Sum of Squares	df	Mean Square	F	Sig.
1 Regression	4957.241	4	1239.310	5.106	.030[a]
Residual	1699.009	7	242.716		
Total	6656.250	11			

a. Predictors : (Constant), X_4, X_1, X_3, X_2

b. Dependent Variable : Y

Coefficients[a]

Model	Unstandardized Coefficients		Standardized Coefficients	t	Sig.
	B	Std. Error	Beta		
1 (Constant)	-102.713	2.07.859		-.694	.636
X_1	.605	.369	.478	1.641	.145

X_2	8.924	5.301	.473	1.684	.136
X_3	1.437	2.2392	.133	.601	.567
X_4	1.361 E-02	.734	.004	.019	.986

Model	95% Confidence Interval for B	
	Lower Bound	Upper Bound
1 (Constant)	-594.220	388.794
X_1	-.267	1.478
X_2	-3.610	21.457
X_3	-4.217	7.093
X_4	-1.722	1.749

a. Dependent Variable : Y

Regression (Stepwise)

Variables Entered/Removed[a]

Model	Variables Entered	Variables Removed	Method
1	X_2		Stepwise (Criteria : Probability-of-F- to-enter ≤ .050, Probability-of-F-to-re move ≥ 100).

a. Dependent Variable : Y

Model Summary

Model	R	R Square	Adjusted R Square	Std. Error of the Estimate
1	.803[a]	.645	.609	15.3811

a. Predictors : (Constant), X_2

ANOVA[2]

Model	Sum of Squares	df	Mean Square	F	Sig.
1. Regression	4290.482	1	4290.482	18.136	.002[a]
Residual	2365.768	10	236.577		
Total	6656.250	11			

a. Predictors : (Constant), X_2

b. Dependent Variable : Y

Coefficients

Model	Unstandardized Coefficients		Standardized Coefficients	t	Sig.
	B	Std. Error	Beta		
1 (Constant)	-90.161	86.741	.803	-1.039	.323
X_2	15.161	3.560		4.259	.002

Model	95% Confidence Interval for B	
	Lower Bound	Upper Bound
1 (Constant)	-283.431	103.110
X2	7.228	23.093

a. Dependent Variable : Y

Excluded Variables[b]

Model	Beta in	*t*	Sig.	Partial Correlation	Collinearity Statistics Tolerance
1 X_1	.392[a]	1.705	.122	.495	.564
X_3	–.042[a]	-.212	.837	-.070	.987
X_4	.011[a]	.056	.957	.019	.999

a. Predictors in the Model : (Constant), X_2

b. Dependent Variable : Y

Regression (Backward)

Variables Entered/Removed[b]

Model	Variables Entered	Variables Removed	Method
1	X_4X_1,X_3,X_2[a]		Enter
2		X_4	Backward (criterion : Probability of F- to-remove ≥ . 100)
3		X_3	Backward (criterion : Probability of F- to-remove ≥ .100).
4		X_1	Backward (criterion : Probability of F- to-remove ≥ .100)

a. All requested variables entered.

b. Dependent Variable : Y

Model	R	R Square	Adjusted R Square	Std. Error of the Estimate
1	.863[a]	.745	.599	15.5793
2	.863[b]	.745	.649	14.5735

3	.855[c]	.731	.672	14.0948
4	.803[d]	.645	.609	15.3811

a. Predictors (Constant), X_4,X_1,X_3,X_2

b. Predictors : (Constant) , X_1,X_3,X_2

c. Predictors : (Constant), X_1,X_2

d. Predictors : (Constant), X_2

ANOVA[e]

Model	Sum of Squares	df	Mean Square	F	Sig.
1 Regression	4957.241	4	1239.310	5.106	.030[a]
Residual	1699.009	7	242.716		
Total	6656.250	11			
2 Regression	4957.157	3	1652.386	7.780	.009[b]
Residual	1699.093	8	212.387		
Total	6656.250	11			
3 Regression	4868.289	2	2434.144	12.253	.003[c]
Residual	1787.961	9	198.662		
Total	6656.250	11			
4 Regression	4290.482	1	4290.482	18.136	.002[d]
Residual	2365.768	10	236.577		
Total	6656.250	11			

a. Predictors (Constant), X_4,X_1,X_3,X_2

b. Predictors : (Constant) , X_1,X_3,X_2

c. Predictors : (Constant), X_1,X_2

d. Predictors : (Constant), X_2

e. Predictors Variable : Y

Coefficients[a]

Model	Unstandardized Coefficient		Standardized Coefficients	t	Sig
	B	Std.Error	Beta		
1 (Constant)	-102.713	207.859		-.494	.636
X_1	.605	.365	.478	1.641	.145
X_2	8.924	5.301	.473	1.684	.136
X_3	1.437	2.392	.133	.601	.567
X_4	1.361 E-02	.734	.004	.019	986
2 (Constant)	-101.610	186.306		-.545	.600
X_1	.606	.345	.478	1.756	.117

X_2	8.919	4.952	.472	1.801	.109
X_3	1.441	2.228	.133	.647	.536
3 (Constant)	.529	95.635		.006	.996
X_1	.497	.292	.392	1.705	.122
X_2	10.267	4.345	.544	2.363	.042
4 (Constant)	-90.161	86.741		-1.039	.323
X_2	15.161	3.560	.803	4.259	.002

Coefficients[a]

Model		95% Confidence Interval for B	
		Lower Bound	Upper Bound
1 (Constant)		-594.220	388.794
X_1		-.267	1.478
X_2		-3.610	21.457
X_3		-4.218	7.093
X_4		-1.722	1.749
2 (Constant)		-531.232	328.012
X_1		-.190	1.401
X_2		-2.501	20.339
X_3		-3.697	6.580
3 (Constant)		-215.811	216.869
X_1		-.162	1.157
X_2		.439	20.095
4 (Constant)		-283.431	103.110
X_2		7.228	23.093

a. Dependent Variable : Y

Excluded Variables[d]

Model		Beta in	t	Sig.	Partial Correlation	Collinearity Statistics Tolerance
2	X_4	.004[a]	.019	.986	.007	.991
3	X_4	.014[b]	.075	.942	.027	.999
	X_3	.133[b]	.647	.536	.223	.755
4	X_4	.011[c]	.056	.957	.014	.999
	X_3	-0.42[c]	-.212	.837	-.070	.987
	X_1	.392[c]	1.705	.122	.494	.564

a. Predictors in the Model : (Constant), X_1,X_3,X_2

b. Predictors in the Model : (Constant), X_1,X_2

c. Predictors in the Model : (Constant), X_2

d. Dependent Variable : Y

Regression (Forward)

Variables Entered/Removed[a]

Model	Variables Entered	Variables Remoed	Method
1	X_2		Forward (Criterion : Probability -of-F- to-enter ≤ .050)

a. Dependent Variable : Y

Model Summary

Model	R	R Square	Adjusted R Square	Std. Error of the Estimate
1	-803[a]	.645	.609	15.3811

a. Predictors : (Constant), X2

ANOVA[b]

Model	Sum of Squares	df	Mean Square	F	Sig.
1 Regression	4290.482	1	4290.482	18.136	.002[a]
Residual	2365.768	10	236.577		
Total	6656.250	11			

a. Predictors : (Constant), X^2

b. Dependent Variable : Y

Coefficients[a]

Model	Unstandardized Coefficients		Standardized Coefficients	*t*	Sig.
	B	Std. Error	Beta		
1 (Constant)	-90.161	86.741		-1.039	.323
X_2	15.161	3.560	.803	4.259	.002

Coefficients[a]

Model	95% Confidence Interval for B	
	Lower Bound	Upper Bound
1 (Constant)	-283.431	103.110
X_2	7.228	23.093

a. Dependent Variable : Y

Excluded Variables[b]

Model	Beta in	t	Sig.	Partial Correlation	Collinearity Statistics Tolerance
1 X_1	.392[a]	1.705	.122	.494	.564
X_3	-.042[a]	-.212	.837	-.070	.987
X_4	.011[a]	.056	.957	.019	.999

a. Predictors in the Model : (Constant), X_2

b. Dependent Variable : Y

Example 14.2

The following data relate to territory wise sales (in lakhs of rupees) (Y), advertising ('000 Rs.) (X_1) and Number of selling agents employed (X_2)

Sales Territory	Y	X_1	X_2
1	100	30	10
2	80	20	8
3	70	30	8
4	120	50	15
5	150	60	20
6	90	20	10
7	80	15	8
8	130	40	10

(*a*) Compute the regression equation.

(*b*) Compute the standard error of estimate.

(*c*) Compute the coefficient of Multiple determination.

(*d*) Test the significance of regression function.

Solution : (SPSS output)

Descriptive Statistics

	Mean	Standard Deviation	*n*
Y	102.5000	28.1577	
X_1	33.1250	15.7973	8
X_2	11.1250	4.2573	

Correlations

	Y	X_1	X_2
Y	1.000	0.879	0.855
X_1	0.879	1.000	0.896
X_2	0.855	0.896	1.0000

Model Summary

R	R Square	Adjusted R Square	Standard error of estimate
0.892	0.796	0.714	15.0525

ANOVA

Source	Sum of Squares	*df*	Mean Square	F	P-Value (Significant)
Regression	447.15	2	2208.558	9.747	0.019
Residual	1132.885	5	226.577		
Total	5550.000	7			

Coefficients

	Unstandardized coefficient		Standardized Coefficient 'Beta'	t	Significant level (P-Value)
	$\hat{\beta}$	Standard Error			
β_0	43.539	16.099		2.704	0.043
β_1	1.022	0.811	0.573	1.260	0.263
β_2	2.256	3.011	0.341	0.749	0.487

The fitting regression relationship is $\hat{Y} = 43.539 + 1.022\, X_1 + 2.256\, X_2$

EXERCISES

1. Define a multiple regression model with assumptions. Explain the uses of multiple regression analysis. Discuss the method of fitting a multiple regression equation and structure of analysis of variance.
2. The following data show the number of bed rooms and prices at which a random sample of 8 Duplex houses sold recently by Metro Builders Private Limited.

Number of Bedrooms x_1	Number of baths x_2	Price (Rs in Lakhs) y
3	2	24
2	1	15
4	3	32
2	2	20
3	2	27
5	3	38
2	1	18
4	2	30

Use the method of least squares to find out a linear equation to predict the price of a Duplex one family house in city area.
Compute the coefficient of multiple determination.
Test the significance of regression function.

3. The following are data on the average weekly profits in lakhs of rupees of five restaurants, their seating capacities and the average daily number of customers (in thousands) dining at the restaurants.

Seating Capacity	Average daily number of customers	Weekly net profit
20	100	1000
30	120	1200
50	100	1200
60	150	1500
80	130	2000

(*a*) Assuming that the regression is linear compute the estimates of β_0, β_1 and β_2

(*b*) Predict the average weekly net-profit of a restaurant with a seating capacity of 60 where the average daily number of customers is 190.

4. The following are data on the percent effectiveness of pain reliever and the amounts of three different medications (in milligrams) present in each capsule.

Medication A x_1	Medication B x_2	Medication C x_3	Percent effective y
15	20	10	47
15	20	20	54
15	30	10	58
15	30	20	66
30	20	10	59
30	20	20	67
30	20	10	71
30	30	20	83
45	20	10	72
45	20	20	82
45	30	10	85
45	30	20	94

Assuming the regression to be linear :

(*i*) Compute the multiple regression equation and test the significance of regression coefficients and also the regression function.

(*ii*) Compute the coefficient of multiple determination R^2 and also adjusted $\overline{R}^2$.

5. What are the assumptions made in the multiple regression model ? What happens when these assumptions are violated ? What are the precautions to be taken in this regard ? Discuss.

6. What are BETA Coefficients ? Explain their uses in multiple regression analysis.
7. Suppose you have the following multiple regression model :

$$\hat{Y}_i = 8 + 5\,X_{1i} + 3\,X_{2i}$$

and $R^2 = 0.60$
   (*a*) Interpret the meaning of slopes.
   (*b*) Interpret the meaning of Y intercept.
   (*c*) What does the coefficient of multiple determination R^2 indicate ?
8. The following analysis of variance table was obtained from a multiple regression model with 2 independent Variables.
   Complete the entries in the table. Determine whether there is a significant relationship between Y two explanatory variables at the 0.05 level of significance.

ANOVA

Source	Degrees of Freedom	Sum of squares	Mean square	F
Regression	—	30	—	
Error	20		—	
Total	22	150		

9. (*a*) Distinguish between interpretations of tests of significance with critical values and P-values in the multiple regression analysis of variance table.
   (*b*) Distinguish between standardised and unstandardised regression coefficient and between R^2 and adjusted R^2.
10. (*a*) What would you interpret from the multiple regression analysis of variance table when the regression function is significant, but not the partial regression coefficient ?
    (*b*) Discuss the testing of regression coefficients in multiple regression analysis. How would you compute the confidence intervals of the regression coefficient ?
    (*c*) Interpret coefficient of partial determination.
    (*d*) How would you determine the contribution of an independent variable to the Regression Model ? Explain.
11. The following data consist of the scores which ten students obtained in an examination, their IQ's and the number of hours they spent studying for the examination.
    (*a*) Assuming that the regression is linear, estimate β_0, β_1 and β_2
    (*b*) Predict the score of a student with an IQ of 108 who studied six hours for the examination.

IQ (x_i)	Number of hours studied (x_i)	Score (y)
112	5	79
126	13	97
100	3	51

114	7	65
112	11	82
121	9	93
110	8	81
103	4	38
111	6	60
124	2	86

12. Write explanatory notes on stepwise, backward and forward methods of selecting explanatory variables.
13. What is a partial 'F' test ? Explain its uses.
14. Given the following information about a trivariate population :

$$\sigma_1 = 3, \sigma_2 = 4, \sigma_3 = 5$$
$$r_{23} = 0.4, r_{31} = 0.6, r_{12} = 0.7$$

Compute :

(*i*) $r_{12.3}$ and $R^2_{1(23)}$

(*ii*) Beta coefficients when X_1 is the dependent variable and X_2 and X_3 are explanatory variables.

15. What is multicollinearity in multiple regression ? Explain its effect on the multiple regression analysis.
16. What is partial correlation ? What does it indicate ? How does it differ from multiple correlation ? How would you test significance of partial and multiple correlation ? Explain.
17. Given the following summary statistics computed from data on three variables X_1 (dependent), X_2 and X_3 for a sample of size 15, make a multiple regression analysis.

$$\Sigma X_1 = 1{,}908 \qquad \Sigma X_1^2 = 1{,}84{,}706$$
$$\Sigma X_2 = 1{,}541 \qquad \Sigma X_2^2 = 1{,}19{,}951$$
$$\Sigma X_3 = 1{,}502 \qquad \Sigma X_3^2 = 1{,}13{,}104$$
$$\Sigma X_1X_2 = 1{,}48{,}344$$
$$\Sigma X_2X_3 = 1{,}15{,}754$$
$$\Sigma X_1X_3 = 1{,}43{,}626$$

18. The following data relate to 12 fast food centres in city. Make a multiple regression analysis.

Sl.No. of Centre	Y Total Sales (000' Rs.)	X_1 Number of advertisements appearing	X_2 Cost of advertismenet in 000'Rs
1	457	10	35
2	386	11	32
3	302	9	30
4	354	10	35

5	462	12	40
6	352	8	30
7	305	6	25
8	406	9	35
9	382	7	30
10	236	6	28
11	328	5	20
12	374	8	28

19. (*a*) What is autocorrelation ? How would you measure and test the significance of autocorrelation ? Discuss.

    (*b*) Explain how would you make regression analysis with indicator predictor variables ?

20. A city super market has experienced a marked change in its sales as a result of a very successful advertising campaign. The management would like to develop a new regression model for its sales. The following data relate the sales position in the 12 weeks since the advertising campaign began.

Time	Sales in Thousand Rs.	Time	Sales in Thousands Rs.
1	4,500	7	19,754
2	3,745	8	33,259
3	5,736	9	50,352
4	4,398	10	65,780
5	5,118	11	86,455
6	8,867	12	1,05,464

(*a*) Fit a linear regression model.

(*b*) Test the serial correlation (autocorrelation) and plot the residuals.

(*c*) Compute the confidence intervals for Y-intercept and slope.

□□□

CHAPTER

15

MULTIVARIATE APPLICATIONS—AN OVERVIEW

15.1 Introduction

In recent years the multivariate statistical tools have been widely applied in all fields of economic and social research in their respective decision making processes. It is seen that in many problems of research interest, a host of dependent and independant variables comes to play their role and thus making the problems more complex, than the problems bivariate model can explain. Advancement of computer technology in formulating computer programs has helped solving complex mathematical problems, creating interest in the minds of researchers to work for a number of explanatory variables satisfactorily explaining the situation at hand.

The management researches in different functional areas of management have increasingly become more scientific and also more problems are being addressed by considering multiple dependent and multiple independent variables. Sales managers make forecast of sales on various product history variables, marketers consider and develop market strategies based on a set of buyer preferences and prefered product options; financial analysts analyse credit risk on a set of predictors; and human resource managers develop future wage policy based on multivariate techniques. An agriculture scientiest forecasts for crop production dependent on various inputs, rainfall, temperature, irrigation facilities, fertilizer practices etc. Economic forecasts and investment decisions depend on multivariate techniques. Develoment planning of a country cannot over look multivariate criteria. Future prediction of fertility and mortality scenario in a country depends on a host of socio-economic, cultural and health variables. In fact foreign policy and strategic defence studies take into account a number of interdependent variables to arrive at a judicious decision.

Multivariate techniques may be classified as (*i*) dependency and (*ii*) interdependancy techniques. Multiple regression and multivariate analysis of variance and discriminant function analysis take into consideration both dependent and independent variables. Alternatively, factor analysis, cluster analysis and multidimensinal scaling make use of variables in that being designated as dependent and independent variables. Each of the multivariate techniques has a specific research question for which it is best suited. Each technique also has certain strengths and weaknesses that should be clearly understood by the analyst before interpreting results.

Before launching an analysis technique, it is important to have a clear understanding of the form and quality of data. The form of data refers to whether the data are nonmetric or metric. The quality of data refers to distributional properties in data— normality, linearity, homoscedasbility, presence of missing observations, presence of outliers, etc. The researcher should consider whether to ignore the missing observations or impute them and also some considerations for the outliers.

In the following we introduce certain multivariate analysis techniques which are useful for business/marketing/social science research studies.

Multiple Regression Analysis

Multiple regression is the most commonly utilised multivariate technique. It examines the relationship between a single metric dependent variable and two or more metric independent variables. The technique relies upon determining the linear relationship with the lowest sum of squared variances ; therefore, assumptions or normality, linearity, and equal variance are carefully observed. The beta coefficients (weights) are the marginal impacts of each variable, and the size of the weight can be interpreted directly. Multiple regression is often used as a forecasting tool.

Discriminant Analysis

The purpose of discriminant analysis is to correctly classify observations or people into homogeneous groups. The independent variables must be metric and must have a high degree of normality. Discriminant analysis builds a linear discriminant function, which can then be used to classify the observations. The overall fit is assessed by looking at the degree to which the group means differ (Wilkes Lambda or D^2) and how well the model classifies. To determine which variables have the most impact on the discriminant function, it is possible to look at partial F values. The higher the partial F, the more impact that variable has on the discriminant function. This tool helps categorize people, like buyers and nonbuyers.

Multivariate Analysis of Variance (MANOVA)

This technique examines the relationship between several categorical independent variables and two or more metric dependent variables. Whereas analysis of variance (ANOVA) assesses the differences between groups (by using t tests for 2 meana nd F tests between 3 or more means), MANOVA examines the dependence relationship between a set of dependnent measures across a set of groups. Typically this analysis is used in experimental design, and usually a hypothesized relationship between dependent measures is used. This technique is slightly different in that the independent variables are categorical and the dependent variable is metric. Sample size is an issue, with

15-20 observations needed per cell. However, too many observations per cell (over 30) and the technique loses its practical significance. Cell sizes should be roughly equal, with the largest cell having less than 1.5 times the observations of the smallest cell. That is because, in this technique, normality of the dependent variables is important. The model fit is determined by examining mean vector equivalents across groups. If there is a significant difference in the means, the null hypothesis can be rejected and treatment differences can be determined.

Factor Analysis

When there are many variables in a research design, it is often helpful to reduce the variables to a smaller set of factors. This is an independence technique, in which there is no dependent variable. Rather, the researcher is looking for the underlying structure of the data matrix. Ideally, the independent variables are normal and continuous, with at least 3 to 5 variables loading onto a factor. The sample size should be over 50 observations, with over 5 observations per variable. Multicollinearity is generally preferred between the variables, as the correlations are key to data reduction. Kaiser's Measure of Statistical Adequacy (MSA) is a measure of the degree to which every variable can be predicted by all other variables. An overall MSA of .80 or higher is very good, with a measure of under .50 deemed poor.

There are two main factor analysis methods : *common factor analysis*, which extracts factors based on the variance shared by the factors, and *principal component analysis*, which extracts factors based on the total variance of the factors. Common factor analysis is used to look for the latent (underlying) factors, where as principal components analysis is used to find the fewest number of variables that explain the most variance. The first factor extracted explains the most variance. Typically, factors are extracted as long as the eigenvalues are greater than 1.0 or the Scree test visually indicates how many factors to extract. The factor loadings are the correlations between the factor and the variables. Typically a factor loading of .4 or higher is required to attribute a specific variable to a factor. An orthogonal rotation assumes no correlation between the factors, whereas an oblique rotation is used when some relationship is believed to exist.

Cluster Analysis

The purpose of cluster analysis is to reduce a large data set to meaningful subgroups of individuals or objects. The division is accomplished on the basis of similarity of the objects across a set of specified characteristics. Outliers are a problem with this technique, often caused by too many irrelevant variables. The sample should be representative of the population, and it is desirable to have uncorrelated factors. There are three main clustering methods ; hierarchical, which is a treelike process appropriate for smaller data sets ; nonhierarchical, which equires specification of the number of clusters a priori, and a combinantion of both. There are 4 main rules for developing clusters ; the clusters should be *different*, they should be *reachable*, they should be *measurable*, and the clusters should be *profitable* (big enough to matter). This is a great tool for market segmentation.

Multidimensional Scaling (MDS)

The purpose of MDS is to transform consumer judgements of similarity into distances represented in multidimensional space. This is a decompositional approach that uses perceptual mapping to present the dimensions. As an exploratory technique, it is useful in examining unrecognized dimensions about products and in uncovering comparative evaluations of products when the basis for comparison is unknown. Typically there must be at least 4 times as many objects being evaluated as dimensions. It is possible to evaluate the objects with nonmetric preference rankings or metric similarities (paired comparison) ratings. Kruskal's Stress measue is a "badness of fit" measure ; a stress percentage of 0 indicates a perfect fit, and over 20% is a poor fit. The dimensions can be interpreted either subjectively by letting the respondents identify the dimensions or objectively by the researcher.

Correspondence Analysis

This technique provides for dimensional reduction of object ratings on a set of attributes, resulting in a perceptual map of the ratings. However, unlike MDS, both independent variables and dependent variables are examined at the same time. This technique is more similar in nature to factor analysis. It is a compositional technique, and is useful when thee are many attributes and many companies. It is most often used in assessing the effectiveness of advertising campaigns. It is also used when the attributes are too similar for factor analysis to be meaningful. The main structural approach is the development of a contingency (crosstab) table. This means that the form of the variables should be nonmetric. The model can be assessed by examining the Chi-square value for the model. Correspondence analysis is diffficult to interpret, as the dimensions are a combination of independent and dependent variables.

Conjoint Analysis

Conjoint analysis is often referred to as "trade-off analysis", in that it allows for the evaluation of objects and the various levels of the attributes to be examined. It is both a compositional technique and a dependence technique, in that a level of preference for a combination of attributes and levels is developed. A part-worth, or utility, is calculated for each level of each attribute, and combinations of attributes at specific levels are summed to develop the overall preference for the attribute at each level. Models can be built which identify the ideal levels and combinations of attributes for products and services.

Canonical Correlation

The most flexible of the multivariate techniques, canonical correlation simultaneously correlates several independent variables and several dependent variables. This powerful technique utilizes metric independnet variables, unlike MANOVA, such as sales, satisfaction levels, and usage levels. It can also utilize nonmetric categorical variables. This technique has the fewest restrictions of any of the multivariate techniques, so the results should be interpreted with caution due to the relaxed assumptions. Often, the dependent variables are related, and the independent variables are related, so finding a relationship is difficult without a technique like canonical correlation.

Structural Equation Modeling

Unlike the other multivariate techniques discussed, structural equation modeling (SEM) examines multiple relationships between sets of variables simultaneously. This represents a family of techniques, including LISREL, latent variable analysis, and confirmaory factor analysis. SEM can incorporate latent variables, which either are not or cannot be measured directly into the analysis. For example, intelligence levels can only be inferred, with direct measurement of variables like test scores, level of education, grade point average, and other related measures. These tools are often used to evaluate many scaled attributes or build summated scales.

Conclusions

Each of the multivariate techniques described above has a specific type of research question for which it is best suited. Each technique also has certain strengths and weaknesses that should be clearly understood by the analyst before attempting to interpret the results of the technique. Current statistical packages (SAS, SPSS, S-Plus, and others) make it increasingly easy to run a procedure, but the results can be disastrously misinterpreted without adequate care.

15.2 Sampling from a multivariate normal population :

Consider a random sample of n observation vector, recorded on p responses of interest. The random data matrix is

$$\underset{(p \times n)}{\underline{X}} = \begin{bmatrix} X_{11} & X_{12} & \dots & X_{1n} \\ X_{21} & X_{22} & \dots & X_{2n} \\ X_{p1} & X_{p2} & \dots & X_{pn} \end{bmatrix} = [\underline{X}_1, \underline{X}_2, \dots, \underline{X}_n]$$

The column vectors $\underline{X}_1, \dots, \underline{X}_n$ represent independent observations from a p-variate normal density function

$$f(x) = f(x_1, x_2, \dots, x_p).$$

$$= |2\pi\,\Sigma|^{-\frac{1}{2}} \exp[(x-\mu)'\,\Sigma^{-1}\,(x-\mu)],$$

with mean vector μ and variance covariance matrix $\underline{\Sigma}$ ($\underline{\Sigma} > \underline{0}$);

$$-\infty < x_i < +\infty,\ i = 1, 2, \dots, p.$$

Results :

$\overline{X} = (\underline{X}_1 + \underline{X}_2 + \dots + \underline{X}_n)/n$ is an unbiased estimator of $\underline{\mu}$ and its covariance matrix is $\frac{1}{n}\underline{\Sigma}$. That is,

$$E(\underline{\overline{X}}) = \underline{\mu},$$

$$\text{Cov}(\overline{X}) = \frac{1}{n}\underline{\Sigma}.$$

An unbiased estimator of Σ is given by

$$\underline{S} = \frac{1}{n-1}\sum_{j=1}^{n} (\underline{X}_j - \underline{\overline{X}})(\underline{X}_j - \underline{\overline{X}})'.$$

The (i, k) entry of $\underline{S}$ is

$$\frac{1}{n-1}\sum_{j=1}^{n}(X_{ij}-\overline{X}_i)(X_{kj}-\overline{X}_k).$$

The sample variance-covariance matrix is represented by

$$\underline{S}=\begin{bmatrix} s_{11} & s_{12} & \cdots & s_{1p} \\ s_{12} & s_{22} & \cdots & s_{2p} \\ s_{1p} & s_{2p} & \cdots & s_{pp}\end{bmatrix}$$

The sample covariance matrix contains p variances and $\frac{p(p-1)}{2}$ different covariances.

Sometimes it is desirable to assign a single numerical value for the variation expressed by $\underline{S}$. This is represented by the determinant $|S|$, which is called the **generalized sample variance**. The generalized sample variance provides one way of writing the information on all variances and covariances as a single number. For instance if

$$\underline{S}=\begin{bmatrix} 12 & -4 \\ -4 & 6\end{bmatrix},$$

the generalized variance

$$\begin{aligned}|S| &= (12)(6)-(-4)(-4)\\ &= 72-16 = 56.\end{aligned}$$

15.2.1 Test of Hypothesis on mean vector ($\underline{\mu}$)

$$H_0 : \underline{\mu} = \underline{\mu}_0$$
$$H_1 : \underline{\mu} \neq \underline{\mu}_0.$$

Compute the statistic T, called Hotelling's T^2- statistic, a generalization of Student's *t*-statistic,

$$T^2 = n(\overline{\underline{X}}-\underline{\mu}_0)'\,\underline{S}^{-1}(\overline{\underline{X}}-\underline{\mu}_0),$$

where $\underset{(p\times 1)}{\overline{\underline{X}}} = \frac{1}{n}\sum_{j=1}^{n}\underline{X}_j,\ \underline{S} = \frac{1}{n-1}\Sigma(\underline{X}_j-\overline{\underline{X}})(\underline{X}_j-\overline{\underline{X}})'$

and $\underset{(p\times 1)}{\underline{\mu}_0} = \begin{bmatrix}\mu_{10}\\ \mu_{20}\\ \vdots \\ \mu_{p0}\end{bmatrix}$

$\frac{1}{n}\underline{S}$ is the estimated covariance matrix of $\overline{\underline{X}}$.

T^2 is distributed as $\frac{(n-1)p}{(n-p)}F_{p,\,n-p}$, where $F_{p,\,n-p}$ denotes a random variable with F- distribution with p and $n-p$ degrees of freedom.

If the observed value of T^2 is too large, that is, $\overline{\underline{X}}$ is too far from $\underline{\mu}_0$, the null hypotheses $H_0 : \underline{\mu} = \underline{\mu}_0$ is rejected.

Thus, reject $H_0 : \underline{\mu} = \underline{\mu}_0$ at α level of significance if

$$T^2 > \frac{(n-1)p}{n-p} F_{\alpha, p, n-p}.$$

Here, $F_{\alpha, p, n-p}$ is the upper (100 α)th percentile of $F_{p, n-p}$ distribution.

Example 15.1. 20 sales promotion officers have the following data on annual salary, attitude scores and the amount of sales performed.

Test the hypothesis

$$H_0 : \underline{\mu} = \begin{pmatrix} 4 \\ 40 \\ 10 \end{pmatrix} \text{ against } H_1 : \underline{\mu} \neq \begin{pmatrix} 4 \\ 40 \\ 10 \end{pmatrix} \text{ at 5\% level of significance.}$$

TABLE 15.1

Sales Officers	X_1 (Annual salary) in lakhs	X_2 Attitude scores	X_3 (Amount of monthly sales)
1	3.7	48.5	9.3
2	5.7	65.1	8.0
3	3.8	47.2	10.9
4	3.2	53.2	12.0
5	3.1	55.5	9.7
6	4.6	36.1	7.9
7	2.4	24.8	14.0
8	7.2	33.1	7.6
9	6.7	47.4	8.5
10	5.4	54.1	11.3
11	3.9	36.9	12.7
12	4.5	58.8	12.3
13	3.5	27.8	9.8
14	4.5	40.2	8.4
15	1.5	13.5	10.1
16	8.5	56.4	7.1
17	4.5	71.6	8.2
18	6.5	52.8	10.9
19	4.1	44.1	11.2
20	5.5	40.9	9.4

Solution

Computer calculations show

$$\underline{\bar{X}} = \begin{bmatrix} 4.640 \\ 45.400 \\ 9.965 \end{bmatrix}, \underline{S} = \begin{bmatrix} 2.879 & 10.002 & -1.810 \\ 10.002 & 199.798 & -5.627 \\ -1.810 & -5.627 & 3.628 \end{bmatrix}$$

and

$$\underline{S}^{-1} = \begin{bmatrix} 0.586 & -0.022 & 0.258 \\ -0.022 & 0.006 & -0.002 \\ 0.258 & -0.002 & 0.402 \end{bmatrix}$$

The computed value of

$$T^2 = 20[4.640-4,\ 45.400-40,\ 9.965-10] \times \begin{bmatrix} 0.586 & -0.022 & 0.258 \\ -0.022 & 0.006 & -0.002 \\ 0.258 & -0.002 & 0.402 \end{bmatrix} \begin{bmatrix} 4.640-4 \\ 45.400-40 \\ 9.965-10 \end{bmatrix}$$

$$= 20[0.640\ \ 5.400\ \ -0.035] \times \begin{bmatrix} 0.586 & -0.022 & 0.258 \\ -0.022 & 0.006 & -0.002 \\ 0.258 & -0.002 & 0.402 \end{bmatrix} \begin{bmatrix} 0.640 \\ 5.400 \\ -0.035 \end{bmatrix}$$

$$= 20[0.640,\ 5.400\ -0.035] \begin{bmatrix} 0.247 \\ 0.018 \\ 0.140 \end{bmatrix} = 20 \times 0.2504$$

$$= 5.008$$

Comparing the observed $T^2 = 5.008$ with the critical value

$$\frac{(n-1)p}{n-p} F_{\alpha,\, p,\, n-p} = \frac{19(3)}{17} F_{0.05,\, 3,\, 17}$$

$$= \frac{57}{17}(3.20) = 10.72$$

As $T^2 = 5.008$ is less than 10. 72, H_0 cannot be rejected as per the given data.

The simultaneous intervals for the means μ_1, μ_2 and μ_3 at $\alpha\%$ level of significance are obtained as

$$\bar{x}_i - \sqrt{\frac{p(n-1)}{n-p} F_{\alpha,\, p,\, n-p}} \sqrt{\frac{s_{ii}}{n}} \le \mu_i \le \bar{x}_i + \sqrt{\frac{p(n-1)}{n-p} F_{\alpha,\, p,\, n-p}} \sqrt{\frac{s_{ii}}{n}},\ i = 1, 2, 3.$$

Given $\bar{X} = \begin{pmatrix} \bar{x}_1 \\ \bar{x}_2 \\ \bar{x}_3 \end{pmatrix} = \begin{pmatrix} 4.640 \\ 5.400 \\ 9.965 \end{pmatrix},$

$$\bar{x}_1 = 4.640 \quad \bar{x}_2 = 5.400 \quad \bar{x}_3 = 9.965$$

From S matrix, we have

$$s_{11} = 2.879$$

$$s_{22} = 199.798$$

$$s_{33} = 3.628$$

Further $\frac{p(n-1)}{n-p} F_{\alpha,\, p,\, n-p}$

$$= \frac{3 \times 19}{17} 3.20$$

$$= 10.72.$$

Therefore, the simultaneous confidence statements with confidence coefficient 0.95 are

$$4.640 - \sqrt{10.72} \sqrt{\frac{2.879}{20}} \le \mu_1 \le 4.640 + \sqrt{10.72} \sqrt{\frac{2.879}{20}}$$

or $3.3978 \le \mu_1 \le 5.8822$

$$5.400-\sqrt{10.72}\sqrt{\frac{199.798}{20}} \le \mu_2 < 5.400+\sqrt{10.72}\sqrt{\frac{199.798}{20}}$$

or $-4.9485 \le \mu_2 \le 15.7485$

$$9.965-\sqrt{10.72}\sqrt{\frac{3.628}{20}} \le \mu_3 \le 9.965+\sqrt{10.72}\sqrt{\frac{3.628}{20}}$$

or $8.5705 \le \mu_3 \le 11.3595$

15.2.2 Test of Hypothesis on equality of two mean vectors :

A T^2 statistic can be developed for testing the equality of two vector means from two multivariate populations.

Consider a random sample of size n_1 from population 1 and n_2 from population 2. The observations on p–variables are summarized as follows.

Sample	Summary Statistics
$\underline{X}_{11}, \underline{X}_{12}, ..., \underline{X}_{1n_1}$	$\overline{\underline{X}}_1 = \frac{1}{n}\sum_{j=1}^{n_1} \underline{X}_{ij}$, $\underline{S}_1 = \frac{1}{n_1-1}\sum(\underline{X}_{ij}-\overline{\underline{X}}_1)(\underline{X}_{ij}-\overline{\underline{X}}_1)'$
$\underline{X}_{21}, \underline{X}_{22}, ..., \underline{X}_{2n_2}$	$\overline{\underline{X}}_2 = \frac{1}{n_2}\sum_{j=1}^{n_2} \underline{X}_{2j}$, $\underline{S}_2 = \frac{1}{n_2-1}\sum(\underline{X}_{2j}-\overline{\underline{X}}_2)(\underline{X}_{2j}-\overline{\underline{X}}_2)'$

Note. Hence the first subscript in the sample refers to the population 1 or 2.

$H_0 : \underline{\mu}_1 = \underline{\mu}_2$ or $\underline{\mu}_1-\underline{\mu}_2 = \underline{0}$

$$H_1 : \underline{\mu}_1 \ne \underline{\mu}_2 \text{ or } \underline{\mu}_1-\underline{\mu}_2 \ne 0, \text{ or } > 0.$$

Assumptions :

1. The sample $X_{\underline{11}}, X_{\underline{12}}, ..., X_{\underline{1n_1}}$ is a random sample of size n_1 from a p-variate normal population with mean vector $\underline{\mu}_1$ and covariance matrix $\underline{\Sigma}_1$.

2. The sample $X_{\underline{21}}, X_{\underline{22}}, ..., X_{\underline{2n_2}}$ is a random sample of size n_2 from a p-variate population with mean vector $\underline{\mu}_2$ and covariance matrix $\underline{\Sigma}_2$

3. Also $\underline{X}_{11}, \underline{X}_{12}, ..., \underline{X}_{1n_1}$ are independent of $\underline{X}_{21}, \underline{X}_{22}, ..., \underline{X}_{2n_2}$

4. $\underline{\Sigma}_1 = \underline{\Sigma}_2 = \underline{\Sigma}$ (same covariance matrix).

As $\underline{S}_1 = \frac{1}{n_1-1}\sum(X_{ij}-\overline{X}_1)(X_{ij}-\overline{X}_1)'$ is an unbiased estimate of $\underline{\Sigma}_1$ and $\underline{S}_2 = \frac{1}{n_2-1}\sum(X_{2j}-\overline{X}_2) \times (X_{2j}-\overline{X}_2)'$ is an unbiased estimate of $\underline{\Sigma}_2$, an estimate of common covariance matrix $\underline{\Sigma}$ can be obtained by pooling information from both the samples. Thus we get

$$\underline{S}_{pooled} = \frac{\sum_{j=1}^{n_1}(X_{ij}-\overline{X}_1)(X_{ij}-\overline{X}_1)' + \sum_{j=1}^{n_2}(X_{2j}-\overline{X}_2)(X_{2j}-\overline{X}_2)'}{n_1+n_2-2}$$

$$= \frac{(n_1-1)\underline{S}_1 + (n_2-1)\underline{S}_2}{n_1+n_2-2}$$

Under the hypothesis $H_0 : \underline{\mu}_1 - \underline{\mu}_2 = \underline{0}$

$$E(\underline{\overline{X}} - \underline{\overline{X}}_2) = E(\underline{\overline{X}}_1) - E(\underline{\overline{X}}_2)$$
$$= \underline{\mu}_1 - \underline{\mu}_2 = 0.$$

Since two samples are independent, $\underline{\overline{X}}_1$ and $\overline{X}_2$ are independent and as such Cov. $(\underline{\overline{X}}_1, \underline{\overline{X}}_2) = \underline{0}$

$$\text{Cov}\,(\underline{\overline{X}}_1 - \underline{\overline{X}}_2) = \text{Cov}(\underline{\overline{X}}_1) + \text{Cov}(\underline{\overline{X}}_2)$$
$$= \frac{1}{n_1}\Sigma + \frac{1}{n_2}\Sigma = \left(\frac{1}{n_1} + \frac{1}{n_2}\right)\Sigma.$$

Thus, an estimator of Cov $(\underline{\overline{X}}_1 - \underline{\overline{X}}_2)$ is $\left(\frac{1}{n_1} + \frac{1}{n_2}\right)\underline{S}_{\text{pooled}}$.

To test the $H_0 : \underline{\mu}_1 - \underline{\mu}_2 = \underline{0}$, an appropriate statistic is

$$T^2 = [\underline{\overline{X}}_1 - \underline{\overline{X}}_2]' \left[\left(\frac{1}{n_1} + \frac{1}{n_2}\right)\underline{S}_{\text{pooled}}\right]^{-1} [\underline{\overline{X}}_1 - \underline{\overline{X}}_2],$$

which is distributed as

$$\frac{(n_1+n_2-2)p}{n_1+n_2-p-1} F_{p,\, n_1+n_2-p-1}$$

Thus, reject H_0, if

$$T^2 > \frac{(n_1+n_2-2)p}{n_1+n_2-p-1} F_{\alpha,\, p,\, n_1+n_2-p-1},$$

where $F_{\alpha,\, p,\, n_1+n_2-p-1}$ is $100\alpha\%$ percentile of F-distribution with p and n_1+n_2-p-1 degrees of freedom.

$100(1-\alpha)\%$ simultaneous confidence intervals for the components of the vectors $\underline{\mu}_1 - \underline{\mu}_2$ of the type $(\mu_{1i} - \mu_{2i})$ are given by

$$\overline{X}_{1i} - \overline{X}_{2i} \pm c\sqrt{\left(\frac{1}{n_1} + \frac{1}{n_2}\right) s_{ii,\,\text{pooled}}}, \text{ for } i = 1, 2, ..., p,$$

Where $c = \sqrt{\frac{(n_1+n_2-2)p}{n_1+n_2-p-1} F_{\alpha,\, p,\, n_1+n_2-p-1}}$

Example 15.2 A random sample of 20 bars of soap were collected from each of two manufacturing companies following two methods of production.

Two characteristics were measured :

X_1 = lather and X_2 = mildness.

The summary statistics for bars produced by methods 1 and 2

$$\underline{\overline{X}}_1 = \begin{bmatrix} 8.3 \\ 4.1 \end{bmatrix}, \underline{S}_1 = \begin{bmatrix} 2 & 1 \\ 1 & 6 \end{bmatrix}$$

$$\underline{\overline{X}}_2 = \begin{bmatrix} 10.2 \\ 3.9 \end{bmatrix}, \underline{S}_2 = \begin{bmatrix} 2 & 1 \\ 1 & 4 \end{bmatrix}$$

$$H_0 : \underline{\mu}_1 - \underline{\mu}_2 = \underline{0} \quad H_1 : \underline{\mu}_1 - \underline{\mu}_2 \neq \underline{0}$$

Solution

Assuming $\Sigma_1 = \Sigma_2$,

$$\underline{S}_{pooled} = \frac{(20-1)\underline{S}_1 + (20-1)\underline{S}_2}{20 + 20 - 2} = \begin{bmatrix} 2 & 1 \\ 1 & 5 \end{bmatrix}$$

$$S^{-1}_{pooled} = \begin{bmatrix} \frac{5}{9} & \frac{-1}{9} \\ \frac{-1}{9} & \frac{2}{9} \end{bmatrix}$$

$$\underline{\overline{X}}_1 - \underline{\overline{X}}_2 = \begin{bmatrix} -1.9 \\ 0.2 \end{bmatrix}$$

$$T^2 = [\underline{\overline{X}}_1 - \underline{\overline{X}}_2]' \left(\frac{1}{n_1} + \frac{1}{n_2}\right)^{-1} \underline{S}^{-1}_{pooled} [\underline{\overline{X}}_1 - \underline{\overline{X}}_2]$$

$$= \left(\frac{1}{20} + \frac{1}{20}\right)^{-1} [-1.9 \ \ 0.2] \begin{bmatrix} \frac{5}{9} & -\frac{1}{9} \\ \frac{-1}{9} & \frac{2}{9} \end{bmatrix} \begin{bmatrix} -1.9 \\ 0.2 \end{bmatrix}$$

$$= (10)\ [-1.0777 \quad 0.2555] \begin{bmatrix} -1.9 \\ 0.2 \end{bmatrix}$$

$$= (10)(2.0987) = 20.987$$

At 5% level of significance, the critical value of T^2 is

$$\frac{(n_1 + n_2 - 2)\,p}{n_1 + n_2 - p - 1} F_{\alpha, p, n_1 + n_2 - p - 1}$$

$$= \frac{(38)(2)}{37} F_{0.05, 2, 37} = \frac{(38)(2)}{37}(3.25)$$

$$= 6.67$$

As $T^2 (= 20.987) > \frac{(n_1 + n_2 - 2)\,p}{n_1 + n_2 - p - 1} F_{0.05, 2, 37} = 6.67,$

the null hypothesis is rejected.

Let us compute 95% simultaneous confidence intervals for the differences in the mean components.

$$\underline{S}_{pooled} = \frac{(n_1 - 1)\,\underline{S}_1 + (n_2 - 1)\,\underline{S}_2}{n_1 + n_2 - 2}$$

$$= \begin{bmatrix} 2 & 1 \\ 1 & 5 \end{bmatrix}$$

$$c^2 = \frac{(n_1 + n_2 - 2)\,p}{n_1 + n_2 - p - 1} F_{\alpha,\, p,\, n_1 + n_2 - p - 1}$$

$$= \frac{38 \times 2}{37} (3.25) = 6.67$$

$$c = 2.5826$$

$$\mu_{11} - \mu_{21} : (8.3 - 10.2) \pm 2.5826 \sqrt{\left(\frac{1}{20} + \frac{1}{20}\right)(2)}$$

or $\quad - 1.9 \pm 2.5826 \times 0.4472$

or $\quad - 1.9 \pm 1.1549$

or $\quad - 3.0549 \le \mu_{11} - \mu_{21} \le - 0.7451$

$$\mu_{12} - \mu_{22} : 0.2 \pm 2.5826 \sqrt{\left(\frac{1}{20} + \frac{1}{20}\right)(5)}$$

or $\quad - 1.6262 \le \mu_{12} - \mu_{22} \le 2.7826$

15.2.3 Paired T^2 – test

Measurements are often recorded under different sets of experimental conditions to know whether responses differ significantly over these sets.

For example, the efficiency of a new innovative programme, new drug or an advertising campaign may be determined by comparing measurements before the treatment (drug/programme/advertising) with those after the treatment administered.

In a single response (univariate) case we have the paired *t*-test. Now if X_{1j} denote the response before the treatment and X_{2j} denote the response after the treatment, on *j*th unit ($j = 1,2, \ldots , n$), define.

$D_j = X_{1j} - X_{2j}$, $j = 1,2, \ldots , n$, an indicator of differential effect of the treatments.

Assuming D_j's to be independent observations from a normal population with mean δ and variance σ_d^2, the variable

$$t = \frac{\overline{D} - \delta}{\frac{s_d}{\sqrt{n}}},$$

where $\quad \overline{D} = \frac{1}{n} \sum_{j=1}^{n} D_j$ and $s_d^2 = \frac{1}{n-1} \sum_{j=1}^{n} (D_j - \overline{D})^2$,

has a *t*-distribution with $(n - 1)$ degrees of freedom.

Thus, to test

$$H_0 : \delta = 0$$

against $\quad H_1 : \delta \ne 0$

we reject H_0 if

$$|t| > t_{\alpha/2\,,\, n-1},$$

where $t_{\alpha/2, n-1}$ is the upper $100\left(\frac{\alpha}{2}\right)$th percentile of a t-distribution with $(n-1)$ degrees of freedom.

A 100 (1–α)% confidence interval for the mean difference δ is provided by

$$\overline{D} - t_{\alpha/2, n-1} \frac{s_d}{\sqrt{n}} \le \delta \le \overline{D} + t_{\alpha/2, n-1} \frac{s_d}{\sqrt{n}}$$

Let us now extend the discussion to multivariate situation with p responses (variables), 2 treatments and n experimental units. Thus, we arrange the observations as

X_{11j} = variable 1 under treatment 1

X_{12j} = variable 2 under treatment 1

⋮

X_{1pj} = variable p under treatment 1

⋮

X_{21j} = variable 1 under treatment 2

X_{22j} = variable 2 under treatment 2

⋮

X_{2pj} = variable p under treatment 2

The paired differences are

$$\left.\begin{aligned} D_{1j} &= X_{11j} - X_{21j} \\ &\vdots \qquad \vdots \\ D_{2j} &= X_{12j} - X_{22j} \\ D_{pj} &= X_{1pj} - X_{2pj} \end{aligned}\right\} j = 1, 2, \ldots, n$$

In matrix rotation

$$\underline{D}'_j = [D_{1j}, D_{2j}, \ldots, D_{pj}], j = 1, 2, \ldots, n$$

$$E(\underline{D}_j) = \underline{\delta} = \begin{bmatrix} \delta_1 \\ \delta_2 \\ \vdots \\ \delta_p \end{bmatrix}$$

and $\quad \text{Cov}(\underline{D}_j) = \underline{\Sigma}_d$

Assumption : $\underline{D}_1, \underline{D}_2, \ldots, \underline{D}_n$ are independent $N_p(\underline{\delta}, \underline{\Sigma}_d)$ random vectors.

In the absence of knowledge about Σ_d, we may make inferences on vector of mean differences $\underline{\delta}$ using T^2-statistic, defined as

$$T^2 = n(\overline{\underline{D}} - \underline{\delta})' \underline{S}_d^{-1} (\underline{D} - \underline{\delta}),$$

where $\quad \overline{\underline{D}} = \frac{1}{n} \sum_{j=1}^{n} \underline{D}_j$

and $\quad \underline{S}_d = \frac{1}{n-1} \sum_{j=1}^{n} (\underline{D}_j - \overline{\underline{D}})(\underline{D}_j - \overline{\underline{D}})'$

T^2 is distributed as

$$\frac{(n-1)p}{n-p} F_{p,\,n-p}$$

To test the null hypothesis $H_0 : \underline{\delta} = \underline{O}$ againt alternative $H_1 : \underline{\delta} \neq \underline{O}$, reject H_0 at α level if

$$T^2 > \frac{(n-1)p}{n-p} F_{\alpha,\,p,\,n-p},$$

where $F_{\alpha,\,p,\,n-p}$ is αth upper percentage of F-distribution with p and $(n-p)$ degrees of freedom.

Example 15.3 Personality and performance of 11 management trainees were evaluated by 2 panel of judges.

TABLE–15.2
Evaluation data

Sample j	1st Panel		2nd Panel	
	X_{11j}	X_{12j}	X_{21j}	X_{22j}
1	6	27	25	15
2	6	23	28	13
3	18	64	36	22
4	8	44	35	29
5	11	30	15	31
6	34	75	44	64
7	28	26	42	30
8	71	24	54	64
9	43	54	34	56
10	33	30	29	20
11	20	14	39	21

Do the two panels agree ?

Solution

The T^2-statistic for testing $H_0 : \delta' = (\delta_1 \quad \delta_2] = [0\,,\ 0]$ is constructed from the difference of paired observations.

$d_{1j} = X_{11j} - X_{21j}$	−19	−22	−18	−27	−4	−10	−14	−17	−9	4	−19
$d_{2j} = X_{12j} - X_{22j}$	12	10	42	15	−1	11	−4	40	−2	10	−7

$$\underline{\bar{d}} = \begin{bmatrix} \bar{d}_1 \\ \bar{d}_2 \end{bmatrix} = \begin{bmatrix} -9.36 \\ 13.27 \end{bmatrix}$$

$$S_d = \begin{bmatrix} 199.26 & 88.38 \\ 88.38 & 418.61 \end{bmatrix}$$

and
$$T^2 = 11\,[-9.36\,,\ 13.27] \begin{bmatrix} 0.0055 & -0.0012 \\ -0.0012 & 0.0026 \end{bmatrix} \begin{bmatrix} -9.36 \\ 13.27 \end{bmatrix}$$
$$= 13.6$$

At $\alpha = 0.05$,

$$\frac{p(n-1)}{n-p} F_{0.05, p, n-p}$$
$$= \frac{2(10)}{9} F_{0.05, 2, 9} = \frac{20}{9}(4.26)$$
$$= 9.47$$

Since $T^2 = 13.6 > 9.47$, we reject H_0 and conclude that two panels of judges differ in their judgement.

15.3 Testing of equality of several multivariate population mean vectors :

Consider random samples, collected from each of g p-variate populations, arranged as

Population 1 : $\underline{X}_{11}, \underline{X}_{12}, \ldots, \underline{X}_{1n_1}$

Population 2 : $\underline{X}_{21}, \underline{X}_{22}, \ldots, \underline{X}_{2n_2}$

:

:

Population g : $\underline{X}_{g_1}, \underline{X}_{g_2}, \ldots, \underline{X}_{gn_g}$

We shall use Multivariate Analysis of variance (MANOVA) to investigate whether the population mean vectors are the same or not.

Assumptions

1. The random samples from different populations are independent.
2. All populations have a common covariance matrix Σ.
3. Each population is multivariate normal.

The assumption of normality may be relaxed by appealing to the Central limit theorem.

Univariate Analysis of Variance (ANOVA) :

We have random samples $X_{ii}, X_{i2}, \ldots X_{i_{n_i}}$ $(i = 1, 2, \ldots, g)$ from g univariate normal populations with mean μ_i and variance σ^2. The samples are independent. The null hypothesis under consideration.

$$H_0 : \mu_1 = \mu_2 = \ldots = \mu_g$$
$$H_1 : \text{Not all } \mu\text{'s are equal}$$

We may visualize μ_i decomposed into

μ_i ↓	=	μ ↓	+	$(\mu_i - \mu)$ ↓
ith population mean		overall mean		ith population effect measured as deviation from over all mean

The null hypothesis can be restarted as

$$H_0 : \tau_1 = \tau_2 = ... = \tau_g = 0,$$

where

$$\tau_i = \mu_i - \mu$$

$$\underset{\text{observation}}{\underset{\downarrow}{X_{ij}}} = \underset{\text{overall mean}}{\underset{\downarrow}{\overline{X}}} + \underset{\text{estimate of } i\text{th population effect}}{\underset{\downarrow}{(\overline{X}_i - \overline{X})}} + \underset{\text{residual}}{\underset{\downarrow}{(X_{ij} - \overline{X}_i)}}$$

Now $(X_{ij} - \overline{X}) = (\overline{X}_i - \overline{X}) + (X_{ij} - \overline{X}_i)$

Squaring and summing with respect to the subscripts

$$\underset{\text{Total sum of squares}}{\underset{\downarrow}{\sum_{i=1}^{g} \sum_{j=1}^{n_i} (X_{ij} - \overline{X})^2}} = \underset{\text{Between (sample) sum of squares}}{\underset{\downarrow}{\sum_{i=1}^{g} n_i (\overline{X}_i - \overline{X})^2}} + \underset{\text{within (sample) sum of squares}}{\underset{\downarrow}{\sum_{i=1}^{g} \sum_{j=1}^{n_i} (X_{ij} - \overline{X})^2}}$$

Table 15.3
Analysis of Variance

Source of Variation	Degrees of freedom	Sum of squares (S.S.)	Mean square (M.S.)	F
Between samples	$g - 1$	SSB $= \Sigma n_i (\overline{X}_i - \overline{X})^2$	$MSB = \dfrac{SSB}{g-1}$	$\dfrac{MSB}{MSW}$
Within samples (Residual)	$\sum_{i=1}^{g} n_i - g$	SSW $= \Sigma\Sigma (X_{ij} - \overline{X}_i)^2$	$MSW = \dfrac{SSW}{\sum_{i}^{g} n_i - g}$	
Total	$\sum_{i=1}^{g} n_i - 1$	TSS $= \Sigma\Sigma (X_{ij} - \overline{X})^2$	–	

The usual F–test rejects

$$H_0 : \tau_1 = \tau_2 = ... = \tau_g = 0, \text{ at level } \alpha, \text{ if}$$

$$F = \frac{MSB}{MSW} > F_{\alpha,\, g-1,\, \sum_{i=1}^{g} n_i - g}$$

Example 15.4. An experiment was run to determine whether four specific firing temperatures affect the density of a certain type of brick. The experiment led to the following data.

TABLE–15.4

Temperature (°F)	Density
100	21.8, 21.9, 21.7, 21.6, 21.7, 21.5, 21.8
125	21.7, 21.4, 21.5, 21.5

150	21.9, 21.8, 21.8, 21.6, 21.5
175	21.9, 21.7, 21.8, 21.7, 21.6, 21.8

Does the firing temperature affect the density of the brick ?

Solution

$$n_1 = 7\ , n_2 = 4\ , n_3 = 5 \text{ and } n_4 = 6$$

Let x_{ij} be the value of jth observation for the ith firing temperature. $i = 1, 2, 3, 4$, $j = 1, 2, ..., n_i$

$$G = \sum_{i=1}^{4} \sum_{j=1}^{n_i} x_{ij} = 15.2$$

Total sum of squares

$$= \Sigma\Sigma (x_{ij} - \bar{x})^2 = \Sigma\Sigma x_{ij}^2 - \frac{(\Sigma\Sigma x_{ij})^2}{\sum_{i=1}^{4} n_i}$$

$$= 10.96 - \frac{(15.2)^2}{22} = 10.96 - 10.5018$$

$$= 0.4582$$

Between sum of squares

$$= \sum_{i=1}^{4} \sum_{j=1}^{n_i} (\bar{x}_i - \bar{x})^2$$

$$= \sum_{i=1}^{4} n_i (\bar{x}_i - \bar{x})^2 = \frac{T_1^2}{n_1} + \frac{T_2^2}{n_2} + \frac{T_3^2}{n_3} + \frac{T_4^2}{n_4} - \frac{G^2}{22},$$

where $T_1 = \sum_{j=1}^{n_1} x_{ij} = 5.0,\ T_2 = \sum_{j=1}^{n_2} x_{2j} = 2.1,$

$$T_3 = \sum_{j=1}^{n_3} x_{3j} = 3.6 \text{ and } T_4 = \sum_{j=1}^{n_4} x_{4j} = 4.5$$

Therefore, Between sum of squares

$$= \frac{(5.0)^2}{7} + \frac{(2.1)^2}{4} + \frac{(3.6)^2}{5} + \frac{(4.5)^2}{6} - \frac{(15.2)^2}{22} = 10.6409 - 10.5018$$

$$= 0.1391$$

TABLE–15.5

Analysis of Variance

Source of Variation	Degrees of freedom	S.S.	M.S.	F	$F_{5\%}$
Between samples	3	0.1391	0.0464	2.62	3.16
Within samples	18	0.3191	0.0177		
Total	21	0.4582			

Conclusion : As the computed value of F = 2.62 is less than the theoretical value of F at 5% level of significance with 3 and 18 degrees of freedom *i.e.* 3.16, the null hypothesis that firing temperatures have no effect on the density of the brick is not rejected.

15.3.1 Mutlivariate Analysis of Variance (MANOVA)

MANOVA Model for comparing of population mean vectors is represented by

$$\underline{X}_{ij} = \underline{\mu} + \underline{\tau}_i + \underline{e}_{ij},$$
$$j = 1, 2, ..., n_i$$

and $$i = 1, 2, ..., g,$$

where $\underline{e}_{ij}$ are indepenent $N_P(\underline{O}, \Sigma)$ variables.

The parameter vector $\underline{\mu}$ is the overall population mean vector, $\underline{\tau}_i$ represents the *i*th population (treatment) effect with

$$\sum_{i=1}^{2} n_i \underline{\tau}_i = \underline{0}$$

As suggested by the model a vector of observations may be decomposed as

$$\underline{X}_{ij} = \overline{\underline{X}} + (\overline{\underline{X}}_i - \overline{\underline{X}}) + (\underline{X}_{ij} - \overline{\underline{X}}_i)$$

Observation = Overall sample mean $\hat{\mu}$ + estimated population (treatment) effect $\hat{\underline{\tau}}_i$ + residual $(\hat{\underline{e}}_{ij})$.

Total sum of squares and cross products matrix

$$= \sum_{i=1}^{g} \sum_{j=1}^{n_i} (\underline{X}_{ij} - \overline{\underline{X}})(\underline{X}_{ij} - \overline{\underline{X}})'$$

Between sum of squares and cross products matrix

$$= \sum_{i=1}^{g} n_i (\overline{\underline{X}}_i - \overline{\underline{X}})(\overline{\underline{X}}_i - \overline{\underline{X}})'$$

Within (residual) sum of squares and cross products matrix

$$= \sum_{i=1}^{g} \sum_{j=1}^{n_i} (X_{ij} - \overline{X}_i)(X_{ij} - \overline{X}_i)'$$

It may be verified that $\underline{W} = \Sigma\Sigma (X_{ij} - \overline{X}_i)(X_{ij} - \overline{X}_i)'$

$$= (n_1 - 1)\underline{S}_1 + (n_2 - 1)\underline{S}_2 + ... + (n_g - 1)\underline{S}_g,$$

where $\underline{S}_i$ is the sample covariance matrix for the *i*th sample.

TABLE–15.6
MANOVA FOR COMPARING POPULATION VECTORS

Source of Variation	Matrix of Sum of Squares and Cross products	Degrees of freedom (*d.f.*)
Between Populations	$B = \Sigma n_i (\overline{\underline{X}}_i - \overline{\underline{X}})(\overline{\underline{X}}_i - \overline{\underline{X}})'$	$g - 1$

Residual	$W = \Sigma\Sigma(\underline{X}_{ij} - \overline{\underline{X}}_i)(\underline{X}_{ij} - \overline{\underline{X}}_i)'$	$\sum_{i=1}^{g} n_i - g$
Total	$B + W = \Sigma\Sigma(\underline{X}_{ij} - \overline{\underline{X}})(\underline{X}_{ij} - \overline{\underline{X}})'$	$\sum_{i=1}^{g} n_i - 1$

To test $H_0 : \underline{\tau}_1 = \underline{\tau}_2 = ... = \underline{\tau}_g = \underline{0}$

We reject H_0 if the ratio of generalized variances

$$\wedge^* = \frac{|\underline{W}|}{|\underline{B} + \underline{W}|} = \frac{|\Sigma\Sigma(\underline{X}_{ij} - \overline{\underline{X}}_i)(\underline{X}_{ij} - \overline{\underline{X}}_i)'|}{|\Sigma\Sigma(\underline{X}_{ij} - \overline{\underline{X}})(\underline{X}_{ij} - \overline{\underline{X}})'|}$$

is too small.

The statistic $\wedge^*$, originally proposed by Wilks, is called **Wilk's lambda**.

The exact distribution of $\wedge^*$ for some special cases are shown below.

TABLE–15.7

Distribution of Wilk's LAMBDA, $\wedge^* = \frac{|W|}{|W + W|}$

Number of Variables	No. of Groups	Sampling distribution for multipvariate normal data
$p = 2$	$g \geq 2$	$\left(\frac{\Sigma n_i - g - 1}{g - 1}\right)\left(\frac{1 - \sqrt{\wedge^*}}{\sqrt{\wedge^*}}\right) \sim F_{2(g-1),\, 2(\Sigma n_i - g - 1)}$
$p \geq 1$	$g = 2$	$\left(\frac{\Sigma n_i - p - 1}{p}\right)\left(\frac{1 - \wedge^*}{\wedge^*}\right) \sim F_{p,\, (\Sigma n_i - p - 1)}$
$p \geq 1$	$g = 3$	$\left(\frac{\Sigma n_i - p - 2}{g - 1}\right)\left(\frac{1 - \sqrt{\wedge^*}}{\sqrt{\wedge^*}}\right) \sim F_{2p,\, 2(\Sigma n_i - p - 2)}$

Bartlett has shown that if H_0 is true and $\Sigma n_i = n$ is large

$$-\left(n - 1 - \frac{(p+g)}{2}\right) l_n \wedge^* = -\left(n - 1 - \frac{(p+g)}{2}\right) l_n \left(\frac{|W|}{|B+W|}\right)$$

has approximately a chi-square distribution with $p(g - 1)$ degrees of freedom.

Thus, if $\sum_{i=1}^{g} n_i$ is large, reject H_0 : at significance level α if

$$-\left(n - 1 - \frac{(p+g)}{2}\right) l_n \left(\frac{|W|}{|B+W|}\right) > \chi^2_{\alpha,\, p(g-1)},$$

where $\chi^2_{\alpha,\, p(g-1)}$ is the upper (100 α)th percentile of a chi-square distribution with $p(g - 1)$ degrees of freedom.

Example 15.5. Consider samples from 3 bivariate populations (Johnson & Wichern, 2003) and observations are arranged as

$$\begin{pmatrix} \begin{bmatrix} 9 \\ 3 \end{bmatrix} & \begin{bmatrix} 6 \\ 2 \end{bmatrix} & \begin{bmatrix} 9 \\ 7 \end{bmatrix} \\ \begin{bmatrix} 0 \\ 4 \end{bmatrix} & \begin{bmatrix} 2 \\ 0 \end{bmatrix} & \\ \begin{bmatrix} 3 \\ 8 \end{bmatrix} & \begin{bmatrix} 1 \\ 9 \end{bmatrix} & \begin{bmatrix} 2 \\ 7 \end{bmatrix} \end{pmatrix}$$

with $\underline{\overline{X}}_1 = \begin{bmatrix} 8 \\ 4 \end{bmatrix}$, $\underline{\overline{X}}_2 = \begin{bmatrix} 1 \\ 2 \end{bmatrix}$, $\underline{\overline{X}}_3 = \begin{bmatrix} 2 \\ 8 \end{bmatrix}$ and $\underline{\overline{X}} = \begin{bmatrix} 4 \\ 5 \end{bmatrix}$

$n_1 = 3$, $n_2 = 2$ and $n_3 = 3$. Test the hypothesis that three bivariate populations have same mean vector, or same treatment effect.

Solution

Following univariate analysis, observations for the first variable may be decomposed into general mean effect, population (treatment) effect and residual such as

$$\begin{pmatrix} 9 & 6 & 9 \\ 0 & 2 & \\ 3 & 1 & 2 \end{pmatrix} = \begin{pmatrix} 4 & 4 & 4 \\ 4 & 4 & \\ 4 & 4 & 4 \end{pmatrix} + \begin{pmatrix} 4 & 4 & 4 \\ -3 & -3 & \\ -2 & -2 & -2 \end{pmatrix} + \begin{pmatrix} 1 & -2 & 1 \\ -1 & 1 & \\ 1 & -1 & 0 \end{pmatrix}$$

Hence,

$$\text{TSS} = \text{SSB} + \text{SSE}$$

$$\Rightarrow \quad 88 = 78 + 10$$

Repeating the technique for the observations on the second variable we have,

$$\begin{pmatrix} 3 & 2 & 7 \\ 4 & 0 & \\ 8 & 9 & 7 \end{pmatrix} = \begin{pmatrix} 5 & 5 & 5 \\ 5 & 5 & \\ 5 & 5 & 5 \end{pmatrix} + \begin{pmatrix} -1 & -1 & -1 \\ -3 & -3 & \\ 3 & 3 & 3 \end{pmatrix} + \begin{pmatrix} -1 & -2 & 3 \\ 2 & -2 & \\ 0 & 1 & -1 \end{pmatrix}$$

As such,

$$\text{TSS} = \text{SSB} + \text{SSE}$$

$$\Rightarrow \quad 72 = 48 + 24$$

As regards the decomposition of cross-products.

Mean Cross product effect : $\frac{1}{8}(9+6+9+0+2+3+1+2)(3+2+7+4+0+8+9+7)$

$$= \frac{32 \times 40}{80} = 160$$

Population (Treatment) Between Cross product

$$= 3(4)(-1) + 2(-2)(-3)(-3) + 3(-2)(3)$$

$$= -12$$

Residual Cross product : $1(-1) + (-2)(-2) + 1(3) + ... + ... + 0(-1) = 1$

Total cross product : $9(3) + 6(2) + 9(7) + 0(4) + ... + 2(7) = 149$

Total (Corrected) Cross product = Total cross product – Mean cross product

$$= 149 - 160 = -11$$

TABLE–15.8
MANOVA

Source of Varisation	Matrix of sum of squares and cross products	Degrees of freedom
Treatment	$\underline{B} = \begin{bmatrix} 78 & -12 \\ -12 & 48 \end{bmatrix}$	3–2 = 2
Residual	$\underline{W} = \begin{bmatrix} 10 & 1 \\ 1 & 4 \end{bmatrix}$	7–2 = 5
Total	$\begin{bmatrix} 88 & -11 \\ -11 & 72 \end{bmatrix}$	7

Now $$\wedge^* = \frac{|W|}{|B+W|} = \frac{\begin{vmatrix} 10 & 1 \\ 1 & 24 \end{vmatrix}}{\begin{vmatrix} 88 & -11 \\ -11 & 72 \end{vmatrix}}$$

$$= \frac{(10)(24)-(1)(1)}{(88)(72)-(-11)(-11)} = \frac{239}{6215} = 0.385$$

In the present example

$$p = 2, g = 3$$
$$H_0 : \underline{\tau}_1 = \underline{\tau}_2 = \underline{\tau}_3 = \underline{0}$$
$$H_1 : \text{Not all } \underline{\tau}_i = \underline{0}$$

An exact test, assuming multivariate normality and equality of covariance matrices can be carried out by computing the test statistic.

$$\frac{1-\sqrt{\wedge^*}}{\sqrt{\wedge^*}} \frac{(\Sigma n_i - g - 1)}{(g-1)}$$

$$= \frac{1-\sqrt{0.0385}}{\sqrt{0.0385}} = \left(\frac{8-3-1}{3-1}\right) = 8.19$$

The percentage point (critical point) of the F-distribution at 1% level of significance with

$$\upsilon_1 = 2(g-1) = 4$$
$$\upsilon_2 = 2(\Sigma n_i - g - 1)$$
$$= 2(8–3–1) = 8$$

degrees of freedom is 7.01.

As the numerical value of the statistic *i.e.* 8.19 is greater than the critical value *i.e.* 7.01, we reject H_0 and conclude that treatment differences/population differences exist.

15.4 Discriminant Analysis

Discriminant analysis along with classification rules are multivariate techniques concerned with **separating** distinct sets of objects/observations and **allocating** new objects/observations to previously defined groups. The need of such techniques becomes a matter of importance in applied research when we may be required to assign a given observation in some optimum fashion to one of several populations. These techniques were first developed in for biological researches when a biologist may like to classify a new specimen as one of several recognized species of a flower. Subsequently it was found its application in other fields of research. For instance in MBA admission to a Business school a condidate may be assigned to the categories 'admit', 'admit conditionally', or 'admission denied' on the basis of a vector of test scores, grades, and ratings. In banking transactions a loan officer may wish to classify loan applicants as low or high credit risks on the basis of certain accounting statements.

Discriminant analysis is a **separatory** procedure which provides a basis to investigate observed differences when causal relationships are not well understood. Classification (allocation) procedures are less exploratory in the sense that they lead to well defined rules which help us in assigning new objects. In discriminant analysis the discriminants are computed numerically in such a way that the collections are separated as much as possible where as in the classification the objects (observations) are sorted into two or more labeled classes with emphasis on deriving a rule that can be used to optionally assign a new object to the labeled classes. However, in practice there seems to be no water- tight compartments between two procedures–separation and allocation.

Discriminant function analysis is used to determine which variables discriminate between two or more naturally occurring classes/groups. For example, an educational researcher may want to investigate which variables discriminate between higher secondary pass outs who decide to go to college for taking up general courses or to join professional institutions. Under these circumstances discriminant analysis could be used to determine. which variable(s) are the best predictors of students' subsequent choices. To consider another example, a mortgage company may like to take a decision whether to approve an applicant's mortgage loan. The decision is based on determining whether the applicants' characteristics are more like those of persons in the past who repaid loans successfully than like those of persons who defaulted. Information on these two groups may be available from past records and would include such factors such as age, income, marital status, outstanding debt, ownership of certain durable goods. Further, a researcher may classify the group of firms according to whether they had eventually failed or did not fail, on the basis of independent variables such as location, financial ratios or management changes.

Thus, to sum up, the **discriminant analysis** determines a linear combination of two or more predictor variables which will best discriminanto between a priori defined groups and **classificatory analysis** develops well defined rules to allocate new objects to different classes/groups.

The concept of *discriminant function* is due to R.A. Fisher (1938), who arrived at *a linear classification statistic involving linear function of the characters by transforming the multivariate observations from two populations* π_1 *and* π_2 *to one-dimensional scale that discriminates between the populations by some measure of maximal separation.* Fisher did not assume the multivariate populations to be multivariate normal, but implicity assumed the populations having common covariance matrix.

Suppose we have two independent random samples of size n_1 and n_2 respectively from two p-variate populations π_1 and π_2 with mean vectors $\underline{\mu}_1$ and $\underline{\mu}_2$ and common covariance matrix $\underline{\Sigma}$. If $\underline{\bar{x}}_1$ and $\underline{\bar{x}}_2$ are the sample mean vectors and $\underline{S}$ is the pooled estimate of $\underline{\Sigma}$, Fisher's discriminant function $\underline{l}'\underline{x}$ is such that its coefficient vector $\underline{l}$ maximizes $\frac{(\underline{l}'\underline{d})^2}{\underline{l}'\underline{S}\underline{l}}$,

where $$\underline{l} = \begin{bmatrix} l_1 \\ l_2 \\ l_3 \end{bmatrix}, \underline{d} = \underline{\bar{x}}_1 - \underline{\bar{x}}_2$$

As such, the linear discriminant function $y = (\underline{\bar{x}}_1 - \underline{\bar{x}}_2)'\,\underline{S}^{-1}\,\underline{x}$

The maximum of the ratio is

$$D^2 = (\underline{\bar{x}}_1 - \underline{\bar{x}}_2)'\,\underline{S}^{-1}_{\text{pooled}}\,(\underline{\bar{x}}_1 - \underline{\bar{x}}_2),$$

which is the sample squared distance between the two means, showing the maximum separation in the samples and is called **Mahalanobis D²-statistic.**

To use the linear discriminant function for **classifying** an observation of unknown population, compute the mean values of the scores for the two populations.

$$\bar{y}_1 = (\underline{\bar{x}}_1 - \underline{\bar{x}}_2)'\,\underline{S}^{-1}\,\underline{\bar{x}}_1$$

and $$\bar{y}_2 = (\underline{\bar{x}}_1 - \underline{\bar{x}}_2)'\,\underline{S}^{-1}\,\underline{\bar{x}}_2$$

The midpoint of these means on the discriminant function scale is

$$\frac{1}{2}(\underline{\bar{x}}_1 - \underline{\bar{x}}_2)'\,\underline{S}^{-1}\,(\underline{\bar{x}}_1 + \underline{\bar{x}}_2)$$

15.4.1 Classification rule

Assign the individual with observation $\underline{x} = \underline{x}_0$ to population π_1 if

$(\underline{\bar{x}}_1 - \underline{\bar{x}}_2)'\,\underline{S}^{-1}\,\underline{x} > \frac{1}{2}(\underline{\bar{x}}_1 - \underline{\bar{x}}_2)'\,\underline{S}^{-1}\,(\underline{\bar{x}}_1 + \underline{\bar{x}}_2)$ and to population π_2 if

$$(\underline{\bar{x}}_1 - \underline{\bar{x}}_2)'\,\underline{S}^{-1}\,\underline{x} \le \frac{1}{2}(\underline{\bar{x}}_1 - \underline{\bar{x}}_2)'\,\underline{S}^{-1}\,(\underline{\bar{x}}_1 + \underline{\bar{x}}_2)$$

Alternatively, as the mean mid point is also a random variable, being based on sample values, it would be more appropriate to compute a single statistic

$$W = (\underline{\bar{x}}_1 - \underline{\bar{x}}_2)'\,\underline{S}^{-1}\,\underline{x} - \frac{1}{2}(\underline{\bar{x}}_1 - \underline{\bar{x}}_2)'\,\underline{S}^{-1}\,(\underline{\bar{x}}_1 + \underline{\bar{x}}_2)$$

and assign $\underline{x} = \underline{x}_0$ to population π_1 if $W > 0$ and otherwise to population π_2.

W is called **Wald-Anderson classification statistic** because of its origin (Wald, 1944) and derivation of sampling properties (Anderson, 1951).

Suppose the populations π_1 and π_2 are multivariate normal with a common covariance matrix $\underline{\Sigma}$. Then, $H_0 : \underline{\mu}_1 = \underline{\mu}_2$ against $H_1 : \underline{\mu}_1 \neq \underline{\mu}_2$ can be tested by using statistic.

$$\frac{n_1 + n_2 - p - 1}{(n_1 + n_2 - 2)\,p}\left(\frac{n_1 n_2}{n_1 + n_2}\right)D^2,$$

which follows a F-distribution with $v_1 = p$ and $v_2 = n_1 + n_2 - p - 1$ degrees of freedom.

If H_0 is rejected, we can conclude that the separation between the two populations π_1 and π_2 is significant.

Note. Significant value for the statistic does not imply that the classification is a good one. The efficiency of classification procedure can be judged independently of the test. However, if the statistic is **not** significant, the search for a useful classification rule may perhaps prove fruitless.

15.4.2 Classification for several groups

Consider methods for classification of an unknown observation to one of k populations $\pi_1, \pi_2, \ldots, \pi_k$. Suppose $k = 3$.

Assume measurements/responses of the independent groups are best described by multinormal random variables with mean vectors $\underline{\mu}_1$, $\underline{\mu}_2$ and $\underline{\mu}_3$ with common covariance matrix Σ.

The mean vectors and covariance matrix are replaced by their usual estimators based on n_1, n_2 and n_3 samples

$$\hat{\underline{\mu}}_j = \underline{\bar{x}}_j \ (j = 1, 2, 3)$$

and pooled estimate

$$\underline{S}_{\text{pooled}} = \frac{1}{n_1 + n_2 + n_3 - 3} \left[(n_1 - 1)\,\underline{S}_1 + (n_2 - 1)\,\underline{S}_2 + (n_3 - 1)\,\underline{S}_3\right]$$

where $\underline{S}_j$ is the covariance matrix for the jth group.

The distinct discriminant statistics are

$$W_{12} = \underline{x}'\,\underline{S}^{-1}\,(\underline{\bar{x}}_1 - \underline{\bar{x}}_2) - \frac{1}{2}(\underline{\bar{x}}_1 + \underline{\bar{x}}_2)'\,\underline{S}^{-1}\,(\underline{\bar{x}}_1 - \underline{\bar{x}}_2)$$

$$W_{13} = \underline{x}'\,\underline{S}^{-1}\,(\underline{\bar{x}}_1 - \underline{\bar{x}}_3) - \frac{1}{2}(\underline{\bar{x}}_1 + \underline{\bar{x}}_2)'\,\underline{S}^{-1}\,(\underline{\bar{x}}_1 - \underline{\bar{x}}_3)$$

$$W_{23} = \underline{x}'\,\underline{S}^{-1}\,(\underline{\bar{x}}_2 - \underline{\bar{x}}_3) - \frac{1}{2}(\underline{\bar{x}}_2 + \underline{\bar{x}}_3)'\,\underline{S}^{-1}\,(\underline{\bar{x}}_2 - \underline{\bar{x}}_3)$$

Because $W_{23} = W_{13} - W_{12}$, it is only necessary to use the statistics W_{12} and W_{13}.

Classification rule

Classify $\underline{x}$ as from

$$\pi_1 : \text{if } W_{12} > 0 \text{ and } W_{13} > 0$$

$$\pi_2 : \text{if } W_{12} < 0 \text{ and } W_{13} > W_{12}$$

$$\pi_3 : \text{if } W_{13} < 0 \text{ and } W_{12} > W_{13}$$

Classification by minimum distance

In case of k populations, the classification rule can be expressed in terms of the Mahalanobis squared distance,

$$D_i^2 = (\underline{x}_0 - \underline{\bar{x}}_i)'\,\underline{S}^{-1}\,(\underline{x}_0 - \underline{\bar{x}}_i)$$

of the unknown observation $\underline{x}_0$ from the mean of the ith sample as :

Assign $\underline{x}_0$ to population i if

$$D_i^2 = \min\,(D_1^2, D_2^2, \ldots, D_k^2)\,.$$

15.4.3 Optimal Classification

The classification rules cannot usually provide an error free method. This is because there may not be a clear distinction between the measured characteristics of populations, which may lead to incorrectly classify a π_2 object as belonging to π_1 or a π_1 object as belonging to π_2.

A good classification procedure should have a few misclassifications. That implies, the probabilities or chances of misclassification should be small.

An optimal classification rule should take into account.

(*i*) prior probabilities of occurrence

(*ii*) cost associated with misclassification.

For instance, if the problem is to classify a firm as financially sound or bankrupt and there is greater likelihood of occurrence of a financially sound firm (because they are large in number) than the bankrupt one, then one should classify a randomly selected firm as nonbankrupt unless the data overwhelmingly favour bankruptcy. Secondly there is the problem of cost. If the classifying a π_1 object wrongly belonging to π_2 is more serious than classifying π_2 object wrongly belonging to π_1, one should be cautious about making the previous assignment. For instance failing to diagnose a potentially failure in a machine may prove more 'costly' than when it is not so.

Let $f_1(\underline{x})$ and $f_2(\underline{x})$ be the probability density of the p-variate random variable $\underline{X}$ for the populations π_1 and π_2 respectively.

An object with associated measurements x is to be assigned to either π_1 or π_2. Let Ω be the sample space containing all possible observations $\underline{x}$. Let R_1 be the set of points Ω for which we classify objects belonging to π_1 and $R_2 = \Omega - R_1$ be the remaining set of points for which we classify objects belonging to π_2.

R_1 and R_2 are mutually exclusive and exhaustive.

Now, the conditional probability P (2 | 1) of classifying the object as π_2 when infact it is from π_1 is

$$P(2|1) = P\left(X \in R_2 | \pi_1\right) = \int_{R_2} f_1(\underline{x})\, d\underline{x}$$

$$P(1|2) = P\left(X \in R_1 | \pi_2\right) = \int_{R_1} f_2(\underline{x})\, d\underline{x}$$

Let p_1 and p_2 be the a priori probabilities of π_1 and π_2 respectively $p_1 + p_2 = 1$

Thus, P (correctly classified as π_1)

= P (observation comes from π_1 and is correctly classified as π_1)

$= P\left(\underline{X} \in R_1 | \pi_1\right) P(\pi_1)$

$= P(1|1)\, p_1$

P (misclassified as π_1)

= P (observation comes from π_2 and is misclassified as π_1)

$$= P\left(\underline{X} \in R_1 | \pi_2\right) P(\pi_2)$$
$$= P(1|2)\, p_2$$

Similarly,

P (correctly classified as π_2)

$$= P(2|2)\, p_2$$

P(misclassified as π_2)

$$= P\left(\underline{X} \in R_2 | \pi_1\right) P(\pi_1)$$
$$= P(2|1)\, p_1$$

The cost of misclassification can be stated by a cost matrix.

		Classify as π_1	Classify as π_2
True population	π_1	0	C (2|1)
	π_2	C (1 | 2)	0

For any rule, the average or **expected cost of misclassification** (ECM) is given by

$$ECM = C(2|1)\, P(2|1)\, p_1 + C(1|2)\, P(1|2)\, p_2$$

For a reasonable classification rule ECM should be **as small as possible.**

Thus, the regions R_1 and R_2 that minimize the ECM are defined by the values of $\underline{x}$ for which the following inequalities hold

$$R_1: \frac{f_1(\underline{x})}{f_2(\underline{x})} \geq \left(\frac{C(1|2)}{C(2|1)}\right)\left(\frac{p_2}{p_1}\right)$$

i.e. $\left(\text{density ratio}\right) \geq (\text{cost ratio}) \left(\text{prior probability ratio}\right)$

$$R_2: \frac{f_1(\underline{x})}{f_2(\underline{x})} < \left(\frac{C(1|2)}{C(2|1)}\right)\left(\frac{p_2}{p_1}\right)$$

Given a new observation $\underline{x}_0$, the density ratio is to be computed at $\underline{x}_0$.

Illustration 1. Suppose $f_1(\underline{x}_0) = 0.4$ and $f_2(\underline{x}_0) = 0.5$; $p_1 = 0.8$ and $p_2 = 0.2$; C (2|1) = 5 units C (1|2) = 10 units.

$$R_1: \frac{f_1(\underline{x})}{f_2(\underline{x})} \geq \left(\frac{10}{5}\right)\left(\frac{0.2}{0.8}\right) = 0.5$$

$$R_2: \frac{f_1(\underline{x})}{f_2(\underline{x})} < \left(\frac{10}{5}\right)\left(\frac{0.2}{0.8}\right) = 0.5$$

Now $\frac{f_1(\underline{x}_0)}{f_2(\underline{x}_0)} = \frac{0.4}{0.5} = 0.8$

As $\frac{f_1(\underline{x}_0)}{f_2(\underline{x}_0)} > 0.5,$

We find that $\underline{x}_0 \in R_1$ and classify it as belonging to π_1.

Illustration 2. Suppose $f_i(\underline{x}) = \dfrac{1}{(2\pi)^{p/2}\,|\Sigma|^{1/2}} \exp.\left[-\dfrac{1}{2}(\underline{x}-\underline{\mu}_i)'\,\Sigma^{-1}\,(\underline{x}_i-\underline{\mu}_i)\right]$ for $i = 1,2$ and $\underline{\mu}_1$, $\underline{\mu}_2$ and Σ are known.

The allocation rule that minimizes the ECM is given by :

Allocate $\underline{x}_0$ to π_1 if

$$(\underline{\mu}_1-\underline{\mu}_2)'\,\Sigma^{-1}\,\underline{x}_0 - \frac{1}{2}(\underline{\mu}_1-\underline{\mu}_2)'\,\Sigma^{-1}\,(\underline{\mu}_1+\underline{\mu}_2) \geq l_n\left[\frac{C(1\,|\,2)}{C\,(2\,|\,1)}\left(\frac{p_2}{p_1}\right)\right]$$

Allocate $\underline{x}_0$ to π_2 otherwise.

In most practical situations the population values such as $\underline{\mu}_1$, $\underline{\mu}_2$ and Σ are unknown and hence these unknown parameters are to be estimated from the samples to construct the classification/allocation rules.

Thus, the estimated minimum ECM rule for two normal populations is stated as follows :

Allocate $\underline{x}_0$ to π_1 if

$$(\bar{\underline{x}}_1-\bar{\underline{x}}_2)'\,\underline{S}^{-1}_{\text{pooled}}\,\underline{x}_0 - \frac{1}{2}(\bar{\underline{x}}_1-\bar{\underline{x}}_2)'\,\underline{S}^{-1}_{\text{pooled}}\,(\bar{\underline{x}}_1+\bar{\underline{x}}_2) \geq l_n\left[\frac{C(1\,|\,2)}{C\,(2\,|\,1)}\left(\frac{p_2}{p_1}\right)\right]$$

Example 15.6 Admission to a business school is based on the undergraduate grade point average (GPA) and graduate management aptitude test (GMAT) scores to decide which applicant should be admitted to the school.

Given data on recent applicants, who have been categorised as π_1 : 'Admit' and π_2 : Not admit, on two variables x_1 = GPA and x_2 = GMAT (*i*) compute the linear discriminant function and (*ii*) if a new applicant has an undergraduate GPA of $x_1 = 3.21$ and GMAT score of $x_2 = 497$, classify whether the applicant belongs to π_1 or π_2.

The summary statistics are

$$n_1 = 32,\ n_2 = 28$$

$$\bar{\underline{x}}_1 = \begin{bmatrix} 3.40 \\ 561.23 \end{bmatrix} \quad \bar{\underline{x}}_2 = \begin{bmatrix} 2.48 \\ 447.07 \end{bmatrix}$$

$$\underline{S}_{\text{pooled}} = \begin{bmatrix} 0.0361 & -2.0188 \\ -2.0188 & 3665.9011 \end{bmatrix}$$

$$\underline{S}^{-1}_{\text{pooled}} = \begin{bmatrix} 28.6096 & 0.0158 \\ 0.0158 & 0.0003 \end{bmatrix}$$

Solution

The linear discriminant function is given by

$$(\bar{\underline{x}}_1-\bar{\underline{x}}_2)'\,\underline{S}^{-1}_{\text{pooled}}\,\underline{x}$$

$$= [3.40-2.48\ ,\ 561.23-447.07]\begin{bmatrix} 28.6096 & 0.0158 \\ 0.0158 & 0.0003 \end{bmatrix}\begin{bmatrix} x_1 \\ x_2 \end{bmatrix}$$

$$= [0.92 \quad 114.16] \begin{bmatrix} 28.6096 & 0.0158 \\ 0.0158 & 0.0003 \end{bmatrix} \begin{bmatrix} x_1 \\ x_2 \end{bmatrix}$$

$$= [28.1246 \quad 0.0488] \begin{bmatrix} x_1 \\ x_2 \end{bmatrix}$$

$$= 28.1246\, x_1 + 0.0488\, x_2$$

Now $\hat{m} = \frac{1}{2}(\bar{x}_1 - \bar{x}_2)' S^{-1} (\bar{x}_1 + \bar{x}_2)$

$$= \frac{1}{2} [0.92 \quad 114.16] \begin{bmatrix} 28.6096 & 0.0158 \\ 0.0158 & 0.0003 \end{bmatrix} \begin{bmatrix} 5.88 \\ 1008.30 \end{bmatrix}$$

$$= \frac{1}{2} [28.1246 \quad 0.0488] \begin{bmatrix} 5.88 \\ 1008.30 \end{bmatrix}$$

$$= \frac{1}{2}(214.5777) = 107.2888$$

For $\underline{x}_0 = \begin{pmatrix} 3.21 \\ 497 \end{pmatrix}$

$$y_0 = 28.1246\, x_1 + 0.0488\, x_2$$

$$= 28.1246\,(3.21) + 0.0488\,(497)$$

$$= 114.5336$$

As $y_0\ (= 114.5336) > \hat{m}\ (= 107.2888)$, assign the applicant with $\underline{x}_0$ to π_1

Alternative method :

Compute sample distances

$$D_1^2(\underline{x}_0) = (\underline{x}_0 - \bar{\underline{x}}_1)' S^{-1} (\underline{x}_0 - \bar{\underline{x}}_1)$$

$$= 2.6580$$

$$D_2^2(\underline{x}_0) = (\underline{x}_0 - \bar{\underline{x}}_2)' \underline{S}^{-1} (\underline{x}_0 - \bar{\underline{x}}_2)$$

$$= 17.1451$$

Since the distance from $\underline{x}'_0 = [3.21, 497]$ to the group mean $\bar{\underline{x}}_1$ is lowest, we assign the applicant to π_1.

15.5 CLUSTER ANALYSIS

A cluster is a group of relatively homogeneous cases or observations. Objects in a cluster are similar to each other. They are also dissimilar to objects outside the cluster, particular objects in other clusters.

Cluster analysis is a classification method that is used to arrange a set of objects into clusters.

The term cluster analysis consists of a number of algorithms (step-by-step rules) and methods for grouping objects of similar kind into respective categories. Researchers in many areas of inquiry often require to organize observed data into meaningful structures, that is to develop taxonomies.

The *cluster analysis is an exploratory data analysis* which aims at sorting different objects into groups in a way that the degree of association between two objects is maximal if they belong to the same group and minimal otherwise. It is used in the data analysis to discover structures in data without providing an explanation/interpretation. In other words it simply discovers the structures in data without explaining why they exist and is essentially a *segmentation analysis or taxonomy analysis* to create groups of objects of clusters in such a way that the profiles of objects in the same cluster are similar and the profiles of objects in different clusters are quite distinct. When an object is associated with another in a cluster, it remains clustered with that object.

The clustering is not based on any statistical significance testing and comprises a 'collection' of different algorithms that put objects into clusters according to well defined rules. It does not presuppose any apriori hypotheses and cluster analysis is *mostly used in exploratory stage of research.*

Clustering techniques have been applied to a wide variety of research problems. In the field of medicine, clustering diseases-cures for diseases or symptoms of diseases can lead to very useful taxonomies. In archaeology, researchers have successfully applied the technique to establish taxonomies of stone tools, funeral objects, etc. The cluster analysis has also found wide applications in biological and social sciences. In the field of biology, the animals can be grouped according to class and families. The people in a township may be classified according to their socio-economic status. In marketing the buyers can be grouped according to buying habits, preferences, etc.

Since similar objects cluster together, one may include one object from each cluster in the ultimate analysis. Thus, the cluster analysis may be regarded *as a data reduction technique* and the main idea behind the cluster analysis is *to identify homogeneous groups.*

Grouping or clustering is different from classification methods where the operational objective is to assign new observations to a known number of groups. The cluster analysis is a more primitive technique where no assumptions are made concerning the number of groups or the group structure and the grouping is done on the basis of similarities or distances (dissimilarities). Cluster analysis is an interdependence technique and makes no distinction between dependent and independent variables. The entire set of interdependent relationships is examined.

15.5.1 Distance Measures

A distant type of measure is often computed to assess the level of similarity or dissimilarity between two objects, besides computation of correlation coefficients and using other techniques.Suppose we have cbserved p-variables on sample objects. The values of ith object (i = 1, 2, ..., n) is denoted by a vector

$$\underline{X}_i = (X_{i1}, X_{i2}, ... X_{ip})$$

Then, the Euclidean distance between the ith and jth object is given by

$$d_{ij} = \sqrt{\sum_{k=1}^{p} (X_{ik} - X_{jk})^2}$$

Note. The Euclidean distances are usually computed from raw data and not from standardized data. The distance between any two objects is not affected by the addition of new objects to the analysis, which may be outliers. However, the distances can be greatly affected by differences in scale among the dimensions from which the distances are computed, generally, it is good practice to transform the dimensions so that they have similar scales.

Squared Euclidean Distance

In order to place progressively greater weight on objects that are further apart we may compute

$$d_{ij} = \sum_{k=1}^{p} (X_{ik} - X_{jk})^2$$

City Block Distance

This distance is simply the absolute difference across dimensions and is computed as

$$d_{ij} = \sum_{k=1}^{p} | X_{ik} - X_{jk} |$$

Minkowski Distance

$$d_{ij} = \left[\sum_{k=1}^{p} | X_{ik} - X_{jk} |^m \right]^{\frac{1}{m}}$$

Note 1. The varying m changes the weight given to larger and smaller differences.

Note 2. Any distance measure $d(P, Q)$ between two points P and Q is valid provided it satisfies the following properties where R is any other intermediate point

$$d(P, Q) = d(Q, P)$$
$$d(P, Q) > 0 \text{ if } P \neq Q$$
$$d(P, Q) = 0 \text{ if } P = Q$$
$$d(P, Q) \leq d(P, R) + d(R, Q), \text{ triangle inequality.}$$

Chebychev Distance

This distance measure may be appropriate in cases when one wants to define two objects as 'different' if they are different on any one of the dimensions. The Chebychev distance is computed as :

$$d_{ij} = \underset{k}{\text{MAX}} | X_{ik} - X_{jk} |$$

Power Distance

Sometimes one may want to increase or decrease the progressive weight that is placed on dimensions on which the respective objects are very different. The **power distance** is computed as :

$$d_{ij} = \left[\Sigma \mid X_{ik} - X_{jk} \mid^p \right]^{\frac{1}{r}},$$

where p and r are well defined parameters. The parameter p controls the progressive weight that is placed on differences on individual dimensions, parameter r controls the progressive that is placed on larger differences between objects. If r and p are equal to 2, then distance is equal to the Euclidean distance.

Another measure of distance is Mahalanobis D^2 defined by $D^2 = (\underline{X}_i - \underline{X}_j)' S^{-1} (\underline{X}_i - \underline{X}_j)$, where X_i and X_j are the vectors of observations recorded on the ith and jth object respectively and $\underline{S}$ is the pooled within group covariance matrix.

15.5.2 Steps for cluster analysis

1. Formulate the problem–select sample objects and the measurable variables that are to be used for clustering technique.
2. Select a distance measure–various ways of computing distance.
3. Select a clustering procedure.
4. Decide on the number of clusters.
5. Map and interpret clusters–draw conclusions.
6. Assess reliability and validity–various methods :

- repeat analysis but use different distance measure.
- repeat analysis but use different clustering technique,
- split the data randomly into two halves and analyze each part separately.
- repeat analysis several times, deleting one variable each time.
- repeat the analysis several times, using a different order each time.

15.5.3 Clustering Procedures

The clustering procedures can be classified into two broad types of clustering :

- Hierarchical clustering.
- Non-Hierarchical clustering.

In heirarchical clustering objects are organized into an hierarchical structure as part of the procedure. The heirarchical cluster may be classified into

- Divisive clustering
- Agglomerative clustering

Divisive clustering is a top-down or decision approach where we start by treating all objects as if they are part of a single large cluster, then divide the cluster into smaller and smaller clusters, until each object constitutes a cluster.

Agglomerative clustering procedure is a bottom-up approach where we start by treating each object as a seperate cluster, then group them into bigger and bigger clusters, until a single cluster is formed consisting of all the objects.

Agglomerative clustering includes *three* methods :

- **Centroid methods.** Clusters are generated that maximize the distance between the centers of clusters (a centroid is the mean value for all the objects in the cluster).
- **Variance methods.** Clusters are generated that minimize the within cluster

variance. For instance, in **Ward's procedure** clusters are generated that minimize the squared Euclidean distance to the center mean.

❐ **Linkage methods.** Objects are clustered based on distance between them.

For example, we have

(i) Single Linkage Method. Cluster objects based on the minimum distance between them (also called the nearest neighbour rule).

(ii) Complete Linkage Method. Cluster objects based on the maximum distance between them (also called farthest neighbour rule).

(iii) Average Linkage Method. Cluster objects based on the average distance between all pairs of objects (one member of the pair must be from a different cluster).

Non-hierarchical clustering techniques are designed to group items, rather than variables, into a collection of K clusters. The number of clusters (K) may either be specified in advance or determined as part of the clustering procedure. K-mean clustering is a non-hierarchical clustering where an initial set of K clusters also called initial seeds is formed intuitively or through arbitrary method. First, determine a cluster center, then group all objects that are within a certain distance, for instance, Sequential Threshold Method (first determine a Cluster Center, then group all objects that are within a predetermined threshold from the center–one cluster is created at a time) Parallel Threshold Method–(simultaneously several cluster centers are determined, then objects that are within a predetermined threshold from the centers are grouped), Optimizing Partitioning method (first a non-hierarchical procedure is run, then objects are reassigned so as to optimize an overall criterion).

After clustering, the objects in the clusters are represented by a diagram, known as **'Dendogram'**.

Hierarchical Clustering Methods

Hierarchical clustering techniques proceed either by a series of successive mergers or successive divisions.

Agglomerative hierarchical methods start with the individual objects. Thus, initially we have as many clusters as objects. First, **most similar** objects are grouped and then these initial groups are merged according to their **similarities**. Eventually, as the similarity **decreases**, all subgroups are fused into a single cluster.

Divisive hierarchical methods work in the opposite direction. Initially the single group of objects are divided into two subgroups such that the objects in one subgroup are **'far from'** the objects in the other. These subgroups are then further subdivided into **dissimilar** subgroups; the process continues until there are as many subgroups as objects; that is, until each object forms a group.

In this section we shall concentrate on linkage methods such as **single linkage** (minimum distance or nearest neighbour), **complete linkage** (maximum distance or farthest neighbour), and **average linkage** (average distance) are discussed. Linkage methods are found to be suitable for clustering items, as well as variables.

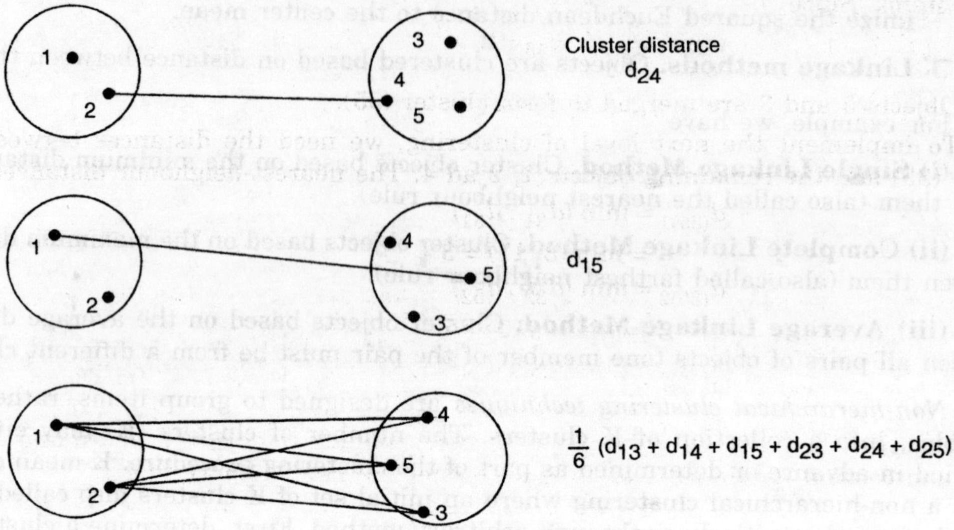

Fig. 15.1 Inter cluster distance (dissimilarity)

Steps in the agglomerative hierarchical clustering algorithm for grouping

N objects (items or variables) :

1. Start with N clusters. Each cluster contains a **single entity**. Form a $N \times N$ symmetric matrix of distances (or similarities) $\underline{D} = \{d_{ik}\}$
2. Search the distance matrix for the nearest (most similar) pair of clusters, say d_{uv}.
3. Merge clusters u and v and label it (uv). Update the entries in the distance matrix by (a) deleting the row and column corresponding to clusters u and v. and (b) adding a row and column giving the distances between cluster (uv) and the remaining clusters.
4. Repeat steps 2 and 3 a total of (N–1) times. All objects will be in a single cluster at termination of the algorithm. Record the identity of clusters that are merged and the levels (distances and similarities) at which the mergers take place.)

Illustration 3. (Single Linkage) : Consider the hypothetical distances between pairs of 5 objects given below

$$\underline{D} = \{d_{ik}\} = \begin{matrix} \\ 1 \\ 2 \\ 3 \\ 4 \\ 5 \end{matrix} \begin{matrix} \begin{matrix} 1 & 2 & 3 & 4 & 5 \end{matrix} \\ \begin{bmatrix} 0 & & & & \\ 9 & 0 & & & \\ 3 & 7 & 0 & & \\ 6 & 5 & 9 & 0 & \\ 11 & 10 & 2 & 8 & 0 \end{bmatrix} \end{matrix}$$

Treat each object as a cluster. The clustering commences by merging the two closest items. Since

$$\min_{i,\,k} \{ d_{ik} \} = d_{53} = 2$$

Objects 5 and 3 are merged to form cluster (35).

To implement the next level of clustering, we need the distances between the cluster (35) and the remaining objects 1, 2 ad 4. The nearest-neighbour distances are

$$d_{(35)1} = \min (d_{31}, d_{51})$$
$$= \min (3, 11) = 3$$
$$d_{(35)2} = \min (d_{32}, d_{52})$$
$$= \min (7, 10) = 7$$
$$d_{(35)4} = \min (d_{34}, d_{54})$$
$$= \min (9, 8) = 8$$

Deleting the rows and columns of D corresponding to objects 3 and 5 and adding a row and column for the cluster (35), we obtain the new distance matrix

$$\begin{array}{c} \\ (35) \\ 1 \\ 2 \\ 4 \end{array} \begin{array}{c} \begin{array}{cccc} 35 & 1 & 2 & 4 \end{array} \\ \begin{bmatrix} 0 & & & \\ 3 & 0 & & \\ 7 & 9 & 0 & \\ 8 & 6 & 5 & 0 \end{bmatrix} \end{array}$$

The **smallest** distance between pairs of clusters is now $d_{(35)1} = 3$ and we merge cluster (1) with cluster (35) to get the next cluster, (135).

Calculating

$$d_{(135)2} = \min (d_{(35)2}, d_{12}) = \min (7, 9)$$
$$= 7$$
$$d_{(135)4} = \min (d_{(35)4}, d_{14})$$
$$= \min (8, 6) = 6$$

The distance matrix for the next level of clustering is

$$\begin{array}{c} \\ (135) \\ 2 \\ 4 \end{array} \begin{array}{c} \begin{array}{ccc} (135) & 2 & 4 \end{array} \\ \begin{bmatrix} 0 & & \\ 7 & 0 & \\ 6 & 5 & 0 \end{bmatrix} \end{array}$$

The minimum nearest neighbor distance between pairs of clusters is $d_{42} = 5$, and we merge objects 4 and 2 to get the cluster (24).

At this point we have two distinct clusters (135) and (24). Their nearest neighbor distance is

$$d_{(135)(24)} = \min (d_{(135)2}, d_{(135)4})$$
$$= \min (7, 6) = 6$$

The final distance matrix becomes

$$\begin{array}{c} \\ (135) \\ (24) \end{array} \begin{array}{c} \begin{array}{cc} (134) & (24) \end{array} \\ \begin{bmatrix} 0 & \\ 6 & 0 \end{bmatrix} \end{array}$$

Consequently, clusters (135) and (24) are merged to form a single cluster of all five objects (12345), when the nearest neighbor distance reaches 6.

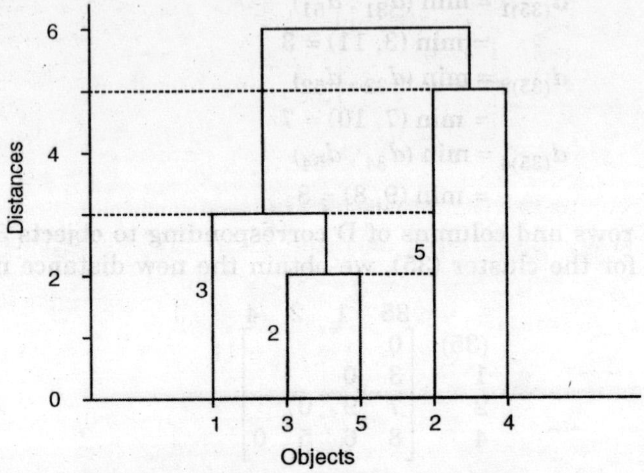

Fig. 15.2 Dendogram (Single linkage).

Illustration 4. (Complete linkage) :

$$\underline{D} = \{d_{ik}\} = \begin{array}{c} \\ 1 \\ 2 \\ 3 \\ 4 \\ 5 \end{array} \begin{array}{c} \begin{array}{ccccc} 1 & 2 & 3 & 4 & 5 \end{array} \\ \begin{bmatrix} 0 & & & & \\ 9 & 0 & & & \\ 3 & 7 & 0 & & \\ 6 & 5 & 9 & 0 & \\ 11 & 10 & 2 & 8 & 0 \end{bmatrix} \end{array}$$

At the first step objects 3 and 5 are merged since they are most similar. This gives the cluster (35). At the second step we compute

$$d_{(35)1} = \max \{d_{31}, d_{51}\}$$
$$= \max \{3, 11\} = 11$$
$$d_{(35)2} = \max \{d_{32}, d_{52}\} = 10$$
$$d_{(35)4} = \max \{d_{34}, d_{54}\} = 9$$

and the modified distance matrix becomes

$$\begin{array}{c} \\ (35) \\ 1 \\ 2 \\ 4 \end{array} \begin{array}{c} \begin{array}{cccc} (35) & 1 & 2 & 4 \end{array} \\ \begin{bmatrix} 0 & & & \\ 11 & 0 & & \\ 10 & 9 & 0 & \\ 9 & 6 & 5 & 0 \end{bmatrix} \end{array}$$

The next merger occurs between the most similar groups 2 and 4 to give the cluster (24).

Then at 3rd step compute

$$d_{(24)(35)} = \max\{d_{2(35)}, d_{4(35)}\}$$
$$= \max\{10, 9\} = 10$$
$$d_{(24)1} = \max\{d_{21}, d_{41}\}$$
$$= 9$$

$$\begin{array}{c} \\ (35) \\ (24) \\ 1 \end{array} \begin{array}{c} \begin{array}{ccc} (35) & (24) & 1 \end{array} \\ \left[\begin{array}{ccc} 0 & & \\ 10 & 0 & \\ 11 & 9 & 0 \end{array}\right] \end{array}$$

The next merger produces the cluster (124)

At the final stage the groups (35) and (124) are merged as the single cluster (12345) at level

$$d_{(124)(35)} = \max\{d_{1(35)}, d_{(24)(35)}\}$$
$$= \max\{11, 10\} = 11$$

The dendogram is shown in Fig. 15.3.

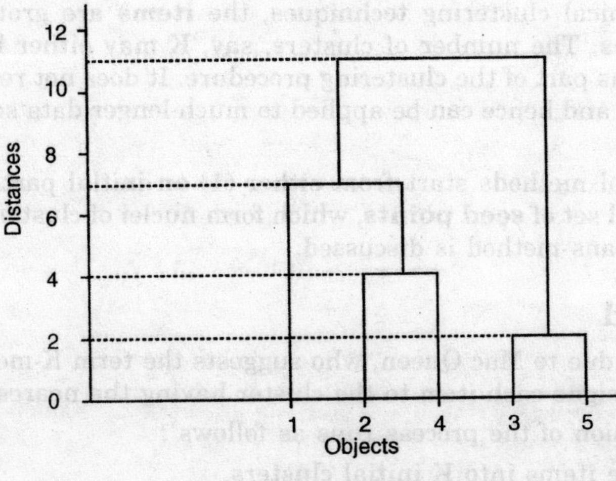

Fig. 15.3 Dendogram

Comparing the dendograms in Fig. 15.2 and Fig. 15.3, one finds that there is difference in allocation of object 1 to previous groups.

Average Linkage

In average linkage procedure we treat the distance between two clusters as the average distance between all pairs of items where one member of a pair belongs to each cluster.

In the first step we begin by searching the distance matrix D = $\{d_{ik}\}$ to find the nearest neighbor objects say u and v. Then, these objects are merged to form the cluster (uv). In the 3rd step, following the general agglomerative algorithm, the distances between (uv) and any other cluster say w are determined by

$$d_{(uv)w} = \frac{\sum_{i} \sum_{k} d_{ik}}{N_{uv} N_{w}},$$

where d_{ik} is the distance between object i in the cluster (uv) and the object k in the cluster w, and $N_{(uv)}$ and N_w are the number of items in cluster (uv) and w respectively.

For average linkage clustering, changes in the assignment of distances (similarities), affect the final configuration of clusters, although relative orderings are preserved.

Note. There are many agglomerative hierarchical clustering procedures besides the single linkage, complete linkage and average linkage and all of them follow the same basic algorithm.

Sources of error and variations are not considered in hierarchical procedures and hence a clustering method will be sensitive to outliers or 'noise points'.

Non hierarchical Clustering Methods

In non-hierarchical clustering techniques, the **items** are grouped into clusters rather than **variables**. The number of clusters, say, K may either be specified in advance or determined as part of the clustering procedure. It does not require computation of matrix of distances and hence can be applied to much longer data sets than hierarchical techniques.

Non-hierarchical methods start from either (1) an initial partition of items into groups or (2) an initial set of **seed points**, which form nuclei of clusters. In the following a more popular K-means method is discussed.

K-means method

This method is due to Mac Queen, who suggests the term K-means for describing his algorithm that assigns each item to the cluster having the nearest centroid (mean).

A simplest version of the process runs as follows :

1. Partition the items into K initial clusters.
2. Proceed through the list of items, assigning an item to the cluster whose centroid (mean) is nearest. Distance is usually computed using Euclideau distance with either standardized or unstandardized observations. Recalculate the centroid for the cluster receiving the new item and for the cluster losing the item.
3. Repeat step 2 until no more assignments take place.

Rather than starting with a partition of all items into K preliminary groups in step 1, we could specify K initial centroids (seed points) and then proceed to step 2.

The final assignment of items of clusters will be somewhat dependent on the initial partition or the initial selection of seed points.

Illustration 5. Suppose we measure two variables X_1 and X_2 for each of four items A, B, C and D and the relevant data are given below :

Items	Observation	
	x_1	x_2
A	5	3
B	–1	1
C	1	–2
D	–3	–2

The objective is to divide these items into K = 2 clusters such that the items within a cluster are closer to one another than the items in different clusters.

To implement the K = 2 means method, we arbitrarily partition the items into two clusters, such as (AB) and (CD), and compute the co-ordinates $(\bar{x}_1, \bar{x}_2)$ of the cluster centroid (mean).

Step 1 :

Cluster	Co-ordinates of Centroid	
	$\bar{x}_1$	$\bar{x}_2$
(AB)	$\frac{5+(-1)}{2} = 2$	$\frac{3+1}{2} = 2$
(CD)	$\frac{1+(-3)}{2} = -1$	$\frac{-2+(-2)}{2} = -2$

Step 2 :

Compute the Euclidean distance of each item from the group centroids and reassign each item to the nearest group.

If an item is moved from the initial configuration, the cluster centroids (means) must be updated before proceeding to compute the squared distances

$$d^2\,(A\,,(AB)) = (5-2)^2 + (3-2)^2 = 10$$
$$d^2\,(A\,,(CD)) = (5+1)^2 + (3+2)^2 = 61$$

Since A is closer to cluster (AB), it is not reassigned.

Further,

$$d^2\,(B\,,(AB)) = (-1-2)^2 + (1-2)^2 = 10$$
$$d^2\,(B\,,(CD)) = (-1+1)^2 + (1+2)^2 = 9$$

Since B is closer to (CD) rather than to (AB), B is reassigned to cluster (CD), forming cluster (BCD) and the following are updated centroid co-ordinates.

Cluster	Co-ordinates of Centroid	
	$\bar{x}_1$	$\bar{x}_2$
A	5	3
(BCD)	–1	–1

Again each item is checked for reassignment. Computing the squared distances gives the following table :

Squared distances to group centroids

Cluster	Item			
	A	**B**	**C**	**D**
A	0	40	41	89
(BCD)	52	4	5	5

We, now, see that each item is assigned to the cluster with the nearest centroid (mean) and the process stops.

The final K = 2 clusters are A and (BCD).

15.6 Principal Component Analysis

In data mining one often encounters situations where there are a large number of variables in the data base and a researcher is fascinated to use multivariate analysis for the purpose. It may so happen (which may be very likely) that subsets of variables are highly correlated with each other. The accuracy and reliability of a classification or prediction model will suffer if you include highly correlated variables or variables that are unrelated to the outcome of interest. Superfluous variables can increase the data-collection and data-processing costs by deploying a model on large data base. The dimensionality of a model is the number of independent or input variables used by the model. One of the key steps in data mining is finding ways to reduce dimensionality without sacrificing accuracy.

Principal Component Analysis (PCA) is a mathematical procedure that transforms a number of (possibly) correlated variables into a 'smaller' number of uncorrelated variables called **principal components** with objective *(i)* to reduce the dimensionality (number of variables) of the database but retain most of the original variability in the data, *(ii)* to identify new meaningful underlying variables. The first principal component accounts for as much of the variability in the data as possible, and each succeeding component accounts for as much of the remaining variability as possible. A principal component analysis performed on a selected data base, is concerned with explaining the variance-covariance structure of a high dimensional random vector through a few linear combinations of the original component variables.

15.6.1 Principal Component Theory

Consider a p-dimensional random vector $\underline{X} = (X_1, X_2, \ldots X_p)'$ with covariance matrix Σ with eigen values $\lambda_1 \geq \lambda_2 \geq \ldots \geq \lambda_p$.

Consider, further the linear combinations

$$Y_1 = \underline{l}'_1 \underline{X} = l_{11} X_1 + l_{12} X_2 + \ldots + l_{p1} X_p$$

$$Y_2 = \underline{l}'_2 \underline{X} = l_{12} X_1 + l_{22} X_2 + \ldots + l_{p2} X_p$$

$$\vdots$$

$$Y_p = \underline{l}'_p \underline{X} = l_{1p} X_1 + l_{2p} X_2 + \ldots + l_{pp} X_p$$

Now, $\quad V(Y_i) = \underline{l}'_i \Sigma \underline{l}_i,\ i = 1, 2, \ldots, p$

$$\text{Cov}(Y_i, Y_k) = \underline{l}'_i \Sigma \underline{l}_k,\ i, k = 1, 2, \ldots, p$$

The principal components are those **uncorrelated** linear combinations $Y_1, Y_2, \dots, Y_p$ whose variances $V(Y_i)$, $i = 1, 2, \dots, p$ are as large as possible.

The first principal component Y_1 has variance $V(Y_1) = \underline{l}'_1 \Sigma \underline{l}_1$, where the coefficients maximize $V(Y_1)$. As the var(Y_1) can be increased by multiplying $\underline{l}_1$ by some constant, it is convenient to restrict attention to coefficient vectors of unit length to eliminate this confusion. That is, $V(Y_1) = \underline{l}' \Sigma \underline{l}_1$ is maximized subject to restriction $\underline{l}'_1 \underline{l}_1 = 1$.

Second principal component $Y_2 = \underline{l}'_2 \underline{X}$ that maximizes $V(Y_2)$ subject to $\underline{l}'_2 \underline{l}_2 = 1$ and $\text{Cov}(\underline{l}'_1 \underline{X}, \underline{l}'_2 \underline{X}) = 0$

Thus, the ith principal component $Y_i = \underline{l}'_i \underline{X}$, where $\underline{l}_i$ maximizes $V(Y_i)$ s.t. $\underline{l}'_i \underline{l}_i = 1$ and $\text{Cov}(\underline{l}'_i X, \underline{l}'_k X) = 0$ for $k < i$.

Note. Let Σ have the **eigen value-eigen vector pairs** (λ_1, e_1), (λ_2, e_2) .... (λ_p, e_p) where $\lambda_1 \geq \lambda_2 \geq \dots \geq \lambda_p \geq 0$

The ith principal component is given by

$$Y_i = \underline{e}'_i \underline{X}$$
$$= e_{1i} X_1 + e_{2i} X_2 + \dots + e_{pi} X_p, \quad i = 1, 2, \dots, p,$$

since $\dfrac{\underline{l}'_i \Sigma \underline{l}_i}{\underline{l}'_i \underline{l}_i}$ is maximized

when $l_i = e_i$, with maximum value λ_i.

$$\text{Thus,} \qquad \max_{l_i \neq 0} \frac{\underline{l}'_i \Sigma \underline{l}_i}{\underline{l}'_i \underline{l}_i} = \lambda_i = \frac{e'_i \Sigma e_i}{e'_i e_i}$$
$$= \text{Var}(Y_i),$$

since $\underline{e}'_i \underline{e}_i = 1$ (because eigen vectors are normalized.)

$$\text{It may be proved that } \sigma_{11} + \sigma_{22} + \dots + \sigma_{pp} = \sum_{i=1}^{p} V(X_i)$$

$$= \lambda_1 + \lambda_2 + \dots + \lambda_p = \sum_{i=1}^{p} V(Y_i),$$

where $\sigma_{ii} = V(X_i)$, $i = 1, 2, \dots, p$.

Thus, total population variance

$$= \sigma_{11} + \sigma_{22} + \dots + \sigma_{pp} = \lambda_1 + \lambda_2 + \dots + \lambda_p.$$

The proportion of total variance due to ith principal component is given by

$$\frac{\lambda_i}{\lambda_1 + \lambda_2 + \dots + \lambda_p}, \quad i = 1, 2, \dots, p.$$

In most of the situations met in practice total population variance, for large p, can be explained by a few principal components. Thus, these principal components which are smaller in number than the original set of p variables without much loss of information. The first principal component corresponding to largest λ_i has the largest variance of all linear combinations of variables.

Note. A square matrix $\underline{A}$ is said to have an eigen value λ, with corresponding eigen vector $\underline{X} \neq \underline{0}$, if

$$\underline{A}\,\underline{X} = \lambda\,\underline{X}$$

We normalize $\underline{X}$ so that it has length one. Therefore $1 = \underline{X}'\,\underline{X}$.

That is, if $\underline{A}\,\underline{X} = \lambda$, we take $\underline{e} = \dfrac{\underline{X}}{\sqrt{\underline{X}'\underline{X}}}$

The eigen values are obtained from the solution of the characteristic equation $|\underline{A} - \lambda\,\underline{I}| = 0$. Suppose λ_1, λ_2 and λ_3 are the characteristic roots of the equation, then λ_1, λ_2 and λ_3 are eigen values. The corresponding eigen vectors $\underline{e}_1$, $\underline{e}_2$ and $\underline{e}_3$ are the normalized solutions of the equations $\underline{A}\,\underline{e}_i = \lambda_i\,\underline{e}_i$.

Illustration 6. Given the matrix

$$A = \begin{bmatrix} 1 & 2 \\ 2 & -2 \end{bmatrix},$$

find the eigen values λ_1 and λ_2 and the associated eigen vectors e_1 and e_2.

The equation $|A - \lambda I| = 0$, gives the roots $\lambda_1 = -3$ and $\lambda_2 = 2$.

To find the eigen vector $\underline{e}_1$ corresponding to $\lambda_1 = -3$, we have

$\underline{A}\,\underline{e}_1 = \lambda\,\underline{e}_1$ with $\lambda = \lambda_1 = -3$.

That is,
$$\begin{bmatrix} 1 & 2 \\ 2 & -2 \end{bmatrix}\begin{bmatrix} e_{11} \\ e_{12} \end{bmatrix} = -3\begin{bmatrix} e_{11} \\ e_{12} \end{bmatrix}$$

or
$$e_{11} + 2e_{12} = -3\,e_{11}$$
$$2e_{11} - 2e_{12} = -3\,e_{12}$$

or
$$4e_{11} - 2e_{12} = 0$$
$$2e_{11} + e_{12} = 0$$

That is,
$$e_{11} = -\frac{1}{2}\,e_{12}$$

There are many solutions for e_{11} and e_{12}

Setting $e_{12} = 1$ (arbitrarily),

$$e_{11} = -\frac{1}{2}$$

Thus
$$\underline{e}_1 = \begin{bmatrix} -\frac{1}{2} \\ 1 \end{bmatrix}$$

For normalizing vector $\underline{e}_1$, we determine the eigen vector so that it has length one. Hence

$$\underline{e}_1 = \begin{bmatrix} \dfrac{-\frac{1}{2}}{\sqrt{\left(-\frac{1}{2}\right)^2 + 1^2}} \\[2ex] \dfrac{1}{\sqrt{\left(-\frac{1}{2}\right)^2 + 1^2}} \end{bmatrix}$$

$$= \begin{bmatrix} -\dfrac{1}{\sqrt{5}} \\ \dfrac{2}{\sqrt{5}} \end{bmatrix}$$

To determine $\underline{e}_2$, set

$A\,\underline{e}_2 = \lambda\,\underline{e}_2$ with $\lambda = \lambda_2 = 2$

Therefore $\begin{bmatrix} 1 & 2 \\ 2 & -2 \end{bmatrix}\begin{bmatrix} e_{21} \\ e_{22} \end{bmatrix} = 2\begin{bmatrix} e_{21} \\ e_{22} \end{bmatrix}$

$$\left.\begin{aligned} e_{21} + 2e_{22} &= 2e_{21} \\ 2e_{21} - 2e_{22} &= 2e_{22} \end{aligned}\right\}$$

That is,

$$\left.\begin{aligned} -e_{21} + 2e_{22} &= 0 \\ 2e_{21} - 4e_{22} &= 0 \end{aligned}\right\}$$

That is, $e_{21} = 2e_{22}$

Now, there are many solutions for e_{21} and e_{22}.

Put $e_{22} = 1$ (arbitrarily)

Then $e_{21} = 2$

Thus, $\underline{e}_2 = \begin{bmatrix} 2 \\ 1 \end{bmatrix}$

When normalized,

$$\underline{e}_2 = \begin{bmatrix} \dfrac{2}{\sqrt{5}} \\ \dfrac{1}{\sqrt{5}} \end{bmatrix}$$

Note. For a symmetric positive definite matrix the eigen values are always greater than or equal to zero.

Illustration 7. Suppose the random variables X_1, X_2 and X_3 have the covariance matrix.

$$\Sigma = \begin{bmatrix} 1 & -2 & 0 \\ -2 & 5 & 0 \\ 0 & 0 & 2 \end{bmatrix}$$

The eigen value–eigen vector pairs are

$\lambda_1 = 5.83 \qquad e'_1 = [.383, -.924, 0]$

$\lambda_2 = 2.00 \qquad e'_2 = [0, 0, 1]$

$\lambda_3 = 0.17 \qquad e'_3 = [.924, .383, 0]$

Therefore the principal components become

$$Y_1 = \underline{e}'_1\,\underline{X} = 0.383\,X_1 - 0.924\,X_2$$

$$Y_2 = \underline{e}'_2\,\underline{X} = X_3$$

$$Y_3 = \underline{e}'_3\,\underline{X} = 0.924\,X_1 + 0.383\,X_2$$

It may be verified that

$$\begin{aligned} V(Y_1) &= \text{Var}\,(0.383\, X_1 - 0.924\, X_2) \\ &= (0.383)^2\ \text{Var}\,(X_1) + (-0.924)^2\ \text{Var}\,(X_2) \\ &\qquad + 2(0.383)\,(-0.924)\ \text{Cov}\,(X_1, X_2) \\ &= 0.147\,(1) + 0.854(5) - (5) - 0.708\,(-2) \\ &= 5.83 = \lambda_1 \end{aligned}$$

$$\begin{aligned} \text{Cov}\,(Y_1, Y_2) &= \text{Cov}\,(0.383\, X_1 - 0.924\, X_2, X_3) \\ &= 0.383\ \text{Cov}\,(X_1, X_3) - 0.924\ \text{Cov}\,(X_2, X_3) \\ &= 0.383\,(0) - 0.924\,(0) = 0 \end{aligned}$$

Further, $\sigma_{11} + \sigma_{22} + \sigma_{33} = 1 + 5 + 2$

$$= \lambda_1 + \lambda_2 + \lambda_3 = 5.83 + 2.00 + 0.17$$

The proportion of total variance accounted for by the first principal component is

$$\frac{\lambda_1}{\lambda_1 + \lambda_2 + \lambda_3} = \frac{5.83}{8} = 0.73.$$

The proportion of total variance accounted for by the first two principal components is

$$\frac{\lambda_1 + \lambda_2}{\lambda_1 + \lambda_2 + \lambda_3} = \frac{5.83\ + 2}{8} = 0.98$$

If we replace the original variables X_1, X_2 and X_3 by Y_1 and Y_2 there will be little loss of information.

Note. If $Y_1 = e'_1 \underline{X}$, $Y_2 = e'_2 \underline{X}$, ... $Y_p = e'_p X$ are the principal components obtained from the covariance matrix Σ, then

$$\rho_{Y_i, X_k} = \frac{e_{ki} \sqrt{\lambda_i}}{\sqrt{\sigma_{kk}}}, \quad i, k = 1, 2, .., p$$

are the correlation coefficients between the components Y_i and the variables X_k; $(\lambda_1, \underline{e}_1)$, $(\lambda_2, \underline{e}_2)$ ...... $(\lambda_p, \underline{e}_p)$ are the eigen value–eigen vector pairs for $\underline{\Sigma}$.

The advantage of the principal component analysis is to analyse the variation expressed along a single continuum rather than in p-dimensional space. The coefficients of the variables in a linear combination would indicate the importance of each variate in the new derived principal component.

Analysis of principal components are more of a means to an end rather than an end in themselves. They may be used in regression analysis or cluster analysis or in factor analysis models.

15.6.2 Sample Principal Components

Let $\underline{x}_1, \underline{x}_2, \ldots, \underline{x}_n$ be a random sample from a p-variate population, with mean vector $\underline{\mu}$ and covariance matrix Σ.

Then $\underline{\bar{x}} = \frac{1}{n} \sum_{j=1}^{n} \underline{x}_j$ and $\underline{S} = \frac{1}{n-1} \sum_{j=1}^{n} (\underline{x}_j - \underline{\bar{x}})(\underline{x}_j - \underline{\bar{x}})'$, where $\underline{x}$ is the sample mean vector and $\underline{S}$ is the ample covariance matrix $\underline{S}$ and the sample correlation matrix $\underline{R}$.

The problem is to construct uncorrelated linear combinations of the measured characteristics that account for much of the variation in the sample. The uncorrelated combinations with largest variances will be called the **sample principal components**.

If $\underline{S} = \{s_{ik}\}$ is the $p \times p$ sample covariance matrix with eigen value-eigen vector pairs $(\hat{\lambda}_1, \hat{e}_1), (\hat{\lambda}_2, \hat{e}_2), \ldots (\hat{\lambda}_p, \hat{e}_p)$, then ith principal component is given by

$$\hat{y}_i = \underline{e}'_i \underline{x} = \hat{e}_{1i} x_1 + \hat{e}_{2i} x_2 + \ldots + \hat{e}_{pi} x_p, \; i = 1, 2, \ldots, p$$

where $\hat{\lambda}_1, \hat{\lambda}_2 \ldots, \hat{\lambda}_p \geq 0$ and $\underline{x}$ is any observation on the variables $X_1, X_2, \ldots, X_p$

Also, sample variance $(\hat{y}_k) = \hat{\lambda}_k$, $k = 1, 2, \ldots, p$.

Sample covariance $(\hat{y}_i, \hat{y}_k) = 0$, $i \neq k$.

Further, total sample variance

$$= \sum_{i=1}^{p} s_{ii} = \hat{\lambda}_1 + \hat{\lambda}_2 + \ldots + \hat{\lambda}_p$$

and

$$r_{\hat{y}_i, x_k} = \frac{\hat{e}_{ki}\sqrt{\hat{\lambda}_i}}{\sqrt{s_{kk}}}; \; i, k = 1, 2, \ldots, p$$

Note

1. The principal components constructed from $\underline{S}$ and $\underline{R}$ are not the same.
2. The observations $\underline{x}_j$ are often centered by subtracting $\bar{\underline{x}}$. It has no effect on the sample covariance matrix S and gives the ith principal component.

$$\hat{y}_i = \hat{\underline{e}}'_i (\underline{x}_i - \bar{\underline{x}}), \; i = 1, 2, \ldots, p.$$

The sample mean of each principal component is zero and the sample variances remain unchanged and are given by $\hat{\lambda}_i$'s.

15.6.3 Standardizing the Sample Principal Components

Sample principal components are not invariant under the change of scale. Therefore, when variables are measured on different scales or on a common scale with widely differing ranges, it is appropriate to standardize the sample values. Thus,

$$\underline{z}_j = \left[\frac{x_{ij} - \bar{x}_1}{\sqrt{s_{11}}}, \frac{x_{2j} - \bar{x}_2}{\sqrt{s_{pp}}} \ldots\ldots, \frac{x_{pj} - \bar{x}_p}{\sqrt{s_{pp}}}\right]', \; j = 1, 2, \ldots, n$$

Also

$$\underline{z} = [\underline{z}_1, \underline{z}_2, \ldots \underline{z}_n] = \begin{bmatrix} z_{11} & z_{12} & \ldots & z_{1n} \\ z_{21} & z_{22} & \ldots & z_{2n} \\ \ldots & \ldots & & \ldots \\ z_{p1} & z_{p2} & \ldots & z_{pn} \end{bmatrix} = \begin{bmatrix} \frac{x_{11} - \bar{x}_1}{\sqrt{s_{11}}} & \frac{x_{12} - \bar{x}_2}{\sqrt{s_{11}}} & \ldots & \frac{x_{1n} - \bar{x}_1}{\sqrt{s_{11}}} \\ \frac{x_{21} - \bar{x}_2}{\sqrt{s_{22}}} & \frac{x_{22} - \bar{x}_2}{\sqrt{s_{22}}} & \ldots & \frac{x_{2n} - \bar{x}_2}{\sqrt{s_{22}}} \\ \ldots & \ldots & & \ldots \\ \ldots & \ldots & & \ldots \\ \frac{x_{p1} - \bar{x}_p}{\sqrt{s_{pp}}} & \frac{x_{p2} - \bar{x}_p}{\sqrt{s_{pp}}} & \ldots & \frac{x_{pn} - \bar{x}_p}{\sqrt{s_{pp}}} \end{bmatrix}$$

It may be verified that

$$\underline{\bar{z}} = 0$$

and sample covariance matrix

$$\underline{S}_z = \frac{1}{n-1} \underline{z}\, \underline{z}'$$

$$= \frac{1}{n-1} \begin{bmatrix} \frac{(n-1)\, s_{11}}{s_{11}} & \frac{(n-1)\, s_{12}}{\sqrt{s_{11}}\sqrt{s_{22}}} & \cdots & \frac{(n-1)\, s_{1p}}{\sqrt{s_{11}}\sqrt{s_{pp}}} \\ \frac{(n-1)\, s_{12}}{\sqrt{s_{11}}\sqrt{s_{22}}} & \frac{(n-1)\, s_{22}}{s_{22}} & \cdots & \frac{(n-1)\, s_{2p}}{\sqrt{s_{22}}\sqrt{s_{pp}}} \\ \cdots & \cdots & & \cdots \\ \frac{(n-1)\, s_{1p}}{\sqrt{s_{11}}\sqrt{s_{pp}}} & \frac{(n-1)\, s_{2p}}{\sqrt{s_{22}}\sqrt{s_{pp}}} & \cdots & \frac{(n-1)\, s_{pp}}{s_{pp}} \end{bmatrix} = \underline{R} \text{ (sample correlation matrix)}$$

Thus, if $\underline{z}_1, \underline{z}_2, \ldots, \underline{z}_n$ are standardized observations with covariance matrix $\underline{R}$, the ith sample principal component is given by

$$\hat{y}_i = \hat{\underline{e}}_i\, \underline{z}$$

$$= \hat{e}_{1i} + z_1 + e_{2i\, z_2} + \ldots + \hat{e}_{pi\, z_p}, \; i = 1, 2, .., p,$$

where $(\hat{\lambda}_i, \hat{e}_i)$ is the ith eigen value—eigen vector pair $\underline{R}$ with

$$\hat{\lambda}_1 \geq \hat{\lambda}_2 \geq \ldots \geq \hat{\lambda}_p$$

Total (standardized) sample variance

$$= p = \hat{\lambda}_1 + \hat{\lambda}_2 + \ldots + \hat{\lambda}_p$$

Thus, the proportion of total sample variance explained by the ith sample principal component is $\frac{\hat{\lambda}_i}{p}$; $i = 1, 2, \ldots p$.

15.7 FACTOR ANALYSIS

15.7.1 Introduction

Factor analysis is a statistical technique to study the inter-relationship among a large number of variables by finding a new set of factors, smaller in number than the original variables so that the factors are common among the original variables. These common factors are sufficient to study the interrelationships of the original variables.

Factor analysis is used to uncover the latent structure (dimension) of a set of variables. It reduces attribute space from a larger number of variables to a smaller number of factors and as such is a 'non-dependent' procedure (that is, it does not assume a dependent variable is specified). The detection of structure in the relationships between variables helps classification of variables. Thus, the factor analysis is applied as a data reduction or structure detection method and was first introduced by Thurstone in 1931.

The principal component analysis is a **data reduction procedure** and the variation in p-dimensional data space is translated into smaller number of components (weighted linear combinations of variables) as per desirability of the researcher, which can explain maximum variation, where as in factor analysis the researcher researches for **common factors,** which are simply artificial mathematical variables, which might not be real, but represent **latent measurement variables**. These common factors indirectly induce observed correlations among the variables.

Both principal component analysis and factor analysis can be viewed as attempts to approximate the covariance matrix $\underline{\Sigma}$. However, the approximation based on the factor analysis model is more elaborate.

Factor analysis is a collection of methods used to examine how underlying constructs influence the responses on a number of measured variables.

There are basically **two types** of **factor analysis** : exploratory and confirmatory.

- ❒ **Exploratory factor analysis** (EFA) attempts to discover the nature of the constructs influencing a set of responses or in other words to uncover the underlying structure of a relatively large set of variables.
- ❒ **Confirmatory factor analysis** (CFA) tests whether a specified set of constructs is influencing responses in a predictive way.

Both types of factor analyses are based on the **common factor model.** Consider the illustration in Fig. 15.4 where the model proposes that each observed response (Measure 1 to Measure 5) is influenced partially by underlying **common factors** (factor 1 and factor 2) and partially by underlying **unique factors**(E1 through E5).

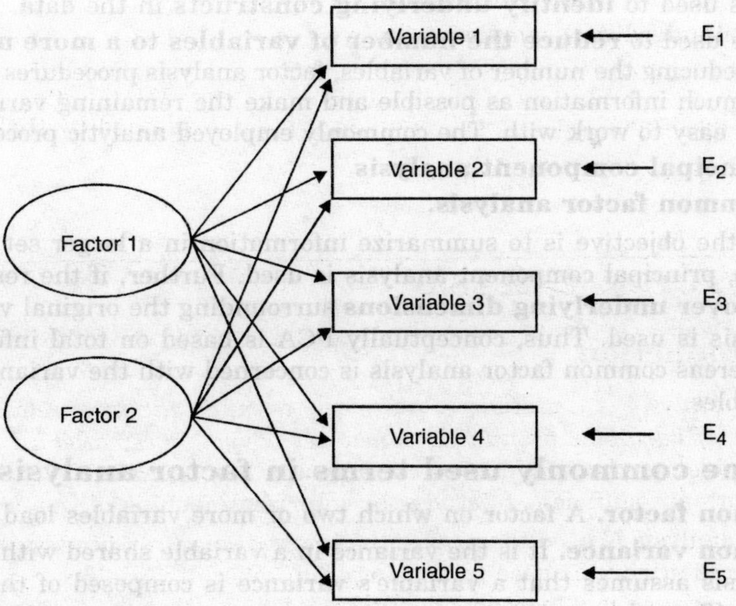

Fig. 15.4 The Common Factor Model

Factor analyses are performed by examining the pattern of correlations (or covariances) between the observed measures. Measures that are highly (either positively or negatively) are likely to be influenced by the same factors, while those that are relatively less likely to be influenced by different factors.

There are different methods of extracting the factors from a set of data such as Principal Components Analysis (PCA), Canonical Factor Analysis (CFA), Principal Factor Analysis (PFA), etc. However the most common and widely used form of factor analysis is by using principal component analysis. The PCA seeks a linear combination of variables such that the maximum variance is extracted from the variables. It then removes this variance and seeks a second linear combination which explains the maximum proportion of the remaining variance, and so on. This is called the **principal axis method** and results in orthogonal (uncorrelated) factors. PCA analyses total (common and unique) variance.

The **principal factor analysis** (PFA), also called **principal axis factoring** (PFA) seeks the least number of factors which can account for the **common variance** (correlation) of a set of variables, where as the common PCA in its full form seeks the set of factors which can account for all the common and unique (specific plus error) variance in a set of variables. PFA uses a PCA strategy but applies it to a correlation matrix in which the diagonal elements are not 1's, as in PCA, but iteratively derived estimates of the communalities. PFA accounts for the covariation among variables where as PCA accounts for the total variance of variables. However data sets, PCA and PFA lead to similar substantive conclusions.

Thus, to sum up, the researchers can use factor analysis mainly for two purposes in data analysis :

(*i*) It is used to **identify underlying constructs** in the data.

(*ii*) It is used to **reduce the number of variables to a more manageable set.** In reducing the number of variables, factor analysis procedures attempt to retain as much information as possible and make the remaining variables meaningful and easy to work with. The commonly employed analytic procedures are

(*i*) **Principal component analysis**

(*ii*) **Common factor analysis.**

When the objective is to summarize information in a larger set of variables into fewer factors, principal component analysis is used. Further, if the researcher is interested to **uncover underlying dimensions** surrounding the original variables common factor analysis is used. Thus, conceptually PCA is based on total information in each variable, whereas common factor analysis is concerned with the variance shared among all the variables.

15.7.2 Some commonly used terms in factor analysis

Common factor. A factor on which two or more variables load.

Common variance. It is the variance in a variable shared with common factors. Factor analysis assumes that a variable's variance is composed of three components– common, specific and error.

Communality

It is the proportion of a variable's variance explained by a factor structure *i.e.* by all the factors jointly. It is the reliability of the indicator. A variable's communality must be estimated prior to performing a factor analysis. It is usually denoted by h^2. Communality for a variable is computed as the sum of squared factor loadings for that variable.

Data matrix

It is a rectangular arrangement of the raw data on n cases over m variables. The most common data matrix is defined with rows for the cases and columns for the variables, and a factor analysis is performed to reduce the dimensionality of the columns (variables).

Data reduction

The purpose is to reduce the number of cases or variables in a data matrix.

Diagonal factoring

This is an orthogonal decomposition of the variance of a set of variables which uses residuals from regression models.

Distance

This is a measure of discrepancy between two observations on a set of variables. The most common measure is the squared Euclidean distance which is the sum of squared differences across a set of variables. Letting m = the number of variables and X_{ij} be the value of the jth variables for the ith case, the squared Euclidean distance between cases k and l is

$$D_{kl}^2 = \sum_{j=1}^{m} (X_{kj} - X_{lj})^2$$

Eigen value : (also called characteristic roots)

The eigen value of a given factor is the variance in a set of variables explained by that factor or component and denoted by **Lambda.**

Equimax

It is an analytic factor rotation criterion which simplifies the rows and columns of a factor matrix.

Factor Loading

This term is used to refer to factor pattern coefficients or structure coefficients.

Factor Matrix

This is a matrix of pattern or structure coefficients in which the factors are presented as columns and the variables are presented as rows.

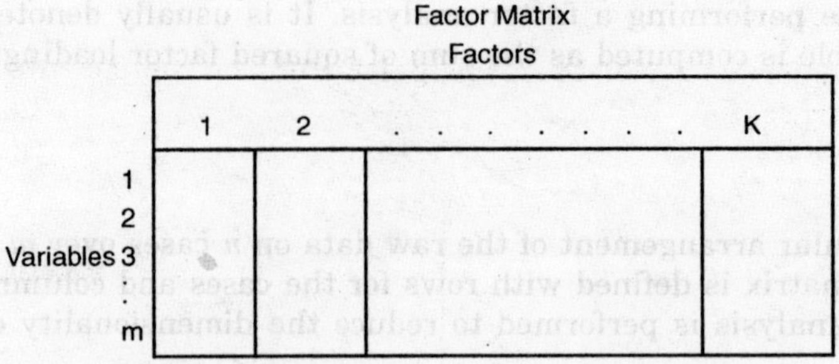

Factor Pattern Coefficients

These are regression coefficients which multiply with factors to produce measured variables according to the common factor model.

Factor Scores

These are linear combinations of variables which are used to estimate the case's scores on the factors or components. Least square estimates of factor scores are the most commonly used.

Factor Structure Coefficient

This is Pearson's correlation between a variable and a factor.

Latent Variable

This is a theoretical variable hypothesized to influence a number of observed variables. Common factor analysis assumes latent variables are linearly related to observed variables. Factors are sometimes construed to be estimates of latent variables.

Loading

This is the correlation between a variable and a factor.

Main Diagonals

These refer to elements in a square matrix ranging from the upper left to the lower left corners of the matrix.

Communality estimates are inserted in the main diagonal of a correlation matrix when performing a factor analysis. When performing a principal component analysis the maindiagonal elements of the correlation matrix will be 1's.

Oblique factors. Correlated factors

Orthogonal decomposition of variables. This results in transforming a set of correlated variables into a set of uncorrelated variables.

Orthogonal factors. Uncorrelated factors.

Q-factor analysis. Factoring the intercase correlation matrix.

R-factor analysis. Factoring the intervariable correlation matrix. This is the most common form of factor analysis.

Rotation of factors

This is a transformation of the principal factors or components in order to approximate simple structure.

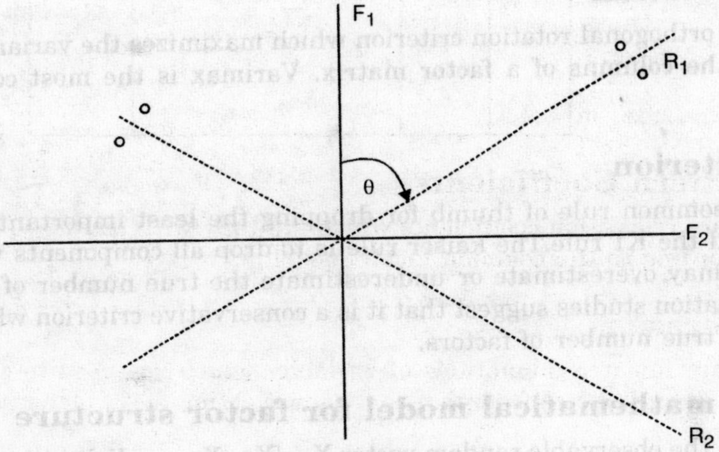

Fig. 15.5

Specific factor. A factor on which only one variable loads.

Specific variance. The component of unique variance which is reliable but **not** explained by common factors.

Quartimax rotation. An othogonal rotational criterion which maximizes the variance of the rows of a factor matrix.

Scree test. It is a graphic method for determining the number of factors. The eigen values are plotted in the sequence of the principal factors. The number of factors is chosen where the plot levels off to a linear decreasing pattern.

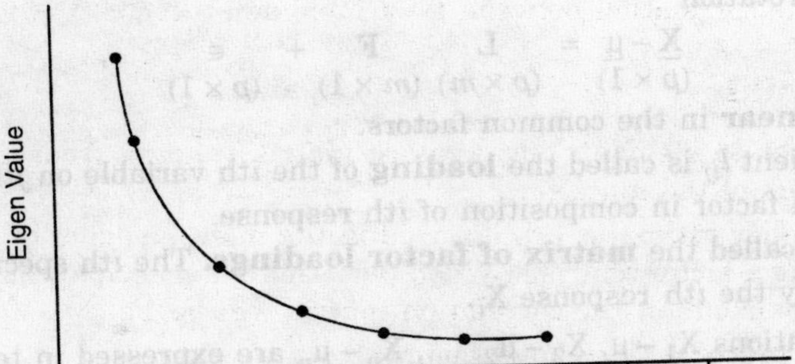

Fig. 15.6 Scree Plot.

Trace. The sum of the main diagonal elements of a square matrix.

Unique Variance. It is the variance of a variable which is not explained by common factors. Unique variance is composed of specific and error variance.

Uniqueness

The uniqueness of a variable is the proportion of a variable's variance that is **not** shared with a factor structure and is given by $1 - h^2$.

Varimax rotation

It is an orthogonal rotation criterion which maximizes the variance of the squared elements in the columns of a factor matrix. Varimax is the most common rotational criterion.

Kaiser Criterion

It is a common rule of thumb for dropping the least important factors from the analysis called the K1 rule.The kaiser rule is to drop all components with eigen values under 1.0. It may overestimate or underestimate the true number of factors; evidence through simulation studies suggest that it is a conservative criterion which usually overestimates the true number of factors.

15.7.3 The mathematical model for factor structure

Suppose the observable random vector $\underline{X} = [X_1, X_2, \ldots X_p]'$ with p components has mean $\underline{\mu}$ and covariance matrix Σ. Assume $\underline{X}$ to have p-variate normal distribution. Further, the components of $\underline{X}$ are linearly dependent upon a few unobservable random variables $F_1, F_2, \ldots, F_m$, called **common factors** and p additional sources of variation $\epsilon_1 \epsilon_2, \ldots \epsilon_p$ called errors, or sometimes, **specific factors.**

In factor analysis **model** is

$$X_1 - \mu_1 = l_{11} F_1 + l_{12} F_2 + \ldots + l_{1m} F_m + \epsilon_1$$
$$X_2 - \mu_2 = l_{21} F_1 + l_{22} F_2 + \ldots + l_{2m} F_m + \epsilon_2$$
$$\ldots\ldots\ldots\ldots\ldots\ldots\ldots\ldots\ldots\ldots\ldots\ldots$$
$$X_p - \mu_p = l_{p1} F_1 + l_{p2} F_2 + \ldots + l_{pm} F_m + \epsilon_p$$

In matrix rotation

$$\underset{(p \times 1)}{\underline{X} - \underline{\mu}} = \underset{(p \times m)}{L} \; \underset{(m \times 1)}{F} + \underset{(p \times 1)}{\epsilon},$$

which is **linear** in the common factors.

The coefficient l_{ij} is called the **loading** of the ith variable on jth factor, reflecting importance of jth factor in composition of ith response.

Thus, $\underline{L}$ is called the **matrix of factor loadings.** The ith specific factor ϵ_i is associated with only the ith response X_i.

The p-deviations $X_1 - \mu, X_2 - \mu_2, \ldots, X_p - \mu_p$ are expressed in terms of $p + m$ random variables $F_1, F_2, \ldots, F_m; \epsilon_1, \epsilon_2, \ldots, \epsilon_p$, which are **unobservable.**

The factor model is distinguished from the regression model in the sense that in the **regression model** $F_1, F_2, \ldots, F_m$ are **observable independent variables.**

In the presence of this number of unobservable quantities direct verification of factor model becomes almost impossible. This necessitates some additional assumptions about the random vectors $\underline{F}$ and $\underline{\epsilon}$ as to certain covariance relationships.

Assumptions

$$E(\underline{F}) = \underline{O};\ \text{Cov}(\underline{F}) = E(\underline{F}\,\underline{F}') = I$$
$$E(\underline{\epsilon}) = \underline{O};$$

$$\text{Cov}(\underline{\epsilon}) = E(\underline{\epsilon}\,\underline{\epsilon}') = \underline{\psi}_{(p\times p)} = \begin{bmatrix} \psi_1 & 0 \ldots\ldots\ldots 0 \\ 0 & \psi_2 \ldots\ldots 0 \\ \ldots\ldots\ldots\ldots & \\ \ldots\ldots\ldots\ldots & \\ 0 & 0 \ldots\ldots \psi_p \end{bmatrix}$$

Further $\underline{F}$ and $\underline{\epsilon}$ are independent so $\text{Cov}(\underline{\epsilon}\,\underline{F}) = E(\underline{\epsilon}\,\underline{F}') = \underline{O}_{(p\times m)}$

The model along with the assumptions constitute the **orthogonal factor model**.

15.7.4 Covariance structure for the Orthogonal Factor Model

The orthogonal factor model simplies a covariance structure for $\underline{X}$.

Thus $\quad \underline{\Sigma} = \text{Cov}(\underline{X}) = E(\underline{X} - \underline{\mu})(X - \mu)'$
$= \underline{L}\,\underline{L}' + \underline{\psi}$

Therefore, $\quad \text{Var}(X_i) = l_{i1}^2 + \ldots + l_{1m}^2 + \psi_i$

$\text{Cov}(X_i, X_k) = l_{i1}\,l_{k1} + \ldots + l_{im}\,l_{km}$

Further, $\text{Cov}(\underline{X}, \underline{F}) = \underline{L}$

or, $\text{Cov}(X_i, F_j) = l_{ij}$

The portion of the variance of the ith variable X_i $\text{Var}(X_i) = \sigma_{ii}$ due to m common factors is called the ith **communality** and due to specific factor is often called **uniqueness** or specific **variance**.

Thus,

$$\text{Var}(X_i) = \sigma_{ii}$$
$$= (l_{i1}^2 + l_{i2}^2 + \ldots + l_{im}^2) + \psi_i$$
$$= \text{Communality} + \text{specific variance}$$

Denoting $\quad h_i^2 = l_{i1}^2 + l_{i2}^2 + \ldots. + l_{im}^2,$

we have $\quad \sigma_{ii} = h_i^2 + \psi_i \ (i = 1, 2, \ldots, p)$

The ith communality is the sum of squares of the loadings of the ith variable on the m common factors.

15.7.5 Method of estimation

Given observations $\underline{x}_1, \underline{x}_2, \ldots \underline{x}_n$ on p correlated variables, factor analysis answers the question whether the model with small number of factors adequately represent the data and in a sense verifies the **covariance relationship.**

The sample covariance matrix $\underline{S}$ is an estimater of population covariance matrix $\underline{\Sigma}$.

If the population matrix $\underline{\Sigma}$ significantly deviates from a diagonal matrix, the factor analysis problem gets significance. The problem then boils down to estimating the factor loadings l_{ij} and specific variances ψ_i. A number of methods of estimation such as principal component (and the related principal factor) method, maximum likelihood method, etc. are available for the purpose. Thus, the solutions can be obtained by one of these methods and can be rotated to simplify the interpretation of factors. In the following section we shall consider the **principal component method** for the factor analysis.

Thus in practice, the number of common factor to be retained in the model is to be increased until a sizeable proportion of total sample variance has been explained. If we deal with factor analysis of $\underline{R}$, it is a usual practice to set m equal to number to eigen values of $\underline{R}$ greater than unity.

Alternatively, we may set m equal to the number of positive eigen values of $\underline{S}$, if the sample covariance matrix is to be factored. However, the best approach would be to retain fewer factors to facilitate satisfactory interpretation of data, thereby providing satisfactory fit to $\underline{S}$ or $\underline{R}$. Some popular criteria for determining the number of factors are :

- **Kaiser Criterian.** The Kaiser rule is to drop all components with eigen values of the correlation matrix under 1.0.
- **Scree plot.** The Cattell scree test plots the components as the X-axis and the corresponding correlation matrix eigen values in descending order as the Y-axis. As one moves to the right, toward later components, the eigen values drop. When the drop ceases and the curve makes an elbow toward less steep decline, Cattll's scree test says to drop all further components after the one starting the elbow. Thus, we use a number of factors equal to the number of eigen values that occur prior to the last major drop in eigen value magnitude.

15.7.6 Rotation methods

Rotation serves to make the output more understandable and is usually necessary to facilitate the interpretation of factors. The sum of eigen values is not affected by rotation, but rotation will alter the eigen values (and percent of variance explained) of particular factors and will change the factor loadings. Since alternative rotations may explain the same variance (have the same total eigen value) but have different factor loadings, and since factor loadings are used to intuit the meaning of factors, this means that different meanings may be ascribed to the factors depending on the rotation–a problem which is sometimes regarded as a drawback of factor analysis.

The researcher may wish to experiment with alternative rotation methods to see which leads to the most interpretable factor structure.

For any given set of correlations and number of factors, there are actually an infinite number of ways that you can define your factors and still account for the same amount of covariance in your measure. Some may be easier to interpret and others not so easier. By rotating factors one attempts to find a factor solution that is equal to that obtained in the initial extraction but which has the simplest interpretation.

There are many different types of rotation categorized into orthogonal rotations, which produce uncorrelated factors and oblique rotations, which produce correlated factors. The best orthogonal rotation is widely believed to be **varimax.**

No rotation comes out as default in SPSS computer package. But it is a good idea to select a rotation method, usually **varimax.** The original, unrotated principal components solution maximizes the sum of squared factor loadings, efficiently creating a set of factors which explain as much of the variance in the original variables as possible.

The amount explained is reflected in the sum of the eigen values of all factors. However **unrotated solutions are hard to interpret because variables tend to load on multiple factors.**

Varimax rotation is an orthogonal rotation of the factor axes to maximize the variance of the squared loadings of a factor (column) on all the variables (rows) in a factor matrix, which has the effect of differentiating the original variables by extracted factor. Each factor will tend to have either large or small loadings of any particular variable. A varimax solution yields results which make it as easy as possible to identify each variable with a single factor. This is the **most common rotation option.**

Quartimax rotation is an orthogonal alternative which minimizes the number of factors needed to explain each variable. This type of rotation often generates a general factor on which most variables are loaded to a high or medium degree. Such a factor structure is usually **not helpful to the research purpose.**

Equimax rotation is a compromise between **Varimax** and **Quartimax** criteria.

The orthogonal rotation criterion maximizes the variance of the rows of a **factor matrix**.

Graphical illustration of factor rotation

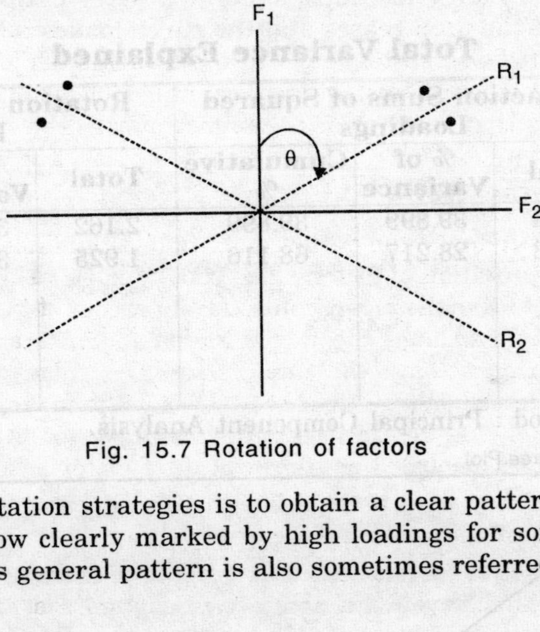

Fig. 15.7 Rotation of factors

The goal of all rotation strategies is to obtain a clear pattern of loadings, that is, factors that are somehow clearly marked by high loadings for some variables and low loadings for others. This general pattern is also sometimes referred to as **simple structure**.

Interpretation of factor structure

Each of the variables (measures) will be linearly related to each of the factors. The strength of relationship is contained in the respective **factor loading**, produced by rotation. This loading can be interpreted as a standardized regression coefficient, regressing the factor on the variables.

Thus, we define a factor by considering the **possible theoretical constructs** that could be responsible for the observed pattern of positive and negative loadings. To ease interpretation we may have the option of multiplying all of the loadings for a given factor –1. This essentially reverses the scale of the factor, allowing, for example, to turn an 'unfriendliness' factor into a 'friendliness' factor.

X_4	1.000	.693
X_5	1.000	.401
X_6	1.000	.802

Extraction Method : Principal Component Analysis.

Total Variance Explained

Component	Initial Eigen values		
	Total	% of Variance	Cumulative %
1	2.394	39.899	39.899
2	1.693	28.217	68.116
3	.930	15.493	83.609
4	.577	9.614	93.224
5	.267	4.453	97.677
6	.139	2.323	100.000

Extraction Method : Principal Component Analysis.

Total Variance Explained

Component	Extraction Sums of Squared Loadings			Rotation Sums of Squared Loadings		
	Total	% of Variance	Cumulative %	Total	% of Variance	Cumulative %
1	2.394	39.899	39.899	2.162	36.030	36.030
2	1.693	28.217	68.116	1.925	32.086	68.116
3						
4						
5						
6						

Extraction Method : Principal Component Analysis.

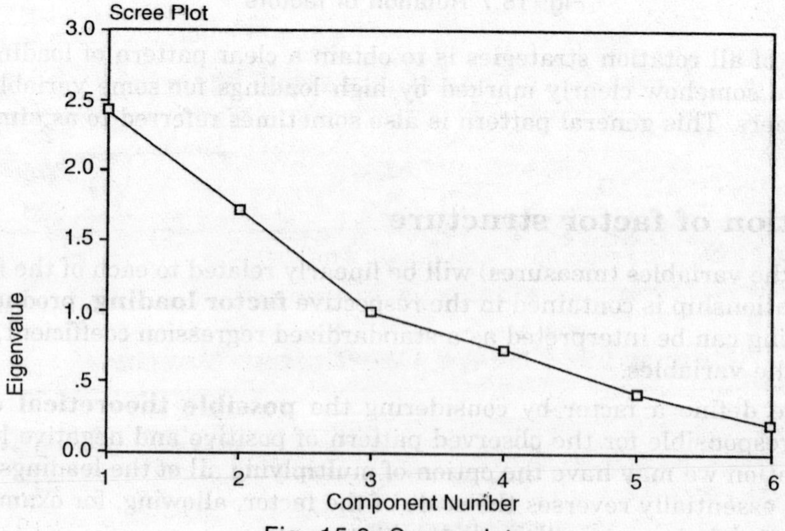

Fig. 15.9. Scree plot.

Component Matrix[a]

	Component	
	1	2
X_1	.733	-.329
X_2	.944	-.1515E-02
X_3	.595	.550
X_4	.596	-.581
X_5	.500	.388
X_6	8.992E-02	.891

Extraction Method : Principal Component Analysis.

(*a*) 2 components extracted.

Rotated Component Matrix[a]

	Component	
	1	2
X_1	.788	.153
X_2	.780	.531
X_3	.170	.792
X_4	.822	-.132
X_5	.185	.605
X_6	-.439	.780

Extraction Method : Principal Component Analysis.

Rotation Method : Varimax with Kaiser Normalization.

(*a*) Rotation converged in 3 iterations.

Component Transformation Matrix

Component	1	2
1	.818	.575
2	.-575	.818

Extraction Method : Principal Component Analysis.

Rotation Method : Varimax with Kaiser Normalization.

Component Score Coefficient Matrix

	Component	
	1	2
X_1	.362	.017
X_2	.327	.219
X_3	.016	.409

3	.930	15.493	83.609	1.278	21.307	83.609
4						
5						
6						

Extraction Method : Principal Component Analysis.

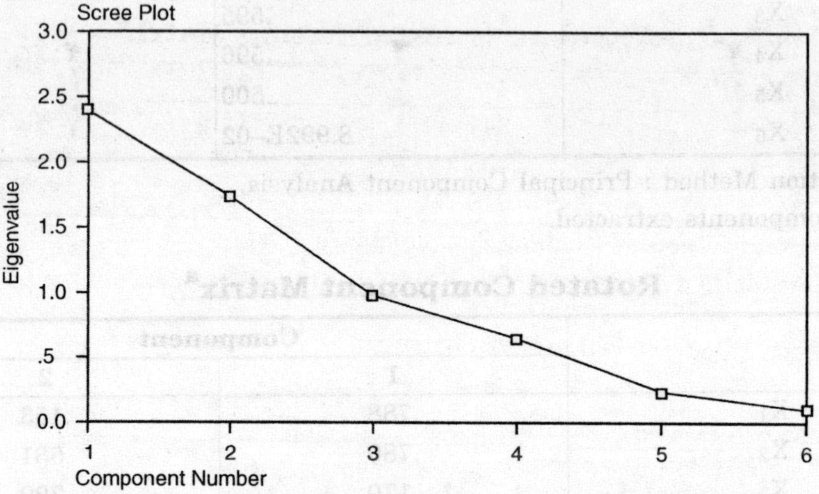

Fig. 15.11

Component Matrix[3]

	Component		
	1	2	3
X1	.733	−.329	−.373
X2	.944	−1.51E−02	.147
X3	.595	.550	−.490
X4	.596	−.581	.127
X5	.500	.388	.713
X6	8.992E−02	.891	−6.002E−02

Extraction Method : Principal Component Analysis.
(*a*) 3 components extracted.

Rotated Component Matrix[a]

	Component		
	1	2	3
X1	.861	.172	−.118
X2	.769	.237	.515
X3	.335	.885	2.673E−02

X4	.761	–.324	.159
X5	7.178E–02	.127	.942
X6	–.352	.772	.293

Extraction Method : Principal Component Analysis.

Rotation Method : Varimax with Kaiser Normalization.

(*a*) Rotation converged in 5 iterations.

Component Transformation Matrix

Component	1	2	3
1	.841	.341	.421
2	–.495	.798	.343
3	–.219	–.496	.840

Extraction Method : Principal Component Analysis.

Rotation Method : Varimax with Kaiser Normalization.

Component Plot in Rotated Space

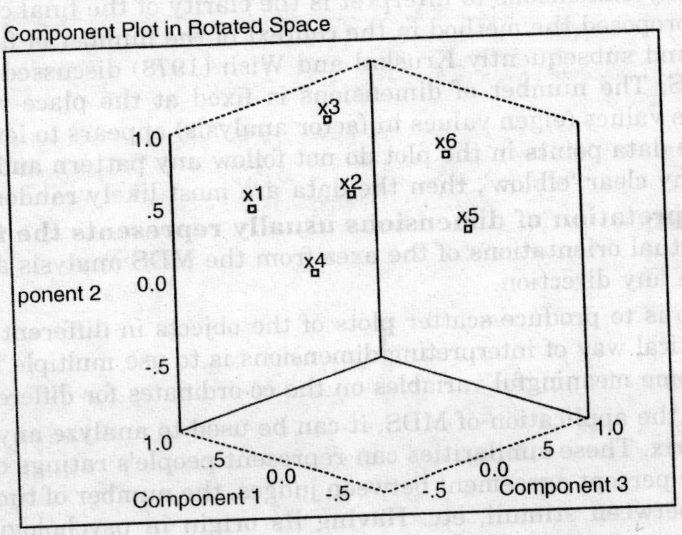

Fig. 15.12

Component Score Coefficient Matrix

	Component		
	1	2	3
X1	.442	.149	–.275
X2	.301	.049	.295
X3	.164	.606	–.227

putation of the sum of squared deviations of the observed distances (or some monotone transformation of those distances) from the reproduced distances. Thus, smaller the stress value, the better is the fit of the reproduced distance matrix to the observed distance matrix.

Kruskal suggests the stress be informally interpreted according to following guidelines :

TABLE 15.9

Stress	Goodness-of-fit
0.20	Poor
0.10	Fair
0.05	Good
.02%	Excellent
0%	Perfect

Goodness of fit refers to the monotone relationship between the similarities and final distancės.

A common way to decide how many dimensions to use is to plot the stress value against different numbers of dimensions. This is called 'scree test'. A second criterion for deciding how many dimensions to interpret is the clarity of the final configuration. Cattell (1966) first proposed the method in the context of the number of factors problems in factor analysis and subsequently Kruskal and Wish (1978) discussed its application of this plot to MDS. The number of dimensions is fixed at the place where the smooth decrease of stress values (eigen values in factor analysis) appears to level off to the right of the plot. If the data points in the plot do not follow any pattern and if the stress plot does not show any clear 'elblow', then the data are most likely random 'noise'.

The interpretation of dimensions usually represents the final step of the analysis. The actual orientations of the axes from the MDS analysis are arbitrary, and can be rotated in any direction.

A first step is to produce scatter plots of the objects in different two dimensional planes. An analytical way of interpreting dimensions is to use multiple regression techniques to regress some meaningful variables on the co-ordinates for different dimensions.

As regards the application of MDS, it can be used to analyze any kind of distance or similarity matrix. These similarities can represent people's ratings of similarities between objects, the percent agreement between judges, the number of times a subject fails to discriminate between stimuli, etc. Having its origin in psychological research the MDS has become popular in marketing research, in order to detect the number and nature of dimensions underlying the perceptions of different brands or products. In general MDS methods allow to ask relatively unobtrusive questions ("how similar is brand A to brand B") and is derive from those questions underlying dimensions without the respondents ever knowing what is the researcher's real interest.

The scatter plot showing the plotting of the reproduced distances for a particular number of dimensions against the observed input data (distances) is referred to as a **'Sheppard diagram".** This plot shows the reproduced distances plotted on the vertical (Y) axis versus the original similarities plotted on the horizontal (X) axis (hence, the generally negative slope). This plot also shows the step function. This line represents the so called **D-hat values,** that is the result of the montone transformation $f(\delta_{ij})$ of the

The Principal Component Method

Let the coveriance structure $\underline{\Sigma}$ be factored into eigen value–eigen vector pairs $(\underline{X}_i, \underline{e}_i)$ with $\lambda_1 \geq \lambda_2 \geq \ldots \geq \lambda_p \geq 0$.

Then $$\underline{\Sigma} = \lambda_1 \underline{e}_1 \underline{e}'_1 + \lambda_2 \underline{e}_2 \underline{e}'_2 + \ldots + \lambda_p \underline{e}_p \underline{e}'_p.$$

This simplified and exact structure for the factor analysis model is available if number of factors (m) is equal to number of variables (p).

The specific variance $\psi_i = 0$, for all i

Thus,we can write,

$$\Sigma_{(p \times p)} = \underline{L}_{(p \times p)} \underline{L}'_{(p \times p)} + \underline{O}_{p \times p}$$
$$= \underline{L}\,\underline{L}'$$

Such exact representation of $\underline{\Sigma}$ is not particularly useful because it deals with as many factors as there are variables and does not allow variations in specific factor $\underline{\in}$.

The factor analysis becomes complicated when we are required to explain the covariance structure with smaller number of common factors. One approach through the Principal Component Analysis is to neglect contribution of smaller eigen values and approximate the covariance matrix.

$$\underline{\Sigma} \cong [\sqrt{\lambda_1}\ \underline{e}_1 \vdots \sqrt{\lambda_2}\ \underline{e}_2 \vdots \ldots \vdots \sqrt{\lambda_m}\ \underline{e}_m] \begin{bmatrix} \sqrt{\lambda_1}\ \underline{e}_1 \\ \cdots\cdots \\ \sqrt{\lambda_2}\ \underline{e}_2 \\ \cdots\cdots \\ \sqrt{\lambda_m}\ \underline{e}_m \end{bmatrix}$$

$$= \underline{L}_{(p \times m)}\ \underline{L}'_{(m \times p)}$$

This approximation assumes that the specific factors are $\underline{\in}$ of minor importance. If specific factor is included in the model, their variances may be denoted by diagonal elements in $\Sigma - \underline{L}\,\underline{L}'$ and thus the $\underline{\Sigma}$ is approximated as

$$\underline{\Sigma} \cong \underline{L}\,\underline{L}' + \underline{\psi},$$

with $$\psi_i = \sigma_{ii} - \sum_{j=1}^{m} l_{ij}^2$$

The foregoing discussion when applied to sample covariance matrix $S = [s_{ij}]$ with centred observations

$$\underline{x}_j - \underline{\bar{x}} = \begin{bmatrix} x_{1j} \\ x_{2j} \\ \vdots \\ x_{pj} \end{bmatrix} - \begin{bmatrix} \bar{x}_1 \\ \bar{x}_2 \\ \vdots \\ \bar{x}_p \end{bmatrix} = \begin{bmatrix} x_{1j} - \bar{x}_1 \\ x_{2j} - \bar{x}_2 \\ \vdots \\ x_{pj} - \bar{x}_p \end{bmatrix}, j = 1, 2, \ldots, n \text{ is given by}$$

$$S = \left(\frac{1}{n-1}\right) \begin{bmatrix} \Sigma (x_{1j} - \bar{x}_1)^2 & \Sigma (x_{ij} - \bar{x}_1)(x_{2j} - \bar{x}_2) & \Sigma (x_{1j} - \bar{x}_1)(x_{pj} - x_p) \\ \Sigma (x_{1j} - \bar{x}_1)(x_{2j} - \bar{x}_2) & \Sigma (x_{2j} - \bar{x}_2)^2 & \Sigma (x_{2j} - \bar{x}_2)(x_{pj} - \bar{x}_p) \\ \cdots\cdots & \cdots\cdots & \cdots\cdots \\ \Sigma (x_{1j} - \bar{x}_1)(x_{pj} - \bar{x}_p) & \Sigma (x_{2j} - \bar{x}_2)(\bar{x}_{pj} - \bar{x}_p) & \Sigma (x_{pj} - \bar{x}_p)^2 \end{bmatrix}$$

In case we like to work with standardized variables

$$z_j = \begin{bmatrix} \dfrac{x_{1j}-\bar{x}_1}{\sqrt{s_{11}}} \\ \dfrac{x_{2j}-\bar{x}_2}{\sqrt{s_{22}}} \\ \vdots \\ \dfrac{x_{pj}-\bar{x}_p}{\sqrt{s_{pp}}} \end{bmatrix}, \text{ where } s_{ii} = \frac{1}{n-1}\sum_{j=1}^{n}(x_{ij}-\bar{x}_i)^2, j = 1, 2, \ldots, n$$

the sample covariance matrix $\underline{S}$ is the sample correlation matrix $\underline{R}$.

The estimates of eigen value-eigen vector pairs are given by $(\hat{\lambda}_1\ \hat{\underline{e}}_1)$, $(\hat{\lambda}_2\ \hat{\underline{e}}_2)$, …., $(\hat{\lambda}_p\ \hat{\underline{e}}_p)$ where $\hat{\lambda}_1 \geq \hat{\lambda}_2 \geq \ldots \hat{\lambda}_p$.

Let $m < p$ be the number of common factors. The matrix of estimated factor leadings $\{\hat{l}_{ij}\}$ is given by

$$\hat{\underline{L}} = \left[\sqrt{\hat{\lambda}_1}\,\hat{\underline{e}}_1 \vdots \sqrt{\hat{\lambda}_2}\,\hat{\underline{e}}_2 \vdots \ldots \vdots \sqrt{\hat{\lambda}_m}\,\hat{\underline{e}}_m\right]$$

The estimated specific variances are provided by the diagonal elements of the matrix $\underline{S} - \hat{\underline{L}}\,\hat{\underline{L}}'$, so

$$\hat{\underline{\Psi}} = \begin{bmatrix} \hat{\Psi}_1 & 0 \ldots\ldots & \ldots 0 \\ 0 & \hat{\Psi}_2 \ldots\ldots & \ldots 0 \\ \ldots\ldots & \ldots\ldots & \ldots \\ \ldots\ldots & \ldots\ldots & \ldots \\ 0 & 0 \ldots\ldots & \hat{\Psi}_p \end{bmatrix}$$

Communalities are estimated as

$$\hat{h}_i^2 = \hat{l}_{i1}^2 + \hat{l}_{i2}^2 + \ldots + \hat{l}_{im}^2$$

The principal component factor analysis of the sample correlation matrix can also be carried out by using $\underline{R}$ in place of $\underline{S}$.

The contribution of the first few factors to the sample variance of the variables is expected to be large. Thus, the contribution to the sample variance s_{ii} from the first common factor is $\hat{l}_{i1}^2$. Hence the contribution to the total sample variance

$$s_{11} + s_{22} + \ldots + s_{pp} = t_r(\underline{S})$$

from the **first** common factor is then

$$\hat{l}_{11}^2 + \hat{l}_{21}^2 + \ldots + \hat{l}_{p1}^2 = (\sqrt{\hat{\lambda}_1}\,\hat{\underline{e}}_1)'\,(\sqrt{\hat{\lambda}_1}\,\hat{\underline{e}}_1),$$
$$= \hat{\lambda}_1,$$

since the eigen vector is $\hat{e}_1$ has unit length *i.e.* $\hat{e}_1'\,\hat{e}_1 = 1$.

In general, the proportion of total sample variance due to jth factor

$$= \frac{\hat{\lambda}_j}{s_{11} + s_{22} + \ldots + s_{pp}}, \text{ for a factor analysis of } \underline{S}$$

$$= \frac{\hat{\lambda}_j}{p}, \text{ for a factor analysis of } \underline{R}.$$

Construction of factor scores

If one needs to perform further additional analysis using the factors as variables, it is necessary to construct factor scores. The score for a given factor is a linear combination of all of the variables, weighted by the corresponding factor loadings. To make the factor scores idealized, we may assign a value of +1 to strongly positive loadings and –1 to strongly negative loadings and a value zero to intermediate loadings. These factor scores can then be used in analysis just like any other variable, remembering that they will be strongly collinear with the variables used to generate them.

Comparison of Factor Analysis with Principal Component Analysis

In factor analysis we are interested in making statements about the factors that are responsible for a set of observed responses, where as in principal component analysis we are interested in performing data reduction, that is the reduce to dimensionality of data (Fig. 15.8).

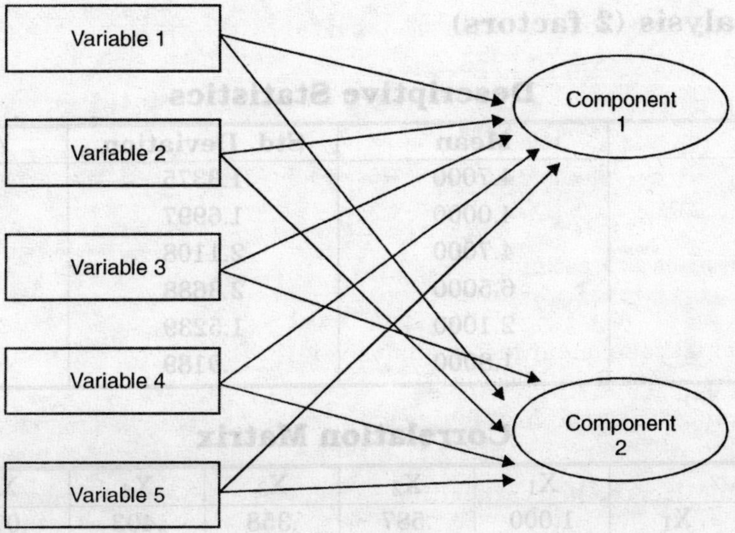

Fig. 15.8 The model for principal component analysis

Example 15.7. The market manager of a newly assembled car company designed a questionnaire to customers' feed back about the new car of six variables

X_1 : Fuel efficiency

X_2 : Life

X_3 : Handling convenience

X_4 : Quality of spares

X_5 : Breakdown rate

X_6 : Price

Respondents	X_1	X_2	X_3	X_4	X_5	X_6
1	7	7	8	9	1	2
2	4	4	6	8	2	1
3	6	2	5	5	1	2
4	3	3	6	2	3	3
5	4	3	5	5	2	2
6	4	4	6	7	2	3
7	3	3	1	8	1	2
8	6	7	5	9	6	2
9	5	3	2	8	1	0
10	5	4	3	4	2	1

The company administered a questionnaire among 10 customers to obtain their opinion on the above variables in the form of scores in the range 0–10. The score 0 means low rating and 10 means high rating.

Perform factor analysis using principal component method.

Factor Analysis (2 factors)

Descriptive Statistics

	Mean	Std. Deviation	Analysis N
X_1	4.7000	1.3375	10
X_2	4.0000	1.6997	10
X_3	4.7000	2.1108	10
X_4	6.5000	2.3688	10
X_5	2.1000	1.5239	10
X_6	1.8000	.9189	10

Correlation Matrix

		X_1	X_2	X_3	X_4	X_5	X_6
Correlation	X_1	1.000	.587	.358	.403	.071	–.235
	X_2	.587	1.000	.465	.580	.515	.071
	X_3	.358	.465	.1000	–.011	.183	.481
	X_4	.403	.580	–.011	1.000	.046	–.308
	X_5	.071	.515	.183	.046	1.000	.254
	X_6	–.235	.071	.481	–.306	.254	1.000

Communalities

	Initial	Extraction
X_1	1.000	.645
X_2	1.000	.890
X_3	1.000	.656

X_4	.401	–.137
X_5	.039	.308
X_6	–.272	.452

Extraction Method : Principal Component Analysis.
Rotation Method : Varimax with Kaiser Normalization.
Component Scores.

Component Score Covariance Matrix

Component	1	2
1	1.000	.000
2	.000	1.000

Extraction Method : Principal Component Analysis.
Rotation Method : Varimax with Kaiser Normalization.
Component Scores.

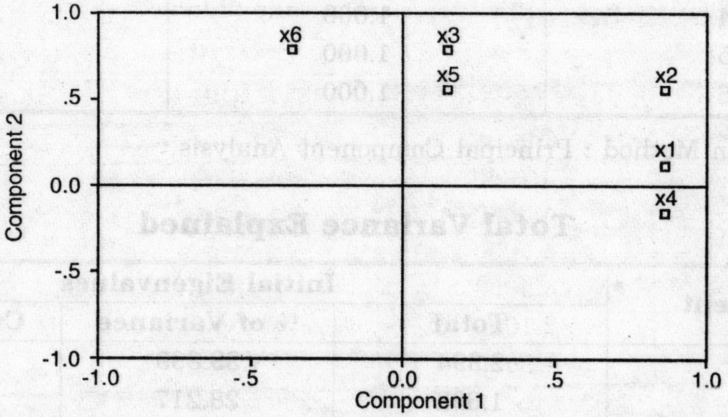

Fig. 15.10

Factor Analysis (3 factors)

Descriptive Statistics

	Mean	Std. Deviation	Analysis N
X1	4.7000	1.3375	10
X2	4.0000	1.6997	10
X3	4.7000	2.1108	10
X4	6.5000	2.3688	10
X5	2.1000	1.5239	10
X6	1.8000	.9189	10

Correlation Matrix

		X1	X2	X3	X4	X5	X6
Correlation	X1	1.000	.587	.358	.403	.071	–.235
	X2	.587	1.000	.465	.580	.515	.071
	X3	.358	.465	1.000	–.011	.183	.481
	X4	.403	.580	–.011	1.000	.046	–.306
	X5	.071	.515	.183	.046	1.000	.254
	X6	–.235	.071	.481	–.306	.254	1.000

Communalities

	Initial	Extraction
X1	1.000	.784
X2	1.000	.912
X3	1.000	.897
X4	1.000	.709
X5	1.000	.909
X6	1.000	.805

Extraction Method : Principal Component Analysis.

Total Variance Explained

Component	Initial Eigenvalues		
	Total	% of Variance	Cumulative %
1	2.394	39.899	39.899
2	1.693	28.217	68.116
3	.930	15.493	83.609
4	.577	9.614	93.224
5	.267	4.453	97.677
6	.139	2.323	100.000

Extraction Method : Principal Component Analysis.

Total Variance Explained

Component	Extraction Sums of SquaredLoadings			Rotation Sums of Squared Loadings		
	Total	% of Variance	Cumulative %	Total	% of Variance	Cumulative %
1	2.394	39.899	39.899	2.152	35.863	35.863
2	1.693	28.217	68.116	1.586	28.440	62.302

X4	.349	–.257	.102
X5	–.106	–.126	.811
X6	–.215	.465	.142

Extraction Method : Principal Component Analysis.

Rotation Method : Varimax with Kaiser Normalization.

Component Scores

Component Score Covariance Matrix

Component	1	2	3
1	1.000	.000	.00
2	.000	1.000	.000
3	.000	.000	1.000

Extraction Method : Principal Component Analysis.

Rotation Method : Varimax with Kaiser Normalization.

Component Scores.

Interpretation. The principal component method of extracting factors shows that three factor solution appears to be more justified in the sense that the third factor explains a significant amount of additional sample variation (15.493% unrotated/21.307% rotated).

The first factor appears to be longeivity factor dominated by X_1 (Fuel efficiency), X_2 (Life) and X_4 (Quality of spares). The second factor represents price (X_6) and handling convenience (X_3) variables, whereas the third factor represents breakdown variable (X_5).

15.8 Multidimensional Scaling

Multidimensional scaling (MDS) consists of multivariate techniques, used to **measure human perceptions and preferences towards some stimuli (objects)**, like products, organisations, places, events, brands and positioning them in a **perceptual space.** From a non-technical point of view, the purpose of multidimensional scaling is to provide a visual representation of the pattern proximities (similarities/distances) among a set of objects. For example, given a matrix of perceived similarities between various brands of, say, air freshness, MDS plots the brands on a map such that brands that are perceived to be similar are placed near each other on the map, and those brands that are perceived to be very different from each other are placed far away from each other on the map.

Multidimensional scaling (MDS) uncovers underlying dimensions based on a series of similarity or distance judgments by subjects. That is, MDS may be thought of as a way of representing subjective attributes in objective scales. A type of *perceptual mapping*, the central MDS output takes the form of a set of scatterplots ("perceptual maps") in which the axes are the underlying dimensions and the points are the products, candidates, opinions, or othes objects of comparison. The objective of MDS is to array points in multidimensional space such that the distances separating points physically on the scatterplot (s) reflect as closely as possible the subjective distances obtained by surveying subjects. That is, MDS shows graphically how different objects of comparison do or do not cluster.

The scale value of each stimulus may be either **metric or non- metric.** The metric data are interval scaled or ratio scaled where as non-metric data are ordinal scaled.

The metric scaling is akin to the principal components concept and non-metric scaling, which is more general, but requires an iterative algorithm for minimizing the objective function measuring the fit of the original and lower-dimensional spaces.

For a set of observed similarities (or distances) between every pair of N items, the problem is to find the representation of the items **in few dimensions** such that inter-item proximities 'nearly match' the original similarities (or distances).

The numerical measure of closeness is called the **stress.**

It is possible to arrange the N items in low dimensional co-ordinate system using only the rank orders of the N(N–1)/2 original similarities (distances) and not their magnitudes. When only this ordinal information is used to obtain a geometric representation, the process is called **nonmetric multidimensional scaling**. If the actual magnitude of the original similarities (distances) are used to obtain a geometric representation in q-dimensions ($q \leq N-1$), the process is called **metric multidimensional scaling.**

The goal of the analysis is **to detect meaningful underlying dimensions** that allow the researcher to explain observed similarities or dissimiarities (distances) between the investigated objects. In general the MDS attempts to arrange 'objects' in a space with a particular number of dimensions so as to reproduce the observed distances, thus explaining the distances in terms of underlying dimensions.

MDS is not so much an exact procedure as rather a way to 'rearrange objects in an efficient manner, so as to arrive at a configuration that best approximates the observed distances. It actually moves objects around in the space defined by the requested number of dimensions, and checks how well the distances between objects can be reproduced by the new configuration. In more technical terms, it uses a function minimization algorithm that evaluates different configurations with the goal of maximising the goodness-of-fit (or minimizing 'lack of fit').

The most common measure that is used to evaluate how well (or poorly) a particular configuration reproduces the observed distance matrix (measure of goodness-of-fit) is the computation of a **'stress'** measure. For instance, the stress value 'Phi' of configuration is defined by

$$\text{Phi} = \Sigma\,\Sigma\,(d_{ij} - f(\delta_{ij}))^2,$$

where d_{ij} stands for the reproduced distances, given the number of dimensions, and δ_{ij} stands for the input data (*i.e.* observed distances).

Next, we divide phi by a scale factor in order to measure the squared discrepanies relative to a sensible measuring stick. The scale factor most commonly used is $\Sigma\,\Sigma d_{ij}^2$. Kruskal, thus, provides the formula for measuring stress as

$$\text{Kruskal stress (Stress 1)} = \sqrt{\frac{\Sigma\,\Sigma\,(d_{ij} - f(\delta_{ij}))^2}{\text{scale factor}}}.$$

The expression $f(\delta_{ij})$ indicates a nonmetric, monotone transformation of the observed input data (distances). Thus, it will attempt to reproduce the general rank ordering of distances between the objects in the analysis.

A number of related measures are commonly used, but all of them result in com-input data. If all reproduced distances fall onto the step line, then the rank ordering of distances (or similarities) would be perfectly reproduced by the respective solution (dimensional model). Deviations from the step line indicate **lack of fit.**

The question arises as to the reasonable number of dimensions to specify. **The more dimensions we use to reproduce the distance matrix, the better is the fit of the reproduced matrix to the observed matrix** (*i.e.* **smaller is the stress**). In-fact, if we use as many dimensions as there are variables, then we can perfectly reproduce the observed distance matrix. Of Course, our goal is to **reduce** the observed complexity of nature, that is, to explain the distance matrix in **terms of fewer underlying dimensions.**

Normally, MDS is used to provide a visual representation of a complex set of relationships that can be scanned at a glance. Since maps on paper are two dimensional objects, this translates technically to finding an optimal configuration of points in 2–dimensional space. However, the best possible configuration in two dimensions may be very poor, highly distorted representation of your data. If so, this will be reflected in a high stress value. When this happens one have his choices : either the MDS as a method of representing data is abandoned or one can increase the number of dimensions.

Two difficulties may arise with increasing the number of dimensions. The first is that even 3–dimensions are difficult to display on paper and are significantly more difficult to comprehend. Four or more dimensions render MDS virtually useless as a method of making complex data more accessible to the human mind.

The second problem is that with increasing dimensions, one must estimate an increasing number of parameters to obtain a decreasing improvement in stress. The result is model of the data that is nearly as complex as the data itself.

Note

Objects and subjects : objects, also called variables or stimuli, are the products, candidates, opinions or other choices to be compared. Subjects are those doing the comparing. Sometimes, the subjects are termed the source and the objects are termed target.

15.8.1 Multidimensional scaling procedure

There are several steps in conducting MDS research :

1. Formulating the problem. What brands do you want to compare ? How many brands do you want to compare ? More than 20 is cumbersome. Less than 8 (4 pairs) will not give valid results. What purpose is the study to be used for ?

2. Obtaining Input Data. Respondents are asked a series of questions. For each product pair they are asked to rate similarity (usually on a 7 point Likert scale from very similar to very dissimilar). The number of questions is a function of the number of brands under comparison and can be calculated as $Q = N (N–1)/2$ where Q is the number of questions and N is the number of brands. This approach is referred to as the "Perception data : direct approach." There are two other approaches. There is the "Perception data : derived approach" in which products are decomposed into attributes which are rated on a semantic differential scale. The other is the "Preference data approach" in which respondents are asked their preference rather than similarity.

3. Running the MDS statistical program. Software for running the procedure is available in most of the better statistical applications programs. Often there is a choice between Metric MDS (which deals with interval or ratio level data), and Non-metric MDS (which deals with ordinal data). The researchers must decide on the number of dimensions they want the computer to create. The more dimensions, the better the statistical fit, but the more difficult it is to interpret the results.

4. Mapping the results and defining the dimensions. The statistical program (or a related module) will map the results. The map will plot each product (usually in two dimensional space). The proximity of products to each other indicate either how similar they are or how preferred they are, depending on which approach was used. The dimensions must be labelled by the researcher. This requires subjective judgement and is often very challenging. However, the results must be interpreted.

5. Test the results for reliability and Validity. Compute R-squared to determine what proportion of variance of the scaled data can be accounted for by the MDS procedure. An R-square of .6 is considered the minimum acceptable level. Other possible tests are Kruskal's Stress, split data tests, data stability tests (i.e. : eliminating one brand), and test-retest reliability.

15.8.2 Some applications of Multidimensional Scaling

Multidimensional scaling is a multivariate technique that takes a table of similarities (or distances) between objects and iteratively places points on a map so that it accurately represents the original similarity table.

Example I. Given a table of distances between a major cities (say) of the country, we may be required to draw a map which located these a cities on it as points in a way that fairly represents the relative distances in the table.

Example II. Suppose that a producer of under arm deodorants wants to know who the closest competitors might be. This knowledge could be helpful in determining how to spend the company's advertising money wisely.

The company might like to make a survey with a random sample of consumers and ask each consumer to rate each of the products on a number of criteria such as fragrance, ability to control wetness, ability to stop odour, ease of application, and lack of leaving residue on clothes.

Next compute the means for each of the brands of deodorants for each of these criteria and then calculate distance between all pairs of brand means. This will give a similarity matrix (in terms of distances between brand means) for the brands under consideration.

Given this table of distances between the brand means, the question arises as to drawing a two-dimensional map, which locates the brands on it as points in a way that fairly represents the relative distances in the similarity matrix.

The focus in MDS boils down to use similarity matrix to find a pair of values (dim 1, dim 2) for each object (brand of deodorant in this case) in such a way that the plotted pair of points on a map accurately represent the original similarity matrix. MDS procedure essentially helps obtain these pairs of points.

Example III. Suppose we are interested in understanding consumer's perceptions of six candy bars on the market. Instead of trying to gather information about consumer's evaluation of the candy bars on a number of attributes, the researcher will instead gather only perceptions of overall similarities or dissimilarities.

The data are gathered by first creating a set of 15 unique pairs of the six candy bars. Respondents are then asked to rank the following candy bar pairs, where rank of 1 is assigned to the pair of candy bars that is most similar and a rank of 15 indicates the pair which is least alike. The results for all pairs of candy bars for one respondent are shown below :

Candy Bar	A	B	C	D	E	F
A	—	2	13	4	3	8
B		—	12	6	5	7
C			—	9	10	11
D				—	1	14
E					—	15
F						—

The respondent's perceptions through rankings show that D and E are most similar than A and B, with E and F the least similar.

Example IV. To study the similarity between cars manufactured by different companies, an investigator collected information on 11 variables, Say, Make, Make model, Base price, Engine type, Engine HP, Top speed, Fuel consumption, etc. Suppose 30 manufacturers were selected and the car selected from each of the manufacturers was the manufacturer's most expensive one.

The measurements on 11 variables were used to compute the distance matrix (between car makes). The MDS procedure can be used to plot pair of points in a 2-dimensional space for easy visualization.

15.8.3 Analysis of Multidimensional Scaling using SPSS Package :

In SPSS, select Analyze, Scale, Multidimensional Scaling (ALSCAL) ; in the Multidimensional Scaling dialog box, enter the objects into the Variable list box (rows and columns will be the same objects, but enter the column headings) ; in the Distances box leave the default as "Square Matrix" (for other, press the Shape key) ; click the Model button and enter the level of measurement (ordinal, interval, or ratio), the conditionality (matrix, row, unconditional), the scaling model (Euclidean distance or individual differences Euclidean distance), and accept or change the default number of dimensions. Click continue and back in the Multidimensional Scaling dialog box, click the Options button and select the output options you want. Under Options you can also change the default stress values for convergence and choose whether to treat negative distances as missing values. Click Continue to exit Options. Click OK in the Multidimensional Scaling dialog to run the analysis.

For technical reasons, the ALSCAL algorithm is more efficient with dissimilarity/distance measures than with similarity/proximity measures. For this reason SPSS requires distance matrices, not similarity matrices. Cells in the matrix must indicate the degree of dissimilarity between pairs represented by the rows and columns of the matrix. If necessay, the researcher should convert similarity matrices into distance matrices before undertaking MDS analysis in SPSS.

SPSS OUTPUT (Example—I)

ALSCAL Procedure Options

Data Options :

Number of Rows (Observations/Matrix) 9

Number of Columns (Variables) 9

Number of Matrices	1
Measurement Level	Ratio
Data Matrix Shape	Symmetric
Type	Dissimilarity
Approach to Ties	Leave Tied
Conditionality	Matrix
Data Cutoff at	000000
Model Options :	
Model	Euclid
Maximum Dimensionality	2
Minimum Dimensionality	2
Negative Weights.....	Not Permitted
Output Options :	
Job Option Header	Printed
Data Matrices	Printed
Configurations and Transformations ...	Plotted
Output Dataset.....	Not Created
Initial Stimulus Coordinates	Computed
Algorithmic Options :	
Maximum Iterations ...	30
Convergence Criterion ...	.00100
Minimum S-stress ...	.00500
Missing Data Estimated by	Ulbounds

Raw (unscaled) Distance (Km) Data for 9 Indian Cities (Subject 1)

	1	2	3	4	5	6	7	8	9
1	.000								
2	1514.000	.000							
3	2453.000	1332.000	.000						
4	1430.000	1829.000	2202.000	.000					
5	334.000	1448.000	2603.000	1225.000	.000				
6	566.000	1220.000	1899.000	1063.000	704.000	.000			
7	1883.000	2006.000	1888.000	488.000	1678.000	1516.000	.000		
8	2019.000	886.000	446.000	1745.000	3157.000	1453.000	1142.000	.000	
9	1033.000	551.000	1854.000	1691.000	1367.000	739.000	2081.000	1408.000	.000

Note : 1. Bangalore 2. Ahmedabad 3. Amritsar 4. Bhubaneswar 5. Chennai 6. Hyderabad 7. Kolkata 8. New Delhi 9. Mumbai.

Iteration history for the 2 dimensional solution (in squared distances)

Young's S-stress formula 1 is used.

1	.24250	
2	.21277	.02973
3	.21211	.00066

Iterations stopped because S-stress improvement is less than .001000

Stress and squared correlation (RSQ) in distances

RSQ values are the proportion of variance of the scaled data (disparities) in the partition (row, matrix, or entire data) which is accounted for by their corresponding distances. Stress value are Kruskal's stress formula 1.

For matrix

Stress = .11492 RSQ = .91681

Configuration derived in 2 dimensions
Stimulus Coordinates Dimension

Stimulus Number	Stimulus Name	1	2
1	BANGALORE	1.2281	.4048
2	AHMEDABAD	-.4244	.9787
3	AMRITSAR	-1.9083	.1532
4	BHUBANESWAR	.4974	-1.1952
5	CHENNAI	1.7649	.0724
6	HYDERABAD	.5158	.1506
7	KOLKATA	-.1211	-1.5573
8	NEWDELHI	-1.7035	-.0433
9	MUMBAI	.1510	1.0362

Optimally scaled data (disparities) for subject 1

	1	2	3	4	5	6	7	8	9
1	.000								
2	1.937	.000							
3	3.138	1.704	.000						
4	1.829	2.340	2.817	.000					
5	.427	1.852	3.330	1.567	.000				
6	.724	1.561	2.429	1.360	.901	.000			
7	2.409	2.566	2.415	.624	2.146	1.939	.000		
8	2.583	1.133	.571	2.232	4.038	1.859	1.845	.000	
9	1.321	.705	2.372	2.163	1.749	.945	2.662	1.801	.000

Derived Stimulus Configuration

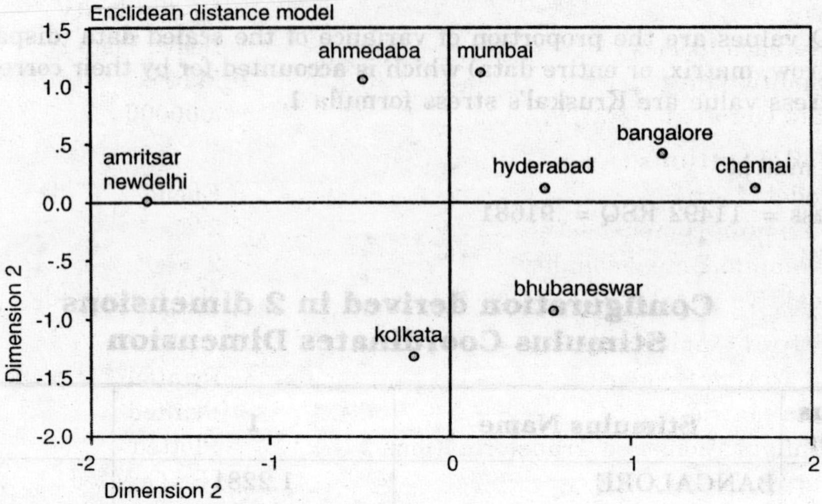

Fig. 15.13

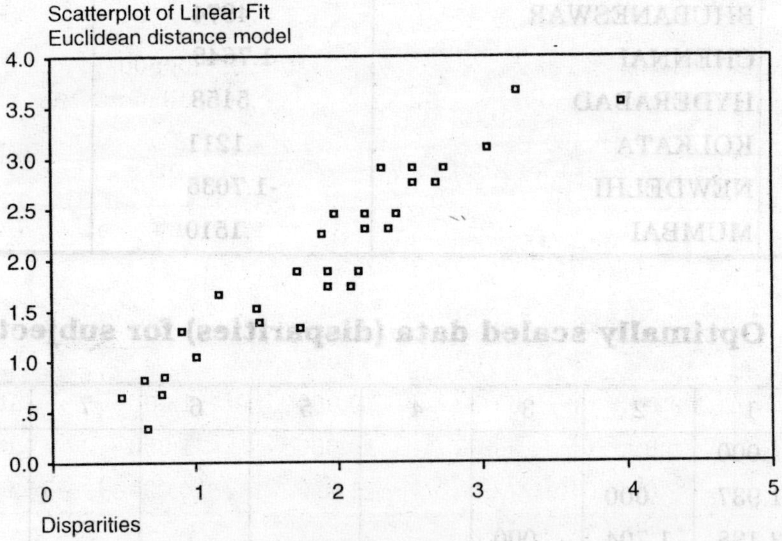

Fig. 15.14

SPSS OUTPUT (Example III)

ALSCAL Procedure Options

Data Options :

Number of Rows (Observations/Matrix)..	6
Number of Columns (Variables) ...	6
Number of Matrices	1

Measurement Level	Ordinal
Data Matrix Shape	Symmetric
Type	Dissimilarity
Approach to Ties	Leave Tied
Conditionality	Matrix
Data Cutoff at	.000000
Model Options :	
Model	Euclid
Maximum Dimensionality ...	2
Minimum Dimensionality ...	2
Negative Weights ...	Not Permitted
Output Options :	
Job Option Header	Printed
Data Matrices	Printed
Configurations and Transformations .	Plotted
Output Dataset	Not Created
Initial Stimulus Coordinates	Computed
Algorithmic Options :	
Maximum Iterations	30
Convergence Criterion	.00100
Minimum S-stress	.00500
Missing Data Estimated by	Ulbounds
Tiestore......	1.5

Raw (unscaled) Data for Subject 1

	1	2	3	4	5	6
1	.000					
2	2.000	.000				
3	13.000	12.000	.000			
4	4.000	6.000	9.000	1.000	.000	
5	3.000	5.000	10.000	1.000	.000	
6	8.000	7,000	11.000	14.000	15.000	.000

Number of parameters is 12. Number of data values is 15

Iteration history for the 2 dimensional solution (in squared distances)

Young's S-stress formula 1 is used,

Iteration	S-stress	Improvement
1	.00490	

Iterations stopped because S-stress is less than .005000

Stress and squared correlation (RSQ) in distances

RSQ values are the proportion of variance of the scaled data (disparities) in the partition (row, matrix, or entire data) which is accounted for by their corresponding distances. Stress values are Kruskal's stress formula 1.

For matrix

Stress = .00366, RSQ = .99992

Configuration derived in 2 dimensions
Stimulus Coordinates

Stimulus Number	Stimulus Name	Dimension	
		1	2
1	A	.2063	.9503
2	B	-.1189	.8071
3	C	-.4406	-1.8678
4	D	1.0589	-.2192
5	E	1.2549	-.0139
6	F	-1.9605	.3435

Optimally scaled data (disparities) for subject 1

	1	2	3	4	5	
1	.000					
2	.355	.000				
3	2.891	2.694	.000			
4	1.447	1.581	2.239	.000		
5	1.425	1.581	2.512	.284	.000	
6	2.239	1.899	2.683	3.071	3.235	.000

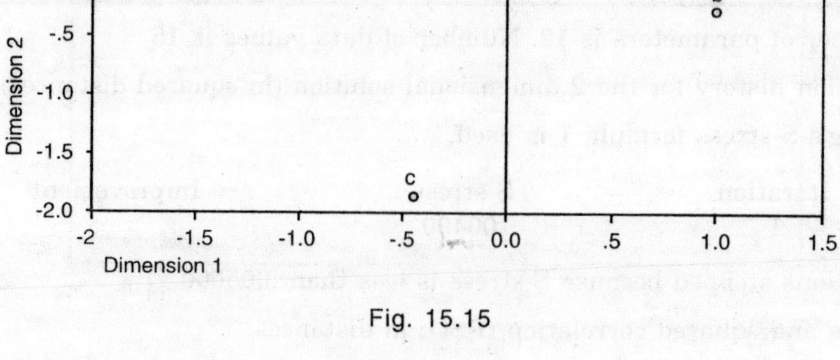

Fig. 15.15

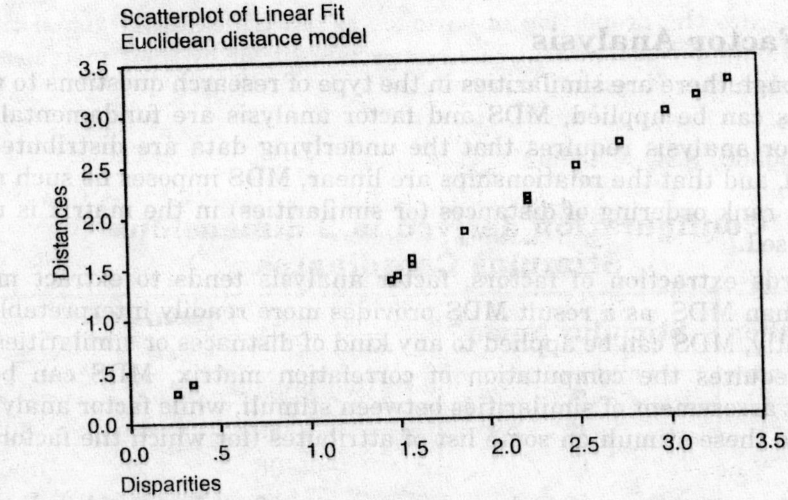

Fig. 15.16

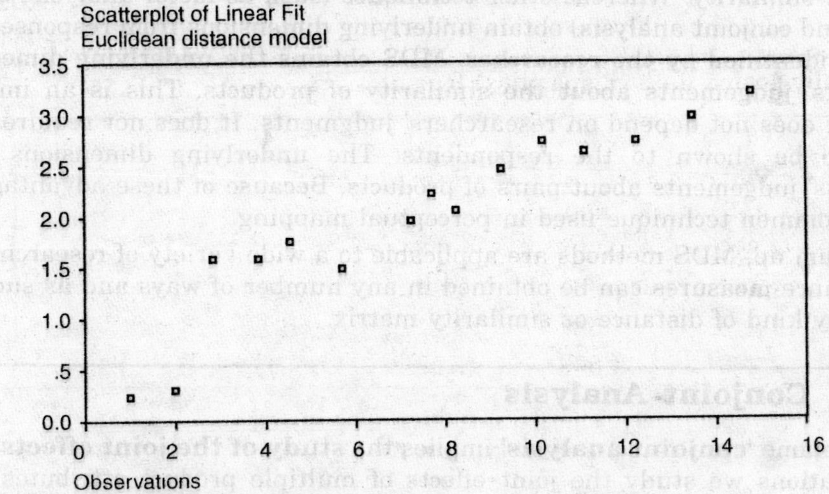

Fig. 15.17

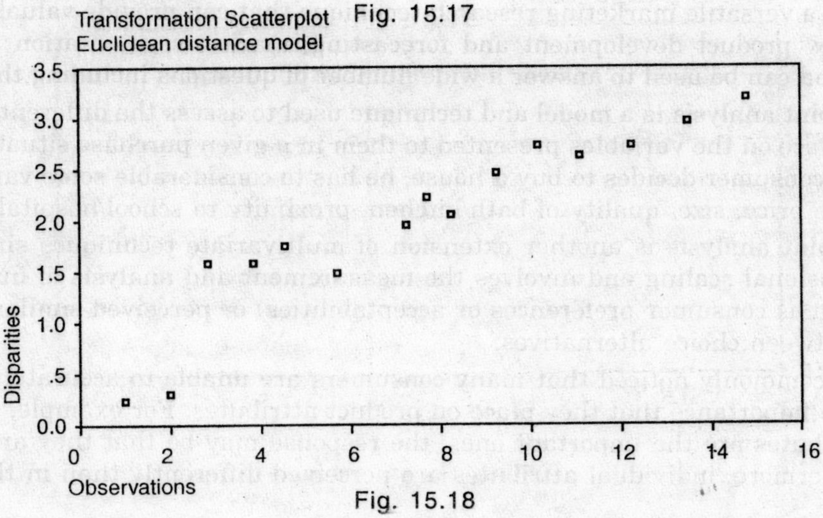

Fig. 15.18

MDS and Factor Analysis

Even though there are similarities in the type of research questions to which these two procedures can be applied, MDS and factor analysis are fundamentally different methods. Factor analysis requires that the underlying data are distributed as multivariate normal, and that the relationships are linear, MDS imposes no such restrictions. As long as the rank ordering of distances (or similarities) in the matrix is meaningful, MDS can be used.

As regards extraction of factors, factor analysis tends to extract more factors (dimensions) than MDS, as a result MDS provides more readily interpretable solutions. Most importantly, MDS can be applied to any kind of distnaces or similarities, while factor analysis requires the computation of correlation matrix. MDS can be based on subjects' direct assessment of similarities between stimuli, while factor analysis requires subjects to rate these stimuli on some list of attributes (for which the factor analysis is performed).

Potential customers are asked to compare pairs of products and make judgements about their similarity. Whereas other techniques (such as factor analysis, discriminant analysis, and conjoint analysis) obtain underlying dimensions from responses to product attributes identified by the researcher. MDS obtains the underlying dimensions from respondents' judgements about the similarity of products. This is an important advantage. It does not depend on researchers' judgments. It does not require a list of attributes to be shown to the respondents. The underlying dimensions come from respondents' judgements about pairs of products. Because of these advantages, MDS is the most common technique used in perceptual mapping.

To sum up, MDS methods are applicable to a wide variety of research designs because distance measures can be obtained in any number of ways and as such MDS can analyse any kind of distance or similarity matrix.

15.9 Conjoint Analysis

The name **'conjoint analysis'** implies the **study of the joint effects.** In marketing applications we study the joint effects of multiple product attributes on product choice. It is a versatile marketing research technique that can provide valuable information for new product development and forecasting, market segmentation and pricing decisions and can be used to answer a wide number of questions including the following.

Conjoint analysis is a model and technique used to assess the different weights individuals place on the variables presented to them in a given purchase situation. For example, if a consumer decides to buy a house, he has to considerable some variables such as purchase price, size, quality of bath/kitchen, proximity to school/hospital etc.

Conjoint analysis is another extension of multivariate techniques similar to the multidimensional scaling and involves the measurement and analysis of human judgements (such as consumer preferences or acceptabilities) or perceived similarities or differences between choice alternatives.

It is commonly noticed that many consumers are unable to accurately determine the relative importance that they place on product attributes. For example, when asked which attributes are the important ones, the response may be that they are all important. Furthermore, individual attributes are perceived differently than in the combinations found in a product. It is difficult for a survey respondent to take a list of attributes and mentally construct the preferred combinations of them. The task is easier if the respondent is presented with combinations of attributes that can be visualized as different product offerings. However, such a survey becomes impractical when there are several attributes that result in a very large number of possible combinations.

Under these circumstances conjoint analysis can facilitate the process. Conjoint analysis is a tool that allows a subset of the possible combinations of product features to be used to determine the relative importance of each feature in the purchasing decision. Conjoint analysis is based on the fact that the relative values of attributes considered jointly can better be measured than when considered in isolation.

In a conjoint analysis, the respondent may be asked to arrange a list of combinations of product attributes in decreasing order of preference. Once this ranking is obtained, a computer is used to find the utilities of different values of each attribute that would result in the respondent's order of preference. This method is efficient in the sense that the survey does not need to be conducted using every possible combination of attributes. The utilities can be determined using a subset of possible attribute combinations.

In management research the most common applications for conjoint analysis are found in market research and product development. Consumers buying a Personal Computer (PC) may evaluate a set of attributes to choose the product that best meets their needs- brands, speed, price, educational values, games, etc. The attributes and features require the buyer to make trade-offs in the final decision making.

Thus, by using conjoint analysis a company can determine the optimal features for their product or service. In addition, conjoint analysis will identify the best advertising message by identifying the features that are most important in product choice.

Conjoint analysis makes use of input from non-metric independent variables. Cross-classification tables help to handle such data. For instance, if there were three prices, three brands, three speeds, two levels of educational values, two categorisis of games we would have $3 \times 3 \times 3 \times 2 \times 2 = 108$ decision levels. A choicest combination to search poses enormous difficulties for the respondents as well as analysts.

The objective of conjoint analysis is to secure part-worths or **utility** scores that represent the importance of each aspect of a product or service in the subjects over all preference ratings. Utility scores are computed from subject's ranking's or ratings of a set of cards, each describing one possible configuration of combined product attributes.

15.9.1 Steps in Developing a Conjoint Analysis

Developing a conjoint analysis involves the following steps :

- Choose product attributes. This may require an explanatory study such as focus group, or it could be done by an expert with thorough market knowledge. The attributes selected are the independent variables, which are called **factors**.
- Choose the values or options for each attribute. The possible values for all attribute are called **factor levels**- different levels of speed factor in MHz for computers, price levels, different brands (measured as discrete variables) etc. The higher number of options/levels used for each attribute, the more burden that is placed on the respondents.

- Define products as a combination of attribute options. The set of combinations of attributes that will be used will be a subset of the possible universe of products.
- Choose the form in which the combinations of attributes are to be presented to the respondents. Options include verbal presentation, paragraph description, and pictorial presentation.
- Decide how responses will be aggregated. There are three choices, that is, use individual responses, pool all responses into a single utility function, or define segments of respondents who have similar preferences.
- Select the technique to be used to analyse the collected data. The part-worth model is one of the simpler models used to express the utilities of the various attributes. There are also vector (linear) models and ideal-point (quadratic) models.

Statistical software specially written for conjoint analysis are available.

Conjoint analysis was first used in early 1970's and has become an important marketing research tool. It is well suited for defining a new product or improving an existing one. It is an effective tool used by researchers to match preference to known characteristics of market segments and design or target a product accordingly.

15.9.2 Conducting Conjoint Analysis

At the outset the researcher must identify the attributes and attribute levels to be used in constructing the stimuli. Attribute levels denote the values assumed by the attributes. The attributes selected should be such that they should influence in a major way in influencing consumer preference and choice. For instance, in the choice of attributes to take purchase decision to buy an automobile, the attributes such as automobile brand, price, petrol mileage, interior space, etc. should be included. The attributes can be decided with the help of knowledgeable persons, experts, business managers, analysis of secondary data and pilot surveys.

Once the salient attributes have been identified, the next step is to take decision on the number of attribute levels, not necesary always equal. The utility or part-worth function for the levels of an attribute may be non-linear. In the previous example the loss of utility in going from low to medium price may be much smaller than the loss in ability in going from medium to a high price. In such cases, at least three levels of price should be used.

The attribute levels selected do affect the consumer evaluation and the researcher should take into account the attribute levels prevalent in the market place and the objectives of the study. The attribute levels should cover approximates the broad range of choice of the consumer.

The respondents/prospective consumers are presented with stimuli that consist of combinations of attribute levels. They are asked to evaluate these stimuli in terms of their desirability. Conjoint procedure rests in assigning values to each levels of each attribute so that the resulting values/utilities attacked to the stimuli, match, as closely as possible, the input evaluations provided by the respondents.

Like multidimensional scaling, conjoint analysis relies on respondents subjective evaluation. However, in MDS the stimuli are products or brands, but in conjoint analysis the stimuli are combination of attribute levels of the attributes determined by the researcher. In MDS the researcher aims at developing a spatial map depicting the stimuli in a multidimensional perceptual space, but in conjoint analysis the researcher seeks to develop the part worth or utility function which describes the utility consumers attach to the levels of each attribute. Two broad approaches are available for conjoint analysis.

- ❒ the pairwise approach
- ❒ the full-profile approach

In pairwise approach also called **two factor approach** the respondents compare and evaluate two attributes at a time for all possible combinations of levels of two attributes. These combinations can be depicted by a matrix. In the full-profile approach, also called **multiple factor evaluation,** full or complete profiles of combinations of attribute levels of all the attributes are constructed. The advantage of the pairewise approach is that it makes it easy for the respondents to provide judgements, but the disadvantage is that it requires more evaluations. Sometimes, the evaluation task may be unrealistic when two attributes are under comparison. In full profile approach the profiles of combinations may be very large and also may not be feasible. However, the number of stimulus profiles can be greatly reduced by means of **fractional factorial design.** Two sets of data may be obtained by using two orthogonal fractions. One, the **estimation set** is used to calculate the part-worth functions for the attribute levels and the other, the hold out set is used to assess the reliability and validity.

As in case of MDS data, the conjoint analysis can either use metric or non-metric data. For non-metric data the respondents are typically required to provide rank order evaluations. But in the metric form the respondents provide ratings, rather than rankings. Ratings are easier and more convenient for the respondents to analyze than rankings, as argued by their advocates. Proponents of ranking data believe that such data accurately reflect the behaviour of consumers in the market place. However, in recent years the rating method is increasingly used.

In conjoint analysis the dependent variable is usually preference or intention to buy, indicated by their ratings/rankings. The conjoint is more flexible in the sense that it can handle other dependent variables such as actual purchase or choice.

In evaluation of profiles the respondents may be asked to provide their preference using a nine point Likert scale i.e. 1 = not preferred, 9 = greatly preferred.

Conjoint Analysis Model

The basic conjoint analysis model may be represented by the formula

$$U(X) = \sum_{i=1}^{m} \sum_{j=1}^{k_i} \alpha_{ij} X_{ij},$$

where $U(X)$ = overall utility of an alternative

α_{ij} = the part worth contribution or utility associated with the jth level ($j = 1, 2, .., k_i$) of the ith attribute ($i = 1, 2, .., m$)

X_{ij} = 1, if the jth level of the ith attribute is present

= 0, otherwise.

The importance of ith attribute is defined in terms of the range of the part worths α_{ij}, across the level of that attribute, as

$$I_i = \text{Max}(\alpha_{ij}) - \text{Min}(\alpha_{ij}), \; i = 1, 2, \ldots m.$$

Next the attribute's importance is normalized to ascertain its importance relative to other attributes,

$$W_i = \frac{I_i}{\sum_{i=1}^{m} I_i}$$

as such $\sum_{i=1}^{m} W_i = 1$

Several methods may be proposed for estimating the basic model, but the one which is gaining popularity is the dummy variable regression model.

Next question arises whether the data should be analysed at individual respondent level or at aggregate level. If an aggregate-level analysis is to be adopted, some procedure of grouping the respondents must be devised.

A common approach is first to estimate individual level part-worth or utility function and then the respondents are clustered on the basis of similarity in their part-worths. Aggregate analysis in then performed for each cluster. Next comes the use of an appropriate model for estimating the parameters under consideration. The method of analysis used in this discussion is done using ordinary least square (OLS) regression with dummy variables, dependent variable being the preference ratings and the independent variables being the dummy variables. It gives the part-worth or utility functions estimated for each attribute along with their relative importance.

Example 15.8

Let us consider the problem when the student consumers are required to evaluate shoes. The qualitative research identified three attributes—the sole, the upper and the price. Each attribute has three levels.

Attributes with Level Number

Sole — Rubber (3) Polyurethane (2), Plastic (1).
Upper — Leather(3), Convas (2) Nylon (1)
Price — Rs. 300 (3), Rs. 1200 (2) Rs. 1500 (1)

The product profiles are all possible combinations of levels of attributes. A typical profile may be [Rubber (sole), Nylon (upper), Rs. 900 (Price)] combination of attribute levels.

Given three attributes each at three levels, there are 3 × 3 × 3 = 27 profiles. To reduce the respondent evaluation task a fractional factorial design was employed, and as such a set of nine profiles were constructed to estimate stimuli set.

TABLE 15.10
Profiles and their Ratings
Attribute Levels

Profile No.	Sole	Upper	Price	Preference Rating
1	1	1	1	9
2	1	2	2	7

3	1	3	3	5
4	2	1	2	6
5	2	2	3	5
6	2	3	1	6
7	3	1	3	5
8	3	2	1	7
9	3	3	2	6

For the use of regression analysis, define dummy variables as follows :

Let the dummy variables be

X_1 , X_2 represent sole

X_3 , X_4 represent upper

X_5 , X_6 represent price

Thus, for sole, the attribute levels were coded as follows :

	X_1	X_2
Level 1 :	1	0
2 :	0	1
3 :	0	0

The levels of other attributes were coded similarly.

The Regression model with dummy variables X_1 , X_2 , X_3 , X_4 , X_5 and X_6 is written as

$$Y = \beta_0 + \beta_1 X_1 + \beta_2 X_2 + \beta_3 X_3 + \beta_4 X_4 + \beta_5 X_5 + \beta_6 X_6 + e,$$

where e is the error term.

The values of dependent variable Y and the dummy variables X_1 , X_2 , ..., X_6 are presented in the Table 15.11.

TABLE 15.11
INPUTS FOR DUMMY REGRESSION

Preference Rating	Sole		Upper		Price	
Y	X_1	X_2	X_3	X_4	X_5	X_6
9	1	0	1	0	1	0
7	1	0	0	1	0	1
5	1	0	0	0	0	0
6	0	1	1	0	0	1
5	0	1	0	1	0	0
6	0	1	0	0	1	0

5	0	0	1	0	0	0
7	0	0	0	1	1	0
6	0	0	0	0	0	1

The estimated OLS regression model is represented as

$$U = b_0 + b_1X_1 + b_2X_2 + b_2X_3 + b_4X_4 + b_5X_5 + b_6X_6.$$

with $b_0 = 4.222$

$b_1 = 1.000$

$b_2 = -0.333$

$b_3 = 1.000$

$b_4 = 0.667$

$b_5 = 2.333$

$b_6 = 1.333$

Given the dummy variable coding, in which the level 3 is the base level, the coefficients may be related to the part-worths.

Each dummy variable coefficient represents the difference in the part-worth for that level minus the partworth for the base level.

Then, for sole

$$\alpha_{11} - \alpha_{13} = b_1$$
$$\alpha_{12} - \alpha_{13} = b_2$$

To solve for the part-worths, put the additional restriction

$$\alpha_{11} + \alpha_{12} + \alpha_{13} = 0$$

On solving $\alpha_{11} = 0.778$

$\alpha_{12} = -0.556$

$\alpha_{13} = -0.222$

For upper, $\alpha_{21} - \alpha_{23} = b_3$

$$\alpha_{22} - \alpha_{23} = b_4$$
$$\alpha_{21} + \alpha_{22} + \alpha_{23} = 0$$

from which $\alpha_{21} = 0.445$, $\alpha_{22} = 0.111$ **and** $\alpha_{23} = -0.556$

Finally, for price

$$\alpha_{31} - \alpha_{33} = b_5$$
$$\alpha_{32} - \alpha_{33} = b_6$$
$$\alpha_{31} + \alpha_{32} + \alpha_{33} = 0$$

From which $\alpha_{31} = 1.111$, $\alpha_{32} = 0.111$, $\alpha_{33} = -1.222$

Sum of ranges of part-worths $= I_1 + I_2 + I_3$

$= \{\text{Max}(\alpha_{1j}) - \text{Min}(\alpha_{1j})\} + \{\text{Max}(\alpha_{2j}) - \text{Min}(\alpha_{2j})\} + \{\text{Max}(\alpha_{3j}) - \text{Min}(\alpha_{3j})\}$

$= [0.778 - (0.556)] + [0.445 - (-0.556)] + [1.111 - (-1.222)] =$ **4.668**

Thus, relative importance of sole

$$= \frac{I_1}{\sum_{i=1}^{3} I_i} = \frac{0.778-(-0.556)}{4.668}$$

$$= \frac{1.334}{4.668} = 0.286$$

Relative importance of upper

$$= \frac{I_2}{\sum_{i=1}^{3} I_i} = \frac{0.445 - \in 0.556)}{4.668}$$

$$= \frac{1.001}{4.668} = 0.214$$

Relative importance of Price

$$= \frac{I_3}{\sum_{i=1}^{3} I_i} = \frac{1.111-(-1.222)}{4.668}$$

$$= \frac{2.333}{4.668} = 0.500$$

Finally, the estimation of the part-worths and the relative importance of the weights, assigned to attributes provide the basis for interpreting the results summerized in TABLE 15.12.

TABLE 15.12
RESULTS OF CONJOINT ANALYSIS

Attribute	Level	Description	Utility	Importance
Sole	3	Rubber	0.778	
	2	Polyurethane	–0.556	0.286
	1	Plastic	–0.222	
Upper	3	Leather	0.445	
	2	Canvas	0.111	0.214
	1	Nylon	–0.556	
Price	3	Rs. 900	1.111	
	2	Rs. 1200	0.111	0.500
	1	Rs. 1500	–1.222	

Assessing Reliability and Validity

The goodness of fit of the estimated model can be tested by using the value of R^2 in the fitting of multiple regression model with dummy variables.

The evaluation for the hold out or validation stimuli can be predicted by the estimated part-worth functions. The predicted evaluations can then be correlated with the input ratings for these profiles obtained from the respondents. If the correlation coefficient is statistically significant, the internal validity is confirmed.

15.10 Correspondence Analysis

Correspondence analysis is a descriptive/exploratory technique designed to analyse simple two way and multi-way tables containing some measure of correspondence between the rows and columns. The results provide information which is similar in nature to those produced by **Factor Analysis** and they allow to explore the structure of categorical variables included in the table.

An important feature of correspondence analysis is the multivariate treatment of the data through simultaneous consideration of multiple categorical variables. The multivariate nature of correspondence analyses can reveal relationships that would not be detected in a series of **pair wise** comparisons of variable. Another feature is the graphical display of row and column points in biplots, which can help in detecting structural relationships among the variable categories and objects (*i.e.* cases). Finally, correspondence analysis has highly flexible data requirements.The only strict data requirement is a rectangular data matrix with non-negative entries.

Correspondence analysis is **most effective if the following conditions are satisfied:**

- The data matrix is large enough, so that visual inspection or simple statistical analysis cannot reveal its structure.
- The variables are homogeneous, so that it makes sense to calculate the statistical distances between the rows or columns.
- The data matrix is a priori "amorphous", *i.e.* its structure is either unknown or poorly understood.

A distinct advantage of correspondence analysis over other methods yielding joint graphical displays is that it produces two dual displays whose row and column geometrics have similar interpretation, facilitating analysis and detection of relationships. In other multivariate approaches to graphical data representation, this duality is **not** present.

The **correspondence analysis (CA) may be defined as a special case of principal component analysis (PCA) of the rows and columns of a table, especially applicable to a cross-tabulation.** Principal component analysis is used for tables consisting of continuous measurement, where as correspondence analysis is applied to contigency tables (*i.e.* cross tabulation). Its primary goal is to transform a table of numerical information into a graphical display, in which each row and each column is depicted as a point.

The usual procedure of analyzing a cross tabulation to employ a chi-square test to test the significance of global association between rows and columns. But this test provides **no information** as to which are the significant individual associations between row-column pairs of the data matrix. Correspondence analysis shows how the variables are related, not just that a relationship exists.

Correspondence analysis is a statistical visualization method for picturing the associations between the levels of a two-way contingency table. The term correspondence denotes a 'system of association's between the elements of two sets.

In a two way contigency table, the observed association of two traits is summarized by cell frequencies and a typical inferential aspect is the study of whether certain levels of one characteristic are associated with some levels of another. Correspondence analysis is a geometric technique for displaying the rows and columns of a two way contingency table as points in a low-dimensional space, such that the positions of the row and column points are consistent with their associations in the tablle. The goal is to have a global view of the data that is useful for interpretation.

Marginal row frequencies :

$$n_{i+} = \sum_{j=1}^{J} n_{ij}, \; i = 1, 2, ..., I$$

Marginal column frequencies :

$$n_{+j} = \sum_{i=1}^{I} n_{ij}, \; j = 1, 2, ..., J$$

Total frequency :

$$n = \sum_{i=j}^{J} \sum_{i=1}^{I} n_{ij} = n_{++}$$

Row profiles

The profile in each row is a vector of conditional densities :

$$\frac{n_{ij}}{n_{i+}}, j = 1, 2, ..., J$$

The complete set of the row profile may be denoted by I × J matrix R.

Matrix of Row Profiles

Rows	Columns			Total
	1	2........................	J	
1	$\frac{n_{11}}{n_{1+}}$	$\frac{n_{12}}{n_{1+}}$	$\frac{n_{1J}}{n_{1+}}$	1
2	$\frac{n_{21}}{n_{2+}}$	$\frac{n_{22}}{n_{2+}}$	$\frac{n_{2J}}{n_{2+}}$	1
3	$\frac{n_{31}}{n_{3+}}$	$\frac{n_{32}}{n_{3+}}$	$\frac{n_{3J}}{n_{3+}}$	1
....	....	....	....	....
I	$\frac{n_{I1}}{n_{I+}}$	$\frac{n_{I2}}{n_{I+}}$	$\frac{n_{IJ}}{n_{I+}}$	1
Column mass	$\frac{n_{+1}}{n_{++}}$	$\frac{n_{+2}}{n_{++}}$	$\frac{n_{+j}}{n_{++}}$	1

Column Profiles

The profile for each column j is a vector of conditional densities $\frac{n_{ij}}{n_{+j}}$ $(i = 1, 2, ..., I)$

The complete set of the column profiles may be denoted by $(i \times j)$ matrix C.

Rows	Columns			Row Mass
	1	2.........................	J	
1	$\frac{n_{11}}{n_{+1}}$	$\frac{n_{12}}{n_{+2}}$	$\frac{n_{1J}}{n_{+J}}$	$\frac{n_{+1}}{n_{1+}}$
2	$\frac{n_{21}}{n_{+1}}$	$\frac{n_{22}}{n_{+2}}$	$\frac{n_{2J}}{n_{+J}}$	$\frac{n_{2+}}{n_{++}}$
3	$\frac{n_{31}}{n_{+1}}$	$\frac{n_{32}}{n_{+2}}$	$\frac{n_{3J}}{n_{+J}}$	$\frac{n_{3+}}{n_{++}}$
:	....	....	....	....
I	$\frac{n_{I1}}{n_{+1}}$	$\frac{n_{I2}}{n_{+2}}$	$\frac{n_{IJ}}{n_{+J}}$	$\frac{n_{I+}}{n_{++}}$
Total	1	1	1	1

Masses

Another fundamental concept in correspondence analysis is the concept of mass. Thus, the mass of the ith row is given by

$$= \frac{\text{Marginal frequency of the } i\text{th row}}{\text{Grand Total}}$$

$$= \frac{n_{i+}}{n}$$

Similarly, the mass of the jth column

$$= \frac{\text{Marginal frequency of the } j\text{th column}}{\text{Grand Total}}$$

$$= \frac{n_{+j}}{n}$$

Correspondence matrix

The correspondence matrix $\underline{P}$ is defined as the original table N divided by the grand total n,

$$P = \left(\frac{1}{n}\right) N$$

Thus, each cell of the correspondence matrix is given by the cell frequency divided by the grand total.

The correspondence matrix shows how one unit of mass is distributed across the cells. The row and column totals of the correspondence matrix are the row mass and column mass respectively.

Cloud of Points N(I) and N(J) :

The cloud of points N(I) is the set of elements of points $i \in I$, whose co-ordinates are the components of the profile and whose mass is $\frac{n_{i+}}{n_{++}}$, $i = 1, 2, ..., I$.

The cloud points N(J) is the set of elements of points $j \in$ J, whose co-ordinates are the components of the profile and whose massis

$$\frac{n_{+j}}{n_{++}} \; (j = 1, 2, \dots \text{J})$$

Distances

A variant of Euclidean distance, called the weighted Euclidean distance, is used to measure and thereby depict the distances between profile points. Here, the weighting of the dimensions of the space and **not** to the weighting of the profiles.

Distance between two rows i and i' is given by

$$d^2 (i , i') = \sum_{j=1}^{\text{J}} \frac{1}{n_{+j}} \left(\frac{n_{ij}}{n_{i+}} - \frac{n_{i'j}}{n_{i'+}} \right)^2$$

In symmetric fashion, the distance between two columns, j and j' is given by

$$d^2 (j , j') = \sum_{i=1}^{\text{I}} \frac{1}{n_{i+}} \left(\frac{n_{ij}}{n_{+j}} - \frac{n_{ij'}}{n_{+j'}} \right)^2$$

The distance thus obtained is called the chi-square distance.

The chi-square distance differs from the Euclidean distance in that each square is weighted by the inverse of the frequency corresponding to each term.

Inertia

Inertia is a term borrowed from the 'moment of inertia' in mechanics.

For the ith row profile

$$\text{Inertia} = m_i \sum_j \frac{(r_{ij} - \bar{r}_j)^2}{\bar{r}_j},$$

where $$r_{ij} = \frac{n_{ij}}{n_{i+}} \text{ and } \bar{r}_j = \frac{n_{+j}}{n}$$

The inertia of the jth column profile is computed similarly.

The total inertia of the contingency table is given by

$$\text{Total inertia} = \frac{\text{Total Pearson chi–square}}{\text{Total sum } n}$$

If the rows and columns in a table are completely independent of each other, the entries in the 2 × 2 table (distribution of mass) can be reproduced from the row and column totals alone, or row and column profiles in the terminology of correspondence analysis. According to well known formula for computing the **chi- square** statistic for two way tables, the expected frequencies in a table where the columns and rows are independent of each other, are equal to the respective column total times the row total, divided by the grand total. Any deviation from the expected values (expected under the hypothesis of the complete independence of the row and column variables) will contribute to the overall **chi-square**. Thus, another way of looking at the correspondence analysis is to consider it a method of decomposing the overall chi-square statistic (or inertia = chi-square/total n) by identifying a small number of dimensions in which the deviations from the expected values can be represented. This is similar to the goal of **factor analysis** where the total variance is decomposed, so as to arrive at a **lower-dimensional** representation of the variables that allows one to reconstruct most of the variance/covariance matrix of variables.

As regards analysis of rows and columns, if we are interested in column totals, then we may plot the column points in a small- dimensional space which satisfactorily reproduces the similarily (or distances) between the relative frequencies for the columns, across the rows, in the cross tabulation. Similar procedures may be adopted, in case we are interested in row totals. In fact it is customary to simultaneously plot the column points and the row points in a single graph to summarize the information in a two-way table.

Note that the dimensions are 'extracted' so as to maximise the distances between the row or column points, and successive dimensions will explain less and less of the overall chi-square value (and thus inertia). Thus the extraction of the dimensions is similar to the extraction of principal components in Factor Analysis. The maximum number of dimensions that can be extracted is minimum of (Number of rows minus 1, Number of columns minus 1).

Quality. The quality column contains information concerning the quality of representation of the respective row point in the co- ordinate system defined by the respective number of dimensions, as chosen by the user. The quality of a point is defined as the ratio of the squared distance of the point from the origin in the chosen number of dimensions, over the squared distance from the origin in the space defined by the maximum number of dimensions (metric is chi-square). By analogy to factor analysis, the quality of a point is similar to the interpretation of the communality for a variable in factor analysis. **Quality Measure** can be interpreted as the proportion of chi-square accounted for" for the respective row, given the respective number of dimensions. A low **quality** means that the current number of dimensions does not well represent the respective row (or column)

Relative Intertia

This represents the proprortion of the total **inertia** accounted for by the respective point and is independent of the number of dimensions chosen by the user. The total inertia of a table qualifies how much variation is present in the row profiles or in the column profiles.

Each row and each column makes a contribution to the total inertia, respectively called row inertia and column inertia.

Note that a particular solution may represent a point very well (high quality) but the same point may not contribute much to the over all inertia.

Relative inertia may also be computed for each dimension and reported for each (row or column) point for each dimension.

Cosine ^{2} (quality or squared correlation with each dimension) : In computational table a column is provided to show the quality for each point by dimension. The sum of values in these columns across the dimensions is equal to the **total quality**. This value may also be interpreted as the correlation of the respective point with the respective dimension. The term **cosine²** refer to the fact that this value is also the squared cosine value value of the angle ϕ, the point makes with the respective dimension. Thus, **Quality** = $\Sigma\, Cos^2\phi$.

The correspondence analysis is an exploratory technique and there is no statistical significance tests involved in the analysis. The primary purpose of the technique is to produce a simplified low- dimensional representation of the information in a large frequency table.

Example 15.9

Suppose it is required to develop a correspondence analysis of smoking habits of different groups of employees in a company. The employees are grouped under Rows as:

1. Senior Managers
2. Junior Managers
3. Senior Employees
4. Junior Employees
5. Part time Employees

The smoking habits are categorized under columns às :

1. None
2. Light
3. Medium
4. Heavy

The following Table 15.13 represents hypothetical data on 200 employees.

TABLE—15.13

	Observed Table : (Frequencies) (Spreadsheet 1 in Workbook 1) Row variables : Var 1(5) Column variables : Var 2(4)				
	1	**2**	**3**	**4**	**Total**
1	5	3	4	3	15
2	4	5	8	4	21
3	25	10	12	4	51
4	18	24	33	13	88
5	10	6	7	2	25
Total	62	48	64	26	200

Row Category	**Column Category**
(Staff group)	(Smoking Categories)
1. Senior Managers	1. None
2. Junior Managers	2. Light
3. Senior Employees	3. Medium
4. Junior or Employees	4. Heavy
5. Part Time Employees	

TABLE—A

	Percentages of Row Totals (Spreadsheet 1 in Workbook1) Row Variables : Var 1(5) Column variables : Var2(4)				
	1	**2**	**3**	**4**	**Total**
1	33.33333	20.00000	26.66667	20.00000	100.0000
2	19.04762	23.80952	38.09524	19.04762	100.0000
3	49.01961	19.60784	23.52941	7.84314	100.0000
4	20.45455	27.27273	37.50000	14.77273	100.0000
5	40.00000	24.00000	28.00000	8.00000	100.0000

TABLE—B

	Percentages of Column Totals (Spreadsheet 1 in Workbook1) Row variables : Var 1 (5) Column variables : Var 2(4)			
	1	**2**	**3**	**4**
1	8.0645	6.2500	6.2500	11.5385
2	6.4516	10.4167	12.5000	15.3846
3	40.3226	20.8333	18.7500	15.3846
4	29.0323	50.0000	51.5625	50.0000
5	16.1290	12.5000	10.9375	7.6923
Total	100.0000	100.0000	100.0000	100.0000

TABLE—C

	Percentages of Total (Spreadsheet 1 in Workbook1) Row variables : VAR 1 (5) Column variables : Var 2(4)				
	1	**2**	**3**	**4**	**Total**
1	2.50000	1.50000	2.00000	1.50000	7.5000
2	2.00000	2.50000	4.00000	2.00000	10.5000
3	12.50000	5.00000	6.00000	2.00000	25.5000
4	9.00000	12.00000	16.50000	6.50000	44.0000
5	5.00000	3.00000	3.50000	1.00000	12.5000
Total	31.00000	24.00000	32.00000	13.00000	100.0000

TABLE—D

	Expected Frequencies (Spreadsheets 1 in Workbook1) Row variable : Var1(5) Column variabes : Var2(4)				
	1	**2**	**3**	**4**	**Total**
1	4.65000	3.60000	4.8000	1.95000	15.0000

2	6.51000	5.04000	6.72000	2.73000	21.0000
3	15.81000	12.24000	16.32000	6.63000	51.0000
4	27.28000	21.12000	28.16000	11.44000	88.0000
5	7.75000	6.00000	8.00000	3.25000	25.0000
Total	62.00000	48.00000	64.00000	26.00000	200.0000

TABLE E

	Contributions to Chi-Square (Spreadsheet 1 in Workbook 1) Row variables : Var1 (5) Column variables : Var 2(4)				
	1	**2**	**3**	**4**	**Total**
1	0.02634	0.100000	0.133333	0.565385	0.82506
2	0.96776	0.000317	0.243810	0.590806	1.80269
3	5.34194	0.409935	1.143529	1.043273	7.93868
4	3.15683	0.392727	0.831875	0.212727	4.59416
5	0.65323	0.000000	0.125000	0.480769	1.25900
Total	10.14610	0.902979	2.477547	2.892960	16.41959

TABLE—F

	Eigenvalues and Inertia for all Dimensions (Spreadsheet 1 in Workbook 1) Input Table (Rows x Columns) : 5 x 4 Total Inertia = 0.8210 Chil² = 16.420 df = 12p = .17283				
Number of Dims.	**Singular Values**	**Elgen Values**	**Perc.of Inertia**	**Cumulative Percent**	**Chi Squares**
1	0.275036	0.075645	92.13991	92.1399	15.12899
2	0.078758	0.006203	7.55536	99.6953	1.24056
3	0.015817	0.000250	0.30474	100.000	0.05004

Note : The maximum number of eigenvalues that can be extracted from the given two-way table is minimum of [Number of rows —1, Number of columns - 1] i.e. 3 (three). If it is decided to to extract (i.e. interpret the maximum number of dimensions that can be expracted, then you can reproduce extactly all the information in the table. It is seen that with a single dimension 92. 14% of the inertia can be explained and with two dimensions 99.70% of the inertia can be explained.

TABLE—G

	Row Coordinates and Contribution to Inertia (Spreadsheet in Workbook1) Input Table (Rows x Columns) : 5 x 4 Standardization : Row and column profiles							
Row Name	**Row Number**	**Coordin Dim.1**	**Cordin. Dim.2**	**Mass**	**Quality**	**Relative Interia**	**Inertia Dim.1**	**Cosine² Dim 1**
1	1	-0.017611	0.231902	0.075000	0.983357	0.050249	0 .000307	0.005638

2	2	0.278383	0.084773	0.105000	0.986501	0.109789	0.107571	0.902785
3	3	-0.394410	0.002512	0.255000	0.999389	0.483488	0.524391	0.999349
4	4	0.224984	-0.0439610	0.440000	0.999621	0.279798	0.294425	0.969567
5	5	-0.210622	-0.076046	0.125000	0.995727	0.076676	0.073306	0.880894

	Row Coordinates and Contributions to Inertia (Spreadsheet 1 in Work book 1) Input Table (Rows x Columns) : 5 x 4 Standardization : Row profiles	
Row Name	**Intertia Dim.2**	**Cosine^2 Dim. 2**
1	0.650254	0.977718
2	0.121650	0.083716
3	0.000259	0.000041
4	0.111296	0.030053
5	0.116540	0.114834

TABLE—H

	Column Coordinates and Contributions to Inertia (Spreadsheet 1 in Workbook1) Input Table (Row x Columns) : 5 x 4 Standardization : Row and column profiles							
Column Name	**Column Number**	**Coordin. Dim.1**	**Coordin. Dim.2**	**Mass**	**Quality**	**Relative Interia**	**Inertia Dim.1**	**Cosine^2 Dim.1**
1	1	-0.404127	0.018011	0.310000	0.999978	0.617927	0.669295	0.997995
2	2	0.115959	-0069368	0.240000	0.970567	0.054994	0.042662	0.714781
3	3	0.191669	-0.040379	0.320000	0.991104	0.150890	0.155407	0.948986
4	4	0.277810	0.184508	0.13000	0.999587	0.176190	0.132635	0.693629

	Column Cordinates and Contributions to Inertia (Spreadsheet 1 in Workbook1) Input Table (Rows x Columns) : 5 x 4 Standardization : Row and column profiles	
Column Name	**Intertia Dim.2**	**Cosine^2 Dim.2**
1	0.016213	0.001982
2	0.186182	0.255787
3	0.08416	0.042118
4	0.713489	0.305958

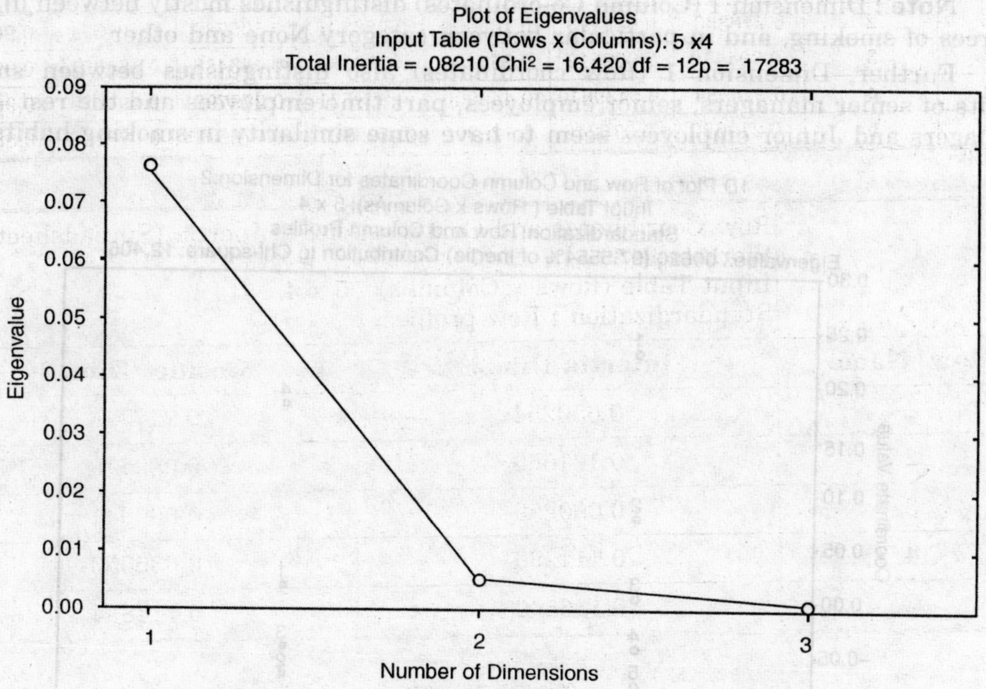

Fig. 15.19

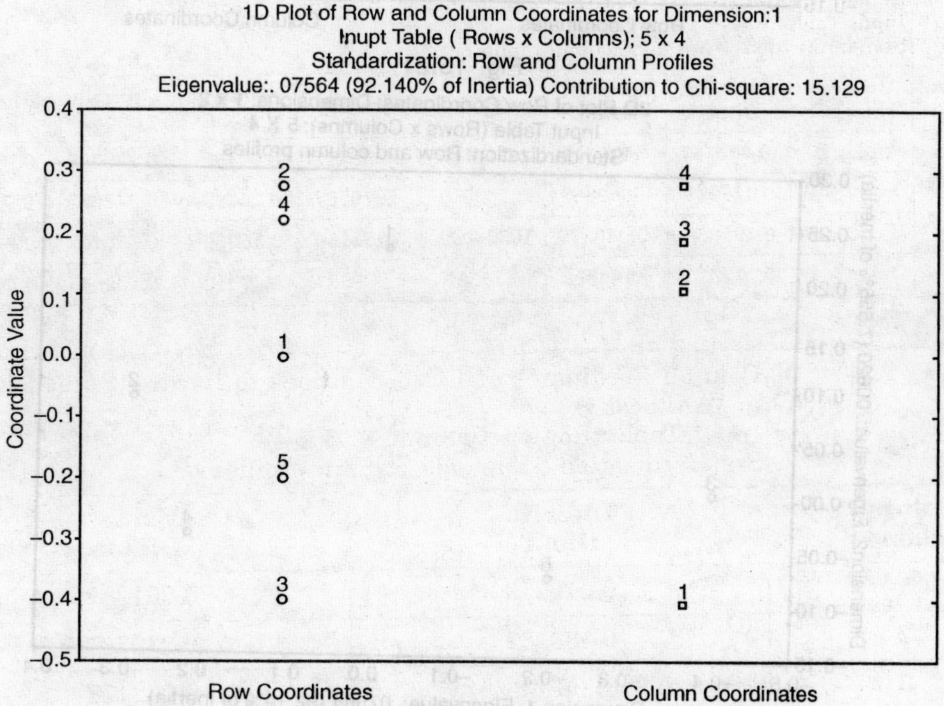

Fig. 15.20

Note : Dimension 1 (Column Co-ordinates) distinguishes mostly between different degrees of smoking, and in particular between category None and other.

Further, Dimension 1 (Row coordinates) also distinguishes between smoking habits of senior managers, senior employees, part time employees and the rest. Junior managers and Junior employees seem to have some similarity in smoking habits.

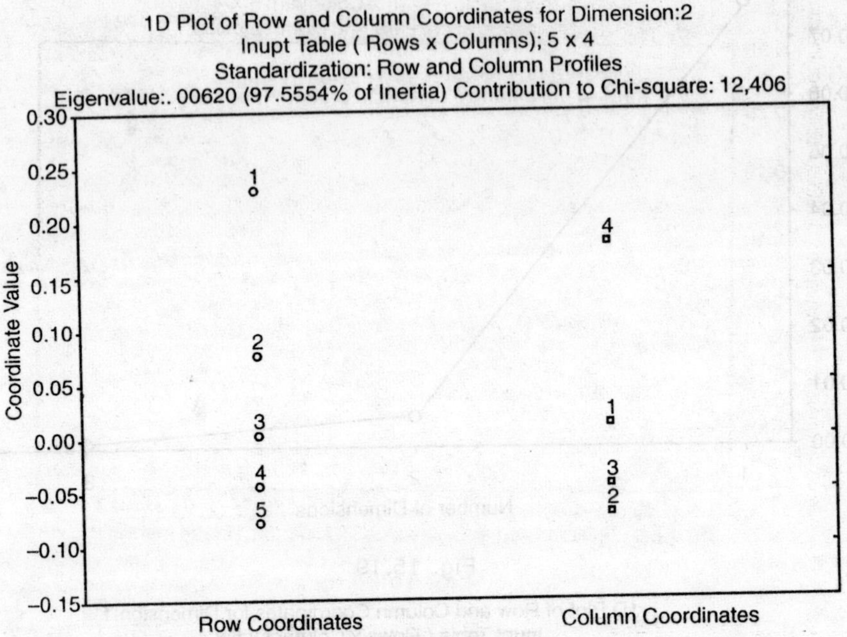

Fig. 15.21

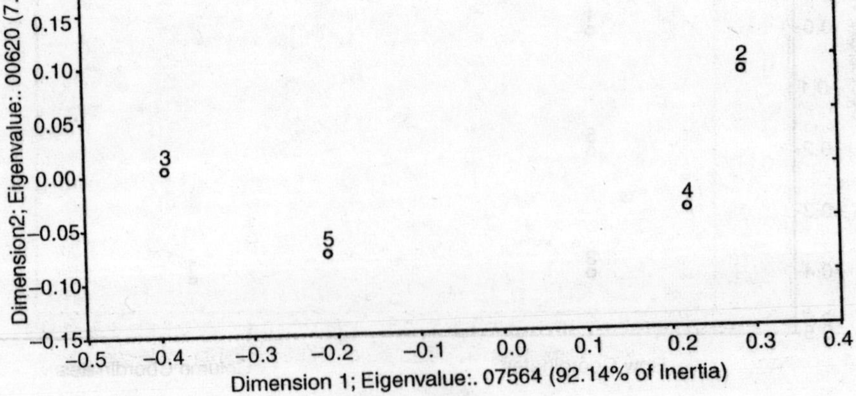

Fig. 15.22

Note : The points corresponding to junior managers and Junior employees fall on the right side of the central axis and the points corresponding to senior employees and part time employees fall on the left side of the central axis, signifying some similar pattern of smoking habits.

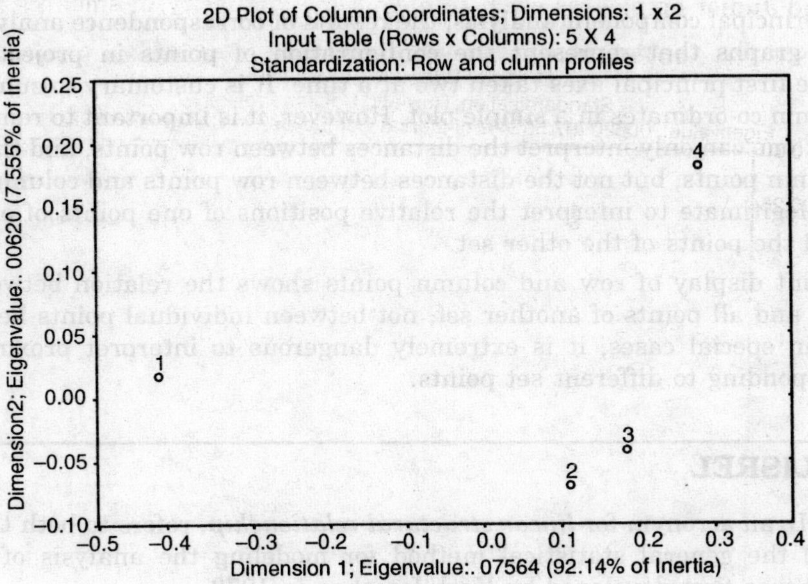

Fig. 15.23

Note : Both Dimension 1 and Dimension 2 considered together, degree of smoking belonging to 'light' and 'medium' categories are distinguished from 'none' and 'heavy' categories.

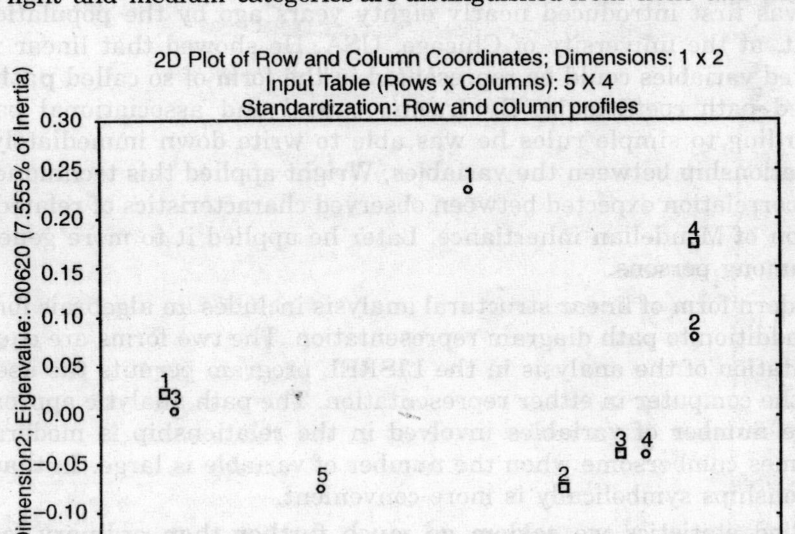

Fig. 15.24

Note : Senior managers stand distinctly and distinguishably as regards smoking habit and degree of smoking amongst others.

Interpretation of graphics

As in principal component analysis, the results of correspondence analysis are represented on graphs that represent the configuration of points in projection planes, formed by the first principal axes taken two at a time. It is customary to summarize the row and column co-ordinates in a simple plot. However, it is important to remember that in such plots, one can only interpret the distances between row points, and the distances between column points, but not the distances between row points and column points. Of course, it is legitimate to interpret the relative positions of one points of one set with respect to all the points of the other set.

The joint display of row and column points shows the relation between a point from one set and all points of another set, not between individual points between each set. Except in special cases, it is extremely dangerous to interpret proximity of two points corresponding to different set points.

15.11 LISREL

LISREL, an acronym for *linear structural relationship*, refers to both the software program and the general statistical method for modeling the analysis of covariance structures. It was first developed by Karl Joreskog in 1973.

LISREL is the most widely referenced package for estimation of the covariance structure model, referred to as 'structural equation modeling' (SEM). Although structural modelling has become a prominent form of data analysis only in last twenty years, the concept was first introduced nearly eighty years ago by the population biologist, Sewell Wright, at the university of Chicago, USA. He showed that linear relationship among observed variables could be represented in the form of so called **path diagrams** and associated path coefficients. By tracing causal and associational paths on the diagram according to simple rules he was able to write down immediately the linear structural relationship between the variables, Wright applied this technique initially to calculate the correlation expected between observed characteristics of related persons on the supposition of Mendelian inhertiance. Later he applied it to more general types of relationship among persons.

The modern form of linear structural analysis includes an algebraic formulation of the model in addition to path diagram representation. The two forms are equivalent and the implementation of the analysis in the LISREL program permits the user to submit the model to the computer in either representation. The path analytic approach is excellent when the number of variables involved in the relationship is moderate, but the diagram becomes cumbersome when the number of variable is large. In that case, writing the relationships symbolically is more convenient.

In applied statistics we seldom go much further than ordinary least squares analysis of data from controlled experiments, group comparisons, or simple prediction studies. Collectively, these procedures make up regression analysis, and the linear mathematical functions on which they depend and referred to as regression models. This basic method of data analsysis is quite suitable for curve-fitting problems in physical science, where an empiricial relationship between an observed dependent variable and a manipulated independent variable must be estimated. It also serves well the purposes of biological investigation in which organisms are assigned randomly to treatment conditions and differences in the average responses among the treatment groups are estimated.

An essential feature of these applications is that only the dependent variable or the observed response is assumed to be subject to measurement error or other uncontrolled variation. That is, there is only one random variable in the picture. The independent variable or treatment level is assumed to be fixed by the experimenter at known predetermined values. The only exception to this formulation is the empirical prediction problem. For that purpose, the investigator observes certain values of one or more predictor variables and wishes to estimate the mean and variance of the distribution of a certain variable among respondents with given values of the predictors. Because the prediction is conditional on these known values, they may be considered fixed quanitites in the regression model. An example is predicting the height that a child will attain at maturity from his or her current height and the known heights of the parents. Even though all of the heights are measured subject to error, only the child's height at maturity is considered a random variable.

Where ordinary regression methods no longer suffice, and indeed give misleading results, is in purely observational studies in which all variables are subject to measurement error or uncontrolled variation and the purpose of the inquiry is to estimate relationships that account for variation among the variables in question. This is the essential problem of data analysis in those fields where experimentation is impossible or impractical and mere empirical prediction is not the objective of the study. It is typical of almost all research in fields such as sociology, economics, ecology, and even areas of physical science such as geology and meteorology. In these fields, the essential problem of data analysis is the estimation of structural relationships between quantitative observed variables. When the mathematical model that respresents these relationships is linear we speak of a linear structural relationship. The various aspects of formulating, fitting, and testing such relationships we refer to as structural equation modelling.

Here comes the importance and utility of LISREL as a tool for data analysis.

❒ LISREL is a powerful alternative to other multivariate techniques, such as multiple regressions, MANOVA, and canonical analysis, which are limited to representing only a single relationship between the dependent and independent variables.

❒ The major advantages of LISREL are that it can estimate multiple and interrelated dependence relationships, and that it can represent unobserved concepts or *latent variables* in those relationships and account for measurement error in the estimation process.

❒ LISREL technique allows for separate relationships for each of a set of dependent variables. It provides an efficient technique for a series of multiple regression equations projected simultaneously.

❒ The general LISREL consists of two sub-models :

(*a*) The measurement model

(*b*) The structural model

The measurement model allows the researcher to use several observed variables as factors of a single unobserved independent or dependent variables. This provides link between the observed scores on measurement instruments and the underlying constructs they are designated to measure. Using confirmatory factor analysis (CFA), the researcher can evaluate the contribution of each manifest variable as well as incorporate how well the overall instrument measures the concept into the estimation of the relationship between dependent and independent variables.

The structural model is the 'path' model that defines the relationships among the unobserved variables. It specifies which latent variables cause changes in the values of other latent variables in the model. However, the development of structural model needs the incorporation of theory, previous experience and other guidelines to assist the research to determine which independent variables predict each dependent variable.

❒ LISREL is viewed as confirmatory rather than exploratory procedure and its flexibility and versatility can be applied to a variety of research objectives.

In the LISREL model, the linear structural relationship and the factor structure are combined into one comprehensive model applicable to observational studies in many fields. The model allows multiple latent constructs indicated by observable explanatory (or exogenous) variables, recursive and nonrecursive relationships between constructs, and multiple latent constructs indicated by observable responses (or endogenous) variables. The connections between the latent constructs compose the structural equation model ; the relationships between the latent constructs and their observable indicators or outcomes compose the factor models. All parts of the comprehensive model may be represented in the path diagram and all factor loadings and structural relationships appear as coefficients of the path.

Nested within the general model are simpler models that the user of the LISREL program may choose as special cases. If some of the variables involved in the structural relationships are observed directly, rather than indicated, part or all of the factor model may be excluded. Conversely, if there are no structural relationships, the model may reduce to a confirmatory factor analysis applicable to the data in question. Finally, if the data arise from a simple prediction problem or controlled experiment in which the independent variable or treatment level is measured without error, the user may specialize to a simple regression model and obtain the standard results of ordinary least-squares analysis.

These specializations may be communicated to the LISREL computer program in three different ways. At the most intuitive, visual level, the user may construct the path diagram interactively on the screen, and specify paths to be included or excluded. The corresponding verbal level is the SIMPLIS command language. It requires only that the user name the variables and declare the relationships among them. The third and most detailed level is the LISREL command language. It is phrased in terms of matrices that appear in the matrix-algebraic representation of the model. Various parameters of the matrices may be fixed or set equal to other parameters, and linear and non-linear constraints may be imposed among them. The terms and syntax of the LISREL command language are explained and illustrated in the LISREL program manuals. Most but not all of these functions are included in the SIMPLIS language ; certain advanced functions are only possible in native LISREL commands.

The essential statistical assumption of LISREL analysis is that random quantities within the model are distributed in a form belonging to the family of elliptical distributions, the most prominent member of which is the multivariate normal distribution. In applications where it is reasonable to assume multivariate normality, the maximum likelihood method of estimating unknowns in the model is justified and usually preferred. Where the requirements of maximum likelihood estimation are not met, as when the data are ordinal rather than measured, the various least squares estimation methods are available. It is important to understand, however, except in those cases where ordinary least squares analysis applies or the weight matrices of other least squares methods are known, that these are large-sample estimation procedures. This is not a serious limitation in observation studies, where samples are typically large. Small-sample theory applies properly only to controlled experiments and only when the model contains a single, univariate or multivariate normal error component.

The operation of reducing the raw data to their sufficient statistics (while cleaning and verifying the validity for the data) is performed by the PRELIS program which accompanies LISREL. PRELIS also computes summary statistics for qualitative data in the form of tetrachoric or polychoric correlation matrices. When thee are several sample groups, and the LISREL model is defined and compared across the groups, PRELIS prepares the sufficient statistics for each sample in turn. Thus, to sum up LISREL is not a general purpose software. It is a program for estimating the coefficients in a set of structural equations. PRELIS is a preprocessor for LISREL and does a fair amount of data screening (including tests of univariate and multivariate normality) it with LISREL.

In many social and psychological or educational research studies where a single sample is involved, the variables are usually measured on a scale with an arbitrary origin. In that case, the overall means of the variables in the sample can be excluded from the analysis, and the fitting of the LISREL model can be regarded simply as an analysis of the covariance structure, in which case the expected covariance matrix implied by the model is fitted to the observed covariance matrix directly. Since the sample covariance matrix is a sufficient statistic under the distribution assumption, the result is equivalent to fitting the data. Again, the analysis is made more manageable because one can examine the residuals from the observed covariances, which are moderate in number, as opposed to analyzing residuals of the original observations in a large sample.

Many of these aspects of the LISREL analysis are brought out in the examples in the PRELIS and LISREL program manuals. In addition, the SIMPLIS manual contains exercises to help the student strengthen and expand his or her understanding of this powerful method of data analysis. Files containing the data of these examples are included with the program and can be analyzed in numerous different ways to explore and test alternative models.

Today, however, LISREL for Windows is no longer limited to SEM. The latest LISREL for Windows includes the following statistical applications.

- LISREL for structural equation modeling.
- PRELIS for data manipulations and basic statistical analyses.
- MULTILEV for hierarchical linear and non-linear modeling.
- SURVEYGLIM for generalized linear modeling.
- CATFIRM for formative inference-based recursive modeling for categorical response variables.
- CONFIRM for formative inference-based recursive modeling for continuous response variables.
- MAPGLIM for generalized linear modeling for multilevel data.

EXERCISES

1. Define Hotelling's T^2-statistic and mention its application.
2. How would you test a hypothesis on equality of two mean vectors ? Explain.
3. Explain the test procedure for testing the equality of several multivariate mean vectors.
4. Describe multivariate analysis of variance (MANOVA).
5. Explain multivariate paired T^2-test.
6. What is discriminant analysis ? Mention its purpose and applications. How does it help in classification ? Explain.
7. Discuss classification of an unknown observation to one of three multivariate populations.
8. How would you determine optimum classification ? Explain.
9. What is cluster analysis ? Mention its applications. Discuss different types of distance measures.
10. Discuss steps for cluster analysis.
11. Explain different clustering procedures.
12. What is a dendogram ? Explain.
13. What is principal component analysis ? Mention its applications.
14. Define factor analysis. Discuss its purpose and application areas. Differentiate between Exploratory factor analysis (EFA) and confirmatory factor analysis (CFA).
15. Differentiate between factor analysis and principal component analysis.
16. What does rotation serve in factor analysis ? Explain different rotation methods.
17. What are the assumptions in factor analysis ? Discuss.
18. What are different methods of extracting the factors from a set of data.
19. Compare and contrast different data reduction techniques. Mention their relative advantages.
20. Explain the following terms :
    (*a*) Common factor
    (*b*) Communality
    (*c*) Eigen value and Eigen vectors
    (*d*) Factor loading
    (*e*) Factor scores
    (*f*) Latent variable
    (*g*) Rotation of factors
    (*h*) Varimax rotation
    (*i*) Kaiser criterion
    (*j*) Scree test
    (*k*) Factors and components
    (*l*) Uniqueness
21. What is multi-dimensional scaling ? What does it achieve ? Explain.
22. Discuss procedures of a multidimensional scaling ?

23. Distinguish between multidimensional scaling and conjoint analysis.

24. Explain the concept of multidimensional scaling in its application to geographical location of cities in a country.

25. Describe applications of conjoint analysis in market research.

26. How would you determine the number of dimensions of the conceptual space of multidimensional scale ?

27. What is correspondence analysis ? Describe its features and applications.

28. Distinguish between correspondence analysis and principal component analysis.

29. Why correspondence analysis is called as exploratory data analysis?

30. Discuss the basics of conjoint analysis.

31. What is LISREL ?

32. Mention the importance of LISREL.

33. Explain advantages of LISREL.

□□□

CHAPTER 16

ANALYSIS AND INTERPRETATION OF DATA

16.1 Introduction

Data do not speak for themselves. They reveal what the analyst can detect. The researcher at the end of hectic days involving the planning, design of research; collection of facts and figures, interwoven with ideas, sits down to build a little world containing all the key elements which enter into his work at hand; to put each in its place in a systematic manner, continually readjusting the framework around the development in each part of it. When analysing data (whether from questionnaires, interviews, focus groups, or whatever) the researcher should always start from review of his research goals. This helps him to organise data and focus his analysis.

The analyst starts with assumption that behind accumulated facts there is something more important than mere facts and figures and the careful thoughtout, well marshalled facts and figures, when related to whole body of data in a systematic manner have significant general meaning of interest from which valid generalizations can be drawn. He is expected to be wiser in belief that no analysis is an end itself, but is a continuous process, nurtured throughout the research understanding and process, though it may look rudimentary and tentative at the start.

The analyst's determination to know what types of data to secure and what techniques to be used to secure them, what sources to tap them, what hypotheses to formulate and how to test them, necessitates and guides subsequent classification and analysis.

The analyst should bear in mind that the facts and figures, in and by do not speak for themselves and in fact look raw and bare, waiting for the analyst to detect. Further, facts and figures are not free and equal and may have many dependents of varying complexities, sources and structures and contain many objective and subjective elements in varying degrees and combinations. Before embarking upon the analysis of data the researcher must have thorough knowledge and background of the data in hand. Without penetrating and insightful knowledge, the analysis is likely to be aimless, if not altogether worthless.

A fruitful early step for the analysis of data would be

- ❒ scrutiny of the assembled data
- ❒ preparation of an outline—a blue print of the study.

16.2 The Outline

An outline is in reality a systematic ordering and classification of the major aspects of the assembled facts and helps in visualizing the whole study as well as relatedness of its various aspects. The whole range of associated and naturally allied facts comes to view of the researcher in the forefront of his responsible intellectual and practical exercises to follow.

A preliminary outline, as comprehensive as data and objectives will permit, should focus on all major factors under contention in the study. At a later time this outline could be condensed and some detailed items could be combined into more general groupings as per requirement.

The sequence of items in the outline should be decided on logical considerations or on objectives of the study or on need for emphasis of certain factors. However, the fixation of the sequenc may be carried out by trial and error techniques to arrive at a convenient position for analysis.

The preparation of outline should not be undertaken in haste and the researcher should not jump into the process with scattered data and incoherent thoughts in mind. Under these circumstances the vital relationships existing between data may escape the notice of the researcher.

In short a careful outline aids in determining whether the basic facts stand in the proper relationship to each other, whether there are serious gaps in the data, and whether the researcher has properly assimilated his facts, keeping in view the research objectives.

After the tentative outline has been prepared the researcher, should consult with some expert who can give frank, honest and careful opinion on the outline as to its deficiencies and errors in logical arrangement. Further, it would also be a good attempt to explain the data and the outline to some person who can understand, but knows little or nothing about the subject under consideration.

If the researcher creates interest of the person in the matter and the person concerned gains insight into the problem, it may be said that the interpreter has developed mastery and expertise over his subject.

As with most other aspects of the study, the **analysis and interpretation should relate to the study objectives and research questions.** The usual analysis approach is to begin with descriptive analysis to explore and gain a 'feel' for the data. The analyst then turns to address specific questions from the study aims or hypotheses, from findings, from studies reported in the literature and also from patterns suggested by the descriptive analysis.

Before the researcher begins analysis, a considerable amount of preparatory work must usually be carried out.

- ❒ Data editing
- ❒ Data cleaning
- ❒ Data coding
- ❒ Data reduction
- ❒ Exploring data
- ❒ Treatment of missing values

16.3 Data Preparation

16.3.1 Data Editing

Even if the study is a well executed one, all data collection activities are monitored to ensure adherence to the data collection protocol and to prompt actions to minimize and resolve missing and questionable data. Monitoring procedures are instituted at the outset and maintained throughout the study, since the faster irregularities can be detected, the greater the likelihood that they can be resolved in a satisfactory manner and the sooner the preventive measures can be instituted.

Nevertheles, there is often need to edit the data both before and after they are computerised. Of course the first step is manual or visual editing. The problems arising out of coding open-ended questions can also be sorted out.

16.3.2 Data Cleaning

Once the data are computerised and verified they are subjected to a series of computer checks to 'clean them.

Range Checks. Range checks compare each data item to the set of usual and permissible values for that variable. Range checks are used to

- ❒ Detect and correct **invalid values**
- ❒ Note and investigate **unusual values**
- ❒ Note **outliers** which may need special statistical treatment, if the presence is correct.
- ❒ Check reasonableness of **distributions** and also note their form, since that will also affect choice of statistical procedures.

Consistency checks. Consistency checks examine each pair (sometimes more) of related data items in relation to set of usual and permissible values for the variables as pair consistency checks are used to

(*i*) Detect and correct impermissible combinations

(*ii*) Note and correct **unusual combinations**

(*iii*) Check consistency of **'denominators'**, and **'missing'** and **'not applicable'** values

(*iv*) Check reasonableness of **joint distributions** (scatter plot)

Inconsistent responses may have noticeable impact on estimates and can alter comparisons across groups.

16.3.3 Data Coding

Data coding means translating information into values for computer entry and statistical analysis.

It is necessary to achieve balance between coding the 'minimum' and coding 'everything'.

- ❒ Coding is much easier when done all at once.
- ❒ One can always subsequently ignore coded distinctions **not** judged as meaningful.
- ❒ Information not coded will be unavailable for analysis
- ❒ More detail → More codes → More programming → More opportunities for error.

16.3.4 Data reduction

Data reduction seeks to reduce the number of variables for analysis by combining single variables into compound variables, that better quantify the construct. For instance, variables-created coding attempt faithfully to reflect the original data (*e.g.* Height, Weight). Often these variables can be used directly for analysis, but it is also often necessary to create additional variables to represent constructs for analysis. For instance, the construct of over weight is often represented by a variable derived from the values for height and weight. Data reduction also implies simplifying a number of possible values to a smaller number and deriving compound variables (*e.g.* 'socio-economic status' derived from education and occupation.

Types of derived variables

In a pure scale all of the items may be intended to measure the same construct. The scale score is usually the sum of the response values for the items, though items with negative aspect (*e.g.* I feel happy in a depression scale) must be inverted. The purpose of deriving a scale score from multiple items is to obtain a more reliable measure of construct than is possible from a single item.

Indexes

An index consists of a group of items that are combined (usually summed) to give a measure of multidimensional construct.

Algorithm

It is a procedure that uses a set of criteria according to specific rules or considerations, *e.g.* major depressive disorder, effective contraception, congenial business environment, etc.

16.3.5 Exploring the data

This requires ingenuity in data handling to get a 'feel' for the data. The analyst inspects the distribution of each variable, examines bivariate scatter plots and cross tabulations to unravel pattern and associations, if any.

The exploration may be directed towards :

- ❒ Observe shape of the distribution—symmetry vs skewness, discontinuities
- ❒ Select—summary statistics appropriate to the distribution and variable types (nominal, ordinal, measurement)

such as Location—mean, median, percentage above certain cut-point
Dispersion—standard deviation, range, quantiles, etc.

- ❒ Look for relationship in data
- ❒ Look within important sub-groups
- ❒ Note the proportion of missing values

16.3.6 Cross Tabulation

Cross tabulation is a technique for comparing two classification variables e.g. gender and promotion to next higher grade, applications of levels of two fertilisers, inocculation and contracting a disease, MBA specialisations and first salary range, advertisement and increase of sales, etc. This technique uses tables having rows and columns that correspond to the levels or values of each variable's categories :

Gender	Promotion to next higher grade Yes	No	Total
M			
F			
Total			Grand Total

The given table has two rows and columns corresponding to gender and promotion to next higher grade. The combination of the variables with their values produces four cells. Each cell contains count of the cases of joint classification.

Cross tabulation creates a **two dimensional table.** The percentages in cross tabulation help comparison of data both row-wise and column-wise. The question arises as to which direction the percentages should be computed. Logically one should compute percentages in the direction of the independent variable. If the independent variable is placed in the row, compute row percentages and if it is in the column, select column percentages.

Certain **guidelines** may be used while computing percentages.

- ❒ Avoid computing average of percentages, unless weighted by the size of the group from which it is derived.
- ❒ Percentages should be logically less than 100. A large percentage say 300 percent should be reported as 3 fold increase.
- ❒ Percentages hide the base. Comparison of percentages with small base will not carry much meaning.
- ❒ Percentage decreases and can never exceed 100 percent.

The number of rows and columns cells is often used to designate the size of the table, such as the one given in Table as 2 × 2 table. The cells are individually identified by row and column numbers. Row and column totals called marginals appear at the bottom and right margins of the table. They show both the counts and percentages of the separate rows and columns.

Cross tabulation is an association table, termed as **contingency table** and helps constructing statistics to test whether the classified variables are independent.

There are a wide variety of statistics available to analyse cross-tabulation. Some cross tabulation statistics are appropriate for nominal (categorical) scales, some for ordinal scales and some interval scales.In order to analyse the cross tabulation appropriately one should be able to recognise what type of data is appropriate for each statistic and to recognise the level of measurement for the scales under analysis.

Table 16.1
CROSSTABS STATISTICS

Level of Measurement (Type of data)	Appropriate CROSSTABS statistics
Nominal	Pearson chi-square, Likelihood Ratio, Phi, Cramer' V, Contingency coefficient, Goodman—Kruskal Tau, Uncertainty coefficient.
Ordinal	Gamma, Tau–*b*, Tau–*c*, Somers' *d*, Spearman correlation.
Interval	Pearson's *r* and Eta (η)

16.3.7 Missing Values

Missing data are a nuisance and can be a problem. It brings changes into analysis and becomes tiresome to explain the findings. In the analysis involving multiple variables, missing value in any variable may call for listwise deletion. Moreover, unless data are missing completely at random, an analysis that makes no adjustment for the missing data will be biased, because certain subgroups will be under represented in the available data. Such bias is a form of selection bias.

Another technique to deal with missing observations is the use of **imputation** techniques. With the development of theory, methods and computing power over the years, analytic methods for handling missing data to minimize their detrimental effects have improved. These methods seek to impute values for the missing item responses in ways that attempt to increase statistical efficiency and reduce bias. Earlier methods of using some average values for the missing ones are now out of favour and in fact these do not reduce the bias, instead tend to introduce additional distortion. More sophisticated methods using complete data cases and predictive models are available in statistical literature.

The complete cases (observations that have no missing values) for the variables of interest serve as the raw materials for the imputations. Factors that are theoretically related to the variables to be imputed and with which they are associated in the complete data cases, are used to develop 'predictive' models for the imputed variables. These models are then applied to the remaining observations, providing predicted ("imputed") values for their missing responses. The resulting imputations are said to be **conditional** on the variables in the model. For instance, suppose there is positive correlation shown by data between blood pressure and age. By conditioning imputations on age, we impute (on average) higher blood pressures to older subjects with missing blood pressure data and lower blood pressures to younger subjects with missing blood pressure data.

Imputation causes least distortion when the proportion of missing data is small, and data are available for variables that are strongly associated with the variable being imputed. However, imputation is most necessary when the proportion of missing data is large.

16.4 Descriptive Analysis

Exploration of data in certain stages becomes descriptive analysis. The problems involved in the statistical analysis are directly related to complexity of the research questions and the related hypotheses. Descriptive Analysis involves methods of

- statistical representation of data
- logical ordering of data,
- so that the question can be raised and answered.

The statistical representation of data invariably needs classifications, frequency distribution or tabulation.

The tabulation in order to have utlity, must have internal logic and order.

The most common summary statistics/descriptive statistics are

- ratios
- percentages
- proportions
- measures of location/averages
- measures of dispersion

A common and simple method of comparing frequencies is the use of ratio. For instance, consider, the age and sex classification of some population, below 15 years of age.

Age	Male (M)	Female (F)	Ratio (F/M)	Proportion of Males (M/(M +F))
0–4	500	450	0.90	0.526 (52.6%)
5–7	250	220	0.88	0.532 (53.2%)
10–14	150	140	0.93	0.517 (51.7%)
Total	900	810	0.90	0.525 (52.6%)

The proportions of males in the groups 0–4, 5–9 and 10–14 are 0.526, 0.532 and 0.517 respectively.

That is, proportion is a fraction where the numerator is one of two observed frequencies and denominator is the sum of the frequencies (*i.e.* M + F).

When proportions are expressed in multiples of 100, they are percentages.

The cross tabulation involving two or more attributes is a formal and economical method of arranging data, so that existence of association/correlation can be detected among the attributes/variables under consideration. It may be underlined here that the information gained through cross-tabulation depends on the logical design of the study and the insightfulness of the investigator.

The recognition of independent and dependent variables and the exploration of cause-effect relationship is aided by cross tabulations and researcher's intuition and deep understanding of the study and survey questions.

The diagrammatical and graphical representation of data are some popular methods for understanding the data and opens up the concealed features in the data, which are of interest to the researcher.

16.5 Analytical Statistics and Inference

The selection of variables and studying their nature play an important role in the analysis of data and form a basis for the rigorous applications of the basic principles of scientific method. **Correlation should be clearly distinguished from causation in the analysis.**

Besides computation of basic statistical derivatives such as frequency distribution, measures of location and dispersion, etc. there are certain important statistics, named as analytical statistics which provide tools for analytical comparison among different frequency distributions, cross tabulations and in the process explore relationship among variables-independent or explanatory and dependent. Differences and coefficients such as coefficients of association, coefficients of correlation, coefficients of regression are some of the analytical statistics widely used and analysed in research studies. In multivariate studies the analytical statistics bring out complex relationship in a multidimensional set up.

Management questions frequently involve relationship between two or more variables. Correlation analysis may be applied to study such relationship.

Parametric Karl Pearson's Correlation requires two continuous variables measured on an interval or ratio scale. The correlation coefficient represents an index of magnitude of relationship. Its sign governs the direction and its square explains the proportion of common variance. Bivariate correlation deals both the variables symmetrically and assumes linear relationship among variables.

Scatter plot of the variables enables the researcher to detect the direction, magnitude and shape of a relationship.

In a multivariate study the correlation matrix is used to display coefficients for more than two variables. This has helped the computation and understanding of the nature of relationships in multiple regression, discriminant analysis, principal component analysis, factor analysis and many multivariate statistical techniques.

Regression analysis provides further insight into relationship of Y and X, by bringing into the concept of dependent and independent (explanatory) variables. When the observed value of X is used in the regression equation to estimate or predict corresponding Y-values, the process is called **simple prediction.**

When more than one explanatory variable is used to compute a regression relationship, the outcome is a multiple regression equation which predicts unobserved dependent variable for given (observed) values of explanatory variables. The discriminant analysis classifies people/objects into categorical groups using metric predictors. The cluster analysis techniques are used for grouping similar objects. The principal component analysis extracts uncorrelated factors from the initial set of variables and factor analysis reduces the number of variables to discover underlying constructs.

Often, the assumptions or the measurement level for the applications of parametric techniques can not be met, non-parametric measures of association are the alternatives. Nominal measures of association are used to assess the strength of relationships in cross-classification tables. They are often used in conjunction with chi-square statistic. Ordinal measures of association include **gamma, Kendall's tau b and tau c** and **Spearman's rho**. None of these statistics require the assumption of normality and most produce a range from –1 to +1.

Analysis of variance techniques partition the total variation in an experiment into components ascribable to different sources of variation. Multivariate analysis of variance assesses the relationship between two or more metric dependent variables and independent classifactory variables.

In market research the conjoint analysis assists the researcher to discover the importance of product or service attributes and level of features that are most desirable. The perceptions about products or services are revealed numerically and geometrically by multidimensional scaling.

After the descriptive analysis comes the evaluation of study hypothesis put to answer the research questions or hypotheses which come out as by products of descriptive analysis or identified during such analysis. One aspect of descriptive analysis and hypothesis testing, especially the latter, is the assessment of the likely influence of random variability (chance) on the data. This leads to need for a more evaluation of potential confounding, other forms of bias and potential alternative explanations for what has been observed. Much of the field of statistics in recent times have grown up to deal with this aspect.

Many events happen in this world quite randomly or due to chance. A researcher with his observations from a population, not entirely known to him, wants to ascertain whether results he gets from sample evidence can be ascribable due to chance alone. His conclusions are based on the application of tests of significance, which are probably the most common procedures for assessing the role of chance.

Suppose a production manager innovates a manufacturing technique and wants to assess whether new manufacturing technique increases production. He brings out two sets of data on production based on old and new techniques and finds some difference. Now, the question arises whether the observed difference is due to chance alone or how likely the observed difference is due to chance. Let us consider another example where the effectiveness of vaccination is studied as to its association with attack due to a disease. The significance test in this situation simply evaluates the strength of numerical evidence of association for discounting chance as a likely sufficient explanation.

The role of chance is played by a suitable probability model, chosen to represent the probability structure of the data and the study design.

The probability model is set up under 'no difference' or 'no association' premises, which is generally a 'null hypothesis' (H_0). If there is sufficient numerical evidence to lead us to reject H_0, then we will decide that the converse is true, *i.e.* there is difference/association. The converse is designated as alternative hypothesis (H_1).

Two kinds of errors are likely to be committed.

Type I error : Erroneously reject H_0 (*i.e.* incorrectly, that data are not consistent with the model)

Type II error : Erroneously fail to reject H_0 (*i.e.* conclude, incorrectly that are consistent with the model)

Type I error is referred to as **significance level.**

Sometimes the underlying probability model tends to be more abstract and under the circumstances asymptotic test may be applied as an approximation, whose accuracy increases with increase in sample size. Typically, asymptotic tests are based on normal (Gaussian) distribution, which is easy to handle and also because of the **central limit theorem.**

Finally statistical analysis and interpretation of data depend on the quality of data and interpreting ability of the analyst who should have sound knowledge about the study at hand and technical expertise.

In this context a few words need to be pointed out about the statistics, statistical analysis and the role of statistician in a general context.

The uncertainty of events is the characteristic phenomenon of this world. Such uncertainty perhaps captured human minds in the dice games played in courts of nobles, kings and emperors in olden days. In dice game same numbers fell more often than others, thus questioning the logic behind such phenomena. Such observations in the field of dice/card games become the starting point the development of theory of chance or probability in later years and ultimately became the backbone of statistical science.

Whether or not, Lord God does not play dice with the universe, the world exists as it does, and the world and the people behave in a certain way. Because the world behaves as it does, things happen. We can observe the things that happen and describe these things by making measurements and these measurements yield statistics (plural). These statistics may be the results of an examination, scores in cricket matches, buying habits of the consumers, production of crop, sales of ice creams in market places, production in factories, etc. It is the object of statistics (singular–as a discipline) to examine them and try to learn from them something useful about the processes that created them, which is usually a difficult job in practice.

The inherent problem lies with the fact that there are many states of the world that can produce a given set of observations. For any given state of the world, one can attempt to work out statistics that would be produced, but it is quite a different matter to start with the statistics and say something about the world that produced them. Because of this it is often the case that what may appear to be conclusion to an unqualified analyst, are just not true and so why many people still associate statistics with lies.

For example, suppose we select a random sample of size 20 from community A and another random sample of size 20 from community B and measure their heights. Suppose the sample average height of persons in community A is 1.65 meters and the sample average height of persons in community B is 1.70 meters. Can you infer that the persons of community B are on the average taller than persons of community A ? We should not jump to such conclusion, primarily because we are drawing samples and also there might be considerable variations in heights in both the communities and further it is possible, some taller persons of the community B might have been included in the sample. If we draw larger samples from both the communities, the difference in heights may be smaller, but still showing that persons in community B are on the average taller, thus making the assertion stronger. In either case, statistics can **not** prove that the persons of community B are taller. However, in larger samples the persons of community A may also come out taller on the average. Statistical analysis is carried out on samples because it is often not possible to measure the entire population. So we take samples and use statistical analysis to draw conclusions about the populations from which these samples are drawn. Statistics from sample can never prove anything about the population. All one can do with statistics is to write down the hypothesis and then look at the data and say whether or not they are consistent with that hypothesis being true, backed by certain probability. 'Statistically significant' results are not truth.

Another instance where statistics is misinterpreted is the case of **mistaking correlation with causation.** If one makes a correlation analysis between 'how long you live and how much you earn', and finds the result is statistically significant, this conclusion is not statistically incorrect, but is not truth. One cannot look at association of this sort and draw conclusions about the cause. To some, this implies that money can by long life. But there are many who can interpret it differently. Economic prosperity can afford to get best possible medical treatment during illness. This is the cause. It is said that some statistician took a random sample of 50 towns and counted number of storks nesting in chimney stacks and the number of births per year and found high correlation. This correlation does not make any sense and the truth is that both these quantities are independently correlated with the size of the town. The bigger is the town, the greater were the numbers of chimney stacks and hence the more storks nests, also the greater were the number of houses and hence people and hence more babies. This discussion points out that an analyst should be careful in distinguishing correlation from causation to get rid of confusion in the analysis.

A statistical analyst is duty bound professionally and ethically to report what the data contain and reveal and nothing else. He is also not expected to be an alchemist who can produce gold out of worthless materials.

16.6 Content Analysis

16.6.1 Content analysis—an Introduction

Content analysis is defined as a research technique for the objective, systematic and quantitative description of manifest content of communication/ research data, procured through interview, questionnaires, schedules and other linguistic expressions, written or oral. It is a research tool focussed on the actual content and internal features of communication messages through media. It is used to determine the presence of certain words, characters, or sentences within texts or sets of texts and quantify this presence in an objective manner. Texts can be broadly defined as books, book chapters, essays, interviews, discussions, newspaper headlines and articles, historical documents, speeches, conversations, advertising, theatre, informal conversation or really any occurrence of communicative language. In business researches content analysis makes use of materials of interest to managers and business studies.

Although communications required for the content analysis are sometimes published, some researchers take recourse to content analysis after asking people to produce some publications, essays, answer to interview questions, diaries, verbal protocols, etc.

Content analysis has been on plays, folklores, religious books, legends, popular music, drama etc. to demonstrate differences in existing cultures and sub-cultures and changes in content may be taken as indicative of changes in public attitude.

Content analysis can indicate pertinent features such as comprehensiveness of coverage or the intentions, biases, prejudices and over sights of authors, publishers, as well as all other persons responsible for the content of materials. It is a **specialised application of coding techniques.**

To sum up content analysis is a method for summarizing any form of content by counting various aspects of the content. This enables a more objective evaluation than comparing content based on the impressions of a listener/observer, for example, impressionistic summary of a TV program is not content analysis.

Content analysis, though often analyses written words, is a quantitative method. **The results of content analysis are numbers and percentages.**

The counting serves two purposes :

❒ to remove much of the subjectivity from summaries.

❒ to simplify the detection of trends.

16.6.2 What is Content ?

The content that is analysed can be in any form to begin with, but is often converted into written words before it is analysed. The original source can be printed publications, broad cast programs, other recordings, the internet or live situations. All this content is something that people have created.

Example of Content :

- **Print media.** Newspaper items, magazine articles, books, catalogues.
- **Other Writings.** Web pages, advertisements, bill boards, posters, etc.
- **Broadcast Media.** Radio programs, news items, TV programs.
- **Other recordings.** Photos, drawings, video, films, music.
- **Live Situations.** Speeches, interviews, plays, concerts.
- **Observations.** Gestures, products in shops.

16.6.3 Media Content and Audience content

The foregoing examples constitute media content. When we get feedback from the audience, the content reduces to **audience content.**

The audience content is classified into :

- Private audience
- Public audience

The private audience includes :

- Open-ended questions in surveys
- Interview transcripts
- group discussions

Public audience content comes from communication between all the audience members, such as :

- Letters to the editor
- Postings to an online discussion forum
- Listeners' responses in talkback radio.

Content analysis is a product of the electronic age. Though content was regularly performed in the 1940's, it became a more credible and frequently used research methods since the mid 1950's as researchers started to focus on concepts rather than simply words, and on semantic relationships rather than just presence.

16.6.4 Uses of content analysis.

Due to the fact that it can be applied to examine any piece of writing or occurrence of recorded communication, content analysis is used in large number of fields, ranging from marketing and media studies, to literature and rhetoric, ethnography and cultural studies, gender and age issues, sociology and political science, psychology and cognitive science, management science as well as other fields of enquiry. Additionally content analysis reflects a close relationship with socio and psycholinguistics and is playing an integral role in the development of artificial intelligence.

The unobtrusive nature of content analysis makes it well suited for strategic management research.

16.6.5 Stages of Content analysis

- ❒ Selecting content for analysis
- ❒ Units of Content
- ❒ Preparing content for coding
- ❒ Counting and weighting
- ❒ Statistical Inference and analysis
- ❒ Drawing conclusions

Selection of content is an important aspect of content analysis. This requires selection of a representative sample of contents. The sampling means sampling body of information—often called **corpus.** As regards decision about sample size, it is necessary to take a very large sample unless one looks for very fine distinctions.

To be able to count content, the corpus needs to be divided into a number of units, roughly similar in size. Although there is no limit to the number of units in corpus, the larger the unit, the fewer the units you need for the corpus. If the units vary greatly in length, the long unit will have a greater chance of including some theme, whose presence one is looking for. If interviews vary greatly in length, a time based unit may be more appropriate than 'per interview.'

Before content analysis can begin it needs to be preserved in a form that can be analysed. For print media, the internet, and mail surveys no **transcription** is needed. However, radio and TV programs, as well as recorded interviews and group discussions, are often trancribed before the content analysis can begin.

Coding in content analysis is the same as coding answers in a survey : summarizing response into groups, reducing the number of different responses to make comparisons easier. Thus, it is required to sort concepts into groups, so that in each group the concepts are both :

- ❒ as similar as possible to each other and
- ❒ as different as possible from concepts in every other group.

The types of audience content most commonly produced from research data, which need coding, are :

- ❒ Open ended response to a question in a survey.
- ❒ Statements produced by consensus groups.
- ❒ Comments from in-depth interviews or group discussions.

In these cases the unit may be either a person or a comment.

In market research organizations, open ended questions are usually coded before the data entry stage. The computer file of results has only the coded data, not the original verbatim answer. Coding is necessary to reduce the data to a manageable mass, but any piece of text can be coded in many different ways. It is therefore important to able to check the coding easily, by seeing the text and the codes on the same sheet of paper.

When all the preparation for the content analysis has been done, the counting is usually the quickest parti-specially if all the data is on a computer file and software is used for the counting.

An important part of any content analysis is to study the content that is not there : what was not said. The content one finds in the analysis can be compared with the content that the analyst (or the audience) expected or it can be compared with another set of content. When one compares two corpora, the content analysis becomes most useful. Making a comparison between two matched sets of data will often produce very interesting results. These comparisons are usually made using cross-tabulation and statistical significance testing.

Different analysts could analyse the same set of content and arrive at completely different conclusions. The focus of the study controls what is noticed in the content. Any content analysis report should begin with a clear explanation of the focus—what was included, what was excluded, and why. This would minimise difference in conclusions. The content analysis cannot boast of including all aspects of the data. Therefore, when reporting content analysis, it is important to select and present some key units of content in the report. Another aspect to note is that the coding principles should be explained in the report.

16.6.6 Advantages of Content Analysis

Content analysis offers several advantages to researchers who consider using it. In particular, content analysis :

- looks directly at communication via texts or transcripts, and hence gets at the central aspect of social interaction.
- can allow for both quantitative and qualitative operations
- can provide valuable historical/cultural insights over time through analysis of texts.
- allows a closeness to text which can alternate between specific categories and relationship and also statistically analyzes the coded form of the text.
- can be used to interpret texts for purposes such as the development of expert systems (since knowledge and rules can both be coded in terms of explicit statements about the relationships among concepts)
- is an unobtrusive means of analyzing interactions
- provides insight into complex models of human thought and language use
- when done well, is considered as a relatively "exact" research method (based on hard facts, as opposed to Discourse Analysis).

16.6.7 Disadvantages of Content analysis

Content analysis

- can be extremely time consuming.
- is subject to increased error, particularly when relational analysis is used to attain a higher level of interpretation.
- is often devoid of theoretical base.
- is inherently reductive, particularly dealing with complex texts.
- tends too often to simply consist of word counts.
- often disregards the context that produced the text, as well as the state of things after the text is produced.
- can be difficult to automate or computerise.

Further, sampling for content analysis may not be perfect and accurate. Different communicators explain or analyse a problem with different criteria or references. Sometimes it may be difficult to objectively and adequately define a category, when categorisation is the basis of content analysis. The information contained in a communication is qualitative in nature which may not necessarily be converted into quantitative data by simply counting the frequencies. Inefficient coding may affect the reliability of content analysis.

16.7 SWOT Analysis

The SWOT (strength, weakness, opportunities and threats) analysis in management/social science research is a very useful tool to identify the strengths, weaknesses, opportunities and threats in relation to a project or group or organisation and how such an assessment will change overtime. This analysis provides a framework for decision making and as a precursor to strategic planning in various kinds of applications. A SWOT analysis is perhaps the most effective and objective way to determine how capable the organisation is when it comes to surviving 'threats' and capitalising on 'opportunity'. Similarty in case of projects, this method is useful when qualitative assessments, for example, the services provided by the project, relationships between beneficiaries/project stakeholders and the implementing agencies or partners, local groups and the project team itself, are being made. **What are the underlying meanings of four words-strength, weaknesses, opportunity and threats ?**

'Strength' refers to all those material and non-material things that are working well in an organisation/project. The deficiencies or those things, which did not work well, are the 'weaknesses', 'opportunities' are the external factors that are readily available to overcome the weaknesses and build on strengths. 'Threats' are those things that constrain or threaten the availability of opportunities for change. Strengths and weaknesses are the internal aspects, while opportunities and threats can be from internal or external sources/factors.

Steps for SWOT Analysis

Step 1

Make a worksheet with four sectors one each for strength, weaknesses, opportunities, and threats such as :

1. Potential Internal Strength

(*a*)

(*b*)

(*c*)

(*d*)

2. Potential Internal Weaknesses.

(*a*)

(*b*)

(*c*)

(*d*)

3. Potential External Opportunities

(*a*)

(*b*)

(*c*)

(*d*)

4. Potential External Threats

(*a*)

(*b*)

(*c*)

(*d*)

Step II :

Discuss and record as many factors as possible for each of the headings in the worksheet.

Step III :

SWOT analysis can be formed by the individual or in groups, for example during a workshop or in a community.

Group techniques are more effective in providing structure, objectivity, clarity and focus to discussions about strategy.

Step IV.

Based on the observations, decisions are taken as regards future course of action to capitalise the opportunities and to overcome threats.

Advantages and limitations

SWOT analysis is a flexible method, which takes into account different views of those involved in joint action. Past mistakes and weaknesses are duly considered. This is one of the easiest ways to solve the complex problems within the shortest time possible. It is easy to communicate ideas, policies and concern to others.

Opportunities and threats are not absolute. What might at first seem to be an opportunity may emerge as the potential threat to the organisation or effective implementation of programmes. Thus, there is need to make a careful and correct judgement of factors that would benefit the organisation.

SWOT's reflect the viewpoint of individuals, which can be misused to justify a previously decided course of action than used as a means for newly carved out ends. SWOT analysis always entails a correct judgement on future course of action.

16.8 PARTICIPATORY RESEARCH

The conventional methods of social research have long relied on questionnaire based interview surveys where random samples are selected from a large population and the respondents are selected to answer questions pertaining to various issues. The questionnaire surveys, however, suffer from many limitations and associated inherent problems. This led to innovation of participatory research, as an alternative method and approach to orthodox positivist research.

The participatory research consists of several approaches and methods. It has a defined methodology and is a systematic learning process, where emphasis is given on cumulative learning by all the participants. If involves the researchers/professionals working alongside the stakeholders, recognising the knowledge, power and strengths of these group processes. The PR is a process which facilitates empowerment of participants towards a change at structural and personal levels.

The participatory research distinguishes between two forms of participation in development scenario

(i) participatory development (ii) participation in development.

The **participatory development** approaches conventional project practice in a more participatory and sensitive manner and is introduced within the pre-determined project framework. Further, it is a **top-down** form of participation in the sense that the management of the project defines where, when and how much the people can contribute towards development through participation.

The **participation in development** is a **bottom up** form of participation in the sense that local people have full control over the process and the project provides for necessary flexibility. It entails efforts to engage in practices that openly and radically encourage people's participation. It is more prevalent with NGOs than with the Government machinery.

Participation includes people's involvement in decision-making processs, in implementing programmes, their sharing in benefits of development programmes and their involvement in efforts to evaluate such programmes.

People's participation is essentially to do with economic and political relationship within wider society ; it is not just a matter of involvement in project activities, but rather the process by which the people are able to organise themselves, through their own organisation, are able to identify their own needs, share in design, implement, and evaluate participatory action.

Participation is an active process by which the beneficiaries or client groups influence the direction and execution of a development project with a view to enhancing their well being in terms of income, personal growth, self reliance or other values they cherish.

Thus, PR can be defined as a family of approaches and methods which ensure people's participation in investigation, planning and action followed by monitoring and evaluation of development activities for increasing their socio-cultural and economic well being and at large, for the societal and institutional transformations. Although, as an approach of learning and action originally developed for rural areas, it is at present widely used in a variety of settings. This approach can be employed successfully at all stages of the development project cycle and in different sectors of the economy.

16.9 Data Analysis by Software Packages

Data analysis in the context of present day sophisticated computing facilities has been revolutionized by the innovation of a number of powerful statistical software packages, *e.g.* SPSS/SAS/STAT, etc. Instruction manuals are available for the professional software packages as regards benefits, features and operational procedures.

SPSS

SPSS is the acronym of **Statistical Package for the Social Sciences.**

- ❐ SPSS is one of the most popular statistical packages which can perform highly complex data manipulation and analysis with simple instructions.

- SPSS is a comprehensive and flexible statistical analysis and data management system. SPSS can take data from almost any type of file and use them to generate tabulated reports, charts, and plots of distributions and trends, descriptive statistics, and conduct complex statistical analysis. It is among the most widely used programs for statistical in social science. It is used by market researchers, government and commercial establishments.
- SPSS package programs is available for both personal and mainframe (or multi-user) computers. SPSS package consists of a set of software tools for data entry, data management, statistical analysis and presentation. SPSS integrates complex data and file management, statistical analysis and reporting functions.
- SPSS makes statistical analysis accessible for the casual user and convenient for the experienced user. The data editor offers of simple and efficient spreadsheet like facility for entering data and browsing the working data file. To invoke SPSS in the windows environment, select the appropriate SPSS icon. There are a number of different types of windows in SPSS.
- The latest version of SPSS, developed by SPSS Inc. is SPSS 16, which works with OS : Windows, Unix and Mac.

SPSS has scores of statistical and mathematical functions, scores of statistical procedures, and a very flexible data handling capability. It can need data in almost any format (*e.g.* numeric, alphanumeric, binary, dollar, date, time formats).

Besides other functions, some of the common functionalistics of SPSS are

- Data transformation/Data Examination
- Descriptive statistics
- Contigency tables
- Correlation
- t-tests
- ANOVA
- MANOVA
- General Linear Model
- Regression
- Nonlinear Regression
- Logistic Regression
- Log linear Regression
- Discriminant Analysis
- Factor Analysis
- Cluster Analysis
- Multidimensional scaling
- Non-parametric Analysis
- Forecasting/Time series
- Graphics and graphical interface, etc.

SAS

The SAS system (orginally **Statistical Analyses System**) is an integrated system of software products provided by SAS Institute.

From traditional analysis of variance and predictive modelling to exact methods and statistical visualization techniques SAS software provides tools for both specialized and enterprise-wise analytical needs.

Increasingly organizations are turning to statistical analysis to guide decision making processes. Using optimal statistical techniques can provide new information that improves processes. SAS software is designed for use by business analysts, statisticians, researchers and engineers.

Statistical procedures in SAS are constantly being updated to reflect the latest advances in statistical methodology, thus enabling one to go beyond the basis for more advanced statistical analysis.

SAS software is designed to handle large data sets from disparate sources, enabling the analyst to take advantage of all data that is available for analysis.

The software products enable the programmer to perform

- ❒ data entry, retrieval, management and mining
- ❒ report writing graphics
- ❒ statistical and mathematical analysis business planning, forecasting and decision support.
- ❒ operations research and project management
- ❒ quality improvement
- ❒ applications development
- ❒ data warehousing
- ❒ Platform independent and remote computing.

In addition, the SAS system integrates with many SAS business solutions that enable large scale software solutions for areas such as human resource management, financial management, business intelligence, customer relationship management and more.

The latest version of SAS system developed by SAS Institute is SAS 9.1.3 service Pack/April 2006. The required operating systems are Windows, IBM mainframe, Unix/Linux.

Key Features

- ❒ **Analysis of variance.** Analysis of variance is a technique for analyzing experimental data. With SAS/STAT software, you can perform analysis of variance for balanced or unbalanced designs, multivariate analysis of variance and repeated measurements analysis of variance.
- ❒ **Regression.** SAS/STAT software's general regression procedure uses least squares to estimate parameters, includes nine different model selection methods and produces a variety of diagnostic measures. More specialized procedures fit generalized linear models, mixed linear models, nonlinear models and quardratic response surface models.
- ❒ **Categorical data analysis.** In categorical data the outcome of interest reflects categories with data often presented in tabular form, known as contingency tables. With SAS/STAT software, you can investigate the association in a contingency table as well as produce measures that indicate the strength of that relationship.

- **Multivariate analysis.** Multivariate analyses encompass a variety of methods for modeling data with two or more response variables or for identifying relationships among several variables without designating particular variables as response or explanatory variables. You can use common factor analysis to explain the correlations among a set of variables in terms of a limited number of unobservable, or latent variables.

SAS/STAT software also includes many other types of analysis, including :

- Survival analysis
- Psychometric analysis
- Cluster analysis
- Nonparametric analysis
- Survey data analysis
- Multiple imputation for missing values
- Study planning.

Note. More about benefits, operations and features about SAS software will be found its manual and software fact sheet.

EXERCISES

1. Explain the relationship between data preparation and data analysis.

2. Discuss different steps for preparation of data for subsequent analysis.

3. 'Data do not speak for themselves'. Elucidate this statement.

4. Explain the difference between descriptive analysis and inferential analysis.

5. Briefly mention different multivariate applications in data anlaysis.

6. Comment on the statements :

(*a*) "Lies, damned lies and statistics".

(*b*) "Statisticians are not alchemists who can produce gold out of worthless materials."

7. (*a*) What is cross-tabulation ? Mention its uses in statistical analysis.

(*b*) What are the statistics available for analysing cross tabulated data ?

8. What is content analysis ? Mention its importance in Business research.

9. Write a note on SWOT analysis.

10. What is participatory research ? Mention its utility.

11. Write notes on :

(*a*) Data editing (*b*) Data cleaning

(*c*) Data coding (*d*) Exploring data

12. Distinguish between types of discrete variables and continuous variables.

13. Explain the need for data reduction.

14. How does missing data create problems in data analysis ? What are the remedies ? Explain.

15. Mention appropriate cross-tabulation statistics for different levels of measurement.

□□□

CHAPTER

17

REPORT WRITING AND ORAL PRESENTATION

17.1 What is a report ?

A Report may be defined as a document in which a given problem is examined for the purpose of conveying information, reporting findings, putting forward ideas and sometimes, making recommendations.

In Oxford English Dictionary **'A report is a statement of the results of an investigation or of any matter on which definite information is required.'**

In a general sense a report is an account of something (information), presented in an organised form and requested by an authorised person, who wants to use that information. It is said to be a communication from some one who has the information to some one who wants to use that information.

A research report is written for a specific audience for a specifice purpose and includes the procedure of collecting data, its subsequent analysis and conclusions obtained by the researcher/writer and also often includes recommendations.

Thus, a research report is defined as a formal communication for a specific audience and contains (*i*) the purpose and/or probelm that necessitates the report. (*ii*) the information dealing with methods of investigation as well as materials and equipments used (*iii*) results, conclusions, limitations and recommendations (if any).

Research reports are a highly structured form of writing often following conventions that have been laid down to produce a common format. Structure and convention in written reports stress the process by which the information was gathered as much as the information itself.

A few key and consistent attributes about all reports are as follows :

- Reports follow conventional organizational patterns.
- Reports are grounded in factual supportable details.

- ❐ Reports address specific readers' needs because they may want to use the information provided by the report.

Thus, the basic orientation of a research report depends on its audience. Before writing the report.

- ❐ the researcher must know his audience.
- ❐ he may have to make assumptions about the composition, background and interest of target readers.

Broadly two types of research reports may be distinguished :

❐ **Technical report :**

suitable for a target audience of researchers, research managers or other people familiar with and interested in the technicalities such as research design, sampling methods, statistical details, etc.

• **Popular report :** suitable for a more general audience, interested mainly in the research findings as it is non-technical in nature.

To sum up, the research report is a means of communication that can be understood, believed and trusted by every one who are likely to be affected by the research and acted upon by the decision maker. The researcher should discuss the major findings, conclusions and recomendations with the key decision makers.

Report writing is a specialised form of written communication. Many of the rules which must be observed when writing a report are therefore, equally applicable to written communication in general.

The research report is the final product after hard work physical as well as intellectual involved throughout the research process beginning from the selection of the problem and research planning and design till the completion of the project through busy field investigation schedules and analysis of voluminous data. The preparation of report is the final stage of the research investigation and its sole purpose is to convey the interested reader/manager/client the purpose of the study and to determine for himself the validity of the findings and conclusions. It is of utmost importance for the researcher to consider his audience before he begins to embark upon fulfilling his responsibility of writing the report so that his report will adequately communicate his research to the readers to whom it is meant. Thus, the researcher while writing the report should keep in mind **'who will read the research report and how will they read it?'**

The quality of presentation of research findings puts an inordinate effect on a reader's mind as to study's quality. On this front the researcher is supposed to be an expert on the subject and he only knows the specifics than no one else. As the report is an authorised one way of communication, it stands on an obligation for maintaining objectives.

The report is expected to be presented in a lucid style and clarity in language, bereft of jargons and should be prepared keeping in view the end users/audience of the product. The research reporting is not a simple task as it may seem in the first reaction, and also not a populist report, but a document exploring new vista of knowledge hither to unknown, to be discussed either in a scientific community or in the committee of planners or among the senior management cadre or for the benefit of the general public.

Long report and short report

Reports differ as to their degree of formality and design. The formal report follows a well delineated and relatively **long format** unlike an informal or **short-report**.

The **short report** is prepared when the problem is well defined and is of limited scope and has simple and straight forward methodology. Further, it has the same standard as that of informal and interim reports and contains only a few pages containing brief statement about the authorization of study, the problem examined, conclusions and recommendations followed by the findings supporting them. The purpose of the short-report is to distribute information quickly in an easy to use format. A letter of transmittal is a vehicle to convey short reports with informal tone, omitting detailed information on the research method, although an overview is appended,

Long reports include–**technical and management reports.** The choice is motivated depending on the audience and the researcher's objectives. The technical report is meant for the audience of researchers where as management report is written mostly in non-technical language for the non-technical manager or client.

The **technical report** includes full documentation and detail.–'What was done and how it was done'. Non-essential materials are avoided but sufficient procedural information should be included to enable some body to replicate it. It has all the elements of a scientific research report including the sources of data, research procedures, sampling design, data collection techniques, methods of data analysis, etc. The report provides background of earlier research theories, findings, conclusions and recommedation before presenting full presentation and analysis of significant data and related specific findings without much technical jargons.

The **management report,** on the other hand, is meant for those having little or no research background, such as managers and clients. As the management report is written for the non- technical audience, the researcher has a prime responsibility to provide lucid statement of research objectives, major findings, conclusions and recommendations, which enable the managers in making decisions. The readers of such category are **not** much interested in methodological details. The style of the report should be so as to encourage quick easy reading and appraisal. The reporting tone may sometimes be journalistic, but should be accurate. **Headlines and underlinings** for putting emphasis about certain points become helpful for the readers, besides in certain cases provision of graphs and pictures in replacing tables. *Liberal use of reporting papers for presenting the reports is advisable with single finding on each page for easy and quick comprehension.*

17.1.1 Objectives

The objectives of a report identify exactly what information it covers, for whom it is written and why it should be produced; these objectives should be clear to the writer long before the process of writing starts.

It may be necessary to keep in mind that the writer should note down the precise details and check regularly until the last stages of production.

The writer should ask himself the following questions :

❐ What does the reader already know about the material of this report ?

❐ How wide is the reader's knowledge of the subject ?

- ❒ Why should the particular reader need this particular report ?
- ❒ What is it necessary to tell the reader ?
- ❒ What will be the reader's expected response ?
- ❒ What from the writer's point of view is the desired response ?
- ❒ How can the writer bridge the gap between what the reader knows already and what the writer wants the reader to know, in order to produce desired response ?

17.1.2 Purpose of Reports

Reports generally have one of the following, sometimes overlapping purposes :

- ❒ to report information, including key aspects of daily activities, meetings, trips, and conferences; to report progress on projects.
- ❒ to analysis information, including data for decision making and data from laboratory studies or field studies.
- ❒ to persuade readers to consider the analysis and accept any recommendations

Regardless of the type of the reports, the writer should consider why it is needed and for whom it is needed. At times, some one needs information to stay informed, make a decision, or justify an action. The content, style and format of reports simplify readers' work.

17.2 Types of Reports.

Reports may be

- ❒ Oral
- ❒ Written

An **oral report** is a piece of face to face communication about something seen or observed and is liable to be changed if repeated.

A written report is relatively more accurate and permanent. It can be referred to again and again by its nature of presentation and is more formal than an oral report.

17.2.1 Formal and Informal Reports

The written report may be classified as

- ❒ Fomal
- ❒ Informal

The primary differences have to do with writer's familiarity with the audience, the amount of documentation in the report and the tone.

Formal reports generally follow a prescribed format such as **Front matter, Body** and **Back (End) matter. Infomal reports** usually run from a few paragraphs to a few pages and is shorter version report having only essential elements such as : **Introduction, Body, conclusions and recommendations.** Because of their brevity, informal reports are customarily written as a letter or as a memorandum and are used for internal purposes and for dealing with routine issues such as task reports, periodic activity reports, progress reports, trip and conference reports, 'to file' (archive) documents.

Deciding whether a report should be informal or formal has less to do with subject of the report than with the readers, and writer's assessment of their information needs. After the writer decides about the intended audience, he can decide whether to write an informal or formal report. For instance, if the research is carried out on high yielding varieties of paddy, the researcher may like to write an informal report to his research team, but a formal one to the funding agency.

In contrast to informal reports, writers of formal reports probably don't have regular contact with their readers. Because the readers may not be familiar with the background, it needs to be included in formal reports, usually making the reports longer and more detailed. These reports need more documentation because the readers may not know the history or sources.

Formal reports generally adhere closely to strict conventions of languages. Most formal reports also have a number of standard sections : such as an abstract and table of contents, end matter such as references and appendices. Because of the extensive front matter in a formal report, it tends to repeat content, something that seldom occurs in an informal report. However, this is usually an advantage rather than a disadvantage because the multiple audience for formal reports read various sections for different purposes. For example, managers focus on conclusions and recommendations so they can make informed decisions. Technical professionals focus on the accuracy and feasibility of the technical details. Individual readers seldom go through the entire report, rather they read the sections to suit to their interests and relevant to their jobs.

What distinguishes a formal report from an informal reporting of information ? The answer lies not in the topics of formal reports, but in the expectations of the audiences for formal reports. In a formal report, the audience expects a methodical presentation of the subject that includes summaries of important points as well as appendices on tangential and secondary points. The audiences for a formal report include professionals specializing in the report's subject matter, professionals not specializing in the report's subject matter, and managers overseeing the report's subject matter.

Organising formal reports

A formal report's audience and purpose influence not only its content but also its organization. Writing for a mixed audience requires the writer to organize the material so that it serves all categories of readers, whatever their different needs.

A well-crafted formal report is formatted such that the report's information is readily accessible to all the audiences. For that reason, formal reports are split into different sections. One way to group these sections is in terms of the **front matter, main text** (body) and **back (end) matter.** The **front matter,** which presents preliminary information for the report, serves to orient all intended audiences to what the report contains. The text portion of the formal report is the report's 'story' and contains the introduction, discussion and conclusion of the report. **The text** delivers a methodical explanation of the report's work to the report's primary audience. The report's **back matter** portion, which cotains the appendices, glossary, and references, serves to provide secondary information to all readers as well as primary information to secondary readers.

Organising Informal Reports

Informal reports dealing with routine issues may be organised into the following categories :

- ❐ Task reports (recommendation, justification, inspection, information, investigation)
- ❐ Periodic activity reports (daily, weekly monthly, quarterly)
- ❐ Progress (interim, status) reports.
- ❐ Trip and conference reports.
- ❐ 'To file' (archive) documents.

17.2.2. Types of formal reports

Formal reports may further be classified as

- ❐ Informational
- ❐ Interpretive/Analytical
- ❐ Presuasive

Informational reports inform data collected or facts observed in an organised form. Reader sees the details of events, activities or conditions. There are no analysis of the situations, no conclusions and no recommendations. They are usuful because they present relevant collected data put together, as required by the management to take appropriate decision.

Analytical reports are written on collected facts to solve problems . Information, thus collected is analysed, conclusions are drawn and recommendations are made.

Persuasive Reports are an extension of analytical reports. The main focus is to sell an idea, a service or a product. Proposals are most common types of persuasive reports.

17.2.3. Some common informal Reports

Progress Reports : Progress reports summarize the progress, status, and projections related to a particular project.

Progress reports (sometimes called status reports or interim reports) are part of almost all long range projects and may also be expected in short-term projects. When a long term project is under implementation, the administration may like to be informed about the progress during the course of running the project. The project may be either the construction of a bridge, buidling complex, installation of a factory or the investigation of some problems. These reports help the officers and workers immediately responsible for the explanation of the project to take stock of what already has been done with an eye on the total money and time available.

Information about the progress answers a variety of readers' questions.

- ❐ How is the project going ?
- ❐ What has been accomplished during this phase of the project ?
- ❐ How much time or effort, money etc. did these tasks take ?

Information about status answers the following questions :

❒ Where are we now ?

❒ How do current activities relate to overall project ?

❒ How does this work affect other phases of the project ?

Information about projections answers some more readers questions :

❒ Are we on schedule to meet our completion date ?

❒ What plans need to be changed or altered ?

❒ What will do in the future ?

A progress report gives the following sequence of information.

❒ Overview : Introduce the project.

❒ Progress : Summarize the porogress to date.

❒ Recommendation : Identify major recommended schedule changes.

❒ Evidence : Provide reasons for changes.

❒ Discussion : Discuss the impact of changes.

The overview of a progress report orients readers to the project, identifying the purposes of both the project and the report. Additionally the overview surveys the project and specifies the dates covered in the report. Some progress reports recommend changes necessitated by the progress or lack of progress.

The frequency of progress report depends on the practice followed by concerned organisation.

If the progress reports are prepared at regular intervals, they are sometimes called **periodic** reports. The proforma may differ from organisation to another.

But in any case the proforma contains the following essential information.

❒ Name of the project

❒ Total work to be completed

❒ Date of starting of the project

❒ Work completed up to date

❒ Work to be completed

❒ Possible date for completion

❒ Remarks including the changes to be incorported and its possible effects

❒ Signature and position of the Reporting Officer.

❒ Date of reporting.

The **final report** will contain the same types of data as the interim report but more numerical details and more extensive analysis of data.

Laboratory Reports : In science and engineering researches a number of experiments are conducted to test a theory, verify the modifications proposed or to examine the validity of research findings.

The writing laboratory reports is considered as essential for any scientific investigation and experiments.

The following points need to be mentioned in a laboratory report

❒ Heading

❒ Experiment No.

- ❒ Date
- ❒ Statement of objects
- ❒ Apparatus used
- ❒ Method or procedure followed
- ❒ Observations
- ❒ Conclusions
- ❒ Signature

Inspection Reports :

Inspection reports may concern with the inspection of

- ❒ a piece of equipment to ascertain whether functioning properly
- ❒ a lot of products to ascertain whether the products conform to quality envisaged.
- ❒ a visit to ascertain whether the program on any subject has been effectively implemented.

Inventory Reports :

Inventory report is a periodical report prepared usually by every business/manufacturing concern **to take stock** of the materials, equipment, furniture, stationery etc. existing to date.

The person who prepares inventory i.e. checks the stock and fills in his observations in a prescribed form.

A specimen form

Sl. No	Item	Stock on hand (Date–)
1.		
2.		
3.		
4.		
:		

Confidential Reports :

In almost all organisations the performance and general conduct of the employees are periodically assessed to keep an eye on their efficiencies. Appropriate forms prepared for organisations are used for the purpose to write the reports, which are generally of confidential nature and referred at proper time for promotion and award of increments. Several characteristics are observed for each individuals, e.g. appearence, character, motivation, relationship, output, expression, integrity/honesty, special achievements, other remark etc. with the help of grades/scales such as excellent, good, average, below average (5-point scale). The report requires the signature of the reporting officer with date and place and subsequent remarks by the senior officers in the cadre. Confidential reports form an essential component of assessment of employees to keep track on their efficiencies and to impose disciplinary actions, if any. Sometimes self assessment forms are used to be countersigned with remarks by the controlling officer and his seniors in the official cadre.

Meeting Minutes :

The record of the proceedings of any deliberative group is usually called the **minutes.** Minutes provide a record of the discussion and decisions that occur at meetings, serving as official (sometimes even legal) records. Beyond their function of official documentation, minutes provide a convenient review of the meeting for people who attended as well as for those who did not.

Preparing the minutes for a meeting requires both organization and attention to long established conventions. The agenda for a meeting can provide you with a basis from which you can organize the information. If the meeting was recorded, you can use the tape to fill in details, you may have missed while taking notes. The emotions and feelings, if any, expressed by members during the course of discussion are generally not recorded.

Ordinarily, unless the minutes are to be published, they should contain mainly a record of what was done at the meeting, not what was said by the members. The minutes should never reflect the Secretary's opinion, favourable or otherwise, on anything said or done. When you are called upon to write the minutes of the meeting, take down the notes carefully and then prepare the draft of the minutes and before giving it a final shape to show them to the Chairman.

When a proposal or resolution is approved by a majority, the name of the proposer and seconder should be recorded along with the votes cast for and against it. The following items are generally given place in the minutes.

- The name of the organizational unit, *e.g.*, Board of Directors, Syndicate meeting, Finance committee, etc.
- The date, time and place of the meeting
- The serial number of the meeting if it is in a series. *e.g.* sixth meeting etc
- Names of members present, those could not attend and special invitees, if any.
- Record of transactions
- Signature of the Secretary and the Chairman.

The minutes need to be read and approved by the members at the next meeting and signed by the chairman. often the minutes are circulated to members before hand for approval. If any member suggests an amendment, the chairman signs the minutes after seeking the approval of the members present at the meeting.

Notices and Agenda :

A meeting whether the general body meeting or a meeting of the smaller groups is to be arranged with the help of a notice circulated among the members eligible to attend the meeting. A meeting is to be called according to some prescribed rules of the body for which the meeting is to be arranged and notice is to be served. The notice must reach members within reasonable time before the meeting and must indicate date, time and place of the meeting.

Agenda is an official list of items to be discussed or business to be transacted at a particular meeting.

An agenda usually accompanies a notice as an annexture or may be circulated separately and contains the following elements.

- ❒ Name of the organisation.
- ❒ Date of circulation.
- ❒ The day, time and place of meeting.
- ❒ The programme of business to be transacted.
- ❒ Background information, if any.
- ❒ Signature of Secretary.

The first item on every agenda is the confirmation of the minutes of the previous meeting and last item any other matter with the permission of the chairman.

Memorandum :

A **memorandum** is a short piece of writing generally used by the officers of an organization for communicating among themselves and sometimes termed **inter-office memorandum.**

The main pupose of the memorandum is to record or convey information and decisions or to make short requests.

A memo serves and ensures quick and smooth flow of information in all directions and helps good business relationships among the officers.

A memo sometimes comes to aid when it is desired to avoid face to face contact with certain colleagues having lapses in their activities against the interest of the organisation. It also serves an important useful function to establish accountability.

Many organisations have printed memo forms to be used by officers in writing the message and its subsequents transmission. It takes comparatively less time compared to writing letters. It contains the designation of the sender, designation of the receiver, reference, date and of course the subject matter. The printed memo should have the name of organisation/department concerned at the top and if the copies are to be submitted to other officers, an indication is to be given at the bottom as in case of letters.

Recommendation Report :

The goal of recommendation report will be to help the reader to solve a problem by presenting results of research and your evaluation of the findings.

In these reports specific actions are suggested to solve a problem that the writer identifies. In addition the report will highlight criteria for decision making in its structure.

In general recommendation reports will answer the following types of questions.

- ❒ Which is better option A or B ? (comparative analysis)
- ❒ Is the project feasible ? (feasibility study)
- ❒ Why does 'x' happen and what can be done about it ? (cause-effect analysis)

Reports for Decision Making :

A sponsor whether he is a manager of a firm or head of an organisation gets the report from the vendor/researcher for taking steps for the implementation of the points raised in the management questions, either in the form of certain suggestions or recommendations.

At the outset, if he is not equipped with sufficient technical knowledge to understand the contents of the report before taking decisions, he may as well appoint a technical committee to go through the report, discuss the incorporated results and study its implications along with the benefits to be accrued therefrom. If the report contains alternative courses of action, these actions should be weighed according to benefits, inherent difficulties for implementation and the possible adverse effects (if any) requiring certain changes in the organisational set up and increased cost, if any.

On the favourable recommendations received from the committee, the manager may go ahead with the implementation and if necessary, after taking into confidence senior officers in the management cadre, experienced workers and public concerns.

Typical Business Reports :

Report	Purpose
Periodic Operating Reports	To monitor and control production, sales, shipping, service, etc.
Situatioal Report	To describe one-time events, such as trips, conferences, and seminars.
Investigative/Informational	To examine problems and supply facts–with little analysis.
Compliance	To respond to government agencies and laws.
Justification/Recommendation	To make recommendations to management and become tools to solve problems and make decisions.
Yardstick	To establish criteria and evaluate alternatives by measuring against the "yardstick" criteria.
Feasibility	To analyze problems and predict whether alternatives will be practical or advisable.
Research Studies	To study problems scientifically by analyzing a problems, developing hypotheses, collecting data, analyzing data, and drawing conclusions.
Proposals	To offer to solve problems, investigate ideas, or sell products and services.

17.2.4 Research Report format

Reports are generally divided into sections. Each section has a specific purpose and often there are specific guidelines for formatting each section.

Generally, a report will include the following sections

- Title page
- Abstract
- Table of contents
- Introduction

- Body
- Recommendations
- References
- Appendices.

However, some distinctions may be made among formats of three types of report :

- Long format report
- Short formal report
- Informal report

The structure of a long formal report may be as follows :

- Title page
- Contents
- Synopsis
- Terms of reference
- Procedure
- Detailed findings
- Conclusions
- Recommendations
- Appendices
- Bibliography/References.

Short formal report is written for internal use in companies/institutions.

The structure of short formal report is as follows :

- Title page
- Terms of reference
- Procedure
- Findings
- Conclusions
- Recommendations
- Appendices

Informal reports are used for internal use, particularly within departments dealing with routine issues. Memorandum format is often used for these reports.

The structure of an informal report is as follows :

- Introduction
- Main section findings
- Final section conclusions and Recommendations.

Note. The headings of the format in formal report varies as per the requirements of the sponsoring authority and the presentation needs and style of the writer of the report.

17.3 Basic components of a research report

Research reports whether short or long have a set of **identifiable components.**

Headings and subheadings are used to divide different sections incorporated in the report. Depending on the type of users, the report may drop or add the sections.

The basic components are :

1. Prefatory particulars :
   - (*i*) Letter of transmittal
   - (*ii*) Title and cover page
   - (*iii*) Authorization letter
   - (*iv*) Summary of study design, findings and recommendations
   - (*v*) Acknowledgements
   - (*vi*) Table of contents
   - (*vii*) List of tables, figures (optional)
   - (*viii*) List of abbreviations
2. Introduction :
   - (*i*) Statement of the problem
   - (*ii*) Research objectives
   - (*iii*) Review of literature
3. Methodology
   - (*i*) Sampling design
   - (*ii*) Research design
   - (*iii*) Data collection techniques
   - (*iv*) Data analysis techniques
   - (*v*) Limitations
4. Research Findings
5. Discussion
6. Conclusions
   - (*i*) Summary and conclusions
   - (*ii*) Recommendations
7. Appendixes/Annexes
8. Bibliography/References

Letter of transmittal

When the relationship between the researcher and the client is formal, it is necessary that a letter of transmittal should be included and more so when the user is a specific client outside the organisation. This should refer to authorities sponsoring the project, their instructions or limitations placed on the study. However, for internal projects, such letter of transmittal may not be necessary.

Title and Cover page

The cover page should contain the title of the report, the name(s) of the author(s)/researcher(s) with his/their title(s)and position(s) the organisation/institution for whom the report is prepared and is publishing the report, and the month and year of publication.

Authorisation letter

When the report is sent to any public organisation, it is an usual practice to include a letter of authorisation showing the sponsoring authority for undertaking the research.

Summary

Summary is a miniature report covering all aspects of the body of the report but in a concise form. The summary should be written only after the first or even the second draft of the report has been completed. It should contain :

- a very brief discription of the problem (WHY this study was needed)–the main objectives (WHAT has been studied)
- the place of study (WHERE)
- the type of study and methods used (HOW)
- major findings and conclusions, followed by
- the major (or all) recommendations.

The summary will be the first part of the study that will be read. Therefore, its writing demands thorough reflection and is time consuming. Several drafts may have to be made, each discussed by the research team as a whole.

Acknowledgements

It is a good practice to thank those who supported the researcher technically or financially in the design and implementation of the study. Also, the employer who has allowed the researcher to invest time in the study and the respondents may be acknowledged. Acknowledgements are usually placed right after the title page or at the end of the report, before the references.

Table of Contents

A table of contents is esential for any report. It provides the reader a quick overview of the major sectors of the report, with page references, so that s(he) can go through the report in a different order or skip certain sections and on the whole it is a rough guide to the content of the report.

Tables, figures and abbreviations

If the report includes tables or figures it is helpful to list these also, in a 'table of contents' type format with page numbers.

If abbreviations or acronyms are used in the report, these should be stated in full in the text the first time they are mentioned. If there are many, they should be listed in alphabetical order as well. The list can be placed before the first chapter of the report.

Introduction

The introduction is a relatively easy part of the report. The introduction is the place for a broad, general view of your material. This includes the **statement of the problem** under study and need for the research project highlighting management questions, followed by more detailed set of objectives.

Research objectives address purpose of the study. The objectives may be research questions and associated investigative questions. In correlational/causal studies the hypothesis statements are to be included. They also indicate clearly the variables of concern and their interrelationships, besides the target group under study. Further operational definitions of certain critical variables may also be required to be mentioned.

Finally it should contain a paragraph on what of researcher hoped to achieve with the results of the study.

The **review of literature** is an important component in any research report. It is ethical to highlight the research work of the torch bearers on the subject of research study, high lighting its connection and effects on initiating the present research and management questions. Background materials included in the report may be preliminary results from experience survey, focus group and other sources or alternatively the secondary data from literature review. The literature mentioned in the report should be organized, integrated or presented in a way that connects logically to the problem. The background also includes definitions and assumptions made in the previous research work.

The Methodology

The methodology may not be explicitly mentioned in short and management reports, but in technical report this should be adequately dealt with. **Sampling design**, if used in the study, states how to reach the target group in the population and the sampling method and also the sample size. Further, major study themes or variables involved in the study may be annexed. The coverage of the **research design** must be adapted to the purpose. In this context, in an experimental study the materials, tests, equipment, control and conditions and other devices should be described in detail.

The section for **data collection techniques** describes the specifics of collecting of data either in field or in experiments, depending in the selected design. All problems connected with field work, training and supervision of field workers and administrative problems are also to be included, along with handling the irregularities, non-response, non- contacts etc. in the field.

Data analysis component of the methodology describes the procedures used for analysing data including statistical tests (if applicable).

It is professionally sound and ethical to state the **limitations of the proposed study** so that quick generalizations are cautioned. If the researcher has deviated from the original study design presented in the research proposal, he should explain to what extent he did so and why. The consequences of this deviation or meeting certain objectives in the study should be indicated. If the quality of some of the data is weak, resulting in possible biases, this should be described as well under the heading 'limitations of the study'.

Research Findings

The systematic presentation of findings in relation to research objectives is the crucial part of the report. The objective is to explain the data rather than draw interpretations or conclusions. The quantitative data can be presented as simply as possible with charts, graphics and tables.

The description of findings should offer a good combination or triangulation of data from qualitative and quantitative components of the study. There are two different ways in which one can present the findings.

(a) *An integrated presentation of all data by objective* : This is a much easy proposition. The integrated presentation will be a compilation of tables, graphs, narrative interpretation and illustrative documentation from in-depth interviews, etc.

(b) *Presentation of data by research instrument* : Sometimes it is easier to analyse the data by instrument and integrate the findings only in the discussion.

Separate analysis is indicated for objectives that are covered by distinct study populations using specific instruments.

The list of data by objective will help the researcher to decide how to organise the presentation of data. The decision concerning **'where to put what'** can be best be made after all data have been fully processed and analysed, and before the writing starts.

When all the data have been analysed, a detailed **outline** has to be made for the presentation of the findings. This will help the decision making on how to organise the data, and is an absolute precondition for optimal division of tasks among group members in the writing process.

A outline should contain

- The headings of the main sections of the report
- The heading of subsections
- The points to be made in each section, and
- A list of tables, figures and/or quotes to illustrate each section

The **outline for the chapter** on findings will predictably be the most elaborate. The first section usually gives a description of the study population. Then, depending on the study design more information on the problem studied is provided. Thereafter, in an analytical study, the degree to which different independent veriables influence the problem will be discussed.

Tables and figures in the text need numbers and clear titles. It is advisable to first use the number of the section to which the table belongs and in the final draft the researcher may decide to number the tables and figures in sequence.

Discussion

The findings are discussed by objective or by cluster of related variables, themes, which should lead to conclusions and possible recommendations. The discussion may include findings from other related studies that support or contradict it.

Summary, conclusions and recommendations

The summary is a brief statement of the essential findings. There may also be sectional summaries, combined into an overall summary. In descriptive research simple summary completes the report, because conclusions and recommendations may not be required.

Findings state facts; conclusions represent inferences drawn from findings with an eye to the objectives.

Conclusions may be presented in a tabular form for easy reading and reference. Recommendations provide a few ideas corrective actions. The conclusions and recommendations should follow logically from the discussion of the findings. As the discussions follow the sequence in which the findings have been presented, the conclusions should logically follow the same order. It makes easy reading for an outsider if the recommendations are again placed in roughly the same sequence as the conclusions. In making recommendations, use not only the finding of the study, but also supportive information from other sources.

In academic research the recommendations include study suggestions, that broaden or test understanding of the subject area.

Appendixes

The appendixes are the place for complex tables, statistical tests, supporting documents, copies of forms and questionnaires, detailed description of the methodology, instructions to field workers and other important evidences incorporated in the report.

The annexes should contain any additional information needed to enable professionals to follow research procedures and data analysis.

Bibliography/References

The use of secondary data requires a bibliography which is a honest declaration of the sources of information and research materials, documents etc. used for the present report.

It is important that the writer gives the precise details of all the work done by other authors which has been **referred** to within the report.

Details of the reference should include

- ❒ author's name and initials
- ❒ date of publication
- ❒ title of the book/research paper/monograph, etc.
- ❒ Name of journal, if any
- ❒ Publisher
- ❒ Place of publication
- ❒ Page number
- ❒ details of journal volume in which the article has appeared.

References should be listed in alphabetical order of the author's name.

Make sure that the references are accurate and comprehensive.

17.4 Report writing process

There are three cardinal rules of report writing :

(*a*) Accuracy

(*b*) Brevity

(*c*) Clarity

However, these are not very easy to be mastered. It must be remembered that **'Hard writing makes easy reading'.** A report writer must constantly strive to make his task as easy as the subject matter permits.

Pre-writing Exercise

Before drafting the report, the report-writer should take out a piece of paper and write down answers to the following questions as pre-writing exercise.

- ❒ Describe the purpose of research undertaken.
- ❒ Describe the most important feature of research.
- ❒ Make a list of anyone who contributed to present research and who could be involved in writing the research report.
- ❒ Compile the list of works by other researchers, which were used in the present research or that is related to the research at hand.
- ❒ Describe the ways in which the present research proves or disproves other researchers' work.
- ❒ Describe the background of this subject.
- ❒ Describe what you expected to find before the research started. How did the project change over time ? How did your results differ from expectations.
- ❒ Describe your results.
- ❒ Describe the consequences of the current research. How will it affect future research in the subject ?

FLOW CHART RESEARCH REPORT

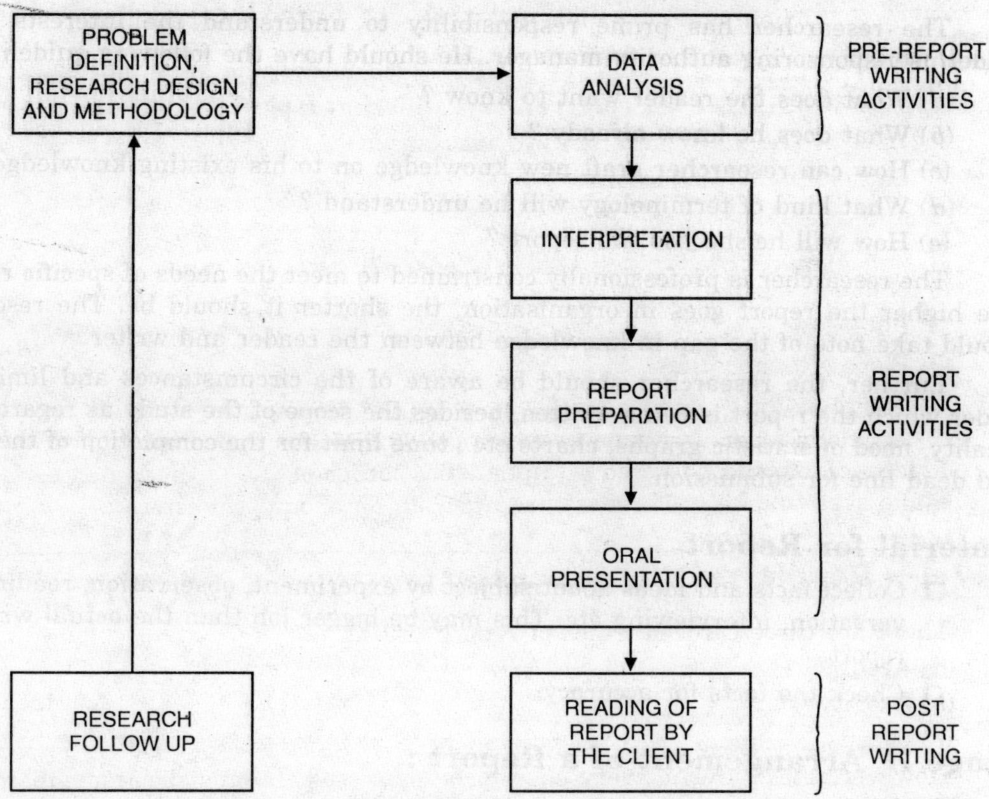

Fig. 17.1

- ❒ Describe the ideal audiences for the research reports.
- ❒ Consider the specific guidelines under which the research is undertaken.

Make a list of sections required to be included in the report.

The report writing method may be classified into four stages.

Stage I : Preparation of Report
Stage II : Arrangement of Report
Stage III : Writing of Report
Stage IV : Revision and finalisation of Report

Stage I : Preparation of Report

At the first step a researcher should, aware of the **'terms of reference'.** That is, he must know exactly **what has been asked to do.** He should establish clearly in his mind the subject, scope and purpose of report. The purpose will generally be a combination of some or all of the following :

- ❒ To give information, either general or detailed
- ❒ To report findings
- ❒ To put forward ideas
- ❒ To recommend a course of action

The researcher has prime responsibility to understand the interests of the reader/user/sponsoring authority manager. He should have the following guidelines :

(*a*) What does the reader want to know ?
(*b*) What does he know already ?
(*c*) How can researcher graft new knowledge on to his existing knowledge ?
(*d*) What kind of terminology will he understand ?
(*e*) How will he/she use the report ?

The researcher is professionally constrained to meet the needs of specific readers. The higher the report goes in organisation, the shorter it should be. The researcher should take note of the gap in knowledge between the reader and writer.

Further, the researcher should be aware of the circumstances and limitations under which the report is being written, besides the scope of the study as regards technicality, need of statistic graphs, charts etc., time limit for the completion of the report and dead line for submission.

Material for Report

- ❒ Collect facts and ideas about subject by experiment, observation, reading, conversation, interviewing etc. This may be bigger job than the actual writing of report.
- ❒ Check the facts for accuracy.

Stage II. Arrangement of a Report :

Observance of the following points will help the researcher to construct a concise, logical and well arranged report.

1. Write down the purpose briefly. This will test the understanding of task and deter from including unnecessary points.

2. Consider collected facts and ideas. Reject any which on second thoughts are neither helpful nor necessary to the purpose at hand. Add notes of any others which now appear essential or desirable.

3. Prepare the outline and review any main division critically. Once the researcher has made the analysis of the data, drawn tentative conclusions and completed statistical significance tests, it is time to develop on outline and consider what the main divisions (major topic headings) should be and to choose section headings (major sub topic headings) for each main division.

4. Decide the order of the main divisions. They will form sections of the report. Number section headings so that they can be easily referred to in any discussion of report.

5. Within each division, arrange material in order which the reader will easily follow. Lead the reader step by step from the known to the unknown. Careful arrangement of material in order is the only way to clarify the complex subject.

6. Make sure that conclusion and recommendations square with facts. Decide whether to group them in a section of their own which will form a natural conclusion to the report.

Alternatively, they may be distributed among the sections to which they belong.

7. Review title and section headings critically. The should identify, and not merely the subject matter under them. Brevity is desirable, but should be precise and with informative words.

8. Consider illustrations to supplement or replace words. A good informative diagram is ofhen worth more than pages of writings.

9. Consider the use of footnotes. Foot notes should be as brief as possible. These may be used to give sources of quotations or references mentioned in the text; and to indicate authorities or sources of information. This may explain passages in the text which may be clear to some readers but not to others.

10. Consider whether the factual details can be taken out of the main divisions and placed in the appendices. Appendices perform functions similar to those of footnotes by removing distracting details and ths enabling the reader to follow main line of thought without interruption. The details may also be summarised in report itself.

11. Prepare a bibliography and check whether the sources referred in preparing the report are duly included. A bibliography documents the sources used by the writer.

Stage III. Writing the report

Before finalising the report it is always advisable to prepare a draft report which is subject to revision. Each writer uses different mechanisms for getting thoughts into written form. While preparing the draft the writer should consider the reading ability of their audience to achieve high readership. High readership is dependent on the topical interest created in the minds of the readers.

Good writing varies with the writing objective. **Research writing** necessitates conveying information in a precise manner and ambiguities, multiple meanings and allusions are required to be avoided. Words and sentences should be carefully organized and edited. This requires to choose words carefully, opting for the known and short rather than the unknown and long.The tone of writing is an important aspect to be looked into when reviewing the writing. The reader can or should be referred to but the researchers should avoid referring to themselves.

When time comes to undertake final proof, it is advisable to put the draft away for some time and relax and then take a final look at the draft for critical examination of all aspects.

The preparation draft needs following points for consideration.

1. Report Style. Decide what the tone of the text should be. A lucid, business-like and balanced exposition is usually desired in business. For scientific and technical reports a challenging or controversial approach may, however, occasionally be justified.

2. Arrangement. Consider whether the writer can help the reader by numbering or lettering paragraphs or items within the sections. Any numbering scheme must be maintained consistently and must be set out on the page so that it is clearly subordinate to the section numbering.

3. Illustrations. Think of illustration while writing, so that reading matter and visual items may be closely linked. Every illustration should be referred at least once in the text and should be accompanied by an identifying caption or title. It is also advisable to number the illustrations for reference.

4. Introduction. The introduction is a must for any report, which may be written last of all. It is the place for a broad, general view of the study material. Details are to be avoided because their best places belong to main sections or appendices.

- ❒ Define subject and indicate broadly its extent, composition and significance.
- ❒ State your purpose and terms of reference, and indicate how far one is able to carry them out.
- ❒ State fully, or summarize the results, conclusions and recommendations.
- ❒ Announce the arrangement of your main sections.
- ❒ Define technical terms and words (jargons) that are intended to be used in a special sense.

On the whole the **writer should try to make the introduction as interesting as one** can.

5. The main sections and appendices. The writer should try to concentrate writing one of the sections/appendices at a time. For each section

- ❒ State facts obtained and indicate sources.
- ❒ Analyse facts.
- ❒ State conclusions and recommendations.
- ❒ Describe procedures followed in investigations or experiments.
- ❒ Refer to, or summarize, matters fully presented in an Appendix.

6. The conclusion :

- ❒ Summarize the discussion in the main sections.

- ❒ Summarize findings and inferences.
- ❒ Make recommendations based on findings and inferences.
- ❒ State clearly what action should be taken.
- ❒ Emphasize finally the significance of the subject matter.
- ❒ Refer briefly to any wider considerations, outside the terms of reference, on which the report may have a bearing.

7. List of references. Each reference should contain full information in the following order :

- ❒ Author
- ❒ Title
- ❒ Edition
- ❒ Place of publication
- ❒ Publisher
- ❒ Date of publication

8. Table of contents. The reader may wish to have a glance at the main headings/subheadings without going right through the report. This is why, a **table of contents should precede the introduction.**

9. Synopsis (Summary). A synopsis or summary of the report precedes the Table of contents and introduction.

Stage IV : Revising and finalising the report :

After the completion of the draft, lay it aside for a day or two, if time permits and try to judge it objectively as though it were work of another author.

This involves a cursory examination of the draft with critical examination of the title, objectives, table of contents, introduction and conclusion in relation to one another. The text should be examined in detail and every statement should be weighed critically. The following questions should be kept in mind when reading the draft.

- ❒ Whether the problem has been formulated scientifically and focussed in right direction ?
- ❒ Whether the hypotheses have been formulated explicitly ?
- ❒ Whether proper considerations have been taken to be apprised of the related literature and discussions among the scientific community to formulate right, meaningful and verifiable hypotheses ?
- ❒ Have all important findings been included ?
- ❒ Do the conclusions logically follow from the findings ? Are there any contradictions ? Have these been discussed and explained ?
- ❒ Are there any overlaps in the draft ?
- ❒ Is it possible to condense the content ?
- ❒ Do data in the text agree with data in tables ? Are they numbered in sequence with clear titles and headings ?
- ❒ Does the summary really summarize the results to serve the purpose of the study ?
- ❒ Have paragraphing, grammar punctuation and spelling checks been taken into account ?

If the illustrations are included in the report, these need to be checked as regards their necessity and clarity, conveying the message clearly and serving the purpose for which they are meant and avoiding longwinded explanations in the text.

Finally before submitting the final report, the writer, if possible, may ask for comments and constructive criticisms from a qualified person, familiar with subject of study.

Report size is another important issue, needing consideration. The size varies depending on the level of authority/management to whom it is submitted for use. For instance, the report submitted to an Executive-level manager may be a shorter one say containing one or two pages compared to an operational–level personnel, for whom the report size may be, say, around 50 pages or so. Of course, there is no hard and fast rule as to the number of pages, but the top level managers need shorter report for perusal.

As a last word, the writer of a research report should adhere to the following :

Style of writing

- ❒ *Proper paragraph structure :* A paragraph should convey a single idea. They should flow nicely, one to the next.
- ❒ *Sentences should not be too long,* say not more than 20 words.
- ❒ *Write in active voice* (Direct speech). The passive voice becomes wordy and boring when used consistently. Use adverbs and adjectives sparingly. Be consistent in use of tenses.
- ❒ *Eliminate Jargons.*
- ❒ *Make no statement that is not based on facts and data.*
- ❒ *Quantify when you have the data to do so.* Avoid 'large' and 'small', instead, say 50%, one third etc.
- ❒ *Be precise and specific in phrasing of findings.*
- ❒ *Inform, not impress. Avoid exaggeration.*
- ❒ *Aim to be logical and systematic in presentation.*

Lay out of the report

A good **physical lay out** is important as it will

- ❒ make a good initial impression
- ❒ encourage the readers and
- ❒ given them an idea of how the material has been organised, so that the reader can make a quick determination of what he will read first.

Particular attention should be paid to make sure that there is

- ❒ An attractive lay out for the title page and a clear table of contents.
- ❒ Consistency in margins and spacing.
- ❒ Consistency in headings and subheadings.
- ❒ Good quality printing and photocopying.
- ❒ Correct drafts carefully for grammatical and spelling mistakes.
- ❒ Numbering of figures and tables, provision of clear titles for tables, and clear headings for columns and rows etc.
- ❒ Accuracy and consistency in quotations and references.

17.5 Guidelines for effective report writing

Introduction

There are a number of characteristics of an effective document. These characteristics can be summarised as follows :

❒ The document should include all the information the readers need. This means including important information to the document as an appendix and cross reference or cite documents that contain less important information.
An effective document should also provide a background section (*e.g.* background theory) if the audience includes readers unfamiliar with the topic. This document should also include a clear description of the writer's methods, as well as a complete statement of the principle findings. These findings include the results, observeations (discussion), and any conclusions.

❒ The document should be structured so that readers can easily locate the information they seek. Some readers are interested in only one or several sections of a document. Other readers might read most of them. But relatively few people will read the whole document from start to finish, like a novel.
To achieve this, discussions should be self-contained, and headings and lists easy to identify. Also for reports, a detailed table of contents should be given.

❒ Your writing should be as concise as you can make it without sacrificing content. One way to shorten a document is to replace long words and phrases with short ones. Short documents are better than long documents.

❒ Workplace writing is meant to get a job done, not to show off your personal style. The reader should be thinking about the subject you are writing about and not about you.

❒ Always acknowledge your use of other people's ideas or words by citing them. This involves referring to information that you may have read by citing the document from which it came (and possibly the section in the document if it is a book).

Steps for Writing

This section discusses the steps commonly used to write effective documents. This involves gathering your ideas, organising them, drafting the document, and finally revising the document.

Generate ideas to include in the document. Before you start writing, you must decide what information the document will contain. One particular method for generating ideas is brainstorming. Brainstorming involves quickly listing all the ideas that might be appropriate for the document. Write ideas quickly without trying to organise them; this organisation will be done next.

Organise your ideas using some kind of outline. This involves ordering your ideas into some structured pattern. Examples of patterns are :

1. Chronological. This pattern is useful if the reader needs to follow your discussion in order to perform a task.

2. Classification. This involves placing items into logical categories.

3. Partitioning. This involves breaking a single entity into its logical components.

Write the draft quickly. This involves quickly turning outline into sentences and paragraphs. Don't worry about individual words and sentences; leave this until the revising stage.

Spend your time revising the draft. After writing the draft, leave the document for as long as possible. When revising the draft, the following areas should be looked at :

1. Comprehensiveness. Have you covered everything in your outline, and have you gone into sufficient detail to make the message clear ?

2. Accuracy. Make sure all your data and statements are accurate.

3. Organisation. Does the information follow a clear and logical order ?

4. Emphasis. Provide the same level of information on each subpoint ? If a certain point needs more clarification than another, then structure the discussion accordingly.

5. Paragraphing. Does each paragraph have a clear topic sentence that summarises the information that follows ? Is the paragraph logically organised and developed ?

6. Style. Check for sentence variety (don't keep using the same phrase over and over), grammar and punctuation mistakes, and awkward sentence constructions.

7. Spelling. Always check for spelling mistakes by using either a spell chcker or having someone else read the document. Spelling errors are almost always visible when someone else reads the document.

Improving Your Writing

The document should follow from one idea to the next smoothly without having to re-read the sentence or paragraph to grasp its meaning. The reader should be able to read the document once without getting lost by what you are saying.

Use informative titles and headings. Titles and headings should be sufficiently precise and easy to read and understand.

Use lists to communicate parallel information. Many sentences become quite long and complicated. Information that is parallel should be presented as a list, either vertically or horizontally. These lists can either be numbered or listed using bullets.

Use introductions to forecast discussions. Because you know the subject better than the reader, you must adequately explain what information you are going to present, how you're going to present it, and why you're presenting it that way. The questions you need to ask yourself are :

1. What is the subject ?
2. What is the purpose of the discussion ?
3. What is the background of the subject ?
4. What is the scope of the discussion ?
5. What is the organisation of the discussion ?
6. What are the key terms that will be used in that discussion ?

Use conculsions to complete discussions. This is done by answering the following questions :

1. What are the main points established in the document ?
2. What should be done next ?

The second question would only need addressing if there is any future work involved.

How to Write Better Paragraphs ?

Effective paragraphs simply state the idea and then explain or defend it. Hence, paragraphs begin with a clear topic sentence, and then support this idea logically. The paragraph should contain certain words and phrases to help the reader make the transition from one sentence to the next. There are four steps in writing an effective paragraph :

1. Begin with a clear topic sentence.
2. Support the topic sentence logically.
3. Emphasise the coherence of the paragraph.
4. Keep paragraphs to a manageable length.

How to Write Better Sentences ?

Style is how you sound when someone reads what you have written. You need to be straightforward, clear, concise, unpretentious, authoritative, and easy to understand. You do not want to be pompous, unclear, and verbose.

• **Use the active and passive voices appropriately.** The active voice focuses on the performer of the action, whereas the passive voice focuses on the recipient of the action. The active voice is usually more precise and less wordy than the passive voice. In general, the active voice is preferable.

• **Use appropriate tense.** Whenever you quote or discuss previously published work (possibly your own), you should use the present tense. Whenever you present your own work (*i.e.* work you did in an experiment), you must use the past tense.

• **Choose appropriate sentence patterns.** There are four types of sentences :

1. Simple. The simple sentence has only one independent clause.

2. Compound. The compound sentence has two independent clauses, linked by a semicolon or by a comma and one of the seven coordinating conjunctions : *and, or, for, nor, so, but,* and *yet.*

3. Complex. The complex sentence has one independent clause and at least one dependent clause.

4. Compound-complex. Th compound-complex sentence has at least two independent clauses and at least one dependent clause.

• **Use modifying elements effectively.** There are two types of modifiers :

1. Restrictive Modifiers
2. Non-restrictive Modifiers

Restrictive modifiers restict the meaning of the word (*i.e.* they make the word more specific). Non-restrictive modifiers simply provide extra information about the word.

• **Keep parallel items parallel.** Do not turn parallel information into sentences. Either use a list, or number each item in the sentence.

How to Choose the Right Word ?

• **Choose simple, clear words and phrases.** Picture yourself speaking on the phone to a good friend. If you would be embarrassed to have the person hear what you have written, change it.

• **Replace fancy words and phrases with plain words and phrases.**

Creating and Integrating Graphics

• **Determine whether you need graphics.** Do not construct tables unless repetitive data must be presented. Do not simply present reams of data because you have them in your workbook; only present the important information.

• **Determine what kind of graphic to use.** If a graph presents that data better than a table (*i.e.* it shows the significance between certain values better), then use a graph.

• **Make the graphic self-sufficient.** Support the figure or table with text to allow the reader to examine the figure without having to read the supporting text to understand its significance. Always label axes on graphs (also giving units).

• **Determine where to put the graphic.** Place the graphic as close to the reference in the text as possible. Normally, it is placed on the same page or the page following.

• **Tie the graphic to the text.** This involves introducing the graphic and explanining its significance, cross-referencing appropriately (*e.g* Figure 1 : *Title of figure*) and referring to the label figure 1, or Fig. 1, in the text. Tables and figures should use separate numbering sequences.

Improving Page Design

There are a number of areas for improving the clarity of the information contained on the page.

❒ Leave adequate margins.

❒ Use appropriate line spacing.

❒ Use appropriate justification.

❒ Use easy-to-read fonts.

❒ Use different members of a single type family.

❒ Use type sizes appropriately.

❒ Use uppercase and lowercase.

❒ Design titles and headings for emphasis and clarity.

❒ Design lists for clarity.

❒ Include page numbers on all pages.

Checklist for report writing

❒ **Title page**

Does this include the :

Title ?

Author's name ?

❐ **Acknowledgements**

Have you acknowledged all sources of help ?

❐ **Contents**

Have you listed all the main sections in sequence ?

Have you included a list of illustrations ?

❐ **Abstract or summary**

Does this state :

The main task ?

The methods used ?

The conclusions reached ?

The recommendations made ?

❐ **Introduction**

Does this include;

Your terms of reference ?

The limits of the report ?

An outline of the method ?

A brief background to the subject matter ?

❐ **Methodology**

Does this include;

The form your enquiry took ?

The way you collected your data ?

❐ **Reports and findings**

Are your diagrams clear and simple ?

Are they clearly labelled ?

Do they relate closely to the text ?

❐ **Discussion**

Have you identified key issues ?

Have you suggested explanations for your findings ?

Have you outlined any problems encountered ?

Have you presented a balanced view ?

❐ **Conclusions and recommendations**

Have you drawn together all of your main ideas ?

Have you avoided any new information ?

Are any recommendations clear and concise ?

❐ **References**

Have you listed all references alphabetically ?

Have you included all the ncessary information ?

Are your references accurate ?

❒ **Appendices**
Have you only included supporting information ?
Does the reader need to read these sections ?
❒ **Writing style**
Have you used clear and concise language ?
Are your sentences short and jargon free ?
Are your paragraphs tightly focused ?
Have you used the active or the passive voice ?
❒ **Layout**
Have you clearly labelled each section ?
Is your labelling consistent throughout the report ?
❒ **Presentation**
Have you left sufficient margin space for binding/feedback ?
Are your headings clear ?
Have you checked your spelling ?
Overall :
❒ What are the main points for consideration ?
❒ What have you done well ?
❒ What needs fine tuning ?

17.6 Data Analysis and writing the report

The writing a research report is logically associated with data analysis and interpretation. The quality and usefulness of the report to facilitate the decision making process is dependent on how efficiently the investigation was carried out, keeping objectives in mind and also how judiciously data were processed, analysed and interpreted.

Some likely steps in data analysis and writing the report are shown in Table–17.1 in a sequence. However the sequence may be changed for convenience according to the needs of the researcher and his team.

TABLE 17.1
Data analysis and writing the report

Questions you must ask	Steps you will take	Important elements of each step
What data have been collected for each research objective ? Are data complete, accurate ?	Prepare data for analysis	Review field experience Make an inventory of data for each objective/study population. Sort data and check quality. Check computer outputs
What do the data look like? How can the data be summarised for easy analysis?	Summarise data and describe variables/identify new variables	Frequency tables, figures, means, proportions, descriptive cross-tabulations, (quantitative data). Coding, listing, summarising data in compilation sheets, flow

		charts, diagrams and narratives (qualitative data)
How can the associations between variables be determined ?	Analyse associations	Analytic cross-tables Measures of association
	Prepare for statistical analysis	Measures of location and dispersion, deciding about Normal distribution and Sampling variation
Do we measure differences of associations between variables ?	Determine the types of statistical analysis	Choosing significance tests–bivariate and multivariate
How can differences between groups be determined ?	Analyse unpaired and paired observations	t-test, chi-square etst **paired t-test, **Analysis of variance
How can associations between numeric variables be determined ?	Implement measures of association	**Scatter diagram, **Regression lines **Correlation coefficient –Linear and Multiple
How should the report be written ?	Write the report and formulate recommendations	Prepare outline for report. Present and interpret data. Draft and redraft. Discuss and summarise conclusions. Formulate recommendations
How should the findings and recommendations be communicated, disseminated and used ?	Present summaries and final report for implementation of recommendations	Discuss summaries and plan for implementation with all stakeholders and knowledgeable experts.

17.7 What is a technical report ?

A technical report is a **formal report** designed to convey technical information in a clear and easily accessible format. It is divided into sections which allow different readers to access different levels of information. It describes the process, progress or results of technical or scientific research or the state of a technical or scientific research problem.

The essence of a successful technical report lies in how accurately and concisely it conveys the intended information to the intended readers.

'Who is going to read the report' should always ring in the ears of a technical report writer. The answer will affect the content and technical level.

The objectives of a report identify exactly what information it covers, for whom it is written and why it should be produced; these objectives should be clear to the writer long before the process of writing starts.

On the identity of the reader will depend not only the approach but also the technical level and the style of writing.

When the objectives of the report are firmly established, the material must be collected; indeed, some of it will probably be already available. Decisions about organising the information can begin now, even if they are only provisional.

As material arrives, it should be put into one of three categories :

1. obviously important information which must go into the report because it is completely relevant to the objectives.
2. borderline information which might be useful to some readers, or which might amplify or substantiate other more important material.
3. information which is interesting (or not) to the writer, but which is not relevant to the objectives of the report.

Technical reports are today a major source of scientific and technical information. They are prepared for internal or wider distribution by many organisations. Technical reports are often prepared for sponsors of research projects. Many organisations collect their technical reports into a formal series.

Reports vary in content and informality and also, of course, may have to follow the outline which is standardised in company templates. Nevertheless, there are widely accepted sections, all of which would appear in a long and very formal report; they must be adopted or amalgamated as the writer thinks appropriate for the reader's needs.

The full format of a long report can be as follows :

❒ Title page
❒ Acknowledgements
❒ Summary
❒ Table of contents
❒ Introduction/Terms of Reference/Scope
❒ Procedure
❒ Findings (the evidence)
❒ Conclusions
❒ References/Bibliography
❒ Appendices

Most technical reports might not need such a detailed breakdown, but it is helpful for writers, to keep the scheme in mind in arranging the information, even if they do not use the headings in full.

17.7.1. Purpose of Technical Report

A technical report may be grouped into a number of sections according to their rhetoric purposes.

❒ Descriptive
❒ Analytical
❒ Comparative
❒ Conclusive
❒ Persuasive
❒ Summaries

This list may not be all inclusive but the aforesaid six elements can be usually found in all technical reports.

Descriptive elements are simple to write. The purpose is to provide reader with a word picture of something, condition or problem associated in your report.

Analytical reports are often more difficult to write and throws a challenging task to writer in explaining the reader often long reasoning process. In order not to lose the attention of the audience, you may reverse the actual process, probably used to arrive at your conclusions. That is, first state your conclusions and then reasons out for believing them to be correct.

There are very few technical problems for which there is only 'right' solution. Develop a comparison matrix, graphical method rating method, tabular method for stating alternative solutions along with their features with pros and cons views. Use of this kind of presentation makes the reader to understand the report better and moreover reduces your job as the technical writer to summarising it in the text of your report.

After the main task of the technical investigation is completed, take the time to assess the results.

Then ask yourself :

- ❒ What can we conclude from what we have just done ?
- ❒ Are the results what we expect ?
- ❒ Are they considerably different or surprising in any way ?
- ❒ Will they require that we change our original plan of attack ? If answer is 'yes', go back to the outline of report.

If you think that the data still fit to have a fresh look, you reformulate your writing plan as well as your technical problem solving procedure. If the plan goes well, write the part of your report by preparing a list to main conclusions you can feel confident in reaching. Now, are these conclusions you can support with your data ? Are the conclusions logical or some audience/reader can find loopholes in them ? After, you have successfully answered these questions, write the conclusive sections of your report within the framework you have decided upon. State the main conclusions first followed by the most telling reasons to arrive at such conclusions.

Technical reports are often persuasive in nature and are written for the purpose of persuading some one to do something, the author of the report desires. The desired action may be inherent suggestion to fund some project or to effect some changes within the organisation or to sell an idea or to sell a product, etc.

Whatever may be the purpose one will have to convince others of the logical reasons behind the preposals.

Persuasive elements usually appear in the conclusions and recommendations part of the report. Remember, you are not trying to convince yourself, you are lying to canvince your primary audience. If you know your audience, your have the first of your persuasion problems solved. Secondly, in persuasion the writer is expected to anticipate objections. It is likely that your solutions may have negative effects somewhere, for example, they may affect the people working in the organisation, may cost more for implementation, may require additional staff to be hired, etc. All these things may seem threatening, but as a writer you should have your techniques and knowlege for meeting these reasonable objectives.

Summaries :

It is said that Sir Winston Churchill has a three part formula for any speech. It runs like this : 'Tell them what you are going to tell them, tell it, then, tell them what you just told them. Translated for our purpose this may be rephased an follows : summarize each main report section, sandwich in the substantive discussion and data, and then reiterate the main points. Although it is wasteful to have repetitions, it is repetition with some purpose. The readers need to be reminded from time to time what the main points are and simultaneously the writer should not deviate from getting into main points under discussion.

Thus, it is a good idea to summarize the report briefly and clearly, to begin each section with a summary or overview the contents of that section.

17.7.2 Audience and Audience Analysis

There are three categories of audience for a technical report, that can usually be identified from the beginning

- ❒ Technical
- ❒ Non-technical
- ❒ Mixed.

Technical audiences are made up of people in the same field as that of the technical report writer. They are people such as engineers, technicians or scientists. They may be people from the same organisation, or they may work outside of it, who are expected to create interest in the report.

Non-technical readers may include advisory boards, financial experts, legal or administrative readers. Their needs will be quite different from the technical readers. They might be looking at certain things which is the job of a technical writer to provide.

The most common audiences include both technical and non- technical readers. Such mixed or multi-layered audiences are more difficult to write for.

However, the design of the report should be such that, if followed, the report will provide each reader with the information he needs to use the report efficiently.

Among the broad categories of audience there is one common thing in the sense that they are busy people, going through a good deal of reading every day and if you hand them a thick, complicated and badly written report, you will alienate them immediately. Thus, it is necessary that report, in order to be usable, should be designed properly. Once the subject of the report has been identified, the first task for the report writer is to identify and analyse the audience, for whom the report is meant. That is , the writer would like to know what is their technical background, what is their function in the organization, what is their interest and finally what level of detail they need from the report for it to be useful to them. Unless the writer takes into account these aspects, his purpose is likely to result in certain failure.

Audience Analysis

Very few technical reports are written for a single, simply identifiable, reader. The audience is usually a complex group of people each with different needs, desires, expectations and back grounds and therefore some thoughts must be given to each if the researcher/writer desires to communicate with him/her.

The Primary Audience

A researcher's first task in audience analysis is to identify the primary audience. This is not necessarily the audience closest to writer in the organisation. His immediate supervisor, who will review his report and send it to others, is obviously an important audience member but is not necessarily the most important. The primary audience will be determined by the nature of the report but will always be that person or group who will make the most important decisions regarding his technical problem. Whoever makes these decisions is the primary audience to whom the researcher/writer needs to address his report.

The Secondary Audience

There will alwyas be many secondary audiences. A researcher/writer's immediate supervisor will often be among these because he must concur with the report before they pass it along to others who may make the final decisions. Examples of other secondary audiences include regulatory agencies, funding agencies, co-workers in the organistation who may be affected by his recommendations and possibly citizen groups who have an interest in the results, his technical problem solutions provide.

It may also be recognized that there may be some audience members who are completely unknown to the researcher, may be interested in the report. As such, the report should be designed in such a way these audiences may be able to gain some useful information from it.

What information do the audiences have ?

The aforesaid audiences have certain information or knowledge, but may not have other information they would need to understand the report. One of the tasks of the technical writer, is to provide whatever information may be missing so that his readers will understand his message. The writer has to do some guessing in this because he may not know all of the people who will read his report. It is therefore, best to include a little more information rather than little less. This must be done carefully so as not to insult the readers by implying that they are more ignorant than they are. In general, the wider the range of knolwedge among his audiences, the more basic information he will need to include.

What will they do with the report ?

Each of the readers will use the report in a somewhat different way. For example, the finance director needs budget figures so that he knows how the proposal in the report may affect the rest of the organisation. A political activist will look for the political effects of the plan proposed in the report. For each main audience group the writer asks himself how they may use his report. If the subject of the report is controversial in nature, he must anticipate some opposing views among some audience members who may attempt to use his report against him. Knowing that in advance is a great advantage and allows the writer to anticipate that criticism and include answers to those objections in the report.

What are their prejudices ?

Most of the audiences may have prejudices of some kind or another. The technical writer having closeness to his current boss probably knows something he likes and something he does not like. If his boss does not like complicated solutions and instead prefer simpler ones, the technical writer must fashion his report accordingly to gain his approval. If it is not possible to find simpler solution, the writer may explain why he cannot find a simpler answer to the technical question.

What are their functions and concerns ?

Apart from theeir personal preferences each of the readers will have concerns that relate to their jobs. This may happen to Production Managers, Finance Directors, Regulatory Specialists, etc. As such, the report must address their concerns if these audience members in the decision making loop. Ignoring any legitimate concern of the audience members belonging to authoritative positions may not get the report approved or even if approved the report may not be supported and implemented by some important members of the team.

How will the report affect them ?

Sometimes human nature in each of audience looks at any proposal from a selfish point of view. Many people are averse to changes and even view changes as threatening. Suggestions to change the way of things that have been done for a long time will almost always meet resistence, specially from those who may have career interest in keeping the things the way as they are. The writer should therefore recommend changes that is really necessary or desirable and less threatening to them.

Time and Money

No matter how widely varied the audiences' interests are, there are two things which every one of them may be expected to understand. These are time and money. His report must answer these two basic questions for every reader.

17.7.3 Structure of Report

The Structure of Technical resport is more detailed and meticulous compared to a general research report. The elements may be broadly categorised as

Front Matter

- ❒ Cover
- ❒ Title page
- ❒ Letter of Transmittal
- ❒ Forwarding Letter
- ❒ Preface
- ❒ Acknowledgements
- ❒ Table of contents
- ❒ List of illustrations
- ❒ List of abbreviations and symbols
- ❒ Abstract/Summary/Synopsis

Main Body (Text)

- Introduction
- Text
- Conclusions
- Recommendations
- References

Back (End) Matter

- Appendices
- Bibliography
- Glossary
- Index.

FRONT MATTER

The front matter to a formal report includes the preliminay information that orients all readers to the content of the report.

Front Cover : Front cover of a formal report is important because it first comes to the notice of the reader. When the report is put flat on a desk, the front cover should contain the report's title and the author's name and date of publication. The front cover have no page number. It is usually made of white or some neutral coloured card. It potects the manuscript from damage and wear and tear and gives the report a real appearance. As the front cover gives the first impression to the reader, it should not be crowded with information, which may distract the reader's attention and mar the attractiveness of the layout.

Title Page : The title page for a formal report often contains the same information as is on the cover. In addition to information provided in the cover page, the title page may contain the following information

- Name of the authority for whom the report is meant.
- Approvals
- Date of the presentation of the report.

Letter of Transmittal : This is the letter to the authority/person who commissioned the report, in which you effectively hand over your work to him. This includes :

- A salutation (*e.g.* Dear Mr. X).
- the purpose of the letter
- the main findings of the report
- any important consideration
- an acknowledgement of any significant help.
- an expression of pleasure or gratitude (*e.g.* thank you for giving us the opportunity to work on this report)

Forwarding letter : It is customarily written by an authority or expert in the field commending the work done by the author on the project.

Preface : This is an introductory statement, which includes explanatory remarks about the report, usually **written** by the **author**, as regards origin, scope, purpose, plan and intended audience. When written by a person other than the author, it is called a forward. The preface or forward is distinet from introduction which deals with subject of work.

Acknowledgements : These mention the names of the persons and organisations who have helped the author in the collecteion of data and preparing the report, but not a lengthier one.

List of Illustrations : A separate list of illustrations is given immediately after the table of contents of the report makes use of a large number of tables and figures. All tables and figures must be named and numbered.

Synopsis/Abstract/Summary : Most reports contain a synopsis which is sometimes termed as abstract or a summary. An abstract gives the content in a condensed form whereas the summary gives the substance of the report.

An abstract is quite different from an introduction. It is a summary of the report in which you include the findings of every section in one or two sentences.

For instance, you can conclude

- the context of the research
- the purpose of the report
- the major findings
- the conclusions
- the main recommendations.

Table of Contents : This is a list of the headings and appendices of the report. Depending on the complexity and length of the report, you should list the tables, figures and appendices separately. Make sure that the correct page numbers are shown opposite the contents.

MAIN BODY

Introduction : Although an abstract or a summary is the first section to be read by the reader and aso contains short introduction about the project, it is always necessary to include introduction in the main body (text) to say what the report is about, what work has already been done on the subject and what new grounds are covered in the present study.

The following guidelines may be observed.

- gives enough background information to provide a context for the report.
- State the purpose of the report.
- Clarify key terms and indicate the scope of the report (*i.e.* what the report will cover).

Body. The content of the body depends on the purpose of the report, and whether it is a report of primary or secondary research.

A report of primary research (based on your own observations and experiments) would include :

- Literature reveiw what other people have written about this topic. The literature review should lead towards your research question.
- Method (summarises what you did and why)

- ❐ Findings or results (describes what you discoverd, observed, etc. in your observations and experiments. Use the past tense.
- ❐ Discussion (discusses and explains your findings and relates them to previous research). Use the present tense generalisations.

A report of secondary research (based on secondary data) would include :

- ❐ Information organised under appropriate topics with sub-headings. It is unlikely that your report will discuss each source separately. You need to synthesise material from different sources under topic headings.
- ❐ Analysis/discussion of the sources you are reporting.

Conclusion. The word conclusion is generally used to describe the concluding remarks at the end of a piece of writing. It sums up the main points of the report and shows the reader that the goal has been reached. The conclusion should clearly relate to the objectives of your report. No surprise should be added by including new information.

Recommendations may be added to the conclusions if needed and appropriate. The conclusions embody the inference derived from the findings where as the function of the recommendations is to suggest the future action. They must be logically derived from the body of your report.

BACK MATTER/END MATTER

The end matter of a report comes after the body. The end matter of a report can be made up of any of several elements. The formality of the report and the needs of the audience influence what is included. Very formal reports include a great deal of end matter; very informal reports usually include none.

Appendices : These present supplementary information to increase readers' knowledge or understanding. What to include depends on the purpose and audience of the document. For example, primary readers who have a technical background benefit from detailed technical data in the body of the report far more than do readers who rely on the writer's technical expertise to summarize pertinent information. For primary readers with background in business rather than technical field, detailed data are appropriately placed in the appendix.

An appendix contains material which is too detailed, technical or complex to include in the body of the report. (*e.g.* specifications, a questionnaire, or a long complex table of figures which is referred to in the report.) Appendices are put at the very end of the report, after everything else. Each appendix should contain different material and should be numbered clearly.

Bibliography/References : Bibliography is a list of serially numbered published and unpublished works which are consulted before or during the preparation of report.

How does it differ from list of references ? The bibliography lists the works which the author has read and to which he is indebted to get ideas or information in general terms, but the purpose of referenes is to point out the specific location or pieces of information in the original source.

The bibliography may include certain literature which may contain works recommended for further study, where as this has no place in the list of references. In bibliography works are mentioned in alphabetical order where as works mentioned in the list

- ❒ Statement of the problem, its purpose and scope
- ❒ Determination of audience to whom report is meant.
- ❒ Collection of data
- ❒ Organization of material for the report
- ❒ An outline.

Reports are prepared at the direction from some quarters. The sponsoring authority often gives clear instructions for the purpose, which are generally called **Terms of reference** that tell the researcher/writer what is required to do. Although the terms of reference guide before the collection of data, it is advisable to give some thoughts in analysing the exact scope of the report.

Often a report is required at a very short notice *e.g.* sales performance of a company's product in the first quarter of a financial year, which may be required to place before the meeting of the heads of departments of an organisation. Such a report needs to be very much elaborative and in such a case you may collect necessary data from the relevant files and arrange and present them in meaningful form. There are also occasions when a committee is formed to find ways and means to boost sales of a product. In such circumstances the researcher/writer may be given ample time and instructions as to nature and extent of coverage and a sample survey may be required to collect information from the consumers and other sources to form a basis for a comprehensive report to be submitted to the committe for its discussion and possible recommendations. As regards reports of routine nature *e.g.* annual financial reports, quarterly reports of purchase and sales, feasibility reports of new ventures etc., models of such reports may be available with the organisation, inviting reports. The writer may use these models for the purpose.

A report is always written with an audience in mind. The terms of reference give clear indication as to who would be the readers.

A technical report may have any of the following six kinds of audience.

- ❒ Superior officer
- ❒ Colleagues of the writer/researcher
- ❒ Subordinate employees
- ❒ Other organisations
- ❒ Share holders
- ❒ Customers and the public

Once the purpose and scope have been specified, the next step is to gather relevant data. The writer must have knowledge about data types and data sources, from which he can gather relevant information.

Next step is the organisation of the material the writer proposes to include in the report. If the writer steps in immediately to start writing the first draft, he may be lost in the mass of data and as a result it may be difficult to adhere to the sequence of ideas possessed by the writer when contemplating to write the report. Random thoughts might trouble him at the writing stage. Thus, the best way for the writer is to prepare the outline of the report before he actually starts writing it.

While constructing the outline, the audience must be kept in mind. Reject the material which is beyond the reader's comprehension or which might not help him to take a decision; while collecting the mateiral this point may be kept in mind so that unnecessary materials are not colleted. While organizing the material the writer should take care of logical ordering of ideas, co-ordinating them with topics and sub-topics, grouping the ideas under one topic/sub-topic, numbering the topics and sub- topics besides using proper words, phrases or sentences to indicate the topics or sub-topics for the outline and avoiding single sub-topic outside the relevant topic.

Making outline : An outline is a framework which helps in organising and planning the presentation of material, gathered by the writer, although there is no set of rules for the purpose. It all depends on the ingenuity of the writer as regards co-ordinating his thoughts and ideas about the project. At the time of writing the text, the writer may well discover certain omissions of materials and inclusion of some irrelevant materials and the writer can detect these omissions and commissions by referring to the outline, already prepared. However, outline is supposed to be flexible by nature and the writer can change it as the writing goes along.

17.8 Technical Writing

Technical writing refers to authoring of informative or instructive content about any technology, procedure, or a process. This presented content should be clear, precise, and provide the specific information sought by its audience.

There are many types of technical documents, such as instruction manuals, online help, analysis documents, the feasibility reports, catering to a wide variety of audience. However, each document caters only to a specific group of audience, called the target audience.

For example, an instruction manual caters to users learning to use an application or a product, whereas a feasibility report helps a manager plan for a project. Therefore, the author of a technical document should address the specific expectations of the specific target audience. Although there are no hard and fast rules about writing technical documents, a few basic steps can help an author save time and write a good document. Before we understand these steps, we should know what qualifies a document to be a good technical document.

Attributes of a Technical Document

The only primary expectation from a technical document for any reader is only information. However, the reader also expects this information to be clear, readable, precise, and complete. A good technical document should deliver all that is expected of it.

Clarity and Readability

Words, sentences, and the overall flow of information in a technical document should be simple and straightforward. This improves clarity of information and allows a reader to spend the least amount of time and effort in reading the document. Undue elaborations and complex sentences reduce the clarity of the document and hence should be avoided under all circumstances by the author.

A well-strcutured document should have logical segmentation of content and continuity of information. Readers find such documents easy to read and can quickly seek specific information from the document.

The language used in the document should also be specific to the target audience. For example, an instructional manual should not contain technical jargon or acronyms that are not commonly used. However, a technical journal for circulation among engineeers can contain technical terms and jargon.

Preciseness and Completeness

Information provided in a technical document should be precise and complete. The author needs to also consider the interests of the target audience and not include any information that would not interest the target audience. For example, a user referring to an online help of a Web application would not be interested in the software components and objects used in the application. This information is best suited for the engineers in-charge of the maintenance of the application.

Authoring a Technical Document

The process of authoring a technical document starts with conception of the topic or subject for the document. The decision to write a document is made based on demand for information on the topic or in anticipation of such a demand.

There are four basic steps in authoring a technical document as listed below :

1. Information gathering
2. Designing or Structuring
3. Authoring
4. Reviewing

Information gathering

In this step, the author collects all possible information about the topic and the audience. This collected information is the foundation for further work on the document. Exhaustive homework at this stage saves the author additional rework at later stages. Therefore, the author should collect precise and complete information about the topic. Any ambiguity in the information should be clarified immediately.

It also pays to do some homework about the audience. Learning about the audience helps the author decide on the presentation style and the complexity level of information that will suit the audience best. For example, when writing a user manual for a banking application, if the audience are business users with prior knowledge in banking, the author need not elaborte on banking terminologies or processes. Author only needs to explain the application and its user interface components including the functionality of the buttons, the information to be entered in the screens asking for user input, how to delete incorrect or unwanted data that is keyed in. However, if the audience were end customers, some background information about banking terminologies and processes would be appropritate.

Designing or Structuring

In this step, author decides on the High Level Design (HLD) or Table of Contents (TOC) of the document. In other words, the author divides the topic into multiple sections and also decides on what and how much information should go into each section.

A well-structured document ensures that the information flows through the document and there are no repetitions or gaps in the document. It also helps busy readers to easlly search of information from the document.

Authoring

This is the step when the author actually writes the document. The author should ideally not have any trouble at this stage, if the strcuture of the document is well defined and the author knows exactly what information should go into the document as he/she has decided in the previous step. He only needs to take care that the language used is clear and correct. The author can also use figures, illustrations, or other graphics to describe complex ideas.

However, if the author feels the needs to revisit the design or finds some gap in information at this stage, then authoring can become complicated. The author would not be wasting time but also compromising on the quality of the document.

Reviewing

To err is human. However experienced, proficient or knowledgeable an author might be, the chances of an error or scope for improvement in a document is never zero. Therefore, the author should always review the document immediately after completion.

Errors can be of many types. Apart from grammatical and typographical errors, there can be technical inaccuracies, format errors, and incorrect ambiguous elements in the document. If necesary, the document should be sent to respective experts to identify and rectify errors.

The primary characteristics of technical writing that differentiate it from other forms of writing are found in structure and choice of language. In general technical writing is highly structured, making extensive use of devices such as numbering of headings, numbered figures and hierarchical arrangement of the components of the document. Choice of language is formal in character.

Technical writing is **not limited to explanatory manuals** that come with technologically complex products. It is also used by major corporations as well as non-profit organisations to explain beliefs, ideas, instructions, mechanics and logistics.

The **foremost requirements** of a technical writing are that the writers must understand that audience and the purpose of a particular document. If the medium does not communicate the information intended *i.e.* what is trying to be conveyed to the audience, then the communication is meaningless.

The **goal of technical writing** is to translate technical ideas into words that the intended audience will understand. However, the technical writer must have an understanding of rhetoric and language in order to write in a way that displays coherence, concision clarity, but also elegance in order to maintain the attention of audience in question. **Audience analysis** is thus a key feature of all technical writing. Format, organisation and style are important in that they make information easy for the reader to follow.

Twelve Basic Guidelines for Technical Writing

These guidelines provide a simple **check list** when writing technical pieces. If they are used, they will improve the quality of the finished product,improving the writer's chance of success.

- ❒ Always use the simplest, most accurate word, phrase, design, or graphic. Never use two words where one will do.
- ❒ Always strive for an attractive, consistent, well-spaced design. The good first impression that this creates is invaluable.
- ❒ Be thorough. Readers won't mind additional details if your design allows for navigating around them.
- ❒ Fill a document's section only with the information that should logically be there.
- ❒ Make sure all sentences in a paragraph lead into each other and that they fully support the topic sentence. These connections should be obvious.
- ❒ Refer to yourself cautiously. Instilling a sense of yourself can help both your writing and your reader but not if your presence obtrudes or shifts the document's focus.
- ❒ Use passive voice only with good reason.
- ❒ Label, refer to, explain, and cite (if necessary) every table, chart, graph, illustration, photo or other graphic you use.
- ❒ Be consistent but not repetitive : use the same name for a person or object every time, but don't start more than two sentences the same way ("This is.....", "This is ...," etc.)
- ❒ Get in the habit of writing more formally than you speak in everyday conversation. It's better to come across a little too stiff than a little too loose.
- ❒ Revise until your writing is free of grammar and punctuation errors. Even common mistakes can severely damage your professional credibility.
- ❒ Pamper your readers. Make your job hard so that you make their's easy.

17.9 Instruction Manual

Instruction manual is a set of instructions or steps used by users to perform tasks whether to execute project, or to write a report or for functioning a process or an equipment in a systematic and methodical manner, without consulting an outside party.

The manuals are of different kinds *e.g.* soft ware manuals, technical manuals, product production manual, course manual, employee training manual, quality manual, technical report writing manual, Project execution manual, etc.

The general guidelines are :

- ❒ Briefly got down all the steps that come to your mind.

- ❐ Instead of explaining task in long paragraphs, break your instruction manual into specific detailed steps. Give as much direction as possible.
- ❐ If one step requires slightly different tasks, create substeps.
- ❐ Continue revising and describing until your written words encompass every step in the most detailed and effective way possible.

17.9.1 Manual for Technical Report Writing

In addition to performing the engineering activities, an engineer has to prepare operating and assembly manuals, requests for proposals (RFP), responses to proposals, research and development reports, and articles for publications. Writing for these specific purposes is called *technical writing.* Technical writing is totally different from creative writing. The difference between the two styles of writing is similar to the difference between a text on Physics and a novel. *A technical report or a paper generally consists of reporting and/or interpretation of data/physical phenomena.* The report should be written in a purely objective and impersonal manner and reflect the writer's effort in addressing a technical problem. The results are to be judged on the basis of engineeering experience and common sense. *Most technical reports are written in third person, past tense. Generous use of the technical terminology is employed.* For the description of the laboratory equipment, scientific laws and the presentation of results, present tense should be employed. *The use of personal pronouns should be avoided.* A technical report generally contains a clear outline of the problem, mathematical equations, drawings, charts, tables and graphs, etc. For completeness purposes, they always require explanations at appropriate locations within the text of the report. Technical reports must be accurate and to the point. Superfluous and unsupported assertions should never be made. Conclusions and recommendations must be based on the results presented in the report. *It must be technically correct and without any ambiguities.* In this respect technical report writing is a hard work.

A report or a technical paper usually consists of the following parts.

1. Title Page
2. Nomenclature
3. Abstract (or Summary)
4. Introduction (or Background)
5. Technical Approach (or Methodology)
6. Description of Experimental Setup and Tools Used
7. Results
8. Conclusions

Explanation

1. Title Page : The title page should contain the title of the project, the authorship and their affiliation and date of submission.

2. Nomenclature : This part of the report is optional. Here all the symbols used should be defined. Alternately, the symbols can be defined in the text where they appear for the first time. For big and complex reports (like a big proposal or final report on a contract, it is suggested that a list of the symbols with appropriate definitions should be provided up front. For reorts with limited objectives (*e.g.* research papers or class reports), it is recommended that the symbols should be defined within the text after they appear for the first time.

3. Abstract : It is a brief summary of the essential content of the technical report. Its length should be about 200 words or less. The abstract usually contains a brief statement of the objectives, the methods used to fulfil those objectives, most significant results, and conclusion. *No graph, sketch, table, or equations should be used or referred to in the abstract.* It is recommended that the abstract be written after the report has been finished. It is imperative that a great deal of attention is paid to the writing of the abstrct. A majority of the readership (like upper administration) of the report will confine their focus to this pat of the report. Only those dealing directly with the subject matter of the report will look into the details.

4. Introduction : The purpose of the introduction is to provide the appropriate background on the subject matter. The introduction should describe the objectives of the work and the method and scope of the investigation, and the reasons for carrying out the work. Appropriate references to any earlier work must be acknowledged. *Usually, figures, sketches, or tables are not presented in the introduction.* Unlike the abstract, there is no upper limit on the length of the introduction, however, an effort to keep it concise is always recommended.

5. Methodology or Technical Approach : This part of the report should identify the theoretical principles and equations used in accomplishing the work. The equations should be numbered and follow the order of the principles they represent. Any supporting sketch of diagram related to the problem should be provided. *Definitely, these are not the diagrams representing the results that you have obtained.* These diagrams must be labeled and should appear after a reference has been made in the text.

A discussion of the sources and the extent of experimental and/or computational uncertainties should be included. *One must be cognizant of the fact that the precision of the measuring device is compatible with the objectives of the investigation.* Similarly, the computational technique that is being used also is stable and does not pollute the results. For example, a scale usually employed in grocery stores cannot accurately measure a microgram of an expensive chemical. A careless inversion of an ill-conditioned matrix can affect the final outcome of a computational experiment.

6. Description of the Experimental Setup or Tools Used : A sketch of the setup with appropriate identification of the components should be included. All the measuring devices and the samples tested should be brifely described. In case it is purely a computational effort, a description of the numericalf methodology or the use of specializated software and the language in which the computer code is written should be provided.

7. Results and Discussion : This is the most important part of the report, where the findings have to be reported. Most of the engineering results are presented in the form of tables, charts, and graphs. Each of these entities should be numbered and provided with a one-line caption. These entities should then be fully described in the text as to what each table and chart stands for and why it is important that it has been included in the report. Appropriate discussion of the results for trends, self-consistency, accuracy, and meeting the original objectives must be provided. **It is the duty**

of the writer to sort out the results in a logical and systematic fashion and convince the reader about their validity. Quantitiative discussion of any errors from the expected results should be clearly pointed out. **Avoid any discussion of irrelevant and insignificant aspect of the results.** (Note. Proposals do not have results sections.)

8. Conclusions. The most significant conclusions reached in the results and discussion section should be summarized herein. These should be listed in the order of their significance and preferably in an itemized form. References to figures or tables should not be included, and no new information should be introduced in this section. However, suggestions for further investigations can be made.

17.10 Technical Proposal

What is proposal ?

A project proposal is an undertaking that has :

❒ short term

❒ definite objective

❒ well defined inputs and outputs.

❒ specific objective realisation within specified costs and quality.

Thus, we may define *a proposal as a written offer from a person/organisation to undertake a project for designing, creating something new or for changing or modifying an existing procedure, method, system or structure within a specified period of time, cost and quality.*

When the objective of the proposal is to modify or create something which requires technical knowlege and skills, it is termed as technical proposal.

Two important skills needed in writing research proposals are :

❒ technical skills

❒ management skills.

Technical skills are needed to conceive research ideas, justify its need, scientific and technical means to satisfy the need. Managerial skills are needed in design and implementation stages and in identification of resources needed to accomplish promised tasks. One of the basic reasons for rejection of many research proposals is due to lack of managerial skill in the initial proposal writing phase. Even technologically sound projects may fail if implementation tasks are ill defined or external factors such as socio-economic and enviromental concerns are not addressed properly. On the other hand, an ill planned project, even if approved on technical merits alone, may lead to major setbacks in implementation as a result of flaws in the planning and writing phase. While good planning may not by itself guarantee smooth running of a project, poor planning will greatly reduce the chance of its success.

Before writing the proposal, identify the sponsor agency and relate your and your employer's interests to the sponsor's current interests.

The formats of most funding agencies are similar with minor variations. More details about the sponsor's funding priorities and application procedures can be found from their websites.

Most funding agencies adapt some kind of appraisal system to evaluate the projects. The appraisal criteria are sponsor agency specific.

Characteristics

Every proposal answers the following among other details :

- What do you plan to do ?
- How will you do it ?
- How much time will you take in completing it ?
- What will it cost ?

The factors which help the acceptance of the proposal are :

- Specify the scope clearly
- Explain the significance of the work undertaken.
- Be realistic when estimating time, budget, material and personnel required.
- Establish your credential as a researcher/research team for accomplishing the task.
- Mention your previous experiences, if any.
- High light the benefits that would accrue to the sponsor
- Keep the proposal short, precise and pointed.
- Use plain and simple language without jargons.
- Ensure that the presentation and the layout are neat and attractive.
- Proofread several times and be sure to execute a spell check.

Types of Proposals

A proposal is a request for support of sponsored research, instruction or extension projects, and generally consists of a cover page, brief project summary, technical or narrative section, biographical sketches of key personnel, and a detailed budget. Most common proposal types include :

Solicited proposals are submitted in response to a specific solicitation issued by a sponsor. Such solicitations, typically called Request for proposals (RFP), Request for quotations (RFQ) or Request for Bids (RFB), etc., are usually specific in their requirements regarding format and technical content, and may stipulate certain award terms and conditions.

Unsolicited proposals are submitted to a sponsor that has not issued a specific solicitation but is believed by the investigator to have an interest in the subject.

Pre-proposals are requested when a sponsor wishes to minimize an applicant's effort in preparing full proposal. Pre-proposals are usually in the form of a *letter of intent or brief abstract.* After the pre-proposal is reviewed, the sponsor notifies the investigator if a full proposal is warranted.

Sometimes a sponsor forms a review committee to review all the pre-proposals and rank them in order of merit to help the sponsor to take a decision as regards the award.

Continuation or Non-competing proposals confirm the original proposal and funding requirements of a multi-year project for which the sponsor has already provided funding for an initial period (normally one year). Continued support is usually contingent on satisfactory work progress and the availability of funds.

Renewal or Non-competing proposals are requests for continued support for an existing project that is about to terminate, and, from the sponsor's view point, generally have the same status as an unsolicited proposal.

Guide to Proposal Writing

Introduction

Experts agree that proposal writing is a process that requires a multitude of steps to be followed in order for the successful submission of a proposal. The term **"proposer"** refers to the persons(s) writing the proposal. The term **"sponsor"** refers to the funding source (*i.e.*, govoernmental sponsor, corporation or foundation). The term **"preproposal phase"** refers to all of the activities leading up to and including the actual submission of a proposal.

Preproposal phase (Pre-research proposal)

Developing Your Proposal Idea

The proposal idea usually comes in two forms : (1) **solicited** or (2) **unsolicited.** A solicited idea is one that has been suggested, at least in general terms, by the funding sponsor. This may include but is not limited to *Request for Proposal, White Paper, Statement of Work, Program Announcement, Request for Information, etc.* An unsolicited proposal is one that is created by the sponsor organization and has no kowledge if it will be of interest to a potential donor. If you are planning to put the time in to write a proposal, please contact the sponsor. This will help you understand the priorities of the sponsor.

Also, focus on these questions when developing your idea.

❒ What is the function of the project you are proposing ?

❒ In what field is your project ?

❒ Who will benefit from your project ?

❒ What are the geographic parameters of your project ?

❒ Do you have an appropriate project team assembled ?

❒ Have your ideas for research been discussed with the seniors/experts ?

Gathering Information

One of the first things you can do after developing your idea is to gather the documentation for it.

You will require background documentation in three areas :

❒ Concept

❒ Program

❒ Finance

If all of this information is not readily available to you, then determine who can help you gather each type of information. The data-gathering process makes the actual writing much easier. By involving other stakeholders in the process, it also helps key people within organisation consider the project's value.

Talk to the Funding Sponsor (if feasible)

Principal Investigators (PI) invest a lot of time and effort in preparing proposals. Determining if the proposal will be seriously considered by the sponsor is an aspect worth exploring. Some agencies will reveal important information not written in the solicitation an understanding of the sponsor's politices and areas of interest. Talk to the peoplee who wrote the Request for Proposal (RFP) and find out who will evaluate and select proposals.

Remember that agencies have funding priorities and so try to gage these issues :

- ❐ Hot Topics
- ❐ Funding Level
- ❐ Competitors
- ❐ Context
- ❐ Attitude toward your work
- ❐ Past relevant works

Visit the Sponsor Website (if available)

Most federal agencies have a website that you can research. Sponsor specific websites are full of insightful tips that can help you organize your thoughts. These websites also indicate whether the proposal can be transmitted electronically as opposed to by mail. In addition, these websites generally have their forms posted so that you can download them.

Scan the Solicitation

If you are submitting a solicited proposal, breifely scan the solicitation to determine if the guidelines meet your project needs and vice versa. Too often, grant writers ignore the sponsor's funding priorities and focus solely on their own needs. However, if you have determined that it does meet your mutual needs, then begin the proposal process by **highlighting** all pertinent information (*i.e.*, facilities and administration restrictions dealing dates, font size, page restrictions, proposal number restrictions per institution, etc.) Begin to develop your personal checklist by identifying key points to insure that you mark-off each section or point as it is completed.

Developing the Budget

Developing your budget early in the process will help you determine how much human, physical and financial resources are needed to carry out your proposed research Budgeting is simply the process of translating the project plan into fiscal terms. Keep the budget realistic and do not pad the numbers. Agencies know the price of most equipment and supplies. Developing the budget early will also help you identify consultants, subcontractors, equipment, etc. to be used in your proposal.

Keep these steps in mind when developing this section :

- ❒ Determine the proposal guidelines (*i.e.*, facilities and administration allowances, etc.) which will govern the preparation and review of the budget.
- ❒ Identify the total costs of the project and estimate the utilization of these during various phases of the project
- ❒ Translate this information into appropriate budget categories and record this on required forms or in a suitable format
- ❒ Redesign your project objectives and procedures in order to propose more realistic goals or use less costly means when your initial figures appear to high.

These ideas are important because additional documents will be requested before proposal submission.

The Proposal Writing Phase :

Reasons for a Good Proposal

- ❒ You have done your homework and not duplicating previous research
- ❒ This project is relevant to the sponsor
- ❒ The purpose of the project will address a critical need
- ❒ You have an effective and feasible approach to solving this problem
- ❒ Something tangible can be anticipated at the end of the project that the justifies the resources requested.
- ❒ The project staff and its organization have the capability, credibility and experience needed to make the project succeed.

There are specific techniques and processes of writing and application that can be acquired with practice and experience. But these, by themselves, are not substitutes for the authority that is evident in applications written by those knowledgeable in their field and excited at the opportunity to create something new. The propossal document is the major means of communcation with potential sponsors thus it bears the considerable burden of simultaneously creating a favourable impression and securing support for your proposed project.

Reasons for a Weak Proposal

- ❒ Lack of technical detail
- ❒ No evidence of innovation
- ❒ No statement of the feasibility question, risk or solution measure
- ❒ Too much background information

Proposal Development Strategies and Writing Tips

Consider these additional strategies and writing tips when developing your proposal :

- ❒ Set a positive tone
- ❒ Use outline formats and listings whenever possible

❒ Use visuals to enhance and explain abstract concepts and relationships
❒ Don't overkill a point
❒ Avoid language such as "might, could, ought, may, should, hope, will consider, it appears"
❒ Take a stand in your proposal
❒ Avoid inflated rhetoric
❒ Avoid unsupported subjective arguments
❒ Do not assume that the reader is familiar with the subject
❒ Sequence your proposal in a logical manner

Proposal development

Developing the project prposal follows the structure of a project.

The distinct structural elements of a project are :

1. Title
2. Introduction
3. Rationale
4. Research method means of objective relization
5. Work program activities, time, resources, indicators and their evaluative norms
6. Budget.

Cover or Title Page

Title gives first impression of a proposal and hence it has to be catchy, small and informative. It shall not be the same as objective, it has to be shorter but at the same time indicates broadly what is being attempted.

This page should include

❒ Title of the proposed project
❒ Name(s) and title(s) of the principal investigater and co-investigators, if any
❒ Proposed project period.
❒ Total cost for the project
❒ Sponsor with addres
❒ Name of the organisation with address.
❒ Month and year of submission
❒ Singnature of the person or any authorised person of the institution/organisation who submits the proposal.

Introduction

The introduction will have the following sub-sections

❒ Background
❒ Problem statement
❒ Initial statement
❒ Objective

Back ground. This section is concerned with background information, urgency, critical gaps in knowledge and need for the present study.

Two pertinent questions help you to develop this section.

❒ What is the context for the proposal ?

❒ Why this needed ?

A review of literature will help you in this regard. Review may suggest :

❒ Past work on the current problem if any and existence of any secondary data.

❒ Ideas for your own work

❒ What not to do

❒ Convince others about your knowledge of past work in the area.

Develop background information leading to the need for the present study. Justification for urgency must be reflected in this.

Problem statements

The background part of introduction deals with a context having a set of problems. In this section, state specific problem of your interest making necessary connection to the context given in the background specify limits that can be studied in the time, resources, budget sought.

State what the project is expected to do in one statement, preferably one sentence. It might be something like the following :

'Technological forecasting of power requirement in the country'

The initial statement clarifies the basic intent. The statement is not precise enough to use as a basis for implementation and needs to be developed into further precise statements in objectives.

Objectives

Care must be taken in writing objectives such that they must be measurable or specifiable in same way so as to know the completion. This will facilitate the intentions clearly and it also sets useful criteria for evaluation purposes.

While writing the objectives try to answer the following questions :

❒ What do you want to achieve ?

❒ The objectives are valuable to whom ?

❒ Are they measureable ?

❒ Are they realistic in terms of time and available resources ?

Each objective must be clear with broad and specific measureable out put and possible to accomplish in the specified time frame.

Rationale

Specify hypothesis corresponding to each of the objectives and involvement of stake holders. This should not be justification for the project, which appears in the introduction.

As a general rule, a formal research should involve a hypothesis, some preliminary information and a strong hunch suggesting the type of outcome you are likely to find. A hypothesis is to be made a careful statement of an idea or hunch. The formal study may be preceded by a simple test from which ideas or hunches may evolve. However, some studies can be purely exploratory.

Remember every study provides a piece of information that did not exist prior to the study. What is important is that the evidence adds a significant body of knolwedge or some practical significance or both. Specify this in this section.

Research Method : This is a technical section and should succeed the rationale section and gives answer to questions on how to realize the objectives. Give approaches in details without ambiguities and references whenever possible. Try to specify how using the listed approaches will solve the problem. Identify the stakeholders, partners or team members. Specify involvement of stakeholders in retail. List all the activities and show methodologies for each activity separately.

Work program

Schedule the work elements listed in the methodology in a sequence indicating the role of each associate. Standard project mangement techniques like flow chart, gnat chart or PERT network can be used to illustrate this. Specify facilities available and additional resources needed and the methods of acquiring resources. Specify time frame activity wise. Give milestones for each objective. Elaborate how the work will be managed. The management arrangements for execution of the project to be specified. This will be important if the project is multi- location or multi-institutional in nature. Most donors require list of equipments with detailed specifications, time, and schedule for procurement and finally the actual users of the equipment. The facilities available at the host institution are to be mentioned clearly. Show that you have not only sufficient scientific and technical skills but also access to facilities and your institution has requisite infrastructure to carry out the project. The chief investigator as the manager of the project has to identify quality resources and manage them efficiently for successful completion. The proposal has to document this aspect. Give detials of training and consultancies needed linking their relevance to the project.

- **Feasibility.** Show that you have not only sufficient scientific and technical skills but also access to facilities and your institution has requisite infrastructure to carryout the project.

- **Activities.** All the activities essential to carry out the project are to be identified through the developmnt of an activity network, which consists of actions and shows :

  – All major activities, and
  – The logical relationships between them.

Note that the activity network is non-linear with multiple feedback loops. Activities begin with actions (verbs). For the identified activities, set the sequence, time and resources needed. This can be done only after identifying all the sub- activities for each of the activities. For each resource, human or non-human, specify availability and cost.

It is unlikely to identify all the resources at the beginning. Keep provision to meet such contingencies during implementation.

• **Partners.** For each associate, clearly specify their role, the work division and the financial details. In a multi disciplinary project, develop activities for each discipline or associate so as to bring clarity of work elements and accountability.

Relate the training/consultancy needs to the project work. Specify when and where the training has to be provided and whether it can be provided within the country or outside.

• **Quality concerns.** One of the serious concerns of planners is quality of research output. Various indicators have been identified and formulated to identify professional quality. Some distinctive concepts should be available to convey quality in professional output, *i.e.* to convey successful and non- successful applications. This has to be peer judgements. If the project is to run successful, it is important to identify indicators for monitoring and evaluation.

• **Monitoring and evaluation.** Sponsor would like to have periodic evaluation reports so as to judge the success of project at various stages and if need be assist in mid term corrections. Logical framework analysis with stress on participatory working (participation of stakeholders and interest groups in planning, monitoring and evaluation) is most widely promoted.

Log frame method as a project management tool helps the participants arrive at agreement on the method to be used and then generate an agreed view of the way in which the project should be managed. The key assumption and risk serve to acknolwege external disturbances during the course of the project. This provides an awareness of source of turbulence with provision for further monitoring and review.

• **Indicators.** Specify quantitative indicators to assess the project progress and achievement. Explain how to assess or measure them. Give indicator to each activity. Provide who and how many will be benefited and try to give quantifiable figures.

For each activity set criteria for performance, *i.e.* give performance indicators and also measure of performance. This will facilitate monitoring of the progress. The key activities and critical parameters for success of project must figure here. Ultimately this information will be used to judge project progress.

Budget

Give year wise and activity wise budget in detail. Justify costly equipment and other facilities. Try to include reasonable inflation while calculating year-wise budget. Give summary budget. Specify budget for each partner if they come from different places and administrative units. In such case, a summary budget for each partner should be provided separately. The various budgets should match the details given in the work program. Avoid over budgeting, as under utilization will be a negative remark.

Once all the project activities costs are listed, then split the costs as per the funding agencies format. Most funding agencies need cost details in three heads, viz. establishment (salaries), recurring and non-recurring, to be specified year-wise.

Include bay windows or activities that can be dropped if the sponsor agency gives reduced sanction. Alternatively, if you feel the cost is high, look into sub-activities of each activity and drop the low priority sub-activities and adjust the project cost.

The fund requirement will be low in the initial phase, rises rapidly during the implementation phase and then falls rapidly at the end. The year-wise splits have to be kept in mind while preparing the budget.

General Tips

- **Sequence.** The sequence of various sections in the project proposal will be same as in the project structure. However, the sequence in which each section is to be written need not be the same as in the structure. The logical sequence which helps in writing the proposal, is described below.

Write the title and key words first. Following this develop rationale and materials and methods. Develop work program including training details. Provide indicators. Give detailed budget and budget abstract. At this stage write introduction giving background information, urgency and need for the present study. Finally wirte the abstract in less than 15 lines.

- **Style of write-up.** The proposal should be easy to read with short sentences. For every break in the continuity of text, a separate paragraph is to be given. The entire text should be written in future tense. The manuscript should be about 25 typed pages typed with double space and with clear one-inch margin on either side.

- **Review.**

❒ Check for safe procedures, environmental concerns, the ethical considerations.

❒ Downplay but do not omit the benefits to your organisations.

❒ If you have to use "we". always be unambiguous, clearly identify which scientist or partner will do what.

❒ Write and sleep on the proposal; then re-read critically. Consult with others; spend time thinking. Listen to comments with patience. Show it to a non-technical person. Try to catch errors, repetitions, and inconsistencies. Get the words right. Edit to shorten and make it clear.

17.11 Oral Presentations

Researchers are often required to present their findings orally before an audience consisting of a small group of persons usually managers of different levels and some interested in the research findings.

Oral presentations, like written presentations can enhance a researcher's reputation within an organization. Therefore, for a researcher it is an opportunity to sell not only his ideas but also his competence in the research topic.

The presentation time is expected not to exceed an hour at the most and normally followed by questions and discussions.

The oral presentations are sometimes termed as briefings and only critical elements are presented without affecting the clarity.

For successful presentation, the written report must be condensed so as to be able to complete full presentation within the stipulated time span. Sometimes, the briefing time is communicated or the researcher may have prior information about it. If the time is severly limited, the need for topical priorities seems obvious.

The researcher, when planning to prepare the presentation, should have in mind as to

- ❒ purpose of briefing.
- ❒ whether it is required for raising concerns about problems uncovered.
- ❒ whether it is required to add to knowledge of audience members.
- ❒ whether it is required to present conclusions and recommendations for decision making.

The researcher, then should develop certain basic strategies for his briefing, which generally contain the following points :

17.11.1 Basic strategies for effective oral presentation

The basic stategies cover two broad aspects :

1. Preparation :

- ❒ Understand the context of presentation.
- ❒ Analyze audience.
- ❒ Understand and articulate presentation's purpose.
- ❒ Choose and shape presentation's content.
- ❒ Organize presentation.

2. Delivery :

- ❒ Choose an appropriate speaking style.
- ❒ Practise an effective delivery style.
- ❒ Select and use visual aids effectively.

In order to **understand the situation or context** of presentation, the researcher should ask himself the following questions :

- ❒ What is the broader concern underlying the need for the presentation ?
- ❒ What primary issues underlie the presentation ?
- ❒ How does presentation relate to these issues ?
- ❒ What is the current situation in the organisation ?
- ❒ What would be the effect of the presentation in the organizational situation
- ❒ In what surroundings the presentation will be made ?

Knowing the situation is as important as knowing the audience and the purpose. In many cases situation will be inextricably bound up with questions of audience attitude and the way the researcher shapes his purpose. Audience attitude frequently results from situational problems or current issues within the organization, besides the content and purpose of the presentation, dictated by the context surrounding the presentation.

Analysis of audience is facilitated by the knowledge of the audience about the subject, their expectations, interest, attitude towards the speaker and the subject, positions in the organisation, educational/cultural background and cultural biases, if any, etc.

Oral presentations must be designed around a **specific purpose.** As the researcher begins his presentation, he must make his purpose clearly evident at the beginning.

By knowing the purpose in the beginning, the audience members can more easily focus their attention on the content presented. A good way to grab audience attention is to develop a title that at the very least, reflects the content of the presentation. If necessary, the researcher should include background material to help the audience grasp his presentation.

Preparing an oral presentation needs proper choice of content. First, the researcher should determine **what information he needs for presentation.** In selecting content the researcher needs to consider a variety of information types : statistics, testimony, cases, illustrations, history, and particularly narratives that help convey the goal he has for the presentation.

Because listening is more difficult than reading, narratives can be particularly effective in retaining the attention of his listeners. The researcher may vary his content and should make sure to include all information, pertaining to the goal of his presentation.

The researcher should organize his presentation having the following guidelines :

- Introduction
- Main body
- Conclusion
- Recommendations

The **Introduction** should clearly tell the audience what the presentation will cover, so that the audience is prepared for what is to come. In planning introduction it is necessary for the researcher to state his goal near the beginning and moreover the opening should be direct, so as to draw the attention of the audience. He should state how he will proceed with presentation ; what main issues will be discussed ; what main ideas have been developed during the research and also should hint about the content. Generally, the introduction should end with a reiteration of the main points in the presentation.

The body should develop each point previewed in the introduction. The researcher should develop each of the main points/issues/ideas raised in the introduction in a chronological sequence, a logical sequence, or a simple topical sequence. This will help the audience to follow the researcher's ideas whether the presentation is informative, an analytical or a persuasive. The important point is that the researcher should demarcate each point in the body so that the audience knows when he has completed one point and begun another.

The **conclusion** should reiterate the ideas presented and reinforce the purpose of the presentation. The conclusion helps the audience understand the significance of the presentation and remember the main points. The conclusions should not be long, but it should leave the audience with a positive feeling about the researcher/speaker and his ideas. Each conclusion is to be followed by the findings to support it. Thus, the design of the conclusion will depend on initial purpose and subsequent findings. A strong conclusion is nearly as important as a strong introduction, as both the beginning and the end will be the parts most likely to be remembered.

Recommendations whenever necessary, should be made and may be followed by reference to the conclusions. Finally after the end of the talk the speaker, as a sign of good manner, should say. **'Thank you'** for the audience. At the end of presentation it may be appropriate to **call for questions** from the audience. Presenting research findings using **power point** or other presentation software requires preparation similar to presenting with non-electronic visual aids.

Speaker's **speaking style** plays an important part in presentation. How a speaker sounds when he speaks is crucial to the success of his presentation. He may have effective content, excellent ideas, accurate supportive statistics, but if the style used in speaking is inappropriate to the occasion, to the audience or to the purpose envisaged, his content will more than likely be ineffective. Thus, it is proper to expect the speaker to sound respectful, confident, courteous and sincere.

Style in delivering oral presentations is also defined by verbal and many non-verbal cues that can either enhance or detract from the presentation. The following guidelines as regards the speaking style may be followed :

- Avoid long, cumbersome and complex sentences. Use phrases and use a variety of sentence lengths.
- Avoid over use of abstract, polysyllabic words and jargons.
- Use sentences that follow natural speech patterns.
- Use short, active voice sentences.
- Avoid memorizing the presentation verbatim

The most effective style is usually a **conversational style.**

Types of Presentation

1. Memorization : It is a risky and time consuming course to follow. Memorization virtually precludes establishing rapport with the audience and adapting to their reaction while the speaker speaks and will sound as if the speaker is reading.

2. Reading a manuscript : This is also not an advisable proposition. The delivery sounds dull and lifeless because most people are not trained to read aloud and therefore do it badly. The speaker becomes focussed on the manuscript rather than on the audience.

3. Extemporaneous presentation : This is audience centered and made from minimal notes or an outline. Extemporareous presentation permits the speaker to be natural, conversational and flexible. It is the best **choice for an organizational setting.** Preparation consists of a draft with complete sentence outline and converting the main points to notes. The main points are fixed sequentially in speaker's mind and then supporting connections are made.

Audiences are not averse to notes and their presence allays fears in the speaker's mind.

Speaker's power and technique of delivery plays an important part in presentation. But there is possible danger in shaping the delivery in the sense that sometimes the presentation overpowers the message. It may be remembered that the research presentation faces audience who are usually responsive managers or research workers with a high level of interest in the research, who do not need to be entertained. Thus the speaker faces real challenge in communicating effectively. The delivery should be restrained. Total appearance of the speaker including dress and posture should be appropriate for the occasion. Speed of speach, clarity of pronounciation, pause, gesture, voice pitch and tone quality play their role in improving the delivery.

Maintaining eye contact with audience and doing so helps listeners involved in what the speaker is saying. If the speaker looks at the ceiling, the floor and the corners of the room, the audience may sense a lack of confidence. Lack of eye contact also tends to lessen the credibility of the speaker. In contrast, consistent eye contact enhances the importance of the message. By looking at the audience, one can ofhen sense the reaction of the audience and make adjustments in presentation, if necessary. Audience members need to feel that the speaker is looking at them. It may be helpful to pickout three people in the audience (left, right and center) and practise looking at them successively as one talks. Even if one is an accomplished speaker, it is helpful to review his performances as one watches a videotape of his presentation. If possible, before presentation recorded speech may be listened to gauge the contents, tone, attitude and clarity. This will be helpful to know whether each sentence can be easily understood, whether the speaker is speaking too rapidly, whether major divisions in the presentation are easily understood and whether any sentences are difficult to understand. Sometimes a researcher may like to rehearse the presentation before team members.

Further, if possible, the speaker should make himself familiar with the room where the presentation is made so that he can have some sense about how loudly he should speak, so that the presentation is audible to the audience. It is necessary to talk clearly and loudly enough for every one to hear.

The audience should not be provided with hand-out material before beginning of the presentation. If so, the audience gets encouraged to read rather than listen. If written materials are provided, they must be co-ordinated with the presentation, and hence have a better chance of keeping audience's attention on what the speaker is presenting.

The speaker in order to make the presentation more clear should select and use visual aids effectively without making them burden on the audience.

To sum up, no matter what type of presentation one is giving, the ultimate success as a speaker and the success of presentation depend on establishing credibility with the audience and finishing presentation in the allotted time.

17.11.2 Audiovisuals

A researcher may make use of a variety of audio visuals in his presentation. The usual **visual aids** are

1. Chalk boards and white boards : These are flexible, inexpensive and require little specific preparation.

2. Handout materials : These ae expensive but can be made more professional. These need more time to prepare and may have distracting impact if not properly used. These may be distributed at the end of presentation, but a better use to refer them during presentation.

3. **Flip charts :** One can show colour, pictures and large letters with flip charts.

4. **Overhead transparencies**

5. **Slides**

6. **Computer-drawn visuals**

7. **Computer animation**

The choice of visual aids is determined by

❐ purpose

❐ size of audience

❐ meeting room condition

- time and budget constraints
- available equipment

17.11.3 Benefits of using visual aids

- They help presenting research output more effectively. Statistical relationships which are difficult to explain verbally, can be shown by pictures and graphs to communicate well.
- These help audience to undestand ideas. The speaker can use visual aids to announce each main point as he begins discussion on that point.
- They help the audience follow the 'train' of thought of the speaker. Power point is an effective tool for developing and presenting outlines to aid listeners.
- They make the presentation more memorable and increase the chances that what the speaker said will be remembered. The continuity and memorability of the speaker's message are also improved with visual aids. The audience can review the point already made by the speaker and relate it to earlier ones and thus improves retention.

17.11.4 How to use visual aids effectively ?

The key to using graphics and visual aids effectively requires using them in a way that make the maximum impact. The speaker should begin the presentation with no aids and then present the aid at the appropriate point in the presentation, give audience a few seconds to comprehend and then comment on the aid. Then, aid should be removed immediately.

- Be sure to speak slowly and deliberately as you explain or use a graphic to avoid confusing your audience. In addition, remember to talk to your audience, keeping eye contact with them, not on your visual aid.
- When you use slides, tell the audience what they will see, show them the slide, give them time to digest what they are seeing, then comment on the slide.
- Turn off the projector lamp between slides. Do not begin talking about another topic while a slide, depicting the past topic, is still showing. Remember : people cannot see and listen at the same time.

17.12 Precis writing and reporting committee findings :

17.12.1. Introduction

In life of the executives/managers or even in general there is great pressure for quick action and disposal of work. We need to shift heaps of information, grasp and present it logically to arrive at a decision. Under such circumstances it is required to present the information in brief and precise manner by making precis of the material under purview. Thus, *a precis is a brief summary and its writing requires to choose words carefully and arrange them skillfully, so that one can put maximum amount of meaning into the minimum space*. In order to summarise another's ideas in your own words, one must understand the ideas thoroughly.

The following facts are worth considering :

- A precis is a short summary
- A precis gives only heart of the passage.
- A precis is written entirely in the words of the person writing it, not in the words the selected passage.
- A precis is written from the point of view of the author whose work is being summarised.

In modern administrative and business organisation, the higher authorities usually set up different committees to help taking decision in certain important matters. A committee consisting a group of members collects relevant information from the existing files and sometimes makes on the spot enquiry or conduct interviews to get additional inputs to arrive at certain conlusions and recommendations after a series of exchange of views and discussions among them. The reports are sometimes so bulky covering a large number of pages that it may be time consuming for busy executives to grasp them to take required steps for implementation. In such cases if the precis of the reports, along with the main reports are submitted before the authorities, it saves time and energy for them to understand the contents of the report and take appropriate timely decisions.

17.12.2 Precis Writing

Precis writing involves summarising a document to extract the maximum amount of information, then conveying this information to a reader in the minimum number of words. In reducing the number of words, it is usually necessary to paraphrase from the original document. Paraphrasing simply means the expressing of ideas from the original document in your own words. When you paraphrase, you should try to write as concisely as possible, cutting out all the unnecessary verbiage, but you must always be very careful not to lose or distort the original meaning.

Guidelines for writing an effective precis :

- Identify the reader and purpose of the precis
- Read the original document
- Underline the key ideas and concepts
- Write a note-form summary of each paragraph
- Write a precis
- Review and edit

Identify the reader and purpose of the precis

This determines how much detail should be included and how formal the precis needs to be. For instance, the precis you make of a textbook chapter for your own study purposes does not have to be as carefully refined as the executive summary of a formal report for an important client.

Read the original document

Read the document carefully to get an overview, then read it again more slowly to identify the main themes and to distinguish the key ideas and concepts from the unimportant ones.

Underline the key ideas and concepts

Each paragraph should have one key topic, which the rest of the paragraph clarifies, supports and develops.

Write a note- form summary of each paragraph

Use the words of the original document, but omit all irrelevant material.

Write a precis

Paraphrase to express the summarised points more concisely and to develop them into coherent sentences, expressing all important points in a generalised form. Eliminate any repetitions or irrelevant details. Limit the size of precis to **one third** of the words contained in the original passage.

Review and edit

Compare your precis with original document and make sure that it emphasises the same points. Ensure that the precise is clear, concise and coherent.

An Example of precis writing :

Original document. Because the ability to communicate effectively plays an important part in an accountant's success on the job, many employers screen prospective accountants for adequate skills in oral and written communication. In fact, one study shows communication skills to be the most important factor in decisions to hire. Employers view the ability to write and speak effectively as even more important than a prospective employee's academic results (66 words).

Action : underline key words or ideas

Action : write note-form summary

- ❒ ability to communicate effectively important to accountant's success
- ❒ important factor in decision to hire
- ❒ employers value communication skills even more than academic results

Action : Use your own words to express these key ideas more concisely and to develop a full sentence paraphrase which conveys the original message accurately and is clear, concise and coherent.

Employers recognise the importance of oral and written communication in accounting, and therefore prefer to hire graduates with effective communication skills. (21 words)

[Note that the words have been changed to express the key ideas more concisely. In changing the words in this way, always make sure the key ideas are not lost or distorted.]

EXERCISES

1. What is a report ? What are the characteristics of good report ? Discuss.
2. Distinguish between long and short report. Who are the audiences for such reports.
3. (*a*) Discuss the basic components of a research report.
   (*b*) Differentiate between formal and informal reports.
   (*c*) Discuss same common informal reports.
4. Discuss four stages report writing techniques.
5. Discuss the salient points for writing a draft report.
6. **Write short notes on :**
   (*a*) Letter of transmittal
   (*b*) Long reports vs short reports
   (*c*) Informal reports.
   (*d*) Style of writing
   (*e*) Lay out of the report.
7. Discuss the relationship between data analysis and writing the report.
8. 'Hard writing makes easy reading'. Illucidate this statement.
9. Discuss the importance of research questions and stakeholders in writing a report.
10. What is a technical report ? Explain its purposes.
11. Discuss the role of audience for technical report.
12. What is audience analysis ? Discuss.
13. What are attributes of a technical document ? Discuss.
14. Describe the structure of Instruction manual.
15. What is a technical proposal ? Explain types of technical proposals.
16. What is a precis ? Explain the guidelines for writing a precis.
17. Distinguish between written report and oral presentation.
18. What are basic strategies for effective oral presentation ?
19. What should be the mindset of the researcher before delivering oral presentation ?
20. How should a researcher organize his presentation ? Explain its different parts.
21. Mention the appropriate speaking style for the researcher to make his presentation.
22. What should be the effective delivery style for the speaker ?
23. Explain briefly different types of presentation.
24. Explain the need a speaker for maintaining eye contact with the audience.
25. Mention different visual aids used in oral presentation. What should be the best choice ?
26. What are benefits of using visual aids ? How can they be effectively used ?

□□□

REFERENCES

1. Aaker, D.A, Kumar, V. Dey, G.S. (2001), Marketing Research, John Wiley and Sons, Inc.
2. Ackoff, R.L (1953) The Design of Social Research, Chicago.
3. Anderson, T.W. (1974) : Introduction to Multivariate Statistical Analysis, Wiley Eastern Private Ltd., New Delhi.
4. Beri, G.C. (2003) : Statistics for Management, Tata McGraw Hill, New Delhi.
5. Borg, I. and Groenen, P (1997) : Modern Multidimensional Scaling : Theory and applications, Springer—Verlag New York, 1997.
6. Cohen, M. and E. Nagel (1934) An Introduction to Logic and Scientific Method, New York.
7. Cochran, W.G. (1953) Sampling Techniques, Wiley, New York.
8. Cooper, D.R. and Schindler, P.S. (2003) : Business Research Methods, Tata McGraw Hill Edition, (8th edition) New Delhi.
9. Dunn, O.J. and Clack, V.A. (1974) : Applied Statistics : Analysis of variance and Regression, New York, Wiley.
10. Federer, W.T. (1955) : Experimental Design, Theory and Application, Mcmillan Publishing Company, Co. Inc.
11. Freund, J.E. and Walpole, R.E. (1987) : Mathematical Statistics, Prentice Hall of India, New Delhi.
12. Gibbons, J.D. (1971) : Non-parametric Statistical Inference, McGraw Hill Book Company, New York.
13. Goode, W.J. and Hatt, P.K. (1952) : Methods in Social Research, McGraw Hill Book Company, Inc., Tokyo.
14. Greenacre, M.J. (1993) : Correspondence analysis in practice, London : Academic Press.
15. Hines, W.W. and Montgomery, D.C. (1990). Probability and Statistics in Engineering and Management Science (3rd edition), John Wiley and Sons.
16. Johnson, R.A. and Wichern, D.W.(1992) Applied Multivariate Statistical Analysis, (3rd Edition), Prentice Hall of India, New Delhi.
17. Johnson, R.A. (2002) Miller & Freund's Probability and Statistics for Engineers, 6th edition, Prentice Hall of India, New Delhi.
18. Kothari, C.R. (2001) : Research Methodology, Wishwa Prakashan.
19. Kruskal, J.B. and M. Wish (1978) Multidimensional scaling, Sage publication.
20. Kyeberg (Jr.) H.E. (1968) : Philosophy of Science—A formal approach, McMillan, N.Y.
21. Linstone, H.A. and Turoff, M.T. (1975) : The Delphi Method Techniques and applications, London, Addison—Wesley.
22. Levin, R.I., Rubin, et.al (1992) : Quantitative Approaches to Management, McGraw Hill Book Company, New York.

23. Levine, D.M., Krehbiel, T.C. and Berenson, M.L. (2001). Business statistics—A first course (2nd edition), Pearson Education, Asia.

24. Louviere, Jordan J. (1988) : Analysing Decision making : Metric conjoint analysis, sage university paper.

25. Malhotra, N.K. (2005) Marketing Research, Prentice Hall of India, New Delhi.

26. Morrison, D.F. (1990) : Multivariate Statistical Methods, McGraw Hill Internal edition, New Delhi.

27. Northrop, F.S.C. (1947) : The Logic of Science and Humanities, McMillan, London.

28. Paneerselvam, R. (2004). Research Methodology, Prentice Hall of India, New Delhi.

29. Riordan, D. and Pauley, S. (2004) : Technical Report Writing To day, Biztantra.

30. Scheffe, H. (1959) Analysis of Variance, John Wile & Sons, New York.

31. Sharma, R.C. and Mohan, Krishna (2002) : Business correspondence and Report Writing, Tata McGraw Hill Publishing Company Ltd.

32. Snedecor, G.W. and Cochran, W.G. (1973) Statistical Methods, 6th edition, Iowa University Press, Iowa, USA.

33. Stake, R.E. (1995) : The art case study research, Thousands Oaks, C.A. : Sage Publication.

34. Sukhatme, P.V., Sukhatme, B.V. and Asok, C. (1984). Sampling theory in surveys with applications, Ind. Soc. Ag. Stat., New Delhi.

35. Swain, A.K.P.C. (2003) A first course in Statistics with applications, Kalyani Publishers, Ludhiana.

36. Swain, A.K.P.C. (2003) Finite Population Sampling : Theory and Methods, South Asia Publishers, New Delhi.

37. Swain, A.K.P.C. (2005) : Probability and Statistics with Engineering and Computer Science Applications, Kalyani Publishers, Ludhiana.

38. Theobald, D.W. (1968) : An Introduction to Philosophy of Science, Methuen, London.

39. Torgerson, W.S. (1958). Theory and Method of Scaling, Wiley, N.Y.

40. Trochim, William (2004) : Research Methods, Biztantra.

41. Walters, A.A. (1970) : An Introduction to Econometrics, Mcmillan (2nd edition), Mcmillan students', Edition, London.

42. Yin, R (1984) : Case study research : Design and methods, Newbury Park, CA: Sage Publication.

43. Yin, R (1994) : Case study research : Design and Methods (2nd edition), Beverly Hills, CA : Sage Publishing.

44. Young, P.V. (2003) : Scientific Social Surveys and Research, Prentice Hill of India, New Delhi.

45. Zikmund, William (2002) : Business Research Methods, Thomson (7th edition)

46. Firestone, W.A. (1987) : Meaning in Method : The Rhetoric of quantitative and qualitative research, Educational Researcher, 16, 16-21.

47. Harvey, M. and Blackmon, K. (2005) : Research Methods for business and Management, Palgrove MacMillan.

□□□

APPENDICES

(STATISTICAL TABLES)

TABLE A–1
Standard Normal Distribution Function

$$\phi(z) = \frac{1}{\sqrt{2\pi}} \int_{-\infty}^{z} e^{-\frac{1}{2}t^2}\, dt$$

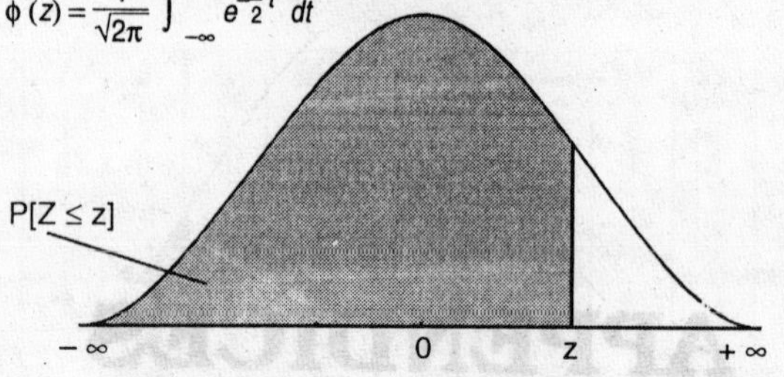

z	0.00	0.01	0.02	0.03	0.04	0.05	0.06	0.07	0.08	0.09
0.0	.5000	.5040	.5080	.5120	.5160	.5199	.5239	.5279	.5319	.5359
0.1	.5398	.5438	.5478	.5517	.5557	.5596	.5636	.5675	.5714	.5753
0.2	.5793	.5832	.5871	.5910	.5948	.5987	.6026	.6064	.6103	.6141
0.3	.6179	.6217	.6255	.6293	.6331	.6368	.6406	.6443	.6480	.6517
0.4	.6554	.6591	.6628	.6664	.6700	.6736	.6772	.6808	.6844	.6879
0.5	.6915	.6950	.6985	.7019	.7054	.7088	.7123	.7157	.7190	.7224
0.6	.7257	.7291	.7324	.7357	.7389	.7422	.7454	.7486	.7517	.7549
0.7	.7580	.7611	.7642	.7673	.7704	.7734	.7764	.7794	.7823	.7852
0.8	.7881	.7910	.7939	.7967	.7995	.8023	.8051	.8078	.8106	.8133
0.9	.8159	.8186	.8212	.8238	.8264	.8289	.8315	.8340	.8365	.8389
1.0	.8413	.8438	.8461	.8485	.8508	.8531	.8554	.8577	.8599	.8621
1.1	.8643	.8665	.8686	.8708	.8729	.8749	.8770	.8790	.8810	.8830
1.2	.8849	.8869	.8888	.8907	.8925	.8944	.8962	.8980	.8997	.9015
1.3	.9032	.9049	.9066	.9082	.9099	.9115	.9131	.9147	.9162	.9177
1.4	.9192	.9207	.9222	.9236	.9251	.9265	.9279	.9292	.9306	.9319
1.5	.9332	.9345	.9357	.9370	.9382	.9394	.9406	.9418	.9429	.9441
1.6	.9452	.9463	.9474	.9484	.9495	.9505	.9515	.9525	.9535	.9545
1.7	.9554	.9564	.9573	.9582	.9591	.9599	.9608	.9616	.9625	.9633
1.8	.9641	.9649	.9656	.9664	.9671	.9678	.9686	.9693	.9699	.9706
1.9	.9713	.9719	.9726	.9732	.9738	.9744	.9750	.9756	.9761	.9767
2.0	.9772	.9778	.9783	.9788	.9793	.9798	.9803	.9808	.9812	.9817
2.1	.9821	.9826	.9830	.9834	.9838	.9842	.9846	.9850	.9854	.9857
2.2	.9861	.9864	.9868	.9871	.9875	.9878	.9881	.9884	.9887	.9890
2.3	.9893	.9896	.9898	.9901	.9904	.9906	.9909	.9911	.9913	.9916
2.4	.9918	.9920	.9922	.9925	.9927	.9929	.9931	.9932	.9934	.9936
2.5	.9938	.9940	.9941	.9943	.9945	.9946	.9948	.9949	.9951	.9952
2.6	.9953	.9955	.9956	.9957	.9959	.9960	.9961	.9962	.9963	.9964
2.7	.9965	.9966	.9967	.9968	.9969	.9970	.9971	.9972	.9973	.9974
2.8	.9974	.9975	.9976	.9977	.9977	.9978	.9979	.9979	.9980	.9981
2.9	.9981	.9982	.9982	.9983	.9984	.9984	.9985	.9985	.9986	.9986
3.0	.9987	.9987	.9987	.9988	.9988	.9989	.9989	.9989	.9990	.9990
3.1	.9990	.9991	.9991	.9991	.9992	.9992	.9992	.9992	.9993	.9993
3.2	.9993	.9993	.9994	.9994	.9994	.9994	.9994	.9995	.9995	.9995
3.3	.9995	.9995	.9995	.9996	.9996	.9996	.9996	.9996	.9996	.9997
3.4	.9997	.9997	.9997	.9997	.9997	.9997	.9997	.9997	.9997	.9998
3.5	.9998	.9998	.9998	.9998	.9998	.9998	.9998	.9998	.9998	.9998

TABLE A–2
Critical Values of t-distribution $P(t > t_\alpha) = \alpha$

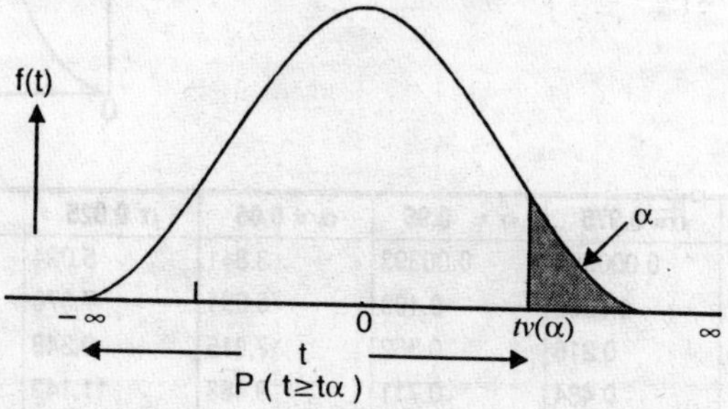

ν	α = 0.10	α = 0.05	α = 0.025	α = 0.01	α = 0.005	ν
1	3.078	6.314	12.706	31.821	63.657	1
2	1.886	2.920	4.303	6.965	9.925	2
3	1.638	2.353	3.182	4.541	5.841	3
4	1.533	2.132	2.776	3.747	4.604	4
5	1.476	2.015	2.571	3.365	4.032	5
6	1.440	1.943	2.447	3.143	3.707	6
7	1.415	1.895	2.365	2.998	3.499	7
8	1.397	1.860	2.306	2.896	3.355	8
9	1.383	1.833	2.262	2.821	3.250	9
10	1.372	1.812	2.228	2.764	3.169	10
11	1.363	1.796	2.201	2.718	3.106	11
12	1.356	1.782	2.179	2.681	3.055	12
13	1.350	1.771	2.160	2.650	3.012	13
14	1.345	1.761	2.145	2.624	2.977	14
15	1.341	1.753	2.131	2.602	2.947	15
16	1.337	1.746	2.120	2.583	2.921	16
17	1.333	1.740	2.110	2.567	2.898	17
18	1.330	1.734	2.101	2.552	2.878	18
19	1.328	1.729	2.093	2.539	2.861	19
20	1.325	1.725	2.086	2.528	2.845	20
21	1.323	1.721	2.080	2.518	2.831	21
22	1.321	1.717	2.074	2.508	2.819	22
23	1.319	1.714	2.069	2.500	2.807	23
24	1.318	1.711	2.064	2.492	2.797	24
25	1.316	1.708	2.060	2.485	2.787	25
26	1.315	1.706	2.056	2.479	2.779	26
27	1.314	1.703	2.052	2.473	2.771	27
28	1.313	1.701	2.048	2.467	2.763	28
29	1.311	1.699	2.045	2.462	2.756	29
inf.	1.282	1.645	1.960	2.326	2.576	inf.

TABLE A–3
Critical values of χ^2_α

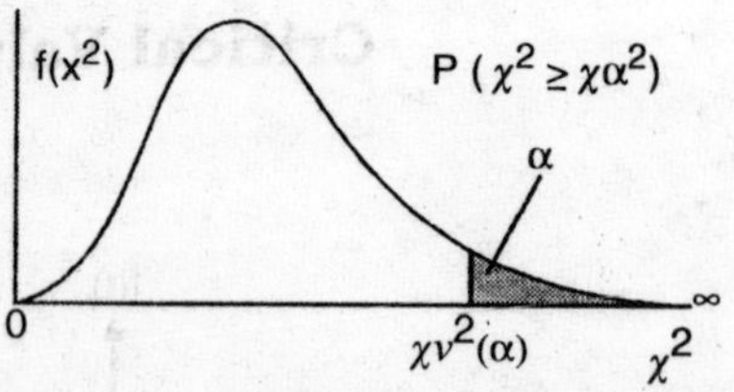

ν	α = 0.995	α = 0.99	α= 0.975	α = 0.95	α = 0.05	α 0.025	α = 0.01	α = 0.005	ν
1	0.0000393	0.000157	0.000982	0.00393	3.841	5.024	6.635	7.879	1
2	0.0100	0.0201	0.0506	0.103	5.991	7.378	9.210	10.597	2
3	0.0717	0.115	0.216	0.352	7.815	9.348	11.345	12.838	3
4	0.207	0.297	0.484	0.711	9.488	11.143	13.277	14.860	4
5	0.412	0.554	0.831	1.145	11.070	12.832	15.056	16.750	5
6	0.676	0.872	1.237	1.635	12.592	14.449	16.812	18.548	6
7	0.989	1.239	1.690	2.167	14.067	16.013	18.475	20.278	7
8	1.344	1.646	2.180	2.733	15.507	17.535	20.090	21.955	8
9	1.735	2.088	2.700	3.325	16.919	19.023	21.666	23.589	9
10	2.156	2.558	3.247	3.940	18.307	20.483	23.209	25.188	10
12	3.074	3.571	4.404	5.226	21.026	23.337	26.217	28.300	12
13	3.565	4.107	5.009	5.892	22.362	24.736	27.688	29.819	13
14	4.075	4.660	5.629	6.571	23.685	26.119	29.141	31.319	14
15	4.601	5.229	6.262	7.261	24.996	27.488	30.578	32.801	15
16	5.142	5.812	6.908	7.962	26.296	28.845	32.000	34.267	16
17	5.697	6.408	7.564	8.672	27.587	30.191	33.409	35.718	17
18	6.265	7.015	8.231	9.390	28.869	31.526	34.805	37.156	18
19	6.844	7.633	8.907	10.117	30.144	32.852	36.191	38.582	19
20	7.434	8.260	9.591	10.851	31.410	34.170	37.566	39.997	20
21	8.034	8.897	10.283	11.591	32.671	35.479	38.932	41.401	21
22	8.643	9.542	10.982	12.338	33.924	36.781	40.289	42.796	22
23	9.260	10.196	11.689	13.091	35.172	38.076	41.638	44.181	23
24	9.886	10.856	12.401	13.484	36.415	39.364	42.980	45.558	24
25	10.520	11.524	13.120	14.611	37.652	40.646	44.314	46.928	25
26	11.160	12.198	13.844	15.379	38.885	41.923	45.642	48.290	26
27	11.808	12.879	14.573	16.151	40.113	43.194	46.963	49.645	27
28	12.461	13.565	15.308	16.928	41.337	44.461	48.278	50.993	28
29	13.121	14.256	16.047	17.708	42.557	45.772	49.588	52.336	29
30	13.787	14.953	16.791	18.493	43.773	46.979	50.892	53.672	30
40	20.706	22.164	24.433	26.509	55.758	59.342	63.691	66.766	40
50	27.991	29.707	32.357	34.764	67.505	71.420	76.154	79.490	50
60	35.535	37.485	40.482	43.118	79.082	83.298	88.379	91.952	60
70	43.275	45.442	48.758	51.739	90.531	95.023	100.425	104.215	70
80	51.172	53.540	57.153	60.391	101.879	106.629	112.329	116.321	80
90	59.196	61.754	65.646	69.126	113.145	118.136	124.116	128.299	90
100	67.328	70.065	74.222	77.929	124.342	129.561	135.807	140.169	100

TABLE A–4 (*a*)
F-Distribution critical points (α = .05)

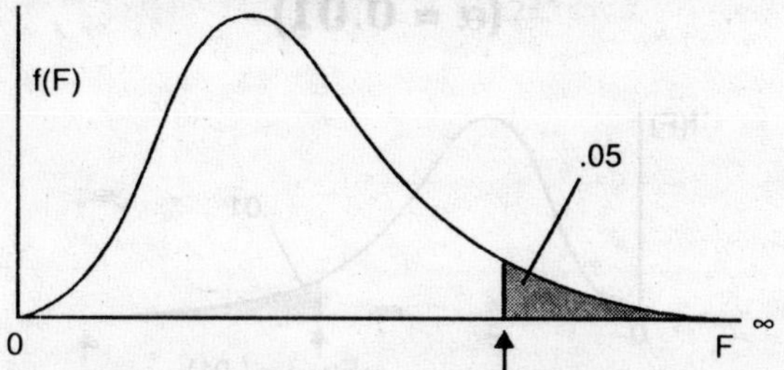

ν_1 / ν_2	1	2	3	4	5	6	7	8	9	10	12	15	20	25	30	40	60
1	161.5	199.5	215.7	224.6	230.2	234.0	236.8	238.9	240.5	241.9	243.9	246.0	248.0	249.3	250.1	251.1	252.2
2	18.51	19.00	19.16	19.25	19.30	19.33	19.35	19.37	19.38	19.40	19.41	19.43	19.45	19.46	19.46	19.47	19.48
3	10.13	9.55	9.28	9.12	9.01	8.94	8.89	8.85	8.81	8.79	8.74	8.70	8.66	8.63	8.62	8.59	8.57
4	7.71	6.94	6.59	6.39	6.26	6.16	6.09	6.04	6.00	5.96	5.91	5.86	5.80	5.77	5.75	5.72	5.69
5	6.61	5.79	5.41	5.19	5.05	4.95	4.88	4.82	4.77	4.74	4.68	4.462	4.56	4.52	4.50	4.46	4.43
6	5.99	5.14,4	76	4.53	4.39	4.28	4.21	4.15	4.10	4.06	4.00	3.94	3.87	3.83	3.81	3.77	3.74
7	5.59	4.74	4.35	4.12	3.97	3.87	3.79	3.73	.68	3.64	3.57	3.51	3.44	3.40	3.38	3.34	3.30
8	5.32	4.46	4.07	3.84	3.69	3.58	3.50	3.44	3.39	3.35	3.28	3.22	3.15	3.11	3.08	3.04	3.01
9	5.12	4.26	3.86	3.63	3.48	3.37	3.29	3.23	3.18	3.14	3.07	3.01	2.94	2.89	2.86	2.83	2.79
10	4.96	4.10	3.71	3.48	3.33	3.22	3.14	3.07	3.02	2.98	2.91	2.85	2.77	2.73	2.70,.	2.66	2.62
11	4.84	3.98	3.59	3.36	3.20	3.09	3.01	2.95	2.90	2.85	2.79	2.72	2.65	2.60	2.57	2.53	2.49
12	4.75	3.89	3.49	3.26	3.11	3.00	2.91	2.85	2.80	2.75	2.69	2.62	2.54	2.50	2.47	2.43	2.38
13	4.67	3.81	3.41	3.18	303	2.92	2.83	2.77	2.71	2.67	2.60	2.53	2.46	2.41	2.38	2.34	2.30
14	4.60	3.74	3.34	3.11	2.96	2.85	2.76	2.70	2.65	2.60	2.53	2.46	2.39	2.34	2.31	2.27	2.22
15	4.54	3.68	3.29	3.06	2.90	2.79	2.71	2.64	2.59	2.54	2.48	2.40	2.33	2.28	2.25	2.20	2.16
16	4.49	3.63	3.24	3.01	2.85	2.74	2.66	2.59	5.54	2.49	2.42	2.35	2.28	2.23	2.19	2.15	2.11
17	4.45	3.59	3.20	2.96	2.81	2.70	2.61	2.55	2.49	2.45	2.38	2.31	2.23	2.18	2.15	2.10	2.06
18	4.41	3.55	3.16	2.93	2.77	2.66	2.58	2.51	2.46	2.41	2.34	2.27	2.19	2.14	2.11	2.06	2.02
19	4.38	3.52	3.13	2.90	2.74	2.63	2.54	2.48	2.42	2.38	2.31	2.23	2.16	2.11	2.07	2.03	1.98
20	4.35	3.49	3.10	2.87	2.71	2.60	2.51	2.45	2.39	2.35	2.28	2.20	2.12	2.07	2.04	1.99	1.95
21	4.32	3.47	3.07	2.84	2.68	2.57	2.49	2.42	2.37	2.32	2.25	2.18	2.10	2.05	2.01	1.96	1.92
22	4.30	3.44	3.05	2.82	2.66	2.55	2.46	2.40	2.34,	2.30	2.23	2.15	2.07	2.02	1.98	1.94	1.89
23	4.28	3.42	3.03	2.80	2.64	2.53	2.44	2.37	2.32	2.27	2.20	2.13	2.05	2.00	1.96	1.91	1.86
24	4.26	3.40	3.01	2.78	2.62	2.51	2.42	2.36	2.30	2.25	2.18	2.11	2.03	1.97	1.94	1.89	1.84
25	4.24	3.39	2.99	2.76	2.60	2.49	2.40	2.34	2.28	2.24	2.16	2.09	2.01	1.96	1.92	1.87	1.82
26	4.23	3.37	2.98	2.74	2.59	2.47	2.39	2.32	2.27	2.22	2.15	2.07	1.99	1.94	1.90	1.85	1.80
27	4.21	3.35	2.96	2.73	2.57	2.46	2.37	2.31	2.25	2.20	2.13	2.06	1.97	1.92	1.88	1.84	1.79
28	4.20	3.34	2.95	2.71	2.56	2.45	2.36	2.29	2.24	2.19	2.12	2.04	1.96	1.91	1.87	1.82	1.77
29	4.18	3.33	2.93	2.70	2.55	2.43	2.35	2.28	2.22	2.18	2.10	2.03	1.94	1.89	1.85	1.81	1.75
30	4.17	3.32	2.92	2.69	2.53	2.42	2.33	2.27	2.21	2.16	2.09	2.01	1.93	1.88	1.84	1.79	1.74
40	4.08	3.23	2.84	2.61	2.45	2.34	2.25	2.18	2.12	2.08	2.00	1.92	1.84	1.78	1.74	1.69	1.64
60	4.00	3.15	2.76	2.53	2.37	2.25	2.17	2.10	2.04	1.99	1.92	1.84	1.75	1.69	1.65	1.59	1.53
120	3.92	307	2.68	2.45	2.29	2.18	2.09	2.02	1.96	1.91	1.83	1.75	1.66	1.60	1.55	1.50	1.43
∞	3.84	3.00	2.61	2.37	2.21	2.10	2.01	1.94	1.88	1.83	1.75	1.67	1.57	1.51	1.46	1.39	1.32

TABLE A–4 (*b*)
F-Distribution Critical Points
(α = 0.01)

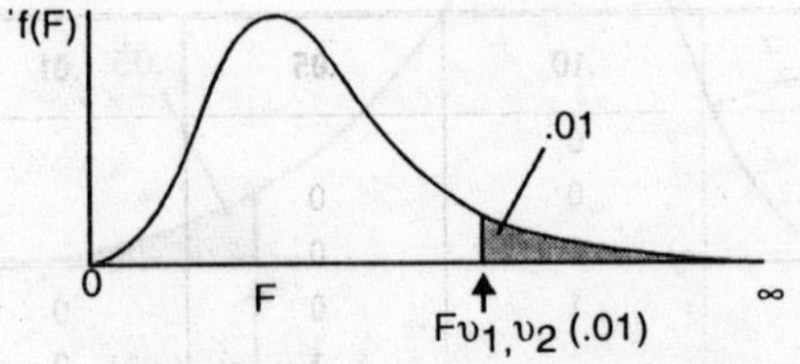

ν_2 \ ν_1	1	2	3	4	5	6	7	8	9	10	12	15	20	25	30	40	60
1	4052.	5000	5403.	5625.	5764.	5859.	5928.	5981.	6023.	6056.	6106.	6157.	6209.	6240	6261	6287.	6313.
2	98.50	99.00	99.17	99.25	99.30	99.36	99.36	99.37	99.39	99.40	99.42	99.43	99.45	99.46	99.47	99.47	99.48
3	34.12	30.82	29.46	28.71	28.24	27.91	27.67	27.49	27.35	27.33	27.05	26.87	26.69	26.58	26.50	26.41	26.32
4	21.20	18.00	16.69	15.98	15.52	15.21	14.89	14.80	14.66	14.55	14.37	14.20	14.02	13.91	13.84	1375	13.65
5	16.26	13.27	12.06	11.39	10.97	10.67	10.46	10.29	10.16	10.05	9.89	9.72	9.55	9.45	9.38	9.29	9.20
6	13.75	10.92	9.78	9.15	8.75	8.47	8.26	8.10	7.98	7.87	7.72	7.56	7.40	7.30	7.23	7.14	7.06
7	12.25	9.55	8.45	7.85	7.46	7.19	6.99	6.84	6.72	6.62	6.47	6.31	6.16	6.06	5.99	5.91	5.82
8	11.26	8.65	7.59	7.01	6.63	6.37	6.18	6.03	5.91	5.81	5.67	5.52	5.36	5.26	5.20	5.12	5.03
9	10.56	8.02	6.99	6.42	6.06	5.80	5.61	5.47	5.35	5.26	5.11	4.96	4.81	4.71	4.65	4.57	4.48
10	10.04	7.56	6.55	5.99	5.64	5.39	5.20	5.06	4.94	4.85	4.71	4.56	4.41	4.31	4.25	4.17	4.08
11	9.65	7.21	6.22	5.67	5.32	5.07	4.89	4.74	4.63	4.54	4.40	4.25	4.10	4.01	3.94	3.86	3.78
12	9.33	6.93	5.95	5.41	5.069	4.82	4.64	4.50	4.39	4.30	4.16	4.01	3.86	3.76	3.70	3.62	3.54
13	9.07	6.70	5.74	5.21	4.86	4.62	4.44	4.30	4.19	4.10	3.96	3.82	3.66	3.57	3.51	3.27	3.34
14	8.86	6.51	5.56	5.04	4.69	4.46	4.28	4.14	4.03	3.94	3.80	3.66	3.51	3.41	3.35	3.27	3.18
15	8.68	6.36	5.42	4.89	4.56	4.32	4.14	4.00	3.89	3.80	3.67	3.52	3.37	3.28	3.21	3.13	3.05
16	8.53	6.23	5.29	4.77	4.44	4.20	4.03	3.89	3.78	3.69	3.55	3.41	3.26	3.16	3.10	3.02	2.93
17	8.40	6.11	5.19	4.67	4.34	4.10	3.93	3.79	3.68	3.59	3.46	3.31	3.16	3.07	3.00	2.92	2.83
18	8.29	6.01	5.09	4.58	4.25	4.01	3.84	3.71	3.60	3.51	3.37	3.23	3.08	2.98	2.92	2.84	2.75
19	8.18	5.93	5.01	4.50	4.17	3.94	3.77	3.63	3.52	3.43	3.30	3.15	3.00	2.91	2.84	2.76	2.67
20	8.10	5.85	4.94	4.43	4.10	3.87	3.70	3.56	3.46	3.37	3.23	3.09	2.94	2.84	2.78	2.69	2.61
21	8.02	5.78	4.87	4.37	4.04	3.81	3.64	3.51	3.40	3.31	3.17	3.03	2.88	2.79	2.72	2.64	2.55
22	7.95	5.72	4.82	4.31	3.99	3.76	3.59	3.45	3.35	3.26	3.12	2.98	2.83	2.73	2.67	2.58	2.50
23	7.88	5.66	4.76	4.26	3.94	3.71	3.54	3.41	3.30	3.21	3.07	2.93	2.78	2.69	2.62	2.54	2.45
24	7.82	5.61	4.72	4.22	3.90	3.67	3.50	3.36	3.26	3.17	3.03	2.89	2.74	2.64	2.58	2.49	2.40
25	7.77	5.57	4.68	4.18	3.85	3.63	3.46	3.32	3.22	3.13	2.99	2.85	2.70	2.60	2.54	2.45	2.36
26	7.72	5.53	4.64	4.14	3.82	3.59	3.42	3.29	3.18	3.09	2.96	2.81	2.66	2.57	2.50	2.42	2.33
27	7.68	5.49	4.60	4.11	3.78	3.56	3.39	3.26	3.15	3.06	2.93	2.78	2.63	2.54	2.47	2.38	2.29
28	7.64	5.45	4.57	4.07	3.75	3.53	3.36	3.23	3.12	3.03	2.90	2.75	2.60	2.51	2.44	2.35	2.26
29	7.60	5.42	4.54	4.04	3.73	3.50	3.33	3.20	3.09	3.00	2.87	2.73	2.57	2.48	2.41	2.33	2.23
30	7.56	5.39	4.51	4.02	3.70	3.47	3.30	3.17	3.07	2.98	2.84	2.70	2.55	2.45	2.39	2.30	2.21
40	7.31	5.18	4.31	3.83	3.51	3.29	3.12	2.99	2.89	2.80	2.66	2.52	2.37	2.27	2.20	2.11	2.02
60	7.08	4.98	4.13	3.65	3.34	3.12	2.95	2.82	2.72	2.63	2.50	2.35	2.20	2.10	2.03	1.94	1.84
120	6.85	4.79	3.95	3.48	3.17	2.96	2.79	2.66	2.56	2.47	2.34	2.19	2.03	1.93	1.86	1.76	1.66
∞	6.63	4.61	3.78	3.32	3.02	2.80	2.64	2.51	2.41	2.32	2.18	2.04	1.88	1.78	1.70	1.59	1.47

TABLE A–5
Critical Values for the Sign Test
(r^*_α)

n \ α	.10	.05	.01
5	0		
6	0	0	
7	0	0	
8	1	0	0
9	1	1	0
10	1	1	0
11	2	1	0
12	2	2	1
13	3	2	1
14	3	2	1
15	3	3	2
16	4	3	2
17	4	4	2
18	5	4	3
19	5	4	3
20	5	5	3
21	6	5	4
22	6	5	4
23	7	6	4
24	7	6	5
25	7	7	5
26	8	7	6
27	8	7	6
28	9	8	6
29	9	9	7
30	10	9	7
31	10	9	7
32	10	9	8
33	11	10	8
34	11	10	9
35	12	11	9
36	12	11	9
37	13	12	10
38	13	12	10
39	13	12	11
40	14	13	11

For $n > 40$, r is approximately normally distributed with mean $n/2$ and variance $n/4$.

TABLE A–6
Critical Values of the Kolmogorov-Smirnov One Sample Test Statistics.

One-Sided Test :											
α =	.10	.05	.025	.01	.005	α =	.10	.05	.025	.01	.005
Two sided Test :											
α =	.20	.01	.05	.02	.01	α =	.20	.10	.05	.02	.01
n = 1	.900	.950	.975	.990	.995	n = 21	.226	.259	.287	.321	.344
2	.685	.776	.842	.900	.929	22	.221	.253	.281	.314	.337
3	.565	.636	.708	.785	.829	23	.216	.247	.275	.307	.330
4	.493	.565	.624	.689	.734	24	.212	.242	.269	.301	.323
5	.447	.509	.563	.627	.669	25	.208	.238	.264	.295	.317
6	.410	.468	.519	.577	.617	26	.204	.233	.259	.290	.311
7	.381	.436	.483	.538	.576	27	.200	.229	.254	.284	.305
8	.358	.410	.454	.507	.542	28	.197	.225	.250	.279	.300
9	.339	.387	.430	.480	.513	29	.193	.221	.246	.275	.295
10	.323	.369	.409	.457	.489	30	.190	.218	.242	.270	.290
11	.308	.352	.391	.437	.468	31	.187	.214	.238	.266	.285
12	.296	.338	.375	.419	.449	32	.184	.211	.234	.262	.281
13	.285	.325	.361	.404	.432	33	.182	.208	.231	.258	.277
14	.275	.314	.349	.390	.418	34	.179	.205	.227	.254	.273
15	.266	.304	.338	.377	.404	35	.177	.202	.224	.251	.269
16	.258	.295	.327	.366	.392	36	.174	.199	.221	.247	.265
17	.250	.286	.318	.355	.381	37	.172	.196	.218	.244	.262
18	.244	.279	.309	.346	.371	38	.170	.194	.215	.241	.258
19	.237	.271	.301	.337	.361	39	.168	.191	.213	.238	.255
20	.232	.265	.294	.329	.352	40	.168	.189	.210	.235	.252
						Approximation for n > 40	$\frac{1.07}{\sqrt{n}}$	$\frac{1.22}{\sqrt{n}}$	$\frac{1.36}{\sqrt{n}}$	$\frac{1.52}{\sqrt{n}}$	$\frac{1.63}{\sqrt{n}}$

TABLE A-7
Critical Values of the Kolmogorov-Smirnov Test Statistic for Two Samples of Equal Size

One-Sided Test :											
α	.10	.05	.025	.01	.005	α =	.10	.05	.025	.01	.005
Two-Sided Test :											
α =	.20	.10	.05	.02	.01	α =	.20	.10	.05	.02	.01
n = 3	2/3	2/3				n = 20	6/20	7/20	8/20	9/20	10/20
4	3/4	3/4	3/4			21	6/21	7/21	8/21	9/21	10/21
5	3/5	3/5	4/5	4/5	4/5	22	7/22	8/22	8/22	10/22	10/22
6	3/6	4/6	4/6	5/6	5/6	23	7/23	8/23	9/23	10/23	10/23
7	4/7	4/7	5/7	5/7	5/7	24	7/24	8/24	9/24	10/24	11/24
8	4/8	4/8	5/8	5/8	6/8	25	7/25	8/25	9/25	10/25	11/25
9	4/9	5/9	5/9	6/9	6/9	26	7/26	8/26	9/26	10/26	11/26
10	4/10	5/10	6/10	6/10	7/10	27	7/27	8/27	9/27	11/27	11/27
11	5/11	5/11	6/11	7/11	7/11	28	8/28	9/28	10/28	11/28	12/28
12	5/12	5/12	6/12	7/12	7/12	29	8/29	9/29	10/29	11/29	12/29
13	5/13	6/13	6/13	7/13	8/13	30	8/30	9/30	10/30	11/30	12/30
14	5/14	6/14	7/14	7/14	8/14	31	8/31	9/31	10/31	11,31	12/31
15	5/15	6/15	7/15	8/15	8/15	32	8/32	9/32	10/32	12/32	12/32
16	6/16	6/16	7/16	8/16	9/16	34	8/34	10/34	11/34	12/34	13/34
17	6/17	7/17	7/17	8/17	9/17	36	9/36	10/36	11/36	12/36	13/36
18	6/18	7/18	8/18	9/18	9/18	38	9/38	10/38	11/38	13/38	14/38
19	6/19	7/19	8/19	9/19	9/19	40	9/40	10/40	12/40	13/40	14/40
						Approximation for n > 40 :	$\frac{1.52}{\sqrt{n}}$	$\frac{1.73}{\sqrt{25n}}$	$\frac{1.92}{\sqrt{n}}$	$\frac{2.15}{\sqrt{n}}$	$\frac{2.30}{\sqrt{n}}$

TABLE A–8
Critical Values of the Kolmogorov-Smirnov Test Statistic for Two Samples of Unequal Size

N_1 = smaller sample size, N_2 = larger sample size, and α.

One-Sided Test :	α	.10	.05	.025	.01	.005
Two-Sided Test :	α	.20	.10	.05	.02	.01
$N_1 = 1$	$N_2 = 9$	17 /18				
	10	9/10				
$N_2 = 2$	$N_2 = 3$	5/6				
	4	3/4				
	5	4/5	4/5			
	6	5/6	5/6			
	7	5/7	6/7			
	8	3/4	7/8			
	9	7/9	8/9	7/8		
	10	7/10	4/15	9/10		
$N_3 = 3$	$N_3 = 4$	3/4	3/4			
	5	2/3	4/5	4/5		
	6	2/3	2/3	5/6		
	7	2/3	5/7	6/7	6/7	
	8	5/3	3/4	3/4	7/8	
	9	2/3	2/3	7/9	8/9	8/9
	10	3/5	7/10	4/5	9/10	9/10
	12	7/12	2/3	3/4	5/6	11/12
$N_4 = 4$	$N_2 = 5$	3/5	3/4	4/5	4/5	
	6	7/12	2/3	3/4	5/6	5/6
	7	17/28	5/7	3/4	6/7	6/7
	8	5/8	5/8	3/4	7/8	7/8
	9	5/9	2/3	3/4	7/9	8/9
	10	11/20	13/20	7/10	4/5	4/5
	12	7/12	2/3	2/3	3/4	5/6
	16	9/16	5/8	11/16	3/4	13/16
$N_5 = 5$	$N_2 = 6$	3/5	2/3	2/3	5/6	5/6
	7	4/7	23/35	5/7	29/35	6/7
	8	11/20	5/8	27/40	4/5	4/5
	9	5/9	3/5	31/45	7/9	4/5
	10	1/2	3/5	7/10	7/10	4/5
	15	8/15	3/5	2/3	11/15	11/15
	20	1/2	11/20	3/5	7/10	3/4

$N_6 = 6$	$N_2 = 7$	23/42	4/7	29/42	5/7	5/6
	8	1/2	7/12	2/3	3/4	3/4
	9	1/2	5/9	2/3	13/18	7/9
	10	1/2	17/30	19/30	7/10	11/15
	12	1/2	7/12	7/12	2/3	3/4
	18	4/9	5/9	11/18	2/3	13/18
	24	11/24	1/2	7/12	5/8	2/3
$N_7 = 7$	$N_2 = 8$	27/56	33/56	5/8	41/56	3/4
	9	31/63	5/9	40/63	5/7	47/63
	10	33/70	39/70	43/70	7/10	5/7
	14	3/7	1/2	4/7	9/14	5/7
	28	3/7	13/28	15/28	17/28	9/14
$N_1 = 8$	$N_2 = 9$	4/9	13/24	5/8	2/3	3/4
	10	19/40	21/40	23/40	27/40	7/10
	12	11/24	1/2	7/2	5/8	2/3
	16	7/16	1/2	9/16	5/8	5/8
	32	13/32	7/16	1/2	9/16	19/32
$N_1 = 9$	$N_2 = 10$	7/15	1/2	26/45	2/3	31/45
	12	4/9	1/2	5/9	11/18	2/3
	15	19/45	22/45	8/15	3/5	29/45
	18	7/18	4/9	1/2	5/9	11/18
	36	13/36	5/12	17/36	19/36	5/9
$N_1 = 10$	$N_2 = 15$	2/5	7/15	1/2	17/30	19/30
	20	2/5	9/20	1/2	11/20	3/5
	40	7/20	2/5	9/20	1/2	
$N_1 = 12$	$N_2 = 15$	23/60	9/20	1/2	11/20	7/12
	16	3/8	7/16	23/48	13/24	7/12
	18	13/36	5/12	17/36	19/36	5/9
	20	11/30	5/12	7/15	31/60	17/30
$N_1 = 15$	$N_2 = 20$	7/20	2/5	13/30	29/60	31/60
$N_1 = 16$	$N_2 = 20$	27/80	31/80	17/40	19/40	41/80
Large-sample approximation		$1.07\sqrt{\frac{m+n}{mn}}$	$1.22\sqrt{\frac{m+n}{mn}}$	$1.36\sqrt{\frac{m+n}{mn}}$	$1.52\sqrt{\frac{m+n}{mn}}$	$1.63\sqrt{\frac{m+n}{mn}}$

Note. *m* and *n* are two sample sizes.

TABLE A–9
Critical Values of the Wilcoxon Signed Ranks Test

n	Two-Tailed Test		One-Tailed Test	
	$\alpha = .05$	$\alpha = .01$	$\alpha = .05$	$\alpha = .01$
5	–	–	0	–
6	0	–	2	–
7	2	–	3	0
8	3	0	5	1
9	5	1	8	3
10	8	3	10	5
11	10	5	13	7
12	13	7	17	9
13	17	9	21	12
14	21	12	25	15
15	25	15	30	19
16	29	19	35	23
17	34	23	41	27
18	40	27	47	32
19	46	32	53	37
20	52	37	60	43
21	58	42	67	49
22	65	48	75	55
23	73	54	83	62
24	81	61	91	69
25	89	68	100	76
26	98	75	110	84
27	107	83	119	92
28	116	91	130	101
29	126	100	140	110
30	137	109	151	120

Note. T = min (T^+, T^-). Reject Ho, if T is less than T_α, where is α is the prescribed level of significance.

TABLE A–10
Critical values of the Rank Sum for the Wilcoxon Signed Rank Sum, Test for Matched Samples.

This table gives critical values for a one-sided test, so that the values of α must be doubled for a two-sided test. For example, if we are testing the null hypothesis that two medians are equal, T = 6, n = 8 and α = .05, we look in the α = .025 column and find a critical value of 4. Since T is above 4, we do not reject the null hypothesis of equality. We reject the null hypothesis if T ≤ the table value.

n	α = .05	α = .025	α = .01	α .005	n	α = .05	α = .025	α = .01	α = .005
5	1	–	–	–	28	130	117	102	92
6	2	1	–	–	29	141	127	111	100
7	4	2	0	–	30	152	137	120	109
8	6	4	2	0	31	163	148	130	118
9	8	6	3	2	32	175	159	141	128
10	11	8	5	3	33	188	171	151	138
11	14	11	7	5	34	201	183	162	149
12	17	14	10	7	35	214	195	174	160
13	21	17	13	10	36	228	208	186	171
14	26	21	16	13	37	242	222	198	183
15	30	25	20	16	38	256	235	211	195
16	36	30	24	19	39	271	250	224	208
17	41	35	28	23	40	287	264	238	221
18	47	40	33	28	41	303	279	252	234
19	54	46	38	32	42	319	295	267	248
20	60	52	43	37	43	336	311	281	262
21	68	59	49	43	44	353	327	297	277
22	75	66	56	49	45	371	344	313	292
23	83	73	62	55	46	389	361	329	307
24	92	81	69	61	47	408	379	345	323
25	101	90	77	68	48	427	397	362	339
26	110	98	85	76	49	446	415	380	356
27	120	107	93	84	50	466	434	398	373

TABLE A–11
Simplified Wilcoxon-Mann-Whitney Rank Sum Test for Two Independent Samples

This table gives the p-value corresponding to the rank sum W of the smaller sample when ranking is done starting from the end when the smaller sample is concentrated. p-values are doubled for **two-sided tests.** For example, suppose we are testing equality of medians for $\alpha = .05$, $n_2 = 6$ and $n_1 = 3$, and that W = 8. The p-value for 8 is .0476, which we double to .0952. Since this is above α we do not reject the null hypothesis.

Larger Sample size $n_2 = 2$
Smaller Sample size n_1

1		2	
W	p	W	p
1	.3333	3	.1667
		4	.3333

Larger Sample Size $n_2 = 3$
Smaller Sample Size n_1

1		2		3	
W	p	W	p	W	p
1	.2500	3	.10000	6	.0500
2	.5000	4	.2000	7	.1000
		5	.4000	8	.2000
		6	.6000	9	.3500
				10	.5000

Larger Sample Size $n_2 = 4$
Smaller Sample Size n_1

1		2		3		4	
W	p	W	p	W	p	W	p
1	.2000	3	.0667	6	.0286	10	.0143
2	4000	4	.1333	7	.0571	11	.0286
3	.6000	5	.2667	8	.1143	12	.0571
		6	.4000	9	.2000	13	.1000
		7	.6000	10	.3143	14	.1714
				11	.4206	15	.2429
				12	.5714	16	.3429
						17	.4429
						18	.5571

Larger Sample Size $n_2 = 5$
Smaller Sample Size n_1

1		2		3		4		5	
W	p	W	p	W	p	W	p	W	p
1	.1667	3	.0476	6	.0179	10	.0079	15	.0040
2	.3333	4	.0952	7	.0357	11	.0159	16	.0079
3	.5000	5	.1905	8	.0714	12	.0317	17	.0159
		6	.2057	9	.1250	13	.0556	18	.0270
		7	.4286	10	.1964	14	.0952	19	.0476
		8	.5714	11	.2857	15	.1429	20	.0754
				12	.3929	16	.2063	21	.1111
				13	.5000	17	.2778	22	.1548
						18	.3651	23	.2103
						19	.4524	24	.2738
						20	.5476	25	.3452
								26	.4206
								27	.5000

TABLE A–11 (Continued)
Simplified Wilcoxon-Mann-Whitney Rank Sum Test for Two Independent Samples

Larger Sample Size $n_2 = 6$
Smaller Sample Size n_1

1		2		3		4		5		6	
W	p	W	p	W	p	W	p	W	p	W	p
1	.1429	3	.0357	6	.0119	10	.0048	15	.0022	21	.0011
2	.2857	4	.0714	7	.0238	11	.0095	16	.0043	22	.0022
3	.4286	5	.1429	8	.0476	12	.0190	17	.0087	23	.0043
4	.5714	6	.2143	9	.0833	13	.0033	18	.0152	24	.0076
		7	.3214	10	.1310	14	.0571	19	.0260	25	.0130
		8	.4286	11	.1905	15	.0857	20	.0411	26	.0206
		9	.5714	12	.2738	16	.1286	21	.0628	27	.0325
				13	.3571	17	.1762	22	.0887	28	.0465
				14	.4524	18	.2381	23	.1234	29	.0660
				15	.5476	19	.3048	24	.1645	30	.0898
						20	.3810	25	.2143	31	.1201
						21	.4571	26	.2684	32	.1548
						22	.5429	27	.3312	33	.1970
								28	.3961	34	.2424
								29	.4654	35	.2944
								30	.5346	36	.3596
										37	.4091
										38	.4686
										39	.5314

Larger Sample Size $n_2 = 7$
Smaller Sample Size n_1

1		2		3		4		5		6		7	
W	p	W	p	W	p	W	p	W	p	W	p	W	p
1	.1250	3	.0278	6	.0083	10	.0030	15	.0013	21	.0006	28	.0003
2	.2500	4	.0556	7	.0167	1	.0061	16	.0025	22	.0012	29	.0006
3	.3750	5	.1111	8	.0333	12	.0121	17	.0051	23	.0023	30	.0012
4	.5000	6	.1667	9	.0583	13	.0212	18	.0088	24	.0041	31	.0020
		7	.2500	10	.0917	14	.0364	19	.0152	25	.0070	32	.0035
		8	.3333	11	.1333	15	.0545	20	.0240	26	.0111	33	.0055
		9	.4444	12	.1917	16	.0818	21	.0366	27	.0175	34	.0087
		10	.5556	13	.2583	17	.1152	22	.0530	28	.0256	35	.0131
				14	.3333	18	.1576	23	.745	29	.0367	36	.0189
				15	.4167	19	.2061	24	.1010	30	.0507	37	.0265
				16	.5000	20	.2636	25	.1338	31	.0688	38	.0364
						21	.3242	26	.1717	32	.0903	39	.0487
						22	.3939	27	.2159	33	.1171	40	.0641
						23	.4636	28	.2652	34	.1474	41	.0825
						24	.5364	29	.3194	35	.1830	42	.1043
								30	.3775	36	.2226	43	.1297
								31	.4301	37	.2669	44	.1500
								32	.5000	38	.3141	45	.1914
										39	.3654	46	.2279
										40	.4178	47	.2675
										41	.4726	48	.3100
										42	.5274	49	.3552
												50	.4024
												51	.4508
												52	.5000

TABLE A–12
Critical values of the Rank Sum for the Mann- Whitney-Wilcoxon Rank Sum Test for Independent Samples.

The tables give values of T_L and T_U for various values of n_1 and n_2 for testing equality of medians in inpedendent samples. For example if the Null Hypothesis is $v_1 = v_2$, $\alpha = .05$, $n_1 = 6, n_2 = 10$ and W = 40, $T_L = 32$ and $T_U = 70$. Since $T_L < W < T_U$, do not reject the null hypothesis.

A–12(*a*) α = 0.25 for a 1-tailed test or α = .05 for a 2-tailed test.

n_2 \ n_1	3	4	5	6	7	8	9	10	11	12
3	–	6	6	7	7	8	8	9	9	10
		18	21	23	26	28	31	33	36	38
4	6	10	11	12	13	14	14	15	16	17
	18	26	29	32	35	38	42	45	48	52
5	6	11	17	18	20	21	22	23	24	26
	21	29	38	42	45	49	53	57	61	64
6	7	12	18	26	27	29	31	32	34	35
	23	32	42	52	57	61	65	70	74	79
7	7	13	20	27	36	38	40	42	44	46
	26	35	45	57	69	74	79	84	89	94
8	8	14	21	29	38	49	51	53	55	58
	28	38	49	61	74	87	93	99	105	110
9	8	14	22	3165	40	51	62	65	68	71
	31	42	53		79	93	109	115	121	127
10	9	15	23	32	42	53	65	78	81	84
	33	45	57	70	84	99	115	132	139	146
11	9	16	24	34	44	55	68	81	96	99
	36	48	61	74	89	105	121	139	157	165
12	10	17	26	53	46	58	71	84	99	116
	38	51	64	79	94	110	127	146	165	184

A–12(*b*) α = .05 for a 1-tailed test or α = .10 for a 2-tailed test.

n_2 \ n_1	3	4	5	6	7	8	9	10	11	12
3	–	6	7	8	8	9	10	11	11	
		18	20	22	25	27	30	32	34	37
4	6	11	12	13	14	15	16	17	18	19
	18	25	28	31	34	37	40	43	46	49
5	7	12	19	20	21	23	24	26	27	28
	20	28	36	40	44	47	51	54	58	62
6	8	13	20	28	29	31	33	35	37	38
	22	31	40	0	55	59	63	67	71	76
7	8	14	21	29	39	41	43	45	47	49
	25	34	44	55	66	71	76	81	86	91
8	9	15	23	31	41	51	54	56	59	62
	27	37	47	59	71	85	90	96	101	106
9	9	16	24	33	43	54	66	69	72	75
	30	40	51	63	76	90	105	111	117	123
10	10	17	26	35	45	56	69	02	06	09
	32	43	54	67	81	96	111	128	134	141
11	11	18	27	37	47	59	72	86	100	104
	34	46	58	71	86	101	117	134	153	160
12	11	19	28	38	49	62	75	89	104	120
	37	49	62	76	91	106	123	141	160	180

TABLE A–13 (*a*)
Critical Values of the Mann -Whitney U (One-Tailed Testing)

n_2	α	n_1 = 3	4	5	6	7	8	9	10	11	12	13	14	15	16	17	18	19	20
3	.05	0	0	1	2	2	3	4	4	5	5	6	7	7	8	9	9	10	11
	.01	–	0	0	0	0	0	1	1	1	2	2	2	3	3	4	4	4	5
4	.05	0	1	2	3	4	5	6	7	8	9	10	11	12	14	15	16	17	18
	.01	–	–	0	1	1	2	3	3	4	5	5	6	7	7	8	9	9	10
5	.05	1	2	4	5	6	8	9	11	12	13	15	16	18	19	20	22	23	25
	.01	–	0	1	2	3	4	5	6	7	8	9	10	11	22	13	14	15	16
6	.05	2	3	5	7	8	10	12	14	16	17	19	21	23	25	26	28	30	32
	.01	–	1	2	3	4	6	7	8	9	11	12	13	15	16	18	19	20	22
7	.05	2	4	6	8	11	13	15	17	19	21	24	26	28	30	33	35	37	39
	.01	0	1	3	4	6	7	9	11	12	14	16	17	19	21	23	24	26	28
8	.05	3	5	8	10	13	15	18	20	23	26	20	31	33	36	39	41	44	47
	.01	0	2	4	6	7	9	11	13	15	17	20	22	24	26	28	30	32	34
9	.05	4	6	9	12	15	18	21	24	27	30	33	36	39	42	45	48	51	54
	.01	1	3	5	7	9	11	14	16	18	21	23	26	28	31	33	36	38	40
10	.05	4	7	11	14	17	20	24	27	31	34	37	41	44	48	51	55	58	62
	.01	1	3	6	8	11	13	16	19	22	24	27	30	33	36	38	41	44	47
11	.05	5	8	12	16	19	23	27	31	34	38	42	46	50	54	57	61	65	69
	.01	1	4	7	9	12	15	18	22	25	28	31	34	37	41	44	47	50	53
12	.05	5	9	13	17	21	26	30	34	38	42	47	51	55	60	64	68	72	77
	.01	2	5	8	11	14	17	21	24	28	31	35	38	42	46	49	53	56	60
13	.05	6	10	15	19	24	28	33	37	42	47	51	56	61	65	70	75	80	84
	.01	2	5	9	12	16	20	23	27	31	35	39	43	47	51	55	59	63	67
14	.05	7	11	16	21	26	31	36	41	46	51	56	61	66	71	77	82	87	92
	.01	2	6	10	13	17	22	26	30	34	38	43	47	51	56	60	65	69	73
15	.05	7	12	18	23	28	33	39	44	50	55	61	66	72	77	83	88	94	100
	.01	3	7	11	15	19	24	28	33	37	42	47	51	56	61	66	70	75	80
16	.05	8	14	19	25	30	36	42	48	54	60	65	71	77	83	89	95	101	107
	.01	3	7	12	16	21	26	31	36	41	46	51	56	61	66	71	76	82	87
17	.05	9	15	20	26	33	39	45	51	57	64	70	77	83	89	96	102	109	115
	.01	4	8	13	18	23	28	33	38	44	49	55	60	66	71	77	82	88	93
18	.05	9	16	22	28	35	41	48	55	61	68	75	82	88	95	102	109	116	123
	.01	4	9	14	19	24	30	36	41	47	53	59	65	70	76	82	88	94	100
19	.05	10	17	23	30	37	44	51	58	65	72	80	87	94	101	109	116	123	130
	.01	4	9	15	20	26	32	38	44	50	56	63	69	75	82	88	94	101	107
20	.05	11	18	25	32	39	47	54	62	69	77	84	92	100	107	115	123	130	138
	.01	5	10	16	22	28	34	40	47	53	60	67	73	80	87	93	100	107	114

TABLE A–13 (*b*)
Critical Values of the Mann-Whitney U (Two-Tailed Testing)

n_2	α	n_1 = 3	4	5	6	7	8	9	10	11	12	13	14	15	16	17	18	19	20
3	.05	–	0	0	1	1	2	2	3	3	4	4	5	5	6	6	7	7	8
	.01	–	0	0	0	0	0	0	0	0	1	1	1	2	2	2	2	3	3
4	0.5	–	0	1	2	3	4	4	5	6	7	8	9	10	11	11	12	13	14
	.01	–	–	0	0	0	1	1	2	2	3	3	4	5	5	6	6	7	8
5	.05	0	1	2	3	5	6	7	8	9	11	12	13	14	15	17	18	19	20
	.01	–	–	0	1	1	2	3	4	5	6	7	7	8	9	10	11	12	13
6	.05	1	2	3	5	6	8	10	11	13	14	16	17	19	21	22	24	25	27
	.01	–	0	1	2	3	4	5	6	7	9	10	11	12	13	15	16	17	18
7	.05	1	3	5	6	8	10	12	14	16	18	20	22	24	26	28	30	32	34
	.01	–	0	1	3	4	6	7	9	10	12	13	15	16	18	19	21	22	24
8	.05	2	4	6	8	10	13	15	17	19	22	24	26	29	31	34	36	38	41
	.01	–	1	2	4	6	7	9	11	13	15	17	18	20	22	24	26	28	30
9	.05	2	4	7	10	12	15	17	20	23	26	28	31	34	37	39	42	45	48
	.01	0	1	3	5	7	9	11	13	16	18	30	22	24	27	29	31	33	36
10	0.5	3	5	8	11	14	17	20	23	26	29	33	36	39	42	45	48	523	55
	.01	0	2	4	6	9	11	13	16	18	21	24	26	29	31	34	37	9	42
11	0.5	3	6	9	13	16	19	23	26	30	33	37	40	44	47	51	55	58	62
	0.1	0	2	5	7	10	13	16	18	21	24	27	30	33	36	39	42	45	48
12	0.5	4	7	11	14	18	22	26	29	33	37	41	45	49	53	57	61	65	69
	0.1	1	3	6	9	12	15	18	21	24	27	31	34	37	41	44	47	51	54
13	.05	4	8	12	16	20	24	28	33	37	41	45	50	54	59	63	67	72	76
	.01	1	3	7	10	13	17	20	24	27	31	34	38	42	45	49	53	56	60
14	.05	5	9	13	17	22	26	31	36	40	45	50	55	59	64	67	74	78	83
	.01	1	4	7	11	15	18	22	26	30	34	38	42	46	50	54	58	63	67
15	.05	5	10	14	19	24	29	34	39	44	49	54	59	64	70	75	80	85	90
	.01	2	5	8	12	26	20	24	29	33	37	42	46	51	55	60	64	69	73
16	.05	6	11	15	21	26	31	37	42	47	53	59	64	70	75	81	86	92	98
	.01	2	5	9	13	18	22	27	31	36	41	45	50	55	60	65	70	74	79
17	.05	6	11	17	22	28	34	39	45	51	57	63	67	75	81	87	93	99	105
	.01	2	6	10	15	19	24	29	34	39	44	49	54	60	65	70	75	81	86
18	.05	7	12	18	24	30	36	42	48	55	61	67	74	80	86	93	99	106	112
	.01	2	6	11	16	21	26	31	37	42	47	53	58	64	70	75	81	87	92
19	.05	7	13	19	25	32	38	45	52	58	65	72	78	85	92	99	106	113	111
	.01	3	7	12	17	22	28	33	39	45	51	56	63	69	74	81	87	93	99
20	.05	8	14	20	27	34	41	48	55	62	69	76	83	90	98	105	112	119	127
	.01	3	8	13	18	24	30	36	42	48	54	60	67	73	79	86	92	99	105

TABLE A–14
Critical Values of *r* of Run Test

Any Observed Value of *r* which is Less than or Equal to the Smaller Value or Greater than or Equal to the Large Value for Given n_1 and n_2 is Significant at $\alpha = 0.05$

n_1 \ n_2	2	3	4	5	6	7	8	9	10	11	12	13	14	15	16	17	18	19	20
2											2	2	2	2	2	2	2	2	2
											—	—	—	—	—	—	—	—	—
3					2	2	2	2	2	2	2	2	2	3	3	3	3	3	3
					—	—	—	—	—	—	—	—	—	—	—	—	—	—	—
4				2	2	2	3	3	3	3	3	3	3	3	4	4	4	4	4
				9	9	—	—	—	—	—	—	—	—	—	—	—	—	—	—
5			2	2	3	3	3	3	3	4	4	4	4	4	4	4	5	5	5
			9	10	10	11	11	—	—	—	—	—	—	—	—	—	—	—	—
6		2	2	3	3	3	3	4	4	5	5	5	5	5	6	6	6	6	6
		—	9	10	11	12	12	13	13	13	13	—	—	—	—	—	—	—	—
7		2	2	3	3	3	4	4	5	5	5	5	5	6	6	6	6	6	6
		—	—	11	12	13	13	14	14	14	14	15	15	15	—	—	—	—	—
8		2	3	3	3	4	4	5	5	5	6	6	6	6	6	7	7	7	7
		—	—	11	12	13	14	14	15	15	16	16	16	16	17	17	17	17	17
9		2	3	3	4	4	5	5	5	6	6	6	7	7	7	7	8	8	8
		—	—	—	13	14	14	15	16	16	16	17	17	18	18	18	18	18	18
10		2	3	3	4	5	5	5	6	6	7	7	7	7	8	8	8	8	9
		—	—	—	13	14	15	16	16	17	17	18	18	18	19	19	19	20	20
11		2	3	4	4	5	5	6	6	7	7	7	8	8	8	9	9	9	9
		—	—	—	13	14	15	16	17	17	18	19	19	19	20	20	20	21	21
12	2	2	3	4	4	5	6	6	7	7	7	8	8	8	9	9	9	10	10
	—	—	—	—	13	14	16	16	17	18	19	19	20	20	21	21	21	22	22
13	2	2	3	4	5	5	6	6	7	7	8	8	9	9	9	10	10	10	10
	—	—	—	—	—	15	16	17	18	19	19	20	20	21	21	22	22	23	23
14	2	2	3	4	5	5	6	7	7	8	8	9	9	9	10	10	10	11	11
	—	—	—	—	—	15	16	17	18	19	20	20	21	22	22	23	23	23	24
15	2	3	3	4	5	6	6	7	7	8	8	9	9	10	10	11	11	11	
	—	—	—	—	—	15	16	18	18	18	19	20	21	22	22	23	23	24	25
16	2	3	4	4	5	6	6	7	8	8	9	9	10	10	11	11	11	12	12
	—	—	—	—	—	—	17	18	19	20	21	21	22	23	23	24	25	25	25
17	2	3	4	4	5	6	7	7	8	9	9	10	10	11	11	11	12	12	13
	—	—	—	—	—	—	17	18	19	20	21	22	23	23	24	25	25	26	26
18	2	3	4	5	5	6	7	8	8	9	9	10	10	11	11	12	12	13	13
	—	—	—	—	—	—	17	18	19	20	21	22	23	24	25	25	26	26	27
19	2	3	4	5	6	6	7	8	8	9	10	10	11	11	12	12	13	13	13
	—	—	—	—	—	—	17	18	20	21	22	23	23	24	25	26	26	27	27
20	2	3	4	5	6	6	7	8	9	9	10	10	11	12	12	13	13	13	14
	—	—	—	—	—	—	17	18	20	21	22	23	24	25	25	26	27	27	28

TABLE A–15
Cumulative Binomial Distribution

n	x|p	.01	.05	.10	.15	.20	.25	.30	.35	.40	.45	.50
2	0	0.9801	0.9025	0.8100	0.7225	0.6400	0.5625	0.4900	0.4225	0.3600	0.3025	0.2500
	1	0.9999	0.9975	0.9900	0.9775	0.9600	0.9375	0.9100	0.8775	0.8400	0.7975	0.7500
	2	1.0000	1.0000	1.0000	1.0000	1.0000	1.0000	1.0000	1.0000	1.0000	1.0000	1.0000
3	0	0.97030	0.85738	0.729	0.61413	0.512	0.42187	0.343	0.27463	0.216	0.16638	0.125
	1	0.99970	0.99275	0.972	0.93925	0.896	0.84375	0.784	0.71825	0.648	0.57475	0.500
	2	1.0000	0.99988	0.999	0.99663	0.992	0.98437	0.973	0.95713	0.936	0.90887	0.875
	3	1.00000	1.00000	1.000	1.00000	1.000	1.00000	1.000	1.00000	1.000	1.00000	1.000
4	0	0.96060	0.81451	0.6561	0.52201	0.4096	0.31641	0.2401	0.17851	0.1296	0.09151	0.0625
	1	0.99941	0.98598	0.9477	0.89048	0.8192	0.73828	0.65517	0.56298	0.4752	0.39098	0.3125
	2	1.00000	099952	0.9963	0.98802	0.9728	0.94922	0.9163	0.87352	0.8208	0.75852	0.6875
	3	1.00000	0.99999	0.9999	0.99949	0.9984	0.99609	0.9919	0.98499	0.9744	0.95899	0.9375
	4	1.00000	1.00000	1.0000	1.00000	1.0000	1.00000	1.0000	1.00000	1.0000	1.00000	1.0000
5	0	0.950090	0.77378	0.59049	0.44371	0.32768	0.23730	0.16807	0.11603	0.07776	0.05033	0.03125
	1	0.99902	0.97741	0.91854	0.83521	0.73728	0.63281	0.52822	0.42842	0.33696	0.25622	0.18750
	2	0.99902	0.99884	0.99144	0.97339	0.94208	0.89648	0.83692	0.76483	0.68256	0.59313	0.50000
	3	1.00000	0.99997	0.99954	0.99777	0.99328	0.98437	0.96922	0.94598	0.91296	0.86878	0.81250
	4	1.00000	1.00000	0.99999	0.99992	0.99968	0.99902	0.99757	0.99475	0.98976	0.98155	0.96875
	5	1.00000	1.00000	1.00000	1.00000	1.00000	1.00000	1.00000	1.00000	1.00000	1.00000	1.00000
6	0	0.94148	0.73509	0.53144	0.37715	0.26214	0.17798	0.11765	0.007542	0.04666	0.02768	0.01563
	1	0.99854	0.96723	0.88573	0.77648	0.65536	0.53394	0.42017	0.31908	0.23328	0.16357	0.10938
	2	0.99998	0.99777	0.98415	0.95266	0.90112	0.8307	0.74431	0.64709	0.54432	0.44152	0.34375
	3	1.00000	0.99991	0.99873	0.99411	0.98304	0.96240	0.92953	0.88258	0.82080	0.74474	0.65625
	4	1.00000	1.00000	0.99994	0.99960	0.99840	0.99536	0.98906	0.97768	0.95904	0.93080	0.89062
	5	1.00000	1.00000	1.00000	0.99999	0.99994	0.99976	0.99927	0.99816	0.99590	0.99170	0.98437
	6	1.00000	1.00000	1.00000	1.00000	1.00000	1.00000	1.00000	1.00000	1.00000	1.00000	1.00000
7	0	0.93207	0.69834	0.47830	0.32058	0.20972	0.13348	0.08235	0.04902	0.02799	0.01522	0.00781
	1	0.99797	0.95562	0.85031	0.71658	0.57672	0.44495	0.32942	0.23380	0.15863	0.10242	0.06250
	2	0.99997	0.99624	0.97431	0.92623	0.85197	0.75641	0.64707	0.53228	0.41990	0.31644	0.22656
	3	1.00000	0.9981	0.99727	0.98790	0.96666	0.92944	0.87396	0.80015	0.71021	0.60829	0.50000
	4	1.00000	0.99999	0.99982	0.99878	0.99533	0.98712	0.97120	0.94439	0.90374	0.84707	0.77344
	5	1.00000	1.00000	0.99999	0.99993	0.99963	0.99866	0.99621	0.99099	0.98116	0.96429	0.93750
	6	1.00000	1.00000	1.00000	1.00000	0.99999	0.99994	0.99978	0.99936	0.99836	0.99626	0.99219
	7	1.00000	1.00000	1.00000	1.00000	1.00000	1.00000	1.00000	1.00000	1.00000	1.00000	1.00000
8	0	0.92274	0.66342	0.43047	0.2749	0.16777	0.10011	0.05765	0.03186	0.01680	0.00837	0.00391
	1	0.99731	0.94276	0.81310	0.65718	0.50332	0.36708	0.25530	0.16913	0.10638	0.06318	0.03516
	2	0.99995	0.99421	0.96191	0.89479	0.79692	0.67854	0.55177	0.42781	0.31539	0.22013	0.14453

n	x|p	.01	.05	.10	.15	.20	.25	.30	.35	.40	.45	.50
	3	1.00000	0.99963	0.99498	0.97865	0.943725	0.88618	0.80590	0.70640	0.59409	0.47696	0.36328
	4	1.00000	0.99998	0.99957	0.99715	0.98959	0.97270	0.94203	0.89391	0.82633	0.73962	0.63672
	5	1.00000	1.00000	0.99998	0.99976	0.99877	0.99577	0.98871	0.97468	0.95019	0.91154	0.85547
	6	1.00000	1.00000	1.00000	0.99999	0.99992	0.99962	0.99871	0.99643	0.99148	0.98188	0.96484
	7	1.00000	1.00000	1.00000	1.00000	1.00000	0.99998	0.99993	0.99977	0.99934	0.99832	0.99609
	8	1.00000	1.00000	1.00000	1.00000	1.00000	1.00000	1.00000	1.00000	1.00000	1.00000	1.00000
9	0	0.91352	0.63025	0.38742	0.23162	0.13422	0.07508	0.04035	0.02071	0.01008	0.00461	0.00195
	1	0.99656	0.92879	0.77484	0.59948	0.43621	0.30034	0.19600	0.12109	0.07054	0.03852	0.01953
	2	0.99992	0.99164	0.94703	0.85915	0.73820	0.60068	0.46283	0.33727	0.23179	0.14950	0.08984
	3	1.00000	0.99936	0.99167	0.96607	0.91436	0.83427	0.72966	0.60889	0.48261	0.36138	0.25391
	4	1.00000	0.99997	0.99911	0.99437	0.98042	0.95107	0.90119	0.82828	0.73343	0.62142	0.50000
	5	1.00000	1.00000	0.99994	0.99937	0.99693	0.99001	0.97471	0.94641	0.90065	0.83418	0.74609
	6	1.00000	1.00000	1.00000	0.99995	0.99969	0.99866	0.99571	0.98882	0.97497	0.95023	0.91016
	7	1.00000	1.00000	1.00000	1.00000	0.99998	0.99989	0.99957	0.99860	0.99620	0.99092	0.98047
	8	1.00000	1.00000	1.00000	100000	1.00000	1.00000	0.99998,0	.99992	0.99974	0.99924	0.99805
	9	1.00000	1.00000	1.00000	1.00000	1.00000	1.00000	1.00000	1.00000	1.00000	1.00000	1.00000
10	0	0.90438	0.59874	0.34868	0.19687	0.10737	0.05631	0.028025	0.01346	0.00605	0.00253	0.00098
	1	0.99573	0.91386	0.73610	0.54430	0.37581	0.24403	0.14931	0.08595	0.04636	0.02326	0.01074
	2	0.99989	0.98850	0.92981	0.82020	0.67780	0.52559	0.38278	0.26161	0.16729	0.09956	0.05469
	3	1.00000	0.99897	0.98720	0.95003	0.87913	0.77588	0.64961	0.51383	0.38228	0.26604	0.17188
	4	1.00000	0.99994	0.99837	0.99013	0.96721	0.92187	0.84973	0.75150	0.63310	0.50440	0.37695
	5	1.00000	1.00000	0.99985	0.99862	0.99363	0.98027	0.95265	0.90507	0.83376	0.73844	0.62305
	6	1.00000	1.00000	0.99999	0.99987	0.99914	0.99649	0.98941	0.97398	0.94524	0.89801	0.82812
	7	1.00000	1.00000	1.00000	0.99999	0.99992	0.99958	0.99841	0.99518	0.98771	0.97261	0.94531
	8	1.00000	1.00000	1.00000	1.00000	1.00000	0.99997	0.99986	0.99946	0.99832	0.99550	0.98926
	9	1.00000	1.00000	1.00000	1.00000	1.00000	1.00000	0.99999	0.99997	0.99990	0.99966	0.99902
	10	1.00000	1.00000	1.00000	1.00000	1.00000	1.00000	1.00000	1.00000	1.00000	1.00000	1.00000
11	0	0.89534	0.56680	0.31381	0.16734	0.08590	0.04224	0.01977	0.00875	0.000363	0.00139	0.00049
	1	0.99482	0.89811	0.69736	0.49219	0.32212	0.19710	0.11299	0.06058	0.00363	0.01393	0.00586
	2	0.99984	0.98476	0.91044	0.77881	0.61740	0.45520	0.31274	0.20013	0.11892	0.06522	0.03271
	3	1.00000	0.99845	0.98147	0.93056	0.83886	0.71330	0.56956	0.42555	0.29628	0.19112	0.11328
	4	1.00000	0.9989	0.99725	0.98411	0.94959	0.88537	0.78970	0.66831	0.53277	0.39714	0.27441
	5	1.00000	0.99999	0.99970	0.99734	0.98835	0.96567	0.92178	0.85132	0.75350	0.63312	0.50000
	6	1.00000	1.00000	0.99998	0.99968	0.99803	0.99244	0.97838	0.94986	0.90065	0.82620	0.72559
	7	1.00000	1.00000	1.00000	0.9997	0.99976	0.99881	0.99571	0.98776	0.97072	0.93904	0.88672
	8	1.00000	1.00000	1.00000	1.00000	0.99998	0.99987	0.99942	0.99796	0.99408	0.98520	0.96720
	9	1.00000	1.00000	1.00000	1.00000	1.00000	0.99999	0.99995	0.99979	0.99927	0.99779	0.99414
	10	1.00000	1.00000	1.00000	1.00000	1.00000	1.00000	1.00000	0.99999	0.99996	0.99985	0.99951
	11	1.00000	1.00000	1.00000	1.00000	1.00000	1.00000	1.00000	1.00000	1.00000	1.00000	1.00000
12	0	0.88638	0.54036	0.28243	0.14224	0.06872	0.03468	0.01384	0.00569	0.00218	0.00077	0.00024

n	x|p	.01	.05	.10	.15	.20	.25	.30	.35	.40	.45	.50
	1	0.99383	0.88164	0.65900	0.44346	0.27488	0.15838	0.08503	0.04244	0.01959	0.00829	0.00317
	2	0.99979	0.98043	0.88913	0.73582	0.55835	0.39068	0.25282	0.15129	0.08344	0.04214	0.01929
	3	1.00000	0.99776	0.97436	0.90779	0.79457	0.64878	0.49252	0.34665	0.22534	0.13447	0.07300
	4	1.00000	0.99982,0	.99567	0.97608	0.92744	0.84236	0.72366	0.58335	0.43818	0.30443	0.19385
	5	1.00000	0.99999	0.99946	0.99536	0.98059	0.94560	0.88215	0.78726	0.66521	0.52693	0.38721
	6	1.00000	1.00000	0.99995	0.99933	0.99610	0.98575	0.96140	0.91537	0.84179	0.73931	0.61279
	7	1.00000	1.00000	1.00000	0.99993	0.99942	0.99722	0.99051	0.97449	0.94269	0.88826	0.80615
	8	1.00000	1.00000	1.00000	0.99999	0.99994	0.99961	0.99831	0.99439	0.98473	0.96443	0.92700
	9	1.00000	1.00000	1.00000	1.00000	1.00000	0.99996	0.99979	0.99915	0.99719	0.99212	0.98071
	10	1.00000	1.00000	1.00000	1.00000	1.00000	1.00000	0.99998	0.99992	0.99968	0.99892	0.99683
	11	1.00000	1.00000	1.00000	1.00000	1.00000	1.00000	1.00000	1.00000	0.99998	0.99993	0.99976
	12	1.00000	1.00000	1.00000	1.00000	1.00000	1.00000	1.00000	1.00000	1.00000	1.00000	1.00000
13	0	0.87752	0.51334	0.25419	0.12091	0.05498	0.02376	0.00969	0.00370	0.00131	0.00042	0.00012
	1	0.99275	0.86458	0.62134	0.39828	0.23365	0.12671	0.06367	0.02858	0.01263	0.00490	0.00171
	2	0.99973	097549.	0.86612	0.69196	0.50165	0.33260	0.20248	0.11319	0.05790	0.02691	0.01123
	3	0.99999	0.99690	0.96584	0.88200	0.74732	0.58425	0.42061	0.27827	0.16858	0.09292	0.04614
	4	1.00000	0.99971	0.99354	0.96584	0.90087	0.79396	0.65431	0.50050	0.35304	0.22795	0.13342
	5	1.00000	0.99998	0.99908	0.99247	0.96996	0.91979	0.83460	0.71589	0.57440	0.42681	0.29053
	6	1.00000	1.00000	0.99990	0.99873	0.99300	0.97571	0.93762	0.87053	0.77116	0.64374	0.50000
	7	1.00000	1.00000	0.99999	0.99984	0.99875	0.99435	0.98178	0.95380	0.90233	0.82123	0.70947
	8	1.00000	1.00000	1.00000	0.99998	0.99983	0.99901	0.99597	0.98743	0.96792	0.93015	0.86658
	9	1.00000	1.00000	1.00000	1.00000	0.99998	0.99987	0.99935	0.99749	0.99221	0.97966	0.95386
	10	100000	1.00000	1.00000	1.00000	1.00000	0.99999	0.99993	0.99965	0.99868	0.99586	0.98877
	11	1.00000	1.00000	1.00000	1.00000	1.00000	1.00000	0.99999	0.99997	0.99986	0.99948	0.99829
	12	1.00000	1.00000	1.00000	1.00000	1.00000	1.00000	1.00000	1.00000	0.99999	0.99997	0.99988
	13	1.00000	1.00000	1.00000	1.00000	1.00000	1.00000	1.00000	1.00000	1.00000	1.00000	1.00000
14	0	0.86875	0.48767	0.22877	0.10277	0.04398	0.01782	0.00678	0.00240	0.00078	0.00023	0.00006
	1	0.99160	0.84701	0.58463	0.35667	0.19791	0.10097	0.04748	0.02052	0.00810	0.00289	0.00092
	2	0.99966	0.96995	0.84164	0.64791	0.44805	0.28113	0.16084	0.08393	0.03979	0.01701	0.00647
	3	0.99999	0.99583	0.95587	0.85349	0.69819	0.52134	0.35517	0.22050	0.12431	0.06322	0.02869
	4	1.00000	0.99957	0.99077	0.95326	0.87016	0.74153	0.58420	0.42272	0.27926	0.16719	0.08978
	5	1.00000	0.99997	0.99853	0.98847	0.95615	0.88833	0.78052	0.64051	0.48585	0.33732	0.21198
	6	1.00000	1.00000	0.99982	0.99779	0.98839	0.96173	0.90672	0.81641	0.69245	0.54612	0.39526
	7	1.00000	1.00000	0.99998	0.99967	0.99760	0.98969	0.96853	0.92466	0.84986	0.74136	0.60474
	8	1.00000	1.00000	1.00000	0.99996	0.99962	0.99785	0.99171	0.97566	0.94168	0.88114	0.78802
	9	1.00000	1.00000	1.00000	1.00000	0.99995	0.99966	0.99833	0.99396	0.98249	0.95738	0.91022
	10	1.00000	1.00000	1.00000	1.00000	1.00000	0.99996	0.99975	0.99889	0.99609	0.98857	0.97131
	11	1.00000	1.00000	1.00000	1.00000	1.00000	1.00000	0.99997	0.99986	0.99939	0.99785	0.99353
	12	1.00000	1.00000	1.00000	1.00000	1.00000	1.00000	1.00000	0.99999	0.99994	0.99975	0.99908
	13	1.00000	1.00000	1.00000	1.00000	1.00000	1.00000	1.00000	1.00000	1.00000	0.99999	0.99994
	14	1.00000	1.00000	1.00000	1.00000	1.00000	1.00000	1.00000	1.00000	1.00000	1.00000	1.00000

TABLE A–16
Cumulative Poisson Distribution–1

λ = 0.1

k	P (x = k)	P (x ≤k)
0	.904837	0.90484
1	0.090484	0.99532
2	0.004524	0.99985
3	0.000151	1.00000
4	0.000004	1.00000

λ = 0.2

k	P(x = k)	P(x ≤ k)
0	0.818731	0.81873
1	0.163746	0.98248
2	0.016375	0.99885
3	0.001092	0.99994
4	0.000055	1.00000

λ = 0.3

k	P(x=k)	P(x ≤k)
0	0.740818	0.74082
1	0.222245	0.96306
2	0.033337	0.99640
3	0.003334	0.99973
4	0.000250	0.99998

λ = 0.4

k	P (x = k)	P (x ≤k)
0	0.670320	0.67032
1	0.268128	0.93845
2	0.053626	0.99207
3	0.007150	0.99922
4	0.000715	0.99994
5	0.000057	1.00000
6	0.000004	1.00000
7	0.000000	1.00000

λ = 0.5

k	P(x = k)	P(x ≤ k)
0	0.606531	0.60653
1	0.303265	0.90980
2	0.075816	0.98561
3	0.012636	0.99825
4	0.001580	0.99983
5	0.000158	0.99999
6	0.000013	1.00000
7	0.000001	1.00000

λ = 0.6

k	P(x=k)	P(x ≤k)
0	0.548812	0.54881
1	0.329287	0.87810
2	0.098786	0.97688
3	0.019757	0.99664
4	0.002964	0.99961
5	0.000356	0.99996
6	0.000036	1.00000
7	0.000003	1.00000

λ = 0.7

k	P (x = k)	P (x ≤k)
0	0.496585	0.49659
1	0.347610	0.84420
2	0.121663	0.96586
3	0.028388	0.99425
4	0.004968	0.99921
5	0.000696	0.99991
6	0.00081	0.99999
7	0.000008	1.00000
8	0.000001	1.00000
9	0.000000	1.00000
10	0.000000	1.00000

λ = 0.8

k	P(x = k)	P(x ≤ k)
0	0.449329	0.44933
1	0.359463	0.80879
2	0.143785	0.95258
3	0.038343	0.99092
4	0.007669	0.99859
5	0.001227	0.99982
6	0.000164	0.99998
7	0.000019	1.00000
8	0.000002	1.00000
9	0.000000	1.00000
10	0.000000	1.00000

λ = 0.9

k	P(x=k)	p(x ≤k)
0	0.406570	0.40657
1	0.365913	0.77248
2	0.164661	0.93714
3	0.049398	0.98654
4	0.011115	0.99766
5	0.002001	0.99966
6	0.0003000	0.99996
7	0.000039	1.00000
8	0.000004	1.00000
9	0.000000	1.00000
10	0.000000	1.00000

Note. λ is the parameter of Poisson distribution.

TABLE A–16 Poisson Distribution-2

λ = 1.0

k	P (x = k)	P (x ≤k)
0	0.367879	0.36788
1	0.367879	0.73576
2	0.183940	0.91970
3	0.061313	0.98101
4	0.015238	0.99634
5	0.003066	0.99941
6	0.000511	0.99992
7	0.000073	0.99999
8	0.000009	1.00000
9	0.000001	1.00000
10	0.000000	1.00000

λ = 1.1

k	P(x = k)	P(x ≤ k)
0	0.332871	0.33287
1	0.366158	0.69903
2	0.201387	0.90042
3	0.073842	0.97426
4	0.020307	0.99456
5	0.004467	0.99903
6	0.000819	0.99985
7	0.000129	0.99998
8	0.000018	1.00000
9	0.000002	1.00000
10	0.000000	1.00000

λ = 1.2

k	P(x=k)	P(x ≤k)
0	0.301194	0.30119
1	0.361433	0.66263
2	0.216860	0.87949
3	0.086744	0.96623
4	0.026023	0.99225
5	0.006246	0.99850
6	0.001249	0.99975
7	0.000214	0.99996
8	0.000032	1.00000
9	0.000004	1.00000
10	0.000000	1.00000

λ = 1.3

k	P (x = k)	P (x ≤k)
0	0.272532	0.27253
1	0.354291	0.85711
2	0.230289	0.85711
3	0.099792	0.95690
4	0.032432	0.98934
5	0.008432	0.99777
6	0.001827	0.99960
7	0.000339	0.99994
8	0.000055	0.99999
9	0.000008	1.00000
10	0.000001	1.00000

λ = 1.4

k	P(x = k)	P(x ≤ k)
0	0.246597	0.24660
1	0.345236	0.59183
2	0.241665	0.83350
3	0.112777	0.94627
4	0.039472	0.98575
5	0.011052	0.99680
6	0.002579	0.99938
7	0.000516	0.99989
8	0.000090	0.99998
9	0.000014	1.00000
10	0.000002	1.00000

λ = 1.5

k	P(x=k)	P(x ≤k)
0	0.223130	0.22313
1	0.334695	0.55783
2	0.251021	0.80885
3	0.125511	0.93436
4	0.047067	0.98142
5	0.014120	0.99554
6	0.003530	0.99907
7	0.000756	0.99983
8	0.000142	0.99997
9	0.000024	1.00000
10	0.000004	1.00000

λ = 1.8

k	P (x = k)	P (x ≤k)
0	0.165299	0.46530
1	0.297538	0.46284
2	0.267784	0.73062
3	0.160671	0.89129
4	0.072302	0.96359
5	0.026029	0.98962
6	0.007809	0.99743
7	0.002008	0.999444
8	0.000452	0.99989
9	0.000090	0.99998
10	0.000016	1.00000
11	0.000003	1.00000
12	0.000000	1.00000
13	0.000000	1.00000

λ = 2.0

k	P(x = k)	P(x ≤ k)
0	0.135335	0.13534
1	0.270671	0.40601
2	0.270671	0.67668
3	0.180447	0.85712
4	0.090224	0.94735
5	0.036089	0.98344
6	0.012030	0.99547
7	0.003437	0.99890
8	0.000859	0.99976
9	0.000191	0.99995
10	0.000038	0.99999
11	0.000007	1.00000
12	0.000001	1.00000
13	0.000000	1.00000

λ = 2.5

k	P(x=k)	P(x ≤k)
0	0.082058	0.08208
1	0.205213	0.28730
2	0.256516	0.54381
3	0.213763	0.75758
4	0.133602	0.89118
5	0.066801	0.95798
6	0.027834	0.98581
7	0.009941	0.99575
8	0.003106	0.99886
9	0.000863	0.99972
10	0.000216	0.99994
11	0.000049	0.99999
12	0.000010	1.00000
13	0.000002	1.00000

TABLE A–16 Poisson Distribution-3

λ = 3.0

k	P (x = k)	P (x ≤k)
0	0.049787	0.04979
1	0.149361	0.19915
2	0.224042	0.42319
3	0.224042	0.64723
4	0.168031	0.81526
5	0.100819	0.91608
6	0.050409	0.96649
7	0.021604	0.98810
8	0.008102	0.99620
9	0.002701	0.99890
10	0.000810	0.99971
11	0.000221	0.99993
12	0.000055	0.99998
13	0.000013	1.00000
14	0.000003	1.00000
15	0.000001	1.00000
16	0.000000	1.00000
17	0.000000	1.00000

λ = 3.5

k	P(x = k)	P(x ≤ k)
0	0.030197	0.03020
1	0.105691	0.13589
2	0.184959	0.32085
3	0.215785	0.53663
4	0.188812	0.72544
5	0.132169	0.85761
6	0.077098	0.93471
7	0.038549	0.97326
8	0.016865	0.99013
9	0.006559	0.99669
10	0.002296	0.99898
11	0.000730	0.99971
12	0.000213	0.99992
13	0.000057	0.99998
14	0.000014	1.00000
15	0.000003	1.00000
16	0.000001	1.00000
17	0.000000	1.00000

λ = 4.0

k	P(x=k)	P(x ≤k)
0	0.018316	0.01832
1	0.073263	0.09158
2	0.146525	0.23810
3	0.195367	0.43347
4	0.195367	0.62884
5	0.156293	0.78513
6	0.104196	0.88933
7	0.059540	0.94887
8	0.029770	0.97864
9	0.013231	0.99187
10	0.005292	0.99716
11	0.001925	0.99908
12	0.000642	0.99973
13	0.000197	0.99992
14	0.000056	0.99998
15	0.000015	1.00000
16	0.000004	1.00000
17	0.0000001	1.00000

λ = 4.5

k	P (x = k)	P (x ≤k)
0	0.011109	0.01111
1	0.049990	0.06110
2	0.112479	0.17358
3	0.168718	0.34230
4	0.189808	0.53210
5	0.170827	0.70293
6	0.128120	0.83105
7	0.082363	0.913411
8	0.046329	0.91341
9	0.023165	0.98291
10	0.010424	0.99333
11	0.004264	0.99760
12	0.001599	0.99919
13	0.000554	0.99975
14	0.000178	0.99993
15	0.000053	0.99998
16	0.000015	0.99999
17	0.000004	1.00000
18	0.000001	1.00000
19	0.000000	1.00000
20	0.000000	1.00000

λ = 5.0

k	P(x = k)	P(x ≤ k)
0	0.006738	0.00674
1	0.033690	0.04043
2	0.084224	0.12465
3	0.140374	0.26503
4	0.175467	0.44049
5	0.175467	0.61596
6	0.143223	0.76218
7	0.104445	0.86663
8	0.065278	0.93191
9	0.036266	0.96817
10	0.018133	0.98630
11	0.008424	0.99455
12	0.003434	0.99798
13	0.001321	0.99930
14	0.000472	0.99977
15	0.000157	0.99993
16	0.000049	0.99998
17	0.000014	0.99999
18	0.000004	1.00000
19	0.000001	1.00000
20	0.000000	1.00000

λ = 5.5

k	P(x=k)	P(x ≤k)
0	0.004087	0.00409
1	0.022477	0.02656
2	0.061812	0.08838
3	0.113323	0.20170
4	0.155819	0.35752
5	0.171401	0.52892
6	0.157117	0.68604
7	0.123449	0.80949
8	0.084871	0.89436
9	0.051866	0.94622
10	0.028526	0.97475
11	0.014263	0.98901
12	0.006537	0.99555
13	0.002766	0.99831
14	0.001087	0.99940
15	0.000 398	0.99980
16	0.000137	0.99994
17	0.000044	0.99998
18	0.000014	0.99999
19	0.000004	1.00000
20	0.000001	1.00000

TABLE A-17 (a)

Upper Percentage points for the Studentized Range Statistic q (5%)

p \ k	2	3	4	5	6	7	8	9	10	11	12	13	14	15	16	17	18	19	20
1	18.0	27.0	32.8	37.1	40.4	43.1	45.4	47.4	49.1	50.6	52.0	53.2	54.3	55.4	56.3	57.2	58.0	58.8	59.6
2	6.09	8.3	9.8	10.9	11.7	12.4	13.0	13.5	14.0	14.4	14.7	15.1	15.4	15.7	15.9	16.1	16.4	16.6	16.8
3	4.50	5.91	6.82	7.50	8.04	8.48	8.85	9.18	9.46	9.72	9.95	10.15	10.35	10.52	10.69	10.84	10.98	11.11	11.24
4	3.93	5.04	5.76	6.29	6.71	7.05	7.35	7.60	7.83	8.03	8.21	8.37	8.52	8.66	8.79	8.91	9.03	9.13	9.23
5	3.64	4.60	5.22	5.67	6.03	6.33	6.58	6.80	6.99	7.17	7.32	7.47	7.60	7.72	7.83	7.93	8.03	8.12	8.21
6	3.46	4.34	4.90	5.31	5.63	5.89	6.12	6.32	6.49	6.65	6.79	6.92	7.03	7.14	7.24	7.34	7.43	7.51	7.59
7	3.34	4.16	4.68	5.06	5.36	5.61	5.82	6.00	6.16	6.30	6.43	6.55	6.66	6.76	6.85	6.94	7.02	7.09	7.17
8	3.26	4.04	4.53	4.89	5.17	5.40	5.60	5.77	5.92	6.05	6.18	6.29	6.39	6.48	6.57	6.65	6.73	6.80	6.87
9	3.20	3.95	4.42	4.76	5.02	5.24	5.43	5.60	5.74	5.87	5.98	6.09	6.19	6.28	6.36	6.44	6.51	6.58	6.64
10	3.15	3.88	4.33	4.65	4.91	5.12	5.30	5.46	5.60	5.72	5.83	5.93	6.03	6.11	6.20	6.27	6.34	6.40	6.47
11	3.11	3.82	4.26	4.57	4.82	5.03	5.20	5.35	5.49	5.61	5.71	5.81	5.90	5.99	6.06	6.14	6.20	6.26	6.33
12	3.08	3.77	4.20	4.51	4.75	4.95	5.12	5.27	5.40	5.51	5.62	5.71	5.80	5.88	5.95	6.03	6.09	6.15	6.21
13	3.06	3.73	4.15	4.45	4.69	4.88	5.05	5.19	5.32	5.43	5.53	5.63	5.71	5.79	5.86	5.93	6.00	6.05	6.11
14	3.03	3.70	4.11	4.41	4.64	4.83	4.99	5.13	5.25	5.36	5.46	5.55	5.64	5.72	5.79	5.85	5.92	5.97	6.03
15	3.01	3.67	4.08	4.37	4.60	4.78	4.94	5.08	5.20	5.31	5.40	5.49	5.58	5.65	5.72	5.79	5.85	5.90	5.96
16	3.00	3.65	4.05	4.33	4.56	4.74	4.90	5.03	5.15	5.26	5.35	5.44	5.52	5.59	5.66	5.72	5.79	5.84	5.90
17	2.98	3.63	4.02	4.30	4.52	4.71	4.86	4.99	5.11	5.21	5.31	5.39	5.47	5.55	5.61	5.68	5.74	5.79	5.84
18	2.97	3.61	4.00	4.28	4.49	4.67	4.82	4.96	5.07	5.17	5.27	5.35	5.43	5.50	5.57	5.63	5.69	5.74	5.79
19	2.96	3.59	3.98	4.25	4.47	4.65	4.79	4.92	5.04	5.14	5.23	5.32	5.39	5.46	5.53	5.59	5.65	5.70	5.75
20	2.95	3.58	3.96	4.23	4.45	4.62	4.77	4.90	5.01	5.11	5.20	5.28	5.36	5.43	5.49	5.55	5.61	5.66	5.71
24	2.92	3.53	3.90	4.17	4.37	4.54	4.68	4.61	4.92	5.01	5.10	5.18	5.25	5.32	5.38	5.44	5.50	5.54	5.59
30	2.89	3.49	3.84	4.10	4.30	4.46	4.60	4.72	4.83	4.92	5.00	5.08	5.15	5.21	5.27	5.33	5.38	5.43	5.48
40	2.86	3.44	3.79	4.04	4.23	4.39	4.52	4.63	4.74	4.82	4.91	4.98	5.05	5.11	5.16	5.22	5.27	5.31	5.36
60	2.83	3.40	3.74	3.98	4.16	4.31	4.44	4.55	4.65	4.73	4.81	4.88	4.94	5.00	5.06	5.11	5.16	5.20	5.24
120	2.80	3.36	3.69	3.92	4.10	4.24	4.36	4.48	4.56	4.64	4.72	4.78	4.84	4.90	4.95	5.00	5.05	5.09	5.13
∞	2.77	3.31	3.63	3.86	4.03	4.17	4.29	4.39	4.47	4.55	4.62	4.68	4.74	4.80	4.85	4.89	4.93	4.97	5.01

TABLE A—17 (b)

Upper Percentage Points for the Studentized Range Statistic q (1%)

p \ k	2	3	4	5	6	7	8	9	10	11	12	13	14	15	16	17	18	19	20
1	90.0	135	164	186	202	216	227	237	246	253	260	266	272	277	282	286	290	294	298
2	14.0	19.0	22.3	24.7	26.6	28.2	29.5	30.7	31.7	32.6	33.4	34.1	34.8	35.4	36.0	36.5	37.0	37.5	37.9
3	8.26	10.6	12.2	13.3	14.2	15.0	15.6	16.2	16.7	17.1	17.5	17.9	18.2	18.5	18.8	19.1	19.3	19.5	19.8
4	6.51	8.12	9.17	9.96	10.6	11.1	11.5	11.9	12.3	12.6	12.8	13.1	13.3	13.5	13.7	13.9	14.1	14.2	14.4
5	5.70	6.97	7.80	8.42	8.91	9.32	9.67	9.97	10.24	10.48	10.70	10.89	11.08	11.24	11.40	11.55	11.68	11.81	11.93
6	5.24	6.33	7.03	7.56	7.97	8.32	8.61	8.87	9.10	9.30	9.49	9.65	9.81	9.95	10.08	10.21	10.32	10.43	10.54
7	4.95	5.92	6.54	7.01	7.37	7.68	7.94	8.17	8.37	8.55	8.71	8.86	9.00	9.12	9.24	9.35	9.46	9.55	9.65
8	4.74	5.63	6.20	6.63	6.96	7.24	7.47	7.68	7.87	8.03	8.18	8.31	8.44	8.55	8.66	8.76	8.85	8.94	9.03
9	4.60	5.43	5.96	6.35	6.66	6.91	7.13	7.32	7.49	7.65	7.78	7.91	8.03	8.13	8.23	8.32	8.41	8.49	8.57
10	4.48	5.27	5.77	6.14	6.43	6.67	6.87	7.05	7.21	7.36	7.48	7.60	7.71	7.81	7.91	7.99	8.07	8.15	8.22
11	4.39	5.14	5.62	5.97	6.25	6.48	6.67	6.84	6.99	7.13	7.25	7.36	7.46	7.56	7.65	7.73	7.81	7.88	7.95
12	4.32	5.04	5.50	5.84	6.10	6.32	6.51	6.67	6.81	6.94	7.06	7.17	7.26	7.36	7.44	7.52	7.59	7.66	7.73
13	4.26	4.96	5.40	5.73	5.98	6.19	6.37	6.53	6.67	6.79	6.90	7.01	7.10	7.19	7.27	7.34	7.42	7.48	7.55
14	4.21	4.89	5.32	5.63	5.88	6.08	6.26	6.41	6.54	6.66	6.77	6.87	6.96	7.05	7.12	7.20	7.27	7.33	7.39
15	4.17	4.83	5.25	5.56	5.80	5.99	6.16	6.31	6.44	6.55	6.66	6.76	6.84	6.93	7.00	7.07	7.14	7.20	7.26
16	4.13	4.78	5.19	5.49	5.72	5.92	6.08	6.22	6.35	6.46	6.56	6.66	6.74	6.82	6.90	6.97	7.03	7.09	7.15
17	4.10	4.74	5.14	5.43	5.66	5.85	6.01	6.15	6.27	6.38	6.48	6.57	6.66	6.73	6.80	6.87	6.94	7.00	7.05
18	4.07	4.70	5.09	5.38	5.60	5.79	5.94	6.08	6.20	6.31	6.41	6.50	6.58	6.65	6.72	6.79	6.85	6.91	6.96
19	4.05	4.67	5.05	5.33	5.55	5.73	5.89	6.02	6.14	6.25	6.34	6.43	6.51	6.58	6.65	6.72	6.78	6.84	6.89
20	4.02	4.64	5.02	5.29	5.51	5.59	5.84	5.97	6.09	6.19	6.29	6.37	6.45	6.52	6.59	6.65	6.71	6.76	6.82
24	3.96	4.54	4.91	5.17	5.37	5.54	5.69	5.81	5.92	6.02	6.11	6.19	6.26	6.33	6.39	6.45	6.51	6.56	6.61
30	3.89	4.45	4.80	5.05	5.24	5.40	5.54	5.65	5.76	5.85	5.93	6.01	6.08	6.14	6.20	6.26	6.31	6.36	6.41
40	3.82	4.37	4.70	4.93	5.11	5.27	5.39	5.50	5.60	5.69	5.77	5.84	5.90	5.96	6.02	6.07	6.12	6.17	6.21
60	3.76	4.28	4.60	4.82	4.99	5.13	5.25	5.36	5.45	5.53	5.60	5.67	5.73	5.79	5.84	5.89	5.93	5.98	6.02
120	3.70	4.20	4.50	4.71	4.87	5.01	5.12	5.21	5.30	5.38	5.44	5.51	5.56	5.61	5.66	5.71	5.75	5.79	5.83
∞	3.64	4.12	4.40	4.60	4.76	4.88	4.99	5.08	5.16	5.23	5.29	5.35	5.40	5.45	5.49	5.54	5.57	5.61	5.65

TABLE A–18
Random Numbers

10480	15011	01536	02011	81647	91646	69179	14194	62590
22368	46573	25595	85393	30995	89198	27982	53402	93965
24130	48360	22527	97265	76393	64809	15179	24830	49340
42167	93093	06243	61680	07856	16376	39440	53537	71341
37570	39975	81837	16656	06121	91782	60468	81305	49684
77921	06907	11008	42751	27756	53498	18602	70659	90655
99562	72905	56420	69994	98872	31016	71194	18738	44013
96301	91977	05463	07972	18876	20922	94595	56869	69014
89579	14342	63661	10281	17453	18103	57704	84378	25331
85475	36857	53342	53988	53060	59533	38867	62300	08158
28918	69578	88231	33276	70997	79936	56865	05859	90106
63553	40961	48235	03427	49626	69445	18663	72695	52180
09429	93969	52636	92737	88974	33488	36320	17617	30015
10365	61129	87529	85689	48237	52267	67689	93394	01511
07119	97336	71048	08178	77233	13916	47564	81056	97735
51085	12765	51821	51259	77452	16308	60756	92144	49442
02368	21382	52404	60268	89368	19885	55332	44849	01188
01011	54092	33362	94904	31273	04146	18594	29852	71585
52162	53916	46369	58586	23216	14513	83149	98736	23495
07056	97628	33787	09998	42698	06691	76988	13062	51851
48663	91245	85828	14346	09172	30168	90229	04734	59193
54164	58492	22421	74103	47070	25306	76468	26384	58151
32639	32363	05597	24200	13363	38005	94342	28728	35806
29334	27001	87637	87308	58731	00256	45834	15398	46557
02488	33062	28834	07351	19731	92420	60952	61280	50001
81525	72295	04839	96423	24678	82651	66566	14778	76797
29676	20591	68086	26432	46901	20849	89768	81536	86645
00742	57392	39064	66432	84673	40027	32832	61362	98947
05366	04213	25669	26422	44407	44048	37937	63904	45766
91921	26418	64117	94305	26766	25940	39972	22209	71500
00582	04711	87917	77341	42206	35126	74087	99547	81817
00725	69884	62797	56170	86324	88072	76222	36086	84637
69011	65795	95876	55293	18988	27354	26575	08625	40801
25976	57948	29888	88604	67917	48708	18912	82271	65424
09763	83473	73577	12908	30883	18317	28290	35797	05998
91567	42595	27958	30134	04024	86385	29880	99730	55536
17955	56349	90999	49127	20044	59931	06115	20542	18059
46503	18584	18845	49618	02304	51038	20655	58727	28168
92157	89634	94824	78171	84610	82834	09922	25417	44137
14577	62765	35605	81263	39667	47358	56873	56307	61607
98427	07523	33362	64270	01638	92477	66969	98420	04880
34914	63976	88720	82765	34476	17032	87589	40836	32427
70060	28277	39475	46473	23219	53416	94970	25832	69975
53976	54914	06990	67245	68350	82948	11398	42878	80287
76072	29515	40980	07391	58745	25774	22987	80059	39911
90725	52210	83974	29992	65831	38857	50490	83765	55657
64364	67412	33339	31926	14883	24413	59744	93251	97473
08962	00358	31662	25388	61642	34072	81249	35648	56891
95012	68379	93526	70765	10592	04542	76463	54328	02349
15664	10493	20492	38391	91132	21999	59516	81652	27195